MISHNAH BERURAH

the classic commentary to

Shulchan Aruch Orach Chayim

comprising the laws of daily Jewish conduct

BY

RABBEINU YISROEL MEIR HA-COHEN

(The Chafetz Chayim)

זצוק"ל

PISGAH FOUNDATION

FELDHEIM PUBLISHERS

JERUSALEM

ספר

משנה ברורה

והוא פירוש יפה ומנופה על

שו"ע אורח חיים

הלכות שבת

אשר חיבר הרב הגאון רשכבה"ג מו"ה **יוסף קארו** זצ"ל

עם חידושי דינים שהשמיט הגאון הנ"ל והמציאם

הגאון מו"ה **משה איסרליש** זצ"ל,

עם נושאי כליהם הלא המה:

באר הגולה מהגאון מו"ה **משה רבקש** זצ"ל מווילנא

באר היטב מהרב המובהק מו"ה **יהודא אשכנזי** זצ"ל דיין טיקטין

שערי תשובה מאת הגאון מו"ה **חיים מרדכי מרגליות** זצ"ל

ובאורי קראתיו בשם **משנה ברורה**, יען כי מתוכו מתברר דברי השו"ע כל דין ודין בטעמו ונימוקו מגמרא ופוסקים ולא יהיה כספר החתום, גם יקבץ בו כל הדינים וההלכות והביאורים המפוזרים בספרי האחרונים מפרשי השו"ע המפורסמים (כמו מא"ר ופמ"ג וברכי יוסף ומאמר מרדכי ורבות כהנה). אשר היו הרבה מהם אחרי הבה"ט ולא הובאו בשע"ת כי אם מעט מזעיר באיזה מקומות כל אלה חוברו פה והכל בלשון צח וקל ובסדר נכון בעז"ה:

עוד צרפתי בצדו כמה ענינים נחוצים ובשם **ביאור הלכה** יכונה ובשמו כן הוא כי בו ביארתי כמה פעמים דברי ההלכה המובא בקיצור בתוך המשנה ברורה בלי ראיה ופה הראיתי בעזה"י את מקורו לעין כל מגמרא ופוסקים, גם יבואר בו לפעמים דברי השו"ע באורך במקום הצריך ביאור;

גם תחת המשנה ברורה הנ"ל פתחתי שער רחב עם פרחים וציצים מצוינים ושמו נאה לו **שער הציון** כי בו יצויין על כל דיבור ודיבור לדעת מכמן מי יצאו הפנינים האלו:

כל אלה חברתי בעזה"י החונן לאדם דעת

ישראל מאיר בר' **אריה זאב הכהן** זלה"ה, מעיר **ראדין**

ירושלים

MISHNAH BERURAH

משנה ברורה

VOLUME I (B)
חלק ראשון (ב)

The laws of tefilin
§ 25 — § 45
הלכות תפילין
סי׳ כ״ה — מ״ה

An English Translation
of *Shulchan Aruch* and *Mishnah Berurah*
with explanatory comments, notes
and facing Hebrew text

This volume edited by

RABBI AVIEL ORENSTEIN

First published 1992
Large edition: ISBN 0-87306-624-3
Regular edition: ISBN 0-87306-623-5

Sole distributors throughout the world

Philipp Feldheim Inc.
200 Airport Executive Park
Spring Valley, NY 10977

Feldheim Publishers Ltd
POB 35002 / Jerusalem, Israel

Printed in Israel

Acknowledgement and thanks

The beautiful illustrated Hebrew edition of Mishnas Soferim which appears in this volume was published by *Mishmereth STaM.* We thank them for their kind permission to use it in our English edition and feel certain that our gratitude will be felt by all those who will use our edition to acquire an understanding of the laws concerning the writing of Torah Scrolls, *tefilin* passages and mezuzos and of the form of the letters.

We wish them continued success and blessing in their commendable and essential work in this important field of activity.

Editor's Note

The editor wishes to point out that in accordance with our policy of providing the reader with the best we can, the Hebrew text of this volume has been taken from a clearer modern and corrected edition which has recently been published. In that edition there are many corrections, some firmly based and some based on judgment, and, in addition, translations are provided for the Yiddish words used by the Mishnah Berurah. Those corrections and translations are entirely the responsibility of the editors of that edition. We have taken our own pains to produce a correct and reliable translation and we are only responsible for what appears in the English text and notes.

It may not be realized that the translation of the Yiddish words appearing in the Mishnah Berurah, particularly the names of fruits and spices, etc. is a most difficult task. The spelling is phonetic and not necessarily the accepted spelling. Many of the words do not appear in any form in a Yiddish dictionary, either because they are old Yiddish words no longer in use taken from early Poskim, because they were local terms or because they are simply vague descriptions. We have done our utmost to solve this problem reliably.

See Volume I(A) for letters of approbation and blessing by leading world Torah authorities and the Editor's Introduction, which describes the principles on which the translation is based.

מפתח ההלכות

הלכות תפילין

TABLE OF CONTENTS*

	Summary of Punctuation Marks and Transliteration Key	x
Section 25:	The laws of *tefilin* in detail To put on a *talis* first; when to don the *tefilin*; what to have in mind when one dons *tefilin*; the order in which to don the *tefilin*; the blessings to be made and when they should be made; making an interruption in between the donning of the arm and of the head *tefilin*; when to take off the *tefilin*	3
Section 26:	The law when one has only one of the *tefilin* units Also: The law when one can only don one of the units	33
Section 27:	The area where /the *tefilin*/ should be donned and the manner in which they should be donned Also: The required length and width for the straps	37
Section 28:	The laws concerning the taking off of the *tefilin* Also: To feel the *tefilin*; the practice of kissing the *tefilin*	61
Section 29:	/Whether one must make a blessing over the taking off of *tefilin*/	65
Section 30:	The time for donning /*tefilin*/ Also: The ruling if one donned *tefilin* before sunset or on Erev Shabbos and when one wishes to depart for the road early	67
Section 31:	The laws /as regards the donning/ of *tefilin* on Shabbos or Yom Tov Also: The laws as regards donning *tefilin* on Chol Ha-Moed	75
Section 32:	The procedure for the writing of the *tefilin* passages The passages to be written and the order required; the number of parchments to be used; the ink to be used; that each letter should be complete and surrounded by blank parchment; to write with the "right" hand; marking out the lines; the kind of parchment required; the processing of the parchment; the practice as regards the parchment to be used for the various passages; if there is a hole or a break in a letter; if a drop of ink fell into a letter; scraping or erasing to correct a letter; how the scribe should act in order to write for the sake of the holiness of *tefilin*; to be meticulous about the letters required to be written and to read the written passages; to test the quill; remedying a passage when a letter is missing or is superfluous; writing on a spot where one scraped away or erased; correcting a letter after other letters have been written; separating letters of a Divine Name; to avoid one letter entering into another; writing when one does not know the passages or without a written copy; the blank space one is required to leave; the making of the rows; the form of the passages, open or closed Also: Sending parchment with a non-Jew, relying on a letter-like sign of holes; what skin may be used for the housings and the straps; to use a single skin for the housings; the squareness of the housings; to make the housings black; the law for the grooves of the housings; the size of the housings; the letter ש required on the housings; the bridge of the housings; the passageway; the manner in which the passages are inserted; if one wrote all four passages for the head *tefilin* on a single parchment or the passages for the arm *tefilin* on separate parchments; if one overlaid the housings with gold, etc.; the sinews for the sewing; the stitches required; the insertion of the straps and their knots	79
Section 33:	The law as regards /the need to/ repair *tefilin* and the law concerning the straps If the skin has become spoiled or the stitches have become severed; what skin may be used for the straps; the color required for the straps; a non-Jew blackening the straps; if the straps became severed Also: If a non-Jew blackened the skin of the housings	213
Section 34:	The order in which the passages should be placed in the *tefilin*. /The practice of/ the meticulous to have two pairs of *tefilin*	229
Section 35:	The law as regards the number of lines /required in the passages/	243
Section 36:	The accuracy /required/ for the writing of /the *tefilin* passages/ Not to deviate from the form of the letter or to write a letter which resembles another letter; that all the letters, except for ה and ק must be a single /coherent/ body; the crownlets required for the letters	245

* *Subtitles added by editor*

Mishnas Soferim:

A brief /account/ of the rules concerning /invalidity because one wrote/ in incorrect order 255
A few additional points, concerning carving around /to form the letter/ 261
The form of the letters 263
Some of the rules concerning /the need for the letter to be/ surrounded by /blank/ parchment 309

Section 37: The time for the donning of *tefilin* 311
That it is a mitzvah to wear *tefilin* all day; the practice of refraining from doing so
Also: The reward for donning *tefilin* and the gravity of neglecting it; the ruling for a child

Section 38: The law as regards who are obliged to /don/ *tefilin* and who are exempt /from doing so/ 317
The law when a person has a disorder in his bowels, is suffering from another illness, is distressed, is not mentally at ease, or cannot avoid breaking wind; the law for women and slaves, a mourner, a bridegroom and his groomsmen, writers of Torah Scrolls, etc. and their brokers, a banned person or a person who is suffering from *tzara'as*; the law for someone who reads Torah
Also: If one has thoughts of lust while wearing *tefilin*; the law on Tishah Be-Av; the law when one is occupied with the performance of a mitzvah; taking off *tefilin* in the presence of one's Torah teacher; the law when one cannot acquire both *tefilin* and a mezuzah

Section 39: Who are fit to write *tefilin* /passages/ and from whom they may be bought 333
The law of *tefilin* which were written by a slave, a woman, a child, a Cuthean, a confirmed sinner, an informer, a convert to Judaism who returned to his former religion or a heretic; the law of *tefilin* found in the possession of a heretic or of a non-Jew; that *tefilin* should be acquired from a qualified person
Also: Someone not fit to write *tefilin* passages doing other things in the production of *tefilin*; purchasing *tefilin*, etc. from gentiles for more than their value; the law when one purchases *tefilin* from an unqualified person; whether *tefilin* need to be examined for validity

Section 40: The law as regards how one should act with respect to the holiness of *tefilin* 349
Hanging up *tefilin*; the laws concerning *tefilin* with reference to marital relations or a chance ejaculation; eating if one is wearing *tefilin*

Section 41: The law concerning how someone who is carrying a burden should act as regards *tefilin* 359

Section 42: Whether it is permitted to alter arm *tefilin* to head /*tefilin*/ 361
Also: Whether it is permitted to alter head *tefilin* to arm *tefilin*; the ruling of a cloth designated for wrapping *tefilin* or in which one wrapped *tefilin* without designating it for *tefilin* and of parchment processed for the sake of use for *tefilin*

Section 43: The law as regards how one should conduct himself with *tefilin* when he enters a lavatory 377
Also: How one should act if he forgot that he had *tefilin* on his head and started to relieve himself; whether one may take a urine bowl in his hand with *tefilin* on his head

Section 44: The prohibition against sleeping /wearing/ *tefilin* 389

Section 45: The law as regards /wearing/ *tefilin* /when one is/ in a graveyard or a bathhouse 393
Also: Wearing *tefilin* within four cubits of a dead person

Glossary 397
Bibliography 403

Summary of punctuation marks, etc. for easy reference:

/ /	editorial insertions; *words within are to be read continuously with text, as if slashes do not exist.*
( )	do not appear in Hebrew text; they are added to set off parenthetical phrases, or for English-Hebrew equivalents of preceding word.
(( ))	parentheses appearing in original Hebrew text.
[ ]	brackets appearing in original Hebrew text.
( )	a gloss in the Shulchan Aruch.
(...)	an omission, in a gloss, of the sources cited in the Hebrew text, or an omission of a gloss explaining a word that has been rendered superfluous by the translation.
1, 2, etc.	begin new paragraphs in the Shulchan Aruch.
(1), (2), etc.	correspond to the sub-paragraphs of the Mishnah Berurah commenting on words *following* the number.
[1*], [2*], etc.	Shulchan Aruch footnotes.
[1], [2], etc.	Mishnah Berurah footnotes.
Sec.	Section.
Par., sub-Par.	Paragraph, sub-Paragraph.

All italic non-foreign words in the Shulchan Aruch are glosses.

Where more than one English page is required to translate a page of Hebrew text, the Hebrew text is printed a second time and that part of the Hebrew text which is not translated on the facing page is reproduced in a fainter impression.

Transliteration Key

Vowels				Letters			
◌ָ	a	◌ַ	a	א (internal)	'	מ	m
◌ֵ	ey,ei,e	◌ֶ	e	בּ	b	נ	n
וֹ	o	◌ָ	a	ב	v	ס	s
וּ	u	◌ֻ	u	ג	g	ע (internal)	'
◌ִי	i	◌ִ	i	ד	d	פּ	p
◌ְ	e (where vocalized)			ה	h	פ	f
				ו	v	צ	tz
				ז	z	ק	k
				ח	ch	ר	r
				ט	t	שׁ	sh
				י	y	שׂ	s
				כּ	k	תּ	t
				כ	ch	ת	s
				ל	l		

MISHNAH BERURAH

משנה ברורה

הלכות תפילין

כה דיני תפילין בפרטות. ובו י"ג סעיפים:

א טור וב"י ורמ"א
יונה ב בית יוסף

א (א) [א]אחר שלבש טלית מצוייץ (א) [א] (ב) יניח תפלין * שמעלין בקודש והמניחין כיס התפלין והטלית לתוך כיס אחת [ב]צריכין ליזהר * שלא יניחו כיס התפלין למעלה כדי (ג) * שלא יפגע

באר היטב

רקנ"ט: (ד) הזהיר במצות ציצית. ויזהר לעשות טלית נאה משום זה אלי ואנוהו ועיין בזוהר שלח לך דהקורא ק"ש בלא ציצית מעיד עדות שקר בעצמו. מ"א. בתשובת הרדב"ז ח"א סימן מ"ה אוסר לרקום פסוקים של תורה בטלית. והמחבר לקט הקמח כתב הראיתי פנים להתיר ע"ש:

(א) יניח תפילין. הרב כנה"ג בשיוריו פסק דמי שאין ידו משגת לקנות ציצית ותפילין דציצית קודם ע"ש והמחבר בני חייא וע"ת והלק"ט ח"א סי' כ"ד ובתשובת יד אליהו סימן מ"א והיד אהרן כולם כאחד חלקו עליו ופסקו דתפילין קודם ע"ש. אם מחויב להחזיר

שערי תשובה

שישנו בראיה אלא אחרים ע"ש: [ג] הזהיר. עבה"ט ומ"ש לענין לרקום פסוקים כו' עיין ביו"ד סימן רפ"ג. ואין נכון לעשות כן ועיין בגינת ורדים כלל א' סי' כ"ה שכתב שמ"מ אם כבר נעשה ורקם פי' ציצית מותר לברך עליו. ויזהר כשישב ע"ג ספסל יגביהו מלדדים ולא ישב על גוף הטלית שד"ת מרוקמים שם ועיין בש"ך ביו"ד שם שנהגו היתר לרקום ע"ש. ועיין בגינת ורדים סי' ק"ו שהבא לשאול אם ירקום על מפות אין מורין כן היתר לכתחלה כ"ש על טלית והביא שם מהרדב"ז. ובלקט הקמח הביא ג"כ מהרדב"ז. וכתב שהסכים בתשובה בדיעבד לברך דמ"ש שם ביורה דעה בשם הרמב"ם אינו בטליתים שלנו שאנו נוהגין בהם קדושה שלא ליכנס בהם לבהכ"ם וכיוצא בו ע"ש. ועיין בא"ר בשם מקור חיים שאף שמצות אין מצילות מיצה"ר מ"מ מצות ציצית מציל ונראה שלמד כן מעובדא דמנחות מעשה באדם אחד כו'. וכן הוא אומר וראיתם אותו וזכרתם את כל מצות ה' כו' אשר אתם זונים אחריהם למען תזכרו וכו' והייתם קדושים ויאמו דברינו בקדושה:
[א] יניח תפילין. עיין בה"ט וכתב בר"י בשם האחרונים שאם אפשר שיהיה לו תפילין בשאלה מאחר ציצית קודמין ע"ש. ועיין לקמן סי' ל"ח ס"ק י"ד[א] לענין תפילין ומזוזה. ונראה דהיינו אם נכון לבו בטוח שיוכל לשאול תפילין שעכ"פ לא יצטרך להחזירם כל זמן שירצה אם לא יזדמנו לו לקנות. ואם לאו אכתי איכא למיחש שמא יצטרך להחזירם טרם יזדמנו לו אחרים ונמצא בטל ממצות תפילין שהיא קודמת למצות ציצית לדברי הפוסקים אלו שהם עיקר לדינא. ועיין ביד אפרים ובשו"ת שאגת אריה סי' כ"ח ובשו"ת שמש צדקה סי' ט"ו וגו"ז. ונראה דאם יש לו תפילין של רש"י אלא שרוצה להניח תפילין של ר"ת ואין לו ציצית הציצית קודמין כיון דרובא דאינשי אין מניחין תפילין דר"ת כלל אבל איפכא לא. ואפילו יש לו של ר"ת אם אין לו של רש"י הם קודמין לציצית שהם העיקר לענין ברכה כמ"ש בסי' ל"ד. ואף שקדושת תפילין של ר"ת גדולה מאד מ"מ לענין לצאת בו י"ח של רש"י קודמים שאדרבה מחמת זה נמנעו רוב העולם מלהניחם לפי שכל א' הוא פעולה מיוחדת כמ"ש בזוהר חדש וכמ"ש בסי' ל"ד ולכן פשוט מי שאינו יכול לקנות שניהם יקנה של רש"י תחלה ואח"כ כשיהיה לו לקנות של ר"ת יקנה. והכי נהוג עלמא וא"כ ה"ה לענין ציצית. וכתב בשלמי צבור בשם תשובות דבר

משנה ברורה

א (א) אחר שלבש וכו'. ואפילו אם הטלית אינו חייב אלא מדרבנן כגון שאולה אחר שלשים יום וכנ"ל בסימן י"ד וכל כה"ג ג"כ יש להקדימו לתפילין [ארה"ח]: (ב) יניח תפילין. ומי שאין ידו משגת לקנות ציצית ותפילין הכריעו (א) האחרונים דתפילין קודמין כי ציצית הוא רק מצוה אם יש לו טלית של ד' כנפות ותפילין הוא חובה ומי שאינו מניחן הוא בכלל פושעי ישראל בגופן וכדלקמן בסימן ל"ז. וכ"ש לענין לקנות תפילין מהודרין וטלית נאה דתפילין קודמין לכו"ע והעולם נכשלין בזה. מי שאין ידו משגת לקנות ציצית ותפילין (ב) אין מחוייב לחזור על הפתחים כדי לקנותן אבל מי שידו משגת אך סומך על מה ששואל מאחרים אחר שילאו בהן כתב הב"ח דעונשו גדול*): (ג) שלא יפגע. פי' אפילו לא יאחוז בהם בידו רק לפי הושטת ידו הם מונחין לפניו תחלה אין מעבירין עליהם (ג) וצריך להקדימן וכל זה דוקא אם רוצה להניח עתה התפילין אבל (ד) אם עדיין אין רוצה להניחם רק לאחר זמן לא שייך בזה אין מעבירין על המצות:

ביאור הלכה

* שמעלין בקודש. על האדם קאי שצריך לילך מדרגא לדרגא ולהתעלות בקדושה כי מתחלה הוא רק מכסה את עצמו בכיסוי של מצוה וע"י התפילין הוא מקשר את עצמו בקשר היחוד והקדושה [א"ר והגר"א וכוון[ב] בזה לתרץ קושית הש"א והדגול מרבבה]: * שלא יניחו. עיין במג"א שכתב דנ"ל דאין קפידא בזה כיון דהתפילין עדיין מונחין בתוך כיסן ומהלבוש והב"ח והט"ז סק"י משמע דאין לחלק בזה וכ"כ בנשמת אדם אף דראייתו נגד המ"א [מתוספות דיומא ל"ג ע"ב ד"ה עבורי מפירוש רבינו אליהו שמצריך למשמש תחלה בשל יד והלא הש"י על פי הרוב מכוסה ואעפ"כ שייך בזה אין מעבירין] היא ראיה חלושה מאוד דטעם מ"א הוא כיון שהתפילין עדיין מונחין בתוך כיסן אין המצוה של הקשירה מזומנת לפניו דהלא צריך לזה מתחלה ליטלן מן הכיס משא"כ התם לענין משמוש דהמשמוש הוא המצוה ואפילו אם הבית יד של הכתונת מכסה את התפילין שייך ג"כ מצוה זו ע"כ שייך בזה אין מעבירין מ"מ קשה מאוד להקל כהמ"א אחרי דרבים חולקין עליו. ואפילו אם אירע לו כן כשהוא יושב בבהכ"נ ברבים ומתבייש עי"ז מסתפיקנא אם יש להקל בזה אחרי דמסיק בנ"א בכלל ס"ח וכן משמע מהפמ"ג במ"ז סק"ה דדינא דאין מעבירין על המצות הוא ד"ת וכבר פסק בשו"ע לעיל סוף סימן י"ג בהג"ה דד"ת אין נדחה מפני כבוד הבריות בכל גווני אם לא בגנאי גדול ולישב בלי טלית אפילו זמן ארוך ס"ל להרמ"א דהוא רק גנאי קטן כמ"ש המ"א שם וכ"ש כאן שהוא על רגעים אחדים עד שיניח הט"ג ואעפ"כ צ"ע: * שלא יפגע וכו'. עיין במ"ב במה שכתב פי' אפילו וכו' ומקורו מהא דיומא ל"ג ע"ב בגמרא וכי עייל להיכל וכו' ומשוך כלפי חוץ וכו' והנה אף דיש לדחות קצת דהכא שהתפילין מונחין בתוך כיס הטלית שעדיין לא הוציאן מן הכיס קיל טפי ואפילו אם נגע בהן בידיו מותר לו לסלק ידו מהן וליטול הטלית וכמש"כ הפמ"ג לדעת המ"א בא"א אות א' ובמ"ז אות י' דלהמ"א מותר לכתחלה להיות מונחין בשוה הש"ר והש"י בתוך התיק ואף אם יארע שיפגע תחלה בהש"ר יסלקנו מידו ויטול תחלה הש"י ואין

בזה

שער הציון

(ה) אחרונים: (ו) אחרונים: (א) א"ר ופמ"ג וח"א ועוד ס"פ: (ב) ע"ת בשם הירו': (ג) כמו שבררתי בבה"ל: (ד) הח"א ומייתי ראיה לזה ממ"א סק"ד ע"ש:

*) גם מלבד שעי"ז אינו מקיים מצות תפילין כדין וגם מברך לבטלה ועובר על לא תשא כי לפעמים הקשר קטן או גדול לפי מדת ראשו והוא מתעצל לתקנו או שחבירו מקפיד על זה וכבר כתב הפמ"ג דתפילין שמונחין שלא במקומן הם כמונחין בכיסן:

הגהות ותיקונים: א) ד': ב) וכוונו:

THE LAWS OF *TEFILIN*

§25: THE LAWS OF *TEFILIN* IN DETAIL

(Contains Thirteen Paragraphs)

1. (1) After having put on a *talis* with *tzitzis* /attached/, (2) one should /now/ don *tefilin*. /This order is necessary/ because one should ascend in holiness.[1*]

Those who place the bag /containing/ the *tefilin* and /also/ the *talis* inside one /larger/ bag, must take care not to place the bag /containing/ the *tefilin* on top. /They must avoid this/ so that (3) they will not encounter /the *tefilin*/

Mishnah Berurah

(1) **After having put on, etc.** Even when the obligation /to insert *tzitzis* in/ the *talis* is merely a Rabbinical one, /the putting on of the *talis*/ should also be given precedence to /the donning of/ the *tefilin*. [*Ar.Hach.*] For example, /if it is/ a borrowed /*talis*/ which has been thirty days /in one's possession (for which *tzitzis* are only required according to Rabbinical law/, as /explained/ above in Sec. 14) or anything analogous.

(2) **One should don *tefilin*.** The Acharonim have decided that if someone cannot afford to buy /both a *talis* with/ *tzitzis* /attached/ and *tefilin*, *tefilin* have precedence. The reason is that /having/ *tzitzis* /attached to one's garment/ is only a mitzvah if one has a *talis* /or other garment/ which has four corners, /whereas the donning of/ *tefilin* is an /absolute/ obligation. If one does not don /*tefilin*/ he is classed among those of Israel who sin with their bodies, as /stated/ below in Sec. 37.

As regards /whether/ one should /rather/ purchase superior *tefilin* or a /more/ attractive *talis*, *tefilin* certainly have precedence according to all /authorities/. /However,/ the public stumble on this /point/.

If someone cannot afford to purchase /neither a *talis* with/ *tzitzis* /attached/ nor *tefilin*, he is not obliged to go from door to door /begging/ in order /to be able/ to purchase them. However, the *Bach* writes that if one is able to afford /their purchase/, but relies on borrowing them from others after they have fulfilled /their own obligation/ with them, his punishment will be severe.[1]

(3) **They will not encounter.** /It should be noted/ in explanation /of this ruling/ that even if one does not take hold of /the *tefilin*/ in his hand, but they are lying first in front of him as he stretches out his hand, he may not bypass them and must give them precedence.

All this only /applies/ if one wishes to don the *tefilin* now. However, if he does not yet wish to don them, but only /some/ time later, /the fact/ that one must not bypass mitzvos is not relevant in such a case /and he may put on the *talis* first/.

1* This relates to the person. When one puts on a *talis* he merely covers himself with a mitzvah covering, whereas by donning *tefilin* he connects himself with the unity and holiness. (Beyur Halachah)

1 It is also common as a result of this that the mitzvah of *tefilin* is not fulfilled in accordance with halachic requirements and one also makes a vain blessing and transgresses "You should not take the Name of the Lord your God in vain". This is because it sometimes happens that the knot of the *tefilin* one borrows has been tied in such a way that the encircling strap is too small or too large for the size of his head and he is too lazy to adjust it or his fellow objects to him doing so. The *P.Mg.* has already written that *tefilin* which are not in their proper place on one's head may just as well be in their bag. (Note added by the author of the Mishnah Berurah, with additional words added for clarity.)

בהם תחלה (ד) * ויצטרך להניחם (ה) קודם הטלית כדי שלא יעבור על המצוה: הגה מיהו אם תפילין מזומנים בידו (ו) ואין לו ציצית (ז) אין צריך להמתין על הציצית אלא מניח תפילין וכשמביאים טלית מעטפו (דברי עצמו): **ב** * ג מי שהוא זהיר בטלית קטן ילבשנו ויניח תפלין (ח) בביתו וילך לבוש בציצית ומוכתר בתפילין לבית הכנסת (ט) ושם יתעטף (ב) [ב] בטלית גדול: הגה והעולם נהגו (י) להתעטף אף בטלית גדול קודם (יא) ולברך עליו ואח"כ מניח התפילין והולך לבהכ"נ: ג ד הרא"ש היה מסדר הברכות עד עוטר ישראל בתפארה (יב) ואז היה מניח תפילין (יג) ומברך עוטר ישראל בתפארה: ד ה צריך שיהיו תפילין עליו (יד) בשעת ק"ש ותפלה: ה (טו) ו יכוין בהנחתם שצונו

באר הגולה

ג זוהר פרשת ואתחנן ד טור ה ברכות י"ד ו ר' יונה פ"ה שם

שערי תשובה

משה שמי שאין ידו משגת לקנות תש"י ותפילין של ראש יקנה של ראש תחלה ע"ש: [ב] בטלית גדול. עבה"ט ובבר"י כתב בשם תשו' מהר"י מולכין כ"י מי שהיה מונח בכיסו טלית של חול ותפילין וטלית של שבת היה למעלה מכל אם יכול להעביר על של שבת וליקח של חול והביא מתוספות דיומא דף ל"ג דלא שייך אין מעבירין כו' אלא כי בעי למעבד תרווייהו ושוב דחה זאת. והבר"י כתב ללמוד מדברי המג"א אלו שהביא הבה"ט דה"ה בזה יכול להעביר על של שבת וליקח את של חול ע"ש. ושם כתב שלדעת האר"י ז"ל אף שהוא

ביאור הלכה

בזה משום חשש דמעביר על המצות אבל כ"ז אין שייך לדינא דהא לדעת המחבר דנקטינן כוותיה וכן פסקו כמעט כל האחרונים [הלבוש והב"ח והט"ז והגר"א והארה"ח דלא כמ"א] אין חילוק בזה שהוא סובר דאפילו אם התפלין מונחין בתוך כיסן שייך בזה אין מעבירין. ובאמת פשוט הוא לענ"ד דגם המ"א מודה בזה ודלא כהפמ"ג דעד כאן לא קשרי המ"א אלא היכא שהתפלין מונחין בכיס בפ"ע שלא נגע בהן כלל בידו רק ע"י כיס וא"א להניחן ע"י כיס משא"כ בזה שהם ממש בידו או שלפי הושטת ידו הם מזומנין לפניו תחלה מה יועיל במה שהם עדיין בתוך הכיס וראיה לדברינו ממ"ש המ"א בעצמו לקמן בסימן כ"ח ס"ק ד' דמש"כ המחבר ועליו של יד פירושו שיתנו קצת לצד מעלה הרי דצריך ליתנו לצד מעלה כדי שיפגע בהם תחלה ולהפמ"ג אין צריך לזה רק שיתן סימן בכריכת הרצועות כדי שיבחין בהם בנגיעתו בם איזו ש"י ואיזו ש"ר ולא יוציא הש"ר תחלה מהתיק וכמ"ש במש"ז אות י' ויש ליישב לדידיה דכוונת הש"ע כדי שלא ישכח ויוציא הש"ר מהתיק ודוחק ואולי זהו כוונת הפמ"ג בעצמו מה שנשאר בצ"ע מלקמן סימן כ"ח סק"ד במ"א. ואולם כ"ז אין נ"מ לדינא לדידן דפסקינן בלא"ה דלא כמ"א אפילו אם הם מונחין בתוך כיסן. היוצא מדברינו דאם הושיט ידו בתוך כיס הטלית ופגע קודם בהתפלין מחויב להוציאן קודם ולהניחן משום אין מעבירין על המצות וכן לענין תפלין יש לו ליזהר לכתחלה להיות מונח הש"י קצת לצד מעלה ולא בשוה ממש כדי שלא לפגוע בתוך הכיס בהשל ראש ברישא כדי שלא יעבור על הדין דאין מעבירין: * ויצטרך להניחם. לכאורה יש לעיין אם פשט הטלית ותפלין רק לפי שעה ודעתו להחזירם תיכף דפסקינן לקמן דאין צריך לחזור ולברך ואח"כ בעת לבישה נזדמן לו התפלין מקודם אם מחויב להניחן תחלה דאולי כיון דלא הסיח דעתו אפשר כאלו הוא עוסק עדיין בהמצוה ופשיטא בעזה"י דאין לחלק בזה מהא דיומא ל"ג ע"ב בתוד"ה עבורי מפירוש ר"א שמפרש מימרא דרבא לענין משמוש דחייב למשמש בשל יד בתחלה מחמת אין מעבירין אף דלענין משמוש קי"ל דאין לברך על המשמוש כי לא נסתלק עדיין מהמצוה וכ"ש בעניינו וא"ל דשם קאי לפי דינא דגמרא דבזמנם היו מברכין על המשמוש ז"א דבעל המימרא דשם הוא רבא ורבא בעצמו סבירא ליה בסוכה מ"ו ע"א דאין לברך על המשמוש ואין לומר דר"א יסבור כמו שרוצה הב"י בסוף הסימן לאמר לדעת הרמב"ם דלהכי השמיט הרמב"ם האי דינא דמשמוש דס"ל דדוקא אם נסתלקו ממקומן ורוצה להחזירם דזה הוא הנחה מחדש ממש ולא פליגי כלל רבא ורבנן דבי ר"א ע"ש דז"א דע"כ הר"א לא ס"ל כן דא"כ ישאר קושית התוספות במקומה כמו שמקשים על רש"י דלמה צריך רבא לאמר ש"מ מדר"ל והלא מקרא נפקא מתחלה וקשרתם והדר ולטוטפות אלא ודאי דלהר"א ע"כ דרבא ס"ל דזה לא מיקרי הנחה או דהר"א ס"ל דמשמוש מיקרי אפילו לא נסתלקו ממנו וכאידך פוסקים ואפ"ה ס"ל לרבא דשייך בזה אין מעבירין אלא ודאי כדכתבינן דאין לחלק בזה: * מי שהוא זהיר וכו'. ר"ל כי כתוב בזוהר שמצוה לילך מפתח ביתו בציצית

באר היטב

על הפתחים כדי לקנות תפילין וציצית תנינא בירושלמי דפאה דאינו מחויב ע"ש ע"ת: (ב) בטלית גדול. ואז אפי' בא לידו הטלית קודם שהניח תפילין א"צ להתעטף בו בביתו כיון שאין דעתו ללבשו כאן מ"א. ועיין הרדב"ז סימן ל"ו. כתב בתשובת מהר"ם מלובלין סימן ל"ד א' נתקשר עצמו בקנס לילך לתהלים קודם אור הבוקר ועתה רוצה לחזור בו מפני שאינו יכול לילך לבהכ"נ בציצית ותפילין הרשות בידו

משנה ברורה

(ד) ויצטרך להניחם. נ"ל פשוט דאם מתפלל בביתו ורוצה להניח טלית ותפילין ובתוך חדר שלפניו מונח התפילין ובתוך חדר אחר מונח הטלית צריך להניח תפלין ברישא כדי שלא יעבור על המצות אחרי דהתפלין מזומנין לפניו תחלה ואף שלא נטל עדיין התפלין בידו [וראיה מהא דיומא ל"ג ע"ב בגמרא וכי עייל להיכל וכו' עיי"ש]: (ה) קודם הטלית. ואם עבר והניחם מידו ונטל הטלית (ה) שוב אסור לעזבו וליטול התפילין: (ו) ואין לו ציצית. אפילו הוא הולך בלי ד' כנפות וכ"ש לפי מנהגנו דכל אחד זהיר בט"ק: (ז) אין צריך. מפני שאין משהין את המצוה (ו) אע"פ שי"ל שיעשה אח"כ יותר מן המובחר מצוה בשעתא חביבא וכן (ז) בתדיר ושאינו תדיר דקי"ל דתדיר קודם אם אין התדיר לפניו א"צ להמתין: **ב** (ח) בביתו. כדי שילא (ח) מפתח ביתו בציצית ותפילין וכמו שהביא הב"י והד"מ בשם הזוהר עי"ש שהוא ענין גדול. ואם יודע שילך דרך מבואות המטונפות או שמצויין נכרים ברחוב (ט) יניחם בחצר בית הכנסת ואם (י) אי אפשר יניחם בביתו ויכסם בכובעו או בידו. ועיין (יא) באחרונים שכתבו במשכים קודם אור הבוקר ובא לבהכ"נ לא שייך אזהרת הזוהר דעדיין לא מטי זמן חיובא. ומ"מ כשיאור היום יותר טוב שילא לחצר בהכ"נ וילבשם שם ויכנס אח"כ לבהכ"נ: (ט) ושם יתעטף. ואע"פ (יב) שבא הט"ג לידו קודם שהניח התפילין א"צ להתעטף בו בביתו כיון שאין דעתו ללבשו כאן: (י) להתעטף. ובמקום שמצויין נכרים ברחוב (יג) יתעטף בחצר בית הכנסת אם אפשר לו: (יא) ולברך עליו. פי' ברכת להתעטף ויכוין לפטור בברכה זו גם הט"ק וכדלעיל בסימן ח' סעיף י"ד עי"ש במ"ב סקכ"ד: ג (יב) ואז היה וכו'. כדי ליתן שבח והודאה בברכה זו גם על התפילין שנקראין פאר שנאמר פארך חבוש עליך וקאי גם על תפלין שהן פאר לישראל כמו שנאמר וראו כל עמי הארץ וגו' ויראו ממך ודרשינן אלו תפילין שבראש: (יג) ומברך עוטר וכו'. ובארה"ח כתב לא ראיתי שנוהגין כן רק מניחין תפלין קודם ברכת השחר או אח"כ כ"א לפי מנהגו רק ראיתי מדקדקים למשמש בתש"י ובש"ר בשעה שמברך ברכה זו: ד (יד) בשעת ק"ש ותפלה. ר"ל לכל הפחות בשעת ק"ש ותפלה וכדלקמן בסימן ל"ז ס"ב ואמרינן בגמרא כל הקורא ק"ש בלי תפלין הרי הוא כאלו מעיד עדות שקר בעצמו ח"ו ופירשו בתוספות לפי שאומר וקשרתם לאות וגו' ואין קושר ואף שבדיעבד יצא ידי ק"ש מ"מ יש לו עבירה תגד אחר שמראה על עצמו שאין רוצה לקיים רצון הש"י והו עדות שקר שמעיד על עצמו ויש עוד פי' אחר עיין בלבוש וכתב בספר חרדים דמזה נלמוד כשאומר ואהבת את ד' וגו' יראה להכניס אהבת הש"י בלבו שלא יהיה כדובר שקר ח"ו. ודע דלא אמרו כן אלא כשעושה כן במזיד שמתעצל להניח תפלין קודם ק"ש אבל מי שאין לו תפלין או כשהוא בדרך ומתמת קור וכיוצא אינו יכול להניח תפלין וכל כה"ג בודאי אין לו לאחר ק"ש במגה מחמת זה. לבוש בסימן כ"ח והעתקתי שם את לשונו עי"ש: ה (טו) יכוין בהנחתם

שער הציון

(ה) פשוט: (ו) מ"א: (ז) פמ"ג: (ח) מ"א: (ט) מ"א: (י) ארה"ח: (יא) א"ר ופמ"ג וארה"ח: (יב) מ"א וארה"ח: (יג) מ"א:

first. /If they do so/ (4) they will have to don them (5) before /putting on/ the *talis*, in order not to bypass the mitzvah.

Gloss: However, if one has tefilin *ready at hand* (6) *and does not have /a* talis *with/* tzitzis */attached/,* (7) *he does not need to wait for /a* talis *with/* tzitzis */attached to be brought/, but should don the* tefilin. *When the* talis *is brought he should wrap /himself in/ it /then/. (...)*

2. Someone who is careful to /wear/ the small *talis*[2*] should put on /the small *talis*/ and don *tefilin* (8) at home. He should /then/ go to the Synagogue wearing /the small *talis* with its/ *tzitzis* /attached/ and crowned with *tefilin*. (9) There, he should wrap himself in the large *talis*.

Gloss: The public have adopted the practice (10) *of wrapping themselves /at*

Mishnah Berurah

(4) **They will have to don them.** If one prays at home and wishes to don a *talis* and *tefilin*, the *tefilin* may be lying in the room in front of him, /whereas/ the *talis* is lying in a different room. It seems to me self-understood that even if he did not yet take the *tefilin* in his hand, he is required to don the *tefilin* first, so as not to bypass mitzvos, since the *tefilin* are ready in front of him /and are encountered by him/ first. [There is proof /of this/ from what /is stated/ in the Gemara in *Yoma* 33b, "When he goes to the Sanctuary, etc."; see there.]

(5) **Before the *talis*.** If one transgressed /in such a case/ and released /the *tefilin*/ from his hand and took up the *talis*, he is thenceforth forbidden to leave /the *talis*/ and take up the *tefilin*.

(6) **And does not have *tzitzis*.** /This ruling applies/ even if one is going about without the /small/ four-cornered /*talis*/. It certainly /applies/ according to our practice, whereby everybody is careful to /wear/ the small *talis*.

(7) **He does not need.** This is because one should not delay /the performance of/ a mitzvah. Even though there are grounds for arguing that one will /be able to/ perform /the mitzvah/ subsequently in a more choice /manner, the performance of/ a mitzvah is /nevertheless/ more cherished /when it is done/ at the time when /the mitzvah arises/.

/This reasoning applies/ likewise when /one must perform a mitzvah/ which is recurrent and /another mitzvah/ which is not /so/ recurrent, in which case we rule that the /more/ recurrent /mitzvah/ has precedence. One does not need to wait /because of this before he performs the less recurrent mitzvah/, if the /requirements of the more/ recurrent /mitzvah/ are not in front of him /then/.

(8) **At home.** /The purpose of this is/ so that he should leave the entrance of his home /wearing a *talis* with/ *tzitzis* /attached/ and *tefilin*. It accords with what the *B.Y.* and the *D.M.* quote from the *Zohar*; see there that this is an important matter.

If one knows that he will be going through dirty alleyways or if there are non-Jews to be found in the street, he should put them on in the courtyard of the Synagogue. If this is impossible, he should don them at home and cover them with his hat or his hand.

See the Acharonim, who write that if one rises early before the morning light and comes to the Synagogue /then/, the admonition of the *Zohar* is not applicable, since /he arrives there when/ the time /for the fulfillment/ of the obligation has not yet arrived. Nevertheless, when the day lights up, it is preferable /for him/ to go out into the courtyard of the Synagogue and put them on there and enter the Synagogue afterwards.

(9) **There, he should wrap himself.** Even if the large *talis* comes into his hand before he has donned the *tefilin*, he does not need to wrap himself in it at home, since he does not intend to put it on there.

(10) **Of wrapping themselves.** In a locality where non-Jews are to be found in the street, one should wrap himself /in the large *talis*/ in the courtyard of the Synagogue if he is able.

2* See Sec. 24, Par. 1.

בהם תחלה (ד) * ויצטרך להניחם (ה) קודם הטלית כדי שלא יעבור על המצוה: הגה מיהו אם תפילין מזומנים בידו (ו) ואין לו ציצית (ז) אין צריך להמתין על הציצית אלא מניח תפילין וכשמביאים טלית מתעטף (דברי עצמו): **ב** * גמי שהוא זהיר בטלית קטן ילבשנו ויניח תפלין (ח) בביתו וילך לבוש בציצית ומוכתר בתפילין לבית הכנסת (ט) ושם יתעטף (ג) [נ] בטלית גדול: הגה והעולם נהגו (י) להתעטף אף בטלית גדול קודם (יא) ולברך עליו ואח"כ מניח התפילין והולך לבהכ"נ: **ג** דהרא"ש היה מסדר הברכות עד עוטר ישראל בתפארה (יב) ואז היה מניח תפילין (יג) ומברך עוטר ישראל בתפארה: **ד** הצריך שיהיו תפילין עליו (יד) בשעת ק"ש ותפלה: **ה** (טו) ויכוין בהנחתם שצונו

ג זוהר פרשת ואתחנן ד טור ה ברכות י"ד ו ר' יונה פ"ה שם

שערי תשובה

משה שמי שאין ידו משגת לקנות תש"י ותפילין של ראש יקנה של ראש תחלה ע"ש: [נ] בטלית גדול. עבה"ט ובבר"י כתב בשם תשו' מהר"י מולכין כ"י מי שהיה מונח בכיסו טלית של חול ותפילין וטלית של שבת היה למעלה מכל אם יכול להעביר על של שבת וליקח של חול והביא מתוספות דיומא דף ל"ג דלא שייך אין מעבירין כו' אלא כי בעי למעבד תרווייהו ושוב דחה זאת. והבר"י כתב ללמוד מדברי המג"א אלו שהביא הבה"ט דה"ה בזה יכול להעביר על של שבת וליקח את של חול ע"ש. וגם כתב שלדעת האר"י ז"ל אף שהוא

ביאור הלכה

בזה משום חשש דמעביר על המצות אבל כ"ז אין שייך לדינא דהא לדעת המחבר דנקטינן כוותיה וכן פסקו כמעט כל האחרונים [הלבוש והב"ח והט"ז והנ"א והארה"ח דלא כמ"א] אין חילוק בזה שהוא סובר דאפילו אם התפלין מונחין בתוך כיסן שייך בזה אין מעבירין. ובאמת פשוט הוא לענ"ד דגם המ"א מודה בזה ודלא כהפמ"ג דעד כאן לא קשרי המ"א אלא היכא שהתפלין מונחין בכיס בפ"ע שלא נגע בהן כלל בידו רק ע"י כיס וא"א להניחן ע"י כיס משא"כ בזה שהם ממש בידו או שלפי הושטת ידו הם מזומנין לפניו תחלה מה יועיל במה שהם עדיין בתוך הכיס וראיה לדברינו ממ"ש המ"א בעצמו לקמן בסימן כ"ח ס"ק ד' דמש"כ המחבר ועליו של יד פירושו שיתנו קצת לצד מעלה הרי דצריך ליתנו לצד מעלה כדי שיפגע בהם תחלה ולהפמ"ג אין צריך לזה רק שיתן סימן בכריכת הרצועות כדי שיבחין בהם בנגיעתו גם איזו ש"י ואיזו ש"ר ולא יוציא הש"ר תחלה מהתיק וכמ"ש במש"ז אות י' ויש ליישב לדידיה דכוונת הש"ע כדי שלא ישכח ויוציא הש"ר מהתיק ודוחק ואולי זהו כוונת הפמ"ג בעצמו מה שנשאר בצ"ע מלקמן סימן כ"ח סק"ד במ"א. ואולם כ"ז אין נ"מ לדינא לדידן דפסקינן בלא"ה דלא כמ"א אפילו אם הם מונחין בתוך כיסן. היוצא מדברינו דאם הושיט ידו בתוך כיס הטלית ופגע קודם בהתפלין מחויב להוציאן קודם ולהניחן משום אין מעבירין על המצות וכן לענין תפלין יש לו ליזהר לכתחלה להיות מונח הש"י קצת לצד מעלה ולא בשוה ממש כדי שלא לפגוע בתוך הכיס בהשל ראש בתחלה כדי שלא יעבור על הדין דאין מעבירין: * ויצטרך להניחם. לכאורה יש לעיין אם פשט הטלית ותפלין רק לפי שעה ודעתו להחזירם תיכף דפסקינן לקמן דאין צריך לחזור ולברך ואח"כ בעת לבישה נזדמן לו התפלין מקודם אם מחויב להניחן תחלה דאולי כיון דלא הסיח דעתו אפשר כאלו הוא עוסק עדיין בהמצוה ופשיטא בעזה"י דאין לחלק בזה מהא דיומא ל"ג ע"ב בתוד"ה עבורי מפירוש ר"א שמפרש מימרא דרבא לענין משמוש דחייב למשמש בשל יד בתחלה מחמת אין מעבירין אף דלענין משמוש קי"ל דאין לברך על המשמוש כי לא נסתלק עדיין מהמצוה וכ"ש בענינינו וא"ל דשם קאי לפי דינא דגמרא דבזמנם היו מברכין על המשמוש ז"א דבעל המימרא דשם הוא רבא ורבא בעצמו סבירא ליה בסוכה מ"ו ע"א דאין לברך על המשמוש ואין לומר דר"א יסבור כמו שרוצה הב"י בסוף הסימן לאמר לדעת הרמב"ם דלהכי השמיט הרמב"ם האי דינא דמשמוש דס"ל דדוקא אם נסתלקו ממקומן ורוצה להחזירם דזה הוא הנחה מחדש ממש ולא פליגי כלל רבא ורבנן דבי ר"א ע"ש דז"א דע"כ הר"א לא ס"ל כן דא"כ ישאר קושית התוספות במקומה כמו שמקשים על רש"י דלמה צריך רבא לאמר ש"ת מדר"ל והלא מקרא נפקא מתחלה וקשרתם והדר ולטוטפות אלא ודאי דלהר"א ע"כ דרבא ס"ל דזה לא מיקרי הנחה או דהר"א ס"ל דמשמוש מיקרי אפילו לא נסתלקו ממנו וכאידך פוסקים ואפ"ה ס"ל לרבא דשייך בזה אין מעבירין אלא ודאי כדכתבינן דאין לחלק בזה: * מי שהוא זהיר וכו'. ר"ל כי כתוב בזוהר שמצוה לילך מפתח ביתו בציצית

באר היטב

על הפתחים כדי לקנות תפילין וציצית תנינא בירושלמי דפאה דאינו מחויב ע"ש ע"ת: (ג) בטלית גדול. ואז אפי' בא לידו הטלית קודם שהניח תפילין א"צ להתעטף בו בביתו כיון שאין דעתו ללבשו כאן מ"א. ועיין הרדב"ז סימן ל"ו. כתב בתשובת מהר"ס מלובלין סימן ל"ד א' נתקשר עצמו בקנס לילך לתהלים קודם אור הבוקר ועתה רוצה לחזור בו מפני שאינו יכול לילך לבהכ"נ בציצית ותפילין הרשות בידו

משנה ברורה

(ד) ויצטרך להניחם. נ"ל פשוט דאם מתפלל בביתו ורוצה להניח טלית ותפילין ובתוך חדר שלפניו מונח התפילין ובתוך חדר אחר מונח הטלית צריך להניח תפלין בראשונה כדי שלא יעבור על המצות אחרי דהתפלין מזומנין לפניו תחלה ואף שלא נטל עדיין התפלין בידו [וראיה מהא דיומא ל"ג ע"ב בגמרא וכי עייל להיכל וכו' עיי"ש]: (ה) קודם הטלית. ואם עבר והניחם מידו ונטל הטלית (ה) שוב אסור לעזבו וליטול התפילין: (ו) ואין לו ציצית. אפילו הוא הולך בלי ד' כנפות וכ"ש לפי מנהגנו דכל אחד זהיר בט"ק: (ז) אין צריך. מפני שאין משהין את המצוה (ו) אע"פ שי"ל שיעשה אח"כ יותר מן המובחר מצוה כשעתא תיבא וכן (ז) בתדיר ושאינו תדיר דקי"ל דתדיר קודם אם אין התדיר לפניו א"צ להמתין: ב (ח) בביתו. כדי שילא (ח) מפתח ביתו בציצית ותפילין וכמו שהביא הב"י והד"מ בשם הזוהר עי"ש שהוא ענין גדול. ואם יודע שילך דרך מבואות המטונפות או שמצויין נכרים ברחוב (ט) יניחם בחצר בית הכנסת ואם (י) אי אפשר יניחם בביתו ויכסם בכובעו או בידו. ועיין (יא) באחרונים שכתבו במשכים קודם אור הבוקר ובא לבהכ"נ לא שייך אזהרת הזוהר דעדיין לא מטי זמן מיובא. ומ"מ כשיאור היום יותר טוב שיצא לחצר בהכ"נ וילבשם שם ויכנס אח"כ לבהכ"נ: (ט) ושם יתעטף. ואע"פ (יב) שבא הט"ג לידו קודם שהניח התפילין א"צ להתעטף בו בביתו כיון שאין דעתו ללבשו כאן: (י) להתעטף. ובמקום שמצויין נכרים ברחוב (יג) יתעטף בחצר בית הכנסת אם אפשר לו: (יא) ולברך עליו. פי' ברכת להתעטף ויכוין לפטור בברכה זו גם הט"ק וכדלעיל בסימן ח' סעיף י"ד עי"ש במ"ב סקכ"ד: ג (יב) ואז היה וכו'. כדי ליתן שבח והודאה בברכה זו גם על התפילין שנקראין פאר שנאמר פארך חבוש עליך וקאי גם על תפלין שהן פאר לישראל כמו שנאמר וראו כל עמי הארץ וגו' ויראו ממך ודרשינן אלו תפילין שבראש: (יג) ומברך עוטר וכו'. ובארה"ח כתב לא ראיתי שנוהגין כן רק מניחין תפלין קודם ברכת השחר או אח"כ כ"א לפי מנהגו רק ראיתי מדקדקים למשמש בתש"י וש"ר בשעה שמברך ברכה זו: ד (יד) בשעת ק"ש ותפלה. ר"ל לכל הפחות בשעת ק"ש ותפלה וכדלקמן בסימן ל"ז ס"ב ואמרינן בגמרא כל הקורא ק"ש בלי תפלין הרי הוא כאלו מעיד עדות שקר בעצמו ח"ו ופירשו בתוספות לפי שאומר וקשרתם לאות וגו' ואין קושר ואף שבדיעבד יצא ידי ק"ש מ"מ יש לו עבירה מצד אחר שמראה על עצמו שאין רוצה לקיים רצון הש"י וזהו עדות שקר שמעיד על עצמו ויש עוד פי' אחר עיין בלבוש וכתב בספר חרדים דמזה נלמוד כשאומר ואהבת את ד' וגו' יראה להכניס אהבת הש"י בלבו שלא יהיה כדובר שקר ח"ו. ודע דלא אמרו כן אלא כשעושה כן במזיד שמתעצל להניח תפלין קודם ק"ש אבל מי שאין לו תפלין או כשהוא בדרך ומחמת קור וצינה אינו יכול להניח תפלין וכל כה"ג בודאי אין לו לאחר ק"ש בזמנה מחמת זה. לבוש בסימן נ"ח והעתקתי שם את לשונו עי"ש: ה (טו) יכוין

בהנחתם

שער הציון

(ה) פשוט: (ו) מ"א: (ז) פמ"ג: (ח) מ"א: (ט) מ"א: (י) ארה"ח: (יא) א"ר ופמ"ג וארה"ח: (יב) מ"א וארה"ח: (יג) מ"א:

home/ in the large talis *as well before /they don* tefilin/ **(11)** *and to make the blessing over it. After that they don* tefilin *and go to the Synagogue.*
3. The *Rosh* would say the /morning/ blessings in order until /he reached the blessing/ *Oteyr Yisra'eyl Be-Sif'arah* (Who crowns Israel with glory). **(12)** Then he would don *tefilin* **(13)** and say the blessing *Oteyr Yisra'eyl Be-Sif'arah.*
4. The *tefilin* must be on one **(14)** when /he reads/ "The Reading of Shema" and /prays the eighteen-blessing/prayer.
5. **(15)** When one dons /*tefilin*/, he should have in mind that the Holy One,

Mishnah Berurah

(11) And to make the blessing over it. I.e., the blessing *Lehisateyf.*

One should have in mind to discharge /his obligation/ by means of this blessing also /as regards the making of a blessing over/ the small *talis.* This is /explained/ above in Sec. 8, Par. 10; see there in the Mishnah Berurah, sub-Par. 24.

(12) Then he would, etc. /He did so/ in order to give praise and thanks by means of this blessing for the *tefilin* as well.

/*Tefilin*/ are described as "a glory" as it is stated,[2] "You should be attired with your glory". (This also refers to *tefilin*, which are a glory to Israel, as /we see/ from the statement,[3] "All the peoples of the earth will see, etc. and they will fear you", which was interpreted /by the Sages/ as /a reference to/ the *tefilin* on one's head.)

(13) And say the blessing *Oteyr*, etc. /The author of/ the *Ar.Hach.* writes, "I have not seen /people/ acting in this way. They only don *tefilin* before /saying/ the morning blessings or subsequently, each one /acting/ according to the practice to which he /is accustomed/. I have merely seen people being careful to handle the arm *tefilin* and head /*tefilin*/ when they say this blessing".

(14) When /he reads/ "The Reading of Shema" and /prays the eighteen-blessing/ prayer. What is meant is /that the *tefilin* should/ at least /be on one/ when /he reads/ "The Reading of Shema" and /prays the eighteen-blessing/ prayer, as /stated/ below in Sec. 37, Par. 2.

/This is because/ it is stated in the Gemara[4] that whenever one reads "The Reading of Shema" without /wearing/ *tefilin* it is as if he testifies false witness against himself, Heaven forfend. The *Tosafos* explain that it is because he says וּקְשַׁרְתָּם לְאוֹת וגו' (and you shall bind them for a sign), /whereas/ he does not /in fact/ bind /them/. Although once it is after the event he will have fulfilled /his obligation/ as regards /the reading of/ "The Reading of Shema", he nevertheless /transgresses/ a transgression from a different angle, since he shows himself unwilling to fufill the Will of *Ha-Sheym*, may He be blessed. This is the false witness that one testifies of himself /if he reads "The Reading of Shema" without wearing *tefilin*/. There is another explanation /of this/; see the *Levush.*

/The author of/ the *Sefer Ha-Chareydim* writes that one can deduce from this that when one says וְאָהַבְתָּ אֵת ד' וגו' (and you should love the Lord), he should see that he introduces the love of *Ha-Sheym*, may He be blessed, into his heart, so that he should not be like a speaker of falsehood, Heaven forfend.

Note that the Sages /of the Gemara/ only made this statement with reference to /an instance/ when one does it in deliberate transgression, being /simply/ neglectful about the donning of *tefilin* before /he reads/ "The Reading of Shema". However, if someone does not have *tefilin* or he is on the road and due to the cold and the chill he is unable to don *tefilin* (or if there are any similar circumstances /because of which he cannot don *tefilin*/), he should definitely not delay, because of this, reading "The Reading of Shema" in its /proper/ time. *Levush* in Sec. 58. There I have quoted his wording; see there.

(15) When one dons /*tefilin*/ he should

2 *Yechezkeyl* 24:17.
3 *Devarim* 28:10. The full verse reads, "All the peoples of the earth will see that the Name of the Lord is readable on you and they will fear you".
4 *Berachos* 14b.

הקב"ה (טז) להניח ארבע פרשיות אלו שיש בהם יחוד שמו ויציאת מצרים על הזרוע כנגד הלב ועל הראש כנגד המוח כדי שנזכור נסים ונפלאות שעשה עמנו שהם מורים על יחודו ואשר לו הכח והממשלה בעליונים ובתחתונים לעשות בהם כרצונו וישתעבד[א] להקב"ה הנשמה שהיא במוח וגם הלב שהוא עיקר התאוות והמחשבות ובזה יזכור הבורא וימעיט הנאותיו [ז]ויניח של יד (ג) [ג] (יז) תחלה (יח) ויברך (ד) [ד] להניח (יט) תפילין ואח"כ יניח של ראש [ח]ולא יברך כ"א ברכה אחת לשתיהם: הגה וי"א לברך על של ראש (כ) על מצות תפילין אפילו לא הפסיק בינתיים (הרא"ש הלכות תפילין) (וכן פשט המנהג בבני אשכנז שמברכין (ה) [ה] שתי ברכות (כא) * וטוב לומר תמיד אחר הברכה השניה ברוך שם כבוד מלכותו לעולם ועד) (מהר"י בן חביב אגור סימן ל"ח): ו [ט]אם (כב) * פגע בשל

ז מנחות ל"ו ח לפירוש רש"י והרי"ף והרמב"ם ותשובת הרשב"א ט תוספות במנחות ל"ה וביומא ל"ג

באר היטב

לחזור דדמי לנדרי שגגה. וכ"ה בכוונת שמה"ט לא היה האר"י מיו"ד ראשונים מפני שהם היו משכימים קודם אור הבוקר והוא לא רצה לילך לביהכ"נ בלא תפילין. וא"ל ה"ל לצאת מבהכ"נ כשיאיר היום ויניח תפילין י"ל דאדהכי והכי יגמרו הקהל ברכות השחר לכן מוטב לבטולי האי מקמי האי וכתב המ"ג וכ"ל דצריך התרה. ועיין בתשובת נחלת שבעה סי' ו' (ובספר אליהו רבה מביא בשם כנה"ג דאפי' כשיש מבואות מטונפות יניחם בביתו ויכסה התפילין. וכן משמע בתשובת מ"ע סימן נ"ט ובזוהר פ' ואתחנן ופ' שלח לך): (ג) תחלה. עיין הרמ"ע מפאנו סי' ק"כ ובתשובת דרכי נועם חלק א"ח סי' ג' שהאריך אם ברכות תפילין צריך להיות מעומד: (ד) להניח תפילין. הלמ"ד בדג"ש ל"ת. ועל מצות יש לברך הוא"ו בפת"ח ל"ח אות כ"ו וכ"כ המ"א. אבל הט"ז כתב בשם אחיו הר"י הלוי שיאמר הוא"ו בחולם לשון רבים דהוי תרי מצות דקאי אתרוייהו על של ראש ושל יד דאית בש"ס תפלה של יד אינו מעכב ש"ר וש"ר אינה מעכבת של יד מוכח מזה דב' מצות הם דאי הוי מצוה א' היו מעכבות זו את זו כדתנן גבי ציצית ד' ציצית מעכבות זו את זה מפני שהם מצוה אחת למדין מזה גבי ציצית מברך מצות ציצית בפת"ח מפני שהן מצוה אחת. ובתפילין מברך מצות בחולם שהן ב' מצות. וה"ה נמי אם אין לו אלא של ראש לבד יברך בפת"ח ע"ש: (ה) שתי ברכות. עיין הלק"ט ח"א

שערי תשובה

לבוש ט"ק יש ללבוש גם טלית גדול קודם התפילין ע"ש: [ג] תחלה. עבה"ט ומי שנוהג להניח של יד מיושב וש"ר מעומד כדעת האר"י ז"ל כתב בדרכי נועם שם כיון דלענין דינא נמי אין חובה לברך ברכת תפילין מעומד ולכן אינו רשאי להחמיר לברך מעומד שלדעת המקובלים הנכון להיות מיושב: [ד] להניח. עבה"ט במג"א מייתי מקרא דמצות ה' ברה. עיין בהגהת תוספות שבת ובשער יוסף על הוריות מ"ש שם בדף כ"ו ובשו"ת חינוך ב"י סי' א' ע"ש: [ה] שתי ברכות. עיין בה"ט. וכתב במחזיק ברכה מי שטעה ובירך על תפילין של יד על מצות תפילין יצא. ואם הוא מבני אשכנז אם נזכר קודם ההידוק מברך להניח קודם הידוק ג"כ ועל של ראש מברך על מצות כ"כ מהר"ש ווינטורה. ובמכתם לדוד חלק עליו וכתב שבבני אשכנז אם נזכר קודם ההידוק יברך להניח ובש"ר לא יברך כלל ואם לא נזכר יברך כשמניח של ראש

משנה ברורה

בהנחתם. כתב הב"ח בסימן ח' טעם לזה מדכתיב והיה לך לאות על ידך וגו' למען תהיה תורת ד' בפיך כי ביד חזקה הוציאך וגו' יורה כי עיקר המצוה וקיומה תלויה בכונה שיכוין בשעת קיום המצוה וכתב הפמ"ג דמ"מ בדיעבד אפילו אם לא כיון רק לשם מצוה בלבד יצא: (טז) להניח ד' פרשיות. (יד) ויש נוהגים מחמת זה לקרות הארבע פרשיות לאחר הנחת תפלין היינו קדש והיה כי יביאך דשמע והיה אם שמוע בלא"ה קורין כל ישראל בשעת ק"ש. ובתפלין דר"ת יאמר כל הד' פרשיות. ומנהג יפה הוא [ארה"ח]: (יז) תחלה. (טו) דכתיב וקשרתם וגו' והדר והיו לטוטפות וגו': (יח) ויברך. ר"ל קודם ההידוק וכדלקמן: (יט) תפילין. הלמ"ד (טז) בדגש: (כ) על מצות. בפת"ח תחת הוא"ו שהוא לשון יחיד ולא יאמר בחול"ם שהוא לשון רבים שהרי לא ניתקנה ברכה זו כ"א לתש"ר בלבד כמו שיתבאר בסימן כ"ו [כן הכריעו (יז) רוב האחרונים דלא כט"ז]: (כא) וטוב לומר. משום חשש ספק ברכה לבטלה כמש"כ בסימן ר"ו ולא שהוא ספק גמור דא"כ איך יברך מספק ברכה לבטלה ויסמוך על שיאמר בשכמל"ו אלא דאנן בני אשכנז סבירא לן להלכה כדעת ר"ת רק (יח) לרווחא דמילתא להוציא עצמינו מידי כל פקפוק נוהגין לומר בשכמל"ו. ויזהר (יט) מאוד שלא לומר ברוך שם רק אחר שיהדק הש"ר על ראשו כראוי דאל"כ יהיה הפסק בין הברכה להנחה ויהיה ברכה זו לבטלה בודאי וצריך לחזור ולברך והעולם נכשלין בזה: ו (כב) פגע וכו'. דוקא פגע

ביאור הלכה

ותפלין וע"כ אם אינו זהיר בט"ק מוכרח ע"י זה ללבוש בביתו קודם התפלין הט"ג אבל אם הוא זהיר בט"ק יוכל לצאת כ"ז ע"י הטלית קטן והט"ג יוכל ללבשו בביהכנ"ס וכ"ש אם ירצה להתעטף גם בט"ג בביתו [מביאור הגר"א]:

* וטוב וכו'. עיין בביאור הגר"א שפסק כהמחבר ובחידושי רע"א כ' עצה שיכוין בעת ברכת להניח אם הלכה כשיטת רש"י אני מכוין שלא לצאת בברכת להניח על הש"ר והוי זה כסת ויוכל לברך על של ראש [ואין זה בכלל גורם ברכה שאינה צריכה דהא מוכרח לעשות כן מפני ספיקא דדינא ועוד טעמים אחרים כמו שכתב בארה"ח] וכבר קדמו העולת תמיד וכפי מה שביאר הפמ"ג את דבריו ובארה"ח משמע ג"כ שמסכים לעצה זו אך בפמ"ג ראיתי שמסיים ע"ז ואין לנהוג כן ואולי טעמו כדי שלא ירגיל האדם את עצמו לפקפק אחר מנהגן של ישראל שנתייסד ע"פ שיטות הרבה מהראשונים: * פגע וכו'. ע' במ"ב כן פסק הט"ז לקמן בסימן תרפ"ד סק"ד דלא כאבודרהם והעתיקו הגרע"א בחידושיו וכן פסק הפמ"ג וכן מוכח לכאורה מדברי הגר"א שם בסוף סי' תרפ"ד שם בסוף ס"ג שציין שם על דין הרמ"א משום דאין משגיחין בחנוכה ולא כתב טעם האבודרהם בעצמו [שהובא במ"א שם] ש"מ דבתפלין אם עבר והניח ש"ר אין צריך לסלקו. ובארה"ח ראיתי שמצדד לפסוק כאבודרהם משום דלכתחלה עשה עבירה ועבר על מה שאמרו דכל שבין עיניך יהיו שתים ע"כ צריך עתה לתקן ולהניח כדין ולא נהירא דהלא באמת קי"ל דהש"י אינו מעכב של ראש הרי דבעלם קיים בזה הש"ר מצותו רק דלא קיים המצוה כתיקונה וא"ל דיסלק הש"ר ויחזור ויניחו ויקיים עתה כתיקונו ז"א דהלא בכל רגע ורגע שהוא נושא התפילין עליו הוא מקיים בזה מצות הש"ת ובודאי אין לנו לומר שיסלק עתה המצוה ממנו כדי שאח"כ יקיים יותר מן המובחר וגדולה מזו אמרו ביבמות ל"ט ע"א דצריך הקטן לייבם ואין ממתינים בגדול עד שיבא ממדינת הים אף דבקרא כתיב והיה הבכור משום דכל שהוי מצוה לא משהינן אף דאם היינו ממתינין לא היינו מבטלין עי"ז העשה בידים רק בגדר שב ואל תעשה וכ"ש כאן שאין לנו לסלק המצוה בידים ממי שעושה אותה כדי שאח"כ יקיים מן המובחר וזה אין לחלק בין שהיה מרוצה לשהייה מועטת וראיה לזה ממג"א סק"ב ואף שמצאתי אח"כ ראיה להיפך והוא בסימן תכ"ו ס"ב בהג"ה ועי"ש בביאור הגר"א בשם תה"ד דמחלק בין ההיא דיבמות משום דהתם שאפשר לבוא לידי דיחוי חדא דגם ע"ז כבר ערערו הפוס' בתשובותיהם [והוא בתשובת עה"ג סימן י"ב ובתשובת פ"י חלק אה"ע סימן ט"ו ובקו"א לתשובת צ"צ סימן קכ"ו[ב]]. ועוד דשם הוא בגדר שב ואל תעשה משא"כ הכא לעקור ממנו העשה בידים נראה דכו"ע מודים בזה וגם ידוע הוא דהגר"א בעצמו הנהיג למהר בקידוש הלבנה ולא להמתין וכמו שכתב במע"ר. ע"כ נראה פשוט דהדין עם רבינו הט"ז וכמו שכתב הא"ר דמאי דהוי הוי וימהר להניח

שער הציון

(יד) ב"ח ושל"ה: (טו) גמרא: (טז) אחרונים: (יז) א"ר ודה"ח וארה"ח עי"ש שכתב כן בשם הרבה אחרונים ועיין בל"ש שהוכיח שהט"ז בעצמו חולק ג"כ על אחיו: (יח) א"ר: (יט) פמ"ג:

הגהות ותיקונים: א) וישעבד: ב) קכ"ז:

Blessed be He, commanded us **(16)** to place the /relevant/ four passages, which contain the uniqueness of His Name and the Exodus from Egypt, on the arm opposite the heart and on the head against the brain, so that we should remember the miracles and wonders which He performed for us. (/The miracles and wonders/ show his uniqueness and that He has the power and the dominion over /the inhabitants of/ the upper /world/ and /the inhabitants of/ the lower /world/ to do with them as He wishes.) /In view of this,/ one will subject to the Holy One, Blessed be He, /both/ the soul, which is /situated/ in the brain, and also the heart, which is the root of the desires and the thoughts. In this /manner/ one will remember the Creator and confine his indulgence.

One should don the arm */tefilin/* **(17)** first **(18)** and make the blessing *Lehaniach* **(19)** *Tefilin*. After that he should don the head */tefilin/*. He should only make one blessing over both of them.

Mishnah Berurah

have in mind. The *Bach* writes a reason in Sec. 8. /to explain from where we learn/ that this /is required/. /He notes/ that it is written,[5] "And it should be for you a sign on your arm, etc., in order that the Torah of the Lord shall be in your mouth, for with a strong arm He took you out, etc." This shows that the essence of the mitzvah and its fulfillment is dependent on application /, i.e./, that one should have in mind /the Torah and the Exodus, etc./ when he fulfils the mitzvah.

The *P.Mg.* writes that, nevertheless, once it is after the event, even if one merely had intent /to don them/ for the sake of the mitzvah only, he will have fulfilled /his obligation/.

(16) To place ... four passages. There are /people/ who are accustomed because of this to read the four passages after they have donned the *tefilin*. I.e., /they read in addition the passages/ *Kadesh* and *Ve-Hayah Ki Yevi'acha*, since /the passages/ *Shema* and *Ve-Haya Im Shamo'a* are in any case read by all Israel when /they read/ "The Reading of Shema".

When /one dons/ the *tefilin* /which accord with the view/ of Rabbeinu Tam, he should say all four passages. This is a commendable practice. [*Ar.Hach.*]

(17) First. For it is written,[6] "And you should bind, etc.", and /only/ after that, "And they should be for *tefilin*, etc."

(18) And make the blessing. I.e., before tightening, as /explained/ below /in Par. 8/.

(19) *Tefilin*. The /letter/ ל /in the word תְּפִלִּין/ has a *dagesh*.

5 *Shemos* 13:9.

6 *Devarim* 6:8. The full verse reads, "And you should bind them for a sign on your arm and they should be for *tefilin* between your eyes".

הקב"ה (טז) להניח ארבע פרשיות אלו שיש בהם יחוד שמו ויציאת מצרים על הזרוע כנגד הלב ועל הראש כנגד המוח כדי שנזכור נסים ונפלאות שעשה עמנו שהם מורים על יחודו ואשר לו הכח והממשלה בעליונים ובתחתונים לעשות בהם כרצונו וישתעבד[א] להקב"ה הנשמה שהיא במוח וגם הלב שהוא עיקר התאוות והמחשבות ובזה יזכור הבורא וימעיט הנאותיו: ז ויניח של יד (ג) [ג] (יז) תחלה (יח) ויברך (ד) [ד] להניח (יט) תפילין ואח"כ יניח של ראש ח ולא יברך כ"א ברכה אחת לשתיהם: הגה וי"א לברך על של ראש (כ) על מצות תפילין אפילו לא הפסיק בינתיים (הרא"ש הלכות תפילין) (וכן פשט המנהג בבני אשכנז שמברכין (ה) [ה] שתי ברכות (כא) * וטוב לומר תמיד אחר הברכה השניה ברוך שם כבוד מלכותו לעולם ועד) (מהר"י בן חביב אגור סימן ל"ח): ו ט אם (כב) * פגע בשל

ז מנחות ל"ו
ח לפירוש רש"י והרי"ף והרמב"ם ותשובת הרשב"א
ט תוספות במנחות ל"ה ויומא ל"ג

באר היטב

לחזור דדמי לנדרי שגגה. וכ"ה בכוונת שמה"ט לא היה האר"י מיו"ד ראשונים מפני שהם היו משכימים קודם אור הבוקר והוא לא רצה לילך לביהכ"נ בלא תפילין. וא"ל ה"ל לצאת מבהכ"נ כשיאיר היום ויניח תפילין י"ל דאדהכי והכי יגמרו הקהל ברכות השחר לכן מוטב לבטולי האי מקמי האי וכתב המ"ג וכ"ל דלריך התרה. ועיין בתשובת נחלת שבעה סי' ו' (ובספר אליהו רבה מביא בשם כנה"ג דאפי' כשיש מבואות מטונפות יניחם בביתו ויכסה התפילין. וכן משמע בתשובת מ"ע סימן כ"ט ובזוהר פ' ואתחנן ופ' שלח לך): (ג) תחלה. עיין הרמ"ע מפאנו סי' ק"כ ובתשובת דרכי נועם חלק א"ח סי' ג' שהאריך אם ברכות תפילין לריך להיות מעומד: (ד) להניח תפילין. הלמ"ד בדג"ש ל"ח. ועל מלות יש לברך הוא"ו בפת"ח ל"ח אות כ"ו וכ"כ המ"א. אבל הט"ז כתב בשם אחיו הר"י הלוי שיאמר הוא"ו בחולם לשון רבים דהוי תרי מלות דקאי אתרוייהו על של ראש ושל יד דאית בש"ס תפלה של יד אינו מעכב ש"ר וש"ר אינה מעכבת של יד מוכח מזה דב' מלות הם דאי הוי מלוה א' היו מעכבות זו את זו כדתנן גבי ליצית ד' ליצית מעכבות זה את זה מפני שהם מלוה אחת למדין מזה גבי ליצית מברך מלות ליצית בפת"ח מפני שהן מלוה אחת. ובתפילין מברך מלות בחולם שהן ב' מלות. וה"ה נמי אם אין לו אלא של ראש לבד יברך בפת"ח ע"ש: (ה) שתי ברכות. עיין הלק"ט ח"א

שערי תשובה

לבוש ט"ק יש ללבוש גם טלית גדול קודם התפילין ע"ש: [ג] תחלה. עבה"ט ומי שנוהג להניח של יד מיושב וש"ר מעומד כדעת האר"י ז"ל כתב בדרכי נועם שם כיון דלענין דינא נמי אין חובה לברך ברכת תפילין מעומד ולכן אינו רשאי להחמיר לברך מעומד שלדעת המקובלים הנכון להיות מיושב: [ד] להניח. עבה"ט במג"א מייתי מקרא דמלות ה' ברה. עיין בהגהת תוספות שבת ובשער יוסף על הוריות מ"ש שם בדף כ"ו ובשו"ת חינוך ב"י סי' א' ע"ש: [ה] שתי ברכות. עיין בה"ט. וכתב במחזיק ברכה מי שטעה ובירך על תפילין של יד על מלות תפילין יצא. ואם הוא מבני אשכנז אם נזכר קודם ההידוק מברך להניח קודם הידוק ג"כ ועל של ראש מברך על מלות כ"כ מהר"ש ווינטורה. ובמכתם לדוד חלק עליו וכתב שבבני אשכנז אם נזכר קודם ההידוק יברך להניח ובש"ר לא יברך כלל ואם לא נזכר יברך כשמניח של ראש

משנה ברורה

בהנחתם. כתב הב"ח בסימן ח' טעם לזה מדכתיב והיה לך לאות על ידך וגו' למען תהיה תורת ד' בפיך כי ביד חזקה הוליאך וגו' יורה כי עיקר המלוה וקיומה תלויה בכונה שיכוין בשעת קיום המלוה וכתב הפמ"ג דמ"מ בדיעבד אפילו אם לא כיון רק לשם מלוה בלבד יצא: (טז) להניח ד' פרשיות. (יד) ויש נוהגים מחמת זה לקרות הארבע פרשיות לאחר הנחת תפלין היינו קדש והיה כי יביאך ושמע והיה אם שמוע בלא"ה קורין כל ישראל בשעת ק"ש. ובתפלין דר"ת יאמר כל הד' פרשיות. ומנהג יפה הוא [א"ר"ת]: (יז) תחלה. (טו) דכתיב וקשרתם וגו' והדר והיו לטוטפות וגו': (יח) ויברך. ר"ל קודם ההידוק וכדלקמן: (יט) תפילין. הלמ"ד (טז) בדגש: (כ) על מצות. בפת"ח תחת הוא"ו שהוא לשון יחיד ולא יאמר בחול"ם שהוא לשון רבים שהרי לא ניתקנה ברכה זו כ"א לתש"ר בלבד כמו שיתבאר בסימן כ"ו [כן הכריעו (יז) רוב האחרונים דלא כט"ז]: (כא) וטוב לומר. משום חשש ספק ברכה לבטלה כמש"כ בסימן ר"ו ולא שהוא ספק גמור דא"כ איך יברך מספק ברכה לבטלה ויסמוך על שיאמר בשכמל"ו אלא דאנן בני אשכנז סבירא לן להלכה כדעת ר"ת רק (יח) לרווחא דמילתא להוציא עצמינו מידי כל פקפוק נוהגין לומר בשכמל"ו. ויזהר (יט) מאוד שלא לומר ברוך שם רק אחר שיהדק הש"ר על ראשו כראוי דאל"כ יהיה הפסק בין הברכה להנחה ויהיה ברכה זו לבטלה בודאי וצריך לחזור ולברך והעולם נכשלין בזה: ו (כב) פגע וכו'. דוקא פגע

ביאור הלכה

ותפלין וע"כ אם אינו זהיר בט"ק מוכרח ע"י זה ללבוש בביתו קודם התפלין הט"ג אבל אם הוא זהיר בט"ק יוכל לצאת כ"ז ע"י הטלית קטן והט"ג יוכל ללבשו בביהכנ"ס וכ"ש אם ירצה להתעטף גם בט"ג בביתו [מביאור הגר"א]:

* וטוב וכו'. עיין בביאור הגר"א שפסק כהמחבר ובחידושי רע"א כ' עלה שיכוין בעת ברכת להניח אם הלכה כשיטת רש"י אני מכוין שלא לצאת בברכת להניח על הש"ר והוי זה כפסק ויוכל לברך על של ראש [ואין זה בכלל גורם ברכה שאינה צריכה דהא מוכרח לעשות כן מפני ספיקא דדינא ועוד טעמים אחרים כמו שכתב בארה"ח] וכבר קדמו העולת תמיד וכפי מה שביאר הפמ"ג את דבריו ובארה"ח משמע ג"כ שמסכים לעצה זו אך בפמ"ג ראיתי שמסיים ע"ז ואין לנהוג כן ואולי טעמו כדי שלא ירגיל האדם את עצמו לפקפק אחר מנהגן של ישראל שנתייסד ע"פ שיטות הרבה מהראשונים: * פגע וכו'. ע' במ"ב כן פסק הט"ז לקמן בסימן תרפ"ד סק"ד דלא כאבודרהם והעתיקו הגרע"א בחידושיו וכן פסק הפמ"ג וכן מוכח לכאורה מדברי הגר"א שם בסוף סי' תרפ"ד שם בסוף ס"ג שציין שם על דין הרמ"א משום דאין משגיחין בחנוכה ולא כתב טעם האבודרהם בעצמו [שהובא במ"א שם] ש"מ דבתפלין אם עבר והניח ש"ר אין צריך לסלקו. ובארה"ח ראיתי שמלדד לפסוק כאבודרהם משום דלכתחלה עשה עבירה ועבר על מה שאמרו דכל שבין עיניך יהיו שתים ע"כ צריך עתה לתקן ולהניח כדין ולא נהירא דהלא באמת קי"ל דהש"י אינו מעכב של ראש הרי דבעלם קיים בזה הש"ר מצותו רק דלא קיים המצוה כתיקונה וא"ל דיסלק הש"ר ויחזור ויניחו ויקיים עתה כתיקונו ז"א דהלא בכל רגע ורגע שהוא נושא התפילין עליו הוא מקיים בזה מצות הש"ת ובודאי אין לנו לומר שיסלק עתה המצוה ממנו כדי שאח"כ יקיים יותר מן המובחר וגדולה מזו אמרו ביבמות ל"ט ע"א דצריך הקטן לייבם ואין ממתינים בגדול עד שיבא ממדינת הים אף דבקרא כתיב והיה הבכור משום דכל שהויי מצוה לא משהינן אף דאם היינו ממתינין לא היינו מבטלין עי"ז העשה בידים רק בגדר שב ואל תעשה וכ"ש כאן שאין לנו לסלק המצוה בידים ממי שעושה אותה כדי שאח"כ יקיים מן המובחר וזה אין לחלק בין שהייה מרובה לשהייה מועטת וראיה לזה ממג"א סק"ב ואף שמצאתי אח"כ ראיה להיפך והוא בסימן תכ"ו ס"ב בהג"ה ועי"ש בביאור הגר"א בשם תה"ד דמחלק בין ההיא דיבמות משום דהתם שאפשר לבוא לידי דיחוי חדא דגם ע"ז כבר ערערו הפוס' בתשובותיהם [והוא בתשובת עה"ג סימן י"ב ובתשובת פ"י חלק אה"ע סימן ט"ו ובקו"א לתשובת צ"צ סימן קכ"ו[ב]]. ועוד דשם הוא בגדר שב ואל תעשה משא"כ הכא לעקור ממנו העשה בידים נראה דכו"ע מודים בזה וגם ידוע הוא דהגר"א בעצמו הנהיג למהר בקידוש הלבנה ולא להמתין וכמו שכתב במע"ר. ע"כ נראה פשוט דהדין עם רבינו הט"ז וכמו שכתב הא"ר דמאי דהוי הוי וימהר להניח

שער הציון

(יד) ב"ח ושל"ה: (טו) גמרא: (טז) אחרונים: (יז) א"ר ודה"ח וארה"ח עי"ש שכתב כן בשם הרבה אחרונים ועיין בל"ש שהוכיח שהט"ז בעצמו חולק ג"כ על אחיו: (יח) א"ר: (יט) פמ"ג:

הגהות ותיקונים: א) וישעבד: ב) קכ"ז:

*Gloss: There are /authorities/ who say that /, in addition,/ one should make over the head /*tefilin*/ the blessing* **(20)** Al Mitzvas Tefilin, *even if he did not make an interruption in between /the donning of the arm* tefilin *and the donning of the head* tefilin*/. (...) (It has in fact become the practice among the Ashkenazic community to make the two blessings.* **(21)** *It is desirable to say always after the second blessing* בָּרוּךְ שֵׁם כְּבוֹד מַלְכוּתוֹ לְעוֹלָם וָעֶד*.) (...)*

6. If /when about to don the *tefilin*/ **(22)** one encountered the head

Mishnah Berurah

(20) ***Al Mitzvas***. /The word מִצְוַת/ has a *pasach* (ַ) underneath the /letter/ ו, which is the singular form. One should not say /the word/ with a cholam (וֹ),[7] which is the plural form, since this blessing was ordained /to be made/ over the head *tefilin* alone, as explained /below/ in Sec. 26. [This is the decision of most of the Acharonim, in contradiction to /the view of/ the *Taz*.]

(21) It is desirable to say. This is because of the fear that one may have /said/ a vain blessing. /When one has in fact said a vain blessing he is required to say this verse,/ as stated in Sec. 206 /, Par. 6/.

/One should/ not /conclude/ that this is /considered/ fully a /case where there is a/ doubt /as to whether or not the blessing should be said/. If /this would be/ so /, then/, in view of the possibility that it may be a vain blessing, one could not /be allowed to/ say the blessing and rely on the /subsequent/ saying of בָּרוּךְ שֵׁם כְּבוֹד מַלְכוּתוֹ לְעוֹלָם וָעֶד. In actual fact, we, of the Ashkenazic community, are of the opinion that the halachic ruling conforms with the view of Rabbeinu Tam /, that this blessing should always be said over the head *tefilin*/. It is only our practice to say בָּרוּךְ שֵׁם כְּבוֹד מַלְכוּתוֹ לְעוֹלָם וָעֶד /because we wish/ to /fulfil our obligation/ comfortably by removing any question of our /conduct being incorrect/.

One should be very careful to say בָּרוּךְ שֵׁם /וכו'/ only after he has /already/ tightened the head *tefilin* on his head properly. Otherwise, it will be an interruption in between /the making of/ the blessing and the donning /of the *tefilin*, so that/ the blessing will definitely become a vain blessing and he will be required to make the blessing again. The public stumble over this.

(22) One encountered, etc. This only /applies/ when one /merely/ encountered /the head *tefilin* first/. However, if one

7 I.e., one should not say מִצְוֹות.

ראש תחלה צריך (כג) להעביר על אותה המצוה ויניח של יד תחלה ואח"כ של ראש: ז יברך (ו) [ו] (כד) להניח בקמץ תחת הה"א ולא בפתח ובדגש: ח כל המצות מברך עליהם עובר לעשייתן (פי' קודם. ויעבר את הכושי פירושו רץ והקדים לפניו) ל לפיכך צריך לברך על התפלה של יד (כה) אחר הנחה על הקיבורת (כו) קודם קשירתם שקשירתם זו היא עשייתן: הגה וכן בשל ראש (כז) קודם (ז) [ז] שמהדקן בראשו (טור): ט (כח) מאסור להפסיק (ח) (כט) בדיבור בין תפלה של יד לתפלה של ראש (ל) * ואם הפסיק מברך על של ראש על מצות תפילין: הגה (לא) * ולדידן דנוהגין לברך שתי ברכות אף אם לא הפסיק צריך (לב) לחזור ולברך על של ראש להניח גם"כ (ט) על מצות (ד"ע):

באר הגולה

י אגור בשם מהרי"ו מולין כ מנחות שם ובכמה דוכתי בש"ס ל רמב"ם פ"ד מהלכות תפלין מ מנחות ל"ו

שערי תשובה

להניח לבד ע"ש: [ו] להניח בקמץ. עבה"ט. ומ"ש בשם הלבוש ול"ח ליתא דאדרבה גם הם הכריעו לומר בקמץ וכתב כן עפ"י הע"ת וכבר השיג עליו בא"ר וא"ר ומור וקציעה הסכימו להב"י לומר בקמץ וכ"כ מהר"מ זכותא בהשגת כת"י על ספר מלת שמורים וכתב כי בקמץ מלשון להניח ברכה אתי שפיר שפירושו שתהיה נחה שם בקיום ובקביעות ע"י הקשר לא תנוד אנה ואנה משא"כ בפתח ודגש שרשו ינח שהוא ג"כ לשון עזיבה. וגם כשהוא בלשון שימה כגון והנחתו לפני ה' אינו אלא שימה גרידא לרגע וארעי ע"ש וקצת מזה כתב ג"כ בא"ר ע"ש: [ז] שמהדקו. עבה"ט. וכתב בשלמי ציבור שצריך ליזהר שלא יהא נחפז לברך על של יד קודם הנחה בקבורת דה"ל קודם דקודם. ואחר הידוק אעפ"י שלא עשה הכריכות לא מיקרי עובר לעשייתן.

באר היטב

סי' ל"ד: (ו) להניח בקמץ. בלבוש ול"ח אות כ"ד ומהר"ס דלונזאנו חלקו על המחבר וס"ל לברך בפתח: (ז) שמהדקו בראשו. היינו ג"כ אחר הנחה על הראש וקודם ההידוק דלא כמו שנוהגין העולם שמברכין קודם הנחה ב"ח מג"א: (ח) בדיבור. אפילו בלשון הקודש. בא"ר שבע וכנה"ג וע"ת. וכתב בספר ברכת אברהם ל"ד דיבור אלא אפי' הניח תפילין של יד בבית א' והלך להניח של ראש בבית אחר אע"פ שבשעת הברכה היה דעתו בכך צריך לברך וכ"כ שכנה"ג וע"ת כתב עליו וצ"ע למעשה ע"ש. ואם רמז בעיניו וקורץ באצבעותיו הוי הפסק בין תפלה של יד לתפלה של ראש הלק"ט ח"א סי' נ"ז. אם הניח תפלין של יד וכשבא להניח של ראש קודם שהגיע הקצילה בבשר אחר שהגיע לאויר הראש הפסיק בדיבור אי אמרינן הכא קלוטה כמי שהונחה דמיא עיין הלק"ט ח"ב סי' מ"ב. מי שהניח תפילין של יד וכרך ג' כריכות העליונות ולא בירך וסח בנתיים מברך שתים כיון דברכות אינן מעכבות מיקרי שפיר סח בין תפלה לתפלה ומברך שתים הלק"ט ח"ב סימן קי"ט: (ט) על מצות. וצריך למשמש בשל

ביאור הלכה

להניח הש"י כדי שיקוי' כ"ז שבין עיניך יהיו שתים ודי בזה: * ואם הפסיק. פשוט דבין אם ההפסק היה ע"י דבור או ע"י היסח הדעת בלבד וכ"ש הוא ע' במ"א סימן ח' סקי"ד ושיעור ההפסק דע"י דיבור הוא אפילו ע"י תיבה אחת ממה שכתב הרא"ש בה"ק דאם ענה אמן בינתיים על איזו ברכה ששמע שצריך לחזור ולברך ועיין במ"א בכלל ה' שמסתפק על הפסק תיבה אחת או ב' בין הברכה לעשיית אותו דבר אם הוי הפסק ותימא שלא שם לבו לדברי הרא"ש אלו. כתב הבה"ט אם הניח תפילין של יד וכשבא להניח של ראש קודם שהגיע הקצילה בבשר אחר שהגיע לאויר הראש הפסיק בדיבור אי אמרינן קלוטה כמי שהונחה דמיא לענין זה עיין בהלק"ט ח"ב סימן מ"ב. ועיין בארה"ח שהשיג עליו בראיה ברורה דכל שלא הידק לא נגמר המצוה וכן כתב בספר עיקרי דינים בשם תפלה לדוד. עוד כתב בבה"ט בשם הלק"ט מי שהניח תפילין של יד וכרך ג' כריכות העליונות ולא בירך וסח בינתיים מברך שתים כיון דברכות אינן מעכבות מיקרי שפיר סח בין תפלה לתפלה ומברך שתים והשיג ע"ז ג"כ הארה"ח דהא אם לבש ט"ק ולא בירך ואח"כ לבש הט"ג יכול לברך ברכה אחת על שניהם כמ"ש בשו"ע [סימן ח' סעיף י] וה"ה בזה חוזר ברכת להניח גם אש"י הקודמת וא"צ לברך רק ברכה אחת להמחבר ע"ש: * ולדידן דנוהגין וכו'. עיין במ"ב בס"ק ל"ב לענין משמוש ודע דהגרע"א מסיק בחידושיו דבסח יברך תחלה על ש"ר על מצות ואח"כ ימשמש בש"י ויחזק הקשר ויברך להניח ובזה יצא ידי שיטת רש"י ור"ת ע"ש:

משנה ברורה

אבל אם הניח ש"ר תחלה או שמצא הש"י שנשמט ממקומו אין להסיר הש"ר דמאי דהוה הוה וימהר להניח ש"י על מקומו ויש חולקין ועיין בביאור הלכה: (כג) להעביר. כיון (כ) דכתיב בקרא מפורש דיד קודם דמתחלה וקשרתם והדר ולטוטפות לפיכך אין משגיחין על העברת המצוה משא"כ לעיל בס"א גבי ציצית ותפלין: ז (כד) להניח בקמץ. שהוא לשון הנחה כמש"כ להניח ברכה אל ביתך ולא בפת"ח שהוא לשון עזיבה כמש"כ אחיכם אחד הניחו אתי [אחרונים]: ח (כה) אחר הנחה וכו'. (כא) דקודם לכן לכתחילה אין ראוי לברך דהוי קודם דקודם וצריך לקרב הברכה לעשיית המצוה בכל מה דאפשר: (כו) קודם קשירתן. ובדיעבד (כב) יברך אפילו אח"כ דמצוה שיש לה משך זמן הוא בכולי יומא: (כז) קודם שמהדקן. כי ההידוק הוא מצות הקשירה וצריך גם כן ליזהר שיהיה הברכה אחר שמונחים על הראש (כג) לא כאותן שמברכין בעודם בידם דא"כ הו"ל קודם דקודם. גם בשעת ברכה של תש"ר יראה (כד) שיהיה מכוסה ראשו בטלית ולא יברך בגילוי הראש: ט (כח) אסור להפסיק. אפילו בדיבור של מצוה (כה) כגון להשיב שלום לרבו וכל כה"ג כי גורם ברכה שאינה צריכה. ואפילו לאותן המניחין (כו) תפילין בחוה"מ בלי ברכה או המניחין תפלין דר"ת אחר שחלץ תפלין דרש"י או (כז) שחלץ תפלין ע"מ להחזירן דהרמ"א בסי"ב פסק דא"צ לחזור ולברך כשמניחן אח"כ אפ"ה עבירה היא להפסיק ביניהן דלכתחלה בעינן שיהיו סמוכין ותכופין זה לזה דכתיב והיה לך לאות על ידך ולזכרון בין עיניך שיהא הויה אחת לשתיהן: (כט) בדיבור. ואפילו (כח) בלשון הקודש ולכתחילה אסור (כט) אפי' להפסיק בשתיקה אם שוהא הרבה שלא לצורך אפילו (ל) לא הסיח דעתו, ואפי' (לא) לרמז בעיניו ולקרוץ באצבעותיו בין התש"י ובין התש"ר ג"כ יש ליזהר לכתחילה. אם הניח תפלין של יד בבית זה ותש"ר בבית אחר והיה דעתו לזה עיין לעיל בסימן ח' סי"ג ומ"ב שם לענין טלית (לב) וה"ה לעניננו: (ל) ואם הפסיק. אפילו (לג) בשוגג: (לא) ולדידן דנוהגין וכו'. כי הטעם שאנו מברכין שתי ברכות על תפילין ולא די בברכת להניח לבד הוא שאנו סוברין דעיקר תיקון הברכות אנו כך היתה בתחלת הנחתם תקנו לברך להניח וקאי נמי על ש"ר וכשמניח הש"ר ומהדקו מברך נמי על מצות שזו היא גמר המצוה הילכך ממילא אם סח והסיח דעתו צריך לחזור ולברך גם להניח על הש"ר [הרא"ש]: (לב) לחזור ולברך. וכנון (לד) שימשמש או בשל יד להזיזו ממקומו ויחזק הקשר ובזה תחזור ברכת להניח גם על הש"י ודומה כאלו הניח עתה הש"י והש"ר תכופים זה לזה (לה) ואם בירך בלא משמוש

שער הציון

(כ) מ"א: (כא) מ"א: (כב) פמ"ג: (כג) ב"ח מ"א: (כד) פמ"ג: (כה) רמב"ס: (כו) מ"א: (כז) ארה"ח: (כח) ב"ש ופשוט: (כט) פמ"ג: (ל) דבהיסח הדעת לכו"ע אפילו בדיעבד חוזר ומברך: (לא) ארה"ח בשם הלק"ט: (לב) א"ר וארה"ח: (לג) פשוט: (לד) מ"א ועיין בארה"ח שהאריך וחיזק שיטת הרז"ה: (לה) פמ"ג וארה"ח:

הגהות ותיקונים: א) וגם:

/tefilin/ first, he must **(23)** bypass the mitzvah and don the arm */tefilin/* first and /don/ the head */tefilin/* subsequently.
7. One should say /the word/ **(24)** לְהָנִיחַ with a *kamatz* (ָ) underneath the /letter/ ה, not with a *pasach* (ַ) /underneath it/ and a *dagesh* /in the letter נ/.
8. /In the case of/ all mitzvos, one must say the blessing over them immediately before they are performed. *(...)* Therefore, one must make the blessing over the arm *tefilin* **(25)** after he has placed them on the biceps, **(26)** before he binds them /to the arm/, since the binding constitutes the performance /of the mitzvah/.

Gloss: Likewise in the case of the head /tefilin, *one should make the blessing/* **(27)** *before he tightens them on his head. (...)*

Mishnah Berurah

/already/ donned the head *tefilin* first or he discovers that his arm *tefilin* have slipped out of place, he should not remove the head *tefilin* /in order to don the arm *tefilin* first/, since what happened /already/ is /a matter/ of the past /and does not concern us/. /In such circumstances/ one should hurry to put the hand */tefilin/* in place. There are authorities/ who dispute /this ruling/. See the Beyur Halachah.

(23) Bypass. This is because it is written explicitly in the verse[6] that the arm */tefilin/* have precedence. For /it is stated/ first, "And you should bind /, etc./" and after that, "for *tefilin* /etc./". Therefore, we are not bothered /in such a case/ about /the need to avoid/ bypassing the mitzvah.

This /reasoning/ does not apply /in the case discussed/ above in Par. 1, which relates to /putting on a *talis* with/ *tzitzis* /attached/ and /donning/ *tefilin*.

(24) לְהָנִיחַ with a *kamatz*. This /vowelling/ implies "placing". For /we find this usage/ in Scripture,[8] "לְהָנִיחַ (to place) blessing in your home".

/One should/ not /say the word/ with a *pasach* (ַ), since that implies "leaving behind". For /we find/ in Scripture,[9] "your one brother הַנִּיחוּ (leave behind) with me". [Acharonim]

(25) After he has placed them. Before that /stage/ it is not proper to make the blessing, initially, since it is /still/ prior to /the stage/ which is /immediately/ before /the performance of the mitzvah/. One is required to /say/ the blessing as close as possible to the /actual/ performance of the mitzvah.

(26) Before he binds them. Once it is after the event /and one did not yet make the blessing/, he may make the blessing even after that. /This is/ because the mitzvah /of wearing *tefilin*/ extends for a period of time, /in fact/ for the entire day.

(27) Before he tightens them. For /in their case/ the tightening is /the fulfillment of/ the mitzvah of binding.

One must also take care that the blessing is /said/ after /the *tefilin*/ are /already/ lying on the head. /He must/ not /act/ like those /people/ who make the blessing when /the *tefilin*/ are still in their hands, as then it is /still/ prior to /the stage/ which is /immediately/ before /the performance of the mitzvah/.

In addition, when /one is making/ the blessing over the head *tefilin*, he must see /to it/ that his head is covered by the *talis* and should not say the blessing with an exposed head.

8 *Yechezkeyl* 44:30.
9 *Bereyshis* 42:33.

ראש תחלה צריך (כג) להעביר על אותה המצוה ויניח של יד תחלה ואח"כ של ראש: ז ׳יברך (ו) [ו] (כד) להניח בקמץ תחת הה"א ולא בפתח ובדגש: ח ׳כל המצות מברך עליהם עובר לעשייתן (פי' קודם. ויעבר את הכושי פירושו רץ והקדים לפניו) ׳לפיכך צריך לברך על התפלה של יד (כה) אחר הנחה על הקיבורת (כו) קודם קשירתם שקשירתם זו היא עשייתן: הגה וכן בשל ראש (כז) קודם (ז) [ז] שמהדקן בראשו (טור): ט (כח) ׳אסור להפסיק (ח) (כט) בדיבור בין תפלה של יד לתפלה של ראש (ל) * ואם הפסיק מברך על של ראש על מצות תפילין: הגה (לא) * ולדידן דנוהגין לברך שתי ברכות אף אם לא הפסיק צריך (לב) לחזור ולברך על של ראש להניח גם[א] (ט) על מצות (ד"ע):

באר הגולה

י אגור בשם מהר"י מולין כ מנחות שם ובכמה דוכתי בש"ס ל רמב"ם פ"ד מהלכות תפלין מ מנחות ל"ו

שערי תשובה

להניח לבד ע"ש: [ו] להניח בקמץ. עבה"ט. ומ"ש בשם הלבוש ול"ח ליתא דאדרבה גם הם הכריעו לומר בקמץ וכתב כן עפ"י הע"ת וכבר השיג עליו בא"ר וא"ר ומור וקציעה הסכימו להב"י לומר בקמץ וכ"כ מהר"מ זכותא בהשגת כת"י על ספר מלת שמורים וכתב כי בקמץ מלשון להניח ברכה אתי שפיר שפירושו שתהיה נחה שם בקיום ובקביעות ע"י הקשר לא תנוד אנה ואנה משא"כ בפתח ודגש שרשו ינח שהוא ג"כ לשון עזיבה. וגם כשהוא בלשון שימה כגון והנחתו לפני ה' אינו אלא שימה גרידא לרגע וארעי ע"ש וקצת מזה כתב ג"כ בא"ר ע"ש: [ז] שמהדקו. עבה"ט. וכתב בשלמי ציבור שצריך ליזהר שלא יהא נחפז לברך על של יד קודם הנחה בקבורת דה"ל קודם דקודם. ואחר הידוק אעפ"י שלא עשה הכריכות לא מיקרי עובר לעשייתן.

באר היטב

סי' ל"ד: (ו) להניח בקמץ. בלבוש ול"ח אות כ"ד ומהר"ס דלונזאנו חלקו על המחבר וס"ל לברך בפתח: (ז) שמהדקו בראשו. היינו ג"כ אחר הנחה על הראש וקודם ההידוק דלא כמו שנוהגין העולם שמברכין קודם הנחה ב"ח מג"א: (ח) בדיבור. אפילו בלשון הקודש. באר שבע וכנה"ג וע"ת. וכתב בספר ברכת אברהם ל"ד דיבור אלא אפי' הניח תפילין של יד בבית א' והלך להניח של ראש בבית אחר אע"פ שבשעת הברכה היה דעתו בכך צריך לברך וכ"כ שכנה"ג וע"ת כתב עליו וצ"ע למעשה ע"ש. ואם רמז בעיניו וקורץ באצבעותיו הוי הפסק בין תפלה של יד לתפלה של ראש הלק"ט ח"א סי' נ"ז. אם הניח תפלין של יד וכשבא להניח של ראש קודם שהגיע הקציצה בבשר אחר שהגיע לאויר הראש הפסיק בדיבור אי אמרינן הכא קלוטה כמי שהונחה דמיא עיין הלק"ט ח"ב סי' מ"ב. מי שהניח תפילין של יד וכרך ג' כריכות העליונות ולא בירך וסח בנתיים מברך שתים כיון דברכות אינן מעכבות מיקרי שפיר סח בין תפלה לתפלה ומברך שתים הלק"ט ח"ב סימן קי"ט: (ט) על מצות. וצריך למשמש בשל

ביאור הלכה

להניח הש"י כדי שיקויי' כ"ז שבין עיניך יהיו שתים ודי בזה: * ואם הפסיק. פשוט דבין אם ההפסק היה ע"י דבור או ע"י היסח הדעת בלבד וכ"ש הוא ע' במ"א סימן ח' סקי"ד ושיעור ההפסק דע"י דיבור הוא אפילו ע"י תיבה אחת ממה שכתב הרא"ש בה"ק דאם ענה אמן בינתיים על איזו ברכה ששמע שצריך לחזור ולברך ועיין בח"א בכלל ה' שמסתפק על הפסק תיבה אחת או ב' בין הברכה לעשיית אותו דבר אם הוי הפסק ותימא שלא שם לבו לדברי הרא"ש אלו. כתב הבה"ט אם הניח תפילין של יד וכשבא להניח של ראש קודם שהגיע הקציצה בבשר אחר שהגיע לאויר הראש הפסיק בדיבור אי אמרינן קלוטה כמי שהונחה דמיא לענין זה עיין בהלק"ט ח"ב סימן מ"ב. ועיין בארה"ח שהשיג עליו בראיה ברורה דכל שלא הידק לא נגמר המצוה וכן כתב בספר עיקרי דינים בשם תפלה לדוד. עוד כתב בבה"ט בשם הלק"ט מי שהניח תפילין של יד וכרך ג' כריכות העליונות ולא בירך וסח בינתיים מברך שתים כיון דברכות אינן מעכבות מיקרי שפיר סח בין תפלה לתפלה ומברך שתים והשיג ע"ז ג"כ הארה"ח דהא אם לבש ט"ק ולא בירך ואח"כ לבש הט"ג יכול לברך ברכה אחת על שניהם כמ"ש בשו"ע [סימן ח' סעיף י] וה"ה בזה חוזר ברכת להניח גם אש"י הקודמת וא"צ לברך רק ברכה אחת להמחבר ע"ש: * ולדידן דנוהגין וכו'. עיין במ"ב בס"ק ל"ב לענין משמוש ודע דהגרע"א מסיק בחידושיו דבסח יברך תחלה על ש"ר על מצות ואח"כ ימשמש בש"י ויחזק הקשר ויברך להניח ובזה יצא ידי שיטת רש"י ור"ת ע"ש:

משנה ברורה

אבל אם הניח ש"ר תחלה או שנפל הש"י שנשמט ממקומו אין להסיר הש"ר דמאי דהוה הוה וימהר להניח ש"י על מקומו ויש חולקין ועיין בביאור הלכה: (כג) להעביר. כיון (כ) דכתיב בקרא מפורש דיד קודם דמתחלה וקשרתם והדר ולטוטפות לפיכך אין מעגימין על העברת המצוה משא"כ לעיל בס"א גבי ציצית ותפלין: ז (כד) להניח בקמץ. שהוא לשון הנחה כמש"כ להניח ברכה אל ביתך ולא בפת"ח שהוא לשון עזיבה כמש"כ אחיכם אחד הניחו אתי [אחרונים]: ח (כה) אחר הנחה וכו'. (כא) דקודם לכן לכתחילה אין ראוי לברך דהוי קודם דקודם וצריך לקרב הברכה לעשיית המצוה בכל מה דאפשר: (כו) קודם קשירתן. ובדיעבד (כב) יברך אפילו אח"כ דמצוה שיש לה משך זמן הוא בכולי יומא: (כז) קודם שמהדקן. כי ההידוק הוא מצות הקשירה וצריך גם כן ליזהר שיהיה הברכה אחר שמונחים על הראש (כג) לא כאותן שמברכין בעודם בידם דא"כ הו"ל קודם דקודם. גם בשעת ברכה של תש"ר יראה (כד) שיהיה מכוסה ראשו בטלית ולא יברך בגילוי הראש: ט (כח) אסור להפסיק. אפילו בדיבור של מצוה (כה) כגון להשיב שלום לרבו וכל כה"ג כי גורם ברכה שאינה צריכה. ואפילו לאותן המניחין (כו) תפילין בחוה"מ בלי ברכה או המניחין תפלין דר"ת אחר שחלץ תפלין דרש"י או (כז) שחלץ תפלין ע"מ להחזירן דהרמ"א בסי"ב פסק דא"צ לחזור ולברך כשמניחן אח"כ אפ"ה עבירה היא להסיח ביניהן דלכתחלה בעינן שיהיו סמוכין ותכופין זה לזה דכתיב והיה לך לאות על ידך ולזכרון בין עיניך שיהא הוייה אחת לשתיהן: (כט) בדיבור. ואפילו (כח) בלשון הקודש ולכתחילה אסור (כט) אפי' להפסיק בשתיקה אם שוהא הרבה שלא לצורך אפילו (ל) לא הסיח דעתו, ואפי' (לא) לרמז בעיניו ולקרוץ באצבעותיו בין התש"י ובין התש"ר ג"כ יש ליזהר לכתחילה. אם הניח תפלין של יד בבית זה ותש"ר בבית אחר והיה דעתו לזה עיין לעיל בסימן ח' סי"ג ומ"ב שם לענין טלית (לב) וה"ה לענינינו: (ל) ואם הפסיק. אפילו (לג) בשוגג: (לא) ולדידן דנוהגין וכו'. כי הטעם שאנו מברכין שתי ברכות על תפילין ולא די בברכת להניח לבד הוא שאנו סוברין דעיקר תיקון הברכות אלו כך היתה בתחלת הנחתם תקנו לברך להניח וקאי נמי על ש"ר וכשמניח הש"ר ומהדקו מברך נמי על מצות שזו היא גמר המצוה הילכך ממילא אם סח והסיח דעתו צריך לחזור ולברך גם להניח על הש"ר [הרא"ש]: (לב) לחזור ולברך. ונכון (לד) שימשמש אז בשל יד להזיזו ממקומו ויחזק הקשר ובזה תחזור ברכת להניח גם על הש"י ודומה כאלו הניח עתה הש"י והש"ר תכופים זה לזה (לה) ואם בירך בלא משמוש ימשמש

שער הציון

(כ) מ"א: (כא) מ"א: (כב) פמ"ג: (כג) ב"ח מ"א: (כד) פמ"ג: (כה) רמב"ס: (כו) מ"א: (כז) ארה"ח: (כח) ב"ש ופשוט: (כט) פמ"ג: (ל) דבהיסח הדעת לכו"ע אפילו בדיעבד חוזר ומברך: (לא) ארה"ח בשם הלק"ט: (לב) א"ר וארה"ח: (לג) פשוט: (לד) מ"א ועיין בארה"ח שהאריך וחיזק שיטת הרז"ה: (לה) פמ"ג וארה"ח:

הגהות ותיקונים: א) וגם:

9. **(28)** It is forbidden to interrupt **(29)** with speech in between /the donning of/ the arm *tefilin* and /the donning of/ the head *tefilin.* **(30)** If one did /in fact/ make an interruption /then/, he should make the blessing *Al Mitzvas Tefilin* over /the donning of/ the head /*tefilin*/.

Gloss: **(31)** *For us, who are accustomed to make two blessings even without having made an interruption /in between, the ruling is that if one did make an interruption in between/ he must* **(32)** *make the blessing* Lehaniach Tefilin *again over /the donning of/ the head /*tefilin*/ and should also /make the blessing/* Al Mitzvas Tefilin */over it/. (...)*

Mishnah Berurah

(28) It is forbidden to interrupt. This even /applies/ to speech for a mitzvah /purpose/, such as returning a greeting to one's /Torah/ teacher or anything similar. /The reason is/ that one would thereby cause an unnecessary blessing to be made.

There are /people/ who don *tefilin* on Chol Ha-Mo'ed without /making/ a blessing /over them/. /There are/ those who don *tefilin* /which accord with the view/ of Rabbeinu Tam, after they have removed the *tefilin* of *Rashi* /, without making a blessing, in conformance with what is stated in Sec. 34, Par. 2/. One may /also/ have removed *tefilin* having in mind to return them /in place/. (The *Rema* rules below in Par. 12 that /in such a case/ one is not required to make the blessing again when he dons them subsequently.) Even /in these cases/ it is nevertheless a transgression to speak in between /the donning of the arm *tefilin* and the donning of the head *tefilin*/. /This is because/ they are required to be /donned/, initially, immediately after and closely following one another /, quite apart from the question of an unnecessary blessing/. For it is stated,[5] /with reference to the *tefilin*/, "And it should be for you a sign on your arm and a reminder between your eyes", /which implies/ that they should both have one /coming to/ be /together/.

(29) With speech. It is even /forbidden to interrupt by speaking/ in the holy tongue.

Initially, it is forbidden /for one/ to interrupt even with silence, by delaying for a long /time in between/ unnecessarily. /This applies/ even if he does not distract his mind /from the mitzvah/. In addition, one should avoid, initially, even suggesting with his eyes or indicating with his fingers in between /the donning of/ the arm *tefilin* and /the donning of/ the head *tefilin*.

/As regards the ruling/ if one donned arm *tefilin* in one building and the head *tefilin* in another building and had this in mind /from the outset/, see above in Sec. 8, Par. 13 and the Mishnah Berurah there. /The ruling/ as regards a *talis* /is given there/ and a corresponding /ruling applies/ in our case.

(30) If one did make an interruption. /I.e.,/ even /if one did so/ in ignorance of /the fact/ that it was a transgression.

(31) For us, who are accustomed, etc. This is because the reason why we make two blessings over the *tefilin*, and do not /consider it/ sufficient to /make/ only the blessing *Lehaniach Tefilin*, is that we are of the opinion that, essentially, the ordainment /of the Sages/ to /say/ these blessings was as follows. They ordained that at the outset when one dons them he must make the blessing *Lehaniach Tefilin,* which relates also to the head /*tefilin*/, and when he dons the head *tefilin* and tightens them he must make, in addition, the blessing *Al Mitzvas Tefilin*, since this is the completion /of the fulfillment/ of the mitzvah. Therefore, it follows that if one talks and distracts his mind /from the mitzvah in between/ he must also make the blessing *Lehaniach Tefilin* again, as well, over the head /*tefilin*/. [The *Rosh*]

(32) Make the blessing ... again. It is proper to handle the hand /*tefilin*/ then /before the blessing/, by moving it from its place and tightening the knot. By these /means/ the blessing *Lehaniach Tefilin* will relate also to the arm /*tefilin*/ and it will be as if he now donned the arm /*tefilin*/ and the head /*tefilin*/ closely following one another. If one made the blessing without handling

י (לג) נאם סח (י) לצורך[1] תפילין (לד) אינו חוזר ומברך * סאם שמע קדיש או קדושה בין תפלה של יד לתפלה של ראש (לה) לא יפסיק (לו) לענות (יא) [ח] עמהם עאלא (לז) שותק ושומע ומכוין למה שאומרים: **יא** פאחר שקשר של יד על הזרוע יניח של ראש (לח) קודם שיכרוך (יב) [ט] הרצועה סביב הזרוע צויש מי שאומר (לט) שאסור להוציא תפלה של ראש (יג) [י] מהתיק עד שתהא תפלה של יד (מ) מונחת: הגה ואף אם שניהם לפניו חוץ לתיק (מא) לא יתקן לפתוח התפלה של ראש עד אחר הנחה של יד (מהרי"א ומהר"י בן חביב) יש מי שכתב להניח של יד מיושב ושל ראש מעומד

נ מרדכי בשם ר"ת ס הרא"ש והטור ע רש"י ספ"ג דסוכ' ור"ת ור"ן ותוספות בברכות פ טור בשם הרא"ש צ תשובת הר"י גיקטילא

באר היטב

יד כשאומר שנית להניח ט"ז: (י) לצורך תפילין. ולכתחילה אסור. מיהו אי לא סגי בלא"ה מותר להסיח מ"א (יא) עמהם. ואפי' לענות אמן על ברכת תפילין שבירך אחר לעצמו אסור דבר שמואל סימן קמ"ב. ואם פסק וענה מחלוקת בין הפוסקים אם חוזר ומברך. וט"ז פסק דא"צ לחזור ולברך. וכ"כ דבר שמואל שם. ועיין בתשובת פנים מאירות חלק א"ח סימן י'. וכתב המ"א ומ"מ דהמניח ח"ה[ג] בלא ברכה רשאי לענות דליכא איסור אלא משום שגורם ברכה והכא אין כאן ברכה ע"ש. לפי"ז מותר לענות קדיש וקדושה ואמן בין תפלה לתפלה בתפילין דר"ת הואיל ואין מברכין עליהם. וכ"כ בהדיא בתשובת דרכי נועם חלק א"ח סי' יו"ד. גם נ"ל אם חבירו מברך על התפילין והוא מכוון לצאת בברכת חבירו וגם חבירו מכוון להוציאו דרשאי לענות קדיש וקדושה וק"ל אבל שיחת חולין לעולם אסור וכ"כ בדרכי נועם שם. ועיין בע"ת ס"ק י"ב. ועיין סי' ל"א ס"ק ג' מש"ש: (יב) הרצועה. ובכוונת[א] איתא שהאר"י ז"ל כרך קודם שהניח של ראש וע"ל סי' כ"ו[ב] ס"ק ט"ו מש"ש: (יג) מהתיק. ויניחם בתיק באופן שא"א לשל ראש שיצא קודם ט"ז. הכנה"ג כתב בשם רבו דאין קפידא אלא כשמניח עצמו מוציאה מן התיק קודם שיניח של יד אבל אדם אחר בעוד שחבירו מניח תפלה של יד מוציאה ומתיר לו תפילין

שערי תשובה

ועיין ב"ח ושו"ת בית יעקב בסי' פ"ח והבאתיו לעיל סי' ח' ע"ש: [ח] עמהם. עיין בה"ט ובפנים מאירות ח"א סי' נ"ט דעתו שמותר לענות אמן אחר ברכת חבירו על התפילין לכתחלה אע"ג דלקדיש וקדושה לא יפסיק מ"מ אמן הוא קבלת דברים שמאמין בה' שלונו להניח תפילין לא הוי הפסק וכיון שלר"ת אף לקדיש וקדושה פוסק יש לסמוך עליו לענין עניית אמן ע"ש. ומ"ש בשם דרכי נועם לענין להפסיק בעניית קדיש וקדושה ואמן בין תש"י לש"ר בתפילין של ר"ת כ"כ בבכור שור בסוטה דף מ"ד ע"ב ע"ש: [ט] הרצועה. עיין בבה"ט בשם האר"י ז"ל וכ"כ הרדב"ז בתשובה ח"ג סי' תרכ"ג וכתב בבר"י שכן המנהג בכל מקום. וכתב בספר מ"מ אמנם נראה שאם אחר שבירך שמע קדיש או קדושה ואם לא יכרוך יהיה לו פנאי להניח של ראש ולענות דיש לעשות כן ועדיף טפי למעבד הכי וכן נהגתי עכ"ל: [י] מהתיק. עיין בבה"ט ועיין לקמן סימן כ"ח מ"ש בשם המג"א. וכתב בבר"י בשם תשובות מהר"י מולכין מי ששכח ולבש ש"ר קודם ש"י אין צריך להסירה כיון דילא ידי מצותה והוכיח כן מב"י סי' כ"ו ע"ש וכ"כ בשאלת יעבץ סי' קכ"ה וזה דלא כבעל הלכות קטנות סי' נ"ג ומ"מ גם הוא כתב שאם לבש ש"ר מפני שלא היה לו ש"י ואח"כ נזדמן לו ש"י א"צ להסיר ש"ר קודם הנחת ש"י ע"ש. ועי' בשלמי צבור בשם מהרח"ו שכתב מורי ז"ל היה נזהר שלא להוציא תש"ר מן הכים עד שיניח ויקשור תש"י סביב הזרוע בקיבורת במקום הקשר ואח"כ לא היה חושש מלהוציא תש"ר אף שעדיין לא הקיף בזרוע עצמו. וכפי הטעם שכתב המ"א אפשר דאף ע"י אחר אין להוציא ש"ר עד שיניח של יד ע"ש. ועי'

ביאור הלכה

* אם שמע קדיש וכו'. עיין במ"ב בס"ק ל"ו דאם פסק וענה חוזר ומברך. ועיין בח"א שכתב בפשיטות דלדידן צריך לברך שתים על הש"ר ולהמחבר לא יברך כ"א ע"מ ובארה"ח הכריע דבזה אפילו לדידן דנוהגין כר"ת לא יברך כ"א ברכה אחת והוא על מצות עי"ש מילתא בטעמא. כתב הבה"ט נ"ל אם חבירו מכוין להוציאו בברכת תפילין וגם הוא מכוין לצאת דרשאי לענות קדיש או קדושה ואינו נראה דהלא יוצא בברכת חבירו אינו עדיף מאם מברך לעצמו ובברכת עצמו אם פסק אפילו לאיש"ר חוזר ומברך ואינו יוצא בברכה ראשונה וא"כ הוא גורם ברכה שאינה צריכה ועיין בא"ר שמוכח כדברינו ועיין בסי' קס"ז ס"ו במ"א סקי"ט ובט"ז סק"ח שם בא"ד ועוד תמוה פסק הרוקח ע"ש. ואפילו הרוקח גופא מודה בענין תפילין כמו שכתב הפמ"ג שם מכל זה נראה דאפילו בדיעבד יש להחמיר בזה ולחזור ולברך ואפילו אם חבירו הניח כבר התפילין שלו בשעה שהוא מפסיק ועכ"פ לכתחלה בודאי אסור להפסיק בזה כיון

משנה ברורה

ימשמש אחר הברכה ועיין בבה"ל מה שכתבנו בשם הגרע"א בזה: י (לג) אם סח. ואפילו (לו) אם סח בין ברכת להניח ובין הנחת התש"י ג"כ דינא הכי: (לד) אינו וכו'. אבל לכתחילה אסור להסיח בין ברכת להניח עד אחר הנחה של ראש (לז) אפילו בדברים שהן לצורך תפילין אם לא היכי שא"א בענין אחר. (לח) אך בחוה"מ שאין מברכין אפשר דיש להקל לכתחילה בדברים שהם לצורך תפילין: (לה) לא יפסיק. ואפילו לענות אמן על ברכה זו גופא כגון לענות אמן על ברכת תפילין שמברך אחר אסור אם לא שחבירו מכוין להוציאו בברכה זו [תשובת ד"ש והגרע"א בחידושיו דלא כפ"מ[ד] עי"ש]: (לו) לענות עמהם. ואם פסק וענה איש"ר או קדושה או ברכו (לט) או שענה אמן על איזה ברכה ששמע (מ) חוזר ומברך ועיין בבה"ל. ובחוה"מ או המניח תפילין דר"ת וכיוצא שמניח בלי ברכה (מא) יש להקל ולהפסיק לעניית איש"ר וקדושה וברכו ואמן אך (מב) אח"כ יזיז הש"י ממקומו קודם שיניח הש"ר כדי שיהיה הוייה אחת לשניהן: (לז) שותק ושומע. דהשתיקה כענייה (מג) לענין לצאת י"ח אבל לא שיחשב כהפסקה: **יא** (לח) קודם שיכרוך. הטעם (מד) כיון שברכת להניח חוזרת גם על של ראש כנ"ל בס"ק ל"א וכ"ש להמחבר לעיל בס"ה דס"ל דאינו מברך אלא אחת ע"כ ימעט ההפסק בכל מה שיוכל והכריכה סביב הזרוע אינה מעיקר הדין ע"כ טוב לאחר אותה עד שיניח של ראש ובספר כוונות האר"י ז"ל כתוב שהיה נוהג לכרוך השבעה כריכות סביב זרועו תחלה [אבל (מה) לא הג' כריכות שעל האצבע] מפני שהוא סובר כיון דלכתחלה גם הכריכות הוא מצוה לפיכך אין זה הפסק (מו) וכן המנהג בכ"מ ועיין בתשובת משכנות יעקב סימן כ"ח דעתו ג"כ כמנהגנו לכרוך קודם על הזרוע לחיזוק דבלא"ה לא מתקיים ואינו נקרא קשירה עי"ש כתב בספר מ"מ אם שמע קדיש וקדושה אחר שבירך על של יד ואם יכרוך לא יהיה לו פנאי להניח ש"ר ולענות יניח ש"ר קודם הכריכות (מז) אם יכול להדק במקלת שלא ימיש התש"י ממקומו: (לט) שאסור וכו'. היינו (מח) אפילו אם ירצה להוציא הש"ר והש"י שניהן בשוה מן התיק דבזה אין מעביר על המצות אפ"ה יש ליזהר כי יש בזה טעם ע"פ הקבלה כמש"כ בב"י וכ"ש להניח הש"י מידו ולהתעסק בהוצאת הש"ר מדינא אסור: (מ) מונחת. ר"ל שתהיה מהודקת יפה על הזרוע ואז מותר (מט) אפי' קודם שעשה השבעה כריכות. ואם אחר יכול להוציא ולתקן ש"ר בעוד שחבירו מניח של יד הפמ"ג מחמיר וארה"ח מיקל עי"ש: (מא) לא יתקן. ר"ל (נ) אפילו אם בעת תיקון הש"ר לא יניח הש"י ג"כ מידו אפ"ה (נא) כשמניח אח"כ הש"ר להניח הש"י הוי כמעביר על המצות

שער הציון

(לו) פמ"ג: (לז) מ"א: (לח) פמ"ג וארה"ח: (לט) הרא"ש בה"ק: (מ) לבוש וב"ל ומ"א וא"ר וח"א ודה"ח דלא כט"ז: (מא) מ"א ודה"ח וארה"ח ועוד הרבה אחרונים ע"ש דלא כא"ר: (מב) ארה"ח: (מג) ט"ז: (מד) ט"ז בשם הרא"ש (מה) פמ"ג: (מו) פמ"ג: (מז) ארה"ח: (מח) ארה"ח: (מט) אחרונים: (נ) פמ"ג: (נא) מ"א:

הגהות ותיקונים: א) ובכוונות: **ב)** כ"ז: **ג)** ומ"מ משמע דהמניח בחו"ה: **ד)** כפמ"א:

הערות והארות: 1) עיין מ"ב סי' קס"ז ס"ק ל"ז לענין אם אינו לצורך אלא רק מענין:

10. (33) If one spoke /in between/ for the sake of /the donning of/ the *tefilin*, (34) he should not make the blessing again.

If one hears *Kadish* or *Kedushah* in between /the donning of/ the arm *tefilin* and /the donning of/ the head *tefilin*, (35) he should not make the interruption (36) of responding /together/ with /the congregation/, but (37) should be silent and listen and apply his mind to what they are saying.

11. After one has bound the arm /*tefilin*/ on the arm, he should don the head /*tefilin*/ (38) before he winds the strap /of the arm *tefilin*/ around the arm.

Mishnah Berurah

/the arm *tefilin*/ he should handle them after the blessing. See the Beyur Halachah, for what we have written about this in the name of the Gaon Rabbi Akiva Eiger.[10]

(33) If one spoke. Even if one spoke in between /the making of/ the blessing *Lehaniach Tefilin* and the donning of the arm *tefilin* this ruling also /applies/.

(34) He should not, etc. However, initially, it is forbidden to speak even of matters which are for the sake of /the donning of/ the *tefilin*, from /when one has said/ the blessing *Lehaniach Tefilin* until after he has donned the head /*tefilin*/, unless in an instance when it is impossible /to act/ otherwise. However, on Chol Ha-Mo'ed, when we do not make a blessing /over the donning of the *tefilin*/, it may be that one may be lenient initially as regards /speaking of/ matters which are for the sake of /the donning of/ the *tefilin*.

(35) He should not make the interruption. Even to respond אָמֵן to this blessing itself /which is made over the donning of the *tefilin*/, such as to respond אָמֵן to the blessing when someone else makes it over /his donning of the/ *tefilin*, is forbidden, unless his fellow has in mind that this blessing should serve for him to fulfil /his obligation/. [Responsa *D.Sh.* and the Gaon Rabbi Akiva Eiger in his *Chidushim*, in contradiction to the *P.M.*; see there.]

(36) Of responding with /the congregation/. If one did interrupt and respond אָמֵן יְהֵא שְׁמֵהּ רַבָּא /וכו'/, with *Kedushah* or /to the call of/ *Barechu* or he responded אָמֵן to some blessing which he heard, he must make the blessing again. See the Beyur Halachah.

If it is Chol Ha-Mo'ed, if one dons the *tefilin* of Rabbeinu Tam or in similar /cases/ where one dons /the *tefilin*/ without /making/ a blessing over them, one may be lenient and make an interruption to respond אָמֵן יְהֵא שְׁמֵהּ רַבָּא /וכו'/, with *Kedushah*, to /the call of/ *Barechu* and אָמֵן. However, he should afterwards move the arm /*tefilin*/, so that they should both have one /coming to/ be[11] /together/.

(37) Should be silent and listen. For /listening in/ silence has the same /ruling/ as responding with respect to the fulfillment of one's obligation, but not /to the extent/ that it is considered an interruption.

(38) Before he winds. The reason /for this follows from the fact/ that the blessing *Lehaniach Tefilin* relates also to the head /*tefilin*/. /This even applies according to the *Rema*,/ as /explained/ above in sub-Par. 31, and it certainly /applies/ according to the author /of the Shulchan Aruch/, who is of the opinion that one should only make one blessing /over both *tefilin*, as stated/ above in Par. 5. In view of this, one must minimize

10 The Gaon concludes that if one made an interruption of speech, he should first make the blessing *Al Mitzvas Tefilin* over the head *tefilin* and, subsequently, he should handle the hand *tefilin* and strengthen the binding and make the blessing *Lehaniach Tefilin*.

11 See sub-Par. 28.

י (לג) נאם סח (י) לצורך[י] תפילין (לד) אינו חוזר ומברך * סאם שמע קדיש או קדושה בין תפלה של יד לתפלה של ראש (לה) לא יפסיק (לו) לענות (יא) [ח] עמהם עאלא (לז) שותק ושומע ומכוין למה שאומרים: **יא** פאחר שקשר של יד על הזרוע יניח של ראש (לח) קודם שיכרוך (יב) [ט] הרצועה סביב הזרוע **צויש מי שאומר (לט) שאסור להוציא תפלה של ראש (יג) [י] מהתיק עד שתהא תפלה של יד (מ) מונחת: הגה ואף אם שניהם לפניו חוץ לתיק (מא) לא יתקן לפתוח התפלה של ראש עד אחר הנחה של יד (מהרי"א ומהר"י בן חביב) יש מי שכתב להניח של יד מיושב ושל ראש מעומד**

נ מרדכי בשם ר"ת ס הרא"ש והטור ע רש"י ספ"ג דסוכ' ור"ת ור"ן ותוספות בברכות פ טור בשם הרא"ש צ תשובת הר"י גיקטילא

באר היטב

יד כשאומר שנית להניח ט"ז: (י) לצורך תפילין. ולכתחילה אסור. מיהו אי לא סגי בלא"ה מותר להסיח מ"א (יא) עמהם. ואפי' לענות אמן על ברכת תפילין שבירך אחר לעצמו אסור דבר שמואל סימן קמ"ב. ואם פסק וענה מחלוקת בין הפוסקים אם חוזר ומברך. וט"ז פסק דא"ל לחזור ולברך. וכ"כ דבר שמואל שם. ועיין בתשובת פנים מאירות חלק א"ח סימן י'. וכתב המ"א ומ"מ דהמניח ח"ה[ג] בלא ברכה רשאי לענות דליכא איסור אלא משום שגורם ברכה והכא אין כאן ברכה ע"ש. לפי"ז מותר לענות קדיש וקדושה ואמן בין תפלה לתפלה בתפילין דר"ת הואיל ואין מברכין עליהם. וכ"כ בהדיא בתשובת דרכי נועם חלק א"ח סי' יו"ד. גם נ"ל אם חבירו מברך על התפילין והוא מכוון לצאת בברכת חבירו וגם חבירו מכוון להוציאו דרשאי לענות קדיש וקדושה וק"ל אבל שיחת חולין לעולם אסור וכ"כ בדרכי נועם שם. ועיין בע"ת ס"ק י"ב. ועיין סי' ל"א ס"ק ג' מש"ש: (יב) הרצועה. ובכוונת[א] איתא שהאר"י ז"ל כרך קודם שהניח של ראש וע"ל סי' כ"ו[ב] ס"ק ט"ו מש"ש: (יג) מהתיק. ויניחם בתיק באופן שא"א לשל ראש שיצא קודם ט"ז. הכנה"ג כתב בשם רבו דאין קפידא אלא כשמניח עלמו מוליאה מן התיק קודם שיניח של יד אבל אדם אחר בעוד שחבירו מניח תפלה של יד מוליאה ומתיר לו תפילין

שערי תשובה

ועיין ב"ח ושו"ת בית יעקב בסי' פ"ח והבאתיו לעיל סי' ח' ע"ש: [ח] עמהם. עיין בה"ט ובפנים מאירות ח"א סי' נ"ט דעתו שמותר לענות אמן אחר ברכת חבירו על התפילין לכתחלה אע"ג דלקדיש וקדושה לא יפסיק מ"מ אמן הוא קבלת דברים שמאמין בה' שלונו להניח תפילין לא הוי הפסק וכיון שלר"ת אף לקדיש וקדושה פוסק יש לסמוך עליו לענין עניית אמן ע"ש. ומ"ש בשם דרכי נועם לענין להפסיק בעניית קדיש וקדושה ואמן בין תש"י לש"ר בתפילין של ר"ת כ"כ בבכור שור בסוטה דף מ"ד ע"ב ע"ש: [ט] הרצועה. עיין בבה"ט בשם האר"י ז"ל וכ"כ הרדב"ז בתשובה ח"ג סי' תרכ"ג וכתב בבר"י שכן המנהג בכל מקום. וכתב בספר מ"מ אמנם נראה שאם אחר שבירך שמע קדיש או קדושה ואם לא יכרוך יהיה לו פנאי להניח של ראש ולענות דיש לעשות כן ועדיף טפי למעבד הכי וכן נהגתי עכ"ל: [י] מהתיק. עיין בבה"ט ועיין לקמן סימן כ"ח מ"ש בשם המג"א. וכתב בבר"י בשם תשובות מהר"י מולכין מי ששכח ולבש ש"ר קודם ש"י אין צריך להסירה כיון דילא ידי מצותה והוכיח כן מב"י סי' כ"ו ע"ש וכ"כ בשאלת יעבץ סי' קכ"ה וזה דלא כבעל הלכות קטנות סי' נ"ג ומ"מ גם הוא כתב שאם לבש ש"ר מפני שלא היה לו ש"י ואח"כ נזדמן לו ש"י א"ל להסיר ש"ר קודם הנחת ש"י ע"ש. ועי' בשלמי צבור בשם מהרח"ו שכתב מורי ז"ל היה נזהר שלא להוציא תש"ר מן הכיס עד שיניח ויקשור תש"י סביב הזרוע בקיבורת במקום הקשר ואח"כ לא היה חושש מלהוציא תש"ר אף שעדיין לא הקיף בזרוע עלמו. וכפי הטעם שכתב המ"א אפשר דאף ע"י אחר אין להוציא ש"ר עד שיניח של יד ע"ש. ועי'

משנה ברורה

יתעמעם אחר הברכה ועיין בבה"ל מה שכתבנו בשם הגרע"א בזה: י (לג) אם סח. ואפילו (לו) אם סח בין ברכת להניח ובין הנחת התש"י ג"כ דינא הכי: (לד) אינו וכו'. אבל לכתחילה אסור להסיח בין ברכת להניח עד אחר הנחה של ראש (לז) אפילו בדברים שהן לצורך תפילין אם לא היכי שא"א בענין אחר. (לח) אך בחוה"מ שאין מברכין אפשר דיש להקל לכתחילה בדברים שהם לצורך תפילין: (לה) לא יפסיק. ואפילו לענות אמן על ברכה זו גופא כגון לענות אמן על ברכת תפילין שמברך אחר אסור אם לא שחבירו מכוין להוציאו בברכה זו [תשובת ד"ש והגרע"א בחידושיו דלא כפ"מ[ד] עי"ש]: (לו) לענות עמהם. ואם פסק וענה איש"ר או קדושה או ברכו (לט) או שענה אמן על איזה ברכה ששמע (מ) חוזר ומברך ועיין בבה"ל. ובחוה"מ או המניח תפילין דר"ת וכיוצא שמניח בלי ברכה (מא) יש להקל ולהפסיק לעניית איש"ר וקדושה וברכו ואמן אך (מב) אח"כ יזיז הש"י ממקומו קודם שיניח הש"ר כדי שיהיה הויה אחת לשניהן: (לז) שותק ושומע. דהשתיקה כעניה (מג) לענין לצאת י"ח אבל לא שיחשב כהפסק: יא (לח) קודם שיכרוך. הטעם (מד) כיון שברכת להניח חוזרת גם על של ראש כנ"ל בס"ק ל"א וכ"ש להמחבר לעיל בס"ה דס"ל דאינו מברך אלא אחת ע"כ ימנע ההפסק בכל מה שיוכל והכריכה סביב הזרוע אינה מעיקר הדין ע"כ טוב לאחר אותה עד שיניח של ראש ובספר כוונות האר"י ז"ל כתוב שהיה נוהג לכרוך השבעה כריכות סביב זרועו תחלה [אבל (מה) לא הג' כריכות שעל האלבע] מפני שהוא סובר כיון דלכתחלה גם הכריכות הוא מלוה לפיכך אין זה הפסק (מו) וכן המנהג בכ"מ ועיין בתשובת משכנות יעקב סימן כ"ח דעתו ג"כ כמנהגנו לכרוך קודם על הזרוע לחיזוק דבלא"ה לא מתקיים ואינו נקרא קשירה עי"ש כתב בספר מ"מ אם שמע קדיש וקדושה אחר שבירך על של יד ואם יכרוך לא יהיה לו פנאי להניח ש"ר ולענות יניח ש"ר קודם הכריכות (מז) אם יכול להדק במקצת שלא ימיש התש"י ממקומו: (לט) שאסור וכו'. הייני (מח) אפילו אם ירצה להוציא הש"ר והש"י שניהן בשוה מן התיק דבזה אין מעביר על המצות אפ"ה יש ליזהר כי יש בזה טעם ע"פ הקבלה כמש"כ בב"י וכ"ש להניח הש"י מידו ולהתעסק בהוצאת הש"ר מדינא אסור: (מ) מונחת. ר"ל שתהיה מהודקת יפה על הזרוע ואז מותר (מט) אפי' קודם שעשה השבעה כריכות. ואם אחר יכול להוציא ולתקן ש"ר בעוד שחבירו מניח של יד הפמ"ג מחמיר וארה"ח מיקל עי"ש: (מא) לא יתקן. ר"ל (נ) אפילו אם בעת תיקון הש"ר לא יניח הש"י ג"כ מידו אפ"ה (נא) כשמניח אח"כ הש"ר להניח הש"י הוי כמעביר על המלות

ביאור הלכה

* אם שמע קדיש וכו'. עיין במ"ב בס"ק ל"ו דאם פסק וענה חוזר ומברך. ועיין בח"א שכתב בפשיטות דלדידן לריך לברך שתים על הש"ר ולהמחבר לא יברך כ"א ע"מ ובארה"ח הכריע דבזה אפילו לדידן דנוהגין כר"ת לא יברך כ"א ברכה אחת והוא על מלות עי"ש מילתא בטעמא. כתב הבה"ט נ"ל אם חבירו מכוין להוציאו בברכת תפילין וגם הוא מכוין לצאת דרשאי לענות קדיש או קדושה ואינו נראה דהלא יוצא בברכת חבירו אינו עדיף מאם מברך לעצמו ובברכת עצמו אם פסק אפילו לאיש"ר חוזר ומברך ואינו יוצא בברכה ראשונה וא"כ הוא גורם ברכה שאינה לריכה ועיין בא"ר שמוכח כדברינו ועיין בסי' קס"ז ס"ו במ"א סקי"ט ובט"ז סק"ח שם בא"ד ועוד תמוה פסק הרוקח ע"ש. ואפילו הרוקח גופא מודה בענין תפילין כמו שכתב הפמ"ג שם מכל זה נראה דאפילו בדיעבד יש להחמיר בזה ולחזור ולברך ואפילו אם חבירו הניח כבר התפילין שלו בשעה שהוא מפסיק ועכ"פ לכתחלה בודאי אסור להפסיק בזה כיון

שער הציון

(לו) פמ"ג: (לז) מ"א: (לח) פמ"ג וארה"ח: (לט) הרא"ש בה"ק: (מ) לבוש ונ"ל ומ"א וא"ר ומ"א ודה"ח דלא כט"ז: (מא) מ"א ודה"ח וארה"ח ועוד הרבה אחרונים ע"ש דלא כא"ר: (מב) ארה"ח: (מג) ט"ז: (מד) ט"ז בשם הרא"ש (מה) פמ"ג: (מו) פמ"ג: (מז) ארה"ח: (מח) ארה"ח: (מט) אחרונים: (נ) פמ"ג: (נא) מ"א:

הגהות ותיקונים: א) ובכוונות: **ב)** כ"ז: **ג)** ומ"מ משמע דהמניח בחו"ה: **ד)** כפמ"א:

הערות והארות: 1) עיין מ"ב סי' קס"ז ס"ק ל"ז לענין אם אינו לצורך אלא רק מענין:

There is /an authority/ who says (39) that it is forbidden to take the head *tefilin* out of the bag until the arm *tefilin* (40) have been donned.

*Gloss: Even if both /*tefilin*/ are in front of him, outside the bag,* (41) *one should not prepare the head* tefilin *by opening them up, until after he has donned the arm /*tefilin*/. (...)*

*There is /an authority/ who writes that one should don the arm /*tefilin*/*

Mishnah Berurah

the interruption as much as he is able. The winding around the arm is not an essential halachic /requirement/. Therefore, it is desirable to postpone it until after one has donned the head /*tefilin*/.

In the work *Kavanos Ha-Ari, Zal*, it is stated that the practice of /the *Ari*, of blessed memory,/ was to wind the seven windings around the arm first [but not the three windings on the finger]. This is because he was of the opinion that, since, initially, the windings are also a mitzvah, /those windings/ are therefore not /considered/ an interruption. This is likewise the practice everywhere. See the responsa *Mishkenos Ya'akov* in Sec. 28. His opinion also /favors/ our practice, that one should wind /the strap/ around the arm first to strengthen /the binding/, for /he argues/ that otherwise /the binding/ will not last and is not describable as binding; see there.

It is stated in the work *M.M.* that if one hears *Kadish* or *Kedushah* after he has made the blessing over the arm /*tefilin*/ and if he will wind /the strap around his arm/ he will not have sufficient /time/ to don the head /*tefilin*/ and /be able to/ respond, he should /then/ don the head /*tefilin*/ before /he does/ the windings, if he can tighten /the bindings of/ the arm *tefilin* somewhat so that /the *tefilin*/ will not move from their place.

(39) That it is forbidden, etc. I.e., even if one wishes to take out both the head /*tefilin*/ and the arm /*tefilin*/ simultaneously from the bag, in which case bypassing a mitzvah is not involved, he must nevertheless avoid it. This is because there is a reason for this, based on the Kabala, as stated by the *B.Y.* One should certainly /not/ release the arm /*tefilin*/ from his hand, to occupy himself with taking out the head /*tefilin*/. This is /even/ forbidden from /the standpoint of binding/ halachah.

(40) Have been donned. I.e., they must be perfectly tight around the arm. Then it is permitted /to take out the head *tefilin*/, even before one has done the seven windings.

As to whether someone else may take out and prepare the head /*tefilin* for his fellow/ while his fellow is /engaged in/ donning the arm /*tefilin*/, the *P.Mg.* rules stringently and the *Ar.Hach.* rules leniently; see there.

(41) One should not prepare. I.e., even if while one prepares the head /*tefilin*/ he also does not release the arm /*tefilin*/ from his hand. Even in such a case, when he subsequently puts down the head /*tefilin* in order/ to don the arm /*tefilin*/, this will involve /a transgression of the prohibition against/ bypassing mitzvos.

(אגור בשם הזוהר סימן פ"ד) (ובמדינות אלו לא נהגו כן אלא (מב) שתיהן (יד) [יא] מעומד: **יב** * [ק]אם מניח תפילין כמה פעמים ביום צריך לברך עליהם (מג) בכל פעם. (מד) [ר]נשמטו (מה) ממקומם וממשמש בהם להחזירם למקומן צריך (טו) [יב] לברך: הגה ואם ממזיר א' מהם יברך כמו שמניח תפלה אחת כדלקמן סי' כ"ו[א] (דברי עצמו) [ש]הזיזם ממקומם אדעתא להחזירם מיד (מו) צריך לברך: הגה * וי"א (טז) [יג] (מז) שלא לברך (טור סימן ח') * והכי נהוג וכבר נתבאר לעיל סימן ח' סעיף י"ד: [ת]מי שמניח תפילין (מח) של יד ובירך ובתחלת (יז) [יד] ההדוק * נפסק הקשר של יד והוצרך

באר הגולה: ק סוכה מ"ו וכרבי ר הרא"ש בשם ר"י והטור ש בית יוסף ת שאלה במהרי"ק קל"ג

שערי תשובה

בתשובת יעבץ ח"ג סי' כ"ו שהבאתי לקמן סי' מ"ס ע"ש: [יא] מעומד. עיין בה"ט ועיין בשו"ת ח"ל סי' ל"ו שהביא מתשובת הרדב"ז דדין שאינו מוזכר ההיפך בש"ס ופוסקים יש לילך אחר דברי קבלה וגם במקום שיש פלוגתא בין הפוסקים דברי קבלה יכריע ע"ש: [יב] לברך. עבה"ט ועיין בשל"ה דמחלק בין מי שלובש תפילין כל היום וגם מו"מ שלו בתפילין שפיר הוי היסח הדעת בנשמטו ע"ש: [יג] שלא לברך. עבה"ט ועי' לקמן סי' נ"ג בבאר היטב סק"ג שהביא מגינת ורדים וכתב דממג"א סי' כ"ה משמע דא"ל לברך. וכבר כתבתי מזה בסי' וא"ו[ב] ע"ש ועיין בפרח שושן כלל א' סי' ט' מ"ש בזה על דברי גינת ורדים ובסי' נ"ג יתבאר בעזהי"ת: [יד] ההדוק. עיין בה"ט ומ"ש וכ"פ המג"א כו' ז"א דהמג"א לאו מטעמא דהט"ז אתי עלה אלא משום טעמא דכתב לעיל בנשמטו דבזה"ז שאין לבוש התפילין רק בזמן תפלה לא הוי היסח הדעת וא"כ לדעת הש"ע והא"ר שכתב לעיל ס"ק ט"ו גם בזה יש לברך. וגם נ"מ במי שלובש תפילין כל היום דגם של"ה מודה כמש"ל. גם דברי המג"א צ"ע מה דמדמה נפסק לנשמטו אליבא דמ"ש של"ה שנראה שלפי הטעם דשל"ה יש לחלק ביניהם. ועיין בא"ר שבנ"ל משמע כהט"ז ויש להקל בספק ברכה. ואם נפסק הקשר ורוצה להניח תפילין אחרים י"ל דהכל מודים

באר היטב

של ראש אין קפידא ע"ש. ועיין בספר משנת חסידים דף נ"ז ובע"ת: (יד) מעומד. כתב הכנה"ג בכללי הפוסקים כל דבר שבעלי קבלה וזוהר חולקין עם הגמרא הלך אחר הגמרא והפוסקים מיהו אם בעלי קבלה מחמירין יש להחמיר ג"כ. ואם לא הוזכר בגמרא ובפוסקים אע"פ שנזכר בקבלה אין אנו יכולין לכוף לנהוג כך ע"ש ובמ"א: (טו) לברך. ושל"ה כתב דלא נהיגי אידנא לברך כשנשמטו ממקומם משום דבשעת תפלה מסתמא אינו מסיח דעתו מהם והוי כחולצן ע"מ להחזירן מ"א. [ובספר אליהו רבה פסק כדעת הש"ע והביא ראיה לדבריו ע"ש]: (טז) שלא לברך. אבל אם חולצן ליכנס לבית הכסא צריך לברך לכ"ע דהא אין רשאי לילך בהם לבה"כ ואידחי ליה וה"ה אם לא היה בדעתו לחזור מיד צריך לברך ב"ח ע"ת ט"ז. וכתב המ"א ואפשר לומר דכשבהכ"ס אינו רחוק כמו בהכ"ס שלהם שהי' בשדה א"צ לברך וא"כ אין חילוק בין בהכ"ס למקום אחר ולכן סתם רמ"א כאן ע"ש. ודע הא דכתב רמ"א וי"א וכו' קאי נמי אהא אם מסירן לגמרי כי לענין זה שוה אם הזיזן ממקומם או הסירן לגמרי ע"ת: (יז) ההדוק. ר"ל קודם שנעשה המצוה כתקנה[ג] מש"ה א"צ לחזור ולברך דעשיית הקשר אינו הפסק כיון שהוא מענין המצוה. וכתב ט"ז מזה יש ללמוד במי שיש בידו תפילין בלא קשר ומברך ועושה קשר ומניח דשפיר עולה לו הברכה שעשה תחלה דעשיית הקשר אינה

ביאור הלכה

שחבירו מוליאו בברכתו: * אם מניח תפילין וכו'. עיין במ"ב במ"ש אם בשעת ברכה היה דעתו וכו' ואף דהמ"א איירי שם לענין ציצית פשוט דה"ה לתפילין דהגמרא במנחות מ"ג מדמי להו להדדי ע"ש: * וי"א שלא לברך. עיין במ"ב שהעתקתי דהחולצן ליכנס לבהכ"ס דצריך לחזור ולברך אף דהמ"א ספוקי מספקא ליה לענין בהכ"ס שלנו שאינם רחוקין כבר כתב הח"א דלא שבקינן פשיטותא דכל הני גדולים [הב"ח והע"ת וט"ז וא"ר] משום ספיקא דמ"א וגם עיקר סברתו דחו אותה עיין בחידושי רע"א ובספר ארצות החיים וכן ראיתי עוד חבל נביאים כולם בסגנון אחד דצריך בזה לחזור ולברך ולכן אף שהפמ"ג והדה"ח העתיקו את דברי המג"א המברך בודאי לא הפסיד ובפרט שהגר"א ז"ל מסכים לדעת המחבר דבכל גווני צריך לחזור ולברך: * והכי נהוג. כתב בארה"ח דאם חלץ התפילין בסתם אם חלץ הש"ל יד והש"ל ראש צריך לחזור ולברך ואם נשאר עליו התש"י או הש"ר אין צריך לברך דעדיין לא אסח דעתיה מן המצוה אבל אם היה בדעתו שלא להחזירו מיד רק לאח"ז אף שנשאר עליו תפלה אחת צריך לחזור ולברך. ולמד כ"ז מלעיל סימן ח' בנשאר עליו ט"ק כן הכא בנשאר עליו תפלה אחת ע"ש. ונראה פשוט דהחולצן בתוך התפלה אפילו בסתמא דינו כחולצן ע"מ להחזירן וא"כ אם חלצן לילך בחוץ להשתין מים אין צריך אח"כ לחזור ולברך: * נפסק הקשר. ואם נפסק הרלועה של

משנה ברורה

המלות: (מב) שתיהן מעומד. עיין במ"א שרולה להכריע דהנחה של יד תהיה מיושב והברכה תהיה בעמידה אבל בא"ר בשם רש"ל בתשובה סימן נ"ח כתב דמי לנו גדול מר"ש מקינון אחר שלמד קבלה היה מתפלל כתינוק בין יומו דמי שלא יכול להשיג סודה על נכון יבוא לקלן בנטיעות ע"כ (נב) יהיה הברכה והנחה בעמידה ובביאור הגר"א הוכיח דגם לפי הזוהר מותר להניח התש"י בעמידה ע"כ אין לזוז מהמנהג. כתב הכנה"ג בכללי הפוסקים כל דבר שבעלי הקבלה והזוהר חולקין עם הגמרא והפוסקים הלך אחר הגמרא והפוסקים מיהו אם בעלי קבלה מחמירין יש להחמיר ג"כ ואם לא הוזכר בגמרא ובפוסקים אע"פ שנזכר בקבלה אין אנו יכולין לכוף לנהוג כך (נג) ודין שאין מוזכר בהיפוך בש"ס ופוסקים יש לילך אחר דברי קבלה וגם במקום שיש פלוגתא בין הפוסקים דברי קבלה יכריע: **יב** (מג) בכל פעם. אפילו אם כשסילקן (נד) היה דעתו להחזירם תיכף ואפילו אם (נה) לא שינה מקומו כלל בינתים. והרמ"א בסמוך פליג ע"ז. ואם בשעת ברכה היה דעתו שאח"כ יסלקם ויחזור ויניחם מוכח מדברי המג"א לעיל בסימן ח' סקט"ז דלכו"ע אין צריך לחזור ולברך: (מד) נשמטו. כתב של"ה הא דלא נהיגי אידנא לברך כשנשמטו ממקומם משום דבשעת תפלה מסתמא אינו מסיח דעתו מהם והוי כחולצן ע"מ להחזירן דפסק ההג"ה בסמוך דאין לחזור ולברך. וא"כ (נו) אותן שהולכין לפעמים עד חלות בתפילין אם נשמטו ראוי לברך. והח"א כתב דאף בשעת התפלה אם נשמטו המברך לא הפסיד. ומ"מ (נז) נראה דלמעט בברכות עדיף: (מה) ממקומן. דוקא כולן או רובן אבל מקצתן אף דצריך להחזירן על מקומן אין צריך לחזור ולברך [ט"ז בסימן ח' סט"ו ועי"ש בפמ"ג]: (מו) צריך לברך. דכיון שהזיזן ממקומן הוי כמו שהסירן לגמרי: (מז) שלא לברך. כיון דהזיזן על דעת לחזור מסה"כ בנשמטו מעצמן אמרינן דתיכף שנשמטו אודה ליה המצוה ולהכי שפיק ליה הרב להמחבר שם. ודע עוד דה"ה (נח) אם הסירם לגמרי אדעתא להחזירם מיד פליג נמי הי"א ואפילו אם (נט) שינה מקומו בינתים ופסקו האחרונים כן. ואם (ס) לא היה בדעתו להחזירו מיד רק לאחר זמן אפילו אם אח"כ נמלך תיכף או שהיה בדעתו להחזירן תיכף ואח"כ (סא) נשתהא הדבר והסיח דעתו בינתים לכו"ע צריך לחזור ולברך. וכן (סב) אם חלצן לכנוס לבהכ"ס אפילו היה דעתו ללבשן תיכף צריך לברך לכו"ע דהא אין רשאי לילך בהם לבית הכסא ואדחי ליה וכמ"ש בסימן ס"ה וכתב הח"א דה"ה כשחולץ שצריך להפיח כיון דאסור להפיח בהן צריך לחזור ולברך: (מח) של יד. וה"ה (סג) בתפילין של ראש דינא הכי:

לא

שער הציון

(נב) וכן הסכים הפמ"ג: (נג) שע"ת: (נד) בב"י: (נה) דאפילו הזיזם חוזר ומברך: (נו) פמ"ג: (נז) פמ"ג: (נח) ע"ת וט"ז וא"ר: (נט) מ"א לעיל בסימן ח' בס"ק י"ח: (ס) מ"א: (סא) פשוט: (סב) עיין בבה"ל שביארתי היטב: (סג) ח"א:

הגהות ותיקונים: א) כ"ו: ב) ח' סקי"ד: ג) כתקונה:

sitting and the head /tefilin/ *standing. (...) (In these countries this is not the practice, but* **(42)** *both /are donned/ standing.)*

12. If one dons *tefilin* several times on /one/ day, he must make the blessing over them **(43)** every time.

(44) If /the *tefilin*/ slipped **(45)** out of place and one handles them /in order/ to put them back in place, he must make the blessing /again/.

Mishnah Berurah

(42) Both standing. See the *M.A.*, who wishes to decide that the donning of the arm /*tefilin*/ should be /done/ sitting, but the blessing should be /made/ standing. However, the *E.R.* writes in the name of the *Rashal*, /who states this/ in a responsum, Sec. 98, that we have no one greater than the *Rash* of Chinon and he, /even/ after studying the Kabala, would pray like a new born babe, since someone who cannot grasp correctly the secrets /of the Kabala/ can come to cut down /growing/ plants.[12] Therefore, /both/ the blessing and the donning should be /done/ standing. The *Beyur Ha-Gra* proves that even according to the *Zohar* it is permitted to don the arm *tefilin* standing. Consequently, one should not deviate from the practice /noted by the *Rema*/.

The *Kn.Hag.* writes among the rules of the Poskim that in any case where the authorities of the Kabala or the *Zohar* dispute /a ruling of/ the Gemara or the Poskim, one must follow the Gemara and the Poskim. However, where the authorities of the Kabala /rule/ more stringently, one should also be stringent. If something is not mentioned in the Gemara or by the Poskim /, then/, even if it is mentioned in the Kabala one cannot enforce /a person/ to act in accordance with it. Where an opposite ruling is not mentioned in the Talmud or by the Poskim, one should follow the words of the Kabala. In addition, where there is a dispute among the Poskim, the words of the Kabala should /be relied on to/ decide /the dispute/.

(43) Every time. /In the opinion of the author of the Shulchan Aruch, he must do so/ even if when he removed them he had in mind to put them back /on/ immediately and even if he did not change his place at all in the meanwhile. The *Rema* disputes this nearby.

If one had in mind when /he made/ the blessing that he would subsequently remove /the *tefilin*/ and don them again, it is evident from the words of the *M.A.* above in Sec. 8, sub-Par. 16 that, according to all /authorities/, it is /then/ unnecessary /for him/ to make the blessing again /when he in fact does so/.

(44) If /the *tefilin*/ slipped. The *Shelah* writes that /the reason/ why it is not the practice at present to make a blessing /over *tefilin*/ when they have slipped out of place is because at the time when one prays one ordinarily does not distract his mind from them. /In view of this,/ it is as if one takes them off in order to put them back on and the gloss rules nearby that /in such a case/ one should not make the blessing again.

According to this /reasoning/, it is proper for those who go about sometimes until midday /wearing/ *tefilin*, to make the blessing /again/ if /the *tefilin*/ have slipped /out of place/. The *Ch.A.* writes that even while one is praying he will not lose if he makes a blessing /over *tefilin*/ when they have slipped /out of place/. Nevertheless, it appears /logical that one should follow the principle/ that it is preferable to minimize /making/ blessings.

(45) Out of place. This only /applies/ if all or most /of the *tefilin* slipped out of place/, but if /merely/ part /of the *tefilin* slipped out of place, then/, even though one is required to put them back in place, he does not need to make the blessing again. [*Taz* in Sec. 8, Par. 15. See the *P.Mg.* there.]

12 See the *Talmud Yerushalmi, Chagigah,* Chapter 2, *Halachah* 1. It is related there that four people entered into the Heavenly secrets. These secrets are described there metaphorically as an orchard. It is stated there that one of them came to cut down growing plants. What is meant is that he began to cut down Torah scholars of promise and persuaded youths to leave the study of Torah and learn a trade instead. From this we know that a person who cannot grasp the Heavenly secrets correctly can become distorted if he follows them.

(אגור בשם הזוהר סימן פ"ד) (ובמדינות אלו לא נהגו כן אלא (מב) שתיהן (יד) [יא] מעומד: יב * ךאם מניח תפילין כמה פעמים ביום צריך לברך עליהם (מג) בכל פעם. (מד) ךנשמטו (מה) ממקומם וממשמש בהם להחזירם למקומן צריך (טו) [יב] לברך: הגה ואם מחזיר א' מהם יברך כמו שמניח תפלה אחת כדלקמן סי' כ"ז[א] (דברי עצמו) שהזיזם ממקומם אדעתא להחזירם מיד (מו) צריך לברך: הגה * וי"א (טז) [יג] (מז) שלא לברך (טור סימן ח' * והכי נהוג וכבר נתבאר לעיל סימן ח' סעיף י"ד:) תמי שמניח תפילין (מח) של יד ובירך ובתחלת (יז) [יד] ההדוק * נפסק הקשר של יד והוצרך

ק סוכה מ"ו וכרבי ר הרא"ש בשם ר"י והטור ש בית יוסף ת שאלה במהרי"ק קל"ג

שערי תשובה

בתשובת יעבץ ח"ג סי' כ"ו שהבאתי לקמן סי' מ"ס ע"ש: [יא] מעומד. עיין בה"ט ועיין בשו"ת ח"ל סי' ל"ו שהביא מתשובת הרדב"ז דדין שאינו מוזכר ההיפך בש"ס ופוסקים יש לילך אחר דברי קבלה וגם במקום שיש פלוגתא בין הפוסקים דברי קבלה יכריע ע"ש: [יב] לברך. עבה"ט ועיין בשל"ה דמחלק בין מי שלובש תפילין כל היום וגם מו"מ שלו בתפילין שפיר הוי היסח הדעת בנשמט ע"ש: [יג] שלא לברך. עבה"ט ועי' לקמן סי' נ"ג בבאר היטב סק"ג שהביא מגינת ורדים וכתב דממג"א סי' כ"ה משמע דא"צ לברך. וכבר כתבתי מזה בסי' וא"ו[ב] ע"ש ועיין בפרח שושן כלל א' סי' ט' מ"ש בזה על דברי גינת ורדים ובסי' נ"ג יתבאר בעזהי"ת: [יד] ההדוק. עיין בה"ט ומ"ש וכ"פ המג"א כו' ז"א דהמג"א לאו מטעמא דהט"ז אתי עלה אלא משום טעמא דכתב לעיל בנשמטו דבזה"ז שאין לבוש התפילין רק בזמן תפלה לא הוי היסח הדעת וא"כ לדעת הש"ע והא"ר שכתב לעיל ס"ק ט"ו גם בזה יש לברך. וגם נ"מ במי שלובש תפילין כל היום דגם של"ה מודה כמש"ל. גם דברי המג"א צ"ע מה דמדמה נפסק לנשמטו אליבא דמ"ש של"ה שנראה שלפי הטעם דשל"ה יש לחלק ביניהם. ועיין בא"ר שבנ"ל משמע כהט"ז ויש להקל בספק ברכה. ואם נפסק הקשר ורוצה להניח תפילין אחרים י"ל דהכל מודים

באר היטב

של ראש אין קפידא ע"ש. ועיין בספר משנת חסידים דף כ"ז ובע"ת: (יד) מעומד. כתב הכנה"ג בכללי הפוסקים כל דבר שבעלי קבלה וזוהר חולקין עם הגמרא הלך אחר הגמרא והפוסקים מיהו אם בעלי קבלה מחמירין יש להחמיר ג"כ. ואם לא הוזכר בגמרא ובפוסקים אע"פ שנזכר בקבלה אין אנו יכולין לכוף לנהוג כך ע"ש ובמ"א: (טו) לברך. ושל"ה כתב דלא נהיגי אידנא לברך כשנשמטו ממקומם משום דבשעת תפלה מסתמא אינו מסיח דעתו מהם והוי כחולצן ע"מ להחזירן מ"א. [ובספר אליהו רבה פסק כדעת הש"ע והביא ראיה לדבריו ע"ש]: (טז) שלא לברך. אבל אם חולצן ליכנס לבית הכסא צריך לברך לכ"ע דהא אין רשאי לילך בהם לבה"כ ואידחי ליה וה"ה אם לא היה בדעתו לחזור מיד צריך לברך ב"ח ע"ת ט"ז. וכתב המ"א ואפשר לומר דכשבהכ"ס אינו רחוק כמו בהכ"ס שלהם שהי' בשדה א"צ לברך וא"כ אין חילוק בין בהכ"ס למקום אחר ולכן סתם רמ"א כאן ע"ש. ודע הא דכתב רמ"א וי"א וכו' קאי נמי אהא אם מסירן לגמרי כי לענין זה שוה אם הזיזן ממקומם או הסירן לגמרי

ע"ת: (יז) ההדוק. ר"ל קודם שנעשה המצוה כתקנה[ג] מש"ה א"צ לחזור ולברך דעשיית הקשר אינו הפסק כיון שהוא מענין המצוה. וכתב ט"ז מזה יש ללמוד במי שיש בידו תפילין בלא קשר ומברך ועושה קשר ומניח דשפיר עולה לו הברכה שעשה תחלה דעשיית הקשר אינה

ביאור הלכה

שחבירו מוליאו בברכתו: * אם מניח תפילין וכו'. עיין במ"ב במ"ש אם בשעת ברכה היה דעתו וכו' ואף דהמ"א איירי שם לענין ציצית פשוט דה"ה לתפילין דהגמרא במנחות מ"ג מדמי להו להדדי ע"ש: * וי"א שלא לברך. עיין במ"ב שהעתקתי דהחולצן ליכנס לבהכ"ס דצריך לחזור ולברך אף דהמ"א ספוקי מספקא ליה לענין בהכ"ס שלנו שאינם רחוקין כבר כתב הח"א דלא שבקינן פשיטותא דכל הני גדולים [הב"ח והע"ת וט"ז וא"ר] משום ספיקא דמ"א וגם עיקר סברתו דחו אותה עיין בחידושי רע"א ובספר ארצות החיים וכן ראיתי עוד חבל נביאים כולם בסגנון אחד דצריך בזה לחזור ולברך ולכן אף שהפמ"ג והדה"ח העתיקו את דברי המג"א המברך בודאי לא הפסיד ובפרט שהגר"א ז"ל מסכים לדעת המחבר דבכל גווני צריך לחזור ולברך: * והכי נהוג. כתב בארה"ח דאם חלץ התפילין בסתם אם חלץ הש"ל יד והש"ל ראש צריך לחזור ולברך ואם נשאר עליו התש"י או הש"ר אין צריך לברך דעדיין לא אסח דעתיה מן המצוה אבל אם היה בדעתו שלא להחזירו מיד רק לאח"ז אף שנשאר עליו תפלה אחת צריך לחזור ולברך. ולמד כ"ז מלעיל סימן ח' בנשאר עליו ט"ק כן הכא בנשאר עליו תפלה אחת ע"ש. ונראה פשוט דהחולצן בתוך התפלה אפילו בסתמא דינו כחולצן ע"מ להחזירן וא"כ אם חלצן לילך בחוץ להשתין מים אין צריך אח"כ לחזור ולברך: * נפסק הקשר. ואם נפסק הרלועה של

משנה ברורה

המלות: (מב) שתיהן מעומד. עיין במ"א שרוצה להכריע דהנחה של יד תהיה מיושב והברכה תהיה בעמידה אבל בא"ר בשם רש"ל בתשובה סימן ל"ח כתב דמי לנו גדול מר"ש מקינון אחר שלמד קבלה היה מתפלל כתינוק בין יומו דמי שלא יכול להשיג סודה על נכון יבוא לקלן בנטיעות ע"כ (נב) יהיה הברכה והנחה בעמידה ובביאור הגר"א הוכיח דגם לפי הזוהר מותר להניח התש"י בעמידה ע"כ אין לזוז מהמנהג. כתב הכנה"ג בכללי הפוסקים כל דבר שבעלי הקבלה והזוהר חולקין עם הגמרא והפוסקים הלך אחר הגמרא והפוסקים מיהו אם בעלי קבלה מחמירין יש להחמיר ג"כ ואם לא הוזכר בגמרא ובפוסקים אע"פ שנזכר בקבלה אין אנו יכולין לכוף לנהוג כך (נג) ודין שאין מוזכר בהיפוך בש"ס ופוסקים יש לילך אחר דברי קבלה וגם במקום שיש פלוגתא בין הפוסקים דברי קבלה יכריע: יב (מג) בכל פעם. אפילו אם כשסילקן (נד) היה דעתו להחזירם תיכף ואפילו אם (נה) לא שינה מקומו כלל בינתים. והרמ"א בסמוך פליג ע"ז. ואם בשעת ברכה היה דעתו שאח"כ יסלקם ויחזור ויניחם מוכח מדברי המג"א לעיל בסימן ח' סקט"ז דלכו"ע אין צריך לחזור ולברך: (מד) נשמטו. כתב של"ה הא דלא נהיגי אידנא לברך כשנשמטו ממקומם משום דבשעת תפלה מסתמא אינו מסיח דעתו מהם והוי כחולצן ע"מ להחזירן דפסק הגה"ה בסמוך דאין לחזור ולברך. וא"כ (נו) אותן שהולכין לפעמים עד חלות בתפילין אם נשמטו ראוי לברך. והח"א כתב דאף בשעת התפלה אם נשמטו המברך לא הפסיד. ומ"מ (נז) נראה דלמעט בברכות עדיף: (מה) ממקומן. דוקא כולן או רובן אבל מקצתן אף דצריך להחזירן על מקומן אין צריך לחזור ולברך [ט"ז בסימן ח' סט"ו ועי"ש בפמ"ג]: (מו) צריך לברך. דכיון שהזיזן ממקומן הוי כמו שהסירן לגמרי: (מז) שלא לברך. כיון דהזיזן על דעת לחזור משא"כ בנשמטו מעלמן אמרינן דתיכף שנשמט אזדא ליה המלוה ולהכי שתיק ליה הרב להמחבר שם. ודע עוד דה"ה (נח) אם הסירם לגמרי אדעתא להחזירם מיד פליג נמי הי"א ואפילו אם (נט) שינה מקומו בינתים ופסקו האחרונים כן. ואם (ס) לא היה בדעתו להחזירו מיד רק לאחר זמן אפילו אם אח"כ לבשן תיכף או שהיה בדעתו להחזירן תיכף ואח"כ (סא) נשתהא הדבר והסיח דעתו בינתים לכו"ע צריך לחזור ולברך. וכן (סב) אם חלצן לכנוס לבהכ"ס אפילו היה דעתו ללבשן תיכף צריך לברך לכו"ע דהא אין רשאי לילך בהם לבית הכסא ואדחי ליה וכמ"ש בסימן ס"ה וכתב הח"א דה"ה כשחולץ שצריך להפיח כיון דאסור להפיח בהן צריך לחזור ולברך: (מח) של יד. וה"ה (סג) בתפילין של ראש דינא הכי:

לא

שער הציון

(נב) וכן הסכים הפמ"ג: (נג) שע"ת: (נד) בב"י: (נה) דאפילו הזיזם חוזר ומברך: (נו) פמ"ג: (נז) פמ"ג: (נח) ע"ת וט"ז וא"ר: (נט) מ"א לעיל בסימן ח' בס"ק י"ח: (ס) מ"א: (סא) פשוט: (סב) עיין בבה"ל שביארתי היטב: (סג) ח"א:

הגהות ותיקונים: א) כ"ו: ב) ח' סקי"ד: ג) כתקונה:

Gloss: If one puts one of /the tefilin *units/ back /in place/, he should make the blessing /or blessings/ that /one makes/ when one dons /only/ one of the* tefilin */units/, as /explained/ below in Sec. 26. (...)*

If one moved /the *tefilin*/ out of place with intent to put them back /in place/ immediately, (46) he must /nevertheless/ make the blessing /again when he puts them back in place/.

Gloss: There are /authorities/ who say (47) *that one should not make the blessing /again in such a case/. (... This is how one should act.*[3*] *This has already been explained above in Sec. 8, Par. 14.)*

If one is donning (48) the arm *tefilin* and has made the blessing and /then/, at the beginning of the tightening /of the *tefilin*/, the knot of the arm /*tefilin*/ becomes severed, he is /of course/ required to make another knot. However, if

Mishnah Berurah

(46) He must make the blessing. For, since he moved them out of place, it is as if he slipped them off completely.

(47) That one should not make the blessing. Since he moved them with intent to put them back.

This does not apply when they slipped /out of place/ of their own accord. /In such circumstances/ we rule that immediately they slipped /out of place/ the mitzvah /over which the blessing was made/ came to an end. That is why the Rav[13] acquiesced to /the ruling of/ the author /of the Shulchan Aruch above/ for such a case.

Note further that, correspondingly, in /a case when/ one slipped off /the *tefilin*/ completely with intent to put them back on immediately, the /authorities quoted by the *Rema*/ also dispute /the ruling of the Shulchan Aruch and exempt him from making a blessing again over the *tefilin* when he puts them back on/. This even /applies/ if he moved from his place in the meanwhile. The Acharonim rule accordingly.

If one did not have in mind to put /the *tefilin*/ back on at once, but only after an interval (even if subsequently he /did/ put them on immediately), or if he had in mind to put them back /in place/ immediately, but subsequently the matter was delayed and he diverted his mind /from them/ in the meanwhile, he is required to make the blessing again, according to all /authorities/.

Likewise, if one took off /the *tefilin*/ to enter a lavatory, he is required to make a blessing again, according to all /authorities/, even if he had in mind to put them on /again/ immediately. For one is not allowed to go into a lavatory with them /on/ and /the mitzvah over which the blessing was made/ was /therefore/ relinquished /when he took them off for this purpose/, in conformance with what is explained /below/, in Sec. 65 /, sub-Par. 2/. The *Ch.A.* writes that, correspondingly, when one takes off /the *tefilin*/ because he must break wind, he is required to make the blessing again /when he puts them back on/, since it is forbidden to break wind with them /on/.

(48) The arm. Correspondingly, the same ruling /applies/ in the case of the head *tefilin*.

3* If one took off the *tefilin* without having anything specific in mind, then if one of them remained on him he will not have distracted his mind from the mitzvah and he should not make a blessing when he dons the other again. If one took off the *tefilin* in the middle of the prayer service, for example, to go out and pass water, then, even if he did not have anything specific in mind it is ruled as if he took them off with intent to put them back on again. Therefore, he should not make the blessing when he puts them back on subsequently. (Beyur Halachah)

13 I.e., the *Rema*.

לעשות * קשר אחר אמנם (מט) לא הסיח דעתו * ^א^אינו צריך לחזור (נ) ולברך ^ב^אם (נא) הותר של יד קודם הנחת של ראש מהדקן וא״צ לחזור ולברך אבל אם הניח של ראש ואחר כך הותר של יד (נב) * מהדק ומברך ^י^מותר לברך על תפילין (נג) שאולין ולא על (יח) (נד) גזולין: ^יג^ (יט) [טו] (נה) ^ד^נהגו העולם שלא לחלוץ תפילין עד אחר קדושת ובא לציון: ויש מי שכתב על ד׳ הקבלה שלא לחלוץ עד שאמר בהם (כ) (נו) שלש קדושות וארבע קדישים דהיינו לאחר קדיש יתום והכי נוהגים המדקדקים: (פתח עינים

א ב״י ב א״ח בשם הרא״ש ג א״ח בשם העיטור ד ב״י

באר היטב

הפסק אבל אם לאחר הדוק התפילין על הזרוע ונעשה המצוה כתקנה[א] אח״כ נפסק הקשר משמע דצריך לברך וט״ז חולק ופסק דכל זמן שלא הניח תש״ר עדיין עוסק במצוה של יד כי א״א לו להניח ש״ר קודם ש״י ולא נגמר עדיין המצוה של יד ולא גרע ממ״ש הש״ע אם הותר של יד קודם הנחת של ראש א״צ לברך ה״ה נמי אם נפסק ג״כ א״צ לברך דהותר ונפסק שוים הם ע״ש וכ״פ המ״א וכתב דלפי מה שכתבתי בס״ק ט״ו בשם של״ה משמע דאפי׳ בנפסק אחר הדוק דא״צ לברך וכ״פ בתשובת הלק״ט ח״ב סי׳ ק״כ ע״ש. ועיין ע״ת ובנחלת צבי ומ״ש היד אהרן: (יח) גזולין. דהוי מצוה הבאה בעבירה וכתב ט״ז אפי׳ ביאוש ושינוי רשות לא מהני. ובשואל שלא מדעת מותר גם בתפילין כמו בטלית אך יקפלם כבראשונה תשובת בנימין זאב סי׳ רל״ט הובא בכנה״ג בני חייא ובע״ת: (יט) נהגו העולם. ויש שאין משהין יותר מן החיוב דצריכין גוף נקי והכל לפי מה שהוא אדם מ״א. והאר״י ז״ל לא חלץ עד אחר ע״כ נקוה. וביום של מילה אין לחלוץ עד אחר המילה מ״א: (כ) ג׳ קדושות. ע״ם הוא וצ״ל ג׳ קדישים וד׳ קדושות. וארבע קדושות הם. ברכו את ה׳ חדא. וקדושת שפה ברורה שניה. וקדושת העמידה. וקדושת ובא לציון. ובמקומות שאומרים קדיש יתום אחר עלינו המה ג״כ ארבע קדישים עיין במט״מ

שערי תשובה

שיברך וכ״כ במח״ב בשם מאמר מרדכי וספר זרע אמת עיי״ש: [טו] נהגו העולם. עיין בה״ט והמקור חיים כתב שלא לחלוץ עד אמירת פסוק והיה ה׳ למלך כו׳ ובספר הכוונות המסודר ממהר״ש וויטל כתב בהגהותיו שיסיר הכריכות מהאצבע וב׳ או ג׳ כריכות מהזרוע ויסיר של ראש ואח״כ של יד

משנה ברורה

(מט) לא הסיח דעתו. ואפילו אם סח בינתיים לצורך ענין אינו הפסק בדיעבד וכדלקמן סימן קס״ז ס״ו. ועיין לעיל בסי׳ ח׳ במ״ב סקכ״ח: (נ) ולברך. דכיון דלא נעשה עדיין מצות הנחה נמצא דלא חלה עדיין הברכה על שום מצוה (סד) ועשיית הקשר אינו מפסיק כיון שהוא מענין המצוה ע״כ חייל הברכה על הנחה שניה. ומזה יש ללמוד במי שיש בידו תפילין בלי קשר ובירך ועשה קשר והניח דבדיעבד שפיר עולה לו הברכה שעשה דעשיית הקשר אינו הפסק. ומשמע מדברי השו״ע דאם לאחר שהידק התפילין על הזרוע נפסק הקשר צריך לחזור ולברך דכבר נגמר מעשה המצוה וה״ל כנשמטו ממקומם דצריך לברך כשמחזירם וכנ״ל (סה) והאחרונים חלקו ע״ז וכתבו דכיון דברכת להניח שבירך קודם הנחת של יד קאי גם על תפילין של ראש כדאיתא לעיל וא״כ כ״ז שלא הניח תש״ר עדיין עסוק במצות[ב] השייך לאותה ברכה ולא נגמר עדיין המצוה שבירך עליו עד שהניח גם הש״ר ע״כ כמו בהותר הקשר של יד קודם הנחת של ראש פסק השו״ע דאינו צריך לחזור ולברך ה״ה נמי אם נפסק הקשר ג״כ אינו צריך לחזור ולברך. ואם נפסק הקשר של ראש או של יד לאחר שכבר הניח הש״ר והדקו צריך לחזור ולברך. ואם אין שם מי שיודע לתקן הקשר והולך לקחת תפילין אחרים (סו) בכל גווני צריך[1] לחזור ולברך דדמי להא דסימן ר״ו ס״ו: (נא) הותר. הקשר. וה״ה אם נשמטו ממקומם ומ״ש הניח ש״ר ר״ל שהדקו דהוא עיקר מצות הנחה וכנ״ל: (נב) מהדק ומברך. דה״ל כנשמטו ממקומם וכן אם הותר הש״ר לאחר הידוקו צריך לחזור ולברך כשמהדקו על ראשו ולפי מה שכתבנו לעיל בשם השל״ה אין לברך אם הותר התפילין בזמן התפלה בכל גווני: (נג) שאולים. ואפילו בשואל שלא מדעת מותר דניחא ליה לאיניש למיעבד מצוה בממוניה רק שיקפלם כבראשונה ולא יוציאם ממקומו הראשון כמו בטלית לעיל בסימן י״ד עי״ש [אחרונים]: (נד) גזולים. דה״ל (סז) מצוה הבאה בעבירה ואפילו (סח) אחר יאוש ואפילו (סט) בדיעבד לא קיים מצות תפילין אך אם מכר התפילין לאחר יאוש לאחר דעת המ״א בתרמ״ט והמחה״ש לעיל בסימן י״א דיוכל השני לברך דלדידיה הוי יאוש ושינוי רשות אכן הט״ז והגר״א בסימן זה כתבו בהדיא דבכל גווני אסור לברך אף דלענין לצאת בהם משמע מדברי הגר״א דיוצא בהם אך לענין הברכה אסור מ״מ משום בוצע ברך דעל ידי לקיחתו יצא הגזילה מרשות הבעלים. אך מי שלקח מהשני הזה נראה דיוכל לברך כן מצאתי במחנה אליעזר לעיל בסימן י״א עי״ש יג (נה) נהגו העולם. ויש (ע) שאין משהין עליהם יותר מן החיוב דצריכין גוף נקי והכל לפי מה שהוא אדם אם אין לו גוף נקי ומתירא שמא יפיח יסלק מיד ועיין סימן ל״ז ס״ב דתשו״ה אין רוב העולם נוהגים להניחם כל היום ובשם האר״י ז״ל כתבו שלא היה חולץ עד אחר ע״כ נקוה לך. וביום שיש בו מילה ראוי שלא לחלוץ עד אחר המילה כי מילה היא אות ותפילין הם אות: (נו) ג׳ קדושות. ט״ס הוא (עא) ובאמת צ״ל ג׳ קדישים וד׳ קדושות. כי ברכו את ד׳ נחשב חדא שהיא דבר שבקדושה וקדושת שפה ברורה שניה וקדושת העמידה וקדושת ובא לציון. ושלשה קדישים הוא ח״ק שקודם ברכו ותלי קדיש שלם שאחר תפלת י״ח וקדיש שלם שאחר ובא לציון. ומ״מ משמע מפמ״ג ושארי אחרונים דבמקומות שנוהגים לומר קדיש יתום בכל יום אחר עלינו טוב שלא לחלוץ עד אחר קדיש יתום. ואנשים שנוהגין לקפל הטלית ותפילין ולהכינם בתיקן בעת אמירת קדיש (עב) לא יפה הן עושין דמחויב יש לכוון בעניית אמש״ר כמבואר לקמן בסימן נ״ו בטור ובשו״ע ואיש״ר הוא עוד במדרגה גבוה יותר מקדושה כמבואר שם במ״ח סק״א ובודאי לא גרע מאשר ברכות דרבנן דאסור לעשות אפי׳ תשמיש

ביאור הלכה

הש״ר או הש״י לאחר שכבר נגמר מצות הנחתם וחלץ את התפילין ותיקנם נראה לכאורה דאם נשאר בם השיעור המבואר לקמן בסי׳ כ״ז ס״ח וי״א דמדינא כשר בלי שום תיקון תו לא הוי כנשמטו ממילא רק כהזיזן מדעתו ע״מ להחזירן דקי״ל דא״צ לחזור ולברך ובאופן שפסולים לגמרי צריך לחזור ולברך דה״ל כנשמטו ואולי כיון דבעת הפסיקה נשאר מהודק על הראש והזרוע מקרי אח״כ בכל גווני כחולצן ע״מ להחזירן ועיין בב״י: * קשר אחר. נ״ל דאין שום חילוק בין אם הקשר מאותה הרצועה או שהולרך ליקח רצועה חדשה דעיקר הברכה היא על התפילין בעצמם: * א״צ לחזור ולברך. עיין במ״ב במה שכתבנו דאם נפסק הקשר ש״ר או הש״י לאחר שכבר הידק הש״ר צריך לחזור ולברך אף דהמג״א כתב דלפי מה שפסק השל״ה בנשמטו שלא לברך א״כ ה״ה בנפסק חדא דדינא דשל״ה הוא דהוי כחולצן ע״מ להחזירן ובחולצן גופא יש ויש הרבה מהראשונים והאחרונים והב״י והגר״א בתוכם דס״ל דצריך לברך ואפילו לדעת רמ״א דס״ל דבחולצן ע״מ להחזיר א״צ לברך הא הרבה פליגי על של״ה עיין בא״ר ובח״א ובפרט בענינינו דהרבה חולקין יש בזה על המ״א דיש לחלק בין זה להיא דהשל״ה דהתם רגיל להשמט בתוך התפלה ע״כ בודאי היה דעתו בשעת ברכה שכשישמט שיתקננו משא״כ בנפסק דלא מצוי וגם בפמ״ג ובדה״ח משמע כן עי״ש ע״כ נ״ל פשוט דהמברך לא הפסיד בזה: * מהדק ומברך. לאו דוקא דהברכה צריך

שער הציון

(סד) ט״ז: (סה) ט״ז והגר״א ופמ״ג: (סו) ארה״ח וש״ת: (סז) מ״א: (סח) הגר״א (סט) מ״א וכמו שפירשו הפמ״ג ע״ש וכן פסק הגר״א בביאורו דלא כע״ת ובמ״א נ״ל עיין סימן תרמ״ט ס״א דשם מבואר דהוא לעיכובא דלא כע״ת ואלו בס״ה שם מבואר כע״ת עי״ש במ״א: (ע) מ״א: (עא) אחרונים: (עב) כנ״ל פשוט.

הגהות ותיקונים: א) כתקונה: ב) במצוה:

הערות והארות: 1) עיין מ״ב סי׳ קמ״ג ס״ק י״ט ובשעה״צ סי׳ תפ״ט אות מ״א ובסי׳ תרל״ט אות צ״ד ובסי׳ תרנ״א אות ע״ד לענין אם בירך על מצוה ולקח חפץ אחר ממין המצוה שבירך עליה:

(49) he has not diverted his mind /from the donning of the *tefilin*/, he does not need **(50)** to make the blessing again.[4*]

If the arm /*tefilin*/ **(51)** becomes undone before one has donned the head /*tefilin*/, he may tighten /the *tefilin* to the arm after he has tied it/ and does not need to make the blessing again.

On the other hand, if one has /already/ donned the head /*tefilin*/ and, subsequently, the arm /*tefilin*/ becomes undone[5*] /, then, after he has tied it/ **(52)** he must tighten /the *tefilin* to the arm/ and make the blessing.

Mishnah Berurah

(49) He has not diverted his mind. Even if one talked in the meanwhile /, but/ for the sake of this matter, this is not considered an interruption, once it is after the event, as /ruled/ below in Sec. 167, Par. 6. See above in Sec. 8, in the Mishnah Berurah, sub-Par. 28.

(50) To make the blessing. For in view of the fact that the mitzvah of donning /the *tefilin*/ was not yet performed, it follows that the blessing did not yet relate to any mitzvah. The forming of the knot is not an interruption, since it is /done/ for the purpose of the mitzvah. Consequently, the blessing relates to the second donning.

From this one can derive that if someone had in his possession *tefilin* without a knot and he made the blessing and formed the knot /subsequently/ and /then/ donned them, the blessing he made will effectually serve for his /obligation/ now that it is after the event, since the forming of the knot is not /considered/ an interruption.

It is implied by the words of the Shulchan Aruch that if the knot became severed after one tightened the *tefilin* on the arm, he must make the blessing again. For /by then/ the mitzvah act was already completed and /the case/ is comparable to /an instance/ when /the *tefilin*/ slipped out of place, in which case one is required to make the blessing when he puts them back /in place/, as /ruled/ above. /However,/ the Acharonim dispute this. They write that in view /of the fact/ that the blessing *Lehaniach Tefilin*, which he said before donning the arm /*tefilin*/, also relates to the head *tefilin*, as /stated/ above, it follows that as long as one has not /yet/ donned the head /*tefilin*/ he is still /considered to be/ occupied with the mitzvos which are relevant to that blessing. /Thus/ the mitzvah /act/ over which he made the blessing is not completed until he has also donned the head /*tefilin*/. Consequently, just as the Shulchan Aruch rules /for an instance/ when the knot of the hand /*tefilin*/ became undone before one donned the head /*tefilin*/ that it is unnecessary to make the blessing again, the same ruling also /applies/ if the knot became severed. In such a case also one is not required to make the blessing again.

If the knot of the head or the arm /*tefilin*/ became severed after one already donned the head /*tefilin*/ and tightened it, he must make the blessing again.

If there is nobody there who knows how to form the knot and he /therefore/ had to take other *tefilin*, he is required to make the blessing again in all cases, since this is comparable to /the case/ of Sec. 206, Par. 6.

(51) Becomes undone. /I.e.,/ if the knot /becomes undone/.

The same ruling /applies/ if /the arm *tefilin*/ slipped out of place /before one donned the head *tefilin*/.

When /the Shulchan Aruch/ states, "one has donned the head /*tefilin*/", it means that he has tightened them, since that is the essential /fulfillment of the/ mitzvah of donning /*tefilin*/, as /stated/ above.

(52) He must tighten and make the blessing. For this is comparable to /the *tefilin*/ having slipped out of place.

Likewise, if /the knot of/ the head /*tefilin*/

4* I.e., even if he was required to take another strap. (Beyur Halachah)

5* I.e., of its own accord. If one undid the knot deliberately and reformed it, a further blessing is unnecessary, in conformance with the ruling of the *Rema* for an instance when one moved the *tefilin*. (Beyur Halachah)

לעשות * קשר אחר אמנם (מט) לא הסיח דעתו * אאינו צריך לחזור (נ) ולברך באם (נא) הותר של יד קודם הנחת של ראש מהדקן וא"צ לחזור ולברך אבל אם הניח של ראש ואחר כך הותר של יד (נב) * מהדק ומברך גמותר לברך על תפילין (נג) שאולין ולא על (יח) (נד) גזולין: **יג** (יט) [טו] (נה) דנהגו העולם שלא לחלוץ תפילין עד אחר קדושת ובא לציון: יש מי שכתב על לד הקבלה שלא לחלוץ עד שאמר בהם (כ) (נו) שלש קדושות וארבע קדישים דהיינו לאחר קדיש יתום והכי נוהגים המדקדקים: (פתח עינים

באר הגולה

א ב"י ב א"ח בשם הראב"ד ג א"ח בשם העיטור ד ב"י

באר היטב

הפסק אבל אם לאחר הדוק התפילין על הזרוע ונעשה המצוה כתקנה[א] אח"כ נפסק הקשר משמע דצריך לברך וט"ז חולק ופסק דכל זמן שלא הניח תש"ר עדיין עוסק במצוה של יד כי א"א לו להניח ש"ר קודם ש"י ולא נגמר עדיין המצוה של יד ולא גרע ממ"ש הש"ע אם הותר של יד קודם הנחת של ראש א"ל לברך ה"ה נמי אם נפסק ג"כ א"ל לברך דהותר ונפסק שוים הם ע"ש וכ"פ המ"א וכתב דלפי מה שכתבתי בס"ק ט"ו בשם של"ה משמע דאפי' בנפסק אחר הדוק דא"ל לברך וכ"פ בתשובת הלק"ט ח"ב סי' ק"כ ע"ש. ועיין ע"ת ובנחלת צבי ומ"ש היד אהרן: (יח) גזולין. דהוי מצוה הבאה בעבירה וכתב ט"ז אפי' ביאוש ושינוי רשות לא מהני. ובשואל שלא מדעת מותר גם בתפילין כמו בטלית אך יקפלם כבראשונה תשובת בנימין זאב סי' רל"ט הובא בכנה"ג בני חייא ובע"ת: (יט) נהגו העולם. ויש שאין משהין יותר מן החיוב דצריכין גוף נקי והכל לפי מה שהוא אדם מ"א. והאר"י ז"ל לא חלץ עד אחר ע"כ נקוה. וביום של מילה אין לחלוץ עד אחר המילה מ"א: (כ) ג' קדושות. ט"ס הוא וצ"ל ג' קדישים וד' קדושות. וארבע קדושות הם. ברכו את ה' חדא. וקדושת שפה ברורה שניה. וקדושת העמידה. וקדושת ובא לציון. ובמקומות שאומרים קדיש יתום אחר עלינו המה ג"כ ארבע קדישים עיין במט"מ

שערי תשובה

שיברך וכ"כ במח"ב בשם מאמר מרדכי וספר זרע אמת עיי"ש: [טו] נהגו העולם. עיין בה"ט והמקור חיים כתב שלא לחלוץ עד אמירת פסוק והיה ה' למלך כו' ובספר הכוונות המסודר ממהר"ש וויטל כתב בהגהותיו שיסיר הכריכות מהאצבע וב' או ג' כריכות מהזרוע ויסיר של ראש ואח"כ של יד

משנה ברורה

(מט) לא הסיח דעתו. ואפילו אם שח בינתיים לצורך ענין אינו הפסק בדיעבד וכדלקמן סימן קס"ז ס"ו. ועיין לעיל בסי' ח' במ"ב סקכ"ח: (נ) ולברך. דכיון דלא נעשה עדיין מצות הנחה גמלא דלא חלה עדיין הברכה על שום מצוה (סד) ועשיית הקשר אינו מפסיק כיון שהוא מענין המצוה ע"כ חייל הברכה על הנחה שניה. ומזה יש ללמוד במי שיש בידו תפילין בלי קשר ובירך ועשה קשר והניח דבדיעבד שפיר עולה לו הברכה שעשה דעשיית הקשר אינו הפסק. ומשמע מדברי השו"ע דאם לאחר שהידק התפילין על הזרוע נפסק הקשר צריך לחזור ולברך דכבר נגמר מעשה המצוה וה"ל כנשמטו ממקומם דצריך לברך כשמחזירם וכנ"ל (סה) והאחרונים חלקו ע"ז וכתבו דכיון דברכת להניח שבירך קודם הנחת של יד קאי גם על תפילין של ראש כדאיתא לעיל וא"כ כ"ז שלא הניח תש"ר עדיין עסוק במצוה[ב] הש"ך לאותה ברכה ולא נגמר עדיין המצוה שבירך עליו עד שהניח גם הש"ר ע"כ כמו בהותר הקשר של יד קודם הנחת של ראש פסק השו"ע דאינו צריך לחזור ולברך ה"ה נמי אם נפסק הקשר ג"כ אינו צריך לחזור ולברך. ואם נפסק הקשר של ראש או של יד לאחר שכבר הניח הש"ר ויהדקו צריך לחזור ולברך. ואם אין שם מי שיודע לתקן הקשר והולך לקחת תפילין אחרים (סו) בכל גווני צריך[1] לחזור ולברך דדמי להא דסימן ר"ו ס"ו: (נא) הותר. הקשר. וה"ה אם נשמטו ממקומם ומ"ש הניח ש"ר ר"ל שהדקו דהוא עיקר מצות הנחה וכנ"ל: (נב) מהדק ומברך. דה"ל כנשמטו ממקומם וכן אם הותר הש"ר לאחר הידוקו צריך לחזור ולברך כשמהדקו על ראשו ולפי מה שכתבנו לעיל בשם השל"ה אין לברך אם הותר התפילין בזמן התפלה בכל גווני: (נג) שאולים. ואפילו בשואל שלא מדעת מותר דניחא ליה לאיניש למיעבד מצוה בממוניה רק שיקפלם כבראשונה ולא יוציאם ממקומו הראשון כמו בטלית לעיל בסימן י"ד עי"ש [אחרונים]: (נד) גזולים. דה"ל (סז) מצוה הבאה בעבירה ואפילו (סח) אחר יאוש ואפילו (סט) בדיעבד לא קיים מצות תפילין אך אם מכר התפילין לאחר יאוש לאחר דעת המ"א בתרמ"ט והמחה"ש לעיל בסימן י"א דיוכל השני לברך דלדידיה הוי יאוש ושינוי רשות אכן הט"ז והגר"א בסימן זה כתבו בהדיא דבכל גווני אסור לברך אף דלענין לצאת בהם משמע מדברי הגר"א דיוצא בהם אך לענין הברכה אסור מ"מ משום בוצע ברך דעל ידי לקיחתו יצא הגזילה מרשות הבעלים. אך מי שלקח מהשני הזה נראה דיוכל לברך כן מצאתי בדמשק אליעזר לעיל בסימן י"א עי"ש יג (נה) נהגו העולם. ויש (ע) שאין משהין עליהם יותר מן החיוב דצריכין גוף נקי והכל לפי מה שהוא אדם אם אין לו גוף נקי ומתירא שמא יפיח יסלק מיד ועיין סימן ל"ז ס"ב דתשו"ה אין רוב העולם נוהגים להניחם כל היום ובשם האר"י ז"ל כתבו שלא היה חולץ עד אחר ע"כ נקוה לך. וביום שיש בו מילה ראוי שלא לחלוץ עד אחר המילה כי מילה היא אות ותפילין הם אות: (נו) ג' קדושות. ט"ס הוא (עא) ובאמת צ"ל ג' קדישים וד' קדושות. כי ברכו את ד' נחשב חדא שהיא דבר שבקדושה וקדושת שפה ברורה שניה וקדושת העמידה וקדושת ובא לציון. ושלשה קדישים הוא ח"ק שקודם ברכו ותלי קדיש שאחר תפלת י"ח וקדיש שלם שאחר ובא לציון. ומ"מ משמע מפמ"ג ושארי אחרונים דבמקומות שנוהגים לומר קדיש יתום בכל יום אחר עלינו טוב שלא לחלוץ עד אחר קדיש יתום. ואנשים שנוהגין לקפל הטלית ותפילין ולהניחן בתיקן בעת אמירת קדיש (עב) לא יפה הן עושין דהתלמוד יש לכוון בעניית אמש"ר כמבואר לקמן בסימן נ"ו בטור ובשו"ע ואיש"ר היא עוד במדרגה גבוה יותר מקדושה כמבואר שם במ"א סק"א ובודאי לא גרע משאר ברכות דרבנן דאסור לעשות אפי' תשמיש

ביאור הלכה

הש"ר או הש"י לאחר שכבר נגמר מצות הנחתם וחלץ את התפילין ותיקנם נראה לכאורה דאם נשאר גם השיעור המבואר לקמן בסי' כ"ז ס"ח וי"א דמדינא כשר בלי שום תיקון תו לא הוי כנשמט ממילא רק כהזזן מדעתו ע"מ להחזירן דקי"ל דא"ל לחזור ולברך ובאופן שפסולים לגמרי צריך לחזור ולברך דה"ל כנשמט ואולי כיון דבעת הפסיקה נשאר מהודק על הראש והזרוע מקרי אח"כ בכל גווני כחולצן ע"מ להחזירן ועיין בב"י: * קשר אחר. נ"ל דאין שום חילוק בין אם הקשר מאותה הרצועה או שהולך ליקח רצועה חדשה דעיקר הברכה היא על התפילין בעצמם: * א"צ לחזור ולברך. עיין במ"ב במה שכתבנו דאם נפסק הקשר ש"ר או הש"י לאחר שכבר הידק הש"ר צריך לחזור ולברך אף דהמג"א כתב דלפי מה שפסק השל"ה בנשמט שלא לברך א"כ ה"ה בנפסק חדא דדינא דשל"ה הוא דהוי כחולצן ע"מ להחזירן ובחולצן גופא יש ויש הרבה מהראשונים והאחרונים והב"י והגר"א בתוכם דס"ל דצריך לברך ואפילו לדעת רמ"א דס"ל דבחולצן ע"מ להחזיר א"ל לברך הא הרבה פליגי על של"ה עיין בא"ר ובח"א ובפרט בעניינו דהרבה חולקין יש בזה על המ"א דיש לחלק בין זה להאיה דהשל"ה דהתם רגיל להשמט בתוך התפלה ע"כ בודאי היה דעתו בשעת ברכה שכשישמט שיתקננו משא"כ בנפסק דלא מצוי וגם בפמ"ג ובדה"ח משמע כן עי"ש ע"כ נ"ל פשוט דהמברך לא הפסיד בזה: * מהדק ומברך. לאו דוקא דהברכה צריך

שער הציון

(סד) ט"ז: (סה) ט"ז והגר"א ופמ"ג: (סו) ארה"ח וש"ת: (סז) מ"א: (סח) הגר"א (סט) מ"א וכמו שפירשו הפמ"ג ע"ש וכן פסק הגר"א בביאורו דלא כע"ת ובמ"א נ"ל עיין סימן תרמ"ט ס"א דשם מבואר דהוא לעיכובא דלא כע"ת ואלו בס"ה שם מבואר כע"ת עי"ש במ"א: (ע) מ"א: (עא) אחרונים: (עב) כנ"ל פשוט.

הגהות ותיקונים: א) כתקונה: ב) במצוה:

הערות והארות: 1) עיין מ"ב סי' קמ"ג ס"ק י"ט ובשעה"צ סי' תפ"ט אות מ"א ובסי' תרל"ט אות צ"ד ובסי' תרנ"א אות ע"ד לענין אם בירך על מצוה ולקח חפץ אחר ממין המצוה שבירך עליה:

One is permitted to make a blessing over **(53)** borrowed *tefilin*, but not over **(54)** stolen /*tefilin*/.

13. **(55)** It is the universal practice not to take off the *tefilin* until after the *kedushah* of /the prayer/ *U-Va Le-Tziyon* /has been said/.

Mishnah Berurah

becomes undone after they were tightened /on the head/, he must make the blessing /*Al Mitzvas Tefilin*/ again when he tightens them on his head.

/Note that/ according to what we have written above in the name of the *Shelah*, if /the knot of/ the *tefilin* becomes undone while /one is engaged/ in prayer, one should not make the blessing /when he dons them again/ in any circumstances.

(53) Borrowed. It is even permitted to borrow them without /the owners'/ knowledge, as a person is pleased if a mitzvah is performed with his possessions. One must only /be careful to/ wind them up /afterwards/ as /they were/ at the outset and not to take them out of their original place, as /is the ruling given/ above for a *talis* in Sec. 14 /, Par. 4/; see there. [Acharonim]

(54) Stolen. For this involves /the fulfillment of/ a mitzvah through a transgression.

/If one used stolen *tefilin*,/ he will not have fulfilled the mitzvah of *tefilin*, even once it is after the event.

/The ruling of the Shulchan Aruch applies/ even after /the owner/ has /already/ despaired /of his *tefilin*/. However, if one sold /stolen/ *tefilin* to someone else after /the owner had/ despaired of them, the *M.A.* in /Sec./ 649 and the *Mach.Hash.* above in Sec. 11 are of the opinion that the /buyer/ is able to make the blessing /over donning them/. /This is because/ for him there was /not only/ despair /on the part of the owner/, but /also/ a change of possession. On the other hand, the *Taz* and the *Gra* write explicitly in this section that to make the blessing is forbidden in all cases. Although it is implied by the words of the *Gra* as regards /the question of whether or not/ one fulfils /his obligation/ by means of such /*tefilin*/ that he does /in fact/ fulfil it, with respect to /the making of/ the blessing, however, /we/ nevertheless /rule that/ it is forbidden, because of /the implication of the verse[14]/, "If a robber makes a blessing /, etc./". /This is due to the fact/ that by his taking /them from the robber/ the stolen /*tefilin*/ left the possession of the owner. On the other hand, if someone acquires /the *tefilin*/ from this second person, it appears that /the third person/ is able to make the blessing /when he dons them/. I found this /stated/ in the *Damesek Eliezer*, above in Sec. 11; see there.

(55) It is the universal practice. There

14 *Tehilim* 10:3.

א ב"י ב א"ח בשם הרא"ש ג א"ח בשם העיטור ד ב"י

לעשות * קשר אחר אמנם (מט) לא הסיח דעתו * [א]אינו צריך לחזור (נ) ולברך [ב]אם (נא) הותר של יד קודם הנחת של ראש מהדקו וא"צ לחזור ולברך אבל אם הניח של ראש ואחר כך הותר של יד (נב) * מהדק ומברך [ג]מותר לברך על תפילין (נג) שאולין ולא על (יח) (נד) גזולין: יג (יט) [טו] (נה) [ד]נהגו העולם שלא לחלוץ תפילין עד אחר קדושת ובא לציון: ויש מי שכתב על פי הקבלה שלא לחלוץ עד שאמר בהם (כ) (נו) שלש קדושות וארבע קדישים דהיינו לאחר קדיש יתום והכי נוהגים המדקדקים: (פתח עינים

באר היטב

הפסק אבל אם לאחר הדוק התפילין על הזרוע ונעשה המצוה כתקנה[א] אח"כ נפסק הקשר משמע דצריך לברך וט"ז חולק ופסק דכל זמן שלא הניח תש"ר עדיין עוסק במצוה של יד כי א"א לו להניח ש"ר קודם ש"י ולא נגמר עדיין המצוה של יד ולא גרע ממ"ש הש"ע אם הותר של יד קודם הנחת של ראש א"צ לברך ה"ה נמי אם נפסק ג"כ א"צ לברך דהותר ונפסק שוים הם ע"ש וכ"פ המ"א וכתב דלפי מה שכתבתי בס"ק ט"ו בשם של"ה משמע דאפי' בנפסק אחר הדוק דא"צ לברך וכ"פ בתשובת הלק"ט ח"ב סי' ק"כ ע"ש. ועיין ע"ת ובנחלת צבי ומ"ש היד אהרן: (יח) גזולין. דהוי מצוה הבאה בעבירה וכתב ט"ז אפי' ביאוש ושינוי רשות לא מהני. ובשואל שלא מדעת מותר גם בתפילין כמו בטלית אך יקפלם כבראשונה תשובת בנימין זאב סי' רל"ט הובא בכנה"ג בני חייא ובע"ת: (יט) נהגו העולם. ויש שאין משהין יותר מן החיוב דצריכין גוף נקי והכל לפי מה שהוא אדם מ"א. והאר"י ז"ל לא חלץ עד אחר ע"כ נקוה. וביום של מילה אין לחלוץ עד אחר המילה מ"א: (כ) ג' קדושות. ט"ס הוא וצ"ל ג' קדישים וד' קדושות. וארבע קדושות הם. ברכו את ה' חדא. וקדושת שפה ברורה שניה. וקדושת העמידה. וקדושת ובא לציון. ובמקומות שאומרים קדיש יתום אחר עלינו המה ג"כ ארבע קדישים עיין במט"מ

שערי תשובה

שיברך וכ"כ במח"ב בשם מאמר מרדכי וספר זרע אמת עיי"ש: [טו] נהגו העולם. עיין בה"ט והמקור חיים כתב שלא לחלוץ עד אמירת פסוק והיה ה' למלך כו' ובספר הכוונות המסודר ממהר"ש וויטל כתב בהגהותיו שיסיר הכריכות מהאלבע וב' או ג' כריכות מהזרוע ויסיר של ראש ואח"כ של יד

משנה ברורה

(מט) לא הסיח דעתו. ואפילו אם שח בינתיים לצורך ענין אינו הפסק בדיעבד וכדלקמן סימן קס"ז ס"ו. ועיין לעיל בסי' ח' במ"ב סקכ"ח: (נ) ולברך. דכיון דלא נעשה עדיין מצות הנחה נמצא דלא חלה עדיין הברכה על שום מצוה (סד) ועשיית הקשר אינו מפסיק כיון שהוא מענין המצוה ע"כ חייל הברכה על הנחה שניה. ומזה יש ללמוד במי שיש בידו תפילין בלי קשר ובירך ועשה קשר והניח דבדיעבד שפיר עולה לו הברכה שנעשה דעשיית הקשר אינו הפסק. ומשמע מדברי השו"ע דאם לאחר שהידק התפילין על הזרוע נפסק הקשר צריך לחזור ולברך דכבר נגמר מעשה המצוה וה"ל כנשמטו ממקומם דצריך לברך כשמחזירם וכנ"ל (סה) והאחרונים חלקו ע"ז וכתבו דכיון דברכה להניח שמברך קודם הנחת של יד קאי גם על תפילין של ראש כדאיתא לעיל וא"כ כ"ז שלא הניח תש"ר עדיין עסוק במצות[1] השייך לאותה ברכה ולא נגמר עדיין המצוה שבירך עליו עד שהניח גם הש"ר ע"כ כמו בהותר הקשר של יד קודם הנחת של ראש פסק השו"ע דאינו צריך לחזור ולברך ה"ה נמי אם נפסק הקשר ג"כ אינו צריך לחזור ולברך. ואם נפסק הקשר של ראש או של יד לאחר שכבר הניח הש"ר והדקו צריך לחזור ולברך. ואם אין שם מי שיודע לתקן הקשר והולך לקחת תפילין אחרים (סו) בכל גווני צריך[1] לחזור ולברך דדמי לההיא דסימן ר"ו ס"ו: (נא) הותר. הקשר. וה"ה אם נשמטו ממקומם ומ"ש הניח ש"ר ר"ל שהדקו דהוא עיקר מצות הנחה וכנ"ל: (נב) מהדק ומברך. דה"ל כנשמטו ממקומם וכן אם הותר הש"ר לאחר הידוקו צריך לחזור ולברך כשמהדקו על ראשו ולפי מה שכתבנו לעיל בשם השל"ה אין לברך אם הותר התפילין בזמן התפלה בכל גווני: (נג) שאולים. ואפילו בשואל שלא מדעת מותר דניחא ליה לאיניש למיעבד מצוה בממוניה רק שיקפלם כבראשונה ולא יוציאם ממקומו הראשון כמו בטלית לעיל בסימן י"ד עי"ש [אחרונים]: (נד) גזולים. דה"ל (סז) מצוה הבאה בעבירה ואפילו (סח) אחר יאוש ואפילו (סט) בדיעבד לא קיים מצות תפילין אך אם מכר התפילין לאחר יאוש לאחר דעת המ"א בתרמ"ט והמחה"ש לעיל בסימן י"א דיוכל השני לברך דלדידיה הוי יאוש ושינוי רשות אכן הט"ז והגר"א בסימן זה כתבו בהדיא דבכל גווני אסור לברך אף דלענין לצאת בהם אך לענין הברכה אסור מ"מ משום בוצע ברך דעל ידי לקיחתו יצא הגזילה מרשות הבעלים. אך מי שלקח מהשני הוא נראה דיוכל לברך כן מצאתי במשק אליעזר לעיל בסימן י"א עי"ש יג (נה) נהגו העולם. ויש (ע) שאין משהין עליהם יותר מן החיוב דצריכין גוף נקי והכל לפי מה שהוא אדם אם אין לו גוף נקי ומתיירא שמא יפיח יסלק מיד ועיין סימן ל"ז ס"ב דמשו"ה אין רוב העולם נוהגים להניחם כל היום ובשם האר"י ז"ל כתבו שלא היה חולץ עד אחר ע"כ נקוה לך. וביום שיש בו מילה ראוי שלא לחלוץ עד אחר המילה כי מילה היא אות ותפילין הם אות: (נו) ג' קדושות. ט"ס הוא (עא) ובאמת צ"ל ג' קדישים וד' קדושות. כי ברכו את ד' נחשב חדא שהיא דבר שבקדושה וקדושת שפה ברורה שניה וקדושת העמידה וקדושת ובא לציון. ושלשה קדישים הוא ח"ק שקודם ברכו וחצי קדיש שאחר תפילת י"ח וקדיש שלם שאחר ובא לציון. ומ"מ משמע מפמ"ג ושארי אחרונים דבמקומות שנוהגים לומר קדיש יתום בכל יום אחר עלינו טוב שלא לחלוץ עד אחר קדיש יתום. ואנשים שנוהגין לקפל הטלית ותפילין ולהניחן בתיקן בעת אמירת קדיש (עב) לא יפה הן עושין דמאוד יש לכוון בעניית איש"ר כמבואר לקמן בסימן נ"ו בטור ובשו"ע ואיש"ר היא עוד במדרגה גבוה יותר מקדושה כמבואר שם במ"א סק"א ובודאי לא גרע משאר ברכות דרבנן דאסור לעשות אפי'

ביאור הלכה

הש"ר או הש"י לאחר שכבר נגמר מצות הנחתם וחלץ את התפילין ותיקנם נראה לכאורה דאם נשאר בם השיעור המבואר לקמן בסי' כ"ז ס"ח וי"א דמדינא כשר בלי שום תיקון תו לא הוי כנשמט ממילא רק כהזזן מדעתו ע"מ להחזירן דקי"ל דא"צ לחזור ולברך ובאופן שפסולים לגמרי צריך לחזור ולברך דה"ל כנשמט ואולי כיון דבעת הפסיקה נשאר מהודק על הראש והזרוע מקרי אח"כ בכל גווני כחולצן ע"מ להחזירן ועיין בב"י: * קשר אחר. נ"ל דאין שום חילוק בין אם הקשר מאותה הרצועה או שהוצרך ליקח רצועה חדשה דעיקר הברכה היא על התפילין בעצמם: * א"צ לחזור ולברך. עיין במ"ב במה שכתבנו דאם נפסק הקשר ש"ר או הש"י לאחר שכבר הידק הש"ר צריך לחזור ולברך אף דהמג"א כתב דלפי מה שפסק השל"ה בנשמט שלא לברך א"כ ה"ה בנפסק חדא דדינא דשל"ה הוא דהוי כחולצן ע"מ להחזירן ובחולצן גופא יש ויש הרבה מהראשונים והאחרונים והב"י והגר"א בתוכם דס"ל דצריך לברך ואפילו לדעת רמ"א דס"ל דבחולצן ע"מ להחזיר א"צ לברך הא הרבה פליגי על של"ה עיין בא"ר ובח"א ובפרט בענינינו דהרבה חולקין יש בזה על המ"א דיש לחלק בין זה לההיא דהשל"ה דהתם רגיל להשמט בתוך התפלה ע"כ בודאי היה דעתו בשעת ברכה שכשישמט שיתקננו משא"כ בנפסק דלא מצוי וגם בפמ"ג ובדה"ח משמע כן עי"ש ע"כ נ"ל פשוט דהמברך לא הפסיד בזה: * מהדק ומברך. לאו דוקא דהברכה צריך

תשמיש

שער הציון

(סד) ט"ז: (סה) ט"ז והגר"א ופמ"ג: (סו) ארה"ח וש"ת: (סז) מ"א: (סח) הגר"א (סט) מ"א וכמו שפירשו הפמ"ג ע"ש וכן פסק הגר"א בביאורו דלא כע"ת ובמ"א נ"ל עיין סימן תרמ"ט ס"א דשם מבואר דהוא לעיכובא דלא כע"ת ואלו בס"ה שם מבואר כע"ת עי"ש במ"א: (ע) מ"א: (עא) אחרונים: (עב) כנ"ל פשוט.

הגהות ותיקונים: א) כתקונה: ב) במצוה:

הערות והארות: 1) עיין מ"ב סי' קמ"ג ס"ק י"ט ובשעה"צ סי' תפ"ט אות מ"א ובסי' תרל"ט אות צ"ד ובסי' תרנ"א אות ע"ד לענין אם בירך על מצוה ולקח חפץ אחר ממין המצוה שבירך עליה:

There is /an authority/ who writes, from the point of view of the Kabala, that one should not take off /the tefilin */until he has said* **(56)** *three* kedushos *and four* kadishim *with them /on/. I.e., /they should only be taken off/ after the* kadish *for an orphan /has been said/. This is how those who are meticulous /in the observance of mitzvos/ act. (...)*

Mishnah Berurah

are /people/ who do not leave /the *tefilin*/ on their /persons/ more than one is obliged /to do/, because /of the fact that/ a clean body is required /for wearing *tefilin*/. Everything depends on what /the situation is in the case/ of the particular individual. If he does not have a clean body and is afraid that he may break wind, he should remove them immediately /he is no longer obliged to wear them/. See Sec. 37, Par. 2 that it is for this /reason/ that most people are not accustomed to leave them on all day.

It is written on the authority of the *Ari*, of blessed memory, that he did not take off /the *tefilin*/ until after /the passage/ *Al Keyn Nekaveh Lecha.*

On a day when there is a circumcision it is proper not to take off /the *tefilin*/ until after the circumcision, for circumcision /serves as/ a sign[15] and *tefilin* also /serve as/ a sign.[16]

(56) Three *kedushos*. This is a scribal error. /The correct reading/ should /in fact/ be three *kadishim* and four *kedushos*.

This is because /the call of/ *Barechu* is considered one /*kedushah*/, as it is a form of sanctification. The *kedushah* /after the words/ שָׂפָה בְרוּרָה is the second. /The final two are/ the *kedushah* of the standing prayer[17] and the *kedushah* of /the prayer/ *U-Va Le-Tziyon.*

The three *kadishim* are the partial *kadish* /said/ before /the call of/ *Barechu*, the partial *kadish* /said/ after the eighteen/-blessing/ prayer and the complete *kadish* /said/ after /the prayer/ *U-Va Le-Tziyon.* Nevertheless, it is implied by the *P.Mg.* and other Acharonim, that in those localities where it is the practice to say daily after /the prayer *Aleynu*/ the *kadish* for an orphan, it is desirable /for one/ not to remove /the *tefilin*/ until after the *kadish* for an orphan /has been said/.

/There are/ people who are accustomed to fold up the *talis* and the *tefilin* and place them in their bag while *Kadish* is being said. These /people/ act improperly, since one must apply himself intensely to the response of /אָמֵן יְהֵא שְׁמֵהּ רַבָּא /וכו', as explained below in Sec. 56 in the *Tur* and the Shulchan Aruch. /The response of אָמֵן יְהֵא שְׁמֵהּ רַבָּא /וכו' is of a still higher level /of holiness/ than *Kedushah*, as stated there by the *M.A.* in sub-Par. 1. It is definitely of no less /importance/ than /the saying of/ other blessings, which are /merely/ a Rabbinical /requirement, and even for them the ruling is/ that it is forbidden to do even light activity while one

15 See *Bereyshis* 17:11.
16 See *Shemos* 13:9 and 16; *Devarim* 6:8 and 11:18.
17 I.e., the eighteen-blessing prayer.

ספר המוסר פ"ד) ה וביום שיש בו ספר תורה נוהגים שלא לחלצם (נז) עד שיחזירו ספר תורה (נח) ויניחוהו (כא) בהיכל: הגה והיינו במקום שמכניסין התורה לאחר ובא לציון גואל אבל לפי מנהג מדינות אלו שמכניסים התורה מיד לאחר הקריאה אין לחלצם רק כמו בשאר ימים (דברי עצמו). ו ביום ראש חודש חולצים אותם קודם תפלת (כב) [טז] (נט) מוסף: הגה (ס) וה"ה בחול המועד ודוקא במקום שאומרים במוסף (כג) (סא) קדושת כתר מיהו נוהגים לסלקם קודם מוסף (סב) בכל מקום (ב"י):

ה בית יוסף ו שם בב"י

כו דין מי שאין לו אלא תפלה אחת. ובו ב' סעיפים:

א א אם אין לו אלא תפלה אחת * מניח אותה שיש לו ומברך עליה שכל אחת מצוה בפני עצמה

א מנחות ל"ח

שערי תשובה

יחלוץ מיושב והטלית יהיה עליו עד שיסיר התפילין ע"ש: [טז] מוסף. עיין בה"ט וכתבו בשם האר"י ז"ל אחר קדיש של חזרת ס"ת שבהיכל והיינו כפי מנהגם להחזיר הס"ת אחרי אשרי ובא לציון כמבואר בסי' תכ"ג ע"ש וכן נוהגין. ודלא כמ"ש בתשובות מ"ע סי' ק"ח לחלוץ אחר תפלת שחרית ע"ש. וכתב הפר"ח סי' תכ"ג שאם השעה דחוקה שאינו מספיק לחלוץ התפילין יזיזם ממקומם לצד אחר דחשיב כמונחים בכיסם כו' ונראה שיש מציאת[א] לענין זה כגון שהוא עומד לבוש בתפילין והציבור כבר התחילו קדושת כתר שאין שהות לחלוץ שכמו רגע שיאחר ישלימו לומר הקדושה. וכתב עוד מי שיצא ידי חובת חזרת מוסף וחזר להניח תפילין והלך לבהכנ"ס שעדיין לא התפללו מוסף דעתי נוטה שיכול לומר כתר עמהם. ומח"ב כתב שנראה לו שיסלק התפילין ויאמר כתר. וכתב בשלמי ציבור מדלא אמר אסור עד שיסלקם ש"מ דדוקא לכתחלה יש לו לסלקם אבל אם היה עסוק בלימודו ולאו אדעתיה וכשהתחילו הציבור הקדושה ננער ממשנתו ושמעה אזנו ואין שהות לחלוץ בהא אזיל ומודה להפר"ח דעונה כתר עמהם ע"ש. ומ"ש בבה"ט בשם הרמ"ע ע"ש בסי' ק"ח שכתב שהמניחין תפילין במנחה יניחו ג"כ במנחת ר"ח כי קדושת ר"ח עולה וירדת אחר תפלת מוסף ולכן יכול ללובשם כל היום ובמח"ב כתב שכן נוהגים ודלא כמ"ש באור לדיקים בשם מהרח"ו שאין כן דעתו. וכן מבואר מדברי הפר"ח דלעיל שאחר מוסף יכול ללובשם. ועיין בדבר שמואל סי' קי"ב בענין שיש נוהגין שלא לחלצן בר"ח ובחה"מ אף במוסף וכתב שם שהלבוש והרדב"ז נתנו טעם שיש לחלצם במוסף ע"ש:

באר היטב

ובשל"ה ובע"ת: (כא) בהיכל. סי' לדבר ויעבור מלכם לפניהם וה' בראשם. והחולץ קודם לכן לא יחלוץ בפני ס"ת אלא יסלק לצדדין מט"מ רש"ל מ"א: (כב) מוסף. אחר חזרת ס"ת בהיכל. ובח"ה יש לחולצן קודם ההלל. והש"ץ אחר ההלל. ובח"ה של סוכות אף הש"ל קודם ההלל מ"א עיין בשכנה"ג. הנוהגין ללבוש כל היום יחזור וילבוש בר"ח אחר תפלת מוסף אבל בח"ה לא יניחם לגמרי אפילו במנחה הרמ"ע: (כג) קדושת כתר. פי' במקום שאנו אומרים נקדש במוסף אומרים בקצת מדינות כתר יתנו לך לכן אין ראוי להיות כתר של תפילין עליו. וכתב ט"ז דהנוהג כן שאינו חולץ מוסף אין לו עליו תלונה מאחר שאין אנו אומרים קדושת כתר יתנו לך ושמעתי בשם גדול א' שלא היה חולצם במוסף ע"ש:

ביאור הלכה

להיות קודם הצידוק וכנ"ל בס"ח. ודע דמשמע מדברי האחרונים דדוקא אם הותר מעצמו שנתרפה הקשר ממילא אבל אם התירו בידים וחזר ותיקנו לדעת הרמ"א לעיל בהזין א"צ לחזור ולברך בזה בכל גווני. נסתפקתי אם פתח התפילין כדי לבדוק הפרשיות ונמצאו כשרים והניחן בתוכו ותפרן כדין דאפשר דצריך לחזור ולברך כשמניחן לכו"ע אף דהיה דעתו בשעת חליצתן לחזור ולהניחן כשימצאו כשרים משום דבאמצע נתבטל מינייהו שם תפילין רק פרשיות ובתים ואינו דומה להותר הקשר או נפסק דתפילין בלי רצועות ג"כ שם תפילין עלייהו משא"כ בזה. וכעין זה יש להסתפק לענין ציצית דזה פשוט אם מצא בטליתו כשהוא לבוש שאחת מציציותיו פסולין מן הדין ותקנו צריך לחזור ולברך כשלובשו דדמי ממש להא דנפסק הקשר אחר גמר קיום המצוה וכן מצאתי בדה"ח אך אם מן הדין הם כשרים אלא שרוצה לפשוט הטלית כדי להטיל בו ציצית אחרים מהודרים ולחזור וללבשו מיד לכאורה נראה דזה נקרא הסח מדעתו ע"מ להחזירו וא"צ לברך שנית וכדלעיל בסימן ח' סי"ד בהג"ה אך יש לדחות דשם נשאר הטלית עם הציצית בשלמותו ולא נתבטל מיניה מצותו משא"כ בזה דנתבטל בינתיים מן הבגד מצות ציצית אפשר דצריך לחזור ולברך שנית לכו"ע ואינו דומה למה דמבואר בארה"ח לעיל בסימן ח' דאם נפסקו הציצית אחר הברכה קודם הלבישה ומטיל בו ציצית אחרים דאין צריך לחזור ולברך דשם הלא היה קודם קיום המצוה וכמבואר בט"ז סקי"ב דמשם למד את דינו משא"כ בזה וצ"ע בכל זה:

* מניח אותה שיש לו וכו'. אפילו אם היא רק של ראש לבד ולא יחוש למה שאמרו כ"ז שבין עיניך יהיו שתים וגם אפילו בעת ק"ש ותפלה מותר לו ללבוש אחת ולא יחוש למה שאומר אח"כ בעצמו בק"ש וקשרתם וגו' והוא אינו מקיים דכל זה דוקא אם יש לו שיכול להניחם משא"כ בזה. ואם הוא מצפה שיביאו לו קודם שיעבור הזמן ק"ש אם הוא איש שדרכו ללבוש תפילין רק בזמן הק"ש ותפלה והוא רוצה עתה ללבשם ולהתפלל בהם בודאי יש לו להמתין עד שיביאו לו השניה ולא יקרא ק"ש ותפילין[ב] בתפלה אחת כיון שעדיין לא עבר הזמן ק"ש אבל אם דרכו ללבוש תפילין אפילו שלא בזמן

משנה ברורה

תשמיש קל בשעה שהוא מברך כמבואר לקמן בסימן קנ"א במ"א סק"ב: (נז) עד שיחזירו. רמז לדבר ויעבור מלכם לפניהם [היינו הס"ת] וד' בראשם [תפילין] ב"י: (נח) ויניחוהו בהיכל. והחולצן קודם עכ"פ יזהר שלא יחלוץ הש"ר בפני הס"ת כדי שלא יגלה ראשו בפניה אלא יסתלק לצדדין ובש"י דליכא גילוי או בתפילין ש"ר תחת הטלית גדול שרי [פמ"ג]: (נט) מוסף. אחר (עג) שהחזירו הס"ת בהיכל ובמקומותינו שמכניסים תיכף אחר הקריאה יחלצם (עד) אחר הקדיש שקודם תפילת מוסף. ובאליהו רבא כתב דבר"ח יחלוץ אחר קדושת ובא לציון קודם שאומר יהי רצון מלפניך וכו' שנשמור חוקיך ולא ימתין מלחלצם עד אחר קדיש כדי שלא להפסיק בין קדיש להתפלה: (ס) וה"ה בחוה"מ. והאחרונים (עה) כתבו כיון די"א שלא להניח כלל בחוה"מ כדלקמן בסימן ל"א ימהר לחלצן קודם הלל והש"ץ אחר הלל ובחוה"מ של סוכות שיש פנאי בעוד שממתינין על האתרוג אף הש"ץ יחלוץ קודם הלל. הנוהגין ללבוש כל היום (עו) יחזור וילבוש בר"ח אחר תפלת מוסף (עז) וא"צ לחזור ולברך אם היה דעתו לזה בשעת חליצתן לפי מה שפסק הרמ"א לעיל בסי"ב ובחוה"מ לא יניחם שוב לגמרי עד הערב. והאנשים המניחין תפילין דר"ת בחוה"מ לא יניחום כלל ובר"ח יוכלו להניחם אחר שיסיים הש"ץ תפלת מוסף או שיסירו התפילין של רש"י קודם ובא לציון ושל ר"ת ילבשו בעת אמירת ובא לציון [פמ"ג]: (סא) קדושת כתר. פי' במקום שאנו אומרים נקדש במוסף אומרים בקצת מקומות כתר יתנו לך לכן אין נכון להיות או כתר של תפילין עליו ואפילו בעת תפלת הלחש ופשוט דאם שכח והתחיל להתפלל בהם לא יחלצם באמצע דאינו רק מנהגא: (סב) בכל מקום. ובט"ז כתב דהנוהג שאינו חולץ במוסף אין עליו תלונה מאחר שאין אנו אומרים קדושת כתר יתנו לך ושמעתי על גדול הדור אחד שלא היה חולצם במוסף אך המתפלל בצבור (עח) בודאי לא ישנה מנהגא דצבורא:

שער הציון

(עג) מ"א בשם הכונות: (עד) מ"א לקמן בסי' תכ"ג וכדפירשתי דלא פליגי: (עה) מ"א וט"ז לקמן בסי' ל"א ושארי אחרוני': (עו) בה"ט: (עז) פשוט: (עח) פשוט:

הגהות ותיקונים: א) מציאות: ב) ויתפלל:

On a day when a Torah Scroll is /taken out from the Sanctuary and read from/, it is the practice not to take off /one's *tefilin*/ **(57)** until the Torah Scroll has been returned **(58)** and placed in the Sanctuary.

This /ruling/ relates to a locality where the Torah /Scroll/ is inserted /in the Sanctuary/ after /the prayer/ U-Va Le-Tziyon */has been said/. However, according to the practice in these countries, whereby the Torah /Scroll/ is inserted /in the Sanctuary/ immediately after the reading /from the Torah/, one must only take off /the* tefilin *at the same stage/ as /he would/ on other days. (...)*

On a day /when it is/ Rosh Chodesh, /the *tefilin*/ must be taken off before the prayer of **(59)** Musaf /is prayed/.

Gloss: /One should act/ **(60)** *correspondingly, on Chol Ha-Mo'ed.*

Mishnah Berurah

says the blessing, as stated below in Sec. 191, in the *M.A.*, sub-Par. 2.

(57) Until ... has been returned. This requirement is alluded to /by the verse/, "And their king will pass in front of them [i.e., the Torah Scroll] and the Lord at the head of them[18] [/i.e.,/ *tefilin*]". *B.Y.*

(58) And placed in the Sanctuary. Someone who takes them off earlier should at least take care not to take off the head /*tefilin*/ in front of the Torah Scroll, so as not to expose his head before it. Instead, he must go aside /before he does so/. In the case of the hand /*tefilin*/, where exposure is not involved, or when the head *tefilin* are underneath the large *talis*, it is permitted /to take them off in front of the Torah Scroll/. [*P.Mg.*]

(59) Musaf. /I.e., they must be taken off/ after the Torah Scroll has been returned to the Sanctuary.

In our localities, where /it is the practice to/ insert /the Torah Scroll in the Sanctuary/ immediately after the reading /from it/, one should take off /the *tefilin*/ after the *kadish* /which is said/ before the Musaf prayer /has been said/. The *Eliyahu Raba* writes that on Rosh Chodesh one should take off /the *tefilin*/ after /having said/ the *kedushah* /of the prayer/ *U-Va Le-Tziyon*, before /the prayer/ יְהִי רָצוֹן מִלְּפָנֶיךָ וכו' שֶׁנִּשְׁמֹר חֻקֶּיךָ וכו'/ is said. One should not wait before taking them off until after the *kadish* /has been said prior to the *Musaf* prayer/, so as not to make an interruption in between /the saying of/ the *kadish* and /the praying of/ the /Musaf/ prayer.

(60) Correspondingly, on Chol Ha-Mo'ed. The Acharonim write that in view /of the fact/ that there are /authorities/ who say that one should not don /*tefilin*/ at all on Chol Ha-Mo'ed, as /stated/ below in Sec. 31,

18 *Michah* 2:13.

ספר המוסר פ"ד) ובְּיוֹם שֶׁיֵּשׁ בּוֹ סֵפֶר תּוֹרָה נוֹהֲגִים שֶׁלֹּא לַחֲלְצָם (נז) עַד שֶׁיַּחֲזִירוּ סֵפֶר תּוֹרָה (נח) וְיַנִּיחוּהוּ (כא) בַּהֵיכָל: הגה והיינו במקום שמכניסין התורה לאחר ובא לציון גואל אבל לפי מנהג מדינות אלו שמכניסים התורה מיד לאחר הקריאה אין לחלצם רק כמו בשאר ימים (דברי עצמו). בְּיוֹם רֹאשׁ חֹדֶשׁ חוֹלְצִים אוֹתָם קֹדֶם תְּפִלַּת (כב) [טו] (נט) מוּסָף: הגה (ס) וה"ה בחול המועד ודוקא במקום שאומרים במוסף (כג) (סא) קדושת כתר מיהו נוהגים לסלקם קודם מוסף (סב) בכל מקום (ב"י): ה בית יוסף ו שם בב"י

כו דין מי שאין לו אלא תפלה אחת. ובו ב' סעיפים:

א אאִם אֵין לוֹ אֶלָּא תְּפִלָּה אַחַת * מַנִּיחַ אוֹתָהּ שֶׁיֵּשׁ לוֹ וּמְבָרֵךְ עָלֶיהָ שֶׁכָּל אַחַת מִצְוָה בִּפְנֵי עַצְמָהּ א מנחות ל"ח

שערי תשובה

יחלוץ מיושב והטלית יהיה עליו עד שיסיר התפילין ע"ש: [טו] מוסף. עיין בה"ט וכתבו בשם האר"י ז"ל אחר קדיש של חזרת ס"ת שבהיכל והיינו כפי מנהגם להחזיר הס"ת אחרי אשרי ובא לציון כמבואר בסי' תכ"ג ע"ש וכן נוהגין. ודלא כמ"ש בתשובות מ"ע סי' ק"ח לחלוץ אחר תפלת שחרית ע"ש. וכתב הפר"ח סי' תכ"ג שאם השעה דחוקה שאינו מספיק לחלוץ התפילין יזיזם ממקומם לצד אחר דחשיב כמונחים בכיסם כו' ונראה שיש מציאת[א] לענין זה כגון שהוא עומד לבוש בתפילין והציבור כבר התחילו קדושת כתר שאין שהות לחלוץ שכמו רגע שיאחר ישלימו לומר הקדושה. וכתב עוד מי שיצא ידי חובת חזרת מוסף וחזר להניח תפילין והלך לבהכנ"ס שעדיין לא התפללו מוסף דעתי נוטה שיכול לומר כתר עמהם. ומח"ב כתב שנראה לו שיסלק התפילין ויאמר כתר. וכתב בשלמי ציבור מדלא אמר אסור עד שיסלקם ש"מ דדוקא לכתחלה יש לו לסלקם אבל אם היה עסוק בלימודו ולאו אדעתיה וכשהתחילו הציבור הקדושה ננער ממשנתו ושמעה אזנו ואין שהות לחלוץ בהא אזיל ומודה להפר"ח דעונה כתר עמהם ע"ש. ומ"ש בבה"ט בשם הרמ"ע ע"ש בסי' ק"ח שכתב שהמניחין תפילין במנחה יניחו ג"כ במנחת ר"ח כי קדושת ר"ח עולה ויורדת אחר תפלת מוסף ולכן יכול ללובשם כל היום ובמח"ב כתב שכן נוהגים ודלא כמ"ש באור לדיקים בשם מהרח"ו שאין כן דעתו. וכן מבואר מדברי הפר"ח דלעיל שאחר מוסף יכול ללובשם. ועיין בדבר שמואל סי' קי"ב בענין שיש נוהגין שלא לחלצן בר"ח ובחה"מ אף במוסף וכתב שם שהלבוש והרדב"ז נתנו טעם שיש לחלצם במוסף ע"ש:

באר היטב

ובשל"ה ובע"ת: (כא) בהיכל. סי' לדבר ויעבור מלכם לפניהם וה' בראשם. והחולץ קודם לכן לא יחלוץ בפני ס"ת אלא יסלק לצדדין מט"מ רש"ל מ"א: (כב) מוסף. אחר חזרת ס"ת בהיכל. ובח"ה יש לחולצן קודם ההלל. והש"ץ אחר ההלל. ובח"ה של סוכות אף הש"ל קודם ההלל מ"א עיין בשכנה"ג. הנוהגין ללבוש כל היום יחזור וילבוש בר"ח אחר תפלת מוסף אבל בח"ה לא יניחם לגמרי אפילו במנחה הרמ"ע: (כג) קדושת כתר. פי' במקום שאנו אומרים נקדש במוסף אומרים בקצת מדינות כתר יתנו לך לכן אין ראוי להיות כתר של תפילין עליו. וכתב ט"ז דהנוהג כן שאינו חולץ מוסף אין לו עליו תלונה מאחר שאין אנו אומרים קדושת כתר יתנו לך ושמעתי בשם גדול א' שלא היה חולצם במוסף ע"ש:

ביאור הלכה

להיות קודם הצידוק וכנ"ל בס"ח. ודע דמשמע מדברי האחרונים דדוקא אם הותר מעצמו שנתרפה הקשר ממילא אבל אם התירו בידים וחזר ותיקנו לדעת הרמ"א לעיל בהזיון א"צ לחזור ולברך בזה בכל גווני. נסתפקתי אם פתח התפילין כדי לבדוק הפרשיות ונמצאו כשרים והניחן בתוכו ותפרן כדין דאפשר דצריך לחזור ולברך כשמניחן לכו"ע אף דהיה דעתו בשעת חליצתן לחזור ולהניחן כשימצאו כשרים משום דבאמצע נתבטל מינייהו שם תפילין רק פרשיות ובתים ואינו דומה להותר הקשר או נפסק דתפילין בלי רצועות ג"כ שם תפילין עלייהו משא"כ בזה. וכעין זה יש להסתפק לענין ציצית דזה פשוט אם מצא בטליתו כשהוא לבוש שאחת מציציותיו פסולין מן הדין ותקנו צריך לחזור ולברך כשלובשו דדמי ממש להא דנפסק הקשר אחר גמר קיום המצוה וכן מצאתי בדה"ח אך אם מן הדין הם כשרים אלא שרוצה לפשוט הטלית כדי להטיל בו ציצית אחרים מהודרים ולחזור וללבשו מיד לכאורה נראה דזה נקרא חלצו מדעתו ע"מ להחזירו וא"צ לברך שנית וכדלעיל בסימן ח' סי"ד בהג"ה אך יש לדחות דשם נשאר הטלית עם הציצית בשלמותו ולא נתבטל מיניה מצותו משא"כ בזה דנתבטל בינתיים מן הבגד מצות ציצית אפשר דצריך לחזור ולברך שנית לכו"ע ואינו דומה למה דמבואר בארה"ח לעיל בסימן ח' דאם נפסקו הציצית אחר הברכה קודם הלבישה ומטיל בו ציצית אחרים דאין צריך לחזור ולברך דשם הלא היה קודם קיום המצוה וכמבואר בט"ז סקי"ב דמשם למד את דינו משא"כ בזה וצ"ע בכל זה:

* מניח אותה שיש לו וכו'. אפילו אם היא רק של ראש לבד ולא יחוש למה שאמרו כ"ז שבין עיניך יהיו שתים וגם אפילו בעת ק"ש ותפלה מותר לו ללבוש אחת ולא יחוש למה שאומר אח"כ בעצמו בק"ש וקשרתם וגו' והוא אינו מקיים דכל זה דוקא אם יש לו שיכול להניחם משא"כ בזה. ואם הוא מצפה שיביאו לו קודם שיעבור הזמן ק"ש אם הוא איש שדרכו ללבוש תפילין רק בזמן הק"ש ותפלה והוא רוצה עתה ללבשם ולהתפלל בהם בודאי יש לו להמתין עד שיביאו לו השניה ולא יקרא ק"ש ותפילין[ב] בתפלה אחת כיון שעדיין לא עבר הזמן ק"ש אבל אם דרכו ללבוש תפילין אפילו שלא בזמן

משנה ברורה

תמיד קל בשעה שהוא מברך כמבואר לקמן בסימן קל"א במ"א סק"ב: (נז) עד שיחזירו. רמז לדבר ויעבור מלכם לפניהם [היינו הס"ת] וה' בראשם [תפילין] ב"י: (נח) ויניחוהו בהיכל. והחולצן קודם עכ"פ יזהר שלא יחלוץ הש"ר בפני הס"ת כדי שלא יגלה ראשו בפניה אלא יסתלק לצדדין ובש"י דליכא גילוי או בתפילין ש"ר תחת הטלית גדול שרי [פמ"ג]: (נט) מוסף. אחר (עג) שהחזירו הס"ת בהיכל ובמקומותינו שמכניסים תיכף אחר הקריאה יחלצם (עד) אחר הקדיש שקודם תפלת מוסף. ובאליהו רבא כתב דבר"ח יחלוץ אחר קדושת ובא לציון קודם שאומר יהי רצון מלפניך וכו' שנשמור חוקיך ולא ימתין מלחלצם עד אחר קדיש כדי שלא להפסיק בין קדיש להתפלה: (ס) וה"ה בחוה"מ. והאחרונים (עה) כתבו כיון די"א שלא להניח כלל בחוה"מ כדלקמן בסימן ל"א יזהר לחלצן קודם הלל והש"ץ אחר הלל ובחוה"מ של סוכות שיש פנאי בעוד שממתינין על האתרוג אף הש"ץ יחלוץ קודם הלל. הנוהגין ללבוש כל היום (עו) יחזור וילבוש בר"ח אחר תפלת מוסף (עז) וא"צ לחזור ולברך אם היה דעתו לזה בשעת חליצתן לפי מה שפסק הרמ"א לעיל בסי"ב ובחוה"מ לא יניחם שוב לגמרי עד הערב. והאנשים המניחין תפילין דר"ת בחוה"מ לא יניחום כלל ובר"ח יוכלו להניחם אחר שיסיים הש"ץ תפלת מוסף או שיסירו התפילין של רש"י קודם ובא לציון ושל ר"ת ילבשו בעת אמירת ובא לציון [פמ"ג]: (סא) קדושת כתר. פי' במקום שאנו אומרים נקדש במוסף אומרים בקצת מקומות כתר יתנו לך לכן אין נכון להיות אז כתר של תפילין עליו ואפילו בעת תפלת הלחש ופשוט דאם שכח והתחיל להתפלל בהם לא יחלצם באמצע דאינו רק מנהגא: (סב) בכל מקום. והט"ז כתב דהנוהג שאינו חולץ במוסף אין עליו תלונה מאחר שאין אנו אומרים קדושת כתר יתנו לך ושמעתי על גדול הדור אחד שלא היה חולצם במוסף אך המתפלל בצבור (עח) בודאי לא ישנה מנהגא דצבורא:

שער הציון

(עג) מ"א בשם הכונות: (עד) מ"א לקמן בסי' תכ"ג וכדפירשתי דלא פליגי: (עה) מ"א וט"ז לקמן בסי' ל"א ושארי אחרוני': (עו) בה"ט: (עז) פשוט: (עח) פשוט:

הגהות ותיקונים: א) מציאות: ב) ויתפלל:

שוס

This only /applies/ in a locality where **(61)** *the* kedushah Keser *is said in the Musaf /service/. However, it is the practice* **(62)** *everywhere to remove /the* tefilin/ *before the Musaf /prayer is prayed/. (...)*

§26: THE LAW WHEN ONE HAS ONLY ONE OF THE *TEFILIN* UNITS

(Contains Two Paragraphs)

1. If one has only one of the *tefilin* units, he should /nevertheless/ don /the unit/ which he does have[1*] and make a blessing over /donning/ it, since /the donning of/ each unit is an independent mitzvah.

Mishnah Berurah

/Par. 2/, one should hasten to take off /the *tefilin* on Chol Ha-Mo'ed/ before /the reading of/ *Haleyl.* The community prayer /should remove the *tefilin*/ after *Haleyl.* On Chol Ha-Mo'ed of Sukkos, when he has time available while /the congregation are/ waiting for /the use of/ the citron, even the community prayer should take off /the *tefilin*/ before /the reading of/ *Haleyl.*

Those whose practice is /to wear *tefilin*/ all day, should put on /the *tefilin*/ again on Rosh Chodesh after the *Musaf* prayer /has been prayed/. They are not required to make the blessing again if they had in mind when they took them off to /put them on again/, according to what the *Rema* rules above in Sec. 12. On Chol Ha-Mo'ed /, however,/ one should not don /the *tefilin*/ again at all /at any time, up/ until night.

Those people who don the *tefilin* /which accord with the view/ of Rabbeinu Tam, should not don them at all on Chol Ha-Mo'ed. On Rosh Chodesh they can don these /*tefilin*/ after the community prayer has concluded the Musaf prayer. Alternatively, they should slip off the *tefilin* /which accord with the view/ of *Rashi* before /the saying of the prayer/ *U-Va Le-Tziyon* and should wear /the *tefilin* which accord with the view/ of Rabbeinu Tam while /the prayer/ *U-Va Le-Tziyon* is said. [*P.Mg.*]

(61) The *kedushah Keser*. I.e., instead of /נְקַדֵּשׁ /וכו', which we say in /the *kedushah* of/ Musaf, /it is the practice/ in some localities to say /כֶּתֶר יִתְּנוּ לְךָ /וכו' (... will give You a crown). Therefore, it is improper for the crown of *tefilin* to be on one then, even at the time when the quiet prayer /is prayed/.

It is self-understood that if one forgot /to take off the *tefilin*/ and began praying with them on, he should not take them off in the middle /of the prayer/, since /to take them off before then/ is only a practice /, but is not a halachic obligation/.

(62) Everywhere. The *Taz* writes that we cannot complain against someone whose practice is not to take off /the *tefilin*/ before the Musaf /service/, in view of /the fact/ that we do not say the *kedushah* /with the wording כֶּתֶר יִתְּנוּ לְךָ /וכו'. /He states that/ he heard /it said/ of a distinguished /scholar/ of the generation that he did not take off /his *tefilin*/ before the Musaf /service/. However, someone who prays /together/ with a congregation should definitely not deviate from the practice of the congregation.

1* I.e., if he will not receive the other unit before the time for reading "The Reading of Shema" has passed or if he is accustomed to wear *tefilin* even when he is not praying. (Beyur Halachah)

ב והוא הדין אם יש לו שתיהם * ג ויש לו (א) (א) שום אונס שאינו יכול להניח אלא אחת מניח אותה שיכול: **ב** ד אם אינו מניח אלא של ראש לבד מברך עליה על מצות תפילין לבד: הגה (ב) ולדידן דנוהגים לברך בכל יום שתי ברכות מברך על של ראש לבד שתי ברכות ואם מניח של יד לבד (ג) מברך להניח לבד (טור):

ב שם מ"ד סברא בתרא דרב חסדא
ג הרא"ש ד רש"י והרי"ף והרמב"ם בפרק ד' מה"ת

כז מקום הנחתן ואופן הנחתן. ובו י"א סעיפים:

א א מקום הנחתן של יד בזרוע (א) [א] (א) שמאל (ב) * בבשר התפוח שבעצם ב שבין (ב) (ג) הקובד"ר ובית השחי ג ויטה התפלה מעט לצד הגוף בענין שכשיכוף זרועו למטה יהיו כנגד לבו ונמצא מקיים והיו הדברים האלה על לבבך: הגה וצריך להניח (ד) * בראש העצם הסמוך (ג) [ב] לקובד"ו

א מנחות ל"ו ל"ז
ב סמ"ק ג מנחות ל"ז

באר היטב

(א) שום אונס. כגון שצריך לצאת לדרך ואינו יכול להתעכב להניח של יד מניח של ראש לבד. כ"כ הרא"ש ועיין מ"א:

(א) שמאל. ואם הניחו בימינו אפי' בדיעבד לא יצא חוט השני סי' כ"ח: (ב) הקובד"ו. בל"א עלינבוגי"ן°: (ג) לקובד"ו. ויש להניח

משנה ברורה

א (א) שום אונס. כגון שיש לו מכה בראשו או בזרועו או (א) שהוא צריך לצאת לדרך ואין השיירא ממתנת עליו עד שיניח שתיהם מניח אותה שיכול. והי מינייהו עדיפא לענין הנחה (ב) י"א דיותר טוב שיניח ש"ר לבד דקדושתו חמורה (ג) וי"א שיניח לע"ע הש"י כדי שלא ישנה הסדר שבתורה (ד) בד"א כשיהיה יכול אח"כ להניח בדרך התפלה השניה אבל אם אח"כ לא יכול להניח התפלה השניה יניח הש"י והש"ר קודם הליכתו מביתו דמשום איחור דרכו לא התירו לו לבטל ממצות תפילין: **ב** (ב) ולדידן דנוהגין וכו'. כמו שביארנו בסימן כ"ה במ"ב ס"ק ל"ב[א] ע"ש: (ג) מברך להניח. עיין בפמ"ג שהביא עוד פוסקים דס"ל דאף על של יד לבד נמי מברך שתי ברכות ולהלכה הסכימו האחרונים דאינו מברך על ש"י אלא להניח לבד (ה) דבלא"ה הרבה ראשונים ס"ל דאפילו על שתיהן נמי אינו מברך אלא אחת. אם (ו) הניח שתיהן ולא בירך דהדין הוא דיברך כ"ז שהן עליו עדיין אם הקדים ברכת ש"ר תחלה ואח"כ ש"י אינו חוזר ומברך אבל לכתחלה אפילו הניח ש"י ולא בירך יברך עליו קודם הנחת של ראש:

א (א) שמאל. מדכתיב (א) ידכה בה"א פירוש יד כהה דהיינו השמאל שהיא תשה וכהה ועוד דרשו מדכתיב וקשרתם וכתבתם מה כתיבה בימין שכן דרך בני אדם אף קשירה בימין וכיון דקשירה בימין ממילא הנחה בשמאל ואם הניחו בימין אף בדיעבד לא יצא [אחרונים]: (ב) בבשר התפוח. והוא המקום הנקרא קיבורת בלשון חז"ל והוא לעיכובא כדילפינן לזה בגמ' מקרא: (ג) הקובד"ו. הנקרא עלינבוגי"ן°: (ד) בראש העצם. אין ר"ל ראש העצם ממש דהתם עדיין נמוך הבשר ועד שיתחיל להיות גבוה (ב) אין מקום תפילין דאין ע"ז שם קיבורת אלא ר"ל בגובה הבשר שבעצם ולא בא הרמ"א בזה לחדש שום דבר רק במה שסיים אבל לא בחצי העצם שסמוך לשחי ור"ל (ג) אף שיש גם שם עדיין מקצת בשר תפוח וגם דעת המחבר הוא כן דדוקא מחצי העצם ולמטה כדמוכח בסעיף ז' ומה שכתב המחבר מתחלה בבשר התפוח שבעצם ע"כ ג"כ דכונתו מחצי העצם ולמטה והגר"א בביאורו הסכים לדינא דכל מקום הקיבורת כשר להניח בו תפילין וכן משמע בפרישה ועב"פ (ד) למטה ממקום הקיבורת פסול לכו"ע ע"כ נכון למנוע ג.להניח תפילין גדולים כי ע"פ הרוב מצוי בתפילין גדולים שסוף הקציצה מונחת למטה ממקום הקיבורת אם לא שיקשרם לכתחלה בחצי העצם העליון וגם זה לא נכון להקל לכתחילה בזה אחרי דדעת המחבר ורמ"א להחמיר בזה. אך אם אין לו כ"א תפילין גדולים טוב יותר שיקשרם בחצי העצם העליון במקום שנמצא עדיין

שערי תשובה

[א] שמאל. עבה"ט ובבית יעקב סי' קמ"ט בסוף מלדד לומר דילא ולא מחוור ומ"ש מבה"ע שהביא הב"י בסימן תרנ"א אין ראיה דהתם באיטר קאי ועיין לקמן ס"ק י"א ע"ש: [ב] לקובד"ו. עיין בה"ט ועיין

ביאור הלכה

ק"ש והוא רוצה עתה ללבוש כדי שלא לבטל מצות תפילין מעליו פשוט דיכול ללבשם תיכף ולברך עליהם אך לענין לקרות בהם ק"ש נראה דיש לו להמתין עד שיביאו לו השניה: * ויש לו שום אונס. המחבר איירי לענין שיהא מותר להניח תפלה אחת לכתחילה אבל בדיעבד אפילו אם הזיד ולא הניח רק אחת יצא ידי אותה שהניח [ב"י]:

* בבשר התפוח. וצריך ליזהר שלא יהיה קצה התפילין למטה מבשר התפוח כמו בשל ראש שצריך ליזהר שלא יהיה קצהו על המצח כדלקמן דהא ילפינן במנחות ל"ז ע"ב גז"ש גובה שביד מגובה שבראש עי"ש: * בראש העצם. עיין במ"א ועיין במחצית השקל ומשמע לכאורה דבשר התפוח נתפשט בכל העצם בשוה והרמ"א אסר להניח התפילין כ"א בחצי בשר התפוח שאצל הקובד"ו ובאמת לפ"ז יפלא מאוד דהאיך סוברים דאין מותר להניח כ"א חצי קיבורת והלא בערכין י"ט ע"ב איתא בהדיא דקיבורת כולה איקרי יד ולענין תפילין איירי שם בגמרא וא"ל דהגהת סמ"ק לא היה לו הגירסא בגמרא קיבורת כולה דהלא כל הראשונים העתיקו לשון זה [עיין בתוספת שבת ל"ב ע"א ובספר יראים לרבינו אליעזר ממיץ ובסה"ת] וכן מוכח ג"כ במנחות ל"ז ע"א דכל הקיבורת כשר דקאמר ידך זה קיבורת בין עיניך זה קדקוד היכא אמרי דבי ר"י מקום שמוחו של תינוק רופס ומדלא מבאר ג"כ את מקום המיוחד שבקיבורת ש"מ דכל הקיבורת כשר וכן הרי"ף והרמב"ם והרא"ש והטור ורי"ו לא הזכירו שום זכר שיחלק את בשר הקיבורת לחצאין ואיך יתפוס הרמ"א דעת הסמ"ק ואין לומר דרק להחמיר חשש לדעתו דהלא לקמן בס"ז משמע דאם נתפשט המכה בכל השטח שמחצי עלס ולמטה פטור תו מתפילין [ועיין במרדכי דעת הר"מ ונוכל לומר דהרמ"א כוון לאפוקי מדעתו אך דינא דהשו"ע לקמן בס"ז קשה] ועזרני ה' שמצאתי בספר התרומה אחר דשקיל וטרי שם ומסכים לדעת ר"ת דמקום התפילין הוא בעצם העליון שהוא בין הקובד"ו ובית השחי כתב וז"ל הלכך בעצם העליון יניח תפילין הוא הנקרא זרוע והוא יד דאורייתא וסמוך לפרק של האציל קצת [אציל הוא קובד"ו] יניחם כי שם היא קיבורת בשר המכונס קרוי קיבורת כמו קיבורא דאיני קיבורא דאיזלי ושם הוא כנגד הלב דכתיב ושמתם את דברי אלה על לבבכם ורב חייא מנח להו כנגד ליבא עכ"ל הנך רואה לעין דעת סה"ת דהתפשטות בשר הקיבורת הוא רק סמוך לקובד"ו ולא מצינו למי מהראשונים שיחלוק עליו בדבר זה התלוי בסברא לבד ובגילוי מלתא ולפ"ז פשוט הוא דסובר הרמ"א והשו"ע לקמן בס"ז דהקיבורת לא נתפשט כ"א עד מקום שמחצי עלס ולמטה וכן משמע בב"ח דפלג זרוע העליונה הוא מן הקיבורת ולמעלה אך לישנא דהמ"א קשה לפ"ז ויש ליישב דר"ל אף שנראה קצת שיש גם שם בשר תפוח אעפ"כ עיקר שם קיבורית[ב] אינו כ"א על מקום שמחצי עלס ולמטה ובביאור הגר"א חולק על פסק השו"ע והרמ"א וסובר דאף מחצי עלס ולמעלה כשר כל שיש בו עדיין מבשר הקיבורת ובפשיטות נוכל לאמר דהוא סבר ג"כ כסה"ת הנ"ל דהעיקר מקום הקיבורת הוא לצד הקובד"ו אך דדעתו דהקיבורת נמשך יותר מחצי העלס: שאין

מתרגם: °מרפק

שער הציון

(א) הרא"ש הובא במ"א: (ב) ישועות יעקב: (ג) א"ר: (ד) מ"א: (ה) א"ר: (ו) פמ"ג: (א) גמרא: (ב) ב"י ומ"א ופמ"ג והגר"א: (ג) מ"א: (ד) וכן הסכים הא"ר ע"ש:

הגהות ותיקונים: **א)** ל"א: **ב)** קיבורת:

Correspondingly, if one has both /*tefilin* units/, but has (1) some compelling /reason/ because of which he can only don one /of them/, he should don the unit which he can[2*] /in fact don/.

2. If one merely dons the head /*tefilin*/ alone, he should solely make over it the blessing *Al Mitzvas Tefilin.*

Gloss: (2) *For us, whose practice is to say two blessings every day /when we don both units/, two blessings should be made over the head /*tefilin *when they are donned/ alone. If we don the arm /*tefilin*/ alone,* (3) *we should solely make the blessing* Lehaniach Tefilin. *(...)*

Mishnah Berurah

§26

(1) Some compelling /reason/. For example, if he has a wound on his head or if he needs to leave for the road and the caravan will not wait for him until he has donned both /units/. He should /then/ don /the unit/ which he is able /to don/.

As to which of /the units/ has preference for being donned /in the latter case/, there are /authorities/ who say that it is better /for one/ to don the head /*tefilin*/ alone, because it has more intense holiness, and /authorities/ who say that /it is better for him/ to don the arm /*tefilin*/ at that moment, so as not to deviate from the order /of the donning given/ in the Torah.[1]

/However, the permission to don only one unit in such circumstances/ only applies if one will be able to don the second *tefilin* unit subsequently on the road, but if one will not be able to don the second *tefilin* unit subsequently, he must don /both/ the arm /*tefilin*/ and the head /*tefilin*/ before he leaves home. For /the Sages/ did not permit one to neglect the mitzvah of *tefilin* because his journey will be delayed /if he dons them/.

(2) For us, whose practice is, etc. /The reason is/ as we have explained in Sec. 25, in the Mishnah Berurah, sub-Par. 31; see there.

(3) We should ... make the blessing *Lehaniach Tefilin.* See the *P.Mg.*, who cites other Poskim who are of the opinion that even over the arm /*tefilin*/ alone one should also make the two blessings. As to the halachic /ruling/, the Acharonim are agreed that one should only make the blessing *Lehaniach Tefilin* alone over the arm /*tefilin*/. /This is/ because /quite/ apart from /the considerations/ here, there are many Rishonim who are of the opinion that even over /the donning of/ both /*tefilin* units/ also one should only make one blessing.

If one has /already/ donned both /units/ and did not make a blessing, the /halachic/ ruling is that he should make the blessings /now/ , as long as they are still on him. /Then,/ if he gave precedence to the blessing for the head /*tefilin*/ first and subsequently /made the blessing over/ the arm /*tefilin*/, he should not make the blessing again. However, initially, /the blessing over the arm *tefilin* should be said first and/ even if one donned the arm /*tefilin*/ without making the blessing, he should make the blessing over /the arm *tefilin*/ before donning the head /*tefilin*/.

2* Even if one dons a single unit in deliberate transgression, he will fulfil his obligation as regards that unit. (Beyur Halachah)

1 See *Devarim* 6:8 and 11:18, where it is implied that the arm *tefilin* should be bound first.

ג והוא הדין אם יש לו שתיהם * ג ויש לו (א) (א) שום אונס שאינו יכול להניח אלא אחת מניח אותה שיכול: ב ד אם אינו מניח אלא של ראש לבד מברך עליה על מצות תפילין לבד: הגה (ב) ולדידן דנוהגים לברך בכל יום שתי ברכות מברך על של ראש לבד שתי ברכות ואם מניח של יד לבד (ג) מברך להניח לבד (טור):

ב שם מ״ד סברא בתרא דרב חסדא ג הרא״ש ד רש״י והרי״ף והרמב״ם בפרק ד׳ מה״ת

כז מקום הנחתן ואופן הנחתן. ובו י״א סעיפים:

א א מקום הנחתן של יד בזרוע (א) [א] (א) שמאל (ב) * בבשר התפוח שבעצם ב שבין (ב) (ג) הקובד״ו ובית השחי ג ויטה התפלה מעט לצד הגוף בענין שכשיכוף זרועו למטה יהיו כנגד לבו ונמצא מקיים והיו הדברים האלה על לבבך: הגה וצריך להניח (ד) * בראש העצם הסמוך (ג) [ב] לקובד״ו

א מנחות ל״ו ל״ז ב סמ״ק ג מנחות ל״ז

באר היטב

(א) שום אונס. כגון שצריך לצאת לדרך ואינו יכול להתעכב להניח של יד מניח של ראש לבד. כ״כ הרא״ש ועיין מ״א:

(א) שמאל. ואם הניחו בימינו אפי׳ בדיעבד לא יצא חוץ השני סי׳ כ״ח: (ב) הקובד״ו. בל״א עלינבוגי״ן°: (ג) לקובד״ו. ויש להניח

שערי תשובה

[א] שמאל. עבה״ט ובבית יעקב סי׳ קמ״ט בסוף מלדד לומר דילא ולא מחוור ומ״ש מבה״ע שהביא הב״י בסימן תרנ״א אין ראיה דהתם בלאיטר קאי ועיין לקמן ס״ק י״א ע״ש: [ב] לקובד״ו. עיין בה״ט ועיין

משנה ברורה

א (א) שום אונס. כגון שיש לו מכה בראשו או בזרועו או (א) שהוא צריך לצאת לדרך ואין השיירא ממתנת עליו עד שיניח שתיהם מניח אותה שיכול. וכי מינייהו עדיפא לענין הנחה (ב) י״א דיותר טוב שיניח ש״ר לבד דקדושתו חמורה (ג) וי״א שיניח לע״ע הש״י כדי שלא ישנה הסדר שבתורה (ד) בד״א כשיהיה יכול אח״כ להניח בדרך התפלה השניה אבל אם אח״כ לא יכול להניח התפלה השניה יניח הש״י והש״ר קודם הליכתו מביתו דמשום איחור דרכו לא התירו לו לבטל ממצות תפילין: ב (ב) ולדידן דנוהגין וכו׳. כמו שביארנו בסימן כ״ה במ״ב ס״ק כ״ב° ע״ש: (ג) מברך להניח. עיין בפמ״ג שהביא עוד פוסקים דס״ל דאף על של יד לבד נמי מברך שתי ברכות ולהלכה הסכימו האחרונים דאינו מברך על ש״י אלא להניח לבד (ה) דבלא״ה הרבה ראשונים ס״ל דאפילו על שתיהן נמי אינו מברך אלא אחת. אם (ו) הניח שתיהן ולא בירך דהדין הוא דיברך כ״ז שהן עליו עדיין אם הקדים ברכת ש״ר תחלה ואח״כ ש״י אינו חוזר ומברך אבל לכתחלה אפילו הניח ש״י ולא בירך יברך עליו קודם הנחת של ראש:

א (א) שמאל. מדכתיב (א) ידכה בה״א פירוש יד כהה דהיינו השמאל שהיא תשה וכהה ועוד דרשו מדכתיב וקשרתם וכתבתם מה כתיבה בימין שכן דרך בני אדם אף קשירה בימין וכיון דקשירה בימין ממילא הנחה בשמאל ואם הניחו בימין אף בדיעבד לא יצא [אחרונים]: (ב) בבשר התפוח. והוא המקום הנקרא קיבורת בלשון חז״ל והוא לעיכובא כדילפינן לזה בגמ׳ מקרא: (ג) הקובד״ו. הנקרא עלינבויגי״ן°: (ד) בראש העצם. אין ר״ל ראש העצם ממש דהתם עדיין נמוך הבשר ועד שיתחיל להיות גבוה (ב) אין מקום תפילין דאין ע״ז שם קיבורת אלא ר״ל בגובה הבשר שבעצם ולא בא הרמ״א בזה לחדש שום דבר רק במה שסיים אבל לא בחצי העצם שסמוך לכתף ור״ל (ג) אף שיש גם שם עדיין מקצת בשר תפוח וגם דעת המחבר הוא כן דדוקא מחצי העצם ולמטה כדמוכח בסעיף ז׳ ומה שכתב המחבר מתחלה בבשר התפוח שבעצם ע״כ ג״כ דכונתו מחצי העצם ולמטה והגר״א בביאורו הסכים לדינא דכל מקום הקיבורת כשר להניח בו תפילין וכן משמע בפרישה ועכ״פ (ד) למטה ממקום הקיבורת פסול לכו״ע ע״כ נכון למנוע מ[ל]הניח תפילין גדולים כי ע״פ הרוב מצוי בתפילין גדולים שסוף הקציצה מונחת למטה ממקום הקיבורת אם לא שיקשרם לכתחלה בחצי העצם העליון וגם זה לא נכון להקל לכתחילה בזה אחרי דדעת המחבר ורמ״א להחמיר בזה. אך אם אין לו כ״א תפילין גדולים טוב יותר שיקשרם בחצי העצם העליון במקום שנמצא עדיין

מתרגם: °מרפק

ביאור הלכה

ק״ש והוא רוצה עתה ללבוש כדי שלא לבטל מצות תפילין מעליו פשוט דיכול ללבשם תיכף ולברך עליהם אך לענין לקרות בהם ק״ש נראה דיש לו להמתין עד שיבאו לו השניה: * ויש לו שום אונס. המחבר איירי לענין שיהא מותר להניח תפלה אחת לכתחילה אבל בדיעבד אפילו אם הזיד ולא הניח רק אחת יצא ידי אותה שהניח [ב״י]:

* בבשר התפוח. וצריך ליזהר שלא יהיה קצה התפילין למטה מבשר התפוח כמו בשל ראש שצריך ליזהר שלא יהיה קצהו על המצח כדלקמן דהא ילפינן במנחות ל״ז ע״ב גז״ש גובה שביד מגובה שבראש עי״ש: * בראש העצם. עיין במ״א ועיין במחצית השקל ומשמע לכאורה דבשר התפוח נתפשט בכל העצם בשוה והרמ״א אסר להניח התפילין כ״א בחצי בשר התפוח שאצל הקובד״ו ובאמת לפ״ז יפלא מאוד דהאיך סוברים דאין מותר להניח כ״א חצי קיבורת והלא בערכין י״ט ע״ב איתא בהדיא דקיבורת כולה איקרי יד ולענין תפילין איירי שם בגמרא וא״ל דהגהת סמ״ק לא היה לו הגירסא בגמרא קיבורת כולה דהלא כל הראשונים העתיקו לשון זה [עיין בתוספת שבת ל״ב ע״א ובספר יראים לרבינו אליעזר ממיץ ובסה״ת] וכן מוכח ג״כ במנחות ל״ז ע״א דכל הקיבורת כשר דקאמר ידך זה קיבורת בין עיניך זה קדקוד היכא אמרי דבי ר״י מקום שמוחו של תינוק רופס ומדלא מבאר ג״כ את מקום המיוחד שבקיבורת ש״מ דכל הקיבורת כשר וכן הרי״ף והרמב״ם והרא״ש והטור ורי״ו לא הזכירו שום זכר שיחלק את בשר הקיבורת לחצאין ואיך יתפוס הרמ״א דעת הסמ״ק ואין לומר דרק להחמיר חשש לדעתו דהלא לקמן בס״ז משמע דאם נתפשט המכה בכל השטח שמחצי עלם ולמטה פטור תו מתפילין [ועיין במרדכי דעת הר״ח ונוכל לומר דהרמ״א כוון לאפוקי מדעתו אך דינא דהשו״ע לקמן בס״ז קשה] ועזרני ה׳ שמצאתי בספר התרומה אחר דשקיל וטרי שם ומסכים לדעת ר״ת דמקום התפילין הוא בעצם העליון שהוא בין הקובד״ו ובית השחי כתב וז״ל הלכך בעצם העליון יניח תפילין הוא הנקרא זרוע והוא יד דאורייתא וסמוך לפרק של האציל קצת [אציל הוא קובד״ו] יניחם כי שם היא קיבורת בשר המכונס קרוי קיבורת כמו קיבורא דאהיני קיבורא דאיזלי ושם הוא כנגד הלב דכתיב ושמתם את דברי אלה על לבבכם ורב חייא מנח להו כנגד ליבא עכ״ל הנך רואה לעין דעת סה״ת דהתפשטות בשר הקיבורת הוא רק סמוך לקובד״ו ולא מצינו למי מהראשונים שיחלוק עליו בדבר זה התלוי בסברא לבד ובגילוי מלתא ולפ״ז פשוט הוא דסובר הרמ״א והשו״ע לקמן בס״ז דהקיבורת לא נתפשט כ״א עד מקום שמחצי עלם ולמטה וכן משמע בב״ח דפלג זרוע העליונה הוא מן הקיבורת ולמעלה אך לישנא דהמ״א קשה לפ״ז ויש ליישב דר״ל אף שנראה קצת שיש גם שם בשר תפוח אעפ״כ עיקר שם קיבורית[ב] אינו כ״א על מקום שמחצי עלם ולמטה ובביאור הגר״א חולק על פסק השו״ע והרמ״א וסובר דאף מחצי עלם ולמעלה כשר כל שיש בו עדיין מבשר הקיבורת ובפשיטות נוכל לאמר דהוא סבר ג״כ כסה״ת הנ״ל דהעיקר מקום הקיבורת הוא נגד הקובד״ו אך דדעתו דהקיבורת נמשך יותר מחצי העלם: שאין

שער הציון

(א) הרא״ש הובא במ״א: (ב) ישועות יעקב: (ג) ארה״ח: (ד) מ״א: (ה) ארה״ח: (ו) פמ״ג: (א) גמרא: (ב) ב״י ומ״א ופמ״ג והגר״א: (ג) מ״א: (ד)וכן הסכים הארה״ח עי״ש:

הגהות ותיקונים: א) ל״א: ב) קיבורת:

§27: THE AREA WHERE /THE *TEFILIN*/ SHOULD BE DONNED AND THE MANNER IN WHICH THEY SHOULD BE DONNED

(Contains Eleven Paragraphs)

1. The area where the arm /*tefilin*/ should be donned is on the (1) left arm, (2) on the swollen flesh over the bone between (3) the elbow and the armpit.

One should incline the *tefilin* unit somewhat towards the body, in such a way that when he bends his arm downwards /the unit/ will be opposite his heart. He will thus fulfil /the requirement/, "And these matters will be on your heart".[1*]

Mishnah Berurah

§27

(1) Left. /We know this/ from /the fact/ that it is written /that they should be on/ ידכה[1] (your arm), with /the letter/ ה /appearing at the end of the word/. The explanation /for this/ is that the feeble[2] arm /is meant/, i.e., the left arm, since that is the weak and feeble /arm/.

/The Sages/ derived this additionally from /the fact/ that it is written,[3] "and you should bind them /, etc.", and immediately afterwards/, "and you should write them". /This implies that just/ as the writing is /meant to be done/ with the right /hand/, since that is how people normally /write/, so is the binding /meant to be done/ with the right /hand/. In view /of the fact/ that the binding is /done/ with the right /hand/ it follows that the donning is /done/ on the left /arm/.

If one donned /*tefilin*/ on his right /arm/, he is not /ruled to/ have fulfilled /his obligation/, although it is now after the event. [Acharonim]

(2) On the swollen flesh. This is the area described as the *kibores* (biceps) in the terminology of the Sages, of blessed memory.

/The need to don the *tefilin* there/ is an essential /requirement/, as the Gemara[4] derives this from a verse.[5]

(3) The elbow. This is called the *elinboygin* /in Yiddish/.

1* *Devarim* 6:6.

1 *Shemos* 13:16.
2 It should be noted that this use of the letter ה implies a female owner of the hand and thus suggests weakness.
3 *Devarim* 6: 8 and 9.
4 *Menachos* 37a.
5 *Devarim* 6:8.

באר הגולה

ב שם מ"ד סברא בתרא דרב חסדא
ג הרא"ש ד רש"י והרי"ף והרמב"ם בפרק ד' מה"ת

ב והוא הדין אם יש לו שתיהם * ג ויש לו (א) (א) שום אונס שאינו יכול להניח אלא אחת מניח אותה שיכול: ב ד אם אינו מניח אלא של ראש לבד מברך עליה על מצות תפילין לבד: הגה (ב) ולדידן דנוהגים לברך בכל יום שתי ברכות מברך על של ראש לבד שתי ברכות ואם מניח של יד לבד (ג) מברך להניח לבד (טור):

כז מקום הנחתן ואופן הנחתן. ובו י"א סעיפים:

א מנחות ל"ו ל"ז
ב סמ"ק ג מנחות ל"ז

א א מקום הנחתן של יד בזרוע (א) [א] (א) שמאל (ב) * בבשר התפוח שבעצם ב שבין (ב) (ג) הקובד"ו ובית השחי ג ויטה התפלה מעט לצד הגוף בענין שכשיכוף זרועו למטה יהיו כנגד לבו ונמצא מקיים והיו הדברים האלה על לבבך: הגה וצריך להניח (ד) * בראש העצם הסמוך (ג) [ב] לקובד"ו

באר היטב

(א) שום אונס. כגון שצריך לצאת לדרך ואינו יכול להתעכב להניח של יד מניח של ראש לבד. כ"כ הרא"ש ועיין מ"א:

(א) שמאל. ואם הניחו בימינו אפי' בדיעבד לא יצא חוץ השני סי' כ"ח: (ב) הקובד"ו. בל"א עלינבוגי"ן°: (ג) לקובד"ו. ויש להניח

משנה ברורה

א (א) שום אונס. כגון שיש לו מכה בראשו או בזרועו או (א) שהוא צריך לצאת לדרך ואין השיירא ממתנת עליו עד שיניח שתיהם מניח אותה שיכול. ומי מינייהו עדיפא לענין הנחה (ב) י"א דיותר טוב שיניח ש"ר לבד דקדושתו מרובה (ג) וי"א שיניח לע"ע הש"י כדי שלא ישנה הסדר שבתורה (ד) כ"ז כשיהיה יכול אח"כ להניח בדרך התפלה השניה אבל אם אח"כ לא יכול להניח התפלה השניה יניח הש"י והש"ר קודם הליכתו מביתו דמשום איסור דרכו לא התירו לו לבטל ממצות תפילין: ב (ב) ולדידן דנוהגין וכו'. כמו שבארנו בסימן כ"ה במ"ב ס"ק ל"כ[א] ע"ש: (ג) מברך להניח. עיין בפמ"ג שהביא עוד פוסקים דס"ל דאף על של יד לבד נמי מברך שתי ברכות ולהלכה הסכימו האחרונים דאינו מברך על ש"י אלא להניח לבד (ה) דבלא"ה הרבה ראשונים ס"ל דאפילו על שתיהן נמי אינו מברך אלא אחת.אם (ו) הניח שתיהן ולא בירך והדין הוא דיברך כ"ז שהן עליו ועדיין אם הקדים ברכת ש"ר תחלה ואח"כ ש"י אינו חוזר ומברך אבל לכתחלה אפילו הניח ש"י ולא בירך יברך עליו קודם הנחת של ראש:

א (א) שמאל. מדכתיב (א) ידכה בה"א פירוש יד כהה דהיינו השמאל שהיא תשה וכהה ועוד דרשו מדכתיב וקשרתם וכתבתם מה כתיבה בימין שכן דרך בני אדם אף קשירה בימין וכיון דקשירה בימין ממילא הנחה בשמאל ואם הניחו בימין אף בדיעבד לא יצא [אחרונים]: (ב) בבשר התפוח. והוא המקום הנקרא קיבורת בלשון חז"ל והוא לעיכובא כדילפינן לה בגמ' מקרא: (ג) הקובד"ו. הנקרא עלינבויג"ן°: (ד) בראש העצם. אין ר"ל ראש העצם ממש דהתם עדיין נמוך הבשר ועד שיתחיל להיות גבוה (ב) אין מקום תפילין דאין ע"ז שם קיבורת אלא ר"ל בגובה הבשר שבעצם ולא בא הרמ"א בזה לחדש שום דבר רק במה שסיים אבל לא בחצי העצם שסמוך לשחי ור"ל (ג) אף שיש גם שם עדיין מקצת בשר תפוח וגם דעת המחבר הוא כן דדוקא מחצי העצם ולמטה כדמוכח בסעיף ז' ומה שכתב המחבר מתחלה בבשר התפוח שבעצם ע"כ ג"כ דכונתו מחצי העצם ולמטה והגר"א בביאורו הסכים לדינא דכל מקום הקיבורת כשר להניח בו תפילין וכן משמע בפרישה ועכ"פ (ד) למטה ממקום הקיבורת פסול לכו"ע ע"כ נכון למנוע מלהניח תפילין גדולים כי ע"פ הרוב מצוי בתפילין גדולים שסוף הקציצה מונחת למטה ממקום הקיבורת אם לא שיקשרם לכתחלה בחצי העצם העליון וגם זה לא נכון להקל לכתחילה בזה אחרי דדעת המחבר ורמ"א להחמיר בזה. אך אם אין לו כ"א תפילין גדולים טוב יותר שיקשרם בחצי העצם העליון במקום שנמצא עדיין

מתרגם: °מרפק

שערי תשובה

[א] שמאל. עבה"ט ובבית יעקב סי' קמ"ט בסוף מלדד לומר דיצא ולא מחוור ומ"ש מבה"ע שהביא הב"י בסימן תרנ"א אין ראיה דהתם באיטר קאי ועיין לקמן ס"ק י"א ע"ש: [ב] לקובד"ו. עיין בה"ט ועיין

ביאור הלכה

ק"ש והוא רוצה עתה ללבוש כדי שלא לבטל מצות תפילין מעליו פשוט דיכול ללבשם תיכף ולברך עליהם אך לענין לקרות בהם ק"ש נראה דיש לו להמתין עד שיביאו לו השניה: * ויש לו שום אונס. המחבר איירי לענין שיהא מותר להניח תפלה אחת לכתחילה אבל בדיעבד אפילו אם הזיד ולא הניח רק אחת יצא ידי אותה שהניח [ב"י]:

* בבשר התפוח. וצריך ליזהר שלא יהיה קצה התפילין למטה מבשר התפוח כמו בשל ראש שצריך ליזהר שלא יהיה קצהו על המצח כדלקמן דקא ילפינן במנחות ל"ז ע"ב גז"ש גובה שביד מגובה שבראש עי"ש: * בראש העצם. עיין במ"א ועיין במחצית השקל ומשמע לכאורה דבשר התפוח נתפשט בכל העצם בשוה והרמ"א אסר להניח התפילין כ"א בחצי בשר התפוח שלצד הקובד"ו ובאמת לפ"ז יפלא מאוד דהאיך סוברים דאין מותר להניח כ"א חצי קיבורת והלא בערכין י"ט ע"ב איתא בהדיא דקיבורת כולה איקרי יד ולענין תפילין איירי שם בגמרא וא"ל דהגהת סמ"ק לא היה לו הגירסא בגמרא קיבורת כולה דהלא כל הראשונים העתיקו לשון זה [עיין בתוספת שבת ל"ב ע"א ובספר יראים לרבינו אליעזר ממיץ ובסה"ת] וכן מוכח ג"כ במנחות ל"ז ע"א דכל הקיבורת כשר דקאמר ידך זה קיבורת בין עיניך זה קדקוד היכא אמרי דבי ר"י מקום שמוחו של תינוק רופס ומדלא מבאר ג"כ את מקום המיוחד שבקיבורת ש"מ דכל הקיבורת כשר וכן הרי"ף והרמב"ם והרא"ש והטור ורי"ו לא הזכירו שום זכר שיחלק את בשר הקיבורת לחצאין ואיך יתפוס הרמ"א דעת הסמ"ק ואין לומר דרק להחמיר חשש לדעתו דהלא לקמן בס"ז משמע דאם נתפשט המכה בכל השטח שמחצי עצם ולמטה פטור מו מתפילין [ועיין במרדכי דעת הר"ח ונוכל לומר דהרמ"א כוון לאפוקי מדעתו אך דינא דהשו"ע לקמן בס"ז קשה] ועזרני ה' שמצאתי בספר התרומה אחר דשקיל וטרי שם ומסכים לדעת ר"ת דמקום התפילין הוא בעצם העליון שהוא בין הקובד"ו ובית השחי כתב וז"ל הלכך בעצם העליון יניח תפילין הוא הנקרא זרוע והוא יד דאורייתא וסמוך לפרק של האציל קצת [אציל הוא קובד"ו] יניחם כי שם היא קיבורת בשר המכונס קרוי קיבורת כמו קיבורא דאיזלי ושם הוא כנגד הלב דכתיב ושמתם את דברי אלה על לבבכם ורב חייא מנח להו כנגד ליבא עכ"ל הנך רואה לעין דעת סה"ת דהתפשטות בשר הקיבורת הוא רק סמוך לקובד"ו ולא מצינו למי מהראשונים שיחלוק עליו בדבר זה התלוי בסברא לבד ובגילוי מלתא ולפ"ז פשוט הוא דסובר הרמ"א והשו"ע לקמן בס"ז דהקיבורת לא נתפשט כ"א עד מקום שמחצי עצם ולמטה וכן משמע בב"ח דפלג זרוע העליונה הוא מן הקיבורת ולמעלה אך לישנא דהמ"א קשה לפ"ז ויש ליישב דר"ל אף שנראה קצת שיש גם שם בשר תפוח אעפ"כ עיקר שם קיבורית[ב] אינו כ"א על מקום שמחצי עצם ולמטה ובביאור הגר"א חולק על פסק השו"ע והרמ"א וסובר דאף מחצי עצם ולמעלה כשר כל שיש בו עדיין מבשר הקיבורת ובפשיטות נוכל לאמר דהוא סבר ג"כ כסה"ת הנ"ל דהעיקר מקום הקיבורת הוא לצד הקובד"ו אך דדעתו דהקיבורת נמשך יותר מחצי העצם: שאין

שער הציון

(א) הרא"ש הובא במ"א: (ב) ישועות יעקב: (ג) ארה"ח: (ד) מ"א: (ה) ארה"ח: (ו) פמ"ג: (א) גמרא: (ב) ב"י ומ"א ופמ"ג והגר"א: (ג) מ"א: (ד)וכן הסכים הארה"ח עי"ש:

הגהות ותיקונים: א) ל"א: ב) קיבורת:

Gloss: One must don /the tefilin/ (4) *at the start of the bone, which is next to the elbow, but not on the /upper/ half of the bone, which is next to the armpit. (...)*

Mishnah Berurah

(4) **At the start of the bone.** /The *Rema*/ does not mean at the actual start of the bone. For there the flesh is still /lying/ low and /the area extending/ until where /the flesh/ begins to be raised is not an area where the *tefilin* /may be donned/, since it is not classed /halachically/ as the biceps. What is /in fact/ meant is the raised part of the flesh on the bone.

The *Rema* does not intend to say anything new by /means of/ this /remark/. The only /new element in the gloss/ is his concluding /remark/, "but not on the /upper/ half of the bone which is next to the armpit". He wishes to rule /out donning the *tefilin* in that area/ even though there is still a little swollen flesh there as well. It is also the opinion of the author /of the Shulchan Aruch/ that /*tefilin*/ may only /be donned in the area/ from halfway along the bone downwards. This is evident from Par. 7. When the author /of the Shulchan Aruch/ writes at first, "on the swollen flesh over the bone", he also must mean from halfway along the bone downwards.

The *Gra* agrees in his *Beyur* with the /halachic/ ruling that the entire area of the biceps is valid for the donning of the *tefilin*. This is likewise implied by the *Perishah*. At any rate, according to all /authorities, the area/ below the area of the biceps is not valid /for this purpose/.

Consequently, it is proper to refrain from donning large *tefilin*, as in most cases, it is common with large *tefilin* that the end of the capsule lies below the area of the biceps. This will not /happen/ if one binds /the *tefilin*/ initially in the upper half of the bone. /However,/ it is also not proper to be lenient /about the use of this solution/ initially, bearing in mind that /both/ the author /of the Shulchan Aruch/ and the *Rema* are of the opinion that one should be stringent about /doing/ so. Nonetheless, if one only has large *tefilin* /available/ he should /rather/ bind them over the upper half of the bone in the area where there is still swollen flesh present.

אבל לא בחצי העצם שסמוך לשחי (סמ״ק) (גידם (ה) * שאין לו יד (ד) [ג] רק זרוע * יניח (ו) * בלא ברכה) (תוספות פרק הקומץ כתבו דגידם חייב ובא״ז כתב דפטור): **ב** (ז) * [ד]המנהג הנכון (ח) שיהא היו״ד של קשר תפלה של יד לצד הלב והתפלה (ט) עליו לצד חוץ. (י) * יש ליזהר שלא תזוז (ה) [ד] יו״ד של הקשר (יא) מהתפלה: **ג** * [ה]המנהג הנכון לתקן שהמעברתא שבה הרצועה עוברת תהא מונחת לצד הכתף (יב) והקציצה לצד היד: **ד** (יג) [ו]לא יהא (יד) דבר (ו) [ה] חוצץ בין תפילין לבשרו לא שנא

ד שם ל״ה לפי׳ הנ״י והסכמ׳ מהרי״ן הביב ה ב״י יוסף ו הרא״ש מההיא דערכין ג׳ וזבחים י״ט

שערי תשובה

במג״א ס״ק ב׳ וכוונת דבריו מבואר היטב ביד אפרים ע״ש: [ג] רק זרוע. עבה״ט ובחות יאיר שם כתב דאם נקטע הקנה פטור אבל גידם מעיקרא כל שנשאר לו בחלק העליון קרוב לכתף מקום להניח תפילין י״ל דחייב להניח דזה הנשאר הוי יד דידיה. ועיין במג״א ושאר אחרונים ובפנים מאירות ח״ג סי׳ י״א ובתפארת צבי סי׳ ב׳. ומחוורתא להניח בלא ברכה ויברך על ש״ר שתים כמ״ש הש״י וכתב בשאגת אריה סי׳ ל״ד דמי שאין לו זרוע דפטור מש״י מ״מ חייב להניח ש״ר ע״ש: [ד] יו״ד. עיין בה״ט וכתב בספר שלמי ציבור שבספר זר זהב הוכיח מהר״י למח מדברי הרב ז״ל דצריך שלא תזוז היו״ד לעולם אפילו בהיותם מונחין בתוך הכיס ועי״כ נוהגים רבים מיראי השם לקשור היוד עם חוט של גיד עם התפלה ואין קושרין אותה עם הרצועה בשעת ההנחה עכ״ל. ולדידי צ״ע דע״י קשירה זו יהיה החוט של גיד סביב התיתורא והוא חוצץ בין הזרוע לתפילין. ואפשר כיון שהחוט הקשור הוא בכלות התיתורא במקום המעברתא לא איכפת לן שם בחציצה רק במקום התיתורא שהפרשיות מונחים דפנים וצ״ע ולענין מ״ש שאין קושרים עם הרצועה ע״ל ס״ק ח׳: [ה] חוצץ. עבה״ט דמביא בשם של״ה דיש לרחוץ מקום הנחת

באר היטב

התפילין על בשר התפוח עיין מ״א: (ד) רק זרוע. מי שנקטעת[א] ידו שמאלית פטור מלהניח בימין תשובת רמ״א סי׳ קנ״ב. ובתשובת שבות יעקב ח״א סי׳ ג׳ חולק והעלה להלכה דיש להניח הגידם שאין לו יד רק זרוע או מי שנברא בידו אחת והוא הימנית להניח על ימינו ויברך שתים על של ראש וילא לכ״ע ע״ש ועיין כנה״ג ובתשו׳ חות יאיר סי׳ קס״ז ובמ״א ס״ק ג׳ ובבי״ע סי׳ קמ״ט: (ה) יוד. בזוהר פ׳ פנחס מחמיר מאוד בזה: (ו) חוצץ. בזבחים דף י״ט מבעיא אי כנה חיה ושערו הוי חצילה לענין בגדי כהונה. וכתב המ״א מיהו בכנה מתה ועפר יש לזהר עכ״פ דבזה לא הוי איבעיא כלל. ובשל״ה

ביאור הלכה

* שאין לו יד. עיין במ״ב ודלא כהפמ״ג שרצה לומר להא״ז דפטור בכל גווני כי לא ראה להא״ז כי לא נדפס בימיו: * יניח וכו׳. ר״ל יניח ביד שמאלו [כן משמע למעיין בא״ז גופא דלא נהירא ליה שם הפירוש של המפרשים דלאחרים קאי הריבוי על החיוב דימין רק על השמאל קאי ואפ״ה פסק שם כת״ק ופטור אפילו בנשאר לו הקיבורת דאיהו מפרש שם אין לו זרוע קאי על הקנה ומה שכתב הרמ״א תוספות פרק הקומץ כתבו דחייב ר״ל אפילו בנשאר לו רק הקיבורת ולפי מה דמסיק התוספות בד״ה קיבורת דזרוע נקרא ממקום הקובד״ו והלאה ולהמ״א לא היה לו הא״ז ולכך הוקשה לו מאד דבריו]: * בלא ברכה. ומהב״ח וב״ל וא״ר והגר״א משמע דצריך לברך ג״כ אחרי דיש לו קיבורת ודה״ח ג״כ מסכים בעיקר הדין לחיוב כמותם אך מ״מ לענין ברכה מצדד להקל ואפילו לא נשאר לו רק מחצי עצם שבין הקובד״ו ובית השחי ולמעלה פשוט דיכול לסמוך בזה על שיטת הגר״א דכל שיש עדיין מקצת מן הקיבורת כשר לתפילין ולא יברך ויותר טוב שיברך שנים על השל ראש [היינו לפי מנהגנו כהרמ״א הנ״ל בסימן כ״ה ולהב״י שם אחת] ויכוין להוציא בזה גם השל יד ואפילו בנשאר לו הקיבורת וכמו שהסכים בשערי תשובה: * המנהג הנכון שיהא היו״ד של קשר וכו׳. עיין בב״י בשם מהר״י ב״ח דמשמע מדבריו דרק עשיית הקשר והיו״ד אשר בו צריך שיהיה דוקא למטה מהתפלה לצד הלב אבל כניסת הרצועה תוך כפל הקשר תבא למעלה מהתפלה והוא הנכון ע״ש אבל בד״מ משמע שיותר טוב כהמנהג שנוהגין שגם תחיבת הרצועה בתוך הקשר והכפל יהיה לימינו שהוא לצד הלב וכן משמע בבה״ג שגם הקשירה גופא צריך שתהיה נגד הלב וכן משמע לשון הרא״ש להמעיין בו היטב בסוף אות י״ב במש״כ ומרחיק הקשר מן מעבורת וכו׳ [ועי״ש במעיו״ט אות כ׳[ב] שכתב ואולי ה״פ וכו׳ וכ״ז דוחק עכ״ל ולענ״ד אין זה דוחק כלל וכן הוא האמת לפי מה שכתב הבה״ג] דמשמע שם דאין להרחיב הרבה את כפל קשר העניבה רק כדי שתהיה הרצועה עוברת בתוכה והכל מעט כדי שיהיה מקום הידוק הרצועה סמוך לתפלה ולא לצד מטה וכ״ש שצריך ליזהר שלא יתרחק הקשר של יו״ד גופא מהתפלה לצד מטה וכמו שכתב בסעיף ג׳ וזהו הכל נכלל במה שאמר הגמרא דהקשר צריך להיות למעלה ולא למטה. והנה מלשון השו״ע לכאורה משמע דסובר כמהריב״ח מדכתב שיהא היו״ד של קשר וכו׳ משמע דמקום שתוחב הרצועה בכפל איננו לצד הלב כ״א לצד חוץ אבל יש לדחות דכונתו רק למעט שלא נעשה כשיטת בעל המאור המובא בב״י שיהא התפלה של יד לצד הלב והקשר לצד חוץ אבל בזה רשות בידו לעשות כמה שירצה. ואע״פ שהעדפנו את המנהג של הד״מ מ״מ הנוהג כמהריב״ח אין למחות בידו כי יש לו על מי לסמוך גם ע״י מנהגו טוב שלא יזוז היו״ד לעולם מהבית משא״כ לפי מה שאנו נוהגין כהד״מ צריך בכל עת שמירה לזה אולם באמת יש לזה עצה אחרת ועיין במה שכתבנו במ״ב: * יש ליזהר. עיין בביאור הגר״א שציין ע״ז כנ״ל ור״ל דדין זה יש לו ג״כ מקור מהגמרא דמוכח שאין להרחיק הקשר מהתפילין וכמו שכתב בעצמו בדבריו הקודמים: * המנהג הנכון

משנה ברורה

עדיין בשר התפוח וילא בזה עכ״פ דעת הגר״א וש״פ ממה שיהיו מונחים למטה ממקום הקיבורת ולא יצא בזה אליבא דכו״ע וגם הברכה יהיה לבטלה: (ה) שאין לו יד. ר״ל שניטל פיסת יד שמאלו עם כל הקנה עד הקובד״ו שנקרא עלינבויגי״ן° אבל אם נשאר קצת מהקנה גם הא״ז מודה להתוספות דחייב בתפילין ויברך ג״כ כן מצאתי בא״ז אשר זכינו מקרוב לאורו: (ו) בלי ברכה. עיין בביאור הלכה. ואם (ה) אין לו יד שמאל כלל או אפילו (ו) קנה הזרוע שלמעלה ממקום הקיבורת נשאר ומקום הקיבורת אין לו כלל פטור מלהניח הש״י אף בימין (ז) ויש מחמירין בזה. וכ״ז (ח) שנעשה גידם בשמאל דהוא מקום הנחת התפילין אבל אם נעשה גידם בימין אפילו נקטע לו כל היד חייב בתפילין ויבקש לאחרים שיניחוהו עליו: **ב** (ז) המנהג הנכון. עיין בביאור הגר״א שכתב דדינא דגמרא הוא לפירוש הגאונים: (ח) שיהא היו״ד וכו׳. עיין בבה״ל שכתבנו שנכון ליזהר שלא ירחיב הרבה את כפל קשר העניבה שהרצועה עוברת בה כדי שתהיה גם מקום הידוק הרצועה סמוך להתפילין לצד הלב: (ט) עליו וכו׳. אין ר״ל שתהיה התפלה מונחת על היו״ד דודאי בעינן שתהא היו״ד אצל התפלה בשוה ולא מתחתיה (ט) רק ר״ל דלפי שהוא מטה התפילין לצד הגוף כמו שכתב ס״א לכן נקרא יו״ד של צד הגוף למטה והתפלה עליו לצד מעלה: (י) יש ליזהר. ובזוהר פ׳ פנחס מחמיר מאוד בענין זה (י) ויש מחמירין דגם כשהן בתוך כיסן צריכין ליזהר בזה שלא תזוז כלל היו״ד ומטעם זה יש נוהגין לקשור היו״ד עם חוט של גיד עם התפלה ונראה לבטל זה דע״י הקשירה יהיה חוט של גיד סביב התיתורא חוצץ בין הזרוע להתפילין ובלבושי שרד כתב דראוי לבטל ג״כ המנהג שקורכין הרצועה במקום הקיבורת תחת התיתורא דהוי ג״כ חציצה: (יא) מהתפלה. (יא) ויתפוס בתיתורא מלמעלה ויהדק היו״ד עם הבית: **ג** (יב) והקציצה וכו׳. ולעטר המניח תפילין תמיד שאינו אוטר או להיפוך ואינו יכול להוציא הרצועה ולקבעה כדין עיין בבה״ל: **ד** (יג) לא יהא וכו׳. דכתיב (יב) על ידך ובמס״ר כתיב בין עיניך: (יד) דבר חוצץ. אפילו (יג) חציצה כל דהוא ונכון ליזהר לכתחילה אפי׳

מתרגם: °מרפק

שער הציון

(ה) תשובת הרמ״א: (ו) ב״ח וא״ר והגר״א ושארי אחרונים: (ז) עיין בתשובת שבו״י ובארה״ח ועכ״פ בלי ברכה: (ח) אחרונים וכן משמע מרש״י מנחות ל״ז ע״א: (ט) יד אפרים: (י) עיין בשע״ת: (יא) שולחן שלמה: (יב) הרא״ש והגר״א בביאורו משמע ג״כ שסובר דלא כהרשב״א: (יג) מ״א:

הגהות ותיקונים: **א)** שנקטעה: **ב)** צ״ל אות ד׳:

(A person with a stump, (5) *who does not have an /entire/ arm, but only an /upper/ arm, should don /the arm* tefilin/ (6) *without /making/ a blessing.) (The* Tosafos ... *write that a person with a stump is obliged /to don the arm* tefilin/ *and the* O.Z. *writes that he is exempt /from doing so/.)*

2. (7) The correct practice is (8) that the /letter/ י, which is /formed/ by the knot of the hand *tefilin*, should /face/ towards the heart and the *tefilin* unit (9) above it towards the outside /of the body/.

Mishnah Berurah

If /he does/ so he will at least fulfil /his obligation/ according to the view of the *Gra* and other Poskim. This is better than having /the *tefilin*/ lie below the area of the biceps. In that case all /authorities/ are agreed that one does not fulfil /his obligation/ and, in addition, the blessing is a vain /blessing/.

(5) **Who does not have an arm.** I.e., if his left hand /together/ with the forearm until the elbow (which is called the *elinboygin* /in Yiddish/) has been removed. However, when some of the forearm remains, the *O.Z.* also agrees with the *Tosafos* that he is obliged /to don the arm/ *tefilin* and should also make the blessing. I discovered this /ruling/ in the *O.Z.*, whose light we have recently been given the privilege /to enjoy/.

(6) **Without a blessing.** See the Beyur Halachah.[6]

If one does not have a left arm at all or even if the end of one's /upper/ arm above the area of the biceps remains, but he does not have the biceps area at all, he is exempt from donning the arm /*tefilin*/. He is even /exempt from donning them/ on the right /arm/. /However,/ there are /authorities/ who are stringent about this.

All these /remarks only apply/ if one became stumped on the left, which involves the area where the *tefilin* must be donned, but if one became stumped on the right /, then/, even if his entire arm has been severed he is obliged to /don/ *tefilin* and must ask others to put them on him.[7]

(7) **The correct practice.** See the *Beyur Ha-Gra*, who writes that this is a ruling of the Gemara, according to the explanation of the Geonim.

(8) **That the י, etc.** See the Beyur Halachah, where we have written that it is proper to take care that the fold of the bow knot through which the strap passes should not be made very wide, so that the place where the strap is tightened will also be close to the *tefilin*, /facing/ towards the heart.

(9) **Above it, etc.** This does not mean that the *tefilin* unit should be placed on top of the /letter/ י /formed by the knot/, since it is definitely necessary for the /letter/ י to be next to the *tefilin* unit at the same level and not underneath it. /The Shulchan Aruch's wording/ merely derives from /the fact/ that one inclines the *tefilin* towards the body, as stated in Par. 1. /The letter/ י /formed by the

6 There the author notes, among other things, that according to our practice to make two blessings it is better for a person with a stump to make both blessings over the head *tefilin* and have in mind that the blessing *Lehaniach Tefilin* should also serve for the arm *tefilin*.

7 In the Beyur Halachah to Par. 6, the author writes that if one's right arm became severed, but the biceps remains, he must now don *tefilin* on it, since now that he has accustomed himself to do actions with his left arm the right arm has become the "left" arm.

אבל לא כמלוי העלם שסמוך לשחי (סמ"ק) (גידם (ה) * שאין לו יד (ד) [ג] רק זרוע * יניח (ו) * בלא ברכה) (תוספות פרק הקומץ כתבו דגידם חייב ובא"ז כתב דפטור): ב (ז) * ^ההמנהג הנכון (ח) שיהא היו"ד של קשר תפלה של יד לצד הלב והתפלה (ט) עליו לצד חוץ. (י) * יש ליזהר שלא תזוז (ה) [ד] יו"ד של הקשר (יא) מהתפלה: ג * ^ההמנהג הנכון לתקן שהמעברתא שבה הרצועה עוברת תהא מונחת לצד הכתף (יב) והקציצה לצד היד: ד (יג) ^ילא יהא (יד) דבר (ו) [ה] חוצץ בין תפילין לבשרו לא שנא

ד שם ל"ה לפי' הנ"י והסכמ' מהרי"ן חביב ה בית יוסף ו הרא"ש מההיא דערכין ג' וזבחים י"ט

שערי תשובה

במג"א ס"ק ב' וכוונת דבריו מבואר היטב ביד אפרים ע"ש: [ג] רק זרוע. עבה"ט ובחות יאיר שם כתב דאם נקטע הקנה פטור אבל גידם מעיקרא כל שנשאר לו בחלק העליון קרוב לכתף מקום להניח תפילין י"ל דחייב להניח דזה הנשאר הוי יד דידיה. ועיין במג"א ושאר אחרונים ובפנים מאירות ח"ג סי' י"א ובתפארת לבי סי' ב'. ומחוורתא להניח בלא ברכה ויברך על ש"ר שתים כמ"ש הש"י וכתב בשאגת אריה סי' ל"ד דמי שאין לו זרוע דפטור מש"י מ"מ חייב להניח ש"ר ע"ש: [ד] יו"ד. עיין בה"ט וכתב בספר שלמי ציבור שבספר זר זהב הוכיח מהר"י למח מדברי הרב ז"ל דצריך שלא תזוז היו"ד לעולם אפילו בהיותם מונחין בתוך הכיס וע"כ נוהגים רבים מיראי השם לקשור היוד עם חוט של גיד עם התפלה ואין קושרין אותה עם הרצועה בשעת ההנחה עכ"ל. ולדידי צ"ע דע"י קשירה זו יהיה החוט של גיד סביב התיתורא והוא חוצץ בין הזרוע לתפילין. ואפשר כיון שהחוט הקשר הוא בכלות התיתורא במקום המעברתא לא איכפת לן שם בחציצה רק במקום התיתורא שהפרשיות מונחים בפנים וצ"ע ולענין מ"ש שאין קושרים עם הרצועה ע"ל ס"ק ח': [ה] חוצץ. עבה"ט דמייתי בשם של"ה דיש לרחוץ מקום הנחת

באר היטב

התפילין על בשר התפוח עיין מ"א: (ד) רק זרוע. מי שנקטעת[א] ידו שמאלית פטור מלהניח בימין תשובת רמ"א סי' קנ"ב. ובתשובת שבות יעקב ח"א סי' ג' חולק והעלה להלכה דיש להניח הגידם שאין לו יד רק זרוע או מי שנברא בידו אחת והוא הימנית להניח על ימינו ויברך שתים על של ראש וילא לכ"ע ע"ש ועיין כנה"ג ובתשו' חות יאיר סי' קס"ז ובמ"א ס"ק ג' ובדי"ע סי' קמ"ט: (ה) יוד. בזוהר פ' פנחס מחמיר מאוד בזה: (ו) חוצץ. בזבחים דף י"ט מבעיא אי כנה חיה ושערו הוי חציצה לענין בגדי כהונה. וכתב המ"א מיהו בכנה מתה ועפר יש לזהר עכ"פ דבזה לא הוי איבעיא כלל. ובשל"ה

ביאור הלכה

* שאין לו יד. עיין במ"ב ודלא כהפמ"ג שרצה לומר להא"ז דפטור בכל גווני כי לא ראה להא"ז כי לא נדפס בימיו: * יניח וכו'. ר"ל יניח ביד שמאלו [כן משמע למעיין בא"ז גופא דלא נהירא ליה שם הפירוש של המפרשים דלאחרים קאי הריבוי על החיוב דימין רק על השמאל קאי ואפ"ה פסק שם כת"ק ופטור אפילו בנשאר לו הקיבורת דאיהו מפרש שם אין לו זרוע קאי על הקנה ומה שכתב הרמ"א תוספות פרק הקומץ כתבו דחייב ר"ל אפילו בנשאר לו רק הקיבורת ולפי מה דמסיק התוספות בד"ה קיבורת דזרוע נקרא ממקום הקובד"ו והלאה והמ"א לא היה לו הא"ז ולכך הוקשה לו מאד דבריו]: * בלא ברכה. ומהב"ח וצ"ל וא"ר והגר"א משמע דצריך לברך ג"כ אחרי דיש לו קיבורת ודה"ח ג"כ מסכים בעיקר הדין לחיוב כמותם אך מ"מ לענין ברכה מצדד להקל ואפילו לא נשאר לו רק מחצי עצם שבין הקובד"ו ובית השחי ולמעלה פשוט דיכול לסמוך בזה על שיטת הגר"א דכל שיש עדיין מקצת מן הקיבורת כשר לתפילין ולא יברך ויותר טוב שיברך שנים על השל ראש [היינו לפי מנהגנו כהרמ"א הנ"ל בסימן כ"ה ולהב"י שם אחת] ויכוין להוציא בזה גם השל יד ואפילו בנשאר לו הקיבורת וכמו שהסכים בשערי תשובה: * המנהג הנכון שיהא היו"ד של קשר וכו'. עיין בב"י בשם מהר"י ב"ח דמשמע מדבריו דרק עשיית הקשר והיו"ד אשר בו צריך שיהיה דוקא למטה מהתפלה לצד הלב אבל כניסת הרצועה תוך כפל הקשר תבא למעלה מהתפלה והוא הנכון ע"ש אבל בד"מ משמע שיותר טוב כהמנהג שנוהגין שגם תחיבת הרצועה בתוך הקשר והכפל יהיה לימינו שהוא לצד הלב וכן משמע בבה"ג שגם הקשירה גופא צריך שתהיה נגד הלב וכן משמע לשון הרא"ש להמעיין בו היטב בסוף אות י"ב במש"כ ומרחיק הקשר מן מעבורת וכו' [ועי"ש במעיו"ט אות כ'[ב] שכתב ואולי ה"פ וכו' וכ"ז דוחק עכ"ל ולענ"ד אין זה דוחק כלל וכן הוא האמת לפי מה שכתב הבה"ג] דמשמע שם דאין להרחיב הרבה את כפל קשר העניבה רק כדי שתהיה הרצועה עוברת בתוכה והכל מטעם כדי שיהיה מקום הידוק הרצועה סמוך לתפלה ולא לצד מטה וכ"ש שצריך ליזהר שלא יתרחק הקשר של יו"ד גופא מהתפלה לצד מטה וכמו שכתב בסעיף ב' וזהו הכל נכלל במה שאמר הגמרא דהקשר צריך להיות למעלה ולא למטה. והנה מלשון השו"ע לכאורה משמע דסובר כמהריב"ח מדכתב שיהא היו"ד של קשר וכו' משמע דמקום שתוחב הרצועה בכפל איננו לצד הלב כ"א לצד חוץ אבל יש לדחות דכונתו רק למעט שלא נעשה כשיטת בעל המאור המובא בב"י שיהא התפלה של יד לצד הלב והקשר לצד חוץ אבל בזה רשות בידו לעשות כמה שירצה. ואע"פ שהעדפנו את המנהג של הד"מ מ"מ הנוהג כמהריב"ח אין למחות בידו כי יש לו על מי לסמוך גם ע"י מנהגו טוב שלא יזוז היו"ד לעולם מהבית משא"כ לפי מה שאנו נוהגין כהד"מ צריך בכל עת שמירה לזה אולם באמת יש לזה עצה אחרת ועיין במה שכתבנו במ"ב: * יש ליזהר. עיין בביאור הגר"א שציין ע"ז כנ"ל ור"ל דדין זה יש לו ג"כ מקור מהגמרא דמוכח שאין להרחיק הקשר מהתפילין וכמו שכתב בעצמו בדבריו הקודמים: * המנהג הנכון

משנה ברורה

עדיין בשר התפוח וילא בזה עכ"פ דעת הגר"א וש"פ ממה שיהיו מונחים למטה ממקום הקיבורת ולא יצא בזה אליבא דכו"ע וגם הברכה יהיה לבטלה: (ה) שאין לו יד. ר"ל שניטל שיעור יד שמאלו עם כל הקנה עד הקובד"ו שנקרא עלינבויגי"ן° אבל אם נשאר קצת מהקנה גם הא"ז מודה לתוספות דחייב בתפילין ויברך ג"כ כן מוכחא בא"ז אשר זכינו מקרוב לאורו: (ו) בלי ברכה. עיין בביאור הלכה. ואם (ה) אין לו יד שמאל כלל או אפילו (ו) קנה הזרוע שלמעלה ממקום הקיבורת נשאר ומקום הקיבורת אין לו כלל פטור מלהניח הש"י אף בימין (ז) ויש מחמירין בזה. וכ"ז (ח) שנעשה גידם בשמאל דהוא מקום הנחת התפילין אבל אם נעשה גידם בימין אפילו נקטע לו כל היד חייב בתפילין ויבקש לאחרים שיניחוהו עליו: ב (ז) המנהג הנכון. עיין בביאור הגר"א שכתב דכונת הגמרא הוא כפירוש הגאונים: (ח) שיהא היו"ד וכו'. עיין בבה"ל שכתבנו שנכון ליזהר שלא ירחיב הרבה את כפל קשר העניבה שהרצועה עוברת בה כדי שתהיה גם מקום הידוק הרצועה סמוך להתפילין לצד הלב: (ט) עליו וכו'. אין ר"ל שתהיה התפלה מונחת על היו"ד דודאי בעינן שתהא היו"ד אצל התפלה בשוה ולא מתחתיה (ט) רק ר"ל דלפי שהוא מטה התפילין לצד הגוף כמו שכתב ס"א לכן נקרא יו"ד של צד הגוף למטה והתפלה עליו לצד מעלה: (י) יש ליזהר. ובזוהר פ' פנחס מחמיר מאוד בענין זה (י) ויש מחמירין דגם כשהן בתוך כיסן צריכין ליזהר בזה שלא תזוז כלל היו"ד ומטעם זה יש נוהגין לקשור היו"ד עם חוט של גיד עם התפלה וראוי לבטל זה דע"י הקשירה יהיה חוט של גיד סביב התיתורא חוצץ בין הזרוע להתפילין ובלבושי שרד כתב דראוי לבטל ג"כ המנהג שכורכין הרצועה במקום הקיבורת תחת התיתורא דהוי ג"כ חציצה: (יא) מהתפלה. (יא) ויתחוך בתיתורא מלמעלה ויהדק היו"ד עם הבית: ג (יב) והקציצה וכו'. ואיטר המניח תפילין ממי שאינו איטר או להיפוך ואינו יכול להוציא הרצועה ולקבעה כדין עיין בבה"ל: ד (יג) לא יהא וכו'. דכתיב (יב) על ידך ובתש"ר כתיב בין עיניך: (יד) דבר חוצץ. אפילו (יג) חציצה כל דהוא ונכון ליזהר לכתחילה אפי'

מתרגם: °מרפק

שער הציון

(ה) תשובת הרמ"א: (ו) ב"ח וא"ר והגר"א ושארי אחרונים: (ז) עיין בתשובת שבו"י ובארה"ח ועכ"פ בלי ברכה: (ח) אחרונים וכן משמע מרש"י מנחות ל"ז ע"א: (ט) יד אפרים: (י) עיין בשע"ת: (יא) שולחן שלמה: (יב) הרא"ש והגר"א בביאורו משמע ג"כ שסובר דלא כהרשב"א: (יג) מ"א:

הגהות ותיקונים: א) שנקטעה: ב) צ"ל אות ד':

(10) One must take care that the /letter/ י /formed/ by the knot does not move away (11) from the *tefilin* unit.

3. The correct practice is to arrange that the passageway through which the strap passes is placed /facing/ towards the shoulder (12) and that the capsule /is placed facing/ towards the hand.

4. (13) There should not be (14) an article interposing between the *tefilin* and

Mishnah Berurah

knot/ which /faces/ towards the body is therefore described as /being/ below and the *tefilin* unit above it as /being/ upwards.

(10) One must take care. The *Zohar*, in the portion of *Pinchas*, is very stringent about this matter.

There are /authorities/ who rule stringently that even when /the *tefilin*/ are inside their bag one must be careful about this /and see to it/ that the /letter/ י /formed by the knot/ will not move /away/ at all /from the *tefilin* unit/.

For this reason, there are people who are accustomed to bind the /letter/ י /formed by the knot/ with a thread of sinew to the *tefilin* unit. It is proper to abolish this /practice/, as in view of this binding the thread of sinew around the rim /of the *tefilin* unit/ will interpose between the arm and the *tefilin*.

The *Levushey Serad* writes that it is also proper to abolish the practice of winding the strap in the area of the biceps underneath the rim /of the *tefilin* unit/, as this also constitutes an interposition.

(11) From the *tefilin* unit. One must cut the rim /of the *tefilin* unit/ at the top and tighten the /letter/ י /formed by the knot/ to the receptacle.

(12) And that the capsule, etc. If a left-handed person dons the *tefilin* of someone who is not left-handed or vice-versa and he is unable to take out the strap and insert it in accordance with the halachic /requirements for him/, see the Beyur Halachah[8] /as to how he should act/.

(13) There should not be, etc. For /with reference to the arm *tefilin*/ it is written[5] /that they must be/ "on your arm". With reference to the head *tefilin* it is written[5] /that they must be/ "between your eyes".

(14) An article interposing. /I.e.,/ even the slightest interposition /is forbidden/.

It is proper to be careful initially that even a live louse does not separate between the

8 The author writes there that he should don the *tefilin* in such a case with the passageway towards the hand and the capsule towards the shoulder.

של יד (טו) לא שנא של ראש: הגה ודוקא בתפילין אבל ברצועות (טז) אין (ז) להקפיד (רשב״א בתשובה סימן תתכ״ז): ה [ז]אדם שהוא (יז) עלול לנזילות ואם יצטרך להניח (יח) תפלה של ראש על בשרו לא יניחם כלל יש להתיר לו להניח תפלה של ראש על (יט) הכובע (ח) [ו] דק הסמוך לראש ויכסם [ח]מפני הרואים: הגה והמניחים כדרך זה לא יברך על של ראש (כ) רק יברך על (ט) של יד להניח (לדעת רשב״א): ך (כא) * [ט]ואטר (כב) יד (י) ימינו אם עושה (כג) כל מלאכתו בשמאל

ז תשובת הריב״ש לדעת הרשב״א ח בית יוסף ט מנחו׳ ל״ז

באר היטב

כתב דיש לרחוץ מקום הנחת תפילין: (ז) להקפיד. מיהו יש להחמיר אפי׳ ברצועות מה ששייך להקשירה בין ברצועות של ראש בין ברצועות היד. ט״ז מ״א ע״ת. בספר דבר שמואל סימן רל״ב כתב תוכחת מגולה על המניחין התפילין ע״ג פאה נכרית הנקרא פארו״קה ועיין בתשובת יד אליהו סי׳ ג׳ שהאריך בזה: (ח) דק. ועל כובע עבה אסור. ואם יש לו מכה ביד אסור להניחם על הבגד משום לך לאות ולא לאחרים לאות אבל מותר להניחו על החלוק[א] אם לא סגי בלא״ה דהא לבוש בגד אחר עליו. מ״א: (ט) של יד. וה״ה אם מניח של יד בדרך זה שלא יברך על ש״י אלא על של ראש. מ״א. וכתב הב״ח מ״מ בשעת ק״ש ותפלה יראה שיהא זולת חציצה ע״ש: (י) ימינו. שנים שהלכו בדרך ואחד מהם אטר ואין לו רק תפילין ממי שאינו אטר יניח התפילין בימין דהיינו הקציצה לצד הכתף והמעברתא לצד היד. וכן להיפוך במי שאינו איטר ומניח תפילין של האיטר מניח בשמאלו הקציצה לצד הכתף והמעברתא לצד היד שבות יעקב ח״א סי׳ ג׳ ע״ש. ועיין בתשובת נחלת שבעה סימן מ״א ובחות יאיר סימן

שערי תשובה

תפילין. ובבר״י כתב שפשוט שהנוהג כן צריך לנגב המקום היטב משום התפילין. וגם אפשר שהם מפסיקים כמו חציצה. והביא מדברי המיימ׳ מהלכות עבודת יוה״כ דלכך בכ״ג עלה ונסתפג כו׳ ונשא ונתן בזה עיי״ש. ונראה דהשל״ה כ״כ לפי שהמשכים לחצות נותן אפר תחת פאר וכשרוצה להניח תפילין צריך לרחוץ המקום משום כבוד התפילין וכן הוא בכתבי האר״י ז״ל ע״ש. ועיין בשו״ת פני אריה בסי׳ ו׳ וסי׳ ז׳ לענין אבק שקורין פוד״ר מה דינו ע״ש: [ו] דק. עבה״ט וכתב בתשב״ץ סי׳ ל׳ אין להניח תפילין על הכובע רק[ב] על ראשו ומותר לכסות אותם בסודרו. והא דאמרינן וראו כל עמי הארץ כו׳ היינו שיהיה בראש במקום שהם נראים יותר וראו כמו ושמעו וכל העם רואים את הקולות ע״ש. ונראה דאף שיש איזה דרשא[ג] בהא דוכל העם רואים דקאי על המלאכים שנבראו מכל דיבור מ״מ פשטא דקרא על שמיעה נאמר

משנה ברורה

בכנה חיה שלא יהא מפסיק בין התפילין לבשר (יד) ועכ״פ בכנה מתה ועפר יש ליזהר וע״כ (טו) יש נוהגין לרחוץ מקום הנחת התפילין. כתב בספר רביד הזהב נראה דמה שרצועה חוצצת לפעמים בין תפילין לבשרו לא מיקרי חציצה דמין במינו אינו חוצץ ומלבושי שרד שהעתקתי לעיל בסק״י משמע דנכון לכתחילה להחמיר בזה: (טו) לא שנא ש״ר. כתב בספר מחזית השקל ורע עלי המעשה של אותן האנשים שמגדלין בלורותיהן מלבד כי הוא דרך שחץ וגאוה עיין מה שכתוב ביו״ד סימן קע״ו[ד] יש בו איסור בהנחת תפילין דכיון דגדולין הרבה ליכא למימר בהו היינו רביתייהו וחוצצים עי״ש ובלאו חציצה נמי בשביל הני שערות המרובים א״א לצמצם שיהיו מהודקין ומונחין על מקומן כדין: (טז) אין להקפיד. והאחרונים כתבו דאין להקל רק במקום הכריכות אבל מה ששייך להקשירה (טז) יש להחמיר אף ברצועות בין בשל יד ובין בשל ראש וכתבו תוכחת מגולה על המניחים התפילין ע״ג פאה נכרית הנקרא פארוק״ה ואפילו אם רק הרצועה מונח על הפאה נכרית. ומ״מ משמע מדברי המ״א והח״א דאם יש לו מכה בראשו ורק במקום שהרצועות מונחים ולא במקום הקציצה מותר לו להניח הרצועות ע״ג סמרטוטין שעל המכה או ע״ג כובע דק ולברך אע״ג שיש חציצה בין הרצועות כיון דבמקום הקציצה אין חציצה וכן בשל יד אם יש לו מכה (יז) אפילו במקום הקף הקשר שסביב ידו מותר לו להניח הקף הקשר ע״ג סמרטוטין ולברך אך בזה יזהר לכסות מלמעלה כדי שיתקיים לך לאות ולא לאחרים לאות: ה (יז) עלול לנזילות. פי׳ (יח) שיש לו מכאוב או (יט) מיחוש בראשו ואם יגלה ראשו יזיק לו הקרירות כיון שהוא אנוס יכול לסמוך על הרשב״א דס״ל דאין חשש בחציצה ולא נאמר בין עיניך אלא לסיים להם מקום ומשום לך לאות ולא לאחרים לאות ליכא בתש״ר דבהו כתיב וראו כל עמי הארץ כי שם ד׳ נקרא עליך. ומ״מ צריך לכסות (כ) מפני הרואים שאינם יודעים שהוא אנוס: (יח) תש״ר על וכו׳. ואם יש לו מכה ביד במקום הנחת הקציצה והמכה (כא) מתפשטת בכל הקיבורת מותר לו להניח (כב) על הרטיה אם לא סגי בלא״ה (כג) ולא יברך דהא דעת רוב הפוסקים דחציצה פוסלת ויברך שתים על הש״ר כדלעיל בסימן כ״ו בהג״ה אך ילבוש על התש״י מלמעלה בגד אחר כדי לכסותם דהא כתיב בהו והיה לך לאות ודרשינן לך לאות ולא לאחרים לאות. ודוקא על רטיה אבל להניח תפילין על חלוקו (כד) י״א דאסור אפילו מש לו מכה ואפילו אם ילבוש עליו בגד אחר: (יט) הכובע דק. אבל על כובע עבה אסור להניחם דלא יוכל לכוין ולמצא מקום שמוח של תינוק רופס: (כ) רק יברך וכו׳. (כה) ויכוין להוציא הש״ר דבלא״ה דעת הרבה פוסקים שאין מברך על שניהם אלא אחת. ועיין בב״ח וע״ת דמשמע מדבריהם דנכון ליזהר שעכ״פ בשעת ק״ש ותפלה יהיה בלי חציצה כלל: ך (כא) ואיטר וכו׳. ועיין לעיל בס״ק י״ב: (כב) יד ימינו. ואפילו (כו) נעשה איטר ע״י שהרגיל עצמו אח״כ ולא נולד כך יניח בימין וכ״ש (כז) אם מן השמים הרגילוהו דהיינו שנולד לו חולי בימינו וניטל הכח ממנו או שנקטע לו כף ידו הימנית וצריך לעשות כל מלאכתו בשמאל בודאי דינו כאיטר גמור ויניח על היד הרצועה ואם חזר לבריאותו ונעשה שולט בשתי ידיו בשוה הרי הוא ככל אדם: (כג) כל מלאכתו. (כח) ה״ה אפילו רק רוב

ביאור הלכה

הנכון לתקן וכו׳. ובכל זה מי שהוא איטר ואין לו רק תפילין של אינו איטר או להיפך יוכל להפך להניח הקציצה לצד הכתף והמעברתא לצד היד כ״כ בתשו׳ שבו״י ובארה״ח כי זה בודאי טוב יותר ממה שיניח כך ויהיה התפילין סמוך ללב ויהיה קשר היו״ד חוצה לה וכמו שכתב הגר״א שהסעיף ב׳ אף שכתב בשו״ע בשם מנהג דינא דגמרא הוא לפי׳ הגאונים ועיין בח״א אות י״ג דלא הזכיר שם עצה זו דשבו״י והוא כתב שם דטוב אם יכול להוציא הרצועה ולהכניסה מצד אחר כדי שתהיה היו״ד סמוך ללב אע״פ שאינו יכול להפוך הקשר של היו״ד שתהיה פניה לצד הבית ועכ״פ לא יתבטל ממצות תפילין עבור זה ויניחם כך ע״ש ור״ל אף דיהיה קשר היו״ד לצד חוץ והתפילין לצד הלב ולענ״ד בודאי טוב יותר לעשות כהשבו״י דזה דינא דגמרא הוא לכמה ראשונים וזה מנהג וכמו שכתב הגר״א ואפילו אם יכול להוציא הרצועה ג״כ יש לעיין דאולי מה שהיו״ד לא יהיה פניו כלפי הבית לא נחשב יו״ד ועכ״פ באינו יכול להוציא יעשה כהשבו״י: * ואיטר יד ימינו. עיין מ״ב במש״כ

שער הציון

(יד) מ״א: (טו) של״ה: (טז) הלבוש וע״ת וט״ז וא״ר וכן משמע ג״כ מהגר״א: (יז) כן מוכח במ״א סק״ו דלהרשב״א אם מכסה בחלוק מלמעלה אין אסור ע״י הסמרטוטין משום חציצה וע״כ יש לסמוך עליו לברך עכ״פ לענין רצועות: (יח) ט״ז: (יט) ח״א: (כ) ט״ז: (כא) דאל״ה יניח על מקום הנשאר בקיבורת ועיין בס״ז ובמשנה ברורה שם: (כב) מ״א וא״ר וח״א: (כג) מ״א וחידושי רע״א ומה שהקיל רע״א אם יש לו הש״י לבד מביאור הגר״א לא משמע כן: (כד) ארה״ח וכן משמע מח״א: (כה) ע״ת: (כו) מ״א: (כז) דגול מרבבה ועיין בבה״ל: (כח) וכן משמע בהרא״ש וביאור הגר״א ובשארי אחרונים:

הגהות ותיקונים: א) צ״ל הסמרטוטין: ב) צ״ל דק: ג) דרשה: ד) קע״ח:

one's flesh, irrespective of whether the arm /*tefilin*/ **(15)** or whether the head /*tefilin* are involved/.

Gloss: This only /applies/ to the tefilin *units /themselves/, but as regards the straps* **(16)** *there is no need to be particular /about this/. (...)*

5 If a person has **(17)** a propensity to severe chills, /so that/ if he would be

Mishnah Berurah

tefilin and the flesh. One must at least be careful that /there is no/ dead louse or earth /in between/. In view of this, there are people who are accustomed to wash the area where the *tefilin* are donned.

It is stated in the work *Revid Ha-Zahav* that the occasional interposition of the strap between the *tefilin* and the flesh does not appear to be classed /halachically/ as an interposition, as /the presence of an object/ of the same material is not /ruled as/ an interposition.[9] /However,/ from /the words of/ the *Levushey Serad*, which I have noted above in sub-Par. 10, it is implied that it is proper initially to be stringent about this.

(15) Or whether the head /*tefilin*/. In the work *Machatzis Ha-Shekel*, /the author/ writes, "I am vexed by the conduct of those people who allow their forelocks to grow. Apart from /the fact/ that this is haughty and arrogant behavior (see what is stated in the *Yoreh De'ah*, Sec. 178[10]), it /also/ involves /the transgression of/ a prohibition, when one dons *tefilin*. For in view of the fact that /the locks of hair/ are very long, one cannot argue that they constitute normal growth and they are /therefore ruled as/ an interposition /between the *tefilin* unit and the flesh/". See there.

/Actually, this practice would/ also /be objectionable/ without /the question of/ the interposition. /For/ because of those numerous hairs it is impossible to adjust /the position of the *tefilin*/ with exactitude so that they will be tightly donned in their /proper/ place, in accordance with halachic /requirements/.

(16) There is no need to be particular. The Acharonim write that one should not be lenient /about this/ except in the place where the coils are, but one should be stringent even with the straps /as regards/ what is relevant to the binding. /This applies/ both with respect to the arm /*tefilin*/ and with respect to the head /*tefilin*/. They write an open rebuke to those who don *tefilin* over a wig, called a *parukah* /in Yiddish/, even if they only /allow/ the strap to lie over the wig.

Nevertheless, it is implied by the words of the *M.A.* and the *Ch.A.* that if one has a wound on his head only in the place where the straps lie, but not in the place where the capsule /is placed/, he is permitted to place the straps over cloth on the wound or over a thin cap and to make the blessing, although there is an interposition between the straps /and the flesh/, since in the place where the capsule /is lying/ there is no interposition. Similarly, in the case of the arm /*tefilin*/, if one has a wound even in the place where the binding encircles around the arm, he is permitted to place the binding which encircles /the arm/ over cloth and to make the blessing. However, with /the arm *tefilin*/, one must be careful to cover /the binding/ from above /in such a case/, so that /the requirement of/, "to you for a sign"[11] /, i.e./, and not to others for a sign, will be fulfilled.

(17) A propensity to severe chills. I.e., if he has a pain or an ache in his head and if he would expose his head the cold would harm him. In view of the fact that he is a victim of circumstances beyond his control, he may rely on the *Rashba*, who is of the opinion that an interposition does not matter and /the words/ "between your eyes"[5] were stated only to define the area /where the *tefilin* must be donned/.

As for /the requirement/, "to you for a

9 It should be noted that both the capsule and the strap are made of leather.
10 This is the correct source. (Editor)
11 *Shemos* 13:9.

של יד (טו) לא שנא של ראש: הגה ודוקא בתפילין אבל ברצועות (טז) אין (ז) להקפיד (רשב"א בתשובה סימן תתכ"ז): ה 'אדם שהוא (יז) עלול לנזילות ואם **יצטרך להניח** (יח) **תפלה של ראש על בשרו לא יניחם כלל יש להתיר לו להניח תפלה של ראש על** (יט) **הכובע** (ח) [ו] **דק הסמוך לראש ויכסם** ח**מפני הרואים**: הגה והמניחים בדרך זה לא יברך על של ראש (כ) רק יברך על (ט) של יד להניח (לדעת רשב"א): ו (כא) * ט**ואטר** (כב) **יד** (י) **ימינו אם עושה** (כג) **כל מלאכתו בשמאל**

ז תשובת הריב"ש לדעת הרשב"א ח בית יוסף ט מנחו' ל"ז

באר היטב

כתב דיש לרחוץ מקום הנחת תפילין: (ז) להקפיד. מיהו יש להחמיר אפי' ברצועות מה ששייך להקשירה בין ברצועות של ראש בין ברצועות היד. ט"ז מ"א ע"ת. בספר דבר שמואל סימן רל"ב כתב תוכחת מגולה על המניחין התפילין ע"ג פאה נכרית הנקרא פארו"קה ועיין בתשובת יד אליהו סי' ג' שהאריך בזה: (ח) דק. ועל כובע עבה אסור. ואם יש לו מכה ביד אסור להניחם על הבגד משום לך לאות ולא לאחרים לאות אבל מותר להניחו על החלוק[א] אם לא סגי בלא"ה דהא לבוש בגד אחר עליו. מ"א: (ט) של יד. וה"ה אם מניח של יד בדרך זה שלא יברך על ש"י אלא על של ראש. מ"א. וכתב הב"ח מ"מ בשעת ק"ש ותפלה יראה שיהא זולת חציצה ע"ש: (י) ימינו. שנים שהלכו בדרך ואחד מהם אטר ואין לו רק תפילין ממי שאינו אטר יניח התפילין בימין דהיינו הקציצה לצד הכתף והמעברתא לצד היד. וכן להיפוך במי שאינו איטר ומניח תפילין של האיטר מניח בשמאלו הקציצה לצד הכתף והמעברתא לצד היד שבות יעקב ח"א סי' ג' ע"ש. ועיין בתשובת נחלת שבעה סימן מ"א ובחות יאיר סימן

שערי תשובה

תפילין. ובבר"י כתב שפשוט שהנוהג כן צריך לנגב המקום היטב משום התפילין. וגם אפשר שהם מפסיקים כמו חציצה. והביא מדברי המיימ' מהלכות עבודת יוה"כ דלכך בכ"ג עלה ונסתפג כו' ונשא ונתן בזה עיי"ש. ונראה דהשל"ה כ"כ לפי שהמשכים לחצות נותן אפר תחת פאר וכשרוצה להניח תפילין צריך לרחוץ המקום משום כבוד התפילין וכן הוא בכתבי האר"י ז"ל ע"ש. ועיין בשו"ת פני אריה בסי' ו' וסי' ז' לענין אבק שקורין פוד"ר מה דינו ע"ש: [ו] דק. עבה"ט וכתב בתשב"ץ סי' ל' אין להניח תפילין על הכובע רק[ב] על ראשו ומותר לכסות אותם בסודרו. והא דאמרינן וראו כל עמי הארץ כו' היינו שיהיה בראש במקום שהם נראים יותר וראו כמו ושמעו וכל העם רואים את הקולות ע"ש. ונראה דאף שיש איזה דרשא[ג] בהא דוכל העם רואים דקאי על המלאכים שנבראו מכל דיבור מ"מ פשטא דקרא על שמיעה נאמר

משנה ברורה

נכונה היא שלא יהא מפסיק בין התפילין לבשר (יד) ועכ"פ בכונה מתה ועפר יש ליזהר ועי"כ (טו) יש נוהגין לרחוץ מקום הנחת התפילין. כתב בספר רביד הזהב נראה דמה שרצועה מונחת לפעמים בין תפילין לבשרו לא מיקרי חציצה דמין במינו אינו חוצץ ומלבושי שרד שהעתקתי לעיל בסק"י משמע דנכון לכתחלה להחמיר בזה: (טו) לא שנא ש"ר. כתב בספר תפלת השקל ורע עלי המעשה של אותן האנשים שמגדלין בלורותיהן מלבד כי הוא דרך שחץ וגאוה עיין מה שכתוב ביו"ד סימן קפ"ו[ד] יש בו איסור בהנחת תפילין דכיון דגדולין הרבה ליכא למימר בהו היינו רביתייהו וחוצצים עי"ש ובלאו חציצה נמי בשביל הני שערות המרובים א"א לנמצם שיהיו מהודקין ומונחין על מקומן כדין: (טז) אין להקפיד. והאחרונים כתבו דאין להקל רק במקום הכריכות אבל מה ששייך להקשירה (טז) יש להחמיר אף ברצועות בין בשל יד ובין בשל ראש וכתבו תוכחת מגולה על המניחים התפילין ע"ג פאה נכרית הנקרא פארוק"ה ואפילו אם רק הרצועה מונח על הפאה נכרית. ומ"מ משמע מדברי המ"א והח"א דאם יש לו מכה בראשו ורק במקום שהרצועות מונחים ולא במקום הקציצה מותר לו להניח הרצועות ע"ג סמרטוטין שעל המכה או ע"ג כובע דק ולברך אע"ג שיש חציצה בין הרצועות כיון דבמקום הקציצה אין חציצה וכן בשל יד אם יש לו מכה (יז) אפילו במקום הקף הקשר שסביב ידו מותר לו להניח הקף הקשר ע"ג סמרטוטין ולברך אך בזה יזהר לכסות מלמעלה כדי שיתקיים לך לאות ולא לאחרים לאות: ה (יז) עלול לנזילות. פי' (יח) שיש לו מכאוב או (יט) מיחוש בראשו ואם יגלה ראשו יזיק לו הקרירות כיון שהוא אנוס יכול לסמוך על הרשב"א דס"ל דאין משום חציצה ולא נאמר בין עיניך אלא לסיים להם מקום ומשום לך **לאות ולא לאחרים לאות ליכא בתש"ר דבהו כתיב וראו כל עמי הארץ כי שם ד' נקרא עליך. ומ"מ צריך לכסות (כ) מפני הרואים שאינם יודעים שהוא אנוס: (יח) תש"ר על וכו'. ואם יש לו מכה ביד במקום הנחת הקציצה והמכה (כא) מתפשטת בכל הקיבורת מותר לו להניח (כב) על הרטיה אם לא סגי בלא"ה (כג) ולא יברך דהא דעת רוב הפוסקים דחציצה פוסלת ויברך שתים על הש"ר כדלעיל בסימן כ"ו בהג"ה אך ילבוש על התש"י מלמעלה בגד אחר כדי לכסותם דהא כתיב בהו והיה לך לאות ודרשינן לך לאות ולא לאחרים לאות. ודוקא על רטיה אבל להניח תפילין על חלוקו (כד) י"א דאסור אפילו בדיש לו מכה ואפילו אם ילבוש עליו בגד אחר: (יט) הכובע דק. אבל על כובע עבה אסור להניחם דלא יוכל לכוין ולמצא מקום שהמוח של תינוק רופס: (כ) רק יברך וכו'. (כה) ויכוין להוציא הש"ר דבלא"ה דעת הרבה פוסקים שאין מברך על שניהם אלא אחת. ועיין בב"ח וע"ת דמשמע מדבריהם דנכון ליזהר שעכ"פ בשעת ק"ש ותפלה יהיה בלי חציצה כלל: ו (כא) ואיטר וכו'. ועיין לעיל בס"ק י"ג: (כב) יד ימינו. ואפילו (כו) נעשה איטר ע"י שהרגיל עצמו אח"כ ולא נולד כך יניח בימין וכ"ש (כז) אם מן השמים הרגילוהו דהיינו שנולד לו חולי בימינו וניטל הכח ממנו או שנקטע לו כף ידו הימנית וצריך לעשות כל מלאכתו בשמאל בודאי דינו כאיטר גמור ויניח על היד הרצועה ואם חזר לבריאותו ונעשה שולט בשתי ידיו בשוה הרי הוא ככל אדם: (כג) כל מלאכתו. (כח) ה"ה אפילו רק רוב**

ביאור הלכה

הנכון לתקן וכו'. ובכל זה מי שהוא איטר ואין לו רק תפילין של אינו איטר או להיפך יוכל להפך להניח הקציצה לצד הכתף והמעברתא לצד היד כ"כ בתשו' שבו"י ובארה"ח כי זה בודאי טוב יותר ממה שיניח כך ויהיה התפילין סמוך ללב ויהיה קשר היו"ד חוצה לה וכמו שכתב הגר"א שהסעיף ב' אף שכתב בשו"ע בשם מנהג דינא דגמרא הוא לפי' הגאונים ועיין בח"א אות י"ג דלא הזכיר שם עצה זו דשבו"י והוא כתב שם דטוב אם יכול להוציא הרצועה ולהכניסה מצד אחר כדי שתהיה היו"ד סמוך ללב אע"פ שאינו יכול להפוך הקשר של היו"ד שתהיה פניה לצד הבית ועכ"פ לא יתבטל ממצות תפילין עבור זה ויניחם כך ע"ש ור"ל אף דיהיה קשר היו"ד לצד חוץ והתפילין לצד הלב ולענ"ד בודאי טוב יותר לעשות כהשבו"י דזה דינא דגמרא הוא לכמה ראשונים וזה מנהג וכמו שכתב הגר"א ואפילו אם יכול להוציא הרצועה ג"כ יש לעיין דאולי מה שהיו"ד לא יהיה פניו כלפי הבית לא נחשב יו"ד ועכ"פ באינו יכול להוציא יעשה כהשבו"י: * ואיטר יד ימינו. עיין מ"ב במש"כ

שער הציון

(יד) מ"א: (טו) של"ה: (טז) הלבוש וע"ת וט"ז וא"ר וכן משמע ג"כ מהגר"א: (יז) כן מוכח במ"א סק"ו דלהרשב"א אם מכסה בחלוק מלמעלה אין אסור ע"י הסמרטוטין משום חציצה וע"כ יש לסמוך עליו לברך עכ"פ לענין רצועות: (יח) ט"ז: (יט) ח"א: (כ) ט"ז: (כא) דאל"ה יניח על מקום הנשאר בקיבורת ועיין בט"ז ובמשנה ברורה שם: (כב) מ"א וא"ר וח"א: (כג) מ"א וחידושי רע"א ומה שהקיל רע"א אם יש לו הש"י לבד מביאור הגר"א לא משמע כן: (כד) ארה"ח וכן משמע מח"א: (כה) ע"ת: (כו) מ"א: (כז) דגול מרבבה ועיין בבה"ל: (כח) וכן משמע בהרא"ש וביאור הגר"א ובשארי אחרונים:

הגהות ותיקונים: א) צ"ל הסמרטוטין: ב) צ"ל דק: ג) דרשה: ד) קע"ח:

required to place (18) the head *tefilin* on his flesh he would not don them at all, he should be permitted to don the head *tefilin* over (19) the thin cap /he wears/ close to the head. /However,/ he should cover them from /the view of/ observers.

Gloss: Those who don /tefilin/ *in this manner should not make a blessing over the head* /tefilin/, (20) *but should only make the blessing* Lehaniach Tefilin *over the arm* /tefilin/. *(...)*

6. /The ruling for/ (21) a left (22) handed person /is as follows/.

If /a left-handed person/ does (23) all his actions with his left /hand/,

Mishnah Berurah

sign"[11] /, i.e./, and not to others for a sign, this does not /relate/ to head *tefilin*, since with reference to them it is stated,[12] "and all the peoples of the earth will see that the Name of God is readable on you". Nevertheless, it is necessary /for him/ to cover them from /the view of/ observers who are not aware /of the fact/ that he is a victim of circumstances beyond his control.

(18) The head *tefilin* on, etc. If one has a wound on his arm in the area where the capsule must be donned and the wound is spread over the entire biceps, he is permitted to don /the *tefilin*/ over the bandage if it is otherwise impossible /for him to don the *tefilin*/. He should not make the blessing, as the majority of Poskim are of the opinion that an interposition disqualifies /the donning/. /Instead,/ he should make two blessings over the head /*tefilin*/, as /follows from what is ruled/ above in Sec. 26, in the gloss /to Par. 2/. However, he must wear another garment above, over the hand *tefilin*, in order to cover them. For with reference to these /*tefilin*/ it is stated,[11] "and they will be to you for a sign", which /the Sages/ interpreted to mean to you for a sign and not to others for a sign.

It is only /permitted to don the *tefilin* in such a case/ over a bandage. As regards donning the *tefilin* over one's shirt, however, there are /authorities/ who say that it is prohibited /for one to do so/ even though he has a wound and even if he wears another garment /to cover/ over /the *tefilin*/.

(19) The thin cap. It is, however, forbidden to don /the *tefilin*/ over a thick cap, for /then/ one will be unable to position and adjust /them/ with exactitude /so that they are in/ the /required/ area, where the brain of a child is soft.

(20) But should only make the blessing, etc. They should have in mind that /the blessing/ should serve /also/ to fulfil /their obligation to make a blessing over/ the head /*tefilin*/. /The reason for this is/ that in any case many Poskim are of the opinion that one should only make one blessing for both /*tefilin*/.

See the *Bach* and the *O.T.* It is implied by their words that the correct /practice/ is /for one/ to take care that /the *tefilin*/ should be /on him/ without any interposition, at least while /he is reading/ "The Reading of Shema" and /praying the eighteen-blessing/ prayer.

(21) A left, etc. See above in sub-Par. 12.

(22) Handed person. Even if one was not born /left-handed, but/ became left-handed through having accustomed himself later /to use his left hand/, he should /nevertheless/ don /the *tefilin*/ on his right /arm/. One should certainly /do so/ if he became accustomed /to use his left hand/ through Heavenly /intervention/, i.e., if he contracted a disease in his right /hand/ and its strength was taken away from it or if his right palm was cut off and he is /now/ required to do all his actions with his left /hand/. /Then/ he definitely has the ruling of a fully left-handed person and he should don the *tefilin* on the crushed arm. If the health of /the right hand/ is restored and he becomes in control /of the use/ of both his hands equally, he will have the same /ruling once more/ as everyone else.

(23) All his actions. The same ruling

12 *Devarim* 28:10.

(כד * מניח בשמאלו שהוא ימין של (יא) [ז] כל אדם ואם (כה) שולט בשתי ידיו מניח בשמאל כל אדם. ואם כותב בימינו ושאר כל מעשיו עושה בשמאלו או כותב בשמאל ושאר כל מעשיו עושה בימין ייא שיניח תפילין ביד (כו) שתש כחא) דבעינן יד כהה * כוי"א שהיד שכותב בה היא (כז) חשובה (יב) ימין לענין זה ומניח תפילין ביד שכנגדה: (הגה (כח) * והכי נהוג): ז לאעפ"י שיש לאדם מכה במקום הנחת תפילין יניח תפילין כי ממקום יש בזרוע להניח שתי תפילין כי העצם הסמוך לבית השחי מחציו (כט) עד הקובד"ו הוא מקום הנחת תפילין: ח נאורך רצועה של יד כדי שתקיף את הזרוע ויקשור ממנה הקשר ותמתח על אצבע אמצעית ויכרוך ממנה על אצבעו (ל) שלשה (יג) כריכות ויקשור סונוהגין העולם לכרוך על הזרוע ששה (לא) או שבעה (יד) כריכות: הגה (לב) ואין לכרוך הרצועה על (טו) [ט] התיתורא כדי לחזקה על היד (מהרי"ל): ט עמקום הנחת

י הרא"ש בשם בעל התרומה כ טור והגהת סמ"ג והגהת מיימוני בשם רבי יחיאל ל ב"י יוסף מלא כתוב מ עירובין צ"ו נ מנחות ל"ה לדעת הרמב"ם בפרק ג' מה"ת וסמ"ג בשם הרי"ף ס ב"י יוסף ע מנחות ל"ו

שערי תשובה

ומפיק ליה בלשון ראיה לדרשא וה"נ בהא דוראו דכל עמי הארץ שיהיה השמיעה ברור אלמא כאלו ראו בעיניהם ממש: [ז] כל אדם. עבה"ט ועיין מ"ש לעיל ס"ק ה' ומדברי הבעה"ע שהביא הב"יב) נראה דס"ל דילא. ובשלמי ציבור כתב וז"ל ומצאתי בספר זר זהב למהר"י למה האריך והרבה בראיות שאיטר יד ימינו אינו רשאי לשנות משאר כל אדם שלא לשנות הסדר העליון ע"ש: [ח] התיתורא. עבה"ט ובברכי יוסף כתב שכתבו בשם מהר"י למח שהרב מהר"ש ויטל העיד שאביו מהרח"ו ז"ל כשהיה עובר הרצועה בזרוע היה מהדק היטב וקושר היו"ד עם התפלה וממשיך הרצועה אצל הזרוע לעשות הכריכות אבל בקיבורת לא עשה שום כריכה כלל ואמר מהרח"ו שכן נהג רבינו האר"י ז"ל ומהר"י למח הוכיח כן מדברי הפוסקים ומדברי הקבלה וכן נהגנו. ועיין מ"ש התשב"ץ ח"ג סי' קי"ח עכ"ל. ובמח"ב כתב על מ"ש כאן שאין לכרוך הרצועה על התיתורא וז"ל העולם נוהגין להיפך כמ"ש האחרונים וכתבו שכן מוכח מדברי גורי האר"י ז"ל. והרב מור וקציעה העיד שהגאון מר אביו היה כורך הרצועה על התיתורא וכתב דטעמו ונימוקו עמו ע"ש. ואני תמה שבמח"ב נראה שמסכים להיפך ממ"ש בבר"י בשם מהר"י למח וכתב וכן נהגנו. ובספר שלמי ציבור ראיתי שכתב בשם ספר זר זהב

באר היטב

קס"ז: (יא) כל אדם. ואם הניחו בימינו שהוא שמאל כל אדם אפילו בדיעבד לא יצא חוט השני סימן כ"א: (יב) ימין. ואם כותב בב' ידיו יניח בשמאל כל אדם. ואם הרגיל עצמו לכתוב בשמאל ועושה כל מלאכתו בימין יניח בשמאל כל אדם עיין מ"א (ועיין בספר אליהו רבה שהשיג על פשרת מ"א ופסק כדעת ש"ע. ומסיים מיהו אדם שאין יכול לכתוב יניח בימין כשעושה כל מעשיו בשמאל): (יג) כריכות. א' בפרק האמצעי וב' בתחתון. האר"י ז"ל: (יד) כריכות. וכ"כ האר"י ז"ל ועיין יד אהרן: (טו) התיתורא. רק יהא תלוי כעין של ראש מהרי"ל. ובשכנה"ג חולק על מהרי"ל בזה וכתב ופוק חזי מאי עמא דבר שכל העולם נוהגים לקשור המעברתא עם הרצועות ע"ש. וכ"כ עטרת זקנים ממשמעות ש"ע מר"י לוריא. וז"ל ישים רצועה של יד על התיתורא של יד מיד אחר הקשירה כדי שלא תזוז ממקומה דאם זזה ממקומה אז היה בא לידי ספק ברכה. ואח"כ יקשור בקיבורת ג' כריכות ובזרוע ד' כריכות ואח"כ יניח של ראש ע"ש וע"ל סימן

משנה ברורה

רוב מלאכתו: (כד) מניח בשמאל. ואם הניחו בימינו שהוא שמאל כל אדם אף בדיעבד לא יצא [חוט השני סימן כ"ח] ועיין בביאור הלכה: (כה) שולט בשתי ידיו. ר"ל שעושה כל המלאכות בשניהם שוה בשוה אבל אם נקל לו לעשות בשמאל אף שיכול לעשות אותם גם בימין זה לא מיקרי שולט בשתי ידיו [כן מוכח לקמן בסימן תרנ"א בש"ת עי"ש]: (כו) שתש כחה). ר"ל דכתיבה אין לה שום מעלה משאר מלאכה יחידית ואזלינן בתר רוב המעשים והיא הנקראת שמאל: (כז) חשובה ימין. דכתיב וקשרתם וכתבתם משמע דאותו יד שכותב בה צריך לקשור את התפילין על היד שכנגדו (כט) מיהו כשלא נולד כן רק אח"כ הרגיל עצמו לכתוב בשמאל ושאר מעשיו עושה בימין יניח בשמאל כל אדם. ואדם (ל) שאין יכול לכתוב לכו"ע אזלינן בתר שאר מלאכות באיזה יד שעושה אותם נקרא ימין: (כח) והכי נהוג. עיין בביאור הלכה: ז (כט) עד הקובד"ו. ר"ל (לא) בבשר התפוח אשר אצל הקובד"ו ולא עד הקובד"ו ממש ואם נתפשט המכה בכל בשר התפוח אשר אצל הקובד"ו (לב) יוכל לסמוך על דעת המקילין להניח בבשר התפוח אשר בחצי העליון של עצם (לג) ואם המכה גדולה ומלטער בהנחת התפילין פטור מלהניח התפילין של יד אפילו נשאר לו מקום הנחה ויניח של ראש לבד וכדלעיל בסימן כ"ו עי"ש ועיין מה שכתבנו בסעיף ה' בס"ק י"ח: ח (ל) שלשה כריכות. שנים (לד) בפרק התחתון ואחד בפרק האמצעי (לה) וי"א דתחלה א' בפרק אמצעי ואח"כ ב' בפרק התחתון. ואותן הכריכות יעשה אחר הנחת השל ראש: (לא) או שבעה. ואנו נוהגין שבעה [אחרונים] ועיין בשע"ת שמסיק דאין לעשות אלו הז' כריכות רק על הזרוע דלא כקצת שנוהגים לעשות ג' כריכות על הקיבורת וד' על הזרוע: (לב) ואין לכרוך. שכבר נתקיים וקשרתם ברצועה שעל המעברתא וכמו בתפילין של ראש שתלוי ברצועה שבתוך המעברתא (לו) וכיון שאין מלוה כלל בכריכה לכן אין להניחה על התיתורא

ביאור הלכה

ואפילו נעשה וכו' כן כתב המג"א סק"ט בשם המרדכי ואף דסיים שם דיש חולקין ע"ז מ"מ מוכח בסוף סק"י להמעיין בו דלדינא הסכים כהדרכי משה וכן פסק הדה"ח. ומה שכתבתי וכ"ש אם מן השמים וכו' כן כתב הדגול מרבבה דבזה כו"ע מודים דנעשה איטר ופשוט דלסברתו ה"ה אם נקטע כף ידו הימנית נעשה בזה איטר וכמו שכתבתי בפנים וראיתי בפמ"ג בסימן תרנ"א שמסתפק בזה ומשמע דלא ברירא ליה סברת הדגמ"ר ומ"מ פשוט דנוכל לסמוך בזה על הדגמ"ר אחרי דאפילו באיטר שנעשה ע"י שהרגיל עצמו ג"כ פסק הד"מ דדינו כאיטר. ודע דלפי מה שכתבנו למעלהג) בנקטע שמאלו ולא נשאר לו כ"א הקיבורת דמעיקר הדין חייב להניח עליה תפילין ה"ה בנקטע יד ימינו ולא נשאר לו כ"א הקיבורת חייב להניח עתה עליה תפילין דעתה אחר שהרגיל עצמו לעשות בשמאל הימין נעשה שמאל: * מניח בשמאלו. עי' במ"ב בשם חוט השני ועיין בשע"ת שכתב דמדברי בעל העיטור שהובא בב"י בסי' תרנ"א נראה דס"ל דילא ודבריו אין מחוורין דכונת הבעל העיטור מש"כ שם דלא גרע מתפילין ר"ל אחרי דבתפילין דינא הכי דמניחן בשמאלו שהוא ימין כל אדם עכ"פ לענין לולב בדיעבד יצא בזה אבל בתפילין גופא בודאי אם היפךד) והניח בימינו שהוא שמאל כל אדם אפילו בדיעבד לא יצא דבאיטר שמאל דידיה הוי כימין כל אדם אח"כ מצאתי בחוט השני שמבאר כן דברי בעהע"ט בראיות כמו שכתבנו: * וי"א שהיד שכותב בה וכו'. מסתימת השו"ע והפוס' משמע דכל כתיבה מהני לזה ולא בעינן שיהיה יכול לכתוב ספרים תפילין ומזוזה גופא כדמשמע לכאורה פשטיה דקרא וכתבתם אך אם אינו יכול לכתוב כתב גמור רק רשימות ותמונות בעלמא לזכרון כמו שאנו קורין (בל"א ליפער) איני יודע אם הוא בכלל כתב לענין זה ועיין ברמב"ם פרק י"א מהלכות שבת דין יו"ד במש"כ ואפילו משני סימניות ובהמ"מ שם וצ"ע. ובאמת בכגון זה בודאי יותר טוב לסמוך על שיטת הגר"א והרוב מהראשונים דס"ל כדיעה הראשונה וכמו שהאריך בכעין זה הארה"ח ע"ש: * והכי נהוג. עיין במ"א שכתב דלדעה זו אפילו אם הוא שולט בשתי ידיו בכתיבה מניח בשמאל כל אדם אף ששאר כל מעשיו עושה בשמאלו ועיין עוד שם שהביא דעת הב"ח שחולק וסובר דדוקא אם כותב בימינו ושאר כל מעשיו עושה בשמאלו שבזה נחשב כשולט בשתי ידיו אבל אם כותב בשמאלו ושאר מלאכתו עושה בימינו

שער הציון

(כט) מ"א: (ל) א"ר: (לא) מ"א והגר"א הסכים לדינא ג"כ הכי: (לב) ח"א: (לג) מ"א ופמ"ג: (לד) מ"א ופמ"ג: (לה) ג"ז במ"ז סק"ח: (לו) ט"ז:

הגהות ותיקונים: א) כחה: ב) בסי' תרנ"א: ג) בס"א: ד) הפך: ה) כחה:

(24) he should don /the *tefilin*/ on his "left" /arm/, which is the right /arm/ for everyone /else/. If **(25)** he has control of both his hands /equally/, he should don /the *tefilin*/ on the left /arm/ for everyone /else/.

If one writes with his right /hand/ and does all his other actions with his left /hand/ or writes with his left /hand/ and does all his other actions with his right /hand/, there are /authorities/ who say that he should don the *tefilin* on the arm **(26)** which is weaker in strength, as it is required /to be donned on/ the feebler arm. Other /authorities/ say that the hand with which he writes is **(27)** considered the "right" /hand/ for this purpose and he should /therefore/ don the *tefilin* on the opposite arm. *(Gloss:* **(28)** *This is how one should act.)*

7. Even if a person has a wound in the area where the *tefilin* must be donned he should don the *tefilin*, as there is a /sufficiently large/ area on the arm for

Mishnah Berurah

/applies/ even if /he does/ only the majority of his actions /with his left hand/.

(24) He should don on his "left". If he donned /the *tefilin*/ on his "right" /arm/, which is the left /arm/ for everyone else, he is not /ruled to/ have fulfilled /his obligation/, although it is now after the event. [*Chut Ha-Shani*, Sec. 28.] See the Beyur Halachah.

(25) He has control of both his hands. I.e., if he does all his actions with either of them with equal /ease/. However, if it is easier for him to act with his left /hand/, although he is able to do his /actions/ with his right /hand/ as well, he is not classed as having control of both his hands /equally/. [This is evident /from what is written/ below in Sec. 651 in the *Sh.T.*; see there.]

(26) Which is weaker in strength. What is meant is that /for determining the "right" arm with respect to *tefilin*/ writing carries no more /weight/ than another specific action. We /therefore/ go according to the majority of actions /and class the hand with which he does them as the "right" hand/. /The other hand/ is described as the "left" hand.

(27) Considered the "right". For it is stated,[3] "and you should bind them" /, and immediately afterwards/, "and you should write them". This implies that with the same hand with which one writes he must /also/ bind the *tefilin* on the opposite arm.

However, if one was not born like that, but merely accustomed himself afterwards to write with the left /hand/ and does his other actions with his right /hand/, he should don /the *tefilin*/ on /the arm which is/ the left /arm/ for everybody else.

When a person is unable to write, all /authorities/ are agreed that we go according to the other actions and the particular arm with which he does them is described as the "right" /arm with respect to the donning of *tefilin*/.

(28) This is how one should act. See the Beyur Halachah.[13]

13 There the author states that if one cannot write proper writing, but mere symbols and signs, it is better to rely on the first opinion. He also writes that if one can do other actions also with the hand with which he writes, although it is easier for him to do them with the other hand, he is classed as having control of both his hands equally according to the first opinion.

(כד) * מניח בשמאלו שהוא ימין של (יא) [ז] כל אדם ואם (כה) שולט בשתי ידיו מניח בשמאל כל אדם. ואם כותב בימינו ושאר כל מעשיו עושה בשמאלו או כותב בשמאל ושאר כל מעשיו עושה בימין י״א שיניח תפילין ביד (כו) שתש כח{א} דבעינן יד כהה * ויי״א שהיד שכותב בה היא (כז) תשובה (יב) ימין לענין זה ומניח תפילין ביד שכנגדה: (הגה (כח) * והכי נהוג): ז לאעפ״י שיש לאדם מכה במקום הנחת תפילין יניח תפילין כי מקום יש בזרוע להניח שתי תפילין כי העצם הסמוך לבית השחי מחציו (כט) עד הקובד״ו הוא מקום הנחת תפילין: ח נאורך רצועה של יד כדי שתקיף את הזרוע ויקשור ממנה הקשר ותמתח על אצבע אמצעית ויכרוך ממנה על אצבעו (ל) שלשה (יג) כריכות ויקשור סונהגין העולם לכרוך על הזרוע ששה (לא) או שבעה (יד) כריכות: הגה (לב) ואין לכרוך הרצועה על (טו) [ח] התיתורא כדי לחזקה על היד (מהרי״ל): ט עמקום הנחת

י הרא״ש בשם בעל התרומה
כ טור והגהת סמ״ג והגהת מיימוני בשם רבי יחיאל ל בית יוסף מלא כתוב
מ עירובין צ״ו
נ מנחות ל״ה לדעת הרמב״ם בפרק ג׳ מה״ת וסמ״ג בשם הרי״ף ס בית יוסף
ע מנחות ל״ו

שערי תשובה

ומפיק ליה בלשון ראיה לדרשא וה״נ בהא דורא דכל עמי הארץ שיהיה השמיעה ברור אצלם כאלו ראו בעיניהם ממש: [ז] כל אדם. עבה״ט ועיין מ״ש לעיל ס״ק א׳ ומדברי הבעה״ע שהביא הב״י{ב} נראה דס״ל דילא. ובשלמי ליבור כתב וז״ל ומצאתי בספר זר זהב למהר״י למה האריך והרבה בראיות שאיטר יד ימינו אינו רשאי לשנות משאר כל אדם שלא לשנות הסדר העליון ע״ש: [ח] התיתורא. עבה״ט ובברכי יוסף כתב שכתבו בשם מהר״י למה שהרב מהר״ש ויטל העיד שאביו מהרח״ו ז״ל כשהיה עובר הרצועה בזרוע היה מהדק היטב וקושר היו״ד עם התפלה וממשיך הרצועה אצל הזרוע לעשות הכריכות אבל בקיבורת לא עשה שום כריכה כלל ואמר מהרח״ו שכן נהג רבינו האר״י ז״ל ומהר״י למה הוכיח כן מדברי הפוסקים ומדברי הקבלה וכן נהגנו. ועיין מ״ש התשב״ץ ח״ג סי׳ קי״ח עכ״ל. ובמח״ב כתב על מ״ש כאן שאין לכרוך הרצועה על התיתורא וז״ל העולם נוהגין להיפך כמ״ש האחרונים וכתבו שכן מוכח מדברי גורי האר״י ז״ל. והרב מור וקליעה העיד שהגאון מר אביו היה כורך הרצועה על התיתורא וכתב דטעמו ונימוקו עמו ע״ש. ואני תמה שבמח״ב נראה שמסכים להיפך ממ״ש בבר״י בשם מהר״י למה וכתב וכן נהגנו. ובספר שלמי ליבור ראיתי שכתב בשם ספר זר זהב

ביאור הלכה

ואפילו נעשה וכו׳ כן כתב המג״א סק״ט בשם המרדכי ואף דסיים שם דיש חולקין ע״ז מ״מ מוכח בסוף סק״י להמעיין בו דלדינא הסכים כהדרכי משה וכן פסק הדה״ח. ומה שכתבתי וכ״ש אם מן השמים וכו׳ כן כתב הדגול מרבבה דבזה כו״ע מודים דנעשה איטר ופשוט דלסברתו ה״ה אם נקטע כף ידו הימנית נעשה בזה איטר וכמו שכתבתי בפנים וראיתי בפמ״ג בסימן תרנ״א שמסתפק בזה ומשמע דלא ברירא ליה סברת הדגמ״ר ומ״מ פשוט דנוכל לסמוך בזה על הדגמ״ר אחרי דאפילו באיטר שנעשה ע״י שהרגיל עצמו ג״כ פסק הד״מ דדינו כאיטר. ודע דלפי מה שכתבנו למעלה{ג} בנקטע שמאלו ולא נשאר לו כ״א הקיבורת דמעיקר הדין חייב להניח עליה תפילין ה״ה בנקטע יד ימינו ולא נשאר לו כ״א הקיבורת חייב להניח עתה עליה תפילין דעתה אחר שהרגיל עצמו לעשות בשמאל הימין נעשה שמאל: * מניח בשמאלו. עי׳ במ״ב בשם חוט השני ועיין בשע״ת שכתב דמדברי בעל העיטור שהובא בב״י בסי׳ תרנ״א נראה דס״ל דילא ודבריו אין מחוורין דכונת הבעל העיטור מש״כ שם דלא גרע מתפילין ר״ל אחרי דבתפילין דינא הכי דמניחן בשמאלו שהוא ימין כל אדם עכ״פ לענין לולב בדיעבד יצא בזה אבל בתפילין גופא בודאי אם היפך{ד} והניח בימינו שהוא שמאל כל אדם אפילו בדיעבד לא יצא דבאיטר שמאל דידיה הוי כימין כל אדם אח״כ מצאתי בחוט השני שמבאר כן דברי בעהע״ט בראיות כמו שכתבנו: * וי״א שהיד שכותב בה וכו׳. מסתימת השו״ע והפוס׳ משמע דכל כתיבה מהני לזה ולא בעינן שיהיה יכול לכתוב ספרים תפילין ומזוזה גופא כדמשמע לכאורה פשטיה דקרא וכתבתם אך אם אינו יכול לכתוב כתב גמור רק רשימות ותמונות בעלמא לזכרון כמו שאנו קורין (בל״א ליפער) איני יודע אם הוא בכלל כתב לענין זה ועיין ברמב״ם פרק י״א מהלכות שבת דין יו״ד במש״כ ואפילו משני סימניות ובהמ״מ שם וצ״ע. ובאמת בכגון זה בודאי יותר טוב לסמוך על שיטת הגר״א והרבה מהראשונים דס״ל כדיעה הראשונה וכמו שהאריך בכעין זה הארה״ח ע״ש: * והכי נהוג. עיין במ״א שכתב דלדעה זו אפילו אם הוא שולט בשתי ידיו בכתיבה מניח בשמאל כל אדם אף שאר כל מעשיו עושה בשמאלו ועיין עוד שם שהביא דעת הב״ח שחולק וסובר דדוקא אם כותב בימינו ושאר כל מעשיו עושה בשמאלו שזה נחשב כשולט בשתי ידיו אבל אם כותב בשמאלו ושאר מלאכתו עושה בימינו

באר היטב

קס״ז: (יא) כל אדם. ואם הניחו בימינו שהוא שמאל כל אדם אפילו בדיעבד לא יצא חוט השני סימן כ״א: (יב) ימין. ואם כותב בב׳ ידיו יניח בשמאל כל אדם. ואם הרגיל עצמו לכתוב בשמאל ועושה כל מלאכתו בימין יניח בשמאל כל אדם עיין מ״א (ועיין בספר אליהו רבה שהשיג על פשרת מ״א ופסק כדעת ש״ע. ומסיים מיהו אדם שאין יכול לכתוב יניח בימין כשעושה כל מעשיו בשמאל): (יג) כריכות. א׳ בפרק האמצעי וב׳ בתחתון. האר״י ז״ל: (יד) כריכות. וכ״כ האר״י ז״ל ועיין יד אהרן: (טו) התיתורא. רק יהא תלוי כעין של ראש מהרי״ל. ובשכנה״ג חולק על מהרי״ל בזה וכתב ופוק חזי מאי עמא דבר שכל העולם נוהגים לקשור המעברתא עם הרצועות ע״ש. וכ״כ עטרת זקנים ממשמעות ש״ע מר״י לוריא. וז״ל ישים רצועה של יד על התיתורא של יד מיד אחר הקשירה כדי שלא תזוז ממקומה דאם זזה ממקומה אז היה בא לידי ספק ברכה. ואח״כ יקשור בקיבורת ג׳ כריכות ובזרוע ד׳ כריכות ואח״כ יניח של ראש ע״ש וע״ל סימן

משנה ברורה

רוב מלאכתו: (כד) מניח בשמאל. ואם הניחו בימינו שהוא שמאל כל אדם אף בדיעבד לא יצא [חוט השני סימן כ״ח] ועיין בביאור הלכה: (כה) שולט בשתי ידיו. ר״ל שעושה כל המלאכות בשניהם שוה בשוה אבל אם נקל לו לעשות בשמאל אף שיכול לעשות אותם גם בימין זה לא מיקרי שולט בשתי ידיו [כן מוכח לקמן בסימן תרנ״א במ״א ע״ש]: (כו) שתש כח{ה}. ר״ל דכתיבה אין לה שום מעלה משאר מלאכה יחידית ואזלינן בתר רוב המעשים והיא הנקראת שמאל: (כז) תשובה ימין. דכתיב וקשרתם וכתבתם משמע דנאותו יד שכותב בה צריך לקשור את התפילין על היד שכנגדו (כט) מיהו כשלא נולד כן רק אח״כ הרגיל עצמו לכתוב בשמאל ושאר מעשיו עושה בימין יניח בשמאל כל אדם. ואדם (ל) שאין יכול לכתוב לכו״ע אזלינן בתר שאר מלאכות באיזו יד שעושה אותם נקרא ימין: (כח) והכי נהוג. עיין בביאור הלכה: ז (כט) עד הקובד״ו. ר״ל (לא) בבשר התפוח אשר לצד הקובד״ו ולא עד הקובד״ו ממש ואם נתפשט המכה בכל בשר התפוח אשר לצד הקובד״ו (לב) יוכל לסמוך על דעת המקילין להניח בבשר התפוח אשר בחצי העליון של עצם (לג) ואם המכה גדולה ומצטער בהנחת התפילין פטור מלהניח התפילין של יד אפילו נשאר לו מקום ויניח של ראש לבד וכדלעיל בסימן כ״ו ע״ש ועיין מה שכתבנו בסעיף ה׳ בס״ק י״ח: ח (ל) שלשה כריכות. שנים (לד) בפרק התחתון ואחד בפרק האמצעי (לה) וי״א דתחלה א׳ בפרק אמצעי ואח״כ ב׳ בפרק התחתון. ואותן הכריכות יעשה אחר הנחת הש״ר ראש: (לא) או שבעה. ואנן נהגינן שבעה [אחרונים] ועיין בשע״ת שמסיק דאין לעשות אלו הז׳ כריכות רק על הזרוע דלא כקצת שנוהגים לעשות ג׳ כריכות על הקיבורת וד׳ על הזרוע: (לב) ואין לכרוך. שכבר נתקיים וקשרתם ברצועה שעל המעברתא וכמו בתפילין של ראש שתלוי ברצועה שבתוך המעברתא (לו) וכיון שאין מצוה כלל בכריכה לכן אין להניחה על התיתורא

שער הציון

(כט) מ״א: (ל) א״ר: (לא) מ״א והגר״א הסכים לדינא ג״כ הכי: (לב) ח״א: (לג) מ״א ופמ״ג: (לד) מ״א ופמ״ג: (לה) ג״ז במ״ז סק״ח: (לו) ט״ז:

הגהות ותיקונים: א) כחה: ב) בסי׳ תרנ״א: ג) בס״א: ד) הפך: ה) כחה:

donning two *tefilin* units. This is because /the part of/ the bone near the armpit, from halfway along it (29) until the elbow, constitutes the area where the *tefilin* may be donned.

8. /The /required/ length for the strap of the arm /*tefilin*/ is sufficient for one /to be able/ to encircle the /upper/ arm, bind the knot with it, stretch it onto the middle finger, wind with it around the finger (30) three coils and /then/ tie it. It is the public practice to wind around the arm six (31) or seven coils /with the strap/.

Gloss: (32) *One should not wind the strap over the rim /of the* tefilin *unit/ in order to strengthen it on the arm. (...)*

Mishnah Berurah

(29) Until the elbow. I.e., the swollen flesh on the side of the elbow, but not /the rest of the flesh/ until the actual elbow.

If the wound has spread throughout the swollen flesh on the side of the elbow, one may rely on the view of those who are lenient /and allow one/ to don /the *tefilin*/ on the swollen flesh over the upper half of the bone.

If it is a large wound and one will suffer if he dons the *tefilin*, he is exempt from donning arm *tefilin* even if he has an area left /on which he can don them/. He should /therefore/ don the head *tefilin* only, as /ruled/ above in Sec. 26; see there. See what we have written /here/ in Par. 5, in sub-Par. 18 /of the Mishnah Berurah/.

(30) Three coils. Two /of the coils should be wound/ in the lower section and one in the middle section /of the finger/. There are /authorities/ who say that one must first /wind/ one /coil/ in the middle section and afterwards two in the lower section /of the finger/.

These coils should be made after the head /*tefilin*/ have been donned.

(31) Or seven. We are accustomed /to wind/ seven /coils/. [Acharonim]

See the *Sha.T.*, who concludes that one should not make these seven coils /anywhere/ except on the /fore/arm, unlike those few /people/ whose practice is to make three coils on the biceps and four on the /fore/arm.

(32) One should not wind. /This is/ because /the requirement of/, "and you should bind",[5] is already fulfilled by the strap on the passageway, just as /it is/ in the case of the head *tefilin*, which is suspended /on the head/ by the strap that is inside the passageway. Since there is no mitzvah whatever in making the coils, they should therefore not be placed over the rim /of the

תפלה של ראש מהתחלת (לג) עיקרי (טז) [ט] השער ממצחו (לד) * עד סוף המקום שמוחו של תינוק רופס: י פצריך שיהיה הקשר מאחורי הראש למעלה (יז) [י] (לה) * בעורף. צצריך לכוין הקציצה

לפירוש הרא"ש
פ שם בגמרא ל"ה
צ הרמב"ם שם פ"ד

באר היטב

כ"ה ס"ק י"ב: (טז) השער. הט"ז פסק דכל התפילין צריכים להיות מונחים במקום שיש קרחה דהיינו שיהא קצה התחתון בעקרי השער. ולא כטועים לומר שהקצה העליון יתחיל ממקום השער ועיקר התפילין מונחים על המצח ועוברים על איסור דאורייתא ומברכין ברכה לבטלה ע"ש. ובתשו' בית יעקב סי' קל"א חולק על הט"ז ופסק מהתחלת עיקרי השער יהא התיתורא יתחיל שם ולא הקציצה ע"ש (כנה"ג): (יז) בעורף.

שערי תשובה

כת"י למהר"י צמח והביא שם דברי מהר"ש וויטל וכתב שאמר לו שהרב אביו עלמו הניח לו תפילין כסדר הזה בפעם ראשונה שלבש שאביו לבשם לו ואמר לו שכן היה נוהג האר"י ז"ל לעשות. וכתב להשיג על המתכוונים לעשות דוגמת שם ש"ין דל"ת יו"ד שיש בזה ספק חשש כשמסלק הרצועה נמצא כאלו מוחקו דוגמת שכתב הלבוש בכתב שמו על דפי הספר אין לפותחו ולסוגרו בשבת וגם הביא מהזוהר ואתחנן ופרשת פנחס דאיתא שם תרין בקשרא חד דהיינו יו"ד וקשר רצועה במעברתא שהם תרין בקשרא חד שאנו קושרין היו"ד עם התפילין והוכיח שאין לעשות כריכות על הקיבורת. ובסוף דבריו כתב שראה בחלום להרב מהרח"ו ז"ל אשר האמת נכון עליו ואמר לי הנה בספר הכוונות בדף עצמו שמ"כ אורך הרצועה תמצא ראיה יותר ברורה והוא נכונה וחזקה והוא שתמצא ענין קשירת תש"י יקשור תחילה תש"י ויקיף ז' כריכות סביב הזרוע כו' (ר"ל שיקשור תחלה היו"ד עם התפלה ש"י וזהו קשירות היו"ד לבד ר"ל ע"י הידוק הרצועה נקשרת היו"ד על התפלה) ותיכף ימשוך הרצועה סביבות הזרוע לעשות ז' כריכות ולא אמרתי כ"א קשירת היו"ד כדברי הרשב"י מן הטעם הכתוב בשמו וכן אמרתי כמ"ש וכן תעשה ע"כ החלום. גם בש"ע ולבוש לא נזכר לשון כריכות אלא קושר קשירה אחת בלבד לצורך היו"ד עכ"ל הר"י צמח. ורבים מיראי ה' אחרי רואם זה חזרו לעשות כדבריו ז"ל עכ"ל. ומכאן תראה שמ"ש בש"ע האר"י שהביא בעט"ז לאו האר"י ז"ל חתם עלה. וכן מ"ש בפע"ח הנדפסת לעשות ג' כריכות בקיבורת כעין ש"ין הוא מהמחברים ואינו עיקר כיון שאינו מתורת מהרח"ו שהוא העיקר. וגם במ"ח כתב שיניח היו"ד על המעברתא ויכרוך עליהם כריכה אחת ומדברי מהר"י צמח נראה דליתא. ואם נאמר דמ"ש כשהיה עובר הרצועה בזרוע והיה מהדק וקושר היו"ד עם התפלה היינו ע"י העברת הרצועה על היו"ד עם התיתורא אלא שזה אין עליו שם כריכה רק שם קשירה שמיד משם ממשיך לזרוע לכרוך הז' כריכות וכן משמע קצת בסוף דבריו הוי א"ש לדברי הבר"י ובמח"ב לא סתרי אהדדי. אך מדברי מהר"י צמח שהבאתי לעיל ס"ק ה'[א] מבואר נגלה שדעתו שלא לקשור אותה עם הרצועה כלל וצ"ל דקשירה דקאמר היינו מחמת ההדוק שמושך הרצועה בהדוק מתקרבת ומתחברת אל התפלה והיינו כדרך הנוהגין לעשות הנקב שבכפילות הרצועה לצד השמאל וכל מה שמושכין הרצועה אינה מתקרבת אלא מתרחקת קצת. ולפ"ז ע"כ מ"ש דקושרין היו"ד עם התפלה אינו ע"י ההדוק רק ע"י העברת הרצועה על היו"ד והמעברתא מקשר אותם יחד וכבר כתבתי דממ"ש ס"ק ה'[א] אינו נראה כן וצ"ע: [ט] השער. עבה"ט ובחנס השיב הבר"י דגם כוונת הט"ז על קצה התחתון מהתפילין דהיינו התיתורא ושוב מצאתי כן בא"ר וכ"כ בשו"ת דברי יוסף סי' ס"ג יניח קצילה של ראש מיושבת ומושכבת על הראש ומהתחלת עיקרי שער הפדחת יניח התיתורא ודלא כגן המלך סי' קנ"ג והביאו בבר"י: [י] בעורף.

משנה ברורה

התיתורא שיש בה קדושה יותר מן הרצועה. והנוהגים להניח הש"ר קודם שכורכים על הזרוע י"א (לז) דיכול לכרוך הרצועה על הקציצה שלא תמוש תש"י ממקומה עד שיניח הש"ר ואח"כ יסירנה ויכרוך השבעה כריכות ומי שבשתי ידיו צרות והתפילין נדים ממקומם עי"ז יכול לכרוך סביב התיתורא כדי לחזקם [ארה"ח]: ט (לג) עיקרי השער. פירוש דבין עיניך לאו ממש הוא דגמרינן גזירה שוה מלא תשימו קרחה בין עיניכם האמור אצל מת מה להלן מקום שעושה קרחה והוא בראש אף כאן מתחיל (לח) מקום תפילין ממקום שיש שייכות קרחה דהיינו ממקום התחלת צמיחת השערות שבראש ורבים נכשלים באיסור זה וטועים לומר שהקצה העליון מתחיל ממקום השיער ועיקר התפילין מונח על המצח ועוברים על איסור דאורייתא דכל התפילין צריכין להיות מונחין במקום שיש קרחה דהיינו שיהיה (לט) אפילו קצה התחתון של התיתורא מונח על מקום התחלת עיקרי השער (מ) אבל אין להשגיח למי שיש לו שערות ארוכות ששוכבים עד חצי המצח להניח שם התפילין כי התחלת מקום התפילין צריך להיות מהתחלת עיקרי השער שבפדחת ולמעלה (מא) ויותר טוב להניח קצת למעלה משיעור זה דהא מקום יש בראש להניח שתי תפילין כדי שלא ישמט למטה על המצח. וכל (מב) המניחן על המצח הוא מנהג קראים ולא עשה המצוה (מג) וכל בעל נפש יזהיר לחביריו וילמדם שלא יכשלו בזה כדי שלא יהיו ח"ו בכלל פושעי ישראל בגופן דזהו קרקפתא דלא מנח תפילין וגם הברכה הוי לבטלה (מד) דתפילין שמונחין שלא במקומן הוי כמונחין בכיסן. ואם נשמטו ממקומן צריך להחזירן תיכף ולענין ברכה עיין לעיל בסימן כ"ה סי"ב: (לד) עד סוף המקום. ר"ל (מה) שקצה המעברתא של התפילין לא יהיה מונח למעלה ממקום שמוחו של תינוק רך: י (לה) בעורף. שהוא (מו) סוף הגלגולת והוא

ביאור הלכה

יניח בשמאל של כל אדם אך המ"א מסיים עליו שאנו אין לנו אלא פסק השו"ע וכן סתמו כהמ"א הרבה מאחרונים שאחריו אך הארה"ח החזיק בדעת הב"ח להלכה והגר"א בביאורו החזיק לגמרי כדעה הראשונה דלא אזלינן כלל בתר כתיבה וא"כ אם כותב בימין ושאר מעשיו עושה בשמאל יניח בימין אך מ"מ נלענ"ד דנוכל להמליץ על העולם דנוהגין כהלכה אליבא דכו"ע ומנהגן של ישראל תורה היא דנ"ל דאפילו לדעה הראשונה ה"מ דביד שכותב בה אין יכול לעשות פעולות האחרות אבל אם באותו יד יכול ג"כ לעשות פעולות האחרות רק שנקל לו לעשות בהיד השני מקרי שולט בשתי ידיו לכו"ע כיון דבהיד השני אינו יכול לכתוב כלל וכל יד יש לה מעלה בפני עצמה ואין זה דומה למה שכתבנו במ"ב סקכ"ה ד"ה שולט. ולמדתי דבר זה מתורתו של הרב שערי תשובה לקמן בסימן תרנ"א לענין לולב שכתב אין לכתיבה שום מעלה לכו"ע רק כשאר פעולה יחידית וכמו בכאן לדעה ראשונה לענין תפילין ואפ"ה כתב שם דזה מיקרי שולט בשתי ידיו מחמת סברא זו וא"כ ה"ה הכא אפי' לדעה הראשונה ולהגר"א שהולך בשיטתם אם כותב בימינו ושאר כל מעשיו עושה בשמאל מחמת שנקל לו יניח התפילין בשמאל כל אדם כנלענ"ד: * עד סוף וכו'. עיין בטור ורבינו ירוחם משמע מינייהו דכל גובה הראש הוא בכלל הזה וכן משמע בסה"ת ובירושלמי שהביא להמעיין בו (והעתיקו בביאור הגר"א) וברמב"ם משמע מפשטא דלישניה דלא ס"ל כן ועיין בב"י וכן בסמ"ק ובכל בו כתבו בפירוש דשיעור הנחת תפילין נמשך בסך הכל עד חצי שפוע הראש ולכן מהנכון מאד ליזהר עכ"פ לכתחלה שלא יהיו התפילין גדולים ביותר כי עי"ז נמשך למעלה על כל גובה הראש ומ"מ בדרך כלל טוב יותר שימשיך התפילין בגובה למעלה משישפילם לצד המצח כי בגובה יוצא עכ"פ לדעת כמה מהראשונים והירושלמי מסייע להו וכנ"ל מה שאין כן לצד המצח ועיין בס' מעשה רב ובהגהות כת"י הגאון ר' אלעזר חרל"פ זצ"ל דמשמע מיניה ג"כ דטוב יותר לכתחלה להמשיך התפילין לצד מעלה כדי שלא ישפלו לצד המצח ומ"מ אפשר דגם המע"ר מודה דלכתחלה לא יגביהם עד סוף גובה הראש כדי לצאת לדעת הסמ"ק והכל בו ג"כ. ודע עוד דאפילו לדעת סה"ת דמכשיר כל גובה הראש לתפילין משמע מיניה שם (לחד פירושא) דעכ"פ אין לעשותן יותר גדולים מארבע אצבעות והיינו עם התיתורא והמעברתא וכמו שכתב בספר בית יעקב וזהו שיעור מקום שני תפילין שבזמן הגמרא ועיין לקמן סימן ל"ב סמ"א שכתב דאין שיעור וכו' מ"מ לכתחלה בודאי נכון ליזהר בזה: * בעורף. עיין משנה ברורה וראיתי במעשה רב שכתב שהקשר צ"ל תחת שפוע הקדקוד ולענ"ד משמע כן בספר התרומה שז"ל הקשר של תפילין צריך

שער הציון

(לז) מ"א וארה"ח: (לח) ט"ז: (לט) אחרונים: (מ) פמ"ג: (מא) הגר"א במע"ר ושולחן שלמה: (מב) גמ' ורמב"ם: (מג) ע"ת: (מד) פמ"ג: (מה) אחרונים: (מו) מ"א:

הגהות ותיקונים: א) ד':

9. The area for the donning of the head *tefilin* unit is from the start of /the area where there are/ (33) hair roots on the forehead (34) until the end of the area where the brain of a baby is soft.

10. The knot behind the head must be above, (35) on the back of the head.

Mishnah Berurah

capsule/, which has more holiness than the strap.

For those /people/ whose practice is to don the head /*tefilin*/ before they wind /the coils/ over the /fore/arm, there are /authorities/ who say that they are allowed to wind the strap over the capsule, so that the arm *tefilin* should not move from its place while they are donning the head /*tefilin*/. They should subsequently remove /the strap from the capsule/ and wind the seven coils.

If someone has narrow sleeves, because of which the *tefilin* move out of place, he is allowed to wind /the strap/ around the rim /of the capsule/ in order to secure /the *tefilin*/. [*Ar.Hach.*]

(33) Hair roots. I.e., /when the Torah states that they should be/ "between your eyes",[5] this is not /meant/ literally. We learn this from the parallel usage /in the verse/, "You should not make baldness between your eyes",[14] stated with reference to /bewailing/ a dead person. Just as there the area which can become bald /is meant/, which is on /top of/ the head, so in our case the area for the *tefilin* /to be donned/ begins from the place where baldness is relevant, i.e., from the place where the hairs of the head begin to grow.

There are many /people/ who stumble over this prohibition /against donning *tefilin* in the wrong area/. They err in assuming that the upper edge /of the *tefilin* unit/ must begin in the area of the hair /roots/, but the main /part of the/ *tefilin* /unit/ may lie on the forehead. They /thus/ transgress a Torah prohibition, as the whole of the *tefilin* /unit/ must lie on the area where /there can be/ baldness. I.e., even the lower edge of the rim must lie on the area from where the hair roots start.

However, if someone has long hair which lies halfway down the forehead, one cannot take this into account /and allow him/ to place the *tefilin* there. For the beginning of the area for /the donning of/ the *tefilin* must be /regarded in all cases as starting/ from where the roots of the hairs start on the front of the head and /continuing/ above that. It is /in fact/ preferable to don /the *tefilin*/ somewhat above this limit, so that it should not slip down below onto the forehead, /bearing in mind/ that there is a /sufficiently large/ area /for donning *tefilin*/ on the head for one /to be able/ to don two *tefilin* units /there/.

Those who don /the *tefilin*/ on the forehead /should know that/ it is a Karaite[15] practice and they do not perform the mitzvah /when they do so/. Every conscientious person should admonish his fellows /about this/ and teach them not to stumble over it, so that they should not be, Heaven forfend, in the category of Jews who have sinned with their bodies. For /a person who dons *tefilin* there/ is /classed as/ a /person with a/ scalp that has not donned *tefilin*. In addition, the blessing /he makes over them/ is a vain /blessing/, since when *tefilin* have been donned in the wrong place it is as if they are /still/ lying in their bag.

If /one's *tefilin*/ have slipped out of place, he must return them immediately /to their proper place/. As regards /whether or not he must make/ a blessing /now/, see above in Sec. 25, Par. 12.

(34) Until the end of the area. What is meant is that the edge of the passageway of the *tefilin* should not be lying above the area where the brain of a baby is soft.

(35) On the back of the head. I.e., /on/ the end of the skull,[16] which is opposite the

14 *Devarim* 14:1.
15 The Karaites were a sect who rejected the teachings of the Rabbis and followed the written Torah literally.
16 It must be underneath the slope of the cranium. (Beyur Halachah).

(לו) שתהא באמצע כדי שתהא כנגד בין העינים וגם הקשר יהיה באמצע העורף ולא יטה לכאן או לכאן [ק]וצריך שיהא המקום שבקשר (לז) שנראה כעין דל"ת לצד (יח) חוץ: הגה וה"ה בקשר של יד צריך ליזהר שלא יתהפך (מרדכי דף נ"ו): יא [ר]צריך שיהיה השחור שברצועות לצד חוץ[1] (לח) [ש]ולא (יט) יתהפכו (לט) בין של יד בין של ראש [ת]ישלשל הרצועות שיהיו תלוים לפניו ויגיעו (מ) עד הטבור (מא) או למעלה ממנו מעט [א]רוחב הרצועות של יד ושל ראש (מב) כאורך שעורה לפחות. אם פיחת (כ) משיעור אורך הרצועות ורחבן [ב]אם אינו מוצא אחרות (מג) מניחן (מד) כמות שהן עד שימצא אחרות כשיעור. [ג]תפילין של ראש (מה) טוב להיותם גלוים ונראים אבל תלמיד בפני רבו (מו) אין דרך ארץ לגלות תפילין בפניו: הגה [יא] ובשל יד (מז) אין להקפיד (מח) אם הם גלוים או מכוסים (מרדכי שם) ונראה לי דעכשיו שאין מניחים אלא בזמן ק"ש ותפלה אפילו תלמיד לפני רבו יכול לגלות אף בשל ראש וכן המנהג שלא ליזהר (ד"ע):

באר הגולה

ק שם בגמרא בפי' רש"י ר שם ברש"י לפירוש השני ש מועד קטן כ"ה ת רא"ש בסוף הלכות תפילין ומרדכי וסמ"ג והתרומה בשם הרי"ף א רמב"ם ספ"ג וסמ"ג וסמ"ק ב ב"י לדעת סמ"ק ורמב"ם ג סא"ח בשם רב האי

שערי תשובה

עיין בה"ט ובכנה"ג כתב בשם שלטי הגבורים שבמרדכי דשבת כתב דהמניח שם למטה מלמיחת השער או[א] הצוואר לא יצא והוי ברכה לבטלה והיינו נמי קנה התחתון של הקשר יהיה למעלה מהתחלת למיחות השערות וכמדומה לי שראיתי בספר קטן כשהקשר שמאחורי הראש הוא בגומא לא יצא י"ח ולא ידעתי מאין יצא לו זה שהרי מלשון הש"ג משמע דבלמיחת שערות תליא מלתא מיהא ודאי דעורף היינו נגד הפנים כמבואר בחולין ומ"מ נראה שיש לעשות כן לכתחלה דבעינן שיהא הדק היטב סביב לראשו. ועיין בעטרת זקנים ס"ס זה וכל שהקשר משפע ויורד בתוך גומא א"א שתהיה הרלועה שסביב הראש מהודקת היטב. וכתב בפנים מאירות חלק ג' סי' ט' מי ששגג ולא הניח תפילין ש"ר במלחו במקום הראוי כמה שנים ועל המלות עשה נתכפר לו בוידוי דברים אך לבו חרד על מלות ל"ת של ברכה לבטלה לפ"ד הרמב"ם שהוא מדאורייתא והוא רולה לקבל תשובה ע"ז ונראה כיון שלדעת התוספות והרא"ש הוא מדרבנן וגם שלפי מנהגינו אומר אחר הברכה בשכמל"ו שזה תיקון שלא יעבור על לא תשא א"כ לא חטא בברכה לבטלה ולכן אף שביטל עשה וצריך עולה לספר[ב] מ"מ מיקרי דורון וא"צ לענות נפשו רק תשובתו נרלה בחרטה ומודה ועוזב ירוחם ע"ש. ונראה מדבריו שאם לא הניח ש"י כתיקונו דלא שייך בהו הלד תיקון אמירת בשכמל"ו יש לו לקבל תשובה על ברכתו לבטלה: [יא] ובש"י אין להקפיד. ובלבוש כתב שיהיו מכוסים משום והיה לך לאות. וכתב בבר"י בשם זקנו מוהר"א אזולאי שיש מדקדקים להאפיל בטלית על הזרוע בשעת הנחת תש"י. וכן ראוי לנהוג עפ"י קבלות[ג] האר"י ז"ל גם עפ"י דרכו גם תש"ר ראוי לכסותה בטלית ע"ש. ועיין במג"א לעיל ריש סימן ח' מ"ש:

באר היטב

שהוא סוף הגלגולת והוא נגד הפנים ולא כ"כ למטה כנגד הגרון: (יח) חוץ. ודלא כמו שנוהגין קלת לעשות ב' דלתי"ן מב' לדדים. מ"א: (יט) יתהפכו. ואם נתהפכו אפי' בשוגג מדת חסידות הוא להתענות ודוקא שמקיף הראש והזרוע אבל מה שמשלשל לפניו ומה שכורך אח"כ ליכא קפידא עי' בשכנה"ג ובע"ת: (כ) משיעור. ועכ"פ לריכין להיות משולשין[ד] לפניו מעט הא ל"ה פסולים לגמרי. מ"א:

משנה ברורה

נגד הפנים ולא כ"כ למטה כנגד הגרון (מז) וטוב שיהיה מונח עיקר הקשר למעלה מן הגומא ועכ"פ יש ליזהר שלא יהיה אפילו מקלת הקשר מונח במקום פנוי משער דשם הוא מפרקת הצואר ולא עורף (מח) ולכן יש ליזהר שתהיה הרצועה המקפת הראש מצומצמת ומהודקת סביב ראשו ולא יהיה הקף הרצועה גדול מהקף הראש דאז איכא תרתי לריעותא חדא דצריכים הידוק ממש דבעינן וקשרתם לאות וגו' וההידוק היא הקשירה שנית דאם הם רפוים סביב היקף ראשו יפול הקציצה לפניו על מצחו או יפול הקשר לאחריו למטה בצוארו ולא יהיו במקומן הראוי להן: (לו) שתהא באמצע. רוחב הראש ולא יטה אותם לצד אחד כדי שיתקיים והיו לטוטפות בין עיניך והרבה מהאחרונים כתבו דאם שינה בזה לא קיים מצות תפילין וצריך ליזהר בזה גם נכון ליזהר לכתחילה (מט) שלא יהיו התפילין גדולין ביותר דאז אי אפשר כמעט שיהיו מהודקין על הראש וגם שיהיו מונחין על מקומן דאם הם מונחין בגובה הראש כדין אינם מהודקין וגם הקשר לא יבא על מקומו כדין וע"ל בסי' ל"ב בסעיף מ"א מש"כ שם: (לז) שנראה כעין ד'. כי שתי רצועות יוצאות מתוך הקשר למטה אותה היוצאת מצד שמאל המניח נמשכת לרחבו כמו גג הדלי"ת ואותה היוצאת לצד ימין נמשכת באורך למטה כמו רגל הדלי"ת [א"ר] ויראה שלא יתהפך הקשר בעשייתו ובלבישתו ועיין לקמן בסימן ל"ב בסעיף נ"ב מה שכתבנו שם: יא (לח) ולא יתהפכו. ואם נתהפכו (נ) מדת חסידות הוא להתענות או (נא) לפדות בצדקה ואין להקפיד שלא יתהפכו אלא מה שמקיף את הראש ואת הקיבורת פי' אבל מה שכורך אח"כ וכן מה שמשתלשל לפניו מהרצועה של תש"ר אין צריך להקפיד כלל שלא יתהפך לפי שאינו מעיקר המצוה ומ"מ (נב) משום נוי המצוה ראוי להפוך שיהיה השחור לצד חוץ אפילו בהמותר: (לט) בין של יד וכו'. הנה בשל יד שהוא רואה כשהוא מניח יכול לראות שלא יתהפך לא הקשר ולא הרצועה ובשל ראש דאינו רואה כשהוא מניח סביב ראשו ימשמש היטיב בידו ממקום הקציצה בכל צד ויבדוק אם מונחין כראוי [ב"ח]: (מ) עד הטבור. ואם הוסיף ע"ז לית לן בה: (מא) או למעלה ממנו. ועיין בחידושי רע"א וכן בארה"ח דמסקי דשל ימין עד הטבור ושל שמאל עד החזה וטור כתב עוד וי"א דשל ימין עד המילה ושל שמאל עד הטבור: (מב) כאורך שעורה. היינו (נג) בקליפתה אבל בלא העוקץ שלה דיש גם עוקצין ארוכים מאד וי"א דדי ברוחב מאורך חטה ופחות מכשעורה (נד) ובמקום הדחק יש לסמוך ע"ז. וכתבו האחרונים דצריך ליזהר מאוד במקום כפל הסידוק שרגיל שהרצועה נתקמטה שם או שנפסקת עד שלא נשאר בה כשיעור: (מג) מניחן וכו'. מפני שיש מכשירין ויש פוסלין אף בדיעבד כמבואר בב"י ע"כ הכריע כן: (מד) כמות שהן. (נה) והאחרונים מסקי דאם פיחת משיעור האורך בשל יד הנזכר לעיל בסעיף ח' יניח בלי ברכה ואם יש כדי לפשוט עד אצבע צרידה (נו) הבריתות אין מעכבין. ובאורך רצועות הש"ר כתב בארה"ח דדוקא אם יש תוך ממה שמקיף הראש עכ"פ כשיעור שני טפחים הא לא"ה יניחן בלא ברכה ולענין רוחב הרצועות השל יד והשל* ראש המתיר ג"כ דאם לא היה רק כדי אורך החטה יניחן בלי ברכה ע"ש. ולענין אם מהני לתקן ברצועות עיין לקמן בסוף סימן ל"ג ובמ"ב שם: (מה) טוב להיותם וכו'. דכתיב וראו כל עמי הארץ וגו' וטוב שגם הקשר יהיה מגולה אבל אין נוהגין כן [א"ר] ובדיעבד (נז) אף אם היו מכוסים לגמרי יצא: (מו) אין ד"א. שהתפילין הם דרך כבוד כדכתיב וראו כל עמי הארץ ואין ד"א להשוות עצמו לרבו ע"כ יכסה אותם בטליתו או בכובעו: (מז) אין להקפיד. ומ"מ לכתחילה (נח) טוב יותר לכסותם: (מח) אם הם גלוים. פי' שאם נקרעו בגדיו

שער הציון

(מז) שע"ת: (מח) עט"ז ומחה"ש: (מט) קש"ע: (נ) מ"א: (נא) ח"א: (נב) פמ"ג: (נג) פמ"ג: (נד) כן משמע בארה"ח: (נה) א"ר בשם ע"ת והפמ"ג וארה"ח וכן משמע מהגר"א: (נו) פמ"ג: (נז) ארה"ח: (נח) א"ר וארה"ח:

הגהות ותיקונים: א) שעל: ב) לכפר: ג) קבלת: ד) משולשלין:

הערות והארות: 1) עיין בה"ל סי' ל"ג ס"ג סוף ד"ה מבחוץ וכו' לענין אם לא יצא ידי מצוה כשהיה השחור לצד פנים:

One must position the capsule **(36)** so that it is in the middle, in order that it should be opposite /the spot/ in between the eyes. The knot must also be in the middle of the back of the head and should not incline to one side or the other.

The portion of the knot **(37)** which appears like /the letter/ ד must be /facing/ outwards.

Gloss: Correspondingly, one must be careful that the knot of the arm /tefilin/ *is not inverted. (...)*

Mishnah Berurah

face, and not so low that it is opposite the throat.

It is desirable that the basic knot should be lying above the depression. One should at any rate be careful that not even part of the knot is lying in the area which is free of hair, as /that area/ is /described as belonging to/ the spine of the throat and not as the back of the head.

Therefore, one must take care that the strap which surrounds the head should be of limited /length/ and tight around his head. The circumference of the /surrounding/ strap should not be larger than the circumference of the head, as then there would be two unfavorable /results/. Firstly, because /then the strap would not be tight and it/ must be made actually tight, in view of the requirement,[5] "and you should bind them for a sign, etc.", the tightening being the binding. Secondly, if the strap is loose around the circumference of the head, the capsule will fall in front of one onto his forehead or the knot behind him will fall down onto /the part of the head behind/ his throat and they will not be in the proper place for them.

(36) So that it is in the middle. /I.e., of/ the width of the head.

One should not incline them to one of the sides. Thus, one will fulfil /the requirement/, "and they should be for *tefilin* between your eyes".[5]

Many Acharonim write that if one deviated from this he will not have fulfilled the mitzvah of *tefilin* and one must /therefore/ be careful about it.

It is also proper to take care initially that the *tefilin* are not very large, since then it is almost impossible for them to be held tightly on the head and also to be lying in the proper place. For if /very large *tefilin*/ are lying on top of the head in accordance with halachic /requirements/ they are not held tightly and, in addition, the knot will not settle in the /proper/ place for it, to conform with the halachah. See below in Sec. 32, Par. 41, for what we have written there.

(37) Which appears like ד. This is because two straps come out of the knot below. The one which comes out of the left side of the donner extends breadthways, like the roof of /the letter/ ד, and the one that comes out of the right side /of the donner/ extends lengthways below, like the leg of /the letter/ ד. [*E.R.*]

One should see that the knot is not inverted when it is formed and when it is worn.

See below in Sec. 32, Par. 52, for what we have written there.

(לו) שתהא באמצע כדי שתהא כנגד בין העינים וגם הקשר יהיה באמצע העורף ולא יטה לכאן או לכאן [ק]וצריך שיהא המקום שבקשר (לז) שנראה כעין דל"ת לצד (יח) חוץ: הגה וה"ה בקשר של יד צריך ליזהר שלא יתהפך (מרדכי דף נ"ו): **יא** [ר]**צריך שיהיה השחור שברצועות לצד חוץ**[1] **(לח)** [ש]**ולא (יט) יתהפכו (לט) בין של יד בין של ראש** [ת]**ישלשל הרצועות שיהיו תלוים לפניו ויגיעו (מ) עד הטבור (מא) או למעלה ממנו מעט** [א]**רוחב הרצועות של יד ושל ראש (מב) כאורך שעורה לפחות.** אם פיחת (כ) משיעור אורך הרצועות ורחבן [ב]אם אינו מוצא אחרות (מג) מניחן (מד) כמות שהן עד שימצא אחרות כשיעור. [ג]תפילין של ראש (מה) טוב להיותם גלוים ונראים אבל תלמיד בפני רבו (מו) אין דרך ארץ לגלות תפילין בפניו: הגה [יא] ושל יד (מז) אין להקפיד (מח) אם הם גלוים או מכוסים (מרדכי שם) ונראה לי דעכשיו שאין מניחים אלא בזמן ק"ש ותפלה אפילו תלמיד לפני רבו יכול לגלות אף בשל ראש וכן המנהג שלא ליזהר (ד"ע):

באר הגולה

ק שם נגמרא נפי' רש"י ר שם נרש"י לפירוש השני ש מועד קטן כ"ה ת רא"ש נסוף הלכות תפילין ומרדכי וסמ"ג והתרומה נשם הרי"ף א רמנ"ס ספ"ג וסמ"ג וסמ"ק ב נ"י לדעת סמ"ק ורמנ"ס ג סא"ח נשם רנ האי

שערי תשובה

עיין בה"ט ובכנה"ג כתב בשם שלטי הגבורים שבמרדכי דשנת כתב דהמניח שם למטה מלמיחת השער או[א] הלווחר לא יצא והוי ברכה לבטלה והיינו נמי קלה התחתון של הקשר יהיה למעלה מהתחלת למיחות השערות וכמדומה לי שראיתי בספר קטן כשהקשר שמאחורי הראש הוא בגומא לא יצא י"ח ולא ידעתי מאין יצא לו זה שהרי מלשון הש"ג משמע דבלמיחת שערות תליא מלתא מיהא ודאי דעורף היינו נגד הפנים כמבואר בחולין ומ"מ נראה שיש לעשות כן לכתחלה דבעינן שיהא הדק היטב סביב לראשו. ועיין בעטרת זקנים ס"ס זה וכל שהקשר משפע ויורד בתוך גומא א"א שתהיה הרלועה שסביב הראש מהודקת היטב. וכתב בפנים מאירות חלק ג' סי' ט' מי ששגג ולא הניח תפילין ש"ר במלחו במקום הראוי כמה שנים ועל המלות עשה נתכפר לו בוידוי דברים אך לבו חרד על מלות ל"ת של ברכה לבטלה לפ"ד הרמב"ם שהוא מדאורייתא והוא רולה לקבל תשובה ע"ז ונראה כיון שלדעת התוספות והרא"ש הוא מדרבנן וגם שלפי מנהגינו אומר אחר הברכה בשכמל"ו שזה תיקון שלא יעבור על לא תשא א"כ לא חטא בברכה לבטלה ולכן אף שביטל עשה ולריך עולה לספר[ב] מ"מ מיקרי דורון וא"ל לענות נפשו רק תשובתו נרלה בחרטה ומודה ועוזב ירוחם ע"ש. ונראה מדבריו שאם לא הניח ש"י כתיקונו דלא שייך בהו הלד תיקון אמירת בשכמל"ו יש לו לקבל תשובה על ברכתו לבטלה: [יא] ובש"י אין להקפיד. ובלבוש כתב שיהיו מכוסים משום והיה לך לאות. וכתב בבר"י בשם זקנו מוהר"א אזולאי שיש מדקדקים להאפיל בטלית על הזרוע בשעת הנחת תש"י. וכן ראוי לנהוג עפ"י קבלות[ג] האר"י ז"ל גם עפ"י דרכו גם תש"ר ראוי לכסותה בטלית ע"ש. ועיין במג"א לעיל ריש סימן ח' מ"ש:

באר היטב

שהוא סוף הגלגולת והוא נגד הפנים ולא כ"כ למטה כנגד הגרון: (יח) חוץ. ודלא כמו שנוהגין קלת לעשות ב' דלתי"ן מב' לדדים. מ"א: (יט) יתהפכו. ואם נתהפכו אפי' בשוגג מדת חסידות הוא להתענות ודוקא שמקיף הראש והזרוע אבל מה שמשלשל לפניו ומה שכורך אח"כ ליכא קפידא עי' בשכנה"ג ובע"ת: (כ) משיעור. ועכ"פ לריכין להיות משולשין[ד] לפניו מעט הא ל"ה פסולים לגמרי. מ"א:

משנה ברורה

נגד הפנים ולא כ"כ למטה כנגד הגרון (מז) וטוב שיהיה מונח עיקר הקשר למעלה מן הגומא ועכ"פ יש ליזהר שלא יהיה אפילו מקלת הקשר מונח במקום פנוי משער דשם הוא מפרקת הצואר ולא עורף (מח) ולכן יש ליזהר שתהיה הרלועה המקפת הראש מלומלמת ומהודקת סביב ראשו ולא יהיה הקף הרלועה גדול מהקף הראש דאז איכא תרתי לריעותא חדא דלריכים הידוק ממש דבעינן וקשרתם לאות וגו' וההידוק היא הקשירה שנית דאם הם רפוים סביב היקף ראשו יפול הקלילה לפניו על מלחו או יפול הקשר לאחריו למטה בלוארו ולא יהיו במקומן הראוי להן: (לו) שתהא באמצע. רוחב הראש ולא יטה אותם ללד אחד כדי שיתקיים והיו לטוטפות בין עיניך והרבה מהאחרונים כתבו דאם שינה בזה לא קיים מלות תפילין ולריך ליזהר בזה גם נכון ליזהר לכתחילה (מט) שלא יהיו התפילין גדולין ביותר דאז אי אפשר כמעט שיהיו מהודקין על הראש וגם שיהיו מונחין על מקומן דאם הם מונחין בגובה הראש כדין אינם מהודקין וגם הקשר לא יצא על מקומו כדין וע"ל בסי' ל"ב בסעיף מ"א מש"כ שם: (לז) שנראה כעין ד'. כי שתי רלועות יולאות מתוך הקשר למטה אותה היולאת מלד שמאל המניח נמשכת לרחבו כמו גג הדל"ת ואותה היולאת ללד ימין נמשכת באורך למטה כמו רגל הדל"ת [א"ר] ויראה שלא יתהפך הקשר בעשייתו ובלבישתו ועיין לקמן בסימן ל"ב בסעיף נ"ב מה שכתבנו שם: **יא** (לח) ולא יתהפכו. ואם נתהפכו (נ) מדת חסידות הוא להתענות או (נא) לפדות בלדקה ואין להקפיד שלא יתהפכו אלא מה שמקיף את הראש ואת הקיבורת פ"א אבל מה שכורך אח"כ וכן מה שמשתלשל לפניו מהרלועה של תש"ר אין לריך להקפיד כלל שלא יתהפך לפי שאינו מעיקר המלוה ומ"מ (נב) משום נוי המלוה ראוי להפוך שיהיה השחור ללד חוץ אפילו בהמותר: (לט) בין של יד וכו'. הנה בשל יד שהוא רואה כשהוא מניח יכול לראות שלא יתהפך לא הקשר ולא הרלועה ובשל ראש דאינו רואה כשהוא מניח סביב ראשו ימשמש היטיב בידו ממקום הקלילה בכל לד וירגיש אם מונחין כראוי [ב"ח]: (מ) עד הטבור. ואם הוסיף ע"ז לית לן בה: (מא) או למעלה ממנו. ועיין בחידושי רע"א וכן בארה"ח דמסקי דשל ימין עד הטבור ושל שמאל עד החזה ובטור כתב עוד וי"א דשל ימין עד המילה ושל שמאל עד הטבור: (מב) כאורך שעורה. היינו (נג) בקליפתה אבל בלא העוקץ שלה דיש בה עוקלין ארוכים מאד וי"א דדי ברוחב מאורך חטה ופחות מכשעורה (נד) ובמקום הדחק יש לסמוך ע"ז. וכתבו האחרונים דלריך ליזהר מאוד במקום כפל ההידוק שרגיל שהרלועה נתקמטה שם או שנפסקת עד שלא נשאר בה כשיעור: (מג) מניחן וכו'. מפני שיש מכשירין ויש פוסלין אף בדיעבד כמבואר בב"י ע"כ הכריע כן: (מד) כמות שהן. (נה) והאחרונים מסקי דאם פיחת משיעור האורך בשל יד הנזכר לעיל בסעיף ח' יניח בלי ברכה ואם יש כדי למשוך עד אלבע לרידה (נו) הכריכות אין מעכבין. ובאורך רלועות הש"ר כתב בארה"ח דדוקא אם יש חוץ ממה שמקיף הראש עכ"פ כשיעור שני טפחים הא לא"ה יניחן בלא ברכה ולענין רוחב הרלועות הש"י והש"ר המתיר ג"כ דאם לא היה רק כדי אורך החטה יניחן בלי ברכה ע"ש. ולענין אם מהני לתקן ברלועות עיין לקמן בסוף סימן ל"ג ובמ"ב שם: (מה) טוב להיותם וכו'. דכתיב וראו כל עמי הארץ וגו' וטוב שגם הקשר יהיה מגולה אבל אין נוהגין כן [א"ר] ובדיעבד (נז) אף אם היו מכוסים לגמרי יצא: (מו) אין ד"א. שהתפילין הם דרך כבוד כדכתיב וראו כל עמי הארץ ואין ד"א להשוות עלמו לרבו ע"כ יכסה אותם בטליתו או בכובע: (מז) אין להקפיד. ומ"מ לכתחילה (נח) טוב יותר לכסותם: (מח) אם הם גלוים. פי' שאם נקרעו בגדיו

שער הציון

(מז) שע"ת: (מח) עט"ז ומחה"ש: (מט) קש"ע: (נ) מ"א: (נא) ח"א: (נב) פמ"ג: (נג) פמ"ג: (נד) כן משמע בארה"ח: (נה) א"ר בשם ע"ת והפמ"ג וארה"ח וכן משמע מהגר"א: (נו) פמ"ג: (נז) ארה"ח: (נח) א"ר וארה"ח:

הגהות ותיקונים: א) שעל: **ב)** לכפר: **ג)** קבלת: **ד)** משולשלין:

הערות והארות: 1) עיין בה"ל סי' ל"ג ס"ג סוף ד"ה מבחוץ וכו' לענין אם לא יצא ידי מצוה כשהיה השחור לצד פנים:

11. The black /side/ of the straps must face outwards **(38)** and they should not be inverted. /This applies/ **(39)** both for /the straps of/ the arm /*tefilin*/ and for /the straps of/ the head /*tefilin*/.

One should let the straps /of the head *tefilin*/ drop so that they hang in front of him and reach **(40)** until the navel **(41)** or above it somewhat.

The width of the straps, /both/ of the arm and of the head /*tefilin*, must be/ at least **(42)** the length of a barley /seed/.

Mishnah Berurah

(38) And they should not be inverted. If /while one donned *tefilin*/ they became inverted, it is an act of piety to fast or to redeem /the fast/ with charity.

One need only be particular that /the part/ which surrounds the head and the biceps once should not be inverted. However, /as regards the part of the strap/ that one winds /around the arm/ subsequently and, likewise, /as regards/ what one lets drop of the strap of the head *tefilin* in front of him, one does not need to be particular at all that it should not be inverted. This is because that /part of the strap/ does not /serve/ for the essential /fulfillment/ of the mitzvah. Nevertheless, so that the mitzvah will be /performed/ attractively, it is proper to turn /the strap/ around so that the black /side/ is towards the outside, even in the case of /the part/ that is permitted /to be inverted/.

(39) Both for the arm /*tefilin*/. Now in the case of the arm /*tefilin*/, where one sees /the strap/ as he dons /the *tefilin*/, one can see /to it/ that neither the knot nor the strap is inverted. In the case of the head /*tefilin*, however/, where one cannot see /the strap/ when he dons it around his head, he should feel /the strap/ well with his hand on all sides from the spot where the capsule /is lying/ and he will /then be able to/ notice if they are lying properly. [*Bach*]

(40) Until the navel. If one makes it longer than this it does not matter.

(41) Or above it. See the *Chidushey R.A.E.* and likewise the *Ar.Hach.*, who conclude that the right /strap should extend/ until the navel and the left /strap/ until the chest. The *Tur* writes in addition that there are /authorities/ who say that the right /strap should extend/ until the place where one is circumcised and the left /strap/ until the navel.

(42) The length of a barley /seed/. I.e., /a barley seed/ with the skin, but without its point, since /barley/ has very long points.

There are /authorities/ who say that a width of /more/ than the length of a wheat /seed/ and less than /the length/ of a barley /seed/ is sufficient. Where there is a pressing /need/ one may rely on this /view/.

The Acharonim write that one must be very careful /about this/ at the place where the tightening is doubled over, for it is common for the strap to be folded there or to be severed to the extent that the required width does not remain.

(לו) שתהא באמצע כדי שתהא כנגד בין העינים וגם הקשר יהיה באמצע העורף ולא יטה לכאן או לכאן ׳וצריך שיהא המקום שבקשר (לז) שנראה כעין דל"ת לצד (יח) חוץ: הגה וה"ה נקשר של יד צריך ליזהר שלא יתהפך (מרדכי דף ל"ו): יא ׳צריך שיהיה השחור שברצועות לצד חוץ׳ (לח) ׳ולא (יט) יתהפכו (לט) בין של יד בין של ראש ׳ישלשל הרצועות שיהיו תלוים לפניו ויגיעו (מ) עד הטבור (מא) או למעלה ממנו מעט ׳רוחב הרצועות של יד ושל ראש (מב) כאורך שעורה לפחות. אם פיחת (כ) משיעור אורך הרצועות ורחבן ׳אם אינו מוצא אחרות (מג) מניחן (מד) כמות שהן עד שימצא אחרות כשיעור. ׳תפילין של ראש (מה) טוב להיותם גלוים ונראים אבל תלמיד בפני רבו (מו) אין דרך ארץ לגלות תפילין בפניו: הגה [יא] ובשל יד (מז) אין להקפיד (מח) אם הם גלוים או מכוסים (מרדכי שם) ונראה לי דעכשיו שאין מניחים אלא בזמן ק"ש ותפלה אפילו תלמיד לפני רבו יכול לגלות אף בשל ראש וכן המנהג שלא ליזהר (ד"ע):

ק שם בגמרא בפי׳ רש"י ר שם ברש"י לפירוש השני ש מועד קטן כ"ה ת רא"ש בסוף הלכות תפילין ומרדכי וסמ"ג והתרומה בשם הרי"ף א רמב"ם ספ"ג וסמ"ג וסמ"ק ב ב"י לדעת סמ"ק ורמב"ם ג סא"ח בשם רב האי

שערי תשובה

עיין בה"ט ובכנה"ג כתב בשם שלטי הגבורים שבמרדכי דשבת כתב דהמניח שם למטה מצמיחת השער או[א] הצוואר לא יצא והוי ברכה לבטלה והיינו נמי קצה התחתון של הקשר יהיה למעלה מהתחלת צמיחות השערות וכמדומה לי שראיתי בספר קטן כשהקשר שמאחורי הראש הוא בגומא לא יצא י"ח ולא ידעתי מאין יצא לו זה שהרי מלשון הש"ג משמע דבצמיחת שערות תליא מלתא מיהא ודאי דעורף היינו נגד הפנים כמבואר בחולין ומ"מ נראה שיש לעשות כן לכתחלה דבעינן שיהא הדק היטב סביב לראשו. ועיין בעטרת זקנים ס"ם זה וכל שהקשר משפע ויורד בתוך גומא א"א שתהיה הרצועה שסביב הראש מהודקת היטב. וכתב בפנים מאירות חלק ג׳ סי׳ ט׳ מי ששגג ולא הניח תפילין ש"ר במצחו במקום הראוי כמה שנים ועל המצות עשה נתכפר לו בוידוי דברים אך לבו חרד על מצות ל"ת של ברכה לבטלה לפ"ד הרמב"ם שהוא מדאורייתא והוא רוצה לקבל תשובה ע"ז ונראה כיון שלדעת התוספות והרא"ש הוא מדרבנן וגם שלפי מנהגינו אומר אחר הברכה בשכמל"ו שזה תיקון שלא יעבור על לא תשא א"כ לא חטא בברכה לבטלה ולכן אף שביטל עשה וצריך עולה לספר[ב] מ"מ מיקרי דורון וא"צ לענות נפשו רק תשובתו נגלה בחרטה ומודה ועוזב ירוחם ע"ש. ונראה מדבריו שאם לא הניח ש"י כתיקונו דלא שייך בהו הלך תיקון אמירת בשכמל"ו יש לו לקבל תשובה על ברכתו לבטלה: [יא] ובש"י אין להקפיד. ובלבוש כתב שיהיו מכוסים משום והיה לך לאות. וכתב בבר"י בשם זקנו מוהר"א אזולאי שיש מדקדקים להאפיל בטלית על הזרוע בשעת הנחת תש"י. וכן ראוי לנהוג עפ"י קבלות[ג] האר"י ז"ל גם עפ"י דרכו גם תש"ר ראוי לכסותה בטלית ע"ש. ועיין במג"א לעיל ריש סימן ח׳ מ"ש:

באר היטב

שהוא סוף הגלגולת והוא נגד הפנים ולא כ"כ למטה כנגד הגרון: (יח) חוץ. ודלא כמו שנוהגין קצת לעשות ב׳ דלתי"ן מב׳ צדדים. מ"א: (יט) יתהפכו. ואם נתהפכו אפי׳ בשוגג מדת חסידות הוא להתענות ודוקא שמקיף הראש והזרוע אבל מה שמשלשל לפניו ומה שכורך אח"כ ליכא קפידא עי׳ בשכנה"ג ובע"ת: (כ) משיעור. ועכ"פ צריכין להיות משולשין[ד] לפניו מעט הא ל"ה פסולים לגמרי. מ"א:

משנה ברורה

נגד הפנים ולא כ"כ למטה כנגד הגרון (מז) וטוב שיהיה מונח עיקר הקשר למעלה מן הגומא ועכ"פ יש ליזהר שלא יהיה אפילו מקצת הקשר מונח במקום פני השער דשם הוא מפרקת הצואר ולא עורף (מח) ולכן יש ליזהר שתהיה הרצועה המקפת הראש מצומצמת ומהודקת סביב ראשו ולא יהיה היקף הרצועה גדול מהיקף הראש דאז איכא תרתי לריעותא חדא דצריכים הידוק ממש דבעינן וקשרתם לאות וגו׳ והידוק היא הקשירה שנית דאם הם רפוים סביב היקף ראשו יפול הקציצה לפניו על מצחו או יפול הקשר לאחריו למטה בצוארו ולא יהיו במקומן הראוי להן: (לו) שתהא באמצע. רוחב הראש ולא יטה אותם לצד אחד כדי שיתקיים והיו לטוטפות בין עיניך והרבה מהאחרונים כתבו דאם שינה בזה לא קיים מצות תפילין וצריך ליזהר בזה גם נכון ליזהר לכתחילה (מט) שלא יהיו התפילין גדולין ביותר דאז אי אפשר כמעט שיהיו מהודקין על הראש וגם שיהיו מונחין על מקומן דאם הם מונחין בגובה הראש כדין אינם מהודקין וגם הקשר לא יבא על מקומו כדין וע"ל בסי׳ ל"ב בסעיף מ"א מש"כ שם: (לז) שנראה כעין ד׳. כי שתי רצועות יוצאות מתוך הקשר למטה אותה היוצאת מצד שמאל המניח נמשכת לרחבו כמו גג הדלי"ת ואותה היוצאת לצד ימין נמשכת באורך למטה כמו רגל הדלי"ת [א"ר] ויראה שלא יתהפך הקשר בעשייתו ובלבישתו ועיין לקמן בסימן ל"ב בסעיף נ"ב מה שכתבנו שם: יא (לח) ולא יתהפכו. ואם נתהפכו (נ) מדת חסידות הוא להתענות או (נא) לפדות בצדקה ואין להקפיד שלא יתהפכו אלא מה שמקיף את הראש ואת הקיבורת פ"א אבל מה שכורך אח"כ וכן מה שמשתלשל לפניו מהרצועה של תש"ר אין צריך להקפיד כלל שלא יתהפך לפי שאינו מעיקר המצוה ומ"מ (נב) משום נוי המצוה ראוי להפוך שיהיה השחור לצד חוץ אפילו במותר: (לט) בין של יד וכו׳. הגה בשל יד שהוא רואה כשהוא מניח יכול לראות שלא יתהפך לא הקשר ולא הרצועה ובשל ראש דאינו רואה כשהוא מניח סביב ראשו ימשמש היטב בידו מתחום הקציצה בכל צד ויראה אם מונחין כראוי [ב"ח]: (מ) עד הטבור. ואם הוסיף ע"ז לית לן בה: (מא) או למעלה ממנו. ועיין בחידושי רע"א וכן במרה"מ דמסקי דשל ימין עד הטבור ושל שמאל עד החזה ובטור כתב עוד וי"א דשל ימין עד המילה ושל שמאל עד הטבור: (מב) כאורך שעורה. היינו (נג) בקליפתה אבל בלא העוקץ שלה דיש גם עוקצין ארוכים מאד וי"א די ברוחב מאורך חטה ופחות מכשעורה (נד) ובמקום הדחק יש לסמוך ע"ז. וכתבו האחרונים דצריך ליזהר מאוד במקום כפל הסידוק שרגיל שהרצועה נתקמטה שם או שנפסקת עד שלא נשאר בה כשיעור: (מג) מניחן וכו׳. מפני שיש מכשירין ויש פוסלין אף בדיעבד כמבואר בב"י ע"כ הכריע כן: (מד) כמות שהן. (נה) והאחרונים מסקי דאם פיחת משיעור האורך בשל יד הנזכר לעיל בסעיף ח׳ יניח בלי ברכה ואם יש כדי לפשוט עד אצבע צרידה (נו) הכריכות אין מעכבין. ובאורך רצועות הש"ר כתב בארה"ח דדוקא אם יש חוץ ממה שמקיף הראש עכ"פ כשיעור שני טפחים הא לא"ה יניחן בלא ברכה ולענין רוחב הרצועות השל יד והשל* ראש החמיר ג"כ דאם לא היה רק כדי אורך החטה יניחן בלי ברכה ע"ש. ולענין אם מהני לתקן ברצועות עיין לקמן בסוף סימן ל"ג ובמ"ב שם: (מה) טוב להיותם וכו׳. דכתיב וראו כל עמי הארץ וגו׳ וטוב שגם הקשר יהיה מגולה אבל אין נוהגין כן [א"ר] ובדיעבד (נז) אף אם היו מכוסים לגמרי יצא: (מו) אין ד"א. שהתפילין הם דרך כבוד כדכתיב וראו כל עמי הארץ ואין ד"א להשוות עצמו לרבו ע"כ יכסה אותם בטליתו או בכובע: (מז) אין להקפיד. ומ"מ לכתחילה (נח) טוב יותר לכסותם: (מח) אם הם גלוים. פי׳ שאם נקרעו בגדיו

שער הציון

(מז) שע"ת: (מח) עט"ז ומחה"ש: (מט) קש"ע: (נ) מ"א: (נא) ח"א: (נב) פמ"ג: (נג) פמ"ג: (נד) כן משמע בארה"ח: (נה) א"ר בשם ע"ת והפמ"ג וארה"ח וכן משמע מהגר"א: (נו) פמ"ג: (נז) ארה"ח: (נח) א"ר וארה"ח:

הגהות ותיקונים: א) שעל: ב) לכפר: ג) קבלת: ד) משולשלין:

הערות והארות: 1) עיין בה"ל סי׳ ל"ג ס"ג סוף ד"ה מבחוץ וכו׳ לענין אם לא יצא ידי מצוה כשהיה השחור לצד פנים:

If straps have less than /the required/ length or width /, then/, if one cannot find others, **(43)** he should don /the *tefilin* with/ these /straps/ **(44)** as they are until he finds others which /do have/ the /required/ measurements.

/In the case of/ the head *tefilin*, **(45)** it is desirable for them to be exposed and visible. However, when a pupil is in the presence of his /Torah/ teacher, **(46)** it is disrespectful /for him/ to expose the *tefilin* before him.

Gloss: For the arm /tefilin/, **(47)** *it is unnecessary to be particular* **(48)** *as to whether they are exposed or covered. (...)*

It appears to me that at present, when we only don /tefilin/ *at the time when /we read/ "The Reading of Shema" and /pray/ the /eighteen-blessing/ prayer, it is even allowed for a pupil to expose /his* tefilin/ *in the presence of his /Torah/ teacher, even /if it is/ the head* /tefilin/. *It is likewise the practice /for a pupil/ not to be careful /about this/. (...)*

Mishnah Berurah

(43) He should don these, etc. This is because there are /authorities/ who rule that they are valid and /authorities/ who disqualify /their validity/ even once it is after the event, as stated by the *B.Y.* This is therefore the decision /of the author of the *B.Y.* and the Shulchan Aruch/.

(44) As they are. The Acharonim conclude that if one has less than the required length for the arm /*tefilin*/ mentioned above in Par. 8, he should don /the *tefilin*/ without /making/ the blessing. /However,/ if there is sufficient /strap/ to stretch until the middle finger, /he may make the blessing, as/ the coils are not essential /for the fulfillment of one's obligation/.

The *Ar.Hach.* writes as regards the length of the straps of the head /*tefilin*/ that /one can/ only /make the blessing/ if apart from /the length/ that surrounds the head there is at least a length of two handbreadths. Otherwise, one should don /the *tefilin*/ without /making/ the blessing. As regards the /required/ width of the straps for the arm and head /*tefilin*/, he is also stringent. /He rules/ that if /the width/ is only as much as the length of a wheat /seed/, one should don /the *tefilin*/ without /making/ a blessing. See there.

As to whether it is of avail to mend the straps, see below at the end of Sec. 33 and in the Mishnah Berurah there.

(45) It is desirable for them to be, etc. For it is written,[12] "And all the peoples of the earth will see, etc.".

It is desirable for the knot also to be exposed, but this is not the practice. [*E.R.*]

Once it is after the event, even if /the head *tefilin*/ were completely covered, one will have fulfilled /his obligation/.

(46) It is disrespectful. /This is/ because /the wearing of/ *tefilin* is of a respect /commanding/ nature, as it is written,[12] "and all the peoples of the earth will see /, etc./", and it is disrespectful /for a pupil/ to equate himself with his /Torah/ teacher.

In view of this, /the pupil/ should cover /the head *tefilin*/ with his *talis* or with a hat.

(47) It is unnecessary to be particular. Nevertheless, initially, it is better to cover them.

(48) As to whether they are exposed. I.e., it does not matter if one's clothes /which are worn over the *tefilin*/ became torn. It is,

כח דיני חליצת התפילין. ובו ג׳ סעיפים:

א [א]חייב אדם למשמש בתפילין (א) בכל (א) [א] שעה (ב) שלא[1] יסיח דעתו מהם [ב]וימשמש (ג) בשל יד (ד) תחלה [ג]וכשיאמר וקשרתם לאות על ידך ימשמש בשל יד וכשיאמר והיו לטוטפות בין עיניך ימשמש בשל ראש: **ב** [ד]תפילין של ראש (ה) חולץ (ב) [ב] תחלה משום דכתיב והיו לטוטפות בין עיניך כל זמן שבין עיניך יהיו שתים [ה]צריך לחלוץ תפילין של ראש (ג) (ו) מעומד [ו]ויניח (ד) [ג] בתיק של ראש (ז) ועליו של יד כדי שכשיבוא להניחם יפגע בשל יד (ח) תחלה: **ג** [ז]מנהג החכמים לנשק התפילין בשעת הנחתן (ט) ובשעת חליצתן:

א מנחות ל״ו ב יומא ל״ג לפי׳ התוספות בשם רבי אליהו ג טור בסימן ס״א ד מנחות שם ה מערכת אלקות ו תו׳ מהרי״א דיומא ז ר״ת בשם רב האי

באר היטב

(א) שעה. פי׳ בכל שעה שנזכר מהם חייב למשמש ב״ח מ״א ע״ל סימן מ״ד ס״ק א׳ ובספר הכוונת הזהיר מאוד בענין היסח הדעת דאין פגם גדול מזה: (ב) תחלה. קודם שמסיר הרצועה מהאצבע. גליא רזיא מ״א. אמר המגיה נ״ל שט״ס הוא במ״א וצ״ל וקודם יסיר הרצועה וכו׳: (ג) מעומד. ה״ה הכריכות של אצבע. ולמנהגינו שמניחין של יד מעומד צריך ג״כ לחולצן מעומד דכהנחתן כך חליצתן. ונהגו לכורכם ככנפים ע״ש כנפי יונה. מט״מ: (ד) בתיק. בתשובת בנימין זאב סי׳ רפ״ט כתב שיעשה הכיס או התיק צר כדי שיהיו זה על זה וכ״כ הב״ח וט״ז סימן כ״ה ס״ק יו״ד. והמ״א כתב דיותר טוב להניחם זה אצל זה ויעשה סימן איזה ש״ר ואיזה ש״י דכיון דש״ר קדושתו חמורה מש״י אסור להניח של יד על ש״ר. אין להניח הרצועה על הבתים אלא על הצדדים. לא יאחוז ברצועות ויגלול התפילין ולא ינערם מן התיק אלא יוציאם בידו ס״ח מ״א:

שערי תשובה

[א] שעה. עבה״ט וכתבו בשם גורי האר״י ז״ל בעת לימוד התורה ותפלה א״צ ליתן דעתו בהתפילין ועיין לקמן סי׳ מ״ד ועיין בשו״ת שאגת אריה סי׳ מ׳ שאוסר היסח הדעת בכל ענין רק כתב שי״ל ששיעור היסח הדעת הוא כפי הילוך מאה אמה כמו שאמרו בשינת ארעי ע״ש. ובאמת שהוא זוטר בשיעורא טפי שאינו אלא חלק ס״ז משעה ולא ניתנה תורה למה״ש. ועיין בסי׳ מ״ד בט״ז שם. ונראה שהעולם סומכין בזה על רבינו יונה והרא״ש והטור דלא הוי היסח הדעת כ״א כשעומד בשחוק וק״ר ומה שהקשה בש״א יש ליישב ועיין במ״א סי׳ מ״ד: [ב] תחלה. עבה״ט ולעיל סימן כ״ה כתבתי בשם הזוהר דכשם שצריך ליכנס לבהכנ״ס מוכתר בתפילין כן צריך לצאת מבהכנ״ס מוכתר בתפילין. ובשלמי צבור כתב שלא מצא בשום מקום בהזוהר שיזהיר בזה. ואולי כוונתו שמאותו הטעם שאמרו בזוהר שיכנס בתפילין משום דאיך יאמר אשתחוה כו׳ כמו כן כשנפטר מרבו ואין זה מספיק ע״ש: [ג] בתיק. עבה״ט ומ״ש בשם המג״א שנהגו להניחם זה אצל זה ויעשה סימן כו׳ ליתא דבמג״א כתב שיניחם זה אצל זה ומ״ש בש״ע ועליו ש״י פי׳ שיתנו קצת לצד מעלה ונהגו לסמן כו׳ ומבואר שיש כאן חסרון איזה תיבות וכצ״ל ונהגו לעשות שני כיסין וצריך לסמן כו׳ וזה מבואר מדסיים בה ואסור לשנות הכיס כו׳ וכן מצאתי שיש מגיהין כן והבה״ט לא הרגיש בזה. ומבואר דאם נותן בכיס א׳ יניח זע״ז[א] וש״י יהיה קצת למעלה כדי שיפגע בו תחלה. ועיין ב״ח שדעתו שלא יעשה שני כיסין אחד לש״י ואחד לש״ר ולכתוב ע״ז יד וע״ז ראש דאתי למטעי להחליף ש״י בש״ר אלא יעשה תיק אחד כו׳ ואפשר דע״ז קאי המג״א דיש עושים ב׳ כיסים ונהגו לסמן כו׳. ומ״ש ב״ח דלא מהני כתיבה דאתי למטעי עיין ביומא דף נ״ה גבי יצא והניחו על כן הזהב שבהיכל כו׳ ר״י הוא דלית ליה כתיבה כו׳ ע״ש. ומ״ש דאין לכרוך הרצועה על הבתים כו׳ עיין במג״א ומ״ש ביד אפרים פירוש נפלא בדברי המג״א ע״ש. ועיין בב״ח שם שדקדק מדברי הטור דמיד כשמסיר ש״ר תחלה יניחו בתיקו ולא ימתין מלהניחו בתיק עד שיסיר גם ש״י שלא יבא לידי שגגה להניח ש״י וש״ר עליו והיינו לפי שיטתו לעשות תיק צר והמג״א לא הביאו כיון שסובר שמניח זע״ז[א] ולכן מי שיש לו תיק צר וכמ״ש הבה״ט בשם הב״ח וט״ז יש לו ליזהר כשחולץ להניח את ש״ר בתיק תיכף כשמסירו כדי דלא ליתי למטעי כמ״ש הב״ח. וכתב מח״ב שבספר אור צדיקים כתב שיש מניחין התפילין כשחולצין על הסידור ואין נכון לעשות כך שלענין שבועה בנק״ח חמור סידור מקדושת תפילין כמ״ש הסמ״ע בח״מ סימן פ״ז[ב] והביאו בסולת בלולה ובסי׳ מ״ה חזר בו לפי שבט״ז ח״מ סי׳ פ״ז השיג על הסמ״ע וכן הח״ל בהגהותיו. וע״ש בש״ך שתמה על הרמ״א שמה:

משנה ברורה

בגדיו לית לן בה (נט) אבל אסור להניחן על הבגד וכנ״ל בס״ה:

א (א) בכל שעה. פי׳ בכל שעה (א) שנזכר בהם חייב למשמש דעל ידי כן נזכר עליהן תדיר ולא יבא לידי היסח הדעת ועוד כדי לתקנם (ב) שלא יזוזו[ג] ממקומן: (ב) שלא יסיח דעתו. ובעת התפלה א״צ למשמש בהם [מ״א לקמן בסימן מ״ד ועיין בפמ״ג]: (ג) בשל יד. דהש״י סמוכה לו למשמשו (ג) ואין מעבירין על המצות: (ד) תחלה. ואח״כ בשל ראש. ואם בעת משמוש הש״ר מצאהו שנשמט ממקומו ונודע לו אז שהש״י ג״כ נשמט ממקומו (ד) צריך להחזיר הש״י תחלה על מקומו מקרא וקשרתם לאות על ידך והדר ולטוטפות בין עיניך וכנ״ל בסימן כ״ה ס״ו: **ב** (ה) חולץ תחלה. אחר (ה) שמסיר ג׳ כריכות מהאצבע: (ו) מעומד. ה״ה הסרת הכריכות של האצבע ולמנהגינו שמניחין של יד ג״כ מעומד (ו) צריך ג״כ לחולצן מעומד דכהנחתן כך חליצתן. ויש מהחכמים שהיו נוהגין לחלוץ התש״ר (ז) ביד שמאל שהיא יד כהה להראות שקשה עליו חליצתן (ח) ואם הוא איטר יד שכל מלאכתו בשמאלו חולצן בימינו כדי שלא לעשות החליצה במהירות: (ז) ועליו של יד. כתב הב״ח וכן הט״ז לעיל בסימן כ״ה סק״י דהיינו שיעשה תיק ארוך וצר שיהיו מונחים זה על גבי זה והמ״א כתב דיותר טוב ליתן התפילין זה בצד זה וכן (ט) נוהגין ומה שכתב המחבר ועליו של יד פירושו שיתנו קצת לצד מעלה כדי לפגוע בהם תחלה ובספר שולחן שלמה כתב לטוב שיהיו התש״י בצד ימין של התיק ג״כ מטעם זה. ויש נוהגין (י) לעשות שני כיסין אחד לשל יד ואחד לש״ר אך גם בשני כיסין יותר טוב שיזהר ליתן הכיס של יד קצת לצד מעלה כדי שיפגע בהם תחלה ולא יעביר על המצות ודעת הט״ז לעיל בסימן כ״ה דגם ע״י כיס שייך מעביר על המצוה ועיין במ״א בסימן כ״ה סק״א. אותן בני אדם הנוהגין לעשות תיקין להתפילין (יא) יש להם לסמן איזה שייך לש״ר ואיזו לשל יד (יב) כדי שיזהר בהם ולא יוציא הש״ר תחלה מהתיק גם (יג) דכיון דש״ר קדושתו חמורה יזהר עי״ז שלא לשנות אח״כ התיק ליתן בו של יד אלא א״כ התנה מתחלה וכדלקמן בסימן מ״ב: (ח) תחלה. ולא יצטרך להעביר על המצות. ונכון (יד) ליזהר שלא יחלוץ של יד עד שיניח ש״ר בתוך התיק כדי שלא ישכח ויניח של יד תחלה בתוך התיק: **ג** (ט) ובשעת חליצתן. כשמקפל התפילין לא יכרוך הרצועות על הבתים (טו) אלא בצדדי הבתים על התיתורא ויש נוהגין לכורכן ככנפים ע״ש כנפי יונה. וכשכורכן על צדדי התפילין (טז) צריך לאחוז התפילין בידו ולגלול הרצועה עליהן ולא לאחוז הרצועה בידו ולגלול התפילין לתוכה. גם (יז) כשנוטל התפילין מכיסן לא ינערם אלא נוטלן בידו מתוך הכיס. תיק תפילין אסור בשל שעטנז כמו מטפחת ספרים (פמ״ג):

אין

שער הציון

(נט) אחרונים: (א) ב״ח והגר״א לקמן בסימן ס״ב[ד] סעיף כ״ה: (ב) פמ״ג בשם מהרא״י: (ג) תוספות ביומא ל״ג ע״ב ד״ה עבורי: (ד) פמ״ג: (ה) מ״א ופמ״ג: (ו) מ״א: (ז) של״ה: (ח) פמ״ג: (ט) ברכי יוסף: (י) מ״א: (יא) מ״א: (יב) פמ״ג: (יג) מ״א: (יד) פמ״ג בשם הב״ח: (טו) מ״א: (טז) (יז) מ״א בשם ס״ח:

הגהות ותיקונים: **א)** זא״ז: **ב)** ס״ק מ׳: **ג)** יזוזו: **ד)** ס״א:

הערות והארות: 1) עיין במ״ב סי׳ צ״ד ס״ק ג׳ לענין חילוק בין היסח הדעת סתמא למטריד דעתו הרבה עד שלבבו פונה מי״ש ועיין שעה״צ ר רנ״ב אות ל״ח אם שייך היסח דעת גם באוחזן בידו:

§28: THE LAWS CONCERNING THE TAKING OFF OF THE *TEFILIN*

(Contains Three Paragraphs)

1. A person is obliged to feel the *tefilin* (1) at all times /while he is wearing them/ (2) so that his mind will not be distracted from them. He should feel (3) the arm /*tefilin*/ (4) first.

When one says /the words/ וּקְשַׁרְתָּם לְאוֹת עַל יָדֶךָ (and you should bind them for a sign on your arm), he should feel the arm /*tefilin*/. When one says /the words/ וְהָיוּ לְטֹטָפֹת בֵּין עֵינֶיךָ (and they should be for *tefilin* between your eyes), he should feel the head /*tefilin*/.

2. The head *tefilin* (5) should be taken off first. This is because it is written,[1*] "and they should be for *tefilin*[2*] between your eyes". /This wording implies that/ as long as /the *tefilin*/ are between your eyes there should be two /*tefilin* units on you/.

One must take off the head *tefilin* (6) standing.

Mishnah Berurah

however, forbidden to place /the *tefilin*/ over a garment, as /stated/ above in Par. /4 and/ 5.

§28

(1) **At all times.** I.e., at all times when he recalls them, he is obliged to feel them.

Through this, one will remember them constantly and will not come to have his mind distracted /from them/. In addition, /it is desirable for one to feel them/ so that he can adjust them /when necessary/, to prevent them moving out of place.

(2) **So that his mind will not be distracted.** While one is praying, he does not need to feel them. [*M.A.* below in Sec. 44. See the *P.Mg.*]

(3) **The arm /*tefilin*/.** /This is/ because the arm /*tefilin*/ are closer to one's feeling /hand/ and one must not bypass the mitzvah /of feeling them and feel the head *tefilin* instead/.

(4) **First.** After that /he should feel/ the head /*tefilin*/.

If while feeling the head /*tefilin*/ he discovers that it has moved out of place and he becomes aware then that the arm /*tefilin*/ have also slipped out of place, he must put the arm /*tefilin*/ back in place first. /We learn this/ from /the fact that it is stated at the beginning of/ the verse,[1*] "and you should bind them for a sign on your arm", and /only/ subsequently, "for *tefilin* between your eyes", as /explained/ above in Sec. 25, Par. 6.

(5) **Should be taken off first.** /I.e.,/ after one has removed the three coils from the /middle/ finger.

(6) **Standing.** The same ruling /applies to/ the removal of the coils on the finger.

According to our practice, which is to don the arm /*tefilin*/ standing as well, one must also take /the arm *tefilin*/ off standing. For /*tefilin*/ are /required/ to be taken off /in the manner/ that they are donned.

There were wise men whose practice was to take off the head *tefilin* with the left hand, which is the weaker hand, /in order/ to show that it was a hardship for them to take them off. If one is left-handed /and does/ all his actions with his left /hand/, he should take /the head *tefilin*/ off with his right /hand/, so as not to do the taking off hurriedly.

1* *Devarim* 6:8.
2* This word implies more than one unit. Hence the deduction which follows.

כח דיני חליצת התפילין. ובו ג׳ סעיפים:

א אחייב אדם למשמש בתפילין (א) בכל (א) [א] שעה (ב) שלאי׳ יסיח דעתו מהם בוימשמש (ג) בשל יד (ד) תחלה גוכשיאמר וקשרתם לאות על ידך ימשמש בשל יד וכשיאמר והיו לטוטפות בין עיניך ימשמש בשל ראש: **ב** דתפילין של ראש (ה) חולץ (ב) [ב] תחלה משום דכתיב והיו לטוטפות בין עיניך כל זמן שבין עיניך יהיו שתים הצריך לחלוץ תפילין של ראש (ג) (ו) מעומד ויניח (ד) [ג] בתיק של ראש (ז) ועליו של יד כדי שכשיבוא להניחם יפגע בשל יד (ח) תחלה: **ג** זמנהג החכמים לנשק התפילין בשעת הנחתן (ט) ובשעת חליצתן:

א מנחות ל״ו ב יומא ל״ג לפי׳ התוספות בשם רבי אליהו
ג טור בסימן ס״א
ד מנחות שם
ה מערכת אלקות
ו תו׳ מההיא דיומא
ז ר״ת בשם רב האי

באר היטב

(א) שעה. פי׳ בכל שעה שנזכר מהם חייב למשמש ב״ח מ״א ע״ל סימן מ״ד ס״ק א׳ ובספר הכוונת הזהיר מאוד בענין היסח הדעת דאין פגם גדול מזה: (ב) תחלה. קודם שמסיר הרצועה מהאצבע. גליא רזיא מ״א. אמר המגיה נ״ל שט״ס הוא במ״א וצ״ל וקודם יסיר הרצועה וכו׳: (ג) מעומד. ה״ה הכריכות של אצבע. ולמנהגינו שמניחין של יד מעומד צריך ג״כ לחולצן מעומד דכהנחתן כך חליצתן. ונהגו לכורכם ככנפים ע״ש כנפי יונה. מט״מ: (ד) בתיק. בתשובת בנימין זאב סי׳ רפ״ט כתב שיעשה הכיס או התיק צר כדי שיהיו זה על זה וכ״כ הב״ח וט״ז סימן כ״ה ס״ק יו״ד. והמ״א כתב דיותר טוב להניחם זה אצל זה ויעשה סימן איזה ש״ר ואיזה ש״י דכיון דש״ר קדושתו חמורה מש״י אסור להניח של יד על ש״ר. אין להניח הרצועה על הבתים אלא על הצדדים. לא יאחוז ברצועות ויגלול התפילין ולא ינערם מן התיק אלא יוציאם בידו ס״ח מ״א:

שערי תשובה

[א] שעה. עבה״ט וכתבו בשם גורי האר״י ז״ל בעת לימוד התורה ותפלה א״צ ליתן דעתו בהתפילין ועיין לקמן סי׳ מ״ד ועיין בשו״ת שאגת אריה סי׳ מ׳ שאוסר היסח הדעת בכל ענין רק כתב שי״ל ששיעור היסח הדעת הוא כפי הילוך מאה אמה כמו שאמרו בשינת ארעי ע״ש. ובאמת שהוא זוטר בשיעורא טפי שאינו אלא חלק ס״ז משעה ולא ניתנה תורה למה״ש. ועיין בסי׳ מ״ד בט״ז שם. ונראה שהעולם סומכין בזה על רבינו יונה והרא״ש והטור דלא הוי היסח הדעת כ״א כשעומד בשחוק וק״ר ומה שהקשה בש״א יש ליישב ועיין במ״א סי׳ מ״ד: [ב] תחלה. עבה״ט ולעיל סימן כ״ה כתבתי בשם הזוהר דכשם שצריך ליכנס לבהכנ״ס מוכתר בתפילין כן צריך לצאת מבהכנ״ס מוכתר בתפילין. ובשלמי צבור כתב שלא מצא בשום מקום בהזוהר שיזהיר בזה. ואולי כוונתו שמאותו הטעם שאמרו בזוהר שיכנס בתפילין משום דאיך יאמר אשתחוה כו׳ כמו כן כשנפטר מרבו ואין זה מספיק ע״ש: [ג] בתיק. עבה״ט ומ״ש בשם המג״א שנהגו להניחם זה אצל זה ויעשה סימן כו׳ ליתא דבמג״א כתב שיניחם זה אצל זה ומ״ש בש״ע ועליו ש״י פי׳ שיתנו קצת לצד מעלה ונהגו לסמן כו׳ ומבואר שיש כאן חסרון איזה תיבות וכצ״ל ונהגו לעשות שני כיסין וצריך לסמן כו׳ וזה מבואר מדסיים בה ואסור לשנות הכיס כו׳ וכן מצאתי שיש מגיהין כן והבה״ט לא הרגיש בזה. ומבואר דאם נותן בכיס א׳ יניח זע״זא) וש״י יהיה קצת למעלה כדי שיפגע בו תחלה. ועיין ב״ח שדעתו שלא יעשה שני כיסין אחד לש״י ואחד לש״ר ולכתוב ע״ז יד וע״ז ראש דאתי למטעי להחליף ש״י בש״ר אלא יעשה תיק אחד כו׳ ואפשר דע״ז קאי המג״א דיש עושים ב׳ כיסים ונהגו לסמן כו׳. ומ״ש ב״ח דלא מהני כתיבה דאתי למטעי עיין ביומא דף נ״ה גבי יצא והניחו על כן הזהב שבהיכל כו׳ ר״י הוא דלית ליה כתיבה כו׳ ע״ש. ומ״ש דאין לכרוך הרצועה על הבתים כו׳ עיין במג״א ומ״ש ביד אפרים פירוש נפלא בדברי המג״א ע״ש. ועיין בב״ח שם שדקדק מדברי הטור דמיד כשמסיר ש״ר תחלה יניחו בתיקו ולא ימתין מלהניחו בתיק עד שיסיר גם ש״י שלא יבא לידי שגגה להניח ש״י וש״ר עליו והיינו לפי שיטתו לעשות תיק צר והמג״א לא הביאו כיון שסובר שמניח זע״זא) ולכן מי שיש לו תיק צר וכמ״ש הבה״ט בשם הב״ח וט״ז יש לו ליזהר כשחולץ להניח את ש״ר בתיק תיכף כשמסירו כדי דלא ליתי למטעי כמ״ש הב״ח. וכתב מח״ב שבספר אור צדיקים כתב שיש מניחין התפילין כשחולצין על הסידור ואין נכון לעשות כך שלענין שבועה בנק״ח חמור סידור מקדושת תפילין כמ״ש הסמ״ע בח״מ סימן פ״זב) והביאו בסולת בלולה ובסי׳ מ״ה חזר בו לפי שבט״ז ח״מ סי׳ פ״ז השיג על הסמ״ע וכן הח״ל בהגהותיו. וע״ש בש״ך שתמה על הרמ״א שמה:

משנה ברורה

בגדיו לית לן בה (נט) אבל אסור להניחן על הבגד וכנ״ל בס״ה:

א (א) בכל שעה. פי׳ בכל שעה (א) שנזכר מהם חייב למשמש דעל ידי כן נזכר עליהן תדיר ולא יבא לידי היסח הדעת ועוד כדי לתקנם (ב) שלא יזוזו׳ ממקומן: (ב) שלא יסיח דעתו. ובעת התפלה א״צ למשמש בהם [מ״א לקמן בסימן מ״ד ועיין בפמ״ג]: (ג) בשל יד. דהש״י סמוכה לו למשמשו (ג) ואין מעבירין על המצות: (ד) תחלה. ואח״כ בשל ראש. ואם בעת משמוש הש״ר מצאהו שנשמט ממקומו ונודע לו אז שהש״י ג״כ נשמט ממקומו (ד) צריך להחזיר הש״י תחלה על מקומו מקרא וקשרתם לאות על ידך והדר ולטוטפות בין עיניך וכנ״ל בסימן כ״ה ס״ו: **ב** (ה) חולץ תחלה. אחר (ה) שמסיר ג׳ כריכות מהאצבע: (ו) מעומד. ה״ה הסרת הכריכות של האצבע ולמנהגינו שמניחין של יד ג״כ מעומד (ו) צריך ג״כ לחולצן מעומד דכהנחתן כך חליצתן. ויש מהחכמים שהיו נוהגין לחלוץ התש״ר (ז) ביד שמאל שהיא כהה להראות שקשה עליו חליצתן (ח) ואם הוא איטר יד שכל מלאכתו בשמאלו חולצן בימינו כדי שלא לעשות המצוה במהירות: (ז) ועליו של יד. כתב הב״ח וכן הט״ז לעיל בסימן כ״ה סק״י דהיינו שיעשה תיק ארוך וצר שיהיו מונחים זה על גבי זה והמ״א כתב דיותר טוב ליתן התפילין זה בצד זה וכן (ט) נוהגין ומה שכתב המחבר ועליו של יד פירושו שיתנו קצת לצד מעלה כדי לפגוע בהם תחלה ובספר שולחן שלמה כתב דטוב שיהיו התש״י בצד ימין של התיק ג״כ מטעם זה. ויש נוהגין (י) לעשות שני כיסין אחד לשל יד וא׳ לש״ר אך גם בשני כיסין יותר טוב שיזהר ליתן הכיס של יד קצת לצד מעלה כדי שיפגע בהם תחלה ולא יעביר על המצות דדעת הט״ז לעיל בסימן כ״ה דגם ע״י כיס שייך מעביר על המצוה ועיין במ״א בסימן כ״ה סק״א. אותן בני אדם הנוהגין לעשות תיקין להתפילין (יא) יש להם לסמן איזה שייך לש״ר ואיזו לשל יד (יב) כדי שיזהר בהם ולא יוציא הש״ר תחלה מהתיק גם (יג) דכיון דש״ר קדושתו חמורה יזהר עי״ז שלא לשנות אח״כ התיק ליתן בו של יד אלא א״כ התנה מתחלה וכדלקמן בסימן מ״ב: (ח) תחלה. ולא יצטרך להעביר על המצוה. ונכון (יד) ליזהר שלא יחלוץ של יד עד שיניח ש״ר בתוך התיק כדי שלא ישכח ויניח של יד תחלה בתוך התיק: **ג** (ט) ובשעת חליצתן. כשמקפל התפילין לא יכרוך הרצועות על הבתים (טו) אלא בצדדי הבתים על התיתורא ויש נוהגין לכורכן ככנפים ע״ש כנפי יונה. וכשכורכן על צדדי התפילין (טז) צריך לאחוז התפילין בידו ולגלול הרצועה עליהן ולא לאחוז הרצועה בידו ולגלול התפילין לתוכה. גם (יז) כשנוטל התפילין מכיסן לא ינערם אלא נוטלן בידו מתוך הכיס. תיק תפילין אסור בשל שעטנז כמו מטפחת ספרים (פמ״ג):

אין

שער הציון

(נט) אחרונים: (א) ב״ח והגר״א לקמן בסימן ס״בד) סעיף כ״ה: (ב) פמ״ג בשם מהרא״י: (ג) תוספות ביומא ל״ג ע״ב ד״ה עבורי: (ד) פמ״ג: (ה) מ״א ופמ״ג: (ו) מ״א: (ז) של״ה: (ח) פמ״ג: (ט) ברכי יוסף: (י) מ״א: (יא) מ״א: (יב) פמ״ג: (יג) מ״א: (יד) פמ״ג בשם הב״ח: (טו) מ״א: (טז) (יז) מ״א בשם ס״ח:

הגהות ותיקונים: א) זא״ז: ב) ס״ק מ׳: ג) יזוזו: ד) ס״א:

הערות והארות: 1) עיין במ״ב סי׳ צ״ד ס״ק ג׳ לענין חילוק בין היסח הדעת סתמא למטריד דעתו הרבה עד שלבבו פונה מי״ש ועיין שעה״צ ס׳ רנ״ב אות ל״ח אם שייך היסח דעת גם באוחזן בידו:

One should put the head /*tefilin*/ in the bag /first/ **(7)** and over it the arm /*tefilin*/, so that when he comes to don /the *tefilin* again/ he will encounter the arm /*tefilin*/ **(8)** first.

3. It is the practice of the wise to kiss the *tefilin* when they don them **(9)** and when they take them off.

Mishnah Berurah

(7) And over it the arm /*tefilin*/. The *Bach* and, likewise, the *Taz* write above, in Sec. 25, sub-Par. 10 that what is meant is that one should make a long and narrow bag, so that /the *tefilin* units/ lie one on top of the other.

The *M.A.* writes that it is preferable to put the *tefilin* units alongside one another. This is /in fact/ the practice. /He explains that/ when the author /of the Shulchan Aruch/ writes, "and over it the arm /*tefilin*/", this means that /the arm *tefilin*/ should be put a little towards the top /of the bag/, so that he will encounter them first.

In the work *Shulchan Shelomoh*, /the author/ writes that it is desirable for the arm *tefilin* to be towards the right of the bag as well, for the same reason.

There are people whose practice is to make two pouches, one for the arm /*tefilin*/ and one for the head /*tefilin*/. However, even if /one has/ two pouches, it is better /for him/ to be careful to put the pouch for the arm /*tefilin*/ a little towards the top /of where they are kept/, so that he will encounter them first and will not /have to/ bypass a mitzvah. /This is/ because in the opinion of the *Taz*, /given/ above in Sec. 25, /the question of/ bypassing mitzvos is relevant even where /the object of the mitzvah/ is in a pouch. See the *M.A.* in Sec. 25, sub-Par. 1.

Those people whose practice is to make cases for the *tefilin* units, must indicate which of /the cases/ belongs to the head /*tefilin*/ and which of them is for the arm /*tefilin*/. They will thus /be able to/ be careful when /they use/ them not to take the head /*tefilin*/ out of the bag first. An additional /reason for doing so/ is that, /bearing in mind/ that the head /*tefilin*/ have a higher degree of holiness /than the arm *tefilin*/, one can thus avoid a subsequent change /in one's usage of/ the /head *tefilin*/ case /to a usage of a lesser holiness/ by putting the arm /*tefilin*/ inside it. /It is prohibited to make such a change,/ unless one made a provision from the outset /to enable him to do so/. /If one made such a provision, however, it is of avail,/ as /ruled/ below in Sec. 42 /, Par. 2/.

(8) First. /Then/ he will not be required to bypass the mitzvah /of donning the head *tefilin*/.

It is proper /for one/ to avoid taking off the arm /*tefilin*/ until he has placed the head /*tefilin*/ inside the bag, so that he will not /come to/ forget /himself/ and place the arm /*tefilin*/ inside the bag first.

(9) And when they take them off. When one folds up the *tefilin* he should not wind the straps over the receptacles, but /should wind them/ on the sides of the receptacles, over the rim. There are /people/ who are accustomed to wind them in /the form of/ wings, to commemorate the dove's wings.[1]

When one winds /the straps/ over the sides of the *tefilin* units he must hold the *tefilin* units in his hand and roll the straps over them and should not hold the straps in his hand and roll the *tefilin* units into them.

In addition, when one takes *tefilin* out of their pouch he should not shake them /out of the pouch/, but should take hold of them with his hand from inside the pouch.

A *tefilin* bag is forbidden /to be made/ with *sha'atneyz*,[2] just like a covering for /holy/ scrolls. ((*P.Mg.*))

1 See *Shabbos* 130a. There it is related that the Romans decreed that a person who dons *tefilin* on his head will have his brain pierced. Elisha did so and was seen by a quaestor. Elisha was pursued by the quaestor and when the quaestor reached Elisha, the latter took them off his head and held them in his hand. The quaestor asked Elisha what he had in his hand and he answered, "A dove's wings". The quaestor stretched out his hand and discovered them to be /in fact/ a dove's wings.

2 I.e., from cloth made out of wool and linen combined together.

כט ובו סעיף אחד:

א (א) (א) ^א^אין לברך שום ברכה כשחולץ תפילין אפי' כשחולצם ערב שבת (ב) בין (ג) השמשות:

ל זמן הנחתן. ובו ה' סעיפים:

א ^א^זמן (א) הנחתן בבוקר משיראה את חבירו ^ב^הרגיל (ב) עמו (א) קצת ברחוק ד' אמות ויכירנו:
ב ^ג^אסור להניח תפילין (ג) בלילה שמא ישכחם (ד) ויישן (ב) [א] בהם. ^ד^אם הניחם (ה) קודם שתשקע החמה וחשכה עליו אפילו הם עליו (ו) כל הלילה (ז) מותר (ח) ואין (ג) [ב] מורין כן. * ^ה^אם לא חלץ תפילין משתשקע חמה מפני שלא היה לו מקום לשמרן (ט) * ונמצאו עליו כדי לשמרן * מותר (ד) ומורין כן: ^ג^ ^ו^היה רוצה (י) לצאת לדרך (יא) בהשכמה (יב) מניחם

באר הגולה

א רא"ש בה"ת בשם ר"ת והתוספות במנחות ל"ו ובכמה דוכתי

א ברכות ט'
ב תוספות בשם הירושלמי ג מנחות ל"ו ד הרמב"ם פ"ד מה"ת ורא"ש בפירוש הגמרא ה שם במנחות ל' ג' הרי"ף ו שם בגמרא

שערי תשובה

[א] בהם. עבה"ט וכתבו האחרונים רמז פסוק אדם ביקר כו' לפי שרש"י פירש שמא יפיח בהם שהוא מעשה בהמה ואינו כבוד לתפילין ותפילין נקראו יקר כדאמרינן במגילה ויקר אלו תפילין וז"ש אדם ביקר ר"ל בתפילין לא^א)^ ילין וצריך להסירם כיון שבעת השינה נמשל כבהמות כו' והוא רמז נאה: [ב] מורין כן. עבה"ט ועיין מ"ש בהלכות ציצית^ב)^ שהאר"י היה נזהר מאד לחולצן אחר

באר היטב

(א) אין לברך. ומטעם זה נכון לחלוץ התפילין בשמאל כי דבר הצריך ברכה נוטל בימין ועיין מ"ש השכנה"ג ובני חייא מיישבו ע"ש: (ג) השמשות. עיין מ"א שהעלה דאם הניחן בשבת לשם מצוה עובר משום בל תוסיף אבל כשמניחם שלא לשם מצוה אין איסור להניחם עיין מ"ש המ"א בסי' ש"ח ס"ק י"א ולפי מה שמחלק כאן לא הקשה שם מידי ולא ידעתי למה לא מתרץ שם כהאי חלוקה וק"ל. עיין בתשובת יד אליהו סי"ט. ובספר יד אהרן:

(א) קצת. דאלו הרבה יכירנו אפי' מרחוק ואינו רגיל כלל לא יכיר אפי' בקרוב מאוד: (ב) בהם. וחיישינן שמא יפיח בשינתו אבל מדאורייתא מותר להניחם בלילה דאנן קי"ל לילה זמן תפילין: (ג) מורין כן. וא"כ ברבים צריך לחולצן מ"א. כתב השכנה"ג מנהגי שביום צום תענית שאחר המנחה אני עומד בקהל עד ערבית שלא להסיר תפילין וטלית עד אחר תפלת ערבית דכיון דלילה זמן תפילין אלא שלכתחלה אין להניחם מאחר שכבר הם עלי משעת המנחה טוב שלא לחלצן עד אחר תפלת ערבית לפיכך בט"ב שמניחין תפילין בתפלת המנחה אין לחלוץ אותם קודם תפלת ערבית ומה שהעם נוהגים לחלוץ אותם היינו טעמא דלאו כ"ע דיני גמירי וחכם הדור אין להם להורות דהא אין מורין כן ע"כ. וכ"כ בל"ח הלכות תפילין אות ע"ט. וכתב ע"ת שדבריו נכונים ע"ש. וכן פסק בהלק"ט ח"א סימן רל"ח ע"ש. אבל מהרי"ל בהלכות ט"ב כתב שהיה חולץ תפילין שלו מיד אחר קדושה למנחה. וכן נראה דעת המ"א שכתב ברבים צריך לחולצן. וכן הכריע בתשובת שבות יעקב ח"ב סימן כ"ד ע"ש: (ד) ומורין כן. וצריך שיאמר שעושה כן כדי לשומרן. אבל לכתחלה אין מורין להניחם בשביל השמירה

ביאור הלכה

צריך שיהא למעלה בעורף ולא למטה במפרקת הצואר:

* אם לא חלץ תפילין משישקעה חמה. ר"ל גמר שקיעה דהוא צאת הכוכבים דאז הוא זמן חליצת תפילין מדינא דאלו בין השמשות אפילו אם היה לו מקום לשמרן אין צריך לחלצן כן מוכח במנחות ל"ו ע"ב אפילו למאן דאית ליה לילה לאו זמן תפילין וכ"ש לדידן דפסקינן לילה זמן תפילין וכן כתב הלבוש והפמ"ג דמורין כן לכתחילה: * ונמצאו עליו כדי לשמרן. עיין במ"א שכתב דצריך שיאמר להם כן שעושה כדי לשמרן וכן מוכח בגמרא ונלאו כל המפרשים [הפמ"ג והמחה"ש והארה"ח] דבגמרא משמע להיפך במעשה דרב אשי עי"ש ולענ"ד נראה פשוט דהוא בא להוסיף על דברי המחבר דאפילו אם באמת אין כונתו בשביל השמירה רק שהוא אומר להם כן שעושה בשביל השמירה כדי שלא יבואו להתיר להניח לכתחילה בלילה ג"כ די בכך וכן מוכח בהדיא שם בגמרא במעשה דרב אשי: * מותר ומורין כן. עיין במ"ב במ"ש דיש מקילין אפילו להניח לכתחילה בשביל השמירה ונ"ל פשוט דאף דמותר לכוין אז במחשבתו שלובשן לשם מצוה וכדמוכח במעשה דר"א

משנה ברורה

א (א) אין לברך. פירוש לאפוקי ממאי דאמרינן [בנידה נ"א ע"ב] דבני מערבא היו מברכין אשר קדשנו במצותיו וצונו לשמור חוקיו בתר דמסלקי תפילין בלילה (א) שהם היו סוברים דלילה לאו זמן תפילין הוא ונפקא להו זה מקרא ושמרת את החוקה הזאת למועדה מימים ימימה ימים ולא לילות אבל לדידן דס"ל דהאי קרא אתי לענין אחר כדאיתא בגמרא ולילה קי"ל דזמן תפילין הוא אך אין להניחם לכתחילה דגזרו שמא יישן בהם ויפיח הילכך אין לברך: (ב) בין השמשות. פי' אף דקי"ל שבת ויו"ט לאו זמן תפילין (ב) וכשירצה להניחן אז לשם מצוה עובר על בל תוסיף מ"מ כיון שאם מניחן עליו בלי כונה לשם מצוה אין בזה איסור מן התורה אלא מדברי סופרים (ג) משום גזירה שמא יצא בהן לר"ה ויש חולקין גם ע"ז כמו שיבואר לקמן בסימן ל"א לפיכך לא שייך ברכה ע"ז כיון שבחליצת התפלה מצד עצמה אין בה מצוה ואינו חולצן^1)^ אלא משום גזירה:

א (א) הנחתן. ר"ל תחלת זמן הנחתן משיראה ותלותן כל היום וכדלקמן בסימן ל"ז עי"ש והטעם (א) דעד זמן הזה חיישינן שמא יישן בהם ובכלל לילה הוא לענין תפילין: (ב) עמו קצת. דאלו הרבה יכירנו אפילו מרחוק ואינו רגיל כלל לא יכיר אפילו בקרוב מאוד: ב (ג) בלילה. ובין השמשות מדברי המג"א משמע דמותר לכתחלה להניח אבל בפמ"ג מסתפק בזה אם לא שלא קיים עדיין מצות תפילין באותו יום דאז יניחם בין^ו)^ השמשות: (ד) ויישן בהם. וחיישינן שמא יפיח בשינתו (ב) אבל מדאורייתא מותר להניחם בלילה דקי"ל לילה זמן תפילין: (ה) קודם וכו'. ר"ל דלא אסרו רבנן רק להניחם לכתחלה בלילה (ג) אבל מכיון שכבר מונחין עליו מבעוד יום לא הצריכום לחלצן: (ו) כל הלילה. פי' כל זמן שאין חולצן (ד) דאלו חולצן פ"א שוב אסור להניחן: (ז) מותר. ר"ל עד זמן שרוצה לישן דאז בהכרח מסירן שאסור לישן שינת קבע בהן וכדלקמן בסימן מ"ד. (ה) ואפשר דבלילה דזמן שינה הוא אפילו שינת עראי אסור מדינא: (ח) ואין מורין כן. הלכה למעשה לאחרים שמא יבואו להניחן לכתחלה וע"כ לא יעשה כן אלא בינו לבין עצמו (ו) אבל לא ברבים דהוא ג"כ כהוראה וע"כ (ז) אין להתפלל בהם תפלת ערבית בתענית צבור ברבים: (ט) ונמצאו עליו. דוקא נמצאו מקילינן ומורין שבשביל השמירה אין צריך לחלוץ אפילו כל הלילה כ"ז שלא ישן (ח) אבל להניחם לכתחלה אסור בשביל השמירה ויש מקילין בזה [ע"ת והגר"א]: ג (י) לצאת לדרך. וקשה לו להניחן אח"כ מפני הקור וכל כה"ג [מ"א]: (יא) בהשכמה. אפילו (ט) קודם עמוד השחר: (יב) מניחם. קודם יציאתו. ויכול (י) לכוין שלובשם

שער הציון

(א) תוס' ב"י: (ב) מ"א לקמן בסימן ל"א: (ג) ב"י: (א) לבוש ופמ"ג: (ב) מ"א: (ג) ב"י: (ד) מנחות ל"ו ע"א: (ה) פמ"ג: (ו) מ"א: (ז) ארה"ח בשם אחרונים: (ח) ב"י וט"ז: (ט) רש"י מנחות ל"ו ע"א: (י) פשוט:

הגהות ותיקונים: א) בל: ב) סי' י"ח ס"ק א': ג) חולצה:

הערות והארות: 1) עיין בה"ל סוף הסימן לענין ברכה:

§29: /WHETHER ONE MUST MAKE A BLESSING OVER THE TAKING OFF OF *TEFILIN*/

(Contains One Paragraph)

1. (1) One should not make any blessing when he takes off *tefilin*. This even /applies/ when one takes off /*tefilin*/ on Erev Shabbos /upon the arrival of/ (2) *beyn ha-shemashos* (in between sunset and the appearance of the stars).

Mishnah Berurah

§29

(1) **One should not make ... blessing.** The explanation /of this ruling is that the author of the Shulchan Aruch wishes thereby/ to reject /the practice/ described [in *Nidah* 51b].

/It is stated there/ that the people of the west[1] would make a blessing /worded/ אֲשֶׁר קִדְּשָׁנוּ בְּמִצְוֹתָיו וְצִוָּנוּ לִשְׁמֹר חֻקָּיו (Who has sanctified us with his commandments and commanded us to observe his statutes) after they removed the *tefilin* at night. They were of the opinion that in the nighttime /the mitzvah of wearing/ *tefilin* does not /apply/. They derived this from a verse[2] /which relates to *tefilin*/ where /it is stated/, "And you shall observe this statute at its appointed time from day to day". /They interpreted this verse to mean that *tefilin* should be worn/ by day and not by night.

However, we are of the opinion that that verse is meant to /teach/ something else, as stated in the Gemara.[3] We /therefore/ rule that in the nighttime /the mitzvah of wearing/ *tefilin* does /apply/ and it follows that one should not make /this/ blessing.

Despite this, one should not don /*tefilin* at night/, initially, as /the Sages/ decreed /a prohibition against it, for fear/ that one may fall asleep /wearing/ them and will /come to/ break wind.

(2) ***Beyn ha-shemashos.*** The explanation /of this observation / is /as follows/.

We rule /in fact/ that Shabbos and Yom Tov are times when /the mitzvah of wearing/ *tefilin* does not /apply/. If one wishes to don /*tefilin*/ then for the sake /of fulfilling/ the mitzvah /of wearing *tefilin*/, he will transgress /the prohibition of/, "You should not add".[4] Even so, /one should/ nevertheless /not make a blessing when he removes the *tefilin* then/, since if he leaves them on his /person/ without having in mind /to do so/ for the sake of the mitzvah /the transgression of/ a Torah prohibition is not involved. /The need to remove them is/ a mere Rabbinical requirement, because /the Sages/ decreed /a prohibition against this/ in case one would go out into a public domain with /the *tefilin* on his person/. There are /authorities/ who also dispute /the existence of this decree/, as explained below in Sec. 31. Consequently, a blessing over /the taking off of the *tefilin* then/ is not applicable, as the taking off of the *tefilin* units itself is not a mitzvah, but one merely takes them off because of the decree /prohibiting one to leave them on/.

1 I.e., the people of the Land of Israel, which is to the west of Babylon.
2 *Shemos* 13:10.
3 *Menachos* 36b.
4 *Devarim* 4:2 and 13:1.

באר הגולה

א רא"ש בה"ת בשם ר"ת והתוספות במנחות ל"ו ובכמה דוכתי

א ברכות ט'
ב תוספות בשם הירושלמי ג מנחות ל"ו ד הרמב"ם פ"ד מה"ת ורא"ש בפירוש הגמרא ה שם במנחות ל' ג' הרי"ף ו שם בגמרא

כט ובו סעיף אחד:

א (א) (א) ^א^אין לברך שום ברכה כשחולץ תפילין אפי' כשחולצם ערב שבת (ב) בין (ב) השמשות:

ל זמן הנחתן. ובו ה' סעיפים:

א ^א^זמן (א) הנחתן בבוקר משיראה את חבירו ^ב^הרגיל (ב) עמו (א) קצת ברחוק ד' אמות ויכירנו: ב ^ג^אסור להניח תפילין (ג) בלילה שמא ישכחם (ד) ויישן (ב) [א] בהם. ^ד^אם הניחם (ה) קודם שתשקע החמה וחשכה עליו אפילו הם עליו (ו) כל הלילה (ז) מותר (ח) ואין (ג) [ב] מורין כן. * ^ה^אם לא חלץ תפילין משקעה חמה מפני שלא היה לו מקום לשמרן (ט) * ונמצאו עליו כדי לשמרן * מותר (ד) ומורין כן: ג ^ו^היה רוצה (י) לצאת לדרך (יא) בהשכמה (יב) מניחם

שערי תשובה

[א] בהם. עבה"ט וכתבו האחרונים רמז פסוק אדם ביקר כו' לפי פרש"י פירש שמא יפיח בהם שהוא מעשה בהמה ואינו כבוד לתפילין ותפילין נקראו יקר כדאמרינן במגילה ויקר אלו תפילין וז"ש אדם ביקר ר"ל בתפילין לא^א)^ ילין וצריך להסירם כיון שבעת השינה נמשל כבהמות כו' והוא רמז נאה: [ב] מורין כן. עבה"ט ועיין מ"ש בהלכות ציצית^ב)^ שהאר"י היה נזהר מאד לחולצן אחר

באר היטב

(א) אין לברך. ומטעם זה נכון לחלוץ התפילין בשמאל כי דבר הצריך ברכה נוטל בימין ועיין מ"ש השכנה"ג ובני חייא מיישבו ע"ש: (ב) השמשות. עיין מ"א שהעלה דאם הניחן בשבת לשם מצוה עובר משום בל תוסיף אבל כשמניחם שלא לשם מצוה אין איסור להניחם עיין מ"ש המ"א בסי' ש"ח ס"ק י"א ולפי מה שמחלק כאן לא הקשה שם

מידי ולא ידעתי למה לא מתרץ שם כהאי חלוקה וק"ל. עיין בתשובת יד אליהו סי"ט. ובספר יד אהרן:

(א) קצת. דאלו הרבה יכירנו אפי' מרחוק ואינו רגיל כלל לא יכיר אפי' בקרוב מאוד: (ב) בהם. וחיישינן שמא יפיח בשינתו אבל מדאורייתא מותר להניחם בלילה דאנן קי"ל לילה זמן תפילין: (ג) מורין כן. וא"כ ברבים צריך לחולצן מ"א. כתב השכנה"ג מנהגי שביום צום תענית שאחר המנחה אני עומד בקהל עד ערבית שלא להסיר תפילין וטלית עד אחר תפלת ערבית דכיון דלילה זמן תפילין אלא שלכתחלה אין להניחם מאחר שכבר הם עלי משעת המנחה טוב שלא לחלצן עד אחר תפלת ערבית לפיכך בט"ב שמניחין תפילין בתפלת המנחה אין לחלוץ אותם קודם תפלת ערבית ומה שהעם נוהגים לחלוץ אותם היינו טעמא דלאו כ"ע דיני גמירי וחכם הדור אין להם להורות דהא אין מורין כן ע"כ. וכ"כ בל"ח הלכות תפילין אות ע"ט. וכתב ע"ת שדבריו נכונים ע"ש. וכן פסק בהלק"ט ח"א סימן רל"ח ע"ש. אבל מהרי"ל בהלכות ט"ב כתב שהיה חולץ תפילין שלו מיד אחר קדושה למנחה. וכן נראה דעת המ"א שכתב ברבים צריך לחולצן. וכן הכריע בתשובת שבות יעקב ח"ב סימן כ"ד ע"ש: (ד) ומורין כן. וצריך שיאמר שעושה כן כדי לשומרן. אבל לכתחלה אין מורין להניחם בשביל השמירה

ביאור הלכה

צריך שיהא למעלה בעורף ולא למטה במפרקת הצואר:

* אם לא חלץ תפילין משישקעה חמה. ר"ל גמר שקיעה דהוא צאת הכוכבים דאז הוא זמן חליצת תפילין מדינא דאלו בין השמשות אפילו אם היה לו מקום לשמרן אין צריך לחלצן כן מוכח במנחות ל"ו ע"ב אפילו למאן דאית ליה לילה לאו זמן תפילין וכ"ש לדידן דפסקינן לילה זמן תפילין וכן כתב הלבוש והפמ"ג דמורין כן לכתחילה: * ונמצאו עליו כדי לשמרן. עיין במ"א שכתב דצריך שיאמר להם כן שעושה כדי לשמרן וכן מוכח בגמרא ונלאו כל המפרשים [הפמ"ג והמחה"ש והארה"ח] דבגמרא משמע להיפך במעשה דרב אשי עי"ש ולענ"ד נראה פשוט דהוא בא להוסיף על דברי המחבר דאפילו אם באמת אין כונתו בשביל השמירה רק שהוא אומר להם כן שעושה בשביל השמירה כדי שלא יבואו להתיר להניח לכתחילה בלילה ג"כ די בכך וכן מוכח בהדיא שם בגמרא במעשה דרב אשי: * מותר ומורין כן. עיין במ"ב במ"ש דיש מקילין אפילו להניח לכתחילה בשביל השמירה ונ"ל פשוט דאף דמותר לכוין אז במחשבתו שלובשן לשם מצוה וכדמוכח במעשה דר"א

משנה ברורה

א (א) אין לברך. פירוש לאפוקי ממאי דאמרינן [בנידה נ"א ע"ב] דבני מערבא היו מברכין אשר קדשנו במצותיו וצונו לשמור חוקיו בתר דמסלקי תפילין בלילה (א) שהם היו סוברים דלילה לאו זמן תפילין הוא ונפקא להו זה מקרא דושמרת את החוקה הזאת למועדה מימים ימימה ימים ולא לילות אבל לדידן דס"ל דהאי קרא אתי לענין אחר כדאיתא בגמרא ולילה קי"ל דזמן תפילין הוא אך אין להניחם לכתחילה דגזרו שמא יישן בהם ויפיח הילכך אין לברך: (ב) בין השמשות. פי' אף דקי"ל שבת ויו"ט לאו זמן תפילין (ב) וכשילה להניחן אז לשם מצוה עובר על בל תוסיף מ"מ כיון שאם מניחן עליו בלי כונה לשם מצוה אין בזה איסור מן התורה אלא מדברי סופרים (ג) משום גזירה שמא ילא בהן לר"ה ויש חולקין גם ע"ז כמו שיבואר לקמן בסימן ל"א לפיכך לא שייך ברכה ע"ז כיון שבחליצת התפלה מצד עצמה אין בה מצוה ואינו חולצן^1)^ אלא משום גזירה:

א (א) הנחתן. ר"ל תחלת זמן הנחתן משיראה ומצותן כל היום וכדלקמן בסימן ל"ז עי"ש והטעם (א) דעד זמן הזה חיישינן שמא יישן בהם ובכלל לילה הוא לענין תפילין: (ב) עמו קצת. דאלו הרבה יכירנו אפילו מרחוק ואינו רגיל כלל לא יכיר אפילו בקרוב מאוד: ב (ג) בלילה. ובין השמשות מדברי המג"א משמע דמותר לכתחלה להניח אבל בפמ"ג מסתפק בזה אם לא שלא קיים עדיין מצות תפילין באותו יום דאז יניחם בין^י)^ השמשות: (ד) ויישן בהם. וחיישינן שמא יפיח בשינתו (ב) אבל מדאורייתא מותר להניחם בלילה דקי"ל לילה זמן תפילין: (ה) קודם וכו'. ר"ל דלא אסרו רבנן רק להניחם לכתחלה בלילה (ג) אבל מכיון שכבר מונחין עליו מבעוד יום לא הצריכום לחלצן: (ו) כל הלילה. פי' כל זמן שאין חולצן (ד) דאלו חולצן פ"א שוב אסור להניחן: (ז) מותר. ר"ל עד זמן שרוצה לישן דאז בהכרח מסירן שאסור לישן שינת קבע בהן וכדלקמן בסימן מ"ד. (ה) ואפשר דבלילה דזמן שינה הוא אפילו שינת עראי אסור מדינא: (ח) ואין מורין כן. הלכה למעשה לאחרים שמא יבואו להניחן לכתחלה וע"כ לא יעשה כן אלא בינו לבין עצמו (ו) אבל לא ברבים דהוא ג"כ כהוראה וע"כ (ז) אין להתפלל בהם תפילת ערבית בתענית צבור ברבים: (ט) ונמצאו עליו. דוקא נמצאו מקילין ומורין שבשביל השמירה אין צריך לחלוץ אפילו כל הלילה כ"ז שלא ישן (ח) אבל להניחם לכתחלה אסור בשביל השמירה ויש מקילין בזה [ע"ת והגר"א]: ג (י) לצאת לדרך. וקשה לו להניחן אח"כ מפני הקור וכל כה"ג [מ"א]: (יא) בהשכמה. אפילו (ט) קודם עמוד השחר: (יב) מניחם. קודם יציאתו. ויכול (י) לכוין שלובשם

שער הציון

(א) תוס' ב"י: (ב) מ"א לקמן בסימן ל"א: (ג) ב"י: (א) לבוש ופמ"ג: (ב) מ"א: (ג) ב"י: (ד) מנחות ל"ו ע"א: (ה) פמ"ג: (ו) מ"א: (ז) ארה"ח בשם אחרונים:
(ח) ב"י וט"ז: (ט) רש"י מנחות ל"ו ע"א: (י) פשוט:

הגהות ותיקונים: א) בל: ב) סי' י"ח ס"ק א': ג) חולצה:

הערות והארות: 1) עיין בה"ל סוף הסימן לענין ברכה:

§30: THE TIME FOR DONNING */TEFILIN/*
(Contains Five Paragraphs)

1. The time (1) for donning */tefilin/* is in the morning, from /the time/ when one can see his fellow, (2) with whom he is somewhat familiar, at a distance of four cubits and recognize him.
2. It is forbidden to don *tefilin* (3) at night, in case one will forget about them (4) and sleep with them /on him/.

If one donned */tefilin/* (5) before sunset and it became dark /before he took them off, then/, even if the */tefilin* remain/ on him (6) all night (7) /he is

Mishnah Berurah

§30

(1) For donning */tefilin/*. I.e., the time for donning */tefilin/* begins from /the time/ when one can see /, etc./. /However,/ the mitzvah of /donning *tefilin* continues to be relevant/ all day, as /stated/ below in Sec. 37; see there.

The reason /why *tefilin* may only be donned from the time when one can see, etc./ is that until that time we are afraid that one may sleep with them /on him/. /Before that time/ is /therefore/ classed as night with respect to /the donning of/ *tefilin.*

(2) With whom he is somewhat. For if /he is/ very /familiar with him/ he will recognize him even from afar, /whereas/ if he is not familiar /with him/ at all he will not recognize him even when he is very close.

(3) At night. /As for/ *beyn ha-shemashos*, it is implied by the words of the *M.A.* that it is permitted to don */tefilin* then/ initially. However, the *P.Mg.* is in doubt about this, unless /it is an instance/ where one has not yet fulfilled the mitzvah of /donning/ *tefilin* that day. In /the latter/ case, /he agrees that/ one should /in fact/ don them /initially, although it is already/ *beyn ha-shemashos.*

(4) And sleep with them. /For if one sleeps with them on him/ we are afraid that he may break wind while he is asleep.

According to Torah law, however, it is permitted to don */tefilin/* at night. For /with respect to Torah law/ we rule that the night is /also/ a time when /the mitzvah of donning/ *tefilin* /applies/.

(5) Before, etc. /The Shulchan Aruch/ wishes to explain that the Sages only forbade one to don */tefilin/* at night initially. However, once one already donned */tefilin* and they have merely remained on him/ from /the time/ when it was still day, /the Sages/ did not require him to take them off.

(6) All night. I.e., as long as he has not /yet/ taken them off, but once he took them off he is thenceforth prohibited to don them /again until the morning/.

(7) /He is acting/ permittedly. What is meant is /that he may leave them on him/ until the time when he wishes to sleep. When that time /arrives, however,/ he is compelled to remove them, since it is forbidden /for one/

כט ובו סעיף אחד:

א (ֹא) (א) אאין לברך שום ברכה כשחולץ תפילין אפי׳ כשחולצם ערב שבת (ב) בין (ג) השמשות:

ל זמן הנחתן. ובו ה׳ סעיפים:

א אזמן (א) הנחתן בבוקר משיראה את חבירו בהרגיל (ב) עמו (ֹא) קצת ברחוק ד׳ אמות ויכירנו: ב גאסור להניח תפילין (ג) בלילה שמא ישכחם (ד) ויישן (ג) [ֹא] בהם. דאם הניחם (ה) קודם שתשקע החמה וחשכה עליו אפילו הם עליו (ו) כל הלילה (ז) מותר (ח) ואין (ג) [ב] מורין כן. * האם לא חלץ תפילין משתשקעה חמה מפני שלא היה לו מקום לשמרן (ט) * ונמצאו עליו כדי לשמרן * מותר (ד) ומורין כן:*ג והיה רוצה (י) לצאת לדרך (יא) בהשכמה (יב) מניחם

באר הגולה

א רא״ש נה״ת בשם ר״ת והתוספות במנחות ל״ו ובכמה דוכתי
א ברכות ט׳
ב תוספות בשם הירושלמי ג מנחות ל״ו ד הרמב״ם פ״ד מה״ת ורא״ש בפירוש הגמרא
ה שם במנחות ל׳
ו הרי״ף ו שם בגמרא

שערי תשובה

[ֹא] בהם. עבה״ט וכתבו האחרונים רמז פסוק אדם ביקר כו׳ לפי שרש״י פירש שמא יפיח בהם שהוא מעשה בהמה ואינו כבוד לתפילין ותפילין נקראו יקר כדאמרינן במגילה ויקר אלו תפילין וז״ש אדם ביקר ר״ל בתפילין לא[א] ילין וצריך להסירם כיון שבעת השינה נמשל כבהמות כו׳ והוא רמז נאה: [ב] מורין כן. עבה״ט ועיין מ״ש בהלכות ציצית[ב] שהאר״י היה נזהר מאד לחולצן אחר מידי ולא ידעתי למה לא מתרץ שם כהאי חלוקה וק״ל. עיין בתשובת יד אליהו סי״ט. ובספר יד אהרן:

באר היטב

(ֹא) אין לברך. ומטעם זה נכון לחלוץ התפילין בשמאל כי דבר הצריך ברכה נוטל בימין ועיין מ״ש השכנה״ג ובני חייא מיישבו ע״ש: (ג) השמשות. עיין מ״א שהעלה דאם הניחן בשבת לשם מצוה עובר משום בל תוסיף אבל כשמניחם שלא לשם מצוה אין איסור להניחם עיין מ״ש המ״א בסי׳ ש״ח ס״ק י״א ולפי מה שמחלק כאן לא הקשה שם

(ֹא) קצת. דאלו הרבה יכירנו אפי׳ מרחוק ואינו רגיל כלל לא יכיר אפי׳ בקרוב מאוד: (ג) בהם. וחיישינן שמא יפיח בשינתו אבל מדאורייתא מותר להניחם בלילה דאנן קי״ל לילה זמן תפילין: (ג) מורין כן. וא״כ ברבים צריך לחולצן מ״א. כתב השכנה״ג מנהגי שביום צום תענית שאחר המנחה אני עומד בקהל עד ערבית שלא להסיר תפילין וטלית עד אחר תפלת ערבית דכיון דלילה זמן תפילין אלא שלכתחלה אין להניחם מאחר שכבר הם עלי משעת המנחה טוב שלא לחלצן עד אחר תפלת ערבית לפיכך בט״ב שמניחין תפילין בתפלת המנחה אין לחלוץ אותם קודם תפלת ערבית ומה שהעם נוהגים לחלוץ אותם היינו טעמא דלאו כ״ע דיני גמירי וחכם הדור אין להם להורות דהא אין מורין כן ע״כ. וכ״כ בל״ח הלכות תפילין אות ע״ט. וכתב ע״ת שדבריו נכונים ע״ש. וכן פסק בהלק״ט ח״א סימן רל״ח ע״ש. אבל מהרי״ל בהלכות ט״ב כתב שהיה חולץ תפילין שלו מיד אחר קדושה למנחה. וכן נראה דעת המ״א שכתב ברבים צריך לחולצן. וכן הכריע בתשובת שבות יעקב ח״ב סימן כ״ד ע״ש: (ד) ומורין כן. וצריך שיאמר שעושה כן כדי לשומרן. אבל לכתחלה אין מורין להניחם בשביל השמירה

ביאור הלכה

צריך שיהא למעלה בעורף ולא למטה במפרקת הצואר:

* אם לא חלץ תפילין משישקעה חמה. ר״ל גמר שקיעה דהוא צאת הכוכבים דאז הוא זמן חליצת תפילין מדינא דאלו בין השמשות אפילו אם היה לו מקום לשמרן אין צריך לחלצן כן מוכח במנחות ל״ו ע״ב אפילו למאן דאית ליה לילה לאו זמן תפילין וכ״ש לדידן דפסקינן לילה זמן תפילין וכן כתב הלבוש והפמ״ג דמורין כן לכתחילה: * ונמצאו עליו כדי לשמרן. עיין במ״א שכתב דצריך שיאמר להם כן שעושה כדי לשמרן וכן מוכח בגמרא וגלאו כל המפרשים [הפמ״ג והמחה״ש והארה״ח] דבגמרא משמע להיפך במעשה דרב אשי עי״ש ולענ״ד נראה פשוט דהוא בא להוסיף על דברי המחבר דאפילו אם באמת אין כונתו בשביל השמירה רק שהוא אומר להם כן שעושה בשביל השמירה כדי שלא יבואו להתיר להניח לכתחילה בלילה ג״כ די בכך וכן מוכח בהדיא שם בגמרא במעשה דרב אשי: * מותר ומורין כן. עיין במ״ב במ״ש דיש מקילין אפילו להניח לכתחילה בשביל השמירה ונ״ל פשוט דאף דמותר לכוין אז במחשבתו שלובשן לשם מצוה וכדמוכח במעשה דר״א

משנה ברורה

א (א) אין לברך. פירוש לאפוקי ממאי דאמרינן [נגידה נ״א ע״ב] דבני מערבא היו מברכין אשר קדשנו במצותיו וצונו לשמור חוקיו בתר דמסלקי תפילין בלילה (א) שהם היו סוברים דלילה לאו זמן תפילין הוא ונפקא להו זה מקרא דושמרת את החוקה הזאת למועדה מימים ימימה ימים ולא לילות אבל לדידן דס״ל דהאי קרא אתי לענין אחר כדאיתא בגמרא ולילה קי״ל דזמן תפילין הוא אך אין להניחם לכתחילה דגזרו שמא יישן בהם ויפיח הילכך אין לברך: (ב) בין השמשות. פי׳ אף דקי״ל שבת ויו״ט לאו זמן תפילין (ג) וכשירלה להניחן אז לשם מצוה עובר על בל תוסיף מ״מ כיון שאם מניחן עליו בלי כונה לשם מצוה אין בזה איסור מן התורה אלא מדברי סופרים (ג) משום גזירה שמא יצא בהן לר״ה ויש חולקין גם ע״ז כמו שיבואר לקמן בסימן ל״א לפיכך לא שייך ברכה ע״ז כיון שבחליצת התפלה מצד עצמה אין בה מצוה ואינו חולצן[1] אלא משום גזירה:

א (א) הנחתן. ר״ל תחלת זמן הנחתן משיראה ומשם כל היום וכדלקמן בסימן ל״ז עי״ש והטעם (א) דעד זמן הזה חיישינן שמא יישן בהם ובכלל לילה הוא לענין תפילין: (ב) עמו קצת. דאלו הרבה יכירנו אפילו מרחוק ואינו רגיל כלל לא יכיר אפילו בקרוב מאוד: ב (ג) בלילה. ובין השמשות מדברי המג״א משמע דמותר לכתחלה להניח אבל בפמ״ג מסתפק בזה אם לא שלא קיים עדיין מצות תפילין באותו יום דאז יניחם בין השמשות: (ד) ויישן בהם. וחיישינן שמא יפיח בשינתו (ב) אבל מדאורייתא מותר להניחם בלילה דקי״ל לילה זמן תפילין: (ה) קודם וכו׳. ר״ל דלא אסרו רבנן רק להניחם לכתחלה בלילה (ג) אבל מכיון שכבר מונחין עליו מבעוד יום לא הצריכום לחלצן: (ו) כל הלילה. פי׳ כל זמן שאין חולצן (ד) דאלו חולצן פ״א שוב אסור להניחן: (ז) מותר. ר״ל עד זמן שרוצה לישן דאז בהכרח מסירן שאסור לישן שינת קבע בהן וכדלקמן בסימן מ״ד. (ה) ואפשר דבלילה דזמן שינה הוא אפילו שינת עראי אסור מדינא: (ח) ואין מורין כן. הלכה למעשה לאחרים שמא יבואו להניחן לכתחלה וע״כ לא יעשה כן אלא בינו לבין עצמו (ו) אבל לא ברבים דהוא ג״כ כהוראה וע״כ (ז) אין להתפלל בהם תפילת ערבית בתענית צבור ברבים: (ט) ונמצאו עליו. דוקא נמצאו מקילין ומורין שבשביל השמירה אין צריך לחלוץ אפילו כל הלילה כ״ז שלא ישן (ח) אבל להניחם לכתחלה אסור בשביל השמירה ויש מקילין בזה [ע״ת והגר״א]: ג (י) לצאת לדרך. וקשה לו להניחן אח״כ מפני הקור וכל כה״ג [מ״א]: (יא) בהשכמה. אפילו (ט) קודם עמוד השחר: (יב) מניחם. קודם יציאתו. ויכול (י) לכוין שלובשם

שער הציון

(א) תוס׳ ב״י: (ב) מ״א לקמן בסימן ל״א: (א) לבוש ופמ״ג: (ב) מ״א: (ג) ב״י: (ד) מנחות ל״ו ע״א: (ה) פמ״ג: (ו) מ״א: (ז) ארה״ח בשם אחרונים: (ח) ב״י וט״ז: (ט) רש״י מנחות ל״ו ע״א: (י) פשוט:

הגהות ותיקונים: א) בל: ב) סי׳ י״ח ס״ק א׳: ג) חולצה:

הערות והארות: 1) עיין בה״ל סוף הסימן לענין ברכה:

acting/ permittedly. (8) /However,/ one should not teach this /ruling/.

If one /is wearing *tefilin* and/ does not take off the *tefilin* /although it is/ after sunset[1*] because he does not have a place where they will be safeguarded, /so that/ (9) they remain on him to be safeguarded, /he is acting/ permittedly.[2*] One may /even/ teach this /ruling/.

3. If one wishes (10) to depart for the road (11) early, (12) he may don /*tefilin*

Mishnah Berurah

to sleep a settled sleep with /*tefilin* on him/, as /stated/ below in Sec. 44. It may be that at night, which is a time when /people/ sleep, it is prohibited halachically /for one to sleep/ even a momentary sleep /with *tefilin* on him/.

(8) /However,/ one should not teach this /ruling/. /I.e., as the/ halachic /ruling/ for others /to follow/ in practice.

/The reason is that people/ may come to don /*tefilin*/ initially /at night/.

In view of this, one should only act in this way when he is by himself, but should not /do it/ in public, as that is also tantamount to teaching /that it is permitted/. Therefore, on a communal fast, one should not pray the Ma'ariv prayer with /*tefilin* on him when he is/ in public.

(9) They remain on him. It is only when /*tefilin*/ have remained /on one/ that we are lenient and teach that for the sake of safeguarding them it is unnecessary to take them off and they may even /be kept on/ all night, as long as one does not sleep. However, it is forbidden to don /*tefilin*/ initially /at night/ for the sake of safeguarding them. There are /authorities/ who are lenient about this.[1] [*O.T.* and the *Gra.*]

(10) To depart for the road. /I.e.,/ and it will be difficult for him to don them later because of the cold or any similar /reason/. [*Ch.A.*]

(11) Early. /This ruling applies/ even /when one leaves/ before dawn.

(12) He may don /tefilin/. /I.e.,/ before his departure.

1* What is actually meant is after the appearance of the stars. During *beyn ha-shemashos* there is no need to remove *tefilin* and one may even teach this. (Beyur Halachah)

2* One may even say that he is keeping them on for this reason, although this is not true, so that people will not come to permit donning them initially at night because he is keeping them on. (Beyur Halachah)

1 According to their view, one is permitted in such a case to have in mind to fulfil the mitzvah when he wears them. However, he should not make a blessing over them then. (Beyur Halachah)

(יג) * וכשיגיע זמנן ימשמש בהם ויברך דליכא למיחש שמא יישן בהם * כיון שהשכים (יד) ויצא (ה) לדרך: **ד** * ז היה בא בדרך ותפילין בראשו (טו) ושקעה עליו (ו) חמה או שהיה יושב בבית המדרש ותפילין בראשו (טז) וקדש עליו היום יניח ידו עליהם עד שיגיע לבית ואם יש בית קרוב לחומה שמשתמרים שם חולצם ומניחם שם: **ה** * ח ויש מי שאומר שאם התפלל (ז) [ג] תפלת ערבית (יז) מבע"י עד שלא הניח תפילין אין לו להניחם אח"כ:

באר הגולה

ז בילה ט"ו לפירוש התוספות ח כתבי מהר"ר ישראל סימן קכ"א

באר היטב

ט"ז: (ה) לדרך. ודוקא הולך ברגליו או רוכב אבל יושב בעגלה אסור להניחן שמא יישן בהם כ"כ לבוש: (ו) חמה. מיירי בחול ואע"ג דאמרינן בסמוך דא"צ לחולצן דלילה זמן תפילין שאני הכא דיש לחוש למי שיפגע בו יטעה לומר שמותר להניח אז תפילין אבל בסמוך מיירי שיושב בביתו. וכן מ"ש אח"ז קדש עליו היום ר"ל קדושת שבת עליו וצריך לחולצן אבל בחול א"צ היינו מאחר שהוא בבית המדרש וליכא חשש טועין ט"ז והע"ת לא כ"כ ע"ש: (ז) תפלת ערבית. אבל אם הוא לא התפלל אע"פ שהציבור התפללו מותר להניח תפילין מ"א:

שערי תשובה

שקיעת החמה עיין שם: [ג] תפלת ערבית. וכתב בבר"י בשם דבר משה בירך על התפילין בלילה או שסבור שהוא יום והיה לילה אין צריך לברך כשיגיע זמן הנחת תפילין עיין שם:

משנה ברורה

שלובשם לשם מצוה כיון דקי"ל לילה זמן תפילין הוא ואפילו (יא) היה לו מקום לשמרן ג"כ מותר ללובשן כיון דליכא למיחש לשמא יישן בהם וכדלקמיה: (יג) וכשיגיע זמנן. דאף דהתירו חז"ל להקדים ההנחה בלילה במקום דליכא למיחש לשינה אפ"ה לענין ברכה לא רצו לתקן לומר וציונו קודם הזמן. ומ"מ (יב) אם קידם ובירך בלילה כשהניחם א"צ לברך שנית בבקר: (יד) ויצא לדרך. ודוקא (יג) הולך ברגליו (יד) או רוכב אבל יושב בעגלה אסור להניח שמא יישן בהם ועיין בבה"ל: ד (טו) ושקעה וכו'. רישא זו (טו) מיירי בחול ולחולצן ולנושאן בידו הוא מתירא שמא יפלו ממנו בדרך והתירו לו להניח ידו עליהם ולכסותם ואע"ג דבס"ב אמרינן דמכיון שהם מכבר עליו א"צ לחולצן שאני הכא (טז) דמי שיפגע בו פן יטעה לומר שמותר להניח אז תפילין אבל בסמוך מיירי שיושב בביתו. והאי ושקעה חמה (יז) פירוש סוף שקיעה דהוא צאת הכוכבים דבבין השמשות א"צ לחולצן ומורין כן למעשה וכ"ז מדינא ובשם האר"י ז"ל כתוב שהיה נזהר לחולצן אחר שקיעת החמה: (טז) וקידש וכו'. ר"ל דנעשה בין השמשות וא"א לו ליטלם בידו לביתו מפני קדושת שבת ולהסתיר אותם שם אי אפשר דבתי מדרשות שלהם היו בשדה מקום שאין משתמר (יח) מפני הגנבים ע"כ התירו לו חכמים לנושאם עליו דרך מלבוש עד ביתו אך צריך לכסותם שלא יראוהו שהוא נושא תפילין עליו בשבת: ה (יט) מבעוד יום. ואפילו עוד היום גדול (כ) קודם שקיעה לפי שסבר עשאו לזמן הזה לילה וזמן שכיבה בק"ש ותפלה של ערבית ואם יניח בו תפילין יסתור ויעשהו יום והרי הן שתי קולות שסותרות זו את זו אך האחרונים (כ) הסכימו להלכה דמחויב להניחן (כא) ובלי ברכה כל זמן שהוא קודם צאת הכוכבים ואם הוא לא התפלל עדיין אע"פ שהצבור התפללו אין בכך כלום ויניחם בברכה (כב) אם הוא עדיין יום כיון שהוא אינו עושה שתי קולות הסותרות זו את זו (כג) ודוקא אם לא הניחן באותו יום כלל אבל אם כבר הניח תפילין רק שרוצה להניח גם עתה אין ראוי להניחם אם הצבור כבר התפללו ערבית:

ביאור הלכה

הנ"ל אעפ"כ לא יברך אז על התפילין וראיה לדברינו דעיקר ראיית הע"ת והגר"א הוא ממה דאיתא שם בברייתא ומתיירא שמא יאבדו וכו' והרי שם ג"כ פסק הברייתא דאין לברך עד שיגיע הזמן וכמו שפסק הטור ושו"ע כהרא"ש ודלא כרבינו פרץ וכמו שכתב הגר"א: * וכשיגיע זמנן. עיין במ"ב במש"כ ומ"מ אם קידם וכו' הוא מחידושי רע"א שכתב דנוכל לסמוך בזה על דעת הר"פ עי"ש ומשמע מזה דבלא השכים ויצא לדרך צריך לחזור ולברך אם בירך על התפילין בלילה ומדברי הברכי יוסף שהובא בשע"ת משמע דבדיעבד בכל גווני אין צריך לחזור ולברך ולא הביא בברכ"י טעם לזה ואולי שבדיעבד נסמוך על שיטת רש"י ורבינו יונה שס"ל דמאי דאמרינן הלכה ואין מורין כן הוא אפילו לענין להניחם לכתחלה אך בשו"ע ס"ב לא פסק כוותייהו וצ"ע למעשה. ומכל זה תבין דמה דנוהגין איזה אנשים בימות החורף להניח תפילין ולברך עליהם תיכף משעלה עה"ש לא שפיר עבדי: * כיון שהשכים ויצא לדרך. עיין במ"ב ועיין בעט"ז ובפמ"ג במ"ז סק"ג שמלדדים לומר דאף בעגלה נראה להתיר ובארה"ח מסכים להמחמירין ונ"ל דאם הוא מתיירא שמא יאבדם ועושה כדי לשמרם בודאי אין להחמיר אף בישב בעגלה אחרי דבלא"ה דעת הע"ת והגר"א להקל במניחן בשביל השמירה: * היה בא בדרך וכו'. עיין במ"ב בס"ק ט"ו ט"ז וה"ה דהוי מצי המחבר למינקט בחד גוונא היה בא בדרך וקידש עליו היום ג"כ לענין שבת וכדלקמן בסימן רס"ו ס"י אלא דנקט לישנא דגמרא ונוכל לאמר דהגמרא אשמועינן רבותא דאף שהוא עומד בתוך קהל ועדה אפ"ה מועיל מה שהוא מניח ידו עליהם ולא חיישינן פן ירגישו בו שהוא נושא עליו תפילין וגם יוצא בם מבה"מ לחוץ בשבת והא דלא נקט הגמרא והמחבר האי בבא דהיה יושב בבה"מ ג"כ לענין חול תירץ הט"ז דבחול אם יושב בבה"מ א"צ להניח ידו עליהם [כ"ז שהוא בבה"מ]דהכל יודעין שם שלבשן מבעוד יום וליכא איסור והמג"א לא ס"ל האי חילוק כן כתבו האחרונים ונ"ל לתרץ לדידיה בפשיטות דאשמועינן הגמרא רבותא דאף בבא בדרך צריך להניח ידו עליהם פן יפגעו בו אנשים ויחשדוהו שהניח תפילין בלילה ואינו דומה להא דס"ג בהיה רוצה לצאת לדרך דמניחם ולא זכרו הפוסקים כלל דצריך להניח ידו עליהם דשאני התם שהוא קרוב לעלות השחר והוא קרוב מאוד להזמן דכדי שיכיר אך א"כ יולד מזה דין חדש דאם השכים כמה שעות קודם אור הבקר ומניחם דצריך להניח ידו עליהם וצ"ע למעשה. והקרוב אלי דלהכי השמיט הרמב"ם האי ברייתא דהשכים לצאת לדרך שתמהו הפוסקים ע"ז משום האי ברייתא דבילה ט"ו ע"א דקאמרה דצריך להניח ידו עליהם ומשמע ליה דפליגי אהדדי בזה ופסק כהאי ברייתא דבילה משום דאביי דהוא בתרא סבר כוותה וכעין זה כתב ג"כ בארה"ח דהברייתות סותרות אהדדי עי"ש: * ויש מי וכו' מבעוד יום וכו'. עיין במ"ב במש"כ לילה וזמן שכיבה בק"ש וכו' הוא משו"ע הגר"ז ומתורץ בזה קלת קושיא של הא"ר שהרי איסור תפילין בלילה אינו משום לילה רק משום שינה וכבסעיף ג' ובזה קלת ניחא ולפ"ז לאותן האנשים הזהירין לקרות עוד הפעם ק"ש בזמנה ואינן קוראין אז אלא כדי לעמוד בתפלה מתוך ד"ת וכדלקמן בסימן רל"ה ס"א אפשר שישתנה זה הדין ועיין. ועיין עוד במ"ב במש"כ דאם הוא לא התפלל עדיין וכו' אם הוא עדיין יום דאם הוא בין השמשות נ"ל דלא יברך אז דבלא"ה הפמ"ג מפקפק על דברי המ"א בסק"ב במש"כ דזמן הנחת תפילין הוא עד צאת הכוכבים הגם דבודאי מחויב להניחן כיון שלא קיים עדיין מצות תפילין דבד"ת ספיקא לחומרא ושמא הוא עדיין יום וכמו שפסק הפמ"ג בא"א עכ"פ הברכות אינן מעכבות:

אסור

שער הציון

(יא) ע"ת ופמ"ג: (יב) חידושי רע"א: (יג) מ"א: (יד) אחרונים: (טו) ט"ז והגר"א לקמן בסימן רס"ו ס"י: (טז) ט"ז: (יז) פמ"ג: (יח) בילה ט"ו: (יט) מפלג מנחה ברכות כ"ז כרבי יהודה עי"ש: (כ) א"ר ופמ"ג: (כא) פמ"ג: (כב) עיין בבה"ל: (כג) פמ"ג:

early/ (13) and when the time when they /should be donned/ arrives he should /then/ feel them and make the blessing /over them/. For in view /of the fact/ that he got up early (14) and is departing for the road, there are no grounds for fear that he may sleep with them /on him/.

4. If one is proceeding on the road and has *tefilin* on his head (15) and the sun has /already/ set or if one is sitting in the *Beys Ha-Midrash* (Torah study hall)

Mishnah Berurah

He may have in mind that he is wearing /the *tefilin*/ for the purpose of /fulfilling/ the mitzvah, since we rule that the night is /in fact/ a time when /the mitzvah of donning/ *tefilin* /applies/.

Even if he has a place where /the *tefilin*/ can be safeguarded he is also permitted to wear them, since there are no grounds for fear that he may sleep with them /on him/, as /stated/ below.

(13) And when the time when they /should be donned/ arrives. /One should only make the blessing then,/ although the Sages, of blessed memory, permitted one to don /*tefilin*/ earlier, when /it is still/ night, in circumstances where there are no grounds for fear that he will sleep /with them on him/. For, despite this, /they were not lenient/ with respect to the blessing, /because/ they did not wish to ordain that one may say /the wording/ וְצִוָּנוּ (and commanded us) prior to the /proper/ time /for donning *tefilin*/.

Nevertheless, if one made the blessing at night when he /actually/ donned them, earlier /than the proper time/, he does not need to make the blessing a second time in the morning.

(14) And is departing for the road. /This ruling/ only /applies/ when one will be going on foot or will be riding /on an animal/, but if he will be sitting in a carriage it is forbidden /for him/ to don /*tefilin* before the proper time/, in case he will /come to/ sleep with them /on him/. See the Beyur Halachah.[2]

(15) And ... has set, etc. This first part /of the paragraph/ relates to a weekday, /in circumstances/ when one is afraid to take off /the *tefilin*/ and hold them in his hand, in case they will drop from him /while he is/ on the road. /The Sages/ permitted one /to continue wearing them in such a case, provided/ he puts his hand over them and covers them.

Although it is ruled in Par. 2 that once /the *tefilin*/ are already on one he does not need to take them off /and also does not need to cover them, the circumstances/ are different /in the case discussed/ here. For /when one is in public/, someone who encounters him[3] may erroneously assume that it is permitted to don *tefilin* then. /The ruling/ nearby /, in Par. 2,/ however, relates to a person who is staying at home.

The /time of/ sunset meant here is the end of sunset, which is when the stars appear. /This follows from the fact/ that during *beyn ha-shemashos* it is unnecessary to take off /*tefilin*/ and that this /ruling/ may /even/ be taught /to others to be followed in/ practice. /However,/ this /relates/ entirely to the /binding halachic/ ruling, but it is stated in the name of the *Ari*, of blessed memory, that he was careful to take off /his *tefilin* immediately/ after the sun had set.

2 The author writes there that when one fears they may get lost and wishes to don them for safeguarding, he need not be stringent about this even if he travels in a carriage sitting.
3 I.e., and does not know that he donned them at the proper time.

(יג) * וכשיגיע זמנן ימשמש בהם ויברך דליכא למיחש שמא יישן בהם * כיון שהשכים (יד) ויצא (ה) לדרך: ד * זהיה בא בדרך ותפילין בראשו (טו) ושקעה עליו (ו) חמה או שהיה יושב בבית המדרש ותפילין בראשו (טז) וקדש עליו היום יניח ידו עליהם עד שיגיע לבית ואם יש בית קרוב לחומה שמשתמרים שם חולצם ומניחם שם: ה * חויש מי שאומר שאם התפלל (ז) [ג] תפלת ערבית (יז) מבע"י עד שלא הניח תפילין אין לו להניחם אח"כ:

ז בילה ט"ו לפירוש התוספות ח כתבי מהר"ר ישראל סימן קכ"א

באר היטב

ט"ז: (ה) לדרך. ודוקא הולך ברגליו או רוכב אבל יושב בעגלה אסור להניחן שמא יישן בהם כ"כ לבוש: (ו) חמה. איירי בחול ואע"ג דאמרינן בסמוך דא"ל לחולצן דלילה זמן תפילין שאני הכא דיש לחוש למי שיפגע בו יטעה לומר שמותר להניח אז תפילין אבל בסמוך איירי שיושב בביתו. וכן מ"ש אח"ז קדש עליו היום ר"ל קדושת שבת עליו וצריך לחולצן אבל בחול א"צ היינו מאחר שהוא בבית המדרש וליכא חשש טועין ט"ז והע"ת לא כ"כ ע"ש: (ז) תפלת ערבית. אבל אם הוא לא התפלל אע"פ שהציבור התפללו מותר להניח תפילין מ"א:

שערי תשובה

שקיעת החמה עיין שם: [ג] תפלת ערבית. וכתב בברכ"י בשם דבר משה בירך על התפילין בלילה או שסבור שהוא יום והיה לילה אין צריך לברך כשיגיע זמן הנחת תפילין עיין שם:

משנה ברורה

שלובשם לשם מצוה כיון דקי"ל לילה זמן תפילין הוא ואפילו (יא) היה לו מקום לשמרן ג"כ מותר ללובשן כיון דליכא למיחש לשמא יישן בהם וכדלקמיה: (יג) וכשיגיע זמנן. דאף דהתירו חז"ל להקדים ההנחה בלילה במקום דליכא למיחש לשינה אפ"ה לענין ברכה לא רצו לתקן לומר וציונו קודם הזמן. ומ"מ (יב) אם קידם ובירך בלילה כשהניחם א"צ לברך שנית בבקר: (יד) ויצא לדרך. ודוקא (יג) הולך ברגליו (יד) או רוכב אבל יושב בעגלה אסור להניח שמא יישן בהם ועיין בבה"ל: ד (טו) ושקעה וכו'. רישא זו (טו) איירי בחול ולחולצן ולנושאן בידו הוא מתירא שמא יפלו ממנו בדרך והתירו לו להניח ידו עליהם ולכסותם ואע"ג דבס"ב אמרינן דמכיון שהם מכבר עליו א"צ לחולצן שאני הכא (טז) דמי שיפגע בו פן יטעה לומר שמותר להניח אז תפילין אבל בסמוך איירי שיושב בביתו. והאי ושקעה חמה (יז) פירוש סוף שקיעה דהוא צאת הכוכבים דבבין השמשות א"צ לחולצן ומורין כן למעשה וכ"ז מדינא ובשם האר"י ז"ל כתוב שהיה נזהר לחולצן אחר שקיעת החמה: (טז) וקידש וכו'. ר"ל דנעשה בין השמשות וא"א לו לישא אותם בידו לביתו מפני קדושת שבת ולהשאיר אותם שם אי אפשר דבתי מדרשות שלהם היו בשדה מקום שאין משומר (יח) מפני הגנבים ע"כ התירו לו חכמים לנושאם עליו דרך מלבוש עד ביתו אך צריך לכסותם שלא יראוהו שהוא נושא תפילין עליו בשבת: ה (יז) מבעוד יום. ואפילו עוד היום גדול (יט) קודם שקיעה לפי שכבר עשאו לזמן הזה לילה וזמן שכיבה בק"ש ותפלה של ערבית ואם יניח בו תפילין יחזור ויעשהו יום והרי הן שתי קולות שסותרות זו את זו אך האחרונים (כ) הסכימו להלכה דמחוייב להניחן (כא) ובלי ברכה כל זמן שהוא קודם צאת הכוכבים ואם הוא לא התפלל עדיין אע"פ שהצבור התפללו אין בכך כלום ויניחם בברכה (כב) אם הוא עדיין יום כיון שהוא אינו עושה שתי קולות הסותרות זו את זו (כג) ודוקא אם לא הניחן באותו יום כלל אבל אם כבר הניח תפילין רק שרוצה להניח גם עתה אין ראוי להניחם אם הצבור כבר התפללו ערבית:

ביאור הלכה

הנ"ל אעפ"כ לא יברך אז על התפילין וראיה לדברינו דעיקר ראיית הע"ת והגר"א הוא ממה דאיתא שם בברייתא ומתיירא שמא יאבדו וכו' והרי שם ג"כ פסק הברייתא דאין לברך עד שיגיע הזמן וכמו שפסק הטור ושו"ע כהרא"ש ודלא כרבינו פרץ וכמו שכתב הגר"א: * וכשיגיע זמנן. עיין במ"ב במש"כ ומ"מ אם קידם וכו' הוא מחידושי רע"א שכתב דנוכל לסמוך בזה על דעת הר"פ עי"ש ומשמע מזה דבלא השכים ויצא לדרך צריך לחזור ולברך אם בירך על התפילין בלילה ומדברי הברכי יוסף שהובא בשע"ת משמע דבדיעבד בכל גווני אין צריך לחזור ולברך ולא הביא בברכ"י טעם לזה ואולי שבדיעבד נסמוך על שיטת רש"י ורבינו יונה שס"ל דמאי דאמרינן הלכה ואין מורין כן הוא אפילו לענין להניחם לכתחלה אך בשו"ע ס"ב לא פסק כוותייהו וצ"ע למעשה. ומכל זה תבין דמה דנוהגין איזה אנשים בימות החורף להניח תפילין ולברך עליהם תיכף משעלה עה"ש לא שפיר עבדי: * כיון שהשכים ויצא לדרך. עיין במ"ב ועיין בעט"ז ובפמ"ג במ"ז סק"ג שמצדדים לומר דאף בעגלה נראה להתיר ובארה"ח מסכים להמחמירין ונ"ל דאם הוא מתיירא שמא יאבדם ועושה כדי לשמרם בודאי אין להחמיר אף בישב בעגלה אחרי דבלא"ה דעת הע"ת והגר"א להקל במניחן בשביל השמירה: * היה בא בדרך וכו'. עיין במ"ב בס"ק ט"ו ט"ז וה"ה דהוי מצי המחבר למינקט בחד גוונא היה בא בדרך וקידש עליו היום ג"כ לענין שבת וכדלקמן בסימן רס"ו ס"י אלא דנקט לישנא דגמרא ונוכל לאמר דהגמרא אשמועינן רבותא דאף שהוא עומד בתוך קהל ועדה אפ"ה מועיל מה שהוא מניח ידו עליהם ולא חיישינן פן ירגישו בו שהוא נושא עליו תפילין וגם יוצא בם מבה"מ לחוץ בשבת והא דלא נקט הגמרא והמחבר האי בבא דהיה יושב בבה"מ ג"כ לענין חול תירץ הט"ז דבחול אם יושב בבה"מ א"צ להניח ידו עליהם [כ"ז שהוא בבה"מ]דהכל יודעין שם שלבשן מבעוד יום וליכא איסור והמג"א לא ס"ל האי חילוק כן כתבו האחרונים ונ"ל לתרץ לדידיה בפשיטות דאשמועינן הגמרא רבותא דאף בבא בדרך צריך להניח ידו עליהם פן יפגעו בו אנשים ויחשדוהו שהניח תפילין בלילה ואינו דומה להא דס"ג בהיה רוצה לצאת לדרך דמניחם ולא זכרו הפוסקים כלל דצריך להניח ידו עליהם דשאני התם שהוא קרוב לעלות השחר והוא קרוב מאוד להזמן דכדי שיכיר אך א"כ יולד מזה דין חדש דאם השכים כמה שעות קודם אור הבקר ומניחם דצריך להניח ידו עליהם וצ"ע למעשה. והקרוב אלי דלהכי השמיט הרמב"ם האי ברייתא דהשכים לצאת לדרך שתמהו הפוסקים ע"ז משום האי ברייתא דבילה ט"ו ע"א דקאמרה דצריך להניח ידו עליהם ומשמע ליה דפליגי אהדדי בזה ופסק כהאי ברייתא דבילה משום דאביי דהוא בתרא סבר כוותה וכעין זה כתב ג"כ בארה"ח דהברייתות סותרות אהדדי עי"ש: * ויש מי וכו' מבעוד יום וכו'. עיין במ"ב במש"כ לילה וזמן שכיבה בק"ש וכו' הוא משו"ע הגר"ז ומתורץ בזה קצת קושיא של הא"ר שהרי איסור תפילין בלילה אינו משום לילה רק משום שינה וכבסעיף ג' ובזה קצת ניחא ולפ"ז לאותן האנשים הזהירין לקרות עוד הפעם ק"ש בזמנה ואינן קוראין אז אלא כדי לעמוד בתפלה מתוך ד"ת וכדלקמן בסימן רל"ה ס"א אפשר שישתנה זה הדין ועיין. ועיין עוד במ"ב במש"כ דאם הוא לא התפלל עדיין וכו' אם הוא עדיין יום דאם הוא בין השמשות נ"ל דלא יברך אז דבלא"ה הפמ"ג מפקפק על דברי המ"א בסק"ב במש"כ דזמן הנחת תפילין הוא עד צאת הכוכבים הגם דבודאי מחויב להניחן כיון שלא קיים עדיין מצות תפילין דבד"ת ספיקא לחומרא ושמא הוא עדיין יום וכמו שפסק הפמ"ג בא"א עכ"פ הברכות אינן מעכבות:

שער הציון

(יא) ע"ת ופמ"ג: (יב) חידושי רע"א: (יג) מ"א: (יד) אחרונים: (טו) ט"ז והגר"א לקמן בסימן רס"ו ס"י: (טז) ט"ז: (יז) פמ"ג: (יח) בילה ט"ו: (יט) מפלג מנחה ברכות כ"ז כרבי יהודה עי"ש: (כ) א"ר ופמ"ג: (כא) פמ"ג: (כב) עיין בבה"ל: (כג) פמ"ג:

אסור

with *tefilin* on his head **(16)** and /notices that/ the day has become sanctified, he should put his hand over them until he reaches home. If there is a building near the wall /of the city/ where they will be safeguarded, he should take them off and leave them there.

5. There is an /authority/ who says that if one prayed the Ma'ariv prayer **(17)** when it was still day before he donned *tefilin*, he should not don /*tefilin*/ subsequently.

Mishnah Berurah

(16) And ... has become sanctified, etc. I.e., if it has become *beyn ha-shemashos* /at the inception of Shabbos/ and he cannot carry them home in his hand /now/ because of the sanctity of Shabbos.

/The ruling of the Shulchan Aruch relates to circumstances where/ one cannot leave /the *tefilin*/ there. (For /in the times/ of /the Sages who gave this ruling/ the *Batei Midrashos* were in the fields, in places which were not safeguarded from thieves.) In view of this, the Sages permitted one to have /the *tefilin*/ on him as clothing until /he reaches/ home. However, he must cover them so that /people/ will not see that he has *tefilin* on him on Shabbos.

(17) When it was still day. /This ruling/ even /applies/ when there is still much of the day /left/ before /sun/set.[4]

/The reason is/ because by /reading/ "The Reading of Shema" and /praying/ the Ma'ariv prayer he already acted /as if/ it is now night and a time when one lies down. If he will don *tefilin* /now/ he will be going back /on this/, acting /as if/ it is day. He will thus /act in accordance with/ two leniencies, /based on conceptions/ which are contradictory to one another.

However, as regards the halachic /ruling/, the Acharonim are agreed that as long as it is /still/ before the stars have appeared, he is /in fact/ obliged to don /*tefilin* then, but he should do so/ without /saying/ a blessing.

If /someone who has not yet donned *tefilin*/ has not yet prayed /the Ma'ariv prayer, then/ even if the congregation have /already/ prayed /the Ma'ariv prayer/ this does not matter at all. He may /therefore/ don /*tefilin* and say/ the blessing, if it is still day.[5] This is because /in such a case/ he is not /himself/ acting /in accordance with/ two leniencies /based on conceptions/ which are contradictory to one another. /However,/ once the congregation have already prayed the Ma'ariv /prayer/, one should only /don *tefilin*/ if he has not /yet/ donned /*tefilin*/ that day at all, but if he has already donned *tefilin* /that day/ and merely wishes to don /*tefilin*/ now as well, it is improper /for him/ to do so.

4 Provided he prayed the prayer after *pelag ha-Minchah.* (Sha'ar Ha-Tziyun No. 19)

5 During *beyn ha-shemashos*, he should don *tefilin* but should not make the blessing. (Beyur Halachah)

לא דין תפילין בשבת ויו"ט. ובו ב' סעיפים:

א אבשבת (א) ויו"ט (א) [א] (ב) * אסור להניח תפילין מפני (ג) שהם עצמם אות ואם מניחים בהם (ד) אות אחר (ה) * היה זלזול לאות שלהם: ב בבחוה"מ גם כן (ג) אסור להניח תפילין מהטעם הזה בעצמו שימי חול המועד (ו) גם הם אות: הגה וי"א שח"מ חייב בתפילין (ב"י בשם הרא"ש) וכן נוהגין בכל גלילות אלו (ז) להניחם במועד ולברך עליהם אלא (ח) שאין מברכים עליהם (ג) בקול רם בבהכ"נ כמו שאר ימות השנה:

באר הגולה: א מנחות ל"ו ועירובין צ"ו ב תשובת הרשב"א בשם התוספות והרא"ש ותשובת מהרי"ק ורשב"י במדרש הנעלם בשיר השירים וספר העתים בשם גאון

לב סדר כתיבת תפילין. ובו נ"ב סעיפים:

א אמצות תפילין שיכתוב ארבע פרשיות שהן קדש לי כל בכור *) עד למועדה והיה כי יביאך עד

*) עד למועדה מימים ימימה כצ"ל.

באר הגולה: א מנחות ל"ד

שערי תשובה

[א] אסור. עבה"ט ועיין סימן ש"ח בט"ז שם ובבר"י כאן כתב דהכי נקטינן שלא לטלטל תפילין בשבת ועיין בפר"ח סימן תצ"ו שכתב אני הלכתי למצרים ודעתי היה לחזור לא"י תוב"ב וביו"ט שני בבוקר בביתי בגנעא הנחתי תפילין וקראתי ק"ש כו' ואח"כ הלכתי לבהכ"נ כו' ע"ש ושם יבואר אי"ה:

באר היטב

(א) אסור. היינו אם מניחן לשם מצוה ואז עובר משום בל תוסיף מ"א ועיין ע"ת: (ב) אסור. עיין בכסף משנה שכתב ונחלקו המפרשים בחה"מ יש מהם אומרים דבכלל י"ט הם ואין מניחין בהם תפילין וי"א שמניחין וכן נראה מדברי רבינו שכתב בפ"י משביתות י"ט כותב אדם תפילין לעצמו וכו' ע"ש. ול"ע שהוא ז"ל כתב להיפך שם בפ"י משביתות י"ט וז"ל אין לו מה יאכל כו' נראה שטעמו מפני שהוא סובר שאין מניחין תפילין בח"ה דבכלל יו"ט הוא עכ"ל הרי שכתב בדעת הרמב"ם שאין מניחין תפילין בחוה"מ הפך מ"ש כאן בהלכות תפילין ול"ע יד אהרן. ועיין ע"ת: (ג) בקול רם. וכתב ט"ז תמוה הוא כלפי שמיא מי מחלקינן בין סתר לגלוי ע"כ שפיר להניחם בלא ברכה. וכ"פ בס' תמים דעים סי' מ' שלא יברך עליהם. ובל"ח כתב הטעם שרבים חולקים שלא לברך בחה"מ ואותן שרצו להעמיד על הדין ולברך הנהיגו לברך בחשאי כדי שלא יבואו לידי מחלוקת זכר לדבר בשכמל"ו. וכתב המ"א שלא ילך בהם ברשות הרבים רק יניחם בבהכ"נ [ובספר אליהו רבה חולק עליו דכיון דמניחן בב"ה ברבים מה לי בהליכתן ברה"ר]. כתב בכתבי מהרא"י סי' ק"ג וב"י הביאו סימן כ"ה דאותו המניח תפילין בח"ה בלא ברכה אפ"ה אסור לדבר ולהסיח בין תפילין לתפילין ע"ש. והיינו שיחת חולין אבל קדיש או קדושה מותר לאותן המניחין בחה"מ בלא ברכה. עיין מ"א בסימן כ"ה ס"ק ט"ו[ב] וס"ק י"ח[ג] ודו"ק. והמחבר יד אהרן כתב דאשתמיט להרב מ"א דברי מהרא"י אלו הואיל וכתב דהמניח בחול המועד בלא ברכה רשאי לענות ע"ש ולא דק דחילוק יש בין להסיח שיחת חולין או לענות קדיש וקדושה. ותמיה בעיני האיך עלה על דעתו שאישתמיט מהמחבר מ"א דברי מהרא"י הא המ"א הביאו בס"ק ט"ו[ב] ע"ש ואדרבה ממנו אישתמיט מ"ש מ"א בס"ק ט"ו[ב] וק"ל. וע"ל סימן כ"ה ס"ק י"א:

ביאור הלכה

* אסור להניח. עיין במ"ב והנה מקור הדין עיין לקמן בסימן ש"ח ס"ד בט"ז ומ"א שם. והנה בדה"ח בהלכות מוקצה סתם להחמיר דאין לטלטלם כ"א לצורך גופם או מקומם וכן משמע בברכי יוסף בסימן זה אמנם בח"א משמע דכדי שלא יפלו וה"ה לכדי שלא יגנבו נמי מותר לטלטלם וכן משמע בהפמ"ג בסימן ש"ח בסק"ג במ"ז עי"ש וכל עלם הדין הזה מבואר בסי' ש"ח דתלוי אם אסור הנחת תפילין בשבת ויו"ט שלא לשם מצוה וא"כ לפי מה שנביא בסמוך דהגר"א הוא ג"כ מהמקילין בזה א"כ ממילא הוא ג"כ מהמקילין לענין טלטול וע"כ בודאי יש להקל בשעת הדחק וכמו שכתבתי בפנים:

* היה זלזול. עיין מה שכתבתי במ"ב והוא שהניחן וכו' הוא ממ"א לעיל בסימן כ"ט אך לא נתבאר בדבריו אם יש בו עכ"פ איסור מדרבנן ועיין בב"ח שמשמע מדבריו דאין איסור בהנחתן אפילו מדרבנן וכוונתו במניחן שלא לשם מצוה דאל"כ בלא"ה איכא בל תוסיף ומהגר"א בביאורו בסימן ש"א סוף סק"ז[ד] משמע ג"כ דבאינו מכוין בהנחתם בשבת ויו"ט לשם מצוה אפילו מדרבנן אינו אסור להניחם:

משנה ברורה

א (א) ויו"ט. (א) ויו"ט שני נמי בכלל לדידן בני חו"ל: (ב) אסור להניח. ואפילו בטלטול (ב) י"א ג"כ דאסור אם לא לצורך גופם או מקומם כשאר כלי שמלאכתו לאיסור וי"א דכדי שלא יפלו או שלא יגנבום נמי מותר לטלטלם ממקום למקום ובמקום הדחק יש להקל ועיין בבה"ל: (ג) שהן עצמם אות. בין הקב"ה ובין ישראל שנאמר כי אות היא ביני וגו' ויו"ט (ג) ג"כ מיקרי אות דבפסח מצרים כתיב אות והוקשו כל מועדי ה' בפ' אמור: (ד) אות אחר. דהיינו תפילין דכתיב בהו והיה לך לאות על ידך: (ה) היה זלזול. וגם עובר משום לאו דבל תוסיף והוא שהניחן לשם מצוה (ד) אבל במניחן שלא לשם מצוה אין בו משום בל תוסיף וגם משום זלזול (ה) אין בו אם לא (ו) שמניחן בפרהסיא דאז אסור מדרבנן (ז) ויש מחמירין בכל גווני אם לא שמונחים בבזיון כגון המוצא תפילין בשבת בשדה מותר ללובשם ולהכניסם לעיר דרך מלבוש כמו שיתבאר לקמן בסימן ש"א: ב (ו) גם הם אות. בפסח אכילת מצה ובסוכה ישיבת הסוכה והי"א ס"ל כיון שמותרין בעשיית מלאכה מן התורה ליכא אות: (ז) להניחן[ה] במועד. והלצת התפילין צ"ל בחוה"מ (ח) קודם הלל. ועכשיו נהגו איזה אנשים לסלקן אחר קדושה של תפלת י"ח (ט) ומ"מ צריכין ליזהר לכוין לשמוע חזרת התפלה: (ח) שאין וכו'. פי' (י) משום דיש מניחים ויש שאינם מניחים או אין מברכים יש לברך בחשאי כדי שלא לבוא לידי מחלוקת וכן (יא) לא ילך בהם בר"ה לבהכ"נ (יב) והאחרונים הסכימו לדעת הט"ז דיותר טוב להניחן בלי ברכה כי הברכות אינן מעכבות וספק ברכות להקל ובפרט שהגר"א ז"ל כתב שאין לדעת הי"א עיקר בש"ס ועכ"פ לענין ברכה בודאי יש להחמיר. גם קודם ההנחה יחשוב בדעתו אם אני מחוייב אני מניחן לשם מצוה ואם לאו אין אני מניחן לשם מצוה ובזה יצא ידי כו"ע דאף להסוברים דחוה"מ אינו זמן תפילין אינו עובר על בל תוסיף כיון שאינו מכוין בהנחתם לשם מצוה ודאי וכ"ש שאין לחוש בזה לאיסור זלזול של אות חוה"מ דזה ג"כ אינו אלא במתכוין לשם מצוה כנ"ל. ותפילין דר"ת אין להניחם בחוה"מ [פמ"ג] עוד כתבו האחרונים [והובאו בארה"ח ע"ש] דאין נכון שבבהכ"נ אחת קצתם יניחו תפילין וקצתם לא יניחו משום לא תתגודדו. ומי שאין מניח תפילין בחוה"מ שמתפלל בבה"מ שמניחין תפילין יש לו ג"כ להניחן ובלי ברכה ולצור שנהגו להניח תפילין אין להם לשנות מנהגם:

שער הציון

ופרשת

(א) ארה"ח בשם רשב"א: (ב) עיין בבה"ל: (ג) אחרונים: (ד) מ"א: (ה) מ"א בסימן כ"ט: (ו) ב"ח בסימן זה ופמ"ג בסימן ש"ח במ"ז סק"ג: (ז) ט"ז בסימן ש"ח סק"ג עי"ש: (ח) ט"ז: (ט) פמ"ג: (י) א"ז ומיישב בזה קושית הט"ז: (יא) מ"א: (יב) פמ"ג ומחה"ש ודה"ח וח"א:

הגהות ותיקונים: א) שחוה"מ: ב) י"ד: ג) י"ז: ד) צ"ל סוף סעיף ד': ה) להניחם:

§31: THE LAWS /AS REGARDS THE DONNING/ OF *TEFILIN* ON SHABBOS OR YOM TOV

(Contains Two Paragraphs)

1. On Shabbos (1) or Yom Tov (2) it is forbidden to don *tefilin*. This is because (3) these /days/ are in themselves a sign /so that/ if one would don (4) another sign on them (5) this would entail contempt for their sign.
2. On Chol Ha-Mo'ed it is also forbidden to don *tefilin* for this same reason, as the days of Chol Ha-Mo'ed (6) are also a sign.

Mishnah Berurah

§31

(1) Or Yom Tov. For us, who /reside/ outside the land of /Israel/, the second day of Yom Tov is also classed as /Yom Tov with respect to this ruling/.

(2) It is forbidden to don. There are /authorities/ who say that even to handle /*tefilin* on Shabbos or Yom Tov/ is also forbidden, unless /one handles the *tefilin*/ because he needs /to use the *tefilin*/ themselves /for a permissible use/ or /because he needs to use/ the place /where they are lying/. This conforms with /the ruling for/ other utensils /which are used on weekdays/ for work one is forbidden /to do on Shabbos or Yom Tov/.

Other /authorities/ say that it is also permitted to handle /*tefilin* to move them/ from place to place, in order that they should be prevented from falling or prevented from being stolen. Where there is a pressing /need/ one may be lenient /, in accordance with their view/. See the Beyur Halachah.

(3) These /days/ are in themselves a sign. /I.e., of the connection/ between the Holy One, Blessed be He, and Israel.

/This is/ because /as regards Shabbos/ it is stated,[1] "For it is a sign between Me, etc." Yom Tov is also classed as a sign, as it is written[2] in connection with the Pesach/-offering/ of Egypt /that it should be/ a sign and /, consequently,/ all the Yamim Tovim of the Lord /are classed as signs, as they/ are compared /to one another/ in the portion *Emor*.[3]

(4) Another sign. I.e., *tefilin*, with respect to which it is written,[4] "And it will be for you a sign on your arm".

(5) This would entail contempt. This would also /involve/ a transgression of the negative injunction, "You should not add".[5]

/However,/ this /ruling only applies/ if one dons /the *tefilin*/ for the sake of /fulfillment of/ the mitzvah, but if one dons them for other than the purpose of /fulfilling/ the mitzvah, /a transgression/ of /the prohibition/, "You should not add", is not involved. In such a case there is also no /question/ of contempt /for the sign of Shabbos or Yom Tov/. /Then the donning is permitted,/ unless one dons them publicly, in which case it is forbidden according to Rabbinical law.

/However,/ there are /authorities/ who are stringent /and forbid one to don *tefilin* on Shabbos or Yom Tov/ in all cases, unless /the *tefilin*/ are lying in disrespect. For example, when *tefilin* are found /lying/ in a field on Shabbos, they permit one to put them on and take them into the city /worn/ as clothing, as explained below in Sec. 301.

(6) Are also a sign. /According to this opinion,/ on /Chol Ha-Mo'ed of/ Pesach the eating of matzah /is a sign/ and on /Chol Ha-Mo'ed of/ Sukkos the living in a *sukah* /is a sign/.

1 *Shemos* 31:13.
2 *Shemos* 12:13.
3 *Va-Yikra* 23:2.
4 *Shemos* 13:9.
5 *Devarim* 4:2 and 13:1.

באר הגולה

א מנחות ל"ו ועירובין צ"ו
ב תשובת הרשב"א בשם התוספות והרא"ש ותשובת מהרי"ק ורשב"י במדרש הנעלם בשיר השירים וספר העתים בשם גאון

לא דין תפילין בשבת ויו"ט. ובו ב' סעיפים:

א אבשבת (א) ויו"ט (א) [א] (ב) * אסור להניח תפילין מפני (ג) שהם עצמם אות ואם מניחים בהם (ד) אות אחר (ה) * היה זלזול לאות שלהם: ב בבחוה"מ גם כן (ג) אסור להניח תפילין מהטעם הזה בעצמו שימי חול המועד (ו) גם הם אות: **הגה וי"א שח"ה[א] חייב בתפילין (ב"י בשם הרא"ש) וכן נוהגין בכל גלילות אלו (ז) להניחם במועד ולברך עליהם אלא (ח) שאין מברכים עליהם (ג) בקול רם בבהכנ"ס כמו שאר ימות השנה:**

לב סדר כתיבת תפילין. ובו נ"ב סעיפים:

א מנחות ל"ד

א אמצות תפילין שיכתוב ארבע פרשיות שהן קדש לי כל בכור *) עד למועדה והיה כי יביאך עד

*) עד למועדה מימים ימימה כצ"ל.

שערי תשובה

[א] אסור. עבה"ט ועיין סימן ש"ח בט"ז שם ובבר"י כאן כתב דהכי נקטינן שלא לטלטל תפילין בשבת ועיין בפר"ח סימן תצ"ו שכתב אני הלכתי למצרים ודעתי היה לחזור לא"י תוב"ב וביו"ט שני בבוקר בביתי בלנעה הנחתי תפילין וקראתי ק"ש כו' ואח"כ הלכתי לבהכנ"ס כו' ע"ש ושם יבואר אי"ה:

באר היטב

(א) אסור. היינו אם מניחן לשם מצוה ואז עובר משום בל תוסיף מ"א ועיין ע"ת: (ב) אסור. עיין בכסף משנה שכתב ונחלקו המפרשים בחה"מ יש מהם אומרים דבכלל י"ט הם ואין מניחין בהם תפילין וי"א שמניחין וכן נראה מדברי רבינו שכתב בפ"י משביתות י"ט כותב אדם תפילין לעצמו וכו' ע"ש. ול"ע שהוא ז"ל כתב להיפך שם בפ"י משביתות י"ט וז"ל אין לו מה יאכל נראה שטעמו מפני שהוא סובר שאין מניחין תפילין בח"ה דבכלל יו"ט הוא עכ"ל הרי שכתב בדעת הרמב"ם שאין מניחין תפילין בחוה"מ הפך מ"ש כאן בהלכות תפילין ול"ע יד אהרן. ועיין ע"ת: (ג) בקול רם. וכתב ט"ז תמוה הוא כלפי שמיא מי מחלקינן בין סתר לגלוי ע"כ שפיר להניחם בלא ברכה. וכ"פ בס' תמים דעים סי' מ' שלא יברך עליהם. ובל"ח כתב הטעם שרבים חולקים שלא לברך בחה"מ ואותן שראו להעמיד על הדין ולברך הנהיגו לברך בחשאי כדי שלא יבואו לידי מחלוקת זכר לדבר בשכמל"ו. וכתב המ"א שלא ילך בהם ברשות הרבים רק יניחם בבהכ"נ [ובספר אליהו רבה חולק עליו דכיון דמניחן בב"ה ברבים מה לי בהליכתן ברה"ר]. כתב בכתבי מהרא"י סי' ק"ג וב"י הביאו סימן כ"ה דאותו המניח תפילין בח"ה בלא ברכה אפ"ה אסור לדבר ולהסיח בין תפילין לתפילין ע"ש. והיינו שיחת חולין אבל קדיש או קדושה מותר לאותן המניחין בחה"מ בלא ברכה. עיין מ"א בסימן כ"ה ס"ק ט"ו[ב] וס"ק י"ח[ג] ודו"ק. והמחבר יד אהרן כתב דאשתמיט להרב מ"א דברי מהרא"י אלו הואיל וכתב דהמניח בחול המועד בלא ברכה רשאי לענות ע"ש ולא דק דחילוק יש בין להסיח שיחת חולין או לענות קדיש וקדושה. ותמיה בעיני האיך עלה על דעתו שאשתמיט מהמחבר מ"א דברי מהרא"י הא המ"א הביאו בס"ק ט"ו[ב] ע"ש ואדרבה ממנו אשתמיט מ"ש מ"א בס"ק ט"ו[ב] וק"ל. וע"ל סימן כ"ה ס"ק י"א:

ביאור הלכה

* אסור להניח. עיין במ"ב והנה מקור הדין עיין לקמן בסימן ש"ח ס"ד בט"ז ומ"א שם. והנה בדה"ח בהלכות מוקצה סתם להחמיר דאין לטלטלם כ"א לצורך גופם או מקומם וכן משמע בברכי יוסף בסימן זה אמנם בח"א משמע דכדי שלא יפלו וה"ה לכדי שלא יגנבו נמי מותר לטלטלם וכן משמע בהפמ"ג בסימן ש"ח בסק"ג במ"ז עי"ש וכל עלם הדין הזה מבואר בסי' ש"ח דתלוי אם אסור הנחת תפילין בשבת ויו"ט שלא לשם מצוה וא"כ לפי מה שנביא בסמוך דהגר"א הוא ג"כ מהמקילין בזה א"כ ממילא הוא ג"כ מהמקילין לענין טלטול וע"כ בודאי יש להקל בשעת הדחק וכמו שכתבתי בפנים:
* היה זלזול. עיין מה שכתבתי במ"ב והוא שהניחן וכו' הוא ממ"א לעיל בסימן כ"ט אך לא נתבאר בדבריו אם יש בו עכ"פ איסור מדרבנן ועיין בב"ח שמשמע מדבריו דאין איסור בהנחתן אפילו מדרבנן וכוונתו במניחן שלא לשם מצוה דאל"כ בלא"ה איכא בל תוסיף ומהגר"א בביאורו בסימן ש"א סוף סק"ז[ד] משמע ג"כ דבאינו מכוין בהנחתם בשבת ויו"ט לשם מצוה אפילו מדרבנן אינו אסור להניחם:

משנה ברורה

א (א) ויו"ט. (א) ויו"ט שני נמי בכלל לדידן בני חו"ל: (ב) אסור להניח. ואפילו בטלטול (ב) י"א ג"כ דאסור אם לא לצורך גופם או מקומם כשאר כלי שמלאכתו לאיסור וי"א דכדי שלא יפלו או שלא יגנבום נמי מותר לטלטלם ממקום למקום ובמקום הדחק יש להקל ועיין בבה"ל: (ג) שהן עצמם אות. בין הקב"ה ובין ישראל שנאמר כי אות היא ביני וגו' ויו"ט (ג) ג"כ מיקרי אות דבפסח מצריכ כתיב אות והוקשו כל מועדי ה' בפ' אמור: (ד) אות אחר. דהיינו תפילין דכתיב בהו והיה לך לאות על ידך: (ה) היה זלזול. וגם עובר משום לאו דבל תוסיף והוא שהניחן לשם מצוה (ד) אבל במניחן שלא לשם מצוה אין בו משום בל תוסיף וגם משום זלזול (ה) אין בו אם לא (ו) שמניחן בפרהסיא דאז אסור מדרבנן (ז) ויש מחמירין בכל גווני אם לא שמונחים בבזיון כגון המוצא תפילין בשבת בשדה מותר ללובשם ולהכניסם לעיר דרך מלבוש כמו שיתבאר לקמן בסימן ש"א:ב (ו) גם הם אות. נפסק אכילת מצה ובסוכה ישיבת הסוכה והי"א ס"ל כיון שמותרין בעשיית מלאכה מן התורה ליכא אות: (ז) להניחן[ה] במועד. ותלית התפילין צ"ל בחוה"מ (ח) קודם הלל. ועכשיו נהגו איזה אנשים לסלקן אחר קדושה של תפילת י"ח (ט) ומ"מ צריכין ליזהר לכוין לשמוע חזרת התפלה: (ח) שאין וכו'. פי' (י) משום דיש מניחים ויש שאינם מניחים או אין מברכים יש לברך בחשאי כדי שלא לבוא לידי מחלוקת וכן (יא) לא ילך בהם בר"ה לבהכ"נ (יב) והאחרונים הסכימו לדעת הט"ז דיותר טוב להניחן בלי ברכה כי הברכות אינן מעכבות וספק ברכות להקל ובפרט שהגר"א ז"ל כתב שאין לדעת הי"א עיקר בש"ס ועכ"פ לענין ברכה בודאי יש להחמיר. גם קודם ההנחה יחשוב בדעתו אם אני מחוייב אני מניחן לשם מצוה ואם לאו אין אני מניחן לשם מצוה ובזה יצא ידי כ"ע דאף להסוברים דחוה"מ אינו זמן תפילין אינו עובר על בל תוסיף כיון שאינו מכוין בהנחתם לשם מצוה ודאי וכ"ש שאין לחוש בזה לאיסור זלזול של אות חוה"מ דזה ג"כ אינו אלא במתכוין לשם מצוה כנ"ל. ותפילין דר"ת אין להניחם בחוה"מ [פמ"ג] עוד כתבו האחרונים [והובאו בארה"ח ע"ש] דאין נכון שבבהכ"נ אחת קצתם יניחו תפילין וקצתם לא יניחו משום לא תתגודדו. ומי שאין מניח תפילין בחוה"מ שמתפלל בבה"מ שמניחין תפילין יש לו ג"כ להניחן ובלי ברכה ולבור שנהגו להניח תפילין אין להם לשנות מנהגם:

ופרשת

שער הציון

(א) ארה"ח בשם רשב"א: (ב) עיין בבה"ל: (ג) אחרונים: (ד) מ"א: (ה) מ"א בסימן כ"ט: (ו) ב"ח בסימן זה ופמ"ג בסימן ש"א במ"ז סק"ג: (ז) ט"ז בסימן ש"א סק"ג עי"ש: (ח) ט"ז: (ט) פמ"ג: (י) א"ז ומיישב בזה קושית הט"ז: (יא) מ"א: (יב) פמ"ג ומחה"ש ודה"ח וח"א:

הגהות ותיקונים: א) שחוה"מ: ב) י"ד: ג) י"ז: ד) צ"ל סוף סעיף ז': ה) להניחם:

Gloss: There are /authorities/ who say that on Chol Ha-Mo'ed one is obliged /to don/ tefilin. *(...) It is in fact the practice in all these regions* **(7)** *to don /*tefilin*/ on /Chol/ Ha-Mo'ed and make blessings over them. However, the blessings over them* **(8)** *are not made aloud in the Synagogue, as /they are/ on other days of the year.*

Mishnah Berurah

The other /authorities, quoted by the *Rema,*/ are of the opinion that since one is permitted to do /the forbidden/ labors on these days according to Torah law, there is no sign /on them of the connection between the Holy One, Blessed be He, and Israel/.

(7) To don */tefilin/* on /Chol/ Ha-Mo'ed. On Chol Ha-Mo'ed, the *tefilin* must be /taken off/ before /the reading of/ *Haleyl.*

At present, it has become the practice of some people to remove /the *tefilin*/ after the *kedushah* of the eighteen/-blessing/ prayer. /Those who do so/ must at any rate take care that they apply /themselves/ to hearing the repetition of the /eighteen-blessing/ prayer /by the community prayer/.

(8) Are not, etc. The explanation /of this practice is as follows/. There are /people/ who don /*tefilin* on Chol Ha-Mo'ed/ and /people/ who do not don /*tefilin* then/ or /don them, but/ do not make a blessing /over the donning/. In view /of this/, one should say the blessing covertly, so that it should not cause contention.

One should, likewise, not go about with /the *tefilin* on him/ in a public area, /on his way/ to the Synagogue.

The Acharonim agree with the view of the *Taz*, that it is preferable to don /*tefilin* on Chol Ha-Mo'ed/ without /making/ a blessing /over them/. This is because /making/ the blessings is not essential /for the fulfillment of one's obligation/ and where one is in doubt as to /whether or not he is required to say/ a blessing, he should /rather/ be lenient /and refrain from doing so/. It is especially /desirable not to make the blessing, in view of what/ the *Gra*, of blessed memory, writes, that the opinion of these /authorities, requiring one to don *tefilin* on Chol Ha-Mo'ed,/ has no basis in the Talmud. At any rate, in so far as /making/ the blessing is concerned, one should definitely be stringent /and refrain from doing so/.

In addition, before one dons /the *tefilin*/ he should think in his mind: "If I am obliged /to don *tefilin*/ I am donning them for the sake of /fulfilling/ the mitzvah. If not, I am not donning them for the sake of a mitzvah". If /one acts in this way/ he will satisfy all /the

לא דין תפילין בשבת ויו"ט. ובו ב' סעיפים:

א אבשבת (א) ויו"ט (א) [א] (ב) * אסור להניח תפילין מפני (ג) שהם עצמם אות ואם מניחים בהם (ד) אות אחר (ה) * היה זלזול לאות שלהם: ב בבחוה"מ גם כן (ג) אסור להניח תפילין מהטעם הזה בעצמו שימי חול המועד (ו) גם הם אות: הגה וי"א שח"ס מייב בתפילין (כ"י בשם הרא"ש) וכן נוהגין בכל גלילות אלו (ז) להניחם במועד ולברך עליהם אלא (ח) שאין מברכים עליהם (ג) בקול רם בבהכנ"ס כמו שאר ימות השנה:

לב סדר כתיבת תפילין. ובו נ"ב סעיפים:

א אמצות תפילין שיכתוב ארבע פרשיות שהן קדש לי כל בכור *) עד למועדה והיה כי יביאך עד *) עד למועדה מימים ימימה כצ"ל.

באר הגולה

א מנחות ל"ו ועירובין ל"ו
ב תשובת הרשב"א בשם התוספות והראב"ד ותשובת מהרי"ק ורשב"י במדרש הנעלם בשיר השירים וספר העתים בשם גאון

א מנחות ל"ד

שערי תשובה

[א] אסור. עבה"ט ועיין סימן ש"א בט"ז שם ובבר"י כאן כתב דהכי נקטינן שלא לטלטל תפילין בשבת ועיין בפר"ח סימן תל"ו שכתב אני הלכתי למצרים ודעתי היה לחזור לא"י תוב"ב וביו"ט שני בבוקר בביתי בנגעא הנחתי תפילין וקראתי ק"ש כו' ואח"כ הלכתי לבהכנ"ס כו' ע"ש ושם יבואר אי"ה:

באר היטב

(א) אסור. היינו אם מניחן לשם מצוה ואז עובר משום בל תוסיף מ"א ועיין ע"ת: (ב) אסור. עיין בכסף משנה שכתב ונחלקו המפרשים בחה"מ יש מהם אומרים דבכלל י"ט הם ואין מניחין בהם תפילין וי"א שמניחין וכן נראה מדברי רבינו שכתב בפ"י משביתות י"ט כותב אדם תפילין לעצמו וכו' ע"ש. ול"ע שהוא ז"ל כתב להיפך שם בפ"י משביתות י"ט וז"ל אין לו מה יאכל נראה שטעמו מפני שהוא סובר שאין מניחין תפילין בח"ה דבכלל יו"ט הוא עכ"ל הרי שכתב בדעת הרמב"ס שאין מניחין תפילין בחוה"מ הפך מ"ש כאן בהלכות תפילין ול"ע יד אהרן. ועיין ע"ת: (ג) בקול רם. וכתב ט"ז תמוה הוא כלפי שמיא מי מחלקינן בין סתר לגלוי ע"כ שפיר להניחם בלא ברכה. וכ"פ בס' תמים דעים סי' מ' שלא יברך עליהם. ובל"ח כתב הטעם שרבים חולקים שלא לברך בחה"מ ואותן שראו להעמיד על הדין ולברך הנהיגו לברך בחשאי כדי שלא יבואו לידי מחלוקת זכר לדבר בשכמל"ו. וכתב המ"א שלא ילך בהם ברשות הרבים רק יניחם בבהכ"נ [ובספר אליהו רבה חולק עליו דכיון דמניחן בב"ה ברבים מה לי בהליכתן ברה"ר]. כתב בכתבי מהרא"י סי' ק"ג וב"י הביאו סימן כ"ה דאותו המניח תפילין בח"ה בלא ברכה אפ"ה אסור לדבר ולהשיח בין תפילין לתפילין ע"ש. והיינו שיחת חולין אבל קדיש או קדושה מותר לאותן המניחין בחה"מ בלא ברכה. עיין מ"א בסימן כ"ה ס"ק ט"ו[ב] וס"ק י"ח[ג] ודו"ק. והמחבר יד אהרן כתב דלאשתמיט להרב מ"א דברי מהרא"י אלו הואיל וכתב דהמניח בחול המועד בלא ברכה רשאי לענות ע"ש ולא דק דחילוק יש בין להשיח שיחת חולין או לענות קדיש וקדושה. ותמיה בעיני האיך עלה על דעתו שאישתמיט מהמחבר מ"א דברי מהרא"י הא המ"א הביאו בס"ק ט"ו[ב] ע"ש ואדרבה ממנו אישתמיט מ"ש מ"א בס"ק ט"ו[ב] וק"ל. וע"ל סימן כ"ה ס"ק י"א:

ביאור הלכה

* אסור להניח. עיין במ"ב והנה מקור הדין עיין לקמן בסימן ש"ח ס"ד בט"ז ומ"א שם. והנה בדה"ח בהלכות מוקצה סתם להחמיר דאין לטלטלם כ"א לצורך גופם או מקומם וכן משמע בברכי יוסף בסימן זה אמנם בח"א משמע דכדי שלא יפלו וה"ה לכדי שלא יגנבו נמי מותר לטלטלם וכן משמע בהפמ"ג בסימן ש"ח בסק"ג במ"ז עי"ש וכל עקר הדין הזה מבואר בסי' ש"ח דתלוי אם אסור הנחת תפילין בשבת ויו"ט שלא לשם מצוה וא"כ לפי מה שנביא בסמוך דהגר"א הוא ג"כ מהמקילין בזה א"כ ממילא הוא ג"כ מהמקילין לענין טלטול וע"כ בודאי יש להקל בשעת הדחק וכמו שכתבתי בפנים: * היה זלזול. עיין מה שכתבתי במ"ב והוא שהניחן וכו' הוא ממ"א לעיל בסימן כ"ט אך לא נתבאר בדבריו אם יש בו עכ"פ איסור מדרבנן ועיין בב"ח שמשמע מדבריו דאין איסור בהנחתן אפילו מדרבנן וכוונתו במניחן שלא לשם מצוה דאל"כ בלא"ה איכא בל תוסיף ומהגר"א בביאורו בסימן ש"א סוף סק"ז[ד] משמע ג"כ דאינו מכוין בהנחתם בשבת ויו"ט לשם מצוה אפילו מדרבנן אינו אסור להניחם:

משנה ברורה

א (א) ויו"ט. (א) ויו"ט שני נמי בכלל לדידן בני חו"ל: (ב) אסור להניח. ואפילו בטלטול (ג) י"א ג"כ דאסור אם לא לצורך גופם או מקומם כשאר כלי שמלאכתו לאיסור וי"א דכדי שלא יפלו או שלא יגנבום נמי מותר לטלטלם ממקום למקום ובמקום הדחק יש להקל ועיין בבה"ל: (ג) שהן עצמם אות. בין הקב"ה ובין ישראל שנאמר כי אות היא ביני וגו' ויו"ט (ג) ג"כ מיקרי אות דבפסח מצרים כתיב אות והוקשו כל מועדי ה' בפ' אמור: (ד) אות אחר. דהיינו תפילין דכתיב בהו והיה לך לאות על ידך: (ה) היה זלזול. וגם עובר משום לאו דבל תוסיף והוא שהניחן לשם מצוה (ד) אבל במניחן שלא לשם מצוה אין בו משום בל תוסיף וגם משום זלזול (ה) אין בו אם לא (ו) שמניחן בפרהסיא דאז אסור מדרבנן (ז) ויש מחמירין בכל גווני אם לא שמונחים בבזיון כגון המוצא תפילין בשבת בשדה מותר ללובשם ולהכניסם לעיר דרך מלבוש כמו שיתבאר לקמן בסימן ש"א: ב (ו) גם הם אות. בפסח אכילת מצה ובסוכה ישיבת הסוכה והי"א ס"ל כיון שמותרין בעשיית מלאכה מן התורה ליכא אות: (ז) להניחן[ה] במועד. ותלילת התפילין צ"ל בחוה"מ (ח) קודם הלל. ועכשיו נהגו איזה אנשים לסלקן אחר קדושה של תפילת י"ח (ט) ומ"מ צריכין ליזהר לכוין לשמוע חזרת התפלה: (ח) שאין וכו'. פי' (י) משום דיש מניחים ויש שאינם מניחים או אין מברכים יש לברך בחשאי כדי שלא לבוא לידי מחלוקת וכן (יא) לא ילך בהם בר"ה לבהכ"נ (יב) והאחרונים הסכימו לדעת הט"ז דיותר טוב להניחן בלי ברכה כי הברכות אינן מעכבות וספק ברכות להקל ובפרט שהגר"א ז"ל כתב שאין לדעת הי"א עיקר בש"ס ועכ"פ לענין ברכה בודאי יש להחמיר. גם קודם ההנחה יחשוב בדעתו אם אני מחויב אני מניחן לשם מצוה ואם לאו אין אני מניחן לשם מצוה ובזה יצא ידי כו"ע דאף להסוברים דחוה"מ אינו זמן תפילין אינו עובר על בל תוסיף כיון שאינו מכוין בהנחתם לשם מצוה ודאי וכ"ש שאין לחוש בזה לאיסור זלזול של אות חוה"מ דזה ג"כ אינו אלא במתכוין לשם מצוה כנ"ל. ותפילין דר"ת אין להניחם בחוה"מ [פמ"ג] עוד כתבו האחרונים [והובאו בארה"ח ע"ש] דאין נכון שבהכ"נ אחת קצתם יניחו תפילין וקצתם לא יניחו משום לא תתגודדו. ומי שאין מניח תפילין בחוה"מ שמתפלל בבה"מ שמניחין תפילין יש לו ג"כ להניחן ובלי ברכה וצבור שנהגו להניח תפילין אין להם לשנות מנהגם:

שער הציון

ופרשת

(א) ארה"ח בשם רשב"א: (ב) עיין בבה"ל: (ג) אחרונים: (ד) מ"א: (ה) מ"א בסימן כ"ט: (ו) ב"ח בסימן זה ופמ"ג בסימן ש"ח במ"ז סק"ג: (ז) ט"ז בסימן ש"ח סק"ג עי"ש: (ח) ט"ז: (ט) פמ"ג: (י) א"ז ומיישב בזה קושית הט"ז: (יא) מ"א: (יב) פמ"ג ומחה"ש ודה"ח וש"א:

הגהות ותיקונים: א) שחוה"מ: ב) י"ד: ג) י"ז: ד) צ"ל סוף סעיף ז': ה) להניחם:

§32: THE PROCEDURE FOR THE WRITING OF THE *TEFILIN* /PASSAGES/

(Contains Fifty Two Paragraphs)

1. The mitzvah of *tefilin* /requires/ one to write four /Torah/ passages. These /passages/ are *Kadesh Li Chal Bechor*,[1*] until /the words/ למועדה מימים ימימה; *Ve-Hayah Ki Yevi'acha*,[2*] until /the words/ כי בחזק יד הוציאנו ד'

Mishnah Berurah

opinions/. /This is/ because even according to those /authorities/ who are of the opinion that Chol Ha-Mo'ed is not a time when /one is obliged to don/ *tefilin*, one will not transgress /the prohibition of/, "You should not add"[5] /, in such a case/, since he does not have in mind when he dons /the *tefilin* that he is doing so/ for the sake of a definite /fulfillment of/ a mitzvah. There are certainly no grounds for concern that /one is transgressing/ a prohibition against being contemptuous of the sign of Chol Ha-Mo'ed when /one acts/ in this way, as such /a prohibition can/ also only /apply/ when one has in mind /to don them/ for the sake /of fulfillment/ of a mitzvah, as /explained/ above.

On Chol Ha-Mo'ed, one should not don the *tefilin* /which accord with the view/ of Rabbeinu Tam. [*P.Mg.*]

The Acharonim write further [and this is quoted by the *Ar.Hach.*; see there] that it is improper if in the same Synagogue some /people do/ don *tefilin* and some /people/ do not don /*tefilin*/. This is because of /the prohibition/, "You should not separate into factions".[6] If someone who /is accustomed/ not to don *tefilin* on Chol Ha-Mo'ed prays in a *Beys Ha-Midrash*[7] (Torah study hall) where /the congregation do/ don *tefilin*, he should also don /*tefilin*/, but without /making/ a blessing /over them/.

Where it is the practice of a congregation to don *tefilin* /on Chol Ha-Mo'ed/, they should not alter their practice.

1* *Shemos* 13:1-10.
2* *Shemos* 13:11-16.

6 *Devarim* 14:1, as interpreted by the Sages, based on a special understanding of the word used.
7 It is common for people to pray in a *Beys Ha-Midrash*.

כי בחוזק יד הוציאנו ה׳ ממצרים (ה) [ה] (א) ופרשת שמע עד ובשעריך ופ׳ והיה אם שמוע עד ב שם
על הארץ: הגה * וצריך (ב) לכתבם (ב) [ב] (ג) * כסדר הזה לכתוב תחלה הקודמת בתורה * ואם שינה
(ד) פסול ולכתחלה יכתוב (ג) [ג] של יד (ה) קודם של ראש: ב ²של ראש יכתוב כל אחת בקלף
לבדה ושל יד כותבן כולם (ו) בקלף (ד) אחד:

באר היטב

(ה) ופרשת שמע. וצריך לכתוב ד׳ דאחד גדולה כמו ד׳ דלתי״ן קטנים כתבי האר״י מ״א: (ב) בסדר[א] הזה. תפילין שנכתבו כסדרן ובאורך הזמן נפסלו שתי פרשיות ראשונות ויש לסופר עוד שתי פרשיות כאותן שנפסלו שהן כשרות מותר לצרפן אל שתי הפרשיות אחרונות שנשארו בכשרותם תשובת עבודת הגרשוני סי׳ ס׳ עיין בכנה״ג. ובתשובת דבר שמואל סי׳ ש״ב: (ג) של יד קודם של ראש. ובעטרת זקנים כתב ול״נ שיכתוב של ראש תחלה וכ״כ האר״י ז״ל בספר הכוונות שיכתוב הש״ל ראש ויתקנו לגמרי וישחירו ואח״כ יכתוב הש״ל יד. ויזהר לכתוב כל הד׳ פרשיות של ראש ויד רצופים ולא יפסיק ביניהם בשום דיבור כלל ע״ש: (ד) א׳. דכתיב והיה לך לאות על ידך דמשמע אות א׳ כלומר בית אחד:

שערי תשובה

[ה] ופרשת שמע. עבה״ט ובענין תמונת האותיות והתגין המבואר שם ראוי לסופרים יראי ה׳ שילמדו אותם איש מפי איש דהיינו שיבחור לעצמו סופר מומחה ובקי שילמדנו מפה לאוזן וגם יראהו באצבע כזה ראה וקדש לא כאלו שסומכים עצמם לכתוב בכוונות קדושות ולא באו בסוד ה׳ רק מה שרואין בספר מלת שמורים וכדומה מספרים שנתחברו בענין זה והם מדמין בעצמם שמוציאין הדבר מתוקן ותעו מדרך השכל כי שכלם קטן מהכיל עומק הדברים. ומי שלא קיבל הענינים על בוריים מוטב שלא יכנים עצמו כלל לזה ויכתוב בלא כוונות. ומ״מ יכול לדקדק לעשות בתמונות האותיות שכתבו סופרים מפורסמים אנשי השם ואנשי מעשה וכמ״ש מהר״ס זכותא ובברכי יוסף ס״ס כ״ה שיש לדקדק במעשה המצות שיהיו כסדרם וכמשפטם אף שאין אתנו יודע רמזיהם וסודותיהם כי המצוה פועלת בסגולה ועושה רושם למעלה אף שנעשית בלתי הכוונה הפרטית רק שצריך לכוין הכוונה הכללית שיכוין שיעשה המעשה הזה עפ״י מצות אלהיו ע״ש שמ״כ בשם זקינו בעל חסד לאברהם זללה״ה בהגהותיו כת״י כנ״ל. ועיין לקמן ס״ק ל״ד: [ב] בסדר[א] הזה. עבה״ט ומ״ש בשם עה״ג ר״ל שהיו לו שני פרשיות שידוע לו שכתבם קודם אלו האחרונים שנשתיירו רק דס״ד כיון שלא נכתבו להצטרף לאלו יהיו פסולין לצרפם קא משמע לן דלא איכפת לן בזה ואפילו ע״א נאמן לומר שידוע שאלו נכתבו קודם אבל אם הוא מסופק אם נכתבו קודם או אח״כ לא תהא כזאת בישראל לצרפן יחד ח״ו עיין שם ובא״ר. ומ״ש בה״ט ועיין דבר שמואל סימן ש״ב הנה בלקה״ק כתב שבד״ש מחמיר בזה וליתא דהדב״ש שם מיירי במולא פרשה מהראשונות פסולה וכתב אחרת תחתיה פסול וגם לדעת עה״ג כן הוא ומחמיר אפילו בספיקו וכמ״ש ומח״ב כתב שהב״י בסימן ל״ג הביא הגהות סמ״ק דבש״ר שנכתבו בד׳ קלפים אין קפידא בקדימה ואין הלכה כן. ועיין בשו״ת הרשב״ץ שרוצה להחזיק בדברי הגהות סמ״ק וסוגיין דעלמא שאין לחלק בין של ראש לשל יד ולכן סופר שכתב כמה פרשיות לתש״ר בב״א ונזהר לכותבן על הסדר ואחר כך נתערבו בענין שאפשר שיקח פרשה ראשונה שנכתבה מאוחר לג׳ מוקדמים טעונין גניזה ואם כתב פרשיות של ראש ונתקלקלה האחרונה יכתוב אחרת תחתיה משא״כ אם נתקלקלה פרשה מהקודמות שצריך לכותבה שנית עם כל הפ׳ שכתב אחריו כ״כ האחרונים עיין שם: [ג] של יד. עבה״ט מ״ש בשם ספר הכוונות וז״ל וגם צריך ליזהר כל מה שיכול לכתוב כל ד״פ ש״ר או ש״י רצופים ולא יפסיק בינתיים בשום דיבור כלל ועיקר ומכ״ש באמצעם ואם הוא זקן או חולה ואינו יכול לכתוב כל הד״פ ביחד יכתוב שלשה פרשיות ראשונות ואחר כך יכתוב הד׳ ואם גם זה קשה עליו לכתוב יכתוב ב״פ הראשונות רצופים עכ״פ ואח״כ יכתוב ב״פ אחרות ביחד אבל בין פרשה ראשונה לשניה לא יפסיק בשום ענין והנה אם כתב ב״פ הראשונות והפסיק קודם שיתחיל לכתוב פרשה שמע יעביר הקולמוס על תיבת וידבר של קדש ועל תיבת והיה של פ״ב ואחר כך יכתוב מפרשה שמע ואילך ועל ידי זה יש קצת חיבור. ואם כבר כתב בתחלה כל השלשה פרשיות והפסיק אז יעביר הקולמוס על תיבת וידבר של פרשה ראשונה ועל תיבת והיה של פרשה שניה ועל תיבת שמע של פרשה שלישית ואחר כך והיה אם שמוע ועי״ז יש קצת חיבור. גם קודם שיתחיל לכתוב יתפלל ויאמר יהר״מ ה׳ או״א שתשרה שכינתך במעשה ידי ותצליחני בכתבי זאת שאני כותב תפילין הללו לשם קדושת מצות תפילין שצונו ה׳ אלהינו ותצילנו מטעות הכתיבה ומטעות הכוונה אמן כן יהי רצון עכ״ל פע״ח הנקרא בפוסקים ספר הכוונות ומהנכון

משנה ברורה

א (א) ופרשת שמע. וצריך לכתוב ד׳ דאחד כל כך גדולה כמו ד׳ דלתי״ן קטנים [מ״א] (א) ואפשר שאין משערין באותו כתב רק כל שיש בו[ב] דלתי״ן קטנים מאד סגי ומשום הכי נוהגין לכתוב רק גדולה משאר דלתי״ן שבאותו כתב: (ב) לכתבם. כל הפרשיות (ב) בין מהש״י ובין מהש״ר: (ג) בסדר[א] הזה. דכתיב והיו הדברים וגו׳ בהוייתן יהו. וכ״ש שצריך ליזהר מטעם זה שיהיה כל פרשה ופרשה גופא נכתבת כסדרה שלא יחסר בה אפילו אות אחת כי לא יהיה לו תקנה אח״כ להשלימה וכדלקמן בסעיף כ״ג: (ד) פסול. היינו התפילין שנעשו מאותן הפרשיות אבל הפרשיות עצמן לא נפסלו כגון אם התחיל לכתוב מפרשת והיה כי יביאך יוכל לצרף לזה פרשת קדש מתפילין אחרים אם (ג) יודע בודאי שנכתב קודם אלו דאל״ה ספק תורה לחומרא וה״ה אם בעת הכתיבה היה כסדרן רק אח״כ נפסל פרשה אחת המוקדמת נתבטל ממילא כל הפרשיות שאחריה ולענין צירוף מפרשיות אחרים ג״כ הדין כנ״ל: (ה) קודם. משום דמוקדם בפסוק וי״א להיפך מפני שש״ר קדושתו חמורה משל יד (ד) ואנו נוהגין כמ״ש הרב בהגה ובדיעבד לכו״ע אין קפידא. כתוב בספר הכוונות שלכתחלה יזהר לכתוב כל הפרשיות ש״ר ושל יד רצופים ולא יפסיק ביניהם בשום דיבור כלל ועי׳ בס״ת: ב (ו) בקלף אחד. מדכתיב והיה לאות על ידך דמשמע אות אחד כלומר בית אחד וכשם שהוא אות אחד מבחוץ כך יש להיות לכתחלה אות א׳ מבפנים שתהיה על קלף אחד אבל בש״ר שיש בו ד׳ בתים צריך שיהיו הפרשיות כתובות בד׳ קלפים וכ״ז רק לכתחלה וכמו שיתבאר הכל לקמן בסעיף מ״ז. ודע דתש״י צריך להיות ג״כ כתוב דוקא (ה) כד׳ עמודים כל פרשה בעמוד אחר

ביאור הלכה

* וצריך לכתבם וכו׳. הג״ה זו איירי לענין קדימת הזמן ולענין קדימת המקום מבואר לקמן בסימן ל״ד בטור וב״י עי״ש: * בסדר[א] הזה. עיין במ״ב והוא מהא״ר והפמ״ג ושארי אחרונים ודעת הט״ז ביו״ד סימן ר״ן דלדברי התוספות מנחות ל״ב ע״א ד״ה דילמא כשר אם אין סידור בהפרשיות של שמע והא״ש אחרי שאין סמוכות בתורה ועיין שם בנה״כ שחולק עליו ועוד ראיתי בס׳ קדושת יו״ט שכ׳ ג״כ דלא כט״ז ואין חילוק בענין סידור בין הפרשיות והאותיות וכ׳ דהתוספות ס״ל דכונת המכילתא הוא לענין סידור המקום שלא יהא נסדרת בהקלף והיה קודם לקדש אבל אם נסדרת אחר קדש אפי׳ אם היא נכתבת תחילה כשר ואנו להלכה לא ס״ל להקל אפילו באופן זה כיון דנכתבת שלא כסדרה וכדמוכח לקמן בסכ״ג וביו״ד בסימן רפ״ח גם מדברי הגר״א בכל אלו מקומות מוכח דס״ל כפסק השו״ע ולא כהתוספות ועיין לקמן בסימן ס״ד בבה״ל שתירצנו בעזה״י את קושית הט״ז בטוב: ואם שינה. שכתב הפרשה המאוחרת בתחלה אפילו אם כתיבתה היה במקומה כגון שהניח חלק הדף אחד וכתב בהדף השני פרשה והיה כי יביאך ואח״כ כתב הפרשה קדש בהדף

שער הציון

(א) פמ״ג: (ב) הסכמת אחרונים כהב״י לקמן בסימן זה: (ג) עה״ג וא״ר ועיין בפמ״ג בסוף אות ב׳ במ״ז שכתב דלא מצרפינן דעת הט״ז ביו״ד בסי׳ ר״ן ס״ק א׳ (שכתב בשם התוס׳ להקל בפ׳ שמע והיה אם שמוע אם פ׳ והיה נכתב קודם שמע) אפילו לס״ם מאחר שלא נזכר כלל דעה זו בשו״ע: (ד) פמ״ג: (ה) רמב״ס:

הגהות ותיקונים: א) כסדר: ב) צ״ל ד׳ דלתי״ן:

ממצרים; (1) the passage of *Shema*,[3*] until /the word/ ובשעריך, and the passage of *Ve-Hayah Im Shamo'a*,[4*] until /the words/ על הארץ.

Gloss: It is necessary (2) *to write /the passages/* (3) *in this order, so that /the passage/ which appears earlier in the Torah is written before /the succeeding passage is written/. If one deviated /from this order when he wrote the passages/* (4) *they are invalid.*

Mishnah Berurah

§32

(1) The passage of *Shema*. One must write the /letter/ ד of /the word/ אחד as large as four small ד /letters/. [*M.A.*]

It may be that /the small ד letters need/ not be assessed in relation to /the size of the rest of/ the script, but as long as /this letter ד/ has /the size of four/ very small ד /letters/ this is sufficient. That is why it is the practice to write /this letter ד/ merely larger than other ד /letters/ of that script.

(2) To write /the passages/. /This applies to/ all the passages, both /the passages/ for the arm /*tefilin*/ and /the passages/ for the head /*tefilin*/.

(3) In this order. /This is/ because it is written[1] /with reference to the writing of the *tefilin* passages/, "And these words should be, etc.". /This implies that just/ as /the words/ are /written in the Torah/ they should be /written for the *tefilin*/.

For this reason, one must certainly be careful that all of the passages are themselves written in the /correct/ order /of the letters/, without even a single letter being missed when /one writes/ them. /Otherwise,/ one will not be /able to/ remedy this subsequently by supplementing /the letter/, as /stated/ below in Par. 23.

(4) They are invalid. I.e., *tefilin* which were made up with these passages /are invalid/.

The passages themselves, however, will not have become invalid. For example, if one began writing from the /second/ passage *Ve-Hayah Ki Yevi'acha*, he may combine with /the three final passages/ a *Kadesh Li Chal Bechor* passage /taken/ from another *tefilin* /unit/. /However, this is only the case/ if he knows definitely that /the passage he combines/ was written before /he wrote/ these /other passages/. Otherwise, /it cannot be used in combination with them, in view of the fact that/ one must be stringent in /a case of/ doubt where Torah law /is involved/.

Correspondingly, if when one wrote /the passages/ they were /written/ in /the correct/ order and one of the earlier passages became invalid only subsequently, all the passages which follow it will /nevertheless/ have ceased automatically to be /valid if one rewrites the earlier passage now/. As regards combining /a passage taken/ from another /set of/ passages /to replace a passage which became invalid/, the ruling is also /the same/ as /stated/ above.[2]

3* *Devarim* 6:4-9.
4* *Devarim* 11:13-21.

1 *Devarim* 6:6.
2 I.e., one must know definitely that it was written after any passage which precedes it in the Torah and before any passage which succeeds it in the Torah which is used in that *tefilin* unit.

כי בחוזק יד הוציאנו ה' ממצרים (א) [א] (א) ופרשת שמע עד ובשעריך ופ' והיה אם שמוע עד על הארץ: הגה * וצריך (ב) לכתבם (ב) [ב] (ג) * כסדר הזה לכתוב תחלה הקודמת בתורה * ואם שינה (ד) פסול ולכתחלה יכתוב (ג) [ג] של יד (ה) קודם של ראש: **ב** בשל ראש יכתוב כל אחת בקלף לבדה ושל יד כותבן כולם (ו) בקלף (ז) אחד: ב שם

באר היטב

(א) ופרשת שמע. וצריך לכתוב ד' דאחד גדולה כמו ד' דלתי"ן קטנים כתבי האר"י מ"א: (ב) בסדר[א] הזה. תפילין שנכתבו כסדרן ובאורך הזמן נפסלו שתי פרשיות ראשונות ויש לסופר עוד שתי פרשיות כאותן שנפסלו שהן כשרות מותר לצרפן אל שתי הפרשיות אחרונות שנשארו בכשרותם תשובת עבודת הגרשוני סי' ס' עיין בכנה"ג. ובתשובת דבר שמואל סי' ש"ב: (ג) של יד קודם של ראש. ובעטרת זקנים כתב ול"נ שיכתוב של ראש תחלה וכ"כ האר"י ז"ל בספר הכוונות שיכתוב הש"ר ויתקנו לגמרי וישמירו ואח"כ יכתוב הש"י. ויזהר לכתוב כל הד' פרשיות של ראש ויד רצופים ולא יפסיק ביניהם בשום דיבור כלל ע"ש: (ד) א'. דכתיב והיה לך לאות על ידך דמשמע אות א' כלומר בית אחד:

שערי תשובה

[א] ופרשת שמע. עבה"ט ובענין תמונת האותיות והתגין המבואר שם ראוי לסופרים יראי ה' שילמדו אותם איש מפי איש דהיינו שיבחור לעצמו סופר מומחה ובקי שילמדו מפה לאוזן וגם יראהו באצבע כזה ראה וקדש לא כאלו שסומכים עצמם לכתוב בכוונות קדושות ולא באו בסוד ה' רק מה שרואין בספר מלא שמורים וכדומה מספרים שנתחברו בענין זה והם מדמין בעצמם שמוציאין הדבר מתוקן ותעו מדרך השכל כי שכלם קטן מהכיל עומק הדברים. ומי שלא קיבל הענינים על בוריים מוטב שלא יכוין עצמו כלל לזה ויכתוב בלא כוונות. ומ"מ יכול לדקדק לעשות בתמונות האותיות שכתבו סופרים מפורסמים אנשי השם ואנשי מעשה וכמ"ש מהר"ס זכותא ובברכי יוסף ס"ק כ"ה שיש לדקדק במעשה המצות שיהיו כסדרם וכמשפטם אף שאין אתנו יודע רמזיהם וסודותיהם כי המצוה פועלת בסגולה ועושה רושם למעלה אף שנעשית בלתי הכוונה הפרטית רק שצריך לכוין הכוונה הכללית שיכוין שיעשה המעשה הזה עפ"י מצות אלהיו ע"ש שמ"כ בשם זקינו בעל חסד לאברהם זללה"ה בהגהותיו כת"י כנ"ל. ועיין לקמן ס"ק ל"ד: [ב] בסדר[א] הזה. עבה"ט ומ"ש בשם עה"ג ר"ל שהיו לו שני פרשיות שידוע לו שכתבם קודם אלו האחרונים שנשתיירו רק דס"ד כיון שלא נכתבו להצטרף לאלו יהיו פסולין לצרפם קא משמע לן דלא איכפת לן בזה ואפילו ע"א נאמן לומר שיודע שאלו נכתבו קודם אבל אם הוא מסופק אם נכתבו קודם או אח"כ לא תהא כזאת בישראל לצרפן יחד ת"ו עיין שם ובא"ר. ומ"ש בה"ט ועיין דבר שמואל סימן ש"ב הנה בלקה"ק כתב שבד"ש מחמיר בזה וליתא דהדב"ש שם מיירי במולא פרשה מהראשונות פסולה וכתב אחרת תחתיה פסול וגם לדעת עה"ג כן הוא ומחמיר אפילו בספיקו וכמ"ש ומח"ב כתב שהב"י בסימן ל"ג הביא הגהות סמ"ק דבש"ר שנכתבו בד' קלפים אין קפידא בקדימה ואין הלכה כן. ועיין בשו"ת הרשב"ץ שרולה להחזיק בדברי הגהות סמ"ק וסוגיין דעלמא שאין לחלק בין של ראש לשל יד ולכן סופר שכתב כמה פרשיות לתש"ר בב"א ונזהר לכותבן על הסדר ואחר כך נתערבו בענין שאפשר שיקח פרשה ראשונה שנכתבה מאוחר לג' מוקדמים טעונין גניזה ואם כתב פרשיות של ראש ונתקלקלה האחרונה יכתוב אחרת תחתיה משא"כ אם נתקלקלה פרשה מהקודמות שצריך לכותבה שנית עם כל הפ' שכתב אחריו כ"כ האחרונים עיין שם: [ג] של יד. עבה"ט מ"ש בשם ספר הכוונות וז"ל וגם צריך ליזהר כל מה שיכול לכתוב כל ד"פ ש"ר או ש"י רצופים ולא יפסיק בינתיים בשום דיבור כלל ועיקר ומכ"ש באמצעם ואם הוא זקן או חולה ואינו יכול לכתוב כל הד"פ ביחד יכתוב שלשה פרשיות ראשונות ואחר כך יכתוב הד' ואם גם זה קשה עליו לכתוב יכתוב ב"פ הראשונות רצופים עכ"פ ואח"כ יכתוב ב"פ אחרות ביחד אבל בין פרשה ראשונה לשניה לא יפסיק בשום ענין והנה אם כתב ב"פ הראשונות והפסיק קודם שיתחיל לכתוב פרשה שמע יעביר הקולמוס על תיבת וידבר של קדש ועל תיבת והיה של פ"ב ואחר כך יכתוב מפרשה שמע ואילך ועל ידי זה יש קצת חיבור. ואם כבר כתב בתחלה כל השלשה פרשיות והפסיק אז יעביר הקולמוס על תיבת וידבר של פרשה ראשונה ועל תיבת והיה של פרשה שניה ועל תיבת שמע של פרשה שלישית ואחר כך והיה אם שמוע ועי"ז יש קצת חיבור. גם קודם שיתחיל לכתוב יתפלל ויאמר יהר"מ ה' או"א שתשרה שכינתך במעשה ידי ותצליחני בכתבי זאת שאני כותב תפילין הללו לשם קדושת מצות תפילין שצונו ה' אלהינו ותצילנו מטעות הכתיבה ומטעות הכוונה אמן כן יהי רצון עכ"ל פע"ח הנקרא בפוסקים ספר הכוונות ומהנכון

משנה ברורה

א (א) ופרשת שמע. וצריך לכתוב ד' דאחד כל כך גדולה כמו ד' דלתי"ן קטנים [מ"א] (א) ואפשר שאין מעכבין באותו כתב רק כל שיש ט' דלתי"ן קטנים מלא סגי ומשום הכי נוהגין לכתוב רק גדולה משאר דלתי"ן שבאותו כתב: (ב) לכתבם. כל הפרשיות (ב) כן מהט"ז וכן מהא"ר: (ג) בסדר[ב] הזה. דכתיב והיו הדברים וגו' בהוייתן יהו. וכ"ש שצריך ליזהר מטעם זה שיהיה כל פרשה ופרשה גופא נכתבת כסדרה שלא יחסר בה אפילו אות אחת כי לא יהיה לו תקנה אח"כ להשלימה וכדלקמן בסעיף כ"ג: (ד) פסול. היינו התפילין שנעשו מאותן הפרשיות אבל הפרשיות עצמן לא נפסלו כגון אם התחיל לכתוב מפרשת והיה כי יביאך יוכל לצרף לזה פרשת קדש מתפילין אחרים אם (ג) יודע בודאי שנכתב קודם אלו דאל"ה ספק תורה לחומרא וה"ה אם בעת הכתיבה היה כסדרן רק אח"כ נפסל פרשה אחת המוקדמת נתבטל ממילא כל הפרשיות שאחריה ולענין צירוף מפרשיות אחרים ג"כ הדין כנ"ל: (ה) קודם. משום דמוקדם בפסוק וי"א להיפך מפני שש"ר קדושתו חמורה משל יד (ד) ואנו נוהגין כמ"ש הרב בהגה ובדיעבד לכו"ע אין קפידא. כתוב בספר הכוונות שלכתחלה יזהר לכתוב כל הפרשיות ש"ר ושל יד רצופים ולא יפסיק ביניהם בשום דיבור כלל ועי' בש"ת: **ב** (ו) בקלף אחד. מדכתיב והיה לאות על ידך דמשמע אות אחד כלומר בית אחד וכשם שהוא אות אחד מבחוץ כך יש להיות לכתחלה אות א' מבפנים שתהיה על קלף אחד אבל בש"ר שיש בו ד' בתים צריך שיהי' הפרשיות כתובות בד' קלפים וכ"ז רק לכתחלה וכמו שיתבאר הכל לקמן בסעיף מ"ז. ודע דתש"י צריך להיות ג"כ כתוב דוקא (ה) בד' עמודים כל פרשה בעמוד אחר

ביאור הלכה

* וצריך לכתבם וכו'. הג"ה זו איירי לענין קדימת הזמן ולענין קדימת המקום מבואר לקמן בסימן ל"ד בטור וב"י ע"ש: * בסדר[א] הזה. עיין במ"ב והוא מהא"ר והפמ"ג ושארי אחרונים ודעת הט"ז ביו"ד סימן ר"ך דלדברי התוספות מנחות ל"ב ע"א ד"ה דילמא כשר אם אין סידור בהפרשיות של שמע והא"ש אחרי שאין סמוכות בתורה ועיין שם בנה"כ שחולק עליו ועוד ראיתי בס' קדושת יו"ט שכ' ג"כ דלא כט"ז ואין חילוק בענין סידור בין הפרשיות והאותיות וכ' דהתוספות ס"ל דכונת המכילתא הוא לענין סידור המקום שלא יהא נסדרת בהקלף והיה קודם לקדש אבל אם נסדרת אחר קדש אפי' אם היא נכתבת תחילה כשר ואנו להלכה לא ס"ל להקל אפילו באופן זה כיון דנכתבת שלא כסדרה וכדמוכח לקמן בסכ"ג וביו"ד בסימן רפ"ח גם מדברי הגר"א בכל אלו מקומות מוכח דס"ל כפסק השו"ע ולא כהתוספות ועיין לקמן בסימן ס"ד בבה"ל שתירצנו בעזה"י את קושית הט"ז בטוב: ואם שינה. שכתב הפרשה המאוחרת בתחלה אפילו אם כתיבתה היה במקומה כגון שהניח חלק הדף אחד וכתב בהדף השני פרשה והיה כי יביאך ואח"כ כתב הפרשה קדש בהדף

שער הציון

(א) פמ"ג: (ב) הסכמת אחרונים כהב"י לקמן בסימן זה: (ג) עה"ג וא"ר ועיין בפמ"ג בסוף אות ב' במ"ז שכתב דלא מצרפינן דעת הט"ז ביו"ד בסי' ר"ך ס"ק א' (שכתב בשם התוס' להקל בפ' שמע והיה אם שמוע אם פ' והיה נכתב קודם שמע) אפילו לס"ם מאחר שלא נזכר כלל דעה זו בשו"ע: (ד) פמ"ג: (ה) רמב"ס:

הגהות ותיקונים: א) כסדר: ב) צ"ל ד' דלתי"ן:

*Initially, one should write /the passages for/ the arm /*tefilin*/* (5) *before /he writes the passages for/ the head /*tefilin*/.*

2. Each one of /the passages for/ the head */tefilin/* should be written on a separate parchment /, whereas the passages for/ the arm */tefilin/* should all be written (6) on a single parchment.

Mishnah Berurah

(5) Before. This is because /the arm *tefilin*/ are /mentioned/ earlier in the verse.

There are /authorities/ who say the opposite, in view /of the fact/ that the head /*tefilin*/ have a more severe holiness than the arm /*tefilin*/. Our practice /conforms/ with what the *Rav*[3] writes in the gloss.

Once it is after the event /, however,/ all /authorities/ are agreed that one need not be particular /about this/.

It is written in the *Sefer Ha-Kavanos* that, initially, one must be careful to write all the passages of the head /*tefilin*/ and of the arm /*tefilin*/ consecutively, without making any interruption of speech at all in between /writing/ them. See the *Sh.T.*

(6) On a single parchment. /This is/ because it is written[4] /with reference to the arm *tefilin* unit/, "And it should be for a sign on your arm". This implies /that it should be/ a single sign /on the arm/; in other words, /it must consist of/ a single housing. Just as it should be a single sign externally, it should likewise be, initially, a single sign internally, /which means/ that /all the passages/ should be /written/ on a single parchment.

On the other hand, in the case of the head /*tefilin* unit/, which consists of four housings, the passages must be written on four parchments.

All this only /applies/ initially, as is explained fully below in Par. 47.

Note that /the passages of/ the arm *tefilin* must also be written specifically on four /separate/ columns, with each passage on a different column.

3 I.e., the *Rema*.
4 *Shemos* 13:16.

ג * [ג]יכתבם (ז) (ה) בדיו [ד] שחור * [ד]בין שיש בו מי עפצים * בין שלא במי עפצים: הגה ולכתחלה יחמיר לכתוב בדיו העשויה (ח) מעשן (ו) עלים או שמנים שרויים במי עפצים (מהרי"ל סי' קי"ט) וכמו שיתבאר בי"ד סי' רע"א. [ה]כתב אפי' (ט) אות א' (י) (ט) בשאר מיני צבעונים או בזהב * הרי אלו פסולין [ו]אם זרק * עפרות זהב על האותיות (יא) * מעביר הזהב וישאר כתב התחתון וכשר אבל אם זרק הזהב

באר הגולה: ג שבת ק"ג ד רמב"ם בפ"א מה"ת והג"מ שם והרא"ש ה שם בגמ' ו ב"י לפירוש הר"י

שערי תשובה

לומר יהי רצון דלעיל ובמלת שמורים נדפס יה"ר באורך עי"ש ולמנקט נפשיה בקצרה עדיף טפי: [ד] שחור. עבה"ט ומ"ש בשם דב"ש לענין סתם יינס עיין שם בסימן קס"ד דמסיים בה מ"מ דבר שבקדושה וכתיבת כמה אזכרות של שם חמור טפי ונכון לקדש עצמנו במותר לנו ולהרחיק מן הכיעור והדומה לו עיין שם. ועיין שם שכתב להסתפק אם מותר לכתוב תו"מ בקולמוס של עוף טמא דשמא כיון שאינו ניכר ממשו של איסור לאחר הכתיבה אינו דומה לעורות ל"ה. ועיין באר עשק סימן ק"ט:

באר היטב

(ה) שחור. עיין בב"י אין להקשות הא ברייתא זו דפ' הבונה אוקימנא לה בפרק הקומץ בס"ת ולא בתפילין ומזוזות על ההיא דאמרינן התם איבעיא להו שתים ושלש ואחת מהו וכו' ומהדרינן כי תניא ההיא בס"ת ע"ש. וכ"כ התוספות בפרק במה מדליקין דס"ת בעי דיו מסוגיא זו דפרק הקומץ עיין ביד אהרן שמיישבו. מותר לכתוב תו"מ בדיו הנעשה מסתם יינם דבר שמואל סי' קס"ב קס"ד. יד אליהו סימן ק"ט: (ו) עלים. כתב מ"א לא ראיתי

ביאור הלכה

ראשון פסול: * יכתבם בדיו שחור. ועיין ברמב"ם פ"א מהלכות תפילין שכתב דההלמ"מ דנאמר שיהיו כותבין בדיו לא נאמר רק למעט שאר מיני צבעונין כגון האדום והירוק וכיוצא בהן משמע דבכל דבר שיעשה ממנו מראה שחור כדיו כשר ורק שיהיה מתקיים וכן כתב בהלכות ס"ת א' מכ' דברים הפוסלים ס"ת הוא אם נכתב בלא שחור העומד. ואם היה המראה דומה למראה הכחול [שקורין בל"א בלאה[°]] נלענ"ד שיש להחמיר בזה וראיה מחולין מ"ז ע"ב ככוחלא כשירה כדיותא טריפה דאף דמהרמב"ם משמע דהלכה לא נאמר רק שיהיה מראה שחור ובררנו לקמן בסימן ל"ג[א] דהרצועות שיש עליה גם כן הלמ"מ דצריכה להיות שחור די בשחרות שהיא ככחול שאני הכא שכיון שהיתה ההלכה שיכתוב בדיו אף דדיו לאו דוקא להרמב"ם וה"ה כל מראה שחור אבל עכ"פ שיהיה מראיתה שחור כמו דיו. וכ"ש לפירוש הרא"ש וש"פ דסוברים שדיו ממש בעינן מראה כחול בודאי איננו בכלל דיו אך צל"ע קצת דא"כ אם היה מראית הדיו דומה למראית העורב ג"כ איננו בכלל דיו וכדמוכח בנדה כ' ע"א דמראית הדיו שחור יותר ממראית העורב דאמר שם שחור כדיו טמאה כעורב הוא בכלל דיהא מכן וטהור וא"כ אמאי אמר במדרש שחורות כעורב אלו האותיות אך אין למדין הלכה מן האגדות א"נ י"ל בדוחק דשחור כעורב הוא שחור ג"כ כדיו אבל כדיו הלח והוא ג"כ טהור כדמוכח שם בגמרא. ואפילו אם טבעו להיות נשחר לגמרי אחר הכתיבה יש לעיין בזה טובא אי כשר בדיעבד דהלא ההלכה נאמר שיהיו כותבין בדיו כדאיתא בירושלמי ולא נאמר שיהיה כתוב הס"ת בדיו ולשון השו"ע ג"כ משמע דבעת הכתיבה יהיה הדיו שחור ויש לפרש עוד דכוונת השו"ע כ"ש שחור אפילו ממי עפצים וקנקנתום ודלא כר"ת וכמו שביאר בב"י וצ"ע: * בין שיש בו מי עפצים. המחבר סתם דבריו ולא פירש ממה לעשותו משום דאפילו אם הוא עשוי מקנקנתום ומי עפצים או מגומא ומי עפצים כשר דמשני מינים ביחד נקרא דיו ודלא כר"ת דאוסר בזה וכמו שביאר בב"י [כן ביאר הגר"א בסימן תרל"א לקמן וגם בסי' זה רמז לזה דלזה לא כתב השו"ע רק שיש בו ולא כתב אפילו אם הדיו הוא מעפצים בלבד ומיושב בזה קושית הפמ"ג] ולזה בא הרמ"א והוסיף דלכתחלה יש להחמיר שלא לעשותו מעורב בקנקנתום או בגומא משום דהוי כתב שאין יוכל להמחק וכמו שנתבאר ביו"ד בסימן רע"א ס"י[ב] דדוקא בדיעבד אם כתבו במי עפצים וקנקנתום כשר [וגומא הוא ג"כ כתב שאין יוכל להמחק וכדאיתא בסוטה דף י"ז במשנה] וכן מוכח ברמב"ם פ"א מהלכות תפילין ה"ד ע"ש ואין כונת הרמ"א לומר דלכתחלה דוקא מעשן ולא מעלים גופייהו [ועיין מ"א וא"ר] דהרי ביו"ד בסי' רע"א הרמ"א גופא כתב דלכתחלה יותר טוב שיעשה מדבר הבא מן העץ אח"כ מלאתי בעזה"י בעולת תמיד שפירש כן. א"נ י"ל דכונת הרמ"א למעט מה שכתב הב"י סתם בדיו שחור דמשמע כ"ש שחור כיון דהוא מתקיים והוא ניכר על הקלף דיו הוא וכמו שכתב בב"י בשם רבינו שמחה ולזה בא הרמ"א והוסיף דלכתחלה יחמיר כדברי רבינו תם דדוקא בא מן העץ: * בין שלא וכו'. עיין לקמן בסימן תרל"א וביו"ד בסימן רע"א שכתב השו"ע דאם כתב במי עפצים וקנקנתום כשר. כתב הפמ"ג מדלא הזכיר גומא משמע דאף אם לא הטיל בהן גומא כשר ועיין עוד בדבריו שמסתפק לדינא אם דוקא ע"י שניהן ביחד כיון דאין בהן גומא או אפילו בכל אחד יכול לעשות דיו כיון שהוא שחור והגר"א בביאורו בסימן זה ובסימן תרל"א פוסק דממי עפצים בלבד או מקנקנתום בלבד פסול אפילו דיעבד דלא מיקרי דיו כ"א משני מינים ביחד מי עפצים וגומא או מי עפצים וקנקנתום ומגומא וקנקנתום יחד בלי תערובת מי עפצים או עשן עלים ושמנים לא ברירא לי דעת הגר"א בזה והגאון מהר"מ בנעט בביאורו על המרדכי מחמיר בזה לכתחלה ובקנקנתום לבד או בגומא לבד מחמיר אפילו בדיעבד כדעת הגר"א ובתשובת משכנות יעקב סימן ל"ז מחמיר אפילו במי עפצים וקנקנתום יחד בלי תערובת גומא עי"ש. והגם דבדיעבד בודאי אין להחמיר ולפסול במי עפצים וקנקנתום יחד נגד פסק השו"ע בסי' תרל"א וביו"ד סימן רע"א עכ"פ לכתחלה בודאי יש ליזהר כדבריו שאם הוא עושה דיו ממי עפצים אפילו אם הוא מערבו עם קנקנתום לא יעשהו בלתי תערובת גומא וה"ה דממי עפצים וגומא בלחוד נמי שפיר דמי ועי"ש בתשובת משכנות יעקב שמביא הרבה פוסקים סייעתא לדבריו גם כתב שם בתשובה דלכתחלה יש לדקדק לעשותו ע"י בישול כדעת הרמב"ן והר"ן הואיל דאפשר: * הרי אלו פסולין. ואם הוא אות ראשון או שכתבו כולו כך ורוצה אח"כ בתו"מ להעביר קולמוס כסדרן עליהן בדיו צ"ע אם מהני פמ"ג במ"ז אות ט"ו והחתם סופר בסימן רנ"ו ביו"ד פסק דמספק פסול דהוא בכלל דיו ע"ג סיקרא עיין בגיטין י"ט ע"א והדין עם הא"ר דלא כהפמ"ג שמספקא בזה עי"ש: * עפרות זהב. וה"ה שאר מיני צבעונין על הדיו דפוסל בזה להכתב ובזה לא שייך תקנתא דמעביר ואף אם ירצה אח"כ להעביר בדיו על הצבעונין והזהב פסק הע"ת והא"ר דלא מהני וזהו שכתב אחר כך על אות מאוכרה אין לו תקנה כלומר אפילו רוצה לחפות בדיו מלמעלה פסול וראיה זו דחה הפמ"ג עי"ש ובאמת לענ"ד יש לעיין בזה אם יש בזה אפילו פסול ספק כמו דיו ע"ג צבע אחרי דכתב התחתון וגם העליון הוא כתב דיו ואין כאן מקום להאריך: * מעביר הזהב. הפרישה כתב עיין ביו"ד סימן רע"ו כתבתי שם בשם ריב"ש דיש לחוש משום כתב מנומר אם יש הרבה אותיות כן בכמה דפין וכן כתב הל"ח והא"ר השיג עליהם דהריב"ש לא

משנה ברורה

אחר: ג (ז) בדיו שחור. ודיו שמראהו דומה למראה הכחול עיין בביאור הלכה: (ח) מעשן עצים. פי' ולא יטיל לתוכו קומא או קנקנתום [שקורין בל"א קופער וואסער[°°]] כי לכתחלה בעינן כתב שיוכל להמחק וע"י קומא או קנקנתום הכתב עומד ואין נמחק וזהו הכל למצוה מן המובחר בלבד אבל לדינא גם הרמ"א מודה דמותר לעשות ממי עפצים וקומא וקנקנתום וכן נוהגין לעשות כהיום ע"י תערובות שלשתן וע"י בישול דהכי עדיף טפי [וכמו שכתב בתשובת משכנות יעקב סי' ל"ז] ועיין במ"א שכתב דבימיו לא ראה ג"כ לאחד מן הגדולים שנהג לעשות בדיו העשוי מעשן עלים ושמנים [אך אפשר דהיו עושין מדיו של קולים כמו שסיים בשם מהרי"ל] וכן פסק בספר גט מקושר ובספר ברכי יוסף לעשות כמנהגינו עכשיו דהדיו העשוי מעשן עלים ושמנים מתקלקל ונמחק בנקל ע"כ אין נוהגין בו עכשיו ודיו העשוי ממי עפצים בלבד בלא קומא [שקורין בל"א גומא] או מקנקנתום בלבד פסול אפילו דיעבד כן כתב הגר"א בביאורו לקמן בסי' תרל"א עי"ש ועיין בבה"ל. מותר (ו) לכתוב תו"מ בדיו הנעשה מסתם יינם ועי' בש"ת ס"ק ד'. דיו אין צריך (ז) לעשות לשמה: (ט) אות אחת. ל"ד דה"ה מקלת האות כגון קוצו של יוד: (י) בשאר מיני צבעונים. שאינם שחור כגון (ח) האדום והירוק וכיוצא בהם: (יא) מעביר

מתרגם: [°] כחול, תכלת [°°]מי נחושת

שער הציון

(ו) באר היטב: (ז) בל"י[ג]: (ח) רמב"ם:

הגהות ותיקונים: א) ס"ג ד"ה הרצועות: ב) ס"ו: ג) אולי צ"ל באר עשק:

3. /The passages/ should be written **(7)** with black ink, irrespective of whether /the ink/ contains gallnut resin or whether it is not /mixed/ with gallnut resin.

Gloss: Initially, one should be stringent and write /the passages/ with ink that is made **(8)** *out of the soot of wood or oils soaked in gallnut resin, (...) as explained in the* Yo.D., *Sec. 271.*

If one wrote even **(9)** one letter **(10)** with another kind of color or in gold, /the passages/ are invalid.

If one threw gold dust over the letters **(11)** one may remove the gold, leaving the underneath script, and /the passage/ will /then/ be valid. However, if one

Mishnah Berurah

(7) With black ink. /As for/ ink whose appearance resembles the color blue, see the Beyur Halachah.[5]

(8) Out of the soot of wood. I.e., one should not insert into /the ink/ gum or vitriol [which is called *kuper vaser* in Yiddish].

This is because, initially, we require writing which can be erased. Gum or vitriol causes writing to be resistant and unerasable.

All these /requirements/ are /required/ solely /in order/ to /fulfil/ the mitzvah in a choice /way/, but the *Rema* also concedes that from /the point of view of binding/ halachah it is permitted to make the ink /for *tefilin* passages/ with gallnut resin, gum and vitriol. It is in fact the practice to make /the ink/ nowadays with a mixture of the three of them and by cooking, because it is preferable /to use/ this /ink/ [as stated in the **responsum** of the *Mishkenos Ya'akov*, Sec. 37].

See the *M.A.*, who writes that in his time he also did not see any of the eminent /Torah scholars/ use in practice ink made out of the soot of wood or oils [although it may be that they made use of the ink of thorns, as he concludes in the name of the *Maharil*]. It is likewise ruled in the work *Geyt Mekushar* and in the work *Birkey Yosef* that one should make /the ink/ in conformance with our present practice, as ink made out of the soot of wood or oil gets spoiled and erased easily. Consequently, it is not the practice /to use such ink/ nowadays.

Ink which is made out of gallnut resin alone, without gum [which is called *guma* in Yiddish], or out of vitriol alone is /ruled as/ invalid even once it is after the event. This is what the *Gra* writes in his *Beyur* below in Sec. 691; see there. See the Beyur Halachah.

It is permitted to write /passages for/ *tefilin* or *mezuzos* with ink made out of /non-Jewish/ wine which is not known /to be libation wine/. See the *Sh.T.*, sub-Par. 4.

It is unnecessary to make the ink /specifically/ for the sake of /the mitzvah/.

(9) One letter. /This wording/ is imprecise, as the same ruling /applies even if one merely wrote/ a part of a letter, such as the tip of the /letter/ י /, with another kind of color or in gold/.

(10) With another kind of color. I.e., /a color/ other than black, such as red, green or a similar /color/.

(11) One may remove the gold.

5 There the author is inclined to be stringent about allowing the use of such ink.

על אות מאזכרות אין לו תקנה לפי שאסור להעביר הזהב משום דהוי * כמוחק את השם: ד * [ז]צריך שלא תדבק שום אות (ז) [ה] (יב) בחברתה*אלא (יג) * כל אות תהיה מוקפת גויל:* הגה ויכתוב (יד) כתיבה תמה שלא יחסר אפילו (טו) קוצו של יו"ד ויהא מתוייג (טז) כהלכתו (טור א"ח) ולכתחלה יכתוב כתיבה גסה קצת שלא יהיו נמחקים מהרה וכן מצוה ליפותן מבחוץ ומבפנים (דברי מרדכי): ה [ח]צריך (יז) שיכתוב בימינו אפילו אם הוא שולט בשתי ידיו [ט]ואם כתב (יח) בשמאל (ח) פסולים. [י]אם אפשר למצוא אחרים כתובים בימין. ואיטר יד שמאל דידיה (יט) הרי (ט) ימין: ו * [כ]אין צריך לשרטט [ל]כי אם (כ) שטה (י) עליונה [מ]ואם אינו יודע ליישר השטה בלא שרטוט

ז מנחות ל"ד ח שם ל"ז ט סה"ת סימן ר"ה והגה' מימון פ"ב מהלכות תפילין בשם סמ"ק י דעת הב"י כ מנחות ל"ב ל תוס' והרא"ש וספר תרומה מההיא דגיטין ומס' סופרים מ הרא"ש בהלכות ספר תורה

באר היטב

לא' מהגדולים שנהג כן ע"ש: (ז) בחברתה. אם האות גדול ונדבק בסופו באופן שאם נגרר מה שנדבק מ"מ ישאר צורת האות כשר. הרד"ך בית א' חדר כ"ב. ומ"א כתב דיש להחמיר. ואם אינו דבוק בעצמו רק התג א' דבוקה בחברתה כשר הרב המאירי. ופרי חדש בא"ע סי' קכ"ה ס"ק י"א כתב דלא נהירא ואף בדיבוק ע"י תג יש לגרור הדבק ע"ש. גם הרלנ"ח מחמיר עיין במ"א. ועיין לקמן סעיף כ"ה מש"ש: (ח) פסולים. היינו בשולט בימין לבד אבל שולט בשתי ידיו אם כתב בשמאל כשר מ"א: (ט) ימין. ואם כתב בימין פסול. כתב רמ"ע סי' ל"ח שאחד כתב בפיו ופסלו אפי' א"א למצוא אחרים מ"א וה"ה כיוצא בזה דלאו דרך כתיבה הוא אפי' ליכא אחרים אין לברך על תפילין שנכתבו בכה"ג ע"ת ע"ש: (י) עליונה. משום דאסור לכתוב

שערי תשובה

וגידים של הטמאים ע"ש: [ה] בחברתה. עבה"ט ודוקא נדבק בסופו אבל בראשו או באמצעיתו מודה הרד"ך דפסול אף בכה"ג עיין בכנה"ג ומ"ש רק התג אחד דבוקה בחברתה ר"ל שהתג של תיבה אחת נוגע עם התג שבתיבה שאצלה ונדבקו זה בזה מכשיר המאירי הואיל וניכר שאינו דבוק ע"י עצמה כן מבואר בכנה"ג. ועיין בסימן ל"ו ביד אפרים מ"ש שם בתגין שבאות אחת נוגעים זה בזה שפסול ושם הטעם משום דהוי שינוי באות דמחזי כאות אחר משא"כ כאן. ונראה דאף בתיבה אחת שנוגעים התגין מאות לאות ליכא הך טעמא ודינו כמו כן להמאירי דכשר ומ"ש בשם הפר"ח נראה דגם המאירי מודה דודאי יש לגרור הדבוק רק כמש"ל דלא נפסל מ"ש להלן קודם שגרר משום

משנה ברורה

הזהב. ואע"ג דכל זמן שאין מעביר פסול דכתב העליון מבטל כתב התחתון (ט) לא מיקרי ע"י ההעברה כתיבה שלא כסדרן כיון שאין כותב כ"א מעביר ונשאר כתב התחתון ממילא: ד (יב) בחבירת'. ואם האות גדול ונדבק בסופו באופן שאם נגרר מה שדבק מ"מ ישאר צורת אות יש מכשירין*ויש פוסלין והסכימו (י) האחרונים להחמיר ע"כ צריך לגרור מקום הדבק ואף (יא) בתפילין ומזוזות מהני תיקון כיון דלא נשתנה צורת האות מקודם: (יג) כל אות. ואפילו האות האחרון מהשיטה צריכה להיות מוקפת גויל מארבע רוחותיה ולעיכובא הוא אפילו בדיעבד וכדלקמן בסוף סעיף ט"ז ואפילו אם יחסר הקפת גויל להקוץ של היוד ג"כ פסול הוא וכדאיתא במנחות דף כ"ט וכל פרטי דין הזה עיין לקמן בסעי' י"ז[א] ובסימן ל"ו: (יד) כתיבה תמה. דהיינו (יב) שלא יכתוב ביתי"ן כפי"ן ביתי"ן זייני"ן נוני"ן זייני"ן וכל כיוצא בזה: (טו) קוצו של יוד. היינו (יג) עוקץ שמאל של יוד וכ"ש אם חסר רגל ימין דפסול ותמונת היוד עיין לקמן בדיני צורת האותיות בסימן ל"ו ומש"כ בשם הפמ"ג: (טז) כהלכתו. באותיות שעטנ"ז ג"ץ וזה הוא רק לכתחלה דבדיעבד כשר לרוב הפוסקים אם לא תייג וכדלקמן בסימן ל"ו ס"ג עי"ש שמבואר שם כל פרטי דיני התיוג: ה (יז) שיכתוב בימינו. דאין דרך כתיבה בשמאל וה"ה לעשות איזה תיקון בשמאל בענין הכתיבה דפסול אבל להפריד נגיעות שבאותיות נראה דכשר אפילו בשמאל דומיא דמכשרינן בתגים הפסולין לזה לקמן בסימן ל"ט עכ"פ בדיעבד עי"ש: (יח) בשמאל. היינו בשולט בימין לבד אבל אם (יד) שולט בשתי ידיו אפילו כתב בשמאלו כשר ואפילו אם שולט בימינו לבד אם אי אפשר למצוא אחרים (טו) יניחם אך לא יברך עליהם. וסופר שכותב בימין וכל מלאכתו בשמאל או להיפך כתב הפמ"ג שנכון לכתחלה שלא לקבלו לסופר ובדיעבד אין לאסור עי"ש הטעם: (יט) הוי ימין. ע"כ אם כתב בימינו פסול כמו בשמאל דעלמא וכנ"ל אם אפשר למצוא אחרים וכתב הרמ"ע מעשה היה במצרים שתפס אחד הקולמוס בשפתיו וכתב בו ופסלו דאין דרך כתיבה בפה לכו"ע וכתב המ"א דפסול אפילו אם א"א למצוא אחרים. ועיין בספר משנת אברהם בשם הגט מקושר ועוד פוסקים דמשוין זה או הכותב ברגלו להכותב ביד שמאל: ו (כ) שיטה עליונה. משום דתפילין אין עליה הלמ"מ לשרטט כמו מזוזה רק (טז) משום דאסור לכתוב ג' תיבות מפסוק בלי שרטוט ע"כ כשמשרטט שיטה עליונה די כי מתם בני אדם יודעים לאמן ידם לכתוב כל השיטות ישרות אחר שכתבו שיטה עליונה וקאמר אין צריך משום דאם ירצה לשרטט כל השיטין כדי לכתוב

ביאור הלכה

לא קאי כלל על דברי הב"י כשזרק זהב על הדיו דבזה לא שייך ענין מנומר כיון דכתב דלמטה קיים אלא הריב"ש קאי על עיקר הדין אם כתב בזהב או בצבעונים עלמן וגררן וכתבן בדיו דבזה שייך ענין מנומר והאריך בזה ועיין בברכי יוסף סי' רע"ו שהסכים לדברי הא"ר וכן הבני יונה ג"כ: * כמוחק את השם. אבל מוחק ממש לא הוי דנשאר כתב התחתון ומשמע מכאן אפילו זרק זהב שלא בקדושת השם אסור למחוק דלא כמה שכתב הש"ך ביו"ד בסימן רע"ו בס"ק י"ב. פמ"ג: * צריך שלא תדבק שום אות בחברתה. ואם התג אחד דבוקה בחברתה בזה יש נ"מ דאם התגין של האות גופא דבק אחד בחבירו דעת הרמ"ע לפסול [והובא דבריו לקמן במ"א[ב] ובא"ר] אך אם גופי האותיות ניכרות כל אחד בפני עצמו רק התג של אות אחד נוגע בתג שבאות שאצלה או מתיבה לתיבה המאירי מיקל בזה והמ"א והפר"ח[1] בא"ע סי' קכ"ה סקי"א מחמירין ג"כ בזה אך הא"ר בסימן זה כתב דיש להחמיר בזה רק בדאפשר והובא דבריו בפמ"ג בא"א [ומה דמדברי שערי תשובה משמע בסק"ז[ג] שיש להחמיר אף להמאירי בדיעבד אם לא תקנן עיינתי בפר"ח שם ומשמע להדיא דלדעת המאירי יש להכשיר אף בלא גרירה בדיעבד] ומ"מ לכתחלה בודאי יש להחמיר ולגרור כדעת הרלב"ח שהביאו המ"א בסק"ג דתיקון מהני אפילו לדידיה ואפילו תגין שנוגעין אחד לחבירו באות גופא נראה דמהני תיקון ואפילו בתו"מ ולא מיקרי שלא כסדרן כיון דחזינן שלא נשתנה צורת אות מקודם עי"ז וכן כתב בספר קסת הסופר: * כל אות תהיה מוקפת גויל. גויל דנקט לאו דוקא דאין כותבין עליו תפילין וכדלקמן בס"ז רק דנקט לישנא דשייך אבל ס"ת ולאו דוקא. ע"ת: * אין צריך לשרטט כ"א שיטה עליונה. ובדיעבד אם לא שירטט אפילו שיטה עליונה לדעת המחבר או מכל צד לדעת הרמ"א תלוי בין שיטת ר"ת ושארי פוס' דלר"ת שכ' דס"ת אין צריכה שירטוט רק בשיטה עליונה לדעת המחבר או מכל צד לדעת הרמ"א ובדיעבד נפסל בזה ומוכרח לומר כן ממסכת סופרים דיריעה שאינה מסורגלת פסולה א"כ ה"ה בתפילין דחד דינא אית להו לשיטתו אבל לפי מה דפסקינן ביו"ד סימן רע"א ס"ה דס"ת צריכה להיות שירטוט בכולה כמו מזוזה א"כ אין לנו ראיה לפסול התפילין בדיעבד אף אם לא שירטט כלל כ"א בביאור הגר"א בקצרה ובדבריו ניחא שלא כתב המחבר לפסול בדיעבד כמו שכתב להדיא ביו"ד בס"ת ומזוזה:

שער הציון

(ט) ע"ת ופמ"ג: (י) מ"א: (יא) פמ"ג: (יב) ב"י: (יג) א"ר ופמ"ג: (יד) מ"א וביאור הגר"א: (טו) א"ר ופמ"ג דלא כלבוש: (טז) ב"י:

הגהות ותיקונים: **א)** ט"ז: **ב)** סי' ל"ו ס"ק ג': **ג)** בסק"ה:

הערות והארות: 1) עיין בה"ל ד"ה צריך וכו' מביא בשם פרי חדש בא"ע, יש לציין שנשמט סע"ק זה ונמצא בדפוסים קדומים:

threw the gold over a letter /of one/ of the Divine Names this cannot be remedied. This is because /then/ it is forbidden to remove the gold, as this would be tantamount to erasing the /Divine/ Name.

4. It is necessary that no letter whatsoever should be stuck (12) to another /letter/, but (13) each letter should be surrounded by /blank/ parchment.

Gloss: One should write (14) *impeccable script, so that even* (15) *the tip of the /letter/* י *is not missing. /The letters/ should have crownlets* (16) *in conformance with halachic /requirements/. (...)*

Initially, one should write a somewhat stout script, so that /the letters/

Mishnah Berurah

Although as long as one has not /yet/ removed /the gold the letters/ are invalid, since the writing on top nullifies the writing underneath, the removal /of the gold/ does not cause /the writing underneath/ to be classed as written in incorrect order. This is because /the removal/ is not /considered/ writing, but is merely /an act of/ removal, and the writing underneath remains of its own accord.

(12) To another. If the letter is large and is stuck at the end /to another letter/ in such a way that if /the part/ that is stuck would be scraped away the form of the letter would nevertheless remain, there are /authorities/ who rule that it is valid /as it is/ and /authorities/ who rule that it is invalid /without correction/. The Acharonim are agreed that one should be stringent /about this/.

Consequently, one must scrape away the place where it is stuck /to the other letter/. This remedy is of avail even in the case of *tefilin* /passages/ and *mezuzos* /, where the letters must have been written in the correct order/, since the form of the letter will not be changed /because of it/ from /what it was/ before.

(13) Each letter. Even the last letter of the line must be surrounded by /blank/ parchment on /all/ four sides. This is an essential /requirement for the validity of the passage/ even once it is after the event, as /stated/ below at the end of Par. 16. Even if a surrounding of /blank/ parchment is lacking /merely/ around the tip of the /letter/ י, /the passage/ is also invalid, as stated in *Menachos* 29/a/.

For all the details concerning this law, see below in Par. 16 /of this section/ and in Sec. 36.

(14) Impeccable script. I.e., one must not write /the letter/ ב /like the letter/ כ, /the letter/ כ /like the letter/ ב, /the letter/ ז /like the letter/ ג, /the letter/ ג /like the letter/ ז or /deviate in/ any similar /way/.

(15) The tip of the /letter/ י. I.e., the prickle on the left of the /letter/ י.

If the leg on the right /of the letter י/ is missing /the passage/ is definitely invalid.

For the symbol of the /letter/ י, see below in Sec. 36, in the laws concerning the form of the letters, and what we have written there in the name of the *P.Mg.*

(16) In conformance with halachic /requirements/. /I.e.,/ the letters שעטנז גץ /must have crownlets/.

This is only an initial /requirement/, as once it is after the event and one did not make the crownlets /the letters/ are /nevertheless/ valid according to the majority of Poskim. This is /ruled/ below in Sec. 36, Par. 3. See there, where all the detailed laws concerning the crownlets are given.

על אות מאזכרות אין לו תקנה לפי שאסור להעביר הזהב משום דהוי * כמוחק את השם:
ד * זצריך שלא תדבק שום אות (ז) [ה] (יב) בחברתה*אלא (יג) * כל אות תהיה מוקפת גויל:
הגה וילכתוב (יד) כתיבה תמה שלא יחסר אפילו (טו) קולו של יו"ד ויהא מתויג (טז) כהלכתו (טור א"ח) ולכתחלה יכתוב כתיבה גסה קלת שלא יהיו נמחקים מהרה וכן מלוה ליפותן מבחוץ ומבפנים (דברי מרדכי):
ה חצריך (יז) שיכתוב בימינו אפילו אם הוא שולט בשתי ידיו טואם כתב (יח) בשמאל (ח) פסולים. יאם אפשר למצוא אחרים כתובים בימין. ואיטר יד שמאל דידיה (יט) הוי (ט) ימין:
ו * כאין צריך לשרטט לכי אם (כ) שטה (י) עליונה מואם אינו יודע ליישר השטה בלא שרטוט

באר הגולה

ז מנחות ל"ד
ח שם ל"ז ט סה"ת סימן ר"ה והגה' מימון פ"ב מהלכות תפילין בשם סמ"ק
י דעת הב"י
כ מנחות ל"ב
ל תוס' והרא"ש וספר תרומה מההיא דגיטין ומס' סופרים מ הרא"ש בהלכות ספר תורה

באר היטב

לא' מהגדולים שנהג כן ע"ש: (ז) בחברתה. אם האות גדול ונדבק בסופו באופן שאם נגרר מה שנדבק מ"מ ישאר צורת האות כשר. הרד"ך בית א' חדר כ"ב. ומ"א כתב דיש להחמיר. ואם אינו דבוק בעצמו רק התג א' דבוקה בחברתה כשר הרב המאירי. ופרי חדש בא"ע סי' קכ"ה ס"ק י"א כתב דלא נהירא ואף בדיבוק ע"י תג יש לגרור הדבק ע"ש. גם הרלנ"ח מחמיר עיין במ"א. ועיין לקמן סעיף כ"ה מש"ש: (ח) פסולים. היינו בשולט בימין לבד אבל שולט בשתי ידיו אם כתב בשמאל כשר מ"א: (ט) ימין. ואם כתב בימין פסול. כתב רמ"ע סי' ל"ח שאחד כתב בפיו ופסלו אפי' א"א למצוא אחרים מ"א וה"ה כיולא בזה דלאו דרך כתיבה הוא אפי' ליכא אחרים אין לברך על תפילין שנכתבו בכה"ג ע"ת ע"ש: (י) עליונה. משום דאסור לכתוב

שערי תשובה

וגידים של הטמאים ע"ש: [ה] בחברתה. עבה"ט ודוקא נדבק בסופו אבל בראשו או באמצעיתו מודה הרד"ך דפסול אף בכה"ג עיין בכנה"ג ומ"ש רק התג אחד דבוקה בחברתה ר"ל שהתג של תיבה אחת נוגע עם התג שבתיבה שאצלה ונדבקו זה בזה מכשיר המאירי הואיל וניכר שאינו דבוק ע"י עצמה כן מבואר בכנה"ג. ועיין בסימן ל"ו ביד אפרים מ"ש שם בתגין שבאות אחת נוגעים זה בזה שפסול ושם הטעם משום דהוי שינוי באות דמחזי כאות אחר משא"כ כאן. ונראה דאף בתיבה אחת שנוגעים התגין מאות לאות ליכא הך טעמא ודינו כמו כן להמאירי דכשר ומ"ש בשם הפר"ח נראה דגם המאירי מודה דודאי יש לגרור הדבוק רק כמש"ל דלא נפסל מ"ש להלן קודם שגרר משום

משנה ברורה

הזהב. ואעפ"כ דכל זמן שאין מעביר פסול דכתב העליון מבטל כתב התחתון (ט) לא מיקרי ע"י ההעברה כתיבה שלא כסדרן כיון שאין כותב כ"א מעביר ונשאר כתב התחתון ממילא: ד (יב) בחבירת'. ואם האות גדול ונדבק בסופו באופן שאם נגרר מה שדבק מ"מ ישאר צורת אות יש מכשירין* ויש פוסלין והסכימו (י) האחרונים להחמיר ע"כ צריך לגרור מקום הדבק ואף (יא) בתפילין ומזוזות מהני תיקון כיון דלא נשתנה צורת האות מקודם: (יג) כל אות. ואפילו האות האחרון מהשיטה צריכה להיות מוקפת גויל מארבע רוחותיה ולעיכובא הוא אפילו בדיעבד וכדלקמן בסוף סעיף ט"ז ואפילו אם יחסר הקפת גויל להקוץ של היוד ג"כ פסול הוא וכדאיתא במנחות דף כ"ט וכל פרטי דין הזה עיין לקמן בסעי' י"ז* ובסימן ל"ו: (יד) כתיבה תמה. דהיינו (יב) שלא יכתוב בית"ין כפי"ן מ"מין וי"וין נו"נין זיי"ן וכל כיוצא בזה: (טו) קוצו של יוד. היינו (יג) עוקץ שמאל של יוד וכ"ש אם חסר רגל ימין דפסול ותמונת היוד עיין לקמן בדיני צורת האותיות בסימן ל"ו ומש"כ בשם הפמ"ג: (טז) כהלכתו. באותיות שעטנ"ז ג"ץ וזה הוא רק לכתחלה דבדיעבד כשר לרוב הפוסקים אם לא תייג וכדלקמן בסימן ל"ו ס"ג עי"ש שמבואר שם כל פרטי דיני התיוג: ה (יז) שיכתוב בימינו. דאין דרך כתיבה בשמאל וה"ה לעשות איזה תיקון בשמאל בענין הכתיבה דפסול אבל להפריד נגיעות שבאותיות נראה דכשר אפילו בשמאל דומיא דמכשרינן באנשים הפסולין לזה לקמן בסימן ל"ט עכ"פ בדיעבד עי"ש: (יח) בשמאל. היינו בשולט בימין לבד אבל אם (יד) שולט בשתי ידיו אפילו כתב בשמאלו כשר ואפילו אם שולט בימינו לבד אם אי אפשר למצוא אחרים (טו) יניחם אך לא יברך עליהם. וסופר שכותב בימין וכל מלאכתו בשמאל או להיפך כתב הפמ"ג שנכון לכתחלה שלא לקבלו לסופר ובדיעבד אין לאסור עי"ש הטעם: (יט) הוי ימין. ע"כ אם כתב בימינו פסול כמו בשמאל דעלמא וכנ"ל אם אפשר למצוא אחרים וכתב הרמ"ע מעשה היה במצרים שתפס אחד הקולמוס בשפתיו וכתב בו ופסלו דאין דרך כתיבה בפה לכו"ע וכתב המ"א דפסול אפילו אם א"א למצוא אחרים. ועיין בספר משנת אברהם בשם הגט מקושר ועוד פוסקים דמשוין זה או הכותב ברגלו להכותב ביד שמאל: ו (כ) שיטה עליונה. משום דתפילין אין עליה הלמ"מ לשרטט כמו מזוזה רק (טז) משום דאסור לכתוב ג' תיבות מפסוק בלי שרטוט ע"כ כשמשרטט שיטה עליונה די כי סתם בני אדם יודעים לאמן ידם לכתוב כל השיטות ישרות אחר שכתבו שיטה עליונה וקאמר אין צריך משום דאם ירצה לשרטט כל השיטין כדי לכתוב

ביאור הלכה

לא קאי כלל על דברי הנ"י כשזרק זהב על הדיו דבזה לא שייך ענין מנומר כיון דכתב דלמטה קיים אלא הריב"ש קאי על עיקר הדין אם כתב בזהב או בצבעונים עלמן וגררן וכתבן בדיו דבזה שייך ענין מנומר והאריך בזה ועיין בברכי יוסף סי' רע"ו שהסכים לדברי הא"ר וכן הבני יונה ג"כ: * כמוחק את השם. אבל מוחק ממש לא הוי דנשאר כתב התחתון ומשמע מכאן אפילו זרק זהב שלא בקדושת השם אסור למחוק דלא כמה שכתב הש"ך ביו"ד בסימן רע"ו בס"ק י"ב. פמ"ג: * צריך שלא תדבק שום אות בחברתה. ואם התג אחד דבוקה בחברתה בזה יש נ"מ דאם התגין של האות גופא דבק אחד בחבירו דעת הרמ"ע לפסול [והובא דבריו לקמן במ"א[ב] ובא"ר] אך אם גופי האותיות ניכרות כל אחד בפני עלמו רק התג של אות אחד נוגע בתג שבאות שאללה או מתיבה לתיבה המאירי מיקל בזה והמ"א והפר"ח[1] בא"ע סי' קכ"ה סקי"א מחמירין ג"כ בזה אך הא"ר בסימן זה כתב דיש להחמיר בזה רק בדאפשר והובא דבריו בפמ"ג בא"א [ומה דמדברי שערי תשובה משמע בסק"ז[ג] שיש להחמיר אף להמאירי בדיעבד אם לא תקנן עיינתי בפר"ח שם ומשמע להדיא דלדעת המאירי יש להכשיר אף בלא גרירה בדיעבד] ומ"מ לכתחלה בודאי יש להחמיר ולגרור כדעת הרלב"ח שהביאו המ"א בסק"ג דתיקון מהני אפילו לדידיה ואפילו תגין שנוגעין אחד לחבירו באות גופא נראה דמהני תיקון ואפילו בתו"מ ולא מיקרי שלא כסדרן כיון דחזינן שלא נשתנה צורת אות מקודם עי"ז וכן כתב בספר קסת הסופר: * כל אות תהיה מוקפת גויל. גויל דנקט לאו דוקא דאין כותבין עליו תפילין וכדלקמן בס"ז רק דנקט לישנא דשייך אבל ס"ת ולאו דוקא. ע"ת: * אין צריך לשרטט כ"א שיטה עליונה. ובדיעבד אם לא שירטט אפילו שיטה עליונה לדעת המחבר או מכל לד לדעת הרמ"א תלוי בין שיטת ר"ת ושארי פוס' דלר"ת שכ' דס"ת אין צריכה שירטוט רק בשיטה עליונה לדעת המחבר או מכל לד לדעת הרמ"א ובדיעבד נפסל בזה ומוכרח לומר כן ממסכת סופרים דיריעה שאינה מסורגלת פסולה א"כ ה"ה בתפילין דחד דינא אית להו לשיטתו אבל לפי מה דפסקינן ביו"ד סימן רע"א ס"ה דס"ת צריכה להיות שירטוט בכולה כמו מזוזה א"כ אין לנו ראיה לפסול התפילין בדיעבד אף אם לא שירטט כלל כ"א בביאור הגר"א בקצרה ובדבריו ניחא שלא כתב המחבר לפסול בדיעבד כמו שכתב להדיא ביו"ד בס"ת ומזוזה:

שער הציון

(ט) ע"ת ופמ"ג: (י) מ"א: (יא) פמ"ג: (יב) ב"י: (יג) א"ר ופמ"ג: (יד) מ"א וביאור הגר"א: (טו) א"ר ופמ"ג דלא כלבוש: (טז) ב"י:

הגהות ותיקונים: א) ט"ז: ב) סי' ל"ו ס"ק ג': ג) בסק"ה:

הערות והארות: 1) עיין בה"ל ד"ה צריך וכו' מביא בשם פרי חדש בא"ע, יש לציין שנשמט סעי"ק זה ונמצא בדפוסים קדומים:

should not become erased quickly. It is also a mitzvah to beautify /the letters both/ on the outside and on the inside. (...)

5. It is necessary **(17)** for one to write /the passages/ with the right /hand/, even if he is ambidextrous. If one wrote them **(18)** with the left /hand/, they are invalid, if it is possible to find others which were written with the right /hand/.

If /a person is/ left-handed, his left /hand/ **(19)** is /considered/ the "right" /hand with respect to this ruling/.

6. It is not necessary to mark out more than **(20)** the top line. /However,/ if one

Mishnah Berurah

(17) For one to write with the right /hand/. /This is/ because it is not normal to write with the left /hand/.

Correspondingly, if some correction with respect to the writing was done with the left /hand, the passage/ is /also/ invalid. However, it seems /logical/ that if one /merely/ separated contacts between letters /, then/, even /if one did so/ with the left /hand the passage/ is valid. This is comparable to /the ruling/ with respect to /separating contacts between letters given/ below in Sec. 39, that /the passage/ is valid, at any rate, once it is after the event, /even/ if people who are disqualified for /the writing of *tefilin* passages did/ it. See there /in sub-Par. 10 of the Mishnah Berurah/.

(18) With the left /hand/. This /applies/ when /the person who wrote the passages/ is only right-handed, but if he is ambidextrous /, then/, although he wrote /the passages/ with his left /hand/ they are valid.

Even if /the person who wrote the passages/ is solely right handed, one may don /*tefilin* which have these passages/ if he cannot find others, but should not make a blessing over them.

The *P.Mg.* writes that when a scribe writes with his right /hand/ and does all /other/ actions with his left /hand/ or vice versa, it is proper not to accept him as a scribe initially. /However,/ once it is after the event, one should not forbid /the use of the passages he wrote/. See the reasons there.

(19) Is the "right" /hand/. Consequently, if he wrote with his /actual/ right /hand the passages/ are invalid, if one can find others, just as /is the case with passages written/ with a normal left /hand/, as /stated/ above.

The *Rema* /of Fano/ writes that there was a case in Egypt where someone grasped the quill with his lips and wrote with it /in this manner/. He /ruled that the writing was/ invalid, as according to all /authorities writing/ with the mouth is not a /normal/ manner of writing. The *M.A.* writes that /passages written with the mouth/ are invalid even if one is unable to find others. See the work *Mishnas Avraham*, /where it is stated/ in the name of the *Geyt Mekushar* and other Poskim that such /writing/ or writing with one's foot is equivalent to writing with the left hand.[6]

(20) The top line. This is because for /the writing of/ *tefilin* /passages/ there is no halachic /requirement which was taught/ to Mosheh (Moses) on /Mount/ Sinai to mark out /the lines/, as /there is for the writing of/ a *mezuzah*. /The marking out which is done for *tefilin* passages/ is only /necessary/ because it is forbidden to write three words of a verse without marking out. Consequently, if one marks out the top line this is sufficient, as generally people are able to guide their hand to write all the lines straight after they have written the top line.

/The author of the Shulchan Aruch/ states /merely/ that it is not necessary /to mark out more/, because if one does /in fact/ wish to mark out all the lines, in order /to be able/ to

6 It follows that according to these Poskim one may use passages written in this way if he does not have others.

(כא) ישרטט כל השורות ולא ישרטט (כב) בעופרת מפני שהמקום השרטוט נשאר צבוע: הגה * וי"א שצריך לשרטט תמיד למעלה ולמטה ומן הצדדים אעפ"י שיודע לכתוב בלא שרטוט * וכן נוהגין: (ברוך שאמר ומרדכי וספר תרומה וסמ"ג): ז הלכה למשה מסיני תפילין על הקלף ולא על הדוכסוסטוס * ולא על הגויל. כותבין על הקלף במקום בשר * ואם שינה פסול מהו קלף ומהו דוכסוסטוס העור בשעת עיבודו חולקין אותו לשנים וחלק החיצון שהוא לצד השער נקרא קלף והפנימי הדבוק לבשר נקרא דוכסוסטוס ולפ"ז כי אמרינן כותבין על הקלף במקום בשר היינו במקום היותר קרוב לבשר דהיינו במקום חבורו כשהוא דבוק לדוכסוסטוס וקלפים שלנו שאין חולקים אותם יש להם דין קלף * וכותבים עליהם לצד בשר שמה שמגררים קליפתו העליונה שבמקום שער אינו אלא כדי מה שצריך * לתקנו ולהחליקו ואפילו אם היו חולקים העור לשנים היה צריך לגרר ממנו כך * ומצד הבשר גורדים הרבה עד שאין נשאר אלא הקלף בלבד: ח * צריך הקלף להיות מעובד (יא) [ו] (כג) בעפצים או בסיד * וצריך שיהיה מעובד לשמו טוב להוציא (כד) בשפתיו (כה) * בתחלת

ג שבת ע"ט ומנחות ל"ב ם לפי' התוספו' והמרדכי בשם רש"י והר"ן בשם הערוך והרא"ש בה"ת והרמב"ם בפרק א' מה"ת ע תוספות וכל הני רבוותא פ ב"י צ מגילה י"ט ק תוס' שם והרא"ש והר"ן ר גיטין כ"ד אפילו לדעת רש"י ש הרא"ש בהל' ס"ת בשם ר' ברוך וסמ"ג בסימן כ"ה

שערי תשובה

שלא כסדרן וכ"ע בפר"ח שם: [ו] בעפצים. עבה"ט ועיין בפנים מאירות ח"ג סי' ל"ב בקלף שלאחר העיבוד חולקין אותו ומושחין אותו בצבע לבן כדי שיהא חלק ולבן ביותר וקצת סופרים רצו לאסור מפני שאינו כותב על הקלף רק על אותו צבע ומפסיק בין הקלף לכתב והשיב שקנאת סופרים הוא זה והבל יפלה פיהם וכתב שמצוה מן המובחר לכתוב על קלף זה משום זה אלי ואנוהו והצבע הזה שמדובק לקלף אינו הפסק וגם כי כל נגאותו אינו חוצץ ע"ש. ונראה שלכתחלה יש להעביר על פניו בחוזק יד מטלית לבן ולקנח היטב ואז מה שאינו מדובק בהקלף מהצבע דבק טוב יסור ממנו ע"י הקנוח הזה ומה שנשאר

באר היטב

פסוק בלא שרטוט וכשמשרטט שטה עליונה דיו עי' מ"א: (יא) בעפצים

ביאור הלכה

* וי"א שצריך וכו'. יש לעיין קצת אם שירטט כל השורות אם צריך ג"כ לשרטט מן הצדדים או לא וספק זה יש להסתפק בס"ת ומזוזה דשם השירטוט כולו הוא לעיכובא ונראה דבדיעבד אין להחמיר בזה אפילו במזוזה כי לא נזכר בכ"מ רק שירטוט בין השיטין וכ"ש לפי מה שנראה מרדכ"ז הובא בפ"ת ביו"ד עיי"ש דטעם השירטוט אפילו במזוזה הוא כדי ליישר השיטין בודאי אין להחמיר בזה. ודע דשירטוט של תפילין לכו"ע אין צריך להיות לשמה כמש"כ הפמ"ג: * וכן נוהגין. וכהיום נהגו הכל לשרטט בכל השיטין ועיין בספר ב"ש שכתב שנ"ל שטוב לשרטט להשיטין לצד השיער ולמעלה ולמטה ולהצדדים ישרטט לצד הבשר: * ולא על הגויל. גויל הוא העור שלא נחלק ולא הוסר ממנו רק השער ותקנו שם ומצד הבשר לא הוסר כלום: * ואם שינה פסול. קאי אכולם ואפילו אם כתב קוצו של יו"ד שלא על הקלף במקום בשר כגון שבמקום אחד לא העביר מהדוכסוסטוס פסול ועיין לקמן: * וכותבים עליהם לצד בשר. ויזהר מאוד שלא יטעה לכתוב לצד השיער דמעכב בדיעבד וסימנו להכיר אחר העיבוד איזה צד הוא סמוך לבשר רואים לאיזה צד שהקלף מתכויץ כשמלהלחין אותו הוא מקום הסמוך לבשר ומ"מ אין לפסול תפילין ישנים מחמת סימן זה דאע"פ שאחר הבחינה נראה שנכתבו לצד השער אנו מעמידים להסופר שכתבם על חזקתו חזקת בקי ומומחה ובודאי כדין כתבם גם סמכינן על המרדכי דמכשיר אם נכתבו לצד השער. א"ר: * לתקנו ולהחליקו. ואם גרד יותר מזה עיין בנשמת אדם כלל י"ג[א] דעתו דלא מיקרי תו קלף ובחתם סופר א"ח תשובה ג' משמע שמקיל בזה: * ומצד הבשר גורדים הרבה. וסימנו לידע שנגרר כל הדוכסוסטוס מקובל בפי הסופרים כל מקום שהוא נמלא בקלף הוא ניכר לכל כי הוא חלק ושאר קלף אינו חלק כ"כ ואותו מקום החלק יכול לקלוף ולהפריש בסכין או במחט ובדיעבד אם לא גרד כל כך עיין במחה"ש שדעתו להחמיר וכן בתשובת משכנות יעקב ובנשמת אדם כתב דאין לפסול התפילין מטעם זה בדיעבד כיון דעכ"פ נגרר מן העור הקליפה הדקה הסמוך לבשר דעליה בודאי חל שם דוכסוסטוס וכן בתשובת ח"ס הנ"ל ובתשובת חסד לאברהם מיקל ג"כ מחמת זה ואף דאין למחות ביד המקיל בדיעבד דיש לו על מי לסמוך מה מאד ראוי להזהיר להסופרים שיזהרו בזה עכ"פ לכתחלה שלא ישאירו על הקלף קודם שיכתבו עליו שום קרום וקליפה דקה במקום הכתיבה ואפילו קליפה דקה כחוט השערה דזה הוי הכל חשש דוכסוסטוס: * צריך הקלף וכו'. והעיבוד הוא הל"מ דבלא זה אין עליו רק שם עור ולא גויל וקלף ודוכסוסטוס פמ"ג. וכל אלו הסעיפין הנאמרין פה לענין עיבוד הוא רק לענין הפרשיות של התפילין וכן לענין כתיבת ספרים ומזוזות [לבד מדעת הרמב"ם לענין מזוזה וכדאיתא ביו"ד בסימן רפ"ח ס"ה] ולענין עור הבתים יתבאר לקמן בסעיף ל"ז: * וצריך וכו' לשמו. ובלא זה פסולין ואם הוא במקום שלא יוכל להשיג תפלין אחרים כ"א אלו שנכתבו על עור המעובד שלא לשמה אף דבס"ת כה"ג נראה דיוכל לברך עליה בצבור אבל בתפילין יניחם כך בלא ברכה ע"ש בפמ"ג. ודע עוד דהפמ"ג[ב] החליט בפשיטות דעיבוד לשמה הוא מדרבנן והביא ראיה לזה מתשובת הרמב"ם שהובא בכ"מ פ"א מהלכות תפילין הלכה י"א וג"מ היכא שספק לן אם נתחלף לו עור בעד עור שלא לשמה י"ל ספיקא דרבנן לקולא אך מתשובת רע"א סי' ב' משמע דהוא סובר שהוא דאורייתא וכן ראיתי לאחד שכתב בשם המג"ב שכתב ג"כ דכל הפוסקים המחמירין בענין עיבוד לשמה ס"ל דהוא דאורייתא ומ"מ נראה *דבשעת הדחק יש להקל בספיקן דבלא"ה יש הרבה מהראשונים דס"ל דא"צ עיבוד לשמן [עיין בתשובת משכנות יעקב או"ח סימן מ"ב] וכעין שכתב בתשובת פרח מ"א בח"ב סימן ק"א הובא בברכי יוסף יו"ד סימן רע"א. ודע עוד דעיבוד סתמא הוי כשלא לשמה תשובת פמ"א סימן מ"ה דכ"מ מתוספות גיטין דף מ"ה בד"ה עיבוד לשמה ובספר בית אהרן יצא לידון בדבר החדש דהאידנא דאין כותבין ברוב על קלף שאר ספרים רק ס"ת הוי סתמא כלשמה ויש לעיין: * בתחילת העיבוד. ואם היה רק סוף העיבוד לשמה עיין לקמן בס"ט שבררנו שם דהט"ז ביו"ד רע"א ס"ג ס"ל דמהני והפמ"א ח"א סימן מ"ה

משנה ברורה

לכתוב יותר ביושר ליפות השיטות הרשות בידו. ואם לא שירטט אפילו שיטה עליונה עיין בביאור הלכה: (כא) ישרטט. פי' לכתחלה משום זה אלי ואנוהו אבל בדיעבד אפילו אם (יז) לא שירטט (יח) וכתב השיטות עקומות אין לפסול התפילין: (כב) בעופרת. (יט) וכן בדיו ובסיקרא וכל כיוצא בזה ואפילו (כ) בין השיטין אסור לשרטט בו וכל זה לכתחלה אבל בדיעבד אין להחמיר כן כתב הל"ח והא"ר ובתשובת דבר שמואל סימן שמ"ב מפקפק בזה מאוד אם משורטט בשום צבע שחור מחמת נגיעת אות באות ע"י השירטוט השחור אם לא דכתב מתחת השירטוט עי"ש: ח (כג) בעפצים או בסיד. ולעיכובא הוא (כא) דלא מיקרי קלף בלא זה רק דיפתרא ויהא העור בסיד עד (כב) שיפול השער מאליו ולא ע"י גרירה ואם הוציאו קודם לכן לא יכתוב עליו דהוי דיפתרא עדיין ופסול ויש (כג) מי שמולין וכתב הסופר שהוציא העורות לאחר ד' ימים ועדיין לא עבר שערות מעליהן נראה דבדיעבד אין קפידא דלא תליא בשער כלל דכיון דהעבר הוית בסיד וניתקן כהוגן לא מיקרי דיפתרא עי"ש: (כד) בשפתיו. ובדיעבד (כד) דיו במחשבה: (כה) בתחלת. ויותר (כה) אין צריך לא להוציא בשפתיו ולא לחשוב שמתעבדים לשמה אלא בתחלתו בלבד (כו) ואפילו נמשך העיבוד כמה ימים דכל הענין על דעת התחלה הוא עושה.

שער הציון

(יז) ב"ח ומוכח מן הטור: (יח) ב"ח הנ"ל: (יט) פמ"ג דלא כהמקילין בדיו: (כ) שם: (כא) מגילה י"ט ושבת ע"ט: (כב) מ"א ופמ"ג: (כג) משבצת נפש סימן ד': (כד) א"ר ופמ"ג: (כה) הרא"ש בה"ק: (כו) פמ"ג:

הגהות ותיקונים: א) י"ד סי' ג': ב) א"א י"ג

is not capable of /writing/ a straight line without marking it out, (21) he should mark out all the rows.

One should not mark out /the rows/ (22) with lead, since /if one does so/ the place of the mark will remain colored.

Gloss: There are /authorities/ who say that one must always mark out above and below and at the sides, even if he is capable of writing /straight lines/ without marking out. This is /in fact/ the practice.[5*] *(...)*

7. There is a halachic /requirement which was taught/ to Mosheh (Moses) on /Mount/ Sinai, that /the passages for/ *tefilin* /must be written/ on *kelaf* /parchment/, not on *duchsustos* /parchment/ and not on *gevil*[6*] /parchment/. One must write /them/ on the *kelaf* /parchment/ on the flesh side. If one deviated /from this in any respect the passages/ are invalid.

This is /the definition of/ *kelaf* /parchment/ and of *duchsustos* /parchment/. When the skin is processed it is split into two. The outer part, which is towards the hair, is called *kelaf* /parchment/ and the inner /part/, which is stuck to the flesh, is called *duchsustos* /parchment/. It follows from

Mishnah Berurah

write straighter to beautify the lines, he is allowed /to do so/.

/As regards the ruling/ if one did not mark out even the top line, see the Beyur Halachah.

(21) **He should mark out.** I.e., initially, because of /the requirement which derives from the verse/, "This is my God and I will glorify Him".[7] However, once it is after the event, the *tefilin* /passages/ should not be /ruled as/ invalid even if one did not mark out the lines and wrote them crooked.

(22) With lead. The same /applies/ to ink, red paint or anything similar. It is even forbidden to mark out with /such materials/ in between the lines.

All these /remarks apply with reference to/ initial /practice/, but once it is after the event one need not be stringent. This is what the *L.Ch.* and the *E.R.* write. /However,/ in the responsa *Devar Shemu'el*, Sec. 362, /the author/ is very uncertain about this /ruling as regards an instance/ when /the line/ is marked out in some black colored /writing material/. This is because the letters will touch one another as a result of the black marked out /line/, unless one writes underneath the marked out /line/. See there.

5* Nowadays it is the practice to mark out all the lines. For *tefilin* passages, the marking out does not have to be done specifically for the sake of the mitzvah. (Beyur Halachah)

6* *Gevil* parchment is skin which has not been split into two. Only the hair is removed from the skin and it is prepared for writing on that side.

7 *Shemos* 15:2. The Sages derived from this verse that one should perform mitzvos in an attractive way.

(כא) ישרטט כל השורות ולא ישרטט (כב) בעופרת מפני שהמקום השרטוט נשאר צבוע: הגה * וי"א שצריך לשרטט תמיד למעלה ולמטה ומן הצדדים אעפ"י שיודע לכתוב בלא שרטוט * וכן נוהגין: (בלוך שאמר ומרדכי וספר תרומה וסמ"ג): ז ¹הלכה למשה מסיני תפילין על הקלף ולא על הדוכסוסטוס * ולא על הגויל. כותבין על הקלף במקום בשר * ואם שינה פסול ᵒמהו קלף ומהו דוכסוסטוס העור בשעת עיבודו חולקין אותו לשנים וחלק החיצון שהוא לצד השער נקרא קלף והפנימי הדבוק לבשר נקרא דוכסוסטוס ולפ"ז כי אמרינן כותבין על הקלף במקום בשר היינו במקום היותר קרוב לבשר דהיינו במקום חבורו כשהוא דבוק לדוכסוסטוס ᵉוקלפים שלנו שאין חולקים אותם יש להם דין קלף * וכותבים עליהם לצד בשר ᵖשמה שמגררים קליפתו העליונה שבמקום שער אינו אלא כדי מה שצריך * לתקנו ולהחליקו ואפילו אם היו חולקים העור לשנים היה צריך לגרר ממנו כך * ומצד הבשר גורדים הרבה עד שאין נשאר אלא הקלף בלבד: ח * ᶜצריך הקלף להיות מעובד (יא) [ו] (כג) בעפצים או ᵖבסיד * ʳוצריך שיהיה מעובד לשמו ʷטוב להוציא (כד) בשפתיו (כה) * בתחלת

באר הגולה

ג שבת ע"ט ומנחות ל"ב ם לפי' התוספו' והמרדכי בשם רש"י והר"ן בשם הערוך והרא"ש בה"ת והרמב"ם בפרק א' מה"ת ע תוספות וכל הני רבוותא פ ב"י צ מגילה י"ט ק תוס' שם והרא"ש והר"ן ר גיטין כ"ד אפילו לדעת רש"י ש הרא"ש בהל' ס"ת בשם ר' ברוך וסמ"ג בסימן כ"ה

שערי תשובה

שלא כסדרן ול"ע בפר"ח שם: [ו] בעפצים. עבה"ט ועיין בפנים מאירות ח"ג סי' ל"ב בקלף שלאחר העיבוד חולקין אותו ומושחין אותו בצבע לבן כדי שיהא חלק ולבן ביותר וקצת סופרים רצו לאסור מפני שאינו כותב על הקלף רק על אותו צבע ומפסיק בין הקלף לכתב והשיב שקנאת סופרים הוא זה והבל יפצה פיהם וכתב שמצוה מן המובחר לכתוב על קלף זה משום זה אלי ואנוהו והצבע הזה שמדובק לקלף אינו הפסק וגם כי כל לנאותו אינו חוצץ ע"ש. ונראה שלכתחלה יש להעביר על פניו בחוזק יד מטלית לבן ולקנח היטב ואז מה שאינו מדובק בהקלף מהצבע דבק טוב יסור ממנו ע"י הקנוח הזה ומה שנשאר

באר היטב

פסוק בלא שרטוט וכשמשרטט שטה עליונה דיו עי' מ"א: (יא) בעפצים

משנה ברורה

לכתוב יותר בנקל ליפות הטיעות הרשות בידו. ואם לא שירטט אפילו שיטה עליונה עיין בביאור הלכה: (כא) ישרטט. פי' לכתחלה משום זה אלי ואנוהו אבל בדיעבד אפילו אם (יז) לא שירטט (יח) וכתב השיטות עקומות אין לפסול התפילין: (כב) בעופרת. (יט) וכן בדיו ובסיקרא וכל כיוצא בזה ואפילו (כ) בין השיטין אסור לשרטט בו וכל זה לכתחלה אבל בדיעבד אין להחמיר כן כתב הל"ח והא"ר ובתשובת דבר שמואל סימן שמ"ב מפקפק בזה מאוד אם משורטט בשום צבע שחור מחמת נגיעת אות באות ע"י השירטוט השחור אם לא דכתב מתחת השירטוט עי"ש: ח (כג) בעפצים או בסיד. ולעיכובא הוא (כא) דלא מיקרי קלף בלא זה רק דיפתרא ויניח העור בסיד עד (כב) שיפול השער מאליו ולא ע"י גרירה ואם הוליאו קודם לכן לא יכתוב עליו דהוי דיפתרא עדיין ופסול ויש (כג) מי שחולק וכתב דסופר שהוליא העורות לאחר ד' ימים ועדיין לא עבר שערות מעליהן נראה דבדיעבד אין קפידא דלא תליא בשער כלל דכיון דכבר הונח בסיד וניתקן כהוגן לא מיקרי דיפתרא עי"ש: (כד) בשפתיו. ובדיעבד (כד) דיו במחשבה: (כה) בתחלת. ויותר (כה) אין לריך לא להוליא בשפתיו ולא לחשוב שמתעבדים לשמה אלא בתחלתו בלבד (כו) ואפילו נמשך העיבוד כמה ימים דכל העושה על דעת ראשונה הוא עושה.

ביאור הלכה

* וי"א שצריך וכו'. יש לעיין קצת אם שירטט כל השורות אם לריך ג"כ לשרטט מן הצדדים או לא וספק זה יש להסתפק בס"ת ומזוזה דשם השירטוט כולו הוא לעיכובא ונראה דבדיעבד אין להחמיר בזה אפילו במזוזה כי לא נזכר בכ"מ רק שירטוט בין השיטין וכ"ש לפי מה שנראה מרדכ"ז הובא בפ"ת ביו"ד עיי"ש דטעם השירטוט אפילו במזוזה הוא כדי ליישר השיטין בודאי אין להחמיר בזה. ודע דשירטוט של תפילין לכו"ע אין לריך להיות לשמה כמש"כ הפמ"ג: * וכן נוהגין. וכהיום נהגו הכל לשרטט בכל השיטין ועיין בספר ב"ש שכתב שנ"ל שטוב לשרטט להשיטין לצד השיער ולמעלה ולמטה ולהצדדים ישרטט לצד הבשר: * ולא על הגויל. גויל הוא העור שלא נחלק ולא הוסר ממנו רק השער ותקנו שם ומצד הבשר לא הוסר כלום: * ואם שינה פסול. קאי אכולם ואפילו אם כתב קולו של יו"ד שלא על הקלף במקום בשר כגון שבמקום אחד לא העביר מהדוכסוסטוס פסול ועיין לקמן: * וכותבים עליהם לצד בשר. ויזהר מאוד שלא יטעה לכתוב לצד השיער דמעכב בדיעבד וסימנו להכיר אחר העיבוד איזה צד הוא סמוך לבשר רואים לאיזה צד שהקלף מתכויץ כשמלחלחין אותו הוא מקום הסמוך לבשר ומ"מ אין לפסול תפילין ישנים מחמת סימן זה דאע"פ שאחר הבחינה נראה שנכתבו לצד השער אנו מעמידים להסופר שכתבם על חזקתו חזקת בקי ומומחה ובודאי כדין כתבם גם סמכינן על המרדכי דמכשיר אם נכתבו לצד השער. א"ר: * לתקנו ולהחליקו. ואם גרד יותר מזה עיין בנשמת אדם כלל י"ג[א] דעתו דלא מיקרי תו קלף ובחתם סופר א"ח תשובה ג' משמע שמקיל בזה: * ומצד הבשר גורדים הרבה. וסימנו לידע שנגרר כל הדוכסוסטוס מקובל בפי הסופרים כל מקום שהוא נמצא בקלף הוא ניכר לכל כי הוא חלק ושאר קלף אינו חלק כ"כ ואותו מקום החלק יכול לקלוף ולהפריש בסכין או במחט ובדיעבד אם לא גרד כל כך עיין במחה"ש שדעתו להחמיר וכן בתשובת משכנות יעקב ובנשמת אדם כתב דאין לפסול התפילין מטעם זה בדיעבד כיון דעכ"פ נגרר מן העור הקליפה הדקה הסמוך לבשר דעליה בודאי חל שם דוכסוסטוס וכן בתשובת ח"ס הנ"ל ובתשובת חסד לאברהם מיקל ג"כ מחמת זה ואף דאין למחות ביד המקיל בדיעבד דיש לו על מי לסמוך מה מאד ראוי להזהיר להסופרים שיזהרו בזה עכ"פ לכתחלה שלא ישאירו על הקלף קודם שיכתבו עליו שום קרום וקליפה דקה במקום הכתיבה ואפילו קליפה דקה כחוט השערה דזה הוי הכל חשש דוכסוסטוס: * צריך הקלף וכו'. והעיבוד הוא הל"מ דבלא זה אין עליו רק שם עור ולא גויל וקלף ודוכסוסטוס פמ"ג. וכל אלו הסעיפין הנאמרין פה לענין עיבוד הוא רק לענין הפרשיות של התפילין וכן לענין כתיבת ספרים ומזוזות [לבד מדעת הרמב"ם לענין מזוזה וכדאיתא ביו"ד בסימן רפ"ח ס"ה] ולענין עור הבתים יתבאר לקמן בסעיף ל"ז: * וצריך וכו' לשמו. ובלא זה פסולין ואם הוא במקום שלא יוכל להשיג תפלין אחרים כ"א אלו שנכתבו על עור המעובד שלא לשמה אף דבס"ת כה"ג נראה דיוכל לברך עליה בלבור אבל בתפילין יניחם כך בלא ברכה ע"ש בפמ"ג. ודע עוד דהפמ"ג[ב] החליט בפשיטות דעיבוד לשמה הוא מדרבנן והביא ראיה לזה מתשובת הרמב"ם שהובא בכ"מ פ"א מהלכות תפילין הלכה י"א וע"מ היכא שספק לן אם נתחלף לו עור בעד עור שלא לשמה י"ל ספיקא דרבנן לקולא אך מתשובת רע"א סי' ב' משמע דהוא סובר שהוא דאורייתא וכן ראיתי לאחד שכתב בשם המג"ב שכתב ג"כ דכל הפוסקים המחמירין בענין עיבוד לשמה ס"ל דהוא דאורייתא ומ"מ נראה *דבשעת הדחק יש להקל בספיקן דבלא"ה יש הרבה מהראשונים דס"ל דא"ל עיבוד לשמן [עיין בתשובת משכנות יעקב או"ח סימן מ"ב] ועיין שכתב בתשובת פרח מ"א בח"ב סימן ק"א הובא בברכי יוסף יו"ד סימן רע"א. ודע עוד דעיבוד סתמא הוי כשלא לשמה תשובת פמ"א סימן מ"ה דכ"מ מתוספות גיטין דף מ"ה בד"ה עיבוד לשמה ובספר בית אהרן יצא לידון בדבר החדש דהאידנא דאין כותבין ברוב על קלף שאר ספרים רק ס"ת הוי סתמא כלשמה ויש לעיין: * בתחילת העיבוד. ואם היה רק סוף העיבוד לשמה עיין לקמן בס"ט שבררנו שם דהט"ז ביו"ד רע"א ס"ג ס"ל דמהני והפמ"א ח"א סימן מ"ה

שער הציון

(יז) ב"ח ומוכח מן הטור: (יח) ב"ח הנ"ל: (יט) פמ"ג דלא כהמקילין בדיו: (כ) שם: (כא) מגילה י"ט ושבת ע"ט: (כב) מ"א ופמ"ג: (כג) משיבת נפש סימן ד': (כד) א"ר ופמ"ג: (כה) הרא"ש בה"ק: (כו) פמ"ג:

הגהות ותיקונים: א) יו"ד סי' ג': ב) א"א י"ג

this that when we rule that one must write on the *kelaf* /parchment/ on the flesh side, what is meant is the side which is nearer to the flesh, i.e., the side where it is joined when it is /still/ stuck to the *duchsustos* /parchment/.

Our parchment, which is of undivided /skin/, has the ruling of *kelaf* /parchment/ and one must write /the *tefilin* passages/ on it /on the side/ towards the flesh. This is because our scraping of the outer skin on the hairy side is only what is required for preparing and smoothing /the parchment and not a removal of the *kelaf* part/ and even if we would divide the skin into two it would be necessary to scrape this /amount/ from it. /On the other hand, on the side/ towards the flesh we scrape away a lot /of the skin/ until only the *kelaf* /parchment/ by itself remains /without the *duchsustos* part/.

8. The parchment must be processed **(23)** with gallnut or with lime.

/The parchment/ must be processed for the sake of /use for *tefilin*/. It is desirable to express **(24)** with one's lips **(25)** at the start of the processing that

Mishnah Berurah

(23) With gallnut or with lime. This is an indispensable requirement, since without this /treatment the skin/ is not describable as parchment, /but/ merely as *diftera* (skin prepared for writing).

One should leave the skin in the lime until the hair falls out on its own and should not /remove the hair/ by scraping. If one took /the skin/ out /of the lime/ before this /had happened/ one should not write /*tefilin* passages/ on it, as it is still /classed as mere/ *diftera* and is invalid. There is /an authority/ who disputes this and writes that if a scribe took the skins out /of the lime/ after four days /, then, although/ the hairs had not yet gone from them, it appears that, now that it is after the event, one need not be particular /not to use them for *tefilin* passages because of this/. /In his opinion the validity of the skins/ is not dependent on /the falling out of/ the hairs at all, as in view /of the fact/ that /the skins/ were already placed in lime and prepared properly they are not describable as /mere/ *diftera*. See there.[8]

(24) With one's lips. Once it is after the event, it is sufficient for one to have thought /this in his mind/.

(25) At the start of. More /than that/, one is not required either to express with his lips or to think /in his mind/ that they are being processed for the sake of /use for *tefilin* passages or a Torah Scroll/, but this is only /necessary/ at the start. This even /applies/ if the processing is continued for several days. /The reason is/ that whenever one /continues/ an action he does so in conformance with his original purpose.

The start of the processing is defined as

8 In the work *Meshivas Nafesh*, Sec. 4.

העיבוד שהוא מעבדו לשם תפילין * או (כו) לשם (יג) [ז] ספר תורה ת אבל אם עיבדה לשם מזוזה (כז) פסול: ט * אם עיבדו א"י * א להרמב"ם פסול (כח) אפילו א"ל ישראל לעבד לשמו ב ולהרא"ש כשר אם ישראל עומד ע"ג וסייעו: (הגה (כט) קצת (יג) בעבודה)א ב"י בשם הרא"ש

ת ב"י ולדעת ר"ת ור"ת דפסלי שלא לשמה
א בפרק א' מה"ת
ב בהלכות ס"ת בשם רבי ברוך

באר היטב

וניח העור בסיד עד שיפול השער מאליו ואם מוליאה קודם לכן לא יכתוב עליו דהוי דיפתרא ב"ש מ"א: (יג) ס"ת. בתשובת עבודת הגרשוני סימן כ"ה אוסר לכתוב תפילין על קלף שנתעבד לשם ס"ת אם לא שיתנה בתחלה שאם ירצה אח"כ לשנות לקדושה קלה שיהא רשות בידו ע"ש. ועיין ביד אהרן מה שהקשה עליו. ועיין בתשובת למח לדק סימן פ"א אי מועיל התנאי למעבד עור לרצועות של תפילין להשתמש במה שישתייר מהעור לתשמיש של חול ודעתו בהא דברצועות מותר ע"ש. ועיין בי"ד סימן רע"א ס"ק ג' כתבתי בשם הטור דתיקון הקלף והשרטוט לא צריך לשמה: (יג) בעבודה. דוקא כשסייעו בעיבוד ואפילו בסוף העיבוד מהני אבל אינו מועיל אם סייעו להשחיר הרצועות. ובדיעבד אפי' לא סייעו כלל כשר ועכ"פ צריך שיאמר

שערי תשובה

מדובק בו הוא נעשה גוש אחד עם הקלף ואינו חולץ ומ"מ נראה שאין להתיר רק משיחה דקה אבל לא אם הוא טוח על פניו ועב קצת: [ז] ס"ת. עיין בה"ט בשם עה"ג ובפנים מאירות ח"ג סי' י"א כתב שנגד הגאון בעל עה"ג השיג עליו מדברי הש"ע והב"י כאן ובעל פנים מאירות הוכיח מהש"ס דמנחות שהדין עם העה"ג עיין שם. אמנם בשאגת אריה סי' מ"ז האריך בזה דעיבוד וכתיבה לשמה מהני מקדושה חמורה לקדושה קלה ולא מיבעיא מש"ר לש"י דמסתברא דחדא מלתא הוא ומהני בין מש"ר לש"י ובין איפכא ואם עיבד לס"ת מהני לתפילין ומזוזות שקלים מקדושת ס"ת. ואם עיבד לתפילין מהני למזוזה ולא לס"ת ואם עיבד למזוזה לא מהני אלא למזוזה לבד וכמ"ש הב"י

משנה ברורה

ותחילת העיבוד (כז) מיקרי כששמים העורות לתוך הסיד ולא בעת *ששורים לתוך המים קודם מפני דזה לא מיקרי עדיין עיבוד: (כו) לשם ס"ת. דקדושתה חמורה מתפילין ובכלל מאתים מנה ואעפ"כ (כח) מותר לשנות לתו"מ אף דקדושתם קלה ממנה אבל לדבר חול אסור לשנותו לבד (כט) אם התנה בפירוש בתחלת עיבודן שיהא מותר לשנותו אף לדבר חול אז מותר לשנותו. והנכון (ל) שינהגו כן הסופרים לכתחלה בעת ששמים העורות לתוך הסיד שיאמרו אני נותן עורות אלו לתוך הסיד לשם קדושת ס"ת ואני מתנה לכשארצה שאוכל לשנותו לכל דבר ולא כמו שנהגו הסופרים שאומרים לשם ס"ת או תפילין או מזוזות או שאר דבר רשות דאז מסתפקים האחרונים אם מהני ועיין בביאור הלכה: (כז) פסול. ולא מהני רק למזוזה בלבד דקדושתה קלה מתפילין ואם עיבד לתפילין מהני (לא) אף למזוזה ולא לס"ת ואם עיבד העור לשם רצועות לא מהני לכתוב פרשיות עליו אם עשה אח"כ קלף מהן דקדושתן חמורה ואפילו לעשות מהן עור בתים יש לומר נמי דפסול דקדושתן חמורה מרצועה [פמ"ג וע"ש עוד מה שכתב בזה]: ט (כח) אפילו. דס"ל להרמב"ם דעכו"ם עושה אדעתא דנפשיה ואף על פי שהעכו"ם אומר שעושה לישראל אין פיו ולבו שוין בזה אבל הרא"ש ס"ל דכיון שהוא עומד ע"ג (לב) בתחלה בעת ששמים העורות לתוך הסיד ואומר לו שיתנם או לתוך הסיד לשמה ולא בעינן הכונה של העכו"ם לזה רק בעת דבעת נתינתם לסיד לית ליה אמעה מועטת בזה ונותנם אדעתא דהכי אבל אם הישראל העומד ע"ג מיסב בלבו לבד לשמה לא מהני ואפילו אומר לו (לג) בפירוש כל שעומד מרחוק ואינו מלמדו לא מהני אפילו להרא"ש: (כט) קצת. אפי' אם לא סייעו רק (לד) בסוף העיבוד ואפילו גם זה הסיוע לא היה רק בשותפות עם העכו"ם כשר וכ"ז למצוה בעלמא אבל בדיעבד להרא"ש כשר (לה) אפילו לא סייעו כלל דעכו"ם אדעתא דישראל המלמדו

ביאור הלכה

מ"ה חולק ע"ז וס"ל דלדינא יש ספק אם נאמר הוכיח סופו על תחילתו וגם בביאור הגר"א לעיל בסימן י"א כתב כן דספק הוא אם נאמר הוכיח סופו על תחלתו עי"ש. ונראה דאעפ"כ אין להחמיר בדיעבד אחרי שיש הרבה מקילים כי גם דעת הגאון מהר"מ בנעט בבאורו על המרדכי להקל בזה עי"ש היטב בסוף הלכות ס"ת בד"ה או יסייע ובפרט דהראיה שמביא הט"ז לדבריו שם ביו"ד רע"א מדמכשרי הגאונים להחזיר אפילו קלף שנתעבד לגמרי שלא לשמה לידי מתוח ולהעביר עליו סיד לשמה וכ"ש בזה מרפסא איגרא [הגה"ה ומכ"ש לפי מה שמצאתי בשם תשובת חב"י דמפרש ההיא דתשובת הגאונים שמתירים להחזיר את העור המעובד לידי מתוח ולהעביר עליו סיד לשמה היינו בעור שאינו מעובד כל צרכו א"כ הרי מבואר בהדיא כדברינו ועיין בקו"א לשו"ע של הגר"ז ולענ"ד נראה דהאי דק המוזכר שם בתשובת הגאונים היינו קלף ממש וכן מוכח שם מדברי הטור וש"ך שם בתחלת הסימן דלא נוכל לדחות דהטור איירי ג"כ בקלף שלא ניתקן כל צרכו במליח לבד או במליח וקמיח ולא עפיץ דזה לא היה מתיר הטור באם אין יכולת וכו' אפילו במקום הדחק ותדע דהטור וגם השו"ע השמיטו שם האי דין ראשון דתשובת הגאונים שמתירין אפילו במליח לבד במקום הדחק ש"מ דלא ס"ל והטעם דס"ל כיון דזהו הלמ"מ כמש"כ הרמב"ם בפ"א מה' תפילין אין להקל בו ע"כ הג"ה] ואולי גם דעת הגר"א כן כמו לענין ספק אם צריך להוציא בפה דוקא דגם שם מביא הגר"א דספק הוא ואעפ"כ לא החמירו רק לכתחלה וכדמוכח מהטוש"ע שכתב טוב להוציא בשפתיו וכדכתב הפמ"ג כן נאמר בזה ומכ"ש לפי דעת הפמ"ג שעיבוד לשמה הוא דרבנן. היוצא מדברינו דאם שכח ליתן העורות לתוך הסיד לשמה ונזכר בתוך עיבודו בעוד שיש עליה עדיין שם דיפתרא שיטלם מן הסיד ויחזור ויתנם לתוך הסיד לשמה כנ"ל ברור בעזה"י. וכ"ז אם הוא מחשב לשמה במעשה העיבוד גופא אבל אם מחשב לשמה בעת תיקון הקלף אח"כ כגון מה שממחים אותו באבן הפימ"ס וכדומה או בעת השירטוט של הסת"מ או ברצועות בעת השחרתן לבד הוא מחשב לשמן זה בודאי לא מהני [ט"ז ביו"ד שם ופמ"ג והסכמת אחרונים] ודע עוד דבהם קי"ל דא"צ כלל שיהא לשמה ואפילו במזוזה דעלם השירטוט הוא הלמ"מ אפ"ה אינה צריכה להיות לשמה אך יש מן האחרונים שמחמירין בדבר לענין שירטוט [הב"ח במזוזה והבני יונה אף בס"ת] אפילו דיעבד ונכון לחוש לדבריהם עכ"פ לכתחלה ועיין בפמ"ג במ"ז סק"ד ותבין את הכל ועיין בפמ"ג שכתב עוד דלפי דברי הב"ח לא יועיל שירטוט אפילו דס"ת למזוזה אבל לפי מאי דאנן פסקינן דס"ת ומזוזה שוין מהני וע"ש עוד דשירטוט דתפילין ומזוזה בודאי לא מהני להב"ח ואף אם שרטטו לשמה כמאן דליתא דמיא אך כבר הכרענו דאין להחמיר בדיעבד. וע"ש בפמ"ג שכתב דכ"ז בסתמא אבל במחשב בהדיא בהשרטוט שלא לשמה אפשר דגרע לד"ה: * או לשם ס"ת. עיין במ"ב במה שכ' ולא כמו שנהגו הסופרים עי"ש הטעם דבדאורייתא קי"ל אין ברירה ולפי מה שכתב הפמ"ג דעיבוד לשמה הוא דרבנן יש להקל בדיעבד. וצ"ע למעשה: * אם עיבדו עכו"ם. ואם עבדן אשה או קטן עיין לקמן בסימן ל"ט במ"ב סק"י: * להרמב"ם וכו' וסייעו. לבאר הדין דסיוע צריך להאריך קצת דהנה הט"ז הביא פה וביו"ד רע"א דסיוע אפילו בסוף מהני והביא ראיה מהחזרת הקלף לסיד עי"ש והפמ"א בסימן מ"ה השיג עליו אחד דאיך נאמר כאן הוכיח סופו על תחלתו כיון דתחלתו עשאו עכו"ם איך נאמר דמשום דבא הישראל לבסוף וסייעו לשמה יוכיח על תחלתו שהיה לשמה ועוד דאפילו בישראל עצמו הביא ראיה דלדינא יש ספק אם נאמר הוכיח סופו על תחלתו עי"ש היטב. ובאמת לפי הבנתו בט"ז יש על הט"ז פליאה גדולה מזו דהאיך הביא הט"ז ראיה מהחזרת הסיד לתוך[ב] הקלף

שער הציון

(כז) טו"י מ"ת בסימן קע"ה עי"ש ומשיג שם על העט"ז שכתב בסימן זה בהפכו: (כח) ב"י ואחרונים ודלא כתשובת עה"ג דמחמיר: (כט) לקמן בסימן מ"ב עי"ש כל פרטי הדינים: (ל) תשובות רע"א בסימן ב' ולקמן בסימן מ"ב בשע"ת עי"ש: (לא) ב"י: (לב) הרא"ש בה"ק: (לג) פמ"ג: (לד) ט"ז: (לה) ש"ך ב"ח ע"ת כנה"ג ומ"א וא"ר וביאורי הגר"א לעיל בסי' י"א לדעת הרא"ש דלא כפנים מאירות בסי' מ"ה שמחמיר בזה ואעפ"כ במקום שעבדנין ישראל מנוייס יתן להישראל כי גם התוס' ס"ל כהרמב"ם:

הגהות ותיקונים: א) צ"ל בעיבודה: ב) צ"ל על:

one is processing it for the sake of /use for/ *tefilin* or (26) for the sake of /use for/ a Torah Scroll. However, if one processed /parchment/ for the sake of /use for/ *mezuzos*, (27) it is invalid /for use for *tefilin*/.

Mishnah Berurah

/the stage/ when one puts the skins into the lime. It is not the stage when one puts them into water, beforehand, since that /stage/ is not yet describable as processing.

(26) For the sake of a Torah Scroll. /This is/ because the holiness of /a Torah Scroll/ is more severe than /the holiness of/ *tefilin* /passages/ and the higher /degree/ includes the lower[9] /degree of holiness/.

Despite /its greater holiness/, one may divert /parchment designed for use in a Torah Scroll/ to /use/ for *tefilin* /passages/ or mezuzos, although these have a lesser /degree of/ holiness. However, it is forbidden to divert /the parchment/ to secular use, unless one stipulated explicitly at the start of the processing that it should be permitted to divert /the parchment/ even to secular use. In the latter case it is /in fact/ permitted to divert it /to secular use/.

The correct practice, initially, is for the scribes to say at the stage when they put the skins into the lime, "I am placing these skins into the lime for the sake of /serving for/ the holiness of a Torah Scroll and I stipulate that, should I so wish, I will be able to divert them to any use." One should not /, however,/ act like those scribes who say /that the skins are being processed/ for the sake of /serving for/ a Torah Scroll, *tefilin* /passages/ or mezuzos or /some/ other, non-mitzvah, usage. For in such a case the Acharonim are in doubt as to whether this is of avail. See the Beyur Halachah.

(27) It is invalid. /In such a case the processing/ is only of avail for /the sake of use for/ mezuzos alone, as the /degree of/ holiness of /mezuzos/ is less than /that of/ *tefilin* /passages/.

/On the other hand,/ if one processed /parchment/ for /the sake of use for/ *tefilin* /passages/, this is of avail even for /one to be permitted to use it for/ mezuzos, but not for /it to be used for/ a Torah Scroll.

If one processed the skin for the sake of /use for *tefilin*/ straps, this is of no avail for the writing of /*tefilin*/ passages on it /to be permitted/, if one later made parchment out of it, as the holiness of /*tefilin* passages/ is /more/ severe. Even if one wishes to prepare skin /to serve/ for housings out of /this skin/, one may argue that it is also invalid /for that purpose/, as the holiness of /the housings/ is /more/ severe than /that of/ the straps. [*P.Mg.*; see further there, what he writes about this.]

9 Lit., "two hundred includes one hundred". I.e., having in mind that the parchment should have the higher degree of holiness automatically involves having in mind that it should also have the lesser degree of holiness.

העיבוד שהוא מעבדו לשם תפילין * או (כו) לשם (יב) [ז] ספר תורה ה׳אבל אם עיבדה לשם מזוזה (כז) פסול: **ט** * אם עיבדו א״י * אלהרמב״ם פסול (כח) אפילו א״ל ישראל לעבד לשמו בולהרא״ש כשר אם ישראל עומד ע״ג וסייעו: (הגה (כט) קלת (יג) בעבודה)[א] ב״י בשם הרא״ש

ת ב״י ולדעת ר״ת ור״ת דפסלי שלא לשמה
א בפרק א׳ מה״ת
ב בהלכות ס״ת בשם רבי ברוך

באר היטב

ויניח העור בסיד עד שיפול השער מאליו ואם מוציאה קודם לכן לא יכתוב עליו דהוי דיפתרא ב״ש מ״א: (יב) ס״ת. בתשובת עבודת הגרשוני סימן כ״ה אוסר לכתוב תפילין על קלף שנתעבד לשם ס״ת אם לא שיתנה בתחלה שאם ירצה אח״כ לשנות לקדושה קלה שיהא רשות בידו ע״ש. ועיין ביד אהרן מה שהקשה עליו. ועיין בתשובת נחת לדק סימן פ״א אי מועיל התנאי למעבד עור לרצועות של תפילין להשתמש במה שישתייר מהעור לתשמיש של חול ודעתו בהא דברצועות מותר ע״ש. ועיין בי״ד סימן רע״א ס״ק ג׳ כתבתי בשם הטור דתיקון הקלף והשרטוט לא צריך לשמה: (יג) בעבודה. דוקא כשסייעו בעיבוד ואפילו בסוף העיבוד מהני אבל אינו מועיל אם סייעו להשחיר הרצועות. ובדיעבד אפי׳ לא סייעו כלל כשר ועכ״פ צריך שיאמר

שערי תשובה

מדובק בו הוא נעשה גוש אחד עם הקלף ואינו חולץ ומ״מ נראה שאין להתיר רק משיחה דקה אבל לא אם הוא טוח על פניו ועב קצת: [ז] ס״ת. עיין בה״ט בשם עה״ג ובפנים מאירות ח״ג סי׳ י״א כתב שנכד הגאון בעל עה״ג השיג עליו מדברי הש״ע והב״י כאן ובעל פנים מאירות הוכיח מהש״ס דמנחות שהדין עם העה״ג עיין שם. אמנם בשאגת אריה סי׳ מ״ז האריך בזה דעיבוד וכתיבה לשמה מהני מקדושה חמורה לקדושה קלה ולא מיבעיא מש״ר לש״י דמסתברא דהדא מלתא הוא ומהני בין מש״ר לש״י ובין איפכא ואם עיבד לס״ת מהני לתפילין ומזוזות שקלים מקדושת ס״ת. ואם עיבד לתפילין מהני למזוזה ולא לס״ת ואם עיבד למזוזה לא מהני אלא למזוזה לבד וכמ״ש הב״י

משנה ברורה

ותחילת העיבוד (כו) תיקרי כשמשים העורות לתוך הסיד ולא בעת *שמשימם לתוך המים קודם מפני דזה לא תיקרי עדיין עיבוד: (כו) לשם ס״ת. דקדושתה חמורה מתפילין ובכלל מאתים מנה ואעפ״כ (כח) מותר לשנות לתו״מ אף דקדושתם קלה ממנה אבל לדבר חול אסור לשנותו לבד (כט) אם התנה בפירוש בתחלת עיבודן שיהא מותר לשנותו אף לדבר חול אז מותר לשנותו. והנכון (ל) שינהגו כן הסופרים לכתחלה בעת שמשימים העורות לתוך הסיד שיאמרו אני נותן עורות אלו לתוך הסיד לשם קדושת ס״ת ואני מתנה לכשארצה שאוכל לשנותו לכל דבר ולא כמו שנהגו הסופרים שאומרים לשם ס״ת או תפילין או מזוזות או שאר דבר רשות דאז מסתפקים האחרונים אם מהני ועיין בביאור הלכה: (כז) פסול. ולא מהני רק למזוזה בלבד דקדושתה קלה מתפילין ואם עיבד לתפילין מהני (לא) אף למזוזה ולא לס״ת ואם עיבד העור לשם רצועות לא מהני לכתוב פרשיות עליו אם עשה אח״כ קלף מהן דקדושתן חמורה ואפילו לעשות מהן עור בתים יש לומר נמי דפסול דקדושתן חמורה מרצועה [פמ״ג וע״ש עוד מה שכתב מזה]: **ט** (כח) אפילו. דס״ל להרמב״ם דעכו״ם עושה אדעתא דנפשיה ואף על פי שהעכו״ם אומר ששומע לישראל אין פיו ולבו שוין בזה אבל הרא״ש ס״ל דכיון שהוא עומד ע״ג (לב) בתחלה בעת שמשים העורות לתוך הסיד ואומר לו שיתנם אז לתוך הסיד לשמה ולא בעינן הכונה של העכו״ם לזה רק בעת רגע נתינתם לסיד לית ליה אשעה מועטת כזה ונותנם אדעתא דהכי אבל אם הישראל העומד ע״ג חישב בלבו לבד לשמה לא מהני ואפילו אומר לו (לג) בפירוש כל שעומד מרחוק ואינו מלמדו לא מהני אפילו להרא״ש: (כט) קצת. אפי׳ אם לא סייעו רק (לד) בסוף העיבוד ואפילו גם זה הסיוע לא היה רק בשותפות עם העכו״ם כשר וכ״ז למצוה בעלמא אבל בדיעבד להרא״ש כשר (לה) אפילו לא סייעו כלל דעכו״ם אדעתא דישראל המלווהו

ביאור הלכה

מ״ה חולק ע״ז וס״ל דלדינא יש ספק אם נאמר הוכיח סופו על תחילתו וגם בביאור הגר״א לעיל בסימן י״א כתב כן דספק הוא אם נאמר הוכיח סופו על תחלתו עי״ש. ונראה דאעפ״כ אין להחמיר בדיעבד אחרי שיש הרבה מקילים כי גם דעת הגאון מהר״מ בנעט בבאורו על המרדכי להקל בזה עי״ש היטב בסוף הלכות ס״ת בד״ה או יסייע ובפרט דהראיה שמביא הט״ז לדבריו שם ביו״ד רע״א מדמכשרי הגאונים להחזיר אפילו קלף שנתעבד לגמרי שלא לשמה לידי מתוח ולהעביר עליו סיד לשמה וכ״ש בזה מרפסא איגרא [הגה״ה ומכ״ש לפי מה שמצאתי בשם תשובת חב״י דמפרש ההיא דתשובת הגאונים שמתירים להחזיר את העור המעובד לידי מתוח ולהעביר עליו סיד לשמה היינו בעור שאינו מעובד כל צרכו א״כ הרי מבואר בהדיא כדברינו ועיין בקו״א לשו״ע של הגר״ז ולענ״ד נראה דהאי דק המוזכר שם בתשובת הגאונים היינו קלף ממש וכן מוכח שם מדברי הטור וש״ך שם בתחלת הסימן דלא נוכל לדחות דהטור איירי ג״כ בקלף שלא ניתקן כל צרכו במליח לבד או במליח וקמיח ולא עפיץ דזה לא היה מתיר הטור באם אין יכולת וכו׳ אפילו במקום הדחק ותדע דהטור וגם השו״ע השמיטו שם האי דין ראשון דתשובת הגאונים שמתירין אפילו במליח לבד במקום הדחק ש״מ דלא ס״ל והטעם דס״ל כיון דזהו הלמ״מ כמש״כ הרמב״ם בפ״א מה׳ תפילין אין להקל בו ע״כ הג״ה] ואולי גם דעת הגר״א כן כמו לענין ספק אם צריך להוציא בפה דוקא דגם שם מביא הגר״א דספק הוא ואעפ״כ לא החמירו רק לכתחלה וכדמוכח מהטוש״ע שכתב טוב להוציא בשפתיו וכדכתב הפמ״ג כן נאמר בזה ומכ״ש לפי דעת הפמ״ג שעיבוד לשמה הוא דרבנן. היוצא מדברינו דאם שכח ליתן העורות לתוך הסיד לשמה ונזכר בתוך עיבודו בעוד שיש עליה עדיין שם דיפתרא שיטלם מן הסיד ויחזור ויתנם לתוך הסיד לשמה כנ״ל ברור בעזה״י. וכ״ז אם הוא מחשב לשמה במעשה העיבוד גופא אבל אם מחשב לשמה בעת תיקון הקלף אח״כ כגון מה שממחים אותו באבן הפימ״ס וכדומה או בעת השירטוט של הסת״מ או ברצועות בעת השחרתן לבד הוא מחשב לשמן זה בודאי לא מהני [ט״ז ביו״ד שם ופמ״ג והסכמת אחרונים] ודע עוד דבהם קי״ל דא״צ כלל שיהא לשמה ואפילו במזוזה דעלם השירטוט הוא הלמ״מ אפ״ה אינה צריכה להיות לשמה אך יש מן האחרונים שמחמירין בדבר לענין שירטוט [הב״ח במזוזה והבני יונה אף בס״ת] אפילו דיעבד ונכון לחוש לדבריהם עכ״פ לכתחלה ועיין בפמ״ג במ״ז סק״ד ותבין את הכל ועיין בפמ״ג שכתב עוד דלפי דברי הב״ח לא יועיל שירטוט אפילו דס״ת למזוזה אבל לפי מאי דאנן פסקינן דס״ת ומזוזה שוין מהני וע״ש עוד דשירטוט דתפילין ומזוזה בודאי לא מהני להב״ח ואף אם שרטטו לשמה כמאן דליתא דמיא אך כבר הכרענו דאין להחמיר בדיעבד. וע״ש בפמ״ג שכתב דכ״ז בסתמא אבל במחשב בהדיא בהשרטוט שלא לשמה אפשר דגרע לד״ה: * או לשם ס״ת. עיין במ״ב במה שכ׳ ולא כמו שנהגו הסופרים עי״ש הטעם דבדאורייתא קי״ל אין ברירה ולפי מה שכתב הפמ״ג דעיבוד לשמה הוא דרבנן יש להקל בדיעבד. וצ״ע למעשה: * אם עיבדו עכו״ם. ואם עבדן אשה או קטן עיין לקמן בסימן ל״ט במ״ב סק״י: * להרמב״ם וכו׳ וסייעו. לבאר הדין דסיוע צריך להאריך קצת דהנה הט״ז הביא פה וביו״ד רע״א דסיוע אפילו בסוף מהני והביא ראיה מהחזרת הקלף לסיד עי״ש והפמ״א בסימן מ״ה השיג עליו אחד דאיך נאמר כאן הוכיח סופו על תחלתו כיון דתחלתו עשאו עכו״ם איך נאמר דמשום דבא הישראל לבסוף וסייעו לשמה יוכיח על תחלתו שהיה לשמה ועוד דאפילו בישראל עצמו הביא ראיה דלדינא יש ספק אם נאמר הוכיח סופו על תחלתו עי״ש היטב. ובאמת לפי הבנתו בט״ז יש על הט״ז פליאה גדולה מזו דהאיך הביא הט״ז ראיה מהחזרת הסיד לתוך[ב] הקלף

שער הציון

(כז) טו״י מ״ת בסימן קע״ה עי״ש ומשיג שם על העט״ז שכתב בסימן זה בהפכו: (כח) ב״י ואחרונים ודלא כתשובת עה״ג דמחמיר: (כט) לקמן בסימן מ״ב עי״ש כל פרטי הדינים: (ל) תשובות רע״א בסימן ב׳ ולקמן בסימן מ״ב בשע״ת עי״ש: (לא) ב״י: (לב) הרא״ש בה״ק: (לג) פמ״ג: (לד) ט״ז: (לה) ש״ך ב״ח ע״ת כנה״ג ומ״א וא״ר וביאורי הגר״א לעיל בסי׳ י״א לדעת הרא״ש דלא כפנים מאירות בסי׳ מ״ה שמחמיר בזה ואעפ״כ במקום שעבדנין ישראל מצויים יתן להישראל כי גם התוס׳ ס״ל כהרמב״ם:

הגהות ותיקונים: א) צ״ל בעיבודה: ב) צ״ל על:

9. If a non-Jew processed /parchment/, it is invalid according to the *Rambam*,[7*] **(28)** even if a Jew instructed him to process it for the sake of /use for *tefilin*/. /However,/ according to the *Rosh*, it is valid /in such a case/, provided that a Jew stood over /the non-Jew while the non-Jew did it/ and /the Jew also/ assisted /the non-Jew/ *(Gloss:* **(29)** *a little with the work)* ...

Mishnah Berurah

(28) Even. For the *Rambam* is of the opinion that a non-Jew acts for his own purposes and although the non-Jew said that he was listening to the Jew, what /a non-Jew/ says and what he thinks are not the same with respect to this /matter/.

The *Rosh*, on the other hand, is of the opinion that in view /of the fact/ that /the Jew/ stood over him at the outset, at the stage when he put the skins into the lime, and told him to place them inside the lime for the sake of /use for *tefilin* passages, this is sufficient/. /For/ the application of the non-Jew for this /purpose/ is not required except at the point when they are placed in the lime and for so short a time he will heed /the Jew/ and place /them there/ with this in mind.

However, if the Jew who stood over him merely thought in his /own/ mind that /the action should be/ for the sake of /use for *tefilin* passages/, this is of no avail. Even if he told /the non-Jew/ explicitly /to do it for the sake of use for *tefilin* passages/, this will have been of no avail, even according to the *Rosh*, whenever he /merely/ stood at a distance and did not guide him.

(29) A little. Even if /the Jew/ did not assist /the non-Jew/ except at the end of the processing and even if this assistance was only /done/ jointly with the non-Jew, /the parchment/ is valid.

/However,/ this /assistance/ is in all respects a mere mitzvah /requirement/, but, once it is after the event, /the parchment/ is valid according to the *Rosh* even if /the Jew/ did not assist /the non-Jew/ at all. For /, in his opinion,/ a non-Jew acts /having in mind/ the purpose /required of him/ by a Jew

7* *Rambam, Hilchos Tefilin* 1:11.

(ל) וכן נוהגין ועיין לעיל (סי' י"א סעיף ב): י גכשמסמנין הנקבים במרצע * כעין אותיות אע"פ שנקל לא"י * לזייף אין חוששין * משום דמרתת הא"י פן יכיר ישראל (לא) בטביעות (יד) עין: יא עור שעיבדו שלא לשמו אם יש תיקון לחזור לעבדו לשמו דיתבאר בטור יור"ד (טו) סימן רע"א: יב * היהיה הקלף מעור בהמה וחיה ועוף (טז) [ח] * הטהורים * אפילו מנבילה וטריפה שלהם אבל לא מעור בהמה וחיה ועוף הטמאים דכתיב למען תהיה * תורת ה' בפיך ממין המותר לפיך ולא מעור דג אפילו הוא טהור משום דנפיש זוהמיה: יג ויהיה הקלף שלם שלא יהא בו נקבים שאין הדיו עובר עליו זדהיינו שלא תהא * האות נראית בו חלוקה (יז) [ט] (לב) לשתים: יד חהסופרים הזריזים

באר הגולה

ג הגהת מיימון מה"ת ד הרב השמיטו שם והטור ביו"ד שם בשם תשו' לגאון מכשיר ה שבת ק"ח ו שם וחולין ק"כ ז הר"י אלכסנדרי"א בסימן ל"ו ח שם

שערי תשובה

סי' ל"ג ע"ש: [ח] הטהורים. עבה"ט וכתב בבכור שור בשבת דף ק"ח מנין שאין כותבין תפילין כו' והוא עפ"י מה שבארנו בשאלה אחת אם מותר לכתוב תפילין ע"ג עור בהמה טהורה שנעבדה ונעשית ע"ז והעלינו לפי מ"ש כאן דבעינן מן המותר (ור"ל שבתשובה שם הוכיח דמותר בפיך ממש בעינן ודלא כמ"ש התוספות דקאי על המין וספר תשובותיו נעלמו מן העין וחבל על דאבדין) אלא אפילו לפירוש התוס' דהכוונה על המין המותר מ"מ יש לאסור דע"ז איתקש למת כו' עיין שם: [ט] לשתים. עבה"ט ועיין בתשובת הגאון

באר היטב

לעובד כוכבים ליתן לתוך הסיד לשמה ועיין באר עשק סי' י"ד. ובהרמ"ע סי' ל"ד: (יד) עין. כתב הג"מ אם נתנו מתחלה בעיבוד לשם קדושה יוכל להניח העובד כוכבים ולהוציאו ולתקנו וא"צ לסייעו עוד עיין מ"א: (טו) סימן רע"א. דיכולין לחזור ולתקנו ע"ש ס"ק א' מש"ש. (טז) הטהורים. בתוספות דסוטה דף י"ז כתבו בשם הירושלמי דאפילו שאר ספרים שיש בהם שמות אסור לכתוב על עור בהמה טמאה מ"א. בתשובת הרמ"ע סימן ל"ז כתב דיש מעלות דשל שליל מלוה מן המובחר ושל חיה יותר משל בהמה ובהמה שחוטה עדיף משל חיה נבילה ע"ש וכ"כ בשכנה"ג ובע"ת. אי בהמה טמאה שנולדה מטהורה אם עורותיה כשר לתו"מ או עור בהמה טהורה שנולדה מטמאה אי פסול לתו"מ עיין בתשובת יד אליהו סימן ב' שהאריך והעלה להחמיר. עור של בהמה רובעת ונרבעת אסור לכתוב תו"מ יד אליהו סימן ל"ה ע"ש: (יז) לשתים. ר"ל דבשעת הכתיבה נסתם

משנה ברורה

לעשות לשמה עביד: (ל) וכן נוהגין. והמנהג לפי דברי אחרונים לכתחלה צריך להיות כך שישים הישראל בעצמו העורות לתוך הסיד לשמה ויאמר לעכו"ס שכל שאר מלאכת העיבוד שיעשה הוא יעשה ג"כ לשמה ויכול העכו"ס אח"כ להוציאו בעצמו ולתקנו וא"צ עוד לעמוד ע"ג ולסייעו עוד. ואם נתן הישראל העורות בעצמו לתוך הסיד לשמה ולא אמר כלום להעכו"ס כתב הפמ"ג דל"ע בזה [כי לפי דברי הב"י ביו"ד בסימן רע"א כשר אפילו לדברי הרמב"ם והב"ח אוסר] אכן לפי דברי הנו"ב בסימן קע"ה עי"ש וביאורי הגאון מהר"מ בנעט על המרדכי סוף הלכות ס"ת יש להקל בדיעבד. ואם סייעו הישראל להעכו"ס קצת בסוף ובזה גמר מלאכת העיבוד ולא אמר לעכו"ס כלל שיעשה לשמה (לו) זה בודאי לא מהני דמסייע אין בו ממש. וה"ה שזה גמר העיבוד לא עשה בעצמו רק בסיוע עם העכו"ס אבל אם גמרו הישראל בעצמו בלא סיוע העכו"ס כגון שהוציא הישראל העורות מן הסיד קודם שנגמר עיבודן וחזר והניחם בתוך הסיד לשמה הט"ז ביו"ד והגאון מהר"מ הנ"ל מקילין בזה ואין למחות ביד הנוהג להקל כדבריהן וכמו שבררנו בביאור הלכה: י (לא) בט"ע. שנתן בסימנין או שאלו הנקבים נעשו יותר מאדם מסלו וי"א (לז) שיכתוב בראש בפנים במקום שאין דרך לעבד הראש וישאר הכתב עד אחר העיבוד ולא יסמן במרצע מתחת משם זיוף ובדיעבד יש להקל כהש"ע: יג (לב) לשתים.

ביאור הלכה

הקלף והרי ע"כ מיגרע גרע דבהחזרת הסיד אפילו לא היה בעיבוד ראשון שום אמירה לעכו"ס מהני כמו שנראה מדברי הטור ביו"ד שם וכאן צריך ע"כ אמירה לעכו"ס דמסייע לבד אין בו ממש אע"כ דכונת הט"ז במש"כ במסייעו אין ר"ל שיעשה איזה מעשה בסיוע העכו"ס דמסייע זו בודאי אין בו ממש אלא ר"ל שיעשה גם הוא איזה מעשה עיבוד בלי העכו"ס וסברת הט"ז לומר דזה בודאי חשיב הזמנה מעלייתא לקדושה כיון דבלא גמר הישראל לא היה עדיין העור מעובד ועד כאן לא החמירו התוספות אלא דתיקון הקלף ושירטוטו זה לא חשיב הזמנה לקדושה כיון דכבר נגמר מלאכת העיבוד אבל בזה שעושה בעיבוד מעשה גמורה דבלא עשייתו לא היה העור נגמר בעיבודו מהני וע"ז הביא ראיה מהחזרת הדק [שהוא קלף כדאיתא בטור] פי' דהלא לענין שבת בודאי אין עיבוד אחר עיבוד וכמו שמבואר בהלכות שבת לענין שאר מלאכות וכאן מהני אע"כ דכאן לא בעינן רק שיעשה מעשה שיהא מוכיח שהיא הזמנה מעלייתא לקדושה א"כ כ"ש כשעושה הגמר בעיבוד עצמו דזה בודאי מיקרי עיבוד אף לענין שבת [וכמו שמוכח בשבת דף ע"ו[א] דפריך היינו מולח היינו מעבד אלמא אף דלא עשה כ"א מליחה בעלמא שעדיין שם עור עליה ולא קלף כדאיתא בשבת דף ע"ט חייב משום עיבוד א"כ כ"ש כשעשה עפיץ לבד דבזה נגמר עליה מלאכת העיבוד להקרא עי"ז קלף ולא דיפתרא דחייב] כ"ש דמיקרי עיבוד לענין לשמה וא"כ אין אנו צריכין לומר יוכיח סופו על תחלתו דבסופו לבד די וממילא אין אנו צריכין ג"כ לומר שילוה לעכו"ס בתחלתו לעשות לשמה ובזה יוסר כל הקושיות מדברי הרב ט"ז. היוצא מדברינו דשני עניני סיוע יש אם עשה פעולה בשותפות העכו"ס ואפי' בתחלתו בזה ודאי לא מהני רק באופן כשאמר לעכו"ס ליתן לתוך הסיד לשמה ואפילו זה לא מהני רק להרא"ש ובזה מיירי השו"ע שכתב וסייעו קצת בעיבודה אבל ודאי אם עשה פעולה בעצמו במלאכת העיבוד אף שתחלת העיבוד עשה העכו"ס כיון דבלא הישראל לא היה נגמר ס"ל להט"ז דמהני אף אם לא אמר להעכו"ס בתחלתו שיעשה לשמה וגם הרמב"ם והתוספות דס"ל דהאמירה להעכו"ס לא מעלה כלל יודו בזה לדברי הט"ז דמהני אח"כ מצאתי בעזה"י להגאון מהר"מ בנעט בביאורו על המרדכי סוף הלכות ס"ת בד"ה או יסייע שמוכח בהדיא מדבריו שם שהיא סובר ג"כ כמו שכתבנו שאפילו לא אמר לעכו"ס מענין לשמה מהני כיון דעשה הישראל פעולה בעצמו במלאכת העיבוד לשמה:

* כעין אותיות. כדי שלא יחליפם העכו"ס בעורות אחרים. ודוקא כעין אותיות אבל נקבים כך לסימן לא מהני [פמ"ג]: * לזייף. שמניח העור ע"ג עור אחר ועושה ג"כ במרצע כעין אותן האותיות. כתב המחה"ש דלריך זהירות מרובה כשמעבד ע"י עכו"ס אומן הוא מניח מטליתין על הנקבים הנמצאין בהקלף ואותן טלאי' קרוב לודאי שלא נתעבדו לשמה שהן מחתיכות עורות שמקלע ונוטל מכל אשר יבא לידו להטיל טלאי ובקושי נכרים אחר העיבוד כ"א נגד השמש: * משום דמרתת. הלא"ה לא שייך בזה סד"ר לקולא [כי לשיטתו לשמה הוא דרבנן] דכל שנהנה בו העכו"ס רגיל וקרוב לודאי הוא. ובמקום דלא נהנה בו העכו"ס ע"י החליפין קי"ל דלא חיישינן לאחלופי [פמ"ג]: * יהיה הקלף מעור בהמה וכו'. עוף משובח ואחריו חיה ואחריו בהמה ושליל יותר טוב שעדיין לא יצא לאויר העולם [אחרונים]: * הטהורים. וטהורה שנולדה מטמאה עיין בתשובת יד אליהו סימן ב' שהאריך והעלה להחמיר אבל טמאה שנולדה מטהורה מתיר לכתוב עליה סת"מ ועיין בתשובת סת"מ הלכות תפילין סי' ל"ו. ועור של איסור הנאה עיין בפמ"ג בס"ק כ"ז: * ואפילו מנבילה וכו'. ואפילו נתנבלה ע"י אחרים כגון נחורות ועקורות. תוספות שבת ק"ח: * תורת ה'. ואפילו שאר ספרים שאינם תנ"ך שיש בהם שמות שאינם נמחקים אסור לכתוב על עור בהמה טמאה ואם הם כתובים רק ברמז לסימן השם י"ל דשרי לכתוב וה"ה ספרי הש"ס ופוסקים כה"ג שרי [פמ"ג]: * האות וכו' חלוקה לשתים. עיין במ"ב סוף ס"ק ל"ב במה שכ' אם לאחר הכתיבה וכו' רואין אם יש בו צורת אות וכו' ואם הנקב שנעשה לאחר הכתיבה הוא רק באמצע עובי האות אפשר דיש לצדד להקל כהט"ז אפילו אם אין בו שיור אות עד המקום ההוא כיון דלא נשתנה צורת האות עי"ז

שער הציון

(לו) פמ"ג: (לז) מ"א:

הגהות ותיקונים: א) ע"ה:

(30) *The practice accords with this /view/. See above (Sec. 11, Par. 2).*

10. Where one makes a letter-like sign of holes /in parchment/ with an awl /, then/, although it is easy for a non-Jew to forge this,[8*] we are not afraid

Mishnah Berurah

who commands him to do it for the sake of /the mitzvah/.

(30) The practice accords with this. /When a non-Jew processes the parchment,/ the practice, initially, according to the words of the Acharonim, must be as follows. The Jew should himself put the skins into the lime for the sake of /use for *tefilin* passages/. He should instruct the non-Jew that all the other acts of the processing which will be done he should also do for the sake of /use for *tefilin* passages/. The non-Jew may subsequently take out /the skins/ himself and prepare them and /the Jew/ no longer needs to stand over him or to assist him further.

If the Jew himself placed the skins into the lime for the sake of /use for *tefilin* passages/, but did not say anything to the non-Jew, the *P.Mg.* writes that study is required /to determine the ruling/ in such a case. [For according to the words of the *B.Y.*, in the *Yo.D.*, Sec. 271, they are valid even according to the view of the *Rambam*, /whereas/ the *Bach* forbids /their use/.] On the other hand, according to the words of the *No.B.* in Sec. 175 (see there) and /according to/ the *Bey'urey Ha-Gaon Maharam Banet* on the *Mordechai*, at the end of the laws concerning a Torah Scroll, one can be lenient /about this/ once it is after the event.

If the Jew helped the non-Jew a little at the end and thereby completed the work of processing, but did not say to the non-Jew at all that he should do /the processing/ for the sake of /use for *tefilin* passages/, this is certainly of no avail. /The reason is/ because assistance is not /regarded as being/ of actual /significance/. /On the other hand,/ this ruling /applies only in an instance/ when /the Jew/ did not do this final processing by himself, but merely with the assistance of the non-Jew. If the Jew finished the processing by himself, however, without the assistance of the non-Jew, the *Taz*, in the *Yo.D.*, and the */Bey'urey/ Ha-Gaon Maharam Banet*, /mentioned/ above, are lenient about it. (For example, if the Jew took the skins out of the lime before their processing was completed and placed them again inside the lime for the sake of /use for *tefilin* passages/.) One should not protest against someone who acts leniently in accordance with their words, as we have explained in the Beyur Halachah.

8* I.e., by placing the perforated skin over another skin and thus duplicating the holes with an awl in this other skin. (Beyur Halachah)

(ל) וכן נוהגין ועיין לעיל (סי' י"א סעיף בן): י גכשמסמנין הנקבים במרצע * כעין אותיות אע"פ שנקל לא"י * לזייף אין חוששין * משום דמרתת הא"י פן יכיר ישראל (לא) בטביעות (יד) עין: **יא** עור שעיבדו שלא לשמו אם יש תיקון לחזור לעבדו לשמו דיתבאר בטור יור"ד (טו) סימן רע"א: **יב** * היהיה הקלף מעור בהמה וחיה ועוף (טז) [ח] * הטהורים * אפילו מנבילה וטריפה שלהם אבל לא מעור בהמה וחיה ועוף הטמאים דכתיב למען תהיה * תורת ה' בפיך ממין המותר לפיך ולא מעור דג אפילו הוא טהור משום דנפיש זוהמיה: **יג** ויהיה הקלף שלם שלא יהא בו נקבים שאין הדיו עובר עליו זדהיינו שלא תהא * האות נראית בו חלוקה (יז) [ט] (לב) לשתים: **יד** חהסופרים הזריזים

באר הגולה

ג הגהת מיימון מה"ת ד הרב השמיטו שם והטור ביו"ד שם בשם תשו' לגאון מכשיר ה שבת ק"ח ו שם וחולין ק"כ ז הר"י אלכסנדריא בסימן ל"ו ח שם

שערי תשובה

סי' ל"ג ע"ש: [ח] הטהורים. עבה"ט וכתב בבכור שור בשבת דף ק"ח מנין שאין כותבין תפילין כו' והוא עפ"י מה שבארנו בשאלה אחת אם מותר לכתוב תפילין ע"ג עור בהמה טהורה שנעבדה ונעשית ע"ז והעלינו לפי מ"ש כאן דבעינן מן המותר (ור"ל שבתשובה שם הוכיח דמותר בפיך ממש בעינן ודלא כמ"ש התוספות דקאי על המין וספר תשובותיו נעלמו מן העין והבל על דאבדין) אלא אפילו לפירוש התוס' דהכוונה על המין המותר מ"מ יש לאסור דע"ז איתקש למת כו' עיין שם: [ט] לשתים. עבה"ט ועיין בתשובת הגאון

באר היטב

לעובד כוכבים ליתן לתוך הסיד לשמה ועיין באר עשק סי' י"ד. ובהרמ"ע סי' ל"ד: (יד) עין. כתב הג"מ אם נתנו מתחלה בעיבוד לשם קדושה יוכל להניח העובד כוכבים ולהוליאו ולתקנו וא"ל לסייעו עוד עיין מ"א: (טו) סימן רע"א. דיכולין לחזור ולתקנו ע"ש ס"ק א' מש"ש. (טז) הטהורים. בתוספות דסוטה דף י"ז כתבו בשם הירושלמי דאפילו שאר ספרים שיש בהם שמות אסור לכתוב על עור בהמה טמאה מ"א. בתשובת הרמ"ע סימן ל"ז כתב דיש מעלות דשל שליל מלוה מן המובחר ושל חיה יותר משל בהמה ובהמה שחוטה עדיף משל חיה נבילה ע"ש וכ"כ בשכנה"ג ובע"ת. אי בהמה טמאה שנולדה מטהורה אם עורותיה כשר לתו"מ או עור בהמה טהורה שנולדה מטמאה אי פסול לתו"מ עיין בתשובת יד אליהו סימן ב' שהאריך והעלה להחמיר. עור של בהמה רובעת ונרבעת אסור לכתוב תו"מ יד אליהו סימן ל"ה ע"ש: (יז) לשתים. ר"ל דבשעת הכתיבה נסתם

ביאור הלכה

הקלף והרי ע"כ מיגרע גרע דבהחזרת הסיד אפילו לא היה בעיבוד ראשון שום אמירה לעכו"ם מהני כמו שנראה מדברי הטור ביו"ד שם וכאן צריך ע"כ אמירה לעכו"ם דמסייע לבד אין בו ממש אע"כ דכונת הט"ז במש"כ במסייעו אין ר"ל שיעשה איזה מעשה בסיוע העכו"ם דמסייע זו בודאי אין בו ממש אלא ר"ל שיעשה גם הוא איזה מעשה עיבוד בלי העכו"ם וסברת הט"ז לומר דזה בודאי חשיב הזמנה מעלייתא לקדושה כיון דבלא גמר הישראל לא היה עדיין העור מעובד ועד כאן לא החמירו התוספות אלא דתיקון הקלף ושירטוטו זה לא חשיב הזמנה לקדושה כיון דכבר נגמר מלאכת העיבוד אבל בזה שעושה בעיבוד מעשה גמורה דבלא עשייתו לא היה העור נגמר בעיבודו מהני וע"ז הביא ראיה מהחזרת הדק [שהוא קלף כדאיתא בטור] פי' דהלא לענין שבת בודאי אין עיבוד אחר עיבוד וכמו שמבואר בהלכות שבת לענין שאר מלאכות וכאן מהני אע"כ דכאן לא בעינן רק שיעשה מעשה שיהא מוכיח שהיא הזמנה מעלייתא לקדושה א"כ כ"ש כשעושה הגמר בעיבוד עצמו דזה בודאי מיקרי עיבוד אף לענין שבת [וכמו שמוכח בשבת דף ע"ו[א] דפריך היינו מולח היינו מעבד אלמא אף דלא עשה כ"א מליחה בעלמא שעדיין שם עור עליה ולא קלף כדאיתא בשבת דף ע"ט חייב משום עיבוד א"כ כ"ש כשעשה עפיץ לבד דבזה נגמר עליה מלאכת העיבוד להקרא עי"ז קלף ולא דיפתרא דחייב] כ"ש דמיקרי עיבוד לענין לשמה וא"כ אין אנו צריכין לומר יוכיח סופו על תחלתו דבסופו לבד די וממילא אין אנו צריכין ג"כ לומר שיאמר לעכו"ם בתחלתו לעשות לשמה ובזה יוסר כל הקושיות מדברי הרב ט"ז. היוצא מדברינו דשני עניני סיוע יש אם עשה פעולה בשותפות העכו"ם ואפי' בתחלתו בזה ודאי לא מהני רק באופן כשאמר לעכו"ם ליתן לתוך הסיד לשמה ואפילו זה לא מהני רק להרא"ש ובזה מיירי השו"ע שכתב וסייעו קצת בעיבודה אבל ודאי אם עשה פעולה בעצמו במלאכת העיבוד אף שתחלת העיבוד עשה העכו"ם כיון דבלא הישראל לא היה נגמר ס"ל להט"ז דמהני אף אם לא אמר להעכו"ם בתחלתו שיעשה לשמה וגם הרמב"ם והתוספות דס"ל דהאמירה להעכו"ם לא מעלה כלל יודו בזה לדברי הט"ז דמהני אח"כ מצאתי בעזה"י להגאון מהר"מ בנעט בביאורו על המרדכי סוף הלכות ס"ת בד"ה או יסייע שמוכח בהדיא מדבריו שם שהוא סובר ג"כ כמו שכתבנו שאפילו לא אמר לעכו"ם מענין לשמה מהני כיון דעשה הישראל פעולה בעצמו במלאכת העיבוד לשמה:
* כעין אותיות. כדי שלא יחליפם העכו"ם בעורות אחרים. ודוקא כעין אותיות אבל נקבים כך לסימן לא מהני [פמ"ג]: * לזייף. שמניח העור ע"ג עור אחר ועושה ג"כ במרצע כעין אותן האותיות. כתב המחה"ש דצריך זהירות מרובה כשמעבד ע"י עכו"ם אומן הוא מניח מטליתין על הנקבים הנמצאין בהקלף ואותן טלאי' קרוב לודאי שלא נתעבדו לשמה שהן מחתיכות עורות שמקלע ונוטל מכל אשר יבא לידו להטיל טלאי ובקושי נכרים אחר העיבוד כ"א נגד השמש: * משום דמרתת. הלא"ה לא שייך בזה סד"ר לקולא [כי לשיטתו לשמה הוא דרבנן] דכל שנהנה בו העכו"ם רגיל וקרוב לודאי הוא. ובמקום דלא נהנה בו העכו"ם ע"י החליפין קי"ל דלא חיישינן לאחלופי [פמ"ג]: * יהיה הקלף מעור בהמה וכו'. עוף משובח ואחריו חיה ואחריו בהמה ושליל יותר טוב שעדיין לא יצא לאויר העולם [אחרונים]: * הטהורים. וטהורה שנולדה מטמאה עיין בתשובת יד אליהו סימן ב' שהאריך והעלה להחמיר אבל טמאה שנולדה מטהורה מתיר לכתוב עליה סת"מ ועיין בתשובת סת"מ הלכות תפילין סי' ל"ו. ועור של איסור הנאה עיין בפמ"ג בס"ק כ"ז:
* ואפילו מנבילה וכו'. ואפילו נתנבלה ע"י אחרים כגון נחורות ועקורות. תוספות שבת ק"ח: * תורת ה'. ואפילו שאר ספרים שאינם תנ"ך שיש בהם שמות שאינם נמחקים אסור לכתוב על עור בהמה טמאה ואם הם כתובים רק ברמז לסימן השם י"ל דשרי לכתוב וה"ה ספרי הש"ס ופוסקים כה"ג שרי [פמ"ג]: * האות וכו' חלוקה לשתים. עיין במ"ב סוף ס"ק ל"ב במה שכ' אם לאחר הכתיבה וכו' רואין אם יש בו צורת אות וכו' ואם הנקב שנעשה לאחר הכתיבה הוא רק באמצע עובי האות אפשר דיש לצדד להקל כהט"ז אפילו אם אין בו שיור אות עד המקום ההוא כיון דלא נשתנה צורת האות

עי"ז

משנה ברורה

לעשות לשמה עכ"ד: (ל) וכן נוהגין. והמנהג לפי דברי אחרונים לכתחלה צריך להיות כך שיפשיט הישראל בעצמו העורות לתוך הסיד לשמה ויאמר לעכו"ם שכל שאר מלאכת העיבוד שיעשה הוא יעשה ג"כ לשמה ויכול העכו"ם אח"כ להוציאו בעצמו ולתקנו וא"צ עוד לעמוד ע"ג ולסייעו עוד. ואם נתן הישראל העורות בעצמו לתוך הסיד לשמה ולא אמר כלום להעכו"ם כתב הפמ"ג דל"ע בזה [כי לפי דברי הב"י ביו"ד בסימן רע"א כשר אפילו לדברי הרמב"ם והב"ח אוסר] אכן לפי דברי הגר"ז בסימן קע"ה ע"ש ובאורי הגאון מהר"מ בנעט על המרדכי סוף הלכות ס"ת יש להקל בדיעבד. ואם סייעו הישראל להעכו"ם קצת בסוף ובזה גמר מלאכת העיבוד ולא אמר לעכו"ם כלל שיעשה לשמה (לו) זה בודאי לא מהני דמסייע אין בו ממש. וה"ה שזה גמר העיבוד לא עשה בעצמו רק בסיוע עם העכו"ם אבל אם גמרו הישראל בעצמו בלא סיוע העכו"ם כגון שהוציא הישראל העורות מן הסיד קודם שנגמר עיבודן וחזר והניחם בתוך הסיד לשמה הט"ז ביו"ד והגאון מהר"מ הנ"ל מקילין בזה ואין למחות ביד הנוהג להקל כדבריהן וכמו שבררנו בביאור הלכה: י (לא) **בט"ע. שנתן בסימנין או שאלו הנקבים נעשו יותר מחדש משלו וי"א (לז) שיכתוב בראש בפנים במקום שאין דרך לעבד הראש וישאר הכתב עד אחר העיבוד ולא יסמן במרצע מחמת חשש זיוף ובדיעבד יש להקל כהש"ע: יג (לב) לשתים.**

שער הציון

(לו) פמ"ג: (לז) מ"א:

הגהות ותיקונים: א) ע"ה:

/that he will do so/. This is because a non-Jew will be afraid /to do so/ in case a Jew will recognize /the forgery/ (31) by discernment.

11. As to /whether/ skin which was processed not for the sake of /use for the mitzvah/ may be remedied by being processed again /, this time/ for the sake of /use for the mitzvah/, this is discussed in the *Tur*, *Yo.D.*, Sec. 271.

12. The parchment must be /made out/ of the skin of a domestic or non-domestic animal or of a bird,[9*] /which is of a kind/ that is /halachically/ clean.[10*] /The parchment/ may even be from a *neveylah*[11*] or a *tereyfah*[11*] of /such an animal or bird/.

However, /one may/ not /make parchment out/ of the skin of an animal, /whether/ domestic or non-domestic, or of a bird, /which is of a kind/ that is /halachically/ unclean. /This is/ because it is written[12*] /in one of the passages dealing with the mitzvah of *tefilin*/, "In order that the teaching of the Lord should be in your mouth". /The Sages explained that what is meant is that the *tefilin* must be made/ out of a kind /of material/ which is permitted to the mouth.[13*]

/One may also/ not /make parchment out/ of the skin of a fish, even if /the fish/ is /of a halachically/ clean /kind/, because /the skin of a fish/ abounds in filth.

13. The parchment should be intact, without having /any/ holes in it over which the ink will not pass. What is meant is that it should not /have holes which will cause/ the letter to appear divided (32) into two /parts/ on /the parchment/.

Mishnah Berurah

(31) By discernment. /I.e., he will be afraid that the Jew will discover the forgery/ by applying /a discerning eye/ or /that he will recognize/ that these holes were made more recently than his.

There are /authorities/ who say that one should write at the top /of the parchment/ on the inside, in an area on top which it is not usual to process, /so that/ the writing will remain until after the processing, and should not make an /identification/ mark with an awl because of the fear of forgery. Once it is after the event one may be lenient, in accordance with /the ruling of/ the Shulchan Aruch.

(32) Into two. /I.e., if a hole/ is so small

9* The skin of a bird is the best for this purpose, after that the skin of a non-domestic animal is to be preferred and after that the skin of a domestic animal. The skin of a fetus is better. (Beyur Halachah)

10* I.e., it must be a kind of animal or bird from which one is permitted to eat.

11* A dead animal or bird is classed as a *neveylah* if it was not slaughtered in accordance with halachic requirements. It is classed as a *tereyfah* if it was slaughtered in accordance with halachic requirements, but had certain wounds or deficiencies. If it had certain more serious wounds or deficiencies it is classed as a *neveylah* even if it was slaughtered in accordance with halachic requirements. Basically, a slaughtered *tereyfah* could not have lived long, in view of its wounds or deficiencies, and a slaughtered *neveylah* could not have lived at all.

12* *Shemos* 13:9.

13* It is forbidden to write even non-Scriptural books on the skin of an unclean kind of animal, if they contain Divine Names which may not be erased. (Beyur Halachah)

עושים שלשה מיני קלפים העב יותר לכתוב בו פרשת שמע שהיא (יח) [י] קטנה (לג) והדק ממנו לפרשת והיה אם שמוע שהיא יותר גדולה ולפרשת קדש ולפרשת והיה כי יביאך שהם ארוכות עושים קלף דק מאד ובזה יתמלאו הבתים בשוה וזהו נוי לתפילין: **טו** [ט]אם (לד) לאחר שנכתב ניקב (לה) בתוך הה"א או המ"ם כשר אפילו ניקב כל תוכו שהנקב ממלא (לו) כל החלל * אבל בירושלמי משמע (לז) שגם בפנים צריך שיהא מוקף קלף. (לח) ניקב רגל פנימי של ה"א אפילו לא נשאר ממנו אלא כל שהוא [י]כשר להרא"ש: הגה אבל שאר פוסקים (לט) מצריכין כמלא אות

באר הגולה

ט מנחות כ"ט לפירוש השני ברש"י ולהרמב"ם בפ"א מה"ת י בפרק קמא דמגילה ה"א[א] כ בהל' ספר תורה וכפי' הא' שברש"י שבמנחות

באר היטב

שהדיו עובר עליו ואין הנקב נרגש בקולמוס אע"פ שנראה נקב דק כנגד השמש כשר ב"ח מ"א שכנה"ג ע"ת אבל הט"ז כתב דבעינן שיהיה שם נקב קטן כ"כ שהדיו סותמו ואינו נראה כלל נגד השמש ע"ש. וכל זה קודם הכתיבה אבל אם ניקב לאחר הכתיבה אפילו נחלק האות לשנים כשר אלא דבעינן תינוק שיוכל לקרותו. ב"ח שכנה"ג ע"ת ט"ז. ועיין סעיף ט"ז ובתשובת מטה יוסף ח"א סימן א' ובתשובת תורת חיים ח"ג בקונטרס עוללות הכרם: (יח) קטנה. ורמ"י כתב שהסופרים שלהם עושין תיקון אחר שכל הקלפים הם שוים באורך א' ובעובי א' אלא שמניחים גליון בפרשיות הקצרות ע"ש. ועפ"ז שמעתי לתרץ מה שהקשה התוספות י"ט במסכת שבת פרק ח' משנה ג' בד"ה שהיא שמע ישראל וכו' ע"ש די"ל דהתנא אתא לאשמעינן דלענין שבת אין צריך שיהיה הקלף עב או עם הגליון כמו בתפילין רק השיעור הוא כדי לכתוב עליו רק פרשת שמע ישראל וא"ל גליון ואף שהקלף הוא דק וק"ל. ועיין בספר יד אהרן ובהלק"ט ח"א סימן

שערי תשובה

בעל אבן העוזר הנדפס בגליון המג"א. ועיין בשו"ת בית אפרים חלק א"ח סי' ג' ומש"ש: [י] קטנה. עבה"ט ובבר"י כתב בשם יד אהרן שיש ט"ס בש"ע וכצ"ל והדק ממנו פרשה והיה כי יביאך שהיא יותר גדולה. ולפ' קדש ולפ' והיה אם שמוע שהם ארוכות עושים קלף דק מאד ע"ש. ובהלכות קטנות סי' רנ"ט כתב דאין צריך להגיה ע"ש ודבריו דחוקים. וגם כי מ"ש ידחק לחוץ פשיטא שזה מקלקל הנוי ביותר וכאן רוצים להשוות הבתים שיהיה נוי לתפילין

משנה ברורה

שהוא קטן כל כך עד שכשמעביר עליו בקולמוס נסתם הנקב בדיו ואין הנקב נרגש בקולמוס כותבין עליו אע"פ שנפל מעט דיו במקום ההוא ונראה נקב דק כנגד השמש (לח) כשר אבל אם ניקב כ"כ שאין הדיו עובר עליו פסול שהאות נראית חלוקה לשתים על ידו ואפילו אם הנקב באמצע עובי האות בגגו או בירכו (לט) ודיו מקיפה מכל צד פסול ואפילו (מ) אם עד מקום הנקב יש צורת אות. וכ"ז קודם כתיבה אבל אם לאחר כתיבה נחלק האות לשתים ע"י נקב רואין (מא) אם יש בו צורת האות עד מקום הנקב כשר וכמו שיתבאר בסמוך בסעיף ט"ז ועיין ביאור הלכה: **יד** (לג) והדק ממנו לפרשת והא"ש. ט"ס וצ"ל לפרשת והיה כי יביאך שהיא יותר גדולה ולפרשת קדש ולפרשת והא"ש שהם ארוכות וכו' [ביאור הגר"א ויד אהרן] ורמ"י כתב שהסופרים שלהם עושים תיקון אחר שכל הקלפים הם שוים באורך א' ובעובי א' אלא שמניחין גליונין מפרשיות הקצרות: **טו** (לד) לאחר שנכתב וכו'. נקדים ב' הקדמות ואח"כ נבאר בעזה"י. א' כל אות צריך שיהא עליו צורתו הראוי לאותו אות וא"ל פסול ובזה (מב) אין חילוק אם לא נכתב כהלכתו או אם אח"כ נתקלקל. ב' כל אות שאין גויל מוקף לה מארבע רוחותיה פסולה ובדין זה יש שני פרטים. א' דוקא אם לא היה מוקף גויל קודם כתיבה אבל (מג) אם לאחר כתיבה נעשה נקב או קרע סמוך לאות מבחוץ ועי"ז אינו מוקף גויל כשר וכמו שיתבאר בסעיף ט"ז בשו"ע. ב' דעת רוב הפוסקים דאין צריך להיות מוקף גויל רק מבחוץ להאותיות ולא בתוכן חוץ מהירושלמי שמחמיר בזה. ועתה נבוא לבאר השו"ע אם לאחר שנכתב ניקב וכו' הטעם דבפנים אין צריך להקפת גויל ולפ"ז אפילו אם הנקב קודם כתיבה כשר (מד) והאי דנקט אם לאחר שנכתב ניקב משום דלכתחלה אין לכתוב אפילו אם הנקב באמצע חללו ואין ממלא את תוכו אבל באמת אם עבר וכתב אפילו אם היה הנקב קודם שנכתב כשר וא"ל שום תקון: (לה) בתוך הה"א. וה"ה (מה) שאר אותיות שיש להן ג' דפנות ויש חלל בתוכו אבל ד' פשוטה וכ"ש וי"ו וכדומה לאו תוך מיקרי: (לו) כל החלל. ואפילו נגע הנקיבה באות גופא כל שנשאר (מו) שריטה דקה מבחוץ כשר דאין שיעור לעובי האותיות: (לז) שגם בפנים וכו'. וא"כ דינו כמבחוץ אם היה הנקב בתוכו (מז) קודם כתיבה פסול ועיין בט"ז ובפמ"ג בשם הלבוש שיש להחמיר כהירושלמי. ודע דלהירושלמי צריך הקפת גויל בכל הצדדים מבפנים כמו מבחוץ ע"כ אם ניקב בתוכו קודם הכתיבה אצל האות ועי"ז אינו מוקף גויל (מח) יש לגרור מעט מבפנים מעובי הקו של האות ויהיה מוקף גויל ועיין בביאור הלכה סוף ד"ה אבל בירושלמי וכו': (לח) ניקב. וה"ה (מט) אם נמחק קצת מהדיו ולא ניקב. ודוקא בה"א פליג הרא"ש ומכשיר אם נשאר כל שהוא בין למעלה מהנקב (נ) ובין למטה דסבר (נא) דאין שיעור להנקודה התלויה בה ואפילו אם כתב מתחלה רגל קצר כזה כשר להרא"ש אבל בשאר אותיות כמו חי"ת וכדומה (נב) גם הרא"ש מודה דהרגל השמאלי דינו כמו רגל ימיני: (לט) מצריכין כמלא וכו'. ומיירי בענין שאין בו חסרון משום הקפת גויל כגון שניקב לאחר

ביאור הלכה

עי"ז ומחדושי רע"א בד"ה אבל שנשאר בל"ע על הט"ז נראה שמפקפק בזה להחמיר ולפי ביאור הלבו"ש בהט"ז נוכל לומר בפשיטות דגם הט"ז יודה בזה להחמיר ולא מיירי הט"ז רק אם יש בו שיור אות עד המקום ההוא וראייתו הוא מסט"ז ומה שהביא מניקב תוכו הוא לאו דוקא עי"ש לכן דין זה צ"ע: * אבל בירושלמי. עיין במ"ב שכתב ודע וכו' ועיין בט"ז שכתב דין מחודש דאף להירושלמי אין פסול כ"א בניקב כל תוכו ולא אם ניקב תוכו מצד א' סמוך לאות ועיין בפמ"ג ובדה"ח דזה לא קאי רק לתירוץ א' של הב"י עי"ש אבל לתירוץ שני שלו שפסק המחבר כוותיה בסמוך סט"ז יהיה הדין להירושלמי אם ניקב בתוכו קודם הכתיבה סמוך להאות אפילו במקצתו פסול ובאמת כן איתא בירושלמי בהדיא בפ' א' דמגילה אמר נדבך ניקב באמצע הבי"ת אם גויל מקיפו מכל צד כשר וא"ל פסול. וכ"ל פשוט שגם כונת הטור כן אלא דבא למעט במה שכתב כל תוכו לאפוקי היכא דניקב עצמיות תוך האות ולא נשארת רק כחוט השערה מוקף גויל חלק מכל צדדיו דכשר. ומדברי הירושלמי הזה נסתר סברת הדה"ח שרצה ליישב את דברי הט"ז סק"ח כי כתב שהטור סובר כתירוץ א' של הב"י ולכן בעינן דוקא כל חללו שמדברי הירושלמי הזה מוכח בהדיא דלא בעינן כל חללו. ומ"מ לדינא במקום הדחק שלא נזדמן לו סופר שיוכל לקלוף בטוב מעט סמוך להנקב כדי שיהיה מוקף גויל נ"ל שיוכל לסמוך על הפוסקים שמכשירין אפילו ניקב כל תוכו כי אף שהט"ז כתב דאפשר שדעת הרמ"א כחומרא של ב' הפירושים המעיין בד"מ הארוך יראה להדיא דדעתו

שער הציון

(לח) ב"ח מ"א וא"ר ופמ"ג ודה"ח: (לט) ט"ז ודה"ח: (מ) כן מוכח מלבושי שרד: (מא) פשוט: (מב) פשוט ומבואר בכמה מקומות: (מג) לקמן בסט"ז: (מד) פמ"ג ולבושי שרד: (מה) פמ"ג: (מו) כדלקמן: (מז)פמ"ג: (מח) פמ"ג: (מט) דה"ח: (נ) שו"ע של הגר"ז: (נא) ב"ח: (נב) מוכח מהרא"ש ועיין בב"י:

הגהות ותיקונים: א) ה"ט:

14. The zealous scribes make three types of parchment /for the head *tefilin*/. A thicker /parchment/, on which to write the passage *Shema*, that is a small /passage/, **(33)** a thinner one than that for the passage *Ve-Hayah Im Shamo'a*, which is larger, and for the passage *Kadesh Li Chal Bechor* and the passage *Ve-Hayah Ki Yevi'achah*, which are long, they make a very thin parchment. In view of this, /all/ the housings /of the *tefilin* unit/ will be filled uniformly and this /gives/ beauty to the *tefilin*.

15. If **(34)** after /a passage/ was written a hole formed **(35)** inside the /letter/ ה

Mishnah Berurah

that when one will pass the quill over it the hole will become blocked with ink and the hole will not be felt by the quill, one may write over it. Although a little ink will sink in that spot and a minute hole will be noticeable against the sun, /the letter/ will /nevertheless/ be valid.

However, if /the parchment/ is perforated with so /large a hole/ that the ink will not pass over it, /then if a letter will be written over the hole the letter/ will be invalid, since the letter will appear to be divided into two because of /the hole/. Even if the hole will be in the middle of the thickness of the letter, in its roof or in its thigh, and there will be ink surrounding it on all sides, /the letter/ will /nevertheless/ be invalid. This /applies/ even if the form of the letter will be /complete/ before the point where there is a hole.

/However,/ all this /only applies/ before /the letter/ is written, but if a letter became split into two by means of a hole after it was written, we examine whether the form of the letter is /complete/ before the point where there is a hole. /If so,/ it is /ruled as/ valid, as explained shortly in Par. 16. See the Beyur Halachah.

(33) A thinner one than that for the passsage *Ve-Hayah Im Shamo'a*. This is a printer's error. /The correct reading/ should be, "for the passage *Ve-Hayah Ki Yevi'achah*, which is larger, and for the passage *Kadesh Li Chal Bechor* and the passage *Ve-Hayah Im Shamo'a*, which are long, etc." [*Beyur Ha-Gra* and *Yad Aharon*].

The *Rami* writes that their scribes employ a different solution. All the parchments are /made/ equally /large/, with the same length and the same thickness, but margins are left /blank/ in /the parchments of/ the short passages.

(34) After /a passage/ was written, etc. We will first give two introductory /explanations/ and after that we will explain /the words of the Shulchan Aruch/, with the help of *Ha-Sheym*, may He be blessed.

1) Every letter must bear the form which is appropriate for that letter. If it does not /do so/ it is invalid. As regards this /requirement/, it makes no difference whether /the letter/ was not written /in the first place/ in conformance with this principle or whether it became spoiled later.

2) Any letter which does not have /blank/ parchment surrounding it on /all/ four sides is invalid. This law has two qualifications.

a) It only /applies/ if the letter was not surrounded by /blank/ parchment at the time when it was written. However, if after it was written a hole or a tear developed near the letter on the outside, in view of which /the letter/ is no /longer/ surrounded by /blank/ parchment, /the letter remains/ valid, as stated in Par. 16 of the Shulchan Aruch.

b) The view of most Poskim is that the letters only need to be surrounded by /blank/ parchment on the outside, but not on the inside, except that the /*Talmud*/ *Yerushalmi* is stringent about this.

We will now proceed to explain the Shulchan Aruch.

The reason /why the Shulchan Aruch states that/ "if after /a passage/ was written a hole formed, etc." is that the inside /of the letter/ does not need to be surrounded by /blank/ parchment. Accordingly, even if the hole was /there/ before /the letter/ was written /the letter/ is /nevertheless/ valid. As for /the fact/ that /the Shulchan Aruch/ words /the ruling/, "If after /a passage/ was written a hole formed", this is because, initially, one should not write /a letter with a hole/, even when the hole will be in the

עושים שלשה מיני קלפים העב יותר לכתוב בו פרשת שמע שהיא (יח) [י] קטנה (לג) והדק ממנו לפרשת והיה אם שמוע שהיא יותר גדולה ולפרשת קדש ולפרשת והיה כי יביאך שהם ארוכות עושים קלף דק מאד ובזה יתמלאו הבתים בשוה וזהו נוי לתפילין: **טו** ᵗאם (לד) לאחר שנכתב ניקב (לה) בתוך הה"א **או המ"ם כשר אפילו ניקב כל תוכו שהנקב ממלא (לו) כל החלל * אבל ʼבירושלמי משמע (לז) שגם בפנים צריך שיהא מוקף קלף. (לח) ניקב רגל פנימי של ה"א אפילו לא נשאר ממנו אלא כל שהוא ʼכשר להרא"ש:** הגה אבל שאר פוסקים (לט) מצריכין כמלא אות

באר הגולה

ט מנחות כ"ט לפירוש השני ברש"י ולהרמב"ם בפ"א מה"ת י בפרק קמא דמגילה ה"א[א] כ בהל' ספר תורה וכפי' הא' שברש"י שבמנחות

באר היטב

שהדיו עובר עליו ואין הנקב נרגש בקולמוס אע"פ שנראה נקב דק כנגד השמש כשר ב"ח מ"א שכנה"ג ע"ת אבל הט"ז כתב דבעינן שיהיה שם נקב קטן כ"כ שהדיו סותמו ואינו נראה כלל נגד השמש ע"ש. וכל זה קודם הכתיבה אבל אם ניקב לאחר הכתיבה אפילו נחלק האות לשנים כשר אלא דבעינן תינוק שיוכל לקרותו. ב"ח שכנה"ג ע"ת ט"ז. ועיין סעיף ט"ז ובתשובת מטה יוסף ח"א סימן א' ובתשובת תורת חיים ח"ג בקונטרס עוללות הכרם: (יח) קטנה. ורמ"י כתב שהסופרים שלהם עושין תיקון אחר שכל הקלפים הם שוים באורך א' ובעובי א' אלא שמניחים גליון בפרשיות הקצרות ע"ש. ועפ"ז שמעתי לתרץ מה שהקשה התוספות י"ט במסכת שבת פרק ח' משנה ג' בד"ה שהיא שמע ישראל וכו' ע"ש די"ל דהתנא אתא לאשמעינן דלענין שבת אין צריך שיהיה הקלף עב או עם הגליון כמו בתפילין רק השיעור הוא כדי לכתוב עליו רק פרשת שמע ישראל וא"צ גליון ואף שהקלף הוא דק וק"ל. ועיין בספר יד אהרן ובהלק"ט ח"א סימן

שערי תשובה

בעל אבן העוזר הנדפס בגליון המג"א. ועיין בשו"ת בית אפרים חלק א"ח סי' ג' ומש"ש: [י] קטנה. עבה"ט ובברכ"י כתב בשם יד אהרן שיש ט"ס בש"ע וכצ"ל והדק ממנו פרשה והיה כי יביאך שהיא יותר גדולה. ולפ' קדש ולפ' והיה אם שמוע שהם ארוכות עושים קלף דק מאד ע"ש. ובהלכות קטנות סי' רנ"ט כתב דאין צריך להגיה ע"ש ודבריו דחוקים. וגם כי מ"ש ידחק לחוץ פשיטא שזה מקלקל הנוי ביותר וכאן רוצים להשוות הבתים שיהיה נוי לתפילין

משנה ברורה

שהוא קטן כל כך עד שכשמעביר עליו בקולמוס נסתם הנקב בדיו ואין הנקב נרגש בקולמוס כותבין עליו אע"פ שנפל מעט דיו במקום ההוא ונראה נקב דק כנגד השמש (לח) כשר אבל אם ניקב כ"כ שאין הדיו עובר עליו פסול שהאות נראית חלוקה לשתים על ידו ואפילו אם הנקב באמצע עובי האות בגגו או בירכו (לט) והדיו מקיפה מכל צד פסול ואפילו (מ) אם עד מקום הנקב יש צורת אות. וכ"ז קודם כתיבה אבל אם לאחר כתיבה נחלק האות לשתים ע"י נקב רואין (מא) אם יש בו צורת האות עד מקום הנקב כשר וכמו שיתבאר בסמוך בסעיף ט"ז ועיין ביאור הלכה: יד (לג) והדק ממנו לפרשת והא"ש. ט"ס וצ"ל לפרשת והיה כי יביאך שהיא יותר גדולה ולפרשת קדש ולפרשת והא"ש שהם ארוכות וכו' [ביאור הגר"א ויד אהרן] ורמ"י כתב שהסופרים שלהם עושים תיקון אחר שכל הקלפים הם שוים באורך א' ובעובי א' אלא שמניחין גליונן מפרשיות הקצרות: טו (לד) לאחר שנכתב וכו'. נקדים ב' הקדמות ואח"כ נבאר בעזה"י. א' כל אות צריך שיהא עליו צורתו הראוי לאותו אות ואל"ה פסול ובזה (מב) אין חילוק אם לא נכתב כהלכתו או אם אח"כ נתקלקל. ב' כל אות שאין גויל מוקף לה מארבע רוחותיה פסולה ובדין זה יש שני פרטים. א' דוקא אם לא היה מוקף גויל קודם כתיבה אבל (מג) אם לאחר כתיבה נעשה נקב או קרע סמוך לאות מבחוץ ועי"ז אינו מוקף גויל כשר וכמו שיתבאר בסעיף ט"ז בשו"ע. ב' דעת רוב הפוסקים דאין צריך להיות מוקף גויל רק מבחוץ להאותיות ולא בתוכן חוץ מהירושלמי שמחמיר בזה. ועתה נבוא לבאר השו"ע אם לאחר שנכתב ניקב וכו' הטעם דבפנים אין צריך להקפת גויל ולפ"ז אפילו אם הנקב קודם כתיבה כשר (מד) והאי דנקט אם לאחר שנכתב ניקב משום דלכתחלה אין לכתוב אפילו אם הנקב באמצע חללו ואין ממלא את תוכו אבל באמת אם עבר וכתב אפילו אם היה הנקב קודם שנכתב כשר ואל"צ שום תקון: (לה) בתוך הה"א. וה"ה (מה) שאר אותיות שיש להן ג' דפנות ויש חלל בתוכו אבל ך' פשוטה וכ"ש וי"ו וכדומה לאו תוך מיקרי: (לו) כל החלל. ואפילו נגע הנקיבה באות גופא כל שנשאר (מו) שריטה דקה מבחוץ כשר דאין שיעור לעובי האותיות: (לז) שגם בפנים וכו'. וא"כ דינו כמבחוץ אם היה הנקב בתוכו (מז) קודם כתיבה פסול ועיין בט"ז ובפמ"ג בשם הלבוש שיש להחמיר כהירושלמי. ודע דלהירושלמי צריך הקפת גויל בכל הצדדים מבפנים כמו מבחוץ ע"כ אם ניקב בתוכו קודם הכתיבה אצל האות ועי"ז איננו מוקף גויל (מח) יש לגרור מעט מבפנים מעובי הקו של האות ויהיה מוקף גויל ועיין בביאור הלכה סוף ד"ה אבל בירושלמי וכו': (לח) ניקב. וה"ה (מט) אם נמחק קצת מהדיו ולא ניקב. ודוקא בה"א פליג הרא"ש ומכשיר אם נשאר כל שהוא בין למעלה מהנקב (נ) ובין למטה דסבר (נא) דאין שיעור להנקודה התלויה בה ואפילו אם כתב מתחלה רגל קצר כזה כשר להרא"ש אבל בשאר אותיות כמו חי"ת וכדומה (נב) גם הרא"ש מודה דהרגל השמאלי דינו כמו רגל ימיני: (לט) מצריכין כמלא וכו'. ומיירי בענין שאין בו חסרון משום הקפת גויל כגון שניקב לאחר

ביאור הלכה

עי"ז ומחדושי רע"א בד"ה אבל שנשאר בנ"ע על הט"ז נראה שמפקפק בזה להחמיר ולפי ביאור הלבו"ש בהט"ז נוכל לומר בפשיטות דגם הט"ז יודה בזה להחמיר ולא מיירי הט"ז רק אם יש בו שיור אות עד המקום ההוא וראייתו הוא מסט"ז ומה שהביא מניקב תוכו הוא לאו דוקא עי"ש לכן דין זה צ"ע: * אבל בירושלמי. עיין במ"ב שכתב ודע וכו' ועיין בט"ז שכתב דין מחודש דאף להירושלמי אין פסול כ"א בניקב כל תוכו ולא אם ניקב תוכו מצד א' סמוך לאות ועיין בפמ"ג ובדה"ח דזה לא קאי רק לתירוץ א' של הב"י עי"ש אבל לתירוץ שני שלו שפסק המחבר כוותיה בסמוך סט"ז יהיה הדין להירושלמי אם ניקב בתוכו קודם הכתיבה סמוך להאות אפילו במקצתו פסול ובאמת כן איתא בירושלמי בהדיא בפ' א' דמגילה אמר נדבך ניקב באמצע הבי"ת אם גויל מקיפו מכל צד כשר וא"ל פסול. ונ"ל פשוט שגם כונת הטור כן אלא דבא למעט במה שכתב כל תוכו לאפוקי היכא דניקב עלמיות תוך האות ולא נשארת רק כחוט השערה מוקף גויל חלק מכל צדדיו דכשר. ומדברי הירושלמי הזה נסתר סברת הדה"ח שרצה ליישב את דברי הט"ז סק"ח כי כתב שהטור סובר כתירוץ א' של הב"י ולכן בעינן דוקא כל חללו שמדברי הירושלמי הזה מוכח בהדיא דלא בעינן כל חללו. ומ"מ לדינא במקום הדחק שלא נזדמן לו סופר שיוכל לקלוף בטוב מעט סמוך להנקב כדי שיהיה מוקף גויל נ"ל שיוכל לסמוך על הפוסקים שמכשירין אפילו ניקב כל תוכו כי אף שהט"ז כתב דאפשר שדעת הרמ"א כחומרא של ב' הפירושים המעיין בד"מ הארוך יראה להדיא דדעתו

שער הציון

(לח) ב"ח מ"א וא"ר ופמ"ג ודה"ח: (לט) ט"ז ודה"ח: (מ) כן מוכח מלבושי שרד: (מא) פשוט: (מב) פשוט ומבואר בכמה מקומות: (מג) לקמן בסט"ז: (מד) פמ"ג ולבושי שרד: (מה) פמ"ג: (מו) כדלקמן: (מז) פמ"ג: (מח) פמ"ג: (מט) דה"ח: (נ) שו"ע של הגר"ז: (נא) ב"ח: (נב) מוכח מהרא"ש ועיין בב"י:

הגהות ותיקונים: א) ה"ט:

or the /letter/ מ, /the letter/ is /nevertheless/ valid. /This applies/ even if the hole formed in the entire inside /of the letter/, so that the hole fills **(36)** the entire space. However, in the */Talmud/ Yerushalmi* it is implied **(37)** that even on the inside /the letters/ must be surrounded by /blank/ parchment.

(38) If a hole formed in the inner leg of /the letter/ ה, /the letter/ is valid according to the *Rosh*, even if only a slight /amount/ remains of /the leg/.

Gloss: However, other Poskim **(39)** *require the equivalent /length/ of a small*

Mishnah Beruran

middle of the space /inside the letter/ and will not fill the inside /of the letter/. However, the truth is that if one transgressed and wrote /a letter with a hole on the inside of the letter, then/, even though the hole was there at the time when /the letter/ was written, /the letter/ is valid and no correction is required.

(35) Inside the /letter/ ה. The same ruling /applies in the case of/ other letters which have three sides and have a space inside them.

However, the simple /elongated letter/ ך or, all the more so, the /letter/ ו or a similar /letter/ is not describable as /having/ an inside.

(36) The entire space. Even if the hole has hit the letter itself /the letter/ is valid, as long as a thin line remains on the outside, since there is no minimum width /required/ for the thickness of the letters.

(37) That even on the inside, etc. If so, the ruling /as regards the inside/ is the same as /the ruling/ as regards the outside, /so that/ if there was a hole on the inside /already/ at the time when /the letter/ was written /the letter/ is invalid.

See the *Taz* and the *P.Mg.*, in the name of the *Levush*, that one should be stringent /about this/, in conformance with /the view of/ the */Talmud/ Yerushalmi.*

Note that according to /the view of/ the */Talmud/ Yerushalmi* it is necessary to have /blank/ parchment surrounding all sides /of the letter/ on the inside, just as on the outside. Consequently, if there was a hole on the inside of the letter at the time when one wrote /the letter/, because of which /the letter/ is not surrounded /on the inside/ with /blank/ parchment, one must scrape off a bit of the thickness of the letter stroke on the inside and it will /then/ be surrounded with /blank/ parchment. See the Beyur Halachah[10] at the end of /the paragraph/ beginning with the words *Aval Ba-Yerushalmi*, etc.

(38) If a hole formed. The same ruling /applies/ if some of the ink was erased and no hole formed.

It is only as regards /the letter/ ה that the *Rosh* disputes /the view of the other Poskim/ and rules that /the letter/ is valid if a slight /amount of the left leg/ remains, irrespective of whether /it remains/ above the hole or below it. /Then it is/ because he is of the opinion that there is no minimum /required/ size for the stroke which is suspended in /the letter ה to form that leg/. /In fact/ according to the *Rosh*, even if one wrote such a brief leg for the /letter/ ה at the outset, it is /nevertheless/ valid. However, as regards other letters, such as /the letter/ ח or similar /letters/, the *Rosh* also concedes that the left leg /of the letter/ has the same ruling as the right leg.

(39) Require the equivalent of, etc. /The Shulchan Aruch and the *Rema*/ are referring to an instance where /the letter/ is defective because /of a lack/ of /blank/ parchment surrounding /the letter/, such as

10 There the author rules that in a time of pressing need one may rely on the Poskim who say that the letter is valid even if at the time of writing there was a hole filling the entire inside.

(יט) קטנה (מ) * והכי הלכתא*(ב"י) (מא) * ל ניקב רגל (מב) הימיני (מג) אם נשתייר ממנו (מד) *מלא אות קטנה *כשר *ואם לאו פסול: טז (מה) * ינפסק אחת מהאותיות הגה (כ) [יא] (מו) * הפשוטות * כגון וי"ו זיי"ן (מז) או שנפסק רגל (הנו"ן) וכיוצא בה (מרדכי ה"ק דף ל"ג) (מח) *אם תינוק שאינו

שם בגמ' דמנחות מרדכי בהקומץ

באר היטב

רנ"ט: (יט) קטנה. היינו יו"ד: (כ) הפשוטות. כגון וי"ו זיי"ן או שנפסק רגל הנו"ן כנ"ל. וכ"כ בע"ת וכ"ה במרדכי וכ"כ המחבר יד אהרן ובקצת נוסחאות כתב או שנפסק רגל האל"ף. והט"ז הרבה

שערי תשובה

וגם מה ענין לקרות לה ארוכה בשביל שדחוקה באמצע. לכן מחוורתא להגיה כמ"ש ביד אהרן כנ"ל: [יא] הפשוטות. עבה"ט וכ"ש שאין לדברי

להקשות עליו והעלה דהך נפסק רגל הא' מקומו אח"כ מיהו אם אנו רואים שלא נשאר צורת אות כתיקונו או נפסק רגל הא' פסול ע"ש

משנה ברורה

לאחר הכתיבה כדבסמוך סט"ז בסופו דאל"ה פסול אפי' אם נשתייר יותר מכמלא אות קטנה גם להרא"ש: (מ) והכי הלכתא. מדבריו אלו משמע דלא להחמיר בלבד פסק כדעת ש"פ אלא דפשיטא ליה דהלכה כוותיהו וא"כ צריך להזהיר מאד להסופרים שנכשלין בזה: ובתפילין ומזוזות דבעינן כסדרן לכאורה לא מהני שום תיקון אפילו התינוק קוראו לאות כיון שאנו רואין שאין לו צורת אות דבלא זה לא מיקרי ה' לפי דעת אלו הפוסקים וכדלקמן בסכ"ה ע"ש. ומ"מ נראה דיש להקל ע"י תיקון ודומיא שהקיל הפמ"ג בכף פשוטה שעשאו מרובע ע"י תיקון עי"ש: (מא) ניקב. וה"ה אם נפסק האות בלא נקב או נמחק קצה האות ומיירי השו"ע בארכו וה"ה אם נפסק קצת מעביו בין ע"י נקיבה או ע"י מחיקה אם נשאר שריטה דקה שחור כמו וי"ו או יו"ד דקה כשר דאין שיעור לעובי האותיות אלא דבניקב בין בעביו בין בארכו בעינן שניקב לאחר הכתיבה וכדלקמן בסט"ז [ממ"א ודה"ח]: (מב) הימיני. של ה"א. כתב הפמ"ג נראה לי דה"ה לשאר אותיות כגון ד' ל' פ' פשוטה צ' פשוטה קו"ף רי"ש או תי"ו או חי"ת [לכאורה בחי"ת בין רגלה הימיני או השמאלין] אם נשאר מהירך הימיני כיו"ד די בכך עכ"ל ועיין לקמן בסימן ל"ו בדיני צורת האותיות באות ל' ופ' פשוטה וצ' פשוטה וקו"ף ובאות תי"ו: (מג) אם נשתייר. היינו מהנקב לצד מעלה ולא מצרפינן ליה מה שלמטה מהנקב אפילו אם תינוק דלא חכים ולא טיפש קראה לאות כיון דאנו רואין שלא נשאר צורת האות כתיקונו וכמו שנתבאר בסמוך בשם הט"ז אבל אם נשתייר מהנקב ולמעלה [או מההפסק ולמעלה אם נפסק האות באמצע] כשיעור אות קטנה כשר ואין צריך להראותו לתינוק וה"ה אם כתב לכתחלה רגל קטנה קצרה כזה דכשר ועיין ביד אפרים ובביאור הלכה: (מד) מלא או"ק. היינו יו"ד ובקוץ התחתון שלו לפי מה דפסק לקמן בסי' ל"ו בב"י דלא מיקרי יו"ד בלא קוץ התחתון: ט"ז (מה) נפסק. י"ל בשני אופנים או מחמת נקב וזה אין כשר כ"א בניקב אח"כ כמו שיתבאר בסמוך בפנים או ע"י שנסדק הדיו במאותו מקום (נג) ובאופן זה היה קאי הדין דשו"ע אפילו אם בתחלת הכתיבה נעשה כן: (מו) הפשוטות. ולפיכך אין מועיל בה אם נשתייר כמלא יו"ד דלדרבה נראית כיו"ד ופסול הלכך בעינן תינוק בזה: (מז) או שנפסק רגל הנו"ן כצ"ל. ופי' נו"ן פשוטה וכיוצא בה כגון כ"ף פשוטה שרגלה קצרה ודומה קצת לדל"ת או לרי"ש [מפמ"ג ודה"ח]: (מח) אם תינוק. עיין בט"ז שכתב דהך נפסק איירי שנפסק קצת מאורך האות ולמטה לגמרי ולא נשאר ממנו רק החלק שקודם ההפסק או תלוי בקריאת התינוק אם ספק לנו אם נשאר כשיעור של האות ההוא אבל אם נשתייר גם למטה מן ההפסק דהיינו שנעשה ההפסק ברחבו של רגל האות ואחר ההפסק נשאר עוד למטה חלק מן הרגל בזה לא מועיל תינוק דהתינוק יצרף מה שלמטה ממנו לחלק העליון ובאמת אין לו צירוף וזה דומה לנפסק רגל הא' אלא צריך לכסות את חלק הנשאר אחר ההפסק ואין זה דומה למש"כ השו"ע כאן דאין צריך לכסות שאר האותיות דבזה ודאי מודה

ביאור הלכה

להקל בניקב כל תוכו: * והכי הילכתא. עיין במ"ב סק"מ שכתב מדבריו וכו' וכן משמע בב"י ועיין בדה"ח בהל' קה"ת בדין כ"ו דמשמע מדבריו דמטעם ספיקא דדינא החמיר הרמ"א ולדבריו שם ניקב כל חללו וניקב רגל השמאלי עד שלא נשתייר בו כמלא או"ק חד דינא אית להו אבל המעי' בד"מ הארוך יראה להדיא מדבריו דמסכים לדעת המרדכי דמקיל בניקב כל חללו א"כ ממילא רגל השמאלי שוה לרגל ימיני לפסול כידוע להמעיין בפוסקים דהא בהא תליא לבד מהב"ח שכתב דהטור מיקל בשניהם: * ניקב רגל הימיני אם נשתייר וכו'. עיין במ"ב בסקמ"א שכ' שם דינא דהמ"א שהביא בשם הר"מ[ב] דאם נשאר בעובי האות כמו וי"ו או יו"ד דקה כשר וכתבנו ע"ז הטעם דאין שיעור לעובי האותיות כ"ז כתבנו לפי מה שכתב הפמ"ג בסימן זה סקי"ו ע"ז דאם נשאר שריטה דקה שחור די בכך משמע לכאורה לפ"ז דאפילו כ"ש כשר ולא יתכן לפ"ז לשון הגמרא להר"מ דהכי איתא שם ניקב יריכו אם נשתייר הימנו כמלא או"ק כשר וא"ל פסול משמע להדיא דאפילו[א] נשתייר כ"ש פסול. אך באמת זה אינו מוכח כ"א לפי שיטתו דהמאירי משא"כ לדידן לא איירי הגמרא כלל בנפסק האות מעוביו עיין בפמ"ג שם ואין צריך שישאר בזה האות כמלא או"ק מ"מ צ"ע אחרי שהמ"א הביאו: * מלא או"ק. ואם זה הכתב הוא מכתב בינוני לכאורה דאין מועיל אם כמלא או"ק הוא מכתב קטן דאל"כ אין שיעור לדבר אבל אם זה הכתב הוא כתב גדול *נראה דבודאי מהני אם כמאו"ק הוא מכתב בינוני: * כשר. עיין במ"ב מה שכ' שאין צריך להראות להתינוק כן משמע מכל האחרונים ה"ה הפרישה והט"ז והפמ"ג ומחה"ש ודה"ח ולא שבקינן פשיטותא דהני גדולים משום ספיקא דיד אפרים ובאמת פליאה נשגבה על דבריו האיך רצה לומר דדעת המ"א ברמ"א הוא כך הלא מד"מ מוכח להדיא וכן בפרישה דדעת המרדכי הוא דלא בעינן בה"א וכה"ג רק כמלא או"ק דאל"כ לא מקשה מידי שם עי"ש ובכאן הלא נרשם ברמ"א בהג"ה בשם מרדכי וכן כתב בהדיא בפמ"ג במ"ז דאף שבד"מ מגלגל לומר דדעת הטור כהמאירי מ"מ בשו"ע סתם כדעת המרדכי וכן בפרישה השיג על הד"מ ומסיק דגם דעת הטור כהמרדכי דלא אמרינן צירוף באות נפסק וא"כ ממילא מוכח מהגמרא דבאות ה' וכדומה די בשיור כמלא או"ק לבד. והטעם בזה נראה פשוט דקים להו לחז"ל באות ה' וכדומה דזה שיעורן בעלם ולכן אין צריך להביא ראיה מהתינוק דהתינוק אין מורגל בזה התמונה דכל אחד כותב לכתחלה אות ארוך והוא דומיא דחי"ת שיתבאר ג"כ לקמן בסכ"ה דאין ראיה מהתינוק משום דאין מורגל בחי"ת של חטוטרות. ומ"מ בדיעבד אם הראוהו להתינוק דלא חו"ט ולא יכול לקרותו יש להחמיר בזה כי ראיתי להשיורי כנה"ג שמלדד לומר דאפי' במקומות דלא משגחינן על תינוק להקל על ידו משגחינן עליו להחמיר ע"ש. ואף דבחי"ת של חטוטרות מבואר לקמן בסוף סכ"ה דקריאתו של תינוק לא מגרע בזה היינו משום דשם אין מורגל כלל בחי"ת של חטוטרות דאפילו אם היה נכתב כתיקונו היה קוראו בב' זייני"ן כמבואר בב"י בסוף סימן ל"ו משא"כ בענינינו:

* ואם לאו פסול. ולא מצרפינן ליה מה שלמטה מהנקב או ההפסק אפילו לא היה פרידתו ניכר להדיא ותינוק דלא חכים ולא טיפש קרי ליה לאות וכ"ז בלא תיקון אבל אם תיקן את הפסקן הדין בזה הכל כמו שביארנו בסמוך:

* נפסק. וה"ה אם מתחילה כתב הסופר איזה אות פשוט ונסתפק לו אם הוא ארוך כשיעור שראוי להיות וא"א לו להגיה דהוה שלא כסדרן מראה לתינוק. ט"ז וא"ר וחידושי רע"א: * הפשוטות וה"ה אם הספק הוא בד' שגגו קצר ונסתפק לנו אם הוא כשיעורו מראה האות להתינוק אחרונים:

* כגון וי"ו זיין. עיין בפמ"ג שמסתפק לומר דבזיין שנפסק די כמלא אות קטנה דבמה שגגו עובר מב' הלדדים מוכח שאינו יו"ד והובא בחידושי רע"א. ועיין בדה"ח בהלכות קה"ת ובשערי אפרים שהשוו שם זיי"ן לוי"ו לדינא. ועכ"פ אם התינוק קראו ליו"ד ודאי פסול. ועיין במה שכתבנו בסעיף ט"ו בשם כנה"ג[ג]. ועיין בב"י בסימן ל"ו באות וא"ו: * אם תינוק. עיין בפמ"ג וא"ר דאם יש כמלא או"ק דידהו כגון וי"ו או נו"ן פשוטה קטנה וניכר יפה

שער הציון

(נג) פמ"ג:

הגהות ותיקונים: א) דאם ב) ר"ת הר' מנחם מאירי: ג) שכנה"ג:

letter[14*] */to remain/* (40) *and this is the halachic /ruling to be followed/. (...)*
(41) If a hole formed in (42) the right leg /of the letter ה, then/, (43) if there

Mishnah Berurah

when the hole formed after /the letter/ was written (in conformity with what is /ruled/ shortly at the end of Par. 16). Otherwise, even if more than the equivalent /length/ of a small letter remains, /the letter/ is invalid according to the *Rosh* as well.

(40) And this is the halachic /ruling to be followed/. The wording of /the *Rema*/ implies that he does not rule in accordance with the view of the other Poskim only /in order/ to be stringent, but he is convinced that the halachic /ruling/ follows their opinion. Consequently, one must admonish the scribes strongly /about this/, as they stumble over it.

In the case of /the passages/ of *tefilin* and mezuzos, /whose letters/ are required /to be written/ in /the correct/ order, it would appear that /if the equivalent length of a small letter does not remain/, no correction whatsoever is of avail. This even /applies/ if a child will read the letter /correctly/. For we see that /the symbol/ does not have the /correct/ form of the letter, as /a symbol/ cannot be described as /a letter/ ה, /if the left leg/ does not have /the required length/, in the opinion of these Poskim. This accords with /the ruling/ below in Par. 25; see there. Nevertheless, it seems that there are grounds for being lenient as regards correction, /as such a correction may be/ compared to the simple /elongated letter/ ך being converted into the square /letter כ/ by means of a correction, concerning which the *P.Mg.* is lenient; see there.

(41) If a hole formed. The same ruling /applies/ if the letter became broken without a hole /having formed/ or if the edge of the letter became erased.

The Shulchan Aruch is referring to the length /of the leg/. Correspondingly, if some of the thickness /of the length/ was interrupted, whether by means of a hole having formed or through erasure /, then/, if a thin black line remains, like a thin /letter/ ו or /letter/ י, /the letter/ is valid, as there is no minimum width /required/ for the thickness of the letter.

However, if a hole formed /in the leg, then/, irrespective of whether it /formed/ in the width or in the length of /the leg/, it is necessary for the hole to have formed after /the letter/ was written /for the letter to be valid/, according to /what is ruled/ below in Par. 16. [From the *M.A.* and *D.Hach.*]

(42) The right. /I.e.,/ of /the letter/ ה.

The *P.Mg.* writes, "It appears to me that the same ruling /applies/ in the case of other letters, such as /the letters/ ד, ל, the simple /elongated/ ף, the simple /elongated/ ץ, ק, ר, ת or ח. [It would appear that in the case of the /letter/ ח /the ruling applies/ both to the right and the left leg.] If /the equivalent length/ of the /letter/ י remains of the right thigh, this is sufficient."

See below in Sec. 36 /, in *Mishnas Soferim/*, in the laws concerning the form of the letters, in /the description of/ the letter ל, the simple /elongated letter/ ף, the simple /elongated letter/ ץ, /the letter/ ק and the letter ת.

(43) If there remains. I.e., from the hole upwards, but one may not combine with it /the part/ that is below the hole /to complete the required size/. This even /applies/ if a child who is neither /especially/ intelligent nor /especially/ simple has read the letter /correctly/, since we see that the form of the letter has not remained as it should be. This conforms with what is explained nearby in the name of the *Taz*.

On the other hand, if there remains above the hole [or above the break, if the letter is broken in the middle] the length of a small letter, /the letter/ is valid and it is unnecessary to show it to a child. Correspondingly, /even/ if one wrote initially a small brief leg of this /size, the letter/ is valid. See the *Yad Efrayim* and the Beyur Halachah.[11]

14* If the script is large, this is measured in accordance with average script and not in accordance with the size of the script actually used. (Beyur Halachah)

11 There the author rules that once it is after the event and one showed it to a child who is neither especially intelligent nor especially simple and he read it incorrectly, one should rule stringently that the letter is invalid.

(יט) קטנה (מ) * והכי הלכתא*(ב"י) (מא) * לניקב רגל (מב) הימיני (מג) אם **נשתייר ממנו** (מד) ***מלא** אות קטנה *כשר *ואם לאו פסול: **טז** (מה) * מנפסק אחת מהאותיות הגה (כ) [יא] (מו) * הפשוטות * כגון וי"ו זיי"ן (מז) או שנפסק רגל (הטו"ן) וכיוצא בה (מרדכי ה"ק דף ל"ב) (מח) *אם תינוק שאינו

שם בגמ' דמנחות מרדכי בהקומץ

שערי תשובה

וגם מה ענין לקרות לה ארוכה בשביל שדחוקה באמצע. לכן מהוורתא להגיה כמ"ש ביד אהרן כנ"ל: [יא] הפשוטות. עבה"ט וכ"ש שאין לדברי להקשות עליו והעלה דהך נפסק רגל הא' מקומו א"כ מיהו אם אנו רואים שלא נשאר צורת אות כתיקונו או נפסק רגל הא' פסול ע"ש

באר היטב

רנ"ט: (יט) קטנה. היינו יו"ד: (כ) הפשוטות. כגון וי"ו זיי"ן או שנפסק רגל הנו"ן כנ"ל. וכ"כ בע"ת וכ"ה במרדכי וכ"כ המחבר יד אהרן ובקצת נוסחאות כתב או שנפסק רגל האל"ף. והט"ז הרבה

ביאור הלכה

להקל בניקב כל תוכו: * והכי הילכתא. עיין במ"ב סק"מ שכתב מדבריו וכו' וכן משמע בב"י ועיין בדה"ח בהל' קה"ת בדין כ"ו דמשמע מדבריו דמטעם ספיקא דדינא החמיר הרמ"א ולדבריו שם ניקב כל חללו וניקב רגל השמאלי עד שלא נשתייר בו כמלא או"ק חד דינא אית להו אבל המעיין בד"מ הארוך יראה להדיא מדבריו דמסכים לדעת המרדכי דמקיל בניקב כל חללו א"כ ממילא רגל השמאלי שוה לרגל ימיני לפסול כידוע להמעיין בפוסקים דהא בהא תליא לבד מהב"ח שכתב דהטור מיקל בשניהם: * ניקב רגל הימיני אם נשתייר וכו'. עיין במ"ב בסקמ"א שכ' שם דינא דהמ"א שהביא בשם הר"מ[ב] דאם נשאר בעובי האות כמו וי"ו או יו"ד דקה כשר וכתבנו ע"ז הטעם דאין שיעור לעובי האותיות כ"ז כתבנו לפי מה שכתב הפמ"ג בסימן זה סקי"ו ע"ז דאם נשאר שריטה דקה שחור די בכך משמע לכאורה לפ"ז דאפילו כ"ש כשר ולא יתכן לפ"ז לשון הגמרא להר"מ דהכי איתא שם ניקב ירכו אם נשתייר הימנו כמלא או"ק כשר וא"ל פסול משמע להדיא דאפילו[א] נשתייר כ"ש פסול. אך באמת זה אינו מוכח כ"א לפי שיטתו דהמאירי משא"כ לדידן לא איירי הגמרא כלל בנפסק האות מעוביו עיין בפמ"ג שם ואין צריך שישאר בזה האות כמלא או"ק מ"מ צ"ע אחרי שהמ"א הביאו: * מלא או"ק. ואם זה הכתב הוא מכתב בינוני לכאורה דאין מועיל אם כמלא או"ק הוא מכתב קטן דאל"כ אין שיעור לדבר אבל אם זה הכתב הוא כתב גדול *נראה דבודאי מהני אם כמאו"ק הוא מכתב בינוני: * כשר. עיין במ"ב מה שכ' שאין צריך להראות להתינוק כן משמע מכל האחרונים ה"ה הפרישה והט"ז והפמ"ג ומחה"ש ודה"ח ולא שבקינן פשיטותא דהני גדולים משום ספיקא דיד אפרים ובאמת פליאה נשגבה על דבריו האיך רצה לומר דדעת המ"א ברמ"א הוא כך הלא מד"מ מוכח להדיא וכן בפרישה דדעת המרדכי הוא דלא בעינן בה"א וכה"ג רק כמלא או"ק דאל"כ לא מקשה מידי שם עי"ש ובכאן הלא נרשם ברמ"א בהג"ה בשם מרדכי וכן כתב בהדיא בפמ"ג במ"ז דאף שבד"מ מלדד לומר דדעת הטור כהמאירי מ"מ בשו"ע סתם כדעת המרדכי וכן בפרישה השיג על הד"מ ומסיק דגם דעת הטור כהמרדכי דלא אמרינן צירוף באות נפסק וא"כ ממילא מוכח מהגמרא דבאות ה' וכדומה די בשיור כמלא או"ק לבד. והטעם בזה נראה פשוט דקים להו לחז"ל באות ה' וכדומה דזה שיעורן בעלם ולכן אין צריך להביא ראיה מהתינוק דהתינוק אין מורגל בזה התמונה דכל אחד כותב לכתחלה אות ארוך והוא דומיא דחי"ת שיתבאר ג"כ לקמן בסכ"ה דאין ראיה מהתינוק משום דאין מורגל בחי"ת של חטוטרות. ומ"מ בדיעבד אם הראוהו להתינוק דלא חו"ט ולא יכול לקרותו יש להחמיר בזה כי ראיתי להשיורי כנה"ג שמלדד לומר דאפי' במקומות דלא משגחינן על תינוק להקל על ידו משגחינן עליו להחמיר ע"ש. ואף דבחי"ת של חטוטרות מבואר לקמן בסוף סכ"ה דקריאתו של תינוק לא מגרע בזה היינו משום דשם אין מורגל כלל בחי"ת של חטוטרות דאפילו אם היה נכתב כתיקונו היה קורא בב' זייני"ן כמבואר בב"י בסוף סימן ל"ו משא"כ בענינינו:
* ואם לאו פסול. ולא מצרפינן ליה מה שלמטה מהנקב או ההפסק אפילו לא היה פרידתו ניכר להדיא ותינוק דלא חכים ולא טיפש קרי ליה לאות וכ"ז בלא תיקון אבל אם תיקן את הפסקן הדין בזה הכל כמו שביארנו בסמוך:
* נפסק. וה"ה אם מתחילה כתב הסופר איזה אות פשוט ונסתפק לו אם הוא ארוך כשיעור שראוי להיות וא"א לו להגיה דהוה שלא כסדרן מראה לתינוק. ט"ז וא"ר וחידושי רע"א: * הפשוטות וה"ה אם הספק הוא בד' שגגו קצר ונסתפק לנו אם הוא כשיעורו מראה האות להתינוק אחרונים:
* כגון וי"ו זיין. עיין בפמ"ג שמסתפק לומר דבזיין שנפסק די כמלא אות קטנה דבמה שגגו עובר מב' הצדדים מוכח שאינו יו"ד והובא בחידושי רע"א. ועיין בדה"ח בהלכות קה"ת ובשערי אפרים שהשוו שם זיי"ן לוי"ו לדינא. ועכ"פ אם התינוק קראו ליו"ד ודאי פסול. ועיין במה שכתבנו בסעיף ט"ו בשם כנה"ג[ג]. ועיין בב"י בסימן ל"ו באות וא"ו: * אם תינוק. עיין בפמ"ג וא"ר דאם יש כמלא או"ק דידהו כגון וי"ו או נו"ן פשוטה קטנה וניכר יפה

משנה ברורה

לאחר הכתיבה כדבסמוך סט"ו בסופו דאל"ה פסול אפי' אם נשתייר יותר מכמלא אות קטנה גם להרא"ש: (מ) והכי הלכתא. מדבריו אלו משמע דלא להחמיר בלבד פסק כדעת ש"פ אלא דפשיטא ליה דהלכה כוותיהו וא"כ צריך להזהיר מאד להסופרים שנכשלין בזה: ובתפילין ומזוזות דבעינן כסדרן לכאורה לא מהני שום תיקון אפילו התינוק קוראו לאות כיון שאנו רואין שאין לו צורת אות דבלא זה לא מיקרי ה' לפי דעת אלו הפוסקים וכדלקמן בסכ"ה ע"ש. ומ"מ נראה דיש להקל ע"י תיקון ודומיא שהקיל הפמ"ג בכף פשוטה שעשאו מרובע ע"י תיקון עי"ש: (מא) ניקב. וה"ה אם נפסק האות בלא נקב או נמחק קצת האות ומיירי השו"ע בארכו וה"ה אם נפסק קצת מעביו בין ע"י נקיבה או ע"י מחיקה אם נשאר שריטה דקה שחור כמו וי"ו או יו"ד דקה כשר דאין שיעור לעובי האותיות אלא דבניקב בין בעביו בין בארכו בעינן שניקב לאחר הכתיבה וכדלקמן בסט"ז [מפמ"א ודה"ח]: (מב) הימיני. של ה"א. כתב הפמ"ג נראה לי דה"ה לשאר אותיות כגון ד' ל' פ' פשוטה נ' פשוטה קו"ף רי"ש או תי"ו או חי"ת [ולכאורה בחי"ת בין רגלה הימיני או השמאלי] אם נשאר מהירך הימיני כיו"ד די בכך עכ"ל ועיין לקמן בסימן ל"ו בדיני צורת האותיות באות ל' ופ' פשוטה ונ' פשוטה וקו"ף ובאות תי"ו: (מג) אם נשתייר. היינו מהנקב לצד מעלה ולא מצרפינן ליה מה שלמטה מהנקב אפילו אם תינוק דלא חכים ולא טיפש קראה לאות כיון דאנו רואין שלא נשאר צורת האות כתיקונו וכמו שנתבאר בסמוך בשם הט"ז אבל אם נשתייר מהנקב ולמעלה [או מההפסק ולמעלה אם נפסק האות באמצע] כשיעור אות קטנה כשר ואין צריך להראותו לתינוק וה"ה אם כתב לכתחלה רגל קטנה קצרה כזה דכשר ועיין ביד אפרים ובביאור הלכה: (מד) מלא או"ק. היינו יו"ד ובקוץ התחתון שלו לפי מה דפסק לקמן בסי' ל"ו בב"י דלא מיקרי יו"ד בלא קוץ התחתון: **ט ז** (מה) נפסק. י"ל בשני אופנים או מחמת נקב וזה אין כשר כ"א בניקב אח"כ כמו שיתבאר בסמוך בפנים או ע"י שנחסר הדיו באותו מקום (נג) ובאופן זה היה קאי הדין דשו"ע אפילו אם בתחלת הכתיבה נעשה כך: (מו) הפשוטות. ולפיכך אין מועיל בה אם נשתייר כמלא יו"ד דאדרבה נראית כיו"ד ופסול הלכך בעינן תינוק בזה: (מז) או שנפסק רגל הנו"ן כצ"ל. ופי' נו"ן פשוטה וכיוצא בה כגון כ"ף פשוטה שרגלה קצרה ודומה קצת לדל"ת או לרי"ש [מפמ"ג ודה"ח]: (מח) אם תינוק. עיין בט"ז שכתב דהך נפסק מיירי שנפסק קצת מאורך האות ולמטה לגמרי ולא נשאר ממנו רק החלק שקודם ההפסק אז תלוי בקריאת התינוק אם ספק לנו אם נשאר כשיעור של האות ההוא אבל אם נשתייר גם למטה מן ההפסק דהיינו שנעשה ההפסק ברחבו של רגל האות ואחר ההפסק נשאר עוד למטה חלק מן הרגל בזה לא מועיל תינוק דהתינוק יצרף מה שלמטה ממנו לחלק העליון ובאמת אין לו צירוף וזה דומה לנפסק רגל הא' אלא צריך לכסות את חלק הנשאר אחר ההפסק ואין זה דומה למש"כ השו"ע כאן דאין צריך לכסות שאר האותיות דבזה ודאי מודה

שער הציון

(נג) פמ"ג:

הגהות ותיקונים: א) דאם ב) ר"ת הר' מנחם מאירי: ג) שכנה"ג:

remains of /the leg/ (44) the equivalent /length/ of a small letter, /the letter/ is valid, but if not, it is invalid.

16. (45) If there is a break in one of the letters, *Gloss: /i.e., a break in one of/* (46) *the simple /letters/, such as /the letters/* ו *or* ז (47) *or a break in the leg (of the /elongated letter/* ן*), etc. (...),* /the ruling is that/ (48) if a child who is

Mishnah Berurah

(44) The equivalent of a small letter. I.e., /the letter/ י /together/ with its lower tip /on the right/. This accords with what is ruled below in Sec. 36 in the *B.Y.*, that /the symbol/ is not describable as the /letter/ י without the lower tip.

(45) If there is a break. This can be understood in two ways.

/One is that it is/ because of a hole. If so /the letter/ is only valid if the hole developed subsequent /to the writing/, as explained nearby inside /the Shulchan Aruch/.

The alternative is /that it is/ due to a lack of ink in that spot. In that case the law /given/ in the Shulchan Aruch relates even to /an instance/ when /the letter/ became like that when it was first written.

(46) The simple /letters/. In view of /the fact/ that /they are simple letters/ it is of no avail for them if the equivalent /length/ of the /letter/ י remains /of them/. On the contrary, /the letter then/ appears like the /letter/ י and is /therefore/ invalid. Consequently, /the reading of/ a child is required /to determine the validity of the letter/ in such a case.

(47) Or a break in the leg of the /elongated letter/ ן. That is what /the correct reading/ should be.

What is meant is the simple /elongated letter/ ן and similar /letters/. For example, the simple /elongated letter/ ך, which has a short leg and somewhat resembles /the letter/ ד or /the letter/ ר. [From the *P.Mg.* and the *D.Hach.*]

(48) If a child. See the *Taz*, who writes that the break which is being discussed is a break of some of the length of the letter, /so that the part/ below /the break is missing/ completely and only the portion /of the letter/ before the break remains. Then, /the validity of the letter/ depends on the reading of a child, if we are in doubt as to whether a sufficient amount of that letter remains.

However, if /some of the letter/ remains below the break as well, it is of no avail for a child /to read it as it is/ in such a case. I.e., /it is of no avail/ when the break formed in the width of the leg of the letter and after the break some of the leg remains, in addition, below it. /This is/ because the child will combine what is below /the break/ with the portion above /, whereas/, in actual fact it is not combinable. The case is /then/ comparable to /a case where/ there is a break /dividing/ the leg of the /letter/ א /from its roof/. Instead, one must cover the portion which remains after the break /before the child reads it/. /The circumstances in such a case/ are /therefore/ not to be compared with /the circumstances/ for which /the author of/ the Shulchan Aruch writes here that it is unnecessary to cover the other letter. /In fact/ in such circumstances /the author of/ the Shulchan Aruch/ definitely concedes

(כח) [יב] (מט) לא חכם (נ) ולא טפש * יודע לקרותו כשר * ואם לאו פסול (נא) ואין צריך לכסות לו שאר (כב) אותיות כמו שנוהגים: הגה * מיהו אם אנו רואים שלא נשאר צורת (כג) (נב) האות כתקונו פסול אע"פ שהתינוק קורא אותו כהלכתו (מרדכי ומהרי"ק שורש ס"ט וריב"ש) יהא דמכשרינן

נ בית יוסף מדברי הרמב"ם ספ"א מהלכות תפילין

באר היטב

והמ"א גורס רגל האחד ע"ש ואין לדבריו הבנה ועיין בספר תורת חיים בקונטרס עוללות הכרם: (כא) לא חכם. כתב הט"ז נ"ל דהך נפסק מיירי שנפסק קצת מאורך האות ולמטה לגמרי ולא נשאר ממנו רק החלק שקודם ההפסק אז תלוי בקריאת התינוק אם ספק לנו אם נשאר כשיעור של האות ההוא אבל אם נשתייר גם למטה מן ההפסק דהיינו שנעשה ההפסק ברחבו של רגל האות ואחר ההפסק נשאר עוד למטה חלק מן הרגל בזה לא מועיל תינוק דהתינוק יצרף מה שלמטה ממנו לחלק העליון ובאמת אין לו צירוף וזה דומה לנפסק רגל הא' אלא צריך לכסות את חלק הנשאר אחר ההפסק ואין זה דומה למ"ש הש"ע כאן דאין צריך לכסות שאר האותיות דבזה ודאי מודה דצריך לכסות. ב"ח פסק דלא מכשרינן ע"י תינוק אא"כ שנכתב מתחלה כהלכתו האות ואח"כ נפסק אבל אם נכתב מתחלה כך לא מהני תינוק אע"ג דליכא נקב ע"ש וט"ז חולק עליו וכתב דאין חילוק בזה דאם אירע שכתב הסופר איזה אות פשוט ונסתפק לו אם הוא ארוך כשיעור שראוי להיות וא"א לו להגיה דהוי שלא כסדרן ודאי מראה לתינוק האות ע"ש. ועיין בתשובת מטה יוסף ח"א סימן א' שהלין בעד הב"ח. ועיין בקונטרס עוללות הכרס: (כב) אותיות. משמע דבין מלפניו ומלאחריו א"צ לכסותו וכ"כ הב"ח בא"ע סימן קכ"ה ע"ש אבל מהרי"ט ח"ב בטי"ד[א] סי' ל"ב כתב דלקמיה קאמר אבל מה שקודם לו צריך לכסות שאם יתחיל מתחלת המקרא סירכיה נקיט ואזיל וכן נהגו עכ"ל. וכתב היד אהרן דאף בתינוק שלא למד באותה פרשה אפ"ה צריך לכסות מה שלפניו דלא כספר גט פשוט סימן קכ"ה ס"ק פ"ג ע"ש: (כג) האות. ז"ל מהרי"ק שורש פ"ט בדין אלפי"ן שאין היו"ד שלהן נוגעת אל עצמה וכן נקודת הפ"א שאין נוגעת לגגה שהוא פסול ואין להכשירו ע"י קריאת התינוק שלא נאמרו דברים הללו אלא היכא שנפסק האות ובציר לה משיעורא כגון וי"ו קטיעה שאנו מסופקים אם הגיע לאורך וי"ו או אם כשיעור יו"ד ולכן תועיל קריאת התינוק דגילוי מילתא בעלמא הוא דאורך וי"ו יש לה מדלא קראה יו"ד אבל היכא דפשיטא שאין האות נשאר בצורתה מה מועיל בראיית התינוק ועינינו רואות שאין האות בצורתה

שערי תשובה

המג"א הבנה עיין ביד אפרים מ"ש ענין נפלא בזה ע"ש: [יב] לא חכם. עבה"ט ועיין בדברי המאירי שהביא הב"י ומ"ש הא"ר ובשאלות ותשובות בית אפרים בזה באורך. מכאן עד ס"ק ל"א עי' ביד אפרים ותמצא ביאור הדברים שהביא המג"א מתשובות הגדולים וכמה הלכתא גברוותא איכא למשמע מינה. וכתב בגינת ורדים כלל ב' סי' ח' סופר שנזדמן לו כף פשוטה להשלים השיטה והמשיך גגה של כף עד שהגיע לבסוף ועי"ז דומה לדלת או לריש גדולה שהוא פסול לכמה פוסקים אפשר להקל בשעת הדחק דמוכחא מלתא ע"י כתיבתה בקולמוס דקה שאינה מאותיות גדולות רק שהאריכוהו להשלים השיטה. ואם אין לו תפילין אחרים יכול לברך על אלו. ואם אירע כן בכף של אלהיך אסור לגוררה ולכותבה מחדש שאפשר כבר קידשה השם ובשאר אותיות ותיבות יכול לגרור כולה ולכותבה מחדש אבל לתקן ע"י שיגרור מקצת הרוחב שיהיה כף פשוטה כתיקונה אין לה הכשר רק בשעת הדחק כמו קודם התיקון ע"ש. ועיין במ"ש המג"א בשם תשובת מהר"י הלוי ומ"ש ביד אפרים בזה. וכתב בברכי יוסף בתמונת הכף פשוטה אם כתב הכ"ף פשוטה בזוית כמו דל"ת פוסל מהר"ש נרבוני. ומהר"ס גלאנטי בתשובה סי' קכ"ד הכשיר וכ"כ מהריק"ש בתשובה כת"י והעיד שראה ס"ת שכתב מהר"ל בן חביב לעצמו והכ"ף עליו בצורת דל"ת. וכ"כ בלקוטי פר"ח א"ח. ועיין בזכרון יוסף סי' ב' אם האריך הסופר קולי היודי"ן יותר מהראוי עד שישוו לרגלי הימנית אין למחוק כל הקוץ ולחזור ולכתבו ובפרט ביו"ד השם ויש די לגרור אריכות הקוץ משיעורו הראוי והרוצה

משנה ברורה

דצריך לכסות וכן הסכמת (נד) האחרונים [דלא כמש"כ בספר ישועות יעקב להקל כשיטת המאירי. ובביאור הגר"א בסימן ל"ו משמע ג"כ כהט"ז דלא מצרפינן להאות מה שלמטה]: (מט) לא חכם. היינו (נה) חכם כ"כ שמבין הענין ומתוך זה הוא אומר האות הנפסק ויהיה מתפרש שפיר אבל אין נקרא חכם אם הוא חכם בהכרת האותיות היטיב ואין מבין מה שכתוב לפניו דזהו ודאי ג"כ כשר: (נ) ולא טיפש. טיפש היינו שאינו יודע לקרות האותיות (נו) וכל שיודע לקרות האותיות אע"ג דאינו בקי כ"כ בצורת האותיות כל שאומר דאין בו צורת אות פסול הוא: (נא) וא"צ לכסות. וכן כתב הלבוש אבל המ"א בשם מהרי"ט כתב דצריך לכסות מה שלפניו שאם יתחיל מתחלת המקרא סרכיה נקיט ואזיל (נז) ואפילו תינוק שלא למד באותה פרשה אפילו הכי צריך לכסות לו מה שלפניו עד תיבה זו (נח) אבל תיבה זו וגם מה שלאחריה א"צ לכסותו כלל בכל גווני: (נב) האות. כגון (נג) אלפי"ן שאין היו"ד שלהן נוגעת אל עצמן וכן נקודת הפ"א שאין נוגעת לגגה וכן לכל אותיות שאינן פשוטות שיש הפסק באמצען שהוא פסול בין אם נעשה זה בעת הכתיבה או לאחר הכתיבה שלא מהני קריאת התינוק אלא היכא שנפסק האות ובציר לה משיעורא ומחמת זה דומה האות במקצת לאות אחר כגון וי"ו קטיעה שאנו מסופקין אם הגיע לאורך וי"ו או כשיעור יו"ד ולכך תועיל קריאת התינוק דגילוי מילתא בעלמא הוא דאורך וי"ו יש לה מדלא קראה יו"ד וה"ה לאות נו"ן פשוטה וכ"ף פשוטה שיש ספק אם יש להם שיעור ארכן או כ' כפופה שדומה במקצת לב"ת וכה"ג שיש להסתפק אם ממונה דומה לאות אחרת אבל היכא שאנו רואין שאין האות נשאר בצורתה מה מועיל בראיית התינוק ועינינו רואין שאין האות בצורתה. ולכן אין להכשיר האל"ף שרגל שמאלו אין נוגע לקו האמצעי בשביל שהתינוק יקראנה אל"ף דמפני הפירוד לא יטעה לומר שהיא עיין הפוכה. וה"ה בפשוטות אם אנו רואים ודאי שאין בו צורת אות לא מהני מה דתינוק קורא אותו

ביאור הלכה

יפה שהיא וי"ו או נו"ן כשר ואין צריך להראות להתינוק: * יודע לקרותו. אז אפילו הוא נקב גדול או הפסק גדול שפרידתו ניכר להדיא כשר וא"צ שום תיקון דלא יהא עדיף מאלו כתב לכתחילה אות קצר כזה דכשר: * ואם לאו. אפילו נעשה ההפסק לאח"כ כגון שקפץ הדיו מהקלף ונשאר רק רושם אדמומית מהחלודה של הדיו ואפילו אם היה ההפסק קטן כ"כ שלא היה פרידתו ניכר להדיא והראה להתינוק גם החלק שלמטה מההפסק וקראו לאות אפ"ה פסול דאין מצרפין לו מה שלמטה כמש"כ הט"ז. וכ"ז לענין שישאר כך בלא תיקון אבל לענין תיקון אם התינוק יודע לקרות האות ע"י צירוף מה שלמטה מהני אפי' בתפילין ומזוזות דבעינן כסדרן דוקא דלא נתבטל ממנו לגמרי שם אות כיון שהתינוק יודע לקרות ע"י צירוף ואפילו נעשה זה ההפסק בעת הכתיבה. וכתב הפמ"ג דכל זה בשלא ניכר להדיא פרידתן אבל אם ניכר להדיא פרידתן אין מועיל לו שום תיקון אפילו נעשה לאחר הכתיבה. ועיין לקמן בסעיף כ"ה בבה"ל מש"כ אודות זה: * מיהו אם אנו רואין וכו'. עיין במ"ב. וכ"ז מיירי ג"כ בלא תיקון אבל לענין תיקון מהני עכ"פ קריאת התינוק ואין חילוק בזה בין פשוטות לכפופות והכל דינא כמו שכתבנו מתחילה. כ"ז בררתי מדברי הפמ"ג בסימן זה בהרבה מקומות ויתר דיני הפרטים לענין תיקון יתבאר

שער הציון

(נד) ה"ה הפמ"ג ודה"ח ושערי אפרים ושארי אחרונים: (נה) ט"ז: (נו) פמ"ג ומחה"ש משמע לכאורה דפליג ע"ז: (נז) בה"ט: (נח) כ"כ במהרי"ט חי"ד ל"ב ועיין בדה"ח הקה"ת ומסתמא לא ראהו דאל"ה היה מביאו: (נט) מלוקט מט"ז ומ"א ופמ"ג ודה"ח ודלא כא"ר:

הגהות ותיקונים: א) צ"ל בחי"ד:

not **(49)** either /especially/ intelligent **(50)** or /especially/ simple is capable of reading it /correctly, the letter/ is valid,[15*] but if not it is invalid.[16*] /When one shows the letter to the child/ **(51)** it is unnecessary to cover the other letters for him, as is the practice.

Mishnah Berurah

that it is necessary to cover and this is likewise the agreed /view/ of the Acharonim. [This contradicts what is stated in the work *Yeshu'os Ya'akov*, that one may be lenient in accordance with the view of the *Me'iri*. In the *Beyur Ha-Gra*, in Sec. 36, it is also implied that one cannot combine /the continuation/ below /the break/ as /part of/ the letter, as is /the view of/ the *Taz*.]

(49) Either intelligent. I.e., /he is not/ so intelligent that he will comprehend the matter /involved/ and say the broken letter so that it makes proper sense through this /comprehension/. However, /a child/ is not described as being /too/ intelligent /for this purpose/ if he is intelligent /enough/ to recognize letters well, but does not comprehend what is written in front of it. Such /a child/ is definitely also valid /for this purpose/.

(50) Or /especially/ simple. By /especially/ simple is meant that he is incapable of reading the letters. If any /child/ is capable of reading the letters, /then,/ even if he is not so familiar with the form of the letters, when he says that any /letter/ does not have the form of the letter it is invalid.

(51) It is unnecessary to cover. The *Levush* writes likewise.

However, the *M.A.*, in the name of the *Maharit*, writes that it is necessary to cover what is in front of /the letter/, since if he will begin from the beginning of the writing he will /read it by/ following his /normal/ habit. Even if the child has not studied that passage, it is nevertheless necessary to cover for him what is in front of /the letter/ until the word /which contains the letter/. On the other hand, that word and what is /written/ after it does not need to be covered at all in any circumstances.

15* This is also of avail if one wrote such a letter at the outset and does not know whether it is long enough. (Beyur Halachah)

16* The same ruling applies when one is in doubt as to whether the roof of a letter ד is long enough. (Beyur Halachah)

(כח) [יב] (מט) לא חכם (נ) ולא טפש * יודע לקרותו כשר * ואם לאו פסול (נא) ואין צריך לכסות לו שאר (נב) אותיות כמו שנוהגים: הגה * מיהו אם אנו רואים שלא נשאר צורת (כג) (נב) האות כתקונו פסול אע"פ שהתינוק קורא אותו כהלכתו (מרדכי ומהרי"ק שורש ס"ט וריב"ש) נהא דמכשרינן

נ בית יוסף מדברי הרמב"ם ספ"א מהלכות תפילין

באר היטב

והמ"א גורס רגל האחד ע"ש ואין לדבריו הבנה ועיין בספר תורת חיים בקונטרס עוללות הכרס: (כח) לא חכם. כתב הט"ז נ"ל דהך נפסק מיירי שנפסק קצת מאורך האות ולמטה לגמרי ולא נשאר ממנו רק החלק שקודם ההפסק אז תלוי בקריאת התינוק אם ספק לנו אם נשאר כשיעור של האות ההוא אבל אם נשתייר גם למטה מן ההפסק דהיינו שנעשה ההפסק ברחבו של רגל האות ואחר ההפסק נשאר עוד למטה חלק מן הרגל בזה לא מועיל תינוק דהתינוק יצרף מה שלמטה ממנו לחלק העליון ובאמת אין לו צירוף וזה דומה לנפסק רגל הא' אלא צריך לכסות את חלק הנשאר אחר ההפסק ואין זה דומה למ"ש הש"ע כאן דאין צריך לכסות שאר האותיות דבזה ודאי מודה דצריך לכסות. ב"ח פסק דלא מכשרינן ע"י תינוק אא"כ שנכתב מתחלה כהלכתו האות ואח"כ נפסק אבל אם נכתב מתחלה כך לא מהני תינוק אע"ג דליכא נקב ע"ש וט"ז חולק עליו וכתב דאין חילוק בזה דאם אירע שכתב הסופר איזה אות פשוט ונסתפק לו אם הוא ארוך כשיעור שראוי להיות וא"א לו להגיה דהוי שלא כסדרן ודאי מראה לתינוק האות ע"ש. ועיין בתשובת מטה יוסף ח"א סימן א' שהלין בעד הב"ח. ועיין בקונטרס עוללות הכרס: (כב) אותיות. משמע דבין מלפניו ומלאחריו א"צ לכסותו וכ"כ הב"ח בא"ע סימן קכ"ה ע"ש אבל מהרי"ט ח"ב בטי"ד[א] סי' ל"ב כתב דלקמיה קאמר אבל מה שקודם לו צריך לכסות שאם יתחיל מתחלת המקרא סירכיה נקיט ואזיל וכן נהגו עכ"ל. וכתב היד אהרן דאף בתינוק שלא למד באותה פרשה אפ"ה צריך לכסות מה שלפניו דלא כספר גט פשוט סימן קכ"ה ס"ק פ"ג ע"ש: (כג) האות. ז"ל מהרי"ק שורש פ"ט בדין אלפי"ן שאין היו"ד שלהן נוגעת אל עצמה וכן נקודת הפ"א שאין נוגעת לגגה שהוא פסול ואין להכשירו ע"י קריאת התינוק שלא נאמרו דברים הללו אלא היכא שנפסק האות ובציר לה משיעורא כגון וי"ו קטיעה שאנו מסופקים אם הגיע לאורך וי"ו או אם כשיעור יו"ד ולכן תועיל קריאת התינוק דגילוי מילתא בעלמא הוא דאורך וי"ו יש לה מדלא קראה יו"ד אבל היכא דפשיטא שאין האות נשאר בצורתה מה מועיל בראיית התינוק ועינינו רואות שאין האות בצורתה

שערי תשובה

המג"א הבנה עיין ביד אפרים מ"ש ענין נפלא בזה ע"ש: [יב] לא חכם. עבה"ט ועיין בדברי המאירי שהביא הב"י ומ"ש הא"ר ובשאלות ותשובות בית אפרים בזה באורך. מכאן עד ס"ק ל"א עי' ביד אפרים ותמצא ביאור הדברים שהביא המג"א מתשובות הגדולים וכמה הלכתא גברוותא איכא למשמע מינה. וכתב בגינת ורדים כלל ב' סי' ח' סופר שנזדמן לו כף פשוטה להשלים השיטה והמשיך גגה של כף עד שהגיע לבסוף ועי"ז דומה לדלת או לריש גדולה שהוא פסול לכמה פוסקים אפשר להקל בשעת הדחק דמוכחא מלתא ע"י כתיבתה בקולמוס דקה שאינה מאותיות גדולות רק שהאריכוהו להשלים השיטה. ואם אין לו תפילין אחרים יכול לברך על אלו. ואם אירע כן בכף של אלהיך אסור לגוררה ולכותבה מחדש שאפשר כבר קידשה השם ובשאר אותיות ותיבות יכול לגרור כולה ולכותבה מחדש אבל לתקן ע"י שיגרור מקצת הרוחב שיהיה כף פשוטה כתיקונה אין לה הכשר רק בשעת הדחק כמו קודם התיקון ע"ש. ועיין במ"ש המג"א בשם תשובת מהר"י הלוי ומ"ש ביד אפרים בזה. וכתב בברכי יוסף בתמונת הכף פשוטה אם כתב הכ"ף פשוטה בזוית כמו דל"ת פוסל מהר"ש נרבוני. ומהר"ס גלאנטי בתשובה סי' קכ"ד הכשיר וכ"כ מהריק"ש בתשובה כת"י והעיד שראה ס"ת שכתב מהר"ל בן חביב לעצמו והכ"ף עליו בצורת דל"ת. וכ"כ בלקוטי פר"ח א"ח. ועיין בזכרון יוסף סי' ב' אם האריך הסופר קולי היודי"ן יותר מהראוי עד שישוו לרגלי הימנית אין למחוק כל הקוץ ולחזור ולכתבו ובפרט ביו"ד השם ויש די לגרור אריכות הקוץ משיעורו הראוי והרולה

משנה ברורה

דצריך לכסות וכן הסכמת (נד) האחרונים [דלא כמש"כ בספר ישועות יעקב להקל כשיטת המאירי. ובביאור הגר"א בסימן ל"ו משמע ג"כ כהט"ז דלא מצרפינן להאות מה שלמטה]: (מט) לא חכם. היינו (נה) חכם כ"כ שמבין הענין ומתוך זה הוא אומר האות הנפסק ויהיה מתפרש שפיר אבל אין נקרא חכם אם הוא חכם בהכרת האותיות היטיב ואין מבין מה שכתוב לפניו דזהו ודאי ג"כ כשר: (נ) ולא טיפש. טיפש היינו שאינו יודע לקרות האותיות (נו) וכל שיודע לקרות האותיות אע"ג דאינו נקי כ"כ בצורת האותיות כל שאומר דאין בו צורת אות פסול הוא: (נא) וא"צ לכסות. וכן כתב הלבוש אבל המ"א בשם מהרי"ט כתב דצריך לכסות מה שלפניו שאם יתחיל מתחלת המקרא סרכיה נקיט ואזיל (נז) ואפילו תינוק שלא למד באותה פרשה אפילו הכי צריך לכסות לו מה שלפניו עד תיבה זו (נח) אבל תיבה זו וגם מה שלאחריה א"צ לכסותו כלל בכל גווני: (נב) האות. כגון (נט) אלפי"ן שאין היו"ד שלהן נוגעת אל עצמן וכן נקודת הפ"א שאין נוגעת לגגה וכן לכל אותיות שאינן פשוטות שיש הפסק באמצען שהוא פסול בין אם נעשה זה בעת הכתיבה או לאחר הכתיבה שלא מהני קריאת התינוק אלא היכא שנפסק האות ובציר לה משיעורא ומחמת זה דומה האות במקצת לאות אחר כגון וי"ו קטיעה שאנו מסופקין אם הגיע לאורך וי"ו או כשיעור יו"ד ולכן תועיל קריאת התינוק דגילוי מילתא בעלמא הוא דאורך וי"ו יש לה מדלא קראה יו"ד וה"ה לאות נו"ן פשוטה וכ"ף פשוטה שיש ספק אם יש להם שיעור ארכן או כ' כפופה שדומה במקצת לבי"ת וכה"ג שיש להסתפק אם תמונתה דומה לאות אחרת אבל היכא שאנו רואין שאין האות נשאר בצורתה מה מועיל בראיית התינוק ועינינו רואין שאין האות בצורתה. ולכן אין להכשיר האל"ף שרגל שמאלו אין נוגע לקו האמצעי בשביל שהתינוק יקראנה אל"ף דמפני הפירוד לא יטעה לומר שהיא עיין הפוכה. וה"ה בפשוטות אם אנו רואים ודאי שאין בו צורת אות לא מהני מה דתינוק קורא אותו

ביאור הלכה

יפה שהיא וי"ו או נו"ן כשר ואין צריך להראות להתינוק: * יודע לקרותו. אז אפילו הוא נקב גדול או הפסק גדול שפרידתו ניכר להדיא כשר וא"צ שום תיקון דלא יהא עדיף מאלו כתב לכתחילה אות קצר כזה דכשר: * ואם לאו. אפילו נעשה ההפסק לאח"כ כגון שקפץ הדיו מהקלף ונשאר רק רושם אדמומית מהחלודה של הדיו ואפילו אם היה ההפסק קטן כ"כ שלא היה פרידתו ניכר להדיא והראה להתינוק גם החלק שלמטה מההפסק וקראו לאות אפ"ה פסול דאין מצרפין לו מה שלמטה כמש"כ הט"ז. וכ"ז לענין שישאר כך בלא תיקון אבל לענין תיקון אם התינוק יודע לקרות האות ע"י צירוף מה שלמטה מהני אפי' בתפילין ומזוזות דבעינן כסדרן דוקא דלא נתבטל ממנו לגמרי שם אות כיון שהתינוק יודע לקרות ע"י צירוף ואפילו נעשה זה ההפסק בעת הכתיבה. וכתב הפמ"ג דכל זה בשלא ניכר להדיא פרידתן אבל אם ניכר להדיא פרידתן אין מועיל לו שום תיקון אפילו נעשה לאחר הכתיבה. ועיין לקמן בסעיף כ"ה בבה"ל מש"כ אודות זה: * מיהו אם אנו רואין וכו'. עיין במ"ב. וכ"ז מיירי ג"כ בלא תיקון אבל לענין תיקון מהני עכ"פ קריאת התינוק ואין חילוק בזה בין פשוטות לכפופות והכל דינא כמו שכתבנו מתחילה. כ"ז בררתי מדברי הפמ"ג בסימן זה בהרבה מקומות ויתר דיני הפרטים לענין תיקון יתבאר

שער הציון

(נד) ה"ה הפמ"ג ודה"ח ושערי אפרים ושארי אחרונים: (נה) ט"ז: (נו) פמ"ג ומחה"ש משמע לכאורה דפליג ע"ז: (נז) בה"ט: (נח) כ"כ במהרי"ט ח"ד ל"ב ועיין בדה"ח הקה"ת ומסתמא לא ראהו דאל"ה היה מביאו: (נט) מלוקט מט"ז ומ"א ופמ"ג ודה"ח ודלא כא"ר:

הגהות ותיקונים: א) צ"ל בחי"ד:

Gloss: However, if we see that the form of **(52)** *the letter has not remained as it should be, /the letter/ is /then/ invalid, even if the child reads it correctly. (...)*

Mishnah Berurah

(52) The letter. For example, /this applies to a letter/ א, whose י /parts/ do not touch it or, likewise, when the stroke of /a letter/ פ does not touch the roof /of the letter/. /It applies/ likewise to all non-simple letters which have a break in the middle of them, in which case /the letter/ is invalid both if /the break/ was formed at the time when /the letter/ was written or if /it was formed/ after it was written.

/The reason is/ that the reading of a child is only of avail where the letter is broken and lacks its /full/ size, because of which the letter partially resembles another letter. For example, /it is of avail in the case of/ a curtailed ו /letter/ concerning which we are in doubt /as to/ whether /or not/ it reaches the /required/ length for the /letter/ ו or /only/ has the size of the /letter/ י. The reading of a child is of avail for this, as it merely reveals that /the letter/ has the length of the /letter/ ו, since /the child/ did not read it as the /letter/ י. The same ruling /applies/ in the case of a simple /elongated letter/ ן or of a simple /elongated letter/ ך, when there is a doubt as to whether /or not/ they have the required length, or /in the case of/ a bent over /letter/ כ which is somewhat similar to the /letter/ ב and in similar cases where there are grounds for doubt as to whether /or not/ the symbol resembles a different letter. However, where we see that the letter has not remained with its /correct/ form, what the child sees cannot help /for the letter to be considered valid, in contradiction to the fact that/ we see with our eyes that the letter does not /in fact/ have the /appropriate/ form.

Consequently, a /letter/ א whose left leg does not touch the middle stroke cannot be ruled as valid because a child reads it as the /letter/ א, as he will not err in saying that it is an upside down /letter/ ע because of the separation. Correspondingly, in the case of simple letters, if we see definitely that the letter does not have the /appropriate/ form, it is of no avail if the child reads it /correctly/ as it is. /The reading of a child/ is only of

(נג) כשנפסק אות דוקא * כשנכתב בכשרות (נד) * ואח"כ נפסק אבל אם (נה) מתחלה כשנכתב היה שם (נו) נקב (כד) ונפסק בו או אם (נז) °רגל הכ"ף הפשוטה או כיוצא בה מגיע לסוף הקלף (נח) בלי הקף (כה) קלף (נט) מתחלתו (ס) פסול:

ס תשובת ר' לוי ן' חביב

באר היטב

עכ"ל וכ"כ הריב"ש סימן ק"ך דלא מהני קריאת התינוק אלא היכא שהפסול הוא משום שזה האות נדמה לאות אחרת אבל היכא שהפסול הוא משום שנפסק צורתו לא מהני לכן אין להכשיר האל"ף שאין רגל השמאלי נוגע לקו האמצעי בשביל שהתינוק יקראנה אל"ף שהרי מפני הפירוד לא יטעה לומר שהוא אות אחרת דהיינו עי"ן הפוכה עכ"ל ועיין סעיף כ"ה: (כד) ונפסק בו. להב"ח שכתבתי בס"ק כ"א אין חילוק בין נפסק בנקב בין נפסק שלא ע"י נקב אלא כשנראה הגויל החלק באמצע האות לא מכשרינן ע"י תינוק אא"כ שנכתב מתחלה כתיקונו ואח"כ נפסק האות אבל אם נכתב כך מתחלה לא מהני תינוק אע"ג דליכא נקב ולהט"ז צריך לומר דכאן איירי דוקא דנפסק ע"י נקב דאז יש חילוק הזה הואיל ואין מוקפת גויל. כי זהו לשון הב"י וא"ת והיכי מכשרינן באיפסק שוס אות בנוקבא והא אמרינן בהקומץ כל אות שאין גויל מוקף לה מד' רוחותיה פסול וי"ל דהא דמכשרינן היינו דוקא בשנפסק אחר שנכתב דכיון דכשנכתבה היתה כשרה שהיה מקיפה גויל מד' רוחותיה אבל כשבתחלת הכתיבה היה שם נקב ונפסקה בו אע"פ שיש בו שיעור אות פסולה משום דמעולם לא הוקפה גויל ע"ש ובט"ז ודו"ק. כתב בתשובת הר"י הלוי אם יש שריטה דקה בתוך האות ואינו עובר מעבר לגויל כשר כיון שאינו נראה אות חלוקה לב' עיין מטה יוסף ח"א סימן א': (כה) קלף. אע"פ שהיא ארוכה

משנה ברורה

אותו כך רק בספק לנו אם יש בו שיעור כראוי מהני וכ"ז בלא תיקון ולענין תיקון עיין בבה"ל: (נג) כשנפסק אות. וה"ה מה דמכשיר לעיל בסט"ו את[ח] ניקב רגל הה"א (ס) אבל בניקב חללו דמכשיר שם המחבר הוא אפילו ניקב קודם הכתיבה ולא נקט שם אם לאחר שנכתב וכו' אלא משום סיפא דניקב רגל: (נד) ואח"כ נפסק. והטעם דלא בעינן מוקף גויל רק בעת הכתיבה ולפ"ז אפילו אם מגיע הנקב מאות לאות שסמוך לו ג"כ כשר אכן הדה"ח בהלכות קה"ת בדין כ"ו[ט] מחמיר בזה ועיין בביה"ל. ודע עוד דבענין נגיעת האותיות אפילו אם יודע בבירור שנעשה לאחר הכתיבה ג"כ פסול [דה"ח שם וכן משמע בב"ש באה"ע בסימן קכ"ה סקכ"ט עי"ש דס"ל ג"כ דצריך לחוש לתי' א' שבב"י בד"ה וא"ת וכו' דאין מחלק בנגיעה בין אם לא הוקף בעת הכתיבה או אח"כ]: (נה) מתחלה. ובספק מתי נעשה הנקב תולין דאחר הכתיבה נעשה דמסתמא אם היה בעת הכתיבה היה הסופר רואהו אם לא שהנקב קטן מאד [דה"ח]: (נו) נקב. דוקא נקב או קרע אף שאין ניכר כלל הפסק ומשום דלא היה מוקף גויל בעת הכתיבה [לבוש"כ] (סא) אבל הפסק בעלמא כשר וא"צ שום תיקון כיון שיש שיעור אות עד מקום הפסק וכדלעיל בסט"ו וסט"ז. ואם נגלאות שריטות דקות מתוך שיעור אות עיין בביאור הלכה בסעיף כ"ה: (נז) רגל. וכ"ש גגי האותיות ולמעלן שאין להם היקף גויל בעת הכתיבה ונקט רגל לרבותא אף דבעת כתיבת סוף הרגל כבר נגמר צורת האות כראוי אפ"ה כל זמן שלא סלק ידו מן האות מיקרי ד"ז בעת הכתיבה ובעינן לכל האות הקפת גויל: (נח) בלי הקף. ואפילו אם היא ארוכה כראוי דהיינו שיש בה שיעור שאפילו אם נגררה קצת למטה ישאר צורת אות מ"מ פסול [מ"א בס"ק כ"א ועיין במ"א סק"ג]: (נט) מתחלתו. אבל אם נחתך הקלף אח"כ ועי"ז אין מוקף גויל כשר: (ס) פסול. (סב) ואם רוצה לתקן יגרר קצת כדי שיהיה מוקף גויל (סג) אבל דיבוק מטלית לא מהני להקפת גויל דבעינן הקפת

ביאור הלכה

אי"ה לקמן בסעיף כ"ה: * כשנכתב בכשרות. ומ"מ דוקא בנפסק ע"י נקב דהב"י בתירוצו השני הוסיף דע"י נקב בעינן ג"כ שנפסק אח"כ אבל בנגיעה אות לאות אף שנכתב בכשרות ונפסק[א] אח"כ פסול כדמשמע בסעיף י"ח. דע"מ משה מא"ת בסי' י"ג[ב] הביאו הגרע"א בחידושיו והדה"ח בהלכות קה"ת בדין כ"ה סובר דגם זה תליא בב' התירוצים שבב"י ולתירוץ ב' כשר אך שצריך לחוש לחומרת ב' התירוצים ונמצא שיש בזה לדבריו ספיקא דדינא. ומהסעיף י"ח אין ראיה כלל דשם מיירי בעת הכתיבה גופא אחר שנגמר צורת האות נגע אות בחבירו משא"כ בזה שכבר סילק ידו. וסברא זו מוכרחת *ממ"ש השו"ע מגיע לסוף הקלף ע"כ דאין סובר כהירושלמי דמכשיר בנגיעת אות לאות אחר שנגמרה צורתה וכמ"ש הפרישה וביאור הגר"א ואעפ"כ כתב לבסוף בלי היקף קלף מתחלתה דוקא משמע דאם נחתך הקלף אח"כ ועי"ז אין מוקף גויל כשר וע"כ הטעם כמו שכתבנו ומתוך מה שציין הגר"א בסי'[ג] י"ח סק"ג עי"ש משמע ג"כ שמפרש להשו"ע דמיירי בעת הכתיבה ואין סותר כלל לסברת תירוץ הב' שזכרו הש"ע בסט"ז. היוצא מדברינו דאין ראיה להחמיר יותר בזה ממה שסובר בעל דה"ח שם עי"ש דהוא ספיקא דדינא ונ"מ לענין להוציא אחרת עי"ש: * ואח"כ נפסק. עיין בב"י ועי' בדה"ח בהלכות קה"ת דין כ"ו[ד] שכתב שם דאף לתירוץ א' של הב"י פוסל חסרון הקף גויל ע"י נקב ורק לחומרא חשש המחבר לתירוץ הב' ומוכח שם לדבריו דלא מחלק המחבר בין ניקב מקודם לניקב אחר הכתיבה רק אם יש עכ"פ הקף גויל לנקב שאצל האות דהנקב אין מבטל הקפת הגויל שסביבו ונמצא שיש הקף גויל עכ"פ אבל אם הנקב מגיע מאות לאות שסמוך לו פסול בכל גווני דזה חשוב כנגיעת אות לאות וכתירוץ א' דנקטינן כוותיה ג"כ בלהחמיר ולהכי פוסל המחבר לעיל לפי הירושלמי אפילו אם לאחר שנכתב ניקב דזה שניקב כל חללו הוי כנגיעת אות לאות עי"ש [כ"ז לפי דעתו אבל הפמ"ג במ"ז סק"ח דעתו דעיקר דינא דהמחבר הוא רק קודם שנכתב עי"ש] ופליאה נשגבה על דברי הדה"ח א"כ למה כתב או אם רגל וכו' בלי היקף קלף מתחלתו אפילו אם הקלף שסמוך להאות נחתך אח"כ צריך להיות פסול לדידיה דשמא הלכה כתירוץ הא' ולא מחלקינן בין קודם לאח"כ ורק בנקב מקילינן משום דיש עכ"פ הקפת גויל סמוך לנקב שאצל האות משא"כ בזה שנחתך לגמרי אלא וודאי דהב"י סובר דאם נעשה הנקב לאחר הכתיבה כשר בכל גווני וכתירוץ הב' דלא בעינן אז מוקף גויל. ועוד נ"ל באמת דכ"ש לפי תירוץ א' של הב"י אינו פוסל חסרון היקף גויל ע"י הנקב כי הנה הב"י הוציא דין זה שכתב בשו"ע מחמת דהוקשה לו היכי מכשרינן בנפסק שוס אות ע"י נקב הא אמרינן כל אות שאין מוקף גויל לה מארבע רוחותיה פסולה ותירץ דלא אמרינן כל אות וכו' רק בשהיה ע"י נגיעת אות לאות אבל לא ע"י נקב א"נ דלא פסלינן מחמת מוקף גויל רק אם בעת הכתיבה לא היתה מוקפת משא"כ כשנכתב בכשרות והב"י העתיק פה לדינא תירוץ הב' והנה לפי דברי הדה"ח הנ"ל שילא לידון בדבר החדש דאף לתירוץ א' בעינן הקפת גויל אך להכי כשר ע"י נקב משום דיש גויל מעבר להנקב סמוך לאות שאצלו וזה חשוב מוקף גויל תמיהני דא"כ אם הרגל הך' מגיע לסוף בלי היקף קלף פסול אפילו לתירוץ א' לדבריו וזה אינו כדמוכח בב"י דתשובת הרלב"ח דפוסל בזה לא אתיא רק כתירוץ ב' ואפילו אם תרצה לדחוק בהב"י דלכו"ע כתב דינא דהרלב"ח אכן מד"מ הארוך מוכח בהדיא דלתירוץ א' כשר בזה ע"ש. אח"כ מצאתי בעזה"י שגם הלבושי שרד משיג בזה על הנו"ב שכתב ג"כ כהדה"ח הנ"ל גם הפמ"ג במ"ז בס"ק י"ג[ו] כתב להדיא דלתירוץ א' של הב"י לא בעינן היקף גויל בנקב ואפילו אם מתחלת הכתיבה היה רגל הך' בלי היקף קלף כשר וא"כ ממילא לפ"ז אפילו אם הנקב מגיע מאות לאות שסמוך לו כשר לדידן כשנעשה אחר הכתיבה ואף שכל זה ברור בעזה"י מ"מ ל"ע *למעשה אחרי שהדה"ח והנו"ב מחמירין בדבר ועכ"פ בהצטרף עוד איזה קולא כגון שהאות גדול יותר משיעור ונקב נעשה בסופו באופן שאפילו אם ינכה מקום הנקב ושיעור דהקפת גויל ג"כ ישאר שיעור הראוי לאותו אות יש לצדד להקל ולצרף לזה דעת הרד"ך שהובא בסימן זה במג"א סק"ג כי אפילו לדעת הדה"ח והנו"ב הנ"ל איננו רק ספיקא דדינא דשמא הלכה כתירוץ א'[ז]. ויותר טוב אם יכול לגרור מעט מעובי הקו של האות ויהיה מוקף גויל דזה מהני בכל

שער הציון

(ס) מפמ"ג ולבו"ש שם לעיל: (סא) חידושי רע"א וש"א: (סב) מ"א בס"ק כ"ז: (סג) פמ"ג בא"א ודה"ח:

הגהות ותיקונים: א) ונדבק: ב) ח': ג) בסעיף: ד) כ"ז: ה) כ"ב: ו) י"ד: ז) ב': ח) אם: ט) כ"ז:

/The ruling/ that (53) when a letter is broken it is valid only /applies/ if it was written validly (54) and subsequently became broken. However, if (55) at

Mishnah Berurah

avail when we are in doubt /as to/ whether /the letter/ has the proper size.

All these /remarks apply/ where no correction /is made/. For /the ruling/ as regards correction, see the Beyur Halachah.[12]

(53) When a letter is broken. The same applies to what is /stated/ above in Par. 15, that if a hole formed in the leg of the /letter/ ה /the letter/ is valid. However, when the author /of the Shulchan Aruch/ rules there that /the letter/ is valid if a hole formed in the space /inside the letter/, this /applies/ even if the hole formed /in that space/ before /the letter/ was written. /The author/ only uses the wording there, "If after /a passage/ was written, etc.," because of /the ruling/ at the end /of the paragraph, as regards an instance/ where a hole formed in the leg.

(54) And subsequently became broken. The reason is that we do not require /a letter to be/ surrounded by /blank/ parchment except at the time when it is written.

According to this, even if the hole reaches from one letter until the letter next to it /the letters/ are also valid. However, the *D.Hach.*, in Laws concerning the reading of the Torah, law 27, is stringent about this. See the Beyur Halachah.[13]

Note further that with reference to the touching of letters, even if one knows clearly that this happened after they were written /the passage/ is also invalid. [*D.Hach.* there. This is likewise implied by the *B.Sh.* in the *Even Ha-Ezer*, Sec. 125, sub-Par. 29. See there, that he is also of the opinion that one must take into account the first explanation of the *B.Y.* in /the paragraph/ beginning with the words וא"ת וכו'. /There the *B.Y.*/ does not differentiate /as regards the ruling/ when /letters/ touch, between /an instance/ when /the letter/ was not surrounded /by blank parchment/ at the time when it was written and /an instance when the touching developed/ subsequently.]

(55) At the outset. When there is a doubt as to when the hole was formed, we assume that it was formed after /the letter/ was written. For, generally, unless the hole is very small, /one may rely on the reasoning that/ if it was there when /the letter/ was written the scribe would have seen it. [*D.Hach.*]

12 The author states there that if a child can read the letter when the part below the break is combined, then, provided the separation of the parts is not clearly evident, correction of the letter is of avail even in the case of *tefilin* passages and mezuzos.

13 There the author adopts the view that one may be lenient in a case where one can combine a further consideration for leniency. For example, when the letter is so large that if one will subtract from the letter the area of the hole and an additional amount, so that what is left of the letter will be surrounded by blank parchment, there will remain sufficient of the letter to be valid. However, it is preferable to scrape off some of the stroke of the letter so that it is in fact surrounded by blank parchment. This will be of avail even in the case of *tefilin* passages and mezuzos.

(נג) כשנפסק אות דוקא * כשנכתב בכשרות (נד) * ואח"כ נפסק אבל אם (נה) מתחלה כשנכתב היה שם (נו) נקב (כד) ונפסק בו או אם (נז) [ס]רגל הכ"ף הפשוטה או כיוצא בה מגיע לסוף הקלף (נח) בלי הקף (כה) קלף (נט) מתחלתו (ס) פסול:

ס תשובת ר' לוי ן' חביב

באר היטב

עכ"ל וכ"כ הריב"ש סימן ק"ך דלא מהני קריאת התינוק אלא היכא שהפסול הוא משום שזה האות נדמה לאות אחרת אבל היכא שהפסול הוא משום שנפסק צורתו לא מהני לכן אין להכשיר האל"ף שאין רגל השמאלי נוגע לקו האמצעי בשביל שהתינוק יקראנה אל"ף שהרי מפני הפירוד לא יטעה לומר שהוא אות אחרת דהיינו עי"ן הפוכה עכ"ל ועיין סעיף כ"ה: (כד) ונפסק בו. להב"ח שכתבתי בס"ק כ"א אין חילוק בין נפסק בנקב בין נפסק שלא ע"י נקב אלא כשנראה הגויל החלק באמצע האות לא מכשרינן ע"י תינוק אא"כ שנכתב מתחלה כתיקונו ואח"כ נפסק האות אבל אם נכתב כך מתחלה לא מהני תינוק אע"ג דליכא נקב ולהט"ז צריך לומר דכאן איירי דוקא דנפסק ע"י נקב דאז יש חילוק הזה הואיל ואין מוקפת גויל. כי זהו לשון הב"י וא"ת והיכי מכשרינן באיפסק שום אות בנוקבא והא אמרינן בהקומץ כל אות שאין גויל מוקף לה מד' רוחותיה פסול וי"ל דהא דמכשרינן היינו דוקא בשנפסק אחר שנכתב דכיון דכשנכתבה היתה כשרה שהיה מקיפה גויל מד' רוחותיה אבל כשבתחלת הכתיבה היה שם נקב ונפסקה בו אע"פ שיש בו שיעור אות פסולה משום דמעולם לא הוקפה גויל ע"ש ובט"ז ודו"ק. כתב בתשובת הר"י הלוי אם יש שריטה דקה בתוך האות ואינו עובר מעבר לגויל כשר כיון שאינו נראה אות חלוקה לב' עיין מטה יוסף ח"א סימן א': (כה) קלף. אע"פ שהיא ארוכה

משנה ברורה

אותו כך רק בספק לנו אם יש בו שיעור כראוי מהני וכ"ז בלא תיקון ולענין תיקון עיין בבה"ל: (נג) כשנפסק אות. וה"ה מה דמכשיר לעיל בסט"ו אח"[ו] ניקב רגל הה"א (ס) אבל בניקב אללו דמכשיר שם המחבר הוא אפילו ניקב קודם הכתיבה ולא נקט שם אם לאחר שנכתב וכו' אלא משום סיפא דניקב רגל: (נד) ואח"כ נפסק. והטעם דלא בעינן מוקף גויל רק בעת הכתיבה ולפ"ז אפילו אם מגיע הנקב מאות לאות שסמוך לו ג"כ כשר אכן הדה"ח בהלכות קה"ת בדין כ"ו[ו] מחמיר בזה ועיין בבה"ל. ודע עוד דבענין נגיעת האותיות אפילו אם יודע בבירור שנעשה לאחר הכתיבה ג"כ פסול [דה"ח שם וכן משמע בב"ש באה"ע בסימן קכ"ה סקכ"ע עי"ש דס"ל ג"כ דצריך לחוש לתי' א' שבב"י בד"ה וא"ת וכו' דאין מחלק בנגיעה בין אם לא הוקף בעת הכתיבה או אח"כ]: (נה) מתחלה. ובספק מתי נעשה הנקב תולין דלאחר הכתיבה נעשה דמסתמא אם היה בעת הכתיבה היה הסופר רואהו אם לא שהנקב קטן מאד [דה"ח]: (נו) נקב. דוקא נקב או קרע אף שאין ניכר כלל ההפסק ומשום דלא היה מוקף גויל בעת הכתיבה [לבוש"ר] (סא) אבל הפסק בעלמא כשר וא"ל שום תיקון כיון שיש שיעור אות עד מקום ההוא וכדלעיל בסט"ו וסט"ז. ואם נמלאות שריטות דקות בתוך שיעור אות עיין בביאור הלכה בסעיף כ"ה (נז) רגל. וכ"ש גגי האותיות ואמצען שאין להם היקף גויל בעת הכתיבה ונקט רגל לרבותא אף דבעת כתיבת סוף הרגל כבר נגמר צורת האות כראוי אפ"ה כל זמן שלא סלק ידו מן האות מיקרי ד"ז בעת הכתיבה ובעינן לכל האות הקפת גויל: (נח) בלי הקף. ואפילו אם היא ארוכה כראוי דהיינו שיש בה שיעור שאפילו אם נגררה קלת למטה ישאר צורת אות מ"מ פסול [מ"א בס"ק כ"א[ה] ועיין במ"א סק"ג]: (נט) מתחלתו. אבל אם נחתך הקלף אח"כ ועי"ז אין מוקף גויל כשר: (ס) פסול. (סב) ואם רוצה לתקן יגרר קלת כדי שיהיה מוקף גויל (סג) אבל דיבוק מטלית לא מהני להקפת גויל דבעינן הקפת

ביאור הלכה

א"ה לקמן בסעיף כ"ה: * כשנכתב בכשרות. ומ"מ דוקא בנפסק ע"י נקב דהב"י בתירוצו השני הוסיף דע"י נקב בעינן ג"כ שנפסק אח"כ אבל בנגיעה אות לאות אף שנכתב בכשרות ונפסק[א] אח"כ פסול כדמשמע בסעיף י"ח. דבר משה מא"ח בסי' י"ג[ב] הביאו הגרע"א בחידושיו והדה"ח בהלכות קה"ת בדין כ"ה סובר דגם זה תליא בב' התירוצים שבב"י ולתירוץ ב' כשר אך שצריך לחוש לחומרת ב' התירוצים ונמלא שיש בזה לדבריו ספיקא דדינא. ומהסעיף י"ח אין ראיה כלל דשם מיירי בעת הכתיבה גופא אחר שנגמר צורת האות נגע אות בחבירו משא"כ בזה שכבר סילק ידו. וסברא זו מוכרחת ממ"ש השו"ע מגיע לסוף הקלף ע"כ דאין סובר כהירושלמי דמכשיר בנגיעת אות לאות אחר שנגמרה צורתה וכמ"ש הפרישה וביאור הגר"א ואעפ"כ כתב לבסוף בלי היקף קלף מתחלתה דוקא משמע דאם נחתך הקלף אח"כ ועי"ז אין מוקף גויל כשר וע"כ הטעם כמו שכתבנו ומתוך מה שציין הגר"א בסי'[ג] י"ח סק"נ עי"ש משמע ג"כ שמפרש להשו"ע דמיירי בעת הכתיבה ואין סותר כלל לסברת תירוץ הב' שזכרו הש"ע בסט"ז. היוצא מדברינו דאין ראיה להחמיר יותר בזה ממה שסובר בעל דה"ח שם עי"ש דהוא ספיקא דדינא ונ"מ לענין להוציא אחרת עי"ש: * ואח"כ נפסק. עיין בב"י ועי' בדה"ח בהלכות קה"ת דין כ"ו[ד] שכתב שם דאף לתירוץ א' של הב"י פוסל חסרון הקף גויל ע"י נקב ורק לחומרא חשש המחבר לתירוץ הב' ומוכח שם לדבריו דלא מחלק המחבר בין ניקב מקודם לניקב אחר הכתיבה רק אם יש עכ"פ הקף גויל לנקב שאצל האות דהנקב אין מבטל הקפת הגויל שסביבו ונמצא שיש הקף גויל עכ"פ אבל אם הנקב מגיע מאות לאות שסמוך לו פסול בכל גווני דזה חשוב כנגיעת אות לאות וכתירוץ א' דנקטינן כוותיה ג"כ בלהחמיר ולהכי פוסל המחבר לעיל לפי הירושלמי אפילו אם לאחר שנכתב ניקב דזה שניקב כל חללו הוי כנגיעת אות לאות עי"ש [כ"ז לפי דעתו אבל הפמ"ג במ"ז סק"ח דעתו דעיקר דינא דהמחבר הוא רק קודם שנכתב עי"ש] ופליאה נשגבה על דברי הדה"ח א"כ למה כתב או אם רגל וכו' בלי היקף קלף מתחלתו אפילו אם הקלף שסמוך להאות נחתך אח"כ צריך להיות פסול לדידיה דשמא הלכה כתירוץ הא' ולא מחלקינן בין קודם לאח"כ ורק בנקב מקילינן משום דיש עכ"פ הקפת גויל סמוך לנקב שאצל האות משא"כ בזה שנחתך לגמרי אלא וודאי דהב"י סובר דאם נעשה הנקב לאחר הכתיבה כשר בכל גווני וכתירוץ הב' דלא בעינן אז מוקף גויל. ועוד נ"ל בעמת דכ"ש לפי תירוץ א' של הב"י אינו פוסל חסרון היקף גויל ע"י הנקב כי הנה הב"י הוציא דין זה שכתב בשו"ע מחמת דהוקשה לו היכי מכשרינן בנפסק שום אות ע"י נקב הא אמרינן כל אות שאין מוקף גויל לה מארבע רוחותיה פסולה ותירץ דלא אמרינן כל אות וכו' רק בשהיה ע"י נגיעת אות לאות אבל לא ע"י נקב א"כ דלא פסלינן מחמת מוקף גויל רק אם בעת הכתיבה לא היתה מוקפת משא"כ כשנכתב בכשרות והב"י העתיק פה לדינא תירוץ הב' והנה לפי דברי הדה"ח הנ"ל שילא לידון בדבר החדש דאף לתירוץ א' בעינן הקפת גויל אך להכי כשר ע"י נקב משום דיש גויל מעבר להנקב סמוך לאות שאללו וזה חשוב מוקף גויל תמיהני דא"כ אם הרגל הך' מגיע לסוף בלי היקף קלף פסול אפילו לתירוץ א' לדבריו וזה אינו כדמוכח בב"י דתשובת הרלב"ח דפוסל בזה לא אתיא רק כתירוץ ב' ואפילו אם תרלה לדחוק בהב"י דלכו"ע כתב דינא דהרלב"ח אכן מד"מ האחרון מוכח בהדיא דלתירוץ א' כשר בזה ע"ש. אח"כ מלאתי בעזה"י שגם הלבושי שרד משיג בזה על הנו"ב שכתב ג"כ כהדה"ח הנ"ל גם הפמ"ג במ"ז בס"ק י"ג[ו] כתב להדיא דלתירוץ א' של הב"י לא בעינן היקף גויל בנקב ואפילו אם מתחלת הכתיבה היה רגל הך' בלי היקף קלף כשר וא"כ ממילא לפ"ז אפילו אם הנקב מגיע מאות לאות שסמוך לו כשר לדידן כשנעשה אחר הכתיבה ואף שכל זה ברור בעזה"י מ"מ ל"ע *למעשה אחרי שהדה"ח והנו"ב מחמירין בדבר ועכ"פ בהלטרף עוד איזה קולא כגון שהאות גדול יותר משיעור ונקב נעשה בסופו באופן שאפילו אם ינכה מקום הנקב ושיעור דהקפת גויל ג"כ ישאר שיעור הראוי לאותו אות יש ללדד להקל ולצרף לזה דעת הרד"ך שהובא בסימן זה במג"א סק"ג כי אפילו לדעת הדה"ח והנו"ב הנ"ל אינו רק ספיקא דדינא דשמא הלכה כתירוץ א'[ז]. ויותר טוב אם יכול לגרור מעט מעובי הקו של האות ויהיה מוקף גויל דזה מהני בכל

שער הציון

(ס) מפמ"ג ולבו"ש שם לעיל: (סא) חידושי רע"א וש"א: (סב) מ"א בס"ק כ"ז: (סג) פמ"ג בא"א ודה"ח:

הגהות ותיקונים: א) ונדבק: ב) ח': ג) בסעיף: ד) כ"ז: ה) כ"ב: ו) י"ד: ז) ב': ח) אם: ט) כ"ז:

the outset when /a letter/ was written there was **(56)** a hole /in the parchment/ and /the letter/ was broken there or if **(57)** the leg of a simple /elongated letter/ ן or a similar /letter/ reached the end of the parchment, **(58)** without /the letter/ being surrounded /by blank parchment/, **(59)** from the outset, **(60)** /the letter/ is invalid.

Mishnah Berurah

(56) A hole. /This ruling/ only /applies in the case of/ a hole or a tear, /in which case it applies/ even if the break is not noticeable at all. /Then the letter is invalid/ because it was not surrounded by /blank/ parchment at the time when it was written. [*Levu. Sr.*]

However, a mere break /in a letter does not prevent the letter being/ valid and no correction is required /for it/, once the letter has the size required /for that letter in the part of the letter which reaches/ until that spot.

This accords with what is /ruled/ above in Par. 15 and 16.

If there are thin scratches within the required length of the letter, see the Beyur Halachah[14] in Par. 25.

(57) The leg. If the roofs of letters and the middles /of letters/ do not have /blank/ parchment surrounding them at the time when /the letters/ are written, /the letters are/ certainly /invalid/. /The author of the Shulchan Aruch/ speaks of the leg to give a wider /ruling, i.e.,/ that /the lack of blank parchment surrounding the end of the leg causes the letter to be invalid/, even though when /one came to/ write the end of the leg the form of the letter was already appropriately completed. /For/ as long as one has not yet left off /writing/ the letter /the continuation/ is nevertheless regarded as being at the time of the writing, /so that/ we require every /part/ of the letter /written/ to be surrounded by /blank/ parchment.

(58) Without being surrounded. Even if /the letter/ is appropriately long, meaning that it has /more than/ the required length, so that even if some of it would be scraped away below the form of the letter would remain, it is nevertheless invalid /as it is/. [*M.A.* in sub-Par. 2. See the *M.A.* in sub-Par. 3.]

(59) From the outset. However, if the parchment was cut subsequently and due to this /the letter/ is /now/ not surrounded by /blank/ parchment, /the letter/ is /still/ valid.

(60) /The letter/ is invalid. If one wishes to remedy /this/, he should scrape off some /of the letter/ so that it will be surrounded by /blank/ parchment. However, gluing a patch /of blank parchment/ is of no avail for /the letter to be considered/ surrounded by /blank/ parchment, as it is necessary for the letter to be surrounded by /a blank part of/ the Torah Scroll, *tefilin* /parchment/ or mezuzah itself.

14 From what the author writes there, it seems that the letter may be corrected if the scratch is so thin that a close look is required to perceive the separation and a child who is neither especially intelligent nor especially simple reads the letter correctly.

יז * [ע]אם נפלה * טפת (סא) דיו (סב) לתוך האות (סג) * ואינה ניכרת (כו) האות אין תקנה (כז) (סד) לגרור (סה) הדיו * וע"י כך יהיה ניכר האות דהוי (סו) חק תוכות * ופסול משום דבעינן וכתב (סז) ולא וחקק וה"ה אם טעה * וכתב דלי"ת במקום רי"ש או בי"ת במקום (כח) כ"ף

ע הרא"ה[א] פרק ב' דגיטין וס' התרומה סימן ר"ה סמ"ג והגה"מ פרק א'

באר היטב

כראוי. מ"א: (כו) האות. ואם היא מחסרה קוצה של אות או שנראה כאילו היא גופה של אות אע"פ שהאות ניכרת להדיא פסול רד"ך וכנה"ג. ופר"ח בא"ע סי' קכ"ה ס"ק ט"ו חולק עליו וכתב ואיני רואה טעם בהוראה זו דאי כשנתעבה הגג או הירך אותו[ב] טפת דיו שנפל בגוף האות מה בכך. ויוכל לתקנו ולחזור לעשות כך בקולמוס ואין כאן חק תוכות וכן כשהקוץ[ג] קטן כל דהו יוצא חוץ לאות באופן שאינו משנה צורת האות כלל וגם האות ניכרת ללא חכם ולא טפש גם בזה נ"ל להכשיר עכ"ל. וכ"נ דעת הע"ת ע"ש. אם נפלה טפת דיו אפי' מחק הטיפה לגמרי וגמר האות ע"י כתיבה פסול דבעי שיהא כל האות ע"י כתיבה רד"ך. נפלה טיפת דיו והיא עשויה כמין חצי אות לא אשכחן מאן דשרי להשלים האות ע"י כתיבה הר"ס אלשקר סימן ה' אבל הב"י בא"ע סי' קכ"ה מכשיר. וכ"פ רמ"א שם ס"ד. כתב מהריק"ש בא"ע סימן קכ"ה דאם עשה תיבה חלוקה שנראה כב' תיבות והיה בלד של החלקים שי"ן של ג' ראשים ועשאה ד' ראשין והאריכה בכך למלאות החלל שבאמצע חלקי התיבה ואח"כ גרר מראשי השי"ן האמצעים ונשארה שי"ן של ג' ראשים עשוים מאליה כשר ולא נראה חק תוכות. ומ"מ יותר טוב למחוק הראש הראשון קודם כתיבת הראש שהאריך בו השי"ן ומהר"ס בן חביב שם ס"ק ל"ה ופר"ח שם ס"ק ט"ו דחו דבריו וכתבו דבכה"ג מיקרי חק תוכות ופסול ע"ש. והתיקון השני עיקר.

אם כתב ב' תיבות בתיבה א' ע"י אות יתירה ביניהם כגון שהיה צריך לכתוב בחוזק יד והוסיף ק' בין תיבת חוזק לתיבת יד כגון זה בחוזקק יד או שכתב בבחוזק שהוסיף ב' בתחלת תיבת בחוזק מותר למחוק הבי"ת והקו"ף שביניהם ואין בכך פיסול משום חק תוכות גט פשוט סימן קכ"ה ס"ק ל"ו. אם נדבק רגל הה"א כחוט השערה דק מאד ותינוק דלא חכם ולא טיפש יודע שהוא ה"א מי שיקל להפריד הרגל לבד לא אמחה בידו הרלנ"ח סי' א' ול"ז. והרד"ך בית א' חל"א ופר"ח בא"ע סימן קכ"ה ס"ק י' חלקו עליו שאין להורות קולא בדבר וראוי לגעור במי שעושה כן. וכ"כ הע"ת מאחר שנראה לעין שלא נשאר צורות האות אע"פ שהוא דק אטו בדק או בעב תלוי אם הוא דבוק מה לי עב או דק. אם נפלה טפת דיו תוך חלל הב' ונראית כפ' או שאין שם ב' עליה או שנפלה לתוך אות אחרת ואין שמה עליה אין תקנה למחוק ב"י. ב' ביתי"ן הסמוכים בתיבה א' שנדבקו בתחתיהן ונפסדה צורת האות למראית העין שאינה ניכרת אם הוא בי"ת או כ"ף אין תקנה לגררה להפריש הדיבוק דמיקרי חק תוכות כי אם במחיקת הרגל השני ויחזור ויכתבנו דבר שמואל סי' פ"ט. אם נטף שעוה ונלקה מותר אע"פ שהאות אינה ניכרת יוכל לגרור השעוה ולסלקה ואין כאן חק תוכות. פר"ח וכ"כ המ"א: (כז) לגרור. אפי' מעביר הקולמוס לאחר שחק תוכו אינו מועיל. ע"ת: (כח) כ"ף. וה"ה איפכא:

משנה ברורה

האות מגוף הסת"מ: **יז** (סא) דיו. וה"ה צבע אחר אם עי"ז נשתנה צורת האות אבל נטף שעוה על האות אף שמכסה להאות ואינה ניכרת אעפ"כ (סד) מותר לסלק דשעוה אין מבטל הכתב ועיין בבה"ל: (סב) לתוך. בין שנגע הטיפה בגוף האות או לא. וה"ה אם נפלה הטפה על קווי האות ממש ונתפשט הטפה גם מבחוץ להאות עד שאינו ניכר האות בתמונתו עי"ז: (סג) ואינה ניכרת. בין שעי"ז נשתנה תמונתה לאות אחרת כגון שנפלה טפה תוך חלל ב' ונראית כפ"א או שאבדה (סה) תמונתה ואין שמה עליה. וה"ה בשאר אותיות ואפילו אם ע"י הטיפה נחסר (סו) רק קוצה של יו"ד בין ימין או (סז) שמאל פסול. ואם מסתפק בהאות אם צורתו עליו או לא מראה (סח) לתינוק דלא חכים ולא טיפש: (סד) לגרור. ואפילו מעביר קולמוס על האות לאחר שחק תוכו אינו מועיל. מ"א: (סה) הדיו. ואפילו אם הטפה (סט) לח עדיין והאות כבר (ע) נתייבש לא אמרינן שהיא ככסוי בעלמא על האות כיון שעכ"פ נפסל צורת האות קודם התיקון: (סו) חק תוכות. פי' שחוקק (עא) התוך של האות וסביבו וממילא נשאר מה שאינו מוחק בצורת אות: (סז) ולא וחקק. וזה ג"כ חקיקה מיקרי כיון שאינו

ביאור הלכה

בכל גווני ואפילו בתו"מ דבעינן כסדרן וכמו שהתיר המ"א לגרור קצה רגל הק' הנוגע לסוף בלי היקף קלף: * **אם נפלה וכו'.** דע דבכל דבר שכתוב בשו"ע דלא מהני גרירה בלבד מחמת פסול דחק תוכות מוכח מסתימת הפוסקים דאין נ"מ בין אם נעשה בעת הכתיבה או לאחר הכתיבה משא"כ פסול מחמת שאינו מוקף גויל תליא בשני התירוצים שבב"י ד"ה וא"ת היכי מכשרינן וכמו שפסק השו"ע בסט"ז וכן איתא בפמ"ג הועתק לקמן בסעיף כ"ה ועיין בס' גט פשוט בסי' קכ"ה בא"ע[1]: * **טיפת דיו.** עיין במ"ב בסק"א[ד] וז"ל סד"ח בדיני קריאת התורה דין ל"ה נטף שעוה על אות בחול יסירנה [ואם הנטיפה היא על אותיות השמות שאין נמחקין אף בחול אסור שהרי יש לחוש שיתקלף קצת מהאות עמו כילד יעשה ירצה לחמם היטיב הגויל מבחוץ נגד מקום הנטיפה ועי"ז יוסר השעוה בנקל ולא יודבק בו מהכתב כלל ש"א בשער ה' דין ז'] ואם בשבת אם נראה האות מתוכה ויכול לקרות כך כשר אך אם הוא מכוסה שאינו נראה מתוך השעוה אם נמצא זה בין גברא לגברא כיון שאין לקרות בע"פ מה שמכוסה בשעוה ואין קורין בחומשים מפני כבוד הציבור וליכא פגמא של ספר דתרי גברא בתרי ספרא לאו פגמא הוא יש להוציא אחרת ואם נמצא באמצע הקריאה יש לקרות המכוסה בע"פ ואחר כך יסיים בה מנין הקרואים כיון דכבר קרא מה שמכוסה בשעוה מותר לקרות להלן בס"ת הזה דאין פסול בזה מה שמכוסה בשעוה עכ"ל ועיין בספר ש"א הנ"ל ובחידושי רע"א בסימן זה. וכתב עוד שם הגרע"א דאומן ישראל המתקן סידור הבלוי ומוכרח לו להניח נייר ולדבקו עם (פא"פ°) על מקום היפה ופוגע בשמות הקדושים שאינם נמחקים דיש בזה חשש איסור מחיקה כיון דא"א לקלפו שיהיה כל האותיות קיימים וגרע יותר משעוה עי"ש שהאריך בזה ומסיק דיעשה האומן כך יניח נייר על כל שם ושם נייר בלי דבק או ידבק מעט בשעוה דלא הוי מחיקה וכנ"ל [ומה דאסור בשבת גרירת השעוה מעל הס"ת הוא מטעם אחר עי"ש] ואח"כ ידבק הנייר (בפא"פ) דיהיה הנייר הב' מדובק על הנייר ראשון שמונח על השם וזה לא הוי מחיקה דאם יקלפו הנייר השני יהיה השם שלם: * **ואינה ניכרת.** עיין במ"ב בס"ק ס"ב[ה] לענין אם נפל על קווי האות ממש וניכר האות דכתבנו שם להקל בזה אף דהפמ"ג במ"ז בס"ק ט"ו מצדד להחמיר בזה מטעם כתב על כתב אם לאו שבעת נפילת הטיפה כבר נתייבש האות עי"ש כבר הושג ע"ז מחמת כמה קושיות עיין בפ"ת אה"ע בסדר גיטין ואף שמיישבו שם קצת מלבד שהוא דוחק גדול אין להחמיר בזה אחרי שרוב הפוסקים מקילין אפילו בכתב על גבי כתב ממש וכ"ש בזה הטפת דיו שנפלה מעצמה שאין שייך שם כתב עליו. ועוד נ"ל בזה עצה אחרת אפילו בכתב על גבי כתב ממש והשני היה שלא לשמה דיעביר עוד קולמוס עליו לשמה וממ"נ מהני ולא מיקרי שלא כסדרן לכאורה מאחר דמעת כתיבה הראשונה צורתו עליו וכמש"כ בס"ק ל"ט במ"א: * **ועי"כ יהיה ניכר האות.** עיין במ"ב[2] במש"כ ומדינא אפילו תיקון לא בעי וכו'. ואם נפלה הטפה מבחוץ סמוך להאות בעת הכתיבה אפילו אם האות ניכרת עדיין ולא נגע עי"ז לאות אחרת מדינא צריך לגרור את הטיפה במקום הנגיעה באות דאל"ה לא מיתחשיב האות מוקף גויל כן משמע מנ"ב בסימן ע"ה עי"ש: * **ופסול משום דבעינן וכתב וכו'.** עיין בס' בית מאיר על אהע"ז בסימן קכ"ה דמחזיק בזה לשיטת הרשב"א דס"ל דאין בזה משום חק תוכות הואיל דמתחילה נעשה אות ע"י כתיבה וכן בטעה וכתב ד' במקום רי"ש ואין בזה רק משום לתא דחק תוכות מדרבנן עי"ש אבל הגרע"א בחידושיו פה חולק ע"ז עי"ש וכן מוכח מש"ס גיטין דף כ' דהוא מדאורייתא: * **וכתב דלי"ת במקום רי"ש.** ה"ה אם נעשה ד' אחר שנגמר כתיבת הרי"ש ג"כ אין להכשיר בחקיקה לפי מה דפסק המחבר בענין טיפת דיו ובענין דביקת אות לאות אפילו אחר שנגמרה דלא כסמ"ק אח"כ מצאתי בחידושי רע"א

מתרגם: °דבק

שער הציון

(סד) מ"א: (סה) מ"א: (סו) מ"א בשם רד"ך: (סז) פמ"ג: (סח) אחרונים בא"ע: (סט) ט"ז: (ע) פמ"ג: (עא) ט"ז:

הגהות ותיקונים: א) הרא"ש: ב) צ"ל באותו: ג) כשקוץ: ד) ס"ק ס"א וז"ל סדה"ח: ה) ס"ז:

הערות והארות: 1) עיין בבה"ל ד"ה אם נפלה וכו' ואם יש ספק בדבר אם יכולים לצרף דעת הסמ"ק להתיר עיין לקמן דף מ"ז בבה"ל סוף ד"ה רגלי הה"א שיכולים לצרף כסניף להתיר: 2) ס"ק ס"ז:

17. If a drop of **(61)** ink fell **(62)** into a letter **(63)** and the letter is not recognizable, one cannot remedy this **(64)** by scraping off **(65)** the ink so that the letter will become recognizable. /The reason is/ because this constitutes **(66)** carving around /to form the letter/. /A letter which is formed in this way/ is invalid, as one is required to write /the letter/ **(67)** and not to carve /it out/.

Correspondingly, if one erred and wrote the /letter/ ר instead of the /letter/

Mishnah Berurah

(61) Ink. The same ruling /applies/ where other coloring matter /fell into a letter/, if as a result of this the form of the letter was altered. However, if wax dripped onto a letter /, then/, even if it covers the letter and /the letter/ is not recognizable one is nevertheless permitted to remove it, as wax does not cancel the writing. See the Beyur Halachah.[15]

(62) Into. /This applies/ irrespective of whether or not the drop /that fell into the letter/ touched the body of the letter. /It applies,/ correspondingly, /even/ if the drop fell onto the actual letter lines and the drop spread out on the outside of the letter as well, to the extent that the symbol of the letter is not recognizable because of it.

(63) And ... is not recognizable. /This applies/ irrespective of whether because of this the symbol was transformed into /that of/ a different letter (for example, if a drop fell into the space of a /letter/ ב and it /now/ appears like the /letter/ פ) or if /the letter merely/ lost its symbol and cannot be described as what it is /meant to represent/. A corresponding /ruling applies/ with respect to other letters. Even if only the tip of the /letter/ י is missing because of the drop, either on the right or on the left, /the letter/ is invalid.

If /after a drop fell on a letter/ one is in doubt as to whether or not the letter has its /proper/ form, one should show it to a child who is neither /especially/ intelligent nor /especially/ simple.

(64) By scraping off. Even if one passes a quill over the letter after he carved around /to form it/, this is of no avail. *M.A.*

(65) The ink. Even if the drop is still moist and the letter has already dried, we do not argue that /the drop/ is like a mere covering over the letter, since the form of the letter is at any rate invalid /now/ until it is corrected.

(66) Carving around /to form the letter/. I.e., carving out the inside of the letter and around it, /so that/ what one does not erase remains of its own accord in the form of the /required/ letter.

(67) And not to carve /it out/. This is also describable as carving out /the letter/, since one does not do an action in the body of the letter.

15 In the Beyur Halachah, the author states that if the wax is on a letter of a Divine Name which may not be erased, the wax must be removed by heating the parchment on the outside. He also describes how one should act if he discovers wax over a letter during the reading from the Torah Scroll on Shabbos.

(סח) **אין תקנה** (סט) למחוק התג לתקן האות משום דהוי כחק (כט) תוכות: **יח** * [פ]מ"ם פתוחה (ע) שנדבק פתיחתה (עא) * ונסתמה אין מועיל לגרור הדבק (עב) ולפותחה משום דהוי (עג) כחק תוכות (עד) [צ]ומה תקנתה שיגרור * כל החרטום ותשאר (עה) כצורת נו"ן כפופה ואח"כ יכתוב מה שגרר

פ תשובת הרא"ש כלל ה' ס' התרומה ומיימון וסמ"ג צ מטור בתשובת הרשב"א המיוחסת להרמב"ן סימן רל"ו וכן הורה מהרי"ן חביב ומהר"ר לוי בנו

באר היטב

(כט) תוכות. ודוקא חקיקה פוסלת בו אבל אם כתב רי"ש דומה לדלי"ת ורוצה להוסיף עליו דיו לעשותו עגול דתהוי רי"ש וכן בעשה רי"ש במקום דלי"ת יש תקנה להוסיף עליו דיו ולעשותו מרובעת ומותר. וה"ה מבי"ת לכ"ף או איפכא נמי דינא הכי וכל זה דיש תקנה לתקנו היינו קודם שכתב אות אחריו אבל לא אח"כ דאז הוה שלא כסדרן ופסול בתפילין. תפילין שנזדמן לסופר

ביאור הלכה

רע"א שהעיר בזה: * מ"ם פתוחה שנדבק. עיין במ"ב שכתב בדין נדבק כחוט השערה דתלוי בדין ה"א ויותר נלענ"ד לומר דאפילו המקילין בדין ה' כמבואר בב"י לקמן בסימן ל"ו מודים בזה דהרי עכ"פ מ"ס סתום הוא ומה לי אם הסתימה דקה או עבה ושם ראייתם הוא מדאמר הגמרא חזינא לספרי דוקני דתלו לכרעיה דה"א משמע דהוא רק למצוה בעלמא אבל עלם תמונת ה"א אין צריך לתלות הכרעא ואעפ"כ לא דמי לחי"ת כמש"כ הגר"א לקמן בביאורו או כמש"כ הרשב"א הנדפס מחדש על מנחות עי"ש משא"כ במ"ס דאין לנו שום ראיה לקראו מ"ס פתוח ע"י שהסתימה היא דקה: * ונסתמה. עיין בט"ז אהע"ז בסי' קכ"ה ס"ד שכתב ודוקא שנסתם המ"ס אחר שנגמר אבל אם סתם המ"ס קודם הגמר בזה יכול לגרור הסיתום כיון שעדיין צריך להוסיף ברגועה המשופעת כמין יו"ד ע"כ יגרור תחלה הדבוק ואח"כ יגמור ע"ש ונראה דלפי דעת הרד"ך שכתבנו במ"ב בס"ק ע"ח[א] גם בזה יש להחמיר: * כל החרטום. נראה לי פשוט דדוקא שנדבק בעת כתיבת החרטום

משנה ברורה

עושה מעשה בגוף האות אלא (עב) יגרור ג"כ קצת מהאות עד שלא ישאר צורתו עליו ואח"כ יתקננו אם לא כתב עדיין אחר אות זו דאל"ה פסול בתו"מ דבעינן כסדרן. וכ"ז הדין דשו"ע הוא מחמת שהאות אינו ניכר ונתבטל עי"ז כתיבה הראשונה אבל אם לא נשתנה צורת האות יכול למחוק טיפת הדיו ואין חילוק בין שנפל הדיו לתוך חלל האות בלבד או גם על האות גופא (עג) ונתעבה גג האות (עד) או גם הירך עי"ז אפ"ה יוכל לתקן ולא מיקרי חק תוכות מאחר שהאות ניכר עדיין. ומדינא אפילו תיקון לא בעי בזה רק יותר טוב שיתקן ע"כ יכול לעשות תיקון זה אפילו בתו"מ דבעינן כסדרן ועיין בבה"ל. ודע עוד דהשו"ע איירי אפילו נפלה הטיפה אחר שנגמר האות וכ"ש אם נפלה קודם שנגמר האות כדין וגמר מתחלה האות ואין ניכר עדיין דבזה (עה) כו"ע סוברים דאין תקנה בגרירת הטפה דהרי לא היה עליו מעולם שם אות רק עתה ע"י גרירה והוי חק תוכות ממש אך אם גרר מתחלה הטפה ורוצה עתה לגמור האות בזה יש דיעות בין הפוסקים דהרד"ך סובר דלא מהני דס"ל דכיון שנפלה הטפה על מקצת האות נתבטל ממנו שם כתיבה והוי כחקיקה בעלמא ומה מהני אף אם יגמר האות ע"י כתיבה וכ"ש אם נפלה על הקלף טפת דיו ממש ונעשה כמין חצי אות דלא שרי להשלים האות ע"י כתיבה והב"י והרמ"א [בהא"ע בסי' קכ"ה ס"ד] מקילין אפילו בזה הדין האחרון וסוברין דלא מיקרי חק תוכות אלא כשגומר האות ע"י חקיקה אך (עו) האחרונים מצדדין להחמיר בזה הדין האחרון אם לא שמושך (עז) הטפת דיו הלחה ומזיזה ממקום למקום עד שעושה ממנה אות שלם דזה הוי כתיבה: (סח) אין תקנה. פי' ע"י המחיקה אין תקנה אבל מותר להוסיף דיו ולעשותו עגול. וכן אם טעה וכתב רי"ש במקום ד' וכו' במקום כ' והוו אותיות עבין אין תקנה שיגררן ויעמידן בתמונת ד' וכו' אבל (עח) מותר להוסיף עליהן דיו ולעשותן בתמונת ד' וכו'. וכן אם טעה וכתב במקום ווי"ן נו"ן פשוטה אין תקנה שיגררו ויעמידו על זיי"ן דזה הוי חק תוכות ממש אלא צריך למוחקן לגמרי וכן אם טעה וכתב (עט) ה"א במקום ד' אין תקנה לגרור הרגל של הה"א וישאר ד' דדומה לסמ"ך וכו' שנפל טפת דיו שם ונתקלקל תמונתו עי"ז דלא מהני גרירת הטפה משום דאין עושה מעשה בגוף האות וה"נ כה"ג אלא צריך לגרור ג"כ קצת הגג עד שישאר כמו וי"ו או לגרור (פ) הירך עד שלא ישאר צורת ד' עליו ואח"כ יתקננו·(פא) כללא דמילתא גורר לא מהני להיות כתיבה בכך ומיקרי חק תוכות אבל כותב מהני שמעבה האות מדלי"ת רי"ש או מרי"ש ד' שכותב הגג. ולענין שלא כסדרן נהפוך הוא גורר כשר כגון בדיבוק אות לאות וכדלקמן דזה לא מיקרי מעשה בגוף האות וכותב פסול. ומה שהתרנו להוסיף דיו ולהעמידן על תמונתן (פב) היינו כשלא כתב האותיות שאחר זה: (סט) למחוק התג. ואפילו אם אח"כ ימשוך ג"כ גגו ותחתיתו של הכ' (פג) לא מהני דבלא"ה צורתה עליה: **יח** (ע) שנדבק. ואם פוסל בזה נגיעה דקה כחוט השערה עיין מה שכתבנו לקמן[ב] לענין ה"א ועיין בבה"ל: (עא) ונסתמה. והוי כמ"ם סתום שמקומו רק בסוף תיבה ולא באמצעותה[ג] (פד) וכן כל אותיות מנצפ"ך הכפולין בא"ב כותב את הראשונות בתחלת התיבה ובאמצעיתה והאחרונות בסוף ואם שינה פסול: (עב) ולפותחה. וה"ה שאר אותיות שנתקלקל תמונתם בעת הכתיבה או אח"כ וע"י הגרירה יעמדו על תמונתם כגון ד' שהמשיך רגלו ודומה לך' פשוטה וכל כה"ג אין מועיל לכן גרירה כיון שאינו עושה מעשה בגוף האות הנשאר אלא ימחוק רגלו וכנ"ל בס"ק ס"ח ואח"כ יתקננו: וה"ה דמהני בזה אם המשיך גגו של האות לרחבה עד שנראה לכל שהוא ד' אבל לעיל בכתב ה"א במקום ד' דכתבנו שם דצריך ג"כ למחוק רגל הד' או גגו מלבד רגל הה"א (פה) לא מהני עלה זו דהמשכת גג הד' דהרי בלא"ה צורתו עליו לכן לא מיקרי זה שום תיקון: (עג) כחק תוכות. דבגוף האות אין עושה שום מעשה אלא גורר הסתימה וה"ה אם טעה (פו) וכתב ה' במקום ב' ויו"ן אין מועיל לגרור הגג לבד מהך טעמא אלא צריך לגררם עד שיבטלם מתמונתם. וכן אם טעה ועשה ך' פשוטה למעלה כעין דל"ת שלפי דעת הרבה מן הפוסקים היא פסולה כמו שיבואר לקמן בסי' ל"ו ג"כ אין מועיל (פז) לגרור התג ולעשותה עגולה דהוי חק תוכות אלא יוסיף עליה דיו ויעשה עגולה. ונראה (פח) דלא מעכב שלא כסדרן בתיקון זה דבלא"ה צורתה עליה: (עד) ומה תקנתה. כל שכתוב בסעיף זה שיש תקנה היינו קודם שכתב אות שאחריו דאל"ה פסול בתו"מ דבעינן בהן כסדרן דוקא לבד מהיכא שנאמר בהדיא דלא מעכב בזה כסדרן: (עה) כצורת נ"כ. כי כתיבת המ' פתוחה הוא בב' כתיבות דהיינו בתחלה כותבין כמו נו"ן כפופה ואח"כ תולין בלדה כמו וי"ו ואח"כ כל שנעשה הפסול בו דהיינו הו' צריך לגוררו כולו אבל הנו"ן שנכתב בהכשר אין צריך לגוררו וה"ה בכל אות שנכתב בב' כתיבות כגון ג' וכיו"ב ונעשה פסול בכתיבה א' (פט) אין צריך לגרור רק אותה לאפוקי ברי"ש שעשאה כמין ד' דבפעם א' נכתב הכל בפסול צריך הכל לגרור:

ורי"ש

שער הציון

(עב) מסעיף י"ח: (עג) ע"ת ופר"ח בא"ע בסימן קכ"ה ופמ"ג בא"א כתב ג"כ דיש מחמירין דהג"ה שם לא שייך לכאן: (עד) פשוט דזה לא הוי כתב ע"ג כתב ועיין בבה"ל: (עה) אפי' הסמ"ק וכמ"ש בב"י: (עו) הפמ"ג בא"א בשם הט"ז בא"ע והגרע"א בחידושיו ועוד ש"א בפ"ת א"ע סי' קכ"ה ס"ח[ד]: (עז) ט"ז בא"ע מובא פה בפמ"ג: (עח) ט"ז ופמ"ג: (עט) פמ"ג בא"א סי' מ"ז ס"ק י"ז[ה]: (פ) פי' כולו דאל"ה שם ד' עליו כנ"ל בסט"ו פמ"ג בא"א בדיני צורת אותיות בסי' ל"ב א"ד: (פא) פמ"ג: (פב) ט"ז: (פג) פמ"ג בפתיחה לסי' ל"ב[ו]: (פד) מ"ס וביאור הגר"א: (פה) פמ"ג בסי' ל"ב בא"א בדיני צורת אותיות אות ד': (פו) פמ"ג בא"א בשם הב"ש סקכ"ו: (פז) מ"א בסקכ"ו: (פח) פמ"ג בא"א שם אות ך': (פט) ט"ז:

הגהות ותיקונים: א) ס"ז: ב) ס"ק פ"ג: ג) באמצעיתה: ד) ס"ד: ה) צ"ל פרמ"ג במש"ז סקי"ז: ו) בא"א סוף הסימן ד"ה השלישי הוא חק תוכות:

ר or the /letter/ נ instead of the /letter/ כ, (68) this /fault/ cannot be remedied

Mishnah Berurah

Instead, one should also scrape off some of the letter until the /proper/ form of /the letter/ does not remain and after that he should correct it /by rewriting it/. /However, this is only of avail/ provided he has not yet written after this letter. Otherwise, /the letter/ is invalid where *tefilin* /passages/ and mezuzos are involved, since /in their case/ it is necessary /for the letters to be written/ in /the correct/ order.

/On the other hand,/ the ruling of the Shulchan Aruch is entirely due to /the fact/ that the letter is /now/ not recognizable and the original writing has been cancelled by /the drop of ink/. However, if the form of the letter has not changed one may erase the drop of ink. It makes no difference whether the ink fell into the space /inside/ the letter alone or /whether it/ also /fell/ onto the letter itself, /so that/ the roof of the letter, or the thigh /of the letter/ as well, became thicker because of it. /In all these cases/ one may nevertheless correct /the letter by erasing/ and it is not describable as carving around /to form the letter/, since the letter is still recognizable. /In fact,/ from the /standpoint of binding/ halachah it is not even necessary to correct /the letter/ in such a case and it is only better to correct it. Consequently, one may make this correction even in the case of *tefilin* /passages/ and mezuzos, where it is necessary /for the letters to be written/ in /the correct/ order. See the Beyur Halachah.

Note further that the Shulchan Aruch is referring even /to an instance when/ the drop fell after the letter was completed. It is certainly /referring to an instance/ when /the drop/ fell before the letter was completed in accordance with halachic /requirements/ and one first finished /writing/ the letter /and corrected it only subsequently, so that the letter/ was not yet recognizable /before it was corrected/. In such a case all /authorities/ are of the opinion that this cannot be remedied by scraping off the drop, for /then the symbol/ was never describable as a letter and would only /become a letter/ now through the scraping. The scraping would /therefore/ be an actual /case of/ carving around /to form the letter/.

However, if /the drop fell before the letter was halachically completed and/ one first scraped off the drop and now wishes to finish off the letter, there are /conflicting/ opinions among the Poskim as to /the ruling in/ such a case. The *Radach* is of the opinion that /the scraping off/ is of no avail. /This is/ because he holds that in view /of the fact/ that the drop fell on part of the letter, /that part/ ceased to be definable as writing, /so that the scraping off of the drop of ink/ is like mere carving around /to form the letter/. /Therefore, the correction/ cannot be of /any/ avail, even if one finishes off the letter by writing. If an actual drop of ink fell onto the parchment and /its impression/ came to resemble part of a letter, it is certainly not allowed to complete the letter by writing /according to his view/. /On the other hand,/ the *B.Y.* and the *Rema* [in the *Even Ha-Ezer* Sec. 125, Par. 4] are lenient even as regards this latter case. In their opinion it is only regarded as carving around /the letter to form it/ when one completes the letter by carving around it. However, the Acharonim adopt a stringent /view/ in the latter case, unless one leads the wet drop of ink and moves it from place to place until he makes a complete letter out of it, as that does constitute writing /even in their opinion/.

(68) This cannot be remedied. I.e., this cannot be remedied by means of erasing. However, it is permitted to add ink /to the

(סח) אין תקנה (סט) למחוק התג לתקן האות משום דהוי כחק (כט) תוכות: **יח** * [פ]מ"ם פתוחה (ע) שנדבק פתיחתה (עא) * ונסתמה אין מועיל לגרור הדבק (עב) ולפותחה משום דהוי (עג) כחק תוכות (עד) [צ]ומה תקנתה שיגרור * כל החרטום ותשאר (עה) כצורת נו"ן כפופה ואח"כ יכתוב מה שגרר

פ תשובת הרא"ש כלל ה' ס' התרומה ומיימון וסמ"ג צ מבואר בתשובת הרשב"א המיוחסת להרמב"ן סימן רל"ו וכן הורה מהרי"ן חביב ומהר"ר לוי בנו

באר היטב

(כט) תוכות. ודוקא חקיקה פוסלת בו אבל אם כתב רי"ש דומה לדלי"ת ורוצה להוסיף עליו דיו לעשותו עגול דתהוי רי"ש וכן בעשה רי"ש במקום דלי"ת יש תקנה להוסיף עליו דיו ולעשותו מרובעת ומותר. וה"ה מבי"ת לכ"ף או איפכא נמי דינא הכי וכל זה דיש תקנה לתקנו היינו קודם שכתב אות אחריו אבל לא אח"כ דאז הוה שלא כסדרן ופסול בתפילין. תפילין שנזדמן לסופר

ביאור הלכה

רע"א שהעיר בזה: * מ"ם פתוחה שנדבק. עיין במ"ב שכתב בדין נדבק כחוט השערה דתלוי בדין ה"א ויותר נלענ"ד לומר דאפילו המקילין בדין ה' כמבואר בב"י לקמן בסימן ל"ו מודים בזה דהרי עכ"פ מ"ם סתום הוא ומה לי אם הסתימה דקה או עבה ושם ראייתם הוא מדאמר הגמרא חזינא לספרי דוקני דתלו לכרעיה דה"א משמע דהוא רק למצוה בעלמא אבל עלם תמונת ה"א אין צריך לתלות הכרעא ואעפ"כ לא דמי לחי"ת כמש"כ הגר"א לקמן בביאורו או כמש"כ הרשב"א הנדפס מחדש על מנחות עי"ש משא"כ במ"ם דאין לנו שום ראיה לקראו מ"ם פתוח ע"י שהסתימה היא דקה: * ונסתמה. עיין בט"ז אהע"ז בסי' קכ"ה ס"ד שכתב ודוקא שנסתם המ"ם אחר שנגמר אבל אם סתם המ"ם קודם הגמר בזה יכול לגרור הסיתום כיון שעדיין צריך להוסיף ברלועה המשופעת כמין יו"ד ע"כ יגרור תחלה הדבוק ואח"כ יגמור ע"ש ונראה דלפי דעת הרד"ך שכתבנו במ"ב בס"ק ס"ח[א] גם בזה יש להחמיר: * כל החרטום. נראה לי פשוט דדוקא שנדבק בעת כתיבת החרטום

משנה ברורה

עושה מעשה בגוף האות אלא (עב) יגרור ג"כ קצת מהאות עד שלא ישאר צורתו עליו ואח"כ יתקננו אם לא כתב עדיין אחר אות זו דאל"ה פסול בתו"מ דבעינן כסדרן. וכ"ז הדין לשו"ע הוא מחמת שהאות אינו ניכר ונתבטל ע"י כתיבה הראשונה אבל אם לא נשתנה צורת האות יכול למחוק טיפת הדיו ואין חילוק בין שנפל הדיו לתוך חלל האות בלבד או גם על האות גופא (עג) ונתעבה גג האות (עד) או גם היריך ע"י אפ"ה יוכל לתקן ולא מיקרי חק תוכות מאחר שהאות ניכר עדיין. ומדינא אפילו תיקון לא בעי בזה רק יותר טוב שיתקן ע"כ יכול לעשות תיקון זה אפילו בתו"מ דבעינן כסדרן ועיין בבה"ל. ודע עוד דהשו"ע מיירי אפילו נפלה הטיפה אחר שנגמר האות וכ"ש אם נפלה קודם שנגמר האות כדין וגמר מתחלה האות ואין ניכר עדיין דבזה (עה) כו"ע מודים דאין תקנה בגרירת הטפה דהרי לא היה עליו מעולם שם אות רק עתה ע"י גרירה והוי חק תוכות ממש אך אם גרר מתחלה הטפה ורוצה עתה לגמור האות בזה יש דיעות בין הפוסקים דהרד"ך סובר דלא מהני דס"ל דכיון שנפלה הטופה על מקצת האות ונתבטל ממנו שם כתיבה והוי כחקיקה בעלמא ומה מהני אף אם יגמר האות ע"י כתיבה וכ"ש אם נפלה על הקלף טפת דיו ממש ונעשה כמין תוי אות דלא שרי להשלים האות ע"י כתיבה והב"י והרמ"א [בהג"ה בסי' קכ"ה ס"ד] מקילין אפילו בזה הדין האחרון ומוכרין דלא מיקרי חק תוכות אלא כשגומר האות ע"י חקיקה אך (עו) האחרונים מלדדין להחמיר בזה הדין האחרון אם לא שמושך (עז) הטפת דיו הלחה ומזיזה ממקום למקום עד שעושה ממנה אות שלם דזה הוי כתיבה: (סח) אין תקנה. פי' ע"י המחיקה אין תקנה אבל מותר להוסיף דיו ולעשותו עגול. וכן אם טעה וכתב רי"ש במקום ד' וכ' במקום ב' והוו אותיות עבין אין תקנה שיגררן ויעמידן בתמונת ד' וב' אבל (עח) מותר להוסיף עליהן דיו ולעשותן בתמונת ד' וב'. וכן אם טעה וכתב במקום זיי"ן נו"ן פשוטה אין תקנה שיגררו ויעמידו על זיי"ן דזה הוי חק תוכות ממש אלא צריך למוחקו לגמרי וכן אם טעה וכתב (עט) ה"א במקום ד' אין תקנה לגרור הרגל של הה"א וישאר ד' דדומה לסמ"ך וב' שנפל טפת דיו שם ונתקלקל תמונתו ע"ז דלא מהני גרירת הטפה משום דאין עושה מעשה בגוף האות וה"נ כה"ג אלא צריך לגרור ג"כ קצת הגג עד שישאר כמו וי"ו או לגרור (פ) הירך עד שלא ישאר צורת ד' עליו ואח"כ יתקננו*(פא) כללא דמילתא גורר לא מהני להיות כתיבה בכך ומיקרי חק תוכות אבל כותב מהני שמעבה האות מדלי"ת רי"ש או מרי"ש ד' שכותב התג. ולענין שלא כסדרן נהפוך הוא גורר כשר כגון בדיבוק אות לאות וכדלקמן דזה לא מיקרי מעשה בגוף האות וכותב פסול. ומה שהתרנו להוסיף דיו ולהעמידן על תמונתן (פב) היינו כשלא כתב האותיות שאחר זה: (סט) למחוק התג. ואפילו אם אח"כ ימשוך ג"כ גגו ותחתיתו של הכ' (פג) לא מהני דבלא"ה צורתה עליה: **יח** (ע) שנדבק. ואם פוסל בזה נגיעה דקה כחוט השערה עיין מה שכתבנו לקמן[ב] לענין ה"א ועיין בבה"ל: (עא) ונסתמה. והוי כמ"ם סתום שמקומו רק בסוף תיבה ולא באמצעותה[ג] (פד) וכן כל אותיות מנצפ"ך הכפולין בא"ב כותב את הראשונות בתחלת התיבה ובאמצעיתה והאחרונות בסוף ואם שינה פסול: (עב) ולפותחה. וה"ה שאר אותיות שנתקלקל תמונתם בעת הכתיבה או אח"כ וע"י הגרירה יעמדו על תמונתם כגון ד' שהמשיך רגלו ודומה לך' פשוטה וכל כה"ג אין מועיל לגן גרירה כיון שאינו עושה מעשה בגוף האות הנשאר אלא ימחוק רגלו וכנ"ל בס"ק ס"ח ואח"כ יתקננו: וה"ה דמהני בזה אם המשיך גגו של האות לרחבה עד שנראה לכל שהוא ד' אבל לעיל בכתב ה"א במקום ד' דכתבנו שם דצריך ג"כ למחוק רגל הד' או גגו מלבד רגל הה"א (פה) לא מהני עלה זו דהמשכת גג הד' דהרי בלא"ה צורתו עליו לכך לא מיקרי זה שום תיקון: (עג) כחק תוכות. דבגוף האות אין עושה שום מעשה אלא גורר הסתימה וה"ה אם טעה (פו) וכתב ח' במקום כ' ויו"ן אין מועיל לגרור הגג לבד מהך טעמא אלא צריך לגררם עד שיתבטל מתמונתם. וכן אם טעה ועשה ך' פשוטה למעלה כעין דל"ת שלפי דעת הרבה מן הפוסקים היא פסולה כמו שיתבאר לקמן בסי' ל"ו ג"כ אין מועיל (פז) לגרור הגג ולעשותה עגולה דהוי חק תוכות אלא יוסיף עליה דיו ויעשה עגולה. ונראה (פח) דלא מעכב שלא כסדרן בתיקון זה דבלא"ה צורתה עליה: (עד) ומה תקנתה. כל שכתוב בסעיף זה שיש תקנה היינו קודם שכתב אות שאחריו דאל"ה פסול בתו"מ דבעינן בהן כסדרן דוקא לבד מיבלא שנזכר בהדיא דלא מעכב בזה כסדרן: (עה) בצורת נ"כ. כי כתיבת המ' פתוחה הוא בב' כתיבות דהיינו בתחלה כותבין כמו נו"ן כפופה ואח"כ תולין גגה כמו וי"ו ואח"כ כל שנעשה הפסול בו דהיינו הו' צריך לגוררו כולו אבל הנו"ן שנכתב בהכשר אין צריך לגוררו וה"ה בכל אות שנכתב בב' כתיבות כגון ג' וכיו"ב ונעשה פסול בכתיבה א' (פט) אין צריך לגרור רק אותה לאפוקי בר"ש שעשאה כמין ד' דבפעם א' נכתב הכל בפסול צריך הכל לגרור: ועי"ש

שער הציון

(עב) מסעיף י"ח: (עג) ע"ת ופר"ח בא"ע בסימן קכ"ה ופמ"ג בא"א כתב ג"כ דיש מחמירין דהג"ה שם לא שייך לכאן: (עד) פשוט דזה לא הוי כתב ע"ג כתב ועיין בבה"ל: (עה) אפי' הסמ"ק וכמ"ש בב"י: (עו) הפמ"ג בא"א בשם הט"ז בא"ע והגרע"א בחידושיו ועוד ש"א בפ"ת א"ע סי' קכ"ה ס"ח[ד]: (עז) ט"ז בא"ע מובא פה בפמ"ג: (עח) ט"ז ופמ"ג: (עט) פמ"ג בא"א סי' מ"ז ס"ק י"ז[ה]: (פ) פי' כולו דאל"ה שם ד' עליו כנ"ל בסט"ו פמ"ג בא"א בדיני צורת אותיות בסי' ל"ב א"ד: (פא) פמ"ג: (פב) ט"ז: (פג) פמ"ג בפתיחה לסי' ל"ב[ו]: (פד) מ"ס וביאור הגר"א: (פה) פמ"ג בסי' ל"ב בא"א בדיני צורת אותיות אות ד': (פו) פמ"ג בא"א בשם הב"ש סקכ"ו: (פז) מ"א בסקכ"ו: (פח) פמ"ג בא"א שם אות ך': (פט) ט"ז:

הגהות ותיקונים: א) ס"ז: ב) ס"ק פ"ג: ג) באמצעיתה: ד) ס"ד: ה) צ"ל פרמ"ג במש"ז סקי"ז: ו) בא"א סוף הסימן ד"ה השלישי הוא חק תוכות:

(69) by erasing the projection to correct the letter, because this is like carving around /to form the letter/.

18. /In the case of/ an open /letter/ מ (70) whose /strokes forming the/ opening have become stuck /together, so that the opening/ (71) has become closed, it is of no avail to scrape off /the bit which causes/ the sticking (72) and

Mishnah Berurah

projection/ and /thus/ make /the letter/ round /there/.

Likewise, if one erred and wrote the /letter/ ר instead of the /letter/ ד or the /letter/ כ instead of the /letter/ ב and they are thick letters, this cannot be remedied by scraping /the letters/ and leaving them with the symbol for the /letter/ ד or the /letter/ ב, but it is permitted to add ink to them and /in that way/ make them into the symbol for the /letter/ ד or the /letter/ ב.

In the same way, if one erred and wrote the simple /elongated letter/ ן instead of the /letter/ ז, this cannot be remedied by scraping off /the bottom of the letter/ and leaving it as the /letter/ ז, as this constitutes actual carving around /the letter to form it/, but one must erase /the ן/ entirely /and then rewrite the letter/.

Similarly, if one erred and wrote the /letter/ ה instead of the /letter/ ד, this cannot be remedied by scraping away the leg of the /letter/ ה, /so that/ the /letter/ ד remains. For this is comparable to /the case of/ a /letter/ ט or a /letter/ ב on which a drop of ink fell, thereby spoiling its symbol. /In the latter case/ it is of no avail to scrape off the drop, because this does not involve doing an action in the letter itself, and the same applies /when one wrote the letter ה instead of the letter ד/. Instead, one must also scrape off some of the roof, until what remains is like the /letter/ ו, or scrape off the thigh, until /the letter/ does not remain with the form of the /letter/ ד, and then he can correct it.

The general rule is that scraping is of no avail to be /regarded as/ writing and is classed as carving around /to form the letter/. On the other hand, writing which /entails/ thickening the letter from the /letter/ ד to the /letter/ ר or /converting/ the /letter/ ר to the /letter/ ד by /adding/ the projection, is of avail.

As regards /disqualification because the letters/ were /written/ in incorrect order, the opposite is the case. /If one corrected an earlier letter by/ scraping it is valid. For example, if /one scraped to separate/ a letter which was stuck to /another/ letter /, these letters are valid/, as /explained/ below, since this is not regarded as an action in the body of the letter. /On the other hand, a correction which involves/ writing /causes/ disqualification /if the next letter has already been written/. /The ruling/ which permits the adding of ink to adjust /the letter/ to the /required/ symbol, applies /only/ when one has not /yet/ written the letters after it.

(69) By erasing the projection. Even if one will subsequently also draw out the roof and the bottom of the /letter/ כ this will be of no avail, as it will /already/ have the /proper/ form of /the letter even/ without this.

(70) Whose ... have become stuck. /As to/ whether a thin touch, /the thickness/ of a hairsbreadth, which /causes/ this invalidates /the letter/, see what we have written below with respect to /the letter/ ה and see the Beyur Halachah.[16]

(71) Has become closed. /Then,/ it is like the closed /letter/ ם which belongs only at the end of a word and not in the middle of /a word/.

Likewise, /in the case of/ all the letters מ, נ, צ, פ, ך, which /appear/ twice in the alphabet, the first /form/ is written at the beginning and in the middle of the word and the final /form/ at the end /of the word/. If one deviated /from this the letter/ is invalid.

(72) And open it. The same ruling /applies in the case of/ other letters whose symbol became spoiled at the time when they were written or subsequently and whose /proper/ symbol can be established through scraping. For example, /it applies/ if the leg of a /letter/ ד continues /until/ it resembles the

16 There the author adopts a stringent view.

(סח) אין תקנה (סט) למחוק התג לתקן האות משום דהוי כחק (כט) תוכות: **יח** * פמ"ם פתוחה (ע) שנדבק פתיחתה (עא) * ונסתמה אין מועיל לגרור הדבק (עב) **ולפותחה משום דהוי (עג) כחק תוכות (עד) צומה תקנתה שיגרור * כל החרטום ותשאר (עה) כצורת נו"ן כפופה ואח"כ יכתוב מה שגרר**

פ תשובת הרא"ש כלל ה' ס' התרומה ומיימון וסמ"ג צ מבואר בתשובת הרשב"א המיוחסת להרמב"ן סימן רל"ו וכן הורה מהרי"ן חביב ומהר"ר לוי בנו

באר היטב

(כט) תוכות. ודוקא חקיקה פוסלת בו אבל אם כתב רי"ש דומה לדלי"ת ורוצה להוסיף עליו דיו לעשותו עגול דתהוי רי"ש וכן בעשה רי"ש במקום דלי"ת יש תקנה להוסיף עליו דיו ולעשותו מרובעת ומותר. וה"ה מדי"ת לכ"ף או איפכא נמי דינא הכי וכל זה דיש תקנה לתקנו היינו קודם שכתב אות אחריו אבל לא אח"כ דאז הוה שלא כסדרן ופסול בתפילין. תפילין שנזדמן לסופר

ביאור הלכה

רע"א שהעיר בזה: * מ"ם פתוחה שנדבק. עיין במ"ב שכתב בדין נדבק כחוט השערה דתלוי בדין ה"א ויותר נלענ"ד לומר דאפילו המקילין בדין ה' כמבואר בב"י לקמן בסימן ל"ו מודים בזה דהרי עכ"פ מ"ם סתום הוא ומה לי אם הסתימה דקה או עבה ושם ראייתם הוא מדאמר הגמרא חזינא לספרי דוקני דתלו לכרעיה דה"א משמע דהוא רק למלוה בעלמא אבל עלם תמונת ה"א אין לריך לתלות הכרעא ואעפ"כ לא דמי לחי"ת כמש"כ הגר"א לקמן בביאורו או כמש"כ הרשב"א הנדפס מחדש על מנחות עי"ש משא"כ במ"ם דאין לנו שום ראיה לקראו מ"ם פתוח ע"י שהסתימה היא דקה: * ונסתמה. עיין בט"ז אהע"ז בסי' קכ"ה ס"ד שכתב ודוקא שנסתם המ"ם אחר שנגמר אבל אם סתם המ"ם קודם הגמר בזה יכול לגרור הסיתום כיון שעדיין לריך להוסיף ברלועה המשופעת כמין יו"ד ע"כ יגרור תחלה הדבוק ואח"כ יגמור ע"ש ונראה דלפי דעת הרד"ך שכתבנו במ"ב בס"ק מ"ח[א] גם בזה יש להחמיר: * כל החרטום. נראה לי פשוט דדוקא שנדבק בעת כתיבת החרטום

משנה ברורה

עושה מעשה בגוף האות אלא (עב) יגרור ג"כ קלת מהאות עד שלא ישאר לורתו עליו ואח"כ יתקנו אם לא כתב עדיין אחר אות זו דאל"ה פסול בתו"מ דבעינן כסדרן. וכ"ז הדין דשו"ע הוא מחמת שהאות אינו ניכר ונתבטל עי"ז כתיבה הראשונה אבל אם לא נשתנה לורת האות יכול למחוק טיפת הדיו ואין חילוק בין שנפל הדיו לתוך חלל האות בלבד או גם על האות גופא (עג) ונתעבה גג האות (עד) או גם הירך עי"ז אפ"ה יוכל לתקן ולא מיקרי חק תוכות מאחר שהאות ניכר עדיין. ומדינא אפילו תיקון לא בעי בזה רק יותר טוב שיתקן ע"כ יכול לעשות תיקון זה אפילו בתו"מ דבעינן כסדרן ועיין בבה"ל. ודע עוד דהשו"ע מיירי אפילו נפלה הטיפה אחר שנגמר האות וכ"ש אם נפלה קודם שנגמר האות כדין וגמר מתחלה האות ואין ניכר עדיין דבזה (עה) כו"ע סוברים דאין תקנה בגרירת הטפה דהרי לא היה עליו מעולם שם אות רק עתה ע"י גרירה והוי חק תוכות ממש אך אם גרר מתחלה הטפה ורולה עתה לגמור האות בזה יש דיעות בין הפוסקים דהרד"ך סובר דלא מהני דס"ל דכיון שנפלה הטפה על תקלת האות נתבטל ממנו שם כתיבה והוי כחקיקה בעלמא ומה מהני אף אם יגמר האות ע"י כתיבה וכ"ש אם נפלה על הקלף טפת דיו ממש ונעשה כמין חצי אות דלא שרי להשלים האות ע"י כתיבה והב"י והרמ"א [בהא"ע בסי' קכ"ה ס"ד] מקילין אפילו בזה הדין האחרון וסוברין דלא מיקרי חק תוכות אלא כשגומר האות ע"י חקיקה אך (עו) האחרונים מגדלין להחמיר בזה הדין האחרון אם לא שמושך (עז) הטפת דיו הלחה ומזיזה ממקום למקום עד שעושה ממנה אות שבס דזה הוי כתיבה: (סח) אין תקנה. פי' ע"י המחיקה אין תקנה אבל מותר להוסיף דיו ולעשותו עגול. וכן אם טעה וכתב רי"ש במקום ד' וכ' במקום ב' והוו אותיות עבין אין תקנה שיגררן ויעמידן בתמונת ד' וב' אבל (עח) מותר להוסיף עליהן דיו ולעשותן בתמונת ד' וב'. וכן אם טעה וכתב במקום ז"ין נו"ן פשוטה אין תקנה שיגררו ויעמידו על ז"ין דזה הוי חק תוכות ממש אלא לריך למוחקו לגמרי וכן אם טעה וכתב (עט) ה"א במקום ד' אין תקנה לגרור הרגל של הה"א וישאר ד' דדומה לסמ"ך וב' שנפל טפת דיו שם ונתקלקל תמונתו עי"ז דלא מהני גרירת הטפה משום דאין עושה מעשה בגוף האות וה"נ כה"ג אלא לריך לגרור ג"כ קלת הגג עד שישאר כמו וי"ו או לגרור (פ) הירך עד שלא ישאר לורת ד' עליו ואח"כ יתקנו.(פא) כללא דמילתא גורר לא מהני להיות כתיבה בכך ומיקרי חק תוכות אבל כותב מהני שמעבה האות מדלי"ת רי"ש או מרי"ש ד' שכותב התג. ולענין שלא כסדרן נהפוך הוא גורר כשר כגון בדיבוק אות לאות וכדלקמן דזה לא מיקרי מעשה בגוף האות וכותב פסול. ומה שהתרנו להוסיף דיו ולהעמידן על תמונתן (פב) היינו כשלא כתב האותיות שאחר זה: (סט) למחוק התג. ואפילו אם אח"כ ימשוך ג"כ גגו ותמתיתו של הכ' (פג) לא מהני דבלא"ה לורתה עליה: יח (ע) שנדבק. ואם פוסל בזה נגיעה דקה כחוט השערה עיין מה שכתבנו לקמן[ב] לענין ה"א ועיין בבה"ל: (עא) ונסתמה. והוי כמ"ם סתום שמקומו רק בסוף תיבה ולא באמצעותה[ג] (פד) וכן כל אותיות מנצפ"ך הכפולין בא"ב כותב את הראשונות בתחלת התיבה ובאמצעיתה והאחרונות בסוף ואם שינה פסול: (עב) ולפותחה. וה"ה שאר אותיות שנתקלקל תמונתם בעת הכתיבה או אח"כ וע"י הגרירה יעמדו על תמונתם כגון ד' שהמשיך רגלו ודומה לך' פשוטה וכל כה"ג אין מועיל להן גרירה כיון שאינו עושה מעשה בגוף האות הנשאר אלא ימחוק רגלו וכנ"ל בס"ק ס"ח ואח"כ יתקנו:[ד] וה"ה דמהני בזה אם המשיך גגו של האות לרחבה עד שנראה לכל שהוא ד' אבל לעיל בכתב ה"א במקום ד' דכתבנו שם דלריך ג"כ למחוק רגל הד' או גגו מלבד רגל הה"א (פה) לא מהני עלה זו דהמשכת גג הד' דהרי בלא"ה לורתו עליו לכך לא מיקרי זה שום תיקון: (עג) כחק תוכות. דבגוף האות אין עושה שום מעשה אלא גורר הסתימה וה"ה אם טעה (פו) וכתב ח' במקום ב' זיי"ן אין מועיל לגרור הגג לבד מהך טעמא אלא לריך לגררם עד שיבטלם מתמונתם. וכן אם טעה ועשה ך' פשוטה למעלה כעין דל"ת שלפי דעת הרבה מן הפוסקים היא פסולה כמו שיבואר לקמן בסי' ל"ו ג"כ אין מועיל (פז) לגרור התג ולעשותה עגולה דהוי חק תוכות אלא יוסיף עליה דיו ויעשה עגולה. ונראה (פח) דלא מעכב שלא כסדרן בתיקון זה דבלא"ה לורתה עליה: (עד) ומה תקנתה. כל שכתוב בסעיף זה שיש תקנה היינו קודם שכתב אות שאחריו דאל"ה פסול בתו"מ דבעינן בהן כסדרן דוקא לבד מהיכא שנבאר בהדיא דלא מעכב בזה כסדרן: (עה) כצורת נ"כ. כי כתיבת המ' פתוחה הוא בב' כתיבות דהיינו בתחלה כותבין כמו נו"ן כפופה ואח"כ תולין בלדה כמו וי"ו וא"כ כל שנעשה הפסול בו דהיינו הו' לריך לגוררו כולו אבל הנו"ן שנכתב בהכשר אין לריך לגוררו וה"ה בכל אות שנכתב בב' כתיבות כגון ג' וכיו"ב ונעשה פסול בכתיבה א' (פט) אין לריך לגרור רק אותה לאפוקי ברי"ש שעשאה כמין ד' דבפעם א' נכתב הכל בפסול לריך הכל לגרור:

ורי"ש

שער הציון

(עב) מסעיף י"ח: (עג) ע"ת ופר"ח בא"ע בסימן קכ"ה ופמ"ג בא"א כתב ג"כ דיש מחמירין דהג"ה שם לא שייך לכאן: (עד) פשוט דזה לא הוי כתב ע"ג כתב ועיין בבה"ל: (עה) אפי' הסמ"ק וכמ"ש בב"י: (עו) הפמ"ג בא"א בשם הט"ז בא"ע והגרע"א בחידושיו ועוד ש"א בפ"ת א"ע סי' קכ"ה ס"ח[ד]: (עז) ט"ז בא"ע מובא פה בפמ"ג: (עח) ט"ז ופמ"ג: (עט) פמ"ג בא"א סי' מ"ז ס"ק י"ז[ה]: (פ) פי' כולו דאל"ה שם ד' עליו כנ"ל בסט"ו פמ"ג בא"א בדיני לורת אותיות בסי' ל"ב א"ד: (פא) פמ"ג: (פב) ט"ז: (פג) פמ"ג בפתיחה לסי' ל"ב[ו]: (פד) מ"ם וביאור הגר"א: (פה) פמ"ג בסי' ל"ב בא"א בדיני לורת אותיות אות ד': (פו) פמ"ג בא"א בשם הב"ש סקכ"ו: (פז) מ"א בסקכ"ו: (פח) פמ"ג בא"א שם אות ך': (פט) ט"ז:

הגהות ותיקונים: א) ס"ז: ב) ס"ק פ"ג: ג) באמצעיתה: ד) ס"ד: ה) צ"ל פרמ"ג במש"ז סקי"ז: ו) בא"א סוף הסימן ד"ה השלישי הוא חק תוכות:

/thus/ open it, because this constitutes (73) carving around /to form the letter/. (74) The remedy is to scrape away the entire nose, /so that/ it will remain (75) with the form of the bent over /letter/ נ, and after that to write /the part/ which one scraped off.[17*]

Mishnah Berurah

simple /elongated letter/ ך and in all similar cases. Scraping is of no avail in these cases, since one does not do an action in the letter itself which remains. Instead, one should erase the leg, as /explained/ above in sub-Par. 68, and correct /the letter/ subsequently.

Correspondingly, in the case of /a letter ד with a leg which is too long/, it is of avail to continue the roof of the letter breadthways until it is apparent to everyone that it is the /letter/ ד.

However, /in the case discussed/ above /in sub-Par. 68/, where one wrote the /letter/ ה instead of the /letter/ ד, concerning which we wrote there that one must also erase the leg of the /letter/ ד or its roof, apart from the leg of the /letter/ ה, this solution of continuing the roof of the /letter/ ד is of no avail. For /even/ without /one doing/ this /the letter ד/ has the form /required/ for it and therefore /the continuation/ is not describable as a correction at all.

(73) Carving around. For one does not do any action in the letter itself, but merely scrapes away the closure.

Correspondingly, for the same reason, if one erred and wrote the /letter/ ח instead of two ז[17] /letters/, it is of no avail merely to scrape away from the roof, but it is necessary to scrape away from /the ז letters/ until their symbol has been cancelled.

Likewise, if one erred and made a single /elongated/ letter ך like the /letter/ ד on top, in which case it is invalid according to the view of many of the Poskim, as explained below in Sec. 36, it is also of no avail to scrape away the projection and round /the top of the letter/, as this constitutes carving around /to form the letter/. Instead, one should add ink to /the letter/ to make it rounded. It appears /logical/ that if this correction /is made the letter/ will not be precluded /from validity because of the requirement that the letters may not be completed/ in incorrect order, as /even/ without /the correction the letter/ has its form.

(74) The remedy is. Whenever it is stated in this paragraph that there is a remedy, this /only applies/ before the letter after /the letter which requires correction/ has been written. Otherwise, where *tefilin* /passages/ or mezuzos are involved /the passage will remain/ invalid, as their /letters/ are required /to be written/ specifically in /the correct/ order. /There are/ exceptions, for which we explicitly specify that /the correction of the letter/ does not preclude /the validity of the passage/ because of /the requirement to write the letters/ in /the correct/ order.

(75) With the form of the bent over נ. This is because writing the open /letter/ מ involves two writings /of letter-like symbols/. I.e., one first writes /a symbol/ resembling a bent over /letter/ נ and subsequently one suspends at its side /a symbol/ resembling a /letter/ ו. Consequently, the entire /part/ in which the invalidity occurs, i.e., the /part which resembles the letter/ ו, must be entirely scraped away. On the other hand, the /part that resembles the letter/ נ, which was written validly, does not need to be scraped away.

Correspondingly, in the case of every letter which is written with two writings /of a symbol/, such as the /letter/ ג, etc., if it became invalid through the writing of one /of the symbols/ it is solely necessary to scrape that /symbol/ away. This contrasts with /the ruling/ in the case of a /letter/ ך which one made like the /letter/ ד, in which case the entire /letter/ was written at once invalidly. /Then/ one must scrape away the entire /letter/.

17* If the strokes became stuck after the letter was written validly, one may also remedy this by scraping away sufficient of the part of the letter that is like the letter נ until the form of the letter has been cancelled and then writing that part again. (Beyur Halachah)

17 It should be noted that the form of the letter ח used in the writing of a Torah Scroll, *tefilin* passage or mezuzah consists of two ז letters joined together.

(עו) * קוּרי"ש שעשאה (עז) כמין דלי"ת * יש להחמיר ולומר דלא סגי כשיגרור הירך לבד או הגג לבד ויחזור ויכתבנו כמין רי"ש * משום דבין הגג ובין הירך נעשו (ל) [יג] בפיסול הלכך צריך לגרור שניהם ואם נדבקה *אות לאות בין קודם שתגמר בין אחר (עח) שנגמרה פסול * ואם יגרר (לא) [יד] והפרידה (עט) * כשר ולא מיקרי (פ) חק תוכות מאחר שהאות עצמה היתה כתובה (פא) כתקונה. (פב) שאם נגעו * רגלי

ק ב"י ממשמעות תשובת הרשב"א ר הרא"ש בהלכות תפילין וס' התרומה והגה"מ ש תשובת הרשב"א ותשובה להרמב"ם סי' רל"ו ות"ה סימן מ"ח

באר היטב

לכתוב בפרשה פשוטה בסוף להשלים משך רוחב השיטה הארוך והמשיך גגה של כף עד שהגיע לסוף השיטה ונמלאת רוחב הגג דומה לדלי"ת גדולה או ריש גדולה מה דינו עיין הר"י הלוי סי' פ"א ועיין ס"ק שלאחר זה. ובתשובת גינת ורדים חא"ח כלל ב' סימן ט'. ובתשובת דבר שמואל סימן קמ"ג: (ל) בפיסול. ר"ל כי כתיבת המ"ם פתוחה היא בב' כתיבות דהיינו מתחלה כותבין כמו נו"ן כפופה ואח"כ תולין מלדה כמו וי"ו א"כ כל שנעשה הפסול בו דהיינו הוי"ו צריך לגרור כולו אבל הנו"ן שנכתבה בהכשר א"צ לגוררה לאפוקי ברי"ש שעשאה כמין דלי"ת דבפעם א' נכתב הכל בפסול צריך לגוררו כולו ולפ"ז ה"ה בכל אות שנכתב בשני כתיבות כמו ב' ונעשה פסול בכתיבה אחת א"צ לגרור אלא אותה ואם כתב מתחלה רי"ש ואח"כ טעה ועשה בו תג כעין דלי"ת סגי ליה כשיגרר התג[ד] או הירך עם התג ויחזור ויכתבנו כמין רי"ש והמחמיר גם בזה תע"ב לבוש ול"ת. רגל הכ"ף צריך להיות כפלים כגג שלא תדמה כרי"ש. בתשובת מהר"י הלוי סימן פ"א כתב אם עשה גג של הכ"ף רחב צריך תיקון למחוק כל הגג אפי' במלת אלהיך יכול למוחקו אך יזהר שלא ימחוק הרגל והמ"א כתב ול"נ שאם יכול למשוך הרגל שיהיה כפלים כמו הגג שפיר דמי עיין ס"ק שלפני זה: (לא) והפרידה כשר. נ"ל דה"ה אם רגל הכ' מגיע לסוף הקלף בלי היקף רשאי לגרר קצת דלא גרע מנדבק אות לאות. כתב הב"ח בא"ע סימן קכ"ה דאם כל אורך האות דבוקה לחברתה לא מהני

שערי תשובה

להחמיר יכול להעביר הקולמוס על הקוץ הנשאר כו' ע"ש: [יג] בפיסול. עבה"ט ומ"ש מתשובת מהר"י הלוי ומג"א עיין בתשובת דבר שמואל סי' קפ"א שכתב שאע"פ שמהר"י הלוי התיר בבירור לגרור הכ' שבמלת אלהיך נראה שעלהיו"ט אם אפשר שיאריכו בתחלה הרגל עד שיהיה יותר מהגגו[ה] ואח"כ יגררו קצת מהגג כדי שישאר ברגל כפלים כפי מעשה צורת האות לכתחלה שבאופן זה אין מוחקים האות כעין חק תוכות עכ"ל. ונראה דס"ל שא"א למשוך כפלים כהגג ממש כמ"ש המ"א חדא דכיון שהמשיכו ברוחב כ"כ עד שכמעט פי שנים ברגלה מסתמא אין ריווח בין השיטות כ"כ. וגם כשימשוך שוב הרגל פי שנים כרחבה יהיה יותר גדול מאד שאין דומה לו באותיות הגדולות לכן כתב שימשיך רק מעט שיהיה ארוך מן הגג קצת ואח"כ יגרור ול"ע אם בכה"ג הגרירה מותרת באותיות השם דשמא כפלים לאו לעיכובא הוא. ועיין ביד אפרים מ"ש בזה על דברי מהר"י הלוי ז"ל ועיין מ"ש בס"ק שלפני זה: [יד] והפרידה. עבה"ט וכתב בר"י שבספר בית

משנה ברורה

(עו) ורי"ש. או וי"ו שעשאו כמין רי"ש וכל כה"ג שנעשה בכתיבה אחת: (עז) כמין ד'. וה"ה בגגו של כ' פשוטה שעשאו רחב עד שנראה כד' או רי"ש ועיין בבה"ל. והסופרים נכשלין בזה בעו"ה: (עח) שנגמרה. האות בארכו כראוי כגון שכתב תיבת לו ונדבק הוי"ו בקלהו להלמ"ד וכל כיוצא בזה ואפילו בנגיעה כל דהו שלא נשתנית עי"ז האות מצורתה אפ"ה פסול דבעינן שיהא האות מוקף גויל. ואם נתפשטו האותיות מכח לחות הדיו שקורין גיפלאסין° עד שנראין כדבוקין ומ"מ נראה שאין האותיות נוגעין כשר ואם האותיות נוגעין אף שנעשה זה לאחר הכתיבה אפ"ה פסול אה"ע בסימן קכ"ה סט"ז בהג"ה ובב"ש עי"ש ועיין לעיל בבה"ל בסוף סט"ז. ואם נמצא דיבוק בין אות לאות כשהוציאו ס"ת לקריאה עיין לקמן בסימן קמ"ג בבה"ל[א] : (עט) כשר. וה"ה אם (ל) רגלי האותיות או גגן ואמצען מגיע לסוף בלי היקף קלף רשאי לגרר קצת דלא גרע מנדבק אות לאות דמהני גרירה. ודע דבזה אין מעכב שלא כסדרן כמבואר לקמן בסכ"ה מאחר דאין מוסיף בגוף האות. ואפילו (לא) באותיות השם שנגמרו ודיבוקן למטה רשאי לגרור: (פ) חק תוכות. ומיירי (לב) שלא נשתנה האות מצורתה ע"י הדיבוקות אבל אם נשתנית האות מצורתה ואין התינוק יכול לקרותה וכ"ש אם נשתנית לצורת אות אחרת כגון וי"ו שנדבק בסופו לנו"ן כפופה דיבוק עב שנראית כצורת ט"ת עד שתינוק דלא חכים ולא טיפש יקרא אותו לט"ת לא מהני גרירת הדיבוק בזה דהוי כמ"ס שנסתמה ומקרי חק תוכות וע"כ צריך לגרור (לג) גם הנו"ן שגם הוא נשתנה מצורתו ונפסל ע"י הדיבוק וכן כל כיוצא בזה: (פא) כתקונה. ונפלה טפת דיו במ"ז אף דנכתבה מתחלה כתקונה נתקלקלה ע"י הטפה ואינה ניכרת תשא"כ בזה דאפילו קודם הגרירה ניכר היטב כל אות בפני עצמה ולפ"ז אם כל אורך האות דבוקה לחברתה לא מהני גרירה, והפר"ח מיקל בזה. ועיין בש"א ובנתיב חיים: (פב) אם נגעו. אבל אם יש הפסק דק אפילו רק כחוט

ביאור הלכה

דהחרטום נעשה בפסול אבל אם נדבק לאחר הכתיבה אין צריך לזה דוקא גרירת החרטום דה"ה דיכול לגרור מהנו"ן עד שיבטלנו מצורת אות. ול"ע אם מהני בזה שנכתב* בכשרות ג"כ גרירת חצי חרטום וזה תלוי אם בעלמא כל החרטום הוא לעיכובא במ"ס או אפשר דהוא רק לכתחילה וצריך עיון: * ורי"ש שעשאה כמין ד' וכו'. ואם עשה גג רחב לך' פשוטה עד שנראה כמו רי"ש כתב המ"א דימשוך הרגל עד שיהיה כפלים כמו הגג [ואם הכפלים הוא לעיכובא או לכתחלה עיין לקמן בסימן ל"ו בדיני צורת אותיות] ואם אין לו מקום למשוך כתב המ"א בשם הרי"ל וכן סתם הפמ"ג בסי' ל"ו[ב] בצורת האותיות דתקונו הוא שימחוק כל הגג דגרירת היתר בודאי לא מהני בזה דהוי ח"ת ממש ואפילו במלת אלהיך יכול למוחקו אך יזהר שלא ימחק הרגל ול"ע הלא דמי לרי"ש שעשאו כמין ד' דפסק השו"ע דצריך לגרור כולו משום דנכתב בפ"א וה"נ דכוותיה ועיין ביד אפרים שמחלק קצת בזה ודוחק אח"כ מצאתי בחידושי רע"א שכתב בפשיטות דדמי לרי"ש שעשאו כמין ד' [ועיין בש"ת בס"ק כ"ב[ג] במה שהעתיק בזה בשם תשובת גינת ורדים ול"ע אם יש לסמוך ע"ז אחרי שכל האחרונים מחמירין דצריך עכ"פ למחוק הגג] אך אי אתרמי כן בך' של אלהיך שעשאו רחב כמין ד' או רי"ש נראה דיש לסמוך להקל דדי במחיקת הגג אם אין לו מקום למשוך הרגל אחרי שגם ברי"ש שעשאו כמין ד' מיקל הפר"ח והביאו המה"ש דדי שיבטלנו מצורת אות וגם הגרע"א בחידושיו הניח דברי השו"ע בזה בצ"ע מחמת אותה הקושיא של הפר"ח (ותמיה שלא זכרו): * יש להחמיר ולומר וכו'. עיין בחידושי רע"א וכה"ג כתב המחה"ש בשם הפר"ח: * משום דבין הגג ובין הירך כו'. כי בפעם א' נכתב הכל כדרך הכותבין ולפ"ז אם מתחלה כתב ריש ואח"כ טעה ועשה בו תג כעין דלי"ת סגי ליה כשיגרור הגג או הירך עם התג ויחזור ויכתבנו כמין ריש. לבוש ופמ"ג: * ואם גרר והפרידה וכו'. אף אם נעשה הדיבוקות קודם שנגמר האות ועיין בביאור הגר"א ובס' שערי אפרים למהרא"ז מרגליות דדין זה דשו"ע יש לפקפק בו ומוכח שם מדעת ש"א בפתחי שערים שלו דאין להקל בו אלא בתפילין ומזוזות דכדיעבד דמי דאם היה צריך מחיקה היה נפסל משום שלא כסדרן אבל בס"ת וכן בתו"מ אם לא כתב עדיין התיבות שאח"ז לא מהני גרירת הדיבוקות לבד אם נדבק קודם שנגמר האות וגמר האות בפסול: * כשר ולא מקרי וכו'. עיין במ"ב במה שכתב ואם רגל וכו' הוא מבואר ממה דקי"ל דמהני גרירה אפילו נדבק האות בתחילתו: * רגלי הה"א וכו'. עיין במ"ב במה שכתב דכל שאין צורת האות וכו' לשון ח"מ בהעה"ז עי"ש. ובמ"ש ואף אם נדבק וכו' באופן שהתינוק יודע שהוא ה"א וכו' כן נראה ברור מדהביא הב"י בסימן זה ובל"ו מקור לזה מדברי מהרי"ק בשורש נ"ה ושלא כמו שכתב בשורש ע"ח ושם הלא איירי בהדיא בהכי כמבואר שם בסוף השורש. וכן הביא מתה"ד ומוכח שם ג"כ הכי דאל"ה לא מקשה

מתרגם: °דליל

שער הציון

(ל) מ"א ופרישה: (לא) פמ"ג ע"ש וכ"ש למעלה: (לב) מ"א ודה"ח בקה"ת: (לג) פמ"ג

הגהות ותיקונים: א) סעיף ד' בה"ל ד"ה אם ובמ"ב שם סקכ"ה: ב) ל"ב: ג) י"ב: ד) הגג: ה) מגגו:

(76) If one made a /letter/ ר **(77)** similar to the /letter/ ד, one should be stringent and assume that it is insufficient to scrape away the thigh /of the letter/ by itself or the roof /of the letter/ by itself and write it again to resemble the /letter/ ר. This is because both the roof and the thigh were made invalidly. One must therefore scrape away both of them[18*] /and then write the letter again/.

If one letter got stuck to /another/ letter, irrespective of whether /this happened/ before /the second letter/ was completed or whether /it happened/ after **(78)** it was completed, they are /both/ invalid. /However,/ if one scrapes away /the link/ and separates /the letters/ **(79)** they are valid. This is not

Mishnah Berurah

(76) If ... a /letter/ ר. Or if one made a /letter/ ו similar to the /letter/ י or /did/ anything /else/ of that nature /when one wrote a letter/ which is formed with one writing.

(77) Similar to the /letter/ ד. The same ruling /applies/ if one made the roof of a simple /elongated letter/ ך wide, to the extent that it appears like the /letter/ ד or /the letter/ ר. See the Beyur Halachah.[18] The scribes stumble over this, among our many sins.

(78) It was completed. /I.e., after/ the letter /was completed/ with its proper length. For example, if one wrote the word לו and the /letter/ ו got stuck to the /letter/ ל at its edge or anything similar.

Even when /there is/ a slight touch, so that the form of the letter is unchanged by it, /the letter/ is nevertheless invalid, as we require the letter to be surrounded by /blank/ parchment.

If the letters spread out due to the wateriness of the ink, known as its fluidity, to the extent that they seem stuck /together/, but it is nevertheless apparent that the letters are not /actually/ touching /one another/, they are valid. /However,/ if the letters touch /one another, then/, even if this came about after they were written they are nevertheless invalid. *Even Ha-Ezer*, Sec. 125, in the gloss to Par. 16 and in the *B.Sh.*; see there. See above in the Beyur Halachah at the end of Par. 16.

If sticking is discovered between letters when one takes out a Torah Scroll to read /from it/, see below in Sec. 143 in the Mishnah Berurah, sub-Par. 25.

(79) They are valid. Correspondingly, if the legs of the letters, their roofs or their middles reach the end /of the parchment/ without being surrounded by /blank/ parchment, one is permitted to scrape off a little. For this is no worse than /an instance where/ one letter is stuck to another, in which case scraping away is of avail.

Note that when this /correction was made the validity/ is not precluded /because of the fact that the letters/ were /made valid/ in incorrect order, as stated below in Par. 25, since /the correction/ does not involve adding to the letter itself. Even in the case of the letters of the /Divine/ Name one is allowed to scrape away /the link/, if they were completed and are stuck below.

18* It follows that if one wrote the letter ר and then added a projection in error, so that the letter now resembles the letter ד, one may merely scrape off either the roof or the thigh together with the projection and then write it again. (Beyur Halachah)

18 It is stated there that if one can, one should remedy this by lengthening the leg to double the length of the roof. If one cannot do so, then, in the case of a letter ך of the word אלקיך, one should be lenient and erase merely the roof and then rewrite it.

(עו) * [ז]ורי"ש שעשאה (עז) כמין דלי"ת * יש להחמיר ולומר דלא סגי כשיגרור הירך לבד או הגג לבד ויחזור ויכתבנו כמין רי"ש * משום דבין הגג ובין הירך נעשו (ל) [יג] בפיסול הלכך צריך לגרור שניהם ואם נדבקה *אות לאות בין קודם שתגמר בין אחר (עח) שנגמרה פסול * ואם [י]גרר (לא) [יד] והפרידה (עט) * כשר ולא מיקרי (פ) חק תוכות מאחר שהאות עצמה היתה כתובה (פא) כתקונה. (פב) [ש]אם נגעו * רגלי

באר הגולה

ק ב"י ממשמעות תשובת הרשב"א ר הרא"ש בהלכות תפילין וס' התרומה והגה"מ ש תשובת הרשב"א ותשובה להרמב"ס סי' רל"ו ות"ה סימן מ"ח

באר היטב

לכתוב בפרשה פשוטה בסוף להשלים משך רוחב השיטה הארוך והמשיך גגה של כף עד שהגיע לסוף השיטה ונמלאת רוחב הגג דומה לדלי"ת גדולה או ריש גדולה מה דינו עיין הר"י הלוי סי' פ"א ועיין ס"ק שלאחר זה. ובתשובת גינת ורדים חא"ח כלל ב' סימן ט'. ובתשובת דבר שמואל סימן קס"ג: (ל) בפיסול. ר"ל כי כתיבת המ"ס פתוחה היא בב' כתיבות דהיינו מתחלה כותבין כמו נו"ן כפופה ואח"כ תולין מלדה כמו וי"ו א"כ כל שנעשה הפסול בו דהיינו הוי"ו צריך לגרור כולו אבל הנו"ן שנכתבה בהכשר א"ל לגוררה לאפוקי ברי"ש שעשאה כמין דלי"ת דבפעם א' נכתב הכל בפסול צריך לגוררו כולו ולפ"ז ה"ה בכל אות שנכתב בשני כתיבות כמו ב' ונעשה פסול בכתיבה אחת א"ל לגרור אלא אותה ואם כתב מתחלה רי"ש ואח"כ טעה ועשה בו תג כעין דלי"ת סגי ליה כשיגרר התג[ד] או הירך עם התג ויחזור ויכתבנו כמין רי"ש והמחמיר גם בזה תע"ב לבוש ול"ח. רגל הכ"ף צריך להיות כפלים כגג שלא תדמה כרי"ש. בתשובת מהר"י הלוי סימן פ"א כתב אם עשה גג של הכ"ף רחב צריך תיקון למחוק כל הגג אפי' במלת אלהיך יכול למוחקו אך יזהר שלא ימחוק הרגל והמ"א כתב ול"נ שאם יכול למשוך הרגל שיהיה כפלים כמו הגג שפיר דמי עיין ס"ק שלפני זה: (לא) והפרידה כשר. נ"ל דה"ה אם רגל הכ' מגיע לסוף הקלף בלי היקף ראשי לגרר קצת דלא גרע מנדבק אות לאות. כתב הב"ח בא"ע סימן קכ"ה דאם כל אורך האות דבוקה לחברתה לא מהני

שערי תשובה

להחמיר יכול להעביר הקולמוס על הקוץ הנשאר כו' ע"ש: [יג] בפיסול. עבה"ט ומ"ש מתשובת מהר"י הלוי ומג"א עיין בתשובת דבר שמואל סי' קפ"ח שכתב שאע"פ שמהר"י הלוי התיר בבירור לגרור הכ' שבמלת אלהיך נראה שעלהיו"ט אם אפשר שיאריכו בתחלה הרגל עד שיהיה יותר מהגגו[ה] ואח"כ יגררו קצת מהגג כדי שישאר ברגל כפלים כפי מעשה צורת האות לכתחלה שבאופן זה אין מותקים האות כעין חק תוכות עכ"ל. ונראה דס"ל שא"א למשוך כפלים כהגג ממש כמ"ש המ"א חדא דכיון שהמשיכו ברוחב כ"כ עד שכמעט פי שנים ברגלה מסתמא אין ריווח בין השיטות כ"כ. וגם כשימשוך שוב הרגל פי שנים כרחבה יהיה יותר גדול מאד שאין דומה לו באותיות הגדולות לכן כתב שימשיך רק מעט שיהיה ארוך מן הגג קצת ואח"כ יגרור ול"ע אם בכה"ג הגרירה מותרת באותיות השם דשמא כפלים לאו לעיכובא הוא. ועיין ביד אפרים מ"ש בזה על דברי מהר"י הלוי ז"ל ועיין מ"ש בס"ק שלפני זה: [יד] והפרידה. עבה"ט וכתב בר"י שבספר בית

משנה ברורה

(עו) ורי"ש. או וי"ו שעשאו כמין רי"ש וכל כה"ג שנעשה בכתיבה אחת: (עז) כמין ד'. וה"ה נגנו של כ' פשוטה שעשאו רחב עד שנראה כד' או רי"ש ועיין בבה"ל. והסופרים נכשלין בזה בעו"ה: (עח) שנגמרה. האות באורכו כראוי כגון שכתב תיבת לו ונדבק הוי"ו בקלהו להלמ"ד וכל כיוצא בזה ואפילו בנגיעה כל דהו שלא נשתנית עי"ז האות מצורתה אפ"ה פסול דבעינן שיהא האות מוקף גויל. ואם נתפשטו האותיות מכח לחות הדיו שקורין גיפלאסין[ס] עד שנראין כדבוקין ומ"מ נראה שאין האותיות נוגעין כשר ואם האותיות נוגעין אף שנעשה זה לאחר הכתיבה אפ"ה פסול א"ע בסימן קכ"ה סט"ז בהג"ה ובב"ש עי"ש ועיין לעיל בבה"ל בסוף סט"ז. ואם נמצא דיבוק בין אות לאות כשהוליאו ס"ת לקריאה עיין לקמן בסימן קמ"ג בבה"ל[א]: (עט) כשר. וה"ה אם (ל) רגלי האותיות או גגן ואמצען מגיע לסוף בלי היקף קלף ראשי לגרר קצת דלא גרע מנדבק אות לאות דמהני גרירה. וה"ע דבזה אין מעכב שלא כסדרן כמבואר לקמן בסכ"ה מאחר דאין מוסיף בגוף האות. ואפילו (לא) באותיות השם שנגמרו ודיבוקן למטה ראשי לגרור: (פ) חק תוכות. ומיירי (לב) שלא נשתנה האות מצורתה ע"י הדביקות אבל אם נשתנית האות מצורתה ואין התינוק יכול לקרותה וכ"ש אם נשתנית לצורת אות אחרת כגון וי"ו שנדבק בסופו לנו"ן כפופה דיבוק עב שנראית כצורת טי"ת עד שתינוק דלא חכים ולא טיפש יקרא אותו לטי"ת לא מהני גרירת הדיבוק בזה דהוי כמ"ס שנסתמה ומקרי חק תוכות וע"כ צריך לגרור (לג) גם הנו"ן שגם הוא נשתנה מצורתו ונפסל ע"י הדיבוק וכן כל כיוצא בזה: (פא) כתקונה. ובנפלה טפת דיו בסי"ז אף דנכתבה מתחלה כתקונה נתקלקלה ע"י הטפה ואינה ניכרת משא"כ בזה דאפילו קודם הגרירה ניכר היטב כל אות בפני עצמה ולפ"ז אם כל אורך האות דבוקה לחברתה לא מהני גרירה . והפר"ח מיקל בזה. ועיין בש"א ובנתיב חיים: (פב) אם נגעו. אבל אם יש הפסק דק אפילו רק כחוט

ביאור הלכה

דהחרטוס נעשה בפסול אבל אם נדבק לאחר הכתיבה אין צריך לזה דוקא גרירת החרטוס דה"ה דיכול לגרור מהנו"ן עד שיבטלנו מצורת אות. ול"ע אם מהני בזה שנכתב* בכשרות ג"כ גרירת חצי חרטוס וזה תלוי אם בעלמא כל החרטוס הוא לעיכובא במ"ס או אפשר דהוא רק לכתחילה וצריך עיון: * ורי"ש שעשאה כמין ד' וכו'. ואם עשה גג רחב לך' פשוטה עד שנראה כמו רי"ש כתב המ"א דימשוך הרגל עד שיהיה כפלים כמו הגג [ואם הכפלים הוא לעיכובא או לכתחלה עיין לקמן בסימן ל"ו בדיני צורת אותיות] ואם אין לו מקום למשוך כתב המ"א בשם הרי"ל וכן סתם הפמ"ג בסי' ל"ו[ב] בצורת האותיות דתקונו הוא שימחוק כל הגג דגרירת היתר בודאי לא מהני בזה דהוי ח"ת ממש ואפילו במלת אלהיך יכול למוחקו אך יזהר שלא ימחק הרגל ול"ע הלא דמי לרי"ש שעשאו כמין ד' דפסק השו"ע דצריך לגרור כולו משום דנכתב בפ"א וה"נ דכוותיה ועיין ביד אפרים שמחלק קצת בזה ודוחק אח"כ מצאתי בחידושי רע"א שכתב בפשיטות דדמי לרי"ש שעשאו כמין ד' [ועיין בש"ת בס"ק כ"ב[ג] במה שהעתיק בזה בשם תשובת גינת ורדים ול"ע אם יש לסמוך ע"ז אחרי שכל האחרונים מחמירין דצריך עכ"פ למחוק הגג] אך אי אתרמי כן בך' של אלהיך שעשאו רחב כמין ד' או רי"ש נראה דיש לסמוך להקל דדי במחיקת הגג אם אין לו מקום למשוך הרגל אחרי שגם ברי"ש שעשאו כמין ד' מיקל הפר"ח והביאו המחה"ש דדי שיבטלנו מצורת אות וגם הגרע"א בחידושיו הניח דברי השו"ע בזה בצ"ע מחמת אותה הקושיא של הפר"ח (ותמיה שלא זכרו): * יש להחמיר ולומר וכו'. עיין בחידושי רע"א וכה"ג כתב המחה"ש בשם הפר"ח: * משום דבין הגג ובין הירך כו'. כי בפעם א' נכתב הכל כדרך הכותבין ולפ"ז אם מתחלה כתב ריש ואח"כ טעה ועשה בו תג כעין דלי"ת סגי ליה כשיגרור הגג או הירך עם התג ויחזור ויכתבנו כמין ריש. לבוש ופמ"ג: * ואם גרר והפרידה וכו'. אף אם נעשה הדביקות קודם שנגמר האות ועיין בביאור הגר"א ובס' שערי אפרים למהרא"ז מרגליות דדין זה דשו"ע יש לפקפק בו ומוכח שם מדעת ש"א בפתחי שערים שלו דאין להקל בו אלא בתפילין ומזוזות דבדיעבד דמי דאם היה צריך מחיקה היה נפסל משום שלא כסדרן אבל בס"ת וכן בתו"מ אם לא כתב עדיין התיבות שאח"ז לא מהני גרירת הדביקות לבד אם נדבק קודם שנגמר האות וגמר האות בפסול: * כשר ולא מקרי וכו'. עיין במ"ב במה שכתב ואם רגל וכו' הוא מבואר ממה דקי"ל דמהני גרירה אפילו נדבק האות בתחילתו: * רגלי הה"א וכו'. עיין במ"ב במה שכתב דכל שאין צורת האות וכו' לשון ח"מ בא"הע"ז עיי"ש. ובמ"ש ואף אם נדבק וכו' באופן שהתינוק יודע שהוא ה"א וכו' כן נראה ברור מדהביא הב"י בסימן זה ובל"ו מקור לזה מדברי מהרי"ק בשורש נ"ה ושלא כמו שכתב בשורש ע"ח ושם הלא איירי בהדיא בהכי כמבואר שם בסוף השורש. וכן הביא מתה"ד ומוכח שם ג"כ הכי דאל"ה לא מקשה

מתרגם: [ס]דליל

שער הציון

(ל) מ"א ופרישה: (לא) פמ"ג ע"ש וכ"ש למעלה: (לב) מ"א ודה"ח בקה"ת: (לג) פמ"ג

הגהות ותיקונים: א) סעיף ד' בה"ל ד"ה אם ובמ"ב שם סקכ"ה: ב) ל"ב: ג) י"ב: ד) הגג: ה) מגגו:

classed as **(80)** carving around /to form the letter/, in view /of the fact/ that the letters themselves were written **(81)** correctly.[19*]

(82) If the leg of **(83)** the /letter/ ה or of /the letter/ ק touches the roof /of the

Mishnah Berurah

(80) Carving around /to form the letter/. /The Shulchan Aruch/ is referring to /an instance/ when the form of the letter is unchanged because of the sticking. However, if the form of the letter has changed and a child cannot read it /for what it is meant to be/ and certainly if it has become transformed into the form of a different letter /the scraping away is of no avail/.

For example, if a /letter/ ו became stuck at the end to a bent over /letter/ נ with a thick link that gives /the two letters together/ the appearance of the form of /the letter/ ט, to the extent that a child who is neither /especially/ intelligent nor /especially/ simple will read it as a ט, the scraping away of the link is of no avail in such a case. This is analogous to /the case of/ an /open letter/ מ which became closed and /the scraping away/ is describable as carving around /to form the letter/. Consequently, one must scrape away the /bent over letter/ נ as well, since it also changed its form and became invalid because of the link. The same /applies/ in all similar cases.

(81) Correctly. /This is not a contradiction to the ruling/ in Par. 17, with respect to a drop of ink which fell /into a letter/. /This is because/ although /in the case discussed there the letter/ was first written correctly, it became spoiled because of the drop and is no /longer/ recognizable. In this case /, however, the circumstances are/ different, since even before the scraping each letter is clearly recognizable by itself.

According to this /explanation/, if the full length of a letter is stuck to another /letter/ scraping is of no avail. The *Pr.Ch.* is lenient about this. See the *Sh.E.* and the *Nesiv Chayim*.

(82) If ... touches. However, if there is a thin gap, even of only a hairsbreadth, /the letter/ is valid /as it is/.

(83) The /letter/ ה. Even if it sticks /to

19* If a letter got stuck to another letter before one completed it, one should only rely on this ruling where erasing the letter and writing it again would make it invalid because it was written in incorrect order. (Beyur Halachah)

(פג) הה״א והקו״ף (לג) בגג (פד) * יגרור (פה) הרגל ויחזור ויכתבנו ואין צריך לגרור כל האות כי הגג כדין נכתב. אם * נגע רגל האל״ף (פו) בגג האל״ף * או (פז) פני האל״ף בפנים בגג שתחתיה (לג) פסול ואין תקנה בגרירה (פח) להפרידה דהוי כחק תוכות אלא * יגרור (פט) כל מה שנעשה בפיסול ויחזור ויכתבנו: הגה וכן הדין (צ) ביו״ד השי״ן והלמ״ד והעי״ן (צא) והפ״א אם נגעו בגוף האות יותר ממקום

שערי תשובה

הרואה למהרש״פ הרבה לתמוה על מג״א במה שכתב שמותר לגרר קלת הרגל מהכ״ף המגיע לסוף הקלף ע״ש וכ׳ בדבר שמואל סי׳ פ״ט שמי שתי״ן הסמוכין בתפילין שנדבקו בשעת כתיבה בתחתיתן זה לזה כאלו רגליהם רגל ישרה ואינה ניכרת עכשיו אם הוא כ״ף או בי״ת והסופר טרם שכתב אות אחר לפניו נתן לב לתקן ולהפריד בראש האחמל בדיבוקו של מטה העלה שם שאע״פ שלכאורה יש לחלק בין ההיא דמהרד״ך בשי״ן שנעשו כמו חיתי״ן עפ״י טיפת דיו דכאן אין הדיבוק משנה אותה לאות אחרת כדינה אלא הפסיד צורת האות באופן שא״א להבחין בינה ובין חברתה מ״מ כיון שע״י הדחק אין הפרש ניכר לעין כל צריך למחוק כל רגל השני עד סוף הרגל הראשון ולחזור ולכותבו ע״ש. ועיין בתשובת דבר שמואל סי׳ רס״ה שכתב לחלק בין דיבק אות לחברתה משום ס״ס שמא לא נפסלה קודם שנגמר עשייתה ושמא תיקון גרירה אינו בכלל כתיבה שלא כסדרן אבל אם נודע שנדבק קודם הוי ספק פלוגתא אם הפירוד ע״י גרירה ככתיבה שלא כסדרן והמנהג שלא למחות לסופרים. ובשי״ן שנפרדו למטה יש להסתפק אפילו אם היו הפרודין כחוט השערה ע״ש ובבר״י כתב שאם נכתבו כתיקון ואח״כ נפרדו וצורת האות ניכרת יכול לתקן ואין בזה שלא כסדרן וכ״מ מדברי הר״י אכסנדרי[א] שהביא הב״י וכ״כ היד אהרן ואף שהדב״ש מגמגם בזה נראה עיקר כמ״ש. וכתב עוד בדבר שמואל בשני תיבות על כן שנכתבו בתיבה אחת וכבר כתב להלן לא מהני מה שיגרור קלת עובי אות הלמ״ד של מלת על וקלת עובי אות הכ״ף של תיבת

באר היטב

גרירה. ואם נשתנה צורת האות על ידי הדביקות הוי כמ״ש שנסתמה. רד״ך עמ״א. ועיין ב״ח שהעלה דאם נמצא דיבוק בס״ת בקריאה דאין צריך להוציא אחרת אפילו נמצא בשבת וי״ט שא״א לגוררו מ״מ אין להוציא אחרת כיון שמעיקר הדין ס״ת יש תקנה לגוררו רק דאיסור שבת רביע עליה וכל הראויה לבילה אין בילה וכו׳ ע״ש. ובשיורי כנה״ג כתב ומנהגינו דאפי׳ בדבוק אות לאות שנמצא בס״ת בשבת או בי״ט להוציא ס״ת אחר ע״ל סימן קמ״ג. ובספר אבן העוזר מחמיר באותיות הנדבקים בתחלת הכתיבה שאין להם תקנה בגרירה עיין שם באריכות בס׳ מגיני ארץ מדפוסי פרופם: (לג) בגג. כל הסעיף זה איירי קודם שכתב אות שלאחריו דאז יש תקנה אבל אחר כך לא דהוי שלא כסדרן ודוקא שלא נשאר צורת אות בלא תיקון אז אסור לתקנה בשכתב לפניה משום דהוי שלא כסדרן אבל אם נשאר צורת אות אפי׳ בלא תיקון יוכל לתקנו אפילו אח״כ דכיון דצורת אות היה ניכר ליכא משום דלא כסדרן ועיין סעיף כ״ה וס״ק כ״ו מש״ש: (לג) פסול. ודוקא שנגעה היו״ד עצמה באל״ף אבל אם קוצה השמאלית של יו״ד

משנה ברורה

השערה (לד) כשר: (פג) הה״א. אף אם נדבק רק כחוט השערה (לה) באופן שהתינוק יודע שהוא ה״א אפ״ה צריך לגרור כל הרגל דכל (לו) שאין צורת אות עליו כמו שנמסרה למשה מסיני אין שם אות עליו וכן בקו״ף לא מהני קריאת התינוק: (פד) יגרור. ולא מהני הפרדה בעלמא משום דהוי כחק תוכות: (פה) הרגל. פי׳ כולו בין בה״א בין בקו״ף כיון שנעשה בפיסול ועיין בבה״ל: (פו) בגג האל״ף. דאין להיו״ד העליון והתחתון ליגע בהגג אלא בדקות שבהם כמו שיתבאר לקמן במ״ב בסימן ל״ו בדיני צורת האותיות: (פז) פני האל״ף. היינו היו״ד העליון והיינו דוקא שנדבקה כולה שנפסדה צורתה אבל אם נתפשט מעט ואינו דק כראוי ליופי הכתיבה אם נשאר הפרש אין בכך כלום ואין צריך שום (לז) תיקון: (פח) להפרידה. פי׳ להפריד את הנגיעה לבדה וישאר האות ממילא כראוי: (פט) כל וכו׳. היינו שיגרור הרגל כולו ולא סגי שיפריד הרגל מעל האל״ף עד שיבטלנו מצורת אות לבד כיון שנכתב כל הרגל בפסול. וכן נדבק יו״ד שעל האל״ף בגג שתחתיו צריך לגרור כל היו״ד ולכותבו מחדש ויש שמחמירין נדבק היו״ד העליון בעת הכתיבה לגרור כל האל״ף עבור זה כי ממילא נכתב אח״כ שאר האות בפסול עי״ז אך בדיעבד נ״ע אם יש להחמיר בזה וכמו שכתבתי בבה״ל: (צ) ביוד״י. דהיינו שהיו״ד נגעה (לח) קו ישר וליכא[ב] צורת יו״ד אבל אין מזיק אם נתנגעה הקו מעט: (צא) והפ״א.

ביאור הלכה

מקשה מידי מן הר״ס אהרא״ש עי״ש. וכן מבואר בהדיא בא״העז סימן קכ״ה סעיף ט״ז בהג״ה דאף שהתינוק קורא לה״א אפ״ה יש לפסול אם לא במקום עיגון עי״ש והפר״ח מחמיר שם אפילו במקום עיגון מטעם שכתבנו וכן כתב המ״א בשם הרד״ך וכן מוכח מיו״ד בסימן רע״ו בב״י ע״ש. ואמנם אם נמצא כן בס״ת שרגל הה״א והקו״ף נגע למעלה ותינוק דלא חכים ולא טיפש קורא כתיקונה נ״ל דאין להוציא אחרת עבור זה דבאמת בדין זה יש פלוגתא דרבוותא כדמוכח להמעיין בב״י אה״ע בסי׳ קכ״ה והראיה מדמכשירין לזה במקום עיגון עי״ש א״כ לענין להוציא אחרת יש לצרף לזה דעת הרמב״ם דמכשיר לקרות בס״ת פסולה והוי ס״ס וכמו שפסק בכיוצא בזה הפמ״ג בסימן קמ״ג והדה״ח בהלכות קה״ת אבל בתפילין לא יהא אלא ספיקא וס״ד לחומרא. ודע עוד דהגר״א בביאורו מסכים לשיטת המרדכי דתליית הה״א [וכ״ש של הקו״ף כדמוכח להמעיין בו] אינו רק למצוה במקום דמנהג הסופרים לעשות החי״ת בחטוטרות וא״כ יש היכר יפה בין חי״ת לה״א ונ״ל פשוט דמה שכתב להקל הוא רק דוקא אם נוגעת רק כחוט השערה ומרחוק תמונת ה״א עליה מדתינוק קוראה ג״כ לה״א דבאמת באופן זה תמונת ה״א ולא חי״ת עליה ורק משום שלא ירחה כחי״ת דהוי בכלל חיתי״ן ההי״ן דתני בברייתא ע״ז דיגנז לכן אם עושין החי״ת בחטוטרות שוב יש היכר ג״כ לכך אין לפסול בדיעבד אבל אם נדבק רגל ה״א להגג דיבוק עב עד שנראית חי״ת ממש בודאי לא נשתנית שם ח׳ לה״א ע״י הסופרים. שוב מצאתי בעזה״י בביאור הגאון מהר״ס בנעט על המרדכי שגם הוא כתב כן בדעת המרדכי וגם התשב״ץ סובר כן והובא בב״י בא״ע בסי׳ קכ״ו ובחידושי רע״א לקמן בסימן ל״ו עי״ש. ומ״מ צ״ע אם יש לסמוך ע״ד המרדכי להקל בזה אפי׳ ע״י הפרדה אחרי שהשו״ע מחמיר בזה. ואין לדחות דהשו״ע איירי במקום דמנהג הסופרים לעשות חי״ת בלא חטוטרות דכשר בזה כמ״ש המ״א לקמן בסימן ל״ו והסכימו לזה האחרונים ולכן מחמיר שם ג״כ בא״העז בענין גט דשם אין מנהג לעשות ח׳ ע״י חטוטרות וא״כ אין היכר בין ה״א לחי״ת ולכך פסול דח״א דהרי השו״ע מחמיר אפילו בקו״ף שע״י נגיעת הרגל להגג אינו משתנה מצורתו כלל וכ״ש בזה ובמקום הדחק ואין תקנה במחיקת האות כגון שכתב שם הקודש אח״ז ובידוע שנעשה נגיעה דקה זה אחר שנגמר האות בהכשר אפשר דיש לצרף לזה דעת הסמ״ק [המובא בטור בדין נפלה טיפת דיו ע״ש] דסובר להקל בזה ע״י גרירה וצ״ע: * יגרור הרגל. עיין במ״ב במ״ש כולו וכו׳ וה״מ שנעשה הנגיעה בעת הכתיבה אבל אם נעשה לאחר הכתיבה אין דין הה״א והקו״ף שוה דבה״א צריך למחוק כל הרגל דאם ישתייר כ״ש עדיין שם ה״א הראשונה עליו להרא״ש כדאיתא בסט״ז[ג] משא״כ בהקו״ף די שיבטלנו מצורת אות. ודע עוד דמ״ש הפמ״ג בסימן ל״ו בא״א אות ח׳ עוד עצה אחרת דהיינו שיגרור קצת מהגג עד שהרגל יהיה חוץ לגג ועי״ז יתבטל צורתו ואח״כ ימשוך גג הקו״ף למעלה מהרגל דהיינו שיעשה מעט הפרש ושפיר דמי כל שאין בזה משום שלא כסדרן עכ״ד הוא איירי בנעשה הנגיעה אח״כ דאל״ה נעשה הרגל בפסול וצריך לגוררו: * נגע רגל האל״ף וכו׳. דע דאין חילוק בין אם נגע בעת הכתיבה או לאח״כ דומיא דנפלה טיפת דיו בסי״ז רק דאם נגע בעת הכתיבה צריך למחוק הרגל כולו ואם נגע אחר שהשלים האות כראוי אין צריך למחוק כל הרגל רק שיבטלנו מצורת אות דומיא דמה שכתב הלבוש והביאו המ״א סוף ס״ק כ״ה עי״ש : * או פני האל״ף וכו׳. עיין במ״א דדוקא אם נדבק עלם היו״ד להאל״ף משא״כ אם רק נגע עוקצה השמאלית של היו״ד להאל״ף כשר*דהא אפילו בלא הקוצה מיקרי יו״ד פי׳ דאף דע״י הנגיעה נחשב כאלו אין לו קוץ להיו״ד הא אין מעכב בזה לענין תיקון וכ׳ ע״ז הפמ״ג ועכ״פ גרירה בעי ודי וא״צ למחוק כל היו״ד: * יגרור כל מה שנעשה בפסול

שער הציון

(לד) ב״ח: (לה) כן מוכח מתשובת מהרי״ק סימן ל״ח דפסק הב״י כוותיה ועי״ש בשורש ע״א ועיין בב״י בריש סימן ל״ו: (לו) ח״מ וב״ש בא״ע בסי׳ קכ״ה: (לז) כנה״ג: (לח) בפמ״ג ולבו״ש:

הגהות ותיקונים: א) אכסנדרני: ב) ולית ליה: ג) בסט״ו:

letter/ (84) one should scrape off (85) the leg and write it again. It is unnecessary to scrape off the entire letter, since the roof was written in accordance with halachic /requirements/.

If the leg of the /letter/ א[20*] touches (86) the roof of the א or if (87) the front of the /letter/ א inside /touches/ the roof underneath it, /the letter/ is invalid. This cannot be remedied by scraping away (88) to separate /the strokes/, since this constitutes carving around /to form the letter/. Instead, one must scrape

Mishnah Berurah

the roof/ only a hairsbreadth, so that a child /who is neither especially intelligent nor especially simple/ knows that it is a ח, it is nevertheless necessary to scrape off the entire leg. For as long as the form of the letter /symbol/ is not the same as /the form of the letter/ which was prescribed to Mosheh (Moses) on /Mount/ Sinai, /the symbol/ is not describable as a letter.

Likewise, /where this happens/ in the case of a /letter/ ק, the reading of a child is of no avail /and the letter must therefore be corrected/.

(84) One should scrape off. Mere separation is of no avail because it is tantamount to carving around /to form the letter/.

(85) The leg. I.e., the entire /leg/, both in the case of /the letter/ ח and in the case of /the letter/ ק, because /the leg/ was formed invalidly. See the Beyur Halachah.[19]

(86) The roof of the א. For the upper and lower י /parts of the א/ may only touch the roof at their thinnest /point/, as explained below in the Mishnah Berurah, Sec. 36 in the laws concerning the form of the letters.

(87) The front of the א. I.e., the upper י /part/.

This /ruling/ only /applies/ if the entire /head of the י part/ is stuck /to the roof/, in which case the /proper/ form /of the א/ has been lost. However, if /the thigh of the י part/ has spread out a little and is not properly thin, as attractive writing /demands, then/, provided there remains a difference /between its thickness and that of the head, the fact that it has spread out/ does not matter at all and no correction is required.

(88) To separate /the strokes/. I.e., to separate the touch alone, /so that/ the letter will remain of itself with its proper /form/.

20* The letter א which is used in a Torah Scroll, *tefilin* passage or a mezuzah consists of a diagonal stroke, described as the roof, with a letter י above it and another letter י below it.

19 There the author notes that if the touch developed after the letter was written, it is then sufficient in the case of the letter ק to take off sufficient of the leg to cancel the form of the letter. He mentions a further solution which also only applies in such a case. This is to remove some of the roof of the ק, so that the leg will not be underneath the roof at all, and then to draw the roof above the leg without them touching.

(פג) הה"א והקו"ף (לג) בגג (פד) * יגרור (פה) הרגל ויחזור ויכתבנו ואין צריך לגרור כל האות כי הגג כדין נכתב. אם * נגע רגל האל"ף (פו) בגג האל"ף * או (פז) פני האל"ף בפנים בגג שתחתיה (לג) פסול ואין תקנה בגרירה (פח) להפרידה דהוי כחק תוכות אלא * יגרור (פט) **כל מה שנעשה בפיסול ויחזור ויכתבנו: הגה וכן הדין (צ) ביו"ד השי"ן והלדי"ק והעי"ן (צא) והפ"א אם נגעו בגוף האות יותר ממקום**

שערי תשובה

הרואה למהרש"פ הרבה לתמוה על מג"א מה שכתב שמותר לגרר קצת הרגל מהכ"ף המגיע לסוף הקלף ע"ש וכ' בדבר שמואל סי' פ"ט שני מתי"ן הסמוכין בתפילין שנדבקו בשעת כתיבה בתחתיתן זה לזה כאלו רגליהם רגל ישרה ואינה ניכרת עכשיו אם הוא כ"ף או מ"ת והסופר טרם שכתב אות אחר לפניו נתן לב לתקן ולהפריד ברגל האחת בדיבקו של מטה העלה שם שאע"פ שלכאורה יש לחלק בין ההיא דמהרד"ך בויי"ן שנעשו כמו חית"ן עפ"י טיפת דיו דכאן אין הדיבוק משנה אותה לאות אחרת כדינה אלא הפסיד צורת האות באופן שא"א להבחין בינה ובין חברתה מ"מ כיון שע"י הדחק אין הפרש ניכר לעין כל צריך למחוק כל רגל השני עד סוף הרגל הראשון ולחזור ולכותבו ע"ש. ועיין בתשובת דבר שמואל סי' רס"ה שכתב לחלק בין דיבק אות לחברתה משום ס"ם שמא לא נפסלה קודם שנגמר עשייתה ושמא תיקון גרירה אינו בכלל כתיבה שלא כסדרן אבל אם נודע שנדבק קודם הוי ספק פלוגתא אם הפירוד ע"י גרירה ככתיבה שלא כסדרן והמנהג שלא למחות לסופרים. ובשיי"ן שנפרדו למטה יש להסתפק אפילו אם היו הפרודין כחוט השערה ע"ש ובבר"י כתב שאם נכתבו כתיקון ואח"כ נפרדו וצורת האות ניכרת יכול לתקן ואין בזה שלא כסדרן וכ"מ מדברי הר"י אכסנדרי[א] שהביא הב"י וכ"כ היד אהרן ואף שהדב"ש מגמגם בזה נראה עיקר כמ"ש. וכתב עוד בדבר שמואל בשני תיבות על כן שנכתבו בתיבה אחת וכבר כתב להלן לא מהני מה שיגרור קצת עובי אות הלמ"ד של מלת על וקצת עובי אות הכ"ף של תיבת

באר היטב

גרירה. ואם נשתנה צורת האות על ידי הדביקות הוי כמ"ס שנסתמה. רד"ך עמ"א. ועיין ב"ח שהעלה דאם נמצא דיבוק בס"ת בקריאה דאין צריך להוציא אחרת אפילו נמצא בשבת וי"ט שא"א לגוררו מ"מ אין להוציא אחרת כיון שמעיקר הדין ס"ת יש תקנה לגוררו רק דאיסור שבת רמיא עליה וכל הראויה לבילה אין בילה וכו' ע"ש. ובשיורי כנה"ג כתב ומנהגינו דאפי' בדבוק אות לאות שנמצא בס"ת בשבת או בי"ט להוציא ס"ת אחר ע"ל סימן קמ"ג. ובספר אבן העוזר מחמיר באותיות הנדבקים בתחלת הכתיבה שאין להם תקנה בגרירה עיין שם בארוכות בס' מגיני ארץ מדפוסי פרופס: (לג) בגג. כל הסעיף זה איירי קודם שכתב אות שלאחריו דאז יש תקנה אבל אחר כך לא דהוי שלא כסדרן ודוקא שלא נשאר צורת אות בלא תיקון אז אסור לתקנה בשכתב לפניה משום דהוי שלא כסדרן אבל אם נשאר צורת אות אפי' בלא תיקון יוכל לתקנו אפילו אח"כ דכיון דצורת אות היה ניכר ליכא משום דלא כסדרן ועיין סעיף כ"ה וס"ק כ"ו מש"ש: (לג) פסול. ודוקא שנגעה היו"ד עצמה באל"ף אבל אם קוצה השמאלית של יו"ד

משנה ברורה

השערה (לד) כשר: (פג) הה"א. אף אם נדבק רק כחוט השערה (לה) באופן שהתינוק יודע שהוא ה"א אפ"ה צריך לגרור כל הרגל דכל (לו) שאין צורת אות עליו כמו שנמסרה למשה מסיני אין שם אות עליו וכן בקו"ף לא מהני קריאת התינוק: (פד) יגרור. ולא מהני הפרדה בעלמא משום דהוי כחק תוכות: (פה) הרגל. פי' כולו בין בה"א בין בקו"ף כיון שנעשה בפיסול ועיין בבה"ל: (פו) בגג האל"ף. דאין להיו"ד העליון והתחתון ליגע בהגג אלא בדקות שבהם כמו שיתבאר לקמן בגו"כ בסימן ל"ו בדיני צורת האותיות: (פז) פני האל"ף. היינו היו"ד העליון והיינו דוקא שנדבקה כולה שנפסדה צורתה אבל אם נתפשט מעט ואינו רק כראוי ליופי הכתיבה אם נשאר הפרש אין בכך כלום ואין צריך שום (לז) תיקון: (פח) להפרידה. פי' להפריד את הנגיעה לבדה וישאר האות ממילא כראוי: **(פט) כל וכו'. היינו שיגרור הרגל כולו ולא סגי שיפריד הרגל מעל האל"ף עד שיבטלנו מצורת אות לבד כיון שנכתב כל הרגל בפסול. וכן בנדבק יו"ד שעל האל"ף בגג שתחתיו צריך לגרור כל היו"ד ולכותבו מחדש ויש שמחמירין בנדבק היו"ד העליון בעת הכתיבה לגרור כל האל"ף עבור זה כי ממילא נכתב אח"כ שאר האות בפסול עי"ז אך בדיעבד צ"ע אם יש להחמיר בזה וכמו שכתבתי בבה"ל: (צ) ביוד"י. דהיינו שהיו"ד נעשה (לח) קו ישר ולית[ב] צורת יו"ד אבל אין מזיק אם נתעבה הקו מעט: (צא) והפ"א.**

ביאור הלכה

מקשה מידי מן הר"ס אהרא"ש עי"ש. וכן מבואר בהדיא באהע"ז סימן קכ"ה סעיף ט"ז בהג"ה דאף שהתינוק קורא לה"א אפ"ה יש לפסול אם לא במקום עיגון עי"ש והפר"ח מחמיר שם אפילו במקום עיגון מטעם שכתבנו וכן כתב המ"א בשם הרד"ך וכן מוכח ביו"ד בסימן רע"ו בב"י ע"ש. ואמנם אם נמצא כן בס"ת שרגל הה"א והקו"ף נגע למעלה ותינוק דלא חכים ולא טיפש קוראה כתיקונה נ"ל דאין להוציא אחרת עבור זה דבאמת בדין זה יש פלוגתא דרבוותא כדמוכח להמעיין בב"י אה"ע בסי' קכ"ה והראיה מדמכשירין לזה במקום עיגון עי"ש א"כ לענין להוציא אחרת יש לצרף לזה דעת הרמב"ס דמכשיר לקרות בס"ת פסולה והוי ס"ס וכמו שפסק בכיוצא בזה הפמ"ג בסימן קמ"ג והדה"ח בהלכות קה"ת אבל בתפילין לא יהא אלא ספיקא וס"ד לחומרא. ודע עוד דהגר"א בביאורו מסכים לשיטת המרדכי דתליית הה"א [וכ"ש של הקו"ף כדמוכח להמעיין בו] אינו רק למצוה במקום דמנהג הסופרים לעשות הח"ת בחטוטרות וא"כ יש היכר יפה בין ח"ת לה"א וכ"ל פשוט דמה שכתב להקל הוא רק דוקא אם נוגעת רק כחוט השערה ומרחוק תמונת ה"א עליה מדתינוק קוראה ג"כ לה"א דבאמת באופן זה תמונת ה"א ולא ח"ת עליה ורק משום שלא יראה כח"ת דהוי בכלל חית"ן ההי"ן דתני בברייתא ע"ז דיגנו לכן אם עושין הח"ת בחטוטרות שוב יש היכר ג"כ לכך אין לפסול בדיעבד אבל אם נדבק רגל ה"א להגג דיבוק עב עד שנראית ח"ת ממש בודאי לא נשתנית שם ח' לה"א ע"י הסופרים. שוב מצאתי בעזה"י בביאור הגאון מהר"ס בנעט על המרדכי שגם הוא כתב כן בדעת המרדכי וגם התשב"ן סובר כן והובא בב"י בא"ע בסי' קכ"ו ובחידושי רע"א לקמן בסימן ל"ו עי"ש. ומ"מ צ"ע אם יש לסמוך ע"ד המרדכי להקל בזה אפי' ע"י הפרדה אחרי שהשו"ע מחמיר בזה. ואין לדחות דהשו"ע איירי במקום דמנהג הסופרים לעשות ח"ת בלא חטוטרות דכשר בזה כמ"ש המ"א לקמן בסימן ל"ו והסכימו לזה האחרונים ולכן מחמיר שם ג"כ באהע"ז בענין גט דשם אין מנהג לעשות ח' ע"י חטוטרות וא"כ אין היכר בין ה"א לח"ת ולכך פסול דז"א דהרי השו"ע מחמיר אפילו בקו"ף שע"י נגיעת הרגל להגג אינו משתנה מצורתו כלל וכ"ש בזה ובמקום הדחק ואין תקנה במחיקת האות כגון שכתב שם הקודש אח"ז ובידוע שנעשה נגיעה דקה זה אחר שנגמר האות בהכשר אפשר דיש לצרף לזה דעת הסמ"ק [המובא בטור בדין נפלה טיפת דיו ע"ש] דסובר להקל בזה ע"י גרירה וצ"ע: * יגרור הרגל. עיין במ"ב במ"ש כולו וכו' וה"מ שנעשה הנגיעה בעת הכתיבה אבל אם נעשה לאחר הכתיבה אין דין הה"א והקו"ף שוה דבה"א צריך למחוק כל הרגל דאט ישתייר כ"ש עדיין שם ה"א הראשונה עליו להרא"ש כדאיתא בסט"ז[ג] משא"כ בהקו"ף די שיבטלנו מצורת אות. ודע עוד דמ"ש הפמ"ג בסימן ל"ו בא"א אות ח' עוד עצה אחרת דהיינו שיגרור קצת מהגג עד שהרגל יהיה חוץ לגג ועי"ז יתבטל צורתו ואח"כ ימשוך גג הקו"ף למעלה מהרגל דהיינו שיעשה מעט הפרש ושפיר דמי כל שאין בזה משום שלא כסדרן עכ"ד הוא מיירי בנעשה הנגיעה אח"כ דאל"ה נעשה הרגל בפסול וצריך לגוררו: * נגע רגל האל"ף וכו'. דע דאין חילוק בין אם נגע בעת הכתיבה או לאח"כ דומיא דנפלה טיפת דיו בסי"ז רק דאם נגע בעת הכתיבה צריך למחוק הרגל כולו ואם נגע אחר שהשלים האות כראוי אין צריך למחוק כל הרגל רק שיבטלנו מצורת אות דומיא דמה שכתב הלבוש והביאו המ"א סוף ס"ק כ"ה עי"ש: * או פני האל"ף וכו'. עיין במ"א דדוקא אם נדבק עצם היו"ד להאל"ף משא"כ אם רק נגע עוקצה השמאלית של היו"ד להאל"ף כשר*דהא אפילו בלא הקוצה מיקרי יו"ד פי' דאף דע"י הנגיעה נחשב כאלו אין לו קוץ להיו"ד הא אין מעכב בזה לענין תיקון וכ' ע"ז הפמ"ג ועכ"פ גרירה בעי ודי וא"צ למחוק כל היו"ד: * יגרור כל מה שנעשה בפסול

שער הציון

(לד) ב"ח: (לה) כן מוכח מתשובת מהרי"ק סימן ל"ח דפסק הב"י כוותיה ועי"ש בשורש ע"א ועיין בב"י בריש סימן ל"ו: (לו) ח"מ וב"ש בא"ע בסי' קכ"ה: (לז) כנה"ג: (לח) בפמ"ג ולבו"ש:

הגהות ותיקונים: א) אכסנדרני: ב) ולית ליה: ג) בסט"ו:

away **(89)** everything that was made invalidly and /then/ write it again.[21*]

Gloss: The same ruling /applies/ **(90)** *in the case of the* י */parts/ of /the letters/* ש, צ, ע **(91)** *and* פ,[22*] *if they touch the body of the letter more than at the point where they should be stuck to it. (...)*

Mishnah Berurah

(89) Everything, etc. I.e., he must scrape away the entire leg and it is not sufficient to separate the leg from the א merely until he has cancelled the /proper/ form of the letter, as the whole leg was written invalidly.

Likewise, when the י /part/ over the /letter/ א is stuck to the roof /of the א/ underneath it, one must scrape off the entire י /part/ and write it anew. There are /authorities/ who are stringent /in a case/ where the upper י /part/ got stuck to the roof at the time when it was written. /They require one/ to scrape off the entire א because of this, as it follows that the rest of the letter was subsequently written invalidly as a result of it. However, once it is after the event, study is required /to determine/ whether one should be stringent about this, as I have written in the Beyur Halachah.

(90) In the case of the י /parts/. I.e., if the י /part/ was made as a /single/ straight stroke and does not have the form of the /letter/ י. However, there is no harm if the stroke /which forms the thigh of the י part/ has thickened a little.

(91) And פ. The same ruling /also applies/ if the left leg of the /letter/ ת is made straight and does not go outwards at the bottom.

See the *Levushey Serad*, who remains in need of /further/ study /to understand/ why scraping is necessary at all /in the case of these י parts, as/ one may continue subsequently and thicken the י /part/ of the ש a little until it has the appropriate /form/. /One can act/ in this manner likewise in the case of the leg of the /letter/ ת /, if its leg was made straight/. See there. It is likewise implied by the *P.Mg.*, in the *M.Z.*, sub-Par. 20, that this solution is of avail even in the case of /a י part of the letter/ א /which was made as a single straight line/. See the final words of the *Levushey Serad.*

All this /only applies/ when one has not /yet/ written the words following it, as, otherwise, correcting the /letter/ ת and /other corrections/ of that nature will definitely be of no avail, since /the corrected letter will have been written/ in incorrect order. This is because now /, before it has been corrected, the symbol/ does not have the form of the /letter/ ת /, etc./.

21* If the touching developed after the letter was completed properly, it is unnecessary to erase the entire leg, but it is sufficient to cancel the form of the letter. (Beyur Halachah)

22* In a Torah Scroll, *tefilin* passage or mezuzah, these letters are written as follows. The letter ש consists of three י letters meeting at a base. The letter צ consists of a bent over letter נ with a letter י on its back. The letter ע has a letter י on its left. The letter פ has an inverted letter י on its left, which continues above the roof to form an inverted letter ו.

דנוקס (בית יוסף): **יט** (צב) * תבתחלת[ו] (לד) [טו] (צג) הכתיבה (צד) יאמר (צה) בפיו (צו) אני כותב לשם קדושת תפילין אמלבד זה (צז) בכל פעם שכותב אזכרה צריך לומר שכותב לשם קדושת השם: *הגה וי"א דסגי כשמחשב שכותב האזכרות לשמן הואיל והוציא (צח) בתחילת הכתיבה בפיו סגי בהכי (הרא"ש ה"ת וס"ת וטור יורה דעה וא"ח) ויש להקל (צט) בדיעבד וכשבא לנמנס לא יכתוב דאינו כותב אז בכוונה (א"ז):

ת הרא"ש בה' ס"ת סמ"ג סי' פ"ה וספר התרומה מהרי"א דגיטין כ"ד[א]
א שם

באר היטב

נוגעה בא"ף כשר דאפי' בלא הקוצה מיקרי יו"ד. עמ"א: (לד) הכתיבה. קודם שיכתוב השם יעיין בקולמוס שיטבלנו טרס שיכתוב אות אחרונה שלפני השם ויקדש הדיו באותו אות ואם צריך דיו טרס שיגמור השם אזי יטבול באותיות שלפני השם שהם לאיס ויגמור השם ואם לא הניח אות לפני השם יעיין

שערי תשובה

כן דמ"מ שלא כסדרן הוי וגם בס"ת אפשר להסתפק משום חק תוכות עיי"ש: [טו] הכתיבה. עבה"ט וכתב בגינת ורדים סימן י' וי"א בכתיבות שם הקדוש עפ"י ספר מלות[ב] שמורים יש לסמוך כי הם נובעים ממקום קדוש רבינו האר"י ז"ל ואין לגמגם מחמת שצריך לכתוב בתחלה אותיות השם חלקים נפרדים ומשתהא בכתיבתו קצת אע"ג דבכתיבה דבת אחת עדיף טפי כדמשמע ביומא ומ"מ בזה שיש צורך בכוונה לקדושת השם וגם בכתיבת אות אחת שהוא עסוק בכתיבתו אין קפידא

משנה ברורה

וה"ה אם רגל השמאלי של התי"ו נעשה ישר ולא (צט) יוצא למטה לחוץ. ועיין בלבושי שרד שנשאר בצ"ע למה צריך כלל גרירה ימשיך אח"כ ויעבה מעט את יו"ד השי"ן עד שיהיה כהוגן וכן כה"ג ברגל התי"ו עי"ש וכן משמע בפמ"ג במ"ז אות כ' דמהני עצה זו אפילו בא"ף ועיין בסוף דברי הלבושי שרד. וכ"ז כשלא כתב התיבות שא"ז דאל"ה בודאי לא מהני תיקון להתי"ו וכה"ג משום שלא כסדרן כיון שאין בו עתה צורת תי"ו: **יט** (צב) בתחלת. דאם יהיה אף אות אחת שלא נכתב לשם תפילין פסול ולא מהני העברת קולמוס לשמה [יו"ד רע"ד] ותחלת ר"ל תחלת כל הפרשיות יאמר אני כותב פרשיות אלו לשם וכו' ומהני זה מדינא אפילו אם הפסיק בין הפרשיות אך מ"מ טוב יותר שיאמר תחלת כל פרשה וכו': (צג) הכתיבה. נראה דה"ה בתיקון האותיות הנפרדות דצריך לשמן הואיל דבלא"ה התפילין הם פסולים דאין עליהם צורת אותיות כראוי: (צד) יאמר. ואם (ק) אחר כותב צריך גם הוא לומר כן אף באמצע כשהוא מתחיל: (צה) בפיו. ולא סגי במחשבה אף בדיעבד [א"ר ופמ"ג] ועיין בחידושי רע"א: (צו) אני כותב וכו'. יש שכתבו דנכון שיאמר אז ג"כ וכל אזכרות שבו לשם קדושת השם דשמא ישכח אח"כ לקדש השם במקומו ועיין בבה"ל: (צז) בכל פעם. ואם כותב ב' אזכרות בלי הפסק (קא) די בקידוש אחד: (צח) בתחילת הכתיבה. (קב) שהוא כותב לשם קדושת תפילין ואף דלא הזכיר בתחלה קדושת האזכרות סגי דמ"מ הרי הזכיר לשם קדושה אבל אם גם בתחלה לא הזכיר בפירוש רק במחשבה בעלמא או שעתה לא קידש את האזכרות אפי' במחשבה אפילו[2] (קג) בדיעבד לא יצא: (צט) בדיעבד. אבל לכתחלה צריך לומר בפירוש בכל פעם שכותב האזכרה לשם קדושת השם (קד) אפילו אם אמר בתחלת הכתיבה וכל האזכרות שבו וכן פסקו

ביאור הלכה

בפסול וכו'. עי' במ"א שכתב היינו כל מה שכתב באותו אות אחר שעשה הנגיעה. ועיין בפמ"ג שביאר דבריו לענין יו"ד העליון דאם נגע יו"ד העליון בא"ף והשלים האות אחר כך דצריך לגרור כל הא"ף ולא מהני בזה גרירת היו"ד ודקדק המ"א זה ממילת כל הכתוב בש"ע ומאד יפלא להוציא דבר חדש כזה מדקדוק קל כזה ועוד דעיקר דינו פירכא דהלא בב"י כתב וז"ל ואם נגע רגל הא"ף בגג הא"ף או פני הא"ף בפני הגג שבתחתיו כתב האגור כולן פסולין ואין תקנה במחיקה או בגרידה [כצ"ל וכן איתא בדרכי משה הארוך] שנקרא חק תוכות ומיהו בגרידה מה שנעשה בפיסול סגי כמו שכתבתי בסמוך גבי רגל ה"א וקו"ף שנוגעין למעלה עכ"ל ומוכח מפשטא דלישנא דומיהו דאתרווייהו קאי וסגי בגרירת היו"ד והרגל ודומיא דרגל ה"א וקו"ף וכן מוכח ג"כ מלשונו יותר בסימן ל"ו וז"ל שם כתב האגור דאם היה היו"ד שלמעלה על הא"ף נוגעת וכו' וכן כתב בשם ר"י אלכסנדרי וכתב עוד שם אם הדביקן שנפסלו אין די להם במחיקת דבק דהוי כחק תוכות אלא צריך לגרור כל היו"ד שנדבקה ולתקנה לכתחלה והועתק זה ג"כ בד"מ הארוך הרי דאף בדביקת היו"ד העליון די בגרירת היו"ד. וכן ממה שסיים שם בב"י בסי' ל"ו זה הדין גופא בגרירת היו"ד בנדבק יו"ד השי"ן והעיי"ן וכו' מוכח ג"כ כמו שכתבנו דלהפמ"ג צריך בזה ג"כ גרירת כל האות כמו בנדבק יו"ד שעל הא"ף. ואין לומר דמיירי הב"י בכל זה שנדבק אחר שהשלים האות כראוי דא"כ למה צריך למחוק כל היו"ד די שיגרור מקצתו עד שיבטלנו להא"ף מצורת אות וכנ"ל וכן בנגע היודי"ן בשאר אותיות וגם בלבוש כתב בהדיא דדין היו"ד העליון והתחתון שוה כמו שהביא הפמ"ג בעצמו [אם לא שנדחה[ג] גם דברי הפמ"ג[ד] ונאמר דהב"י והד"מ וגם הלבוש מיירי שכתב מתחלה את עלם האות ואח"כ היו"ד שלמעלה ובעת השלמתו נדבק בהקו העקום של הא"ף] ולולי דברי הפמ"ג היה נלענ"ד דהמ"א קאי על רגל התחתון של הא"ף ובא לבאר כונת השו"ע במה שכתב כל דהיינו שיגרור כל הרגל כיון שנכתב זה בכתיבה אחת אחר עשיית הנגיעה ולא סגי שיגרור מקצתו עד שיבטלנו להא"ף מצורת אות וה"ה בנדבק יו"ד העליון אבל עכ"פ די בגרירת כל היו"ד ואין צריך לגרור מה שנכתב אח"כ כיון שנכתב בשני כתיבות ולא חשש המ"א לבאר זה דכבר ביאר זה המחבר בתחילת הסעיף [ובפרט מה שכתב הפמ"ג בדיני צורת האותיות באות א' שהט"ז בא"ע סימן קכ"ה סובר ג"כ כהמ"א דיש חילוק בנדבק יו"ד העליון ליו"ד התחתון דהיינו רגל הא"ף וכונתו להט"ז שם בסק"י שחולק על הב"י והרמ"א בדין נפילת דיו והשלים האות ע"י כתיבה וסובר דכל אות[ה] ע"י כתיבה בעינן ולא שיעשה ממילא ומזה דייק הפמ"ג דה"ה דצריך להט"ז להחמיר גם בדין זה לענ"ד אין זה ראיה כלל דשם טעמו הוא דבעינן כל האות ע"י כתיבה ולא שיעשה ממילא משא"כ בזה דלא נעשה ממילא אפשר דדמי זה לאם היה כותב הגג והרגל ואח"כ היה כותב היו"ד ולא דמי לדלי"ת במקום רי"ש דצריך לגרור כולו דשם עשה הכל בכתיבה אחת וכמו שכתב הט"ז בס"ק י"ז משא"כ בענינינו לכאורה שתי כתיבות הם] גם בספר לדוד אמת להבעל ברכי יוסף אין מחלק בנדבק יו"ד העליון לתחתון אמנם אח"כ ראיתי עוד באיזה אחרונים שאחר הפמ"ג שנראה מדעתם ג"כ כהפמ"ג דדעת המ"א לחלק בין נדבק יו"ד העליון לתחתון ע"כ בודאי לכתחילה צריך להחמיר ולגרור כל מה שנעשה בפסול אחר שעשה הנגיעה דהיינו אפילו רגל התחתון של הא"ף וכה"ג בשאר האותיות דקחשיב פה בהג"ה ובדיעבד יש לעיין אם יש להחמיר בזה אחרי דמסתימת ל' הב"י והד"מ בסי' ל"ו והלבוש לא משמע כן וכנ"ל. ואח"כ מצאתי בחידושי רע"א שרמז לעיין בתשובת מהר"י הלוי אחיו של הט"ז ועיינתי שם ומצאתי שגם הוא פשיטא ליה דבנגיעת יודי"ן שעל האלפי"ן א"צ לגרור רגל התחתון שתחת הקו ועי"ש מה שכתב לענין יו"ד העליון אך לענין קו העקום (דהיינו מה שקורא בשו"ע גג הא"ף) סבירא ליה שם דצריך לגוררו דמיקרי שנעשה בפסול ע"י הדיבוק שנתדבק להיו"ד עי"ש אם לא היכא דכתב מתחלה את הקו העקום ורגל התחתון ואח"כ השלים ליו"ד שע"ג ונתדבק בו דאז לכו"ע אין צריך לגרור רק היו"ד דהרי הקו נכתב בכשרות. נחזור לענינינו דלכתחלה נכון לחוש להחמיר לגרור אפילו רגל התחתון ובדיעבד אם לא גרר רגל התחתון נראה דאין להחמיר ולענין קו העקום יש לעיין דלכאורה מסתימת לשון הב"י והד"מ והלבוש הנ"ל משמע דהיו"ד צריך למחוק ולא הקו וצ"ע למעשה: * **בתחלת וכו'**. עיין במ"ב במה שכתב דנכון שיאמר וכל אזכרות שבו כן כתב הט"ז ביו"ד רע"ד[ו] ס"א הביאו הפמ"ג בפה וכתב דלכתחלה גם הט"ז מודה דצריך בכל פעם לקדש אזכרה אף דקידש בתחלת הכתיבה ולא מועיל זה אלא לענין דיעבד. ולפלא שלא הביא דהל"ח בהלכות ס"ת פליג וסובר דאפילו דיעבד לא מהני ועיין בברכי יוסף ביו"ד רע"ד[ו] שמחמיר בזה. ועכ"פ נ"ל דאם יש לו ספק באיזה שם אי קידש או לא ויודע שבתחלת הכתיבה אמר וכל אזכרות שבו דיש להקל עיין בפמ"ג שמסתפק על הקידוש אי היא דאורייתא או דרבנן ואפילו לדעת הדבר שמואל הובא שם בברכי יוסף דס"ל דמה שצריך לקדש האזכרות לשמן הוא דאורייתא עכ"פ יש לצרף דעת הט"ז לזה ולהקל בזה כן נלענ"ד:

אז

שער הציון

(צט) בפמ"ג ולבו"ש: (ק) פשוט: (קא). (קב). (קג). (קד) הכל בפמ"ג:

הגהות ותיקונים: א) כ"ד: ב) מצת: ג) צ"ל שנדחוק: ד) להשמיט תיבות, גם דברי הפמ"ג: ה) האות: ו) רע"ו:

הערות והארות: 1) עיין במ"ב ס"ק כ"ה לענין אם נמשך כמה ימים: 2) עיין במ"ב ס"ק כ"ד ובסי' י"א ס"ק ד' ובבה"ל סי' י"ד ס"ב ד"ה בלי כוונה, לענין לשמה במחשבה:

19. **(92)** At the beginning **(93)** of the writing **(94)** /the scribe/ should say **(95)** with his mouth, **(96)** "I am writing for the sake of the holiness of *tefilin*". Apart from this, **(97)** every time that he writes a Divine Name, he must say that he is writing for the sake of the holiness of the Name.

Gloss: There are /authorities/ who say that it is sufficient if he thinks /mentally/ that he is writing the Divine Names for the sake of /the holiness of the Name/. /According to them,/ since he expressed /the purpose of his writing/ with his mouth **(98)** *at the beginning of the writing, this is sufficient. (...)* **(99)** *Once it is after the event one may be lenient.*

When one is drowsy he should not write /the passages/, as then he will not be writing with intent. (...)

Mishnah Berurah

(92) At the beginning. /This is/ because if there will be even one letter which was not written for the sake of /the holiness of/ *tefilin*, /the passage/ will be invalid. Passing a quill /over the letters subsequently/ for the sake of /the holiness of *tefilin*/ will be of no avail. [*Yo.D.* /, Sec./ 274]

By "at the beginning", /the Shulchan Aruch/ means that at the beginning /of the writing/ of all the passages /the scribe/ should say, "I am writing these passages for the sake, etc." This is of avail halachically, even if he makes an interruption between /the writing of/ the passages. However, it is nevertheless better for him to say at the beginning of each passage /, "I am writing this passage/, etc."

(93) Of the writing. It appears /logical/ that, correspondingly, the correction of separate letters is also required /to be done/ for the sake of /the holiness of *tefilin*/. For if they are not /corrected/ the *tefilin* /passage/ will be invalid, as the letters /concerned/ do not have the proper form.

(94) /The scribe/ should say. If someone else writes /part of the passages/, he must also say this when he begins /writing/, even /though he starts writing/ in the middle /of a passage/.

(95) With his mouth. It is not enough to think /this in one's mind/. Even once it is after the event /mere thought is not ruled to have been of avail/. [*E.R.* and *P.Mg.*] See the *Chidushey* Rabbi Akiva Eiger.

(96) "I am writing, etc." There are /authorities/ who write that it is correct /practice/ to say then in addition, "and /am writing/ all the Divine Names in /the passages/ for the sake of the holiness of the Name". /The reason is/ that one may forget subsequently to sanctify a name at the point where /he writes/ it. See the Beyur Halachah.[20]

(97) Every time. If one writes two Divine Names without an interruption, one sanctification is sufficient.

(98) At the beginning of the writing. /I.e.,/ that he is writing for the sake of the holiness of *tefilin*. /In their opinion/ this is enough even if he did not mention the holiness of the Divine Names at the beginning, since he at any rate specified /that he is writing/ for the sake of holiness.

However, if even at the beginning /the scribe/ did not specify explicitly /with his mouth that he was writing for the sake of the holiness of *tefilin*, but/ only /had this/ merely in mind, or if he did /specify this then explicitly, but did/ not sanctify the Divine Names even mentally /when he actually wrote them/, he is not /ruled to have/ fulfilled /his obligation/, although it is now after the event.

(99) Once it is after the event. However, initially, every time one writes a Divine Name, he must say explicitly /with his mouth that he is doing so/ for the sake of the holiness of the Name. This even /applies/ if he said at the beginning of the writing /that he is writing for the sake of the holiness of *tefilin*/ and /is writing/ all the Divine Names in /the passages for the sake of the holiness of the Name/. The Acharonim in fact rule /accordingly/.

20 The author states there that this addition at the beginning is only of avail once it is after the event. He rules that one should not rely on the addition in a case when he is in doubt as to whether or not he sanctified any Divine Name at the time when he wrote it.

כ [ב]צריך לדקדק בחסרות ויתרות שאם (ק) חסר * או יתר (קא) אות אחת פסולים ונמצאו המניחים אותם מברכים בכל יום ברכה לבטלה וגם שרוי בכל יום בלא מצות תפילין ונמצא עונש הסופר (קב) מרובה לכן צריך להיות מאוד ירא שמים (קג) וחרד לדבר השם המתעסק בכתיבת תפילין ותיקונן: **כא** [ג]כל פרשה אחר שיכתבנה (קד) יקראנה היטב בכוונה ודקדוק פעמים ושלש ויחזור ויקראנה קודם שיתננה בתוך ביתה כדי שלא תתחלף פרשה בפרשה: **כב** [ד]טוב לנסות הקולמוס (קה) קודם שיתחיל לכתוב הפרשה שלא יהא עליו דיו יותר מדאי ויפסיד וכן יזהר קודם שיכתוב כל שם לקרות כל (קו) מה שכתב כדי שלא יבאו[ב] לידי גניזה (קז) על ידו: **כג** [ה]אם מצא שחסר אות אחת * אין לו (קח) תקנה שאם כן היו כתובין שלא כסדרן ופסולין משום דכתיב והיו (קט) בהוייתן יהו * ואם יתר (קי) אות אחת יש לו תקנה על ידי (קיא) שיגרור אותה אם היא בסוף תיבה או בתחלתה [ו]אבל אם היא באמצע תיבה לא משום דכשיגרור יהיה (קיב) נראה כשתי (לה) [טז] תיבות: **כד** [ז]מותר לכתוב על

ב הרא"ש בספר תקון תפילין וכתיבתן ג הר"י אלכסנדריא[א] ד שם ה טור בשם מכילתין והרמב"ם פרק א' מהלכות תפילין והר"י אלכסנדריא[א] וספר א"ח ו הר"י אלכסנדריא[א] ז הרמב"ם וסא"ח בשם ר' יונה

שערי תשובה

בזה וגם אין חילוק אם יתחיל מסופה לתחלתה כו' ע"ש: [טז] תיבות. עבה"ט ועיין בדבר שמואל סימן שנ"ד שהביא דברי הב"י והרמב"ם ומבואר בדבריו במלת לאבותיך אם בא למחוק הוא"ו והמיותרת אפשר שצריך למחוק [נ"ל למשוך] בתחלה הבי"ת הקודמת לה הגג והתחתית שתהיה סמוכה להתי"ו והוא"ו תבא אל תוכה ואז ימחקנה להוא"ו. אבל אם ימחוק קודם מיד יפסול משום שתיבת לאבותיך יהיה

באר היטב

אם יש אות או תג שצריכה דיו כדי שיקדש הדיו קודם שיכתוב השם ב"ש מ"א. וסדר כתיבת השם דרך סוד עיין בעטרת זקנים ובגינת ורדים חא"ח כלל ב' סי' יו"ד וי"א: (לה) תיבות. כתב הב"י בשם הריא"ם דלפעמים תיקון מהני ליתר אות כגון לאבותיך מלא בוי"ו שאחר

ביאור הלכה

או יתר אות אחת. ואם אות היתר לא היה מחובר לשום תיבה רק שעמד בין תיבה לתיבה או בין השיטין אם נפסל התפילין משום זה עיין בנו"ב חיו"ד ח"א בסי' ע"ד שמקיל בזה והשער אפרים בשער ה' בפ"ש חולק עליו ומסכים עם רש"ל שמחמיר בזה: * אין לו תקנה. עיין במ"ב דאל"ה יגרוד וכו' ר"ל דמתחלה יגרוד ואח"כ יכתוב מה שחסר ממנו ולהלן דאל"ה ל"ע כיון דבעת הכתיבה לא נכתב כסדרן*): * ואם יתר וכו'. עי' במ"ב בשם הפמ"ג לענין תיבה כפולה דלפעמים טוב יותר למחוק הראשונה כדי לחוש אף לדעת ר"ת עי"ש ועי"ש עוד במ"ז סק"כ

משנה ברורה

האחרונים: **כ** (ק) חסר או יתר. אפילו אם התיבה לא נשתנה לקריאתה בזה כגון במלא וחסר וכדלקמן: (קא) אות אחת. ואפילו אם קוצו של יו"ד חסר מעכב כדאיתא מנחות כ"ט א': (קב) מרובה. מלבד עון גזל החמור: (קג) וחרד לדבר השם. ראיתי להעתיק פה לשון הלבוש הצריך מאד לענינינו דז"ל ולא כמו שעושין עכשיו כמה סופרים שמניחין נערים המתלמדין לכתוב תפילין כדי שירגילום בכתב ואח"כ רואה הסופר אם נכתבו כהלכתן בחסירותן ויתירותן וסגי ליה בהכי ואח"כ מניחין אותן בבתים ומוכרין אותם ומחשבין להם הסופרים אותן המעות בשכר הלימוד להנער ומראים להם פני היתר לומר הרי אנו בזה כגומלי חסדים עם הנערים העניים ללמוד להם מלאכת הכתיבה בחנם והיא מלאכת ה' אבל אני אומר יצא שכרם בהפסדם ואדרבה לא טוב המה עושים בעמם כי הנער נער ואין יודע בין ימינו לשמאלו ואין לו שום כונה בעולם רק הם כמתעסקים בכתיבה ליפות הכתב ולא לשום קדושה ושום כונת מצוה בעולם והרי עונש הסופר מרובה מאד שמכשיל את הבריות שמניחין אותן התפילין הפסולין [וכדלעיל בסעיף י"ט] ולא עוד כדי להשביח את מקחו יאמר הסופר לכל אני כתבתים ובכוונה כתבתים וכו' וכל העושין כן בודאי עתידין ליתן את הדין ולקבל עונשין הרבה מאוד ועליהם נאמר ארור עושה מלאכת ה' רמיה ע"כ יזהר כל סופר ויתרחק מזה וטוב לו דלשמן האמור אלא תפילין אין הכונה לשם בעל התפילין כמו גבי גט דצריך לשם האיש והאשה רק לשם קדושת תפילין עי"ש וקיים ע"ז ומן הראוי למי שיש כח בידו למנות כותבי תפילין מהוגנים אנשי אמת שונאי בצע בעלי תורה יראי אלקים וחרדים על דברו בכל עיר כמו שממנים שוחטים ובודקים שלא יאמינו לכל הסופרים שאין כוונתם אלא להרויח ממון ע"י כתיבה ותיקון יפה בעשיית התפילין ואף כי גם כוונה זו טובה היתה לייפות המצוה בנויה זה דוקא אם היה להם כוונה קדושה ג"כ אבל בזה אינם נזהרים ודי בזה עכ"ל הטהור. וכתב בספר ב"ש יכתוב אותיות טובים ותמימות ולא שבורות ובמתון ובכוונה גדולה ולא ימהר אדם בכתיבתו כדי להרויח ממון הרבה כי אותו ריוח ילך לאיבוד ולדיראון ויפסיד נשמתו כי הוא מחטיא את הרבים וכל מי שכותב תפילין טובים וכשרים כפי יכולתו שכרו כפול ומכופל וניצול מדינה של גיהנם. וכתב בס"ח סי' פ"ה[ג] ולדקתו עומדת לעד זה המזכה רבים כגון המלמד לירא השם תיקון תפילין לתקן לאחרים ועיין בסימן ל"ט מתי אדם ראוי לכתוב תפילין: **כא** (קד) יקראנה היטב. שאם ימצא איזה אות חסר באיזה פרשה לא היא לבדה נפסלה אלא גם כל מה שאחריה משום שיהיו שלא כסדרן וכדלעיל בריש הסימן: **כב** (קה) קודם שיתחיל. אינו ר"ל בתחלת הפרשה דוקא אלא (קה) קודם שיתחיל לכתוב בהפרשה: (קו) מה שכתב. באותה (קו) פרשה ולא שלפניה: (קז) על ידו. וכשטובל הקולמוס לכתוב בו את השם (קז) לא יתחיל לכתוב אותו מיד שלא יפסידנו ברבוי דיו או אולי יש עליו שער ולא יצא הכתב מיושר וגם משום שצריך (קח) לקדש הדיו שעל הקולמוס טרם שיכתוב השם לכן יכוין להניח אות אחת מלכתוב קודם השם ובאותו אות יתחיל לכתוב ואם לא עשה כן יתפש אחר אות או תג שצריכה דיו וימלאנה וכותב את השם ואם צריך דיו קודם שיגמור השם או יטבול באותיות שלפני השם שהם לחים עדיין ויגמור השם אבל לא יטבול באותיות השם עצמן (קט) ויש מקילין לטבול באותיות השם עצמן דבזיון ליכא כיון שהוא כדי להשלים בו את השם. ואם האותיות שלפניו אינם לחין אזי יטבול מחדש ויתפש אחר אות או תג שצריכין דיו וכנ"ל וכ"ז הוא למצוה ולא לעיכובא בדיעבד: **כג** (קח) תקנה. בהשלמה ומיירי שמכאן עד סוף הפ' יש שמות שאינם נמחקין דאל"ה יגרוד עד סופה: (קט) בהויתן יהו. פי' כסדר שנכתבות בתורה יהיו כתובין: (קי) אות אחת. ואם כתב (קי) תיבה יתירה יגררנה ויוכל להניח המקום חלק [אם אין לו אותיות מהתיבות שלפניה שיהיה יוכל להמשיכן במקום ההוא] ואין (קיא) החלק פוסל כל שאין במקומו כשיעור הריוח שבין פרשה לפרשה שהוא כדי ט' אותיות. ולפעמים יש תקנה אפילו בזה כגון שיכול להמשיך האות מן התיבה שלפניה כדי למעט הריוח של ט' אותיות. ויותר מזה דבאופן זה שיפסל התפילין מחמת הריוח או אפילו אם בסיום התיבה שלפניה (קיב) יש שם ה"א או קו"ף יוכל להמשיך גגן כדי למעט הריוח ואע"פ שע"י ההמשכה לא יהיה הרגל של הה"א והקו"ף בסופה אין קפידא בדיעבד. וכתב הפמ"ג דבתיבה כפולה טוב יותר למחוק השניה דתיבה הראשונה כדין נכתב. ואם קודם הראשונה יש אות שיכול למושכו טוב יותר שימחוק תיבה הראשונה כדי לחוש אף לדעת ר"ת דשיעור פרשה הוא ג' אותיות: (קיא) שיגרור. ולא מיפסל הפרשה משום חק תוכות כיון שאינו עושה מעשה בגוף התיבות והאותיות: (קיב) נראה כב' תיבות. ופעמים שתיקון מועיל ע"י שיגררנה וימשיך

*) שוב ראיתי שז"א וראיה מק"ש לקמן בסימן ס"ד ס"א בבה"ל ד"ה בד"א עי"ש:

שער הציון

(קה) א"ר ול"ח: (קו) א"ר: (קז) יו"ד רע"ו ס"ד: (קח) ב"ש: (קט) ש"ך יו"ד רע"ד הובא בפמ"ג: (קי) מ"א: (קיא) מ"א: (קיב) מ"א:

הלות

הגהות ותיקונים: א) אכסנדרני: **ב)** יבואו: **ג)** ס"ה:

20. One must be meticulous about /letters/ which are left out and /letters/ which are /written/ in full. For if one **(100)** leaves out or adds **(101)** a single letter /in deviation from the traditional lettering of the passages/, they are invalid.

It follows that /if one did deviate in this manner/, those /people/ who don /the *tefilin* which contain/ the /passages/ involved make a vain blessing every day and, in addition, they dwell each day without /having fulfilled/ the mitzvah of *tefilin*. Thus the punishment /due to/ the scribe /who wrote them/ **(102)** is severe.

Therefore, a person who engages in the writing /of passages/ of *tefilin* or their correction must be very Heaven fearing **(103)** and anxious for the word of *Ha-Sheym* /to be fulfilled/.

Mishnah Berurah

(100) Leaves out or adds. /This applies/ even if the reading of the word is unchanged by this. For example, /it applies in the case of vowel letters which are sometimes written/ in full and /sometimes/ left out, as /explained/ below.

(101) A single letter. Even if /only/ the tip of a /letter/ י /, which forms its right leg,/ is lacking, this precludes /the passage being ruled as valid/, as stated in *Menachos* 29a.

(102) Is severe. /I.e.,/ apart from /the fact that this involves/ the grave iniquity of robbery.

(103) And anxious for the word of *Ha-Sheym*. I felt /that it is desirable/ to quote here the wording of the *Levush*. It is very necessary /to note what he writes, because of its relevance/ to the matter /discussed/ here.

This is his wording: "One should not /act/ as several scribes do nowadays. They leave youths who are training /to write/ to write *tefilin* /passages/, in order to get them accustomed to write. Afterwards, the scribes inspect /them to see/ whether they are written in conformance with the halachah, as regards /the letters/ which are /required to be/ left out and /the letters/ which are /required to be written/ in full, and they satisfy themselves with that. They subsequently place /the passages/ in the /*tefilin*/ housings and sell them. The scribes credit the youths with the money /received towards the payment/ of their tuition fees. In justification, they adopt the argument that they thus practice kindness towards the poor youths by teaching them the art of writing, which is work for *Ha-Sheym*, without charge. However, I say that their gain is offset by their loss and, on the contrary, they act improperly towards their fellowmen. For a youth is /merely/ a youth and cannot distinguish between his right and his left. He has no intent whatever /when he writes/. He merely engages in the writing /wishing/ to beautify the script, but not for /the sake of/ any holiness or any mitzvah intent at all. It follows that the punishment /due/ to the scribe is extremely severe, as the people who don those invalid *tefilin* will stumble because of him [as /follows from what is stated/ above in Par. 19]. Furthermore, in order to boost his commodity, the scribe will tell everyone that he wrote /the passages himself/ and he wrote them with /the correct/ intent, etc. Whoever does this is definitely destined to face judgment and receive very severe punishment. /The verse,/ 'Cursed is he who does the work of *Ha-Sheym* deceitfully,'[21] is applicable to such /a

21 *Yirmeyahu* 48:10.

כ בצריך לדקדק בחסרות ויתרות שאם (ק) חסר * או יתר (קא) אות אחת פסולים ונמצאו המניחים אותם מברכים בכל יום ברכה לבטלה וגם שרוי בכל יום בלא מצות תפילין ונמצא עונש הסופר (קב) מרובה לכן צריך להיות מאוד ירא שמים (קג) וחרד לדבר השם המתעסק בכתיבת תפילין ותיקונן: **כא** גכל פרשה אחר שיכתבנה (קד) יקראנה היטב בכוונה ודקדוק פעמים ושלש ויחזור ויקראנה קודם שיתננה בתוך ביתה כדי שלא תתחלף פרשה בפרשה: **כב** דטוב לנסות הקולמוס (קה) קודם שיתחיל לכתוב הפרשה שלא יהא עליו דיו יותר מדאי ויפסיד וכן יזהר קודם שיכתוב כל שם לקרות כל (קו) מה שכתב כדי שלא יבאו[ב] לידי גניזה (קז) על ידו: **כג** האם מצא שחסר אות אחת * אין לו (קח) תקנה שאם כן היו כתובין שלא כסדרן ופסולין משום דכתיב והיו (קט) בהוייתן יהו * ואם יתר (קי) אות אחת יש לו תקנה על ידי (קיא) שיגרור אותה אם היא בסוף תיבה או בתחלתה ואבל אם היא באמצע תיבה לא משום דכשיגרור יהיה (קיב) נראה כשתי (לה) [טז] תיבות: **כד** ומותר לכתוב על

באר הגולה

ב הרא"ש בספר תקון תפילין וכתיבתן
ג הר"י אלכסנדריא[א]
ד שם ה טור בשם מכילתין והרמב"ם פרק א' מהלכות תפילין והר"י אלכסנדריא[א] וספר א"ח
ו הר"י אלכסנדריא[א]
ז הרמב"ם וסא"ח בשם ר' יונה

שערי תשובה

בזה וגם אין חילוק אם יתחיל מסופה לתחלתה כו' ע"ש: [טז] תיבות. עבה"ט ועיין בדבר שמואל סימן שנ"ד שהביא דברי הב"י והרמב"ם ומבואר בדבריו במלת לאבותיך אם בא למחוק הוא"ו והמיותרת אפשר שצריך למחוק [צ"ל למשוך] בתחלה הבי"ת הקודמת לה הגג והתחתית שתהיה סמוכה להתי"ו והוא"ו תבא אל תוכה ואז ימחקנה להוא"ו. אבל אם ימחוק קודם מיד יפסול משום שתיבת לאבותיך יהיה

באר היטב

אם יש אות או תג שצריכה דיו כדי שיקדש הדיו קודם שיכתוב השם ב"ש מ"א. וסדר כתיבת השם דרך סוד עיין בעטרת זקנים ובגינת ורדים חא"ח כלל ב' סי' יו"ד וי"א: (לה) תיבות. כתב הב"י בשם הריא"ם דלפעמים תיקון מהני ליתר אות כגון לאבותיך מלא בוי"ו שאחר

ביאור הלכה

או יתר אות אחת. ואם אות היתר לא היה מחובר לשום תיבה רק שעמד בין תיבה לתיבה או בין השיטין אם נפסל התפילין משום זה עיין בנו"ב חיו"ד ח"א בסי' ע"ד שמקיל בזה והשער אפרים בשער ה' בפ"ש חולק עליו ומסכים עם רש"ל שמחמיר בזה: * אין לו תקנה. עיין במ"ב דאל"ה יגרוד וכו' ר"ל דמתחלה יגרוד ואח"כ יכתוב מה שחסר ממנו ולהלן דאל"ה ל"ע כיון דבעת הכתיבה לא נכתב כסדרן*): * ואם יתר וכו'. עי' במ"ב בשם הפמ"ג לענין תיבה כפולה דלפעמים טוב יותר למחוק הראשונה כדי לחוש אף לדעת ר"ת עי"ש ועי"ש עוד במ"ז סק"כ

משנה ברורה

האחרונים: כ (ק) חסר או יתר. אפילו אם התיבה לא נשתנה לקריאתה בזה כגון מלא וחסר וכדלקמן: (קא) אות אחת. ואפילו אם קוצו של יו"ד חסר מעכב כדאיתא מנחות כ"ט א': (קב) מרובה. מלבד עון גזל המתור: (קג) וחרד לדבר השם. ראיתי להעתיק פה לשון הלבוש הצריך מאד לענינינו דז"ל ולא כמו שעושין עכשיו כמה סופרים שמניחין נערים המתלמדין לכתוב תפילין כדי שירגילום בכתב ואח"כ רואה הסופר אם נכתבו כהלכתן בחסירותן ויתירותן וסגי ליה בהכי ואח"כ מניחין אותן בבתים ומוכרין אותם ומתכוין להם הסופרים אותן המעות בשכר הלימוד להנער ומראים להם פני היתר לומר הרי אנו בזה כגומלי חסדים עם הנערים העניים ללמוד להם מלאכת הכתיבה בחנם והיא מלאכת ה' אבל אני אומר יצא שכרם בהפסדם ואדרבה לא טוב המה עושים בעתם כי הנער נער ואין יודע בין ימינו לשמאלו ואין לו שום כונה בעולם רק הם כמתעסקים בכתיבה ליפות הכתב ולא לשום קדושה ושום כונת מצוה בעולם והרי עונש הסופר מרובה מאד שמכשיל את הבריות שמניחין אותן התפילין הפסולין [וכדלעיל בסעיף י"ט] ולא עוד כדי להשביח את מקחו יאמר הסופר לכל אני כתבתים ובכוונה כתבתים וכו' וכל העושין כן מודאי עתידין ליתן את הדין ולקבל עונשן הרבה מאוד ועליהם נאמר ארור עושה מלאכת ה' רמיה ע"כ יזהר כל סופר ויתרחק מזה וטוב לו דלשמן האמור אצל תפילין אין הכונה לשם בעל התפילין כמו גבי גט דצריך לשם האיש והאשה רק לשם קדושת תפילין עי"ש וסיים ע"ז ומן הראוי למי שיש כח בידו למנות כותבי תפילין מהוגנים אנשי אמת שונאי בצע בעלי תורה יראי אלקים וחרדים על דברו בכל עיר כמו שממנים שוחטים ובודקים שלא יאמינו לכל הסופרים שאין כוונתם אלא להרויח ממון ע"י כתיבה ותיקון יפה בעשיית התפילין ואף כי גם כוונה זו טובה היתה לייפות המצוה בנוייה זה דוקא אם היה להם כוונה קדושה ג"כ אבל בזה אינם נזהרים ודי בזה עכ"ל הטהור. וכתב בספר ב"ש יכתוב אותיות טובים ותמימות ולא שבורות ובמתון ובכוונה גדולה ולא ימהר אדם בכתיבתה כדי להרויח ממון הרבה כי אותו ריוח ילך לאיבוד ולדיראון ויפסיד נשמתו כי הוא מחטיא את הרבים וכל מי שכותב תפילין טובים וכשרים כפי יכולתו שכרו כפול ומכופל וניצול מדינה של גיהנם. וכתב בס"ח סי' פ"ה[ג] ולדקתו עומדת לעד זה המזכה רבים כגון המלמד לירא השם תיקון תפילין לתקן לאחרים ועיין בסימן ל"ט מתי אדם ראוי לכתוב תפילין: **כא** (קד) יקראנה היטב. שאם ימצא איזה אות חסר באיזה פרשה לא היא לבדה נפסלה אלא גם כל מה שאחריה משום שיהיו שלא כסדרן וכדלעיל בריש הסימן: **כב** (קה) קודם שיתחיל. אינו ר"ל בתחלת הפרשה דוקא אלא (קה) קודם שיתחיל לכתוב בהפרשה: (קו) מה שכתב. באותה (קו) פרשה ולא שלפניה: (קז) על ידו. וכשטובל הקולמוס לכתוב בו את השם (קו) לא יתחיל לכתוב אותו מיד שלא יפסידנו ברבוי דיו או אולי יש עליו שער ולא יצא הכתב מיושר וגם משום שצריך (קח) לקדם הדיו שעל הקולמוס טרם שיכתוב השם לכן יכוין להניח אות אחת מלכתוב קודם השם ובאותו אות יתחיל לכתוב ואם לא עשה כן יתפס אחר אות או תג שצריכה דיו וימלאנה וכותב את השם ואם צריך דיו קודם שיגמור השם אז יטבול באותיות שלפני השם שהם לחים עדיין ויגמור השם אבל לא יטבול באותיות השם עצמן (קט) ויש מקילין לטבול באותיות השם עצמן דבזוי ליכא כיון שהוא כדי להשלים בו את השם. ואם האותיות שלפניו אינם לחין אזי יטבול מחדש ויתפס אחר אות או תג שצריכין דיו וכל"ז הוא למצוה ולא לעיכובא בדיעבד: **כג** (קח) תקנה. בהשלמה ותיירי שמכאן עד סוף הפ' יש שמות שאינם נמחקין דאל"ה יגרוד עד סופה: (קט) בהויתן יהו. פי' כסדר שנכתבות בתורה יהיו כתובין: (קי) אות אחת. ואם כתב (קי) תיבה יתירה יגררנה ויוכל להניח המקום חלק [אם אין לו אותיות מהתיבות שלפניה שיהיה יוכל להמשיכן במקום הפנוי] ואין (קיא) החלק פוסל כל שאין במקומו כשיעור הריוח שבין פרשה לפרשה שהוא כדי ט' אותיות. ולפעמים יש תקנה אפילו בזה כגון שיכול להמשיך האות מן התיבה שלפניה כדי למעט הריוח של ט' אותיות. ויותר מזה דבאופן זה שיפסל התפילין מחמת הריוח אז אפילו אם בסיום התיבה שלפניה (קיב) יש שם ה"א או קו"ף יוכל להמשיך גגן כדי למעט הריוח ואע"פ שע"י ההמשכה לא יהיה הרגל של הה"א והקו"ף בסופה אין קפידא בדיעבד. וכתב הפמ"ג דבתיבה כפולה טוב יותר למחוק השניה דתיבה הראשונה כדין נכתב. ואם קודם הראשונה יש אות שיכול למושכו טוב יותר שימחוק תיבה הראשונה כדי לחוש אף לדעת ר"ת דשיעור פרשה הוא ג' אותיות: (קיא) שיגרור. ולא מיפסל הפרשה משום חק תוכות כיון שאינו עושה מעשה בגוף התיבות והאותיות: (קיב) נראה כב' תיבות. ופעמים שתיקון מועיל ע"י שיגררנה וימשיך

*) שוב ראיתי שז"א וראיה מק"ש לקמן בסימן ס"ד ס"א בבה"ל ד"ה בד"א עי"ש:

שער הציון

(קה) א"ר ול"ח: (קו) א"ר: (קז) יו"ד רע"ו ס"ד: (קח) ב"ש: (קט) ש"ך יו"ד רע"ד הובא בפמ"ג: (קי) מ"א: (קיא) מ"א: (קיב) מ"א:

הגהות ותיקונים: א) אכסנדרני: ב) יבואו: ג) ס"ה:

21. Each passage **(104)** must be read well two or three times with application and meticulous /care/, after it has been written. One must read /the passage/ again before he puts it inside its housing, so that one passage will not be interchanged with another.
22. It is desirable to test the quill **(105)** before one begins to write the passage, so that it should not have too much ink on it and spoil /the letter/.

Mishnah Berurah

person/. Consequently, every scribe should avoid and shun such /behavior/ and /then/ it will be well for him. /One must bear in mind/ that the requirement that *tefilin* must be /prepared/ for the sake of /, etc./ does not mean /that they must be prepared/ for the sake of the owner of the *tefilin*, as /is the case/ with a letter of divorce, which must be /written/ for the sake of the husband and the wife /involved/. /What is meant is/ solely /that they must be prepared/ for the sake of the holiness of *tefilin*". See there.

/The *Levush*/ concludes after this: "It is proper for someone who has the power in his hands /to do so/, to appoint writers of *tefilin* /passages/ in every city who are respectable and trustworthy, hate corruption, possess Torah /knowledge/, are God fearing and are anxious for the word of /*Ha-Sheym* to be fulfilled/, just as /these qualities are sought when/ one appoints slaughterers and examiners /of the slaughtered animals/. One should not have faith in all scribes, as /there are scribes who/ only intend to earn money through beautiful writing and production in the preparation of the *tefilin*. Although this intention, which /promotes/ beautification of /the performance of/ the mitzvah by /making/ attractive /*tefilin* available/, is also desirable, it is only /of value/ if /the scribes/ have intent for holiness as well. However, as regards /this latter intention/ they are not careful. These /remarks/ should be sufficient /to teach one to be careful when he purchases *tefilin*/."

This is his commendable wording.

It is stated in the work *B.Sh.*, "One should write letters which are good, whole and not broken. /He should also write/ with patience and with intense intent. A person should not hurry when he writes /the passages/, in order to earn a lot of money, as the profit /from/ this will become a loss and /cause him/ disgrace and he will forfeit his soul, as he will /thereby/ cause many /people/ to sin. Whoever writes good and valid *tefilin* /passages/ in accordance with his ability will have his reward doubled and redoubled and will be delivered from the visitation of *Geyhinom*."

It is stated in the *S.Ch.*, Par. 65 /with reference to the verse/, "And his righteousness will last forever,"[22] that /the verse refers/ to someone who benefits the many, such as a person who teaches those who fear *Ha-Sheym* how to produce *tefilin*, so that they should prepare them for others.

See Sec. 39, /as to/ when a person is /regarded as/ fit to write *tefilin* /passages/.

(104) Must be read well. For if some letter is found to be missing in any passage /and is added later/, not only /that passage/ will be invalid, but also every /passage/ that follows it. This is because /all that follows/ will have been /written/ in incorrect order. This conforms with what is /ruled/ above at the beginning of the section.

(105) Before one begins. /The Shulchan Aruch/ does not mean /that one must do so/ specifically at the beginning of the passage,

22 *Tehilim* 111:3; 112:3.

כ [ב]צריך לדקדק בחסרות ויתרות שאם (ק) חסר * או יתר (קא) אות אחת פסולים ונמצאו המניחים אותם מברכים בכל יום ברכה לבטלה וגם שרוי בכל יום בלא מצות תפילין ונמצא עונש הסופר (קב) מרובה לכן צריך להיות מאוד ירא שמים (קג) וחרד לדבר השם המתעסק בכתיבת תפילין ותיקונן: **כא** [ג]כל פרשה אחר שיכתבנה (קד) יקראנה היטב בכוונה ודקדוק פעמים ושלש ויחזור ויקראנה קודם שיתנגה בתוך ביתה כדי שלא תתחלף פרשה בפרשה: **כב** [ד]טוב לנסות הקולמוס (קה) קודם שיתחיל לכתוב הפרשה שלא יהא עליו דיו יותר מדאי ויפסיד **וכן יזהר קודם שיכתוב כל שם לקרות כל (קו) מה שכתב כדי שלא יבאו[ב] לידי גניזה (קז) על ידו: כג [ה]אם מצא שחסר אות אחת * אין לו (קח) תקנה שאם כן היו כתובין שלא כסדרן ופסולין משום דכתיב והיו (קט) בהוייתן יהו** * ואם יתר (קי) אות אחת יש לו תקנה על ידי (קיא) שיגרור אותה אם היא בסוף תיבה או בתחלתה [ו]אבל אם היא באמצע תיבה לא משום דכשיגרור יהיה (קיב) נראה כשתי (לה) [טז] תיבות: **כד** [ז]מותר לכתוב על

באר הגולה

ב הרא"ש בספר תקון תפילין וכתיבתן
ג הר"י אלכסנדריא[א])
ד שם ה טור בשם מכילתין והרמב"ם פרק א' מהלכות תפילין והר"י אלכסנדריא[א]) וספר א"ח
ו הר"י אלכסנדריא[א])
ז הרמב"ם וסא"ח בשם ר' יונה

שערי תשובה

בזה וגם אין חילוק אם יתחיל מסופה לתחלתה כו' ע"ש: [טז] תיבות. עבה"ט ועיין בדבר שמואל סימן שנ"ד שהביא דברי הב"י והרמב"ם ומבואר בדבריו במלת לאבותיך אם בא למחוק הוא"ו והמיותרת אפשר שצריך למחוק [נ"ל למשוך] בתחלה הבי"ת הקודמת לה הגג והתחתית שתהיה סמוכה להתי"ו והוא"ו תבא אל תוכה ואז ימחקנה להוא"ו. אבל אם ימחוק קודם מיד יפסול משום שתיבת לאבותיך יהיה

באר היטב

אם יש אות או תג שצריכה דיו כדי שיקדש הדיו קודם שיכתוב השם ב"ש מ"א. וסדר כתיבת השם דרך סוד עיין בעטרת זקנים ובגינת ורדים חא"ח כלל ב' סי' יו"ד וי"א: (לה) תיבות. כתב הב"י בשם הריא"ם דלפעמים תיקון מהני ליתר אות כגון לאבותיך מלא בוי"ו שאחר

ביאור הלכה

או יתר אות אחת. ואם אות היתר לא היה מחובר לשום תיבה רק שעמד בין תיבה לתיבה או בין השיטין אם נפסל התפילין משום זה עיין בנו"ב חיו"ד ח"א בסי' ע"ד שמקיל בזה והשער אפרים בשער ה' בפ"ש חולק עליו ומסכים עם רש"ל שמחמיר בזה: * אין לו תקנה. עיין במ"ב דאל"ה יגרוד וכו' ר"ל דמתחלה יגרוד ואח"כ יכתוב מה שחסר ממנו ולהלן דאל"ה צ"ע כיון דבעת הכתיבה לא נכתב כסדרן*): * ואם יתר וכו'. עי' במ"ב בשם הפמ"ג לענין תיבה כפולה דלפעמים טוב יותר למחוק הראשונה כדי לחוש אף לדעת ר"ת עי"ש ועי"ש עוד במ"ז סק"כ

משנה ברורה

האחרונים: **כ** (ק) חסר או יתר. אפילו אם התיבה לא נשתנה לקריאתה בזה כגון במלא וחסר וכדלקמן: (קא) אות אחת. ואפילו אם קוצו של יו"ד חסר מעכב כדאיתא מנחות כ"ט א': (קב) מרובה. מלבד עון גזל האמור: (קג) וחרד לדבר השם. ראיתי להעתיק פה לשון הלבוש הצריך מאד לענינינו דז"ל ולא כמו שעושין עכשיו כמה סופרים שמניחין נערים המתלמדין לכתוב תפילין כדי שירגילו בכתב ואח"כ רואה הסופר אם נכתבו כהלכתן בחסירותן ויתירותן וסגי ליה בהכי ואח"כ מניחין אותן בבתים ומוכרין אותם ומחשבין להם הסופרים אותן המעות בשכר הלימוד להנער ומראים להם פני היתר לומר הרי אנו בזה כגומלי חסדים עם הנערים העניים ללמוד להם מלאכת הכתיבה בחנם והיא מלאכת ה' אבל אני אומר יצא שכרם בהפסדם והדרבה לא טוב המה עושים בעמם כי הנער נער ואין יודע בין ימינו לשמאלו ואין לו שום כונה בעולם רק הם כמתעסקים בכתיבה ליפות הכתב ולא לשום קדושה ושום כונת מצוה בעולם והרי עונש הסופר מרובה מאד שמכשיל את הבריות שמניחין אותן התפילין הפסולין [וכדלעיל בסעיף י"ט] ולא עוד כדי להשבים את מקחו יאמר הסופר לכל אני כתבתים ובכוונה כתבתים וכו' וכל העושין כן בודאי עתידין ליתן את הדין ולקבל עונשין הרבה מאוד ועליהם נאמר ארור עושה מלאכת ה' רמיה ע"כ יזהר כל סופר ויתרחק מזה וטוב לו דלשמן האמור אבל תפילין אין הכונה לשם בעל התפילין כמו גבי גט דצריך לשם האיש והאשה רק לשם קדושת תפילין עי"ש וסיים ע"ז ומן הראוי למי שיש כח בידו למנות כותבי תפילין המוגגים אנשי אמת שונאי בצע בעלי תורה יראי אלקים וחרדים על דברו בכל עיר כמו שממנים שוחטים ובודקים שלא יאמינו לכל הסופרים שאין כונתם אלא להרויח ממון ע"י כתיבה ותיקון יפה בעשיית התפילין ואף כי גם כוונה זו טובה היתה לייפות המצוה בנויה זה דוקא אם היה להם כוונה קדושה ג"כ אבל בזה אינם נזהרים ודי בזה עכ"ל הטהור. וכתב בספר ב"ש יכתוב אותיות טובים ותמימות ולא שבורות ובמתון ובכוונה גדולה ולא ימהר אדם בכתיבתה כדי להרויח ממון הרבה כי אותו ריוח ילך לאיבוד ולדיראון ויפסיד נשמתו כי הוא מחטיא את הרבים וכל מי שכותב תפילין טובים וכשרים כפי יכולתו שכרו כפול ומכופל ויגול מדינה של גיהנם. וכתב בס"ח סי' פ"ה[ג] ולדקתו עומדת לעד זה המזכה רבים כגון המלמד לירא השם תיקון תפילין לתקן לאחרים ועיין בסימן ל"ט מתי אדם ראוי לכתוב תפילין: **כא** (קד) יקראנה היטב. שאם ימצא איזה אות חסר באיזה פרשה לא היא לבדה נפסלה אלא גם כל מה שאחריה משום שיהיו שלא כסדרן וכדלעיל בריש הסימן: **כב** (קה) קודם שיתחיל. איו ר"ל בתחלת הפרשה דוקא **אלא (קה) קודם שיתחיל לכתוב בהפרשה: (קו) מה שכתב. באותה (קו) פרשה ולא השלפניה: (קז) על ידו. וכשטובל הקולמוס לכתוב בו את השם (קז) לא יתחיל לכתוב אותו מיד שלא יפסידנו ברבוי דיו או אולי יש עליו שער ולא יצא הכתב מיושר וגם משום שצריך (קח) לקדש הדיו שעל הקולמוס טרם שיכתוב השם לכן יכוין להניח אות אחת מלכתוב קודם השם ובאותו אות יתחיל לכתוב ואם לא עשה כן יחפש אחר אות או תג שצריכה דיו וימלאנה וכותב את השם ואם צריך דיו קודם שיגמור השם אז יטבול באותיות שלפני השם שהם לחים עדיין ויגמור השם אבל לא יטבול באותיות השם עצמן (קט) ויש מקילין לטבול באותיות השם עצמן דבזיון ליכא כיון שהוא כדי להשלים בו את השם. ואם האותיות שלפניו אינם לחין אזי יטבול מחדש ויחפש אחר אות או תג שצריכין דיו וכנ"ל וכ"ז הוא למצוה ולא לעיכובא בדיעבד: כג (קח) תקנה. בהשלמה ומיירי שמכאן עד סוף הפ' יש שמות שאינם נמחקין דאל"ה יגרוד עד סופה: (קט) בהוויתן** יהו. פי' כסדר שנכתבים בתורה יהיו כתובין: (קי) אות אחת. ואם כתב (קי) תיבה יתירה יגררנה ויוכל להניח המקום חלק [אם אין לו אותיות מהתיבות שלפניה שיהיה יוכל להמשיכן במקום ההוא] ואין (קיא) החלק פוסל כל שאין במקומו כשיעור הריוח שבין פרשה לפרשה שהוא כדי ט' אותיות. ולפעמים יש תקנה אפילו בזה כגון שיכול להמשיך האות מן התיבה שלפניה כדי למעט הריוח של ט' אותיות. ויותר מזה דבאופן זה שיפסל התפילין מחמת הריוח אז אפילו אם בסיום התיבה שלפניה (קיב) יש שם ה"א או קו"ף יוכל להמשיך גגן כדי למעט הריוח ואע"פ שע"י ההמשכה לא יהיה הרגל של הה"א והקו"ף בסופה אין קפידא בדיעבד. וכתב הפמ"ג דבתיבה כפולה טוב יותר למחוק השניה דתיבה הראשונה כדין נכתב. ואם קודם הראשונה יש אות שיכול למושכו טוב יותר שימחוק תיבה הראשונה כדי לחוש אף לדעת ר"ת דשיעור פרשה הוא ג' אותיות: (קיא) שיגרור. ולא מיפסל הפרשה משום חק תוכות כיון שאינו עושה מעשה בגוף התיבות והאותיות: (קיב) נראה כב' תיבות. ופעמים שתיקון מועיל ע"י שיגררנה וימשיך

*) שוב ראיתי שז"א וראיה מק"ש לקמן בסימן ס"ד ס"א בבה"ל ד"ה בד"א עי"ש:

שער הציון

(קה) א"ר ול"ח: (קו) א"ר: (קז) יו"ד רע"ו ס"ד: (קח) ב"ש: (קט) ש"ך יו"ד רע"ד הובא בפמ"ג: (קי) מ"א: (קיא) מ"א: (קיב) מ"א:

הגהות ותיקונים: א) אכסנדרני: ב) יבואו: ג) ס"ה:

One must likewise be careful before he writes any /Divine/ Name to read everything **(106)** that he has /already/ written /of the passage/, so that it will not come to require *genizah* **(107)** because of him.

23. If one discovered that he left out one letter, this cannot be **(108)** remedied. For if /he will add it now, the letters/ will have been written in incorrect order and will /therefore/ be invalid. This is because it is written,[23*] "And these ... should be", /which implies that/ **(109)** /the letters/ should be /written in the order/ in which they occur /in the passages/.

Mishnah Berurah

but before he begins to write in that passage.

(106) That he has written. /I.e.,/ of that passage and not of /the passage/ that precedes it.

(107) Because of him. When one dips the quill /in ink in order/ to write the /Divine/ Name with it, he should not begin to write /the Name/ immediately, so that he will not spoil it through excess ink. /Alternatively, this is necessary because the quill/ may have hair on it and /then/ the writing will not come out straight. In addition, /he must wait/ because it is necessary to sanctify the ink on the quill before one writes the /Divine/ Name.

Therefore, one should contrive to leave one letter unwritten before the /Divine/ Name and begin to write with that letter /after he has dipped the quill in ink/. If one did not do this, he should search for a letter or a crownlet which needs /more/ ink and fill it and /then/ write the /Divine/ Name. If one requires ink before he has completed /writing/ the /Divine/ Name, he should then dip /the quill/ in the letters before the /Divine/ Name which are still wet and complete the /Divine/ Name. (However, he should not dip /the quill/ in the letters of the /Divine/ Name themselves. There are /authorities/ who /rule/ leniently, that he may /even/ dip /the quill/ in the letters of the /Divine/ Name themselves. /They argue/ that contempt /for the Name/ is not involved, since /one does/ so in order to complete /the writing of/ the /Divine/ Name with /the ink/.) If the letters before /the Name/ are not wet, one should then dip /the quill/ anew /in the ink/ and search for a letter or crownlet which requires ink, as /explained/ above.

/However,/ all this is /merely/ a mitzvah /requirement/, but is not essential /for the validity/ once it is after the event.

(108) Remedied. /I.e.,/ by supplementing /the letter/.

/The Shulchan Aruch/ is speaking of /an instance/ when from that point until the end of the passage there are /Divine/ Names which are not erasable. Otherwise, one may scrape off /all that has been written/ until the end /and then rewrite it/.

(109) /The letters/ should be /written

23* *Devarim* 6:6.

כ [ב] צריך לדקדק בחסרות ויתרות שאם (ק) חסר * או יתר (קא) אות אחת פסולים ונמצא המניחים אותם מברכים בכל יום ברכה לבטלה וגם שרוי בכל יום בלא מצות תפילין ונמצא עונש הסופר (קב) מרובה לכן צריך להיות מאוד ירא שמים (קג) וחרד לדבר השם המתעסק בכתיבת תפילין ותיקונן: **כא** [ג] כל פרשה אחר שיכתבנה (קד) יקראנה היטב בכוונה ודקדוק פעמים ושלש ויחזור ויקראנה קודם שיתגנה בתוך ביתה כדי שלא תתחלף פרשה בפרשה: **כב** [ד] טוב לנסות הקולמוס (קה) קודם שיתחיל לכתוב הפרשה שלא יהא עליו דיו יותר מדאי ויפסיד וכן יזהר קודם שיכתוב כל שם לקרות כל (קו) מה שכתב כדי שלא יבאו[ב] לידי גניזה (קז) על ידו: **כג** [ה] אם מצא שחסר אות אחת * אין לו (קח) תקנה שאם כן היו כתובין שלא כסדרן ופסולין משום דכתיב והיו (קט) בהווייתן יהו * ואם יתר (קי) אות אחת יש לו תקנה על ידי (קיא) שיגרור אותה אם היא בסוף תיבה או בתחלתה [ו] אבל אם היא באמצע תיבה לא משום דכשיגרור יהיה (קיב) נראה כשתי (לה) [טז] תיבות: **כד** [ז] מותר לכתוב על

באר הגולה

ב הרא"ש בספר תקון תפילין וכתיבתן ג הר"י אלכסנדריא[א] ד שם ה טור בשם מכילתין והרמב"ם פרק א' מהלכות תפילין והר"י אלכסנדריא[א] וספר א"ח ו הר"י אלכסנדריא[א] ז הרמב"ם וסא"ח בשם ר' יונה

שערי תשובה

בזה וגם אין חילוק אם יתחיל מסופה לתחלתה כו' ע"ש: [טז] תיבות. עבה"ט ועיין בדבר שמואל סימן שנ"ד שהביא דברי הב"י והרמב"ם ומבואר בדבריו במלת לאבותיך אם בא למחוק הוא"ו והמיותרת אפשר שצריך למחוק [נ"ל למשוך] בתחלה הבי"ת הקודמת לה הגג והתחתית שתהיה סמוכה להתי"ו והוא"ו תבא אל תוכה ואז ימחקנה להוא"ו. אבל אם ימחוק קודם מיד יפסול משום שתיבת לאבותיך יהיה

באר היטב

אם יש אות או תג שצריכה דיו כדי שיקדש הדיו קודם שיכתוב השם ב"ש מ"א. וסדר כתיבת השם דרך סוד עיין בעטרת זקנים ובגינת ורדים חא"ח כלל ב' סי' יו"ד וי"א: (לה) תיבות. כתב הב"י בשם הריא"ם דלפעמים תיקון מהני ליתר אות כגון לאבותיך מלא בוי"ו שאחר

ביאור הלכה

או יתר אות אחת. ואם אות היתר לא היה מחובר לשום תיבה רק שעמד בין תיבה לתיבה או בין השיטין אם נפסל התפילין משום זה עיין בנו"ב חיו"ד ח"א בסי' ע"ד שמקיל בזה והשער אפרים בשער ה' בפ"ש חולק עליו ומסכים עם רש"ל שמחמיר בזה: * אין לו תקנה. עיין במ"ב דאל"ה יגרוד וכו' ר"ל דמתחלה יגרוד ואח"כ יכתוב מה שחסר ממנו ולהלן דאל"ה ל"ע כיון דבעת הכתיבה לא נכתב כסדרן*): * ואם יתר וכו'. עי' במ"ב בשם הפמ"ג לענין תיבה כפולה דלפעמים טוב יותר למחוק הראשונה כדי לחוש אף לדעת ר"ת עי"ש ועי"ש עוד במ"ז סק"כ

משנה ברורה

האחרונים: כ (ק) חסר או יתר. אפילו אם התיבה לא נשתנה לקריאתה בזה כגון במלא וחסר וכדלקמן: (קא) אות אחת. ואפילו אם קוצו של יו"ד חסר מעכב כדאיתא מנחות כ"ט א': (קב) מרובה. מלבד עון גזל הממון: (קג) וחרד לדבר השם. ראיתי להעתיק פה לשון הלבוש הצריך מאד לענינינו דז"ל ולא כמו שעושין עכשיו כמה סופרים שמניחין נערים המתלמדין לכתוב תפלין כדי שירגילום בכתב ואח"כ רואה הסופר אם נכתבו כהלכתן בחסירותן ויתירותן וסגי ליה בהכי ואח"כ מניחין אותן בבתים ומוכרין אותם ומחשבין לאם הסופרים אותן המעות בשכר הלימוד להנער ומראים להם פני היתר לומר הרי אנו בזה כגומלי חסדים עם הנערים העניים ללמוד להם מלאכת הכתיבה בחנם והיא מלאכת ה' אבל אני אומר יצא שכרם בהפסדם ואדרבה לא טוב המה עושים בעמם כי הנער נער ואין יודע בין ימינו לשמאלו ואין לו שום כונה בעולם רק הם כמתעסקים בכתיבה ליפות הכתב ולא לשום קדושה ושום כונת מצוה בעולם והרי עונש הסופר מרובה מאד שמכשיל את הבריות שמניחין אותן התפלין הפסולין [וכדלעיל בסעיף י"ט] ולא עוד כדי להשביח את מקחו יאמר הסופר לכל אני כתבתים ובכוונה כתבתים וכו' וכל העושין כן עתידין ליתן את הדין ולקבל עונשן הרבה מאוד ועליהם נאמר ארור עושה מלאכת ה' רמיה ע"כ יזהר כל סופר ויתרחק מזה וטוב לו דלשתן המחור אבל תפלין אין הכונה לשם בעל התפלין כמו גבי גט דצריך לשם האיש והאשה רק לשם קדושת תפלין עכ"ל וכ"כ ע"ז ומן הראוי למי שיש כח בידו למנות כותבי תפלין מהוגנים אנשי אמת שונאי בצע בעלי תורה יראי אלקים וחרדים על דברו בכל עיר כמו שממנים שוחטים ובודקים שלא יאמינו לכל הסופרים שאין כוונתם אלא להרויח ממון ע"י כתיבה ותיקון יפה בעשיית התפלין ואף כי גם כונה זו טובה היתה ליפות המצוה בעיניו זה דוקא אם היה להם כונה קדושה ג"כ אבל בזה אינם נזהרים ודי בזה עכ"ל הטהור. וכתב בספר ב"ש יכתוב אותיות טובים ותמימות ולא שבורות ובמתון ובכוונה גדולה ולא ימהר אדם בכתיבתה כדי להרויח ממון הרבה כי אותו ריוח ילך לאיבוד ולדיראון ויפסיד נשמתו כי הוא מכשיל את הרבים וכל מי שכותב תפלין טובים וכשרים כפי יכולתו שכרו כפול ומכופל וניצול מדינה של גיהנם. וכתב במ"א סי' פ"ה וצדקתו עומדת לעד זה המזכה רבים כגון המלמד ליראי השם תיקון תפלין לתקן לאחרים ועיין בסימן ל"ט מתי אדם ראוי לכתוב תפלין: **כא** (קד) יקראנה היטב. שאם ימצא איזה אות חסר באיזה פרשה לא היא לבדה נפסלה אלא גם כל מה שאחריה משום שיהיו שלא כסדרן וכדלעיל בריש הסימן: **כב** (קה) קודם שיתחיל. אינו ר"ל בתחלת הפרשה דוקא אלא (קה) קודם שיתחיל לכתוב בהפרשה: (קו) מה שכתב. באותה (קו) פרשה ולא שלפניה: (קז) על ידו. וכשטובל הקולמוס לכתוב בו את השם (קז) לא יתחיל לכתוב אותו מיד שלא יפסידנו ברבוי דיו או אולי יש עליו שער ולא יצא הכתב מיושר וגם משום שצריך (קח) לקדש הדיו שעל הקולמוס טרם שיכתוב השם לכן יכוין להניח אות אחת מלכתוב קודם השם ובאותו אות יתחיל לכתוב ואם לא עשה כן יתפש אחר אות או תג שצריכה דיו ויתלהנה וכותב את השם ואם צריך דיו קודם שיגמור השם אז יטבול באותיות שלפני השם שהם לחים עדיין ויגמור השם אבל לא יטבול באותיות השם עצמן (קט) ויש מקילין לטבול באותיות השם עצמן דבזוי ליכא כיון שהוא כדי להשלים בו את השם. ואם האותיות שלפניו אינם לחין אזי יטבול מתחלה ויתפש אחר אות או תג שצריכין דיו וכנ"ל וכ"ז הוא למצוה ולא לעיכובא בדיעבד: **כג** (קח) תקנה. כהשלמה ומיירי שמכאן עד סוף הפ' יש שמות שאינם נמחקין דאל"ה יגרוד עד סופה: (קט) בהוויתן יהו. פי' כסדר שנכתבות בתורה יהיו כתובין: (קי) אות אחת. ואם כתב (קי) תיבה יתירה יגררנה ויוכל להניח המקום חלק [אם אין לו אותיות מהתיבות שלפניה שיהיה יוכל להמשיך במקום ההוא] ואין (קיא) החלק פוסל כל שאין במקומו כשיעור הריוח שבין פרשה לפרשה שהוא כדי ט' אותיות. ולפעמים יש תקנה אפילו בזה כגון שיכול להמשיך האות מן התיבה שלפניה כדי למעט הריוח של ט' אותיות. ויותר מזה דבאופן זה שיפסל התפלין מחמת הריוח אז אפילו אם בסיום התיבה שלפניה (קיב) יש שם ה"א או קו"ף יוכל להמשיך גגן כדי למעט הריוח ואע"פ שע"י ההמשכה לא יהיה הרגל של הה"א והקו"ף בסופה אין קפידא בדיעבד. וכתב הפמ"ג דבתיבה כפולה טוב יותר למחוק השניה דתיבה הראשונה כדין נכתב. ואם קודם הראשונה יש אות שיכול למושכו טוב יותר שימחוק תיבה הראשונה כדי לחוש אף לדעת ר"ת דשיעור פרשה הוא ג' אותיות: (קיא) שיגרור. ולא מיפסל הפרשה משום חק תוכות כיון שאינו עושה מעשה בגוף התיבות והאותיות: (קיב) נראה כב' תיבות. ופעמים שתיקון מועיל ע"י שיגררנה וימשיך

*) שוב ראיתי שז"א וראיה מק"ש לקמן בסימן ס"ד ס"א בבה"ל ד"ה בד"א עי"ש:

שער הציון

הלוח

(קה) א"ר ול"ח: (קו) א"ר: (קז) יו"ד רע"ו ס"ד: (קח) ב"ש: (קט) ש"ך יו"ד רע"ד הובא בפמ"ג: (קי) מ"א: (קיא) מ"א: (קיב) מ"א:

הגהות ותיקונים: א) אכסנדרני: ב) יבואו: ג) ס"ה:

If one added **(110)** one /superfluous/ letter, this can be remedied by means of **(111)** scraping it away, if it is at the end of a word or at the beginning /of a word/. However, if it is in the middle of a word this cannot be /done/, because when one has scraped it away /the word/ will **(112)** appear like two words.

Mishnah Berurah

in the order/ in which they occur. I.e., they must be written in the order in which they are written in the Torah.

(110) One letter. If one wrote a superfluous word he may scrape it off and may leave the spot blank [if he does not have a letter of the word before it which he is able to continue into that spot]. Blank /space/ does not invalidate /a passage/, as long as the /blank/ spot does not have the width of the interval /required/ between passages, i.e., sufficient for /the writing of/ nine letters. Sometimes one may even have a remedy in /the latter/ case, i.e., when one is able to continue the /last/ letter of the preceding word in order to make the interval less than /is required for the writing of/ nine letters. Moreover, in circumstances where the *tefilin* /passage/ will /otherwise/ be invalid because of the interval, then, even if at the conclusion of the word before /the interval/ there is a /letter/ ה or a /letter/ ק, one may continue the roof /of the letter/ in order to lessen the interval. Although through this continuation the leg of the /letter/ ה or of the /letter/ ק will not be at the end /of the letter/, one does not need to be particular about this once it is after the event /and one is faced with such a situation/.

The *P.Mg.* writes that when a word /has been written/ twice it is preferable to erase the second /word/, since the first word was written in conformance with halachic /requirements/. /However,/ if /the last letter of the first word cannot be continued and/ before the first /word/ there is a letter which can be continued /to shorten the interval/, it is preferable to erase the first word. /It is desirable to shorten the interval/ in order to take into account even the view of Rabbeinu Tam, that the /required/ width for /the interval between/ passages is /merely sufficient to write/ three letters.

(111) Scraping ... away. The passage will not become invalid because of /the fact that one may not/ carve around /to form a letter/, since /this scraping away/ does not involve doing an action to the actual words or letters /of the passage/.

(112) Appear like two words. Sometimes, remedying can be of avail /in such a case/. /This is so/ where one can scrape off /the superfluous letter/ and continue the letter before it to fill its place.

מקום (לו) [יז] (קיג) הגרר ועל מקום המחק אפילו אזכרה ^חולא ימחוק בעודו לח אלא ייבשנו יפה כי אז יגרר בקל ולא ישאר לו שום רושם: כה (קיד) ^טכל אות שהיא כתובה שלא כתקנה (קטו) ואין צורתה (לז) עליה כגון נגע (קטז) רגל האל"ף (לח) [יח] בגג האל"ף או פני האל"ף בפנים בגג שתחתיה או

ח הר"י אלכסנדריא[א]
ט הגהות מיימון פ"א ופרק ב' ומהרי"ק בשורש ס"ט ותרומת הדשן סימן מ"ח והר"י אלכסנדריא[א]

באר היטב

שיגרור הוי"ו ימשוך הב' שלפניה באופן שיהיה ממולא החלק של מקום הגרר אבל בב' נסתפק כגון הוליאך[ב] שכתבו ביו"ד או מלות מלא בוי"ו ואם ימחוק היו"ד או הוי"ו יוכל אח"כ להמשיך חלק התחתון ולא העליון אי כשר או לא. ומסיים הב"י ומ"מ כל שנראית כשתי תיבות פסולה. וכ"כ הלבוש שיש להחמיר בזה וכתב המ"א דאם בתחלת הכתיבה ממשיך רגל התחתון של הנו"ן והלד"י וכותב האות הסמוך בתוכו כזה פני ארצי מותר דהוי ממש כתיבה אחת דלא כהרנ"ח ח"ב סי' ע"ח. עיין כנה"ג. וביד אהרן. ואם כתב תיבה יתירה מתקנה. ואם יהיה חלק ט' אותיות דכשיגררנה יהיה פרשה במקום שאין פרשה פסול. אבל מותר למשוך הה"א אע"פ שלא יצא רגל בסופו מ"א. מלא וי"ו או יו"ד יתירה יגרור אותה ויעבה קצת האות שלפניה או שלאחריה שאין בזה משום שינוי אות. עיין מ"א וביד אהרן (עיין בספר אליה רבה בעניינים האלה בשם כנה"ג ושו"ת רדב"ז): (לו) הגרר. הגרר מקרי כשגררו יבש והמחק מיקרי שמחקו לח: (לז) עליה. ובכל הני אפי' תינוק יוכל לקרותם פסול: (לח) בגג. דאז צריך לגררה כולה כמ"ש סעיף י"ח:

שערי תשובה

חלוק ונראה כשני תיבות ושוב לא יועיל מה שימשוך אחר כך כיון שהפיסול נראה לעין כל יש בתיקון הכתיבה ותוספות הדיו בהמשכה משום כתיבה שלא כסדרן. ומ"ש הבה"ט ואם יהיה חלוק[ג] יש קיצור בהעתקת דברי המג"א וע"ש שכוונתו דהיכי שצריך לגרור תיבה יתירה אז אם כשיגרור יהיה חלק ט' אותיות ויפסלו התפילין וכדי שלא לפוסלם אם בסיום התיבה שלפניו יש שם ה"א או קו"ף ימשוך הגג של הה"א או הקו"ף. ואעפ"י שעל ידי ההמשכה[ד] יהיה הרגל של הה"א או הקו"ף בסופה אין קפידה בדיעבד ע"ש. ולפי מ"ש בשם הדב"ש לכאורה גם בזה היה צריך להמשיך קודם שיגרור ואם כן צריך להמשיך למעלה מן התיבה המיותרת בעוד התיבה כתובה וזה קלקול האות הוא. ואפשר שבזה שאין הפסול רק משום חלק ט' אותיות אין צריך לעשות כן ויכול להמשיך אח"כ ואין בזה משום שלא כסדרן. ונראה שיש לגרור תחלה ב' או ג' אותיות מן התיבה המיותרת ולהמשיך הה"א ואחר כך יגרור השאר וא"כ לא היה כאן פסול מעולם כלל. ועיין בשו"ת מ"ב[ה] שרצה ללמוד לענין נוני"ן המנוזרין מהא דנמלא תיבות כפולות בתפילין ומ"ש עליו בשערי אפרים שער ה' בפתחי שערים שם דבתפילין אי הוי שלא כסדרן מיירי אבל ודאי מ"מ צריך למחוק ולהסיר התיבה המיותרת משם ע"ש: [יז] הגרר. עבה"ט ועיין בדבר שמואל סימן קנ"ד שכתב שאין לתלות תיבה אחת בין השיטין בכתיבת התפילין ומזוזות אף במקום שהכתיבה כסדרה בין המוקדמת למאוחרת חדא דגם זה מיקרי שלא כסדרן מחמת שינוי. וגם מפני שדרך כתיבתן להיות דקה. בלי ריוח הרבה בין שיטה לשיטה לכך אין תולין ע"ש שהביא מתשובת הר"ן סי' ל"ט ועיין בגינת ורדים כלל ב' סימן ד' באמצע התשובה שאם נזדמן להסופר שהשיטה דחוקה מהכיל התיבות שיעור לה אין להתיר שיתלה תיבה אחת למעלה בין השיטות ואחר כך ירד לכתוב כסדר השיטה. ושם כתב דלדעת רש"י תפילין ומזוזות חמירי טפי ואפילו בתליית אות אחת מחזי כמנומר ע"ש: [יח] בגג. עבה"ט

משנה ברורה

האות שלפניה שתמלא מקומה כגון (קיג) לאבותיך שכתב מלא וי"ו אחר הב' יגררנה וימשוך הב' שלפניה שתמלא מקומה. וכן אם התיקון תלוי בכ"ף או דלי"ת או רי"ש שאפשר להמשיכן מעט למלא מקום אות היתרה שנגררה אבל אם האותיות שאפשר להמשיכן הן אחר האות היתרה שא"א להמשיכן לאחוריהן עד שיגרר מהם תחלה כגון שאר שכתוב בתורה שכתבה מלא וי"ו אחר האל"ף שא"א למשוך הרי"ש לאחריה עד שיגרר רגלה תחלה ונמצא שביטל צורתה וכשמתקנה אח"כ נמצא כותב שלא כסדרן ואין תקנה אח"כ יכול למלאות מקומו ע"י (קיד) שיעבה קצת האות שלפניה ושלאחריה שאין בזה משום שינוי האות משא"כ כשהאותיות שאפשר להמשיכן הן לפני האות היתרה אזי אפשר להמשיכן הרבה מבלי שיגרע מהם כלום. אך יש להסתפק (קטו) במלות הראשון שדינו להיות חסר וכתבו מלא ומחק אח"כ הוי"ו אם מועיל אריכת הלדי"ק למטה אח"כ או דילמא כל עוד שאינו מאריך האות למעלה נחשב כשני תיבות אע"פ שסמכה מלמטה וכן נתן שמשפטו להיות חסר וכן הולאך אם כתבו מלא ביו"ד בין לדי"ק לאל"ף בכל אלו יש להסתפק אם יש להם תיקון בהאריך האות שלפניו למטה ומ"מ כל שנראה כב' תיבות פסולה אבל אם בתחלת הכתיבה ממשיך (קטז) רגל התחתון של הנו"ן והלד"י וכותב האות הסמוכה לתוכה כגון פני או ארצי כשר כיון דבתיבה אחת נכתבו ומ"מ לכתחלה אין נכון לעשות כן להבליע אות בתוך אות כי יש מחמירין בזה: כד (קיג) הגרר. הגרר מיקרי כשגררו משנתיבש והמחק מיקרי כשמחקו בעודו לח ומש"כ ולא ימחוק עלה טובה קמ"ל ועיין בפמ"ג שכתב דאם ישאר שום רושם דיו אפי' בדיעבד יש חשש בזה ואפילו תיבה בעלמא דלא אזכרה אסור לכתוב על מקום זה: כה (קיד) כל אות וכו'. סעיף זה יבואר בו דין שלא כסדרן וענייניו ארוכין והכלל בקצרה בדין זה יש בו ג' פרטים [א] אם יש קלקול באיזה אות בין שנעשה זה בעת הכתיבה או שנעשה לאחר הכתיבה [פמ"ג בפתיחה] אם נר' לעין כל שאין צורתו עליו כגון יו"ד שחסר לו רגלו הימני או שי"ן שחסר לו יו"ד אחד וכל כי האי גוונא שחסר באות איזה דבר עד שעי"ז אין תמונתו עליו אפילו אין נדמה משום זה לאות אחר וכתב לפניו לא מהני ליה שום תיקון ואפילו אם אירע שהתינוק קראו לאות אפ"ה פסול משום שלא כסדרן וכ"ש אם ע"י קלקולו וחסרונו נדמה לאות אחר כגון דלי"ת דומה לרי"ש או ב' דומה לכ' או חי"ת שברגל שמאלו יש הפסק בין הרגל להגג ונראה כה"א או לדי"ק שיש בו הפסק במקום נגיעת היו"ד לעצמותו ונראה לעין כל כיו"ד ונו"ן וכל כה"ג שאין משגיחין על התינוק ולא מהני ליה תיקון [ב] אם ע"י קלקולו וחסרונו לא נפסד מצורתו לגמרי כגון שיש הפסק דק (קיז) באיזה אות באמצעו ועדיין עיקר צורתו עליו או כגון שלא היו היודי"ן שעל האלפי"ן והשיני"ן ורגלי התוי"ן נוגעים בגוף האות אם תינוק דלא חו"ט מכירם אף דלא מתכשר האות עי"ז משום דאין צורתו עליו בשלימות עכ"פ מהני זה דנשאר עליו עיקר צורתו לענין שיהא מותר לתקנו ולא יקרא שלא כסדרן. ויש עוד אופן שלישי שאע"פ שעיקר צורתו יש עליו ותינוק קוראו לאות אפ"ה לא מהני ליה שום תיקון כגון אות שנפסל באיזה דבר (קיח) שתיקונו הוא לגרור מקצתו ולכותבו מחדש [כגון רגל הה"א והקו"ף שנגעו למעלה אפילו נגיעה דקה כחוט השערה שתיקונו הוא לגרור כל הרגל ולכותבו מחדש דלא מהני ליה הפרדה בעלמא משום חק תוכות וכן נגע רגל האל"ף בגג האל"ף וכה"ג וכנ"ל בסעיף י"ח] ואירע שקודם תיקונו כתב לפניו בזה לא יועיל שום תיקון דהא צריך לגרור כל מה שנכתב בפסול וא"כ מה שמתקנה אח"כ הוי שלא כסדרן. ועתה נתחיל לבאר בעזה"י את הסעיף. כל אות שהיא כתובה וכו' וה"ה אם נתקלקלה (קיט) אח"כ: (קטו) ואין צורתה עליה. פי' שנראה לעין כל שאין צורתה עליה כלל ואף דבנגעה רגל האל"ף בגג האל"ף או פני האל"ף בגגו או רגל ה"א וקו"ף הנוגעין למעלה ניכר עליו עדיין עיקר צורת האות ותינוק יקראהו לאות אפ"ה כיון שפסול זה אין תיקונו כ"א ע"י גרירת כל מה שנעשה בפסול וכנ"ל בסעיף י"ח תמילא נתבטל צורתו לגמרי ואם יתקנם אח"כ הוי שלא כסדרן: (קטז) רגל האל"ף.

וה"ה

שער הציון

(קיג) ב"י: (קיד) מ"א בשם הרדב"ז: (קטו) ב"י: (קטז) מ"א: (קיז) פמ"ג בא"א: (קיח) ב"י: (קיט) פמ"ג בפתיחה:

הגהות ותיקונים: א) אכסנדרני: ב) הוצאך: ג) חלק: ד) חסר תיבת לא: ה) נו"ב:

24. It is permitted to write on a spot **(113)** where one scraped away and on a spot where one erased. One may even /write/ a Divine Name /there/.

One should not erase while /the ink/ is still wet, but should dry it properly, as then it can be scraped away easily and will not leave any impression.

Mishnah Berurah

For example, if one wrote /the word/ לאבותיך with the /letter/ ו after the /letter/ ב written in full, he should scrape off /the letter ו/ and continue the /letter/ ב before it to fill its place. /This applies/ likewise if the correction is dependent on /the letters/ כ, ד or ך, which can be continued a little /in order/ to fill the place of the superfluous letter which is scraped off.

On the other hand, if the letters which can be continued are after the superfluous letter, it is impossible /to continue them to fill the interval/. /For/ to continue them towards the back /is impossible,/ unless one scrapes away from them first /and cancels their form, and then the letters will come to be written in incorrect order/. (/However,/ one can fill an /erased/ area by somewhat thickening the letter before it and /the letter/ after it, because this does not involve a change in /the form of/ the letters.) For example, /in the case of the word/ שאר written in the Torah, if one wrote it with the /letter/ ו in full after the א, it is impossible to continue the /letter/ ר towards the back unless one scrapes off the leg first. This would result in the form /of the letter ר/ being cancelled, /so that/ when one would correct it subsequently he would be writing /the letter after the letters which follow it and they would therefore be written/ in incorrect order. /It follows that/ after /continuing the letter backwards/ the correction would be of no /avail/. /The situation/ is different when those letters which can be continued are before the superfluous letter, as then they can be continued considerably without detracting from their /form/ at all.

However, it is doubtful /whether continuation of the letter is of avail/ in the case of the first /appearance of the word/ מצות[23] /in the passage *Kadesh Li Chal Bechor*/, which according to the law must be /written with the letter ו/ left out /after the letter צ/, if one /in fact/ wrote /the letter ו/ in full and afterwards erased the /letter/ ו. /The question is/ whether lengthening the /stroke of the letter/ צ at the bottom subsequently is of avail or whether as long as one does not lengthen the letter at the top /the letters of the word which will remain after the ו was erased/ will be considered as two words, even though they were brought close at the bottom. /This applies/ likewise /in the case of the word/ נתן,[24] for which the rule is that it must be /written with the letter ו/ left out /after the letter נ/, and /the word/ הוצאך,[25] if one wrote it /incorrectly/ in full with the /letter/ י in between the /letter/ צ and the /letter/ א. In all these /cases/ it is doubtful whether /the passage/ can be corrected by lengthening /the stroke/ at the bottom of the letter before /the erased letter/. At any rate, whenever /the letters which remain after a letter was erased/ look like two words /the passage/ is invalid.

However, if at the outset when one wrote /the word/ one continued the lower leg of the /letter/ נ or of the /letter/ צ and wrote the adjoining letter inside it, /the passage/ is valid, since /the letters/ were written in one word. For example, /if one did so in the case of the words/ פני or ארצי. Nevertheless, initially, it is not proper to do this, thus enclosing one letter inside /another/ letter, as there are /authorities/ who are stringent about it.

(113) Where one scraped away. /A spot/

23 I.e., in the verse *Shemos* 13:6.
24 I.e., in the verse *Devarim* 11:17.
25 I.e., in the verse *Shemos* 13:9.

מקום (לו) [יז] (קיג) הגרר ועל מקום המחק אפילו אזכרה חולא ימחוק בעודו לח אלא ייבשנו יפה כי אז יגרר בקל ולא ישאר לו שום רושם: **כה** (קיד) טכל אות שהיא כתובה שלא כתקנה (קטו) ואין צורתה (לז) עליה כגון נגע (קטז) רגל האל"ף (לח) [יח] בגג האל"ף או פני האל"ף בפנים בגג שתחתיה או

ח הר"י אלכסנדריא[א]
ט הגהות מיימון פ"א ופרק ב' ומהרי"ק בשורש ס"ט ותרומת הדשן סימן מ"ח והר"י אלכסנדריא[א]

באר היטב

שיגרור הוי"ו ימשוך הב' שלפניה באופן שיהיה ממולא החלק של מקום הגרר אבל בל' נסתפק כגון הוליאך[ב] שכתבו ביו"ד או מלות מלא בוי"ו ואם ימחוק היו"ד או הוי"ו יוכל אח"כ להמשיך חלק התחתון ולא העליון אי כשר או לא. ומסיים הב"י ומ"מ כל שנראית כשתי תיבות פסולה. וכ"כ הלבוש שיש להחמיר בזה וכתב המ"א דאם בתחלת הכתיבה ממשיך רגל התחתון של הנו"ן והלד"י וכותב האות הסמוך בתוכו כזה פני ארצי מותר דהוי ממש כתיבה אחת דלא כהרנ"ח ח"ב סי' ע"ח. עיין כנה"ג. וביד אהרן. ואם כתב תיבה יתירה מתקנה. ואם יהיה חלק ט' אותיות דכשיגררנה יהיה פרשה במקום שאין פרשה פסול. אבל מותר למשוך הה"א אע"פ שלא יצא רגל בסופו מ"א. מלא וי"ו או יו"ד יתירה יגרור אותה ויעבה קצת האות שלפניה או שלאחריה שאין בזה משום שינוי אות. עיין מ"א וביד אהרן (עיין בספר אליה רבה בעניינים האלה בשם כנה"ג ושו"ת רדב"ז): (לו) הגרר. הגרר מקרי כשגררו יבש והמחק מיקרי שמחקו לח: (לז) עליה. ובכל הני אפי' תינוק יוכל לקרותם פסול: (לח) בגג. דאז צריך לגררה כולה כמ"ש סעיף י"ח:

שערי תשובה

חלוק ונראה כשני תיבות ושוב לא יועיל מה שימשוך אחר כך כיון שהפיסול נראה לעין כל יש בתיקון הכתיבה ותוספות הדיו בהמשכה משום כתיבה שלא כסדרן. ומ"ש הבה"ט ואם יהיה חלוק[ג] יש קילור בהעתקת דברי המג"א וע"ש שכוונתו דהיכי שצריך לגרור תיבה יתירה אז אם כשיגרור יהיה חלק ט' אותיות ויפסלו התפילין וכדי שלא לפוסלם אם בסיום התיבה שלפניו יש שם ה"א או קו"ף ימשוך הגג של הה"א או הקו"ף. ואעפ"י שעל ידי ההמשכה[ד] יהיה הרגל של הה"א או הקו"ף בסופה אין קפידה בדיעבד ע"ש. ולפי מ"ש בשם הדב"ש לכאורה גם בזה היה צריך להמשיך קודם שיגרור ואם כן צריך להמשיך למעלה מן התיבה המיותרת בעוד התיבה כתובה וזה קלקול האות הוא. ואפשר שבזה שאין הפסול רק משום חלק ט' אותיות אין צריך לעשות כן ויכול להמשיך אח"כ ואין בזה משום שלא כסדרן. ונראה שיש לגרור תחלה ב' או ג' אותיות מן התיבה המיותרת ולהמשיך הה"א ואחר כך יגרור השאר וא"כ לא היה כאן פסול מעולם כלל. ועיין בשו"ת מ"ב[ה] שרצה ללמוד לענין נוני"ן המנוזרין מהא דנמלא תיבות כפולות בתפילין ומ"ש עליו בשערי אפרים שער ה' בפתחי שערים שם דבתפילין אי הוי שלא כסדרן מיירי אבל ודאי מ"מ צריך למחוק ולהסיר התיבה המיותרת משם ע"ש: [יז] הגרר. עבה"ט ועיין בדבר שמואל סימן קנ"ד שכתב שאין לתלות תיבה אחת בין השיטין בכתיבת התפילין ומזוזות אף במקום שהכתיבה כסדרה בין המוקדמת למאוחרת חדא דגם זה מיקרי שלא כסדרן מחמת שינוי. וגם מפני שדרך כתיבתן להיות דקה. בלי ריוח הרבה בין שיטה לשיטה לכך אין תולין ע"ש שהביא מתשובת הר"ן סי' ל"ט ועיין בגינת ורדים כלל ב' סימן ד' באמצע התשובה שאם נזדמן להסופר שהשיטה דחוקה מהכיל התיבות שיעור לה אין להתיר שיתלה תיבה אחת למעלה בין השיטות ואחר כך ירד לכתוב כסדר השיטה. וגם כתב דלדעת רש"י תפילין ומזוזות חמירי טפי ואפילו בתליית אות אחת מחזי כמנומר ע"ש: [יח] בגג. עבה"ט

משנה ברורה

האות שלפניה שתמלא מקומה כגון (קיג) לאפוקי שכתב מלא וי"ו אחר הב' יגררנה וימשוך הב' שלפניה שתמלא מקומה. וכן אם התיקון תלוי בכ"ף או דלי"ת או רי"ש שאפשר להמשיכן מעט למלא מקום אות היתרה שנגררה אבל אם האותיות שאפשר להמשיכן הן אחר האות היתרה שא"א להמשיכן לאחוריהן עד שיגרר מקום תחלה כגון שאר שכתוב בתורה שכתבה מלא וי"ו אחר האל"ף שא"א למשוך הרי"ש לאחריה עד שיגרר רגלה תחלה ונמצא שביטל צורתה וכשמתקנה אח"כ נמצא כותב שלא כסדרן ואין תקנה אח"כ יכול למלאות מקומו ע"י (קיד) שיעבה קצת האות שלפניה ושלאחריה שאין בזה משום שינוי האות מאח"כ כשהאותיות שאפשר להמשיכן הן לפני האות היתרה אזי אפשר להמשיכן הרבה מבלי שיגרע משם כלום. אך יש להסתפק (קטו) במלות הראשון שדינו להיות חסר וכתבו מלא ומחק אח"כ הוי"ו אם מועיל אריכת הלמ"ד למטה אח"כ או דילמא כל עוד שאינו מאריך האות למעלה נחשב כשני תיבות אע"פ שסמוכה תלמטם וכן נתן שמתמעו להיות חסר וכן הואלך אם כתבו מלא ביו"ד בין לדי"ק לאל"ף בכל אלו יש להסתפק אם יש להם תיקון בהאריך האות שלפניו למטה ומ"מ כל שנראה כב' תיבות פסולה אבל אם בתחלת הכתיבה ממשיך (קטז) רגל התחתון של הנו"ן והלמ"ד וכותב האות הסמוכה לתוכה כגון פני או אלהי כשר כיון דבתיבה אחת נכתבו ומ"מ לכתחלה אין נכון לעשות כן להבליע אות בתוך אות כי יש מחמירין בזה: **כד** (קיג) הגרר. הגרר מיקרי כשגררו משנתיבש והמחק מיקרי כשמחקו בעודו לח ומש"כ ולא ימחוק עלה טובה קמ"ל ועיין בפמ"ג שכתב דאם ישאר שום רושם דיו אפי' בדיעבד יש חשש בזה ואפילו תיבה בעלמא דלא אזכרה אסור לכתוב על מקום זה: **כה** (קיד) כל אות וכו'. סעיף זה יבואר בו דין שלא כסדרן ועניניו ארוכין ואכלול בקצרה בדין זה יש בו ג' פרטים [א] אם יש קלקול באיזה אות בין שנעשה זה בעת הכתיבה או שנעשה לאחר הכתיבה [פמ"ג בפתיחה] אם נר' לעין כל שאין צורתו עליו כגון יו"ד שחסר לו רגלו הימני או שי"ן שחסר לו יו"ד אחד וכל כי האי גונא שחסר באות איזה דבר עד שעי"ז אין תמונתו עליו אפילו אין נדמה משום זה לאות אחר וכתב לפניו לא מהני ליה שום תיקון ואפילו אם אירע שהתינוק קראו לאות אפ"ה פסול משום שלא כסדרן וכ"ש אם ע"י קלקולו וחסרונו נדמה לאות אחר כגון דלי"ת דומה לרי"ש או ב' דומה לכ' או חי"ת שברגל שמאלו יש הפסק בין הרגל להגג ונראה כה"א או לדי"ק שיש בו הפסק במקום נגיעת היו"ד לעצמותו ונראה לעין כל כיו"ד ונו"ן וכל כה"ג שאין משגיחין על התינוק ולא מהני ליה תיקון [ב] אם ע"י קלקולו וחסרונו לא נפסד מצורתו לגמרי כגון שיש הפסק דק (קיז) באיזה אות באמצעו ועדיין עיקר צורתו עליו או כגון שלא היו היודי"ן שעל האלפי"ן והשיני"ן ורגלי התוי"ן נוגעים בגוף האות אם תינוק דלא חו"ט מכירם אף דלא מתכשר האות עי"ז משום דאין צורתו עליו בשלימות עכ"פ מהני זה דנשאר עליו עיקר צורתו לענין שיהא מותר לתקנו ולא יקרא שלא כסדרן. ויש עוד אופן שלישי שאע"פ שעיקר צורתו יש עליו ותינוק קוראו לאות אפ"ה לא מהני ליה שום תיקון כגון אות שנפסל באיזה דבר (קיח) שתיקונו הוא לגרור מקצתו ולכותבו מחדש [כגון רגל הה"א והקו"ף שנגעו למעלה אפילו נגיעה דקה כחוט השערה שתיקונו הוא לגרור כל הרגל ולכותבו מחדש דלא מהני ליה הפרדה בעלמא משום חק תוכות וכן נגע רגל האל"ף בגג האל"ף וכה"ג וכנ"ל בסעיף י"ח] ואירע שקודם תיקונו כתב לפניו בזה לא יועיל שום תיקון דהא צריך לגרור כל מה שנכתב בפסול וא"כ מה שמתקנה אח"כ הוי שלא כסדרן. ועתה נתחיל לבאר בעזה"י את הסעיף. כל אות שהיא כתובה וכו' וה"ה אם נתקלקלה (קיט) אח"כ: (קטו) ואין צורתה עליה. פי' שנראה לעין כל שאין צורתה עליה כלל ואף דנגעה רגל האל"ף בגג האל"ף או פני האל"ף בגגו או רגל ה"א וקו"ף הנוגעין למעלה ניכר עליו עדיין עיקר צורת האות ותינוק יקראהו לאות אפ"ה כיון שפסול זה אין תיקונו כ"א ע"י גרירת כל מה שנעשה בפסול וכנ"ל בסעיף י"ח ממילא נתבטל צורתו לגמרי ואם יתקנם אח"כ הוי שלא כסדרן: (קטז) רגל האל"ף.

וה"ס

שער הציון

(קיג) ב"י: (קיד) מ"א בשם הרדב"ז: (קטו) ב"י: (קטז) מ"א: (קיז) פמ"ג בא"א: (קיח) ב"י: (קיט) פמ"ג בפתיחה:

הגהות ותיקונים: א) אכסנדרני: ב) הוצאך: ג) חלק: ד) חסר תיבת לא: ה) נו"ב:

25. (114) Whenever a letter was written /in a *tefilin* passage/ incorrectly

Mishnah Berurah

is described as "/a spot/ where one scraped away" if one scraped away /the letter from there/ after it had dried and as "/a spot/ where one erased" if one erased /the letter from there/ when it was still wet.

/When the Shulchan Aruch/ states that one should not erase /while the ink is still wet/, it is giving us good advice /and not a binding ruling/.

See the *P.Mg.*, who writes that if any impression of ink remains there are grounds for concern as regards /the validity of what is written on it/ even once it is after the event. /In fact,/ even an ordinary word, which is not a Divine Name, is forbidden to be written on that spot.

(114) Whenever a letter, etc. In this paragraph, the law /with respect to the writing of letters/ in incorrect order is explained. The details concerning this /law/ are extensive. I will summarize them in brief.

There are three cases where this law is involved.

[1] If there is a fault in some letter, irrespective of whether it formed at the time it was written or whether it formed after it was written [*P.Mg.* in his opening /discourse/].

/Then,/ if it is apparent to everyone that /the letter/ does not have its /required/ form, even if it does not resemble another letter because of /the fault/, and one has /already/ written ahead /of the letter/, no correction whatsoever will be of any avail for it. For example, /this applies/ if a /letter/ י lacks the right leg or a /letter/ ש[22*] lacks one of its י /parts/ and in any similar instance where something is missing from a letter to the extent that because of it /the letter/ does not have its /correct/ symbol. /In such cases,/ even if a child happened to read the letter /correctly/ it will nevertheless /remain/ invalid /after it has been corrected/. /This is/ because /after correction the letter will become invalid for a different reason, that it was written/ in incorrect order.

If as a result of the fault or defect /the letter/ resembles a different letter, one may certainly not take into account /the fact that/ a child /reads it for what it is meant to be/ and /it is self-understood that/ correction is of no avail for it. For example, if a /letter/ ד resembles the /letter/ ר, if a /letter/ ב resembles the /letter/ כ, if a /letter/ ה has a break in its left leg between the leg and the roof and appears like the /letter/ ה or if a /letter/ צ[22*] has a break where the י /part/ touches the body /of the letter, so that/ it appears to everybody like a /letter/ י and a /letter/ נ, and in all similar cases.

[2] If as a result of the fault or defect /the letter/ has not lost its form completely.

/We are referring to a case when/ if a child who is neither /especially/ intelligent nor /especially/ simple recognizes /the letter for what it is meant to be/ the letter is not ruled as valid because of this, as it does not fully have its /correct/ form. Even so, /the fact/ that its form essentially remains is at any rate of avail with respect to the permissibility of correcting /the letter, so that/ it will not be regarded /after the correction as if it was written/ in incorrect order. /One/ example is if there is a thin break in the middle of some letter, but essentially it still has its form. /Another/ example is when the י /parts/ of the א[20*] /letters/ or of the ש[22*] /letters/ or the legs of the ת /letters/ are not touching the body of the letter.

There is, in addition, a third instance /where this law is relevant/. /In this instance/ although /the letter/ has its form essentially and a child will read the letter /correctly/, no correction whatsoever will be of avail for it, notwithstanding. This is the case if a letter has become invalid for some reason because of which /it is necessary/ to scrape away some of /the letter/ and write it anew /in order/ to correct it. [For example, when the /left/ leg of a /letter/ ה or /the leg/ of a /letter/ ק touches /the roof/ above, even

מקום (לו) [יז] (קיג) הגרר ועל מקום המחק אפילו אזכרה [ח]ולא ימחוק בעודו לח אלא ייבשנו יפה כי אז יגרר בקל ולא ישאר לו שום רושם: כה (קיד) [ט]כל אות שהיא כתובה שלא כתקנה (קטו) ואין צורתה (לז) עליה כגון נגע (קטז) רגל האל"ף (לח) [יח] בגג האל"ף או פני האל"ף בפנים בגג שתחתיה או

ח הר"י אלכסנדריא[א]
ט הגהות מיימון פ"א ופרק ב' ומהרי"ק בשורש ס"ט ותרומת הדשן סימן מ"ח והר"י אלכסנדריא[א]

באר היטב

שיגרור הוי"ו ימשוך הב' שלפניה באופן שיהיה ממולא החלק של מקום הגרר אבל בל' נסתפק כגון הוליאך[ב] שכתבו ביו"ד או מלות מלא בוי"ו ואם ימחוק היו"ד או הוי"ו יוכל אח"כ להמשיך חלק התחתון ולא העליון אי כשר או לא. ומסיים הב"י ומ"מ כל שנראית כשתי תיבות פסולה. וכ"כ הלבוש שיש להחמיר בזה וכתב המ"א דאם בתחלת הכתיבה ממשיך רגל התחתון של הנו"ן והלד"י וכותב האות הסמוך בתוכו כזה פני ארצי מותר דהוי ממש כתיבה אחת דלא כהרנ"ח ח"ב סי' ע"ח. עיין כנה"ג. וביד אהרן. ואם כתב תיבה יתירה מתקנה. ואם יהיה חלק ט' אותיות דכשיגררנה יהיה פרשה במקום שאין פרשה פסול. אבל מותר למשוך הה"א אע"פ שלא יצא רגל בסופו מ"א. מלא וי"ו או יו"ד יתירה יגרור אותה ויעבה קצת האות שלפניה או שלאחריה שאין בזה משום שינוי אות. עיין מ"א וביד אהרן (עיין בספר אליה רבה בענינים האלה בשם כנה"ג ושו"ת רדב"ז): (לו) הגרר. הגרר מקרי כשגררו יבש והמחק מיקרי שמחקו לח: (לז) עליה. ובכל הני אפי' תינוק יוכל לקרותם פסול: (לח) בגג. דאז צריך לגררה כולה כמ"ש סעיף י"ח:

שערי תשובה

חלוק ונראה כשני תיבות ושוב לא יועיל מה שימשוך אחר כך כיון שהפיסול נראה לעין כל יש בתיקון הכתיבה ותוספות הדיו בהמשכה משום כתיבה שלא כסדרן. ומ"ש הבה"ט ואם יהיה חלוק[ג] יש קילור בהעתקת דברי המג"א וע"ש שכוונתו דהיכי שצריך לגרור תיבה יתירה אז אם כשיגרור יהיה חלק ט' אותיות ויפסלו התפילין וכדי שלא לפוסלם אם בסיום התיבה שלפניו יש שם ה"א או קו"ף ימשוך הגג של הה"א או הקו"ף. ואעפ"י שעל ידי ההמשכה[ד] יהיה הרגל של הה"א או הקו"ף בסופה אין קפידה בדיעבד ע"ש. ולפי מ"ש בשם הדב"ש לכאורה גם בזה היה צריך להמשיך קודם שיגרור ואם כן צריך להמשיך למעלה מן התיבה המיותרת בעוד התיבה כתובה וזה קלקול האות הוא. ואפשר שבזה שאין הפסול רק משום חלק ט' אותיות אין צריך לעשות כן ויכול להמשיך אח"כ ואין בזה משום שלא כסדרן. ונראה שיש לגרור תחלה ב' או ג' אותיות מן התיבה המיותרת ולהמשיך הה"א ואחר כך יגרור השאר וא"כ לא היה כאן פסול מעולם כלל. ועיין בשו"ת מ"ב[ה] שרצה ללמוד לענין נוני"ן המנוזרין מהא דנמלא תיבות כפולות בתפילין ומ"ש עליו בשערי אפרים שער ה' בפתחי שערים שם דבתפילין אי הוי שלא כסדרן מיירי אבל ודאי מ"מ צריך למחוק ולהסיר התיבה המיותרת משם ע"ש: [יז] הגרר. עבה"ט ועיין בדבר שמואל סימן קנ"ד שכתב שאין לתלות תיבה אחת בין השיטין בכתיבת התפילין ומזוזות אף במקום שהכתיבה כסדרה בין המוקדמת למאוחרת חדא דגם זה מיקרי שלא כסדרן מחמת שינוי. וגם מפני שדרך כתיבתן להיות דקה. בלי ריוח הרבה בין שיטה לשיטה לכך אין תולין ע"ש שהביא מתשובת הר"ן סי' ל"ט ועיין בגינת ורדים כלל ב' סימן ד' באמצע התשובה שאם נזדמן להסופר שהשיטה דחוקה מהכיל התיבות שיעור לה אין להתיר שיתלה תיבה אחת למעלה בין השיטות ואחר כך ירד לכתוב כסדר השיטה. ושם כתב דלדעת רש"י תפילין ומזוזות חמירי טפי ואפילו בתליית אות אחת מחזי כמנומר ע"ש: [יח] בגג. עבה"ט

משנה ברורה

האות שלפניה שתמלא מקומה כגון (קיג) לאבותיך שכתב מלא וי"ו אחר הב' יגררנה וימשוך הב' שלפניה שתמלא מקומה. וכן אם התיקון תלוי בכ"ף או דל"ת או רי"ש שאפשר להמשיכן מעט למלא מקום אות היתרה שנגררה אבל אם האותיות שאפשר להמשיכן הן אחר האות היתרה שא"א להמשיכן לאחוריהן עד שיגרר מהם תחלה כגון שאר שכתוב בתורה שכתבה מלא וי"ו אחר האל"ף שא"א למשוך הרי"ש לאחריה עד שיגרר רגלה תחלה ונמצא שביטל צורתה וכשמתקנה אח"כ נמצא כותב שלא כסדרן ואין תקנה אח"כ יכול למלאות מקומו ע"י (קיד) שיעבה קצת האות שלפניה ושלאחריה שאין בזה משום שינוי האות תשא"כ כשהאותיות שאפשר להמשיכן הן לפני האות היתרה אזי אפשר להמשיכן הרבה מבלי שיגרע מהם כלום. אך יש להסתפק (קטו) במלות הראשון שדינו להיות חסר וכתבו מלא ומחק אח"כ הוי"ו אם מועיל אריכת הלדי"ק למטה אח"כ או דילמא כל עוד שאינו מאריך האות למעלה נחשב כשני תיבות אע"פ שסמוכה מלמטה וכן נתן שמשפטו להיות חסר וכן הולאך אם כתבו מלא ביו"ד בין לדי"ק לאל"ף בכל אלו יש להסתפק אם יש להם תיקון בהאריך האות שלפניו למטה ומ"מ כל שנראה כב' תיבות פסולה אבל אם בתחלת הכתיבה ממשיך (קטז) רגל התחתון של הנו"ן והלד"י וכותב האות הסמוכה לתוכה כגון פני או ארצי כשר כיון דבתיבה אחת נכתבו ומ"מ לכתחלה אין נכון לעשות כן להבליע אות בתוך אות כי יש מחמירין בזה: כד (קיג) הגרר. הגרר מיקרי כשגררו משנתיבש והמחק מיקרי כשמחקו בעודו לח ומש"כ ולא ימחוק עלה טובה קמ"ל ועיין בפמ"ג שכתב דאם ישאר שום רושם דיו אפי' בדיעבד יש חשש בזה ואפילו תיבה בעלמא דלא אזכרה אסור לכתוב על מקום זה: כה (קיד) כל אות וכו'. סעיף זה יבואר בו דין שלא כסדרן ועניניו ארוכין ואכלול בקצרה בדין זה יש בו ג' פרטים [א] אם יש קלקול באיזה אות בין שנעשה זה בעת הכתיבה או שנעשה לאחר הכתיבה [פמ"ג בפתיחה] אם נר' לעין כל שאין צורתו עליו כגון יו"ד שחסר לו רגלו הימני או שי"ן שחסר לו יו"ד אחד וכל כי האי גונא שחסר באות איזה דבר עד שעי"ז אין תמונתו עליו אפילו אין נדמה משום זה לאות אחר וכתב לפניו לא מהני ליה שום תיקון ואפילו אם אירע שהתינוק קראו לאות אפ"ה פסול משום שלא כסדרן וכ"ש אם ע"י קלקולו וחסרונו נדמה לאות אחר כגון דל"ת דומה לרי"ש או ב' דומה לכ' או ת"ח שברגל שמאלו יש הפסק בין הרגל להגג ונראה כה"א או צדי"ק שיש בו הפסק במקום נגיעת היו"ד לעצמותו ונראה לעין כל כיו"ד ונו"ן וכל כה"ג שאין משגיחין על התינוק ולא מהני ליה תיקון [ב] אם ע"י קלקולו וחסרונו לא נפסד מצורתו לגמרי כגון שיש הפסק דק (קיז) באיזה אות באמצעו ועדיין עיקר צורתו עליו או כגון שלא היו היודי"ן שעל האלפי"ן והשיני"ן ורגלי התוי"ן נוגעים בגוף האות אם תינוק דלא חו"ט מכירם אף דלא מתכשר האות עי"ז משום דאין צורתו עליו בשלימות עכ"פ מהני זה דנשאר עליו עיקר צורתו לענין שיהא מותר לתקנו ולא יקרא שלא כסדרן. ויש עוד אופן שלישי שאע"פ שעיקר צורתו יש עליו ותינוק קוראו לאות אפ"ה לא מהני ליה שום תיקון כגון אות שנפסל באיזה דבר (קיח) שתיקונו הוא לגרור מקצתו ולכותבו מחדש [כגון רגל הה"א והקו"ף שנגעו למעלה אפילו נגיעה דקה כחוט השערה שתיקונו הוא לגרור כל הרגל ולכותבו מחדש דלא מהני ליה הפרדה בעלמא משום חק תוכות וכן נגע רגל האל"ף בגג האל"ף וכה"ג וכנ"ל בסעיף י"ח] ואירע שקודם תיקונו כתב לפניו בזה לא ילוייר שום תיקון דהא צריך לגרור כל מה שנכתב בפסול וא"כ מה שמתקנה אח"כ הוי שלא כסדרן. ועתה נתחיל לבאר בעזה"י את הסעיף. כל אות שהיא כתובה וכו' וה"ה אם נתקלקלה (קיט) אח"כ: (קטו) ואין צורתה עליה. פי' שנראה לעין כל שאין צורתה עליה כלל ואף דבנגעה רגל האל"ף בגג האל"ף או פני האל"ף בגגו או רגל ה"א וקו"ף הנוגעין למעלה ניכר עליו עדיין עיקר צורת האות ותינוק יקראהו לאות אפ"ה כיון שפסול זה אין תיקונו כ"א ע"י גרירת כל מה שנעשה בפסול וכנ"ל בסעיף י"ח ממילא נתבטל צורתו לגמרי ואם יתקנם אח"כ הוי שלא כסדרן: (קטז) רגל האל"ף.

וה"ה

שער הציון

(קיג) ב"י: (קיד) מ"א בשם הרדב"ז: (קטו) ב"י: (קטז) מ"א: (קיז) פמ"ג בא"א: (קיח) ב"י: (קיט) פמ"ג בפתיחה:

הגהות ותיקונים: א) אכסנדרני: ב) הוצאך: ג) חלק: ד) חסר תיבת לא: ה) נו"ב:

(115) and does not have its /proper/ form, if one went back and corrected it after /other letters/ were written ahead of it, this is /classed as/ writing in incorrect order and /the passage/ is invalid.

For example, /one cannot correct the letter for this reason/ if **(116)** the leg of a /letter/ א[20*] touches the roof of the /letter/ א or if the front of a /letter/ א

Mishnah Berurah

/if it is/ a slender touch of a hairsbreadth. /In such a case the fault/ must be corrected by scraping off the entire leg and writing it anew. Mere separation will be of no avail, in view of /the fact that one may not/ carve around /to form a letter/. A like /example/ is when the leg of a /letter/ א touches the roof of the א. There are similar cases which are /described/ above in Par. 18.] If in such circumstances one happened to write ahead of /the letter/ before he corrected it, no correction whatsoever is conceivable. For /in order to correct the letter/ one is required to scrape off all that was written invalidly and, consequently, when he will correct /the letter/ subsequently this will constitute /writing the letter/ in incorrect order.

We will now begin, with the help of *Ha-Sheym*, to explain the paragraph.

/The Shulchan Aruch writes,/ "Whenever a letter was written, etc." The same ruling /applies/ if /the letter/ became spoiled subsequently.

(115) And does not have its form. I.e., if everyone can see that it does not have its /proper/ form at all.

/Now/ when the leg of a /letter/ א[20*] touches the roof of the א or the front of a /letter/ א /touches/ its roof or the leg of a /letter/ ה or of a /letter/ ק touches /the roof of the letter/ above, the essential form of the letter is still recognizable and a child will read the letter /for what it is meant to be/. Even so, /it can/ nevertheless /not be corrected if one has already written ahead/. This is because this invalidity can only be corrected by scraping away all that was done invalidly, as /explained/ above in Par. 18. It /therefore/ follows /that before one is able to correct the letter/ its form will have been completely lost, /so that/ if he subsequently corrects it this will constitute /writing the letter/ in incorrect order.

(116) The leg of a /letter/ א. This ruling

שהיה רגל הה"א או רגל הקו"ף (קיז) נוגעים או שהיתה * אות אחת חלוקה לשתי אותיות כגון (קיח) צד"י שכתב (לט) יו"ד נו"ן או שי"ן שכתבה (קיט) עי"ן יו"ד (קכ) או חי"ת שני זייני"ן ואחר שכתב לפניו חזר ותקנם הוי שלא כסדרן ופסולין אבל להפריד האותיות הדבוקות אחר שכתב לפניהם שפיר דמי דכיון שהאות צורתה עליה כשמפרידה מחבירתה לא הוי ככותב והוא הדין שאם לא היו מקצת (קכא) יודי"ן שעל האלפי"ן והשיני"ן והעיני"ן ורגלי התוי"ן נוגעין בגוף האות (קכב) ותינוק דלא חכים ולא טיפש

באר היטב

(לט) יו"ד נו"ן. וה"ה אם לא עשה רגל הימין של יו"ד אבל אם לא עשה לה רגל שמאל יכול לתקנם דשם יו"ד עליה. ב"י מ"א:

משנה ברורה

וה"ה כל הני דכתב רמ"א בהג"ה סוף סי"ח הנ"ל: (קיז) נוגעים אפילו (קכ) נגיעה דקה כחוט השערה: (קיח) צד"י שכתב. פי' (קכא) שחלק היו"ד מהנו"ן כ"כ עד שנראה כשני אותיות וכן בכל אינך לכן אפילו אם אירע דתינוק קראו כהלכתו אין יכול לתקנן אח"כ שכיון שעינינו רואות שיש להן צורת אותיות אחרות א"כ כשמתקנם אח"כ הרי זה כתיבה מחדש ושלא כסדרן. וה"ה אפילו אם אין להם צורת אותיות אחרות רק שנראה לעין הכל שאין לה עיקר צורתה (קכב) כגון יו"ד שלא עשה לה רגל הימיני או אל"ף שחסר לה היו"ד העליון וכל כה"ג אין יכול לתקנם אח"כ אבל אם לא עשה להיו"ד רגל שמאלי אף דאם ישאר כך פסול דאיננו יו"ד כראוי לפי דעת רוב הפוסקים כדלקמן בסי' ל"ו מ"מ כיון דיש לה עיקר צורתה דאפילו בלא עוקץ שם יו"ד עליה לכן יכול לתקנה ואין בזה משום שלא כסדרן: (קיט) עי"ן יו"ד. וה"ה מ"ם (קכג) פתוחה שכתבו כ"ו בלי משיכת הגג שביניהם: (קכ) או חי"ת שני זייני"ן. אפילו אם עשה חוטרא על גביהן רק שאין נוגעים זה לזה למעלה (קכד) וניכר להדיא פרידתן ה"ז הפסידה עיקר צורתה שנראה כשני זייני"ן: (קכא) יודי"ן שעל האלפי"ן. וה"ה אם היה הפסק באיזה אות באמצעו [פמ"ג בא"א בפתי']: (קכב) ותינוק וכו'. פי' לכן אפילו אם פרידתן ניכר להדיא [דהיינו תומ"י כשרואה אותן] יכול לתקנם דהרי לא הפסיד עדיין האות עיקר צורתה מדקראה התינוק לאות [כן כתב הגרע"א בחידושיו ודלא כפמ"ג שהחמיר בזה ועיין בבה"ל]

ביאור הלכה

שכתב שם מעשה בסופר אחד שכתב השמרו ב"פ ומחק וא"ו א' והשמר ב' ומשך הרי"ש עד וא"ו שניה והכשיר זה עי"ש. ולדעת הפמ"ג הנ"ל גם לכתחלה צריך לעשות כך. וכתב שם עוד דאפילו היה תיבה ב' תיבה אחרת שאינה מענין תפילין כלל וכה וא"ו לבסוף וגרר כנ"ל נמי כשר דמה בכך ואף דנפסל תחלה שוא"ו מרוחק הרבה לאבותיך נמי כ"ז שלא תיקן ומשך הב' נראה כב' תיבות. ולי צ"ע בזה דהלא בעינן שיכתוב לשמן דהיינו לשם קדושת תפילין ולעיכובא הוא אף בדיעבד וכדלעיל בסעיף י"ט ואף את"ל דכיון בזה התיבה לשמן מי יאמר דמהני בזה אחרי דאין התיבה הזו מענין תפילין כלל וצ"ע: * אות אחת וכו' ראיתי לאיזה אנשים שפוסלין בזה אם נמצא הפסק דקה מן הדקה שאינה ניכרת עד שיסתכל בה היטב ומקורם הוא מדברי הפמ"ג בא"א במה דכתב דבכל זה לא מהני תיקון אפילו אם אין ניכר פרידתן להדיא ועיין ג"כ שם באות ל"ו ולענ"ד *נראה שמדינא אין להחמיר בזה ואברר זה בעזה"י בכמה ראיות והוא. א' מדברי הרי"א שמקור דין זה נובע ממנו שזה לשונו בב"י אם כתב בתו"מ אות א' חלוקה לשתי אותיות כגון לד"י שכ' יו"ד נו"ן וכו' וכן כתב הרא"ש על ה"א וקו"ף שדבקו בתפילין שאין להם תקנה בתיקון וכו' ועיין במ"א בס"ק ל"ו שכתב דבכל הני אפי' התינוק יכול לקרותו פסול כיון שנראה כשני אותיות ועיין בפמ"ג שם ולדבריו איירי הרי"א והמ"א אף דאין ניכר להדיא פרידתן והנה מלבד שהוא דוחק גדול בדברי המ"א כמו שאברר לבסוף יקשה קושיא עצומה לפ"ז בדברי הרי"א דא"כ מה ראיה מייתי לזה מקו"ף דהא ע"כ טעם הקו"ף דלא מהני תיקון ובשאר אותיות שאינם נוגעין שלא הפסידו עיקר צורתן מהני תיקון כמו שכתב הרי"א בעצמו ע"כ הטעם כמו שכתב הב"י מתחלה בשם תה"ד משום דתיקונו הוא ע"י מחיקה וע"כ יתבטל עיקר צורתו לעין הכל א"כ אין ראיה מזה לצד"י שכתבה יו"ד נו"ן ולא היתה ניכר פרידתו להדיא עד שיסתכל בהן היטיב ותינוק קראה לאות ואף דיכול לדחוק ולחלק דשאני צ"די מיו"ד ושי"ן[א] שאינם נוגעין משום דבעלם הם ב' אותיות אחרות כ"ז שלא חברן ביחד ע"כ יקרא זה כשאר אות שהפסיד עיקר צורתו עכ"פ אין ראיה לזה מקו"ף וכ"ש דק"ו ליכא א"ו דכוונת הרי"א לפוסלו הוא דוקא כשחלקו עד שניכר ונראה לעין כשני אותיות ע"כ מייתי שפיר ראיה מקו"ף שבעת הכתיבה לא נדמה לאות אחרת ע"י דיבוקו וגם בעת התיקון שצריך למחקו מתחלה עד שיתבטל צורתו ג"כ לא תדמה עי"ז לאות אחרת ואפ"ה פסול לתקן וכ"ש בלד"י שכתב יו"ד נו"ן והוא נראה לעין הכל כשני אותיות שבודאי אין להם עדיין שום תמונה של לד"י שאין יכול לחברן אח"כ ובזה איירי ג"כ המ"א שכתב דלא מהני קריאת התינוק בזה היינו כיון שנראה לעין הכל כב' אותיות א"כ הפסיד הל"די עיקר צורתו והוי כאל"ף שחסר לו יו"ד אחד אבל אם אין ניכר פרידתו עד שמסתכל בה היטיב מותר לתקנה דעדיין עיקר צורתו עליו והתינוק יקראנו לאות והוי כמו יו"ד ושי"ן[א] שאין נוגעין דמהני שם קריאת התינוק. ובזה מיושב ג"כ לשונו שכתב בכל הני אפילו תינוק וכו' כיון שנראה כשתי אותיות ולא כתב כיון שהם שתי אותיות דליהוי משמע משום דבעלם הם שתי אותיות כ"ז שלא חברם כסברת הפמ"ג א"ו כיון דלעין הרואה לא ניכר להדיא הפרדתה עד שמסתכל בה היטיב וגם התינוק יקראנה לאות מיקרי עי"ז עיקר צורתה עליה ויכול לתקן אותה. גם מלשון הרי"א והשו"ע משמע כמו שכתבנו דאיירי דניכר ונראה לעין הפרדתן מדכתבו לד"י שכתבו יו"ד נו"ן וכו' ולא כתבו שיש הפסק במקום חיבור היו"ד להנו"ן. וגם בספר עולת תמיד משמע ג"כ דמיירי שניכר לעין הכל כשני אותיות ע"ש. (הג"ה ודע עוד דמה שכתב הרי"א כיון שקודם שנתקנו היה להם שם אותה האות ולא שם אחר כיון שקודם תקנתן ינוקא דלא חכים ולא טיפש מלי קרי להו וכו' טעם א' הוא וכיון השני מברר להראשון דמזה ראיה דעדיין שמה עליה משא"כ בלד"י שכתבה יו"ד נו"ן דניכר להדיא הפרדתן בודאי אין מלוי שיקראנה התינוק לצד"י כיון שנראה כב' אותיות ונתבטל עיקר צורתה. ולאות שאמת כדברי אעתיק לך לשון הד"מ הארוך שז"ל ור"י אלכסנדרי כתב אם כתב אות אחת וחלקו לב' אותיות כגון וכו' אבל אם היה הפירוד בשאר אותיות שאין הפירוד מדמה אותן לאות אחרת כגון אות אל"ף או תי"ו שלא חיברן מותר לתקנן מאחר דבלא תיקון תינוק דלא חכים ולא טיפש יכול לקרותן עכ"ל הנך רואה דעיקר הטעם דמכשירין ביו"ד ושי"ן שלא נגעו היינו משום דתינוק יכול לקרותה משא"כ בלד"י שכתבה יו"ד נו"ן מסתמא לא יהיה יכול התינוק לקרותה כיון שנראה לעין הכל כב' אותיות ומה שכתב המ"א בכל הני אפילו תינוק וכו' היינו אפילו אי אתרמי שאיזה תינוק קראה לד"י אפ"ה פסולה משום דעינינו רואות דאין צורתה עליה כלל ע"כ הג"ה). ואף דמדברי הט"ז בס"ק כ"א[ב]ו דמפרש דאיירי בלא עשה לו חטוטרות משמע דאיירי המחבר במה שכ' בחי"ת שני זייני"ן אפילו בלא ניכר להדיא פרידתן דדומיא דסיפא דמיירי בלא ניכר להדיא אך דשם איירי בחוטרא לכך מהני תיקון וכאן בלא חוטרא ומסתמא ה"ה בכל הני דקחשיב המחבר דברי הט"ז גופא מוקשים מאד אחד דלשון המחבר שלפנינו משמע דברישא עיקר הפסול בחי"ת הוא משום דניכר להדיא פרידתו מדכ' בסיפא אך אין ניכר וכו' משמע דמתחלה מיירי בניכר להדיא ועוד דהמעיין בב"י בסוף סימן ל"ו בד"ה מ"כ אם חוטרא וכו' בסוף דבריו יראה להדיא דפסול אף ביש לו חטוטרות ומשטחיות לשונו שם משמע דאפילו תינוק לא היה מהני לזה דאין עליו שם אות כלל משום דניכר להדיא פרידתו ונראה כשני זייני"ן וא"כ מזה גופא אדרבא ג"כ ראיה לדברינו דמיירי המחבר בכל שאר דבריו ברישא ג"כ דוקא בניכר להדיא פרידתן דמשום זה אבד האות את עיקר צורתו ונראה כשני אותיות אחרות משא"כ בלא ניכר להדיא פרידתן עדיין שמו עליו וזהו טעמו של הי"א שהקיל בחוטרא דחי"ת שלא היה ניכר פרידתן ועוד אפשר לומר לענין דינא דבאות לד"י וכל כה"ג גם הט"ז מודה לכל מה שהכרחנו דבלא ניכר להדיא פרידתן יוכל לתקן דעדיין שמו עליו ורק בחי"ת סובר הט"ז כיון שאין חטוטרות עליו מוכח דהוא ב' זייני"ן ולכן אף שעשאן בקירוב כ"כ שלא היה ניכר להדיא פרידתן אבד את שמו. וכן משמע קצת בתה"ד בסימן מ"ח [הובא בב"י בד"ה כתוב בהגה"מ] שכתב שם דהא דכתב הרא"ש דרגל ה"א וקו"ף הנוגעין למעלה בתפילין שצריך לכותבן כסדרן אין ראיה דפליג אהר"ס דמכשיר לתקן ביודי"ן שעל האלפי"ן דנוגעין לגוף האות דשאני הני דאין להם תקנה במחיקה לחודה וכו' וכתב עוד שם דאפשר דהרא"ש קאי נמי אהא דכתב בתר הכי דצריכין היודי"ן שעל האלפי"ן והשיני"ן להיות דבוקין ור"ל דבהני נמי אי אפשר לתקן בתפילין ופליג אהר"ס וכתב הב"י דהמעיין

שער הציון

(קכ) כנ"ל בס"ק ל"ה: (קכא) עיין בבה"ל: (קכב) מ"א: (קכג) א"ר: (קכד) ביארנו בבה"ל:

הגהות ותיקונים: א) של השי"ן: **ב)** כ': **ג)** כ' ו':

/touches/ inside on the roof underneath it or if the leg of a /letter/ ה or the leg of a /letter/ ק **(117)** touches /the roof of the letter/.

/This is also the case/ if one letter is divided into two letters, such as where **(118)** a /letter/ צ[22*] is written /as/ a /letter/ י and a /letter/ נ, a/letter/ ש[22*] is

Mishnah Berurah

/applies/ likewise in all the /cases/ described by the *Rema* in the gloss above, at the end of Par. 18.

(117) Touches. /I.e.,/ even with a slight touch of a hairsbreadth.

(118) A צ is written. I.e., if one divided the י /part of the צ/ from the נ /part of the צ/ to the extent that it appears like two letters. /A corresponding division is meant/ likewise in all the other /cases/.

Therefore /, once one has already written ahead of the letter/, even if a child happened to read it as it should be /read/ one is unable to correct it subsequently. For in view /of the fact/ that we see with our eyes that it has the form of other letters, it follows that when it is corrected subsequently this will involve writing /the correct letter/ anew and in incorrect order.

Correspondingly, even if /the faulty letters/ do not have the form of other letters, but it is apparent to everyone that they do not have their essential form, they cannot be corrected subsequently /if one has already written ahead of them/. For example, /this applies in the case of/ a /letter/ י for which one did not make a right leg or /in the case/ of a /letter/ א[20*] which lacks the upper י /part/ and in all similar cases.

/Now/ if one did not make a left leg to a /letter/ י and it remains like that /the letter/ is invalid, since it is not a proper י according to the view of the majority of Poskim, as /explained/ below in Sec. 36. However, despite this, /the ruling as regards correction is/ nevertheless /different where the left leg is lacking/. /For/ in view /of the fact/ that /such a י/ has its essential form, as even without the /left leg/ prickle /the symbol/ is describable as a י, one is therefore able to correct it /even if he has written ahead/ and /the correction/ does not involve /writing the letter/ in incorrect order.

שהיה רגל הה"א או רגל הקו"ף (קיז) נוגעים או שהיתה * אות אחת חלוקה לשתי אותיות כגון (קיח) צד"י שכתב (לט) יו"ד נו"ן או שי"ן שכתבה (קיט) עי"ן יו"ד (קכ) או חי"ת שני זייני"ן ואחר שכתב לפניו חזר ותקנם הוי שלא כסדרן ופסולין אבל להפריד האותיות הדבוקות אחר שכתב לפניהם שפיר דמי דכיון שהאות צורתה עליה כשמפרידה מחבירתה לא הוי ככותב והוא הדין שאם לא היו מקצת (קכא) יודי"ן שעל האלפי"ן והשיני"ן והעייני"ן ורגלי התוי"ן נוגעין בגוף האות (קכב) ותינוק דלא חכים ולא טיפש

באר היטב

(לט) יו"ד נו"ן. וה"ה אם לא עשה רגל הימין של יו"ד אבל אם לא עשה לה רגל שמאל יכול לתקנס דשם יו"ד עליה. ב"י מ"א:

ביאור הלכה

שכתב שם מעשה בסופר אחד שכתב השמרו השמרו ב"פ ומחק וא"ו א' והשמר ב' ומשך הרי"ש עד וא"ו שניה והכשיר זה עי"ש. ולדעת הפמ"ג הנ"ל גם לכתחלה צריך לעשות כך. וכתב שם עוד דאפילו היה תיבה ב' תיבה אחרת שאינה מענין תפילין כלל וזה וא"ו לבסוף וגרר כנ"ל נמי כשר דמה בכך ואף דנפסל תחלה שוא"ו מרוחק הרבה לאבותיך נמי כ"ז שלא תיקן ומשך הב' נראה כב' תיבות. ולי צ"ע בזה דהלא בעינן שיכתוב לשמן דהיינו לשם קדושת תפילין ולעיכובא הוא אף בדיעבד וכדלעיל בסעיף י"ט ואף את"ל דכיוון בזה התיבה לשמן מי יאמר דמהני בזה אחרי דאין התיבה הזו מענין תפילין כלל וצ"ע: * אות אחת וכו' ראיתי לאיזה אנשים שפוסלין בזה אם נמצא הפסק דקה מן הדקה שאינה ניכרת עד שיסתכל בה היטב ומקורם הוא מדברי הפמ"ג בא"א במה דכתב דבכל זה לא מהני תיקון אפילו אם אין ניכר פרידתן להדיא ועיין ג"כ שם באות ל"ו ולענ"ד נראה שמדינא אין להחמיר בזה ואברר זה בעזה"י בכמה ראיות והוא. א' מדברי הרי"א שמקור דין זה נובע ממנו שזה לשונו בב"י אם כתב בתו"מ אות א' חלוקה לשתי אותיות כגון צד"י שכ' יו"ד נו"ן וכו' וכן כתב הרא"ש על ה"א וקו"ף שדבקו בתפילין שאין להם תקנה בתיקון וכו' ועיין במ"א בס"ק ל"ו שכתב דבכל הני אפי' התינוק יכול לקרותו פסול כיון שנראה כשני אותיות ועיין בפמ"ג שם ולדבריו איירי הרי"א והמ"א אף דאין ניכר להדיא פרידתן והנה מלבד שהוא דוחק גדול בדברי המ"א כמו שאברר לבסוף יקשה קושיא עצומה לפ"ז בדברי הרי"א דא"כ מה ראיה מייתי לזה מקו"ף דהא ע"כ טעם הקו"ף דלא מהני תיקון ובשאר אותיות שאינם נוגעין שלא הפסידו עיקר צורתן מהני תיקון כמו שכתב הרי"א בעצמו ע"כ הטעם כמו שכתב הב"י מתחלה בשם תה"ד משום דתיקונו הוא ע"י מחיקה וע"כ יתבטל עיקר צורתו לענין הכל א"כ אין ראיה מזה לצד"י שכתבה יו"ד נו"ן ולא היתה ניכר פרידתו להדיא עד שיסתכל בהן היטיב ותינוק קראה לאות ואף דיכול לדחוק ולחלק דשאני צ"די מיו"ד ושי"ן[א] שאינם נוגעין משום דבעלם הם ב' אותיות אחרות כ"ז שלא חברן ביחד ע"כ יקרא זה כשאר אות שהפסיד עיקר צורתו עכ"פ אין ראיה לזה מקו"ף וכ"ש דק"ו ליכא א"ו דכוונת הרי"א לפוסלו הוא דוקא כשחלקו עד שניכר ונראה לעין כשני אותיות ע"כ מייתי שפיר ראיה מקו"ף שבעת הכתיבה לא נדמה לאות אחרת ע"י דיבוקו וגם בעת התיקון שצריך למחקו מתחלה עד שיתבטל צורתו ג"כ לא תדמה עי"ז לאות אחרת ואפ"ה פסול לתקן וכ"ש בצד"י שכתב יו"ד נו"ן והוא נראה לעין הכל כשני אותיות שבודאי אין להם עדיין שום תמונה של צד"י שאין יכול לחברן אח"כ ובזה מיירי ג"כ המ"א שכתב דלא מהני קריאת התינוק בזה היינו כיון שנראה לעין הכל כב' אותיות א"כ הפסיד הצ"די עיקר צורתו והוי כאל"ף שחסר לו יו"ד אחד אבל אם אין ניכר פרידתו עד שמסתכל בה היטיב מותר לתקנה דעדיין עיקר צורתו עליו והתינוק יקראנו לאות והוי כמו יו"ד ושי"ן[א] שאין נוגעין דמהני שם קריאת התינוק. ובזה מיושב ג"כ לשונו שכתב בכל הני אפילו תינוק וכו' כיון שנראה כשתי אותיות ולא כתב כיון שהם שתי אותיות דליהוי משמע משום דבעלם הם שתי אותיות כ"ז שלא חברם כסברת הפמ"ג א"ו כיון דלעין הרואה לא ניכר להדיא הפרדתה עד שמסתכל בה היטיב וגם התינוק יקראנה לאות מיקרי עי"ז עיקר צורתה עליה ויכול לתקן אותה. גם מלשון הרי"א והשו"ע משמע כמו שכתבנו דאיירי דניכר ונראה לעין הפרדתן מדכתבו צד"י שכתבו יו"ד נו"ן וכו' ולא כתבו שיש הפסק במקום חיבור היו"ד להנו"ן. וגם בספר עולת תמיד משמע ג"כ דמיירי שניכר לעין הכל כשני אותיות ע"ש. (הג"ה ודע עוד דמה שכתב הרי"א כיון שקודם שנתקנו היה להם שם אותה האות ולא שם אחר כיון שקודם תקנתן יונקא דלא חכים ולא טיפש מלי קרי להו וכו' טעם א' הוא וכיון השני מברר להראשון דמזה ראיה דעדיין שמה עליה משא"כ בצד"י שכתבה יו"ד נו"ן דניכר להדיא הפרדתן בודאי אין מלוי שיקראנה התינוק לצד"י כיון שנראה כב' אותיות ונתבטל עיקר צורתה. ולאות שאמת כדברי אעתיק לך לשון הד"מ הארוך שז"ל ור"י אלכסנדרני כתב אם כתב אות אחת וחלקו לב' אותיות כגון וכו' אבל אם היה הפירוד בשאר אותיות שאין הפירוד מדמה אותן לאות אחרת כגון אות אל"ף או תי"ו שלא חיברן מותר לתקנן מאחר דבלא תיקון תינוק דלא חכים ולא טיפש יכול לקרותן עכ"ל הנך רואה דעיקר הטעם דמכשירין ביו"ד ושי"ן שלא נגעו היינו משום דתינוק יכול לקרותה משא"כ בצד"י שכתבה יו"ד נו"ן מסתמא לא יהיה יכול התינוק לקרותה כיון שנראה לעין הכל כב' אותיות ומה שכתב המ"א בכל הני אפילו תינוק וכו' היינו אפילו אי אתרמי שאיזה תינוק קראה לצ"י אפ"ה פסולה משום דעינינו רואות דאין צורתה עליה כלל ע"כ הג"ה). ואף דמדברי הט"ז בס"ק כ"א[ב] דמפרש דאיירי בלא עשה לו חטוטרות משמע דאיירי המחבר במה שכ' בחי"ת שני זייני"ן אפילו בלא ניכר להדיא פרידתן דדומיא דסיפא דמיירי בלא ניכר להדיא אך דשם איירי בחוטרא לכך מהני תיקון וכאן בלא חוטרא ומסתמא ה"ה בכל הני דקחשיב המחבר דברי הט"ז גופא מוקשים מאד אחד דלשון המחבר שלפנינו משמע דברישא עיקר הפסול בחי"ת הוא משום דניכר להדיא פרידתו מדכ' בסיפא אך אין ניכר וכו' משמע דמתחלה מיירי בניכר להדיא ועוד דהמעיין בב"י בסוף סימן ל"ו בד"ה מ"כ אם חוטרא וכו' בסוף דבריו יראה להדיא דפסול אף דיש לו חטוטרות ומשטחיות לשונו שם משמע דאפילו תינוק לא היה מהני לזה דאין עליו שם אות כלל משום דניכר להדיא פרידתו ונראה כשני זייני"ן וא"כ מזה גופא אדרבא ג"כ ראיה לדברינו דמיירי המחבר בכל שאר דבריו ברישא ג"כ דוקא בניכר להדיא פרידתן דמשום זה אבד האות את עיקר צורתו ונראה כשני אותיות אחרות משא"כ בלא ניכר להדיא פרידתן עדיין שמו עליו וזהו טעמו של הי"א שהקיל בחוטרא דחי"ת שלא היה ניכר פרידתן ועוד אפשר לומר לענין דינא דבאות צד"י וכל כה"ג גם הט"ז מודה לכל מה שהכרחנו דבלא ניכר להדיא פרידתן יוכל לתקן דעדיין שמו עליו ורק בחי"ת סובר הט"ז כיון שאין חטוטרות עליו מוכח דהוא ב' זייני"ן ולכן אף שעשאן בקירוב כ"כ שלא היה ניכר להדיא פרידתן אבד את שמו. וכן משמע קצת בתה"ד בסימן מ"ח [הובא בב"י בד"ה כתוב בהגה"מ] שכתב שם דהא דכתב הרא"ש דרגל ה"א וקו"ף הנוגעין למעלה בתפילין שצריך לכותבן כסדרן אין ראיה דפליג אהר"ס דמכשיר לתקן ביודי"ן שעל האלפי"ן דנוגעין לגוף האות דשאני הני דאין להם תקנה במחיקה לחודה וכו' וכתב עוד שם דאפשר דהרא"ש קאי נמי אהא דכתב בתר הכי דצריכין היודי"ן שעל האלפי"ן והשיני"ן להיות דבוקין ור"ל דבהני נמי אי אפשר לתקן בתפילין ופליג אהר"ס וכתב הב"י דהמעיין

משנה ברורה

וה"ה כל הני דכתב רמ"א בהג"ה סוף סי"ח הנ"ל: (קיז) נוגעים אפילו (קכ) נגיעה דקה כחוט השערה: (קיח) צד"י שכתב. פי' (קכא) שחלק היו"ד מהנו"ן כ"כ עד שנראה כשני אותיות וכן בכל אינך לכן אפילו אם אירע דתינוק קראו כהלכתו אין יכול לתקן אח"כ שכיון שעינינו רואות שיש לכן צורת אותיות אחרות א"כ כשמתקנם אח"כ הרי זה כתיבה מחדש ושלא כסדרן. וה"ה אפילו אם אין להם צורת אותיות אחרות רק שנראה לעין הכל שאין לה עיקר צורתה (קכב) כגון יו"ד שלא עשה לה רגל הימיני או אל"ף שחסר לה היו"ד העליון וכל כה"ג אין יכול לתקנם אח"כ אבל אם לא עשה להיו"ד רגל שמאלי אף דאם ישאר כך פסול דאינו יו"ד כראוי לפי דעת רוב הפוסקים כדלקמן בסי' ל"ו מ"מ כיון דיש לה עיקר צורתה דאפילו בלא עוקץ שם יו"ד עליה לכן יכול לתקנה ואין בזה משום שלא כסדרן: (קיט) עי"ן יו"ד. וה"ה מ"ם (קכג) פתוחה שכתבו כ"ו[ג] בלי משיכת התג שביניהם: (קכ) או חי"ת שני זייני"ן. אפילו אם עשה חוטרא על גביהן רק שאין נוגעים זה לזה למעלה (קכד) וניכר להדיא פרידתן ה"ז הפסידה עיקר צורתה שנראה כשני זייני"ן: (קכא) יודי"ן שעל האלפי"ן. וה"ה אם היה הפסק באיזה אות באמצעו [פמ"ג בא"א בפתי']: (קכב) ותינוק וכו'. פי' לכן אפילו אם פרידתן ניכר להדיא [דהיינו תומ"י כשראה אותן] יכול לתקנם דהרי לא הפסיד עדיין האות עיקר צורתה מדקראה התינוק לאות [כן כתב הגרע"א בחידושיו ודלא כפמ"ג שהחמיר בזה ועיין בבה"ל]

שער הציון

(קכ) כנ"ל בס"ק ל"ה: (קכא) עיין בבה"ל: (קכב) מ"א: (קכג) א"ר: (קכד) ביארנו בבה"ל:

הגהות ותיקונים: א) של השי"ן: ב) כ': ג) כ' ו':

written /as/ (119) a /letter/ ע and a /letter/ י (120) or a /letter/ ח[24*] /is written as/ two ז /letters/.

However, when letters are stuck /together/, it is perfectly /in order/ to separate them after one has written /other letters/ ahead of them. For, in view /of the fact/ that the letters have their /proper/ form, separating one from the other is not like writing.

Correspondingly, if some of (121) the י /parts/ on the א[20*] /letters/, ש[22*] /letters/ and ע[22*] /letters/ and the legs of ה /letters/ are not touching the body of the letter (122) and a child who is neither /especially/ intelligent nor

Mishnah Berurah

(119) A /letter/ ע and a /letter/ י. The same ruling /applies/ if an open /letter/ מ is written as a /letter/ כ and a /letter/ ו, without the link between them having been drawn.
(120) Or a ח two ז /letters/. Even if one made a crown over them and they only do not touch one another above, with their separateness being clearly apparent, /the symbol/ lacks the essential form /of the letter ח/, as it appears like two ז /letters/.
(121) The י /parts/ on the א /letters/. The same ruling /applies/ if there is a break in the middle of some letter. [*P.Mg.*, in the *E.A.*, in the opening /discourse/.]
(122) And a child, etc. What is meant is that in view of this, even if their separation is clearly apparent [i.e., immediately and directly when one sees them] one is /nevertheless/ able to correct them. This is because the letter has not yet lost its essential form, /as we see/ from /the fact/ that a child has read the letter /correctly/. [The Gaon Rabbi Akiva Eiger writes this in his *Chidushim*, in contradiction to the *P.Mg.* who is stringent about this. See the Beyur Halachah.[26]]

24* In a Torah Scroll, *tefilin* passage or mezuzah, the letter ח consists of two ז letters joined together.

26 From the Beyur Halachah, it is clear that the ruling allowing one to correct these letters when the separation is clearly apparent may only be relied on in a time of pressing need. The author adds there that if the gap is very wide and is visible to everyone from a distance, the letter cannot be corrected even if a child reads it correctly. On the other hand, if the gap is so fine that it is only visible against the sun, correction is not required and one should certainly not disqualify the passage.

* מכירם שאע"פ שכתב לפניהם יכול לחזור ולתקנם דכיון דצורת האות היתה ניכרת ליכא משום כתבן שלא כסדרן (קכג) ויש מי שאומר דה"ה אם חוטרא (מ) דחי"ת למעלה אין נוגעין זל"ז אך אין ניכר (קכד) להדיא פרידתן אע"פ שהתינוק קורא שני זייני"ן (קכה) מותר להדביקם: **כו** * י אם אותיות של שם (קכו) דבוקות (מא) יכול (קכז) להפרידם: **כז** כ אותיות ותיבות (מב) [יט] (קכח) שנמחקו קצת אם רישומן ניכר כל כך

י מרדכי בשם ר"י והרא"ש בתשובה כ תרומת הדשן

באר היטב

(מ) דחי"ת. תפילין שחי"ת שלהם כמין ד' וז' כזה ד׳ז או איפכא כזה ז׳ד אין לפוסלם ויגרור מן הד' עד שיעשנה ז' ולא הוי שלא כסדרן עיין מ"א סימן ל"ו ס"ק ג' וכן כתבתי בתשובה על תפילין שנמלאו מלת בניכס בשני כפין כזה בניככס דיגרור כ"ף השניה מכל וכל ויאריך כ"ף ראשונה עד שיגיע סמוך למ"ס אבל לא יגרור המ"ס ויעשה מן הכ"ף השניה מ"ס דהוי שלא כסדרן שכנה"ג בהגהת הטור ועיין תשובת דרכי נועם סימן א' ובעבודת הגרשוני סי' פ"ב. אם עשה חי"ת כדעת רש"י כזה ח כשרה ואפילו האריך בה בסוף שטה עד שאינה מרובעת אפ"ה כשרה מ"א בסימן ל"ו ס"ק ג': (מא) יכול להפרידם. מעשה שהיה רגל הנו"ן פשוטה דבוק לגגה של ה"א המכוונת תחתיה והיתה הה"א מעיקר שם הנכבד והנורא יש להכשיר בשעת הדחק ע"י גרירת קצת רגל הנו"ן ובלבד שלא יגע הסכין באותה נקודה אחרונה המדובקת אות הנו"ן עם הה"א הקדושה. שיורי כנה"ג: (מב) שנמחקו קצת.

שערי תשובה

ועיין ביד אפרים בפירוש דברי המג"א בזה: [יט] שנמחקו. עבה"ט ובתשב"ץ ח"א סימן קכ"ו ות"ג סימן קל"ג אוסר העברת קולמוס על השם. וכתב בבר"י שבתה"ד סימן מ"ח לא משמע כן. אך בדברי הרמב"ן והריטב"א והר"ן בגיטין

משנה ברורה

אבל אם אין פרידתן ניכר להדיא עד שמסתכל בה אין צריך להראות להתינוק. ומ"מ אם אירע שהראה להתינוק ולא קרא לו אות הולכין אחריו להחמיר ואין יכול לתקן [כמ"ש הפמ"ג]: (קכג) ויש מי שאומר. אין כאן מחלוקת (קכה) רק חידוש דין: (קכד) להדיא. דאם היה ניכר להדיא ה"ז הפסידה עיקר צורתה וכמו שכתבנו בס"ק ק"כ: (קכה) מותר להדביקם. דאין התינוק מורגל בחי"ת כזה דאפילו המוכשר כתיקונו יקראהו ב' זייני"ן: **כו** (קכו) דבוקות. בין למעלה ובין (קכו) למטה וה"מ שנדבקו בעת הכתיבה אבל אם נדבקו לאחר גמר הכתיבה אסור להפרידם ועיין בבה"ל: (קכז) להפרידם. ואין בו משום איסור מחיקה כיון שמתקן בזה וכ"ש אם היו דבוקות לאותיות אחרות דמותר להפריד האותיות האחרות מהם בכל גווני ובלבד שיזהר שלא יגע הסכין באותה נקודה אחרונה המדובקת עם השם [בה"ט בשם שכנה"ג ומ"ש בשעת הדחק זה אינו להמעיין שם]: **כז** (קכח) שנמחקו קצת. פי' שהלך מעל האותיות קצת מראה הדיו שלהן. ואם (קכז) בתחלת הכתיבה לא היה הדיו שחור אלא דומה ללבן שהוכהה מראיתו או לאדום וצריך להעביר עליהם קולמוס הוי שלא כסדרן אבל בהאי דהשו"ע לא מיקרי שלא כסדרן (קכח) כיון שגם עכשיו הכתב הוא כשר ומה שמוסיף עליו אינו אלא משמרו שלא יתמחק יותר. וה"ה כשנתקלף לגמ הדיו קיים אבל אם קפץ כל הדיו מהקלף ולא נשאר רק רושם אדמומית (קכט) מתולדה של הדיו כשמעביר קולמוס עליהן ה"ז כותב שלא כסדרן ולפיכך אם נקלף מתחלת אורך (קל) הוי"ו קצת דיו ונשאר רק רושם התולדה באותו מקום וצריכין להראותו לתינוק אם יש בחלק העליון שיעור וי"ו צריך לכוות להחלק התחתון שלא יצרפהו התינוק ודומיא דמה שכתבנו לעיל בס"ק מ"ח. ודע עוד דדעת הפמ"ג הוא דאפילו נשאר מתמות דיו רק שנקלף שחרות העליון ונשאר אדום הוי שלא כסדרן דאודם אין כשר לתפילין אבל התפס סופר בחיו"ד בסי' רכ"ו פליג עליו וסובר דאם השינוי לאדמומית הוא מחמת יושן הרי הוא כשר שהרי הוא נכתב בדיו

ביאור הלכה

דהמעיין שם בדבריו יראה דיותר מסתבר לו להתה"ד כתירוצו הראשון דלא פליג אהר"ס ולא קאי הרא"ש אהא דכתב בתר הכי וא"כ נחזי אנן הרי הרא"ש כלל בדין זה אח"כ ג"כ היודי"ן שאחורי הלד"י דז"ל שם הנקודה שעל האל"ף שהיא כמין יו"ד צריך שתגע בו וכן היו"ד שבתוך השי"ן והעיי"ן ואחורי הלד"י ואם לא נגעה בו נשתנית צורת האות ומפשטא דלישנא דהתה"ד והב"י משמע דלא קאי הרא"ש כלל במה דסובר שאין להם שום תקנה אהא דכתב בתר הכי ומה דנקט התה"ד יודי"ן שעל האלפי"ן והשיני"ן לבד אטו כי רוכלא ליחשיב וליזיל תדע דלא נקט ג"כ יודי"ן שעל העייני"ן ורגלי התוי"ן. והאיר הקב"ה עיני ומצאתי יותר מפורש בתה"ד סימן ר"ל שמסתפק שם בגט שלא היו נוגעין היו"ד שבאל"ף ושבשי"ן ושאחורי הלד"י והיו סמוכות בקירוב עד שהתינוק קראם יפה ע"ש ומשמע שם בהדיא דבכל אלו שם אות עליה כיון דניכר האות אפילו לתינוק רק נפסלו בתפילין ומזוזות ומסתפק שם לפסלם אפילו בגט משום דבעינן לכתוב האותיות כמו שנתנו למשה מסיני כל האותיות מחוברין גוף אחד חוץ מן הה"א וקו"ף א"כ נראה ברור לפ"ז דלפי מה דקי"ל דלענין שלא כסדרן בתו"מ מותר לתקן ביוד"י השי"ן והעי"ן שאינם נוגעין משום דכיון דהתינוק קורא לאות שם אות עליו ומיקרי עדיין עיקר צורתו עליו א"כ ה"ה נמי ביו"ד שאחורי הלד"י. נחזור לעניינו דמכל אלו שהוכחנו מוכח להדיא דאם ההפסק היה דק שלא היתה ניכר פרידתו להדיא עד שמסתכל בה היטיב והתינוק קוראם יפה אפילו אם אירע כה"ג בלד"י בין היו"ד שאחוריו להנו"ן שלו וכל כה"ג מותר לתקן דלא מיקרי זה אות שחלוק לב' אותיות*[ואפשר דאין צריך ג"כ להראות להתינוק באופן זה דבודאי יקרא יפה ודומיא דחי"ת שכתב השו"ע דלא מעכב בו ראית התינוק. אך לכתחלה בודאי נכון להראות להתינוק]. וכן ראיתי עוד באיזה אחרונים שמלמדים להקל בלא ניכר להדיא הפרדתן והתינוק קוראה לאות ע"כ נ"ל דבמקום הדחק יש לסמוך על כל זה להקל שיהא מותר לתקן ודלא כהפמ"ג. ודע עוד דאם ההפסק דק מאד עד שאין נרא' רק כנגד השמש כשר אפילו לדברי הפמ"ג וא"ל שום תיקון דבודאי לא גרע הפסק מאם היה נקב כזה באותו מקום ולענין נקב הלא קי"ל דנקב שהדיו עובר עליו אינו נקב ואפי' נרא' כנגד השמש וכמ"ש לעיל במ"ב ס"ק ל"ב ובודאי אפי' אם איתרע זה בלד"י בין היו"ד לנו"ן וכה"ג ג"כ לא חשיב נקב דאל"ה אמאי אמרו (בשבת ק"ח ע"א) כותבין תפילין על גבי עור של עוף טהור אף דהעור מלחולי מחלחל משום דהוי רק נקב שהדיו עובר עליו ליחוש דילמא איתרמי הנקב בלד"י בין היו"ד לנו"ן או בשי"ן במקום שמחלקו לעיי"ן זיי"ן וכה"ג א"ו דנקב כזה לא חשיב נקב כלל. והרוצה להחמיר בהפסק דק כזה די שיחמיר להצריכו תיקון אבל חלילה לפסול התפילין משום זה: * **מכירם שאע"פ וכו'**. הנה מפשטא דלישנא דהשו"ע מוכח דמיירי אף בניכר להדיא הפרדתו וכמו שהוכיח הגרע"א בחידושיו דלא כהפמ"ג בא"א בסוף צורת האותיות ומה שהביא הפמ"ג ראיה לזה ממה שכתב הב"י בסוף סימן ל"ו בד"ה מ"כ וכו' ודאי אי הוה מופרד להדיא עד שנראה כשני זייני"ן וכו' המעיין יראה דאין ראיה כלל דשם ה"ט כיון שנראה כשני זייני"ן בטל ממנה עיקר תמונתה והוא אות שחלוק לשתי אותיות הכתוב בשו"ע מקודם ולא אמרינן דהסתטורות מוכיח עליה משא"כ בזה דע"י שניכר להדיא הפרדתה לא אבד עדיין ממנה עיקר תמונתה כ"ז שאינה חלוקה כ"כ עד שהתינוק לא יכיר תמונתה גם לפי מה שהוכחנו למעלה דאות שחלוק לשני אותיות מיירי דוקא בניכר להדיא הפרדתה ממילא מוכח דדין זה דסיפא איירי ג"כ בכה"ג דאפילו ניכר להדיא מהני תיקון ועכ"פ נראה לסמוך ע"ז בשעת הדחק להקל דמהני תינוק לענין תיקון וכמו שכתב הגרע"א בחידושיו דהורה כן למעשה בשעת הדחק ומה שכתב לבסוף וצ"ע לדינא נ"ל שהוא מלשון הפמ"ג שם בפתיחה בסוף דבריו שמסיים שם וצ"ע דאל"כ יסתור א"ע שכתב שהורה כן למעשה. אך מ"מ נ"ל בפשיטות דאף הגרע"א מודה היכא שהפסקו גדול כ"כ עד שניכר ונראה לעין כל מרחוק דבזה הרי אנו רואין שאבד צורתו לגמרי ולא עדיף מלד"י שכתבו יו"ד נו"ן ולא מהני לזה תינוק. וכעין זה ראיתי באחרונים שהביאו בשם תשובת פמ"א ח"ב סימן ט"ז שכתב אם ברחוק מכירים שהוא ריוח ואינו מגיע לגוף האות לדעת הב"י בסימן ל"ו ברחוק ד"א ולדעת הב"ח ברחוק אמה בזה ודאי אין לסמוך על תינוק אבל אם נרחק לכל מר כדאית ליה אנו רואין שהוא אל"ף ושי"ן רק כשמקרבין עינינו רואין ריוח ותינוק קורא אל"ף או שי"ן שפיר נוכל לסמוך עליו עכ"ל: * **אם אותיות של שם וכו'**. עיין במ"ב שכתב וה"מ שנדבקו וכו' נוב"י בחיו"ד בסימן קס"ט וכמ"ש שם הטעם דשמא הלכה כתי' ב' של הב"י דלא בעי מוקף גויל רק בעת הכתיבה וג"ל פשוט דאם מסתפק אימת נעשה הדיבוק יכול להפרידו מטעם ס"ס דשמא נעשה בעת הכתיבה ואת"ל דנעשה אח"כ שמא הלכה כתירוץ א' של הב"י לעיל בסט"ז דבנגיעה אין חילוק ואפילו להמחמירין בס"ס

באיסור

שער הציון

(קכה) ט"ז: (קכו) פמ"ג: (קכז) מ"א: (קכח) ב"י: (קכט) מ"א: (קל) פמ"ג:

/especially/ simple can recognize /the letters, then/ even if one /already/ wrote /other letters/ ahead of them he may go back and correct them. For in view /of the fact/ that the form of the letters is recognizable /without the correction/, this does not involve writing in incorrect order.

(123) There is /an authority/ who says that, correspondingly, if /the parts of/ the crown of a /letter/ ח[24]* above do not touch one another, but their separation is not **(124)** clearly apparent /, then/, although a child reads /the symbol as/ two ז /letters/ **(125)** it is permitted to stick them /together/.

26. If letters of a /Divine/ Name **(126)** are stuck /together/, one may **(127)** separate them.

Mishnah Berurah

However, if the separation of /the letter strokes/ is not clearly apparent until one gazes at /the letter/, it is unnecessary[27] to show it to a child /to determine whether or not it still has the required form/. Nevertheless, if one happened to show it to a child and he did not read the letter /correctly/, one is unable to correct /the letter in such a case./ /This is because/ we follow /the reading of a child/ where stringency /is involved/. [This accords with what the *P.Mg.* writes.]

(123) There is /an authority/ who says. There is no dispute /about this/. /The Shulchan Aruch/ merely /words it in this way because/ it is a novel ruling.

(124) Clearly. If it is clearly apparent it will have lost its essential form, as we have written in sub-Par. 120.

(125) It is permitted to stick them /together/. /The reason is/ that a child is not accustomed to /read/ such a ח. Even /a child/ who is perfectly trained /to read/ will read it as two זs.

(126) Are stuck. /I.e.,/ irrespective of whether /they are stuck together/ above or below.

/However,/ this ruling /only applies/ if they were stuck /together/ at the time when they were written, but if they got stuck /together/ after the writing was finished it is forbidden to separate them. See the Beyur Halachah.[28]

(127) Separate them. This does not involve /a transgression of/ the prohibition against erasing /the Divine Name/, since by /the separation/ one improves /the writing/.

If /letters of a Divine Name/ are stuck to other letters, it is certainly permitted to separate the other letters from them in all circumstances, except that one must be careful that the knife does not touch the last point which is stuck to the Name. [*B.Heyt.* in the name of the *Sh.Kn.Hag.* As regards his wording, "in a time of pressing /need/," this is not /borne out/ by study /of what is written/ there.]

27 In the Beyur Halachah, the author writes that initially it is definitely proper to show it to a child.
28 The author rules there that where one is in doubt as to whether they got stuck together while they were being written or after the writing was finished one may also separate them.

* מכירם שאע"פ שכתב לפניהם יכול לחזור ולתקנם דכיון דצורת האות היתה ניכרת ליכא משום כתבן שלא כסדרן (קכג) ויש מי שאומר דה"ה אם חוטרא (מ) דחי"ת למעלה אין נוגעין זל"ז אך אין ניכר (קכד) להדיא פרידתן אע"פ שהתינוק קורא שני זייני"ן (קכה) מותר להדביקם: **כו** * אם אותיות של שם (קכו) דבוקות (מא) יכול (קכז) להפרידם: **כז** ^י^ אותיות ותיבות (מב) [יט] (קכח) שנמחקו קצת אם רישומן ניכר כל כך

י מרדכי בשם ר"י והרא"ש בתשובה כ תרומת הדשן

באר היטב

(מ) דחי"ת. תפילין שחי"ת שלהם כמין ד' וז' כזה ד"ז או איפכא כזה ד"ז אין לפוסלם ויגרור מן הד' עד שיעשנה ז' ולא הוי שלא כסדרן עיין מ"א סימן ל"ו ס"ק ג' וכן כתבתי בתשובה על תפילין שנמצאו מלת בניכם בשני כפין כזה בניככם דיגרור כ"ף השניה מכל וכל ויאריך כ"ף ראשונה עד שיגיע סמוך למ"ס אבל לא יגרור המ"ס ויעשה מן הכ"ף השניה מ"ס דהוי שלא כסדרן שכנה"ג בהגהת הטור ועיין תשובת דרכי נועם סימן א' ובעבודת הגרשוני סי' פ"ב. אם עשה חי"ת כדעת רש"י כזה ח כשרה ואפילו האריך בה בסוף שטה עד שאינה מרובעת אפ"ה כשרה מ"א בסימן ל"ו ס"ק ג': (מא) יכול להפרידם. מעשה שהיה רגל הנו"ן פשוטה דבוק לגגה של ה"א המכוונת תחתיה והיתה הה"א מעיקר שם הנכבד והנורא יש להכשיר בשעת הדחק ע"י גרירת קצת רגל הנו"ן ובלבד שלא יגע הסכין באותה נקודה אחרונה המדובקת אות הנו"ן עם הה"א הקדושה. שיורי כנה"ג: (מב) שנמחקו קצת.

שערי תשובה

ועיין ביד אפרים בפירוש דברי המג"א בזה: [יט] שנמחקו. עבה"ט ובתשב"ץ ח"א סימן קכ"ו וח"ג סימן קל"ג אוסר העברת קולמוס על השם. וכתב בבר"י שבתה"ד סימן מ"א לא משמע כן. אך בדברי הרמב"ן והריטב"א והר"ן בגיטין

משנה ברורה

אבל אם אין פרידתן ניכר להדיא עד שמסתכל בה אין צריך להראות להתינוק. ומ"מ אם אירע שהראה להתינוק ולא קרא לו אות הולכין אחריו להחמיר ואין יכול לתקן [כמ"ש הפמ"ג]: (קכג) ויש מי שאומר. אין כאן מחלוקת (קכה) רק חידוש דין: (קכד) להדיא. דאם היה ניכר להדיא ה"ז הפסידה עיקר צורתה וכמו שכתבנו בס"ק ק"כ: (קכה) מותר להדביקם. דאין התינוק מורגל בחי"ת כזה דאפילו המוכשר כתיקונו יקראהו ב' זייני"ן: **כו** (קכו) דבוקות. בין למעלה ובין (קכו) למטה וה"מ שנדבקו בעת הכתיבה אבל אם נדבקו לאחר גמר הכתיבה אסור להפרידם ועיין בבה"ל: (קכז) להפרידם. ואין בו משום איסור מחיקה כיון שמתקן בזה וכ"ש אם היו דבוקות לאותיות אחרות דמותר להפריד האותיות האחרות מהם בכל גווני ובלבד שיזהר שלא יגע הסכין באותה נקודה אחרונה המדובקת עם השם [בה"ט בשם שכנה"ג ומ"ש בשעת הדחק זה אינו להמעיין שם]: **כז** (קכח) שנמחקו קצת. פי' שהלך מעל האותיות קצת מראה הדיו שלהן. ואם (קכז) בתחלת הכתיבה לא היה הדיו שחור אלא דומה ללבן שהוכהה מראיתו או לאדום וצריך להעביר עליהם קולמוס הוי שלא כסדרן אבל בהאי דהשו"ע לא מיקרי שלא כסדרן (קכח) כיון שגם עכשיו הכתב הוא כשר ומה שמוסיף עליו אינו אלא משמרו שלא יתמחק יותר. בד"א כשמקצת לבע הדיו קיים אבל אם קפץ כל הדיו מהקלף ולא נשאר רק רושם אדמומית (קכט) מהחלודה של הדיו כשמעביר קולמוס עליהן ה"ז כותב שלא כסדרן ולפיכך אם נקלף ממקצת אורך (קל) הוי"ו קצת דיו ונשאר רק רושם החלודה באותו מקום וצריכין להראותו להתינוק אם יש בחלק העליון שיעור וי"ו צריך לכסות להחלק התחתון שלא יצרפהו התינוק ודומיא דמה שכתבנו לעיל בס"ק מ"ח. ודע עוד דדעת הפמ"ג הוא דאפילו נשאר ממשות דיו רק שנקלף שחרות העליון ונשאר אדום הוה שלא כסדרן דאודם אין כשר לתפילין אבל החתם סופר בחיו"ד בסי' רנ"ו פליג עליו וסובר דאם השינוי לאדמומית הוא מחמת יושן הרי הוא כשר שהרי הוא נכתב בדיו

ביאור הלכה

דהמעיין שם בדבריו יראה דיותר מסתבר לו להתה"ד כתירוצו הראשון דלא פליג אהר"ס ולא קאי הרא"ש אהא דכתב בתר הכי וא"כ נחזי אנן הרי הרא"ש כלל בדין זה אח"כ ג"כ היודי"ן שאחורי הלד"י דז"ל שם הנקודה שעל האל"ף שהיא כמין יו"ד לריך שתגע בו וכן היו"ד שבתוך השי"ן והעיי"ן ואחורי הלד"י ואם לא נגעה בו נשתנית לורת האות ומפשטא דלישנא דהתה"ד והב"י משמע דלא קאי הרא"ש כלל במה דסובר שאין להם שום תקנה אהא דכתב בתר הכי ומה דנקט התה"ד יודי"ן שעל האלפי"ן והשיני"ן לבד אטו כי רוכלא ליחשיב וליזיל תדע דלא נקט ג"כ יודי"ן שעל העייני"ן ורגלי התוי"ן. והאיר הקב"ה עיני ומלאתי יותר מפורש בתה"ד סימן ר"ל שמסתפק שם בגט שלא היו נוגעין היו"ד שבאל"ף ושבשי"ן ושאחורי הלד"י והיו סמוכות בקירוב עד שהתינוק קראם יפה ע"ש ומשמע שם בהדיא דבכל אלו שם אות עליה כיון דניכר האות אפילו לתינוק רק נפסלו בתפילין ומזוזות ומסתפק שם לפסלם אפילו בגט משום דבעינן לכתוב האותיות כמו שנתנו למשה מסיני כל האותיות מחוברין גוף אחד חוץ מן הה"א וקו"ף א"כ נראה ברור לפ"ז דלפי מה דקי"ל דלענין שלא כסדרן בתו"מ מותר לתקן ביוד"י השי"ן והעי"ן שאינם נוגעין משום דכיון דהתינוק קוראו לאות שם אות עליו ומיקרי עדיין עיקר לורתו עליו א"כ ה"ה נמי ביו"ד שאחורי הלד"י. נחזור לענינינו דמכל אלו שהוכחנו מוכח להדיא דאם ההפסק היה דק שלא היתה ניכר פרידתו להדיא עד שמסתכל בה היטיב והתינוק קוראם יפה אפילו אם אירע כה"ג בלד"י בין היו"ד שאחוריו להנו"ן שלו וכל כה"ג מותר לתקן דלא מיקרי זה אות שחלוק לב' אותיות* [ואפשר דאין לריך ג"כ להראות להתינוק באופן זה דבודאי יקרא יפה ודומיא דחי"ת שכתב השו"ע דלא מעכב בו ראית התינוק. אך לכתחלה בודאי נכון להראות להתינוק]. וכן ראיתי עוד באיזה אחרונים שמלדדים להקל בלא ניכר להדיא הפרדתן והתינוק קוראה לאות ע"כ נ"ל דבמקום הדחק יש לסמוך על כל זה להקל שיהא מותר לתקן ודלא כהפמ"ג. ודע עוד דאם ההפסק דק מאד עד שאין נרא' רק כנגד השמש כשר אפילו לדברי הפמ"ג וא"ל שום תיקון דבודאי לא גרע הפסק מאם היה נקב כזה באותו מקום ולענין נקב הלא קי"ל דנקב שהדיו עובר עליו אינו נקב ואפי' נרא' כנגד השמש וכמ"ש לעיל במ"ב ס"ק ל"ב ובודאי אפי' אם איתרע זה בלד"י בין היו"ד לנו"ן וכה"ג ג"כ לא חשיב נקב דאל"ה אמאי אמרו (בשבת ק"ח ע"א) כותבין תפילין על גבי עור של עוף טהור אף דהעור חלחולי מחלחל משום דהוי רק נקב שהדיו עובר עליו ליחוש דילמא איתרמי הנקב בלד"י בין היו"ד לנו"ן או בשי"ן במקום שמחלקו לעיי"ן זיי"ן וכה"ג א"ו דנקב כזה לא חשיב נקב כלל. והרולה להחמיר בהפסק דק כזה די שיחמיר להלריכו תיקון אבל חלילה לפסול התפילין משום זה: * **מכירם שאע"פ וכו'**. הנה מפשטא דלישנא דהשו"ע מוכח דמיירי אף בניכר להדיא הפרדתו וכמו שהוכיח הגרע"א בחידושיו דלא כהפמ"ג בא"א בסוף לורת האותיות ומה שהביא הפמ"ג ראיה לזה ממה שכתב הב"י בסוף סימן ל"ו בד"ה מ"כ וכו' ודאי אי הוה מופרד להדיא עד שנראה כשני זייני"ן וכו' המעיין יראה דאין ראיה כלל דשם ה"ט כיון שנראה כשני זייני"ן בטל ממנה עיקר תמונתה והוא אות שחלוק לשתי אותיות הכתוב בשו"ע מקודם ולא אמרינן דהחטוטרות מוכיח עליה משא"כ בזה דע"י שניכר להדיא הפרדתה לא אבד עדיין ממנה עיקר תמונתה כ"ז שאינה חלוקה כ"כ עד שהתינוק לא יכיר תמונתה גם לפי מה שהוכחנו למעלה דאות שחלוק לשני אותיות מיירי דוקא בניכר להדיא הפרדתה ממילא מוכח דדין זה דסיפא איירי ג"כ בכה"ג דאפילו ניכר להדיא מהני תיקון ועכ"פ נראה לסמוך ע"ז בשעת הדחק להקל דמהני תינוק לענין תיקון וכמו שכתב הגרע"א בחידושיו דהורה כן למעשה בשעת הדחק ומה שכתב לבסוף וצ"ע לדינא נ"ל שהוא מלשון הפמ"ג שם בפתיחה בסוף דבריו שמסיים שם וצ"ע דא"ל"כ יסתור א"ע שכתב שהורה כן למעשה. אך מ"מ נ"ל בפשיטות דאף הגרע"א מודה היכא שהפסקו גדול כ"כ עד שניכר ונראה לעין כל מרחוק דבזה הרי אנו רואין שאבד לורתו לגמרי ולא עדיף מלד"י שכתבו יו"ד נו"ן ולא מהני לזה תינוק. וכעין זה ראיתי באחרונים שהביאו בשם תשובת פמ"א ח"ב סימן ע"ז שכתב אם ברחוק מכירים שהוא ריוח ואינו מגיע לגוף האות לדעת הב"י בסימן ל"ו ברחוק ד"א ולדעת הב"ח ברחוק אמה בזה ודאי אין לסמוך על תינוק אבל אם נרחק לכל מר כדאית ליה אנו רואין שהוא אל"ף ושי"ן רק כשמקרבין עינינו רואין ריוח ותינוק קורא אל"ף או שי"ן שפיר נוכל לסמוך עליו עכ"ל: * **אם אותיות של שם וכו'**. עיין במ"ב שכתב וה"מ שנדבקו וכו' עב"י בחיו"ד בסימן קס"ט וכמ"ש שם הטעם דשמא הלכה כתי' ב' של הב"י דלא בעי מוקף גויל רק בעת הכתיבה וצ"ל פשוט דאם מסתפק אימת נעשה הדיבוק יכול להפרידו מטעם ס"ס דשמא נעשה בעת הכתיבה ואת"ל דנעשה אח"כ שמא הלכה כתירוץ א' של הב"י לעיל בסט"ז דבנגיעה אין חילוק ואפילו להמחמירין בס"ס באיסור

שער הציון

(קכה) ט"ז: (קכו) פמ"ג: (קכז) מ"א: (קכח) ב"י: (קכט) מ"א: (קל) פמ"ג:

27. If letters or words are **(128)** somewhat erased /, then/, if their impression is

Mishnah Berurah

(128) Somewhat erased. I.e., if some of the appearance of the ink has gone from the letters.

If from the beginning, when /the letters/ are written, the ink is not black, but resembles white with a darkened appearance or red, it is /then/ necessary to pass a quill over /the letters to make them black/. /Therefore, if one does so,/ it will constitute /writing/ in incorrect order /and the passage will remain invalid/. However, in the case /discussed/ by the Shulchan Aruch, /the passing of the quill over the letters/ is not classed as /writing/ in incorrect order. For /in that case/ the writing is valid even as it is and /the reason/ that one adds /ink/ to it is only to protect it from becoming more erased. /On the other hand,/ this /only/ applies when part of the coloring of the ink /still/ remains, but if all the ink has sprung away from the parchment and nothing remains but a reddish impression from mold /caused/ by the ink /, then/, passing the quill over /the letters/ will be /regarded as/ writing in incorrect order.

/Now/ if some ink from part of the length of a /letter/ ו has peeled away and only an impression of the mold remains in that place, one needs to show /the letter/ to a child /who is neither especially intelligent nor especially simple to determine/ whether /or not/ the upper part has the /required/ length of a ו. It follows /from what is stated above that/ one must cover the bottom part /in such a case/ so that the child will not combine it /with the upper part/. This corresponds with what we have written above in sub-Par. 48.

Note further that in the view of the *P.Mg.*, even if the substance of the ink remains and only the upper blackness has peeled off, /so that/ it remains /tinged/ red, /passing a quill over the letters/ will constitute /writing them/ in incorrect order, as /the color/ red is invalid for *tefilin* /passages/. However, the *Chasam Sofer*, /writing with reference to a Torah Scroll/ in the part /which relates to the/ *Yo.D.*, Sec. 256, disputes this. He is of the opinion that if the change to a red /tinge/ is because of age, /the writing/ is valid, since /the letter/ was written with /valid/ ink. /He

שתינוק דלא חכים ולא טיפש יכול לקרותם מותר להעביר קולמוס עליהם להטיב הכתב ולחדשו ולא הוי שלא (מג) כסדרן: **כח** ליש ליזהר (קכט) שלא יכנס ראש הלמ"ד (מד) [כ] (קל) **באויר הה"א** (קלא) **או החי"ת אפילו** (קלב) **בלא נגיעה:** **כט** מאם אין הפרשיות (קלג) שגורות בפיו צריך שיכתוב (קלד) מתוך (מה) הכתב: **ל** נאינו רשאי לכתוב אלא א"כ (קלה) יודע לקרות: **לא** סאם אינו כותב (קלו) מתוך (מו) הכתב לא יכתוב (קלז) על פה שמקרא אותו אחר אלא אם כן יחזור הוא (קלח) ויקרא בפיו: **לב** עצריך להניח חלק (קלט) למעלה כדי גגה (מז) של למ"ד: הגה (שיהיו גם הם מוקפים גויל) (תשובת מהרי"ל סימן קל"ד וב"י) ולמטה כשיעור כ"ף וגו"ן (קמ) פשוטה ובתחלתן וסופן פאין צריך להניח (קמא) כלל: הגה מיהו נהגו הסופרים להניח (קמב) קלת בתחלה וסוף (אגור רוקח) וצריך להניח בין כל תיבה ותיבה כמלא (מח) (קמג) אות וכן בין השיטים כמלא (קמד) שיטה ובין כל אות כמלא (קמה) חוט השערה כמו גם"ת וכמו שיתבאר בטור יו"ד גם צריך להניח (קמו) מעט חלק בין פסוק (מט) לפסוק: **לג** צינשה

באר הגולה

ל תשובת הריב"ש לדעת הרמב"ם בפ"ב דגיטין מ מגילה י"ח מנחות ל"ב נ פרק קמא דמסכת סופרים ס ספר התרומה קל"ח והמרדכי בהל' קטנות ע סמ"ק והרא"ש פ הרא"ש בסדר תיקון תפילין צ הרא"ש שם וסמ"ג וסמ"ק וס' התרומה סימן ר"ה

שערי תשובה

דף י"ט גבי מלאכת מחשבת נראה כן וצריך להתיישב למעשה ע"ש: [כ] באויר

באר היטב

אבל אם בתחלת הכתיבה לא היה הדיו שחור אלא דומה ללבן שהוכהה מראיתו או לאודם וצריך להעביר עליו קולמוס הוי שלא כסדרן מ"א:

(מג) כסדרן. ודוקא כשקלת לבע הדיו קיים אבל אם קפלה כל הדיו מהקלף ולא נשאר רק רושם אדמומית מהתלודה של הדיו הוי שלא כסדרן. מ"א: (מד) באויר הה"א. ואם נכנס לתוך ד' ונראית כה' פסול הרמ"א בא"ע סימן קכ"ה ססי"ח. ועיין במ"א שסיים בזה"ל וכתב בכנה"ג שיש מכשירים לגמרי ע"כ. ולוח עליו ככרוכיא המחבר יד אהרן שאינו כן ולא מלינו מי שמיקל בזה ע"ש: (מה) הכתב. ואם מקלת הפרשה שגורה בפיו מותר לכתוב אותה מקלת בע"פ ב"ח דלא כב"י: (מו) הכתב. משמע דכשכותב מתוך הכתב א"ל לקרות כל תיבה ול"ע דבי"ד סימן רע"ד ס"ב משמע דאע"פ כן לריך לקרות. וכתב המ"א ואפשר דעתו להקל בתפילין. אבל הב"ח פסק דאפי' בכותב מפי הכתב לריך שיקרא כל תיבה ותיבה קודם שיכתבנה וכ"פ הע"ת וכ"ה בשכנה"ג: (מז) של למ"ד. וב"ח פסק שלריך להניח שיעור חלי ליפורן למעלה מראש של למ"ד. ועיין ט"ז דה"ה למטה: (מח) אות. ובדיעבד אינו מעכב אא"כ נראים כאחד ע"פ תינוק דלא חכים. ט"ז וע"ת וכ"פ הכנה"ג: (מט) לפסוק. ומ"א פסק שלא להניח חלק כלל וכן בין שיטה לשיטה א"ל ע"ש ועיין בד"מ ובע"ת. (ובספר אליהו

משנה ברורה

ולהכי נאמר ההלכה לכתוב בדיו להורות דלריכה היא רק להכתב בדיו וכן דרכו של רוב דיו לכשיזקין יכהה מראיתו ויתהפך קלת לאדמדם ונעשית כעין מרא"ה [שקורין בל"א ברא"ן°] מ"מ טוב להעבירו בקולמוס ואפילו בשמות הקדושים קרוב לודאי דמותר כדיו ע"ג דיו דאין כאן מחיקה ואם נשתנה לאודם ממש שאין כן דרכן של סתם דיו או אפילו רק לאדמומית רק שנשתנה מיד מהר לאחר הכתיבה אין תקנה לאותה ס"ת שנראה שאינו מחמת יושן ועל כרחך יש חסרון בעיקר הדיו שנעשית מסממנים אחרים וע"כ פסול מעיקרא כי לא נכתב בדיו ובשמות אסור להעביר עליו דיו וכו' עי"ש שמאריך בכ"ז מילתא בטעמא: **כח** (קכט) שלא יכנס. אפילו כל שהוא ראש הלמ"ד בשורה שלמעלה הימנה וה"ה (קלא) בך' פשוטה וכדומה שלא יכנס בשורה שלמטה באות ט' וע' וכדומה: (קל) באויר הה"א. וה"ה באויר אל"ף או (קלב) תי"ו וכדומה וכ"ש שיזהר שלא יכנס (קלג) באויר ד' או רי"ש שלא יראה כה"א וכדלקמיה: (קלא) או החי"ת. וה"ה אם נכנס ראש למ"ד לתוך אויר של כ' פשוטה וכדלקמיה בס"ק קל"ב [תשובת מהרי"ס מבריסק[א] בסי' ח' עי"ש וכן הקיל בזה הגאון רע"א בחידושיו בדיעבד]: (קלב) בלא נגיעה. דבנגיעה בלא"ה פסול משום חסרון הקפת גויל. ומשמע מלשון השו"ע דכתב שיש ליזהר דדוקא לכתחלה אבל לא לעיכובא בדיעבד וה"מ שלא (קלד) נכנס בענין שיפסד לורת האות עי"ז כגון שנכנס רק מעט אבל אם נכנס כ"כ בענין שנשתנה לורת האות שתינוק דלא חכים ולא טיפש אם נכסה לו שיטה התחתונה שלא יהא נראה רק ראש הלמ"ד ולא גוף הלמ"ד לא יכיר האות מה הוא הוי שינוי לורת האות ופסול [וגם לא יצוייר בו תיקון משום שלא כסדרן] וכ"ש אם נכנס ראש הלמ"ד בתוך חלל ד' או רי"ש ונראית כה"א דפסול ואינו (קלה) מועיל בזה קריאת התינוק כהוגן שהרי עינינו רואות שנשתנה עי"ז לאות אחר: **כט** (קלג) שגורות בפיו. דהיינו בעת שהוא (קלו) מתחיל לכתוב מתחלה עדיין אין בקי בקריאתן בע"פ כראוי ובפרט במלא וחסר: (קלד) מתוך הכתב. או מפי מקריא כדי שלא יטעה. ואם מקלת הפרשה שגורה בפיו (קלו) מותר לכתוב אותו מקלת בע"פ. ועיין בב"ח שכתב דמ"מ מצוה מן המובחר לכתוב בכל גווני מתוך הכתב: **ל** (קלה) יודע לקרות. (קלח) דאל"ה בקל יכול לטעות ואינו מרגיש: **לא** (קלו) מתוך הכתב. משמע דכשכותב מתוך הכתב א"ל להוציא בפה ומיירי דוקא כששגורות לו ג"כ ואז לא חיישינן שמא יטעה [כן כתב המ"א וא"ר לתרץ דלא תקשה מהא להא דביו"ד בסי' רע"ד ס"ב ועיין בפמ"ג שכן כוונת המ"א] אבל (קלט) הרבה מאחרונים חלקו ע"ז ופסקו דבכל גווני לריך להוציא התיבה מפיו קודם שיכתבנה והטעם כתב הב"ח דכך היא מלות כתיבת סת"ם כדי שתהא קדושת הבל קריאת כל תיבה ותיבה היולא מפי הקורא נמשכת על האותיות כשכותב אותן בקלף וכ"ז לכתחלה (קמ) אבל בדיעבד אין נפסל בכל גווני אם לא טעה: (קלז) ע"פ שמקרא וכו'. ואפילו (קמא) הוא שגור בפיו ג"כ: (קלח) ויקרא בפיו. כל תיבה ותיבה קודם שיכתבנה כדי שלא יטעה וכ"ש אם הוא (קמב) כותב ע"פ בלי מקריא: **לב** (קלט) למעלה. מהשיטות כדי גגה של למ"ד ונ"ל דהיינו מכתב בינוני אפילו הוא כותב רק כתב קטן [דהלא אמרו במנחות ל"א[ב] במלא אטבא דקשרי ופירשו הראשונים שהוא כדי לכתוב גגה של וכו' הנ"ל ואם איתא דיש חילוק מה היה שיעורם ואפשר לדחות בדוחק דהגמרא לא איירי רק בכותב כתב בינוני]: (קמ) פשוטה. ועוד משהו להקפת גוילם וטעם לכל זה כדי שכשיזדמן לו לתפס שיהיה לו מקום לזה וי"א דלריך להניח עוד למעלה מגגה של למ"ד ולמטה מך' ונו"ן[ג] פשוטה כדי חלי ליפורן וזה רק לכתחלה: (קמא) כלל. רק משהו להקפת גוילם: (קמב) קצת. היינו קלת יותר מהקפת גויל. ויש מחמירין דלכתחלה לריך בתחלה קלף כדי לגלול כל הפרשה כמו מזוזה: (קמג) אות. קטנה שהוא יו"ד ובדיעבד אין לפסול אא"כ נראית כתיבה אחת לתינוק דלא חו"ט: (קמד) שיטה. וי"א דאין לריך להניח אלא בס"ת וכן נהגו הסופרים שאין מדקדקין בזה: (קמה) חוט השערה. היינו רק לכתחלה אבל בדיעבד אין לפסול אא"כ נראית התיבה חלוקה לשתים וכמו שנתבאר כ"ז ביו"ד בסי' רע"ד[ג] לענין ס"ת: (קמו) מעט חלק

מתרגם: °אוס

שער הציון

(קלא) כנה"ג: (קלב) בשער אפרים שער ה' באות ח': (קלג) מ"א: (קלד) כנה"ג בשם המהרי"ט ודה"ח בהל' קה"ת וא"ר בסי' קמ"ג והשער אפרים הנ"ל: (קלה) מהרי"ט הנ"ל: (קלו) ב"ח: (קלז) מ"א: (קלח) לבוש: (קלט) ע"ת והב"ח והשכנה"ג והגר"א: (קמ) ב"י: (קמא) והראיה ממרע"ה עיין בב"י: (קמב) ב"י:

הגהות ותיקונים: א) מהרי"ם פאדווה: ב) ל"ב: ג) רע"ד:

discernible to the extent that a child who is neither /especially/ intelligent nor /especially/ simple is able to read them, it is permitted to pass a quill over them to improve the writing and renew it. This is not /regarded as writing them/ in incorrect order.

28. One must take care **(129)** that the top of the /letter/ ל does not enter **(130)** into the space of the /letter/ ה **(131)** or of the /letter/ ח, even **(132)** without touching /the strokes of the letter/.

Mishnah Berurah

maintains/ that the halachah /which requires one/ to write with ink was given /solely/ as a teaching that /the letter/ should be written with ink only. /He points out that/ it is usual for most ink to darken its appearance as it ages and to alter somewhat to reddish, /so that/ it comes to resemble the hue [which is called *bran* in Yiddish /, i.e., brown/]. Nevertheless, it is desirable to pass a quill over /the letters when they have become this color/. Even in the case of the Divine Names it is almost definitely permitted /to pass a quill over the letters/, in accordance with /the ruling that it is permitted to pass/ ink over ink, since this does not involve erasure. /However,/ if /the appearance of the ink/ has changed to actual red, which is not usual for normal ink, or even if it has only /changed/ to reddish, but the change was immediate, shortly after the writing, the Torah Scroll involved cannot be remedied. For /then/ it seems /clear/ that /the change/ did not /come about/ because of age and there must perforce be a defect in the ink's essential /composition/, so that it /must have been/ made from other materials /which are invalid/. Consequently, /the writing/ was invalid from the outset, as it was not written with /valid/ ink. /In such a case/ it is forbidden to pass ink over /the letters/ of /Divine/ Names. See /what he writes/ about this there at length, with reasoned argument.

(129) That ... does not enter. /I.e.,/ even a slight /portion/ of the top of the ל /should not enter/ into the row above it.

Correspondingly, in the case of the simple /elongated letter/ ך or a similar /letter, one must take care/ that it does not enter into the row below it into /the space of/ the letters ט or ע or similar /letters/.

(130) Into the space of the /letter/ ה. Correspondingly, /it should not enter into/ the space of the /letter/ א or of the /letter/ ת or of a similar /letter/.

One should certainly take care that /the top of the letter ל/ does not enter into the space of the /letter/ ד or of the /letter/ ר, so that /the letter/ should not appear like the /letter/ ה, as /stated/ below.

(131) Or of the /letter/ ח. The same ruling /applies/ as regards the top of /the letter/ ל entering the space of the simple /elongated letter/ ך, in accordance with /what is stated/ below in sub-Par. 132. [Responsum of *Maharim* of Brisk (Brest-Litovsk), in Sec. 8; see there. /This follows/ likewise /from the words of/ the Gaon *R.A.E.*, who is lenient about this in his *Chidushim* /as regards the ruling/ once it is after the event.]

(132) Without touching. For if /the letters/ touch, /the passage/ is in any case invalid, because /then, the fulfillment of the requirement that the letters must be/ surrounded by /blank/ parchment is lacking.

It is implied by the wording /of the author/ of the Shulchan Aruch, who writes /concerning this matter/ that one must take care, that /the need to do so/ is merely an initial /requirement/, but is not essential /for the validity/ once it is after the event. This is /only/ the case if /the top of the letter ל/ has not entered /into a letter/ in such a way that the letter has lost its /required/ form because of it, such as when it has only entered a little. However, it may have entered so much that /it has caused/ the form of the letter to be changed /to the extent/ that /the change/ is /regarded halachically as/ a change in the form of the letter and /then the letter/ is invalid. /I.e., if the form has changed/ so /much/ that a child who is neither /especially/ intelligent nor /especially/ simple will not recognize what the letter is /meant to be/ (if the lower line is covered for him, so that only the top of the /letter/ ל, and not the body of the ל, is visible). [There is also no question of

שתינוק דלא חכים ולא טיפש יכול לקרותם מותר להעביר קולמוס עליהם להטיב הכתב ולחדשו ולא הוי שלא (מג) כסדרן: **כח** ׳יש ליזהר (קכט) שלא יכנס ראש הלמ״ד (מד) [כ] (קל) באויר הה״א (קלא) או החי״ת אפילו (קלב) בלא נגיעה: **כט** ׳אם אין הפרשיות (קלג) שגורות בפיו צריך שיכתוב (קלד) מתוך (מה) הכתב: **ל** ׳אינו רשאי לכתוב אלא א״כ (קלה) יודע לקרות: **לא** ׳אם אינו כותב (קלו) מתוך (מו) הכתב לא יכתוב (קלז) על פה שמקרא אותו אחר אלא אם כן יחזור הוא (קלח) ויקרא בפיו: **לב** ׳צריך להניח חלק (קלט) למעלה כדי גגה (מז) של למ״ד: הגה (שיהיו גם הם מוקפים גויל) (תשובת* מהרי״ל סימן קל״ד וב״ש) ולמטה כשיעור כ״ף (קמ) פשוטה ובתחלתן וסופן ׳אין צריך להניח (קמא) כלל: הגה מיהו נהגו הסופרים להניח (קמב) קלת בתחלה וסוף (אגור רוקח) וצריך להניח בין כל תיבה ותיבה כמלא (מח) (קמג) אות וכן בין השיטים כמלא (קמד) שיטה ובין כל אות כמלא (קמה) חוט השערה כמו בס״ת וכמו שיתבאר בטור יו״ד גם צריך להניח (קמו) מעט חלק בין פסוק (מט) לפסוק: **לג** ׳יעשה

ל תשובת הריב״ש לדעת הרמב״ם בפ״ב דגיטין מ מגילה י״ח מנחות ל״ב נ פרק קמא דמסכת סופרים ס ספר התרומה קל״ח והמרדכי בהל׳ קטנות ע סמ״ק והרא״ש פ הרא״ש בסדר תיקון תפילין צ הרא״ש שם וסמ״ג וסמ״ק וס׳ התרומה סימן ר״ה

שערי תשובה

דף י״ט גבי מלאכת מחשבת נראה כן וצריך להתיישב למעשה ע״ש: [כ] באויר

באר היטב

אבל אם בתחלת הכתיבה לא היה הדיו שחור אלא דומה ללבן שהוכהה מראיתו או לאודם וצריך להעביר עליו קולמוס הוי שלא כסדרן מ״א:

(מג) כסדרן. ודוקא כשקלת לבע הדיו קיים אבל אם קפלה כל הדיו מהקלף ולא נשאר רק רושם אדמומית מהחלודה של הדיו הוי שלא כסדרן. מ״א: (מד) באויר הה״א. ואם נכנס לתוך ד׳ ונראית כה׳ פסול הרמ״א בא״ע סימן קכ״ה סקי״ח. ועיין במ״א שסיים בזה״ל וכתב בכנה״ג שיש מכשירים לגמרי ע״כ. ולוח עליו ככרוכיא המחבר יד אהרן שאינו כן ולא מלינו מי שמיקל בזה ע״ש: (מה) הכתב. ואם מקלת הפרשה שגורה בפיו מותר לכתוב אותה מקלת בע״פ ב״ח דלא כב״י: (מו) הכתב. משמע דכשכותב מתוך הכתב א״ל לקרות כל תיבה ול״ע דבי״ד סימן רע״ד ס״ב משמע דאע״פ כן לריך לקרות. וכתב המ״א ואפשר דעתו להקל בתפילין. אבל הב״ח פסק דאפי׳ בכותב מפי הכתב לריך שיקרא כל תיבה ותיבה קודם שיכתבנה וכ״פ הע״ת וכ״ה בשכנה״ג: (מז) של למ״ד. וב״ח פסק שלריך להניח שיעור חלי ליפורן למעלה מראש של למ״ד. ועיין ט״ז דה״ה למטה: (מח) אות. ובדיעבד אינו מעכב אא״כ נראים כאחד ע״פ תינוק דלא חכים. ט״ז וע״ת וכ״פ הכנה״ג: (מט) לפסוק. ומ״א פסק שלא להניח חלק כלל וכן בין שיטה לשיטה א״ל ע״ש ועיין בד״מ ובע״ת. (ובספר אליהו

משנה ברורה

ולהכי נאמר ההלכה לכתוב בדיו להורות דלריכה היא רק להכתב בדיו וכן דרכו של רוב דיו לבשוקין יכהה מראיתו ויתהפך קלת לאדמדם ונעשית כעין מראה [שקורין בל״א ברא״ן°] מ״מ טוב להעבירו בקולמוס ואפילו בשמות הקדושים קרוב לודאי דמותר כדיו ע״ג דיו דאין כאן מחיקה ואם נשתנה לאודם ממש שאין כן דרכן של סתם דיו או אפילו רק לאדמומית רק שנשתנה מיד מהר לאחר הכתיבה אין תקנה לאותה ס״ת שנראה שאינו מחמת יושן ועל כרחך יש חסרון בעיקר הדיו שנעשית מסממנים אחרים וע״כ פסול מעיקרא כי לא נכתב בדיו ובשמות אסור להעביר עליו דיו וכו׳ עי״ש שמאריך בכ״ז מילתא בטעמא: **כח** (קכט) שלא יכנס. אפילו כל שהוא ראש הלמ״ד בשורה שלמעלה הימנה וה״ה (קלא) כף׳ פשוטה וכדומה שלא יכנס בשורה שלמטה באות ט׳ ונ׳ וכדומה: (קל) באויר הה״א. וה״ה באויר אל״ף או (קלב) תי״ו וכדומה וכ״ש שיזהר שלא יכנס (קלג) באויר ד׳ או רי״ש שלא יראה כה״א וכדלקמיה: (קלא) או החי״ת. וה״ה אם נכנס ראש למ״ד לתוך אויר של כ׳ פשוטה וכדלקמיה בס״ק קל״ב [תשובת מהרי״ם מבריסק׳א בסי׳ ה׳ עי״ש וכן הקיל בזה הגאון רע״א בחידושיו בדיעבד]: (קלב) בלא נגיעה. דבנגיעה בלא״ה פסול משום חסרון הקפת גויל. ומשמע מלשון השו״ע דכתב שיש ליזהר דדוקא לכתחלה אבל לא לעיכובא בדיעבד וה״מ שלא (קלד) נכנס בענין שיפסד לורת האות עי״ז כגון שנכנס רק מעט אבל אם נכנס כ״כ בענין שנשתנה לורת האות שתינוק דלא חכים ולא טיפש אם נכסה לו שיטה התחתונה שלא יהא נראה רק ראש הלמ״ד ולא גוף הלמ״ד לא יכיר האות מה הוא הוי שינוי לורת האות ופסול [וגם לא יצוייר בו תיקון משום **שלא כסדרן] וכ״ש אם נכנס ראש הלמ״ד בתוך אלל ד׳ או רי״ש ונראית כה״א דפסול ואינו (קלה) מועיל בזה קריאת התינוק כהוגן שהרי עינינו רואות שנשתנה עי״ז לאות אחר: כט (קלג) שגורות בפיו. דהיינו בעת שהוא (קלו) מתחיל לכתוב מסתמא עדיין אין בקי בקריאתן בע״פ כראוי ובפרט במלא וחסר: (קלד) מתוך הכתב. או מפי מקריא כדי שלא יטעה. ואם מקלת הפרשה שגורה בפיו (קלז) מותר לכתוב אותו מקלת בע״פ. ועיין בב״ח שכתב דמ״מ מלוה מן המובחר לכתוב בכל גווני מתוך הכתב: ל (קלה) יודע לקרות. (קלח) דאל״ה בקל יכול לטעות ואינו מרגיש: לא (קלו) מתוך הכתב. משמע דכשכותב מתוך הכתב א״ל להוליא בפה ומיירי דוקא כששגורות לו ג״כ ואז לא חיישינן שמא יטעה [כן כתב המ״א וא״ר לתרץ דלא תקשה מהא להא דהיו״ד׳ בסי׳ רע״ד ס״ב ועיין בפמ״ג שכן כוונת המ״א] אבל (קלט) הרבה מאחרונים חלקו ע״ז ופסקו דבכל גווני לריך להוליא התיבה מפיו קודם שיכתבנה והטעם כתב הב״ח דכך היא מלות כתיבת סת״מ כדי שתהא קדושת הבל קריאת כל תיבה ותיבה היולא מפי הקורא נמשכת על האותיות כשכותב אותן בקלף וכ״ז לכתחלה (קמ) אבל בדיעבד אין נפסל בכל גווני אם לא טעה: (קלז) ע״פ שמקרא וכו׳. ואפילו (קמא) הוא שגור בפיו ג״כ: (קלח) ויקרא בפיו. כל תיבה ותיבה קודם שיכתבנה כדי שלא יטעה וכ״ש אם הוא (קמב) כותב ע״פ בלי מקריא: לב (קלט) למעלה. מהשיטות כדי גגה של למ״ד ונ״ל דהיינו מכתב בינוני אפילו הוא כותב רק כתב קטן [דהלא אמרו במנחות ל״א׳ב כמלא אטבא דספרי** ופירשו הראשונים שהוא כדי לכתוב גגה של וכו׳ הנ״ל ואם איתא דיש חילוק מה היה שיעורם ואפשר לדחות בדוחק דהגמרא לא איירי רק בכותב כתב בינוני]: (קמ) פשוטה. ועוד משהו להקפת גוילם וטעם לכל זה כדי שכשיזדמן לו לכתבם שיהיה לו מקום לזה וי״א דלריך להניח עוד למעלה מגגה של למ״ד ולמטה מך׳ ונו״ן* פשוטה כדי חלי ליפורן וזה רק לכתחלה: (קמא) כלל. רק משהו להקפת גוילם: (קמב) קלת. היינו קלת יותר מהקפת גויל. ויש מחמירין דלכתחלה לריך בתחלה קלף כדי לגלול כל הפרשה כמו תזוזה: (קמג) אות. קטנה שהוא יו״ד ובדיעבד אין לפסול אא״כ נראית כתיבה אחת לתינוק דלא חו״ט: (קמד) שיטה. וי״א דאין לריך להניח אלא בס״ת וכן נהגו הסופרים שאין מדקדקין בזה: (קמה) חוט השערה. היינו רק לכתחלה אבל בדיעבד אין לפסול אא״כ נראית התיבה חלוקה לשתים וכמו שנתבאר כ״ז ביו״ד בסי׳ רע״ז׳ג לענין ס״ת: (קמו) מעט חלק

מתרגם: °אוס

שער הציון

(קלא) כנה״ג: (קלב) בשער אפרים שער ה׳ באות ח׳: (קלג) מ״א: (קלד) כנה״ג בשם המהרי״ט ודה״ח בהל׳ קה״ת וא״ר בסי׳ קמ״ג והשער אפרים הנ״ל: (קלה) מהרי״ט הנ״ל: (קלו) ב״ח: (קלז) מ״א: (קלח) לבוש: (קלט) ע״ת והב״ח והשכנה״ג והגר״א: (קמ) ב״י: (קמא) והראיה ממרע״ה עיין בב״י: (קמב) ב״י:

הגהות ותיקונים: א) מהרי״ם פאדווה: ב) ל״ב: ג) רע״ד:

29. If one does not /know/ the passages (133) fluently, he must write them (134) from a written /copy/.
30. One is not allowed to write /the passages/ unless (135) he is capable of reading /them/.
31. If one does not write (136) from a written /copy/ , he should not write (137) according to the oral reading of someone else, unless he repeats (138) the reading with his mouth.
32. One must leave blank (139) above /each written line/, sufficient /space/ for /writing/ the roof of the /letter/ ל.

Gloss: (So that /the ל *letters/ will also be surrounded by /blank/ parchment.) (...)*

Mishnah Berurah

correcting this, because /a correction would be considered writing/ in incorrect order.]

If the top of the /letter/ ל has entered into the space of the /letter/ ד or of the /letter/ ר, /so that/ it appears like a /letter/ ה, this certainly invalidates /the passage/. In such a case it is of no avail if a child /who is neither especially intelligent nor especially simple/ reads it correctly, as we see with our eyes that as a result of this /entry the letter/ has been transformed into a different letter.

(133) Fluently. I.e., at the time when one begins to /undertake the/ writing /of these passages/. Generally /, at that time/, one is still not properly familiar with their wording by heart. /One is then/ especially /unfamiliar with the letters/ which are /to be written/ in full or are /to be/ left out.

(134) From a written /copy/. Alternatively, in order to avoid error, /one may also write/ the passages /after hearing them/ from the mouth of a reader.

If one /knows/ a part of the passage fluently, he is permitted to write that part by heart.

See the *Bach*, who writes that at any rate, /in order to fulfil/ the mitzvah in a choice way, one should write from a written /copy/ in all circumstances.

(135) He is capable of reading. For, otherwise, he can easily err without sensing this.

(136) From a written /copy/. It is implied /by the wording of the Shulchan Aruch/ that if one writes from a written /copy/ it is unnecessary /for him/ to pronounce /what he writes/ with his mouth. This relates solely /to a case/ where he also /knows the passages/ fluently. Then we are not afraid that he will err. [This is what the *M.A.* and the *E.R.* write to reconcile /this ruling/, so that it should not conflict with what is /ruled/ in the *Yo.D.*, Sec. 274, Par. 2. See the *P.Mg.*, /who explains/ that this is what the *M.A.* means.]

However, many of the Acharonim dispute this. They rule that in all circumstances one must pronounce the word with his mouth before he writes it.

The *Bach* writes as the reason that the mitzvah of writing Torah Scrolls, *tefilin* /passages/ and mezuzos /requires/ this, so that the holiness of the sound of the reading, /in the case/ of each individual word that issues from the mouth of the reader, should be conducted to the letters as he writes them on the parchment.

/It should be noted that/ all this is /only required/ initially, but, once it is after the event, /even if one did not pronounce the words, the passage/ is not /ruled to be/ invalid, whatever the circumstances, provided /that the writer/ did not err.

(137) According to the oral reading, etc. /I.e.,/ even if /the other person/ also /knows the passage/ fluently.

(138) The reading with his mouth. /I.e.,/ each individual word before it is written, so that he will not err.

/One should/ certainly /say the reading with his mouth/ if he writes by heart, without someone reading /the passage for him/.

(139) Above. /I.e., one must leave blank/ above the lines sufficient /space to contain/ the roof of the /letter/ ל.

It appears to me that what is meant is /a space which is sufficiently large for the roof of the letter ל of/ average/-sized/ script, even if one is only writing /the passage/ with small script. [For /the Sages/ in fact stated in *Menachos* 32/a, that the space should be/ equivalent to /the width of/ a book clasp. The

שתינוק דלא חכים ולא טיפש יכול לקרותם מותר להעביר קולמוס עליהם להטיב הכתב ולחדשו ולא הוי שלא (מג) כסדרן: **כח** [ל]יש ליזהר (קכט) שלא יכנס ראש הלמ"ד (מד) [כ] (קל) באויר הה"א (קלא) או החי"ת אפילו (קלב) בלא נגיעה: **כט** [ס]אם אין הפרשיות (קלג) שגורות בפיו צריך שיכתוב (קלד) מתוך (מה) הכתב: **ל** [ע]אינו רשאי לכתוב אלא א"כ (קלה) יודע לקרות: **לא** [ס]אם אינו כותב (קלו) מתוך (מו) הכתב לא יכתוב (קלז) על פה שמקרא אותו אחר אלא אם כן יחזור הוא (קלח) ויקרא בפיו: **לב** [צ]צריך להניח חלק (קלט) למעלה כדי גגה (מז) של למ"ד: הגה (שיהיו גם הם מוקפים גויל) (תשובת* מהרי"ל סימן קל"ד וב"ש) ולמטה כשיעור כ"ף ונו"ן (קמ) פשוטה ובתחלתן וסופן [פ]אין צריך להניח (קמא) כלל: הגה מיהו נהגו הסופרים להניח (קמב) קצת בתחלה וסוף (אגור רוקח) וצריך להניח בין כל תיבה ותיבה כמלא (מח) (קמג) אות וכן בין השיטים כמלא (קמד) שיטה ובין כל אות כמלא (קמה) חוט השערה כמו בס"ת וכמו שיתבאר בטור יו"ד גם צריך להניח (קמו) מעט חלק בין פסוק (מט) לפסוק: **לג** [צ]יעשה

באר הגולה

[ל] תשובת הריב"ש לדעת הרמב"ם בפ"ב דגיטין [מ] מגילה י"ח מנחות ל"ב [נ] פרק קמא דמסכת סופרים [ס] ספר התרומה קל"ח והמרדכי בהל' קטנות [ע] סמ"ק והרא"ש [פ] הרא"ש בסדר תיקון תפילין [צ] הרא"ש שם וסמ"ג וסמ"ק וס' התרומה סימן ר"ה

שערי תשובה

דף י"ט גבי מלאכת מחשבת נראה כן וצריך להתיישב למעשה ע"ש: [כ] באויר

באר היטב

אבל אם בתחלת הכתיבה לא היה הדיו שחור אלא דומה ללבן שהוכהה מראיתו או לאודם וצריך להעביר עליו קולמוס הוי שלא כסדרן מ"א:

(מג) כסדרן. ודוקא כשקלת לבע הדיו קיים אבל אם קפלה כל הדיו מהקלף ולא נשאר רק רושם אדמומית מהחלודה של הדיו הוי שלא כסדרן. מ"א: (מד) באויר הה"א. ואם נכנס לתוך ד' ונראית כה' פסול הרמ"א בא"ע סימן קכ"ה סס"ח. ועיין במ"א שסיים בזה"ל וכתב בכנה"ג שיש מכשירים לגמרי ע"כ. ולוח עליו ככרוכיא המחבר יד אהרן שאינו כן ולא מלינו מי שמיקל בזה ע"ש: (מה) הכתב. ואם מקלת הפרשה שגורה בפיו מותר לכתוב אותה מקלת בע"פ ב"ח דלא כב"י: (מו) הכתב. משמע דכשכותב מתוך הכתב א"צ לקרות כל תיבה וצ"ע דבי"ד סימן רע"ד ס"ב משמע דאע"פ כן צריך לקרות. וכתב המ"א ואפשר דעתו להקל בתפילין. אבל הב"ח פסק דאפי' בכותב מפי הכתב צריך שיקרא כל תיבה ותיבה קודם שיכתבנה וכ"פ הע"ת וכ"ה בשכנה"ג: (מז) של למ"ד. וב"ח פסק שצריך להניח שיעור חצי ציפורן למעלה מראש של למ"ד. ועיין ט"ז דה"ה למטה: (מח) אות. ובדיעבד אינו מעכב אא"כ נראים כאחד ע"פ תינוק דלא חכים. ט"ז וע"ת וכ"פ הכנה"ג: (מט) לפסוק. ומ"א פסק שלא להניח חלק כלל וכן בין שיטה לשיטה א"צ ע"ש ועיין בד"מ ובע"ת. (ובספר אליהו

משנה ברורה

ולהכי נאמר ההלכה לכתוב בדיו להורות דצריכה היא רק להכתב בדיו וכך דרכו של רוב דיו לכשיזקין יכהה מראיתו ויתהפך קצת לאדמדם ונעשית כעין מרהה [שקורין בל"א ברא"ן°] מ"מ טוב להעבירו בקולמוס ואפילו בשמות הקדושים קרוב לודאי דמותר בדיו ע"ג דיו דאין כאן מחיקה ואם נשתנה לאודם ממש שאין כן דרכן של סתם דיו או אפילו רק לאדמומית רק שנשתנה מיד מהר לאחר הכתיבה אין תקנה לאותה ס"ת שנראה שאינו מחמת יושן ועל כרחך יש חסרון בעיקר הדיו שנעשית מסממנים אחרים וע"כ פסול מעיקרא כי לא נכתב בדיו ובשמות אסור להעביר עליו דיו וכו' עי"ש שמאריך בכ"ז מילתא בטעמא: **כח** (קכט) שלא יכנס. אפילו כל שהוא ראש הלמ"ד בשורה שלמעלה הימנה וה"ה (קל) בך' פשוטה וכדומה שלא יכנס בשורה שלמטה באות ט' ונ' וכדומה: (קל) באויר הה"א. וה"ה באויר אל"ף או (קלב) חי"ו וכדומה וכ"ש שיזהר שלא יכנס (קלג) באויר ד' או רי"ש שלא יראה כה"א וכדלקמיה: (קלא) אר החי"ת. וה"ה אם נכנס ראש למ"ד לתוך אויר של כ' פשוטה וכדלקמיה בס"ק קל"ג [תשובת מהרי"ט מבריסק° בסי' ח' עי"ש וכן הקיל בזה הגאון רע"א בחידושיו בדיעבד]: (קלב) בלא נגיעה. דבנגיעה בלא"ה פסול משום חסרון הקפת גויל. ומשמע מלשון השו"ע דכתב שיש ליזהר דדוקא לכתחלה אבל לא לעיכובא בדיעבד וה"מ שלא (קלד) נכנס בענין שיפסד צורת האות עי"ז כגון שנכנס רק מעט אבל אם נכנס כ"כ בענין שנשתנה צורת האות שתינוק דלא חכים ולא טיפש אם נכסה לו שיטה התחתונה שלא יהא נראה רק ראש הלמ"ד ולא גוף הלמ"ד לא יכיר האות מה הוא הוי שינוי צורת האות ופסול [וגם לא יועיל בו תיקון משום שלא כסדרן] וכ"ש אם נכנס ראש הלמ"ד בתוך חלל ד' או רי"ש ונראית כה"א דפסול ואינו (קלה) מועיל בזה קריאת התינוק כהוגן שהרי עינינו רואות שנשתנה עי"ז לאות אחר: **כט** (קלג) שגורות בפיו. דהיינו בעת שהוא (קלו) מתחיל לכתוב מתחלה עדיין אין בקי בקריאתן בע"פ כראוי ובפרט במלא וחסר: (קלד) מתוך הכתב. או מפי מקריא כדי שלא יטעה. ואם מקצת הפרשה שגורה בפיו (קלז) מותר לכתוב אותו מקצת בע"פ. ועיין בב"ח שכתב דמ"מ מצוה מן המובחר לכתוב בכל גווני מתוך הכתב: **ל** (קלה) יודע לקרות. (קלח) דאל"ה בקל יכול לטעות ואינו מרגיש: **לא** (קלו) מתוך הכתב. משמע דכשכותב מתוך הכתב א"צ להוציא בפה ומיירי דוקא כששגורות לו ג"כ ואז לא חיישינן שמא יטעה [כן כתב המ"א וא"ר לתרץ דלא תקשה מהא דהיו"ד בסי' רע"ד ס"ב ועיין בפמ"ג שכן כוונת המ"א] אבל (קלט) הרבה מאחרונים חלקו ע"ז ופסקו דבכל גווני צריך להוציא התיבה מפיו קודם שיכתבנה והטעם כתב הב"ח דכך היא מצות כתיבת סת"ת כדי שתהא קדושת הבל קריאת כל תיבה ותיבה היוצא מפי הקורא נמשכת על האותיות כשכותב אותן בקלף וכ"ז לכתחלה (קמ) אבל בדיעבד אין נפסל בכל גווני אם לא טעה: (קלז) ע"פ שמקרא וכו'. ואפילו (קמא) הוא שגור בפיו ג"כ: (קלח) ויקרא בפיו. כל תיבה ותיבה קודם שיכתבנה כדי שלא יטעה וכ"ש אם הוא (קמב) כותב ע"פ בלי מקריא: **לב** (קלט) למעלה. מהשיטות כדי גגה של למ"ד וצ"ל דהיינו מכתב בינוני אפילו הוא כותב רק כתב קטן [דהלא אמרו במנחות ל"א° כמלא אטבא דספרי ופירשו הראשונים שהוא כדי לכתוב גגה של וכו' הנ"ל ואם איתא דיש חילוק בזה היה שיעורם ואפשר לדחות בדוחק דהגמרא לא איירי רק בכותב כתב בינוני]: (קמ) פשוטה. ועוד משהו להקפת גוילם וטעם לכל זה כדי שכשיזדמן לו לכתבם שיהיה לו מקום לזה וי"א דצריך להניח עוד למעלה מגגה של למ"ד ולמטה מך' ונו"ן* פשוטה כדי חצי ציפורן וזה רק לכתחלה: (קמא) כלל. רק משהו להקפת גוילם: (קמב) קצת. היינו קצת יותר מהקפת גויל. ויש מחמירין דלכתחלה צריך בתחלה קלף כדי לגלול כל הפרשה כמו מזוזה: (קמג) אות. קטנה שהוא יו"ד ובדיעבד אין לפסול אא"כ נראית כתיבה אחת לתינוק דלא חו"ט: (קמד) שיטה. וי"א דאין צריך להניח אלא בס"ת וכן נהגו הסופרים שאין מדקדקין בזה: (קמה) חוט השערה. היינו רק לכתחלה אבל בדיעבד אין לפסול אא"כ נראית התיבה חלוקה לשתים וכמו שנתבאר כ"ז ביו"ד בסי' רע"ז[ג] לענין ס"ת: (קמו) מעט חלק

מתרגם: °מוס

שער הציון

(קלא) כנה"ג: (קלב) בשער אפרים שער ה' באות ח': (קלג) מ"א: (קלד) כנה"ג בשם המהרי"ט ודה"ח בהל' קה"ת וא"ר בסי' קמ"ג והשער אפרים הנ"ל: (קלה) מהרי"ט הנ"ל: (קלו) ב"ח: (קלז) מ"א: (קלח) לבוש: (קלט) ע"ת והב"ח והשכנה"ג והגר"א: (קמ) ב"י: (קמא) והראיה ממרע"ה עיין בב"י: (קמב) ב"י:

הגהות ותיקונים: א) מהרי"ם פאדווה: ב) ל"ב: ג) רע"ד:

Below /the written line, one must leave blank/ a wide /enough space/ for /writing the tail of/ **(140)** the simple /elongated letters/ ך and ן.

At the beginning and at the end /of the written lines/, it is unnecessary to leave /any blank space/ **(141)** at all.

Gloss: Nevertheless, it has become the practice of the scribes to leave **(142)** *a little /blank space/ at the beginning and at the end /of the lines/. (...)*

It is necessary to leave /blank space/ between each of the words, adequate for /writing/ **(143)** *a letter. Likewise, between the lines, /one must leave blank/ adequate /space/ for /writing/* **(144)** *a line. Between each letter, /one must leave blank/ adequate /space/ of* **(145)** *a hairsbreadth. This accords with /what is required/ for a Torah Scroll, as stated in the part /of the Shulchan Aruch/,* Yoreh De'ah. *One should also leave* **(146)** *a small /additional/ blank /space/ in between the verses.*

Mishnah Berurah

Rishonim explain that /the width described/ is sufficient for writing the roof of, etc. as /stated/ above. It there would be a difference with respect to /the width required, dependent on the size of the script used/, how would the width they /give reconcile with this/? One may counter /this proof/ with a forced /argument/ that the Gemara only speaks of /the width required/ when one writes average/-sized/ script.]

(140) The simple /elongated/. /One must also leave blank/ a further bit /of space/, so that /if one writes them/ they /will be/ surrounded by /blank/ parchment.

The reason for all this is so that if one will happen /to need/ to write them, he will have the place to /do/ so.

There are /authorities/ who say that one must leave additional /blank space/, above /what is required for writing/ the roof of the /letter/ ל /above the lines/ and below /what is required for writing the tail of/ the simple /elongated letters/ ך and ן /below the lines/. /This additional blank space must be the width/ of half a fingernail. This is only an initial /requirement/.

(141) At all. /One must/ only /leave blank/ a bit /of space, in order/ to have /blank/ parchment surrounding /the writing/.

(142) A little. I.e., a little more than /is required for the writing/ to be surrounded by /blank/ parchment.

There are /authorities/ who rule stringently that, initially, one must /leave/ sufficient /blank space/ at the beginning of the parchment for wrapping the entire passage, as /is required in the case of/ a mezuzah.

(143) A letter. /What is meant is/ a small /letter/, i.e., the /letter/ י.

Once it is after the event, one should not rule /the passage/ to be invalid, unless /two words/ appear like a single word to a child who is neither /especially/ intelligent nor /especially/ simple.

(144) A line. There are /authorities/ who say that it is only necessary /to leave this width when writing/ a Torah Scroll.

It is likewise the practice of the scribes not to be particular about this /except in the case of a Torah Scroll/.

(145) A hairsbreadth. This is only an initial /requirement/, but once it is after the event one should not rule /the passage/ to be invalid /because of the space between letters/, unless a word appears divided into two.

All this accords with what is explained in the *Yo.D.*, Sec. 274, with respect to /the writing of/ a Torah Scroll.

(146) A small blank /space/. However,

השורות שוות שלא תהא אחת נכנסת (קמז) ואחת יוצאת ולפחות [א]יזהר שלא יכתוב (קמח) * ג' אותיות חוץ (נ) לשיטה (קמט) ואם כתבם (קנ) לא פסל: **לד** * [ר]ב' אותיות שהם (קנא) * תיבה א' לא יכתוב חוץ לשיטה: **לה** (קנב) [ש]אותיות השם (קנג) צריך שיהיו כולם (נא) בתוך הדף ולא יצא (קנד) מהם כלל חוץ לדף: **לו** * [ת]יעשה (קנה) כל פרשיותיה (קנו) פתוחות חוץ מפרשה אחרונה הכתובה בתורה

ק סמ"ק והגה"מ פ"ב מהס"א דמנחות
ר טור ב"ד רע"ג
ש שם ת הרא"ש
שם והמרדכי וא"ח
והרמב"ם בפרק ג'

באר היטב

רבה פסק כדעת רמ"א דצריך להניח חלק בין פסוק לפסוק והביא ראיה מן ספר ברוך שאמר שכתב להדיא כן וכן בין שיטה לשיטה ע"ש): (נ) לשיטה. וב"ד סימן רע"ג פסק כהרמב"ם דלא קפדינן אלא שלא יכתוב רוב התיבה חוץ לשיטה ואם התיבה בת ח' אותיות מותר לכתוב החלי חוץ לשיטה. וכתב המ"א ואפשר דבא ללמוד כאן דשני אותיות מותר לכתוב אפי' בתיבה בת ג' אותיות דבזה הרמב"ם מודה ע"ש. ואני אומר דמסעי' שאח"ז ידעינן זאת מדכתב ב' אותיות שהם תיבה אחת וכו' משמע ב' אותיות שאינן תיבה אחת מותר אפי' בתיבה בת ג' וק"ל: (נא) בתוך הדף ולא יצא מהם כלל חוץ. כתב הרב בעל באר שבע בתשובה סוף ספרו דף נ"ב ע"ב מדנקט כפל לשון משמע אפילו בדיעבד פסול אפילו בשאר שמות שאינן נמחקין ואפילו הנטפל לשם מאחריו פסול אם יצא חוץ לשיטה כנ"ל להלכה ולא למעשה ע"כ. והמ"א הקשה עליו דהש"ך בי"ד סימן רע"ו ס"ו כתב דקצת פוסקים מכשירין כשתלה מקצת השם ע"ש ס"ק ה' משמע לכאורה דכ"ש כשיצא חוץ לשיטה דהא איסור תליה נזכר בגמרא ואיסור זה לא נזכר בגמרא בהדיא רק הוא מדברי ר"ת ומנ"ל לפסול בדיעבד. ובמ"ב סימן כ"ז

שערי תשובה

הה"א. עבה"ט ועיין ט"ז שהקשה על הש"ע שכתב שיש ליזהר דהא אפי' בדיעבד פסול ועיין בשו"ת מקום שמואל שהביא מש"ע אה"ע סי' קכ"ה דגם שם משמע דוקא לכתחלה רק אם נשתנה צורת האות עי"ז פסול בדיעבד ולכן דעתו להקל בלמ"ד של ולעבדו שנכנס ראשה לתוך ה"א של ולאהבה ולא נגעה רק נכנס לאוירא

משנה ברורה

חלק. אבל המ"א בשם כמה אחרונים והגר"א בביאורו הכריעו דאין צריך להניח חלק יותר מבין תיבה לתיבה באמצע פסוק [ודלא כמ"ש הש"ך ביו"ד רע"ד סק"ו ע"ש]: **לג** (קמז) ואחת יוצאת. ואפילו (קמג) אות אחת (קמד) משום זה אלי ואנוהו: (קמח) ג' אותיות. מדלא חילק משמע דאפילו אם אלו הג' אותיות הם מיעוט התיבה אסור וביו"ד סימן רע"ג פסק כהרמב"ם דלא קפדינן אלא שלא יכתוב רוב התיבה חוץ לשיטה ואם התיבה בת ח' אותיות מותר לכתוב החציה חוץ לשיטה ועיין בש"ך שם שכתב שיש להחמיר כהך דהכא ועיין בא"ר (קמה) שדעתו דעכ"פ בתפילין שהגליונות קצרים יש להחמיר: (קמט) ואם כתבם. (קמו) בין שהיה הבליטה בתחלת השיטה או בסופה: (קנ) לא פסל. ואפילו אם כתב (קמז) תיבה שלמה חוץ לשיטה כל שניכר שהיא נקריית עם אותה השיטה ולא עם העמוד האחר שבצדה: **לד** (קנא) תיבה אחת. ואם התיבה היא בת שלש מותר לכתוב ממנה שתי אותיות חוץ לשיטה אף שהם רוב התיבה יו"ד סימן רע"ג ועיין בבה"ל: **לה** (קנב) אותיות השם. (קמח) אפילו שאר שמות שאינם נמחקין (קנג) צריך וכו'. המ"א בשם הגאון מהר"ר יצחק מפוזנא [וכן הע"ת והא"ר וכמה מהאחרונים] אסיק דדוקא לכתחלה אבל בדיעבד אין להחמיר ומ"מ אם אירע כן בס"ת הורה למחוק כל השורות העליונות אם אין בהם שום שם משמות שאינם נמחקין ולמשוך אותם שיהיו שוות עם השם דמאחר דאפשר לתקוני לא מיקרי דיעבד אבל אם היה שם למעלה איזה שם או (קמט) בתפילין ומזוזות דא"א למחוק משום שלא כסדרן כשר כך בלי תיקון ויש (קנ) מחמירין אפילו בדיעבד והסכים עמהם הגרע"א והדה"ח. אך אם (קנא) בשורות העליונות אות האחרון כ'ד'ר' ובדומה שיכול למושכן כולהו מודו דבין בס"ת ובין בתו"מ ימשוך אותן כדי שיהיו שוות עם האות מהשם שיצא חוץ לשיטה ואין בזה משום שלא כסדרן. וכן אם לא כתב עוד רק שורה אחת (קנב) ובשורה שניה נמשך השם חוץ לשיטה יעשה שרטוטים אחרים ויתכסם שיהיו ארוכים עד סוף השם ובשביל שורה הראשונה אין קפידא. ודע עוד דבאותיות הנטפלות להשם (קנג) הסכמת אחרונים דאין להחמיר בדיעבד ביוצא חוץ לשיטה: (קנד) מהם כלל. אפילו (קנד) אות אחת ואפשר דאף רובו כבולו אבל מקצת האות לית לן בה ואם יצא השם כולו חוץ לגליון העמוד כשר בדיעבד ואינו דומה ליוצא אות אחד חוץ לשיטה דמה שיוצא לחוץ הוא משוב כתליה וקי"ל ביו"ד רע"ו דמקצת השם אין תולין משא"כ בזה כן כתב הבני יונה והגרע"א בחידושיו בסי' זה מחמיר גם בזה עי"ש אבל בביאור הגר"א מוכח בהדיא כהבני יונה להקל: **לו** (קנה) כל פרשיותיה. ר"ל מהתפילין של יד הואיל והן נכתבות בקלף אחד וצריך בהן פתוחה וסתומה דהיינו שכשמניח מקום חלק בסוף שיטה אחרונה של פרשה ראשונה כדי ט' אותיות ומתחיל פרשה שלאחריה בראש השיטה בדף הב' הרי פרשה שלאחריה נקרא פתוחה כמו שבס"ת נקראת פרשה המתחלת בראש השיטה פרשה פתוחה לכו"ע כשיש ריוח כדי ט' אותיות לפניה בשיטה הקודמת לה או בסוף שיטה אחרונה שבדף הקודם אבל בתש"ר שהפרשיות נכתבין על ד' קלפים אין להקפיד בהן בפתוחות וסתומות אך נהגו לכתחלה להקפיד בזה כ"כ האחרונים ועיין בבה"ל במה שכ' בשם הפמ"ג בזה: (קנו) פתוחות חוץ וכו'. מפני שג' ראשונות שהם קדש והיה כי יביאך שמע הם פתוחות בתורה ופרשת והיה אם שמוע סתומה לפיכך צריך לכתוב בתפילין ג"כ ככה. דהיינו שיניח מקום חלק כדי ט' אותיות בסוף שיטה אחרונה שבפ' קדש כדי שבפ' והיה כי יביאך שיתחיל בראש השיטה הא' שבדף הב' תהיה הפרשה פתוחה כמו שהיא בתורה וכן אחר פ' והיה כי יביאך כדי שפ' שמע תהיה פתוחה אבל פ' והיה אם שמוע יעשה סתומה ואופן סתימתה יבואר לקמיה. ופרשת קדש אף דבתורה היא פתוחה מחמת שהוא מפסיק בריוח ט' אותיות בשורה הקודמת לה וכאן אין שייך זה דהיא פרשה

ביאור הלכה

באיסור מהיקה יש להקל בזה לפי מה שכתב שם הנוב"י דבמוחק מקצת אות ועדיין נשאר צורתו עליו אין חייב בזה משום מוחק ורק מדרבנן ע"ש. אח"כ מצאתי כן בעזה"י בספר ישועות יעקב עי"ש: * ג' אותיות. עיין במ"ב ומקורו מהא דש"ך יו"ד בסימן רע"ג סק"ד עיי"ש ועיין בביאור הגר"א דמשמע שהוא מסכים גם כן להש"ך דהמחבר סתם פה כהרא"ש ועיין במ"א והשמטתי תירוצו משום קושית הבה"ט עי"ש והפמ"ג הקשה ג"כ זה אמנם דלא לשויה ח"ו לרבינו המ"א כטועה אמרתי שיש ליישב דמסעיף ל"ד אין ראיה להקל בזה דאפשר דלא מיעט רק דמותר לכתוב אות אחת מן התיבה של שתי אותיות חוץ לשיטה אף שהוא חצי התיבה וכמו שכתב הגר"א לדעת הרמב"ם [ודלא כהלבוש שמחמיר בזה עי"ש בטעמו] אבל ב' אותיות מן תיבה של שלש אותיות דהם רוב התיבה הו"א דאסור וכמו שכתב הגר"א באמת לדעת הרמב"ם לזה קמ"ל המחבר דשתי אותיות מותר בכל גווני כנ"ל בכוונתו: * שתי אותיות וכו'. אבל לכתוב אות אחת ממנה חוץ לשיטה מותר. כל האחרונים דלא כלבוש: * תיבה אחת. עיין במ"ב כן כתב הרא"ש בה"ק ופסק ביו"ד כוותיה ועיין במ"א בס"ק מ"ו שכתב דאף הרמב"ם מודה בזה להקל והגר"א בביאורו כתב שלדעת הרמב"ם אסור בזה: * יעשה כל פרשיותיה. עיין במ"ב

שער הציון

(קמג) ב"ח: (קמד) ביאור הגר"א: (קמה) והובא ג"כ בפמ"ג: (קמו) מוכח מהפרישה דלא מחלק בזה לענין דיעבד: (קמז) אחרונים: (קמח) מ"א: (קמט) פמ"ג לדעת המ"א והוא בעצמו הניח עיקר הדין בצ"ע לקמן בסימן קמ"ט[ב]: (קנ) הב"ש בשם מהרא"י וגם תשובת הרמב"ם שהובא[ג] ביו"ד רע"ו בד"ה ובשם התשב"ץ עי"ש: (קנא) פמ"ג: (קנב) פמ"ג: (קנג) מ"א בשם מ"ב וט"ז יו"ד רע"ו וכמה אחרונים: (קנד) פמ"ג:

הגהות ותיקונים: א) ולפחות יזהר: ב) קמ"ג מש"ז סק"ב: ג) בב"י:

33. One should make the rows of even /length/, without one /of them/ stopping short and **(147)** one /of them/ protruding. One should at least take care not to write **(148)** three letters outside the line. **(149)** If one did write /three letters outside the line/, **(150)** this does not cause invalidity.
34. If two letters constitute **(151)** one word they should not be written outside the line.[25*]
35. **(152)** The letters of the /Divine/ Name **(153)** must all be within the column

Mishnah Berurah

the *M.A.*, in the name of several Acharonim, and the *Gra*, in his *Beyur*, decide that it is unnecessary to leave more blank /space between verses/ than /one leaves/ between words in the middle of a verse. [/This is/ in contradiction to what the *Shach* writes in the *Yo.D.*, /Sec./ 274, sub-Par. 6; see there.]

(147) One protruding. /I.e.,/ even if /the protrusion of only/ one letter /is involved/.

/This requirement is/ because of /the teaching of the verse/, "This is my God and I will glorify him".[29]

(148) Three letters. From /the fact/ that /the Shulchan Aruch/ does not differentiate, it is implied that this is forbidden even if these three letters constitute the smaller part of the word.

/However,/ in the *Yo.D.*, Sec. 273, /the Shulchan Aruch/ rules in accordance with /the view of/ the *Rambam*,[30] that we need only be concerned not to write most of the word outside the line. /According to that view,/ if the word is of eight letters, one may write half of it outside the line. See the *Shach* there, who writes that one should be stringent, in conformance with /the ruling/ here. See the *E.R.*, who is of the opinion that at any rate as regards *tefilin* /passages/, which have narrow margins, one should be stringent /about this/.

(149) If one did write /three letters/. /This applies/ irrespective of whether the projection is at the beginning of the line or at the end of it.

(150) This does not cause invalidity. Even if one wrote a complete word outside the line /the passage is not invalid/, as long as it is evident that it /must be/ read with that line and not with the other column at the side of it.

(151) One word. If a word is of three /letters/, it is permitted to write two of its letters outside the line, although they /constitute/ the greater part of the word. *Yo.D.*, Sec. 273. See the Beyur Halachah.

(152) The letters of the /Divine/ Name. This even /applies in the case of/ other /forms of the Divine/ Name[31] which are not erasable.

(153) Must, etc. The *M.A.*, in the name of the Gaon, our teacher and Rabbi, Rabbi Yitzchak of Posen [and this is likewise /the ruling of/ the *O.T.*, the *E.R.* and several Acharonim] concludes that this is only an initial /requirement/, but, once it is after the event, one need not be stringent /about this/.

Nevertheless, he rules that if in the case of a Torah Scroll /a Divine Name/ happened /to be written outside the column/, one should erase all the higher rows, if they do not have any Names which are /Divine/ Names that may not be erased, and /then/ extend them so that they are of even /length/ with /the row that has/ the /Divine/ Name. For in view /of the fact/ that /in such a case/ one is able to remedy /the fault the situation/ is not describable as being after the event. However, if there is some /Divine/ Name /written/ above there /, in the case of a Torah Scroll,/ or where *tefilin* /passages/ or *mezuzos* are involved (in which case one cannot erase /the writing above in any circumstances/, because /the Divine Name will then have been written/ in incorrect order), /the writing/ is valid as it is, without correction.

There are /authorities/ who are stringent /about this/, even once it is after the event. The Gaon *R.A.E.* and the *D.Hach.* agree with them.

25* It is permitted to write one letter of such a word outside the line. (Beyur Halachah)

29 *Shemos* 15:2.
30 *Rambam, Hilchos Sefer Torah* 7:5 and 6.
31 I.e., Names other than the Tetragrammaton.

השורות שוות שלא תהא אחת נכנסת (קמז) ואחת יוצאת ולפחות [א]יזהר (קמח) שלא יכתוב * ג' אותיות חוץ (ג) לשיטה (קמט) ואם כתבם (קנ) לא פסל: **לד** * [ב]ב' אותיות שהם (קנא) * תיבה א' לא יכתוב חוץ לשיטה: **לה** (קנב) [ש]אותיות השם (קנג) צריך שיהיו כולם (נא) בתוך הדף **ולא יצא** (קנד) **מהם** כלל חוץ לדף: **לו** * [ת]**יעשה** (קנה) **כל פרשיותיה** (קנו) פתוחות חוץ מפרשה אחרונה הכתובה בתורה

ק סמ"ק והגה"מ פ"ב מהה"ל דמנחות
ר טור ב"ד רע"ג
ש שם ת הרא"ש שם והמרדכי וא"ח והרמב"ם בפרק ג'

באר היטב

רבה פסק כדעת רמ"א דצריך להניח חלק בין פסוק לפסוק והביא ראיה מן ספר ברוך שאמר שכתב להדיא כן וכן בין שיטה לשיטה ע"ש): (ג) לשיטה. ובי"ד סימן רע"ג פסק כהרמב"ם דלא קפדינן אלא שלא יכתוב רוב התיבה חוץ לשיטה ואם התיבה בת ח' אותיות מותר לכתוב החצי חוץ לשיטה. וכתב המ"א ואפשר דבא ללמוד כאן דשני אותיות מותר לכתוב אפי' בתיבה בת ג' אותיות דבזה הרמב"ם מודה ע"ש. ואני אומר דמסעי' שאח"ז ידעינן זאת מדכתב ב' אותיות שהם תיבה אחת וכו' משמע ב' אותיות שאינן תיבה אחת מותר אפי' בתיבה בת ג' וק"ל: (נא) בתוך הדף ולא יצא מהם כלל חוץ. כתב הרב בעל באר שבע בתשובה סוף ספרו דף נ"ב ע"ב מדנקט כפל לשון משמע אפילו בדיעבד פסול אפילו בשאר שמות שאינן נמחקין ואפילו הנטפל לשם מאחריו פסול אם יצא חוץ לשיטה כנ"ל להלכה ולא למעשה ע"כ. והמ"א הקשה עליו דהש"ך בי"ד סימן רע"ו ס"ו כתב דקצת פוסקים מכשירין כשתלה מקצת השם ע"ש ס"ק ה' משמע לכאורה דכ"ש כשיצא חוץ לשיטה דהא איסור תליה נזכר בגמרא ואיסור זה לא נזכר בגמרא בהדיא רק הוא מדברי ר"ת ומנ"ל לפסול בדיעבד. ובמ"ב סימן כ"ז

שערי תשובה

הה"א. עבה"ט ועיין ט"ז שהקשה על הש"ע שכתב שיש ליזהר דהא אפי' בדיעבד פסול ועיין בשו"ת מקום שמואל שהביא מש"ע אה"ע סי' קכ"ה דגם שם משמע דוקא לכתחלה רק אם נשתנה צורת האות עי"ז פסול בדיעבד ולכן דעתו להקל בלמ"ד של ולעבדו שנכנס ראשה לתוך ה"א של ולאהבה ולא נגעה רק נכנס לאוירא

משנה ברורה

חלק. אבל המ"א בשם כמה אחרונים והגר"א בביאורו הכריעו דאין צריך להניח חלק יותר מכדי תיבה לתיבה באמצע פסוק [ודלא כמ"ש הש"ך ביו"ד רע"ד סק"ו וע"ש]: **לג** (קמז) ואחת יוצאת. ואפילו (קמג) אות אחת (קמד) משום זה אלי ואנוהו: (קמח) ג' אותיות. מדלא חילק משמע דאפילו אם אלו הג' אותיות הם מיעוט התיבה אסור וביו"ד סימן רע"ג פסק כהרמב"ם דלא קפדינן אלא שלא יכתוב רוב התיבה חוץ לשיטה ואם התיבה בת ח' אותיות מותר לכתוב החציה חוץ לשיטה ועיין בש"ך שם שכתב שיש להחמיר כאן דהכא ועיין בא"ר (קמט) שדעתו דעכ"פ בתפילין שהגליונות קצרים יש להחמיר: (קמט) ואם כתבם. (קנ) בין שהיה הגליונה בתחלת השיטה או בסופה: (קנ) לא פסל. ואפילו אם כתב (קנא) תיבה שלמה חוץ לשיטה כל שניכר שהיא נקריאת עם אותה השיטה ולא עם העמוד האחר שבצדה: **לד** (קנא) תיבה אחת. ואם התיבה היא בת שלש מותר לכתוב ממנה שתי אותיות חוץ לשיטה אף שהם רוב התיבה יו"ד סימן רע"ג ועיין בבה"ל: **לה** (קנב) אותיות השם. (קנב) אפילו שאר שמות שאינם נמחקין (קנג) צריך וכו'. המ"א בשם הגאון מהר"ר יצחק מפוזנא [וכן הע"ת והא"ר וכמה מהאחרונים] אסיק דדוקא לכתחלה אבל בדיעבד אין להחמיר ומ"מ אם אירע כן בס"ת הורה למחוק כל השורות העליונות אם אין בהם שום שם משמות שאינם נמחקין ולמשוך אותם שיהיו שוות עם השם דמאחר דאפשר לתקוני לא מיקרי דיעבד אבל אם היה שם למעלה איזה שם או (קמט) בתפילין ומזוזות דא"א למחוק משום שלא כסדרן כשר כן בלי תיקון ויש (קנ) מחמירין אפילו בדיעבד והסכים עמהם הגרע"א והדה"ח. אך אם (קנא) בשורות העליונות אות האחרון כ'ד'ר' וכדומה שיכול למושכן כולהו מודו דבין בס"ת ובין בתו"מ ימשוך אותן כדי שיהיו שוות עם האות מהשם שיצא חוץ לשיטה ואין בזה משום שלא כסדרן. וכן אם לא כתב עוד רק שורה אחת (קנב) ובשורה שניה משך השם חוץ לשיטה יעשה שרטוטים אחרים וימשכם שיהיו ארוכים עד סוף השם ובשביל שורה הראשונה אין קפידא. ודע עוד דבאותיות הנטפלות להשם (קנג) הסכמת אחרונים דאין להחמיר בדיעבד ביוצא חוץ לשיטה: (קנד) מהם כלל. אפילו (קנד) אות אחת ואפשר דאף רובו ככולו אבל מקצת האות לית לן בה ואם יצא השם כולו חוץ לגליון העמוד כשר בדיעבד ואינו דומה ליוצא אות אחד חוץ לשיטה דמה שיוצא לחוץ הוא חשוב כתליה וקי"ל ביו"ד רע"ו דמקצת השם אין תולין משא"כ בזה כן כתב הבני יונה והגרע"א בחידושיו בסי' זה מחמיר גם בזה עי"ש אבל בביאור הגר"א מוכח בהדיא כהבני יונה להקל: **לו** (קנה) כל פרשיותיה. ר"ל מהתפילין של יד הואיל והן נכתבות בקלף אחד ושייך בהן פתוחה וסתומה דהיינו שכשמניח מקום חלק בסוף שיטה אחרונה של פרשה ראשונה כדי ט' אותיות ומתחיל פרשה שלאחריה בראש השיטה בדף הב' הרי פרשה שלאחריה נקרא פתוחה כמו שבס"ת נקראת פרשה המתחלת בראש השיטה פרשה פתוחה לכו"ע כשיש ריוח כדי ט' אותיות לפניה בשיטה הקודמת לה או בסוף שיטה אחרונה שבדף הקודם אבל בתש"ר שהפרשיות נכתבין על ד' קלפים אין להקפיד בהן בפתוחות וסתומות אך נהגו לכתחלה להקפיד בזה כ"כ האחרונים ועיין בבה"ל במה שכ' בשם הפמ"ג בזה: (קנו) פתוחות חוץ וכו'. מפני שג' ראשונות שהם קדש והיה כי יביאך שמע הם פתוחות בתורה ופרשת והיה אם שמוע סתומה לפיכך צריך לכתוב בתפילין ג"כ ככה. דהיינו שיניח מקום חלק כדי ט' אותיות בסוף שיטה אחרונה שבפ' קדש כדי שבפ' והיה כי יביאך שיתחיל בראש השיטה הא' שבדף הב' תהיה הפרשה פתוחה כמו שהיא בתורה וכן אחר פ' והיה כי יביאך כדי שפ' שמע תהיה פתוחה אבל פ' והיה אם שמוע יעשה סתומה ואופן סתימתה יתבאר לקמיה. ופרשת קדש אף דבתורה היא פתוחה מחמת שהוא תפסיק בריוח ט' אותיות בשורה הקודמת לה וכאן אין שייך זה דהיא פרשה

ביאור הלכה

באיסור מחיקה יש להקל בזה לפי מה שכתב שם הנוב"י דבמוחק מקצת אות ועדיין נשאר צורתו עליו אין חייב בזה משום מוחק ורק מדרבנן ע"ש. אח"כ מצאתי כן בנוב"י בספר ישועות יעקב ע"ש: * ג' אותיות. עיין במ"ב ומקורו מהא דש"ך יו"ד בסימן רע"ג סק"ד עי"ש ועיין בביאור הגר"א דמשמע שהוא מסכים גם כן להש"ך דהמחבר סתם פה כהרא"ש ועיין במ"א והשמטתי מילתו משום קושית הפמ"ג עי"ש והפמ"ג הקשה ג"כ זה אמנם דלא נשויה מ"ו לגבינו המ"א בטוענה אחרי שיש ליישב דמסעיף ל"ד אין ראיה להקל בזה דאפשר דלא מיעט רק דמותר לכתוב אות אחת מן התיבה של שתי אותיות חוץ לשיטה אף שהוא חצי התיבה וכמו שכתב הגר"א לדעת הרמב"ם [ודלא כהלבוש שמחמיר בזה עי"ש בטעמו] אבל ב' אותיות מן תיבה של שלש אותיות דהם רוב התיבה הו"א דאסור וכמו שכתב הגר"א באמת לדעת הרמב"ם לזה קמ"ל המחבר דשתי אותיות מותר בכל גווני כנ"ל בכוונתו: * שתי אותיות וכו'. אבל לכתוב אות אחת ממנה חוץ לשיטה מותר. כל האחרונים דלא כלבוש: * תיבה אחת. עיין במ"ב כן כתב הרא"ש בה"ק ופסק בו"ד כוותיה ועיין במ"א בס"ק מ"ו שכתב דאף הרמב"ם מודה בזה להקל והגר"א בביאורו כתב שלדעת הרמב"ם אסור בזה: * יעשה כל פרשיותיה. עיין במ"ב

שער הציון

(קמג) ב"ח: (קמד) ביאור הגר"א: (קמה) והובא ג"כ בפמ"ג: (קמו) מוכח מהפרישה דלא מחלק בזה לענין דיעבד: (קמז) אחרונים: (קמח) מ"א: (קמט) פמ"ג לדעת המ"א והוא בעצמו הניח עיקר הדין בצ"ע לקמן בסימן קמ"ט[ב]: (קנ) הב"ש בשם מהרא"י וגם תשובת הרמב"ם שהובא[ג] ביו"ד רע"ו בד"ה ובשם התשב"ץ עי"ש: (קנא) פמ"ג: (קנב) פמ"ג: (קנג) מ"א בשם מ"ב וט"ז יו"ד רע"ו וכמה אחרונים: (קנד) פמ"ג:

הגהות ותיקונים: א) ולפחות יזהר: ב) קמ"ג מש"ז סק"ב: ג) בב"י:

and there should not be any protrusion **(154)** of these /letters/ at all outside the column.

36. One should make **(155)** all the passages of /the *tefilin* in the form of/

Mishnah Berurah

However, if in the higher rows the last letter is the /letter/ ב, the /letter/ ד or the /letter/ ר or a similar /letter/, which can be extended, all /authorities/ are agreed that both in the case of a Torah Scroll and in the case of *tefilin* /passages/ or mezuzos one should /in fact/ extend them so that /the rows/ will /end/ evenly with the letter of the /Divine/ Name which went outside the line. This does not involve /writing/ in incorrect order. Likewise, if one has not yet written /many rows, but/ only a single /other/ row, and /already/ in the second row he extended the /Divine/ Name outside the line, he should make a different marking out /of the rows/ and extend them so that their length /continues/ until the end of the /Divine/ Name /which has been extended/. As for the first row /, which will now be shorter than the others/, one need not be concerned /about this/.

Note further that in the case of letters which are affixed to the /Divine/ Name, the Acharonim are agreed that one need not be stringent, once it is after the event, if they protrude outside the line.

(154) Of these /letters/ at all. /I.e.,/ even of a single letter.

It may be that /one must even apply the rule that/ the greater part is like the whole /and not allow the greater part of a letter to protrude/. However, we need not be concerned if /the smaller/ part of a letter protrudes.

If the entire /Divine/ Name protrudes outside into the margin of the column, /the passage/ is valid now that it is after the event. This is not comparable to a single letter /of the Divine Name/ protruding outside the line. /This is/ because what protrudes outside is considered a suspension and it is ruled in the *Yo.D.*, /Sec./ 276 that one may not suspend part of the /Divine/ Name. This does not apply in such a case /, where the entire Name protrudes/. This is stated by the *Benei Yonah.* /On the other hand,/ the Gaon *R.A.E.* in his *Chidushim* on this section is stringent about such a case as well; see there. However, from the *Beyur Ha-Gra*, it is clearly evident /that the *Gra* agrees/ with /the view of/ the *Benei Yonah*, that one may be lenient /with respect to this/.

(155) All the passages of /the *tefilin*/. What is meant is /all the passages/ of the arm *tefilin*, since they are written on a single parchment and /the question of/ being /in the form of/ open or closed /passages/ is relevant in their case. I.e., if one leaves a blank area, sufficient for /the writing of/ nine letters, at the end of the last line of the first passage and starts /writing/ the following passage at the beginning of the line on the second column, this following passage is called an open /passage/. This is comparable to /the ruling for/ a Torah Scroll, where a passage which starts at the beginning of a line is called an open passage according to all /authorities/, when there is an interval sufficient for /the writing of/

השורות שוות שלא תהא אחת נכנסת (קמז) ואחת יוצאת ולפחות יזהר[א] שלא יכתוב (קמח) * ג' אותיות חוץ (נ) לשיטה (קמט) ואם כתבם (קנ) לא פסל: לד * [ב]ב' אותיות שהם (קנא) * תיבה א' לא יכתוב חוץ לשיטה: לה (קנב) [ש]אותיות השם (קנג) צריך שיהיו כולם (נא) בתוך הדף ולא יצא (קנד) מהם כלל חוץ לדף: לו * [ת]יעשה (קנה) כל פרשיותיה (קנו) פתוחות חוץ מפרשה אחרונה הכתובה בתורה

ק סמ"ק והגה"מ פ"ב מהפיא דמנחות ר טור ב"י רע"ג ש שם ת הרא"ש שם והמרדכי וא"ח והרמב"ם בפרק ג'

באר היטב

רבה פסק כדעת רמ"א דצריך להניח חלק בין פסוק לפסוק והביא ראיה מן ספר ברוך שאמר שכתב להדיא כן וכן בין שיטה לשיטה ע"ש): (נ) לשיטה. ובי"ד סימן רע"ג פסק כהרמב"ם דלא קפדינן אלא שלא יכתוב רוב התיבה חוץ לשיטה ואם התיבה בת ח' אותיות מותר לכתוב החצי חוץ לשיטה. וכתב המ"א ואפשר דבא ללמוד כאן דשני אותיות מותר לכתוב אפי' בתיבה בת ג' אותיות דבזה הרמב"ם מודה ע"ש. ואני אומר דמסעי' שאח"ז ידעינן זאת מדכתב ב' אותיות שהם תיבה אחת וכו' משמע ב' אותיות שאינן תיבה אחת מותר אפי' בתיבה בת ג' וק"ל: (נא) בתוך הדף ולא יצא מהם כלל חוץ. כתב הרב בעל באר שבע בתשובה סוף ספרו דף נ"ב ע"ב מדנקט כפל לשון משמע אפילו בדיעבד פסול אפילו בשאר שמות שאינן נמחקין ואפילו הנטפל לשם מאחריו פסול אם יצא חוץ לשיטה כנ"ל להלכה ולא למעשה ע"כ. והמ"א הקשה עליו דהש"ך בי"ד סימן רע"ו ס"ו כתב דקצת פוסקים מכשירין כשתלה מקצת השם ע"ש ס"ק ה' משמע לכאורה דכ"ש כשיצא חוץ לשיטה דהא איסור תליה נזכר בגמרא ואיסור זה לא נזכר בגמרא בהדיא רק הוא מדברי ר"ת ומנ"ל לפסול בדיעבד. ובמ"ב סימן כ"ז

שערי תשובה

הה"א. עבה"ט ועיין ט"ז שהקשה על הש"ע שכתב שיש ליזהר דהא אפי' בדיעבד פסול ועיין בשו"ת מקום שמואל שהביא מש"ע אה"ע סי' קכ"ה דגם שם משמע דוקא לכתחלה רק אם נשתנה צורת האות עי"ז פסול בדיעבד ולכן דעתו להקל בלמ"ד של ולעבדו שנכנס ראשה לתוך ה"א של ולאהבה ולא נגעה רק נכנס לאוירא

משנה ברורה

חלק. אבל המ"א בשם כמה אחרונים והגר"א בביאורו הכריעו דאין צריך להניח חלק יותר מבין תיבה לתיבה באמצע פסוק [ודלא כמ"ש הש"ך ביו"ד רע"ד סק"ו ע"ש]: לג (קמז) ואחת יוצאת. ואפילו (קמג) אות אחת (קמד) משום זה אלי ואנוהו: (קמח) ג' אותיות. מדלא חילק משמע דאפילו אם אלו הג' אותיות הם מיעוט התיבה אסור וביו"ד סימן רע"ג פסק כהרמב"ם דלא קפדינן אלא שלא יכתוב רוב התיבה חוץ לשיטה ואם התיבה בת ס' אותיות מותר לכתוב החציה חוץ לשיטה ועיין בש"ך שם שכתב שיש להחמיר כהך דהכא ועיין בא"ר (קמה) שדעתו דעכ"פ בתפילין שהגליונות קצרים יש להחמיר: (קמט) ואם כתבם. (קמו) בין שהיה הבליטה בתחלת השיטה או בסופה: (קנ) לא פסל. ואפילו אם כתב (קמז) תיבה שלמה חוץ לשיטה כל שניכר שהיא נקרית עם אותה השיטה ולא עם העמוד האחר שבצדה: לד (קנא) תיבה אחת. ואם התיבה היא בת שלש מותר לכתוב ממנה שתי אותיות חוץ לשיטה אף שהם רוב התיבה יו"ד סימן רע"ג ועיין בבה"ל: לה (קנב) אותיות השם. (קמח) אפילו שאר שמות שאינם נמחקין (קנג) צריך וכו'. המ"א בשם הגאון מהר"ר יצחק מפוזנא [וכן הע"ת והא"ר וכמה מהאחרונים] אסיק דדוקא לכתחלה אבל בדיעבד אין להחמיר ומ"מ אם אירע כן בס"ת הורה למחוק כל השורות העליונות אם אין בהם שום שם משמות שאינם נמחקין ולמשוך אותם שיהיו שוות עם השם דמאחר דאפשר לתקוני לא מיקרי דיעבד אבל אם היה שם למעלה איזה שם או (קמט) בתפילין ומזוזות דא"א למחוק משום שלא כסדרן כשר כך בלי תיקון ויש (קנ) מחמירין אפילו בדיעבד והסכים עמהם הגרע"א והדה"ח. אך אם (קנא) בשורות העליונות אות האחרון כד"ר וכדומה שיכול למושכן כולהו מודו דהדין בס"ת ובין בתו"מ ימשוך אותן כדי שיהיו שוות עם האות מהשם שיצא חוץ לשיטה ואין בזה משום שלא כסדרן. וכן אם לא כתב עוד רק שורה אחת (קנב) ובשורה שניה מתחת השם חוץ לשיטה יעשה שרטוטים אחרים ויתמכם שיהיו ארוכים עד סוף השם ובשביל שורה הראשונה אין קפידא. ודע עוד דבאותיות הנטפלות להשם (קנג) הסכמת אחרונים דאין להחמיר בדיעבד ביוצא חוץ לשיטה: (קנד) מהם כלל. אפילו (קנד) אות אחת ואפשר דאף רובו ככולו אבל מקצת האות לית לן בה ואם יצא השם כולו חוץ לגליון העמוד כשר בדיעבד ואינו דומה ליוצא אות אחד חוץ לשיטה דמה שיוצא לחוץ הוא חשוב כתליה וקי"ל ביו"ד רע"ו דמקצת השם אין תולין משא"כ בזה כן כתב הבני יונה והגרע"א בחידושיו בסי' זה מחמיר גם בזה עי"ש אבל בביאור הגר"א מוכח בהדיא כהבני יונה להקל: לו (קנה) כל פרשיותיה. ר"ל מהתפילין של יד הואיל והן נכתבות בקלף אחד ושייך בהן פתוחה וסתומה דהיינו שכשמניח מקום חלק בסוף שיטה אחרונה של פרשה ראשונה כדי ט' אותיות ומתחיל פרשה שלאחריה בראש השיטה בדף הב' הרי פרשה שלאחריה נקראת פתוחה כמו שבס"ת נקראת פרשה המתחלת בראש השיטה פרשה פתוחה לכו"ע כשיש ריוח כדי ט' אותיות לפניה בשיטה הקודמת לה או בסוף שיטה אחרונה שבדף הקודם אבל בתש"ר שהפרשיות נכתבין על ד' קלפים אין להקפיד בהן בפתוחות וסתומות אך נהגו לכתחלה להקפיד בזה כ"כ האחרונים ועיין בבה"ל במה שכ' בשם הפמ"ג בזה: (קנו) פתוחות חוץ וכו'. מפני שג' ראשונות שהם קדש והיה כי יביאך שמע הם פתוחות בתורה ופרשת והיה אם שמוע סתומה לפיכך צריך לכתוב בתפילין ג"כ ככה. דהיינו שיניח מקום חלק כדי ט' אותיות בסוף שיטה אחרונה שבפ' קדש כדי שבפ' והיה כי יביאך שיתחיל בראש השיטה הא' שבדף הב' תהיה הפרשה פתוחה כמו שהיא בתורה וכן אחר פ' והיה כי יביאך כדי שפ' שמע תהיה פתוחה אבל פ' והיה אם שמוע יעשה סתומה ואופן סתימתה יבואר לקמיה. ופרשת קדש אף דבתורה היא פתוחה מחמת שהוא מפסיק בריוח ט' אותיות בשורה הקודמת לה וכאן אין שייך זה דהיא

פרשה

ביאור הלכה

באיסור מחיקה יש להקל בזה לפי מה שכתב שם הנוב"י דבמוחק מקצת אות ועדיין נשאר צורתו עליו אין חייב בזה משום מוחק ורק מדרבנן ע"ש. אח"כ מצאתי כן בעזה"י בספר ישועות יעקב עי"ש: * ג' אותיות. עיין במ"ב ומקורו מהא דש"ך יו"ד בסימן רע"ג סק"ד עיי"ש ועיין בביאור הגר"א דמשמע שהוא מסכים גם כן להש"ך דהמחבר סתם פה כהרא"ש ועיין במ"א והשמטתי תירוצו משום קושית הבה"ט עי"ש והפמ"ג הקשה ג"כ זה אמנם דלא לשויה ח"ו לרבינו המ"א כטועה אמרתי שיש ליישב דמסעיף ל"ד אין ראיה להקל בזה דאפשר דלא מיעט רק דמותר לכתוב אות אחת מן התיבה של שתי אותיות חוץ לשיטה אף שהוא חצי התיבה וכמו שכתב הגר"א לדעת הרמב"ם [ודלא כהלבוש שמחמיר בזה עי"ש בטעמו] אבל ב' אותיות מן תיבה של שלש אותיות דהם רוב התיבה הו"א דאסור וכמו שכתב הגר"א באמת לדעת הרמב"ם לזה קמ"ל המחבר דשתי אותיות מותר בכל גווני כנ"ל בכוונתו: * שתי אותיות וכו'. אבל לכתוב אות אחת ממנה חוץ לשיטה מותר. כל האחרונים דלא כלבוש: * תיבה אחת. עיין במ"ב כן כתב הרא"ש בה"ק ופסק ביו"ד כוותיה ועיין במ"א בס"ק מ"ו שכתב דאף הרמב"ם מודה בזה להקל והגר"א בביאורו כתב שלדעת הרמב"ם אסור בזה: * יעשה כל פרשיותיה. עיין במ"ב

שער הציון

(קמג) ב"ח: (קמד) ביאור הגר"א: (קמה) והובא ג"כ בפמ"ג: (קמו) מוכח מהפרישה דלא מחלק בזה לענין דיעבד: (קמז) אחרונים: (קמח) מ"א: (קמט) פמ"ג לדעת המ"א והוא בעצמו הניח עיקר הדין בצ"ע לקמן בסימן קמ"ט[ב]: (קנ) הב"ש בשם מהרא"י וגם תשובת הרמב"ם שהובא[ג] ביו"ד רע"ו בד"ה ובשם התשב"ץ עי"ש: (קנא) פמ"ג: (קנב) פמ"ג: (קנג) מ"א בשם מ"ב וט"ז יו"ד רע"ו וכמה אחרונים: (קנד) פמ"ג:

הגהות ותיקונים: א) ולפחות יזהר: ב) קמ"ג משי"ש סק"ב: ג) בב"י:

(156) open /passages/, apart from the passage which is written last in the

Mishnah Berurah

nine letters before it in the preceding line or at the end of the last line on the previous column.

However, in the case of the head *tefilin*, for which the passages are written on four /separate/ parchments, one need not be concerned about their being /in the form of/ open or closed /passages/. Notwithstanding, it has become the practice to be particular about this, initially. This is what the Acharonim write. See what we have written about this in the Beyur Halachah in the name of the *P.Mg.*

(156) Open /passages/, apart, etc. This is because the first three /passages/, which are *Kadesh Li Chal Bechor, Ve-Hayah Ki Yevi'acha* and *Shema*, are /written in the form of/ open /passages/ in the Torah and the passage *Ve-Hayah Im Shamo'a* is /written in the form of/ a closed /passage there/. Therefore, one must write /these passages/ for *tefilin* also in this /manner/.

This involves leaving a blank space, sufficient for /the writing of/ nine letters, at the end of the last line of the passage *Kadesh Li Chal Bechor*, so that the passage *Ve-Hayah Ki Yevi'acha*, which will begin at the beginning of the first line of the second column, will be /in the form of/ an open passage, as it is in the Torah. /One should do/ likewise after the passage *Ve-Hayah Ki Yevi'acha*, so that the passage *Shema* will be /in the form of/ an open /passage/. However, the passage *Ve-Hayah Im Shamo'a* one should make /in the form of/ a closed /passage/. The manner in which it is made /in the form of a/ closed /passage/ is described below.

Although in the Torah the passage *Kadesh Li Chal Bechor* is /written in the form of/ an open /passage/ because there is an interval /of blank space sufficient for the writing/ of nine letters at /the end of/ the row which precedes it, this /form/ is not relevant in our

שהיא והיה אם שמוע שיעשנה סתומה (קנז) ואם שינה (נג) [כא] פסול: (קנח) (ויש מכשירים (קנט) בכולם פתוחות) מהר"ס פלדו"ה סי' פ"ז א' בשם אורחות חיים וב"י בשם העיטור (קס) ובמדינות אלו (קסא) נוהגים אף פרשת והיה אם שמוע בראש השיטה כשאר הפרשיות א ולכן נהגו שפרשת (נג) [כב] קדש לי והיה כי יביאך

א בית יוסף

שערי תשובה

ע"ש בסי' י"ג ואין להקל בזה כי אם בשעת הדחק: [כא] פסול. עבה"ט ועיין ביד אפרים ובשו"ת בית אפרים חלק א"ח סימן ב' בביאור דברי הט"ז בזה ועיין במג"א ס"ק מ"ח שמ"ש ובדיעבד אם עשאה סתומה כשר הוא ט"ס וצ"ל אם עשאה פתוחה וכמ"ש ביד אפרים שצ"ל קודם ושייך קודם תיבות וכתב הב"ח והוא נמשך לתירוצו דלפי שבסתומה יש מחלוקת לכך נהגו בפתוחה ואם עשה פתוחה בדיעבד כשר אף להרמב"ם כמ"ש בתשובת אא"ז מהר"ס מפאדו"ה וכן הוא באמת בד"מ ס"ק יו"ד בשם מהר"מ די"ל מ"ש הרמב"ם ואם שינה פסול אס"ת קאי וע"ש ואם ירצו לעשות סתומה גם כן נפלגו בפלוגתא דרבוותא ולכן נהגו בפתוחה ושגם על כ"פ בדיעבד כשר ועיין בט"ז שמביא שם דברי מהר"ס מפאדו"ה והזכיר בד"מ ועיין בפ"מ שעמד על דברי המג"א בזה דמאי קא משמע לן ועיין במחצית השקל שפירש כפשוטו. אבל המעיין בד"מ יראה שכוונת המג"א כמ"ש. ועיין בגינת ורדים כלל ב' סימן ג' וסימן ד' שנחלקו בזה דפרשת והיה אם שמוע שהיא עשויה פתוחה והיינו לפי מנהגם כהב"י ע"ש: [כב] קדש. עבה"ט (מ"ש שאין לעשות בשביל זה ב' זוגות תפילין ועיין מ"ש לקמן ס"ק ס"ז) ומ"ש בה"ט לענין תפילין דר"ת ועיין בתשובת נ"ב מה"ת סימן ה' שכתב גם כן שלא ישנה בתפילין של רבינו תם פרשה שמע כלל ויתחיל מראש שיטה כיון שצריך להניח חלק פרשה והיה א"ש עד אחר כתיבת שמע אם כן בשעת כתיבת שמע ניכר תיכף שאין סמוכות בתורה ואין כאן מקום לטעות עיין שם. ועיין בא"ר שכתב ג"כ דבתפילין של רבינו תם יעשה כולם פתוחות ואף שכותב שמע אחר והיה א"ש *) מ"מ יניח כשיעור ט' אותיות אחר על הארץ. ועיין בתשו' רש"ל. והתשובה ממהר"י שוילין הוא בעהמ"ח נחלה ליהושע ונדפס בתשובותיו סימן א'. וכתב בשו"ת ח"ל סימן נ"ט דלפי מנהג האשכנזים עכשיו שכותבין ג"פ ראשונות שיהיו פתוחות לכ"ע והרביעית פתוחה להרא"ש ליכא חשש זה שהתפילין שבראשו והס"ת שעולה לקרות סתרי אהדדי דדוקא בראשונות כגון קדש והיה כי יביאך שהם סמוכות שייך הך חששא משא"כ בשמע והיה א"ש שאינם סמוכות. וגם דהאידנא כל ס"ת שלנו הם עשוים בפתוחות וסתומות עפ"י דעת הרמב"ם ע"ש ודבריו שם תמוהים מ"ש ואי בעית למיחש לסברת מהר"י דילאון מה לי כתובה ע"ד הרמב"ם או הרא"ש לדברי כולם התפילין היפך הס"ת שבס"ת סתומה ובפרשה פתוחה ע"ש. וזה תימא דבשלמא לפי מנהג מדינות אלו שכתב הרמ"א שעושין גם הרביעית פתוחה אליבא דכ"ע שפיר משא"כ לפי מ"ש שם מנהג האשכנזים שהרביעית פתוחה להרא"ש וא"כ זה כמנהג שכתב הב"י שמתחילין בראש שיטה והיא סתומה להרמב"ם. ואע"ג דלהרא"ש פתוחה היא בע"כ עבדינן הכי. וא"כ העולה לס"ת שכתובה ע"ד הר"מ אין חשש כלל שהפתוחה שבוהיה א"ש היא סתומה להרמב"ם ולהרמב"ם הוא שוה עם הפ' שבס"ת. גם תמהני על מ"ש שם וכתבו האחרונים דטעמם משום שלא אפשר לעשות סתומה לכ"ע לכן בחרו לעשותה פתוחה כו' והמעיין יראה שהמג"א כ"כ על המנהג שכתב רמ"א שנוהגין בפתוחות דהיינו שמתחילין והיה א"ש מראש

*) נ"ל והיה א"ש אחר שמע

באר היטב

כתב אם כתב אלהינו בלא יו"ד מותר לתלות היו"ד מאחר שאינה מהשם עצמו א"כ כ"ש אם יצא הנטפל לשם חוץ לשיטה דכשר והגאון מהור"ר יצחק אב"ד דק"ק פוזנא הורה למחוק בספר תורה כל השורות העליונות ולמשוך אותם שיהיו שוות עם השם מאחר דאפשר לתקוני לא מיקרי דיעבד אבל אם יש שם בשיטות העליונות שאסור למחקו כשר בדיעבד עכ"ל המגן אברהם. וה"ה נמי בתפילין דאסור למחקו משום דהוי שלא כסדרן כשר בדיעבד. והמחבר הלכה ברורה טעה שגיאה גדולה במה שכתב ואני תמה הרי הוי שלא כסדרן עיין שם ס"ק מ"א. ועיין בב"י בי"ד סימן רע"ו שהביא תשובת הרמב"ם וכתב בה בלשון הזה על ספר תורה שנמצא בה ה' כתוב קצתו תוך השיטה וקצתו חוץ לשיטה הראוי אצלי להחליף אותה היריעה ולגונזה ואחר חלופה יקראו בה בציבור לכתחלה עכ"ל נראה דס"ל להרמב"ם דפסול אפילו בדיעבד. והמחבר יד אהרן האריך והעלה דלענין מעשה אין ולאו ורפיא בידיה. ועיין בתשובת גינת ורדים חלק אורח חיים כלל ב' סימן כ"ט. ובספר משנה למלך בפ"ה מהלכות תפילין: (נג) פסול. עיין ט"ז מה שמיישב דעת הרמב"ם מפרק הקומץ והוכיח דאפילו בדיעבד בעי סתומה. ודבריו המה קצת מגומגמים אבל תוכן דבריו הוא דילמא האי דאין מורידין הא מורידין עושין קאי אתפילין אלא ודאי דבתפילין נמי פסול בפתוחות. ואינו נראה לפענ"ד דאם כן באידך מקשן נמי נימא הכי דמקשה בסמוך הא מורידין עושין והא בעי שירטוט ואי לפי דעתו מה ק"ל הלא הרמב"ם פסק בפ"ז דס"ת בעי שירטוט ואם כן נימא נמי דטעמא דאין מורידין קאי אס"ת אלא ודאי נ"ל דלא ס"ל לתלמודא האי סברא דא"כ למה ליה למיתני כלל תפילין א"כ י"ל הכא נמי דאי קאי אתפילין לחודיה ל"ל למיתני כלל ס"ת וכך הוא הוכחה הלימא מסייע. ובזה יתורץ רש"י שם במ"ש בד"ה הכא סתומות. בספר תורה. הכא פתוחות במזוזה כו' למה נקט בראשונה בס"ת ולא נקט תפילין אלא ודאי דבתפילין י"ל דפתוחות כשר בדיעבד ולא קשיא מתפילין רק הקושיא הוא מס"ת למה נקט. גם בשירטוט כתב רש"י ובתפילין לא בעי שירטוט נקט נמי רש"י תפילין לחוד להורות דקושיא הוא למה נקט תפילין ודו"ק: (נג) קדש. אבאר לפניך מקור המחלוקת למען יתברר כבר זכרנו שצריך לעשות ג' פרשיות דהיינו קדש והיה כי יביאך שמע פתוחה. והפרשה ד' שהיא והיה א"ש סתומה. רק שיש מחלוקת

ביאור הלכה

מש"כ בשם האחרונים לענין תפי' של ראש וא"כ לפי דבריהם אפילו אם התחיל ראש כל פרשה באמצע שיטה כשר אף דבעלמא היא סתומה להרמב"ם אבל לפי דברי הפמ"ג בא"א אות מ"ט עי"ש אפשר דיש להחמיר בזה אפילו בדיעבד דהלא עי"ז באותו קלף גופא ניכר שהיא סתומה ומה לנו לקלף פרשה הקודמת לה אך אם לא הניח חלק ט' אותיות בסוף כל פרשה בתש"ר נל"פ דיש להקל בזה כסתימת שארי אחרונים אף דגם בזה מפקפק הפמ"ג שם ומטעם דכיון דכל פרשה הוא

משנה ברורה

(קנה) פרשה ראשונה מ"מ כיון שהוא מתחילה בראש שיטה ואין כתוב לפניה כלום היא נקראת פתוחה דאין כתב אחר סותמה: (קנז) ואם שינה. בין שעשאה מסתומה פתוחה או מפתוחה סתומה: (קנח) ויש מכשירין. ר"ל (קנו) בדיעבד וטעמם שאף שבתורה פ' והיה אם שמוע היא סתומה מ"מ כיון שבתורה אינה סמוכה כלל לפרשת שמע אין זה נחשב שינוי מה שהריוח שבינה לפרשת שמע הוא פתוח ולא סתום כמו שסתום הריוח שלפניה בתורה כיון שגם בתורה יש בינה לפרשת שמע שבתורה ריוח הרבה פתוח (קנז) וכן הסכימו האחרונים: (קנט) בכלם פתוחות. ולהיפך אם עשה איזו פרשה מהשלש פרשיות סתומה לכו"ע פסול כ"כ (קנח) האחרונים עוד (קנט) כתבו דדוקא אם עשה לפרשת והיה א"ש פרשה פתוחה כשר לדעה זו אבל אם אין לפניה ריוח כלל בינה לפרשת שמע לא בדף שלה ולא בדף של פרשת שמע דהיינו שהתחיל אותה בראש שיטה העליונה שבדף ולא הניח ריוח כלל לפניה באותה שיטה ולא בסוף שיטה של פ' שמע או שהניח ריוח ואין בו כשיעור ריוח שבין פרשה לפרשה דהיינו כדי לכתוב ט' אותיות ה"ז נחשב שינוי גמור ממה שהיא כתובה בתורה ופסול לכו"ע אפילו בפרשה זו. ובסוף פרשת והיה א"ש אין צריך להניח שום ריוח וכן נוהגין לסיים על הארץ בסוף שיטה התחתונה: (קס) ובמדינות אלו וכו'. ואף דלכתחלה מצוה לעשות אותה סתומה גם להיש מכשירים וא"כ המנהג הזה הוא שלא כהוגן מ"מ העתיקו הרמ"א דכיון שהעיקר הוא שבדיעבד כשר בכל ענין וא"א לעשותה סתומה לד"ה יש להחזיק במנהג הזה כדי שלא להוציא לעז על הראשונים וכ"כ המ"א בשם הל"ח אבל מדברי הלבוש והגר"א משמע שיותר טוב לעשות כמה שכתוב בשו"ע: (קסא) נוהגים אף וכו'. וכן (קס) בתפילין של ר"ת יעשה ג"כ כולם פתוחות ואף שכותב והיה

שער הציון

(קנה) ב"י: (קנו) הגר"א: (קנז) הגר"א וישועת יעקב וש"א דלא כט"ז: (קנח) לבוש ופמ"ג ורע"א והגר"ז: (קנט) לבוש ומ"א וא"ר: (קס) א"ר ושע"ת

הגהות ותיקונים: א) ע"ז:

Torah, i.e., /the passage/ *Ve-Hayah Im Shamo'a*, which he should make /in the form of/ a closed /passage/. **(157)** If one deviated /from this the *tefilin*/ are invalid.

(158) *(There are /authorities/ who rule that /the* tefilin/ *are valid* **(159)** *when*

Mishnah Berurah

case, as it is the first passage. Nevertheless, since it begins at the beginning of a line and there is nothing written before it, it is classed as /written in the form of/ an open /passage/, since other writing does not make it of closed /form/.

(157) If one deviated. /This applies/ irrespective of whether one made a /passage which is meant to be in/ closed /form in/ open /form/ or a /passage which is meant to be in/ open /form in/ closed /form/.

(158) There are /authorities/ who rule that /the *tefilin*/ are valid. I.e., once it is after the event /and one wrote them in that way/.

Their reason is that although in the Torah the passage *Ve-Hayah Im Shamo'a* is /written in the form of/ a closed /passage, the fact/ that the interval between it and the passage *Shema* is in open /form/ and not in closed /form/, in the way that the interval before /this passage/ is in closed /form/ in the Torah, is nevertheless not considered a deviation. This is because in the Torah /the passage *Ve-Hayah Im Shamo'a*/ is in no way adjacent to the passage *Shema*. /It can therefore be regarded as being in open form in relation to the passage *Shema*/ in the Torah as well, since there is an extensive interval between it and the passage *Shema* as /it is written/ in the Torah, /which makes it in/ open /form/.

The Acharonim likewise agree /with this reasoning/.

(159) When all /the passages/ were /made in the form of/ open /passages/. In the opposite case, if one made some passage of the three passages /which are meant to be in open form/ in closed /form/, it is invalid according to all /authorities/. This is what the Acharonim write.

/The Acharonim/ write further that, /even/ according to this opinion, the only /deviation which is valid in the case of/ the passage *Ve-Hayah Im Shamo'a* is if one made it /in the form of/ an open passage. However, if /one wrote it/ without any interval before it, between it and the passage *Shema*, neither on its own column nor on the column of the passage *Shema*, this is considered a complete deviation from how /the passage/ is written in the Torah. I.e., if one started /writing the passage/ at the beginning of the top line on the column without having any interval before it, /either/ on that line or at the end of the /last/ line of the passage *Shema*, or /even/ if one left an interval, but it does not have the /required/ length for an interval between passages, which is, sufficient for the writing of nine letters. /In such a case/ even this passage is invalid, according to all /authorities/.

At the end of the passage *Ve-Hayah Im Shamo'a* it is unnecessary to leave any interval. It is in fact the practice to conclude /by writing the final words/ על הארץ at the end of the bottom line /of the column/.

א בית יוסף

שה"א והיה אם שמוע שיעשנה סתומה (קנז) ואם שינה (נג) [כא] פסול: (קנח) (ויש מכשירים (קנט) בכולם פתוחות) מהר"ם פאדו"ה סי' פ"ז[א] בשם אורחות חיים וב"י בשם העיטור (קס) ובמדינות אלו (קסא) נוהגים אף פרשת והיה אם שמוע בראש השיטה כשאר הפרשיות [א]ולכן נהגו שפרשת (נג) [כב] קדש לי והיה כי יביאך

שערי תשובה

ע"ש בסי' י"ג ואין להקל בזה כי אם בשעת הדחק: [כא] פסול. עבה"ט ועיין ביד אפרים ובשו"ת בית אפרים חלק א"ח סימן ב' בביאור דברי הט"ז בזה ועיין במג"א ס"ק מ"ח שמ"ש ובדיעבד אם עשאה סתומה כשר הוא ט"ס וצ"ל אם עשאה פתוחה וכמ"ש ביד אפרים שצ"ל קודם ושייך קודם תיבות וכתב הב"ח והוא נמשך לתירוצו דלפי שבסתומה יש מחלוקת לכך נהגו בפתוחה ואם עשה פתוחה בדיעבד כשר אף להרמב"ם כמ"ש בתשובת אא"ז מהר"ם מפאדו"ה וכן הוא באמת בד"מ ס"ק יו"ד בשם מהר"מ די"ל מ"ש הרמב"ם ואם שינה פסול אס"ת קאי וע"ש ואם ירצו לעשות סתומה גם כן נפלגו בפלוגתא דרבוותא ולכן נהגו בפתוחה ושגם על כ"פ בדיעבד כשר ועיין בט"ז שמביא שם דברי מהר"ם מפאדו"ה והזכיר בד"מ ועיין בפ"ת שעמד על דברי המג"א בזה דמאי קא משמע לן ועיין במחצית השקל שפירש כפשוטו. אבל המעיין בד"מ יראה שכוונת המג"א כמ"ש. ועיין בגינת ורדים כלל ב' סימן ג' וסימן ד' שנחלקו בזה דפרשת והיה אם שמוע שהיא עשויה פתוחה והיינו לפי מנהגם כהב"י ע"ש: [כב] קדש. עבה"ט (מ"ש שאין לעשות בשביל זה ב' זוגות תפילין ועיין מ"ש לקמן ס"ק ס"ז) ומ"ש בה"ט לענין תפילין דר"ת ועיין בתשובת נ"ב מה"ת סימן ה' שכתב גם כן שלא ישנה בתפילין של רבינו תם פרשה שמע כלל ויתחיל מראש שיטה כיון שצריך להניח חלק פרשה והיה א"ש עד אחר כתיבת שמע אם כן בשעת כתיבת שמע ניכר תיכף שאין סמוכות בתורה ואין כאן מקום לטעות עיין שם. ועיין בא"ר שכתב ג"כ דבתפילין של רבינו תם יעשה כולם פתוחות ואף שכותב שמע אחר והיה א"ש *) מ"מ יניח כשיעור ט' אותיות אחר על הארץ. ועיין בתשו' רש"ל. והתשובה ממהר"י שוילין הוא בעהמ"ח נחלה ליהושע ונדפס בתשובותיו סימן א'. וכתב בשו"ת ח"ל סימן נ"ט דלפי מנהג האשכנזים עכשיו שכותבין ג"פ ראשונות שיהיו פתוחות לכ"ע והרביעית פתוחה להרא"ש ליכא חשש זה שהתפילין שבראשו והס"ת שעולה לקרות סתרי אהדדי דדוקא בראשונות כגון קדש והיה כי יביאך שהם סמוכות שייך הך חששא משא"כ בשמע והיה א"ש שאינם סמוכות. וגם דהאידנא כל ס"ת שלנו הם עשוים בפתוחות וסתומות עפ"י דעת הרמב"ם ע"ש ודבריו שם תמוהים מ"ש ואי בעית למימש לסברת מהר"י דילאון מה לי כתובה ע"ד הרמב"ם או הרא"ש לדברי כולם התפילין היפך הס"ת שבס"ת סתומה ובפרשה פתוחה ע"ש. וזה תימא דבשלמא לפי מנהג מדינות אלו שכתב הרמ"א שעושין גם הרביעית פתוחה אליבא דכ"ע שפיר משא"כ לפי מ"ש שם מנהג האשכנזים שהרביעית פתוחה להרא"ש וא"כ זה כמנהג שכתב הב"י שמתחילין בראש שיטה והיא סתומה להרמב"ם. ואע"ג דלהרא"ש פתוחה היא בע"כ עבדינן הכי. וא"כ העולה לס"ת שכתובה ע"ד הר"מ אין חשש כלל שהפתוחה שבוהיה א"ש היא סתומה להרמב"ם ולהרמב"ם הוא שוה עם הפ' שבס"ת. גם תמהני על מ"ש שם וכתבו האחרונים דטעמם משום שלא אפשר לעשות סתומה לכ"ע לכן בחרו לעשותה פתוחה כו' והמעיין יראה שהמג"א כ"כ על המנהג שכתב רמ"א שנוהגין בפתוחות דהיינו שמתחילין והיה א"ש מראש

*) נ"ל והיה א"ש אחר שמע

באר היטב

כתב אם כתב אלהינו בלא יו"ד מותר לתלות היו"ד מאחר שאינה מהשם עצמו א"כ כ"ש אם יצא הנטפל לשם חוץ לשיטה דכשר והגאון מהור"ר יצחק אב"ד דק"ק פוזנא הורה למחוק בספר תורה כל השורות העליונות ולמשוך אותם שיהיו שוות עם השם מאחר דאפשר לתקוני לא מיקרי דיעבד אבל אם יש שם בשיטות העליונות שאסור למחקו כשר בדיעבד עכ"ל המגן אברהם. וה"ה נמי בתפילין דאסור למחקו משום דהוי שלא כסדרן כשר בדיעבד. והמחבר הלכה ברורה טעה שגיאה גדולה במה שכתב ואני תמה הרי הוי שלא כסדרן עיין שם ס"ק מ"א. ועיין בב"י בי"ד סימן רע"ו שהביא תשובת הרמב"ם וכתב בה בלשון הזה על ספר תורה שנמצא בה ה' כתוב קלתו תוך השיטה וקלתו חוץ לשיטה הראוי אללי להחליף אותה היריעה ולגונזה ואחר חלופה יקראו בה בציבור לכתחלה עכ"ל נראה דס"ל להרמב"ם דפסול אפילו בדיעבד. והמחבר יד אהרן האריך והעלה דלענין מעשה אין ולאו ורפיא בידיה. ועיין בתשובת גינת ורדים חלק אורח חיים כלל ב' סימן כ"ט. ובספר משנה למלך בפ"ה מהלכות תפילין: (נב) פסול. עיין ט"ז מה שמיישב דעת הרמב"ם מפרק הקומץ והוכיח דאפילו בדיעבד בעי סתומה. ודבריו המה קצת מגומגמים אבל תוכן דבריו הוא דילמא האי דאין מורידין הא מורידין עושין קאי אתפילין אלא ודאי דבתפילין נמי פסול בפתוחות. ואינו נראה לפענ"ד דאם כן באידך מקשן נמי נימא הכי דמקשה בסמוך הא מורידין עושין והא בעי שירטוט ואי לפי דעתו מה ק"ל הלא הרמב"ם פסק בפ"ז דס"ת בעי שירטוט ואם כן נימא נמי דטעמא דאין מורידין קאי אס"ת אלא ודאי צ"ל דלא ס"ל לתלמודא האי סברא דא"כ למה ליה למיתני כלל תפילין א"כ י"ל הכא נמי דאי קאי אתפילין לחודיה ל"ל למיתני כלל ס"ת וכך הוא הוכחה הלימא מסייע. ובזה יתורץ רש"י שם במ"ש בד"ה הכא סתומות. בספר תורה. הכא פתוחות במזוזה כו' למה נקט בראשונה בס"ת ולא נקט תפילין אלא ודאי דבתפילין י"ל דפתוחות כשר בדיעבד ולא קשיא מתפילין רק הקושיא הוא מס"ת למה נקט. גם בשירטוט כתב רש"י ובתפילין לא בעי שירטוט נקט נמי רש"י תפילין לחוד להורות דקושיא הוא למה נקט תפילין ודו"ק: (נג) קדש. אבאר לפניך מקור המחלוקת למען יתברר כבר זכרנו שצריך לעשות ג' פרשיות דהיינו קדש והיה כי יביאך שמע פתוחה. והפרשה ד' שהיא והיה א"ש סתומה. רק שיש מחלוקת

ביאור הלכה

מש"כ בשם האחרונים לענין תפי' של ראש וא"כ לפי דבריהם אפילו אם התחיל ראש כל פרשה באמצע שיטה כשר אף דבעלמא היא סתומה להרמב"ם אבל לפי דברי הפמ"ג בא"א אות מ"ט עי"ש אפשר דיש להחמיר בזה אפילו בדיעבד דהלא עי"ז באותו קלף גופא ניכר שהיא סתומה ומה לנו לקלף פרשה הקודמת לה אך אם לא הניח חלק ט' אותיות בסוף כל פרשה בתש"ר נל"פ דיש להקל בזה כסתימת שארי אחרונים אף דגם בזה מפקפק הפמ"ג שם ומטעם דכיון דכל פרשה הוא

משנה ברורה

(קנה) פרשה ראשונה מ"מ כיון שהוא מתחילה בראש שיטה ואין כתוב לפניה כלום היא נקראת פתוחה דאין כתב אחר סותמה: (קנז) ואם שינה. בין שעשאה מסתומה פתוחה או מפתוחה סתומה: (קנח) ויש מכשירין. ר"ל (קנו) בדיעבד וטעמם שאף שבתורה פ' והיה אם שמוע היא סתומה מ"מ כיון שבתורה אינה סמוכה כלל לפרשת שמע אין זה נחשב שינוי מה שהריוח שבינה לפרשת שמע הוא פתוח ולא סתום כמו שסתום הריוח שלפניה בתורה כיון שגם בתורה יש בינה לפרשת שמע שבתורה ריוח הרבה פתוח (קנז) וכן הסכימו האחרונים: (קנט) בכלם פתוחות. ולהיפך אם עשה איזו פרשה מהשלש פרשיות סתומה לכו"ע פסול כ"כ (קנח) האחרונים עוד (קנט) כתבו דדוקא אם עשה לפרשת והיה א"ש פרשה פתוחה כשר לדעה זו אבל אם אין לפניה ריוח כלל בינה לפרשת שמע לא בדף שלה ולא בדף של פרשת שמע דהיינו שהתחיל אותה בראש שיטה העליונה שבדף ולא הניח ריוח כלל לפניה באותה שיטה ולא בסוף שיטה של פ' שמע או שהניח ריוח ואין בו כשיעור ריוח שבין פרשה לפרשה דהיינו כדי לכתוב ט' אותיות ה"ז נחשב שינוי גמור ממה שהיא כתובה בתורה ופסול לכו"ע אפילו בפרשה זו. ובסוף פרשת והיה א"ש אין צריך להניח שום ריוח וכן נוהגין לסיים על הארץ בסוף שיטה התחתונה: **(קס) ובמדינות אלו וכו'.** ואף לכתחלה מצוה לעשות אותה סתומה גם להיש מכשירים וא"כ המנהג הזה הוא שלא כהוגן מ"מ העתיקו הרמ"א דכיון שהעיקר הוא שבדיעבד כשר בכל ענין וא"א לעשותה סתומה לד"ה יש להחזיק בהמנהג הזה כדי שלא להוציא לעז על הראשונים וכ"כ המ"א בשם הל"ח אבל מדברי הלבוש והגר"א משמע שיותר טוב לעשות כמה שכתוב בשו"ע: **(קסא) נוהגים אף וכו'.** וכן (קס) בתפילין של ר"ת יעשה ג"כ כולם פתוחות ואף שכותב והיה

שער הציון

(קנה) ב"י: (קנו) הגר"א: (קנז) הגר"א וישועת יעקב וש"א דלא כט"ז: (קנח) לבוש ופמ"ג ורע"א והגר"ז: (קנט) לבוש ומ"א וא"ר: (קס) א"ר ושע"ת

הגהות ותיקונים: א) ע"ז:

all /the passages/ were /made in the form of/ open /passages/.) ... **(160)** *In these countries* **(161)** *it is the practice /to start writing/ even the passage* Ve-Haya Im Shamo'a *at the beginning of the line, like the other passages.*

In view of this, it is the practice for the passages, *Kadesh Li Chal Bechor,*

Mishnah Berurah

(160) In these countries, etc. /Now,/ initially, it is a mitzvah to make it /in the form of/ a closed /passage/, even according to /the authorities/ who rule that /the *tefilin/* are valid /if it is made in open form/, and it follows that this practice is improper. Nevertheless, the *Rema* records it, since the prevailing /ruling/ is that once it is after the event /the passage/ is valid either way and it is /also/ impossible to make it /in the form of/ a closed /passage in a way/ that /satisfies/ all opinions. One should /, therefore,/ persist with this practice so as not to cast aspersions on the earlier /*tefilin,* for which this passage was made in open form/.

The *M.A.* likewise writes this in the name of the *L.Ch.* However, from the words of the *Levush* and of the *Gra*, it is implied that it is better to act as stated by /the author of/ the Shulchan Aruch.

(161) It is the practice /to start writing/ even, etc. Likewise, in the case of *tefilin* /made according to the view/ of Rabbeinu Tam, one should also make all /the passages/ in open /form/. /According to this view/ one must write /the passage/ *Ve-Hayah Im Shamo'a* after /the passage/

ופרשת שמע (קסב) מתחילין בראש שיטה ובסוף קדש לי ובסוף והיה כי יביאך * מניחים חלק כדי לכתוב (קסג) ט׳ אותיות ובסוף שמע אין מניחים חלק * ואם מניחים הוא פחות מכדי לכתוב ט׳ אותיות ופרשת [כג] והיה אם שמוע מתחילים באמצע שיטה עליונה ומניח לפניה חלק כדי לכתוב ט׳ אותיות ונמצא ששלשה פרשיות

באר היטב

בצורת פתוחה וסתומה. דלהרא״ש מבואר בי״ד סימן רע״ה דכל שיש חלק בשיטה ומתחיל לכתוב באמצע שיטה. וכן בכותב ומניח בסוף שיטה חלק ומתחיל הפרשה שאחריה בראש שיטה שניה זהו פתוחה. ושיעור החלק היא כדי שיוכל לכתוב ט׳ אותיות. וסתומה הוי כל שמניח חלק באמצע שיטה כשיעור הנ״ל ויתחיל לכתוב בסוף השיטה היא עצמה. וה״ה אם סיים הפ׳ בסוף שיטה יניח שיטה א׳ חלק ויתחיל בשיטה שלישית. והרמב״ם כתב בזה״ל פרשה פתוחה יש לה ב׳ צורות אם גמר באמצע השיטה מניח שאר השיטה פנוי כשיעור הנ״ל ומתחיל הפרשה שהיא פתוחה מתחלת השיטה השניה (זהו כמו להרא״ש) ואם לא נשאר כשיעור פנוי או גמר בסוף השיטה יניח שיטה שאחריה פנוי ומתחיל הפתוחה מתחלת שיטה ג׳ (וזהו להרא״ש סתומה). פרשה סתומה יש לה ג׳ צורות אם גמר באמצע מניח ריוח כשיעור ומתחיל בסוף שיטה עצמה תיבה אחת (זהו כמו להרא״ש). ואם לא נשאר כשיעור ט׳ אותיות ולכתוב תיבה א׳ בסוף יניח הכל פנוי ויניח מעט ריוח מראש שיטה שניה ויתחיל לכתוב הפרשה סתומה מאמצע שיטה הב׳ (אפשר גם להרא״ש כן). ואם גמר בסוף השיטה מניח בתחלת שיטה שניה כשיעור הריוח ומתחיל לכתוב מאמצע השיטה וזו הפ׳ סתומה (וזהו להרא״ש פתוחה) נמצאת אומר שפ׳ פתוחה תחילתה בתחילת שיטה לעולם וסתומה תחלתה מאמצע שיטה לעולם עכ״ל. וכתב הב״י היאך יעשו בתפילין שילאו ידי כולם אם לעשות הג׳ פתוחות דהיינו שישאר בתחילתן שיעור ויתחיל הפ׳ באמצע שיטה לא ילא ידי הרמב״ם דס״ל מתחיל באמצע שיטה מיקרי סתומה. ואם ישאיר חלק בסוף כל פ׳ א״כ הוי אף אחרונה פתוחה דהא כל שיש חלק בסוף הפרשה עושה את הפרשה שלאחריו פתוחה על כן נוהגים בא״י שפוסקים כהרמב״ם שעושים בדרך זה. ב׳ פרשיות ראשונות מתחילות מראש הדף ומסיימין בסוף הדף באמצע שיטה ופ׳ ג׳ שהיא שמע מתחלת בראש הדף ומסיימת בסופה ופרשה ד׳ מתחלת מאמצע שיטה. נמצא ג׳ פרשיות ראשונות לדעת הרמב״ם פתוחה כי הראשונה אע״פ שאין חלק לפניה מיקרי פתוחה כמו בראשית דהוי פשוט פתוחה לדעת הרמב״ס. וב׳

שערי תשובה

שיטה דהוי פתוחה לכ״ע וכמש״ל ס״ק כ״ב[א]. (ועיין שם מ״ש בפירוש דברי המג״א ובאמת שתירוצו צ״ע דמה הפסד היה כאן אם היו עושין כמ״ש הב״י ומה בכך שלא יהיה סתומה לכ״ע עכ״פ ילא י״ח סתומה להרמב״ם ונראה שכוונתו כיון שא״א להעמיד על קו הדין שיהיה סתומה לכ״ע חששו לתקלה שכ״א ימצא לו ענין אחר ויש לחוש שמא לא יניח חלק כט׳ אותיות בסוף שמע ויתחיל מראש שיטה דזה אינו לא פתוחה ולא סתומה כמ״ש המג״א א״כ ולכן הנהיגו בפתוחה לכ״ע דלא עביד דטעו שהרי גם הג׳ פרשיות ראשונות כתבן בפתוחות אליבא דכ״ע ויכתוב גם זה כן) אבל לפי המנהג שכתב הח״ל שהאשכנזים נוהגים עכשיו והיא כשיטת הב״י א״צ לסברא זו של המג״א כלל דמה שעושין פתוחה להרא״ש אינו משום ברירה ורצון לעשות פתוחה רק מצד ההכרח דכיון שחוששין טובא לדעת הרמב״ם כשרוצים לצאת ידי חובת סתומה להרמב״ם א״א כ״א כשיעשה ע״ד זה להניח חלק כשיעור ט׳ אותיות בשיטה העליונה. ואף שזו פתוחה לדעת הרא״ש בע״כ סומכין לומר דבדיעבד כשר בפתוחה וא״צ לתירוץ המג״א שבחרו בפתוחה וצ״ע וראיתי בשיורי ברכה שהביא דברי הח״ל דבתפילין שנהגו ג׳ כהרמב״ם והד׳ להרא״ש פתוחה אין לחוש למ״ש הב״י בשם הר״י דיליאון כו׳ משום דא״א לעשות סתומה לכ״ע. ובין להרמב״ם ובין להרא״ש התפילין היפך הס״ת וכתב שמו׳ ישעיה בסאן בתשובה כת״י תמה עליו דהקורא בס״ת לדעת הרמב״ם לא סתרי כו׳ ולא היתה כוונתם לעשות פתוחה להרא״ש אלא לעשות סתומה להרמב״ם ע״ש והיא ע״ד שכתבתי אלא שלא העתיק דברי הח״ל יפה שאין דעת הח״ל להתיר מהאי טעמא דמה בכך שא״א לצאת בתפילין כאלו לתורה באמת יחלוץ אותם ולא יעלה כ״א בתפילין לדעת כ״א בתורה שנכתבה ג״כ עפ״י דעתו רק שבא לומר כלפי שאמר האיש ההוא שלא לעלות לס״ת הכתובה לדעת הרמב״ם בתפילין כאלו וע״ז השיגו דא״כ גם בס״ת הכתובה להרא״ש לא יעלה. ואמנם באמת בלא״ה ז״א דלא שייך רק בקדש והיה כ״י כמש״ל אך דמ״מ קשיא מ״ש דבס״ת הכתובה לדעת הרמב״ם סתרי אהדדי דהא ליתא ואדרבא בפשיטות היה לו להשיג על האומר שאסור לקרות בס״ת להרמב״ם דז״א דאדרבא להרמב״ם הס״ת ותפילין שוים הם לפי המנהג זה שהד׳ פתוחה להרא״ש וממילא היא סתומה להרמב״ם וגם בתורה היא סתומה. וגם מש״ל דהביא תירוץ המג״א להך מנהגא וליתא אלא למנהג הרמ״א. ומ״ש עוד בשיורי ברכה בשם מהרי״ב הנ״ל לק״מ ויש לדחות ע״ש: [כג] והיה א״ש מתחילין באמצע שיטה כו׳. וכתב הרדב״ז חלק ב׳ סי׳ קנ״ד שאם התחיל בשיטה שניה ג״כ באמצע כמו בשיטה ראשונה ושאר השיטין התחיל מראש הדף צריכה גניזה וכותב אחרת. ואם אירע טעות בפרשה ראשונה צריך לגנוז כל התפלה ע״ש והביאו

משנה ברורה

והיה א״ש אחר שמע כדלקמן בסימן ל״ד במ״ב סק״ג יניח כשיעור ט׳ אותיות אחר על הארץ וכשכותב פרשת שמע מתחיל בתחלת העמוד בראש השיטה: (קסב) מתחילין בראש וכו׳. דזה עושה אותה לפתוחה לכו״ע כשהשאיר חלק כדי ט׳ אותיות בסוף שיטה התחתונה בעמוד הקודם ואם לא התחיל בראש השיטה אלא הניח מעט ריוח (קסא) אפילו פחות מט׳ אותיות הרי פרשה זו נקראת סתומה להרמב״ם ופסולה אפילו דיעבד ובפמ״ג [אות כ״ו] כתב דאפי׳ אם לא המשיך לפנים בראש קדש או והיה כ״י או שמע רק אות אחת או שתים ג״כ י״ל דפסול וצ״ע בזה ובספר מאמר מרדכי משמע דאין להחמיר בזה בדיעבד ועכ״פ לכתחלה יש ליזהר בזה מאוד [ואם השאיר כשיעור תיבת אשר נ״ל דיש להחמיר אפילו בדיעבד דהרי בשיעור זה בוודאי יש כששה אותיות קטנות ויותר וכמו שכתב המחה״ש והרי לדעת הט״ז מצטרף מדינא לכו״ע להקרא סתומה אפילו לא היה הריוח שלמעלה ולמטה רק כשיעור ט׳ אותיות קטנות ע״י צירוף וכמו שכתב הפמ״ג הרי דמה שכתב הרמב״ם ויניח מעט ריוח וכו׳ הוא שיעור קטן מאוד] ע״כ אם רואה שהתחיל הפרשה אפילו אות אחת לפנים שלא במקום שירטט מתחילה ירא לעשות גם שאר השורות באופן זה: (קסג) ט׳ אותיות. כתבו האחרונים דלכתחילה צריך להניח כדי ג׳ תיבות אשר (קסב) ע״כ צריך להניח ג״כ ריוח מלא ב׳ אותיות קטנות מלבד הט׳ אותיות דהא

דין

ביאור הלכה

בקלף בפ״ע נחשבת כפרשת קדש בתש״י דנחשבת פתוחה מלד שאין כתוב לפניה כלום בתפילין: * מניחים חלק כדי לכתוב ט״א. ואם שכח להניח כמלא ט״א בסוף פרשת קדש ופרשת והיה כי יביאך מבואר בלבוש דפסול וכתב הא״ר דמיירי הכא בשעבר והתחיל שיטה ראשונה בראש הדף לכן הוא פסול דתו אין כאן פתוחה אבל לכתחלה עלתו כשנזדמן לו כן שיתחיל לכתוב בתחלת שיטה שניה שהיא נמי פתוחה לדעת הרמב״ם ואף דלא ישתייר מנין השורות הנזכרים בסימן ל״ה הא קי״ל שם דאם שינה לא פסל. אכן לפי מה שראיתי עתה בספר משנת אברהם שכתב דהיכא דמשייר ריוח שני שיטין בין פרשה לפרשה אף לדעת הרא״ש ז״ל היא פתוחה נ״ל בזה שישייר ריוח בתחלת הפרשה שני שיטין דאם ישייר רק שיטה א׳ הלא לדעת הרא״ש תפילין שלו הם פסולין דהיא פרשה סתומה והשלשה פרשיות בעינן שיהא פתוחות לעיכובא לד״ה כמו שכתבו האחרונים ואף דבדיעבד אם לא שייר רק ריוח שיטה א׳ אין לפסול התפילין דבעיקר הדין קי״ל כהרמב״ם בזה מ״מ לכתחלה בודאי י״ש ילא ידי הכל. כתב הפמ״ג יש לשאול אם הניח חלק ט״א ואכלוה עכברים או תולעת מקום החלק ואין שם קלף חלק כלל אם כשר כה״ג או לאו ע״ש דמסתפק בזה גם בתש״ר ולפי מה שכ׳ לעיל בתחלת הסעיף בשם האחרונים בש״ר בודאי יש להקל: * ואם מניחים הוא פחות וכו׳. לאו לעיכובא קאמר אלא דלכתחלה ס״ל

שער הציון

(קסא) כן משמע בביאור הגר״א וכ״כ ש״א ואפשר דמודו ג״כ להפמ״ג דאפילו רק איזה אותיות: (קסב) הב״ח ולבוש:

הגהות ותיקונים: א) כ״א:

Ve-Hayah Ki Yevi'acha and the passage *Shema* **(162)** to be started at the beginning of the line. At the end of /the passage/ *Kadesh Li Chal Bechor* and at the end of /the passage/ *Ve-Hayah Ki Yevi'acha* /it is the practice/ to leave a blank /space/ sufficient for the writing of **(163)** nine letters.[26*] At the end of /the passage/ *Shema* a blank /space/ is not left and if it is left it is /made/ less than is sufficient for the writing of nine letters. The passage *Ve-Hayah Im Shamo'a* is started in the middle of the highest line and a blank /space/ is left beforehand, sufficient for the writing of nine letters. Thus, three passages are

Mishnah Berurah

Shema /has already been written/, as /stated/ below in Sec. 34, in the Mishnah Berurah, sub-Par. 3 /, but in a space left before that passage/. Even so /, when one writes it/, he should leave a width /of blank parchment/ sufficient for /the writing of/ nine letters after /the final words of the passage/ על הארץ. When he writes the passage *Shema*, he should commence at the start of the column, at the beginning of the line.

(162) To be started at the beginning, etc. For this makes /the passage/ in open /form/ according to all /authorities, provided/ one left a blank /space/, sufficient for /the writing of/ nine letters, at the end of the bottom line /of the passage/ in the previous column.

If one did not commence /writing the passage/ at the beginning of the line, but left a little interval /of blank space/, even /if it is/ less than /is required for the writing of/ nine letters /, then/, according to the *Rambam*, this passage is now describable as a /passage/ in closed /form/ and is /ruled as/ invalid even once it is after the event. The *P.Mg.* [in sub-Par. 26] writes that even if one only went into /the line sufficiently for the writing of/ one or two letters before /he commenced writing the passage/ *Kadesh Li Chal Bechor, Ve-Hayah Ki Yevi'acha* or *Shema* there are also grounds for arguing that it is invalid and this requires study. In the work *Ma'amar Mordechai*, it is implied that one need not be stringent about this, once it is after the event. At any rate, initially, one should be very careful about it. [If one left a width /sufficient/ for /the writing of/ the word אשר, it appears to me that one must be stringent even once it is after the event. For this width definitely contains /sufficient for the writing/ of six or more small letters, as stated by the *Mach. Hash.* /One must, therefore, bear in mind/, as stated by the *P.Mg.*, that according to the view of the *Taz*, even when the intervals /of blank space/ above /at the beginning of the passage/ and below /at the end of the preceding passage/ are merely sufficient for /the writing of/ nine small letters after being combined, /the intervals/ combine halachically according to all /Rishonim to cause the passage/ to be classed as /being/ in closed /form/. /From this it follows/ that when the *Rambam*[27*] writes that one must leave a small interval, etc. /when one wishes to make the new passage in closed form/, a very small width /is meant/.]

Consequently, if one sees that he commenced /writing/ a passage /further/ in, not at the point from where he marked out /the line/ at the outset /, then/, even /where the width involved is only sufficient for the writing of/ a single letter, he should see that he makes the other rows also in this way /and start writing them from the corresponding point/.

(163) Nine letters. The Acharonim write that, initially, one must leave sufficient /space/ for /writing/ the word אשר three /times/. Consequently, one must also leave adequate space for /writing/ two small letters apart from /the space for writing/ the nine letters, since between words one is

26* If one did not leave sufficient space for the writing of nine letters, then, now that it is after the event, he should leave blank a space of two lines at the beginning of the following passage. (Beyur Halachah)

הם פתוחות בין להרמב"ם בין להרא"ש ופרשה אחרונה היא (קסד) סתומה * לדעת הרמב"ם:
לז (קסה) * ב עור הבתים צריך להיות * מעור בהמה חיה ועוף (קסו) * טהורים ג אפילו מנבילה

ב שם כ"ח
ג שם ק"ח

באר היטב

פרשיות שאחרי הראשונה נעשו פתוחות מכח שיעור החלק שלפניהם דהיינו החלק מפ' שלפניה בסופה עושה פ' שאחריה פתוחה והיא מתחלת בראש שיטה וזהו בין להרמב"ם בין להרא"ש רק מה שמתחילין פרשה הד' באמצע שיטה מיקרי פתוחה לדעת הרא"ש ואנן בעינן סתומה אבל להרמב"ם הוי זה סתומה ובזה יבואר לך דברי המחבר. וכתב ט"ז דיש לפנינו דרך אחרת שנעשה לצאת ידי הרמב"ם והרא"ש ונקדים תחלה בהא דכתב הרמב"ם בגורה ב' דסתומה דאם לא נשאר מן השיטה כדי להניח ריוח כשיעור ולכתוב בסוף שיטה תיבה אחת יניח הכל פנוי ויניח מעט ריוח מראש שיטה שניה וכו' ושם כתבתי דאפשר דגם להרא"ש כן ע"ש א"כ הרוצה לעשות יעשה בדרך זה דפרשה א' וב' יתחיל בראש הדף וישייר בסוף חלק כדי ט' אותיות רק פרשה ג' יתחיל ג"כ בראש דף וישייר פחות מט' אותיות והפרשה ד' יעשה ג"כ תחלת הדף ריוח קצת אבל פחות מט' אותיות נמצא הפרשה הד' סתומה להרמב"ם ולהרא"ש דלהרמב"ם מיקרי זה מתחיל באמצע וגם להרא"ש אין כאן פתוחה כיון שאין כאן במקום א' חלק כשיעור. וא"ל דלא יניח בסוף פרשה ג' כלל ובתחלת פרשה ד' יניח פחות מכשיעור זה אינו דעכ"פ בעינן ריוח בין פרשה לפרשה כשיעור ט' אותיות בין בסתומה בין בפתוחה אלא דכאן אי אפשר לעשותו במקום א' דאז הוי פתוחה ע"כ חלקנו השיעור לב' חלקים עכ"ל ט"ז. וכ"כ הרמ"ע מפאנו סימן נ"ו ועיין בשיורי כנה"ג בהגהת ב"י סעיף כ"ו. ואין לעשות בשביל ספק ב' זוגות תפילין ב"י. וכתב הב"י שגדול א' פסל כל התפילין במדינתו שהיו עשויות לדעת הרא"ש. כי ס"ת שלהם היו הפרשיות לדעת הרמב"ם א"כ העולה בתורה ותפילין בראשו סתרי אהדדי עיין מ"א. ואמרתי אחכמה לדעת מה יעשה בתפילין של ר"ת בענין פתוחות

משנה ברורה

בין תיבה לתיבה צריך להניח מלא אות קטנה (קסג) ובדיעבד יש להקל כשמניח רק כמלא ט' אותיות קטנות [דהיינו יודי"ן] וכמשמעות השו"ע כאן וכתב הפמ"ג דמשערין הריוח של הט' אותיות כפי אותו הכתב וכל השיעור הזה הוא (קסד) בין לפתוחה או לסתומה: (קסד) סתומה לדעת הרמב"ם. ואף דלדעת הרא"ש היא פתוחה מ"מ אנו עושין כך כי א"א לעשות בתפילין צורת סתומה שילא בה אליבא דכו"ע כי סתומה שאנו נוהגין לעשות בס"ת דהיינו שמסיים הפרשה שלפניה באמצע שיטה ומפסיק כדי ט' אותיות ואח"כ מתחיל הפרשה שאחריה ג"כ באותה השיטה והיא נקראת סתומה אליבא דכו"ע דסתומה מלפניה ומלאחריה וא"א לעשותה פה בתפילין דכל פרשה הוא בעמוד אחר וכן אם ירצה להניח שיטה אחת חלק בתחלת פרשת והיה א"ש ולהתחילה בראש שיטה שנייה זה ג"כ איננה סתומה לכו"ע דהיא רק להרא"ש ולא להרמב"ם דלדידיה היא פתוחה וכיון שא"א לעשותה סתומה לד"ה נהגו כהרמב"ם לפי שכן עיקר אף בס"ת אם א"א לעשות לד"ה כמ"ש ביו"ד סימן ער"ה. ובט"ז המציא עצה לעשותה סתומה שילא אליבא דכו"ע דהיינו שבפרשה או"ב יעשה הכל כמו שכתוב בשו"ע רק שבפרשה שמע בסופה יניח ריוח פחות מכדי ט' אותיות (קסה) קטנות וכן יניח ריוח פחות מט' אותיות קטנות בתחלת פרשת והיה א"ש דעי"ז שאין לה ט' אותיות במקום אחד כ"א ע"י צירוף היא נקראת סתומה לכו"ע וכ"כ בתשובת הרמ"ע מפאנו ובביאור הגר"א וכן משמע מפמ"ג שגם הוא נהג לעשות כן. ודע דבדיעבד אפילו אם שייר ריוח כט' אותיות גדולות מכל צד ג"כ כשר דלהרמב"ם היא סתומה ולהרא"ש היא פתוחה וכתבנו לעיל בס"ק קנ"ח בשם האחרונים' דהסכימו דהלכה כהיש מכשירין הנ"ל ויש מהגדולים שנהגו לעשות כן לכתחילה ונכרא נכרא ופשטיה ועיין בבה"ל: לז (קסה) עור הבתים. וה"ה (קסו) עור התיתורא והמעברתא כיון שמחובר ותפור בהבתים: (קסו) טהורים. דכתיב למען תהיה תורת ה' בפיך מן המותר בפיך

ביאור הלכה

דלא נכון לעשות כן דזה מורה קצת על פרשה שלאחריה שתהיה פתוחה אבל בדיעבד אפילו אם הניח בה חלק כדי ג"פ אשר אפ"ה לא נתבטל שם סתומה מפרשת והיה א"ש כיון שלא התחילה בראש שיטה דכלל הדבר להרמב"ם דנקטינן כוותיה העיקר להלכה דסתומה היא כל שמתחלת מאמצע שיטה כן כתוב בספר מאמר מרדכי ושארי אחרונים וכן מוכח בב"י ביו"ד סימן ער"ה במש"כ בשם הר"י אסכנדרני[א] שם וכן בביאור הגר"א כאן. ודע דבזה דאיירינן השתא ששייר בסוף שמע כדי ט' אותיות דעת רוב האחרונים וכמעט כולם [אפילו אותם החולקים על הט"ז וס"ל דלא מהני צירוף] שאפילו אם לא הניח ריוח בתחלת והיה א"ש כדי ט' אותיות אפ"ה מקרי סתומה לדעת הרמב"ם: * לדעת הרמב"ם. עיין במ"ב במה שכתבנו בשם הט"ז בזה והגר"ז כתב דלכתחלה יש למנוע מלעשות כעצת הט"ז וכתב הטעם דמהרבה פוסקים מוכח דלא ס"ל כלל הסברא דצירוף [ור"ל מדכתבו שאין תקנה לעשות סתומה לד"ה וגם מה שהקשה הב"י בהלכות מזוזה סי' רפ"ח על הא דהרא"ש והטור שם אבל א"כ יהיה ראיה מהרא"ש והטור לט"ז וע"כ דכוונתו מהאחרונים שבסימן זה שלא מצאו עצה לעשות כד"ה] וא"כ אין כאן פתוחה ולא סתומה ופסולה ומוטב לעשות כעצת השו"ע שיהיה עכ"פ כשר בדיעבד בודאי וכן בספר מאמר מרדכי מפקפק בדינו של הט"ז מטעם דמסתפק שם אם מהני צירוף. ומ"מ בודאי אין למנוע הנוהג כהט"ז כי יש ראיה לדינו מהרא"ש והטור כמו שכתב הגר"א וכן הגאון רמ"ע מפאנו כ"כ והובא בחידושי רע"א ושארי אחרונים כמו שכתבתי במ"ב. והנה כ"ז שכ' בהשו"ע הוא לענין תפילין דרש"י ולענין תפילין של ר"ת בענין פתוחות וסתומות דלדידיה פרשה ד' הוא קודם לפ' ג' ג"כ יתנהג באחד מאלו הג' אופנים דהיינו או שיעשה כולן פתוחות וכמש"כ במ"ב ס"ק קס"א וכמו שאנו נוהגין במדינתינו לענין תפילין דרש"י וכמו שכתב בהג"ה והנוהג כהמחבר יעשה כך פרשת קדש והיה כי יביאך מתחיל בראש שיטה ובסוף קדש לי מניחים חלק ט' אותיות ובסוף והיה כי יביאך אין מניחים חלק ואם מניחים הוא פחות מט' אותיות ואח"כ מתחיל פרשת שמע בקצה הקלף דהוא בעמוד הרביעי דהא בעינן כסדרן וכשכותבה הוא מתחילה בראש שיטה ואח"כ חוזר לעמוד ג' לכתוב פרשת והיה א"ש ומתחילה באמצע שיטה עליונה שמניח לפניה חלק ט' אותיות ובסופה משייר חלק כדי ט' אותיות כדי שפרשת שמע שאחריה תהיה פתוחה עי"ז נמצא שפרשת קדש לי ופרשת והיה כי יביאך ופרשת שמע הם פתוחות בין להרמב"ם ובין להרא"ש ופרשת והיה א"ש היא סתומה לדעת הרמב"ם ולהרב ט"ז ג"כ הכל כנ"ל רק דלדידיה ישייר בסוף והיה כי יביאך פחות מכדי ט' אותיות קטנות וכן בריש פרשת והיה א"ש יניח ריוח פחות מכדי ט' אותיות קטנות שעי"ז תקרא פרשת והיה אם שמוע סתומה לכו"ע: * עור הבתים. עיין במ"ב במש"כ וה"ה עור התיתורא וכו' ע"כ הסופרים שמניחים בין הבית להתיתורא עורות ישנים אשר מאשפות ירימו וממנעלים קרועים ידעו כי עבירה היא בידם אחרי שהוא מחובר להבית צריך להיות דוקא מעור כשר כמוהו ממש כ"כ בספר לשכת הסופר ולכתחלה בודאי הדין עמו אך לענין דיעבד יש לעיין לפי מה דכתב הפמ"ג לקמן בסעיף מ"ז דמה דהצריך רמ"א לדבק כשר הוא למצוה ולא לעיכובא כיון דהדיבוק אינו מעכב ממילא אין קפידא במה מדבק וא"כ לכאורה ה"נ בענינינו לא דמי לעור התיתורא והמעברתא דחיובן הוא מלד הדין ע"כ בעינן שיהיו טהורים משא"כ בזה וצ"ע: * מעור בהמה וכו'. ועיין בד"מ שכתב דאין עושין מעור הדג משום דאיבעיא דלא איפשטא בשבת ק"ח ולכאורה יש לעיין דהלא הרמב"ם כתב הטעם שאין כותבין על עור הדג מפני שאין הזוהמא פוסקת בעיבודה משמע מזה דשאר עור פוסק הזוהמא על ידי העיבוד וא"כ הרמב"ם שפוסק דעור הבית מותר על עור שאינו מעובד יהיה מותר אפילו על עור הדג ויש לדחות: * טהורים. עיין במ"ב ע"כ אם נתהוה לו איזה ספק בעור הבתים אם הוא טהור יש להחמיר דספיקא דאורייתא הוא ואפילו ברלועות יש להחמיר פמ"ג[ב] בס"ק כ"ז ומשמע שחזר ממה שכתב בפתיחתו להלכות תפילין בענין זה ע"ש. גם מה שכתב שם בפתיחה דעור הבית ש"י שצריך להיות מעור טהורה הוא מדרבנן בעלמא גם זה אינו לענ"ד דלפ"ז הו"ל להגמרא לתרץ דקאי לש"י דאין בו סי"ן

שער הציון

(קסג) א"ר והגר"א ופמ"ג: (קסד) הגר"א וש"א: (קסה) פמ"ג: (קסו) מרדכי בה"ק הלכות תפילין:

הגהות ותיקונים: א) אכסנדרני: ב) משב"ז:

/written in the form of/ open /passages/, both according to /the view of/ the *Rambam*[27*] and according to /the view of/ the *Rosh*, and the final passage is /written in the form of/ **(164)** a closed /passage/ according to the view of the *Rambam*.

Mishnah Berurah

required to leave adequate /space/ for /writing/ a small letter. /However,/ once it is after the event, if one only left adequate /space/ for /the writing of/ nine small letters [i.e., י /letters/], one can be lenient, as implied by the Shulchan Aruch here.

The *P.Mg.* writes that we assess the interval /required/ for /the writing/ of nine letters in accordance with the script /used/ in the particular /passages/. This entire width applies both as regards /a passage which must be written/ in open /form/ and as regards /a passage which must be written/ in closed /form/.

(164) A closed /passage/ according to the view of the *Rambam*. Although, according to the view of the *Rosh* it is /in the form of/ an open /passage/, we nevertheless /write it/ in this way, because /, unlike in a Torah Scroll/, it is impossible to make a *tefilin* /passage/ in the form of a closed /passage/ which will satisfy /the requirements for such a form/ according to all /Rishonim/. /The form of/ the closed /passages/ which we are accustomed to make in a Torah Scroll involves concluding the preceding passage in the middle of the line, interrupting /with an interval of blank space/, sufficient for /the writing of/ nine letters, and, subsequently, beginning the following passage also on the same line. /A passage started in this manner/ is classed as being in closed /form/ according to all /Rishonim/, as there is closure before /the started passage/ and after /the previous passage/. /However,/ it is impossible to do this in our case, where *tefilin* /passages/ are involved, as each passage is /written/ on a different column.

Likewise, if one wishes to leave one line blank at the beginning of the passage *Ve-Hayah Im Shamo'a* and begin /writing/ it at the beginning of the second line, it will also not be /in the form of/ a closed /passage/ according to all /Rishonim/. /Then/ it will only be /in the form of a closed passage/ according to the *Rosh*, but not according to the *Rambam*, as /in the opinion of the latter/ it will /in fact/ be /in the form of/ an open /passage/.

Since it is impossible to make it /in the form of/ a closed /passage in a way/ which /satisfies the views of/ all /Rishonim/, it has become the practice to /follow the view of/ the *Rambam*. This is because /the *Rambam*'s view/ is the prevailing /view which must be followed/ even in the case of a Torah Scroll, when it is impossible to act /in a way/ which /satisfies/ all /Rishonim/, as stated in the *Yo.D.*, Sec. 275.

The *Taz* devised a solution whereby one can make /the passage/ in closed /form in a manner/ that satisfies all /Rishonim/. /His solution/ is that the first and second passage should be prepared entirely in accordance with what is stated in the Shulchan Aruch. The only /difference is/ that at the end of the passage *Shema*, one should leave an interval /of blank space/ that is insufficient for /the writing of/ nine small letters and should likewise leave an interval at the beginning of the passage *Ve-Hayah Im Shamo'a* that is insufficient for /the writing of/ nine small letters. /He maintains/ that by virtue of /the

27* See *Rambam, Hilchos Sefer Torah* 8:1 and 2.

הם פתוחות בין להרמב"ם בין להרא"ש ופרשה אחרונה היא (קסד) סתומה * לדעת הרמב"ם: ב שם כ"ח

לז (קסה) * [ב]עור הבתים צריך להיות * מעור בהמה חיה ועוף (קסו) * טהורים [ג]אפילו מנבילה ג שם ק"ח

באר היטב

פרשיות שאחרי הראשונה נעשו פתוחות מכח שיעור החלק שלפניהם דהיינו החלק מפ' שלפניה בסופה עושה פ' שאחריה פתוחה והיא מתחלת בראש שיטה וזהו בין להרמב"ם בין להרא"ש רק מה שמתחילין פרשה הד' באמצע שיטה מיקרי פתוחה לדעת הרא"ש ואנן בעינן סתומה אבל להרמב"ם הוי זה סתומה ובזה יבואר לך דברי המחבר. וכתב ט"ז דיש לפנינו דרך אחרת שנעשה לצאת ידי הרמב"ם והרא"ש ונקדים תחלה בהא דכתב הרמב"ם בצורה ב' דסתומה דאם לא נשאר מן השיטה כדי להניח ריוח כשיעור ולכתוב בסוף שיטה תיבה אחת יניח הכל פנוי ויניח מעט ריוח מראש שיטה שניה וכו' ושם כתבתי דאפשר דגם להרא"ש כן ע"ש א"כ הרוצה לעשות יעשה בדרך זה דפרשה א' וב' יתחיל בראש הדף וישייר בסוף חלק כדי ט' אותיות רק פרשה ג' יתחיל ג"כ בראש דף וישייר פחות מט' אותיות והפרשה ד' יעשה ג"כ תחלת הדף ריוח קצת אבל פחות מט' אותיות נמצא הפרשה הד' סתומה להרמב"ם ולהרא"ש דלהרמב"ם מיקרי זה מתחיל באמצע וגם להרא"ש אין כאן פתוחה כיון שאין כאן במקום א' חלק כשיעור. וא"ל דלא יניח בסוף פרשה ג' כלל ובתחלת פרשה ד' יניח פחות מכשיעור זה אינו דעכ"פ בעינן ריוח בין פרשה לפרשה כשיעור ט' אותיות בין בסתומה בין בפתוחה אלא דכאן אי אפשר לעשותו במקום א' דאז הוי פתוחה ע"כ חלקנו השיעור לב' חלקים עכ"ל ט"ז. וכ"כ הרמ"ע מפאנו סימן כ"ו ועיין בשיורי כנה"ג בהגהת ב"י סעיף כ"ו. ואין לעשות בשביל ספק ב' זוגות תפילין ב"י. וכתב הב"י שגדול א' פסל כל התפילין במדינתו שהיו עשויות לדעת הרא"ש. כי ס"ת שלהם היו הפרשיות לדעת הרמב"ם א"כ העולה בתורה ותפילין בראשו סתרי אהדדי עיין מ"א. ואמרתי אחכמה לדעת מה יעשה בתפילין של ר"ת בענין פתוחות

משנה ברורה

בין תיבה לתיבה צריך להניח מלא אות קטנה (קסג) ובדיעבד יש להקל כשמניח רק כמלא ט' אותיות קטנות [דהיינו יודי"ן] וכמשמעות השו"ע כאן וכתב הפמ"ג דמשערין הריוח של הט' אותיות כפי אותו הכתב וכל השיעור הזה הוא (קסד) בין לפתוחה או לסתומה: (קסד) סתומה לדעת הרמב"ם. ואף דלדעת הרא"ש היא פתוחה מ"מ אנו עושין כך כי א"א לעשות בתפילין צורת סתומה שלא בא אליבא דכו"ע כי סתומה שאנו נוהגין לעשות בס"ת דהיינו שמסיים הפרשה שלפניה באמצע שיטה ומפסיק כדי ט' אותיות ואח"כ מתחיל הפרשה שאחריה ג"כ באותה השיטה והיא נקראת סתומה אליבא דכו"ע דסתומה מלפניה ומלאחריה וא"א לעשותה פה בתפילין דכל פרשה הוא בעמוד אחר וכן אם ירצה להניח שיטה אחת חלק בתחלת פרשת והיה א"ש ולהתחילה בראש שיטה שנייה זה ג"כ אינה סתומה לכו"ע דהיא רק להרא"ש ולא להרמב"ם דלדידיה היא פתוחה וכיון שא"א לעשותה סתומה לד"ה נהגו כהרמב"ם לפי שכן עיקר אף בס"ת אם א"א לעשות לד"ה כמ"ש ביו"ד סימן ער"ה. ובט"ז תמציא עצה לעשותה סתומה שלא אליבא דכו"ע דהיינו שבפרשה או"ב יעשה הכל כמו שכתוב בשו"ע רק שבפרשה שמע בסופה יניח ריוח פחות מכדי ט' אותיות (קסה) קטנות וכן יניח ריוח פחות מט' אותיות קטנות בתחלת פרשת והיה א"ש דעי"ז שאין לה ט' אותיות במקום אחד כ"א ע"י צירוף היא נקראת סתומה לכו"ע וכ"כ בתשובת הרמ"ע מפאנו ובביאור הגר"א וכן משמע מפמ"ג שגם הוא נהג לעשות כן:וידע דבדיעבד אפילו אם שייר ריוח כט' אותיות גדולות מכל לד ג"כ כשר דלהרמב"ם היא סתומה ולהרא"ש היא פתוחה וכתבנו לעיל בס"ק קנ"ח בשם האחרוני' דהסכימו דהלכה כהים מכשירין הנ"ל ויש מהגדולים שנהגו לעשות כן לכתחילה ונראה נהרא ופשטיה ועיין בבה"ל: **לז** (קסה) עור הבתים. וה"ה (קסו) עור התיתורא והמעברתא כיון שמחובר ותפור בהבתים: (קסו) טהורים. דכתיב למען תהיה תורת ה' בפיך מן המותר בפיך

ביאור הלכה

דלא נכון לעשות כן דזה מורה קצת על פרשה שלאחריה שתהיה פתוחה אבל בדיעבד אפילו אם הניח בה חלק כדי ג"פ אשר אפ"ה לא נתבטל שם סתומה מפרשת והיה א"ש כיון שלא התחילה בראש שיטה דכלל הדבר להרמב"ם דנקטינן כוותיה העיקר להלכה דסתומה היא כל שמתחלת מאמצע שיטה כן כתוב בספר מאמר מרדכי ושארי אחרונים וכן מוכח בב"י ביו"ד סימן ער"ה במש"כ בשם הר"י אסכנדרני[א] שם וכן בביאור הגר"א כאן. ודע דבזה דאיירינן השתא ששייר בסוף שמע כדי ט' אותיות דעת רוב האחרונים וכמעט כולם [אפילו אותם החולקים על הט"ז וס"ל דלא מהני לירוף] שאפילו אם לא הניח ריוח בתחלת והיה א"ש כדי ט' אותיות אפ"ה מקרי סתומה לדעת הרמב"ס: * לדעת הרמב"ם. עיין במ"ב במה שכתבנו בשם הט"ז בזה והגר"ז כתב דלכתחלה יש למנוע מלעשות כעלת הט"ז וכתב הטעם דמהרבה פוסקים מוכח דלא ס"ל כלל הסברא דלירוף [ור"ל מדכתבו שאין תקנה לעשות סתומה לד"ה וגם מה שהקשה הב"י בהלכות מזוזה סי' רפ"ח על הא דהרא"ש והטור שם אבל א"כ יהיה ראיה מהרא"ש והטור לט"ז וע"כ דכוונתו מהאחרונים שבסימן זה שלא מצאו עצה לעשות כד"ה] וא"כ אין כאן פתוחה ולא סתומה ופסולה ומוטב לעשות כעלת השו"ע שיהיה עכ"פ כשר בדיעבד בודאי וכן בספר מאמר מרדכי מפקפק בדינו של הט"ז מטעם דמסתפק שם אם מהני לירוף. ומ"מ בודאי אין למנוע הנוהג כהט"ז כי יש ראיה לדינו מהרא"ש והטור כמו שכתב הגר"א וכן הגאון רמ"ע מפאנו כ"כ והובא בחידושי רע"א ושארי אחרונים כמו שכתבתי במ"ב. והנה כ"ז שכ' בהשו"ע הוא לענין תפילין דרש"י ולענין תפילין של ר"ת בענין פתוחות וסתומות דלדידיה פרשה ד' הוא קודם לפ' ג' ג"כ יתנהג באחד מאלו הג' אופנים דהיינו או שיעשה כולן פתוחות וכמש"כ במ"ב ס"ק קס"א וכמו שאנו נוהגין במדינתינו לענין תפילין דרש"י וכמו שכתב בהג"ה והנוהג כהמחבר יעשה כך פרשת קדש והיה כי יביאך מתחיל בראש שיטה ובסוף קדש לי מניחים חלק ט' אותיות ובסוף והיה כי יביאך אין מניחים חלק ואם מניחים הוא פחות מט' אותיות ואח"כ מתחיל פרשת שמע בקלה הקלף דהוא בעמוד הרביעי דהא בעינן כסדרן וכשכותבה הוא מתחילה בראש שיטה ואח"כ חוזר לעמוד ג' לכתוב פרשת והיה א"ש ומתחילה באמצע שיטה עליונה שמניח לפניה חלק ט' אותיות ובסופה משייר חלק כדי ט' אותיות כדי שפרשת שמע שאחריה תהיה פתוחה עי"ז נמצא שפרשת קדש לי ופרשת והיה כי יביאך ופרשת שמע הם פתוחות בין להרמב"ם ובין להרא"ש ופרשת והיה א"ש היא סתומה לדעת הרמב"ם ולהרב ט"ז ג"כ הכל כנ"ל רק דלדידיה ישייר בסוף והיה כי יביאך פחות מכדי ט' אותיות קטנות וכן בריש פרשת והיה א"ש יניח ריוח פחות מכדי ט' אותיות קטנות שעי"ז תקרא פרשת והיה אם שמוע סתומה לכו"ע: * עור הבתים. עיין במ"ב במש"כ וה"ה עור התיתורא וכו' ע"כ הסופרים שמניחים בין הבית להתיתורא עורות ישנים אשר מאשפות ירימו וממנעלים קרועים ידעו כי עבירה היא בידם אחרי שהוא מחובר להבית צריך להיות דוקא מעור כשר כמוהו ממש כ"כ בספר לשכת הסופר ולכתחלה בודאי הדין עמו אך לענין דיעבד יש לעיין לפי מה דכתב הפמ"ג לקמן בסעיף מ"ז דמה דהצריך רמ"א לדבק כשר הוא למצוה ולא לעיכובא כיון דהדיבוק אינו מעכב ממילא אין קפידא במה מדבק וא"כ לכאורה ה"נ בענינינו לא דמי לעור התיתורא והמעברתא דחיובן הוא מלד הדין ע"כ בעינן שיהיו טהורים משא"כ בזה וצ"ע: * מעור בהמה וכו'. ועיין בד"מ שכתב דאין עושין מעור הדג משום דאיבעיה דלא איפשטא בשבת ק"ח ולכאורה יש לעיין דהלא הרמב"ם כתב הטעם שאין כותבין על עור הדג מפני שאין הזוהמא פוסקת בעיבודה משמע מזה דשאר עור פוסק הזוהמא על ידי העיבוד וא"כ הרמב"ם שפוסק דעור הבית מותר על עור שאינו מעובד יהיה מותר אפילו על עור הדג ויש לדחות: * טהורים. עיין במ"ב ע"כ אם נתהוה לו איזה ספק בעור הבתים אם הוא טהור יש להחמיר דספיקא דאורייתא הוא ואפילו ברלועות יש להחמיר פמ"ג[ב] בס"ק כ"ז ומשמע שחזר ממה שכתב בפתיחתו להלכות תפילין בענין זה ע"ש. גם מה שכתב שם בפתיחה דעור הבית ש"י שלריך להיות מעור טהורה הוא מדרבנן בעלמא גם זה אינו לענ"ד דלפ"ז הו"ל להגמרא לתרץ דקאי לש"י דאין בו

שער הציון

(קסג) א"ר והגר"א ופמ"ג: (קסד) הגר"א וש"א: (קסה) פמ"ג: (קסו) מרדכי בה"ק הלכות תפילין:

סי"ן

הגהות ותיקונים: א) אכסנדרני: ב) משב"ז:

37. **(165)** The skin /used/ for /making/ the housings must be the skin of a domestic or non-domestic animal or of a bird, which is **(166)** /halachically/

Mishnah Berurah

fact/ that /the passage/ is not /preceded by an interval of blank space which is sufficient for the writing of/ nine letters in /any/ one place, but only /has sufficient space for writing nine letters/ once one combines /the intervals in both places, the passage/ is classed as being in closed /form/ according to all /Rishonim/. This is also stated in a responsum of the *Rema* of Fano and in the *Beyur Ha-Gra*. It is likewise implied by the *P.Mg.* that he also acted in accordance with this /solution/.

Note that once it is after the event, even if one left an interval /of blank space sufficient for the writing/ of nine large letters on each of the /blank/ ends /preceding the passage *Ve-Hayah Im Shamo'a* the *tefilin*/ are also valid. /This follows/ according to /the view of/ the *Rambam*, because /the following passage/ is /classed as being/ in closed /form/. /Although/ according to the *Rosh* it is /classed as being/ in open /form/, we have written above in sub-Par. 158, citing the Acharonim, that the agreed halachic /ruling/ follows /the authorities cited/ above, who rule /that *tefilin*/ are valid /, once it is after the event, if all its passages have been written in the form of open passages/. There were eminent people who adopted the practice /of making them all open, even/ initially. Every river follows its /natural/ course.[32] See the Beyur Halachah.[33]

(165) The skin for the housings. The same ruling /applies/ to the skin /used/ for /making/ the bridge and for /making/ the passageway, since they are joined and sewn to the housing.

(166) /Halachically/ clean. For it is written,[12*] "In order that the teaching of the Lord should be in your mouth". /The Sages explained that what is meant is that the law of the Lord must be written on/ what is permitted to your mouth. Since the letter ש,

32 I.e., each person should follow the custom of his community.

33 The author notes there that there are authorities who question the solution of the *Taz* and think it better to follow the ruling of the Shulchan Aruch. However, he concludes that one should not prevent someone acting in accordance with the view of the *Taz*.

או טרפה שלהם ירשאי לעשות (נד) (קסז) מקלף או מעור (נה) (קסח) שליל: הגה וכן הרצועות יכול (קסט) לעשותן מקלף ועור שליל (מרדכי דף ל"ד) הצריך שיהיה (קע) * מעובד לשמו (קעא) * היכא (נו) [כד] דאפשר: **לח** * יעשה ד' בתים (נז) [כה] (קעב) * מעור אחד לשל ראש

ד טור בשם ספר התרומה ה שם וסמ"ג והרא"ש בהלכות ס"ת מצריכין עיבוד לשמה והרמב"ם לא מצריך ו מנחות ל"ד

באר היטב

וסתומות הואיל ופרשה ד' הוא קודם לפרשה ג'. הנה זהו פשיטא. להרב ב"י פרשת קדש והיה כי יביאך מתחילין בראש שיטה ובסוף קדש לי מניחים חלק ט' אותיות ובסוף והיה כי יביאך אין מניחים חלק ואם מניחים הוא פחות מט' אותיות. ופרשת והיה אם שמוע מתחילים באמצע שיטה עליונה ומניח לפניה חלק ט' אותיות. ובסוף פרשת והיה אם שמוע מניח חלק כדי ט' אותיות. ופרשת שמע מתחיל בראש שיטה. נמצא פרשת קדש לי ופרשת והיה כי יביאך ופרשת שמע הם פתוחות בין להרמב"ם בין להרא"ש ופרשת והיה אם שמוע היא סתומה לדעת הרמב"ם. ולהרב ט"ז פרשת קדש לי ופרשת והיה כי יביאך מתחילין בראש שיטה. ובסוף קדש לי מניחים חלק כדי ט' אותיות. ובסוף והיה כי יביאך מניחים חלק פחות מט' אותיות ופרשת והיה אם שמוע יניח ריוח בראשה פחות משיעור ט' אותיות ובסופה מניח חלק שיעור ט' אותיות. והפרשה שמע מתחיל בראש שיטה וק"ל. אך את זה צל"ע לפי מה שכתב המ"א בסימן ל"ד ס"ק ב' ומ"מ צריך לכותבן כסדרן כמ"ש סימן ל"ב ס"א לכן צריך שיניח חלק פרשת והיה אם שמוע ויכתוב פרשת שמע בקצה הקלף ואח"כ יכתוב פרשת והיה אם שמוע באמצע עכ"ל א"כ כשמניח בסוף פרשת והיה כי יביאך חלק פחות מט' אותיות להרב ט"ז או לא מניח חלק כלל להרב ב"י ואח"כ יתחיל לכתוב פרשת שמע בקצה הקלף בראש שיטה וזהו להרמב"ם פתוחה אבל להרא"ש סתומה ועיין בצורה ב' להרמב"ם דפתוחות. ולאחר עיון ראיתי דלאו כלום היא דלאחר שבא והיה אם שמוע למעלה יתוקן אז ונעשה פתוחה וזהו מהני כמבואר בי"ד סימן רע"ה סעיף א' בהג"ה ועיין הרמ"ע מפאנו סימן ל"ז ועיין ע"ת ובתשובת רמ"א סי' כ"ה: (נד) מקלף. ולכתחלה ישים הקלף במי קליפות של עפצים שקורין בל"א לו"א שמעבדין בהן העורות. מ"א: (נה) שליל. והוא מן המובחר: (נו) דאפשר. ואם אין לו קלף אחר יניחם בלא ברכה ב"ח והמ"א כתב דכדאי הוא הרמב"ם לסמוך עליו ולברך ע"ש. וע"ל סי' ט' סק"ז[א] מש"ש: (נז) מעור א'.

שערי תשובה

בבר"י: [כד] דאפשר. עבה"ט ועיין במשאת משה סי' א' שכתב ליישב שיטת הרמב"ם ע"ש: [כה] מעור א'. עבה"ט ועיין בשו"ת בית אפרים חלק א"ח סימן א' וסי' ב' אם נעשה מעור א' מחותך מצדדיו אחר שמקפלים אותו ואח"כ תולים

משנה ברורה

וכיון (קסז) דאות שי"ן שהוא מרמז על שם שדי נקמט בעור התפילין הוא בכלל תורת ה'. ואין חילוק (קסח) בין הש"ר או הש"י: (קסז) מקלף. ואע"פ שהוא דק שפיר מיקרי עור: (קסח) שליל. דגם עורו נקרא עור (קסט) ואע"ג דהוא נקרא בשר לענין טומאה מ"מ לא גרע מעור עוף: (קסט) לעשותן מקלף. רק שישחירם דרצועות שחורות הלמ"מ: (קע) מעובד לשמו. ואם העיבוד היה רק לרצועות (קע) לא מהני להבתים דקדושתן חמורה: (קעא) היכא דאפשר. כי הרמב"ם ס"ל (קעא) דלא בעי כלל עיבוד עור הבתים דאדרבה יותר חזק הוא כשלא נתעבד משום הכי כשר אפילו עור שאינו מעובד כלל וכ"ש דלא בעי עיבוד לשמה ורוב הפוסקים חולקים עליו ומצרכי עיבוד וגם לשמה ופסק השו"ע דהיכא דאפשר בעי לשמה אבל היכא דלא אפשר למצוא חיפוי הבתים מעור המעובד לשמה מותר לסמוך על דברי הרמב"ם מלהתבטל ממצות תפילין (קעב) וכשימצא אח"כ מעור המעובד לשמה יגנוז הבתים אלו ויעשה מעור המעובד לשמה ונחלקו האחרונים אם לע"ע יניחם בברכה או בלא ברכה והברכי יוסף הסכים להמ"א דיוכל לברך ועיין בבה"ל: **לח** (קעב) מעור אחד. ותחיכת עור תפורים יחד

ביאור הלכה

שי"ן ומש"כ הפמ"ג בזה הוא דוחק גדול אלא נראה פשוט דס"ל להגמרא דכיון דהל"מ הוא אפילו על התפירות שיהיו נתפרין הבתים דוקא בגידין טהורין כ"ש על הבתים גופייהו שיהיו מעור טהור ולא צריך לזה הא דרב יוסף וכעין זה כתב רש"י מנחות מ"ב ע"ב ד"ה פסולות עי"ש ואין זה בכלל אין דנין ק"ו מהלכה דגילוי מילתא בעלמא הוא ואחר דקמקשה הגמרא והאמר אביי שי"ן של תפילין וכו' היה יכול לתרץ דקאי על ש"י ולהקשות ע"ז מהברייתא דקמקשה השתא אך לא רצה להאריך בזה וכמו שכתבו כעין זה בכללי הש"ס עיין בגליון הש"ס להגרע"א והנלענ"ד כתבתי: * **מעובד לשמו**. ועיבוד זה לכו"ע לאו מהלמ"מ הוא ומה דצריך עיבוד הוא משום לשמה דכל דבר קדושה בעינן לשמה פמ"ג בא"א ס"ק י"ב[ב]: * **היכא דאפשר**. עיין במ"א שכתב דאם אין לו קלף אחר יכול לברך ע"ז דכדאי הוא הרמב"ם לסמוך עליו ולברך דגם רש"י ס"ל כן עי"ש. ולכאורה אין מיקל המ"א לענין ברכה רק באם הי' מעובד ושלא לשמה אבל לא בשאינו מעובד כלל דזה לא מצינו לרש"י. איברא ממה דגילה לנו הגר"א את מקורו דהרמב"ם מהא דעירובין נ"ו דעור הבתים הוא כעין עור קמיע שהוא עור שאינו מעובד כלל וחזינן מזה דסוגיין כת"ק דרשב"ג ולא כרשב"ג עי"ש א"כ ממילא מוכח דלרש"י שהוא פוסק כת"ק דרשב"ג מותר אפילו עור שאינו מעובד כלל דאל"ה אמאן תרמייה' האי סוגיא דעירובין. מ"מ לענ"ד צ"ע אעיקרא דדינא אם יש לסמוך על המ"א שמיקל לענין ברכה אף שהברכי יוסף הסכים עמו ודלא כב"ח וא"ר דהלא הגר"א כתב בביאורו בסימן ל"ג סוף ס"ג דדברי הרמב"ם שמיקל בזה לענין לשמה לכאורה צ"ע דהלא הוא עצמו כתב אם חיפן עו"ג להבתים או תפרן פסול מפני שעשייתן ככתיבתן מפני השי"ן [ור"ל א"כ הכא נמי יהיה העור מעובד לשמה מפני השי"ן] ותירץ ע"ז דהרמב"ם אזיל לשיטתו דלא מצריך עיבוד לכל כתב שבקדושה שהרי במזוזה לא מצריך עיבוד אלא בס"ת ובתפילין [וכוונת הגר"א עיבוד לשמה אינו מצריך במזוזה אבל עיבוד מצריך כמו שכתב הרמב"ם בהדיא בהלכות תפילין בפ"א] וא"כ לפ"ז לפי מאי דאנן פסקינן לקמן בסימן ל"ט ס"ב דעשיית הבתים הוא ככתיבה מפני השי"ן וכדאיתא בטור ופסקינן נמי ביו"ד רפ"ח לענין מזוזה דלא כוותי' דהרמב"ם דאף דהשו"ע שם כתב רק דצריכה עיבוד לשמה לכתחילה כל האחרונים חלקו ע"ז עיין בט"ז שם ואפילו להש"ך שם עכ"פ בלא ברכה וגם הגר"א כתב שם דכל הפוסקים חולקים אהרמב"ם א"כ למה נקיל הכא דיהא מותר לברך בעור שאינו מעובד לשמה וצ"ע למעשה. ואם יזדמן איזה ספק בהעיבוד דעור הבתים יש להקל דהוי כעין ס"ס כן משמע מהפמ"ג במ"ז ס"ק ל"א: * **יעשה ד' בתים** וכו'. עיין במ"א בשם הב"ח דע"י תפירה לא חשיב כעור אחד ועיין במחה"ש דה"ה דיבוק להב"ח ובהגהות הגר"א לאזהר כתב דע"י דיבוק לכו"ע מהני ובא"ם שהבאתי במ"ב כתב להיפוך ולפי מה דנמצא בא"ז משמע דשניהן שוין וכמו שיתבאר אח"כ. כתב במחה"ש דה"ה הנעשים מעור אחד אלא שחותכים ממנו רצועות ומ"מ באמצע נשארו מחוברים ואח"כ שוב מחברים הרצועות יחד ובזה נעשו הבתים לדעת הב"ח פסולים כיון דעכ"פ קרועים בכל צדדי הבית ולדידיה התפירה וה"ה הדבק אינו עושה חיבור עכ"ל אמנם בפמ"ג כתב וז"ל בס"ק נ"ב וראוי לעשות הכל מעור אחד ממש ודיעבד הסופרים חותכין למעלה ולמטה מחובר עכ"ל וצ"ל דהביא ראיה להסופרים דזה מיקרי עור אחד ולא הוי בכלל שנים או שלשה זכרונות דהא כל חילם של המחמירים דס"ל עור אחד הוא לעיכובא הוא משום דאפשר תפילין דמי לגט ובגט פסק בהע"ז סימן ק"ל סעיף ז' בהג"ה דדיבוק הוא חשש פסול משום ספר אחד אמר רחמנא ולא שנים או שלשה ספרים וה"ה בענינינו והלא לענין גיטין גופא מסיק הגמרא שם בדף כ' ע"ב דהיכא דמעורה שרי משום דהוא מיקרי עדיין ספר אחד ע"כ נראה דבזה לכו"ע מהני תפירה או דבק ולא דמי למה דהביא במחה"ש בריש סימן ל"ג בשם המרדכי דהתם מיירי שנשאר כך בלי תיקון ומצאתי בפתחי תשובה על או"ח בריש סימן ל"ג שגם הוא מצדד כן אך לא הביא הראיה שלנו ולפ"ז פשוט דאפילו אם נעשה נקב קטן בהעור במקום הריבוע כמו שרגיל אפ"ה לא אבד ממנו שם עור אחד עי"ז ואפילו אם נתקלקל הריבוע עי"ז מהני תיקון אח"כ: * **מעור אחד**. עיין במ"ב מש"כ כי יש מחמירין דלא חשיב חבור היינו הב"ח וכן בספר ביאור

שער הציון

(קסז) שבת כ"ח ע"ב: (קסח) פמ"ג: (קסט) ב"י: (קע) פמ"ג: (קעא) ט"ז ובתוספת ביאור: (קעב) ב"ח:

הגהות ותיקונים: א) סק"ו: ב) י"ג:

clean.[28*] It may even be from a *neveylah*[11*] or *tereyfah*[11*] of /such an animal or bird/.

One is allowed to make /the housings/ **(167)** out of parchment or out of the skin of **(168)** a fetus.

Gloss: Likewise, /as regards/ the straps, one is able **(169)** *to make them out of parchment or the skin of a fetus. (...)*

/The skin used for the housings/ must be **(170)** processed for the sake of /use for the mitzvah/ **(171)** where possible.

38. One must make four housings, **(172)** from a single skin, for the head /*tefilin*/ and a single housing[29*] for the arm /*tefilin*/.

Mishnah Berurah

which alludes to the name ש-ד-י, is folded out in the skin of the *tefilin* /housing/, it is classed as /an article on which/ "the teaching of the Lord" /is written/.

There is no difference /in this respect/ between /the skin to be used for/ the head /*tefilin*/ and /the skin to be used for/ the arm /*tefilin*, although the latter does not have any letter on it/.

(167) Out of parchment. Although /parchment/ is thin, it is fully describable as skin.

(168) A fetus. For the skin /of a fetus/ is also classed as skin. Although it is classed as meat with respect to /the laws of/ uncleanness, it is nevertheless no less /acceptable/ than the skin of a bird /for the making of *tefilin*/.

(169) To make them out of parchment. The only /provision is/ that one must blacken them, as /the fact that/ the straps must be black is a halachic /requirement which was taught/ to Mosheh (Moses) on /Mount/ Sinai.

(170) Processed for the sake of /use for the mitzvah/. If the processing /of the skin/ was /done/ merely for /the sake of use for *tefilin*/ straps, this is of no avail /for it to be used/ for the housings, which have a more severe holiness.

(171) Where possible. /The reason for this ruling/ is that the *Rambam*[34] is of the opinion that the skin for the housings does not need to be processed at all, as, on the contrary, /the skin/ is stronger when it has not been processed. In view of this, even skin which has not been processed at all is valid /for this purpose/ and /the skin one uses/ is certainly not required to have been processed for the sake of /use for the mitzvah/. /On the other hand,/ the majority of Poskim disagree with him and require /the skin/ to be processed and also /require it to be done/ for the sake of /use for the mitzvah/. The Shulchan Aruch /therefore/ rules that where possible it is necessary /to process the skin/ for the sake of /use for the mitzvah/.

However, where it is impossible /for one/ to find for the covering of the housings skin which was processed for the sake of /use for the mitzvah/, it is permitted to rely on the words of the *Rambam* /and it is preferable to do so/ rather than to be idle about /the fulfillment of/ the mitzvah of *tefilin*. When he subsequently finds skin which was processed for the sake of /use for the mitzvah/, he should put away these housings in the *genizah* and make /others/ out of the skin which was processed for the sake of /use for the mitzvah/. The Acharonim are divided as to whether now, /when he must/ don these /*tefilin* which were made with skin which was not processed for the sake of use for the mitzvah/, he should /do so/ with a blessing or without a blessing. The *Birkey Yosef* agrees with the *M.A.*, that he may make the blessing. See the Beyur Halachah.[35]

(172) From a single skin. /As for/ pieces of skin sewn together, the *M.A.* adopts the

28* One must be stringent when one is in doubt as to whether or not the skin of the *tefilin* unit or of its straps is of a halachically clean animal or bird. (Beyur Halachah)
29* Of a single skin. (Beyur Halachah)

34 *Rambam, Hilchos Tefilin* 3:15.
35 The author writes there that the application of this ruling requires further study. However, in a case when there is some doubt as regards the processing for the sake of use for the mitzvah, one may be lenient.

* ובית אחד לשל יד: **לט** ׳תפילין בין ש״ר בין של יד הלכה למשה מסיני (קעג) * שיהיו מרובעות * בתפרן ובאלכסונן דהיינו (קעד) שיהיו ריבוען מכוון ארכו כרחבו (קעה) כדי שיהיה להם אותו אלכסון שאחז״ל כל אמתא בריבועא אמתא ותרי חומשא באלכסונא (קעו) וצריך לרבע מקום (קעז) מושבן

באר הגולה

ז שם ל״ה ותוספות ורמב״ם בפ״ג ורא״ש ושאר פוסקים

באר היטב

אבל בתתיכות תפורות יחד לא חשיב עור א׳. ובתוספות דמנחות דף ל״ב ע״א ד״ה דילמא להשלים משמע דחשיב

משנה ברורה

מגדר המ״א דחשובים כעור אחד וכ״כ בתשובת ח״ס או״ח סימן ה׳ שיש להקל בתפורות ואם היו רק דבוקות בדבק מחמיר שם אבל בח״א משמע דה״ה אם הם דבוקות בדבק וכן משמע בא״ז וכן נתפשט עתה המנהג במדינותינו ומ״מ לכתחילה ראוי ונכון לעשותו מעור אחד ממש כי יש מחמירין וסוברין דלא מהני בחתיכות תפורות יחד או מדובקות בדבק ועיין בח״א דעכ״פ צריכין שיהיו הד׳ בתים פרודות זה מזה ולא יהיו מדובקין ולא כמו שעושין הסופרים שמדבקין ע״י דבק רק שלמעלה עושין סימנים כמו חריץ בעלמא דל״ע אם להכשיר אפילו בדיעבד דממ״נ אם אנו חושבין ע״י דיבוק עור אחד א״כ אין לנו אלא בית אחד ובתוכו ד׳ מחילות דפסול ואם אין הדבק עושה עור אחד ויש כאן ד׳ בתים עם ד׳ חריצים דהדיבוק כנפרד דמי א״כ התפילין גופייהו נעשו משתי עורות ופסולים ובאמת טוב הוא שאפילו העושין מעור אחד ממש יהיו תפיליהן פרודות דשמא הדיבוק חבור וכן התפילין של הגר״א היו פרודות ועיין בבה״ל: **לט** (קעג) שיהיו מרובעות. ואם לא עשה מרובעות מעכב בדיעבד [הרמב״ם פ״ג מהלכות תפילין עי״ש] ומ״מ אם אין לו תפילין אחרים (קעג) יניחם לע״ע בלא ברכה וכשיזדמן לו תפילין אחרים יניחם ועיין בבה״ל: (קעד) שיהיו ריבוען. של התפירות וכ״ל פשוט דצריך להיות התפירות מרובע (קעד) בין למעלה ובין למטה ואף דלא ברירא לי לענין דיעבד מ״מ לכתחילה בודאי יש ליזהר בזה: (קעה) כדי שיהי׳ וכו׳. פי׳ בריבוע גמור (קעה) שארכו כרחבו ממש שיערו חכמים כל השיעור שיש לו יש לו באלכסון ב׳ חומשים נוסף על אותו השיעור וגם כאן צריך שיהיה מרובע ממש אבל אם לא יהיה מרובע ממש לא יהיה באלכסון שלו כשיעור ב׳ חומשים תוספות אלא שיעור אחר. וע״כ (קעו) ימדדנו בד׳ קוים וידע אם הוא מרובע דהיינו תחלה ימדוד קו אחד באורך וקו אחד ברוחב שיהי׳ שוה אך שמא באמצעו שוה ובצדדיו מתמעט לכן ימדדנו עוד בשני קוים באלכסונו שיהיו שוים ב׳ קוי האלכסון ג״כ: (קעו) וצריך לרבע וכו׳. וגם זה הוא מהלמ״מ לדעת רוב הפוסקים. וגם זה הוא (קעז) בריבוע גמור כמו בתפירה ואף (קעח) דמרובע ממש במלאכת הבתים דהיינו שיהיה בתכלית השלמות הוא כמעט מן הנמנע מ״מ כל מה דאפשר לו לאדם (קעט) לעשות בענין זה בודאי חייב הוא לעשות ועיין בט״ז: (קעז) מושבן. והוא התיתורא דהיינו שיתוך המעברתא מב׳ צדדיו כדי שיהא ניכר ריבוע התיתורא וכדלקמן בסמ״ז. וצריך להשגיח מאד ע״ז כי כל זה מעכב אפילו בדיעבד וגם (קפ) יש להשגיח בענין התפירה כי מחמת שהסופרים עושין נקבים גדולים קצת נמשך החוט לצדדין ועי״ז אין התפירות שוות בריבוע זה נכנס וזה יוצא. והתיתורא צריכה להיות מרובע (קפא) בין מלמעלה ובין מלמטה (קפב) ועכשיו בעו״ה הרבה שאין משגיחין על תפיליהן שיהיו מרובעין כדין אפילו המדקדקין במצות יש שאין משגיחין

ביאור הלכה

ביאור מרדכי ובתשובות רע״א סימן י״א מצדדים לומר דספק אם דיבוק הוא חיבור ורא״יתם הוא מהא דפסק הרמ״א באהע״ז סימן ק״ל בהג״ה בשם א״ז לגבי גט דהוא ספק גירושין ומסתמא ה״ה לענינינו. והנה כעת שזכינו לאור של האור זרוע הגדול שנדפס בימינו מצאתי וראיתי בסימן קע״ו שכתב דאם כתב תפילין בשני דפין בעור אחד ואפילו בשני עורות ודבקם יחד בין ע״י תפירה או דבק כשר ושם ג״כ הלא בשם א״ז הוא וע״כ שמחלק בין גט לתפילין ואח״כ חפשתי עוד ומצאתי בסימן זה בד״מ שמביא הא דא״ז וז״ל כתב בא״ז דאם כתב תפילין בשני דפין בעור אחד ואפילו בב׳ עורות ודבקם יחד כשר עכ״ל*ושם באהע״ז ק״ל ס״ז הלא מייתי הרמ״א בד״מ שלו וכן בשו״ע הא דא״ז לגבי גט דהוא ספק וע״כ דיש חילוק בין גט ובין תפילין או דשם משום חומר אשת איש לא רצה הא״ז לסמוך על הראיות שהביא בסימן קע״ו שם. וגם ברש״י מגילה ח׳ ע״ב משמע לכאורה דמהני תפירה בגידין בתפילין ומזוזות וע״כ לענין הפרשיות דאי לענין תפירת התפילין גופא לאחר שניתן הפרשיות בהן מאי שייך מזוזה אך אפשר דאולי באמת מזוזה דנקט רש״י לאו בדוקא הוא אכן בריטב״א שם במגילה מצאתי בהדיא שכתב דמהני תפירה לשני עורות בין בתפילין ובין במזוזה*ובודאי לא גרע בענינינו עשיית הבתים מהפרשיות גופא דמהני בהם חיבור וכדמוכח בביאור הגר״א וע״כ אף דמצינו ביו״ד סימן רפ״ח ס״ד דסתם המחבר כדעת הרמב״ם דתפירה לא מהני למזוזה מ״מ העושה הבתים ע״י תפירה או דבק יש לו על מי לסמוך היינו הסה״ת שסיים לבסוף דרך טוב ונכון לעשות מעור אחד והאור זרוע הגדול שהביאו הד״מ להלכה בסימן זה והריטב״א במגילה וגם לפי חד תירוץ התוס׳ שם במנחות ויוכל להיות דגם הרמב״ם שס״ל דתפירה לא מהני לפרשיות של המזוזה מ״מ לעשיית הבתים גם הוא מודה דמה שמחברם ע״י התפירה לא מיחשב זה שנים או שלשה זכרונות [הג״ה ולענ״ד היה נראה עוד לאמר דלא מיעטה התורה במה שאמרה זכרון אחד ולא שנים או שלשה זכרונות רק שלא יעשה ד׳ בתים מד׳ עורות כל עור ועור בפני עצמו לגמרי היינו הבית עם תיתורא שלו לפרשה אחת וכן לכל לפרשה ופרשה דאז הוא כל בית ובית לזכרון בפ״ע להאדם זה מיעטה לנו התורה וכונת חז״ל במה שאמרו עור אחד היינו שיהיו כל הבתים קבועין בעור אחד ולא יהא כל בית ובית קים בפני עצמו וכן משמע קצת ל׳ המכילתא ע״ש אבל מן הראשונים לא משמע כן דא״כ אפילו לא חיברן בתפירה כל בית לחבירו רק במה שקבען בתיתורא אחת נחשב זכרון אחד ולא הוזכר קולא זו בשום פוסק ואדרבה ברש״י ושארי פוסקים לייר כל אחד אופן עשייתו מעור אחד ממש שמע מיניה דס״ל מכיון שנזכר בגמרא עור אחד בעינן שיהיה ממש עור אחד או עכ״פ ע״י תפירה לאידך פוסקים ע״כ הג״ה] גם הגר״א בביאורו פי״ח דכלים כתב דמהני תפירה לעשותו חיבור [ובסימן זה בביאורו משמע קצת שהוא נוטה להחמיר] ועיין בקובץ על הרמב״ם מש״כ בזה מברייתא דגיטין דהוא מחלוקת רשב״א ורבנן והלכה כרבנן דלא חשיב חבור ועיין בישועות יעקב בהגהת נכדו מש״כ בזה גם יש לדחות דהוא סתם במתניתין ומחלוקת בברייתא והלכה כסתם מתניתין ויש לעיין בזה בכללי ההלכות ומ״מ לכתחילה בודאי מי שאפשר לו טוב להחמיר לעשותו מעור אחד כדי לצאת ידי כל החששות במ״ע דאורייתא: * ובית אחד. ר״ל מעור אחד כן מוכח מלשון הרי״ף עי״ש: * שיהיו מרובעות. עיין במ״ב והוא מהישועות יעקב. אך לענ״ד לע״ג בדין זה כי הוא ז״ל העתיק מתחילה דברי הע״ת והא״ר שכתבו דבדליכא תפילין אחרים אין להחמיר בדיעבד כ״א בהתפירות אם אינם מרובעות אבל לא בהבתים ותמה עליהם דאפילו בהתפירות אם אינם מרובעות טוב יותר להניח מלבטל לגמרי מצות תפילין ובאמת פשוט שדעתם ג״כ כן הוא דיניחם וילא בזה עכ״פ לדעת רש״י עיין ברא״ש בה״ק אך שכונת הע״ת להמעיין בו יראה להדיא דבבתים אם אינם מרובעים כראוי וליכא תפילין אחרים יוכל לברך עליהם אבל בתפירות יניחם בלי ברכה ועיין בהגהת ברוך שאמר שכתב ג״כ דבהבתים אם אינם מרובעין בריבוע גמור ובאלכסון גמור אעפ״כ אין לפסול עי״ש שמשמע מלשונו דיוכל לברך עליהם. אך למעשה נ״ל דאין לסמוך ע״ז לענין ברכה והדין עם הישועת יעקב אחרי דדעת הרבה מהראשונים והוא השימושא רבא[1] והרי״ף [אך הרי״ף לא אמר כ״א בתש״ר וזהו רק להמרדכי אבל בסה״ת פי׳ פירוש אחר בדברי הרי״ף עי״ש שהסכים דגם להרי״ף אין לחלק בין הש״י להש״ר] והרמב״ם והרא״ש והסה״ת ועוד כמה פוסקים דההלכה נאמרה גם לענין הבתים ועיין מה שנכתוב בסמוך לענין אם מקולקל קצת מהריבוע: * בתפרן. עיין בפמ״ג שנשאר בצ״ע מחמת דעת רש״י וצירף לזה ג״כ דעת הרמב״ם ובאמת המעיין בפ״ג בה״א ובה״ח[א]

ירלה

שער הציון

(קעג) ישועות יעקב: (קעד) עיין לקמן בב״י בד״ה כתב הר״י אלכסנדרני כילד יעשה וכו׳ לענין התיתורא ומסתמא ה״ה לענין התפירה: (קעה) ט״ז: (קעו) פמ״ג: (קעז) הרא״ש בה״ק בסדר תיקון בקלרה: (קעח) מעיו״ט וא״ר: (קעט) פמ״ג: (קפ) חיי אדם: (קפא) ב״י לקמן בשם הר״י אלכסנדרני עי״ש ול״ע אם כוונתו לעיכובא בדיעבד: (קפב) מחה״ש:

הגהות ותיקונים: א) ט״ס וצ״ל ובה״י:

הערות והארות: 1) בבה״ל שיהיו מרובעות מביא דעת הרי״ף ובהרי״ף שלפנינו ל״מ רק המרדכי וספר התרומה משמו, וכבר עמד בזה הב״י בסימן זה ד״ה וכה יעשה יקח דפוס של עץ:

39. Both for the head *tefilin* and for the arm /*tefilin*/, there is a halachic /requirement which was taught/ to Mosheh (Moses) on /Mount/ Sinai, **(173)** that /the *tefilin*/ must be square at the sewing and at the diagonals. This means **(174)** that the square must have equal /sides/, with its length identical

Mishnah Berurah

view that they are considered like a single skin. It is likewise stated in a responsum of the *Ch.S.*, *O.Ch.*, Sec. 5, that one can be lenient with sewn /pieces of skin/. /On the other hand,/ where /pieces of skin/ are merely stuck /together/ with glue, /the *Ch.S.*/ is stringent /about this/ there. However, it is implied by the *Ch.A.* that if they are stuck /together/ with glue the same ruling /applies as if they would be sewn together/ and this is likewise implied by the *O.Z.* It has also become the widespread practice now in our countries /to rely on this view/. Nevertheless, initially, it is proper and correct to make /the housings/ out of what is actually one skin, for there are /authorities/ who are stringent and are of the opinion that sewing pieces together or sticking them /together/ with glue is of no avail[36] /for them to be considered a single skin/.

See the *Ch.A.*, /who is of the opinion/ that it is at any rate necessary for the four housings to be separated from one another and not stuck /together/. /One should/ not act like those scribes who stick /them together/ with glue and only make indications externally resembling mere grooves. Study is required /to determine/ whether /the *tefilin*/ are /then/ valid, even once it is after the event, as however one argues /this cannot be justified/. If we consider /the skin/ as one skin, because /the pieces of skin/ have been stuck /together/, it follows that /if the four housings are stuck together/ we only have one housing with four partitions inside it, which is invalid. /On the other hand,/ if /we assume that/ the sticking /together of the pieces of skin/ does not make /them into/ a single skin, so that the stuck /housings/ are like four separate housings with four grooves, it follows that the *tefilin* /housings/ themselves have been made from two /or more/ skins and are invalid /for that reason/. It is in fact desirable even for those who make /the housings/ from actually one skin to have /the housings of/ the *tefilin* separated, in case the sticking is /classed as/ a join. /The housings of/ the *tefilin* of the *Gra* were in fact separated. See the Beyur Halachah.

(173) That /the *tefilin*/ must be square. If one did not make /the *tefilin*/ square, this precludes /them being ruled as valid even/ once it is after the event [*Rambam, Hilchos Tefilin* 3/:1/; see there]. Nevertheless, if one does not have other *tefilin*, he should don them now, without /making/ a blessing /over them/, and /then/ when he happens /to obtain/ other *tefilin* he should don those. See the Beyur Halachah.

(174) That the square. /I.e.,/ at the sewing.

It seems to me self-understood that the sewing must be square both on top and underneath. Although /the ruling/ as regards once it is after the event is not clear to me, one should nevertheless definitely be careful about this initially.

36 If the skin is cut into strips that remain joined to one another and one subsequently sews or sticks the strips together, this is considered a single skin. Accordingly, if a small hole forms in the skin where it is square the skin will still be classed as a single skin and even if the square has become spoiled the repair will be of avail. (Beyur Halachah)

* ובית אחד לשל יד: **לט** [א]תפילין בין ש"ר בין של יד הלכה למשה מסיני (קעג) * שיהיו מרובעות * בתפרן ובאלכסונן דהיינו (קעד) שיהיו ריבוען מכוון ארכו **כרחבו** (קעה) **כדי שיהיה להם אותו אלכסון שאחז"ל כל אמתא בריבועא אמתא ותרי חומשא באלכסונא** (קעו) **וצריך לרבע מקום** (קעז) **מושבן**

ז שם ל"ה ותוספות ורמב"ם בפ"ג ורא"ש ושאר פוסקים

באר היטב

אבל בחתיכות תפורות יחד לא חשיב עור א'. ובתוספות דמנחות דף ל"ב ע"א ד"ה דילמא להשלים משמע דחשיב

ביאור הלכה

ביאור מרדכי ובתשובות רע"א סימן י"א מלדדים לומר דספק אם דיבוק הוא חיבור וראייתם הוא מהא דפסק הרמ"א באהע"ז סימן ק"ל בהג"ה בשם א"ז לגבי גט דהוא ספק גירושין ומסתמא ה"ה לענינינו. והנה כעת שזכינו לאור של האור זרוע הגדול שנדפס בימינו מצאתי וראיתי בסימן קע"ו שכתב דאם כתב תפילין בשני דפין בעור אחד ואפילו בשני עורות ודבקם יחד בין ע"י תפירה או דבק כשר ושם ג"כ הלא בשם א"ז הוא וע"כ שמחלק בין גט לתפילין ואח"כ חפשתי עוד ומצאתי בסימן זה בד"מ שמביא הא דא"ז וז"ל כתב בא"ז דאם כתב תפילין בשני דפין בעור אחד ואפילו בב' עורות ודבקם יחד כשר עכ"ל*ושם באהע"ז ק"ל ס"ז הלא מייתי הרמ"א בד"מ שלו וכן בשו"ע הא דא"ז לגבי גט דהוא ספק וע"כ דיש חילוק בין גט ובין תפילין או דשם משום חומר אשת איש לא רצה הא"ז לסמוך על הראיות שהביא בסימן קע"ו שם. וגם ברש"י מגילה ח' ע"ב משמע לכאורה דמהני תפירה בגידין בתפילין ומזוזות וע"כ לענין הפרשיות דאי לענין תפירת התפילין גופא לאחר שניתן הפרשיות בהן מאי שייך מזוזה אך אפשר דאולי באמת מזוזה דנקט רש"י לאו בדוקא הוא אכן בריטב"א שם במגילה מצאתי בהדיא שכתב דמהני תפירה לשני עורות בין בתפילין ובין במזוזה*ובודאי לא גרע בענינינו עשיית הבתים מהפרשיות גופא דמהני בהם חיבור וכדמוכח בביאור הגר"א וע"כ אף דמלינו ביו"ד סימן רפ"ח ס"ד דסתם המחבר כדעת הרמב"ם דתפירה לא מהני למזוזה מ"מ העושה הבתים ע"י תפירה או דבק יש לו על מי לסמוך היינו הסה"ת שסיים לבסוף דרך טוב ונכון לעשות מעור אחד והאור זרוע הגדול שהבאו הד"מ להלכה בסימן זה והריטב"א במגילה וגם לפי חד תירוץ התוס' שם במנחות ויוכל להיות דגם הרמב"ם שס"ל דתפירה לא מהני לפרשיות של המזוזה מ"מ לעשיית הבתים גם הוא מודה דמה שמחברם ע"י התפירה לא מיחשב זה שנים או שלשה זכרונות [הג"ה ולענ"ד היה נראה עוד לאמר דלא מיעטה התורה במה שאמרה זכרון אחד ולא שנים או שלשה זכרונות רק שלא יעשה ד' בתים מד' עורות כל עור ועור בפני עצמו לגמרי היינו הבית עם תיתורא שלו לפרשה אחת וכן לכל לפרשה ופרשה דאז הוא כל בית ובית לזכרון בפ"ע להאדם זה מיעטה לנו התורה וכונת חז"ל במה שאמרו עור אחד היינו שיהיו כל הבתים קבועין בעור אחד ולא יהא כל בית ובית כים בפני עצמו וכן משמע קצת ל' המכילתא ע"ש אבל מן הראשונים לא משמע כן דא"כ אפילו לא חיברן בתפירה כל בית לחבירו רק במה שקבען בתיתורא אחת נחשב זכרון אחד ולא הוזכר קולא זו בשום פוסק ואדרבה ברש"י ושארי פוסקים לייר כל אחד אופן עשייתו מעור אחד ממש שמע מיניה דס"ל מכיון שנזכר בגמרא עור אחד בעינן שיהיה ממש עור אחד או עכ"פ ע"י תפירה לאידך פוסקים ע"כ הג"ה] גם הגר"א בביאורו פי"ח דכלים כתב דמהני תפירה לעשותו חיבור [ובסימן זה בביאורו משמע קצת שהוא נוטה להחמיר] ועיין בקובץ על הרמב"ם מש"כ בזה מברייתא דגיטין דהוא מחלוקת רשב"א ורבנן והלכה כרבנן דלא חשיב חבור ועיין בישועות יעקב בהגהת נכדו מש"כ בזה גם יש לדחות דהוא סתם במתניתין ומחלוקת בברייתא והלכה כסתם מתניתין ויש לעיין בזה בכללי ההלכות ומ"מ לכתחילה בודאי מי שאפשר לו טוב להחמיר לעשותו מעור אחד כדי לצאת ידי כל החששות במ"ע דאורייתא: * **ובית אחד**. ר"ל מעור אחד כן מוכח מלשון הרי"ף עי"ש: * **שיהיו מרובעות**. עיין במ"ב והוא מהישועות יעקב. אך לענ"ד לע"ג בדין זה כי הוא ז"ל העתיק מתחילה דברי הע"ת והא"ר שכתבו דבדליכא תפילין אחרים אין להחמיר בדיעבד כ"א בהתפירות אם אינם מרובעות אבל לא בהבתים ותמה עליהם דאפילו בהתפירות אם אינם מרובעות טוב יותר להניח מלבטל לגמרי מצות תפילין ובאמת פשוט שדעתם ג"כ כן הוא דיניחם ויצא בזה עכ"פ לדעת רש"י עיין ברא"ש בה"ק אך שכונת הע"ת להמעיין בו יראה להדיא דבבתים אם אינם מרובעים כראוי וליכא תפילין אחרים יוכל לברך עליהם אבל בתפירות יניחם בלי ברכה ועיין בהגהת ברוך שאמר שכתב ג"כ דבהבתים אם אינם מרובעין בריבוע גמור ובאלכסון גמור אעפ"כ אין לפסול עי"ש שמשמע מלשונו דיוכל לברך עליהם. אך למעשה נ"ל דאין לסמוך ע"ז לענין ברכה והדין עם הישועת יעקב אחרי דדעת הרבה מהראשונים והוא השימושא רבא[1] והרי"ף [אך הרי"ף לא אמר כ"א בתש"ר וזהו רק להמרדכי אבל בסה"ת פי' פירוש אחר בדברי הרי"ף עי"ש שהסכים דגם להרי"ף אין לחלק בין הש"י להש"ר] והרמב"ם והרא"ש והסה"ת ועוד כמה פוסקים דההלכה נאמרה גם לענין הבתים ועיין מה שנכתוב בסמוך לענין אם מקולקל קצת מהריבוע: * **בתפרן**. עיין בפמ"ג שנשאר בצ"ע מחמת דעת רש"י וצירף לזה ג"כ דעת הרמב"ם ובאמת המעיין בפ"ג בה"א ובה"ח[א] יראה

משנה ברורה

מלדד הט"ז דחשובים כעור אחד וכ"כ בתשובת ח"ס או"ח סימן ה' שיש להקל בתפורות ואם היו רק דבוקות בדבק מחמיר שם אבל בח"א משמע דה"ה אם הם דבוקות בדבק וכן משמע בא"ז וכן נתפשט עתה המנהג במדינותינו ומ"מ לכתחילה ראוי ונכון לעשותו מעור אחד ממש כי יש מחמירין וסוברין דלא מהני בחתיכות תפורות יחד או מדובקות בדבק ועיין בח"א דעכ"פ צריכין שיהיו הד' בתים פרודות זה מזה ולא יהיו מדובקין ולא כמו שעושין הסופרים שמדבקין ע"י דבק רק שלמעלה עושין סימנים כמו חריץ בעלמא דצ"ע אם להכשיר אפילו בדיעבד דמכ"ג אם אנו חושבין ע"י דיבוק עור אחד א"כ אין לנו אלא בית אחד ובתוכו ד' מחילות דפסול ואם אין הדבק עושה עור אחד ויש כאן ד' בתים עם ד' מרלים והדיבוק כנפרד דמי א"כ התפילין גופייהו נעשו משתי עורות ופסולים ובאמת טוב הוא שאפילו העושין מעור אחד ממש יהיו תפיליהן פרודות דשמא הדיבוק חבור וכן התפילין של הגר"א היו פרודות ועיין בבה"ל: **לט** (קעג) שיהיו מרובעות. ואם לא נעשה מרובעות מעכב בדיעבד [הרמב"ם פ"ג מהלכות תפילין עי"ש] ומ"מ אם אין לו תפילין אחרים (קעג) יניחם לע"ע בלא ברכה וכשיזדמן לו תפילין אחרים יניחם ועיין בבה"ל: (קעד) שיהיו ריבוען. של התפירות וכ"ל פשוט דצריך להיות התפירות מרובע (קעד) בין למעלה ובין למטה ואף דלא ברירא לי לענין דיעבד מ"מ לכתחילה בודאי יש ליזהר בזה: (קעה) **כדי שיהי' וכו'**. פי' בריבוע גמור (קעה) שארכו כרחבו ממש שיערו חכמים כל השיעור שיש לו יש לו באלכסון ב' חומשים נוסף על אותו השיעור וגם כאן צריך שיהיה מרובע ממש אבל אם לא יהיה מרובע ממש לא יהיה באלכסון שלו כשיעור ב' חומשים תוספות אלא שיעור אחר. וע"כ (קעו) ימדדנו בד' קוים וידע אם הוא מרובע דהיינו תחלה ימדוד קו אחד באורך וקו אחד ברוחב שיהי' שוה אך שמא באמצעו שוה ובצדדיו מתמעט לכן ימדדנו עוד בשני קוים באלכסונו שיהיו שוים ב' קוי האלכסון ג"כ: (קעו) **וצריך לרבע וכו'**. וגם זה הוא מהלמ"מ לדעת רוב הפוסקים. וגם זה הוא (קעז) בריבוע גמור כמו בהתפירה ואף (קעח) דמרובע ממש במלאכת הבתים דהיינו שיהיה בתכלית השלמות הוא כמעט מן הנמנע מ"מ כל מה דאפשר לו לאדם (קעט) לעשות בענין זה בודאי חייב הוא לעשות ועיין בע"ד: (קעז) **מושבן**. והוא התיתורא דהיינו שיחתוך המעברתא מב' צדדיו כדי שיהא ניכר ריבוע התיתורא וכדלקמן בסמ"ד. וצריך להשגיח מאד ע"ז כי כל זה מעכב אפילו בדיעבד וגם (קפ) יש להשגיח בענין התפירה כי מחמת שהסופרים עושין נקבים גדולים קצת נמשך החוט לצדדין ועי"ז אין התפירות שוות בריבוע זה נכנס וזה יוצא. והתיתורא צריכה להיות מרובע (קפא) בין מלמעלה ובין מלמטה (קפב) ועכשיו בעו"ה הרבה שאין משגיחין על תפיליהן שיהיו מרובעין כדין אפילו המדקדקין במצות יש שאין משגיחין

שער הציון

(קעג) ישועות יעקב: (קעד) עיין לקמן בב"י בד"ה כתב הר"י אלכסנדרי כילד יעשה וכו' לענין התיתורא ומסתמא ה"ה לענין התפירה: (קעה) ט"ז: (קעו) פמ"ג: (קעז) הרא"ש בה"ק בסדר תיקון בקלרה: (קעח) מעיו"ט וא"ר: (קעט) פמ"ג: (קפ) חיי אדם: (קפא) ב"י לקמן בשם הר"י אלכסנדרי עי"ש וצ"ע אם כוונתו לעיכובא בדיעבד: (קפב) מחה"ש:

הגהות ותיקונים: א) ט"ס וצ"ל ובה"י:

הערות והארות: 1) בבה"ל שיהיו מרובעות מביא דעת הרי"ף ובהרי"ף שלפנינו ל"מ רק המרדכי וספר התרומה משמו, וכבר עמד בזה הב"י בסימן זה ד"ה וכה יעשה יקח דפוס של עץ:

to its breadth, **(175)** so that it has the diagonal /which corresponds with/ what the Sages, of blessed memory, said, "For every cubit /of the length/ of a square there is one and two fifths of a cubit in /the length of/ the diagonal".

(176) One must make square /the base/ **(177)** on which /the *tefilin*/ rest

Mishnah Berurah

(175) So that ... has, etc. I.e., in the case of a perfect square, whose length is exactly the same as its breadth, the Sages determined that whatever length /the side of the square/ has, its diagonal will have two fifths more than that length. Now /the square of the *tefilin*/ must also be actually square. If, however, it is not actually square, its diagonal will not have this length of two fifths more /than the length of the sides of the square/, but a different length.

Consequently, one must measure /the square/ by /checking/ four /of its/ lines and will /thus/ know whether it is /in fact/ square. I.e., he should first measure one length line and one breadth line /to check/ that they are equal. However, in case they are equal in the center, but get smaller at the sides, he should therefore measure a further two lines, its diagonals, so /that he confirms/ that the two diagonal lines are also equal.

(176) One must make square, etc. In the opinion of the majority of Poskim, this is also a halachic /requirement which was taught/ to Mosheh (Moses) on /Mount/ Sinai.

In the case /of the base/ also a perfect square /is required/, just as with the sewing. Although an actual square in the formation of the housing, i.e., which will be /square/ with absolute precision, is almost unattainable, a person is nevertheless definitely obliged to do whatever he is able to do in this matter. See the *I.D.*

(177) On which /the *tefilin*/ rest. This /means/ the bridge.

I.e., one must cut the passageway on both sides, so that the square of the bridge will be recognizable, as /stated/ below in Par. 44.

One must be extremely heedful that this /has been attended to/, as if all this /has not been done/ this will preclude /the *tefilin* being ruled as valid/, even once it is after the event.

One must also be heedful with respect to /the squareness of/ the sewing. This is because owing to /the fact/ that the scribes make somewhat large holes, the thread is pulled to the sides and in view of this the stitches are not in even /lines/, in /the form of/ a square, /but/ one is towards the inside and one towards the outside.

The bridge must be square both on top and underneath.

Nowadays, among our many sins, there are many who are not heedful about their *tefilin* being square in accordance with halachic /requirements/. Even /among/ those who are meticulous in /the observance of/ mitzvos, there are /some/ who are only heedful about the top of the housings being

(נח) [כו] (קעח) וגם הבתים: הגה אבל גובה הבתים * אין להקפיד אם הוא יותר מרחבן וארכן (ב"י בשם אשרי וסמ"ק ומרדכי ורמב"ם פ"ג) ח עשאם מרובעות ואחר זמן[1] (קעט) * נתקלקל ריבוען (קפ) יש מי שאומר (קפא) * שצריך לרבען: הגה (קפב) ויעשה כל הד' בתים בשוה שלא יהא אחד גדול מחבירו (ב"ש):
מ ט עור (קפג) הבתים (קפד) מצוה לעשותו (נט) [כז] (קפה) שחור (וע"ל (קפו) סימן ל"ג) * י חריץ שבין בית לבית צריך שיגיע עד התפר י ואם לא הגיע כשרה (קפז) והוא שיהיה (קפח) ניכר החריץ

ח מלא בשם שמושא רבא בתשו' אשכנזים ט הרא"ש וספר התרומה והמרדכי בשם ר"י מההיא דמנחות ל"ה י שם בגמרא כ הרמב"ם

באר היטב

עור א' ע"י תפירה: (נח) וגם הבתים. דלא כמו שנוהגים קצת לעשות של יד עגולה בראשו רק שמרבע התיתורא מלמטה מרדכי מ"א ועיין מ"ש הע"ת: (נט) שחור. וכתב ב"ח משמע עיכובא ליכא. ולענ"ד אין להקל ובמקום דלא אפשר יש לסמוך ארוב פוסקים המקילין שלא

שערי תשובה

עליו עור מצד המעברתא לצד שכנגדו וכן אם עשה ד' בתים וחיברם ע"י תפירה ועוד כמה דינים בענין בית החילון שאינה רואה את האויר ע"ש באורך ועיין בבגדי כהונה סי' א' בענין זה: [כו] וגם הבתים. עבה"ט וכתב בבר"י בשם בית יהודה ח"ג סי' פ"ח אם מחמת אויר שבין הבתים כשיתיבש העור נתרחבים הבתים וכשיהדקם ימלא הרבוע מכוון כשרים ע"ש: [כז] שחור. עבה"ט וכתב

משנה ברורה

כ"א על ראש הבתים שיהיו מרובעין ואין משגיחין על התיתורא ועל התפירות שהוא ג"כ מעיקר הדין והוא דבר הנקל לתקן: (קעח) וגם הבתים. דלא (קפג) כמו שנוהגין קצת לעשות של יד עגולה בראשו רק שמרבע התיתורא מלמטה אלא בין הש"י ובין הש"ר יהיו מרובעים. והכוונה בהש"ר (קפד) כשהארבעה בתים יחד יהיו מרובעים ולא כל אחד בפני עצמו. וריבוע הבתים צ"ל (קפה) בכל משך גובהן וגם הריבוע יהיה ע"י הבתים עצמן ולא (קפו) ע"י ד"א שמטיח עליהם ועיין לקמן ס"ק קפ"ה: (קעט) נתקלקל ריבוען. כגון שנתעקמו הבתים זה פונה למזרח וזה למערב או שנתקלקל חודי הבתים לגמרי עד שנעשה עגול או שנתקלקל התיתורא או התפירה עד שאבדו ריבוען: (קפ) יש מי שאומר. אין (קפז) חולק בזה ודרך המחבר כן בהרבה מקומות וכמש"כ לעיל בס"ק קכ"ג: (קפא) שצריך לרבען. דכיון דריבוען הוא הלמ"מ (קפח) בכל שעתא בעינן שיהיו מרובעין ומ"מ (קפט) אין צריך למודדן בכל יום אם ריבועם קיים שמעמידים אותם על חזקתם אם לא שרואה שנתקלקל ואם (קצ) נתעקם התיתורא אף שבעצם הוא מרובע רק מחמת התעקמות התיתורא נראית כמו שאינו מרובע יחזור ויתקן: (קפב) ויעשה. ובדיעבד (קצא) אפילו אחד רחב מחבירו כשר: מ (קפג) הבתים. וכ"ש (קצב) שידקדק שהשי"ן יהיה שחור ולפעמים מחמת רוב יושנו נקלף ממנו השחרות: (קפד) מצוה וכו'. משמע דבדיעבד אינו לעיכובא ויש פוסקים דס"ל דהוא הלמ"מ כמו הרצועות ולעיכובא הוא אפילו בדיעבד ובביאור הגר"א משמע שהוא מצדד כן להלכה וכן בישועות יעקב וכן משמע בא"ר ובשכנה"ג ד"ש להחמיר אם לא במקום דלא אפשר יש לסמוך אדברי המקילין כדי שלא להתבטל ממצות תפילין: (קפה) שחור. והשחרות טוב יותר שיהיה בצבע שחור שאין בו מתם כלל והתפילין יהיו שחורים רק בחוצא בעלמא ומ"מ המשחירין במין גלאנ"ץ° שא"א לקלפו אע"פ שיכולין להסיר מן הקלף ע"י פירורין דקין (קצג) אין להחמיר בדיעבד ועיין במה שכ' בסעיף מ"ה בבה"ל בשם הפמ"ג שדעתו ג"כ דאין להחמיר בזה אכן מה שחדשו סופרי זמנינו שמשחירין בטיחה שיכולין לקלוף בשלימות מכל צד מן התפילין וצורתו כמו נייר שחור זהו פסול [מספר נשמת אדם ושהסכים אתו הגאון בעל בית מאיר דלא כנב"י עי"ש]: (קפו) סי' ל"ג. בס"ד בהג"ה ועי"ש במ"ב דהרמ"א קאזיל לשיטת המחבר הכא דהוא רק מצוה בעלמא ולפי מה שכ' באות קפ"ד יש לעיין בזה: (קפז) והוא שיהיה וכו'. אבל אם אינו ניכר מבחוץ (קצד) אף שמבפנים יש ד' בתים וכל פרשה ופרשה מונחת בית בפ"ע לא מהני: (קפח) ניכר החריץ. אבל שריטה או רשימה בעלמא לא מהני כלל

ביאור הלכה

יראה להדיא דדעת הרמב"ם דריבוע התפירות הוא הלכה למשה מסיני ואפשר דקאי רק על ריבוע התיתורא והוא דוחק גדול ובביאור הגר"א כתב ג"כ להדיא דדעת כל הגאונים דריבוע התיתורא וגם התפירות הוא הלמ"מ. ע"כ אין לזוז ממה שכתב הישועות יעקב שיניח בלי ברכה בעת הדחק: * אין להקפיד. דריבוע לא נאמר אלא על אורך ורוחב: * נתקלקל ריבוען. עיין במ"ב. דע דגדר קלקול ריבוע הבתים פשיטא לי דלא בעינן שיתקלקלו ברוב משך גובהן ואפילו במיעוטן סגי ואפילו אם עשאם גדולים מאוד ולא אמרינן דל מהכא היתרון וישאר שיעור תפילין בלי זה דומיא דיש מקילין בענין הקפת גויל אם יש שיעור אות בלא זה ואמינא לה מהא דקי"ל בזבחים ס"ב ע"א דריבוע המזבח מעכב וקיי"ל ג"כ דאפילו פגימת המזבח פוסל והוא מטעם ריבוע כדאיתא בתוספת סוכה מ"ט ע"א ד"ה שכל ולא בעינן דוקא שיפגם רוב המזבח אלא אפילו בכזית או בכטפח לכל מר כדאית ליה בחולין י"ח ע"א עי"ש בגמרא וא"ל דשם מטעם דיש שיעור למזבח משא"כ בזה דאין שיעור לגובה התפילין דז"א דשם הלא ג"כ קיי"ל דמדת קומתו אין מעכב כדאיתא שם בגמרא וא"כ אם לא היה עושה הגובה רק עד למעלה ממקום הסובב ושם היה עושה הקרנות ג"כ היה יוצא בדיעבד ואפ"ה כיון דעתה בנה בקומה הזו בעינן שיהיה למעלה מרובע כדמוכח בזבחים נ"ד ע"ד[א] תוד"ה רב אמר וא"כ ה"ה בענינינו לענין תפילין. גם פשיטא לי דלאו דוקא אם נתקלקל במקום חודו של הזוית למעלה דה"ה אם נתקלקל ונפגם במקום אחר מדפני הבית מבחוץ עד שאבד ריבועו עי"ז וג"כ מהא דמזבח הנ"ל דפשוט דפסול פגימת המזבח הוא בכל מקום מדפנותיו ולאו דוקא במקום חודו ולפ"ז אם מחמת רוב יושנן של התפילין ניכר לכל שאחד מדפנותיו נכנס לפנים ואינו עומד במקום הראוי לו נראה דצריך לתקנם. גם פשיטא לי דע"י פגימה קטנה שנתהוה בהבתים כשיעור חגירת ליפורן ואפשר אפילו מעט יותר מזה לא אזל מניה עי"ז שם ריבוע ואפילו אם נאמר דבעת עשייה יש להסופר ליזהר אפילו בחסרון משהו באיזה מקום דעכ"פ אינו מרובע בשלימות מ"מ בדיעבד שנתקלקל לא אזל שם ריבוע ע"י חסרון משהו וראיה מהא דמשני בחולין י"ח הא באבנא הא בסידא פי' באבנא דכתיב אבנים שלמות פוסל אפילו בחגירת ליפורן אבל בסיד דלא כתיב בו שלמות לכך בעינן שיחסר שיעור חשוב כטפח או כזית עי"ש הרי דאף דלגבי מזבח דקי"ל דריבוע מעכב וגם שם צריך ריבוע גמור שיהא שוה אף באלכסונו וכדמוכח שם בזבחים ס"ב ע"ב מהא דכתיב סביב שיהא כל צדדיו שוין וכדפירש"י שם ואפ"ה כשר בסיד אלא ע"כ דע"י פגימה כחגירת ליפורן לא אבד עי"ז שם ריבוע. ואפילו אם הפגימה קטנה שנתהוה בהתפילין היה במקום חודו של הזוית למעלה דאלת"ה לישני הא והא בסידא וכאן מיירי במקום חודו ואף דיש לבע"ד לחלוק דלגבי מזבח דגדול בשיעורו לא נחשב בו פגימה מועטת דליזיל מיניה עי"ז שם ריבוע משא"כ בענינינו מ"מ נלע"ד דהדין עמי דאלת"ה יקשה ר"ח שם עוד פגימה שפוסלת בחגירת ליפורן כגון בריבוע התפילין ודומיא שכתב הט"ז בסימן תרמ"ה ס"ד[ב] ע"ש. כי מיבעיא לי עלם שיעור קלקול הריבוע עד כמה נקרא בענינינו דזה ברור דלא נוכל לומר לענין תפילין דוקא אם חסרון הריבוע היה בטפח כמו שפסק הרמב"ם שם לענין מזבח דכל התפילין אינם מחזיקין כך ואולי אם נתמעך הריבוע של התפילין מעט יותר מחגירת ליפורן נקרא בענינינו ג"כ קלקול הריבוע וצ"ע: * שצריך. עיין במ"ב לענין התעקמות התיתורא העתקתי מספר לשכת הסופר והביא שם ראיה ע"ז דרש"י פירש במנחות ל"ה ע"א תפילין שיהא מרובעין בתפרן היינו שלא ימשוך חוט התפירה הרבה שלא תכוון ותתמעט הריבוע עי"ש ומה לי אם נתעקם מחמת התפירה או מחמת עצמו ואף שיש קצת לחלק בזה עכ"ל: * חריץ שבין בית לבית וכו' ואם לא הגיע כשרה. עיין בח"א דמשמע מיניה דאפילו הנוהגין לעשות התפילין ע"י דיבוק הד' עורות אפ"ה מהני בדיעבד אם מדבק לבסוף הד' בתים ביחד ומשייר מלמעלה רק מעט שיהיו החריצין ניכרין

מתרגם: °צבע מבריק.

שער הציון

(קפג) מ"א: (קפד) תוס' מנחות ל"ה ע"א עי"ש: (קפה) עבודת היום והדין עמו כמו שביארתי בע"ה בבה"ל: (קפו) נו"ב בסי' א': (קפז) חיי אדם: (קפח) ט"ז: (קפט) מחה"ש: (קצ) לשכת הסופר בשם שולחן שלמה: (קצא) מוכח מלבוש: (קצב) חיי אדם: (קצג) עיין בש"ת: (קצד) רש"י במנחות ל"ד ע"ב ד"ה ואם:

הגהות ותיקונים: א) ע"א: **ב)** ט"ס צ"ל סק"ד:

הערות והארות: 1) עיין בה"ל סי' ל"ג ס"ב ד"ה לחוש וכו' לענין סברת הרמב"ם והפוסקים אם ס"ל דבנתקלקל צריך לרבען:

(178) and also the housings /of the *tefilin* must be made square/.

Gloss: However, /as regards/ the height of the housings, one need not be particular if it is more than their length and their breadth. (...)

If one made /*tefilin*/ square and after a time (179) their squareness became spoiled, (180) there is /an authority/ who says (181) that one must make them square /again/.

Gloss: (182) *One must make all four housings /of the head* tefilin/ *uniform, so that one is not larger than the other. (...)*

Mishnah Berurah

square, but are not heedful about /the squareness of/ the bridge and the sewing, whose /squareness/ is also an essential halachic /requirement/ and is an easy matter to correct.

(178) And also the housings. /This is/ in contradiction to the practice of some /people/, who make the arm /*tefilin* housing/ round at the top and only make the bridge square at the bottom. /In actual fact,/ both the arm /*tefilin* housing/ and the head /*tefilin* housings/ must be square.

What is meant in the case of the head /*tefilin*/ is that the four housings together should /form/ a square and not that each one /of the housings/ by itself /should be square/.

The squareness of the housings must be along the entire extent of the height. The square must also be /formed/ by the housings themselves and not by something else plastered over them. See below in sub-Par. 185.

(179) Their squareness became spoiled. For example, if the housings became warped, /so that/ one of them has turned eastwards and another westwards, if the edges of the housings became spoiled completely, so that they have become rounded, or if the bridge or the sewing became spoiled, so that they have lost their squareness.[37]

(180) There is /an authority/ who says. Nobody disputes this. It is usual for the author /of the Shulchan Aruch to use/ this /wording even in such cases/ in many places. This corresponds with what we have written above in sub-Par. 123.

(181) That one must make them square /again/. For in view /of the fact/ that their squareness is a halachic /requirement which was taught/ to Mosheh (Moses) on /Mount/ Sinai, it is necessary for them to be square all the time.

Nevertheless, it is unnecessary to measure /the *tefilin*/ every day /to determine/ whether the square is intact. /This is/ because we rely on the presumption /that no change has taken place/, unless one sees that they have become spoiled.

If the bridge has become warped /, then/, although the bridge is actually square, but merely appears not square because of the warpedness, one should adjust it /until it appears square/ again.

(182) One must make. Once it is after the event, even if one /of them/ is wider than the other /the *tefilin*/ are /nevertheless/ valid.

37 The squareness is considered spoiled even if only the smaller part has become spoiled and even if what is left unspoiled has the required size by itself. Even if the squareness is not impaired at the edges but somewhere else on the outside of the *tefilin*, they are also invalid. If the impairment is merely the thickness of a fingernail, it is unnecessary to repair the *tefilin*, even if the impairment is on one of the edges on top. (Beyur Halachah)

(נח) [כו] (קעח) וגם הבתים: הגה אבל גובה הבתים * אין להקפיד אם הוא יותר מרחבן וארכן (ב"י בשם אשרי וסמ"ק ומרדכי ורמב"ם פ"ג) עשאם מרובעות ואחר זמן (קעט) * נתקלקל ריבוען (קפ) יש מי שאומר (קפא) * שצריך לרבען: הגה (קפב) ויעשה כל הד' בתים בשוה שלא יהא אחד גדול מחבירו (ב"ש):

מ ט עור (קפג) הבתים (קפד) מצוה לעשותו (נט) [כז] (קפה) שחור (וע"ל (קפו) סימן ל"ג) * י חריץ שבין בית לבית צריך שיגיע עד התפר כ ואם לא הגיע כשרה (קפז) והוא שיהיה (קפח) ניכר החריץ

באר הגולה: ח מלא בשם שמושא רבא בתשו' אשכנזים ט הרא"ש וספר התרומה והמרדכי בשם ר"י מההיא דמנחות ל"ה י שם בגמרא כ הרמב"ם

באר היטב

עור א' ע"י תפירה: (נח) וגם הבתים. דלא כמו שנוהגים קצת לעשות של יד עגולה בראשו רק שמרבע התיתורא מלמטה מרדכי מ"א ועיין מ"ש הע"ת: (נט) שחור. וכתב ב"ח משמע עיכובא ליכא. ולענ"ד אין להקל ובמקום דלא אפשר יש לסמוך ארוב פוסקים המקילין שלא

משנה ברורה

כ"א על ראש הבתים שיהיו מרובעין ואין משגיחין על התיתורא ועל התפירות שהוא ג"כ מעיקר הדין והוא דבר הנקל לתקן: (קעח) וגם הבתים. דלא (קפג) כמו שנוהגין קצת לעשות של יד עגולה בראשו רק שמרבע התיתורא מלמטה אלא בין הש"י ובין הש"ר יהיו מרובעים. והכוונה בהש"ר (קפד) כשהארבעה בתים יחד יהיו מרובעים ולא כל אחד בפני עצמו. וריבוע הבתים צ"ל (קפה) בכל משך גובהן וגם הריבוע יהיה ע"י הבתים עצמן ולא (קפו) ע"י ד"א שמטיח עליהם ועיין לקמן ס"ק קפ"ה: (קעט) נתקלקל ריבוען. כגון שנתעקמו הבתים זה פונה למזרח וזה למערב או שנתקלקל חודי הבתים לגמרי עד שנעשה עגול או שנתקלקל התיתורא או התפירה עד שאבדו ריבוען: (קפ) יש מי שאומר. אין (קפז) חולק בזה ודרך המחבר כן בהרבה מקומות וכמש"כ לעיל בס"ק קכ"ג: (קפא) שצריך לרבען. דכיון דריבוען הוא הלמ"מ (קפח) בכל שעתא בעינן שיהיו מרובעין ומ"מ (קפט) אין צריך למודדן בכל יום אם ריבועם קיים שמעמידים אותם על חזקתם אם לא שרואה שנתקלקל ואם (קצ) נתעקם התיתורא אף שבעצם הוא מרובע רק מחמת התעקמות התיתורא נראית כמו שאינו מרובע יחזור ויתקן: (קפב) ויעשה. ובדיעבד (קצא) אפילו אחד רחב מחבירו כשר: **מ** (קפג) הבתים. וכ"ש (קצב) שידקדק שהשי"ן יהיה שחור ולפעמים מחמת רוב יושנו נקלף ממנו השחרות: (קפד) מצוה וכו'. משמע דבדיעבד אינו לעיכובא ויש פוסקים דס"ל דהוא הלמ"מ כמו הרצועות ולעיכובא הוא אפילו בדיעבד ובביאור הגר"א משמע שהוא מצדד כן להלכה וכן בישועות יעקב וכן משמע בא"ר ובשכנה"ג דיש להחמיר אם לא במקום דלא אפשר יש לסמוך אדברי המקילין כדי שלא להתבטל ממצות תפילין: (קפה) שחור. והשחרות טוב יותר שיהיה בצבע שחור שאין בו ממש כלל והתפילין יהיו שחורים רק בחזותא בעלמא ומ"מ המשחירין במין גלאנ"ץ ° שא"א לקלפו אע"פ שיכולין להסיר מן הקלף ע"י פירורין דקין (קלג) אין להחמיר בדיעבד ועיין במה שכ' בסעיף מ"א בבה"ל בשם הפמ"ג שדעתו ג"כ דאין להחמיר בזה אכן מה שחדשו סופרי זמנינו שמשחירין בטיחה שיכולין לקלוף בשלימות מכל צד מן התפילין וצורתו כמו נייר שחור זהו פסול [מספר נשמת אדם והסכים אתו הגאון בעל בית מאיר דלא כנב"י עי"ש]: (קפו) סי' ל"ג. בס"ד בהג"ה ועי"ש במ"ב דהרמ"א קאזיל לשיטת המחבר הכא דהוא רק מצוה בעלמא ולפי מה שכ' באות קפ"ד יש לעיין בזה: (קפז) והוא שיהיה וכו'. אבל אם אינו ניכר מבחוץ (קלד) אף שמבפנים יש ד' בתים וכל פרשה ופרשה מונחת בית בפ"ע לא מהני: (קפח) ניכר החריץ. אבל שריטה או רשימה בעלמא לא מהני כלל

שערי תשובה

עליו עור מצד המעברתא לצד שכנגדו וכן אם עשה ד' בתים וחיברם ע"י תפירה ועוד כמה דינים בענין בית החילון שאינה רואה את האויר ע"ש באורך ועיין בבגדי כהונה סי' א' בענין זה: [כו] וגם הבתים. עבה"ט וכתב בבר"י בשם בית יהודה ח"ג סי' פ"ח אם מחמת אויר שבין הבתים כשיתיבש העור נתרחבים הבתים וכשיהדקם ימלא הרבוע מכוון כשרים ע"ש: [כז] שחור. עבה"ט וכתב

ביאור הלכה

יראה להדיא דדעת הרמב"ם דריבוע התפירות הוא הלכה למשה מסיני ואפשר דקאי רק על ריבוע התיתורא והוא דוחק גדול ובביאור הגר"א כתב ג"כ להדיא דדעת כל הגאונים דריבוע התיתורא וגם התפירות הוא הלמ"מ. ע"כ אין לזוז ממה שכתב הישועות יעקב שיניח בלי ברכה בעת הדחק: * אין להקפיד. דריבוע לא נאמר אלא על אורך ורוחב: * נתקלקל ריבוען. עיין במ"ב. דע דגדר קלקול ריבוע הבתים פשיטא לי דלא בעינן שיתקלקלו ברוב משך גובהן ואפילו במיעוטן סגי ואפילו אם עשאם גדולים מאוד ולא אמרינן דל מהכא היתרון וישאר שיעור תפילין בלי זה דומיא דיש מקילין בענין הקפת גויל אם יש שיעור אות בלא זה ואמינא לה מהא דקי"ל בזבחים ס"ב ע"א דריבוע המזבח מעכב וקיי"ל ג"כ דאפילו פגימת המזבח פוסל והוא מטעם ריבוע כדאיתא בתוספת סוכה מ"ט ע"א ד"ה שכל ולא בעינן דוקא שיפגם רוב המזבח אלא אפילו בכזית או בכטפח לכל מר כדאית ליה בחולין י"ח ע"א עי"ש בגמרא וא"ל דשם מטעם דיש שיעור למזבח משא"כ בזה דאין שיעור לגובה התפילין דז"א דשם הלא ג"כ קיי"ל דמדת קומתו אין מעכב כדאיתא שם בגמרא וא"כ אם לא היה עושה הגובה רק עד למעלה ממקום הסובב ושם היה עושה הקרנות ג"כ היה יוצא בדיעבד ואפ"ה כיון דעתה בנה בקומה הזו בעינן שיהיה למעלה מרובע כדמוכח בזבחים נ"ד ע"ד[א] תוד"ה רב אמר וא"כ ה"ה בענינינו לענין תפילין. גם פשיטא לי דלאו דוקא אם נתקלקל במקום חודו של הזוית למעלה דה"ה אם נתקלקל ונפגם במקום אחר מדפני הבית מבחוץ עד שאבד ריבועו עי"ז וג"כ מהא דמזבח הנ"ל דפשוט דפסול פגימת המזבח הוא בכל מקום מדפנותיו ולאו דוקא במקום חודו ולפ"ז אם מחמת רוב יושנן של התפילין ניכר לכל שאחד מדפנותיו נכנס לפנים ואינו עומד במקום הראוי לו נראה דצריך לתקנם. גם פשיטא לי דע"י פגימה קטנה שנתהוה בהבתים כשיעור חגירת ליפורן ואפשר אפילו מעט יותר מזה לא אזל מניה עי"ז שם ריבוע ואפילו אם נאמר דבעת עשייה יש להסופר ליזהר אפילו בחסרון משהו באיזה מקום דעכ"פ אינו מרובע בשלימות מ"מ בדיעבד שנתקלקל לא אזל שם ריבוע ע"י חסרון משהו וראיה מהא דמשני בחולין י"ח הא באבנא הא בסידא פי' באבנא דכתיב אבנים שלמות פוסל אפילו בחגירת ליפורן אבל בסיד דלא כתיב בו שלמות לכך בעינן שיחסר שיעור חשוב כטפח או כזית עי"ש הרי דאף דלגבי מזבח דקי"ל דריבוע מעכב וגם שם צריך ריבוע גמור שיהא שוה אף באלכסונו וכדמוכח שם בזבחים ס"ב ע"ב מהא דכתיב סביב שיהא כל סבידיו שוין וכדפירש"י שם ואפ"ה כשר בסיד אלא ע"כ דע"י פגימה כחגירת ליפורן לא אבד עי"ז שם ריבוע. ואפילו אם הפגימה קטנה שנתהוה בהתפילין היה במקום חודו של הזוית למעלה דאלת"ה לישני הא והא בסידא וכאן מיירי במקום חודו ואף דיש לבע"ד לחלוק דלגבי מזבח דגדול בשיעורו לא נחשב בו פגימה מועטת דליזיל מיניה עי"ז שם ריבוע משא"כ בענינינו מ"מ נלענ"ד דהדין עמי דאלת"ה יחשוב ר"ח שם עוד פגימה שפוסלת בחגירת ליפורן כגון בריבוע התפילין ודומיא שכתב הט"ז בסימן תרמ"ה ס"ד[ב] ע"ש. כי מיבעיא לי עלם שיעור קלקול הריבוע עד כמה נקרא בענינינו דזה ברור דלא נוכל לומר לענין תפילין דוקא אם חסרון הריבוע היה בטפח כמו שפסק הרמב"ם שם לענין מזבח דכל התפילין אינם מחזיקין כך ואולי אם נתמעך הריבוע של התפילין מעט יותר מחגירת ליפורן נקרא בענינינו ג"כ קלקול הריבוע וצ"ע: * שצריך. עיין במ"ב לענין התעקמות התיתורא העתקתי מספר לשכת הסופר והביא שם ראיה ע"ז דרש"י פירש במנחות ל"ה ע"א תפילין שיהא מרובעין בתפרן היינו שלא ימשוך חוט התפירה הרבה שלא תכוון ותתמעט הריבוע עי"ש ומה לי אם נתעקם מחמת התפירה או מחמת עצמו ואף שיש קצת לחלק בזה עכ"ל: * חריץ שבין בית לבית וכו' ואם לא הגיע כשרה. עיין בח"א דמשמע מיניה דאפילו הנוהגין לעשות התפילין ע"י דיבוק הד' עורות אפ"ה מהני בדיעבד אם מדבק לבסוף הד' בתים ביחד ומשייר מלמעלה רק מעט שיהיו החריצין ניכרין

מתרגם: ° לבע מבריק.

שער הציון

(קפג) מ"א: (קפד) תוס' מנחות ל"ה ע"א עי"ש: (קפה) עבודת היום והדין עמו כמו שביארתי בע"ה בבה"ל: (קפו) נו"ב בסי' א': (קפז) חיי אדם: (קפח) ט"ז: (קפט) מחה"ש: (קצ) לשכת הסופר בשם שולחן שלמה: (קצא) מוכח מלבוש: (קצב) חיי אדם: (קלג) עיין בש"ת: (קלד) רש"י במנחות ל"ד ע"ב ד"ה ואם:

הגהות ותיקונים: א) ע"א: ב) ט"ס צ"ל סק"ד:

הערות והארות: 1) עיין בה"ל סי' ל"ג ס"ב ד"ה לחוש וכו' לענין סברת הרמב"ם והפוסקים אם ס"ל דבנתקלקל צריך לרבען:

40. The skin **(183)** of the housings **(184)** it is a mitzvah to make **(185)** black. (*See below* **(186)** *in Sec. 33.*)

The grooves /of the head *tefilin*/ in between one housing and the other must reach to the sewing. If they do not reach /to the sewing the *tefilin*/ are /nevertheless/ valid, **(187)** provided that **(188)** the grooves are recognizable,

Mishnah Berurah

(183) Of the housings. One should certainly be meticulous that the /letter/ ש /on the housing/ should be black. Sometimes, as a result of considerable age, the blackness peels off it.

(184) It is a mitzvah, etc. /This wording/ implies that, once it is after the event, /if the skin of the housings was not made black/ this does not preclude /them from being ruled as valid/. /However,/ there are Poskim who are of the opinion that /for their skin to be black/ is a halachic /requirement which was taught/ to Mosheh (Moses) on /Mount/ Sinai, as /is the case for the skin of/ the straps, and /the blackness/ is /therefore/ essential /for their validity/, even once it is after the event. In the *Beyur Ha-Gra*, it is implied that /the author/ adopts /their view/ as the halachic /ruling/ and the *Yeshu'os Ya'akov* /does so/ likewise. It is likewise implied by the *E.R.* and the *Sh.Kn.Hag.* that one should be stringent /about this/, except where that is impossible. /In the latter case/, one may rely on the view of the lenient /authorities/, so as not to be idle about /the fulfillment of/ the mitzvah of *tefilin*.

(185) Black. It is preferable that the blackness should be from black paint which has no substance at all, /so that/ the *tefilin* should only have a mere appearance of blackness. Nevertheless, if one blacked /the housings/ with a kind of polish which cannot be peeled off /, then/, even if it can be removed from the hide by /removing/ fine particles, one should not be stringent /and invalidate the *tefilin*/ where it is /already/ after the event. See what we have written in Par. 48 in the Beyur Halachah in the name of the *P.Mg.*, who is also of the opinion that one should not be stringent about this. On the other hand, there is an innovation of present-day scribes, to black /the housings/ with a plaster which can be peeled off whole from every side of the *tefilin* and has a form like black paper. This /plaster makes the *tefilin*/ invalid. [From the work *Nishmas Adam.* The Gaon who is the author of the /work/ *Beis Meir* agrees with him. This is in contradiction /to the view/ of the *No.Biy.* See there.]

(186) In Sec. 33. /I.e.,/ in Par. 4, in the gloss.

See the Mishnah Berurah there, that the *Rema* follows the view of the author /of the Shulchan Aruch, stated/ here, that /the blacking/ is only a mere mitzvah /requirement/. /However,/ according to what we have written in sub-Par. 184, this /requires/ study.

(187) Provided that ... are, etc. However, if they are not recognizable on the outside /, then/, even though on the inside there are four housings and each individual passage is lying in its own housing, this is of no avail /for the *tefilin* to be valid/.

(188) The grooves are recognizable. However, a mere scratch or mark is of no

כדי שיהיו ד' ראשיה נראין לכל: **מא** (קפט) * [ל]אורך ורחב הבתים * וגובהן * אין לו (ס) שיעור: **מב** * [מ]שי"ן של תפילין (קצ) הלכה למשה מסיני שיעשה בעור הבתים של ראש (קצא) כמין שי"ן (קצב) בולטת (קצג) מקמטי (סא) העור אחד מימינו ואחד משמאלו (קצד) [נ]של (סב) ימין המניח של ג' ראשים ושל שמאל המניח של (סג) ארבע ראשים: הגה מיהו אם היפך (קצה) אינו נפסל (מרדכי וסמ"ק ותוס' פרק הקומץ): **מג** * [ס]חריץ (קצו) של שי"ן דהיינו חודה למטה (קצז) יגיע עד מקום התפר:

באר הגולה

ל העיטור בשם הד"ף וסמ"ג וסא"ח בשם רב האי גאון מ מנחות ל"ה ב תוס' שם בשם שמושא רבא והרא"ש והמנהיג ס מנחות ל"ה לפי' הי"מ שהביא הרא"ש

שערי תשובה

בשו"ת נודע ביהודה סי' א' שיש סופרים אומנים מטיחים טיחה עבה על הבתים וע"י שמנים שפירטו"ש הם שחורים בתכלית ההידור אין לחוש משום שא"ר דכל לנאותו אינו חוצץ דכל השייך לשחרות להשחיר בכלל לנאותו הוא. וגם בשעה שהוא מטיח הטיח העב אין חשש משום מחיקת השי"ן שהרי אין שם רק השי"ן לבד וגם דהליפוי לנוי אינו מבטל ולכן תפילין דמארי עלמא הם ויש בהם משום ואנוהו. ואעפ"כ יש להחמיר שלא יהיה הטיח עב יותר מעור הבתים. וגם פשיטא שצריך שרבוע הבתים יהיה בבתים עצמם בלא הטיח ואם עושה הרבוע ע"י הטיח הוא שלא כדין. וגם יש לאסור שלא לתת לתוך הטיח הזה עלספיל שחוק דבעינן

באר היטב

יתבטל תורת תפילין שכנה"ג עיין ע"ת: (ס) שיעור. ומ"מ יש לחוש לדברי הגאונים שלא לעשותן קטנים מרוחב שני אצבעות בין של יד בין של ראש. ב"י ב"ח ל"ח מ"א. והיינו התיתורא למטה. ויש למחות בעוברי דרכים שמתקנים להם תפילין קטנים מאוד כי מבורר מש"ס שצריכים להיות רחבים יותר מאצבע ואם לאו פסולין הם ע"ת ע"ש: (סא) העור. ולא ע"י דפוס ט"ז וב"ח ע"ת עמ"א: (סב) ימין המניח. ואם הוא איטר לא ישנה ובתר ימין ושמאל דעלמא אזלינן מ"א: (סג) ד' ראשים. ב"ח וע"ת והרמ"ע פסקו דצריך ליזהר שלא יגעו היודי"ן למטה בשי"ן ומ"א פסק דצריכים ליגע היודי"ן למטה בשי"ן ע"ש וכ"פ הרמ"א סעיף מ"ג:

ביאור הלכה

ניכרין אך דמצריך הח"א ליזהר שיהיו החריצין עכ"פ בעגם הבדלת הבתים ולא בהגלאנק° לבד ובתשובת ח"ס סימן ה' משמע דהנוהגין לעשות תפיליהן ע"י דיבוק לא מהני אפילו החריצין ניכרות אלא יהיו מובדלות לגמרי ואז יזהר שיהיה ריבוען קיים כי מצוי שע"י ההבדל נאבד הריבוע ומנהג העולם במדינתינו כהח"א וכן משמע בספר ישועות יעקב ומ"מ כל י"ש יזהר לכתחלה לעשות הבתים נפרדים וכמו שכתב הח"א גופא דלכתחילה פשיטא דנכון לעשות כן. והנה אם לא יהיו מדובקים כלל מצוי לפעמים שנתקלקל הריבוע בהמשך הזמן עי"ז ע"כ אפשר שטוב יותר שידבק מעט בשיפולי הבית אצל תיתורא בין בית לבית והנה יש עוד אופן שידבק מעט העורות שבין בית לבית ואם העורות לא יגיעו זה לזה יתן לתוכם חתיכת קלף דק עם דבק שיתחברם יחדיו ולדי הבתים וכן בראשי הבתים לא יהיה מדובק כלל ובזה יהיה עדיין כל החריצים מינכר היטב וגם ריבוען יהיה קיים אך באופן זה צריך ליזהר מאוד תמיד שלא לנתק בחוזק בית אחד מחבירו כדי שלא יקרע עי"ז העור שבין בית לבית: * אורך ורוחב הבתים וכו'. עיין בעירובין צ"ג[א] ע"ב בגמרא ועיין היטב ברא"ש בה"ק בסדר תיקון תפילין בקצרה מה שכתב לענין שיעור התפילין ובביאור הגר"א בסעיף זה ועכ"פ נלענ"ד דאפילו לפי דעת השו"ע דסתם להלכה דאין להם שיעור מ"מ לפי מה דמוכח שם בגמרא דבראש וכן ביד אין מקום רק להניח שני תפילין ולא שלשה יש ליזהר עכ"פ שלא ללבוש תפילין פעם קטנים מאוד ופעם שיהיו גדולים שלשה פעמים כמו הראשונים כגון שבפעם הראשון היו כשיעור אצבע וחצי על אצבע וחצי ובפעם שני היו ד' אצבעות וחצי על ד' אצבעות וחצי וכה"ג דממ"נ או דתפילין הראשונים היו קטנים מכשיעור או דתפילין השניים מונחים שלא במקום תפילין ועיין לקמן בסימן רל"ג ס"א שאין לעשות תרתי דסתרי אפילו שלא ביום אחד. ואף דיש לדחות דבזמן הגמרא היו תפיליהם ממוצעים כאצבעיים ויותר משא"כ בזה אבל א"כ אזדא ראית הרא"ש שם והשו"ע דפסק דלא כהרא"ש לא נזכר באחרונים שיהיה מחמת זה כ"א מטעם אחר עיין בב"י ובביאור הגר"א. והנכון לאדם שיהיו תפיליו תמיד ממוצעים דהיינו לא פחות משיעור אצבעיים ולא יותר מד' על ד' אצבעות והיינו עם התיתורא ומעברתא דבזה יצא עכ"פ מדינא ידי הכל: * וגובהן. עיין במ"א: * אין לו שיעור. ועיין בספר שולחן שלמה שכתב דמ"מ לא יעשה התפילין גדולים עד מאוד שעי"ז לא יהיה באפשר להניחן על מקום נמיחת השערות וכן בשל יד שלא יבוא להניחן קצת על החצי עצם שסמוך לבית השחי או במקום שאינו בשר התפוח עכ"ל ועיין מה שכתבתי לעיל בסימן כ"ז ס"ט בבה"ל: * שי"ן של תפילין הלמ"מ וכו' כמין שי"ן. עיין במ"ב דאפילו כתב שלנו וכו' אלא דוגמא הוא מהב"ח עי"ש ולפ"ז יש לעיין במה דפסק הכ"א דאם יש קצת הפסק בין היו"ד להשי"ן דהיינו שאין מגיע בשולו התחתון דמעכב בדיעבד כמו בס"ת דלכאורה להב"ח אפשר דרק לכתחלה צריך ליזהר ולא לעיכובא וצ"ע. * חריץ של שי"ן וכו' יגיע עד מקום התפר. ובדיעבד עי' במ"ב דיש להקל וכ"כ בד"מ בשם הא"ז דאין לחוש ומה שכתב הד"מ דמברוך שאמר משמע שמחמיר לפסלו בב"ש שלפנינו ליתא ואדרבה בהג"ה שם הביא להקל בדיעבד:

מתרגם: °נולן, מבריק

משנה ברורה

(קנה) כי עכ"פ צריך הבדל מעט בין הבתים שיהיו החריצין ניכרים ממש וכן הח"א מיאן במעשה הסופרים שמדבקין הבתים וטחין את כל הבית בטיח או בגלאנ"ץ° רק שעושין רושם בהגלאנ"ץ° ומה גם דלכתחלה בעינן שיהי' החריץ מגיע עד למטה ועיין בבה"ל וכ"ש הסופרים שתולין עור על הד' בתים ורושמין בו חריצין בסכין שתהיה נראה כארבעה בתים דפסול (קנו) דעי"ז נעשה תפילה של יד: **מא** (קפט) אורך ורוחב. ומ"מ נכון לחוש לדברי הגאונים שסוברין שלכתחילה לא יעשה אותן קטנים מאצבעיים על אצבעיים והיינו עם התיתורא ועיין בע"ת שכתב דאם אין מחזיק עם התיתורא רק כאצבע על אצבע אפילו בדיעבד פסול וכן פסק בספר ביאור מרדכי ועיין בספר א"ר שלמד עליהם זכות ומ"מ סיים דכל בעל נפש יזהר לעשות התיתורא רחב ב' אצבעיים ולבד כל אלו מצוי מאוד באלו התפילין הקטנים שפרשיותיהן גרועות עד מאד מצד דחק המקום כאשר בעיני ראיתי הרבה מהם ע"כ השומר נפשו ישמור מהם: **מב** (קצ) הלמ"מ. ואם נתקלקל השי"ן ואינו ניכר (קנז) צריך לתקנו מחדש דומיא דאם נתקלקל ריבוע המבואר בסמוך: (קצא) כמין שי"ן. ומשמע (קנח) באחרונים דתמונת שיני"ן שלנו שאנו עושין בתפילין די דלא בעינן דוקא כתב סת"מ ממש אלא דוגמא ומנהג סופרים כהיום באיזה מקומות להדר ולעשותן בכתב אשורית ממש: (קצב) בולטת וכו'. ואם עשה השי"ן בקלף אחר והדביק בדבק על הבית (קנט) פסול: (קצג) מקמטי[ב] העור. דהיינו שמקמט העור במלקט ע"י כפילה שכופל מהעור עד שנעשו סעיפי השי"ן. ולעשותן ע"י דפוס דהיינו שעל הדפוס מקוק שי"ן בולטת ודוחק הדפוס בעור הבית ונעשה תואר שי"ן עיין בט"ז ומ"א דמשמע דלכתחילה טוב למנוע מזה ובכנה"ג בשם תשובת הרמ"ע כתב דזהו יותר הידור וכן המנהג פשוט כהיום לעשותן בדפוס מפני שעי"ז יש לה תואר שי"ן בתוליותיה וזויתיה יותר משי"ן המקומטת מהעור: (קצד) של ימין המניח. ואין (ר) חילוק בזה בין איטר לאחר דבתר ימין ושמאל דעלמא אזלינן: (קצה) אינו נפסל. אבל (רא) אם עשה בשני הצדדים רק שי"ן של שלשה ראשים או ארבעה פסול וכ"ש אם חיסר לגמרי שי"ן אחד: **מג** (קצו) של שי"ן. (רב) בין דימין ובין דשמאל: (קצז) יגיע וכו'. דהיינו עד התיתורא ממש ובדיעבד וכן

שער הציון

(קנה) שע"ת: (קנו) גמרא: (קנז) שולחן שלמה וש"א: (קנח) הב"ח והרמ"ע וע"ת: (קנט) ישועות יעקב ות' רע"א סי' י"א וש"א: (ר) מ"א: (רא) פמ"ג: (רב) הגר"ז ופשוט:

הגהות ותיקונים: א) צ"ה: ב) מקמטי:

so that the four tops are evident to everybody.

41. For **(189)** the length and the breadth of the housings and their height there is no minimum requirement.

42. The /letter/ ש on the *tefilin* /housings/ **(190)** is a halachic /requirement which was taught/ to Mosheh (Moses) on /Mount/ Sinai. /The requirement is/ that one should make in the skin of the housings of the head /*tefilin*/ **(191)** a sort of /letter/ ש, **(192)** which protrudes **(193)** from the folds of the skin,

Mishnah Berurah

avail at all. This is because there must at least be a little separation between the housings, so that the grooves must be actually recognizable. The *Ch.A.* likewise rejects the conduct of scribes who stick the housings /together/ and smear the entire /group of/ housings with plaster or polish, except that they make a mark in the polish, especially because, initially, it is necessary for the groove to reach until the bottom. See the Beyur Halachah.[38]

The scribes who stretch skin over the four housings and mark grooves in it with a knife, so that it appears like four housings, certainly /act improperly/. For /then the *tefilin* unit/ is invalid, since as a result of this it becomes an arm *tefilin* unit.

(189) The length and the breadth. Nevertheless, it is proper to take into account the words of the Geonim who are of the opinion that, initially, one should not make them smaller than two fingerbreadths, i.e., /together/ with the bridge.

See the *O.T.*, who writes that if /together/ with the bridge /the *tefilin* unit/ only measures a fingerbreadth by a fingerbreadth, it is invalid even once it is after the event. This is also ruled by the work *Beyur Mordechai.* See the work *E.R.*, whose /author/ finds justification /for the validity of such *tefilin*/. He nevertheless concludes that every conscientious person should be careful to make the bridge two fingerbreadths wide. Apart from all these /considerations/, it is very common with such small *tefilin* units for their passages to be very inferior, due to the crampedness of the space /available for them/. I have noticed this with many of them with my own eyes. Consequently, a person who protects his soul should beware of them.

(190) Is a halachic /requirement which was taught/ to Mosheh (Moses) on /Mount/ Sinai. If the /letter/ ש became spoiled and is not recognizable, one must form it anew, just as when the square became spoiled /one is required to remedy this/, as explained nearby.

(191) A sort of ש. It is implied by the Acharonim that our symbol for the /letter/ ש, that we make on the *tefilin* /housing/, is adequate. /This is/ because it is not specifically necessary for the actual script /which is used/ for Torah Scrolls, *tefilin* /passages/ and mezuzos to be used, but a counterpart /of that script may also be used/. Nowadays, it is the practice of scribes in some places to enhance /their *tefilin*/ by making /the letter ש/ with actual Assyrian script.[39]

(192) Which protrudes. If one made the /letter/ ש with a different /piece of/ hide and stuck it with glue onto the housing, it is invalid.

(193) From the folds of the skin. I.e., one

38 The author discusses there methods whereby the grooves will be clearly noticeable and the squareness will be preserved.
39 I.e., the script used in a Torah Scroll, etc.

באר הגולה

כדי שיהיו ד' ראשיה נראין לכל: **מא** (קפט) * לאורך ורחב הבתים * וגובהן * אין לו (ס) שיעור: **מב** * משי"ן של תפילין (קצ) הלכה למשה מסיני שיעשה בעור הבתים של ראש (קצא) כמין שי"ן (קצב) בולטת (קצג) מקמטי (סא) העור **אחד מימינו ואחד משמאלו** (קצד) נשל (סב) ימין המניח של ג' ראשים ושל שמאל המניח של (סג) ארבע ראשים: הגה מיהו אם היפך (קצה) אינו נפסל (מרדכי וסמ"ק ותוס' פרק הקומץ): **מג** * סחריץ (קצו) של שי"ן דהיינו חודה למטה (קצז) יגיע עד מקום התפר:

ל ,העיטור בשם רי"ף וסמ"ג וקא"ח נ בשם רב האי גאון מ מנחות ל"ה ב תוס' סם בשם שמושא רבא והרא"ש והמנהיג ס מנחות ל"ה לפי' הי"מ שהביא הרא"ש

שערי תשובה

בשו"ת נודע ביהודה סי' א' שיש סופרים אומנים מטיחים טיחה עבה על הבתים וע"י שמנים שפירטו"ש הם שחורים בתכלית ההידור אין לחוש משום שא"ר דכל לנאותו אינו חוצץ דכל השייך לשחרות להשחיר בכלל לנאותו הוא. וגם בשעה שהוא מטיח הטיח העב אין חשש משום מחיקת השי"ן שהרי אין שם רק השי"ן לבד וגם דהליפוי לנוי אינו מבטל ולכן תפילין דמארי עלמא הם ויש בהם משום ואנוהו. ואעפ"כ יש להחמיר שלא יהיה הטיח עב יותר מעור הבתים. וגם פשיטא שצריך שרבוע הבתים יהיה בבתים עצמם בלא הטיח ואם עושה הרבוע ע"י הטיח הוא שלא כדין. וגם יש לאסור שלא לתת לתוך הטיח הזה עלם פיל שחוק דבעינן

באר היטב

יתבטל תורת תפילין שכנה"ג עיין ע"ת: (ס) שיעור. ומ"מ יש לחוש לדברי הגאונים שלא לעשותן קטנים מרוחב שני אצבעות בין של יד בין של ראש. ב"י ב"ח ל"ח מ"א. והיינו התיתורא למטה. ויש למחות בעוברי דרכים שמתקנים להם תפילין קטנים מאוד כי מבורר מש"ס שצריכים להיות רחבים יותר מאצבע ואם לאו פסולין הם ע"ת ע"ש: (סא) העור. ולא ע"י דפוס ט"ז וב"ח ע"ת עמ"א: (סב) ימין המניח. ואם הוא איטר לא ישנה ובתר ימין ושמאל דעלמא אזלינן מ"א: (סג) ד' ראשים. ב"ח וע"ת והרמ"ע פסקו דצריך ליזהר שלא יגעו היודי"ן למטה בשי"ן ומ"א פסק דצריכים ליגע היודי"ן למטה בשי"ן ע"ש וכ"פ הרמ"א סעיף מ"ג:

ביאור הלכה

ניכרין אך דמצריך הח"א ליזהר שיהיו החריצין .עכ"פ בעלם הבדלת הבתים ולא בהגלאנך° לבד ובתשובת ח"ס סימן ה' משמע דהנוהגין לעשות תפיליהן ע"י דיבוק לא מהני אפילו החריצין ניכרות אלא יהיו מובדלות לגמרי ואז יזהר שיהיה ריבוען קיים כי מצוי שע"י ההבדל נאבד הריבוע ומנהג העולם במדינתינו כהח"א וכן משמע בספר ישועות יעקב ומ"מ כל י"ש יזהר לכתחלה לעשות הבתים נפרדים וכמו שכתב הח"א גופא דלכתחילה פשיטא דנכון לעשות כן. והנה אם לא יהיו מדובקים כלל מצוי לפעמים שנתקלקל הריבוע בהמשך הזמן עי"ז ע"כ אפשר שטוב יותר שידבק מעט בשיפולי הבית אצל תיתורא בין בית לבית והנה יש עוד אופן שידבק מעט העורות שבין בית לבית ואם העורות לא יגיעו זה לזה יתן לתוכם חתיכת קלף דק עם דבק שיתחברו יחדיו ולדי הבתים וכן בראשי הבתים לא יהיה מדובק כלל ובזה יהיה עדיין כל החריצים מינכר היטב וגם ריבוען יהיה קיים אך באופן זה צריך ליזהר מאוד תמיד שלא לנתק בחוזק בית אחד מחבירו כדי שלא יקרע עי"ז העור שבין בית לבית: * **אורך ורוחב הבתים וכו'**. עיין בעירובין צ"ג[א] ע"ב בגמרא ועיין היטב ברא"ש בה"ק בסדר תיקון תפילין בקצרה מה שכתב לענין שיעור התפילין ובביאור הגר"א בסעיף זה ועכ"פ נלענ"ד דאפילו לפי דעת השו"ע דסתם להלכה דאין להם שיעור מ"מ לפי מה דמוכח שם בגמרא דבראש וכן ביד אין מקום רק להניח שני תפילין ולא שלשה יש ליזהר עכ"פ שלא ללבוש תפילין פעם קטנים מאוד ופעם שיהיו גדולים שלשה פעמים כמו הראשונים כגון שבפעם הראשון היו כשיעור אצבע וחצי על אצבע וחצי ובפעם שני היו ד' אצבעות וחצי על ד' אצבעות וחצי וכה"ג דממ"נ או דתפילין הראשונים היו קטנים מכשיעור או דתפילין השניים מונחים שלא במקום תפילין ועיין לקמן בסימן רל"ג ס"א שאין לעשות תרתי דסתרי אפילו שלא ביום אחד. ואף דיש לדחות דבזמן הגמרא היו תפיליהם ממוצעים כאצבעיים ויותר משא"כ בזה אבל א"כ אזדא ראית הרא"ש שם והשו"ע דפסק דלא כהרא"ש לא נזכר באחרונים שיהיה מחמת זה כ"א מטעם אחר עיין בב"י ובביאור הגר"א. והנכון לאדם שיהיו תפיליו תמיד ממוצעים דהיינו לא פחות משיעור אצבעיים על אצבעיים ולא יותר מד' על ד' אצבעות והיינו עם התיתורא ומעברתא דבזה יצא עכ"פ מדינא ידי הכל: * **וגובהן**. עיין במ"א: * **אין לו שיעור**. ועיין בספר שולחן שלמה שכתב דמ"מ לא יעשה התפילין גדולים עד מאוד שעי"ז לא יהיה באפשר להניחן על מקום צמיחת השערות וכן בשל יד שלא יבוא להניחן קצת על החצי עלם שסמוך לבית השחי או במקום שאינו בשר התפוח עכ"ל ועיין מה שכתבתי לעיל בסימן כ"ז ס"ט בבה"ל: * **שי"ן של תפילין הלמ"מ וכו' כמין שי"ן**. עיין במ"ב דאפילו כתב שלנו וכו' אלא דוגמא הוא מהב"ח עי"ש ולפ"ז יש לעיין במה דפסק הכ"א דאם יש קצת הפסק בין היו"ד להשי"ן דהיינו שאין מגיע בשולו התחתון דמעכב בדיעבד כמו בס"ת דלכאורה להב"ח אפשר דרק לכתחלה צריך ליזהר ולא לעיכובא וצ"ע. * **חריץ של שי"ן וכו' יגיע עד מקום התפר**. ובדיעבד עי' במ"ב דיש להקל וכ"כ בד"מ בשם הא"ז דאין לחוש ומה שכתב הד"מ דמברוך שאמר משמע שמחמיר לפסלו בב"ש שלפנינו ליתא ואדרבה בהג"ה שם הביא להקל בדיעבד: וכן

משנה ברורה

(קנה) כי עכ"פ צריך הבדל מעט בין הבתים שיהיו החריצין ניכרים ממש וכן הח"א מיאן במעשה הסופרים שמדבקין הבתים וטחין את כל הבית בטיח או בגלאנ"ך° רק שעושין רושם בהגלאנ"ך° ומה גם דלכתחלה בעינן שיהי' החריץ מגיע עד למטה ועיין בבה"ל וכ"ש הסופרים שתולין עור על הד' בתים ורושמין בו חריצין באופן שתהיה נראה כארבעה בתים דפסול (קנו) דעי"ז נעשה תפילה של יד: **מא** (קפט) אורך ורוחב. ומ"מ נכון לחוש לדברי הגאונים שסוברין שלכתחילה לא יעשה אותן קטנים מאצבעיים על אצבעיים והיינו עם התיתורא ועיין בע"ת שכתב דאם אין מחזיק עם התיתורא רק כאצבע על אצבע אפילו בדיעבד פסול וכן פסק בספר ביאור מרדכי ועיין בספר א"ר שלמד עליהם זכות ומ"מ סיים דכל בעל נפש יזהר לעשות התיתורא רחב ב' אצבעיים ובגד כל אלו מצוי מאוד באלו התפילין הקטנים שפרשיותיהן גרועות עד מאד מגד דחק המקום כאשר בעיני ראיתי הרבה מהם ע"כ השומר נפשו ישמור מהם: **מב** (קצ) הלמ"מ. ואם נתקלקל השי"ן ואינו ניכר (קנז) צריך לתקנו מחדש דודאי דאם נתקלקל ריבוע המבואר בסמוך: (קצא) כמין שי"ן. ומשמע (קנח) באחרונים דתמונת שי"ן שלנו שאנו עושין בתפילין די דלא בעינן דוקא כתב סת"ם ממש אלא דוגמא ומנהג סופרים כהיום באיזה מקומות להדר ולעשותן בכתב אשורית ממש: (קצב) בולטת וכו'. ואם עשה השי"ן בקלף אחר והדביק בדבק על הבית (קנט) פסול: (קצג) מקמטי[ב] העור. דהיינו שמקמט העור במלקט ע"י כפילה שכופל מהעור עד שנעשו סעיפי השי"ן. ולעשותן ע"י דפוס דהיינו שעל הדפוס חקוק שי"ן בולטת ודוחק הדפוס בעור הבית ונעשה תואר שי"ן עיין בט"ז ומ"א דמשמע דלכתחילה טוב למנוע מזה ובכנה"ג בשם תשובת הרמ"ע כתב דזהו יותר הידור וכן המנהג פשוט כהיום לעשותן בדפוס מפני שעי"ז יש לה תואר שי"ן בחוליותיה וזיונה יותר משי"ן המקומטת מהעור: (קצד) של ימין המניח. ואין (ר) חילוק בזה בין איטר לאחר דבתר ימין ושמאל דעלמא אזלינן: (קצה) אינו נפסל. אבל (רא) אם עשה בשני הצדדים רק שי"ן של שלשה ראשים או ארבעה פסול וכ"ש אם חיסר לגמרי שי"ן אחד: **מג** (קצו) של שי"ן. (רב) בין דימין ובין דשמאל: (קצז) יגיע וכו'. דהיינו עד התיתורא ממש ובדיעבד

מתרגם: °נולן, מבריק

שער הציון

(קנה) שע"ת: (קנו) גמרא: (קנז) שולחן שלמה וש"א: (קנח) הב"ח והרמ"ע וע"ת: (קנט) ישועות יעקב ות' רע"א סי' י"א וש"א: (ר) מ"א: (רא) פמ"ג: (רב) הגר"ז ופשוט:

הגהות ותיקונים: א) צ"ה: ב) מקמטי:

one on the right/-hand side/ and one on the left/-hand side/. /The letter ש/ **(194)** on the right of the donner should have three tops and /the letter ש/ on the left of the donner should have four tops.

Gloss: However, if one interchanges them **(195)** */the* tefilin/ *are not invalid. (...)*

43. The groove **(196)** of the /letter/ ש, i.e., its edge below, **(197)** should reach the place of the sewing.

Mishnah Berurah

should fold the skin with a clamp by doubling, bending over the skin until the parts of the /letter/ ש are formed.

See the *Taz* and the *M.A.* /as to/ whether one may make /the letter ש/ by means of a mold. I.e., /if one may use/ a mold which has a depressed /letter/ ש engraved in it, by forcing the mold against the skin of the housing /so that/ the outline of a /letter/ ש will be formed /from the skin/. It is implied /there/ that, initially, it is desirable to refrain from /making the letter ש in/ this /way/. The *Kn.Hag.*, on the authority of a responsum of the *Rema* /of Fano/, writes that this is more enhancing /to the *tefilin*/. It is /in fact/ the widespread practice nowadays to make /the letter ש on the *tefilin*/ with a mold, since through this /method/ it has the outline of a /letter/ ש with its joints and ז[40] /letters/ to a greater extent than a /letter/ ש which is folded out of the skin.

(194) On the right of the donner. There is no difference in this respect between a left-handed person and someone else, since we follow what is generally the "right" and the "left".

(195) /The *tefilin*/ are not invalid. However, if one made on both sides only a /letter/ ש of three heads or /only a letter ש of/ four /heads, the *tefilin*/ are invalid. They are certainly /invalid/ if one completely left out one ש /letter/.

(196) Of the ש. /I.e.,/ both of the /letter ש/ on the right and of the /letter ש/ on the left.

(197) Should reach, etc. I.e., /the edge of the letter ש should reach/ actually until the bridge.

Once it is after the event, /the *tefilin*/ are valid even if /the letter ש/ does not reach /the

40 I.e., the crownlets of the letter ש.

הגה * וכן (קצח) היו"ד שבשי"ן * צריך (קצט) ליגע למטה בשולי השי"ן (סמ"ג) ולא ימשוך השי"ן הרבה אלא (ר) * שגם שולי השי"ן יהא נראה על התפר (ברוך שאמר): **מד** [ע]תיתורא (סד) דתפילין הלכה למשה מסיני והיינו (רא) * שישים עור למטה לכסות פי הבתים ונראה כעין דף של גשר הנקרא תיתורא [פ]מעברתא דתפילין הלכה למשה מסיני והיינו שעור התיתורא (רב) יהא ארוך מצד אחד ויעשה בו המעברתא כיצד יתחכנו בשני צדדים שלא תהא רחבה כמו רוחב התיתורא כדי (רג) שיהא ניכר ריבוע התיתורא ובאותה מעברתא עוברת הרצועה ועל שם כך נקראת מעברתא גם בתפילין של יד יעשה תיתורא ומעברתא. * [צ]יגלגל כל פרשה (רד) מסופה לתחלתה (רה) * [ק]וכורכם (רו) בקלף (סה) קטן [ר]ויש מקפידין מלכורכן אלא (רז) בקלף כשר (רח) [ש]והלכה למשה מסיני שיכרוך עליה שער בהמה או חיה הטהורים: הגה (רט) ונוהגין לכרוך שער על הפרשה ואחר כך כורכין עליו קלף כשר ומוזים וכורכים עליו שער (אגור סימן מ"ה) [ת]ונהגו שיהיה שער (רי) של עגל [א]ואם לא מצא של עגל כורך בשל פרה או של שור ורוחץ השער היטב בתחלה עד שיהא נקי (ריא) [ב]קצת שער זה צריך שיראה (ריב) חוץ

באר הגולה

ע שם בגמרא פ שם צ רמב"ם בפרק ג' מה"ת הרא"ש והמרדכי וספר התרומה מההיא דהקומץ בענין מזוזה ק הרא"ש בשם שמושא רבא ר סמ"ק וסא"ח והגהת מיימוני פ"ג מה"ת ש שבת כ"ח וקי"ח ת שמושא רבא ורמב"ם א הר"י אלכסנדרני ב זוהר פרשה בא

באר היטב

(סד) דתפילין. המחבר כתב סתמא דהיינו שישים עור למטה ולא ביאר שיהא התיתורא מעור הבתים או אפי' מעור בפני עצמו כמו שנהגו הסופרים עכשיו אלא מדסתם משמע דכל גוונא כשר וכ"כ הרא"ש והטור דבכל גוונא כשר עיין ע"ת: (סה) קטן. ואם לא כרכם כשר

משנה ברורה

(רג) כשר אפילו לא הגיע כל שיש צורת השי"ן עליו: (קצח) היו"ד שבשי"ן. יש מהגדולים שמחלקין בין שי"ן הימיני להשמאלי שבשמאלי אדרבה ידקדק שלא יגעו היודי"ן בשולי השי"ן למטה אבל המ"א פסק דאין לחלק בין הימיני להשמאלי ובהשמאלי בעינן שעני היודי"ן יהיו נוגעין למטה בשוליה וכ"כ הפמ"ג דכן ראוי לעשות וכ"כ בברכי יוסף בשם מהר"י עי"ש וכ"פ שארי אחרונים עוד כתב הפמ"ג דיראה שיהיה על השיני"ן צורת יודי"ן לא קוין פשוטין בעלמא: (קצט) ליגע למטה. דבלא"ה אין שם שי"ן עליו ולעיכובא הוא אפילו בדיעבד ובשי"ן השמאלי אם אחד נוגע ואחד אינו נוגע פסול ועיין בבה"ל: (ר) שגם שולי השי"ן. ר"ל תודיהן של השיני"ן והטעם דצריך שיהא כל השי"ן נראה לקיים מה דכתיב וראו כל עמי הארץ כי שם ה' נקרא עליך וא"ר אלעזר[א] אלו תפילין שבראש שם ה' נקרא ר"ת שי"ן ובדיעבד אם נכנס מעט לתוך התיתורא עד שאין לו עי"ז תמונת שי"ן כראוי צ"ע ועיין בבה"ל: **מד** (רא) שישים וכו'. ואפילו לדעת הסוברים דהבתים צריכים להיות כולם מעור אחד ממש מ"מ לא בעינן שיהא התיתורא והמעברתא עם הבתים מעור אחד אלא אפילו אם הוא עור בפני עצמו כשר (רד) וזהו שכתב המחבר שישים וכו'. ומ"מ אם באפשרי טוב להדר גם בזה לצאת דעת המחמירין בזה ועיין בבה"ל: (רב) יהא ארוך. ואם נפסקה (רה) מותר לתופרה: (רג) שיהא ניכר. כי גם התיתורא צריכה מדין להיות מרובע וכמו שכתבנו למעלה בסעיף ל"ט: (רד) מסופה לתחלתה. בעת שנותנה לבית (רו) כמו מזוזה שנגללת מאחד כלפי שמע ולא להיפך מטעם שנתבאר ביו"ד סי' רפ"ח: (רה) וכורכם וכו'. ר"ל לכתחלה אבל אם לא כרכם כשר בדיעבד אם אין לו אחרים ועיין במחלית השקל ובבה"ל: (רו) בקלף קטן. וה"ה במטלית בגד אם אין לו קלף [פמ"ג] ועיין בביאור הגר"א: (רז) בקלף כשר. ר"ל אבל לא מנבלה וה"ה טמאה אבל במטלית גם לדיעה זו שפיר דמי ועיין בב"י שכתב בטעם הדבר דכיון שהוא מניח קלף צריך להיות דוקא מן המותר לפיך כמו לבתים ולרצועות ובביאור הגר"א מפקפק בדין זה: (רח) והלמ"מ. לכן אם לא כרך השיער עליה (רז) פסול אף שכרך עליה קלף: (רט) ונוהגין לכרוך וכו'. כי י"א שיכרוך השער על גוף הפרשה ואח"כ יכרוך הקלף למעלה וי"א להיפך לכך נוהגין לקיים דברי שניהם ועיין בביאור הגר"א שכתב דמדינא אין קפידא איזו קודם: (רי) של עגל. כדי שיזכור מעשה עגל ולא יחטא וגם כדי לכפר על עון זה וכתב הא"ר דמזה הטעם טוב לעשות כל תיקון תפילין מעור עגל ולאפוקי מאותן שעושין הרצועות מעור תיש: (ריא) קצת שער. עיין במ"א ועיין בחידושי רע"א שהספרים שהשער היוצא יהיה פחות מאורך שעורה: (ריב) חוץ לבתים. י"א שיהיה אצל הבית שמונח בו פרשת קדש וי"א אצל והיה א"ש (רח) וטוב שיצא מפרשת והיה א"ש בצד הפונה לפרשת

ביאור הלכה

* וכן היו"ד שבשי"ן. בד"מ הארוך איתא היודי"ן שבשי"ן ונראה שזו הגירסא היה ג"כ לפני המ"א בהגהת שו"ע הזה ולכך הביא ראיה ממנו לסברתו דאין לחלק בין שי"ן הימיני להשמאלי. ודע דמח"א משמע דספוקי מספקא ליה לדינא אי כהב"ח וסייעתו או כהמ"א ע"כ נ"ל אף דאנו מכריעין במ"ב דלכתחילה יותר טוב שיגעו גם היודי"ן שבשי"ן השמאלי לשולו התחתון מ"מ בדיעבד אין להחמיר בהם לפסול אחרי דלדעת הרבה גדולים גם לכתחילה לא יגעו וכן הפמ"ג לא כתב רק דכן ראוי לעשות כהמ"א אם לא היכא דיו"ד אחד נוגע ואחד אינו נוגע דאז ממ"נ פסול וכמו שכתב הח"א. ודע עוד דלפי דברי הגדולים שסוברים דשי"ן שמאלי לא יגעו היודי"ן שלו בשולו ה"ה דגם היודי"ן שלו גופייהו לא יהיה להם תמונת יו"ד כמו בהשי"ן של ג' ראשים אלא יהיו כמין קוין פשוטים אכן לפי פסק המ"א שאין לחלק בין הימין להשמאל גם בזה אין לחלק. ואם עשה בשי"ן של ד' ראשים [ומכש"כ בשל ג' ראשים] קוין פשוטין והן מגיעין עד שוליהן הוא תרתי דסתרי [פמ"ג] ופסול: * צריך ליגע למטה וכו'. עיין הטעם במ"ב והוא מהמ"א דצריך ליכתב כמו בס"ת אחרי דהוא הלמ"מ ולפ"ז נראה דהוא הדין אם אינו נוגע יו"ד בהקו שלו ג"כ אפשר דעיכובא הוא וכ"ש אם לא היה יו"ד כלל רק קו פשוט ואפילו אם שאר הקווין נעשין כהלכה ביודי"ן על ראשיהן רק קו א' לא היה כדין וכ"ש כולם לבד בהשי"ן של ד' ראשין דשם אם היו הקוין פשוטין בלא ראשין אין להחמיר בדיעבד דיש לסמוך על הגדולים המקילין וכנ"ל: * שגם שולי השי"ן. עיין במ"ב לענין דיעבד ובס' עבודת היום משמע דבדיעבד אין להחמיר ואיני יודע מקור לזה ואולי הוא מיירי שלא אבד תמונתו עי"ז ורק מקצת חודו נכנס לתוכו אבל אם נכנס מעט מהשי"ן גופא לתוך המעברתא גם הוא מודה ול"ע: * שישים וכו'. עיין במ"ב ומש"כ לצאת וכו' היינו דעת רש"י וגם הרמב"ם ס"ל כרש"י כמו שכתב בכ"מ ואף דהגאונים פליגי ע"ז וגם הר"י ורא"ש ומרדכי וטור סבירי כוותם וגם מנהג העולם כוותייהו מ"מ טוב להדר לצאת גם דעתם ואף דברא"ש ומרדכי משמע שיותר טוב שלא לעשות מעור אחד עם הבתים עיין הטעם בדבריהם ותראה שזה הקלקול לא שייך בזמנינו למי שיודע אומנות הבתים. והגרע"א הפריז על המידה שהעתיק דברי הריק"ש דמשמע מיניה דהוא מחזיק כן מצד הדין ורק שהעולם לא נהגו כן ובאמת לענ"ד ז"א כמו שכתבנו דרבים פליגי עלייהו: * יגלגל כל פרשה וכו'. הוא למצוה ולא לעיכובא [אחרונים בסעיף מ"ז]: * וכורכם בקלף קטן. עיין במ"ב והטעם דהרא"ש והטור וש"פ ס"ל דלאו הלמ"מ הוא ושנוהגין בגרפת ואשכנז שלא לכרוך עליו דבר לבד השער אלא דלכתחילה חש השו"ע לדברי הרמב"ם שכתב שהוא הלמ"מ ועיין בא"ר דמשמע מיניה דמותר ג"כ לברך אם אין לו אחרים ושלא כמחה"ש שנסתפק

שער הציון

(רג) פמ"ג והגר"ז וע' בבה"ל: (רד) ביאור הגר"א ופמ"ג דלא כבה"ט: (רה) מאיר ע"ם בשם דבר שמואל: (רו) הרא"ש בה"ק: (רז) כן מוכח מהרא"ש בה"ק וכן מביאור הגר"א ושארי אחרונים: (רח) של"ה:

הגהות ותיקונים: א) ברכות דף ו' ע"א כתוב ר' אליעזר הגדול:

Gloss: Likewise, (198) *the* י */part/ of the /letter/* ש[22*] *is required* (199) *to touch below at the bottom of the* ש. *(...)*

One should not extend the /letter/ ש *excessively, but just* (200) *so that the bottom of the* ש *also is visible on the sewing. (...)*

44. The bridge (*tisura*) of the *tefilin* is a halachic /requirement which was taught/ to Mosheh (Moses) on /Mount/ Sinai. /The requirement/ is (201) to put skin underneath to cover the opening of the housings. /This skin/ resembles the slab /spanning/ a bridge, which is called a *tisura* /in Aramaic/.

The passageway (*mabarta*) of the *tefilin* is a halachic /requirement which was taught/ to Mosheh (Moses) on /Mount/ Sinai. /The requirement/ is that

Mishnah Berurah

bridge/, as long as it has the form of a ש.

(198) The י **of the** ש**.** There are eminent /authorities/ who differentiate between the /letter/ ש on the right /of the donner/ and /the letter ש/ on the left /of the donner/. /They maintain/ that in the case of /the letter ש/ on the left /of the donner/, on the contrary, one should take pains /to see/ that the י /parts/ do not reach the bottom of the /letter/ ש below. However, the *M.A.* rules that one should not differentiate between the /letter ש/ on the right /of the donner/ and the /letter ש/ on the left /of the donner/ and in the case of the /letter ש/ on the left /of the donner as well/ we require the two י /parts/ to touch below at the bottom /of the letter ש/. The *P.Mg.* likewise writes that it is proper to make /the letter ש on the left of the donner/ in this /way/ and the *Birkey Yosef* /also/ writes this in the name of the *Mahariy*; see there. The other Acharonim /also/ rule likewise.

The *P.Mg.* writes further that one should see that the ש /letters/ are /composed/ of י forms, not mere plain strokes.

(199) To touch below. For, otherwise, it cannot be termed a /letter/ ש. This is an essential /requirement/ even once it is after the event.

In the case of the /letter/ ש on the left /of the donner/, if one /of the י parts/ touches /the bottom/ and one does not touch /the bottom, the *tefilin/* are invalid. See the Beyur Halachah.[41]

(200) So that the bottom of the ש **also.** I.e., the edge of the ש.

The reason /for this/ is that the entire /letter/ ש must be visible. /It is also necessary/ so that one can fulfil what is written,[42] "And all the peoples of the earth will see that the Name of the Lord is readable on you", /concerning which/ Rabbi Elazar said, "This is /a reference to/ the *tefilin* on the head". By "the Name of the Lord is readable", the ש, /which is/ the first letter /of the Name ש-ד-י is indicated/.

Once it is after the event, if /the letter/ enters a little into the bridge, to the extent that because of this it does not have the proper symbol of the /letter/ ש, study is required /to determine whether the *tefilin* are valid/. See the Beyur Halachah.

(201) To put, etc. Even according to the opinion of those /authorities/ who think that the housings /of the head *tefilin*/ must all be from an actual single skin, it is nevertheless unnecessary for the bridge and the passageway to be /made together/ with the housings from the same skin, but even if they are /from/ an independent skin /the *tefilin*/ are valid. This /explains why/ the author /of the Shulchan Aruch/ writes "to put, etc."

41 The author writes there that if the strokes of the letter ש are ordinary straight strokes and touch the bottom of the ש, the letter is invalid. He notes that the letter ש must conform with all the requirements of the letter ש for a Torah Scroll, except that if the left ש is written with straight strokes one need not be stringent once it is after the event.

42 *Devarim* 28:10.

הגה * וכן (קצח) היו"ד שבשי"ן * צריך (קצט) ליגע למטה בשולי השי"ן (סמ"ג) ולא ימשוך השי"ן הרבה אלא (ר) * שגם שולי השי"ן יהא נראה על התפר (ברוך שאמר): **מד** ^ע תיתורא (סד) דתפילין הלכה למשה מסיני והיינו (רא) * שישים עור למטה לכסות פי הבתים ונראה כעין דף של גשר הנקרא תיתורא ^פ מעברתא דתפילין הלכה למשה מסיני והיינו **שעור התיתורא** (רב) **יהא ארוך מצד אחד ויעשה בו המעברתא כיצד יחתכנו בשני צדדים שלא תהא רחבה כמו רוחב התיתורא כדי** (רג) **שיהא ניכר ריבוע התיתורא ובאותה מעברתא עוברת הרצועה ועל שם כך נקראת מעברתא גם בתפילין של יד יעשה תיתורא ומעברתא. *** ^צ **יגלגל כל פרשה** (רד) **מסופה לתחלתה** (רה) * ^ק **וכורכם** (רו) **בקלף** (סה) **קטן** ^ר **ויש מקפידין מלכורכן אלא** (רז) **בקלף כשר** (רח) ^ש והלכה למשה מסיני שיכרוך עליה שער בהמה או חיה הטהורים: הגה (רט) ונוהגין לכרוך שער על הפרשה ואחר כך כורכין עליו קלף כשר ואוחזים וכורכים עליו שער (אגור סימן מ"ה) ^ת ונהגו שיהיה שער (רי) של עגל ^א ואם לא מצא של עגל כורך בשל פרה או של שור ורוחץ השער היטב בתחלה עד שיהא נקי (ריא) ^ב קצת שער זה צריך שיראה (ריב) חוץ

באר הגולה

ע שם בגמרא פ שם
צ רמב"ם בפרק ג' מה"ת הרא"ש והמרדכי וספר התרומה מההיא דהקומץ בענין מזוזה
ק הרא"ש בשם שמושא רבא ר סמ"ק וסא"ח והגהת מיימוני פ"ג מה"ת
ש שבת כ"ח וקי"ח
ת שמושא רבא ורמב"ם
א הר"י אלכסנדרני
ב זוהר פרשה בא

באר היטב

(סד) דתפילין. המחבר כתב סתמא דהיינו שישים עור למטה ולא ביאר שיהא התיתורא מעור הבתים או אפי' מעור בפני עצמו כמו שנהגו הסופרים עכשיו אלא מדסתם משמע דכל גוונא כשר וכ"כ הרא"ש והטור דבכל גוונא כשר עיין ע"ת: (סה) קטן. ואם לא כרכם כשר

משנה ברורה

(רג) כשר אפילו לא הגיע כל שיש לורת השי"ן עליו: (קצח) היו"ד שבשי"ן. יש מהגדולים שמחלקין בין שי"ן הימיני להשמאלי שבשמאלי אדרבה ידקדק שלא יגעו היודי"ן בשולי השי"ן למטה אבל המ"א פסק דאין לחלק בין הימיני להשמאלי ובהשמאלי בעינן שגם היודי"ן יהיו נוגעין למטה בשוליה וכ"כ הפמ"ג דכן ראוי לעשות וכ"כ בברכי יוסף בשם מהרי"ו עי"ש וכ"פ שארי אחרונים עוד כתב הפמ"ג דילפא שיהיה על השי"ן לורת יודי"ן לא קוין פשוטין בעלמא: (קצט) ליגע למטה. דבלא"ה אין שם שי"ן עליו ולעיכובא הוא אפילו בדיעבד ובשי"ן השמאלי אם אחד נוגע ואחד אינו נוגע פסול ועיין בבה"ל: (ר) שגם שולי השי"ן. ר"ל תוליכן של השיני"ן והטעם דצריך שיהא כל השי"ן נראה לקיים מה דכתיב וראו כל עמי הארץ כי שם ה' נקרא עליך וא"ר אליעזר^א אלו תפילין שבראש שם ה' נקרא ר"ת שי"ן ובדיעבד אם נכנס מעט לתוך התיתורא עד שאין לו עי"ז תמונת שי"ן כראוי צ"ע ועיין בבה"ל: **מד** (רא) שישים וכו'. ואפילו לדעת המוברים דהבתים צריכים להיות כולם מעור אחד ממש מ"מ לא בעינן שיהא התיתורא והמעברתא עם הבתים מעור אחד אלא אפילו אם הוא עור בפני עצמו כשר (רד) וזהו שכתב המחבר שישים וכו'. **ומ"מ אם באפשרי טוב להדר גם בזה לצאת דעת המחמירין בזה ועיין בבה"ל: (רב) יהא ארוך. ואם נפסקה (רה) מותר לתופרה: (רג) שיהא ניכר. כי גם התיתורא צריכה מדין להיות מרובע וכמו שכתבנו למעלה בסעיף ל"ט: (רד) מסופה לתחלתה. בעת שנותנה לביתה (רו) כמו מזוזה שנגללת מאחד כלפי שמע ולא להיפך מטעם שנתבאר ביו"ד סי' רפ"ח: (רה) וכורכם וכו'. ר"ל לכתחלה אבל אם לא כרכם כשר בדיעבד אם אין לו אחרים ועיין במחצית השקל ובבה"ל: (רו) בקלף קטן. וה"ה בחתיכת בגד אם אין לו קלף [פמ"ג] ועיין בביאור הגר"א: (רז) בקלף כשר. ר"ל אבל לא מבהמה וחיה טמאה אבל במטלית גם לדיעה זו שפיר דמי ועיין בב"י שכתב בטעם הדבר דכיון שהוא מביא קלף צריך להיות דוקא מן המותר לפיך כמו לבתים ולרצועות ובביאור הגר"א מפקפק בדין זה:** (רח) והלמ"מ. לכן אם לא כרך השיער עליה (רז) פסול אף שכרך עליה קלף: (רט) ונוהגין לכרוך וכו'. כי י"א שיכרוך השער על גוף הפרשה ואח"כ יכרוך הקלף למעלה וי"א להיפך לכך נוהגין לקיים דברי שניהם ועיין בביאור הגר"א שכתב דמדינא אין קפידא איזו קודם: (רי) של עגל. כדי שיזכור מעשה עגל ולא יחטא וגם כדי לכפר על עון זה וכתב הא"ר דמזה הטעם טוב לעשות כל תיקון תפילין מעור עגל ולאפוקי מאותן שעושין הרצועות מעור תיש: (ריא) קצת שער. עיין במ"א ועיין בחידושי רע"א שהסכים שהשער היוצא יהיה פחות מאורך שעורה: (ריב) חוץ לבתים. י"א שיהיה אצל הבית שמונח בו פרשת קדש וי"א אצל והיה א"ש (רח) וטוב שיצא מפרשת והיה א"ש בצד הפונה לפרשת

ביאור הלכה

* **וכן היו"ד שבשי"ן.** בד"מ הארוך איתא היודי"ן שבשי"ן ונראה שזו הגירסא היה ג"כ לפני המ"א בהגהת שו"ע הזה ולכך הביא ראיה ממנו לסברתו דאין לחלק בין שי"ן הימיני להשמאלי. ודע דמח"א משמע דספוקי מספקא ליה לדינא אי כהב"ח וסייעתו או כהמ"א ע"כ נ"ל אף דאנו מכריעין במ"ב דלכתחילה יותר טוב שיגעו גם היודי"ן שבשי"ן השמאלי לשולו התחתון מ"מ בדיעבד אין להחמיר בהם לפסול אחרי דלדעת הרבה גדולים גם לכתחילה לא יגעו וכן הפמ"ג לא כתב רק דכן ראוי לעשות כהמ"א אם לא היכא דיו"ד אחד נוגע ואחד אינו נוגע דאז ממ"נ פסול וכמו שכתב הח"א. ודע עוד דלפי דברי הגדולים שסוברים דשי"ן שמאלי לא יגעו היודי"ן שלו בשולו ה"ה דגם היודי"ן שלו גופייהו לא יהיה להם תמונת יו"ד כמו בהשי"ן של ג' ראשים אלא יהיו כמין קוין פשוטים אכן לפי פסק המ"א שאין לחלק בין הימין להשמאל גם בזה אין לחלק. ואם עשה בשי"ן של ד' ראשים [ומכש"כ בשל ג' ראשים] קוין פשוטין והן מגיעין עד שוליהן הוא תרתי דסתרי [פמ"ג] ופסול: * **צריך ליגע למטה וכו'.** עיין הטעם במ"ב והוא מהח"א דצריך ליכתב כמו בס"ת אחרי דהוא הלמ"מ ולפ"ז נראה דהוא הדין אם אינו נוגע יו"ד בהקו שלו ג"כ אפשר דעיכובא הוא וכ"ש אם לא היה יו"ד כלל רק קו פשוט ואפילו אם שאר הקווין נעשין כהלכה ביודי"ן על ראשיהן רק קו א' לא היה כדין וכ"ש כולם לבד בהשי"ן של ד' ראשין דשם אם היו הקוין פשוטין בלא ראשין אין להחמיר בדיעבד דיש לסמוך על הגדולים המקילין וכנ"ל: * **שגם שולי השי"ן.** עיין במ"ב לענין דיעבד ובס' עבודת היום משמע דבדיעבד אין להחמיר ואיני יודע מקור לזה ואולי הוא מיירי שלא אבד תמונתו עי"ז ורק מקצת חודו נכנס לתוכו אבל אם נכנס מעט מהשי"ן גופא לתוך המעברתא גם הוא מודה ול"ע: * **שישים וכו'.** עיין במ"ב ומש"כ לצאת וכו' היינו דעת רש"י וגם הרמב"ם ס"ל כרש"י כמו שכתב בכ"מ ואף דהגאונים פליגי ע"ז וגם הר"י ורא"ש ומרדכי וטור סבירי כמותם וגם מנהג העולם כוותייהו מ"מ טוב להדר לצאת גם דעתם ואף דברא"ש ומרדכי משמע שיותר טוב שלא לעשות מעור אחד עם הבתים עיין הטעם בדבריהם ונראה שזה הקלקול לא שייך בזמנינו למי שיודע אומנות הבתים. והגרע"א הפריז על המידה שהעתיק דברי הריק"ש דמשמע מיניה דהוא מחזיק כן מצד הדין ורק שהעולם לא נהגו כן ובאמת לענ"ד ז"א כמו שכתבנו דרבים פליגי עלייהו: * **יגלגל כל פרשה וכו'.** הוא למצוה ולא לעיכובא [אחרונים בסעיף מ"ז]: * **וכורכם בקלף קטן.** עיין במ"ב והטעם דהרא"ש והטור וש"פ ס"ל דלאו הלמ"מ הוא ושנוהגין בגרפת ואשכנז שלא לכרוך עליו דבר לבד השער אלא דלכתחילה חש השו"ע לדברי הרמב"ם שכתב שהוא הלמ"מ ועיין בא"ר דמשמע מיניה דמותר ג"כ לברך אם אין לו אחרים ושלא כמחה"ש שנסתפק

שער הציון

(רג) פמ"ג והגר"ז וע' בבה"ל: (רד) ביאור הגר"א ופמ"ג דלא כבה"ט: (רה) מאיר ע"ם בשם דבר שמואל: (רו) הרא"ש בה"ק: (רז) כן מוכח מהרא"ש בה"ק וכן מביאור הגר"א ושארי אחרונים: (רח) של"ה:

הגהות ותיקונים: א) ברכות דף ו' ע"א כתוב ר' אליעזר הגדול:

the skin of the bridge **(202)** should be longer on one side and in /the extra length/ one should make the passageway. /It is prepared as follows./ /The extra length/ is cut on both sides, so that its width is not the same as the width of the bridge, in order **(203)** that the squareness of the bridge will be evident. Through this passageway the strap passes and for this reason it is called the passageway.

One should also make a bridge and a passageway in the arm *tefilin.*

One should roll up each passage **(204)** from the end to the beginning,[30*] **(205)** and should wrap /the passages/ **(206)** in a small /piece of/ parchment. There are /people/ who are particular to avoid wrapping them in other than **(207)** valid parchment.

Mishnah Berurah

Despite this, if feasible, it is desirable to enhance /the fulfillment of the mitzvah/ in this respect as well, /in order/ to satisfy the view of those /authorities/ who are stringent about this. See the Beyur Halachah.

(202) Should be longer. If it became severed it is permitted to sew it.

(203) That ... will be evident. This is because the bridge is also required to be square, from the /standpoint of binding/ halachah, as we have written above in Par. 39.

(204) From the end to the beginning. /I.e.,/ when one puts it in its housing.

/This ruling/ accords with /the ruling for/ a mezuzah, which must be rolled up from /the word/ אחד towards /the word/ שמע and not in the opposite /way/, for the reason given in the *Yo.D.*, Sec. 288.

(205) And should wrap, etc. What is meant is /that this is/ an initial /requirement/. If, however, one did not wrap /the passages, then,/ now that it is after the event, /the *tefilin*/ are /nevertheless/ valid, if one does not have other /*tefilin*/. See the *Machatzis Ha-Shekel* and the Beyur Halachah.[43]

(206) In a small parchment. Correspondingly, /one may also use/ a piece of cloth if he does not have a /piece of/ parchment. [*P.Mg.*] See the *Beyur Ha-Gra.*

(207) Valid parchment. I.e., but not /with skin/ from a domestic or non-domestic unclean animal. However, as regards /the use of/ a patch of material /for this purpose/, that is perfectly /in order/ even according to this opinion.

See the *B.Y.*, who writes as the reason for the /requirement/, that in view /of the fact/ that one introduces parchment, it must be exclusively from what is permitted to one's mouth, just like /what is used for/ the housings and the straps.

The *Beyur Ha-Gra* questions the ruling /that valid parchment is required for this purpose/.

30* This is a mitzvah, but if one did not do it the *tefilin* are not invalid. (Beyur Halachah)

43 There the author discusses making a blessing over such *tefilin*. The *E.R.* implies that one may in fact make the blessing.

הגה * וכן (קצח) היו"ד שבשי"ן * צריך (קצט) ליגע למטה בשולי השי"ן (סמ"ג) ולא ימשוך השי"ן הרבה אלא (ר) * שגם שולי השי"ן יהא נראה על הספר (ברוך שאמר): מד ע תיתורא (סד) דתפילין הלכה למשה מסיני והיינו (רא) * שישים עור למטה לכסות פי הבתים ונראה כעין דף של גשר הנקרא תיתורא פ מעברתא דתפילין הלכה למשה מסיני והיינו שעור התיתורא (רב) יהא ארוך מצד אחד ויעשה בו המעברתא כיצד יחתכנו בשני צדדים שלא תהא רחבה כמו רוחב התיתורא כדי (רג) שיהא ניכר ריבוע התיתורא ובאותה מעברתא עוברת הרצועה ועל שם כך נקראת מעברתא גם בתפילין של יד יעשה תיתורא ומעברתא. * צ יגלגל כל פרשה (רד) מסופה לתחלתה (רה) * ק וכורכם (רו) בקלף (סה) קטן ר ויש מקפידין מלכורכן אלא (רז) בקלף כשר (רח) ש והלכה למשה מסיני שיכרוך עליה שער בהמה או חיה הטהורים: הגה (רט) ונוהגין לכרוך שער על הפרשה ואחר כך כורכין עליו קלף כשר ומחזירים וכורכים עליו שער (אגור סימן מ"ה) ת ונהגו שיהיה שער (רי) של עגל א ואם לא מצא של עגל כורך בשל פרה או של שור ורוחץ השער היטב בתחלה עד שיהא נקי (ריא) ב קצת שער זה צריך שיראה (ריב) חוץ

באר הגולה

ע שס נגמרא פ שס צ רמנ"ס נפרק נ' מה"ת הרא"ש והמרדכי וספר התרומה מההיא דהקומץ בענין מזוזה ק הרא"ש נשס שמושא רנא ר סמ"ק וסא"ח והגהת מיימוני פ"ג מה"ת ש שנת כ"ח וקי"ח ת שמושא רנא ורמנ"ס א הר"י אלכסנדרני ב זוהר פרשה נא

באר היטב

(סד) דתפילין. המחבר כתב סתמא דהיינו שישים עור למטה ולא ביאר שיהא התיתורא מעור הבתים או אפי' מעור בפני עצמו כמו שנהגו הסופרים עכשיו אלא מדסתם משמע דכל גוונא כשר וכ"כ הרא"ש והטור דבכל גוונא כשר עיין ע"ת: (סה) קטן. ואם לא כרכם כשר

משנה ברורה

(רג) כשר אפילו לא הגיע כל שיש צורת השי"ן עליו: (קצח) היו"ד שבשי"ן. יש מהגדולים שמחלקין בין שי"ן הימיני להשמאלי שבשמאלי אדרבה ידקדק שלא יגעו היודי"ן בשולי השי"ן למטה אבל המ"א פסק דאין לחלק בין הימיני להשמאלי ובעינן שבשני היודי"ן יהיו נוגעין למטה בשולים וכ"כ הפמ"ג דכן ראוי לעשות וכ"כ בברכי יוסף בשם מהרי"ו ע"ש וכ"פ שארי אחרונים עוד כתב הפמ"ג דירא שיהיה על השי"ן צורת יודי"ן לא קוין פשוטין בעלמא: (קצט) ליגע למטה. דבלא"ה אין שם שי"ן עליו ולעיכובא הוא אפילו בדיעבד ובשי"ן השמאלי אם אחד נוגע ואחד אינו נוגע פסול ועיין בבה"ל: (ר) שגם שולי השי"ן. ר"ל מוליכן של השי"ן והטעם דצריך שיהא כל השי"ן נראה ולקיים מה דכתיב וראו כל עמי הארץ כי שם ה' נקרא עליך וא"ר אליעזר א אלו תפילין שבראש שם ה' נקרא ר"ת שי"ן ובדיעבד אם נכנס מעט לתוך התיתורא עד שאין לו עי"ז תמונת שי"ן כראוי צ"ע ועיין בבה"ל: מד (רא) שישים וכו'. ואפילו לדעת הסוברים דהבתים צריכים להיות כולם מעור אחד ממש מ"מ לא בעינן שיהא התיתורא והמעברתא עם הבתים מעור אחד אלא אפילו אם הוא עור בפני עצמו כשר (רד) וזהו שכתב המחבר שישים וכו'. ומ"מ אם באפשרי טוב להדר גם בזה לצאת דעת המחמירין בזה ועיין בבה"ל: (רב) יהא ארוך. ואם נפסקה (רה) מותר לתופרה: (רג) שיהא ניכר. כי גם התיתורא צריכה מדין להיות מרובע וכמו שכתבנו למעלה בסעיף ל"ט: (רד) מסופה לתחלתה. בעת שמונחה לפניו (רו) כמו מזוזה שנגללת מאחד כלפי שמע ולא להיפך מטעם שנתבאר ביו"ד סי' רפ"ח: (רה) וכורכם וכו'. ר"ל לכתחלה אבל אם לא כרכם כשר בדיעבד אם אין לו אחרים ועיין במחצית השקל ובבה"ל: (רו) בקלף קטן. וה"ה במטלית בגד אם אין לו קלף [פמ"ג] ועיין בביאור הגר"א: (רז) בקלף כשר. ר"ל אבל לא מבהמה וחיה טמאה אבל במטלית גם לדיעה זו שפיר דמי ועיין בב"י שכתב בטעם הדבר דכיון שהוא תמיד קלף צריך להיות דוקא מן המותר לפיך כמו לבתים ולרצועות ובביאור הגר"א מפקפק בדין זה: (רח) והלמ"מ. לכן אם לא כרך השיער עליה (רז) פסול אף שכרך עליה קלף: (רט) ונוהגין לכרוך וכו'. כי י"א שיכרוך השער על גוף הפרשה ואח"כ יכרוך הקלף למעלה וי"א להיפך לכך נוהגין לקיים דברי שניהם ועיין בביאור הגר"א שכתב דמדינא אין קפידא איזו קודם: (רי) של עגל. כדי שיזכור מעשה עגל ולא יחטא וגם כדי לכפר על עון זה וכתב הא"ר דמזה הטעם טוב לעשות כל תיקון תפילין מעור עגל ולאפוקי מאותן שעושין הרצועות מעור תיש: (ריא) קצת שער. עיין במ"א ועיין בחידושי רע"א שהסכים שהשער היוצא יהיה פחות מאורך שעורה: (ריב) חוץ לבתים. י"א שיהיה אצל הבית שמונח בו פרשת קדש וי"א אצל והיה א"ש (רח) וטוב שילא מפרשת והיה א"ש בצד הפונה לפרשת

ביאור הלכה

* וכן היו"ד שבשי"ן. בד"מ הארוך איתא היודי"ן שבשי"ן ונראה שזו הגירסא היה ג"כ לפני המ"א בהגהת שו"ע הזה ולכך הביא ראיה ממנו לסברתו דאין לחלק בין שי"ן הימיני להשמאלי. ודע דמח"א משמע דספוקי מספקא ליה לדינא אי כהב"ח וסייעתו או כהמ"א ע"כ נ"ל אף דאנו מכריעין במ"ב דלכתחילה יותר טוב שיגעו גם היודי"ן שבשי"ן השמאלי לשולו התחתון מ"מ בדיעבד אין להחמיר בהם לפסול אחרי דלדעת הרבה גדולים גם לכתחילה לא יגעו וכן הפמ"ג לא כתב רק דכן ראוי לעשות כהמ"א אם לא היכא דיו"ד אחד נוגע ואחד אינו נוגע דאז מת"כ פסול וכמו שכתב הח"א. ודע עוד דלפי דברי הגדולים שסוברים דשי"ן שמאלי לא יגעו היודי"ן שלו בשולו ה"ה דגם היודי"ן שלו גופייהו לא יהיה להם תמונת יו"ד כמו בהשי"ן של ג' ראשים אלא יהיו כמין קוין פשוטים אכן לפי פסק המ"א שאין לחלק בין הימין להשמאל גם בזה אין לחלק. ואם עשה בשי"ן של ד' ראשים [ומכש"כ בשל ג' ראשים] קוין פשוטין והן מגיעין עד שוליהן הוא תרתי דסתרי [פמ"ג] ופסול: * צריך ליגע למטה וכו'. עיין הטעם במ"ב והוא מהח"א דצריך ליכתב כמו בס"ת אחרי דהוא הלמ"מ ולפ"ז נראה דהוא הדין אם אינו נוגע יו"ד בהקו שלו ג"כ אפשר דעיכובא הוא וכ"ש אם לא היה יו"ד כלל רק קו פשוט ואפילו אם שאר הקווין נעשין כהלכה ביודי"ן על ראשיהן רק קו א' לא היה כדין וכ"ש כולם לבד בהשי"ן של ד' ראשין דשם אם היו הקוין פשוטין בלא ראשין אין להחמיר בדיעבד דיש לסמוך על הגדולים המקילין וכנ"ל: * שגם שולי השי"ן. עיין במ"ב לענין דיעבד ובס' עבודת היום משמע דבדיעבד אין להחמיר ואיני יודע מקור לזה ואולי הוא מיירי שלא אבד תמונתו עי"ז ורק מקצת חודו נכנס לתוכו אבל אם נכנס מעט מהשי"ן גופא לתוך המעברתא גם הוא מודה וצ"ע: * שישים וכו'. עיין במ"ב ומש"כ לצאת וכו' היינו דעת רש"י וגם הרמב"ם ס"ל כרש"י כמו שכתב בכ"מ ואף דהגאונים פליגי ע"ז וגם הר"י ורא"ש ומרדכי וטור סבירי כוותהו וגם מנהג העולם כוותייהו מ"מ טוב להדר לצאת גם דעתם ואף דברא"ש ומרדכי משמע שיותר טוב שלא לעשות מעור אחד עם הבתים עיין הטעם בדבריהם ונראה שזה הקלקול לא שייך בזמנינו למי שיודע אומנות הבתים. והגרע"א הפריז על המידה שהעתיק דברי הריק"ש דמשמע מיניה דהוא מחזיק כן מצד הדין ורק שהעולם לא נהגו כן ובאמת לענ"ד ז"א כמו שכתבנו דרבים פליגי עלייהו: * יגלגל כל פרשה וכו'. הוא למצוה ולא לעיכובא [אחרונים בסעיף מ"ז]: * וכורכם בקלף קטן. עיין במ"ב והטעם דהרא"ש והטור וש"פ ס"ל דלאו הלמ"מ הוא ושנוהגין בצרפת ואשכנז שלא לכרוך עליו דבר לבד השער אלא דלכתחילה חש השו"ע לדברי הרמב"ם שכתב שהוא הלמ"מ ועיין בא"ר דמשמע מיניה דמותר ג"כ לברך אם אין לו אחרים ושלא כמחה"ש שנסתפק

שער הציון

(רג) פמ"ג והגר"ז וע' בבה"ל: (רד) ביאור הגר"א ופמ"ג דלא כבה"ט: (רה) מאיר ע"ס בשם דבר שמואל: (רו) הרא"ש בה"ק: (רז) כן מוכח מהרא"ש בה"ק וכן מביאור הגר"א ושארי אחרונים: (רח) של"ה:

הגהות ותיקונים: א) ברכות דף ו' ע"א כתוב ר' אליעזר הגדול:

(208) A halachah /was taught/ to Mosheh (Moses) on /Mount/ Sinai, /requiring one/ to wind around /the passages/ the hair of a domestic or non-domestic /halachically/ clean animal.

Gloss: **(209)** *It is the practice to wind hair around the passages /first/. Subsequently, valid parchment is wrapped around them and /then/ hair is wound around them again. (...)*

It is the practice to /use/ the hair **(210)** of a calf /for winding around the passages/. If one did not obtain /the hair/ of a calf, he should wind /around them the hair/ of a cow or of a bull.

One should first wash the hair thoroughly until it is clean.

(211) Some of this hair must be visible **(212)** outside the housings.

Mishnah Berurah

(208) A halachah /was taught/ to Mosheh on /Mount/ Sinai. Therefore, if one did not wind the hair around /the passages the *tefilin*/ are invalid, even if one wrapped parchment around them.

(209) It is the practice to wind, etc. This is because there are /authorities/ who say that one should wind the hair around the passage itself and subsequently wrap the parchment over it and /authorities/ who say the opposite. It is therefore the practice to /act in a manner which/ satisfies both views.

See the *Beyur Ha-Gra*, who writes that according to binding /halachah/ one need not be particular as to which is /done/ first.

(210) Of a calf. /The hair of a calf is used/ so that one will remember the affair of the /golden/ calf /in the wilderness/ and will not sin and also in order to atone for that sin.

The *E.R.* writes that for this reason it is desirable to make all the /constituent parts/ of the *tefilin* from calfskin. This is a rejection of /the practice of/ those who make the straps out of goatskin.

(211) Some of ... hair. See the *M.A.*

See the *Chidushey R.A.E.*, who agrees that the hair which goes out /of the housings/ should be less than the length of a barley /seed/.

(212) Outside the housings. There are /authorities/ who say that it should be /visible/ next to the housing in which the passage *Kadesh Li Chal Bechor* is lying and /authorities/ who say /that it should be visible/ next to /the housing of the passage/ *Ve-Hayah Im Shamo'a*. It is desirable that it should go out from /the housing of/ the passage *Ve-Hayah Im Shamo'a* on the side

(סו) לבתים: **מה** [ג]יתן כל פרשה בבית שלה * שתהא (ריג) זקופה מעומד (סז) [כח] בביתה: **מו** * [ד]יהיה הגליון עליון תחלה שזהו שורה עליונה וגליון תחתון (ריד) לצד פה הבתים: הגה וראש הפרשה יהיה מונח לצד ימין הקורא שאם בא לפתחן ולקרותן יהיו מונחים לפניו (רטו) כהלכתן: (תרומת הדשן ובית יוסף בשם אורחות חיים): **מז** [ה]אם כתב כל הארבעה פרשיות בקלף אחד כשרים (רטז) אפילו אין ריוח ביניהם ובלבד שיהא חוט (ריז) או משיחה בין כל בית ובית. [ו]של יד כותב הארבעה פרשיות בקלף א' וגולל אותן מסופן לתחלתן וכורך קלף עליהם ושער עגל ומכניסן בביתם כמו של ראש. * [ז]אם כתבם על ארבעה קלפים [כט] והניחם (ריח) בארבעה בתים יצא * והוא שיטלה (פי' יכסה) עור על ארבעה בתים שיהיו נראים כבית אחד: הגה (ריט) והמנהג לדבקם בדבק שיהא הכל כקלף אחד ויזהרו ליטול (רכ) דבק (סח) כשר׳ (ברוך שאמר ואגור סי' ג"ז): **מח** * [ח]אם צפה הבתים בזהב (רכא) או בעור בהמה טמאה פסולים: **מט** [ט]הלכה למשה מסיני שיהיו תפילין נתפרים (רכב) בגידי (סט) [ל] בהמה וחיה (רכג) טהורים [י]וטוב לתפור (רכד) בגידי שור: **נ** [כ]אין לקנות גידים מא"י משום (רכה) דחיישינן

ג הרא"ש בסדר ת"ה והמרדכי לדעת רש"י והר"י אלכסנדרני וספר א"ח ד שם ה מנחות ל"ד ו שם ז שם ח סנהדרין מ"ח ט שבת כ"ח וק"ח י שמושא רבא וכ"י וספר התרומה כ אגור בשם מהר"י מולין

שערי תשובה

מן המותר בפיך עיין שם: [כח] בביתה. עבה"ט וכתב בנו"ב מה"ת דאף שר"ת חולק וס"ל שתהיה שוכבת מ"מ א"ל להניח שתי זוגות תפילין דשאני סדר הנחתן דאיכא רב האי גאון וכמה גאונים דקיימי בשיטת ר"ת ע"ש. ואפשר לומר דבכאן אף לר"ת אין פסול בדיעבד בזה משא"כ לענין סדר הנחתם דודאי עכובא בדיעבד הוא אליבא דר"ת ולכן צריך לצאת דעתו בזה. ועוד נראה שהמנהג של ב' זוגות תפילין יש לו יסוד מונח עפ"י הזוהר וחכם הרזים האר"י ז"ל שאלו ואלו דא"ח ולכן החזיקו בזה כל יראי השם וחושבי שמו משא"כ בשאר מחלוקת הפוסקים כל דסוגיין דעלמא כחד מינייהו הנח להם לישראל כו'. ומי שרוצה להיות חכם בעיניו דעה האחרת ורוצה לצאת י"ח של דעה זו ע"ז אמרו כל המתיהר כו' ודי בזה: [כט] והניחם בד' בתים כו'. וכתב בבר"י בשם בית יהודה ח"ג סי' ע"ו דלאו דוקא הניחם בדיעבד אלא כיון שכתבו בד' קלפים חשוב דיעבד ומותר להניחם לכתחלה ע"ש. וכתב עוד שאם נמצא[א] בפרשה רביעית מותר לכותבה בקלף לבד דהוי כדיעבד ואם נכתבה פרשה אחת בש"ר שלא כסדר עיין שו"ת הר"ש בן הרשב"ץ סימן תרל"ב ע"ש: [ל] בהמה. עבה"ט ובנו"ב מ"ת[ב] ב' חולק ג"כ עליו וכתב שזה תלוי בטאלדורו"ש המבואר בסי'[ג] כ' וכיון שטאלדורו"ש אין הב"י מכשיר לכתחלה איך יוסיף להכשיר בני מעיים וע"ש שכתב בטאלדור"ש שהב"י מתיר בשעת הדחק ואני חושש אפילו בשעת הדחק שהרי הל"מ הוא גידין והטאלדורו"ש

באר היטב

בדיעבד אם אין לו אחרים ב"ח מ"א: (סו) לבתים. וטוב שיניח אצל פרשת והיה אם שמוע בצד הפונה לפרשת קדש של"ה עמ"א: (סז) בביתה. ובדיעבד אין לפסול בשביל זה ע"ת עמ"א: (סח) כשר. מבהמה טהורה: (סט) בהמה. ולוקחין מהעקב שהם לבנים ואם הם קשים מרככין באבנים עד שיעשו כפשתן וטוין אותם ושוזרין אותם

ביאור הלכה

בזה: * שתהא זקופה מעומד. עיין בשע"ת מה שכ' בשם הנוב"י דאין לחוש לשיטת ר"ת שפוסק דוקא בשכיבה וכן משמע בביאור הגר"א: * יהיה הגליון וכו' לצד פה הבתים. ואם היפך יש מאחרונים שפוסלין אף דיעבד: * אם כתבם וכו' והניחם בארבעה בתים וכו'. עיין בפמ"ג שכתב דלדעת המחבר אם הם כולם בבית אחד אפילו לכתחלה א"צ לדבק וע"ז הוסיף רמ"א וכתב והמנהג וכו' ר"ל דאפילו בבית אחד לכתחילה מצוה לדבקם: * והוא שיטלה עור. עיין בפמ"ג דיכסה בהעור גם על מקום השי"ן שלא יראה החוצה דאל"ה יש בו חשש בל תוסיף בהש"י דאין צריך לשי"ן: * ציפה הבתים וכו'. עיין במ"ב בשם הפמ"ג וכתב עוד הא עור כשר ע"ג עור כשר ושי"ן נראה כשר אע"פ שאין בית רואה אויר כיון שהשי"ן נראה ולפ"ז כ"ש אותן שעושין צבע עב שמלהיב תפילין דאין לחוש

משנה ברורה

לפרשת קדש: **מה** (ריג) זקופה. כדרך קריאתה וכדרך שמעמידין ס"ת בהיכל ובדיעבד אם נתנה שם מושכבת אין לפסול התפילין בשביל זה כ"כ הב"י בשם הר"י בן חביב וכ"כ הב"ח ועיין במ"א ונראה דמ"מ על להבא צריך לתקן דהיינו שיוציאם ויניחם כהלכה: **מו** (ריד) לצד פה. דאל"ה יעמדו האותיות הפוכות נגד הקורא: (רטו) כהלכתן. שהרי מלינו שסדר הנחתן בבתים ג"כ הם מסודרים לפני ימין הקורא אשר הוא עומד נגד המניח שיהיה קורא כסדר מתחלה פ' קדש של ימינו ואח"כ פ' והיה כ"י ושאר הפרשיות כמש"כ בסי' ל"ד ע"כ צריך להיות סוף הגלילה שהוא ראש הפרשה ג"כ מצד ימין נגדו: **מז** (רטז) אפי' אין וכו'. ר"ל וכ"ש כשיש ריוח בין הפרשיות שיוכל לחתכם וישתייר כדי היקף גויל לכל אחת דשפיר דמי אף דבעת הכתיבה כתבן בקלף אחד וכתבו האחרונים אע"ג דכשאין ריוח ביניהם יהיה מוכרח להניח כל פרשה בביתה שלא בזקיפה אפ"ה כשר כי הזקיפה אינה אלא למצוה [כן מתבאר הפירוש לפי מש"כ הב"י בשם מהרי"א ומהר"י בן חביב וכן הסכים הב"ח ועיין במ"א בשם הד"מ]: (ריז) או משיחה. ר"ל דכיון שכתב הפרשיות בעור אחד צריך להפסיק בחוט או משיחה או בגיד כמו שאנו נוהגין בין בית לבית כדי לתת היכר שהבתים מובדלים אבל בכתב הפרשיות על ד' עורות א"צ לתת כלום בין בית לבית ויש פוסקים דבכל גווני צריך לתת הבדל בין הבתים וכן יש לנהוג כמו שכתב המחבר לקמן בסעיף כ"א ויעביר חוט וכו' ומ"מ לענין דיעבד כתב הט"ז דאינו מעכב שם שהעיקר כסברא הראשונה: (ריח) בארבעה בתים. וכ"ש אם הניחם בבית אחד דעפי עדיף: (ריט) והמנהג וכו'. ר"ל אם הניחם בבית אחד אף דבודאי יצא מ"מ לכתחלה מצוה לדבקם. כתבו האחרונים דאף שלכתחלה מצוה לכתוב הד' פרשיות של יד בקלף אחד מ"מ אם כבר כתב בד' קלפים חשוב כדיעבד ומותר להניחם לכתחלה אם מדביקם מקודם ואם נמצא טעות בפרשה רביעית מותר לכותבה בקלף לבד אפילו לכתחלה ולהדביקה דזה הוי כדיעבד: (רכ) דבק כשר. ר"ל מבהמה טהורה. וכתב בפמ"ג דזה רק למצוה אבל לא לעיכובא כיון דהדיבוק אינו מעכב מתילא אין קפידא במה מדבק: **מח** (רכא) או בעור. פי' שעשה עור מתחלה מבהמה טהורה ואח"כ ציפה על אותו עור מבהמה טמאה אפ"ה פסולים ואפילו חוץ במקום השי"ן שהשי"ן נראה [פמ"ג] ועיין בבה"ל: **מט** (רכב) בגידי בהמה. ולוקחין מהעקב שהם לבנים ואם הם קשים מרככים באבנים עד שיעשו כפשתן וטווין אותם ושוזרין אותם ודעת המ"א בסוף ס"ק ס"ו דבעינן בזה הטוייה לשמה והא"ר ופמ"ג מפקפקין בזה: (רכג) טהורים. אפילו מנבילות וטריפות שלהם: (רכד) בגידי שור. ואם אין לו יקח מגידי בהמה דקה אבל מטמאה אפילו בדיעבד פסול וצ"ע אם מותר לתפור בגיד הנשה [אחרונים]: **נ** (רכה) דחיישינן וכו'. ודוקא (רע) כשהוא הולך לבתי הנכרים לקנות מהם גידין וגם ידוע לו שמקצת מן הנכרים הנוטלין הגידין מבהמה טמאה לכן אע"פ שהרוב נוטלין מטהורה כיון שהוא הולך אצל נכרי בשעה שהם קבועין בבתיהם אין הולכין אחר הרוב שכל קבוע כמחצה על מחצה דמי אבל אם העו"ג הביא לשוק מותר לקנות ממנו שכיון שפירש מקביעותו אמרינן כל דפריש מרובא פריש (רי) אם לא שמוכרין שם בשוק בחנויות אז הוזרין לקביעותן וכן אם אין ידוע שמקצתן

שער הציון

(רע) מ"א: (רי) פ"ח ומה"ש:

הגהות ותיקונים: א) חסר תיבת טעות: ב) סי': ג) בסעיף:

45. One should insert each passage in its housing so that it will stand (213) erect inside its housing.

46. The top margin should be /inserted/ first, since that is the first line, and the bottom margin /should be/ (214) towards the opening of the housing.

Gloss: The beginning of the passage should be lying on the right side of the reader, so that if he comes to open it and to read it it will be lying in front of him (215) *as required. (...)*

47. If one wrote all four passages /of the head *tefilin*/ on a single parchment, they are valid, (216) even if there is no space between them, provided there is a thread (217) or a string between each of the housings.

Mishnah Berurah

which faces /the housing of/ the passage *Kadesh Li Chal Bechor.*

(213) Erect. /I.e.,/ just as it is read and just as a Torah Scroll is stood in the Sanctuary.

Once it is after the event and one put in /a passage/ in a lying /position/, one should not invalidate the *tefilin* because of this. This is what the *B.Y.* writes in the name of the *Ri Ben Chaviv* and the *Bach* likewise writes this. See the *M.A.* It appears /to me/ that, nevertheless, one must remedy this for the future. I.e., one must take /the passage/ out and put it in as the halachah /demands/.

(214) Towards the opening. Otherwise, the letters will be standing upside-down opposite the reader.

(215) As required. For we find as regards the order in which /the passages/ are placed inside the housings as well, that they are arranged before the right of a reader who stands opposite the person who is donning them, so that he will /be able to/ read them in order. /I.e.,/ first the passage *Kadesh Li Chal Bechor* /appears/, which is on his right, and after that the passage *Ve-Hayah Ki Yevi'acha* and the other passages, as explained in Sec. 34. Consequently, the end of the rolled-up /parchment/, which is the beginning of the passage, must also be on the right side /of a reader who stands/ opposite /the donner/.

(216) Even if there is no, etc. What is meant by this is that it is certainly perfectly /in order/ if there is a /sufficiently large/ space between the passages for one to be able to cut them off with sufficient /blank/ parchment remaining to surround each one /of them/, although at the time of writing one wrote them on a single parchment.

The Acharonim write that although when there is no space between them one will be compelled to place each passage in its housing not erect, /the *tefilin*/ will nevertheless be valid. This is because the /need to insert them/ erect is merely a mitzvah /, but not an essential requirement/. [It follows that this is the explanation, from what the *B.Y.* writes in the name of the *Mahariya* and the *Mahariy ben Chaviv.* The *Bach* likewise agrees /with this/. See the *M.A.* in the name of the *D.M.*]

(217) Or a string. What is meant by this is that in view /of the fact/ that one wrote the passages on a single parchment, one is required to make an interruption of a thread, a string or a sinew, as is our practice, between one housing and the other, in order to provide an indication that the housings are divided. If, however, one wrote the passages on four /separate/ skins, it is unnecessary to put anything between one housing and the other.

There are /authorities/ who rule that it is necessary in all cases to make a division between the housings and that is how one should act. This accords with what the author /of the Shulchan Aruch/ writes below in Par. 51, "One should pass the ... thread, etc." Nevertheless, as regards /the ruling/ once it is after the event, the *Taz* writes that /a thread, etc./ there is not essential /for validity/ as the prevailing /view/ is the first opinion.

(סו) לבתים: מה ׳יתן כל פרשה בבית שלה * שתהא (ריג) זקופה מעומד (סז) [כח] בביתה: מו * ׳יהיה הגליון עליון תחלה שזהו שורה עליונה וגליון תחתון (ריד) לצד פה הבתים: הגה ורחש הפרשה יהיה מונח נגד ימין הקורא שאם בא לפתחן ולקורא יהיו מונחים לפניו (רטו) כהלכתן: (תרומת הדשן ובית יוסף בשם אורחות חיים): מז ׳אם כתב כל הארבעה פרשיות בקלף אחד כשרים (רטז) אפילו אין ריוח ביניהם ובלבד שיהא חוט (ריז) או משיחה בין כל בית ובית. ׳של יד כותב הארבעה פרשיות בקלף א׳ וגולל אותן מסופן לתחלתן וכורך קלף עליהם ושער עגל ומכניסן בביתם כמו של ראש. * ׳אם כתבם על ארבעה קלפים [כט] והניחם (ריח) בארבעה בתים יצא * והוא שיטלה (פי׳ יכסה) עור על ארבעה בתים שיהיו נראים כבית אחד: הגה (ריט) והמנהג לדבקם בדבק שיהא הכל כקלף אחד ויזהרו ליטול (רכ) דבק (סח) כשר* (ברוך שאמר ואגור סי׳ נ״ז): מח * ׳אם צפה הבתים בזהב (רכא) או בעור בהמה טמאה פסולים: מט ׳הלכה למשה מסיני שיהיו תפילין נתפרים (רכב) בגידי (סט) [ל] בהמה וחיה (רכג) טהורים ׳וטוב לתפור (רכד) בגידי שור: נ ׳אין לקנות גידים מא״י משום (רכה) דחיישינן

ג הרא״ש בסדר ת״ת והמרדכי לדעת רש״י והר״י אלכסנדרני וספר א״ח ד שם ה מנחות ל״ד ו שם ז שם ח סנהדרין מ״ח ט שבת כ״ח וק״ח י שמושא רבא וג״י וספר התרומה כ אגור בשם מהר״י מולין

שערי תשובה

מן המותר בפיך עיין שם: [כח] בביתה. עבה״ט וכתב בנו״ב מה״ת דאף שר״ת חולק וס״ל שתהיה שוכבת מ״מ א״ל להניח שתי זוגות תפילין דשאני סדר הנחתן דאיכא רב האי גאון וכמה גאונים דקיימי בשיטת ר״ת ע״ש. ואפשר לומר דכאן אף לר״ת אין פסול בדיעבד בזה משא״כ לענין סדר הנחתם דודאי עכובא בדיעבד הוא אליבא דר״ת ולכן צריך לצאת דעתו בזה. ועוד נראה שהמנהג של ב׳ זוגות תפילין יש לו יסוד מונח עפ״י הזוהר וחכם הרזים האר״י ז״ל שאלו ואלו דא״ח ולכן החזיקו בזה כל יראי השם וחושבי שמו משא״כ בשאר מחלוקת הפוסקים כל דסוגיין דעלמא כחד מינייהו הנח להם לישראל כו׳. ומי שרוצה להיות חכם בעיניו דעה האחרת ורוצה לצאת י״ח של דעה זו ע״ז אמרו כל המתיהר כו׳ ודי בזה: [כט] והניחם בד׳ בתים כו׳. וכתב בבר״י בשם בית יהודה ח״ג סי׳ ע״ו דלאו דוקא הניחם בדיעבד אלא כיון שכתבו בד׳ קלפים חשוב דיעבד ומותר להניחם לכתחלה ע״ש. וכתב עוד שאם נמצא[א] בפרשה רביעית מותר לכותבה בקלף לבד דהוי כדיעבד ואם נכתבה פרשה אחת בש״ר שלא כסדר עיין שו״ת הר״ש בן הרשב״ץ סימן תרל״ב ע״ש: [ל] בהמה. עבה״ט ובנו״ב מ״ת[ב] ב׳ חולק ג״כ עליו וכתב שזה תלוי בטאלדורו״ש המבואר בסי׳[ג] כ׳ וכיון שטאלדורו״ש אין הב״י מכשיר לכתחלה איך יוסיף להכשיר בני מעיים וע״ש שכתב בטאלדור״ש שהב״י מתיר בשעת הדחק ואני חושש אפילו בשעת הדחק שהרי הל״מ הוא גידין והטאלדורו״ש

באר היטב

בדיעבד אם אין לו אחרים ב״ח מ״א: (סו) לבתים. וטוב שיניח אלא פרשת והיה אם שמוע בצד הפונה לפרשת קדש של״ה עמ״א: (סז) בביתה. ובדיעבד אין לפסול בשביל זה ע״ת עמ״א: (סח) כשר. מבהמה טהורה: (סט) בהמה. ולוקחין מהעקב שהם לבנים ואם הם קשים מרככין באבנים עד שיעשו כפשתן וטווין אותם ושוזרין אותם

ביאור הלכה

בזה: * שתהא זקופה מעומד. עיין בשע״ת מה שכ׳ בשם הנוב״י דאין לחוש לשיטת ר״ת שפוסק דוקא בשכיבה וכן משמע בביאור הגר״א: * יהיה הגליון וכו׳ לצד פה הבתים. ואם היפך יש מאחרונים שפוסלין אף דיעבד: * אם כתבם וכו׳ והניחם בארבעה בתים וכו׳. עיין בפמ״ג שכתב דלדעת המחבר אם הם כולם בבית אחד אפילו לכתחלה א״צ לדבק וע״ז הוסיף רמ״א וכתב והמנהג וכו׳ ר״ל דאפילו בבית אחד לכתחילה מצוה לדבקם: * והוא שיטלה עור. עיין בפמ״ג דיכסה בהעור גם על מקום השי״ן שלא יראה החוצה דאל״ה יש בו חשש בל תוסיף בהש״י דאין צריך לשי״ן: * ציפה הבתים וכו׳. עיין במ״ב בשם הפמ״ג וכתב עוד הא עור כשר ע״ג עור כשר ושי״ן נראה כשר אע״פ שאין בית רואה אויר כיון שהשי״ן נראה ולפ״ז כ״ש אותן שעושין צבע עב שמצהיב תפילין דאין לחוש

משנה ברורה

לפרשת קדש: מה (ריג) זקופה. כדרך קריאתה וכדרך שמעמידין ס״ת בהיכל ובדיעבד אם נתנה שם מושכבת אין לפסול התפילין בשביל זה כ״כ הב״י בשם הר״י בן חביב וכ״כ הב״ח ועיין במ״א ונראה דמ״מ על להבא צריך לתקן דהיינו שיוציאם ויניחם כהלכה: מו (ריד) לצד פה. דאל״ה יעמדו האותיות הפוכות נגד הקורא: (רטו) כהלכתן. שהרי מלינו שסדר הנחתן בבתים ג״כ הם מסודרים לפני ימין הקורא אשר הוא עומד נגד המניח שיהיה קורא כסדר מתחלה פ׳ קדש של ימינו ואח״כ פ׳ והיה כי יביאך ושאר הפרשיות כמש״כ בסי׳ ל״ד ע״כ צריך להיות סוף הגלילה שהוא ראש הפרשה ג״כ מצד ימין נגדו: מז (רטז) אפי׳ אין וכו׳. ר״ל וכ״ש כשיש ריוח בין הפרשיות שיוכל לחתכם ויתחייר כדי שיקף גויל לכל אחת דשפיר דמי אף דבעת הכתיבה כתבן בקלף אחד וכתבו האחרונים אע״ג דכשאין ריוח ביניהם יהיה מוכרח להניח כל פרשה בביתה שלא מוקיפה אפ״ה כשר כי הזקיפה אינה אלא למצוה [כן מתבאר הפירוש לפי מש״כ הב״י בשם מהרי״א ומהר״י בן חביב וכן הסכים הב״ח ועיין במ״א בשם הד״מ]: (ריז) או משיחה. ר״ל דכיון שכתב הפרשיות בעור אחד צריך להפסיק בחוט או משיחה או בגיד כמו שאנו נוהגין בין בית לבית כדי לתת היכר שהבתים מובדלים אבל בכתב הפרשיות על ד׳ עורות א״צ לתת כלום בין בית לבית ויש פוסקים דבכל גווני צריך לתת הבדל בין הבתים וכן יש לנהוג כמו שכתב המחבר לקמן בסעיף נ״ח ויעביר חוט וכו׳ ומ״מ לענין דיעבד כתב הט״ז דאינו מעכב שם שהעיקר כסברא הראשונה: (ריח) בארבעה בתים. וכ״ש אם הניחם בבית אחד דטפי עדיף: (ריט) והמנהג וכו׳. ר״ל אם הניחם בבית אחד אף דבודאי יצא מ״מ לכתחלה מצוה לדבקם. כתבו האחרונים דאף שלכתחלה מצוה לכתוב הד׳ פרשיות של יד בקלף אחד מ״מ אם כבר כתב בד׳ קלפים חשוב כדיעבד ומותר להניחם לכתחלה אם מדביקם מקודם ואם נמצא טעות בפרשה רביעית מותר לכותבה בקלף לבד אפילו לכתחלה והדביקה דזה הוי כדיעבד: (רכ) דבק כשר. ר״ל מבהמה טהורה.* וכתב בפמ״ג דזה רק למצוה אבל לא לעיכובא כיון דהדיבוק אינו מעכב ממילא אין קפידא במה מדבק: מח (רכא) או בעור. פי׳ שעשה עור מתחלה מבהמה טהורה ואח״כ ליפה על אותו עור מבהמה טמאה אפ״ה פסולים ואפילו חתך במקום השי״ן שהשי״ן נראה [פמ״ג] ועיין בבה״ל: מט (רכב) בגידי בהמה. ולוקחין מהעקב שהם לבנים ואם הם קשים מרככים באבנים עד שיעשו כפשתן וטווין אותם ושוזרין אותם ודעת המ״א בסוף ס״ק ס״ו דבעינן בזה הטוייה לשמה והא״ר ופמ״ג מפקפקין בזה: (רכג) טהורים. אפילו מנבילות וטריפות שלהם: (רכד) בגידי שור. ואם אין לו יקח מגידי בהמה דקה אבל מנבלות אפילו בדיעבד פסול וכ״ע אם מותר לתפור בגיד הנשה [אחרונים]: נ (רכה) דחיישינן וכו׳. ודוקא (רכו) כשהוא הולך לבתי הנכרים לקנות מהם גידין וגם ידוע לו שמקצת מן הנכרים הנותנין הגידין מבהמה טמאה לכן אע״פ שהרוב נוטלין מטהורה כיון שהוא הולך אצל נכרי בשעה שהם קבועין בבתיהם אין הולכין אחר הרוב שכל קבוע כמחצה על מחצה דמי אבל אם הנכרי הביא לשוק מותר לקנות ממנו שכיון שפירש מקביעותו אמרינן כל דפריש מרובא פריש (רי) אם לא שמוכרין שם בשוק בחנויות או חוזרין לקביעותן וכן אם אין ידוע שמקצתן

שער הציון

(רט) מ״א: (רי) פ״ח ומה״ש:

הגהות ותיקונים: א) חסר תיבת טעות: ב) סי׳: ג) בסעיף:

For the arm /*tefilin*/, one should write the four passages on a single parchment. One should roll them up from the end to the beginning, wrap parchment over them and /wind/ calf hair /around them/ and insert them inside their housing, as /one does in the case/ of the head /*tefilin*/. If one wrote them on four parchments and placed them **(218)** in four housings he will have fulfilled /halachic requirements/, provided that he covered *(...)* over the four housings with skin, so that they appear like a single housing. 31*

Gloss: **(219)** *The practice is to stick them /together/ with glue so that they are all like a single parchment. One must be careful to take* **(220)** *kosher glue /for the purpose/. (...)*

48. If one overlaid the housings with gold **(221)** or with the skin of an unclean animal, they are invalid.

49. A halachah /was taught/ to Mosheh (Moses) on /Mount/ Sinai, /requiring/ the *tefilin* to be sewn **(222)** with the sinews of a **(223)** /halachically/

Mishnah Berurah

(218) In four housings. One certainly /fulfils halachic requirements/ if he places them in a single housing, which is more preferred.

(219) The practice, etc. I.e., if one places them in a single housing. Although he will definitely have fulfilled /halachic requirements in any case/, it is nevertheless a mitzvah, initially, to stick them /together/.

The Acharonim write that although, initially, it is a mitzvah to write the four passages of the arm /*tefilin*/ on a single parchment, if one already wrote them on four parchments this is at any rate considered as after the event. It is /therefore/ permitted /for one/ to put them /in the housing/ initially /in such a case/, provided he sticks them /together/ beforehand.

If one finds an error in the fourth passage, it is permitted to write /that passage/ on a parchment by itself even initially, and stick it /to the rest/, as this is /also regarded/ as /a situation/ where it is after the event.

(220) Kosher glue. I.e., /glue/ from a /halachically/ clean animal.

The *P.Mg.* writes that this is only a mitzvah /requirement/, but is not a preclusive /condition for the validity of the *tefilin*/. For it follows from /the fact/ that the sticking /itself/ is not a preclusive /requirement/, that there /can be/ no insistence as regards what /one uses/ for the sticking.

(221) Or with the skin. I.e., if one first prepared skin from a /halachically/ clean animal and subsequently overlaid that skin with /the skin/ of an unclean animal, /the housings/ are nevertheless invalid. /This applies/ even if one cut out /the invalid covering/ over the area of the ש /letters/, so that the ש /letters/ are visible. [*P.Mg.*] See the Beyur Halachah.[44]

(222) With the sinews of a ... animal, domestic. /It is the practice/ to take /sinews/ from the heel, as they are white. If they are hard, they are softened with stones until they become like linen. They should be spun and intertwined. In the opinion of the *M.A.*, /stated/ at the end of sub-Par. 66, this spinning is required /to be done/ for the sake of /use for the mitzvah/. The *E.R.* and the *P.Mg.* query this.

(223) /Halachically/ clean. /The sinews may/ even /be taken/ from a *neveylah*[11*] or a *tereyfah*[11*] /of such an animal/.

31* If there is a letter ש on the four housings, it must also be covered over with skin. (Beyur Halachah)

44 It is stated there that if one overlaid the housings with valid skin leaving the letter ש visible, the *tefilin* are valid.

ג הרא״ש בסדר ת״ה והמרדכי לדעת רש״י והר״י אלכסנדרני וספר א״ח ד שם ה מנחות ל״ד ו שם ז שם ח סנהדרין מ״ח ט שבת כ״ח וק״ח י שמושא רבא ונ״י וספר התרומה כ באגור בשם מהר״י מולין

(סו) לבתים: מה [ג] יתן כל פרשה בבית שלה * שתהא (ריג) זקופה מעומד (סז) [כח] בביתה: מו * [ד] יהיה הגליון עליון תחלה שזהו שורה עליונה וגליון תחתון (ריד) לצד פה הבתים: הגה וראש הפרשה יהיה מונח נגד ימין הקורא שאם בא לפתחן ולקוראן יהיו מונחים לפניו (רטו) כהלכתן: (תרומת הדשן ומ״ת יוסף בשם אורחות חיים): מז [ה] אם כתב כל הארבעה פרשיות בקלף אחד כשרים (רטז) אפילו אין ריוח ביניהם ובלבד שיהא חוט (ריז) או משיחה בין כל בית ובית. [ו] של יד כותב הארבעה פרשיות בקלף א׳ וגולל אותן מסופן לתחלתן וכורך קלף עליהם ושער עגל ומכניסן בביתם כמו של ראש. * [ז] אם כתבם על ארבעה קלפים [כט] והניחם (ריח) בארבעה בתים יצא * והוא שיטלה (פי׳ יכסה) עור על ארבעה בתים שיהיו נראים כבית אחד: הגה (ריט) והמנהג לדבקם בדבק שיהא הכל כקלף אחד ויזהרו ליטול (רכ) דבק (סח) כשר (ברוך שאמר ואגור סי׳ נ״ז): מח * [ח] אם צפה הבתים בזהב (רכא) או בעור בהמה טמאה פסולים: מט [ט] הלכה למשה מסיני שיהיו תפילין נתפרים (רכב) בגידי (סט) [ל] **בהמה וחיה** (רכג) **טהורים** [י] **וטוב לתפור** (רכד) **בגידי שור: נ** [כ] **אין לקנות גידים מא״י משום** (רכה) **דחיישינן**

שערי תשובה

מן המותר בפיך עיין שם: [כח] בביתה. עבה״ט וכתב בנו״ב מה״ת דאף שר״ת חולק וס״ל שתהיה שוכבת מ״מ א״צ להניח שתי זוגות תפילין דשאני סדר הנחתן דאיכא רב האי גאון וכמה גאונים דקיימי בשיטת ר״ת ע״ש. ואפשר לומר דכאן אף לר״ת אין פסול בדיעבד בזה משא״כ לענין סדר הנחתם דודאי עכובא בדיעבד הוא אליבא דר״ת ולכן צריך לצאת דעתו בזה. ועוד נראה שהמנהג של ב׳ זוגות תפילין יש לו יסוד מונח עפ״י הזוהר וחכם הרזים האר״י ז״ל שאלו ואלו דא״ח ולכן החזיקו בזה כל יראי השם וחושבי שמו משא״כ בשאר מחלוקת הפוסקים כל דסוגיין דעלמא כחד מינייהו הנח להם לישראל כו׳. ומי שרוצה להיות חכם בעיניו דעה האחרת ורוצה לצאת י״ח של דעה זו ע״ז אמרו כל המתיהר כו׳ ודי בזה: [כט] והניחם בד׳ בתים כו׳. וכתב בבר״י בשם בית יהודה ח״ג סי׳ ע״ו דלאו דוקא הניחם בדיעבד אלא כיון שכתבו בד׳ קלפים חשוב דיעבד ומותר להניחם לכתחלה ע״ש. וכתב עוד שאם נמצא[א] בפרשה רביעית מותר לכותבה בקלף לבד דהוי כדיעבד ואם נכתבה פרשה אחת בש״ר שלא כסדר עיין שו״ת הר״ש בן הרשב״ץ סימן תרל״ב ע״ש: [ל] בהמה. עבה״ט ובנו״ב מ״ת[ב] ב׳ חולק ג״כ עליו וכתב שזה תלוי בטאלדורו״ש המבואר בסי׳[ג] כ׳ וכיון שטאלדורו״ש אין הב״י מכשיר לכתחלה איך יוסיף להכשיר בני מעיים וע״ש שכתב בטאלדור״ש שהב״י מתיר בשעת הדחק ואני חושש אפילו בשעת הדחק שהרי הל״מ הוא גידין והטאלדורו״ש

באר היטב

בדיעבד אם אין לו אחרים ב״ח מ״א: (סו) לבתים. וטוב שיניח אצל פרשת והיה אם שמוע בצד הפונה לפרשת קדש של״ה עמ״א: (סז) בביתה. ובדיעבד אין לפסול בשביל זה ע״ת עמ״א: (סח) כשר. מבהמה טהורה: (סט) בהמה. ולוקחין מהעקב שהם לבנים ואם הם קשים מרככין באבנים עד שיעשו כפשתן וטווין אותם ושוזרין אותם

ביאור הלכה

בזה: * שתהא זקופה מעומד. עיין בשע״ת מה שכ׳ בשם הנו״ב דאין לחוש לשיטת ר״ת שפוסק דוקא בשכיבה וכן משמע בביאור הגר״א: * **יהיה הגליון וכו׳ לצד פה הבתים.** ואם היפך יש מאחרונים שפוסלין אף דיעבד: * **אם כתבם וכו׳ והניחם בארבעה בתים וכו׳.** עיין בפמ״ג שכתב דלדעת המחבר אם הם כולם בבית אחד אפילו לכתחלה א״צ לדבק וע״ז הוסיף רמ״א וכתב והמנהג וכו׳ ר״ל דאפילו בבית אחד לכתחילה מצוה לדבקם: * **והוא שיטלה עור.** עיין בפמ״ג דיכסה בהעור גם על מקום השי״ן שלא יראה החוצה דאל״ה יש בו חשש בל תוסיף בהש״י דאין צריך לשי״ן: * **ציפה הבתים וכו׳.** עיין במ״ב בשם הפמ״ג וכתב עוד הא עור כשר ע״ג עור כשר ושי״ן נראה כשר אע״פ שאין בית רואה אויר כיון שהשי״ן נראה ולפ״ז כ״ש אותן שעושין צבע עם שמלהיב תפילין דאין לחוש

משנה ברורה

לפרשת קדש: מה (ריג) זקופה. כדרך קריאתה וכדרך שמעמידין ס״ת בהיכל ובדיעבד אם נתנה שם מושכבת אין לפסול התפילין בשביל זה כ״כ הב״י בשם הר״י בן חביב וכ״כ הב״ח ועיין במ״א ונראה דמ״מ על להבא צריך לתקן דהיינו שיוציאם ויניחם כהלכה: מו (ריד) לצד פה. דאל״ה יעמדו האותיות הפוכות נגד הקורא: (רטו) כהלכתן. שהרי מצינו שסדר הנחתן בבתים ג״כ הם מסודרים לפני ימין הקורא אשר הוא עומד נגד המניח שיהיה קורא כסדר מתחלה פ׳ קדש של ימינו ואח״כ פ׳ והיה כ״י ושאר הפרשיות כמש״כ בסי׳ ל״ד ע״כ צריך להיות סוף הגלילה שהוא ראש הפרשה ג״כ מצד ימין נגדו: מז (רטז) אפי׳ אין וכו׳. ר״ל וכ״ש כשיש ריוח בין הפרשיות שיוכל לחתכם וישייר כדי היקף גויל לכל אחת דשפיר דמי אף לדעת הכמיבה כתבן בקלף אחד וכתבו האחרונים אע״ג דכשאין ריוח ביניהם יהיה מוכרח להניח כל פרשה בביתה שלא בזקיפה אפ״ה כשר כי הזקיפה אינה אלא למצוה [כן מתבאר הפירוש לפי מש״כ הב״י בשם מהרי״א ומהר״י בן חביב וכן הסכים הב״ח ועיין במ״א בשם הד״מ]: (ריז) או משיחה. ר״ל דכיון שכתב הפרשיות בעור אחד צריך להפסיק בחוט או משיחה או בגיד כמו שאנו נוהגין בין בית לבית כדי לתת היכר שהבתים מובדלים אבל בכתב הפרשיות על ד׳ עורות א״צ לתת כלום בין בית לבית ויש פוסקים דבכל גווני צריך לתת הבדל בין הבתים וכן יש לנהוג כמו שכתב המחבר לקמן בסעיף כ״ח ויעביר חוט וכו׳ ומ״מ לענין דיעבד כתב הט״ז דאינו מעכב שם שהעיקר כסברא הראשונה: (ריח) בארבעה בתים. וכ״ש אם הניחם בבית אחד דעדיף: (ריט) והמנהג וכו׳. ר״ל אם הניחם בבית אחד אף דבודאי יצא מ״מ לכתחלה מצוה לדבקם. כתבו האחרונים דאף שלכתחלה מצוה לכתוב הד׳ פרשיות של יד בקלף אחד מ״מ אם כבר כתב בד׳ קלפים חשוב כדיעבד ומותר להניחם לכתחלה אם מדקדק מקודם ואם נמצא טעות בפרשה רביעית מותר לכותבה בקלף לבד אפילו לכתחלה והדביקה דוה הוי כדיעבד: (רכ) דבק כשר. ר״ל מבהמה טהורה. וכתב בפמ״ג דזה רק למצוה אבל לא לעיכובא כיון דהדיבוק אינו מעכב ממילא אין קפידא במה מדבק: מח (רכא) או בעור. פי׳ שעשה עור מתחלה מבהמה טהורה ואח״כ ליפה על אותו עור מבהמה טמאה אפ״ה פסולים ואפילו אתך במקום השי״ן שהשי״ן נראה [פמ״ג] ועיין בבה״ל: מט (רכב) בגידי בהמה. ולוקחין מהעקב שהם לבנים ואם הם קשים מרככים באבנים עד שיעשו כפשתן וטווין אותם ושוזרין אותם ודעת המ״א בסוף ס״ק ס״ו דבעינן בזה הטויה לשמה והא״ר ופמ״ג מפקפקין בזה: (רכג) טהורים. אפילו מנבלות וטריפות שלהם: **(רכד) בגידי שור. ואם אין לו יקח מגידי בהמה דקה אבל מטמאה אפילו בדיעבד פסול וצ״ע אם מותר לתפור בגיד הנשה [אחרונים]: נ (רכה) דחיישינן וכו׳. ודוקא (רט) כשהוא הולך לבתי הנכרים לקנות מהם גידין וגם ידוע לו שמקצת מן הנכרים הנוטלין הגידין מבהמה טמאה לכן אע״פ שהרוב נוטלין מטהורה כיון שהוא הולך אצל נכרי בשעה שהם קבועין בבתיהם אין הולכין אחר הרוב שכל קבוע כמחצה על מחצה דמי אבל אם העו״ג הביא לשוק מותר לקנות ממנו שכיון שפירש מקביעותו אמרינן כל דפריש מרובא פריש (רי) אם לא שמוכרין שם בשוק בחנויות אז חוזרין לקביעותן וכן אם אין ידוע שמקצתן**

שער הציון

(רט) מ״א: (רי) פ״ח ומה״ש:

הגהות ותיקונים: א) חסר תיבת טעות: **ב)** סי׳: **ג)** בסעיף:

clean animal, domestic or non-domestic. It is desirable to sew /the *tefilin*/ **(224)** with the sinews of a bull.

50. One should not buy sinews /for *tefilin*/ from a non-Jew, because **(225)** we are afraid that they may be from an unclean animal.

Mishnah Berurah

(224) With the sinews of a bull. If one does not have /the sinews of a bull/ he should take the sinews of a small animal. However, /the sinews/ of an unclean animal are /ruled as/ invalid /for this purpose/ even once it is after the event.

Study is required to determine whether /or not/ it is permitted to sew with the sinew of the sciatic nerve.[45] [Acharonim]

(225) We are afraid, etc. This only /applies/ if one goes to non-Jewish houses to buy sinews from them and he also knows that some of the non-Jews take sinews from unclean animals. In view of /these facts/, even if the majority take them from /halachically/ clean /animals/, we do not go according to what the majority /of sinews/ are /to regard the sinews as being from a halachically clean animal/. /This is/ because he goes to the non-Jew when /the non-Jews/ are in a "fixed"[46] /position/ in their homes /and we rule that/ whenever /the doubt relates to what is taken from/ a "fixed" /group, we regard the possibilities/ as equal.

However, if the non-Jew brings /sinews/ to the marketplace, it is /then/ permitted to buy them from him. For in view /of the fact/ that /the non-Jew/ separated from his "fixed" /position/, we assume that whoever separated /from his fixed position/ separated[47] from the majority /who take the sinews from halachically clean animals/. There is an exception /to this rule/, where they sell /the sinews/ in the marketplace in shops, as then they return to a "fixed" /position/.

Likewise, if it is not known that some of

45 This sinew is forbidden to be eaten. Consequently, it may be forbidden to use it for the sewing. See Par. 12.

46 I.e., both those that take them from halachically clean animals and those that take them from unclean animals are in a fixed and known position, so that the doubt relates to the fixed position from which the sinews were taken.

47 In such a case we begin to consider the doubt in the marketplace, when the seller of the sinews already separated from his fixed position. Then the doubt relates to the seller only, whether he is of the majority or not. We assume that he belongs to the majority.

שמא של בהמה טמאה הם. * ל מקום שאין גידין מצויים תופרים (רכו) בטאליאדור"ש שעושים מן הקלף (רכז) עד שיזדמנו להם גידים: **נא** * מ יתפור שלשה תפירות (רכח) בכל (ע) [לא] צד ג וחוט התפירה יהיה סובב (רכט) משתי רוחות ס ויעביר חוט התפירה בין כל בית ובית: הגה (רל) מיהו אם לא עשה רק י' תפירות או פחות מזה אינו נפסל (מרדכי) ע ויש מי שאומר שי"ב תפירות אלו יהיו (עא) (רלא) בחוט אחד: **נב** פ יכניס הרצועה תוך המעברתא (רלב) * ויעשה קשר (רלג) כמין דלי"ת בשל ראש וכמין יו"ד בשל יד להשלים אותיות שד"י עם השי"ן שבשל ראש: הגה ונוהגים (רלד) להעביר עור על הבית של יד לרוחב הזרוע ויהיה דמנו כרוחב הבית (טור) ולא יעשה הקשרים (רלה) אלא לאחר שעשה השי"ן מתפילין ואח"כ יעשה הדלי"ת ואח"כ היו"ד כסדר אותיות השם:

באר הגולה

ל העיטור מ שימושא רבא נ הרמב"ם והרא"ש לפי' השימושא רבא ס תוס' במנחות ל"ד והרא"ש והמרדכי ע הר"י אכסנדרני פ מנחות ל"ה בפירוש רש"י

באר היטב

מ"א. בני מעיים דקים ויבשים כמין חוטים של גידים גידים גמורים הם ומותר לתפור בהם ס"ת ותו"מ הלק"ט ח"א סימן רע"ג והיד אהרן חולק עליו: (ע) לד. טעם לי"ב תפירות נגד שבטי ישראל ואם עשה י"ד נגד מנשה ואפרים טוב עיין ע"ת והאר"י ז"ל כתב ע"פ הסוד דוקא י"ב. הרמ"ע מפאנו סימן ל"ח כתב אם אין התפירה בתוך הבית רק בתוך המעברתא פסול אבל בב"י בשם הרא"ש ורש"י והמרדכי משמע דלא בעי תפירה תוך הבית רק סמוך לבית ע"ש מ"א: (עא) בחוט א'. ואם נפסק החוט בשעת עשיה פסולות דבעי שיהא חוט א' ב"י בשם הריא"ס. וכתב ט"ז דלא בא למעט אם חזר וקשר במקום הפסיקה אלא שיהא בדיבוק יחד ולא נפסק ביניהם. וכתב ב"ח דוקא אם נפסק החוט פסול דניכר שפסק החוט אבל אם החוט קלר יגמור התפירה בחוט אחר לכתחלה והכי נהוג:

שערי תשובה

עור הוא שהוא הקלף ועור לתפירה לא שמענו וכו'. וע"ש שהעלה שאין לתפור בגידי עוף טהור כי מי יכריע איזה מהם קרוי גידין ואיזה מהם חוטי' ואיזה מהם ורידין ואיזה מהם מיתרים ולכן אין היתר לקחת גידי עוף לתפילין ע"ש: [לא] לד. עבה"ט וכו' עיין בבר"י שמ"כ לאחד קדוש מה שרוב העולם אין בתפיליהם חריצים עד למטה ולא חוט התפירה עובר בין בית לבית ושמעתי שהטעם שע"י החריצים מתקלקל רבועם ובפרט אם חוט התפירה עובר שגם הוא מפריד רבועם ברוב הימים ומה גם אם הם במקום חם ושרב והרבוע הל"מ והחריצים פלוגתא דאמוראי ופוק חזי מעמא[א] דבר. ואפשר שסמכו על סמ"ק שכתב דוקא כשכתב על קלף א' אבל על ד' קלפים א"ל וע"ש וכתב עוד בבר"י שבבית דוד סי' כ"ח למד זכות על הסופרים שנהגו לעשות הבית ש"ר בלי חריץ רק רשימה כל דהו. ונחלקו עליו רבני הדור כאשר נדפס בח"ב מכנה"ג ח"מ אחר סי' רפ"ט ובכהונת עולם ע"ש. ועיין בבגדי כהונה סי' א' שכתב ג"כ דאם אין חריצים רק שעושים רושם שהרואה יסבור שהם חריצים פסולים. כי לכל הדיעות צריך הבדל מעט בין הבתים שיהיה החריצים ניכרים ממש:

משנה ברורה

שמקלתן נוטלין אותן מבהמה טמאה ג"כ מותר לקנות מהם בכל ענין שרוב גידין הם מבהמות טהורות אך כ"ז בגידין שאינן טויין אבל בגידין טויין דעת המ"א דאסור לקנות מהם אפילו הוא יודע שהם מבהמה טהורה שכיון שהוא הלמ"מ צריך שתהיה עשייתן לשמה וטויית הגידין זו היא עשייתן ונכרים לאו בני לשמה נינהו וכבר כתבנו דהא"ר ופמ"ג מפקפקים אי בעי כלל בזה טוייה לשמה: (רכו) בטאליאדור"ש. הם חוטין הנעשים מן הקלף ובמקום הדחק ס"ל כיון דמינו הוא הם כגידין עלמן וכשרים לתפור בהם סת"ס: (רכז) עד שיזדמנו. כדי שלא להתבטל ממלות תפילין וכשיזדמן לו גידים יתירם ויתפור בגידים ויש מאחרונים (ריא) שחוששין שלא ללאת בהם אפילו בשעת הדחק שהרי הלמ"מ הוא גידין והטאליאדור"ש עור הוא שהוא הקלף ועור לתפירה לא שמענו ולפי"ז (ריב) אם אין לו גידים אחרים עכ"פ לא יברך עליהם וכן בני מעיים דקים ויבשים כמין חוטים של גידים אין לתפור בהם דהלמ"מ הוא דוקא גידים (ריג) עוד כתבו שאין לתפור בגידי עוף טהור כי מי יכריע איזה מהם קרוי גידין ואיזה מהם חוטין ואיזה מהם ורידין ואנן גידין בעינן: **נא** (רכח) בכל צד. טעם לי"ב תפירות נגד י"ב שבטי ישראל ולא בעינן תפירה תוך הבית (ריד) רק סמוך להבית (רטו) ואין תופרין כתופר בגדים בשפת הבגד בלי שיור אלא משייר מן התיתורא חוץ להתפירה (רטז) וצריך שעור הבתים מלמטה לפיו יהיו יוצאים מכל ארבע רוחותיהם עד שיהיו מגיעים תחת נקבי התפירה כדי שיתפור עור הבתים מכל צד עם התיתורא ולא כהסופרים המקלרין עור של הבתים שאינו עובר הלאה תחת נקבי התפירה ואינה נתפרת כלל עם התיתורא רק שמדבקין הבית בתוך הארובה של התיתורא והברוך שאמר כתב שפסל כמה תפילין מחמת זה אלא צריך לתפור יחד העור של הבתים עם התיתורא: (רכט) משתי רוחות. ר"ל שכל התפירה יהא מסובבת משני לדדין פנים ואחור (ריז) נמלא תופר בב' מחטין אחת יוצאה לאחור ואחת נכנסת לגד פנים: (רל) מיהו אם וכו'. וכן (ריח) אם לא העביר חוט התפירה אינו מעכב בדיעבד ועיין לעיל בס"ק רי"ז: (רלא) בחוט אחד. ואם נפסק (ריט) י"א דיכול לקושרו (רכ) וי"א דיטלנו כולו משם ויחזור ויתפור מחדש בחוט אחר שכיון שנפסק בשעת התפירה ניכר שהחוט קלוש ועומד ליפסק ואינו כלום אבל כשהחוט קלר מתחלתו ואינו נפסק לכו"ע יכול (רכא) לקשור לו חוט אחר לגמור התפירה וכתב הפמ"ג דאם אין לו גידין אחרים יש לסמוך על סברה הראשונה ולקשור חוט שנפסק וכ"ז (רכב) אם נפסק באמצע התפירה אבל אם נפסק אחר התפירה עיין לקמן סימן ל"ג ס"ג: **נב** (רלב) ויעשה קשר. וקשר של תפילין (רכג) הוא הלכה למשה מסיני ונראה שצריך לעשותו לשמה ולא יעשהו קטן [פמ"ג]: (רלג) כמין ד'. ויש שעושין קשר כמ"ם סתומה שנראה כשני דלתי"ן משני לדדין רגלו של זה בצד ראשו של זה ועיין בספר תפארת אריה שהביא בשם תשובה מאהבה והסכים עמו לדינא דאלו העושים קשר של דלי"ת מכוון יותר לדינא. גם לא יעשה קשר העשוי להשמט אנה ואנה כמו שביארתי בבה"ל. כתב א"ר מעשה באחד שראה אחר תליית התפילין שהותר הקשר ש"י והוריתי לחזור ולהניחן ולקרות ק"ש בלי ברכה דהא מלות תפלין כל היום עכ"ל וטעמו דלשיטות רש"י דס"ל דהיו"ד הוא הלמ"מ לא יצא עדיין ידי המלוה: (רלד) להעביר. הטעם לפי שהתפילין ש"י משימין אותם תחת הבגדים ונפסדים ומתגלגלים ומתקלקלין לכך נהגו להעביר רלועה זו עליהן לתוקן ועכשיו שאלו הארלות לא נהגו בזה [א"ר ע"ש]: (רלה) אלא לאחר וכו'. ר"ל כן נכון לכתחלה ואי איתרמי שהותר הקשר ש"י א"ל רק לתקנו ולא להתיר הש"י:

ביאור הלכה

וגם השי"ן נראה היטב עכ"ל וזהו שכתבנו במ"ב ס"ק קפ"ה בשמו: * מקום שאין וכו' עד שיזדמנו וכו'. ועיין במ"ב שכתבנו דכשיזדמן לו גידים יתירם וכו' דאם לא יתירם נראה לכאורה דלא מהני כיון שכבר תפור ועומד ועיין לקמיה: * יתפור וכו'. שמעתי בשם אחד הגדולים שהזהיר שלא לדבק התיתורא בדבק קודם התפירה דדבק חשיב חיבור כתפירה וכמו שכ' בסעי' מ"ז בהג"ה ובב"י שם עי"ש וא"כ אפשר דתפירה שאח"כ לא חשיבא כלום וההלכה ל"מ נאמר רק על התפירה ולא על דיבוק ול"ע בזה: * ויעשה קשר וכו'. עיין בפ"ת שהביא בשם בעל העיטור דמלוה שיהיה קשר ולא עניבה עי"ש. וחדשים מקרוב באו שעושין קשר שיוכל להשמט אותו אנה ואנה כדי למעט טרחה אם ירלו להקטינו או להגדילו ולא שפיר עבדי דקשר כזה לא עדיף מעניבה כנ"ל פשוט:

שער הציון

(ריא) נ"ב מ"ת סי' ב': (ריב) פשוט: (ריג) שם: (ריד) מ"א: (רטו) רא"ש וא"ר: (רטז) אחרונים: (ריז) ב"י: (ריח) ט"ז: (ריט) ט"ז ולכאורה מוכח בביאור הגר"א שגם הוא סובר כן: (רכ) ב"ח ומ"א: (רכא) א"ר: (רכב) ב"ח: (רכג) גמרא:

הגהות ותיקונים: א) מאי עמא:

In a locality where sinews are not available they should sew /the *tefilin*/ (226) with thongs which are formed from parchment, (227) until they happen to /obtain/ sinews.

51. One should sew three stitches (228) on each side. The sewing thread should

Mishnah Berurah

/the non-Jews/ take /sinews/ from unclean animals, it is also permitted to buy from them in all circumstances, since the majority of sinews are /taken/ from /halachically/ clean animals.

On the other hand, all this /only applies/ with respect to unspun sinews, but as regards spun sinews, the *M.A.* is of the opinion that it is forbidden to buy them from /non-Jews/, even when one knows that they are from a /halachically/ clean animal. For in view /of the fact/ that /the use of these sinews/ is a halachic /requirement which was taught/ to Mosheh (Moses) on /Mount/ Sinai, /the sinews/ are required to be prepared for the sake of /use for the mitzvah/. It is the spinning of the sinews which constitutes their preparation and non-Jews have no relevance to /doing the spinning/ for the sake of /use for the mitzvah/. We have already stated that the *E.R.* and the *P.Mg.* query whether spinning /the sinews/ for the sake of /the mitzvah/ is required at all.

(226) With thongs. These are narrow strips which are made from parchment. /The author of the Shulchan Aruch/ is of the opinion that in a case of pressing /need we rule that/ they are like sinews themselves, since they are of the /same/ kind, and they are /therefore/ valid for sewing Torah Scrolls, *tefilin* and mezuzos.

(227) Until ... happen. /One should do so/ in order not to be idle from /the performance of/ the mitzvah of *tefilin*. When he happens to obtain sinews he should undo /the thongs/ and sew with sinews /instead/.

There are Acharonim who are afraid /that thongs may not be used and are of the opinion/ that one should not fulfil /his obligation/ with them even in a time of pressing /need/. /They reason/ that /the use of/ sinews is a halachic /requirement which was taught/ to Mosheh (Moses) on /Mount/ Sinai, whereas the thongs are /merely/ skin, as they are from parchment, and we have /received/ no teaching that skin /can be used/ for the sewing. Accordingly, if one does not have other sinews /, but only thongs,/ he should at any rate not make a blessing over /the *tefilin*/. One should likewise not sew with thin dry intestines, which resemble sinew threads, as the halachic /requirement which was taught/ to Mosheh on /Mount/ Sinai specifically /requires/ sinews.

/The Acharonim/ write further that one should not sew with the sinews of a /halachically/ clean bird. This is because /with a bird/ we are unable to determine which of these /parts/ are called sinews, which of them threads and which of them veins and we require /specifically/ sinews /for this purpose/.

(228) On each side. The reason for the twelve stitches is to correspond with the twelve tribes of Israel.

We do not require sewing inside the housing, only close to the housing. One should not sew like someone who sews garments, /who sews/ at the edge of the garment without /leaving/ a margin, but must leave /some/ of the bridge beyond the sewing.

שמא של בהמה טמאה הם. * ימקום שאין גידין מצויים תופרים (רכו) בטאליאדור"ש שעושים מן הקלף (רכז) עד שיזדמנו להם גידים: **נא** * מיתפור שלשה תפירות (רכח) בכל (ע) [נא] צד יוחוט התפירה יהיה סובב (רכט) משתי רוחות סויעביר חוט התפירה בין כל בית ובית: הגה (רל) מיהו אם לא עשה רק י' תפירות או פחות מזה אינו נפסל (מרדכי) עויש מי שאומר שי"ב תפירות אלו יהיו (עא) (רלא) בחוט אחד: **נב** פיכניס הרצועה תוך המעברתא (רלב) * ויעשה קשר (רלג) כמין דל"ת כשל ראש וכמין יו"ד בשל יד להשלים אותיות שד"י עם השי"ן שבשל ראש: הגה ונוהגים (רלד) להעביר עור על הבית של יד לרוחב הזרוע ויהיה רחבו כרוחב הבית (טור) ולא יעשה הקשרים (רלה) אלא לאחר שעשה השי"ן מתפילין ואח"כ יעשה הדל"ת ואח"כ היו"ד כסדר אותיות השם:

ל העיטור מ שימושא רבא נ הרמב"ם והרא"ש לפי' השימושא רבא ס תוס' במנחות ל"ד והרא"ש והמרדכי ע הר"י אלכסנדרני פ מנחות ל"ה בפירוש רש"י

באר היטב

מ"א. בני מעיים דקים ויבשים כמין חוטים של גידים גידים גמורים הם ומותר לתפור בהם ס"ת ותו"מ הלק"ט ח"א סימן רע"ג והיד אהרן חולק עליו: (ע) לד. טעם לי"ב תפירות נגד שבטי ישראל ואם עשה י"ד נגד מנשה ואפרים טוב עיין ע"ת והאר"י ז"ל כתב ע"פ הסוד דוקא י"ב. הרמ"ע מפאנו סימן ל"ח כתב אם אין התפירה בתוך הבית רק בתוך המעברתא פסול אבל בב"י בשם הרא"ש ורש"י והמרדכי משמע דלא בעי תפירה תוך הבית רק סמוך לבית ע"ש מ"א: (עא) בחוט א'. ואם נפסק החוט בשעת עשיה פסולות דבעי שיהא חוט א' ב"י בשם הריא"ס. וכתב ט"ז דלא בא למעט אם חזר וקשר במקום הפסיקה אלא שיהא בדיבוק יחד ולא נפסק ביניהם. וכתב ב"ח דוקא אם נפסק החוט פסול דניכר שפסק החוט אבל אם החוט קצר יגמור התפירה בחוט אחר לכתחלה והכי נהוג:

שערי תשובה

עור הוא שהוא הקלף ועור לתפירה לא שמענו וכו'. וע"ש שהעלה שאין לתפור בגידי עוף טהור כי מי יכריע איזה מהם קרוי גידין ואיזה מהם חוטי' ואיזה מהם ורידין ואיזה מהם מיתרים ולכן אין היתר לקחת גידי עוף לתפילין ע"ש: [נא] לד. עבה"ט וכו' עיין בבר"י שמ"כ לאחד קדוש מה שרוב העולם אין בתפיליהם חריצים עד למטה ולא חוט התפירה עובר בין בית לבית ושמעתי שהטעם שע"י החריצים מתקלקל רבועם ובפרט אם חוט התפירה עובר שגם הוא מפריד רבועם ברוב הימים ומה גם אם הם במקום חם ושרב והרבוע הל"מ והחריצים פלוגתא דאמוראי ופוק חזי מעמא[א] דבר. ואפשר שסמכו על סמ"ק שכתב דוקא כשכתב על קלף א' אבל על ד' קלפים א"צ וע"ש וכתב עוד בבר"י שבבית דוד סי' כ"ח למד זכות על הסופרים שנהגו לעשות הבית ש"ר בלי חריץ רק רשימה כל דהו. ונחלקו עליו רבני הדור כאשר נדפס בח"ב מכנה"ג ח"מ אחר סי' רפ"ט ובכהונת עולם ע"ש. ועיין בבגדי כהונה סי' א' שכתב ג"כ דאם אין חריצים רק שעושים רושם שהרואה יסבור שהם חריצים פסולים. כי לכל הדיעות צריך הבדל מעט בין הבתים שיהיה החריצים ניכרים ממש:

משנה ברורה

שמקלפין נוטלין אותן מבהמה טמאה ג"כ מותר לקנות מהם בכל ענין שרוב גידין הם מבהמות טהורות אך כ"ז בגידין שאינן טוויין אבל בגידין טוויין דעת המ"א דאסור לקנות מהם אפילו הוא יודע שהם מבהמה טהורה מכיון שהוא הלמ"מ צריך שתהיה עשייתן לשמה וטוויית הגידין זו היא עשייתן ונכרים לאו בני לשמה נינהו ובכל כתבנו דהא"ר ופמ"ג מפקפקים אי בעי כלל בזה טוויה לשמה: (רכו) בטאליאדור"ש. הם חוטין הנעשים מן הקלף ובמקום הדחק ס"ל כיון דמינו הוא הם כגידין עצמן וכשרים לתפור בהם עמ"ש. (רכז) עד שיזדמנו. כדי שלא להתבטל ממצות תפילין וכשיזדמן לו גידים יתירם ויתפור בגידים ויש מאחרונים (ריא) שמחמירין שלא לצאת בהם אפילו בשעת הדחק שהרי הלמ"מ הוא גידין והטאליאדור"ש עור הוא שהוא הקלף ועור לתפירה לא שמענו ולפי"ז (ריב) אם אין לו גידים אחרים עכ"פ לא יברך עליהם וכן בני מעיים דקים ויבשים כמין חוטים של גידים אין לתפור בהם דהלמ"מ הוא דוקא גידים (ריג) עוד כתבו שאין לתפור בגידי עוף טהור כי מי יכריע איזה מהם קרוי גידין ואיזה מהם חוטין ואיזה מהם ורידין ולכן גידין בעינן: **נא** (רכח) בכל צד. טעם לי"ב תפירות נגד י"ב שבטי ישראל ולא בעינן תפירה תוך הבית (ריד) רק סמוך להבית (רטו) ואין תופרין כתופר בגדים בשפת הבגד בלי שיור אלא משייר מן התיתורא חוץ להתפירה (רטז) וצריך שעור הבתים מלמטה לפיו יהיו יוצאים מכל ארבע רוחותיהם עד שיהיו מגיעים תחת נקבי התפירה כדי שיתפור עור הבתים מכל צד עם התיתורא ולא כהסופרים המקצרין עור של הבתים שאינו עובר הלאה תחת נקבי התפירה ואינה נתפרת כלל עם התיתורא רק שמהדקין הבית בתוך הארובה של התיתורא והערוך שאמר כתב שפסל כמה תפילין מחמת זה אלא צריך לתפור יחד העור של הבתים עם התיתורא: (רכט) משתי רוחות. ר"ל שכל התפירה יהא מסובבת משני לצדדין פנים ואחור (ריז) נמצא תופר בב' מחטין אחת יוצאת לאחור ואחת נכנסת לצד פנים: (רל) מיהו אם וכו'. וכן (ריח) אם לא העביר חוט התפירה אינו מעכב בדיעבד ועיין לעיל בס"ק רי"ז: (רלא) בחוט אחד. ואם נפסק (ריט) י"א דיכול לקושרו (רכ) וי"א דיטלנו כולו משם ויחזור ויתפור מחדש בחוט אחר שכיון שנפסק בשעת התפירה ניכר שהחוט קלוש ועומד ליפסק ואינו כלום אבל כשהחוט קצר מתחלתו ואינו נפסק לכו"ע יכול (רכא) לקשור לו חוט אחר לגמור התפירה וכתב הפמ"ג דאם אין לו גידין אחרים יש לסמוך על סברא הראשונה ולקשור חוט שנפסק וכ"ז (רכב) אם נפסק באמצע התפירה אבל אם נפסק אחר התפירה עיין לקמן סימן ל"ג ס"ב: **נב** (רלב) ויעשה קשר. וקשר של תפילין (רכג) הוא הלכה למשה מסיני ונראה שצריך לעשותו לשמה ולא יעשהו קטן [פמ"ג]: (רלג) כמין ד'. ויש שעושין קשר כמ"ם סתומה שנראה כשני דלתי"ן משני לצדדין רגלו של זה נגד גגו של זה ועיין בספר תפארת אריה שהביא בשם תשובה מהר"ם והסכים עמו לדינא דאלו העושים קשר של דל"ת מכוון יותר לדינא. גם לא יעשה קשר העשוי להשמט אנה ואנה כמו שביארתי בבה"ל. כתב א"ר מעשה באחד שראה אחר תפלת התפילין שהותר הקשר ש"י והוריתי לחזור ולהכינן ולקרות ק"ש בלי ברכה דהא מצות תפלין כל היום עכ"ל וטעמו דלשיטת רש"י דס"ל דהיו"ד הוא הלמ"מ לא יצא עדיין ידי המצוה: (רלד) להעביר. הטעם לפי שהתפילין ש"י משימין אותם תחת הבגדים ונפסדים ומתקלקלין לכך נהגו להעביר רצועה זו עליהן לתקן ועכשיו באלו הארצות לא נהגו בזה [א"ר ע"ש]: (רלה) אלא לאחר וכו'. ר"ל כן נכון לכתחלה ואי איתרמי שהותר הקשר ש"י א"צ רק לתקנו ולא להתיר הש"י:

ביאור הלכה

וגם השי"ן נראה היטב עכ"ל וזהו שכתבנו במ"ב ס"ק קפ"ה בשמו: * מקום שאין וכו' עד שיזדמנו וכו'. ועיין במ"ב שכתבנו דכשיזדמן לו גידים יתירם וכו' דאם לא יתירם נראה לכאורה דלא מהני כיון שכבר תפור ועומד ועיין לקמיה: * יתפור וכו'. שמעתי בשם אחד הגדולים שהזהיר שלא לדבק התיתורא בדבק קודם התפירה דדבק חשיב חיבור כתפירה וכמו שכ' בסעי' מ"ז בהג"ה ובב"י שם עי"ש וא"כ אפשר דתפירה שאח"כ לא חשיבא כלום וההלכה ל"מ נאמר רק על התפירה ולא על דיבוק וצ"ע בזה: * ויעשה קשר וכו'. עיין בפ"ת שהביא בשם בעל העיטור דמצוה שיהיה קשר ולא עניבה עי"ש. וחדשים מקרוב באו שעושין קשר שיוכל להשמט אותו אנה ואנה כדי למעט טרחה אם ירצו להקטינו או להגדילו ולא שפיר עבדי דקשר כזה לא עדיף מעניבה כנ"ל פשוט:

שער הציון

(ריא) נ"ב מ"ת סי' ב': (ריב) פשוט: (ריג) שם: (ריד) מ"א: (רטו) רא"ש וא"ר: (רטז) אחרונים: (ריז) ב"י: (ריח) ט"ז: (ריט) ט"ז ולכאורה מוכח בביאור הגר"א שגם הוא סובר כן: (רכ) ב"ח ומ"א: (רכא) א"ר: (רכב) ב"ח: (רכג) גמרא:

הגהות ותיקונים: א) מאי עמא:

surround /the skin/ (229) in both directions. One should pass the sewing thread between each of the housings.

Gloss: (230) *Nevertheless, if one did not make /more/ than a mere ten stitches or less than that, /the* tefilin/ *are not invalid. (...)*

There is /an authority/ who says that these twelve stitches should be /sewn/ (231) with a single thread.

52. One should insert the strap inside the passageway (232) and should make

Mishnah Berurah

It is necessary for the skin of the housings below the openings to go outwards on all four sides, until it reaches underneath the holes of the sewing, so that one will /be able to/ sew the skin of the housings /together/ with the bridge on all sides. /One should/ not /act/ like the scribes who make the skin of the housings /too/ short, so that it does not pass onwards underneath the holes of the sewing and is not sewn at all /together/ with the bridge. They merely fasten the housings inside the opening of the bridge. The *Baruch She-Amar* writes that he disqualified several *tefilin* units because of this. Instead, one must sew the skin of the housings together with the bridge.

(229) In both directions. What is meant is that all the sewing must surround /the skin/ on both sides, front and back. One will thus be sewing with two /runs of the/ needle, one going out to the back and one coming inwards.

(230) Nevertheless, if, etc. Likewise, if one did not pass the sewing thread /between each of the housings/, this is not essential /for the validity of the *tefilin*/, once it is after the event. See above in sub-Par. 217.

(231) With a single thread. If /the thread/ became severed, there are /authorities/ who say that one may tie it and /authorities/ who say that one must take the entire /thread/ out of there and go back and sew anew with a different thread. /The latter authorities reason/ that in view /of the fact/ that it became severed during the sewing, it is evident that the thread is weak and ready to sever and is not /worth/ anything. (However, where the thread was short from the outset and is not severed, all /authorities/ are agreed that one may tie another thread to it /to have a long enough thread/ to finish the sewing.) The *P.Mg.* writes that if one does not have other sinews he may rely on the first opinion and tie /another thread to/ the severed thread.

All this /applies/ if /the thread/ became severed in the middle of the sewing, but if it became severed after the sewing, see below in Sec. 33, Par. 2.

(232) And should make a knot. The knot of the *tefilin* is a halachic /requirement which was taught/ to Mosheh (Moses) on /Mount/ Sinai. It seems /logical to assume/ that it must be done for the sake of /the mitzvah/ and should not be done by a child. [*P.Mg.*]

שמא של בהמה טמאה הם. * ל מקום שאין גידין מצויים תופרים (רכו) בטאליאדור"ש שעושים מן הקלף (רכז) עד שיזדמנו להם גידים: **נא** * מ יתפור שלשה תפירות (רכח) בכל (ע) [לא] צד נ וחוט התפירה יהיה סובב (רכט) משתי רוחות ס ויעביר חוט התפירה בין כל בית ובית: הגה (רל) מיהו אם לא עשה רק י' תפירות או פחות מזה אינו נפסל (מרדכי) ע ויש מי שאומר שי"ב תפירות אלו יהיו (עא) (רלא) בחוט אחד: **נב** פ יכניס הרצועה תוך המעברתא (רלב) * ויעשה קשר (רלג) כמין דלי"ת בשל ראש וכמין יו"ד בשל יד להשלים אותיות שד"י עם השי"ן שבשל ראש: הגה ונוהגים (רלד) להעביר עור על הבית של יד לרוחב הזרוע ויהיה רחבו כרוחב הבית (טור) ולא יעשה הקשרים (רלה) אלא לאחר שעשה השי"ן מתפילין ואח"כ יעשה הדלי"ת ואח"כ היו"ד כסדר אותיות השם:

באר היטב

מ"א. בני מעיים דקים ויבשים כמין חוטים של גידים גמורים הם ומותר לתפור בהם ס"ת ותו"מ הלק"ט ח"א סימן רע"ג והיד אהרן חולק עליו: (ע) לד. טעם לי"ב תפירות נגד שבטי ישראל ואם עשה י"ד נגד מנשה ואפרים טוב עיין ע"ת והאר"י ז"ל כתב ע"פ הסוד דוקא י"ב. הרמ"ע מפאנו סימן ל"ח כתב אם אין התפירה בתוך הבית רק בתוך המעברתא פסול אבל בב"י בשם הרא"ש ורש"י והמרדכי משמע דלא בעי תפירה תוך הבית רק סמוך לבית ע"ש מ"א: (עא) בחוט א'. ואם נפסק החוט בשעת עשיה פסולות דבעי שיהא חוט א' ב"י בשם הריא"ס. וכתב ט"ז דלא בא למעט אם חזר וקשר במקום הפסיקה אלא שיהא בדיבוק יחד ולא נפסק ביניהם. וכתב ב"ח דוקא אם נפסק החוט פסול דניכר שפסק החוט אבל אם החוט קצר יגמור התפירה בחוט אחר לכתחלה והכי נהוג:

שערי תשובה

עור הוא שהוא הקלף ועור לתפירה לא שמענו וכו'. וע"ש שהעלה שאין לתפור בגידי עוף טהור כי מי יכריע איזה מהם קרוי גידין ואיזה מהם חוטי' ואיזה מהם ורידין ואיזה מהם מיתרים ולכן אין היתר לקחת גידי עוף לתפילין ע"ש: [לא] לד. עבה"ט וכו' עיין בבר"י שמ"כ לאחד קדוש מה שרוב העולם אין בתפיליהם חריצים עד למטה ולא חוט התפירה עובר בין בית לבית ושמעתי שהטעם שע"י החריצים מתקלקל רבועם ובפרט אם חוט התפירה עובר שגם הוא מפריד רבועם ברוב הימים ומה גם אם הם במקום חם ושרב והרבוע הל"מ והחריצים פלוגתא דאמוראי ופוק חזי מעמא[א] דבר. ואפשר שסמכו על סמ"ק שכתב דוקא כשכתב על קלף א' אבל על ד' קלפים א"צ וע"ש וכתב עוד בבר"י שבבית דוד סי' כ"ח למד זכות על הסופרים שנהגו לעשות הבית ש"ר בלי חריץ רק רשימה כל דהו. ונחלקו עליו רבני הדור כאשר נדפס בח"ב מכנה"ג ח"מ אחר סי' רפ"ט ובכהונת עולם ע"ש. ועיין בבגדי כהונה סי' א' שכתב ג"כ דאם אין חריצים רק שעושים רושם שהרואה יסבור שהם חריצים פסולים. כי לכל הדיעות צריך הבדל מעט בין הבתים שיהיה החריצים ניכרים ממש:

ביאור הלכה

וגם השי"ן נראה היטב עכ"ל וזהו שכתבנו במ"ב ס"ק קפ"ה בשמו: * מקום שאין וכו' עד שיזדמנו וכו'. ועיין במ"ב שכתבנו דכשיזדמן לו גידים יתירם וכו' דאם לא יתירם נראה לכאורה דלא מהני כיון שכבר תפור ועומד ועיין לקמיה: * יתפור וכו'. שמעתי בשם אחד הגדולים שהזהיר שלא לדבק התיתורא בדבק קודם התפירה דדבק חשיב חיבור כתפירה וכמו שכ' בסעי' מ"ז בהג"ה ובב"י שם עי"ש וא"כ אפשר דתפירה שאח"כ לא חשיבא כלום וההלכה ל"מ נאמר רק על התפירה ולא על דיבוק ול"ע בזה: * ויעשה קשר וכו'. עיין בפ"ת שהביא בשם בעל העיטור דמצוה שיהיה קשר ולא עניבה עי"ש. וחדשים מקרוב באו שעושין קשר שיוכל להשמט אותו אנה ואנה כדי למעט טרחה אם ירצו להקטינו או להגדילו ולא שפיר עבדי דקשר כזה לא עדיף מעניבה כנ"ל פשוט:

משנה ברורה

שמקלפין ומוכרין אותן מבהמה טמאה ג"כ מותר לקנות מהם בכל ענין שרוב גידין הם מבהמות טהורות אך כ"ז בגידין שאינן טווין אבל בגידין טווין דעת המ"א דאסור לקנות מהם אפילו הוא יודע שהם מבהמה טהורה שכיון שהוא הלמ"מ צריך שתהיה עשייתן לשמה וטויית הגידין זו היא עשייתן וגוים לאו בני לשמה נינהו וכבר כתבנו דהא"ר ופמ"ג מפקפקים אי בעי כלל שום טויה לשמה: (רכו) בטאליאדור"ש. הם חוטין הנעשים מן הקלף ובמקום הדחק ס"ל כיון דמינו הוא הם כגידין עצמן וכשרים לתפור בהם סת"ם: (רכז) עד שיזדמנו. כדי שלא להתבטל ממצות תפילין וכשיזדמן לו גידים יתירם ויתפור בגידים ויש מאחרונים (ריא) שמחמירין שלא לנהוג כלל אפילו בשעת הדחק שסברי הלמ"מ הוא גידין והטאליאדור"ש עור הוא שהוא הקלף ועור לתפירה לא שמענו ולפי"ז (ריב) אם אין לו גידים אחרים עכ"פ לא יברך עליהם וכן בני מעיים דקים ויבשים כמין חוטים של גידים אין לתפור בהם דהלמ"מ הוא דוקא גידים (ריג) עוד כתבו שאין לתפור בגידי עוף טהור כי מי יכריע איזה מהם קרוי גידין ואיזה מהם חוטין ואיזה מהם ורידין ואין גידין בעינן: **נא** (רכח) בכל צד. טעם לי"ב תפירות נגד י"ב שבטי ישראל ולא בעינן תפירה תוך הבית (ריד) רק סמוך להבית (רטו) ואין תופרין כתופר בגדים בשפת הבגד בלי שיור אלא משייר מן התיתורא חוץ להתפירה (רטז) וצריך שעור הבתים מלמטה לפיו יהיו יוצאים מכל ארבע רוחותיהם עד שיהיו מגיעים תחת נקבי התפירה כדי שיתפור עור הבתים מכל צד עם התיתורא ולא כהסופרים המקצרין עור של הבתים שאינו עובר הלאה תחת נקבי התפירה ואינה נתפרת כלל עם התיתורא רק שמהדקין הבית בתוך האלובה של התיתורא והברוך שאמר כתב שפסול כמה תפילין מחמת זה אלא צריך לתפור יחד העור של הבתים עם התיתורא: (רכט) משתי רוחות. ר"ל שכל התפירה יהא מסובבת משני צדדין פנים ואחור (ריז) נמצא תופר בב' נקבין אחת יוצאת לאחור ואחת נכנסת לצד פנים: (רל) מיהו אם וכו'. וכן (ריח) אם לא העביר חוט התפירה אינו מעכב בדיעבד ועיין לעיל בס"ק רי"ז: (רלא) בחוט אחד. ואם נפסק (ריט) י"א דיכול לקושרו (רכ) וי"א דיטלנו כולו משם ויחזור ויתפור מחדש בחוט אחר שכיון שנפסק בשעת התפירה ניכר שהחוט קלוש ועומד ליפסק ואינו כלום אבל כשהחוט קצר מתחלתו ואינו נפסק לכו"ע יכול (רכא) לקשור לו חוט אחר לגמור התפירה וכתב הפמ"ג דאם אין לו גידין אחרים יש לסמוך על סברא הראשונה ולקשור חוט שנפסק וכ"ז (רכב) אם נפסק באמצע התפירה אבל אם נפסק אחר התפירה עיין לקמן סימן ל"ג ס"ב: **נב** (רלב) ויעשה קשר. וקשר של תפילין (רכג) הוא הלכה למשה מסיני ונראה שצריך לעשותו לשמה ולא יעשהו קטן [פמ"ג]: (רלג) כמין ד'. ויש שעושין קשר כמ"ם סתומה שנראה כשני דלתי"ן משני צדדין רגלו של זה בצד ראשו של זה ועיין בספר תפארת אריה שהביא בשם תשובה מאהבה והסכים עמו לדינא דאלו העושים קשר של דלי"ת מכוון יותר לדינא. גם לא יעשה קשר העשוי להשמט אנה ואנה כמו שביארתי בבה"ל. כתב א"ר מעשה באחד שראה אחר חליצת התפילין שהותר הקשר ש"י והוריתי לחזור ולהניחן ולקרות ק"ש בלי ברכה דהא מצות תפלין כל היום עכ"ל וטעמו דלשיטת רש"י דס"ל דהיו"ד הוא הלמ"מ לא יצא עדיין ידי המצוה: (רלד) להעביר. הטעם לפי שהתפילין ש"י משימין אותם תחת הבגדים ומתנדנדים ונפסדים ומתקלקלין לכך נהגו להעביר רצועה זו עליהן לחזקן ועכשיו באלו הארצות לא נהגו בזה [א"ר ע"ש]: (רלה) אלא לאחר וכו'. ר"ל כן נכון לכתחלה ואי איתרמי שהותר הקשר ש"ר א"צ רק לתקנו ולא להתיר הש"י:

שער הציון

(ריא) נ"ב מ"ת סי' ב': (ריב) פשוט: (ריג) שם: (ריד) מ"א: (רטו) רא"ש וא"ר: (רטז) אחרונים: (ריז) ב"י: (ריח) ט"ז: (ריט) ט"ז ולכאורה מוכח בביאור הגר"א שגם הוא סובר כן: (רכ) ב"ח ומ"א: (רכא) א"ר: (רכב) ב"ח: (רכג) גמרא:

באר הגולה

ל העיטור מ שימושא רבא נ הרמב"ם והרא"ש לפי' השימושא רבא ס תוס' במנחות ל"ד והרא"ש והמרדכי ע הר"י אלכסנדרני פ מנחות ל"ה בפירוש רש"י

הגהות ותיקונים: א) מאי עמא:

a knot (233) resembling a /letter/ ד in /the case of the strap of/ the head /*tefilin*/ and resembling a /letter/ י in /the case of the strap of/ the arm /*tefilin*/. /These letters serve/ to complete the letters /of the Divine Name/ ש־ד־י, /together/ with the /letter/ ש of the head /*tefilin* unit/.

Gloss: It is the practice (234) *to pass /a strip of/ skin over the housing of the arm /*tefilin*/ along with the width of the arm. Its width should be /the same/ as the width of the housing. (...)*

One should not make the knots (235) *except after he has /already/ made the /letter/ ש of the /head/* tefilin. *After that he should make the ד /knot/ and subsequently the י /knot, so that the letters are formed/ in the order of the letters of this /Divine/ Name.*

Mishnah Berurah

(233) **Resembling a ד.** There are /people/ who make a knot like the closed /letter/ ם, which looks like two ד /letters/ from both sides, the leg of the one being alongside the head of the other. See the work *Tif'eres Aryeih*. /The author/ cites in the name of the /work/ *Teshuvah Mey-Ahavah*, that those who make a knot /in the shape/ of the /letter/ ד conform more precisely with halachic /requirements/. He agrees with him that /this is/ the halachic /ruling to be followed/.

One should also not make a knot which is likely to slip to and fro, as I have explained in the Beyur Halachah.

The *E.R.* writes, "There was an incident, where someone saw after having taken off his *tefilin* that the knot of the arm *tefilin* was undone. I ruled that he should don them again without making a blessing and should read 'The Reading of Shema' /with them on/, since the mitzvah of /donning/ *tefilin* /can be fulfilled/ at any /time during/ the day". His reason /for this ruling/ was that according to the view of *Rashi*, who is of the opinion that the י/-like knot on the arm *tefilin*/ is a halachic /requirement which was taught/ to Mosheh (Moses) on /Mount/ Sinai, /this person/ had not yet fulfilled the mitzvah.

(234) **To pass.** The reason is because the arm *tefilin* are put underneath one's clothes and move /to and fro/ and /therefore/ get worn away and spoiled. It therefore became the practice to pass this strap over them to strengthen them.

Nowadays, in these countries, this is not the practice. [*E.R.*; see there.]

(235) **Except after, etc.** What is meant by this /ruling/ is that this is /how it is/ proper /to act/ initially. /However,/ if the knot of the head /*tefilin*/ became undone, it is only necessary to remedy that /knot/ and /one need/ not undo /the knot of/ the arm /*tefilin*/.

לג דין תיקוני תפילין ודין הרצועות. ובו ה׳ סעיפים:

א [א]אם (א) נתקלקל עור של שני בתים (ב) מבתי הראש (ג) * זה אצל זה [ב]אם התפילין (ד) ישנים פסולים ואם הם (ה) חדשים כשרים כל זמן שעור מושב הבתים (א) [א] (ו) קיים: הגה גם הבתים צריכין להיות קיימים אלא שנקרעו קצת (ב״י) וי״א להיפך דישנים כשרים ובחדשים פסולים (רש״י והרא״ש) ונ״ל דיש להחמיר (ז) לפסול בשניהם: [ג]ואלו הם חדשים כל זמן שאם היו מושכים אותם ברצועות (ח) הבית מתפשט (ב) ונפתח נקרא חדש אם אינו נפתח נקרא ישן ואם נתקלקלו שנים זה שלא כנגד זה (ט) * ראשון (ג) ושלישי כשרים אפילו הם ישנים ואם נתקלקלו (י) ג׳ בתים (יא) בכל ענין (ד) פסולים: **ב** [ד]אם נפסקו תפירות התפילין (יב) * להרמב״ם אם היו שתי התפירות זו בצד זו או שנפסקו ג׳ תפירות אפילו (יג) זו שלא כנגד זו הרי אלו פסולים בד״א בישנים אבל בחדשים כל זמן

א מנחות ל״ה לפי׳ הראשון ברש״י ורא״ש והמרדכי ונ״י ב לפירוש הרי״ף שם בגמ׳ ורמב״ם בפ״ג מהלכות תפילין ג שם בגמרא ד כן פי׳ הרמב״ם מההיא דמנחות בפרק ג׳ מה״ת

שערי תשובה

[א] קיים. עבה״ט ובשו״ת פני יהושע חלק א״ח סימן יו״ד כתב בבית תפילין דוקא. וזהו שכתב רמ״א גם הבתים צריכין להיות קיימים אלא שנקרעו קצת פי׳ שנקרעו בין בית לבית אבל הצדדים צריכין להיות שלימים:

באר היטב

(א) קיים. ר״ל התיתורא אבל ב״י פירש ל״נ היינו לומר דבעי שיהיה שלימים מכל שאר צדדים דלא מכשרינן אלא כשנקרעו בין בית לבית (ב) ונפתח. ולדידן אין שייך זה: (ג) ושלישי. ונשאר בית א׳ שלם ביניהם אבל שנים הסמוכים אע״פ שאין הקרעים סמוכים אלא שזה בצד זה והשני בצד אחר מיקרי זה אצל זה ט״ז: (ד) פסולים. אפילו חדשים דכשר בב׳ אפילו בזה אצל זה מ״מ בג׳ פסולים:

ביאור הלכה

* זה אצל זה. עיין במ״ב במה שכתב וכ״ש אם שניהם באויר אחד וכו׳ עיין בב״י ול״ע במה שהביא שם דהנ״י סבר ג״כ כלישנא קמא דרש״י דהמעיין בו בפנים בד״ה שתים ובד״ה אבל יראה להדיא דס״ל להנ״י דתלוי רק באוירין ולדידיה אם הקרע באויר אחד אפילו הוא בב׳ דפנות כשר ולהיפך אם היו בשני אוירין כגון שנעשה הקרע בבית ראשון מצד שמאלו ובבית השלישי מצד ימינו פסול דזה מיקרי לדידיה זה כנגד זה וכ״ש אם הבית השלישי נעשה בו קרע בשני דופנותיו זה מיקרי לדידיה שלשה אוירין מה דלא ס״ל לרש״י לכל זה לא בלישנא קמא ולא בלישנא בתרא ואולי דהב״י מביא רק ראיה למה דסבר רש״י בל״ק דאם נעשה קרע בבית ראשון משמאלו ובבית שני ג״כ משמאלו דהוא פסול דהנ״י סבר ג״כ בזה כוותיה דהרי הוא ב׳ אוירין ודלא כלישנא בתרא ול״ע: * ראשון ושלישי. עיין במ״ב במש״כ ואפילו אם נעשה הקרע בשתי דפנותיו כן כתב הפמ״ג בא״א לדעת המג״א דסבר כן והוכיח ג״כ מהשו״ע מדנקט לבסוף אם נתקלקלו ג׳ בתים משמע אבל לא ג׳ דפנות עי״ש ולא קי״ל כלישנא בתרא דרש״י דמחמיר בזה גם מהגר״א בביאורו משמע דדעת הש״ע רק כל״ק דרש״י וכתב שכן דעת כל הפוסקים וכן בשארי אחרונים ראיתי כן לכן סתמתי כן ולא כהט״ז שמצדד להחמיר בזה: * להרמב״ם וכו׳. עיין במ״ב במה שכתב אבל ש״פ וכו׳ עיין לעיל בסוף סימן ל״ב בב״י שם ד״ה ואם נפסקה התפירה וכו׳ בסוף דבריו שכתב ולענין הלכה במקום דלא אפשר יש לסמוך על דברי המיקל כדי שלא להתבטל ממצות תפילין משמע מזה דדעתו דכל הני פוסקים דהביא מתחלה והם הרא״ש וסה״ת וסמ״ג כולם מקילין ופליגי אהא דהרמב״ם וס״ל דבפסיקת ב׳ תפירות מותר בכל ענין [ובאמת לא ידעתי דלמא גם הם מחמירין ומה דנקטו ג׳ משום דבג׳ אפילו תיקון התפירה במקום ההוא לא מהני וצריך לתפור מחדש אח״כ מצאתי בביאורי מהרש״ל על הסמ״ג שכתב באמת שכן הוא דעתם ואפשר דדעת הב״י דא״כ הוא דסברי כהרמב״ם היה להם להזכיר שום חילוק לדינא בין חדשות וישנות ובין זה כנגד זה לשלא כנגד זה ועוד אחרי שהרא״ש והערוך וסייעתו מפרשי המימרא דר״ה ור״ח במנחות שלא לענין תפירות מנין להו להחמיר בשתי תפירות] וכן הבין הא״ר דעת הב״י בזה ובאמת לפעמים הרמב״ם מיקל יותר מהם כגון בנפסק ג׳ תפירות בחדשים דהרמב״ם מיקל אפילו בלי תיקון כלל ולדידהו צריך תפירה מחדש בזה בין בחדשים ובין בישנים[א] ופשוט דכל זה כלל הב״י שם במה שכתב דיש לסמוך במקום דלא אפשר על המיקל. ומה שכתב אח״כ הרמ״א ע״ז וי״א דבחדשים פסולים וכו׳ ונרשם ע״ז רש״י והטור והרא״ש לאו דהם ס״ל כן דהא לדידהו אין חילוק כלל בתפירה בין חדשות לישנות[א] וכנ״ל דלא איירי הגמרא לענין תפירה רק דר״ל לפי סברתם דלעיל דגרסי בגמרא היפוך מדברי הרמב״ם לענין חדשות וישנות יהיה א״כ לפי פירושו שמפרש המימרא דר״ה ור״ח לענין תפירות היפוך

משנה ברורה

א (א) נתקלקל. פי׳ שנפסק ונעשה קרע: (ב) מבתי הראש. אבל אם נעשה קרע (א) בהבית של יד פסול לכו״ע בכל ענין אף שהתיתורא קיימת ולא דמי לשל ראש דנשתייר בו עוד עכ״פ איזה בתים שלימים: (ג) זה אצל זה. ר״ל דהבתים הם סמוכים זה לזה (ב) אפילו אם אין הקרעים סמוכים כגון שקרע אחד בהבית השני בדופנו הימיני וקרע השני בהבית הג׳ לא שנא בדופנו הימיני (ג) או השמאלי ואפילו אם קרע זה למעלה (ד) וזה למטה וכ״ש אם שניהם באויר אחד זה כנגד זה דפסול: (ד) ישנים פסולים. דכבר נתקלקלו (ה) מחמת יושנן ויש אומרים ס״ל להיפך דבחדשים איגלאי מילתא דעור מקולקל הוא כיון דבזמן מועט נקרעו ואפילו היכא דלא שייכי (ו) אלו הטעמים כגון שנעשה הקרע ע״י סכין וכיו״ב יש להחמיר. ומ״מ לידד בספר פ״ת דדיבוק מהני אם אנו יודעין שאין העור מקולקל אף לאלו דנוהגין לעשות תפילין מעור אחד ע״ש: (ה) חדשים כשרים. ואפילו הקרע בשני הבתים (ז) בשני דפנותיהם: (ו) קיים. היינו התיתורא אבל בב״י פירש דבעי שיהיו שלימין מכל הצדדין דלא מכשרינן אלא מה שנקרע מבפנים בין בית לבית וזהו ג״כ דעת רמ״א שהעתיקו להלכה וכתב דגם הבתים צריכים להיות קיימים אלא שנקרעו קצת פי׳ שנקרעו בין בית לבית אבל הצדדים צריכים להיות שלמים ואפילו קרע בבית אחד אם (ח) נעשה מבחוץ לבד ג״כ יש להחמיר: (ז) לפסול בשניהם. ע״כ יש לפסול מה שרגילין (ט) הסופרים כשעושין הד׳ בתים ונותנין אותו בדפוס חותכין מן העור בין בית לבית כדי שלא יהא נכוץ ובולטת[ב] ותחפין מקום החתך מבפנים כדי שיהיה נראה מבחוץ שלם: (ח) הבית מתפשט. והו לאותן שעושין המעברתא מהעור שעשו ממנו הבתים אבל לדידן שהמעברתא עור בפני עצמו (י) אין שייך לגמר כן: (ט) ראשון ושלישי. ר״ל דבזה מיקרי זה שלא כנגד זה ואפילו אם נעשה (יא) הקרע בהבית השלישי בשני דפנותיו כשר כיון שיש בית שלם מפסיק ביניהן אבל אם נעשה הקרע בבית ב׳ וג׳ אף דקרע אחד בבית אחד מימינו וקרע השני בבית השני משמאלו אעפ״כ מיקרי זה כנגד זה כיון דשני הבתים הם סמוכים להדדי וכנ״ל בסק״ב[ג]: (י) ג׳ בתים. אפילו בכל בית (יב) רק דופן אחד: (יא) בכל ענין. בין לרבות (יג) אפילו חדשים דהכשרנו לעיל בב׳ אפילו בזה אצל זה מ״מ בג׳ פסול: **ב** (יב) להרמב״ם. אבל שארי פוסקים פליגי עליה ומקילים בכל גווני בשתי תפירות ובשלשה תפירות שנפסקו מחמירים דאפילו תיקון במקום ההפסק לא מהני דגלוי הוא כשניכר התיקון בשלשה מקומות בין בחדשים ובין בישנים וצריך לחזור ולתפור מחדש וכמו שנתבאר בטור וב״י לעיל בסוף סימן ל״ב ע״ש: (יג) זו שלא וכו׳.

אפילו

שער הציון

(א) ש״ת: (ב) ט״ז: (ג) מחצית השקל וישועות יעקב: (ד) מרדכי והובא בב״י: (ה) ט״ז: (ו) מחצית השקל עי״ש: (ז) פרי מגדים בא״א אות ג׳: (ח) כן מוכח מדה״ח: (ט) מרדכי: (י) ט״ז: (יא) פמ״ג בא״א: (יב) מוכח בגמרא: (יג) ט״ז:

הגהות ותיקונים: א) בישנים, לישנות, וישנות: ב) ובולט: ג) בסק״ג:

§33: THE LAW AS REGARDS /THE NEED TO/ REPAIR *TEFILIN* AND THE LAW CONCERNING THE STRAPS

(Contains Five Paragraphs)

1. If the skin (1) has become spoiled /in the case/ of two housings, (2) among the housings of the head /*tefilin*/, and (3) one is alongside the other /, the ruling is as follows/. If the *tefilin* are (4) old they are invalid. /However/, if they are (5) new they are valid, as long as the skin on which the housings rest is (6) intact.

Gloss: The housings must also be intact and merely slightly torn. (...)

*There are /authorities/ who say the opposite, that /in such a case/ old /*tefilin*/ are valid, but if /the* tefilin*/ are new they are invalid. (...) It appears to*

Mishnah Berurah

§33

(1) **Has become spoiled.** What is meant is that it became severed and a tear formed.

(2) **Among the housings of the head /*tefilin*/.** However, if a tear formed in the housing of the arm /*tefilin*/, it is invalid according to all /authorities/ in all cases, even if the bridge is intact. /A tear in the housing of the arm *tefilin*/ is not comparable to /tears in the housings of/ the head /*tefilin*/, in which case at any rate some of the housings /of the head *tefilin*/ still remain whole.

(3) **One is alongside the other.** I.e., if the /spoiled/ housings are adjacent to one another.

/This ruling applies/ even if the tears are not adjacent. For example, /it applies/ if one tear is in the second housing on its right wall and the second tear is in the third housing, regardless of whether it is on the right or the left wall. /The ruling also applies/ even if one tear is higher up and the other lower down. If both of /the tears/ are in the same space, against one another, /the *tefilin*/ are certainly invalid.

(4) **Old they are invalid.** /This is/ because they have already become spoiled as a result of their age. The /authorities/ who say /the opposite/ reason that, on the contrary, in the case of new /*tefilin*/ it becomes evident that the skin /used/ was impaired, since it tore in a short time.

Even when these reasons /for invalidating the *tefilin*/ are not relevant, such as when the tear was formed by a knife, etc., one should /nevertheless/ be stringent. Nevertheless, in the work *P.T.*, /the author/ adopts /the view/ that gluing is of avail if one knows that the skin is not impaired, even for those /people/ who are accustomed to make the *tefilin* from a single skin /only/; see there.

(5) **New they are valid.** This even /applies/ if the tear of both housings is in both their walls.

(6) **Intact.** I.e., /if/ the bridge /of the *tefilin* is intact/.

However, the *B.Y.* explains that /the outer surfaces of the housings/ are required to be whole on all sides. For we only rule /the *tefilin*/ to be valid where the tear is on the inside, in between the housings. This is also the view of the *Rema*, who records this as the halachic /ruling/ by writing that the housings must also be intact and merely slightly torn. He means that there may /only/ be a tear in between the housings, but the sides /of the housings/ must be whole. Even if there is a tear in a single housing only

לג דין תיקוני תפילין ודין הרצועות. ובו ה׳ סעיפים:

א אמנחות ל״ה לפי׳ הראשון ברש״י ורא״ש והמרדכי וכ״י
ב לפירוש הרי״ף שם בגמ׳ ורמב״ם בפ״ג מהלכות תפילין
ג שם בגמרא ד כן פי׳ הרמב״ם מההיא דמנחות בפרק ג׳ מה״ת

א אאם (א) נתקלקל עור של שני בתים (ב) מבתי הראש (ג) * זה אצל זה באם התפילין (ד) ישנים פסולים ואם הם (ה) חדשים כשרים כל זמן שעור מושב הבתים (א) [א] (ו) קיים: הגה גם הבתים צריכין להיות קיימים אלא שנקרעו קצת (ב״י) וי״א להיפך בישנים כשרים ובחדשים פסולים (רש״י והרא״ש) וכ״ל דיש להחמיר (ז) לפסול בשניהם: גואלו הם חדשים כל זמן שאם היו מושכים אותם ברצועות (ח) הבית מתפשט (ב) ונפתח נקרא חדש אם אינו נפתח נקרא ישן ואם נתקלקלו שנים זה שלא כנגד זה (ט) * ראשון (ג) ושלישי כשרים אפילו הם ישנים ואם נתקלקלו (י) ג׳ בתים (יא) בכל ענין (ד) פסולים: **ב** דאם נפסקו תפירות התפילין (יב) * להרמב״ם אם היו שתי התפירות זו בצד זו או שנפסקו ג׳ תפירות אפילו (יג) זו שלא כנגד זו הרי אלו פסולים בד״א בישנים אבל בחדשים כל זמן

שערי תשובה

[א] קיים. עבה״ט ובשו״ת פני יהושע חלק א״ח סימן יו״ד כתב בבית תפילין

באר היטב

(א) קיים. ר״ל התיתורא אבל ב״י פירש ל״נ היינו לומר דבעי שיהיה שלימים מכל שאר לדדים דלא מכשרינן אלא כשנקרעו בין בית לבית דוקא. וזהו שכתב רמ״א גם הבתים צריכין להיות קיימים אלא שנקרעו קצת פי׳ שנקרעו בין בית לבית אבל הצדדים צריכין להיות שלימים: (ב) ונפתח. ולדידן אין שייך זה: (ג) ושלישי. ונשאר בית א׳ שלם ביניהם אבל שנים הסמוכים אע״פ שאין הקרעים סמוכים אלא שזה בצד זה והשני בצד אחר מיקרי זה אצל זה ט״ז: (ד) פסולים. אפילו חדשים דכשר בב׳ אפילו בזה אצל זה מ״מ בג׳ פסולים:

ביאור הלכה

* זה אצל זה. עיין במ״ב במה שכתב וכ״ש אם שניהם באויר אחד וכו׳ עיין בב״י וצ״ע במה שהביא שם דהנ״י סבר ג״כ כלישנא קמא דרש״י דהמעיין בו בפנים בד״ה שתים ובד״ה אבל יראה להדיא דס״ל להנ״י דתלוי רק באוירין ולדידיה אם הקרע באויר אחד אפילו הוא בב׳ דפנות כשר ולהיפך אם היו בשני אוירין כגון שנעשה הקרע בבית ראשון מצד שמאלו ובבית השלישי מצד ימינו פסול דזה מיקרי לדידיה זה כנגד זה וכ״ש אם הבית השלישי נעשה בו קרע בשני דופנותיו זה מיקרי לדידיה שלשה אוירין מה דלא ס״ל לרש״י לכל זה לא בלישנא קמא ולא בלישנא בתרא ואולי דהב״י מביא רק ראיה למה דסבר רש״י בל״ק דאם נעשה קרע בבית ראשון משמאלו ובבית שני ג״כ משמאלו דהוא פסול דהנ״י סבר ג״כ בזה כוותיה דהרי הוא ב׳ אוירין ודלא כלישנא בתרא וצ״ע: * ראשון ושלישי. עיין במ״ב במש״כ ואפילו אם נעשה הקרע בשתי דפנותיו כן כתב הפמ״ג בא״א לדעת המג״א דסבר כן והוכיח ג״כ מהשו״ע מדנקט לבסוף אם נתקלקלו ג׳ בתים משמע אבל לא ג׳ דפנות עי״ש ולא קי״ל כלישנא בתרא דרש״י דמחמיר בזה גם מהגר״א בביאורו משמע דדעת הש״ע רק כל״ק דרש״י וכתב שכן דעת כל הפוסקים וכן בשארי אחרונים ראיתי כן לכן סתמתי כן ולא כהט״ז שמצדד להחמיר בזה: * להרמב״ם וכו׳. עיין במ״ב במה שכתב אבל ש״פ וכו׳ עיין לעיל בסוף סימן ל״ב בב״י שם ד״ה ואם נפסקה התפירה וכו׳ בסוף דבריו שכתב ולענין הלכה במקום דלא אפשר יש לסמוך על דברי המיקל כדי שלא להתבטל ממצות תפילין משמע מזה דדעתו דכל הני פוסקים דהביא מתחלה והם הרא״ש וסה״ת וסמ״ג כולם מקילין ופליגי אהא דהרמב״ם וס״ל דבפסיקת ב׳ תפירות מותר בכל ענין [ובאמת לא ידעתי דלמא גם הם מחמירין ומה דנקטו ג׳ משום דבג׳ אפילו תיקון התפירה במקום ההוא לא מהני וצריך לתפור מחדש אח״כ מצאתי בביאורי מהרש״ל על הסמ״ג שכתב באמת שכן הוא דעתם ואפשר דדעת הב״י דא״כ הוא דסברי כהרמב״ם היה להם להזכיר שום חילוק לדינא בין חדשות וישנות ובין זה כנגד זה לשלא כנגד זה ועוד אחרי שהרא״ש והערוך וסייעתו מפרשי המימרא דר״ה ור״ח במנחות שלא לענין תפירות מנין להו להחמיר בשתי תפירות] וכן הבין הא״ר דעת הב״י בזה ובאמת לפעמים הרמב״ם מיקל יותר מהם כגון בנפסק ג׳ תפירות בחדשים דהרמב״ם מיקל אפילו בלי תיקון כלל ולדידהו צריך תפירה מחדש בזה בין בחדשים ובין בישנים[א] ופשוט דכל זה כלל הב״י שם במה שכתב דיש לסמוך במקום דלא אפשר על המיקל. ומה שכתב אח״כ הרמ״א ע״ז וי״א דבחדשים פסולים וכו׳ וגרסם ע״ז רש״י והטור והרא״ש לאו דהם ס״ל כן דהא לדידהו אין חילוק כלל בתפירה בין חדשות לישנות[א] וכנ״ל דלא איירי הגמרא לענין תפירה רק דר״ל לפי סברתם דלעיל דגרסי בגמרא היפוך מדברי הרמב״ם לענין חדשות וישנות[א] יהיה א״כ לפי פירושו שמפרש המימרא דר״ה ור״ח לענין תפירות היפוך

משנה ברורה

א (א) נתקלקל. פי׳ שנפסק ונעשה קרע: (ב) מבתי הראש. אבל אם נעשה קרע (א) בהבית של יד פסול לכו״ע בכל ענין אף שהתיתורא קיימת ולא דמי לשל ראש דנשתייר בו עוד עכ״פ איזה בתים שלימים: (ג) זה אצל זה. ר״ל דהבתים הם סמוכים זה לזה (ב) אפילו אם אין הקרעים סמוכים כגון שקרע אחד בהבית השני בדופנו הימיני וקרע השני בהבית הג׳ לא שנא בדופנו הימיני (ג) או השמאלי ואפילו אם קרע זה למטה וזה למעלה (ד) וכ״ש אם שניהם באויר אחד זה כנגד זה דפסול: (ד) ישנים פסולים. דכבר נתקלקלו (ה) מחמת יושנן ויש אומרים ס״ל להיפך דבחדשים איגלאי מילתא דעור מקולקל הוא כיון דבזמן מועט נקרעו ואפילו היכא דלא שייכי (ו) אלו הטעמים כגון שנעשה הקרע ע״י סכין וכיו״ב יש להחמיר. ומ״מ לידד בספר פ״ת דדיעבד מהני אם אנו יודעין שאין העור מקולקל אף נאלו דנוהגין לעשות תפילין מעור אחד ע״ש: (ה) חדשים כשרים. ואפילו הקרע בשני הבתים (ז) בשני דפנותיהם: (ו) קיים. היינו התיתורא אבל בב״י פירש דבעי שיהיו שלימין מכל הצדדין דלא מכשרינן אלא מה שנקרע מבפנים בין בית לבית וזהו ג״כ דעת רמ״א שהעתיקו להלכה וכתב דגם הבתים צריכים להיות קיימים אלא שנקרעו קצת פי׳ שנקרעו בין בית לבית אבל הצדדים צריכים להיות שלמים ואפילו קרע בבית אחד אם (ח) נעשה מבחוץ לבד ג״כ יש להחמיר: (ז) לפסול בשניהם. ע״כ יש לפסול מה שרגילין (ט) הסופרים כשעושין הד׳ בתים ונותנין אותו בדפוס חותכין מן העור בין בית לבית כדי שלא יהא נכווץ ובולטת[ב] ומחפין מקום החתך מבפנים כדי שיהיה נראה מבחוץ שלם: (ח) הבית מתפשט. זהו לאותן שעושין המעברתא מהעור שעשו ממנו הבתים אבל לדידן שהמעברתא עור בפני עצמו (י) אין שייך לומר כן: (ט) ראשון ושלישי. ר״ל דבזה מיקרי זה שלא כנגד זה ואפילו אם נעשה (יא) הקרע בהבית השלישי בשני דפנותיו כשר כיון שיש בית שלם מפסיק ביניהן אבל אם נעשה הקרע בבית ב׳ וג׳ אף דקרע אחד בבית אחד מימינו וקרע השני בבית השני משמאלו אעפ״כ מיקרי זה כנגד זה כיון דשני הבתים הם סמוכים להדדי וכנ״ל בסק״ב[ג]: (י) ג׳ בתים. אפילו בכל בית (יב) רק דופן אחד: (יא) בכל ענין. בא לרבות (יג) אפילו חדשים דהכשרנו לעיל בב׳ אפילו בזה אצל זה מ״מ בג׳ פסול: **ב** (יב) להרמב״ם. אבל שארי פוסקים פליגי עליה ומקילים בכל גווני בשתי תפירות ובשלשה תפירות שנפסקו מחמירים דאפילו תיקון במקום ההפסק לא מהני דגנאי הוא כשניכר התיקון בשלשה מקומות בין בחדשים ובין בישנים וצריך לחזור ולתפור מחדש וכמו שנתבאר בטור וב״י לעיל בסוף סימן ל״ב ע״ש: (יג) זו שלא וכו׳.

אפילו

שער הציון

(א) ש״ת: (ב) ט״ז: (ג) מחצית השקל וישועות יעקב: (ד) מרדכי והובא בב״י: (ה) ט״ז: (ו) מחצית השקל עי״ש: (ז) פרי מגדים בא״א אות ג׳: (ח) כן מוכח מדה״מ: (ט) מרדכי: (י) ט״ז: (יא) פמ״ג בא״א: (יב) מוכח בגמרא: (יג) ט״ז:

הגהות ותיקונים: **א)** בישנים, לישנות, וישנות: **ב)** ובולט: **ג)** בסק״ג:

me that one should be stringent (7) *and invalidate /the* tefilin/ *in both cases.*

/As to/ what /*tefilin*/ are /considered/ new /with respect to this matter, the following rule applies/. As long as (8) the housings would spread out and open if one would pull them with the straps they are describable as new, but if /the housings/ would not open out they are describable as old.

If two /housings of the head *tefilin*/ which are not next to one another have become spoiled /, i.e., if they are/ (9) the first /housing/ and the third /housing, the *tefilin*/ are valid, even if they are old.

If (10) three housings /of the head *tefilin*/ have become spoiled, /the *tefilin*/ are invalid (11) in all cases.

2. If the stitches of the *tefilin* have become severed /, then/, (12) according to the *Rambam*[1*] /the following ruling applies/. If the two /severed/ stitches are at the side of one another or if three stitches have become severed, even if (13) one is not next to the other, /the *tefilin*/ are invalid. /However,/ this only applies in the case of old /*tefilin*/, but in the case of new /*tefilin*/, as long as

Mishnah Berurah

which has formed on the outside, one should also be stringent.

(7) And invalidate in both cases. When they make the four housings and put them into a mold, the scribes are accustomed to cut from the skin in between the housings, so that it should not shrink and protrude. They /then/ cover the area of the cut from the inside so that it appears whole from the outside. In view /of the ruling of the gloss/, one should invalidate /such *tefilin*/.

(8) The housings would spread out. This /criterion/ is /applicable/ for those who make the passageway /of the *tefilin*/ from the skin with which the housings are made. However, for us who /make/ the passageway from another skin, this rule is not relevant.

(9) The first and the third. What is meant is that these are classed as /two housings/ which are not next to one another. Even if the tear formed in the third housing on both walls /the *tefilin*/ are /nevertheless/ valid, since there is a whole housing separating them.

However, if the tear formed in the second and third housings /, then/, even if the one tear, in one of the housings, is on the right and the other tear, in the other housing, is on the left, they are nonetheless classed as /tears in two housings/ which are next to one another, since the two housings are adjacent to one another, as /explained/ above in sub-Par. 3.

(10) Three housings. /This ruling also applies/ even if in each housing only one wall /has become spoiled/.

(11) In all cases. /This wording/ is intended to include /within the scope of this ruling/ even new /*tefilin*/. /With respect to such *tefilin* the Shulchan Aruch/ rules above that when two /of the housings have become spoiled the *tefilin* remain/ valid, even if one /of the spoiled housings/ is alongside the other. Nevertheless, when three /housings have become spoiled, new *tefilin*/ are /also/ invalid.

(12) According to the *Rambam*. However, the other Poskim dispute /this ruling/. They are lenient in all circumstances where two stitches /have become severed/. Where three stitches have become severed they /rule/ stringently, that even a repair in the place where they have separated is of no avail. /The reason is/ that it is unbecoming when the repair is noticeable in three places, irrespective of whether /the *tefilin*/ are new or old. One must /therefore/ sew them again anew /in such a case/, as explained in the *Tur* and the *B.Y.* above, at the end of Sec. 32; see there.

(13) One is not, etc. /This ruling applies/ even if each one is on a different side.

1* *Rambam, Hilchos Tefilin* 3:18.

שעור (יד) מושב הבתים קיים כשרים. ואלו הן חדשים כל שאוחזין מקצת העור שנקרע תפרו ותולין בו התפילין והוא חזק ואינו נפסק ואם אין ראוי לתלות בו אלא הוא נפסק הרי אלו ישנות: הגה וי״א דבחדשים פסולים ובישנים כשרים (רש״י והטור והרא״ש) וטוב (טו) * לחוש לשתי הסברות כן נ״ל: **ג** * ה‏עור הרצועות צריך שיהיה מעור בהמה חיה ועוף (טז) הטהורים (יז) * ו‏וצריך שיהיה מעובד (ה) [ג] (יח) לשמו * ז‏רצועות בין מעור בין מקלף כשרות * ח‏הלכה למשה מסיני שיהיו * הרצועות (יט) שחורות

השגת הראב״ד והרמב״ם בפרק ג׳ וספר התרומה סימן ק״ל ז מרדכי ח מנחות ל״ה

באר היטב

(ה) לשמו. ויעבדו לשמן. ואם העבידם לשמן אינו מועיל למה שלא עבדם לשמן תשובת דבר שמואל סי׳ ז׳ ט״ו ע״ש. ובתשובת באר עשק סי׳ יו״ד

שערי תשובה

של יד שנקרע קצת פסול לכ״ע עיין שם: [ג] לשמו. עבה״ט והנה הקדים הסדר והקדים תשובת דב״ש ואח״כ תשובת ב״ע והפוך הוא כי הב״ע יצא ראשונה בענין זה אם הרצועות מעובד שלא לשמה ע״י שהישראל ישחור אותם לשמה אבל אין מסכימים עמו הגאונים בעל דב״ש ובעל גדולי תרומה ומהר״י הלוי וכל גדולי ווינציא ואטליא וכולם חתמו על פסק ונדפס בדב״ש סי׳ י״ט שחלילה לעשות כן והרצועות פסולים ולא יצאו י״ח בהשחרה לשמה ע״ש. ועיין בשו״ת נ״ב מ״ת סימן נ׳ בענין רצועות תפילין שמושחין העורות בשומן דגים הנקרא פיש טרהאן אין בו חשש מן המותר בפיך כיון דהמשיחה אינה עיקר הצבע השחור רק להצליל הצבע לחוצה ולרכך העור קצת ואם לא היה רך ג״כ היה שחור וכשר לרצועות. ואם הצבע שחור עצמו נעשה מן דבר הטמא צ״ע קצת. וצבע תכלת שהוא מחלזון תלוי בפלוגתת רש״י והרמב״ם ע״ש:

משנה ברורה

אפילו כל אחד בצד אחר: (יד) מושב הבתים. היינו התיתורא וכנ״ל וגם בזה (יד) דעת רמ״א כמו בהג״ה לעיל דגם הבתים צריכים להיות קיימים אלא שסמך אלמעלה: (טו) לחוש. ר״ל להחמיר מחמת זה לכתחלה בשתיהם אך במקום שא״א למצוא תפילין אחרים ולא לחזור ולתפור תפילין אלו יש לסמוך על (טו) המקילין בפסיקת התפירות בין בחדשות ובין בישנות[א] בין בב׳ תפירות ובין (טז) בשלש אך בשלש יזהר שלא יברך עליהם ועיין בביאור הלכה: ג (טז) הטהורים. דלא הוכשרה למלאכת שמים אלא טהורה בלבד. גמ׳: (יז) וצריך. כל האי (יז) צריך לעיכוב׳ הוא אפילו בדיעבד: (יח) לשמו. ואפי׳ הרמב״ם דמיקל בבתים וכמבואר לעיל בסימן ל״ב סעיף ל״ז מודה הכא וטעם לזה עיין בלבוש ובמ״א. והשחרה צריך ג״כ שיהיה לשמה ואם לא עיבדן לשמן אינו מועיל אפילו אם ישחירן אח״כ לשמן [תשובת דבר שמואל סימן ז׳ ט״ו ע״ש ובתשובת ב״ע כתב דהשחרה לשמה מהני ועיין בתשובת רע״א דהסכים לדינא כהדב״ש הנ״ל והרעיש על המקילין בזה עי״ש]: (יט) שחורות. עיין בברוך שאמר דמשמע מדבריו דמצוה להשחירן עד שיהיו שחורות כעורב. ודע דאם נתישנו (יח) ונתמעך מהן השחרות צריך להשחירן מחדש וכדלעיל בסימן ל״ב סל״ט ובמקום הידוק

ביאור הלכה

הדין ממה שכתב הוא ומצאתי זה באחרונים ופשוט: * לחוש. עיין במ״ב במש״כ יש לסמוך וכו׳ הוא מהא״ר בשם הב״י הנ״ל שהעתיקו להלכה ופשוט דגם בג׳ תפירות יש לסמוך במקום הדחק וכמו שכתבתי במ״ב ובין בחדשות ובין בישנות אחרי דבלא״ה לא יברך עליהם למה לא יקיים מצות תפילין מחמת ספק לדעה המכשרת. אח״כ מצאתי בדה״ח משמע ג״כ שמיקל בכל גווני במקום הדחק אך הוא כתב דלא יברך עליהם ול״נ דבב׳ תפירות יש לסמוך במקום הדחק ארוב פוסקים דפליגי אהרמב״ם ומקילין בזה ועל פי כ״ז כתבתי דברי שבפנים. ואולם בעיקרא דדינא דפסיקת התפירות יש לענ״ד עיון רב לכאורה לפי מאי דקי״ל דתפירה בגידין הוא הל״מ והרמב״ם משמע דריבוע התפירה הוא ג״כ הל״מ ויש מחמירין עוד יותר בזה מריבוע הבתים עיין לעיל בסימן ל״ב ס״מ[ב] בביאור הגר״א שם א״כ לפי מאי דפסק השו״ע לעיל בסימן ל״ב דאם עשאן מרובעין ואח״ז נתקלקל ריבוען דצריך לתקנן ופסולין כ״ז שלא תקנן וכדמשמע שם בסל״ט בט״ז אמאי מיקל הכא הרמב״ם בנפסקו ג׳ תפירות בחדשים הא ממילא נתקלקל הריבוע דע״פ רוב יש גם תפירות בכל צד אם לא דנאמר דאיירי הכא דוקא בשלא היו הג׳ תפירות בצד אחד וס״ל דזה מיקרי עדיין מרובעות בתפרן אבל אם נתקלקל ריבוע התפירות ע״י פסיקת הגידין כגון שנפסק זוית התפירה אימא לך דאפילו ע״י פחות משלשה מיפסל אמנם א״כ היה לו להרמב״ם והפוסקים לחלק בזה ומדלא הזכירו שום רמז חילוק בכל זה משמע דכשר בכל גווני וא״כ ש״מ דלא ס״ל להא דלעיל בעשאם מרובעות ואח״כ נתקלקל ריבוען ואולי י״ל דזהו ג״כ כונת הרמב״ם במה שכתב כ״ז שפני טבלא קיימת שטבלא הוא טבלא מרובעת כדפירש הערוך הביאו הרא״ש בהל״ק והכונה יהיה כ״ז שריבוע התפירה קיים וכמו שכתבנו מתחלה ולכאורה פירוש זה מכוון יותר ממה שפירשו הם דהכונה בזה כ״ז שהתיתורא קיים דמה ענין קיום התיתורא לקלקול התפירה וצ״ע בכל זה: * עור הרצועות וכו׳ הטהורים. עיין במ״ב וכתב הפמ״ג בפתיחתו איני יודע אם מה״ת או מדרבנן ונ״מ להקל בספיקן אם אינו יודע אם טהורה או טמאה גם בעיבוד[1] לשמה אם יש ספק נראה להקל דהוה דרבנן וספיקו לקולא. ועיי״ש עוד לענין חיפוי עור תפילה של יד ועיין ברמב״ם פ״ג מהלכות תפילין הלכה ט״ו דכלל את החיפוי והרצועה בחדא גוונא ועיין לעיל בסי׳ ל״ב בט״ז ס״ק כ״ז ובפמ״ג שם: * וצריך שיהיה מעובד לשמו. עיין במ״ב במש״כ דאם לא עידן לשמה אינו מועיל אח״כ ההשחרה לשמה דלא כהבאר עשק וראיתי בספר דמשק אליעזר ס״ק י״א שר״ל דהגר״א סובר כהבאר עשק עיי״ש ובאמת נ״ל פשוט דאינו כן רק דכונת הגר״א דכיון דחזינן דלויתה התורה שיהיה העור מתוקן כל צרכו אפילו בהשחרות עאכ״ו בעצם התיקון של העור דהיינו העיבוד שצריך שיהיה בו ואין זה בכלל ק״ו מהלכה דאין זה אלא גילוי מילתא וזה מדוקדק מאוד בלשון הגר״א שכתב אח״: וזהו שכתב המ״א ונ״ל וכו׳ רצונו בזה לתרץ מה שהקשה הפמ״ג על המ״א עי״ש דלדברי הדמשק אליעזר יקשה מאוד לשון המ״א דכתב עיבוד והשחרה דבהשחרה בלבד די וסברא זו שכתבתי למדתיה מתוך דברי ספר התרומה הובא בב״י לענין השחרה לשמה שכתב דהשחרה היא כשאר תיקוני העור הגרועין שאחר העיבוד עי״ש. ודע עוד דנלענ״ד דלדעת הרמב״ם דעיבוד לשמה אינה אלא מדרבנן אפילו אם יסבור ג״כ כספר התרומה שצריך השחרה לשמה עכ״פ אינה אלא מדרבנן דהלא טעמו של ספר התרומה הוא כיון שעיקר השחרה הוא הלכה למ״מ לכך ממילא צריך לשמה כמבואר בב״י א״כ עיבוד נמי הלא עיקר העיבוד הוא הלמ״מ כמבואר בפמ״ג בא״א בתחילת סי׳ ל״ב ואעפ״כ העיבוד לשמה אינו אלא מדרבנן כמו שהאריך בזה הפמ״ג שם בסימן ל״ב כנלע״ד: * רצועות בין מעור וכו׳ כשרות. וקלף המעובד לסת״ס צ״ע אי מותר לעשות רצועה מזה [פמ״ג בפתיחה לסימן ל״ב עי״ש]: * הלכה למשה מסיני וכו׳. ולעיכובא הוא אפילו בדיעבד הרמב״ם בפ״ג ה״א והולך לבאר זה דיש הלכה שהוא רק למצוה בעלמא כבשבת דף ע״ט ע״ב עי״ש: * הרצועות שחורות. בין הש״ר או הש״י רמב״ם שם ומסתפקנא אם מה״ת די בכל אחד עד כדי שיעורו והשאר הוא למצוה ולנוי בעלמא או דילמא כיון דהיא מחוברת כולה כחדא צריכה להיות כולה שחור וקצת ראיה לזה מקושית הגמרא מנחות ל״ה ע״א קתני מיהת בין ירוקין וכו׳ דלא משני בהיתר על השיעור ולא היה מקשה עוד אי מבפנים וכו׳ ויש לדחות דס״ל להגמרא דלא היה הברייתא מתיר עכ״פ מדרבנן לצבוע בשני גווני מצד אחד משום דמחזי כמנומר עיין במ״א סק״ז וצ״ע. גם איני יודע אם ההל״מ קאי ג״כ על חתיכת הרצועה שנכנסת בהמעברתא ולכתחילה לא מסתפקנא דחייב להשחיר דילמא מתהפך הבית מזה המקום עיין בגמרא שם אך בדיעבד אולי דמי למה שבפנים ועיין ברמב״ם בפ״ג מה״ת הי״ד. וגדר השחרות עיין בברוך שאמר שכתב שישחירו פ״א ואח״כ כשיתייבש קצת אז ישחירו פעם שנית וכן פעם שלישית עד שיהיה העור שחור לכל הצורך ממש כעורב ונ״ל דזהו רק למצוה בעלמא אבל מדינא כל שחל עליו שם שחור סגי ליה ולפ״ז אפילו אם היה מראיתו דומה למראה הכחול [שקורין בלא״ה] ג״כ כשר וראיה לזה מנידה דף י״ט ע״א במראות הדמים דאם היה שחור כחרת טמא כיהה מכן אפילו היה שחור ככחול טהור וכדפירש״י שם אלמא דמראית

שער הציון

(יד) לבושי שרד: (טו) א״ר בשם הב״י: (טז) דה״ח עי״ש ובבה״ל: (יז) רמב״ם פ״ג מהלכות תפילין הלכה ט״ו ולעיל בסימן ל״ב בב״י ד״ה ומש״כ רבינו שהרא״ש כתב וכו׳ ובהרבה מקומות (יח) ב״ח בסי׳ ל״ב:

הגהות ותיקונים: א) בישנות: **ב)** סעיף ל״ט

הערות והארות: 1) עיין לעיל בסל״ב ס״ח בבה״ל ד״ה וצריך, לענין לשמה אם מה״ת או מדרבנן:

the skin (14) on which the housings rest is intact /the *tefilin*/ are valid.

/As to/ what /*tefilin*/ are /considered/ new /with respect to this matter, the following rule applies/. /*Tefilin* are describable as new/ as long as the skin with the torn stitch would be strong and would not become severed, if one would take hold of some /of it/ and suspend the *tefilin* with it. /However,/ if /the skin/ is not fit for suspending /the *tefilin*/, but would become severed /if one did so, the *tefilin*/ are /considered/ old.

*Gloss: There are /authorities/ who say that in the case of new /*tefilin*/ they are invalid /, whereas/, in the case of old /*tefilin*/ they are valid. (...) It is desirable* (15) *to take into account both views. So it appears to me.*

3. The skin of the straps must be of the skin of a domestic or non-domestic animal or of a bird, (16) which is /halachically/ clean. (17) It must be processed2* (18) for the sake of /use for the mitzvah/.

Mishnah Berurah

(14) On which the housings rest. I.e., the bridge /of the *tefilin*/, as /explained/ above.

With respect to this case also the *Rema* is of the opinion /stated/ in the gloss above, that the housings must also be intact, but he relied that /it would be understood that what he wrote/ above /also applies here/.

(15) To take into account. I.e., one should be stringent initially because of this in both cases. However, where it is impossible to find other *tefilin* or to sew these *tefilin* again, one may rely on /the authorities/ who are lenient when the stitches have become severed, both in the case of new /*tefilin*/ and in the case of old /*tefilin*/ and both when two stitches are involved and when three /stitches/ are involved. Only, when three /stitches/ are involved, one should take care not to make a blessing over /the *tefilin*/. See the Beyur Halachah.

(16) Which is /halachically/ clean. /This is/ because only /halachically/ clean /animals or birds/ alone are allowed /to serve/ a heavenly function. Gemara[1]

(17) It must be. By "must", in all these /cases/, an essential /requirement is meant/. /If the requirement is not complied with, this/ even /precludes validity/ once it is after the event.

(18) For the sake of /use for the mitzvah/. Even the *Rambam*, who is lenient /about this/ with respect to the housings, as explained above in Sec. 32, Par. 37 /, in the Mishnah Berurah, sub-Par. 171/, concedes

2* The strap must also be cut off from the skin for the sake of use for the mitzvah of *tefilin*. (Beyur Halachah)

1 *Shabbos* 28b.

שעור (יד) מושב הבתים קיים כשרים. ואלו הן חדשים כל שאוחזין מקצת העור שנקרע תפרו ותולין בו התפילין והוא חזק ואינו נפסק ואם אין ראוי לתלות בו אלא הוא נפסק הרי אלו ישנות: הגה וי״א דבחדשים פסולים ובישנים כשרים (רש״י והטור והרא״ש) וטוב (טו) * לחוש לשתי הסברות כן נ״ל: ג * ^ה^עור הרצועות צריך שיהיה מעור בהמה חיה ועוף (טז) הטהורים (יז) * ^ו^וצריך שיהיה מעובד (ה) [ג] (יח) לשמו . * ^ז^רצועות בין מעור בין מקלף כשרות * ^ח^הלכה למשה מסיני שיהיו * הרצועות (יט) שחורות

השגת״ה והרמב״ם בפרק ג׳ וספר התרומה סימן ק״ז מרדכי ח מנחות ל״ה

באר היטב

(ה) לשמו. וישחירם לשמן. ואם השחירם לשמן אינו מועיל למה שלא עבדם לשמן תשובת דבר שמואל סי׳ ז׳ ט״ו ע״ש. ובתשובת באר עשק סי׳ יו״ד

שערי תשובה

של יד שנקרע קצת פסול לכ״ע עיין שם: [ג] לשמו. עבה״ט והנה הקדים הסדר והקדים תשובת דב״ש ואח״כ תשובת ב״ע והפוך הוא כי הב״ע יצא ראשונה בענין זה אם הרצועות מעובד שלא לשמה ע״י שהישראל ישחור אותם לשמה אבל אין מסכימים עמו הגאונים בעל דב״ש ובעל גדולי תרומה ומהר״י הלוי וכל גדולי ווינציא ואטליא וכולם חתמו על פסק ונדפס בדב״ש סי׳ י״ט שחלילה לעשות כן והרצועות פסולים ולא יצאו י״ח בהשחרה לשמה ע״ש. ועיין בשו״ת נ״ב מ״ת סימן ג׳ בענין רצועות תפילין שמושחין העורות בשומן דגים הנקרא פיש טראן אין בו חשש מן המותר בפיך כיון דהמשיחה אינה עיקר הצבע השחור רק להצליל הצבע לחזותא ולרכך העור קצת ואם לא היה רך ג״כ היה שחור וכשר לרצועות. ואם הצבע שחור עצמו נעשה מן דבר הטמא צ״ע קצת. וצבע תכלת שהוא מחלזון תלוי בפלוגתת רש״י והרמב״ם ע״ש:

משנה ברורה

אפילו כל אחד בצד אחר: (יד) מושב הבתים. היינו התיתורא וכנ״ל וגם בזה (יד) דעת רמ״א כמו בהג״ה לעיל דגם הבתים צריכים להיות קיימים אלא שסמך אלמעלה: (טו) לחוש. ר״ל להחמיר מתחלה זה לכתחלה בשתיהם אך במקום שא״א למצוא תפילין אחרים ולא לחזור ולהפור תפילין אלו יש לסמוך על (טו) המקילין בפסיקת התפירות בין בחדשות ובין בישנות^א)^ בין בב׳ תפירות ובין (טו) בשלש אך בשלש יזהר שלא יברך עליהם ועיין בביאור הלכה: ג (טז) הטהורים. דלא הוכשרה למלאכת שמים אלא טהורה בלבד. גמ׳: (יז) וצריך. כל האי (יז) צריך לעיכוב׳ הוא אפילו בדיעבד: (יח) לשמו. ואפי׳ הרמב״ם דמיקל בבתים וכמבואר לעיל בסימן ל״ב סעיף ל״ז מודה הכא וטעם לזה עיין בלבוש ובמ״א. וההשחרה צריך ג״כ שיהיה לשמה ואם לא עיבדן לשמן אינו מועיל אפילו אם ישחירן אח״כ לשמן [תשובת דבר שמואל סימן-ז׳ ט״ו עי״ש ובתשובת ב״ע כתב דהשחרה לשמה מהני ועיין בתשובת רע״א דהסכים לדינא כהדב״ש הנ״ל והרעיש על המקילין בזה עי״ש]: (יט) שחורות. עיין בברוך שאמר דמשמע מדבריו דמצוה להשחירן עד שיהיו שחורות כעורב. ודע דאם נתישנו (יח) ונתמעך מהן השחרות צריך להשחירן מחדש וכדלעיל בסימן ל״ב סל״ט ובמקום הידוק

ביאור הלכה

הדין ממה שכתב הוא ומצאתי זה באחרונים ופשוט: * לחוש. עיין במ״ב במש״כ יש לסמוך וכו׳ הוא מהא״ר בשם הב״י הנ״ל שהעתיקו להלכה ופשוט דגם בג׳ תפירות יש לסמוך במקום הדחק וכמו שכתבתי במ״ב ובין בחדשות ובין בישנות אחרי דבלא״ה לא יברך עליהם למה לא יקיים מצות תפילין מחמת ספק לדעה המכשרת. אח״כ מצאתי בדה״ח משמע ג״כ שמיקל בכל גווני במקום הדחק אך הוא כתב דלא יברך עליהם ול״נ דבב׳ תפירות יש לסמוך במקום הדחק ארוב פוסקים דפליגי אהרמב״ם ומקילין בזה ועל פי כ״ז כתבתי דברי שבפנים. ואולם בעיקרא דדינא דפסיקת התפירות יש לענ״ד עיון רב לכאורה לפי מאי דקי״ל דתפירה בגידין הוא הל״מ ומהרמב״ם משמע דריבוע התפירה הוא ג״כ הל״מ ויש מחמירין עוד יותר בזה מריבוע הבתים עיין לעיל בסימן ל״ב ס״מ^ב)^ בביאור הגר״א שם א״כ לפי מאי דפסק השו״ע לעיל בסימן ל״ב דאם עשאן מרובעין ואח״ז נתקלקל ריבוען דצריך לתקנן ופסולין כ״ז שלא תקנן וכדמשמע שם בסל״ט בט״ז אמאי מיקל הכא הרמב״ם בנפסקו ג׳ תפירות בחדשים הא ממילא נתקלקל הריבוע דע״פ רוב יש גם תפירות בכל צד אם לא דנאמר דאיירי הכא דוקא בשלא היו הג׳ תפירות בצד אחד וס״ל דזה מיקרי עדיין מרובעות בתפרן אבל אם נתקלקל ריבוע התפירות ע״י פסיקת הגידין כגון שנפסק זוית התפירה אימא לך דאפילו ע״י פחות משלשה מיפסל אמנם א״כ היה לו להרמב״ם והפוסקים לחלק בזה ומדלא הזכירו שום רמז חילוק בכל זה משמע דכשר בכל גווני וא״כ ש״מ דלא ס״ל להא דלעיל בעשאם מרובעות ואח״כ נתקלקל ריבוען ואולי י״ל דזהו ג״כ כונת הרמב״ם במה שכתב כ״ז שפני טבלא קיימת שטבלא הוא טבלא מרובעת כדפירש הערוך הביאו הרא״ש בהל״ק והכונה יהיה כ״ז שריבוע התפירה קיים וכמו שכתבנו מתחלה ולכאורה פירוש זה מכוון יותר ממה שפירשו הם דהכונה בזה כ״ז שהתיתורא קיים דמה ענין קיום התיתורא לקלקול התפירה וצ״ע בכל זה: * עור הרצועות וכו׳ הטהורים. עיין במ״ב וכתב הפמ״ג בפתיחתו איני יודע אם מה״ת או מדרבנן ונ״מ להקל בספיקן אם אינו יודע אם טהורה או טמאה גם בעיבוד^1)^ לשמה אם יש ספק נראה להקל דהוה דרבנן וספיקו לקולא. ועיי״ש עוד לענין חיפוי עור תפילה של יד ועיין ברמב״ם פ״ג מהלכות תפילין הלכה ט״ו דכלל את החיפוי והרצועה בחדא גוונא ועיין לעיל בסי׳ ל״ב בט״ז ס״ק כ״ז ובפמ״ג שם: * וצריך שיהיה מעובד לשמו. עיין במ״ב במש״כ דאם לא עידבן לשמה דלא כהבאר עשק וראיתי בספר דמשק אליעזר ס״ק י״א שר״ל דהגר״א סובר כהבאר עשק עיי״ש ובאמת נ״ל פשוט דאינו כן רק דכונת הגר״א דכיון דחזינן דלויתה התורה שיהיה העור מתוקן כל צרכו אפילו בהשחרה אעכ״ו בעצם התיקון של העור דהיינו העיבוד שצריך שיהיה בו ואין זה בכלל ק״ו מהלכה דאין זה אלא גילוי מילתא וזה מדוקדק מאוד בלשון הגר״א שכתב אח״: וזהו שכתב המ״א ונ״ל וכו׳ רצונו בזה לתרץ מה שהקשה הפמ״ג על המ״א עי״ש דלדברי הדמשק אליעזר יקשה מאוד לשון המ״א דכתב עיבוד והשחרה דבהשחר: בלבד די וסברא זו שכתבתי למדתיה מתוך דברי ספר התרומה הובא בב״י לענין השחרה לשמה שכתב דהשחרה היא כשאר תיקוני העור הגרועין שאחר העיבוד עי״ש. ודע עוד דנלענ״ד דלדעת הרמב״ם דעיבוד לשמה אינה אלא מדרבנן אפילו אם יסבור ג״כ כספר התרומה שצריך השחרה לשמה עכ״פ אינה אלא מדרבנן דהלא טעמו של ספר התרומה הוא כיון שעיקר השחרה הוא הלכה למ״מ לכך ממילא צריך לשמה כמבואר בב״י א״כ עיבוד נמי הלא עיקר העיבוד הוא הלמ״מ כמבואר בפמ״ג בא״א בתחילת סי׳ ל״ב ואעפ״כ העיבוד לשמה אינו אלא מדרבנן כמו שהאריך בזה הפמ״ג שם בסימן ל״ב כנלע״ד: * רצועות בין מעור וכו׳ כשרות. וקלף המעובד לספ״ס ל״ע אי מותר לעשות רצועה מזה [פמ״ג בפתיחה לסימן ל״ב עי״ש]: * הלכה למשה מסיני וכו׳. ולעיכובא הוא אפילו בדיעבד הרמב״ם בפ״ג ה״א והאורך לצאר זה דיש הלכה שהוא רק למצוה בעלמא כשבת דף ע״ט ע״ב עי״ש: * הרצועות שחורות. בין הש״ר או הש״י רמב״ם שם ומסתפקנא אם מה״ת די בכל אחד עד כדי שיעורו והשאר הוא למצוה ונוי בעלמא או דילמא כיון דהיא מחוברת כולה כחדא צריכה להיות כולה שחור וקצת ראיה לזה מקושית הגמרא מנחות ל״ה ע״א קתני מיהת בין ירוקין וכו׳ דלא משני בהיתר על השיעור ולא היה מקשה עוד אי מבפנים וכו׳ ויש לדחות דס״ל להגמרא דלא היה הברייתא מתיר עכ״פ מדרבנן לצבוע בשני גווני מצד אחד משום דמחזי כמגומר עיין במ״א סק״ז וצ״ע. גם איני יודע אם ההל״מ קאי ג״כ על חתיכת הרצועה שנכנסת בהמעברתא ולכתחילה לא מסתפקנא דחייב להשחיר דילמא מתהפך הבית מזה המקום עיין בגמרא שם אך בדיעבד אולי דמי למה שבפנים ועיין ברמב״ם בפ״ג מה״ת הי״ד. וגדר השחרות עיין בברוך שאמר שכתב שישחירו פ״א ואח״כ כשיתייבש קצת אז ישחירו פעם שנית וכן פעם שלישית עד שיהיה העור שחור לכל הצורך ממש כעורב ונ״ל דזהו רק למצוה בעלמא אבל מדינא כל שחל עליו שם שחור סגי ליה ולפ״ז אפילו אם היה מראיתו דומה למראה הכחול [שקורין בלא״ה] ג״כ כשר וראיה לזה מנידה דף י״ט ע״א במראות הדמים דאם היה שחור כחרת טמא כיהה מכן אפילו היה שחור ככחול טהור וכדפירש״י שם אלמא דמראית

שער הציון

(יד) לבושי שרד: (טו) א״ר בשם הב״י: (טז) דה״ח עי״ש ובבה״ל: (יז) רמב״ם פ״ג מהלכות תפילין הלכה ט״ו ולעיל בסימן ל״ב בב״י ד״ה ומש״כ רבינו שהרא״ש כתב וכו׳ ובהרבה מקומות (יח) ב״ח בסי׳ ל״ג:

הגהות ותיקונים: א) בישנות: **ב)** סעיף ל״ט

הערות והארות: 1) עיין לעיל בסל״ב ס״ח בבה״ל ד״ה וצריך, לענין לשמה אם מה״ת או מדרבנן:

The straps are valid irrespective of whether they are of hide or of parchment.

There is a halachic /requirement which was taught/ to Mosheh (Moses) on /Mount/ Sinai, that the straps /of the *tefilin*/ must be /made/ **(19)** black

Mishnah Berurah

that /for the straps it is in fact required/. For the reason for this, see the *Levush* and the *M.A.*

The blackening must also be done for the sake of /use for the mitzvah/. /However,/ if one did not process the straps for the sake of /use for the mitzvah/, it is of no avail even if one blackens them subsequently for the sake of /use for the mitzvah/. [Responsa of the *Devar Shemu'el*, Sec. 7:15; see there. In the responsa of the *B.A.*, /the author/ writes that /even if one did not process them for the sake of use for the mitzvah/, blackening for the sake of /use for the mitzvah/ is of avail. See the responsa of *R.A.E.* who agrees with the *Dev. Sh.*, /mentioned/ above, as regards the halachic /ruling/ and storms against those who are lenient about this; see there.]

(19) Black. See the *Baruch She-Amar*. It is implied by his words that it is a mitzvah to blacken them until they have the blackness of a raven.[2]

Note that if /the straps/ have aged and their blackness has disintegrated, one must blacken them anew, in conformance with /what is ruled/ above in Sec. 32, Par. 39. In

2 Once it is after the event, as long as it has become classed as black, the strap is valid. A blue color is also valid. (Beyur Halachah)

(כ) * מבחוץ אבל מצד פנים (כא) יעשה מאיזה צבע שירצה חוץ מאדום שמא יאמרו שמדם חטטיו נצבעו והאדימו: ד (כב) [ט]טוב שישחירם ישראל לשמן ולא א"י: הגה * ומיהו בדיעבד כשר אם השחיר עור הבתים (כג) * אבל הרצועות * אפילו בדיעבד (ו) (כד) * פסול (מלא כתוב): ה * אם נפסקה הרצועה

ט ספר התרומה קל"א י מנחות ל"ה

באר היטב

כתב דהשחרה לשמה מהני: (ו) פסול. כי מה שיהיו הבתים שחורים אינו הל"מ א"כ לא הוי השחרות רק תיקון בעלמא וכשר ע"י נכרי משא"כ

משנה ברורה

הקשר מלוי מאד להתמעך השחרות ויש ליזהר בזה מאד: (כ) מבחוץ. לצד השער שהוא מקום החלק. ואם השחירם מבפנים לא מהני וצריך לחזור ולהשחירם מבחוץ ועיין בביאור הלכה: (כא) יעשה. ר"ל אם ירצה לצבוע אותן אבל אין מחוייב לצבען בשום צבע דאף להרמב"ם צריך להשחירן גם מבפנים כמו שהבתים הם שחורין אין אנו נוהגין כהרמב"ם בזה כמבואר בב"י וד"מ: ד (כב) טוב וכו'. אבל בדיעבד כשר לדידיה (יט) אפילו ע"י א"י דס"ל דאפילו ברצועות לא בעינן השחרות כלל לשמן ורמ"א בהג"ה חולק עליו וס"ל דברצועות דהשחרות הוא הל"מ צריך השחרות לשמן וממילא בא"י דאינו עושה לשמה פסול ודינו כדלעיל בסימן ל"ב לענין קלף עי"ש אבל בעור הבתים דלרוב פוסקים שחרותו הוא למצוה בעלמא ולא לעיכובא וכדלעיל בסימן ל"ב ס"מ ולכך לא בעינן ביה ג"כ השחרות לשמן בדיעבד וה"ל להרמ"א לכתוב הגהתו בלשון י"א אך שמלינו כמה פעמים כיולא בזה: (כג) אבל הרצועות וכו'. אם עשאן נכרי או אפילו ישראל אך שלא לשמן והטעם כנ"ל בס"ק כ"ב. וכ"ש בכל דבר שצריך בתפילין גופא לעיכובא כמו עשיית הבית והשי"ן שלו בכל פרטיו שיהיה כדין או תפירתו או עשיית (ג) הקשר שלו דכל אלו הוא הל"מ אם עשאן ישראל שלא לשמן פסול וכתב הפמ"ג דיש למנוע מלמסור ר"ז (כח) יע"י קטן אפי' אם (כב) גדול יעמוד ע"ג ויזהירו לעשות לשמה וכן שלא לעשותם ע"י אשה וכל הפסולין המבואר לקמן בסימן ל"ט עי"ש בסעיף א' וב'. והשחרת הרצועות דזה אינו בגוף התפילין מותר ע"י אשה דהיא יודעת לעשות לשמה כמו איש אבל ע"י א"י וקטן אינו מותר עד שיעמוד אחר על גבם וכדלעיל לענין קלף בסימן ל"ב עי"ש במ"ב: (כד) פסול. כתב המ"א

ביאור הלכה

דמראית כחול הוא בכלל שחור וכן בחולין דף מ"ז לענין ריאה דאם שחרותה דומה לכחול וכדאיתא ברמב"ם בפ"ז מהלכות שחיטה הלכה י"ט שחורה ככחול אלמא דאף מראה כחול הוא בכלל שחור ומ"מ לכתחילה בודאי מצוה להשחירו שיהיה שחור ממש וכמ"ש הב"ש. ועיין במש"כ לעיל בסימן ל"ב ס"ג לענין שחרות הדיו דשם בעינן שיהי' שחור ממש עי"ש. ודע דבמה שכתבנו שם יוסר קושיא אחת שראיתי לגאון אחד שנתקשה על הרמב"ם למה לא נאמר ההלכה סתם שיהיו כותבין בדבר השחור ולדברינו ניחא דשחור סתם היה משמע אפילו אם הוא שחור רק ככחול ודוק: * מבחוץ. עיין מ"ב כן מוכח מרש"י דף ל"ה ע"ב ד"ה ונוייהן דאלת"ה אלא דצריך לצבוע סתם המקום שרולה ללבשו לצד חוץ וזהו כונת הגמרא במה שמשני כאן מבחוץ ממה פסיקא ליה לרש"י דצובע אותו מקום החלק שיהא קרי ליה בשביל זה ונוייהן הי"ל לרש"י לפרש סתמא אותו מקום שהוא חלק ונוי ילבשנו למעלה וממילא יוכרח האדם לצבוע שחור אותו מקום מחמת ההל"מ וכן איתא בטור כמ"ש וראיתי בפמ"ג שכתב אם השחיר עכו"ם הרצועה ואין לו רצועה אחרת יוכל להשחיר מצד השני דנהי דגמירי שחורות אבל לא דוקא מצד השער וכונתו אם יהפך הרצועה וילבש השחור לצד חוץ וכן ביאר הדה"ח את דבריו ולפ"ז מה שמשני שם הגמרא בע"א כאן מבחוץ תלוי רק בהמקום שלובש מצד חוץ ומה שאמרו שם בגמרא ונוייהן לבר שחור וחלק הוא למצוה מן המובחר בלבד והביא ראיה לזה מרש"י זו ד"ה ונוייהן ובאמת לכאורה משמע להיפך ואף אם תדחה דברינו עכ"פ אין ראיה מרש"י לדבריו אך מהרמב"ם בה"ת הי"ד משמע קצת כדבריו ומ"מ לכתחילה בודאי גם הוא מודה כמו שכתב בעצמו. ודע דלדברי הפמ"ג ילמח לפעמים חומרא גדולה אם יהי' מונח הרצועה במקום הקף הקשר בצד השחור למטה לא ילא בזה ידי המצוה והוי ברכה לבטלה ולפי הנראה שדבר זה במחלוקת שנוי עיין לעיל בסימן כ"ז בא"ר שכן כתב בשם גליון המרדכי ולענ"ד דהב"י פליג ע"ז וס"ל דלא עבר רק על ונוייהן לבר ולכך אפילו איתהפך אח"כ נמי אסור עי"ש בא"ר ודוק: * ומיהו בדיעבד וכו'. ועיין בפמ"ג שהביא בשם הב"ח דיש להחמיר בזה אם יש לו תפילין אחרים ונ"ל פשוט דבבתים בודאי יש לסמוך ולהקל אם יחזור הישראל וישחירם לשמן וכמו שכתב המג"א דבלא"ה יש הרבה ספיקות בזה וכמו שכתב הדגמ"ר ולבושי שרד עי"ש: * אבל הרצועות. הטעם כתב סה"ת כיון דעלם השחרות הוא הל"מ לשמה ג"כ בעינן כמו דבעינן לשמה בשעת טוויה בלילית ולביעה בתכלת. ולפ"ז נראה לכאורה דה"ה עלם עשיית הרלועה דהיינו חתיכתה מהעור ג"כ בעינן לשמה ומלאתי שכן כתב בעמק הלכה: * אפילו בדיעבד וכו'. עיין במ"ב במש"כ וכ"ש וכו' עיין לקמן בסימן ל"ט ס"ב דכל אלו שהם בכלל עשיית גוף התפילין הם בכלל כתיבת התפילין עי"ש במ"א א"כ פשוט דעכ"פ לא גריעי מהשחרת הרלועות דבעי שיהי' לשמן וראיתי בס' מגן האלף שכתב דהרמב"ם ע"כ לא ס"ל לדינו דספר התרומה שהרי כתב בפ"ג מה"ת ס"א[א] אין עושין תפילין אלא ישראל וכו' לפיכך אם חיפן העו"ג או תפרן פסולות וכו' וא"א דבעי לשמן תיפוק ליה דלא היה לשמן שהרי הרמב"ם ס"ל דבכל דבר שלריך לשמה אינו מועיל בעכו"ם אפילו ישראל עוע"ג ולפי מה שכתב הגרע"א בחידושיו בסי' ל"ט על קושית המג"א כעין זה עי"ש אזדא ראיתו ובפרט לפי מה שמלדד הפמ"ג בסי' ל"ב ס"ק ל"ב דכתיבה לשמה הוא מדרבנן נ"מ לכמה דברים עיין בפתיחת הפמ"ג בהלכות ק"ש ובלא"ה אין להקל למעשה נגד הכרעת רמ"א ואולי דמה שאינן נזהרין הסופרים בכל זה לחשוב לשמה היינו משום דסתמא לשמה קאי כיון שכבר נעבד לשמה אבל גם זה אינו דהרי בתליית לילית בהבגד איתא לעיל בסימן י"ד דאם הטיל ישראל לילית בבגד בלא כונה דאין לברך עליה אף דשם כבר נטוו החוטין לשם לילית אפ"ה לא אמרינן דסתמא לשמה קאי וכן לענין כתיבת סת"מ ג"כ אפילו בדיעבד לא מהני בסתמא וכדמוכח בסי' ל"ב סי"ט עי"ש ומש"כ בסעיף ח' טוב להוליא וכו' היינו דבדיעבד סגי במחשבה אבל לא בסתמא ואולי דכיון דבעל התרומות בעלמו לא ברירא ליה דין זה כמבואר בב"י אם למידין זה מלילית או לא די אם נחמיר בזה בדיעבד לענין אם עשאן עכו"ם וכן ישראל שחישב שלא לשמן אבל לא בסתמא ול"ע. ואף דלא ברירא לן למפסל משום זה דיעבד מ"מ לכתחילה בודאי לריך לעשות כל עשיית הבתים והשי"ן ותפירתם ועשיית הרלועות והשחרתם בפירוש לשמה. ודע דמה שכתבנו לענין השחרת הרלועות דמותר ע"י קטן כשאחר עוע"ג אף דהפמ"ג בתחלת הפתיחה בל"ב רלה להחמיר בזה אכן במקומו בסי' זה במ"ז או"ק ה' ובל"ט בא"א או"ק ו' חזר מזה והתיר ומלאתי כן בעזה"י בהדיא בתשובת מהר"ס לובלין סי' ס"ח דהשחרת הרלועות אינו בכלל תיקון עשייה. ומש"כ דע"י עכו"ם כשאחר עוע"ג מותר אף דיש לפקפק בזה עיין לעיל בסי' י"א במה שתמה הדגמ"ר על השו"ע דמתיר בטוויה להרא"ש ע"י עכו"ם וא"כ ה"נ מ"מ נלענ"ד דאין להחמיר בזה בדיעבד אחרי שהתרומה[ב] גופא לא פסיקא ליה דינו כ"כ: * פסול. עיין במ"ב במש"כ שהאחרונים השיגו על עלת המ"א ואעפ"כ נ"ל דאם ישראל השחיר הרלועות בפעם ראשון ולא חישב בהן לשמן רק בסתמא בזה אפשר דנוכל לסמוך על המ"א שישחירו שנית בפירוש לשמן ודיו דהוא כעין ס"ם ולכאורה היה נ"ל עלה אחרת דהיה מועיל לכו"ע אף אם השחירו עכו"ם בפעם ראשונה דכל עיקר קושיתם על המ"א הוא דהו"ל דיו ע"ג דיו עתה יצבענו מתחלה על המראה השחור במראה סיקרא או ירוק ולבן וכה"ג ואחי מראה זו ומבטל להשחור כדאמרינן גיטין י"ט סיקרא ע"ג דיו דהוא מוחק ואח"כ יצבע מלמעלה במראה שחור לשמן ודיו ואע"ג דאמרינן שם וכי מפני שאנו מדמין וכו' שאני הכא דתו הוי כעין ס"ם דלבעל התרומה עלמו לא פסיק ליה וכנ"ל אך עכ"ז ל"ע דילמא דוקא כתב דיו ע"ג כתב סיקרא מבטל העליון להתחתון דכתב דיו עדיף לכו"ע משא"כ בלבע שחור ע"ג לבע סיקרא וכדומה דילמא הלבע התחתון עדיף והעושה כן בשבת אינו חייב משום לובע ובדידן נמי הלבע העליון השחור אינו חשוב לבטל בשלימות הלבע שהיה תחתיו מתחילה שישאר רק שם שחור עליו וכמו דאמרינן שם בסיקרא ע"ג דיו עי"ש בגמרא בגיטין י"ט ול"ע: * אם נפסקה וכו' ובשל יד כדי שתקיף וכו'. כתב המחלית השקל דלריך אחר התפירה מתחלה למתוח ביושר הרלועה השלימה עד האלבע ואח"כ יחזור עם הרלועה הנקשר למטה ויכרוך הזרוע כמנהג דעד האלבע לריך להיות בלא קשירה ובספר שנות חיים להגאון מהר"ש קלוגר כתב דאין העולם נוהגין כדבריו והדין עמהם עי"ש גם בתשובת מהר"ס

שער הציון

(יט) מ"א: (כ) פמ"ג בסוף ל"ב קודם הפתיחה: (כא) שם לענין הקשר והשאר לקמן בסי' ל"ט ס"ב במ"א: (כב) לקמן בסי' ל"ט ובאחרונים:

הגהות ותיקונים: א) הט"ז: **ב)** שבעל התרומה:

הערות והארות: 1) עיין בה"ל סי' י"א ס"ב ד"ה טוואן כו' לענין קטן בן י"ג שלא הביא ב' שערות:

(20) on the outside. However, on the inside, **(21)** one may make them any color he wishes, with the exception of red. /Red is forbidden/ in case /people/ would say that /the straps/ became stained from the blood of his scabs and /therefore became/ red.

4. (22) It is desirable that a Jew should blacken /the straps/ for the sake of /use for the mitzvah of *tefilin*/ and not that a non-Jew /should blacken them/.

Mishnah Berurah

the place where the knot is tightened it is very common for the blackness to disintegrate. One must be very careful about this.

(20) On the outside. /I.e.,/ on the hair side, which is the smooth part.

If one blackened /the straps only/ on the inside, this is of no avail and one must blacken them again, /this time/ on the outside. See the Beyur Halachah.

(21) One may make. I.e., if he wishes to color them. One is not, however, obliged to color them with any color. Although according to the *Rambam*[3] one is required to blacken them on the inside as well, just as the housings are /required to be made/ black, we do not act in accordance with the *Rambam*'s /view/ with respect to this /matter/, as stated by the *B.Y.* and the *D.M.*

(22) It is desirable, etc. However, once it is after the event, /the straps/ are valid according to /the view of the author of the Shulchan Aruch/ even if /they were blackened/ by a non-Jew. /This is/ because he is of the opinion that even in the case of the straps the blackening is not at all required /to be done/ for the sake of /use for the mitzvah/.

The *Rema* disputes his /view/ in the gloss. He is of the opinion that since the blackening in the case of the straps is a halachic /requirement which was taught/ to Mosheh (Moses) on /Mount/ Sinai, it is necessary for the blackening /to be done/ for the sake of /use for the mitzvah/. It follows that if /it was done/ by a non-Jew, who will not have done it for the sake of /use for the mitzvah, the straps/ are invalid. /According to him/ the /same/ ruling /applies/ for /the blackening of the straps by a non-Jew/ as is /given/ above in Sec. 32 /, Par. 9/ with respect to /the processing of/ the parchment /used for *tefilin* passages/; see there. However, in the case of the skin of the housings, the blackening, according to the majority of Poskim, is a mere mitzvah /requirement/ and is not essential /for validity/, as /ruled/ above in Sec. 32, Par. 40. For this /reason/, once it is after the event, we also do not require the blackening of this /skin to have been done/ for the sake of /use for the mitzvah/. The *Rema* should have written the gloss with the wording, "There are /authorities/ who say /, etc./", but we find a similar /deviation from this principle/ several times.

3 *Rambam, Hilchos Tefilin* 3:14.

באר הגולה

(כ) * מבחוץ אבל מצד פנים (כא) יעשה מאיזה צבע שירצה חוץ מאדום שמא יאמרו שמדם חטטיו נצבעו והאדימו: ד (כב) [ט]טוב שישחירם ישראל לשמן ולא א"י: הגה * ומיהו בדיעבד כשר אם השחיר עור הבתים (כג) * אבל הרצועות * אפילו בדיעבד (ו) (כד) * פסול (מלא כתוב): ה * [י]אם נפסקה הרצועה

ט ספר התרומה קל"א י מנחות ל"ה

באר היטב

כתב דהשחרה לשמה מהני: (ו) פסול. כי מה שיהיו הבתים שחורים אינו הל"מ א"כ לא הוי השחרות רק תיקון בעלמא וכשר ע"י נכרי משא"כ

משנה ברורה

הקשר מצוי מאד להתמעך השחרות ויש ליזהר בזה מאד: (כ) מבחוץ. לצד השער שהוא מקום החלק. ואם השחירם מבפנים לא מהני וצריך לחזור ולהשחירם מבחוץ ועיין בביאור הלכה: (כא) יעשה. ר"ל אם ירצה לצבוע אותן אבל אין מחוייב לצבען בשום צבע דאף דלהרמב"ם צריך להשחירן גם מבפנים כמו שהבתים הם שחורין אין אנו נוהגין כהרמב"ם בזה כמבואר בב"י וד"מ: ד (כב) טוב וכו'. אבל בדיעבד כשר לדידיה (יט) אפילו ע"י א"י דס"ל דאפילו ברצועות לא בעינן השחרות כלל לשמן ורמ"א בהג"ה חולק עליו וס"ל דברצועות דהשחרות הוא הל"מ צריך השחרות לשמן וממילא בא"י דאינו עושה לשמה פסול ודינו כדלעיל בסימן ל"ב לענין קלף עי"ש אבל בעור הבתים דלרוב פוסקים שחרותו הוא למצוה בעלמא ולא לעיכובא וכדלעיל בסימן ל"ב מ"מ ולכך לא בעינן ביה ג"כ השחרות לשמן בדיעבד וה"ל להרמ"א לכתוב הגהתו בלשון י"א אך שמצינו כמה פעמים כיוצא בזה: **(כג) אבל הרצועות וכו'.** אם עשאן נכרי או אפילו ישראל אך שלא לשמן והטעם כנ"ל בס"ק כ"ב. וכ"ש בכל דבר שצריך בתפילין גופא לעיכובא כמו עשיית הבית והשי"ן שלו בכל פרטיו שיהיה כדין או תפירתו או עשיית (כ) הקשר שלו דכל אלו הוא הלמ"מ אם עשאן ישראל שלא לשמן פסול וכתב הפמ"ג דיש למנוע מלעשות כ"ז (כא)[1] ע"י קטן אפי' אם (כב) גדול יעמוד ע"ג ויצוהו לעשות לשמה וכן שלא לעשותם ע"י אשה וכל הפסולין המבואר לקמן בסימן ל"ט עי"ש בסעיף א' וב'. והשחרת הרצועות דזה איננו בגוף התפילין מותר ע"י אשה דהיא יודעת לעשות לשמה כמו איש אבל ע"י א"י וקטן אינו מותר עד שיעמוד אחר על גבם וכדלעיל לענין קלף בסימן ל"ב עי"ש בס"ט: **(כד) פסול.** כתב המ"א

ביאור הלכה

דמראית כחול הוא בכלל שחור וכן בחולין דף מ"ז לענין ריאה דאם שחרותה דומה לכחול וכדאיתא ברמב"ם בפ"ז מהלכות שחיטה הלכה י"ט שחורה ככחול אלמא דאף מראה כחול הוא בכלל שחור ומ"מ לכתחילה בודאי מצוה להשחירו שיהיה שחור ממש וכמ"ש הב"ש. ועיין במש"כ לעיל בסימן ל"ב ס"ג לענין שחרות הדיו דשם בעינן שיהי' שחור ממש עי"ש. ודע דבמה שכתבנו שם יוסר קושיא אחת שראיתי לגאון אחד שנתקשה על הרמב"ם למה לא נאמר ההלכה סתם שיהיו כותבין בדבר השחור ולדברינו ניחא דשחור סתם היה משמע אפילו אם הוא שחור רק ככחול ודוק: * **מבחוץ.** עיין מ"ב כן מוכח מרש"י דף ל"ה ע"ב ד"ה ונוייהן דאלת"ה אלא דצריך לצבוע סתם המקום שרוצה ללבשו לצד חוץ וזהו כונת הגמרא במה שמשני כאן מבחוץ ממה פסיקא ליה לרש"י דצובע אותו מקום החלק שיהא קרי ליה בשביל זה ונוייהן הי"ל לרש"י לפרש סתמא אותו מקום שהוא חלק וגוי ילבשנו למעלה וממילא יוכרח האדם לצבוע שחור אותו מקום מחמת ההל"מ וכן איתא בטור כמ"ש וראיתי בפמ"ג שכתב אם השחיר עכו"ם הרצועה ואין לו רצועה אחרת יוכל להשחיר מצד השני דנהי דגמירי שחורות אבל לא דוקא מצד השער וכונתו אם יהפך הרצועה וילבש השחור לצד חוץ וכן ביאר הדה"ח את דבריו ולפ"ז מה שמשני שם הגמרא בע"א כאן מבחוץ תלוי רק בהמקום שלובש מצד חוץ ומה שאמרו שם בגמרא ונוייהן לבר שחור וחלק הוא למצוה מן המובחר בלבד והביא ראיה לזה מרש"י זו ד"ה ונוייהן ובאמת לכאורה משמע להיפך ואף אם תדחה דברינו עכ"פ אין ראיה מרש"י לדבריו אך מהרמב"ם בה"ת הי"ד משמע קצת כדבריו ומ"מ לכתחילה בודאי גם הוא מודה כמו שכתב בעצמו. ודע דלדברי הפמ"ג יצמח לפעמים חומרא גדולה אם יהי' מונח הרצועה במקום הקף הקשר בצד השחור למטה לא יצא בזה ידי המצוה והוי ברכה לבטלה ולפי הנראה שדבר זה במחלוקת שנוי עיין לעיל בסימן כ"ז בא"ר שכן כתב בשם גליון המרדכי ולענ"ד דהב"י פליג ע"ז וס"ל דלא עבר רק על ונוייהן לבר ולכך אפילו איתהפך אח"כ נמי אסור עי"ש בא"ר ודוק: * **ומיהו בדיעבד וכו'.** ועיין בפמ"ג שהביא בשם הב"ח דיש להחמיר בזה אם יש לו תפילין אחרים ונ"ל פשוט דבבתים בודאי יש לסמוך ולהקל אם יחזור הישראל וישחירם לשמן וכמו שכתב המג"א דבלא"ה יש הרבה ספיקות בזה וכמו שכתב הדגמ"ר ובלבושי שרד עי"ש: * **אבל הרצועות.** הטעם כתב סה"ת כיון דעצם השחרות הוא הל"מ לשמה ג"כ בעינן כמו דבעינן לשמה בשעת טוויה בציצית וצביעה בתכלת. ולפ"ז נראה לכאורה דה"ה עצם עשיית הרצועה דהיינו חתיכתה מהעור ג"כ בעינן לשמה ומצאתי שכך כתב בעמק הלכה: * **אפילו בדיעבד וכו'.** עיין במ"ב במש"כ וכ"ש וכו' עיין לקמן בסימן ל"ט ס"ב דכל אלו שהם בכלל עשיית גוף התפילין הם בכלל כתיבת התפילין עי"ש במ"א א"כ פשוט דעכ"פ לא גריעי מהשחרת הרצועות דבעי שיהי' לשמן וראיתי בס' מגן האלף שכתב דהרמב"ם ע"כ לא ס"ל לדינו דספר התרומה שהרי כתב בפ"ג מה"ת ה"א[א] אין עושין תפילין אלא ישראל וכו' לפיכך אם חיפן העו"ג או תפרן פסולות וכו' וא"א דבעי לשמן תיפוק ליה דלא היה לשמן שהרי הרמב"ם ס"ל דבכל דבר שצריך לשמה אינו מועיל בעכו"ם אפילו ישראל עומ"ג ולפי מה שכתב הגרע"א בחידושיו בסי' ל"ט על קושית המג"א כעין זה עי"ש אזדא ראיתו ובפרט לפי מה שמצדד הפמ"ג בסי' ל"ב ס"ק ל"ב דכתיבה לשמה הוא מדרבנן נ"מ לכמה דברים עיין בפתיחת הפמ"ג בהלכות ק"ש ובלא"ה אין להקל למעשה נגד הכרעת רמ"א ואולי דמה שאין נזהרין הסופרים בכל זה לחשוב לשמה היינו משום דסתמא לשמה קאי כיון שכבר נעבד לשמה אבל גם זה אינו דהרי בתליית ציצית בהבגד איתא לעיל בסימן י"ד דאם הטיל ישראל ציצית בבגד בלא כונה דאין לברך עליה אף דשם כבר נטוו החוטין לשם ציצית אפ"ה לא אמרינן דסתמא לשמה קאי וכן לענין כתיבת סת"מ ג"כ אפילו בדיעבד לא מהני בסתמא וכדמוכח בסי' ל"ב סי"ט עי"ש ומש"כ בסעיף ח' טוב להוציא וכו' היינו דבדיעבד סגי במחשבה אבל לא בסתמא ואולי דכיון דבעל התרומות בעצמו לא ברירא ליה דין זה כמבואר בב"י אם למידין זה מציצית או לא די אם נחמיר בזה בדיעבד לענין אם עשאן עכו"ם וכן ישראל שחישב שלא לשמן אבל לא בסתמא וצ"ע. ואף דלא ברירא לן למפסל משום זה דיעבד מ"מ לכתחילה בודאי צריך לעשות כל עשיית הבתים והשי"ן ותפירתם ועשיית הרצועות והשחרתם בפירוש לשמה. ודע דמה שכתבנו לענין השחרת הרצועות דמותר ע"י קטן כשאחר עומ"ג אף דהפמ"ג בתחלת הפתיחה בל"ב רצה להחמיר בזה אבל במקומו בסי' זה במ"ז או"ק ה' ובל"ט בא"א או"ק ו' חזר מזה והתיר ומצאתי כן בעזה"י בהדיא בתשובת מהר"ם לובלין סי' ס"ח דהשחרת הרצועות אינו בכלל תיקון עשייה. ומש"כ דע"י עכו"ם כשאחר עומ"ג מותר אף דיש לפקפק בזה עיין לעיל בסי' י"א במה שתמה הדגמ"ר על השו"ע דמתיר בטוייה להרא"ש ע"י עכו"ם וא"כ ה"נ מ"מ נלענ"ד דאין להחמיר בזה בדיעבד אחרי שהתרומה[ב] גופא לא פסיקא ליה דינו כ"כ: * **פסול.** עיין במ"ב במש"כ שהאחרונים השיגו על עצת המ"א ואעפ"כ נ"ל דאם ישראל השחיר הרצועות בפעם ראשון ולא חישב בהן לשמן רק בסתמא בזה אפשר דנוכל לסמוך על המ"א שישחירו שנית בפירוש לשמן ודיו דהוא כעין ס"ס ולכאורה היה נ"ל עצה אחרת דהיה מועיל לכו"ע אף אם השחירו עכו"ם בפעם ראשונה דכל עיקר קושיתם על המ"א הוא דהו"ל דיו ע"ג דיו עתה יצבענו מתחלה על המראה השחור במראה סיקרא או ירוק ולבן וכה"ג ואתי מראה זו ומבטל להשחור כדאמרינן גיטין י"ט סיקרא ע"ג דיו דהוא מוחק ואח"כ יצבע מלמעלה במראה שחור לשמן ודיו ע"ג סיקרא לכו"ע חייב ואע"ג דאמרינן שם וכי מפני שאנו מדמין וכו' שאני הכא דתו הוי כעין ס"ס דלבעל התרומה עצמו לא פסיק ליה וכנ"ל אך עכ"ז צ"ע דילמא דוקא כתב דיו ע"ג כתב סיקרא מבטל העליון להתחתון דכתב דיו עדיף לכו"ע משא"כ בצבע שחור ע"ג צבע סיקרא וכדומה דילמא הצבע התחתון עדיף והעושה כן בשבת אינו חייב משום צובע ובדידן נמי הצבע העליון השחור אינו חשוב לבטל בשלימות הצבע שהיה תחתיו מתחילה שישאר רק שם שחור עליו וכמו דאמרינן שם בסיקרא ע"ג דיו עי"ש בגמרא בגיטין י"ט וצ"ע: * **אם נפסקה** וכו' ובשל יד כדי שתקיף וכו'. כתב המחצית השקל דצריך אחר התפירה מתחלה למתוח ביושר הרצועה השלימה עד האצבע ואח"כ יחזור עם הרצועה הנקשר למטה ויכרוך הזרוע כמנהג דעד האצבע צריך להיות בלא קשירה ובספר שנות חיים להגאון מהר"ש קלוגר כתב דאין העולם נוהגין כדבריו והדין עמהם עי"ש גם בתשובת מהר"ס

שער הציון

(יט) מ"א: (כ) פמ"ג בסוף ל"ב קודם הפתיחה: (כא) שם לענין הקשר והשאר לקמן בסי' ל"ט ס"ב במ"א: (כב) לקמן בסי' ל"ט ובאחרונים:

הגהות ותיקונים: א) הט"ז: ב) שבעל התרומה:

הערות והארות: 1) עיין בה"ל סי' י"א ס"ב ד"ה טוואן כו' לענין קטן בן י"ג שלא הביא ב' שערות:

*Gloss: However, once it is after the event, /*tefilin*/ are valid if /a non-Jew/ blackened the skin of the housings.* (23) *On the other hand, where the straps /were blackened by a non-Jew/* (24) *they are invalid, even now that it is after the event. (...)*

Mishnah Berurah

(23) On the other hand, where the straps, etc. /I.e.,/ if a non-Jew did /the blackening of the straps/ or even if a Jew /did it/, but did not /do it/ for the sake of /use for the mitzvah, they are invalid/. The reason is as /explained/ above in sub-Par. 22.

/In the case of/ all matters that are essentially required for /the validity of/ the *tefilin* themselves, if a Jew did them without /having in mind to do them/ for the sake of /use for the mitzvah, the *tefilin*/ are certainly invalid. /This applies to requirements/ such as the forming of the housing and its /letter/ ש, with all the details /required/ for this to be /done/ in accordance with halachic /requirements/, the sewing of /the *tefilin*/ or the forming of the knot of /the *tefilin*/. For these are all halachic /requirements which were taught/ to Mosheh (Moses) on /Mount/ Sinai.

The *P.Mg.* writes that one should avoid all these /matters/ being done by a child, even if a grown person stands over him and enjoins him to do them for the sake of /use for the mitzvah/. One should likewise not have them done by a woman or any of those /categories of people/ listed below in Sec. 39 who are disqualified /to prepare *tefilin*/; see there in Par. 1 and 2. As for the blackening of the straps, which is not /a matter that is done/ to the *tefilin* themselves, it is permitted /to have it done/ by a woman, since /a woman/ is capable of doing /something/ for the sake of /use for the mitzvah/, just like a man. However, /to have it done/ by a non-Jew or a child is not permitted, unless someone else stands over him[4] /and enjoins him to do it for the sake of use for the mitzvah/, as /explained/ above with respect to /the processing of/ parchment in Sec. 32; see there in Par. 9.

(24) They are invalid. The *M.A.* writes

4 It appears from the Beyur Halachah that in the case of a non-Jew this is only permitted once it is after the event.

(כה) ◦יש מתירים (ז) (כו) לתפור (כז) מצד פנים ◦וי"א מה שמקיף ממנה הראש ובשל יד כדי שתקיף הזרוע לקשור התפלה עם הזרוע וכדי שתמתח עד (ח) (כח) אצבע אמצעית ויכרוך ממנה על אותו אצבע ג' כריכות ויקשור אין להם תקנה לא בקשירה ולא בתפירה וכל יתרון האורך שהוא בשביל שכורך הרצועה כמה פעמים סביב הזרוע ובשל ראש מה שתלוי ממנה * אין התפירה והקשירה פוסלים בה. ◦ובשעת הדחק יש לסמוך על (כט) המתירים כדי שלא (ט) יתבטל ממצות תפילין:

לד סדר הנחת הפרשיות בתפילין והמהדרים אשר להם ב' זוגות תפילין ובו ד' סעיפים:

א (א) * ◦סדר הנחתן בבתים לרש"י והרמב"ם קדש משמאל (א) (ב) המניח בבית החיצון ואחריו

באר הגולה

כ תוספות והרא"ש בשם ר"ת ל תרומת הדשן וספר התרומה מ בית יוסף
א מנחות ל"ד לפירוש רש"י שם ורמב"ם בפרק ג' ובשמושא רב' וסמ"ג והמרדכי בשם כתב מא"י תפילין שנמלאו בנפילת חומה שע"ג קבר יחזקאל ורבי יונה ורמב"ן ורשב"א בתשובת רמב"ן סימן רל"ד:]

באר היטב

ברצועות דהל"מ שיהיו שחורות הוי זה כמו טויה דציצית דפסול בנכרי וכ"ל דאם חזר ישראל והשחירם לשמן כשר מ"א: (ז) לתפור. דוקא בגידין ודוקא לתפור לצד פנים אבל לקשור או לתפור לצד חוץ פסול ואם נפסקה המעברתא מותר לתופרה דבר שמואל סימן רי"א: (ח) אצבע. ר"ל שתמתח הרצועה כפשוטא בלא כריכות וט"ז מחמיר לכתחלה אפי' נפסקה הרצועה לאחר שנקשר ממנה סביב הראש רק מה שתלויה לפניו עד הטבור ברצועה ימין ובשמאל עד החזה דאסור לתפור: ע"ש באורך: (ט) יתבטל. ולא יברך דברכות אינן מעכבות ט"ז. ועי' בתשו' שבות יעקב ח"א סימן א'. וע"ל סימן ט' ס"ק ו' מש"ש [וכתב בספר אליה רבה דדוקא מה שמקיף הראש והזרוע אבל מה שתולה ממנו מותר בדיעבד בתפירה אף שלא בשעת הדחק ומ"ש ב"י דמהרמב"ם משמע דאסור לא משמע הכי בכסף משנה. וכן פסק בספר זכרון לר"י הכהן]:

(א) המניח. ובאיטר אזלינן בתר ימין ושמאל דעלמא מ"א:

משנה ברורה

דאם חזר ישראל והשחירן לשמן כשר והביא ראיה לזה והפמ"ג ושארי אחרונים השיגו על ראיתו ונשארו בדין זה בצ"ע ונתן הפמ"ג לזה עצה אחרת שישחיר בצד השני של הרצועות לשמן דאף שהושחרו משני צדדים כשר כמבואר בס"ג ויהפך הצד שהושחר לשמן למעלה וכ"ז הוא אם אין לו רצועות אחרות וכמו שביארנו בבה"ל: ה (כה) יש מתירים. אפי' בתוך השיעור שמקיף הראש והקיבורת: (כו) לתפור. דוקא תפירה (כג) אבל קשירה בתוך שיעור הנ"ל לכו"ע פסול מן התורה דכתיב וקשרתם ודרשו חז"ל קשר תם דהיינו הרצועה שקושר בה התפילין תהא תמה ושלימה ולא קשורה. גם התפירה הוא (כד) דוקא בגידין ולא בחוטין. כ' בתשובת דבר שמואל אם נפסקה המעברתא מותר לתופרה: (כז) מצד פנים. כדי שלא יהיה מינכר מבחוץ כלל וכ"ש אם מקום התפירה כנוס לתוך המעברתא דשרי לדעה זו: (כח) אצבע. ר"ל שתמתח הרצועה בלא כריכות דזהו שיעור אורך הרצועה של יד וכנ"ל בסימן כ"ז ס"ח והטעם דהקיל בשל ראש עיין בד"מ: (כט) המתירים. היינו דמותר אפילו לתפור בגידים בתוך השיעור שמקיף הראש והקיבורת (כה) ותוך לשיעור הזה מותר אפילו לקשור וכ"ש לתפור בחוטים אבל בכל זה (כו) אין יכול לברך עליהם כי (כז) מעיקר הדין צריך להחמיר כהי"א דספק תורה לחומרא אך כדי שלא יבטל לגמרי את המצוה יניחם עד שימצא אחרים ועיין בט"ז שפוסק דגם ברצועה של ראש אין יכול לברך עליה עד שיהיה הרצועה של ימין עד הטבור ושמאל עד החזה שלימה בלי קשירה ותפירה אבל בספר א"ר הכריע להלכה דבין בש"ר ובין בש"י לבד מה שיש בתוך השיעור שמקיף הראש והקיבורת יכול לתופרו אף שלא בשעת הדחק ולברך עליהם (כח) אך שיזהר לתפור מצד פנים שלא יהיה מינכר התפירות מבחוץ דאם הוא מינכר לא עדיף מקשר וגם (כט) שיהיה בגידין אבל בחוטין או קשירה אסור אפילו בש"ר וכן פסק בספר ישועות יעקב ובדרך החיים. ומ"מ אם יכול להשיג רצועה שלמה בודאי נכון להחמיר לכתחלה כהט"ז כי כמה מאחרוני זמנינו העתיקו דבריו להלכה אך במקום הדחק בודאי יכול לסמוך על כל הגאונים הנ"ל ולברך ובפרט אם נשאר בהש"ר שני טפחים תלוים לבד מה שמקיף הראש בודאי יש לסמוך להקל דמהני תפירה ועיין לעיל בסי' כ"ז במ"ב ס"ק מ"ד. אם נפסקה הרצועה ברחבה ולא נשאר כשיעור שעורה הניח הפמ"ג בצ"ע אי רשאי לתפור ועיין לעיל בסימן כ"ז ס"ק מ"ב מש"כ שם:

א (א) סדר הנחתן. דע דלכו"ע (א) אם החליף איזה פרשה שנתנה שלא בביתה המיוחד לה פסולין אף דיש ד' פרשיות בד' בתים וכ"ש אם נתן שתי פרשיות (ג) בבית אחד: (ב) המניח. ואפילו (ג) אם המניח

ביאור הלכה

מהר"ם מרוטנבורג אחרונים בסימן ד' השיג עליו דעיקר קפידא על השיעור שתשאר כ"כ כדי למתוח ולכרוך ואף דלאחר הכריכה סביב הזרוע נשאר הקשירה למעלה מהאצבע לא חיישינן אך זאת נסתפק דלא יהיה הקשירה על האצבע גופא כיון שגם שם שייך קשירה עי"ש באריכות. ומ"מ לענ"ד לכתחילה טוב שיתפור אותו המקום בגידין ומצד פנים שלא יהיה מינכר כי אפילו אם נחוש לחומרת המחה"ש דזה מיקרי תוך השיעור מ"מ נראה פשוט שבודאי נוכל לסמוך בזה על ר"ת ושארי ראשונים דמקילין בתפירה. ודע דמה שאיזה אנשים מחברין הרצועה מניה וביה בלא תפירה זה לא עדיף מקשר ואפשר דגריעא ממנה: * אין התפירה והקשירה וכו'. ומ"מ יש נ"מ בין הדל יד לשל ראש דבשל ראש אם ישאר כך ולא יחברנה לה הרצועה שנפסקה לא בקשירה ולא בתפירה בודאי אסור לו לברך על התפילין ולא נוכל להכשיר במה שנשאר גרדומין דהיינו הרצועה השנייה וכמו בציצית לעיל בסימן י"ב דהרי מסקינן במנחות ל"ה ע"ב דברצועות פסול גרדומין [ומ"מ מחויב להניח התפילין אם נאבד הרצועה ואין לו שום עצה דשמא הלכה כהשיטות שסוברים דהאי וכמה שיעורייהו אשל יד קאי עיין ב"י לעיל בסימן כ"ז אך באמת בזה יש לו עצה אחרת דיכול להתיר הקשר ולמשוך הרצועה לשני הצדדים ויוכל בשעת הדחק לצאת בזה אם ישאר שני טפחיים[א] לכאן ולכאן עי"ש בסימן כ"ז במ"ב ומ"מ נ"מ מכל זה לענין אם נפסקו שני הרצועות משני הצדדים ולא נשאר כ"א מה שמקיף הראש] ובשל יד אפילו אם לא יחבר כלל מותר לברך על התפילין וכדלעיל בסימן כ"ז ס"ח ולפ"ז בודאי מהני תפירה אפילו בחוטים ומצד חוץ או קשר אך כ"ז אם לא היה עושה הז' כריכות ולדידן דמנהגינו לעשות כריכות כבר כתבנו שטוב שיתפרנו בגידין ומצד פנים כדי לצאת בזה חשש של המחה"ש:

* סדר הנחתן. עיין במ"ב ופשוט דאפילו בשל יד כגון היכא שאין לו תש"י ויש לו ב' תש"ר דמבואר לעיל דטולה עור על אחד מהם דוקא אם מונחין שם כסדר כמבואר בב"י [עיין בב"ח שמתוכו מתבאר דברי הב"י] שהסכים דהאי דינא דאם החליף פרשיותיהם פסולין קאי נמי אשל יד ולכאורה ה"ה דאם כתבן על ארבע קלפים ונתנן בבית אחד דיוצא בזה אפילו אם לא דבקו כמבואר בסימן ל"ב סמ"ז בב"י שצריך לזהר נמי שיהי' מונחין דוקא כסדר קדש מימין[ב] וכו' או אפשר דהכא לא מינכר כ"כ חילופן כמו בקלף אחד בש"י שכותב והיה אחר שמע וגם להסמ"ק יפול ספק זה דאפשר דאף הסמ"ק יודה בזה שהוא פסול כיון שהם ד' קלפים או אפשר דלהסמ"ק לא נאמר כלל דין קביעות מקום להפרשיות הוא

שער הציון

(כג) מ"א: (כד) מ"א והגר"א ושאר הרבה אחרונים דלא כהא"ר: (כה) כן מצדד הפמ"ג לשיטה זו וכ"כ המאמר מרדכי: (כו) ט"ז: (כז) פמ"ג: (כח) רבינו ירוחם: (כט) כן איתא ברבינו ירוחם בשם רבותיו שהחזיק הא"ר שיטתו לדינא וכ"כ בישועת יעקב ובדה"ח סתם בזה: (א) מנחות ל"ה: (ב) פמ"ג בסי' מ"ב סק"ב: (ג) מ"א:

הגהות ותיקונים: א) טפחים: ב) משמאל:

5. If the strap became severed, **(25)** there are /authorities/ who permit one **(26)** to sew it **(27)** on the side /facing/ inwards. /On the other hand,/ there are /authorities/ who say that there can be no remedy, either by binding or by sewing, for /the part/ of /the strap/ that surrounds the head. /According to them there can also be no such remedy/ in the case of the arm /*tefilin*, for the part of the length of the strap/ necessary to surround the upper arm to bind the *tefilin* unit to the upper arm and /the additional length/ necessary for /the strap/ to be stretched until the middle **(28)** finger and wound around that finger /to form/ three coils and /then/ bound.[3*] /As for/ all the remaining

Mishnah Berurah

that if a Jew blackened them again /and did it/ for the sake of /use for the mitzvah/, they are /then/ valid. He brings proof for this /ruling/. /However,/ the *P.Mg.* and other Acharonim criticize his proof and remain in need of /further/ study to /establish the correctness of/ this ruling.

The *P.Mg.* gives another solution /to make the straps valid/. /His suggestion is/ that one should blacken the other side of the straps for the sake of /use for the mitzvah/. /This is possible/ because /the straps/ are valid even if they are blackened on both sides, as /follows from what is/ stated in Par. 3. One must /subsequently/ invert the side which has been blackened for the sake of /use for the mitzvah, so that it is/ on top /facing outwards/.

All this applies if one does not have other straps, as we have explained in the Beyur Halachah.

(25) There are /authorities/ who permit. These /authorities/ even /permit it/ within the length /required/ to surround the head and /within the length required to surround/ the biceps.

(26) To sew it. They only /permit/ sewing /the strap/, but if one binds /the strap/ within the aforementioned length it is invalid, according to all /authorities/, by Torah law. /This is/ because it is written[5] וקשרתם (and you should bind them), and the Sages, of blessed memory, interpreted /this to read as/ קשר תם (a perfect binding). This /indicates/ that the strap with which one binds the *tefilin* must be perfect and whole and not bound.

In addition, the sewing must be /done/ specifically with sinews and not with threads.

In the responsa *Devar Shemu'el*, it is stated that if the passageway /of the *tefilin*/ became severed it is permitted to sew it.

(27) On the side /facing/ inwards. /This is required/ so that /the sewing/ will not be recognizable from the outside at all.

If the place where it is sewn will be inserted inside the passageway /of the *tefilin* the sewing/ is certainly allowed, according to this opinion.

(28) Finger. I.e., for the strap to be stretched without the coils /around the arm

3* In the Beyur Halachah, the author of the Mishnah Berurah concludes that in the additional length of strap which is used until the middle finger so that one can also wind the customary coils around the arm, it is desirable to sew with sinews and on the side facing inwards.

5 *Devarim* 6:8.

(כה) [כ]יש מתירים (ז) (כו) לתפור (כז) מצד פנים [ו]וי״א מה שמקיף ממנה הראש ובשל יד כדי שתקיף הזרוע לקשור התפלה עם הזרוע וכדי שתמתח עד (ח) (כח) אצבע אמצעית ויכרוך ממנה על אותו אצבע ג׳ כריכות ויקשור אין להם תקנה לא בקשירה ולא בתפירה וכל יתרון האורך שהוא בשביל שכורך הרצועה כמה פעמים סביב הזרוע ובשל ראש מה שתלוי ממנה * אין התפירה והקשירה פוסלים בה. [מ]ובשעת הדחק יש לסמוך על (כט) המתירים כדי שלא (ט) יתבטל ממצות תפילין:

לד סדר הנחת הפרשיות בתפילין והמהדרים אשר להם ב׳ זוגות תפילין ובו ד׳ סעיפים:

א (א) * [א]סדר הנחתן בבתים לרש״י והרמב״ם קדש משמאל (א) (ב) המניח בבית החיצון ואחריו

באר הגולה: כ תוספות והרא״ש בשם ר״ת ל תרומת הדשן וספר התרומה מ בית יוסף א מנחות ל״ד לפירוש רש״י שם ורמב״ם בפרק ג׳ ובתשובה רב׳ וסמ״ג והמרדכי בשם כתב מא״י תפילין שנמצאו בנפילה בימה שע״ג קבר יחזקאל ורבי יונה ורמב״ן ורשב״א בתשובת רמב״ן סימן רל״ד:]

באר היטב

ברצועות דהל״מ שיהיו שחורות הוי זה כמו טויה דציצית דפסול בנכרי וכ״ל דאם חזר ישראל והשחירם לשמן כשר מ״א: (ז) לתפור. דוקא בגידין ודוקא לתפור לצד פנים אבל לקשור או לתפור לצד חוץ פסול ואם נפסקה המעברתא מותר לתופרה דבר שמואל סימן רי״א: (ח) אצבע. ר״ל שתמתח הרצועה כפשוטה בלא כריכות וט״ז מחמיר לכתחלה אפי׳ נפסקה הרצועה לאחר שנקשר ממנה סביב הראש רק מה שתלויה לפניו עד הטבור ברצועה ימין ובשמאל עד החזה דאסור לתפור:

ע״ש באורך: (ט) יתבטל. ולא יברך דברכות אינן מעכבות ט״ז. ועי׳ בתשו׳ שבות יעקב ח״א סימן א׳. וע״ל סימן ט׳ ס״ק ו׳ מש״ש [וכתב בספר אליה רבה דדוקא מה שמקיף הראש והזרוע אבל מה שתולה ממנו מותר בדיעבד בתפירה אף שלא בשעת הדחק ומ״ש ב״י דמהרמב״ס משמע דאסור לא משמע הכי בכסף משנה. וכן פסק בספר זכרון לר״י הכהן]:

(א) המניח. ובאיטר אזלינן בתר ימין ושמאל דעלמא מ״א:

משנה ברורה

דאם חזר ישראל והשחירן לשמן כשר והביא ראיה לזה והפמ״ג ושארי אחרונים השיגו על ראיתו ונשארו בדין זה בצ״ע ונתן הפמ״ג לזה עצה אחרת שישחיר בצד השני של הרצועות לשמן דאף שהושחרו משני לצדדים כשר כמבואר בפמ״ג ויהפך הצד שהושחר לשמן למעלה וכ״ז הוא אם אין לו רצועות אחרות וכמו שאמרנו בבה״ל: ה (כה) יש מתירים. אפי׳ בתוך השיעור שמקיף הראש והקיבורת: (כו) לתפור. דוקא תפירה (כג) אבל קשירה בתוך שיעור הנ״ל לכו״ע פסול מן התורה דכתיב וקשרתם ודרשו חז״ל קשר תם דהיינו הרצועה שקושר בה התפילין תהא תמה ושלימה ולא קשורה. גם התפירה הוא (כד) דוקא בגידין ולא בחוטין. כ׳ בתשובת דבר שמואל אם נפסקה המעברתא מותר לתופרה: (כז) מצד פנים. כדי שלא יהיה מינכר מבחוץ כלל וכ״ש אם מקום התפירה כנוס לתוך המעברתא דשרי לדעה זו: (כח) אצבע. ר״ל שתמתח הרצועה בלא כריכות דזהו שיעור אורך הרצועה של יד וכנ״ל בסימן כ״ז ס״ח והטעם דהקיל בשל ראש עיין בד״מ: (כט) המתירים. היינו דמותר אפילו לתפור בגידים בתוך השיעור שמקיף הראש והקיבורת (כה) וחוץ לשיעור הזה מותר אפילו לקשור וכ״ש לתפור בחוטים אבל בכל זה (כו) אין יכול לברך עליהם כי (כז) מעיקר הדין צריך להחמיר כהי״א דספק תורה לחומרא אך כדי שלא יבטל לגמרי את המצוה יניחם עד שימצא אחרים ועיין בט״ז שפוסק דגם ברצועה של ראש אין יכול לברך עליה עד שיהיה הרצועה של ימין עד הטבור ושמאל עד החזה שלימה בלי קשירה ותפירה אבל בספר א״ר הכריע להלכה דדין בש״ר ודין בש״י לבד מה שיש בתוך השיעור שמקיף הראש והקיבורת יכול לתופרו אף שלא בשעת הדחק ולברך עליהם (כח) אך שיזהר לתפור מצד פנים שלא יהיה מינכר התפירות מבחוץ דאם הוא מינכר לא עדיף מקשר וגם (כט) שיהיה בגידין אבל בחוטין או קשירה אסור אפילו בש״ר וכן פסק בספר ישועות יעקב ובדרך החיים. ומ״מ אם יכול להשיג רצועה שלמה בודאי נכון להחמיר לכתחלה כהט״ז כי כמה מאחרוני זמנינו העתיקו דבריו להלכה אך במקום הדחק בודאי יכול לסמוך על כל הגאונים הנ״ל ולברך ובפרט אם נשאר בהש״ר שני טפחים תלוים לבד מה שמקיף הראש בודאי יש לסמוך להקל דמהני תפירה ועיין לעיל בסי׳ כ״ז במ״ב ס״ק מ״ד. אם נפסקה הרצועה ברחבה ולא נשאר כשיעור שעורה הניח הפמ״ג בצ״ע אי רשאי לתפור ועיין לעיל בסימן כ״ז ס״ק מ״ב מש״כ שם:

א (א) סדר הנחתן. דע דלכו״ע (א) אם החליף איזה פרשה שנתנה שלא בביתה המיוחד לה פסולין אף דיש ד׳ פרשיות בד׳ בתים וכ״ש אם נתן שתי פרשיות (ב) בבית אחד: (ב) המניח. ואפילו (ג) אם המניח

ביאור הלכה

מהר״ם מרוטנבורג אחרונים בסימן ד׳ השיג עליו דעיקר קפידא על השיעור שתשאר כ״כ כדי למתוח ולכרוך ואף דלאחר הכריכה סביב הזרוע נשאר הקשירה למעלה מהאצבע לא חיישינן אך זאת נסתפק דלא יהיה הקשירה על האצבע גופא כיון שגם שם שייך קשירה עי״ש באריכות. ומ״מ לענ״ד לכתחילה טוב שיתפור אותו המקום בגידין ומצד פנים שלא יהיה מינכר כי אפילו אם נחוש לחומרת המהר״ם דזה מיקרי תוך השיעור מ״מ נראה פשוט שבודאי נוכל לסמוך בזה על ר״ת ושארי ראשונים דמקילין בתפירה. ודע דמה שאיזה אנשים מחברין הרצועה מניה וביה בלא תפירה זה לא עדיף מקשר ואפשר דגריעא ממנה: * אין התפירה והקשירה וכו׳. ומ״מ יש נ״מ בין השל יד לשל ראש דבשל ראש אם ישאר כך ולא יחברנה לה הרצועה שנפסקה לא בקשירה ולא בתפירה בודאי אסור לו לברך על התפילין ולא נוכל להכשיר במה שנשאר גרדומין דהיינו הרצועה השנייה וכמו בציצית לעיל בסימן י״ב דהרי מסקינן במנחות ל״ה ע״ב דברצועות פסול גרדומין [ומ״מ מחויב להניח התפילין אם נאבד הרצועה ואין לו שום עצה דשמא הלכה כהשיטות שסוברים דהאי וכמה שיעורייהו אשל יד קאי עיין ב״י לעיל בסימן כ״ז אך באמת בזה יש לו עצה אחרת דיכול להתיר הקשר ולמשוך הרצועה לשני הצדדים ויוכל בשעת הדחק לצאת בזה אם ישאר שני טפחיים[א] לכאן ולכאן עי״ש בסימן כ״ז במ״ב ומ״מ נ״מ מכל זה לענין אם נפסקו שני הרצועות משני הצדדים ולא נשאר כ״א מה שמקיף הראש] ובשל יד אפילו אם לא יחבר כלל מותר לברך על התפילין וכדלעיל בסימן כ״ז ס״ח ולפ״ז בודאי מהני תפירה אפילו בחוטים ומצד חוץ או קשר אך כ״ז אם לא היה עושה הז׳ כריכות ולדידן דמנהגינו לעשות כריכות כבר כתבנו שטוב שיתפרנו בגידין ומצד פנים כדי לצאת בזה חשש של המהר״ם:

* סדר הנחתן. עיין במ״ב ופשוט דאפילו בשל יד כגון היכא שאין לו תש״י ויש לו ב׳ תש״ר דמבואר לעיל דטולה עור על אחד מהם דוקא אם מונחין שם כסדר כמבואר בב״י [עיין בב״ח שמתוכו מתבאר דברי הב״י] שהסכים דהאי דינא דאם החליף פרשיותיהם פסולין קאי נמי אשל יד ולכאורה ה״ה דאם כתבן על ארבע קלפים ונתנן בבית אחד דיולא בזה אפילו אם לא דבקו כמבואר בסימן ל״ב סמ״ז בב״י שצריך לזהר נמי שיהי׳ מונחין דוקא כסדר קדש מימין[ב] וכו׳ או אפשר דהכא לא מינכר כ״כ חילופן כמו בקלף אחד בש״י שכותב והיה אחר שמע וגם להסמ״ק יפול ספק זה דאפשר דאף הסמ״ק יודה בזה שהוא פסול כיון שהם ד׳ קלפים או אפשר דלהסמ״ק לא נאמר כלל דין קביעות מקום להפרשיות

הוא

שער הציון

(כג) מ״א: (כד) מ״א והגר״א ושאר הרבה אחרונים דלא כהא״ר: (כה) כן מלדד הפמ״ג לשיטה זו וכ״כ המאמר מרדכי: (כו) ט״ז: (כז) פמ״ג: (כח) רבינו ירוחם: (כט) כן איתא ברבינו ירוחם בשם רבותיו שהחזיק הא״ר שיטתו לדינא וכ״כ בישועת יעקב ובדה״ח סתם בזה: (א) מנחות ל״ה: (ב) פמ״ג בסי׳ מ״ב סק״ב: (ג) מ״א:

הגהות ותיקונים: א) טפחים: ב) משמאל:

length /of the strap of the arm *tefilin*/, which /serves/ for the strap to be wound several times around the arm, and, in the case of the head /*tefilin*/, what hangs of /the strap/, sewing or binding does not invalidate it. In a time of pressing /need/, one may rely on (29) the permitting /authorities/, in order to avoid being idle about /the performance of/ the mitzvah of *tefilin*.

Mishnah Berurah

being made/. For this is the required length for the strap of the arm /*tefilin*/, as /stated/ above in Sec. 27, Par. 8.

/As regards/ the reason for the leniency /with respect to the length which one must not bind or sew/ in the case of /the straps of/ the head /*tefilin*/, see the *D.M.*

(29) The permitting /authorities/. I.e., /the authorities who are of the opinion/ that it is permitted to sew with sinews even within the length /of strap/ that surrounds the head and /within the length of strap that surrounds/ the biceps and that beyond this length it is permitted even to bind /the strap/ and certainly to sew it with threads.

However, in all such cases, one cannot make a blessing over /the *tefilin*/. This is because the ruling, essentially, is that one must be stringent, in conformance with /the view of those authorities/ who say /that there can be no such remedy except for the remaining part of the strap/. /This follows from the fact/ that where a doubt /relates/ to Torah law one must be stringent. It is simply in order not to be completely idle from /the performance of/ the mitzvah that one should don /*tefilin* with such straps/ until he finds others.

See the *Taz*, who rules that in the case of the strap of the head /*tefilin*/ as well, one cannot make a blessing over /the *tefilin*/ unless the right strap until the navel and the left /strap/ until the chest are whole, without binding or sewing.

On the other hand, in the work *E.R.*, /the author/ decides that, halachically, both in the case of the head /*tefilin*/ and in the case of the arm /*tefilin*/, one may sew /the straps/ and make a blessing over /*tefilin* which use these straps/, even when it is not a time of pressing /need/. It is only /prohibited to do so for the parts of the straps/ that are within the length which surrounds the head and /within the length which surrounds/ the

(כה) [כ]יש מתירים (ז) (כו) לתפור (כז) מצד פנים [ל]וי"א מה שמקיף ממנה הראש ובשל יד כדי שתקיף הזרוע לקשור התפלה עם הזרוע וכדי שתמתח עד (ח) (כח) אצבע אמצעית ויכרוך ממנה על אותו אצבע ג' כריכות ויקשור אין להם תקנה לא בקשירה ולא בתפירה וכל יתרון האורך שהוא בשביל שכורך הרצועה כמה פעמים סביב הזרוע ובשל ראש מה שתלוי ממנה * אין התפירה והקשירה פוסלים בה. [מ]ובשעת הדחק יש לסמוך על (כט) המתירים כדי שלא (ט) יתבטל ממצות תפילין:

כ תוספות והרא"ש בשם ר"ת ל תרומת הדשן וספר התרומה מ בית יוסף א מנחות ל"ד לפירוש רש"י שם ורמב"ם בפרק ג' ובשמושא רב' וסמ"ג והמרדכי בשם כתב מא"י תפילין שנמצאו בנפילה בימה שע"ג קבר יחזקאל ורבי יונה ורמב"ן ורשב"א בתשובת רמב"ן סימן רל"ד:

לד סדר הנחת הפרשיות בתפילין והמהדרים אשר להם ב' זוגות תפילין ובו ד' סעיפים:

א (א) * [א]סדר הנחתן בבתים לרש"י והרמב"ם קדש משמאל (א) (ב) המניח בבית החיצון ואחריו

באר היטב

ברצועות דהל"מ שיהיו שחורות הוי זה כמו טויה דציצית דפסול בנכרי וכ"ל דאם חזר ישראל והשחירם לשמן כשר מ"א: (ז) לתפור. דוקא בגידין ודוקא לתפור לצד פנים אבל לקשור או לתפור לצד חוץ פסול ואם נפסקה המעברתא מותר לתופרה דבר שמואל סימן רי"א: (ח) אצבע. ר"ל שתמתח הרצועה כפשוטה בלא כריכות וט"ז מחמיר לכתחלה אפי' נפסקה הרצועה לאחר שנקשר ממנה סביב הראש רק מה שתלויה לפניו עד הטבור ברצועה ימין ובשמאל עד החזה דאסור לתפור: ע"ש באורך: (ט) יתבטל. ולא יברך דברכות אינן מעכבות ט"ז. ועי' בתשו' שבות יעקב ח"א סימן א'. וע"ל סימן ט' ס"ק ו' מש"ש [וכתב בספר אליה רבה דדוקא מה שמקיף הראש והזרוע אבל מה שתולה ממנו מותר בדיעבד בתפירה אף שלא בשעת הדחק ומ"ש ב"י דמהרמב"ס משמע דאסור לא משמע הכי בכסף משנה. וכן פסק בספר זכרון לר"י הכהן]:

(א) המניח. ובאיטר אזלינן בתר ימין ושמאל דעלמא מ"א:

משנה ברורה

דאם חזר ישראל והשחירן לשמן כשר והמ"א רחיה לזה והפמ"ג ושאר אחרונים השיגו על ראיתו ונשארו בדין זה בצ"ע ונתן הפמ"ג לזה עצה אחרת שישחיר בצד השני של הרצועות לשמן דאף שהושחרו משני צדדים כשר כמבואר בס"ג ויהפך הצד שהושחר לשמן למעלה וכ"ז הוא אם אין לו רצועות אחרות וכמו שביארנו בבה"ל: ה (כה) יש מתירים. אפי' בתוך השיעור שמקיף הראש והקיבורת: (כו) לתפור. דוקא תפירה (כג) אבל קשירה בתוך שיעור הנ"ל לכו"ע פסול מן התורה דכתיב וקשרתם ודרשו חז"ל קשר תם דהיינו הרצועה שקושר בה התפילין תהא תמה ושלימה ולא קשורה. גם התפירה הוא (כד) דוקא בגידין ולא בחוטין. כ' בתשובת דבר שמואל אם נפסקה המעברתא מותר לתופרה: (כז) מצד פנים. כדי שלא יהיה מינכר מבחוץ כלל וכ"ש אם מקום התפירה כנוס לתוך המעברתא דשרי לדעה זו: (כח) אצבע. ר"ל שתמתח הרצועה בלא כריכות דזהו שיעור אורך הרצועה של יד וכנ"ל בסימן כ"ז ס"ח והטעם דהקיל בשל ראש עיין בד"מ: (כט) המתירים. היינו דמותר אפילו לתפור בגידים בתוך השיעור שמקיף הראש והקיבורת (כה) וחוץ לשיעור הזה מותר אפילו לקשור וכ"ש לתפור בחוטים אבל בכל זה (כו) אין יכול לברך עליהם כי (כז) מעיקר הדין צריך להחמיר כסי"א דספק תורה לחומרא אך כדי שלא יבטל לגמרי את המצוה יניחם עד שימצא אחרים ועיין בט"ז שפוסק דגם ברצועה של ראש אין יכול לברך עליה עד שיהיה הרצועה של ימין עד הטבור ושמאל עד החזה שלימה בלי קשירה ותפירה אבל בספר א"ר הכריע להלכה דדין בש"ר וכן בש"י לבד מה שיש בתוך השיעור שמקיף הראש והקיבורת יכול לתופרו אף שלא בשעת הדחק ולברך עליהם (כח) אך שיזהר לתפור מצד פנים שלא יהיה מינכר התפירות מבחוץ דאם הוא מינכר לא עדיף מקשר וגם (כט) שיהיה בגידין אבל בחוטין או קשירה אסור אפילו בש"ר וכן פסק בספר ישועות יעקב ובדרך החיים. ומ"מ אם יכול להשיג רצועה שלמה בודאי נכון להחמיר לכתחלה כהט"ז כי כמה מאחרוני זמנינו העתיקו דבריו להלכה אך במקום הדחק בודאי יכול לסמוך על כל הגאונים הנ"ל ולברך ובפרט אם נשאר בהש"ר שני טפחים תלוים לבד מה שמקיף הראש בודאי יש לסמוך להקל דמהני תפירה ועיין לעיל בסי' כ"ז במ"ב ס"ק מ"ד. אם נפסקה הרצועה ברחבה ולא נשאר כשיעור שעורה הניח הפמ"ג בצ"ע אי רשאי לתפור ועיין לעיל בסימן כ"ז ס"ק מ"ב מש"כ שם:

ביאור הלכה

מהר"ס מרוטנבורג אחרונים בסימן ד' השיג עליו דעיקר קפידא על השיעור שתשאר כ"כ כדי למתוח ולכרוך ואף דלאחר הכריכה סביב הזרוע נשאר הקשירה למעלה מהאצבע לא חיישינן אך זאת נסתפק דלא יהיה הקשירה על האצבע גופא כיון שגם שם שייך קשירה עי"ש באריכות. ומ"מ לענ"ד לכתחילה טוב שיתפור אותו המקום בגידין ומצד פנים שלא יהיה מינכר כי אפילו אם נחוש לחומרת המחה"ש דזה מיקרי תוך השיעור מ"מ נראה פשוט שבודאי נוכל לסמוך בזה על ר"ת ושארי ראשונים דמקילין בתפירה. ודע דמה שאיזה אנשים מחברין הרצועה מניה וביה בלא תפירה זה לא עדיף מקשר ואפשר דגריעא ממנה: * אין התפירה והקשירה וכו'. ומ"מ יש נ"מ בין הש"ל יד לש"ל ראש דבש"ל ראש אם ישאר כך ולא יחברנה לה הרצועה שנפסקה לא בקשירה ולא בתפירה בודאי אסור לו לברך על התפילין ולא נוכל להכשיר במה שנשאר גרדומין דהיינו הרצועה השנייה וכמו בציצית לעיל בסימן י"ב דהרי מסקינן במנחות ל"ה ע"ב דברצועות פסול גרדומין [ומ"מ מחויב להניח התפילין אם נאבד הרצועה ואין לו שום עצה דשמא הלכה כהשיטות שסוברים דהאי וכמה שיעורייהו אשל יד קאי עיין ב"י לעיל בסימן כ"ז אך באמת בזה יש לו עצה אחרת דיכול להתיר הקשר ולמשוך הרצועה לשני הצדדים ויוכל בשעת הדחק לצאת בזה אם ישאר שני טפחיים[א] לכאן ולכאן עי"ש בסימן כ"ז במ"ב ומ"מ נ"מ מכל זה לענין אם נפסקו שני הרצועות משני הצדדים ולא נשאר כ"א מה שמקיף הראש] ובשל יד אפילו אם לא יחבר כלל מותר לברך על התפילין וכדלעיל בסימן כ"ז ס"ח ולפ"ז בודאי מהני תפירה אפילו בחוטים ומצד חוץ או קשר אך כ"ז אם לא היה עושה הז' כריכות ולדידן דמנהגינו לעשות כריכות כבר כתבנו שטוב שיתפרנו בגידין ומצד פנים כדי לצאת בזה חשש של המחה"ש:

* סדר הנחתן. עיין במ"ב ופשוט דאפילו בשל יד כגון היכא שאין לו תש"י ויש לו ב' תש"ר דמבואר לעיל דטולה עור על אחד מהם דוקא אם מונחין שם כסדר כמבואר בב"י [עיין בב"ח שמתוכו מתבאר דברי הב"י] שהסכים דהאי דינא דאם החליף פרשיותיהם פסולין קאי נמי אשל יד ולכאורה ה"ה דאם כתבן על ארבע קלפים ונתנן בבית אחד דיולא בזה אפילו אם לא דבקו כמבואר בסימן ל"ב סמ"ז בב"י שצריך לזהר נמי שיהי' מונחין דוקא כסדר קדש מימין[ב] וכו' או אפשר דהכא לא מינכר כ"כ חילופן כמו בקלף אחד בש"י שכותב והיה אחר שמע וגם להסמ"ק יפול ספק זה דאפשר דאף הסמ"ק יודה בזה שהוא פסול כיון שהם ד' קלפים או אפשר דלהסמ"ק לא נאמר כלל דין קביעות מקום להפרשיות

א (א) סדר הנחתן. דע דלכו"ע (א) אם החליף איזה פרשה שנתנה שלא בביתה המיוחד לה פסולין אף דיש ד' פרשיות בד' בתים וכ"ש אם נתן שתי פרשיות (ב) בבית אחד: (ב) המניח. ואפילו (ג) אם המניח הוא

שער הציון

(כג) מ"א: (כד) מ"א והגר"א ושאר הרבה אחרונים דלא כהא"ר: (כה) כן מלדד הפמ"ג לשיטה זו וכ"כ המאמר מרדכי: (כו) ט"ז: (כז) פמ"ג: (כח) רבינו ירוחם: (כט) כן איתא ברבינו ירוחם בשם רבותיו שהחזיק הא"ר שיטתו לדינא וכ"כ בישועת יעקב ובדה"ח סתם בזה: (א) מנחות ל"ה: (ב) פמ"ג בסי' מ"ב סק"ב: (ג) מ"א:

הגהות ותיקונים: א) טפחים: ב) משמאל:

§34: THE ORDER IN WHICH THE PASSAGES SHOULD BE PLACED IN THE *TEFILIN*. /THE PRACTICE OF/ THE METICULOUS TO HAVE TWO PAIRS OF *TEFILIN*

(Contains Four Paragraphs)

1. (1) The order /in which the passages/ should be placed in the housings is /as follows/.

According to *Rashi* and the *Rambam*,[1*] /the passage/ /*Kadesh Li Chal Bechor* should be /placed on the side/ towards the left (2) of the donner, in the

Mishnah Berurah

biceps. However, one must be careful to sew /the strap/ on the side /facing/ inwards, so that the stitches are not noticeable from the outside, since if they are noticeable /the sewing/ is no better than binding. In addition, /the sewing/ must be /done/ with sinews, but /the use of/ threads or of binding is forbidden even for /the straps of/ the head /*tefilin*/. This is likewise ruled in the work *Yeshu'os Ya'akov* and in the /work/ *Derech Ha-Chayim*.

Nevertheless, if one is able to obtain a whole strap it is definitely proper to be stringent /about this/, initially, in conformance with /the view of/ the *Taz*. This is because several Acharonim of our time have transcribed his words as the halachic /ruling/. However, in a case of pressing /need/, one may definitely rely on all the Geonim who are /quoted/ above and may make the blessing /over *tefilin* with sewn straps/. /This applies/ especially, if for /the strap/ of the head /*tefilin*/ two handbreadths /of unsewn strap/ remain hanging, apart from what surrounds the head. /Then/ one may definitely rely on the leniency that sewing is of avail. See above in Sec. 27, in the Mishnah Berurah, sub-Par. 44.

If the strap is severed at the width and the width of a barley /seed/ does not remain /of it/, the *P.Mg.* remains in need of /further/ study /to determine/ whether /or not/ one is allowed to sew it. See above in Sec. 27, sub-Par. 42, for what we have written there.

§34

(1) The order /in which the passages/ should be placed. Note that, according to all /authorities/, if one altered /the place of/ any passage and put it in other than the housing which is meant for it, /the *tefilin* unit/ is invalid. /This applies/ even when the four passages /of the unit are divided and placed/ into the four housings and it certainly /applies/ if one put two passages in a single housing.

(2) Of the donner. /With respect to this matter,/ even when the donner is left-

1* *Rambam* 3:5 and 6.

כי יביאך בבית שני ושמע בבית השלישי והיה אם שמוע בבית הרביעי שהוא בית החיצון לימינו (ג) (ג) [ב]ולר"ת בבית השלישי והיה אם שמוע ובבית הרביעי שהוא החיצון שמע. ומנהג העולם (ד) כרש"י והרמב"ם: **ב** [ג]ירא שמים יצא ידי שניהם ויעשה שתי זוגות תפילין (ה) ויניח (ג) [א] (ו) שניהם * ויכוין בהנחתם (ז) באותם שהם אליבא דהלכתא אני יוצא ידי חובתי והשאר הם

ב תוספות שם ופירוש ר"ת ורבינו האי ג סמ"ג וסמ"ק וספר התרומה

שערי תשובה

[א] שניהם. עבה"ט ועיין במלת שמורים שדעתו לברך על תפילין דר"ת וליתא וע"ד שכתב האר"י ז"ל שאין לברך על ש"ר שקדושתם חמורה וק"ו בשל ר"ת עיין באגרת הרמ"ז סי' ה' ועיין לעיל סימן כ"ה בבה"ט ס"ק י"א בשם דרכי נועם וכ"כ בבכור שור ועיין בבכור שור דף קי"ח שאעפ"י שאין מברכים על של ר"ת מ"מ אין להפסיק בין תש"י לתפילין ש"ר ע"ש ועיין בפנים מאירות ח"א סימן ס"ז שהמניח תפילין של ר"ת בלא ברכה וקורא בהם ק"ש רשאי להפסיק באמצע הפרק מפני הכבוד ומ"מ לא ישיח שיחה בטלה ע"ש ונראה להחמיר להפסיק אף מפני הכבוד ועיין לקמן סימן ס"ו. ונראה דלכתחלה אין להפסיק בשהות ג"כ ועיין סימן ס"ה. ונהגו ללבוש תפילין של ר"ת במנחה שכך נהג האר"י קודם שעשה תפילין של שימושא רבא וכך נהג מהרח"ו ואף שלפי סוד הדברים[א] כיון שהם עשו כן בודאי כדבריהם כן היא ואנחנו לא נדע כ"כ בר"י. ועיין לקמן סימן ל"ח שאין להניח תפילין דר"ת בימי אבלו ובט"ב במנחה שכתב במג"א סימן תקנ"ה שהמניח דר"ת יניח במנחה גם כן. ועיין שם בשיורי כנה"ג בשם תשובת הרמ"ע ומ"ש ע"ז ע"ש ומ"ש בשם השבות יעקב שאם ש"ר נכתב ע"פ דעת רש"י יש להניח ש"ר תחלה עיין שם שמבואר שיברך שתי הברכות על ש"ר כמ"ש בהג"ה ס"ס כ"ו ושל יד דר"ת יניח בלא ברכה ואם של יד הוא לדעת רש"י מברך עליו להניח לבד

באר היטב

(ג) ולר"ת. ומ"מ צריך לכותבן כסידרן כמ"ש סימן ל"ב ס"א לכן צריך שיניח חלק פרשת והיה אם שמוע ויכתוב פרשת שמע בקצה הקלף ואח"כ יכתוב פרשת והיה אם שמוע באמצע מ"א. וע"ל סימן ל"ב ס"ק נ"ג מש"ש: (ג) שניהם. והנוהג כן להניח ב' זוגות ביחד יניח של רש"י למטה ושל ר"ת למעלה ט"ז וכ"כ האר"י ז"ל שיכנים תחלה של רש"י ויעמידם נגד הכתף ואחריהם של ר"ת נגד היד ושניהם על הקיבורת ויניח בראשו של רש"י למטה ושל ר"ת יותר למעלה ושניהם במקום הראוי לתפילין. והרצועות דר"ת יהיו תחת רצועות דרש"י מכוסה בה שלא יתגלו רק רצועות דרש"י. ותפילין דר"ת יהיו קטנים מתפילין דרש"י. עיין ספר הכוונת תפילין פרק יו"ד י"ב. [ועיין בספר אליה רבה שדחה דברי ט"ז וראייתו] מי שמניח תפילין של יד של דעת ר"ת ותפילין של ראש כדעת רש"י והרמב"ם אם יוצא י"ח פסק שבות יעקב ח"א סימן ב' דאינו יוצא אליבא דכ"ע. אבל בשעת הדחק מותר להניחם כך דהא בשעת הדחק יוצא אם מניח אחת לבד. ומ"מ לא

משנה ברורה

הוא איטר אזלינן בתר ימין ושמאל דעלמא: (ג) ולר"ת. כתבו הפוסקים דגם ר"ת (ד) מודה דבעינן כתיבתן כסדר שהם כתובין בתורה שהוא קדש והיה כי יביאך שמע והיה אם שמוע אלא דפליג ארש"י לענין הנחתן בבתים וע"כ הרוצה לכתוב תפילין לדעת ר"ת יכתוב בשל יד שהם בקלף אחד קדש והיה כי יביאך ויניח חלק והיה אם שמוע ויכתוב שמע ואח"כ יכתוב והיה אם שמוע ובש"ר יכתבם בארבע קלפים כסדר ממש ויסדרם בבתים. קדש. והיה כי. והיה אם. שמע. ולענין דיני פתוחות וסתומות בהתפילין איך להתנהג לדעתו כבר ביארנו לעיל בע"ה בסימן ל"ב עי"ש: (ד) כרש"י והרמב"ם. וכתב בב"י ושאר אחרונים דכן עיקר וכן הסכים הגר"א בביאורו: **ב** (ה) ויניח וכו'. והנוהג (ה) כן להניח ב' זוגות תפילין יניח של רש"י למטה נגד הפנים ושל ר"ת למעלה. וכ"כ האר"י ז"ל שיכניס תחלה של רש"י ויעמידם נגד הכתף ואחריהם של ר"ת נגד היד ושניהם על הקיבורת ויניח בראשו של רש"י למטה ושל ר"ת יותר למעלה ושניהם במקום הראוי לתפילין והרצועות דר"ת יהיה מכוסה תחת רצועות דרש"י שלא יתגלו רק רצועות דרש"י ותפילין דר"ת יהיו קטנים מתפילין דרש"י עיין ספר הכוונת תפילין פרק י' י"ב. מי שמניח תפילין של יד של דעת ר"ת ותש"ר כדעת רש"י והרמב"ם אם יוצא ידי חובתו פסק שבות יעקב ח"א סי' ב' דאינו יוצא אליבא דכו"ע אבל בשעת הדחק מותר להניחם כך דהא בשעת הדחק יוצא אם מניח אחת לבד ומ"מ לא יברך רק על אותו שנכתבה ע"פ מנהגינו כדעת רש"י והרמב"ם ואם של ראש נכתבה ע"פ דעת רש"י יש להניח של ראש תחילה ובשחולץ חולץ של יד תחלה עי"ש: (ו) שניהם. יחד על היד ויברך (ו) ויהדקם בבת אחת וה"ה בשל ראש כדי שתהיה הנחת שתיהם סמוך להברכה: (ז) באותם שהם וכו'. דלא (ז) יוכל לכוין בשתיהם בעת ההידוק שמהדקן יחד לשם תפילין דהרי אחד מהם אינו תפילין וי"א עוד דיש בזה (ח) משום בל תוסיף עכ"פ

ביאור הלכה

בש"י כיון דאפשר לכותבן בקלף אחד וצ"ע: * **ויכוין בהנחתם באותם שהם וכו'.** עיין במ"א שכתב דדוקא בזה אבל בשני זוגי תפילין כשרים עובר על בל תוסיף ומה שאמרו בסנהדרין פ"ט דאם עשה עוד בית אחד והניחו גבי הד' בתים האי לחודיה קאי היינו בשכתב פרשה אחרת דלא שייכי כלל לתפילין ועיין בפמ"ג שביאר דל"ד פרשה אחרת דה"ה אם כתב פרשה אחת מד' פרשיות והניחה בבית ההוא ג"כ אמרינן האי לחודיה קאי והאי לחודיה קאי [הג"ה הנה אף דלכאורה בודאי הדין עמו שהרי הד' פרשיות מעכבין זה את זה וא"כ כל זמן דלא כתב כל הד' עדיין תפילין פסולין הם ולא שייכי כלל לאלו הכשרין וכן משמע בביאור הגר"א מ"מ קשה לי מאד על דברי הפמ"ג שפירש כן את דברי המ"א דהרי המ"א הביא סיוע לדבריו מדברי הב"י בשם המ"מ והוא לקמן בסימן תרנ"א ומוכח שם בהדיא מדברי המגיד משנה דאם נטל מין אחר לבד הד' מינין אמרינן האי לחודיה קאי והאי לחודיה קאי ואם נטל לבד הד' מינין עוד לולב אחד או אתרוג אחד עבר על בל תוסיף ומדמה שם זה לשני זוגי תפילין דעובר על ב"ת עי"ש והלא שם ג"כ קי"ל דארבע מינין שבלולב מעכבין זה את זה כמו בד' פרשיות שבתפילין ואעפ"כ לא הצריך המ"מ לענין בל תוסיף שיטול כל הד' מינין כפולין אע"כ דסובר דכיון דמין ההוא הוא מהמינין הכשרים לצאת בזה ידי המצוה אית בזה משום בל תוסיף א"כ ה"נ בענינינו וא"כ יראה דמ"ש במ"א פרשה אחרת הוא בדוקא ומה שהקשה הפמ"ג על זה עיין במחה"ש שיישב זה אמנם דברי מחה"ש גם כן קשה מאוד להולמם דלדידיה דפרשה אחת מהד' בתים עובר על ב"ת יקשה מ"ש תפילין אלו הפסולין מפרשה אחת שבבית חמישי שבהם ג"כ כתוב ב' פרשיות דכשרים לכו"ע ואפשר משום דיש לחלק דעל הקציצה הזו מונח כבר שם פסול דהוחלף פרשיותיה בתוכה משא"כ שם דלא נגמר עדיין הפרשיות שלה ע"כ] ועיין שם במשנה ובגמרא דמוכח דאף אם מכוין להוסיף על התורה בזה אעפ"כ לא עבר על ב"ת וא"כ לכאורה קשה למה הצריך הטוש"ע שיכוין בהנחתם שיהיו התפילין השניים כרצועה בעלמא בלא"ה כיון שתפילין פסולים הם לא שייך בזה ב"ת (אח"כ מצאתי במחה"ש שהקשה קושיא זו) והנראה לי בזה דעצה זו אינה כדי שעי"ז לא יהי' עליו הלאו דבל תוסיף רק דהלא ידוע שהרא"ש סובר דמצות צריכות כונה וכמו שהביא הטור בשמו בסימן סמ"ך והכא הצריך הטור בשמו שיניח שניהם ויהדקם בבת אחת וכמו שפי' המ"א בסק"ד וא"כ איך יעשה בהכונה הצריכה להמצוה אם לא יכוין כלל בודאי לא יצא ידי המצוה ואם יכוין סתמא בההידוק הזה שהוא רוצה בזה לקיים מצות תפילין ג"כ לא יצא בזה להרבה פוסקים כיון שאחד מהם אינו תפילין כלל [והרי זה דומה למקדש שתי נשים כאחת והיתה אחת שפחה או נכרית שאינה ראויה לקידושין דהרמב"ם ובעל הלכות סוברין דאף הראויה אינה מקודשת עיין באה"ע סי' מ"א בב"י ובשו"ע ס"ד ובחו"מ שם סק"ד וה' וגם הרא"ש מסתפק בזה כמבואר בב"י שם וגם הכא הלא ב"ש קאיירינן דרוצה לצאת ידי כל הדיעות] ואם ירצה לברור לזוג אחד ויאמר שבאלו רוצה לקיים ובאלו אינו רוצה אינו יודע איזה הכשרים שיברר לקיים בהם המצוה

שער הציון

(ד) ב"י ומ"א: (ה) בה"ט: (ו) מ"א: (ז) עיין בביאור הלכה: (ח) בב"ח משמע דהוא בב"ת מדאורייתא ולט"ז ולמחה"ש עכ"פ מדרבנן:

הגהות ותיקונים: א) חסר תיבות לא יתכנו תפילין דר"ת לבד:

external housing. /The passage/ *Ve-Hayah Ki Yevi'acha* /should be placed/ after it in the second housing. /The passage/ *Shema* /should be placed/ in the third housing and /the passage/ *Ve-Hayah Im Shamo'a* in the fourth housing, which is the external housing /on the side/ towards the right /of the donner/.

(3) According to Rabbeinu Tam, /the passage/ *Ve-Hayah Im Shamo'a* /should be placed/ in the third housing and /one should place the passage/ *Shema* in the fourth housing, which is the external housing.

The practice of the /Jewish/ world (4) follows /the view of/ *Rashi* and the *Rambam*.

2. A Heaven fearing person should fulfil /his obligation according to/ both

Mishnah Berurah

handed, we go according to what is ordinarily the "right" and the "left".

(3) According to Rabbeinu Tam. The Poskim write that even Rabbeinu Tam acknowledges that it is necessary for the writing of /the passages to be done/ in the order in which they are written in the Torah. This /order/ is *Kadesh Li Chal Bechor, Ve-Hayah Ki Yevi'acha, Shema* and *Ve-Hayah Im Shamo'a*. He only differs with *Rashi* over the placing of /the passages/ in the housings.

Consequently, if one wishes to write *tefilin* /passages/ which accord with the view of Rabbeinu Tam /, then, when he writes the passages/ for the arm /*tefilin*/, which are /written/ on a single parchment /, he should act as follows/. He should /first/ write /the passage/ *Kadesh Li Chal Bechor* and /then the passage/ *Ve-Hayah Ki Yevi'acha*. /After that,/ he should leave blank /a space for writing the passage/ *Ve-Hayah Im Shamo'a* and /proceed to/ write /the passage/ *Shema*. Subsequently, he should write /the passage/ *Ve-Hayah Im Shamo'a* /in the blank space which he left for it/. In the case of the head /*tefilin*/, he should write /the passages/ on four parchments in the actual order /of their appearance in the Torah/ and /then/ arrange them in the housings /in the order/ *Kadesh Li Chal Bechor, Ve-Hayah Ki Yevi'acha, Ve-Hayah Im Shamo'a* and *Shema*.

/As to/ how one should act with respect to the law concerning the opening and closing of the *tefilin* /passages when one writes *tefilin* passages/ according to the view of /Rabbeinu Tam/, we have already explained this above, with the help of *Ha-Sheym*, in Sec. 32 /, sub-Par. 161/; see there.

(4) Follows *Rashi* and the *Rambam*. It is stated by the *B.Y.* and other Acharonim

כי יביאך בבית שני ושמע בבית השלישי והיה אם שמוע בבית הרביעי שהוא בית החיצון לימינו (ג) (ג) [ב]ולר"ת בבית השלישי והיה אם שמוע ובבית הרביעי שהוא החיצון שמע. ומנהג העולם (ד) כרש"י והרמב"ם: ב [ג]ירא שמים יצא ידי שניהם ויעשה שתי זוגות תפילין (ה) ויניח (ג) [א] (ו) שניהם * ויכוין בהנחתם (ז) באותם שהם אליבא דהלכתא אני יוצא ידי חובתי והשאר הם

ב תוספות שם ופירוש ר"ח ורבינו האי ג סמ"ג וסמ"ק וספר התרומה

שערי תשובה

[א] שניהם. עבה"ט ועיין במלת שמורים שדעתו לברך על תפילין דר"ת וליתא וע"ד שכתב האר"י ז"ל שאין לברך על ש"ר שקדושתם חמורה וק"ו בשל ר"ת עיין באגרת הרמ"ז סי' ה' ועיין לעיל סימן כ"ה בבה"ט ס"ק י"א בשם דרכי נועם וכ"כ בבכור שור ועיין בבכור שור דף קי"ח שאעפ"י שאין מברכים על של ר"ת מ"מ אין להפסיק בין תש"י לתפילין ש"ר ע"ש ועיין בפנים מאירות ח"א סימן ס"ז שהמניח תפילין של ר"ת בלא ברכה וקורא בהם ק"ש רשאי להפסיק באמצע הפרק מפני הכבוד ומ"מ לא ישיח שיחה בטלה ע"ש ונראה להחמיר להפסיק אף מפני הכבוד ועיין לקמן סימן ס"ו. ונראה דלכתחלה אין להפסיק בשהות ג"כ ועיין סימן ס"ה. ונהגו ללבוש תפילין של ר"ת במנחה שכך נהג האר"י קודש שעשה תפילין של שימושא רבא וכך נהג מהרח"ו ואף שלפי סוד הדברים[א] כיון שהם עשו כן בודאי כדבריהם כן היא ואנחנו לא נדע כ"כ בר"י. ועיין לקמן סימן ל"ח שאין להניח תפילין דר"ת בימי אבלו ובט"ב במנחה שכתב במג"א סימן תקנ"ה שהמניח דר"ת יניח במנחה גם כן. ועיין שם בשיורי כנה"ג בשם תשובת הרמ"ע ומ"ש ע"ז ע"ש ומ"ש בשם השבות יעקב שאם ש"ר נכתב ע"פ דעת רש"י יש להניח ש"ר תחלה עיין שם שמבואר שיברך שתי הברכות על ש"ר כמ"ש בהג"ה ס"ם כ"ו ושל יד דר"ת יניח בלא ברכה ואם של יד הוא לדעת רש"י מברך עליו להניח לבד

באר היטב

(ג) ולר"ת. ומ"מ לריך לכותבן כסידרן כמ"ש סימן ל"ב ס"א לכן לריך שיניח חלק פרשת והיה אם שמוע ויכתוב פרשת שמע בקלה הקלף ואח"כ יכתוב פרשת והיה אם שמוע באמלע מ"א. וע"ל סימן ל"ב ס"ק כ"ג מש"ש: (ג) שניהם. והנוהג כן להניח ב' זוגות ביחד יניח של רש"י למטה ושל ר"ת למעלה ט"ז וכ"כ האר"י ז"ל שיכנים תחלה של רש"י ויעמידם לצד הכתף ואחריהם של ר"ת לצד היד ושניהם על הקיבורת ויניח בראשו של רש"י למטה ושל ר"ת יותר למעלה ושניהם במקום הראוי לתפילין. והרלועות דר"ת יהיו תחת רלועות דרש"י מכוסה בה שלא יתגלו רק רלועות דרש"י. ותפילין דר"ת יהיו קטנים מתפילין דרש"י. עיין ספר הכוונת תפילין פרק יו"ד י"ב. [ועיין בספר אליה רבה שדחה דברי ט"ז וראייתו] מי שמניח תפילין של יד של דעת ר"ת ותפילין של ראש כדעת רש"י והרמב"ם אם יולא י"א פסק שבות יעקב ח"א סימן ב' דאינו יולא אליבא דכ"ע. אבל בשעת הדחק מותר להניחם כך דהא בשעת הדחק יולא אם מניח אחת לבד. ומ"מ לא

ביאור הלכה

בש"י כיון דאפשר לכותבן בקלף אחד ול"ע: * ויכוין בהנחתם באותם שהם וכו'. עיין במ"א שכתב דדוקא בזה אבל בשני זוגי תפילין כשרים עובר על בל תוסיף ומה שאמרו בסנהדרין פ"ט דאם עשה עוד בית אחד והניחו גבי הד' בתים האי לחודיה קאי היינו בשכתב פרשה אחרת דלא שייכי כלל לתפילין ועיין בפמ"ג שביאר דל"ד פרשה אחרת דה"ה אם כתב פרשה אחת מד' פרשיות והניחה בבית ההוא ג"כ אמרינן האי לחודיה קאי והאי לחודיה קאי [הג"ה הנה אף דלכאורה בודאי הדין עמו שהרי הד' פרשיות מעכבין זה את זה וא"כ כל זמן דלא כתב כל הד' עדיין תפילין פסולין הם ולא שייכי כלל לאלו הכשרין וכן משמע בביאור הגר"א מ"מ קשה לי מאד על דברי הפמ"ג שפירש כן את דברי המ"א דהרי המ"א הביא סיוע לדבריו מדברי הב"י בשם המ"מ והוא לקמן בסימן תרנ"א ומוכח שם בהדיא מדברי המגיד משנה דאם נטל מין אחר לבד הד' מינין אמרינן האי לחודיה קאי והאי לחודיה קאי ואם נטל לבד הד' מינין עוד לולב אחד או אתרוג אחד עבר על בל תוסיף ומדמה שם זה לשני זוגי תפילין דעובר על ב"ת עי"ש והלא שם ג"כ קי"ל דארבע מינין שבלולב מעכבין זה את זה כמו בד' פרשיות שבתפילין ואעפ"כ לא הצריך המ"מ לענין בל תוסיף שיטול כל הד' מינין כפולין אע"כ דסובר דכיון דמין ההוא הוא מהמינין הכשרים לצאת בזה ידי המצוה אית בזה משום בל תוסיף א"כ ה"נ בענינינו וא"כ ירא[ה] דמ"ש במ"א פרשה אחרת הוא בדוקא ומה שהקשה הפמ"ג על זה עיין במחה"ש שיישב זה אמנם דברי מחה"ש גם כן קשה מאוד להולמם דלדידיה דפרשה אחת מהד' בתים עובר על ב"ת יקשה מ"ש תפילין אלו הפסולין מפרשה אחת שבבית חמישי שבהם ג"כ כתוב ב' פרשיות דכשרים לכו"ע ואפשר משום דיש לחלק דעל הקציצה הזו מונח כבר שם פסול דהוחלף פרשיותיה בתוכה משא"כ שם דלא נגמר עדיין הפרשיות שלה ע"כ] ועיין שם במשנה ובגמרא דמוכח דאף אם מכוין להוסיף על התורה בזה אעפ"כ לא עבר על ב"ת וא"כ לכאורה קשה למה הצריך הטוש"ע שיכוין בהנחתם שיהיו התפילין השניים כרצועה בעלמא בלא"ה כיון שתפילין פסולים הם לא שייך בזה ב"ת (אח"כ מצאתי במחה"ש שהקשה קושיא זו) והנראה לי בזה דעלה זו אינה כדי שעי"ז לא יהי' עליו הלאו דבל תוסיף רק דהלא ידוע שהרא"ש סובר דמצות צריכות כונה וכמו שהביא הטור בשמו בסימן סמ"ך והכא הצריך הטור בשמו שיניח שניהם ויהדקם בבת אחת וכמו שפי' המ"א בסק"ד וא"כ איך יעשה בהכונה הצריכה להמצוה אם לא יכוין כלל בודאי לא יצא ידי המצוה ואם יכוין סתמא בההידוק הזה שהוא רוצה בזה לקיים מצות תפילין ג"כ לא יצא בזה להרבה פוסקים כיון שאחד מהם אינו תפילין כלל [והרי זה דומה למקדש שתי נשים כאחת והיתה אחת שפחה או נכרית שאינה ראויה לקידושין דהרמב"ם ובעל הלכות סוברין דאף הראויה אינה מקודשת עיין באה"ע סי' מ"א בב"י ובשו"ע ס"ד ובחו"מ שם סק"ד וה' וגם הרא"ש מסתפק בזה כמבואר בב"י שם וגם הכא הלא בי"ש קאיירינן דרוצה לצאת ידי כל הדיעות] ואם ירצה לברור לזוג אחד ויאמר שבאלו רוצה לקיים ובאלו אינו רוצה אינו יודע איזה הכשרים שיברר לקיים בהם המצוה

משנה ברורה

הוא איטר אולינן בתר ימין ושמאל דעלמא: (ג) ולר"ת. כתבו הפוסקים דגם ר"ת (ד) מודה דבעינן כתיבתן כסדר שהם כתובין בתורה שהוא קדש והיה כי יביאך שמע והיה אם שמוע אלא דפליג ארש"י לענין הנחתן בבתים וע"כ הרוצה לכתוב תפילין לדעת ר"ת יכתוב בשל יד שהם בקלף אחד קדש והיה כי יביאך ויניח חלק והיה אם שמוע ויכתוב שמע ואח"כ יכתוב והיה אם שמוע ובש"ר יכתבם בארבע קלפים כסדר ממש ויסדרם בבתים. קדש. והיה כי. והיה אם. שמע. ולענין דיני פתוחות וסתומות בהתפילין איך להתנהג לדעתו כבר ביארנו לעיל בע"ה בסימן ל"ב עי"ש: (ד) כרש"י והרמב"ם. וכתב בב"י ושאר אחרונים דכן עיקר וכן הסכים הגר"א בביאורו: ב (ה) ויניח וכו'. והנוהג (ה) כן להניח ב' זוגות תפילין יניח של רש"י למטה לצד הפנים ושל ר"ת למעלה. וכ"כ האר"י ז"ל שיכנים תחלה של רש"י ויעמידם לצד הכתף ואחריהם של ר"ת לצד היד ושניהם על הקיבורת ויניח בראשו של רש"י למטה ושל ר"ת יותר למעלה ושניהם במקום הראוי לתפילין והרלועות דר"ת יהיה מכוסה תחת רלועות דרש"י שלא יתגלו רק רלועות דרש"י ותפילין דר"ת יהיו קטנים מתפילין דרש"י עיין ספר הכוונת תפילין פרק י' י"ב. מי שמניח תפילין של יד של דעת ר"ת ותש"ר כדעת רש"י והרמב"ם אם יולא ידי חובתו פסק שבות יעקב ח"א סי' ב' דאינו יולא אליבא דכו"ע אבל בשעת הדחק מותר להניחם כך דהא בשעת הדחק יולא אם מניח אחת לבד ומ"מ לא יברך רק על אותו שנכתבה ע"פ מנהגינו כדעת רש"י והרמב"ם ואם של ראש נכתבה ע"פ דעת רש"י יש להניח של ראש תחילה וכשחולץ חולץ של יד תחלה עי"ש: (ו) שניהם. יחד על היד ויברך (ו) ויהדקם בבת אחת וה"ה בשל ראש כדי שתהיה הנחת שתיהם סמוך להברכה: (ז) באותם שהם וכו'. דלא (ז) יוכל לכוין בשתיהם בעת ההידוק שמהדקן יחד לשם תפילין דהרי אחד מהם אינו תפילין וי"א עוד דיש בזה (ח) משום בל תוסיף עכ"פ

שער הציון

(ד) ב"י ומ"א: (ה) בה"ט: (ו) מ"א: (ז) עיין בביאור הלכה: (ח) בב"ת משמע דהוא בב"ת מדאורייתא ולט"ז ולמחה"ש עכ"פ מדרבנן:

הגהות ותיקונים: א) חסר תיבות לא יתכנו תפילין דר"ת לבד:

/opinions/. He should /therefore/ make two pairs of *tefilin* /, one to conform with each opinion,/ (5) and don (6) both of them.

When one dons /the two pairs/, he should have in mind (7) that /the pair/ which /in fact/ conforms with halachic /requirements/ he is /wearing to/

Mishnah Berurah

that this is /in fact/ the prevailing /view/. The *Gra* likewise agrees /with this/ in his *Beyur*.

(5) And don, etc. A person who acts in this way, donning two pairs of *tefilin* /simultaneously/, should don below, towards the face, /the *tefilin* which accord with the view/ of *Rashi* and above /, towards the back of the head, the *tefilin* which accord with the view/ of Rabbeinu Tam.

This conforms with what the *Ari*, of blessed memory, writes. /He states/ that one should first slip on /the arm *tefilin* which accord with the view/ of *Rashi* and place them towards the shoulder. Subsequently, /he should place the arm *tefilin*, which accord with the view/ of Rabbeinu Tam, towards the hand. Both of these /units must be/ on the biceps. On his head, he should place below /, i.e., towards the face, the *tefilin* which accord with the view/ of *Rashi* and higher /, i.e., towards the back of the head, the *tefilin* which accord with the view/ of Rabbeinu Tam. Both of these /units must be/ in the area which is fit for /the donning of/ *tefilin*. The straps of /the *tefilin* which accord with the view of/ Rabbeinu Tam should be covered, underneath the straps of /the *tefilin* which accord with the view of/ *Rashi*, so that only the straps of /the *tefilin* which accord with the view of/ *Rashi* are exposed. The *tefilin* /which accord with the view/ of Rabbeinu Tam should be smaller than the *tefilin* /which accord with the view/ of *Rashi*. (See *Sefer Ha-Kavanos, Tefilin,* Chapter 10 and 12.)

If someone dons arm *tefilin* /which accord/ with the view of Rabbeinu Tam and head *tefilin* /which accord/ with the view of *Rashi* and the *Rambam*, /the question arises as to/ whether /or not/ he fulfils his obligation. The *Shevus Ya'akov* rules in Part 1, Sec. 2 that he does not fulfil /his obligation and this applies/ according to all /authorities/. However, when there is a pressing /need/ it is permitted to don this /combination/, since when there is a pressing /need/ one will fulfil /part of his obligation/ if he dons one /*tefilin* unit/ alone. Nevertheless, he should only make a blessing over /the unit/ whose /passages/ have been written in conformance with our practice, which /follows/ the view of *Rashi* and the *Rambam*. If /the passages of/ the head /*tefilin*/ have been written in conformance with the view of *Rashi* /, then, when he puts on the *tefilin*/ he should don the head /*tefilin*/ first and when he takes off /the *tefilin*/ he should take off the arm /*tefilin*/ first. See there.

(6) Both of them. /I.e., he should don both of them/ together on the arm, /first/ making the blessing and /then/ fastening them simultaneously, and /should act/ correspondingly with the head /*tefilin*/, so that both /pairs/ are donned closely /following his making of/ the blessing.

(7) That /the pair/ which, etc. /This is/ because one is unable to have in mind at the time he fastens /the *tefilin*/ that he is fastening /the units of/ both /pairs to serve/ together for the sake /of his fulfillment of the mitzvah/ of *tefilin*, since /in fact/ one of /the pairs/ is not /valid/ *tefilin*. Some /authorities/ argue further that this would involve /a transgression of the prohibition/, "You should not add",[1] at least according to Rabbinical Law.

1 *Devarim* 4:2 and 13:1. One transgresses this prohibition if he adds to the mitzvos of the Torah.

כרצועות (ד) (ח) * בעלמא כי מקום יש בראש להניח שתי תפילין וכן בזרוע ד ואם אינו יודע לכוין (ה) המקום ולהניח (ט) שניהם יחד (י) יניח (יא) כדברי האחד (יב) של יד ושל ראש [ויסלקם מיד] ויניח האחרים על סמך ברכה הראשונה [וי"א שאם] (יג) ה לא יוכל להניח בבת אחת יניח של רש"י

ד שם בסמ"ג והתרומה ה ב"י בשם תשובת אשכנזים וכאשר הגהתי בפנים כן הוא בב"י וסמ"ג

באר היטב

יברך רק על אותו שנכתבה ע"פ מנהגינו כדעת רש"י והרמב"ם. ואם של ראש נכתבה ע"פ דעת רש"י יש להניח של ראש תחלה וכשחולץ חולץ של יד תחלה ע"ש: (ד) בעלמא. שהרי ממ"נ אחד מהם פסול אבל אם הניח ב' זוגות תפילין כשרים עובר על בל תוסיף מ"א. ועיין ט"ז שהאריך והיד אהרן הקשה עליו: (ה) המקום וכו' וי"א שאם לא יוכל וכו'. נ"ע דהיינו מליעתא ועוד דגם ברישא דרישא שיודע לכוין המקום אינו מברך אלא על א' מהם וי"ל דה"ק דברישא קאמר שמניח שניהם יחד על היד ויברך ויהדקם בבת אחת וה"ה בש"ר ואח"כ קאמר ואם אינו יודע לכוין המקום ולהניח שניהם יחד פי' כשיהדקם בבת אחת לא יוכל לכוין המקום וצריך לקשרם זא"ז יניח כדברי א' ש"י וש"ר ויניח האחרים על סמך ברכה. ולא גרסינן ויסלקם מיד. ואח"כ כתב וי"א שאם לא יוכל וכו' פירוש אפילו בזא"ז לא יוכל להניחם

משנה ברורה

מדרבנן: (ח) בעלמא. שהרי ממ"נ אחד מהם פסול וכנ"ל בס"ק א' ודוקא (ט) בזה אינו עובר על בל תוסיף שיש בזה שתים למעליותא א' שאחד מהם הוא פסול ב' שכל אחד עומד בפ"ע אבל אם הניח ב' זוגות תפילין כשרים או שהתפילין של ראש עשה של ה' בתים בין (י) שעשהו מתחלה של ה' או שעשהו (יא) של ד' וחיבר לו אח"כ עוד בית אחד עבר בזה על הלאו דבל תוסיף ועיין בביאור הגר"א שמשמע מדבריו דאפילו אם הבית החמישי לא חיבר אותו לגמרי עם הד' בתים רק בקשירה בעלמא אפ"ה פסל להתפילין עי"ז וממילא עבר הלאו דבל תוסיף: (ט) שניהם יחד. פי' כשיהדק שניהם (יב) בבת אחת לא יוכל לכוין המקום שיהיה כל אחד מונח על מקומו כדין ע"כ צריך לקשרם עכ"פ תיכף זה אחר זה בלי הפסק ויהיה מועיל הברכה שבירך מתחלה גם על תפילין השניים וזהו מה שכתב המחבר בסמוך ויניח האחרים על סמך וכו' דהיינו שיניח הזוג השני אצל הזוג הראשון וכנ"ל אך שלא בהנחה אחת: (י) יניח. כדברי האחד של יד ושל ראש ויניח האחרים על סמך ברכה ראשונה (יג) ואם לא יוכל וכו' כנ"ל ולא גרסינן ויסלקם מיד: (יא) כדברי האחד. (יד) המחבר סתם דבריו ולפי הכרעת (טו) האחרונים טוב יותר שיסמוך הברכה להתפילין דרש"י: (יב) ש"י וש"ר. להמחבר בברכה אחת ולפי מנהגינו בב' ברכות וכנ"ל בסימן כ"ה ואח"כ יניח אצלם זוג שניה. ואעפ"כ (טז) שמפסיק ביניהם בהנחת הש"ר של הזוג הראשון וגם כהברכה שמברך עליה לפי מנהגינו אפ"ה ש"ד דהשני ברכות על תרוייהו קאי אבל לא יוכל להניח מתחלה השתים של יד משתי הזוגות ואח"כ השתים של ראש דנמצא (יז) מפסיק בין הש"י להש"ר בהנחת השניים: (יג) לא יוכל. פי' אפילו בזה אחר זה לא יוכל להניח בב"א כגון שיש לו מכה ואין לו מקום לשתיהן או שמתביים מפני הבריות המלעיגין עליו יניח של רש"י ויברך עליהם וכו' דהם (יח) העיקר לדינא ושל ר"ת יניח אחר התפלה כדי לצאת לד"ה

ביאור הלכה

המצוה לכך קאמר שיכוין סתם באותם שהם עשויים כתיקונם וכו' והרי זה כמו שאומר שם הראויה תתקדש לי עי"ש והמעיין בלשון הטור יראה מוכח כדברינו דמה שכתב אח"כ ואין בזה משום בל תוסיף מילתא אחריתא היא דאל"ה מה שמסיים אח"כ דלא מיקרי בל תוסיף דבר יתר הוא כמו שכתבו המפרשים ומה שכתב אח"כ והשאר הם כרצועות בעלמא פי' דאל"ה היה הפסק בין הנחה של יד לשל ראש מהזוג הכשר והרא"ש בעצמו כתב כן וכן מצאתי בעזה"י ברבינו ירוחם בהדיא ובמ"א כלל ס"ח דין כ"ג לכאורה משמע דכשמניח תפילין דרש"י ור"ת בבת אחת מוכרח הוא לכוין מחמת ספיקא דאל"ה יעבור על בל תוסיף אך מדברי המחה"ש משמע כמו שכתבנו דרק מדרבנן מפני שנראה כמוסיף וגם מדברי הגר"א כפי מה שמשמע מביאורו דמסכים להשיטות דמפרשי דמה שאמרו בסנהדרין האי לחודיה וכו' היינו שלא לעבור ג"כ על בל תוסיף ושם הלא איירי אפילו במתכוין להוסיף על המצוה וכנ"ל מהמשנה. ובאמת כל דבריו שם צ"ע במה שכתב שם לבסוף דאם נוטל הלולב כמה פעמים ביום ויאמר דמן התורה בא הקבלה ע"ז דעובר על בל תוסיף דבדברי התוספות ר"ה כ"ז[א] ע"ב מוכח להדיא דאפילו אם יכוין לקיים בזה בכל פעם המ"ע דלולב ג"כ אין עובר וכן ביאר החינוך ג"כ בהדיא ואפשר דדעת המ"א בכל זה לחלק בין אם מכוין בסתמא לקיים המ"ע בכל פעם ובין אם יאמר שבאה כן הקבלה ע"ז ודוחק דהמכוין לקיים מ"ע מוכרח הוא לומר כן ג"כ וצ"ע ודע עוד דלאידך פוסקים דסברי דלא אמרינן כלל האי לחודיה קאי לענין בל תוסיף עיין בתו' סוכה ל"א אתי שפיר מש"כ הטוש"ע ויכוין בהנחתם וכו' כפשוטו דאל"ה עובר על בל תוסיף. ודע עוד דממה שייען לנו המחבר שנעשה דוקא שני זוגות תפילין אם נרצה לצאת אליבא דכו"ע משמע דאסור ליתן שמע והיה אם שמוע בבית ג' וכן בבית הרביעי לצאת בזה ממ"נ [ועיין תוספות ר"ה כ"ז ע"ב ד"ה ומנא תימרו] משום איסור בל תוסיף ופוסל עי"ז את התפילין לגמרי ואפילו אם יאמר בפירוש שאינו רוצה לצאת רק בהפרשיות שהם ע"פ דין והשאר יהיו כקלף בעלמא ג"כ לא מהני ולא דמי למה שהתיר פה בשו"ע בשני זוגי תפילין דכל חד וחד לחודיה קאי וכמו שכתבנו במ"ב בסק"ח ועיין בסמוך: * בעלמא. עיין במ"ב שאם הניח ב' זוגות וכו' הוא מל"ח וב"ח ומ"א וביאור הגר"א דלא כהט"ז. ובס' ת"י מביא ראי' להט"ז מירושלמי דהמוצא תפילין אמנם מצאתי בס' התרומה שמביא להירו' הזה ופי' בו פירוש אחר [והגר"א העתיקו בביאורו בסי' כ"ז ס"ט] ומוכח שם דס"ל להיפוך. ועיין בא"ר שהוכיח מהגמ' דעירובין דאפי' אם מכוין שלא לצאת רק באחד אעפ"כ עבר בזה על בל תוסיף והשיג בזה על הב"ח. אמנם לפי מה שכתב המ"א בסימן תרנ"א דלדידן דקי"ל מצות צריכות כונה אפילו בזמנו אינו עובר אלא כשמכוין לאוסופי ניחא בזה דברי הב"ח דהלא הוא קאי להרא"ש והרא"ש סובר דמצות צריכות כונה כמו שכתב הטור בסימן סמ"ך אך הא"ר לשיטתו אזיל דהשיג שם בזה על המ"א מדברי הרא"ש גופא אמנם מה שמשמע מדברי הב"ח דאפילו בה' בתים אינו עובר על בל תוסיף רק במכוין לקיים מצות תפילין בה' בתים ומשמע דאם יכוין שהבית החמישי לא יהיה רק כרצועה בעלמא דאינו עובר על בל תוסיף לא הסכימו הרבה עמו בזה עיין בספר נהר שלום ובספר דמשק אליעזר שהעתמים זה בכוונות[ב] הגר"א דלהב"ח אינו מתיישב לשון הטור (ובאמת נוכל לאמר כונת הגר"א בפשיטות דקשה ליה קושית הב"ח הא גם בב' זוגות איכא ב"ת אבל לפי זה ניחא דהכוונה במש"כ דלא מיקרי בל תוסיף היינו כשקובע הפסול אצל הכשר ודוק) גם לפי דברי הב"ח יקשה למה לא יעצו שיתן ב' פרשיות בכל אחד ויתנה וכמו שכתבנו בתחלה אחרי דהוא מיקל אפילו בבית של ה' בתים דהוא כמו ה' פרשיות בפשיטות [ואפשר משום דיש הפסק בין הפרשיות והבתים ועיין במרדכי ריש הלכות תפילין] ואפשר דבאמת גם הב"ח יודה דלא מהני תנאי בבית של ה' בתים אך מה שנשאר לבסוף בדוחק על הטור וגם לשונו לא יהיה מתיישב כ"כ. וכ"ז לענין בל תוסיף אבל לענין פסול בודאי גם הב"ח מודה דפסול בה' בתים בכל גווני אף בתנאי לפי הטעם המבואר שם בסנהדרין פ"ט ע"א דכל בית חיצון שאינו רואה את האויר פסול. ודע עוד דפשוט בהפוסקים דאפילו אם לא קבע בהבית החמישי ההוא שום פרשה אפ"ה פסול מטעם דאמר שם בגמרא דהבית החיצון אינו רואה את האויר. ומש"כ במ"ב בשם הגר"א דאף ע"י הקשירה בעלמא מיפסל עיין בספר דמש"א מש"כ ע"ז אמנם מה שכתב בדברי רבינו אבל אם הוא קשור וכו' לא נהירין דברי הדמש"א כלל בזה דמה מצוה שייך בקשירת הבית החמישי וגם מוכח בדברי הגר"א בסימן תרנ"א סי"ד דלרבנן דא"ל אגד מדינא אינו עובר בבל תוסיף. ולענ"ד כוונת הגר"א בפשיטות דכמו שם לר' יהודה דכיון דלריך אגד הד' מינים ממילא מועיל האגד שיעבור על ידו גופא הלאו דבל תוסיף ה"נ כיון שע"י קשירת הבית החמישי מיפסל הד' בתים משום בית החיצון שאינו רואה את האויר ממילא עבר ע"י

שער הציון

(ט) מ"א וביאור הגר"א: (י) (יא) סנהדרין פ"ט ע"א עי"ש: (יב) מ"א: (יג) פמ"ג לגירסת המ"א: (יד) (טו) עיין בט"ז ובפמ"ג בא"א סק"ו: (טז) מ"א ופמ"ג: (יז) יד אפרים: (יח) ב"י והגר"א ופמ"ג:

הגהות ותיקונים: א) כ"ח: **ב)** בכוונת:

fulfil his obligation and /he regards/ the other /pair/ as (8) mere straps. /It is possible to don the two pairs/ because there is place on the head for donning two *tefilin* /units simultaneously/ and there is likewise /place/ on the upper arm /for donning two *tefilin* units simultaneously/.

If one is incapable of placing /the units/ on the /correct/ place and donning /the units of/ (9) both /pairs/ together /there/, (10) he should don /*tefilin*/

Mishnah Berurah

(8) Mere. For, irrespective of whatever /is in fact the correct ruling/, one of /the pairs/ is invalid, as /follows/ from what is /stated/ above in sub-Par. 1.

It is only /because of the special circumstances/ in this case that /the donning of both pairs/ does not /entail/ transgression of /the prohibition/, "You should not add".[1] /The reason is/ that /with respect to this matter/ there are two favorable /factors/, 1) that one of /the pairs/ is invalid and 2) that each one /of the pairs/ is independent /of the other/. If, however, one donned two valid pairs of *tefilin* or if one made the head *tefilin* with five housings (irrespective of whether he made them initially with five /housings/ or /whether/ he made them /first/ with four /housings/ and joined one more housing to them subsequently) /and then donned them/, he will, by /doing/ so, have transgressed the negative injunction of, "You should not add".

See /what/ the *Beyur Ha-Gra* /writes with reference to this/. It is implied by his words that even if one did not join a fifth housing completely to the four housings, /but/ only /connected it/ by mere tying, this nevertheless serves to invalidate the *tefilin*. It follows that /if one dons these *tefilin*/ he will transgress the negative injunction of "You should not add".

(9) Both together. I.e., if when one would fasten both of them simultaneously he would be unable to place /the units/ on the correct place, so that each one of them would be lying in its /proper/ place in accordance with halachic /requirements/. Consequently, /he should not bind them simultaneously, but/ he must at least bind them in immediate succession without interruption. /Then,/ the blessing he makes in the beginning will be of avail for /the unit from/ the second /pair of/ *tefilin* as well.

This is what the author /of the Shulchan Aruch means/ when he writes nearby, "and /then/ don the other /pair/ relying on, etc." I.e., he should don the second pair close to the first pair, as /explained/ above, except /that he should/ not /don both of them/ with one donning.

(10) He should don /*tefilin*/ which conform with the view of one /of these

כרצועות (ד) (ח) * בעלמא כי מקום יש בראש להניח שתי תפילין וכן בזרוע ד ואם אינו יודע לכוין (ה) המקום ולהניח (ט) שניהם יחד (י) יניח (יא) כדברי האחד (יב) של יד ושל ראש [ויסלקם מיד] ויניח האחרים על סמך ברכה הראשונה [וי"א שאם] (יג) ה לא יוכל להניח בבת אחת יניח של רש"י

ד שם בסמ"ג והתרומה ה ב"י בשם תשובת אשכנזים ולאשר הגהתי בפנים כן הוא בב"י וסמ"ג

באר היטב

יברך רק על אותו שנכתבה ע"פ מנהגינו כדעת רש"י והרמב"ם. ואם של ראש נכתבה ע"פ דעת רש"י יש להניח של ראש תחלה וכשחולץ חולץ של יד תחלה ע"ש: (ד) בעלמא. שהרי ממ"נ אחד מהם פסול אבל אם הניח ב' זוגות תפילין כשרים עובר על בל תוסיף מ"א. ועיין ט"ז שהאריך והיד אהרן הקשה עליו: (ה) המקום וכו' וי"א שאם לא יוכל וכו'. נ"ע דהיינו מציעתא ועוד דגם ברישא דרישא שיודע לכוין המקום אינו מברך אלא על א' מהם ונ"ל דה"ק דברישא קאמר שמניח שניהם יחד על היד ויברך ויהדקם בבת אחת וה"ה בש"ר ואח"כ קאמר ואם אינו יודע לכוין המקום ולהניח שניהם יחד פי' כשיהדקם בבת אחת לא יוכל לכוין המקום וצריך לקשרם זא"ז יניח כדברי א' ש"י וש"ר ויניח האחרים על סמך ברכה. ולא גרסינן ויסלקם מיד. ואח"כ כתב וי"א שאם לא יוכל וכו' פירוש אפילו בזא"ז לא יוכל להניחם

משנה ברורה

מדרבנן: (ח) בעלמא. שהרי ממ"נ אחד מהם פסול וכנ"ל בס"ק א' ודוקא (ט) בזה אינו עובר על בל תוסיף שיש בזה שתים למעליותא א' שאחד מהם הוא פסול ב' שכל אחד עומד בפ"ע אבל אם הניח ב' זוגות תפילין כשרים או שהתפילין של ראש עשה של ה' בתים בין (י) שעשהו מתחלה של ה' או שעשהו (יא) של ד' וחיבר לו אח"כ עוד בית אחד עבר בזה על הלאו דבל תוסיף ועיין בביאור הגר"א שמשמע מדבריו דאפילו אם הבית החמישי לא חיבר אותו לגמרי עם הד' בתים רק בקשירה בעלמא אפ"ה פסל להתפילין עי"ז וממילא עבר הלאו דבל תוסיף: (ט) שניהם יחד. פי' כשיהדק שניהם (יב) בבת אחת לא יוכל לכוין המקום שיהיה כל אחד מונח על מקומו כדין ע"כ צריך לקשרם עכ"פ תיכף זה אחר זה בלי הפסק ויהיה מועיל הברכה שבירך מתחלה גם על תפילין השניים וזהו מה שכתב המחבר בסמוך ויניח האחרים על סמך וכו' דהיינו שיניח הזוג השני אצל הזוג הראשון וכנ"ל אך שלא בהנחה אחת: (י) יניח. כדברי האחד של יד ושל ראש ויניח האחרים על סמך ברכה ראשונה (יג) ואם לא יוכל וכו' כצ"ל ולא גרסינן ויסלקם מיד: (יא) כדברי האחד. (יד) המחבר סתם דבריו ולפי הכרעת (טו) האחרונים טוב יותר שיסמוך הברכה להתפילין דרש"י: (יב) ש"י וש"ר. להמחבר בברכה אחת ולפי מנהגינו בב' ברכות וכנ"ל בסימן כ"ה ואח"כ יניח אצלם זוג שניה. ואע"פ (טז) שמפסיק ביניהם בהנחת הש"ר של הזוג הראשון וגם בהברכה שמברך עליה לפי מנהגינו אפ"ה ש"ד דהשני ברכות על תרווייהו קאי אבל לא יוכל להניח מתחלה השתים של יד משתי הזוגות ואח"כ השתים של ראש דנמצא (יז) מפסיק בין הש"י להש"ר בהנחת השניים: (יג) לא יוכל. פי' אפילו בזה אחר זה לא יוכל להניח בב"א כגון שיש לו מכה ואין לו מקום לשתיהן או שמתביישׁ מפני הבריות המלעיגין עליו יניח של רש"י ויברך עליהם וכו' דהם (יח) העיקר לדינא ושל ר"ת יניח אחר התפלה כדי לצאת לד"ה

ביאור הלכה

המצוה לכך קאמר שיכוין סתם באותם שהם עשויים כתיקונם וכו' והרי זה כמו שאומר שם הראויה תתקדש לי עי"ש והמעיין בלשון הטור יראה מוכח כדברינו דמה שכתב אח"כ ואין בזה משום בל תוסיף מילתא אחריתא היא דאל"ה מה שמסיים אח"כ דלא מיקרי בל תוסיף דבר יתר הוא כמו שכתבו המפרשים ומה שכתב אח"כ והשאר הם כרצועות בעלמא פי' דאל"ה היה הפסק בין הנחה של יד לשל ראש מהזוג הכשר והרא"ש בעצמו כתב כן וכן מצאתי בעזה"י ברבינו ירוחם בהדיא ובח"א כלל ס"ח דין כ"ג לכאורה משמע דכשמניח תפילין דרש"י ור"ת בבת אחת מוכרח הוא לכוין מחמת ספיקא דאל"ה יעבור על בל תוסיף אך מדברי המחה"ש משמע כמו שכתבנו דרק מדרבנן מפני שנראה כמוסיף וגם מדברי הגר"א כפי מה שמשמע מביאורו דמסכים להשיטות דמפרשי דמה שאמרו בסנהדרין האי לחודיה וכו' היינו שלא לעבור ג"כ על בל תוסיף ושם הלא איירי אפילו במתכוין להוסיף על המצוה וכנ"ל מהמשנה. ובאמת כל דבריו שם צ"ע במה שכתב שם לבסוף דאם נוטל הלולב כמה פעמים ביום ויאמר דמן התורה באה הקבלה ע"ז דעובר על בל תוסיף דבדברי התוספות ר"ה כ"ז[א] ע"ב מוכח להדיא דאפילו אם יכוין לקיים בזה בכל פעם המ"ע דלולב ג"כ אין עובר וכן ביאר החינוך ג"כ בהדיא ואפשר דדעת הח"א בכל זה לחלק בין אם מכוין בסתמא לקיים המ"ע בכל פעם ובין אם יאמר שבאה כן הקבלה ע"ז ודוחק דהמכוין לקיים מ"ע מוכרח הוא לומר כן ג"כ וצ"ע ודע עוד דלאידך פוסקים דסברי דלא אמרינן כלל האי לחודיה קאי לענין בל תוסיף עיין בתו' סוכה ל"א אתי שפיר מש"כ הטוש"ע ויכוין בהנחתם וכו' כפשוטו דאל"ה עובר על בל תוסיף. ודע עוד דממה שייען לנו המחבר שנעשה דוקא שני זוגות תפילין אם נרצה לצאת אליבא דכו"ע משמע דאסור ליתן שמע והיה אם שמוע בבית ג' וכן בבית הרביעי לצאת בזה ממ"נ [ועיין תוספות ר"ה כ"ז ע"ב ד"ה ומנא תימרו] משום איסור בל תוסיף ופוסל עי"ז את התפילין לגמרי ואפילו אם יאמר בפירוש שאינו רוצה לצאת רק בהפרשיות שהם ע"פ דין והשאר יהיו כקלף בעלמא ג"כ לא מהני ולא דמי למה שהתיר פה בשו"ע בשני זוגי תפילין דכל חד וחד לחודיה קאי וכמו שכתבנו במ"ב בסק"ח ועיין בסמוך: * בעלמא. עיין במ"ב שאם הניח ב' זוגות וכו' הוא מל"ח וב"ח ומ"א וביאור הגר"א דלא כהט"ז. ובס' ת"י מביא ראי' להט"ז מירושלמי דהמוצא תפילין אמנם מצאתי בס' התרומה שמביא להירו' הזה ופי' בו פירוש אחר [והגר"א העתיקו בביאורו בסי' כ"ז ס"ט] ומוכח שם דס"ל להיפוך. ועיין בא"ר שהוכיח מהגמ' דעירובין דאפי' אם מכוין שלא לצאת רק באחד אעפ"כ עבר בזה על בל תוסיף והשיג בזה על הב"ח. אמנם לפי מה שכתב המ"א בסימן תרנ"א דלדידן דקי"ל מצות צריכות כונה אפילו בזמנו אינו עובר אלא כשמכוין לאוסופי ניחא בזה דברי הב"ח דהלא הוא קאי להרא"ש והרא"ש סובר דמצות צריכות כונה כמו שכתב הטור בסימן סמ"ך אך הא"ר לשיטתו אזיל דהשיג שם בזה על המ"א מדברי הרא"ש גופא אמנם מה שמשמע מדברי הב"ח דאפילו בה' בתים אינו עובר על בל תוסיף רק במכוין לקיים מצות תפילין בה' בתים ומשמע דאם יכוין שהבית החמישי לא יהיה רק כרצועה בעלמא דאינו עובר על בל תוסיף לא הסכימו הרבה עמו בזה עיין בספר נהר שלום ובספר דמשק אליעזר שהעמיס זה בכוונת[ב] הגר"א דלהב"ח אינו מתיישב לשון הטור (ובאמת נוכל לאמר כונת הגר"א בפשיטות דקשה ליה קושית הב"ח הא גם בב' זוגות איכא ב"ת אבל לפי זה ניחא דהכוונה במש"כ דלא מיקרי בל תוסיף היינו כשקובע הפסול אצל הכשר ודוק) גם לפי דברי הב"ח יקשה למה לא יעלו שיתן ב' פרשיות בכל אחד ויתנה וכמו שכתבנו בתחלה אחרי דהוא מיקל אפילו בבית של ה' בתים דהוא כמו ה' פרשיות בפשיטות [ואפשר משום דיש הפסק בין הפרשיות והבתים ועיין במרדכי ריש הלכות תפילין] ואפשר דבאמת גם הב"ח יודה דלא מהני תנאי בבית של ה' בתים אך מה שנשאר לבסוף בדוחק על הטור וגם לשונו לא יהיה מתיישב כ"כ. וכ"ז לענין בל תוסיף אבל לענין פסול בודאי גם הב"ח מודה דפסול בה' בתים בכל גווני אף בתנאי לפי הטעם המבואר שם בסנהדרין פ"ט ע"א דכל בית חיצון שאינו רואה את האויר פסול. ודע עוד דפשוט בהפוסקים דאפילו אם לא קבע בהבית החמישי ההוא שום פרשה אפ"ה פסול מטעם דאמר שם בגמרא דהבית החיצון אינו רואה את האויר. ומש"כ במ"ב בשם הגר"א דאף ע"י הקשירה בעלמא מיפסל עיין בספר דמש"א מש"כ ע"ז אמנם מה שכתב בדברי רבינו אבל אם הוא קשור וכו' לא נהירין דברי הדמש"א כלל בזה דמה מצוה שייך בקשירת הבית החמישי וגם מוכח בדברי הגר"א בסימן תרנ"א סי"ד דלרבנן דא"ל אגד מדינא אינו עובר בבל תוסיף. ולענ"ד כוונת הגר"א בפשיטות דכמו שם לר' יהודה דכיון דצריך אגד הד' מינים ממילא מועיל האגד שיעבור על ידו גופא הלאו דבל תוסיף ה"נ כיון שע"י קשירת הבית החמישי מיפסל הד' בתים משום בית החיצון שאינו רואה את האויר ממילא עבר ע"י

שער הציון

(ט) מ"א וביאור הגר"א: (י) (יא) סנהדרין פ"ט ע"א עי"ש: (יב) מ"א: (יג) פמ"ג לגירסת המ"א: (יד) (טו) עיין בט"ז ובפמ"ג בא"א סק"ו: (טז) מ"א ופמ"ג: (יז) יד אפרים: (יח) ב"י והגר"א ופמ"ג:

הגהות ותיקונים: א) כ"ח: ב) בכוונת:

(11) which conform with the view of one /of these authorities, both/ (12) the arm and the head /*tefilin* units/ [and remove them immediately], and /then/ don the other /pair/, relying on the blessing /he made/ at first.

[There are /authorities/ who say that if] (13) one is unable to don /both pairs/ simultaneously, he should don /the pair which conforms with the

Mishnah Berurah

authorities, both/ the arm and the head /*tefilin* units/, and /then/ don the other /pair/, relying on the blessing /he made/ at first. If one is unable, etc. This is what /the correct reading/ should be. We do not accept the reading /which has been added in brackets/, "and remove them immediately".

(11) Which conform with the view of one. The author /of the Shulchan Aruch/ does not specify /that any one of the pairs has precedence/. /However,/ according to the decision of the Acharonim, it is preferable to /make/ the blessing close to /the donning of/ the *tefilin* which /accord with the view/ of *Rashi*.

(12) The arm and the head /*tefilin* units/. According to the author /of the Shulchan Aruch/ one blessing /should be made/ and according to our practice two blessings, as /explained/ above in Sec. 25. Subsequently, one should don the second pair /of *tefilin*/ close to these /*tefilin*/.

Although /this practice involves/ making an interruption in between /the donning of the two arm *tefilin* units/, by /one's/ donning of the head /*tefilin*/ of the first pair and also by /one's/ making of the blessing over /the head *tefilin*/, in accordance with our practice, this is nevertheless /regarded as/ perfectly in order. /This is/ because the two blessings relate to both /pairs/. One may not, however, don the two arm /*tefilin* units/ of both pairs first and subsequently the two head /*tefilin* units/, as he would thereby be interrupting /, in contravention of the halachah,/ in between /the donning/ of the arm /*tefilin*/ and /the donning/ of the head /*tefilin*/, by his donning /of the arm *tefilin*/ of the second /pair/.

(13) One is unable. I.e., if even by /placing them on him/ one after the other he would be unable to don them simultaneously. For example, if he has a wound and does not have /enough/ place /left/ for both of them or if he would be embarrassed because people would mock him. /Then/ he should don /the pair which accords with the view/ of *Rashi* and make a blessing over it, etc., as this is /the pair which accords with/ the prevailing halachic view.

He should don /the pair which accords with the view/ of Rabbeinu Tam after the prayer /service/, in order to fulfil /his obligation/ according to all /authorities/. See the Beyur Halachah, where we have

ויברך עליהם ויהיו עליו בשעת ק"ש ותפלה (יד) ואחר התפלה * יניח של ר"ת בלא ברכה ויקרא בהם (טו) שמע והיה אם שמוע: ג לא יעשה (טז) כן אלא מי שמוחזק ומפורסם (ו) [ב] (יז) בחסידות: ד (יח) * לא יניח * ב' הזוגות (ז) [ג] (יט) בכיס אחד שהאחד מהם (כ) * הוא חול ואסור להניחו

ו שם ז טור בשם אביו ורבו ר"ת וא"ח בשם הר"י מקורביל

שערי תשובה

ועל ש"ר שהוא של ר"ת לא יברך כלל: [ב] בחסידות. עבה"ט ובברכי יוסף כתב שבמקומותינו רוב תופסי התורה ומקלת בעלי בתים מניחים דר"ת גם כן ולא מיחזי כיוהרא. אבל של שימושא רבא אין להניח רק המוחזק בחסידות ועיין במח"ב שיש מי שכתב דבקושי התירום. ואמנם מהרח"ו בשערי קדושה כתב בכלל המלוה לעשות תפילין משימושא רבא ומ"מ כתבו בשם הרמ"ז שאין להניח רק במנחה וכן נהג הרמ"ז להניח תפילין אלו של אלבעים כו' ובעת קריאת שמו"ת כ"כ מוהר"ר ישעיה באסאן בתשובותיו הנקראים לחמי תודה עיין שם. ועיין במח"ב בשם מכתם לדוד סי' ד' דאם אין לו של רש"י רק של ר"ת ילבשם גם שחרית בלא ברכה ובמנחה אעפ"י שיש לו של רש"י לא יניח אלא של ר"ת על דרך האמת ולא יברך וכתב במח"ב בשם אור לדיקים קבלתי ממורי ז"ל שלא להניח תפילין בע"ש כי כבר נתנולץ קדושת שבת עכ"ל. וכ"כ בסוף שומר אמונים בתשובה סימן ז' ומזה מבואר שעל תפילין דר"ת קאמר שג"כ אין להניחם במנחה בע"ש ועיין לקמן סימן ל"ז. וכתב בבר"י מי שנוהג ללבוש תפילין במנחה והושיט ידו אל הכיס ונזדמנו לו תפילין דרש"י לפי מש"ל סימן כ"ה יכול להחזירן לכיס וללבוש של ר"ת כמנהגו ואין בזה משום מעבירין כו': [ג] בכיס אחד. עבה"ט ובמח"ב כתב בשם זרע

באר היטב

בבת אחת כגון שיש לו מכה או שמתבייש בפני הבריות מ"א. ועיין דרכי נועם חלק א"ח סימן ב' ובספר בני חייא: (ו) בחסידות. נשאלתי על איש אחד שהיה נוהג להניח תפילין של ר"ת לאחר התפלה בפרהסיא בפני הקהל אי מחזי כיוהרא פסק בתשובת מהר"ש הלוי דמיחזי כיוהרא ולריך שיבטל מנהגו. וכ"כ בתשובת שבות יעקב ח"ב סימן מ"ד שאפילו אם מקלת עושין יש בו משום יוהרא. ואם מניחן בפני אדם גדול שאין נוהג להניחם כי אם בקרב ביתו ודאי מחזי כיוהרא ע"ש: (ז) כיס אחד. אסור להחליף הכיסים וכ"ש הבתים והרלועות

ביאור הלכה

על ידו גופא הלאו דבל תוסיף והכי מוכח פשטא דסוגיא שם להמעיין בו ובמה שפירש הגר"א המימרא דרבי זירא דאיירי אפילו בקישור ולא בחיבור ממש ניחא מאוד מה דקאמר כל בית החילון שאינו רואה ולא קאמר כל בית הרביעי אלא דאכתי חילון הוא: * יניח של ר"ת. נ"ל דגם בזה לריך ליזהר לכוין שאינו עושה כן רק משום ספיקא ובזה לכו"ע לא עבר על בל תוסיף ובל תגרע דאם יכוין סתם בזה לקיים מ"ע דתפילין הגם דאין בזה משום ב"ת דהאי לחודיה קאי וכו' עכ"פ שמא באמת הדין כרש"י ותפילין אלו פסולים דהחליף פרשיותיה וכמו שכתב הרא"ש והטור ונמלא דעובר בזה על בל תגרע דהלא מבואר בסמ"ג ל"ת שס"ה דהעושה ג' טוטפות בתפילין עובר על בל תגרע וה"נ דכוותיה דהלא אין לו רק שתי פרשיות שקבועין במקומן ואין לחלק דהתם עכ"פ ג' כשרין הן ויש ע"ז רק שם מגרע משא"כ כאן ע"י שקבועין קלת פרשיות בהקלילה שלא במקומן נאמר דהקלילה כולה מיקרי קלילה פסולה ואין עליה שם מגרע ז"א דהלא שם בודאי אין על הקלילה שם תפילין כלל דהלא קי"ל דארבע טוטפות מעכבין זה את זה ואפ"ה נכלל זה בלאו דלא תגרע. ולהיפך אין לחלק דשם גרע מעיקר התפילין משא"כ כאן דז"א אחד דכיון שלא הניחה במקומה הוי ג"כ כמו שחיסרה ועוד דמי גרע זה מדמים הניתנין במתן אחד במקום דלריכין מתן ב' שהן ד' דאמרינן בעירובין דף ק' ע"א ובר"ה כ"ז[א] דעובר על בל תגרע אף דקי"ל בזבחים בפ' ב"ש דבדיעבד כיפר עכ"פ הלא גרע הלכתחלה במלות השם [הג"ה וזה הוא תוכחת מגולה להאדם הרולה להתרשל ממ"ע לפעמים במלות בדבר שהוא רק לכתחלה] ק"ו בזה דהוא לעיכובא אף בדיעבד ועוד דהלא כתב הרמב"ם בספר המלות שלו דלאו זה הוא בין אם מגרע מהכתוב בתורה ובין אם הוא מגרע מהמקובל בע"פ וה"נ כיון דמקובל לנו בע"פ שסדר הנחתם הוא כך והוא משנה בודאי הוא מגרע בזה אם לא שנאמר כמש"כ העט"ז בשם המקובלים דאלו ואלו כשרים הם אבל אנו רואין שהטוש"ע וכל הפוסקים לא קיבלו דבר זה להלכה וידוע דכל היכא שהפוסקים חולקים עם המקובלים הדין כהפוסקים וכן הוכיח הגאון ר' ברוך פרענקיל בהגהותיו מן הגמרא ועוד שירא שמים המניח תפילין דר"ת הוא רולה ללאת ידי כל הדיעות ולא שעי"ז יפול בחשש ספקא דאורייתא ע"כ הנכון לעשות כמו שכתבנו שיכוין בפירוש שאינו מניחן רק משום ספיקא ואפילו סתמא לא מהני בזה דהא קי"ל בר"ה כ"ז ע"ב לעבור בזמנו לא בעי כונה ואף דשם איירי הענין לענין בל תוסיף פשוט דה"ה לענין בל תגרע ועיין בט"ז בסוף סימן תרנ"א ואין לאמר דכאן מיקרי שלא בזמנה משום דכבר ילא בתפילין דרש"י והוא דומה ללולב דפסק שם הט"ז דאינו עובר על בל תגרע אח"כ אם נוטל ג' מינים אם לא שיכוין בס בפירוש לשם מלוה דשאני התם דמדאגבהיה נפיק ביה משא"כ בתפילין דעלם זמנן הוא כל היום והוא מברך עליהן בכל פעם שמניחן ולא גרע עכ"פ מכבור דמסיק שם בר"ה דמיקרי כל היום זמנו או בברכת כהנים אלו מתרמי ליה לבורא אחרינא אף דבדוחק יש לחלק מ"מ הדרך היותר נכון הוא כמו שכתבתי ובפרט דיש דיעות בפוסקים דסברי דחיוב תפילין מן התורה הוא להיותן עליו כל היום עיין בספר ישועות יעקב בודאי מיקרי כל היום זמנו. וכתבתי זה לאפוקי ממה שראיתי לאחד שכתב היפך זה ולא עיין בזה כל הלורך. ויש עוד הרבה דברים שמלאתי אח"כ בפתיחה להפמ"ג בענינא דבל תוסיף ואכ"מ להעתיקם: * לא יניח. עיין במ"ב והוא מהמג"א ועיין לקמן בסימן מ"ב ס"ג דכל דיניהם שייך לכאן ונראה דאפילו אם עשיית הכיס היה על דעת אחד אם קודם שהניח בפעם האחד עקר בפירוש הזמנתו הראשונה דמהני ואין זה בכלל לא אתי דיבור ומבטל מעשה דהעשייה זו לא נחשב רק הזמנה בעלמא עיין סנהדרין מ"ח ואכ"מ להאריך: * שתי הזוגות. ומיירי שהזוג שנתייחד לו הכיס מתחלה הוא בלי תיק ואפילו אם הוא בתיק ופעמים בדרך ערא הם מונחין בו בלי תיק נתקדש עי"ז וכדאיתא מגילה כ"ו ע"ב בגמרא מרים הו"א וכו' עי"ש אבל אם הוא בתיק תמיד הרי הכיס אין נעשה על ידו כ"א תשמיש דתשמיש ולית בו קדושה. ולכאורה ירא דדוקא אם התיק מכסה גם המעברתא והתיתורא דגם הם מכלל גוף הקדושה דלא חשיב במגילה דף כ"ו לתשמישי קדושה בתפילין רק התיק והרלועה וגם משנת כ"ח ע"ב והא אמר אביי שי"ן של תפילין וכו' ועיין אח"כ מלאתי כעין זה במרדכי בהלכות תפילין: * הוא חול. עיין במ"ב והעתקתי כ"ז מבה"ט בשם תשובת ד"נ ולע"ק לדינא במש"כ דאם[ד] לא הניחן וכו' דיכול להחליפם דפשוט דמקורו

משנה ברורה

ועיין בביאור הלכה שהוכחנו דמאוד לריך להזהר שלא יכוין בהנחתם רק משום ספקא ולא בסתמא לשם מלוה: (יד) ואחר התפלה. היינו כדין המבואר לעיל בסימן כ"ה סי"ג ולא כאלו החוללין תפילין דרש"י ומניחין דר"ת תיכף לאחר קדושה של י"ח ובאמת מלבד שעושין שלא כדין המבואר לעיל סימן כ"ה סי"ג גם לריך לכוין בתפלת י"ח להש"ץ לא[ב] לעסוק בדבר אחר [פמ"ג]: (טו) שמע והיה א"ש. אבל א"ל [ג]פ' ליצית כי חששא דשמא העיד עדות שקר (יט) כבר תיקן בב' פרשיות ועיין בפמ"ג דמשמע מיניה דכן יש לנהוג המניח תפילין דר"ת שיניחנו רק לאחר שסילק דרש"י. ופשוט דמי שלובש כל היום תפילין שנכון יותר שילבוש תפילין דרש"י: ג (טז) כן. היינו אפילו אם ירלה להניחם רק אחר התפלה וכתב הבה"ט באיש אחד שהיה נוהג להניח תפילין דר"ת לאחר התפלה בפרהסיא בפני הקהל אי מחזי כיוהרא פסק בתשובת מהר"ש הלוי דמחזי כיוהרא ולריך שיבטל מנהגו וכ"כ בתשו' שבות יעקב ח"ב סימן מ"ד שאפילו אם מקלת עושין יש בו משום יוהרא ואם מניחן בפני אדם גדול שאין נוהג להניחן כ"א בקרב ביתו ודאי מחזי כיוהרא ע"ש: (יז) בחסידות. שכיון שהעולם נוהגין כרש"י נראה[?] כיוהרא מי שחושש להחמיר ע"ע בזה אם אינו מוחזק שמחמיר ע"ע ג"כ בשאר דברים: ד (יח) לא יניח. ומיירי שהזמין הכיס מתחלה רק לדעת אחד מהם (כ) אבל אם נעשה מתחלה להניח בו שניהם שרי: (יט) בכיס אחד. של תפילין כדמפרש אבל בתיק הטלית מותר להניח שניהם אפילו הם בלא תיק דהרי התיק מיוחד גם לדבר חול דהוא הטלית: (כ) הוא

שער הציון

(יט) פמ"ג: (כ) מ"א:

הגהות ותיקונים: א) כ"ח: ב) צ"ל ולא: ג) חסר תבת לומר: ד) ואם:

הערות והארות: 1) עיין בה"ל סי' רס"ב ס"ב ד"ה בגדים נאים וכו' לענין יוהרא כשעושה בבית:

view/ of *Rashi* and make a blessing over it and should have these /*tefilin*/ on him at the time when /he reads/ "The Reading of Shema" and /prays the eighteen-blessing/ prayer. /Then,/ (14) after the prayer /service/, he should don /the *tefilin* which conform with the view/ of Rabbeinu Tam, without /making/ a blessing, and, with them /on/, he should read /the passages/ (15) *Shema* and *Ve-Hayah Im Shamo'a.*

Mishnah Berurah

shown that one must be very careful when he dons them not to have in mind more than /the removal of any/ doubt /as to whether he in fact fulfilled the mitzvah of *tefilin*/. /However,/ he should not /don them/ unqualifiedly for the sake of /the fulfillment of/ a mitzvah.

(14) After the prayer, etc. I.e., in accordance with the ruling given above in Sec. 25, Par. 13. /One should/ not /act/ like those who take off the *tefilin* /which accord with the view/ of *Rashi* and /then/ don those /which accord with the view/ of Rabbeinu Tam immediately after the *kedushah* of the eighteen/-blessing prayer/. Actually, quite apart from /the fact/ that they act in contravention of the ruling given above in Sec. 25, Par. 13, /their behavior is/ also /objectionable for a different reason/. /This is because/ one is required to apply himself /then/ to /hearing the repetition of/ the eighteen/-blessing/ prayer by the community prayer and should not occupy himself with anything else. [*P.Mg.*]

(15) *Shema* and *Ve-Hayah Im Shamo'a.* However, he does not need /to read/ the passage /dealing with the mitzvah/ of *tzitzis*, as he will have already remedied the fear that he may have testified false testimony[2] by /his reading of/ the two /other/ passages.

See the *P.Mg.* It is implied by him that someone who dons *tefilin* /which accord with the view/ of Rabbeinu Tam should /in fact/ act in this way. /I.e.,/ he should don them only after he has removed /the *tefilin* which accord with the view/ of *Rashi.*

It is self-understood that when someone wears *tefilin* all day it is more proper for him to wear *tefilin* /which accord with the view/ of *Rashi.*

2 See Sec. 25, sub-Par. 14 of the Mishnah Berurah.

ויברך עליהם ויהיו עליו בשעת ק"ש ותפלה (יד) ואחר התפלה * יניח של ר"ת בלא ברכה ויקרא בהם (טו) שמע והיה אם שמוע: **ג** ילא יעשה (טז) כן אלא מי שמוחזק ומפורסם (ו) [ב] (יז) בחסידות: **ד** (יח) * ילא יניח * ב' הזוגות (ז) [ג] (יט) בכיס אחד שהאחד מהם (כ) * הוא חול ואסור להניחו

ו שם ז טור בשם אביו ורבו ר"מ וא"ח בשם הר"י מקורבל

שערי תשובה

ועל ש"ר שהוא של ר"ת לא יברך כלל: [ב] בחסידות. עבה"ט ובברכי יוסף כתב שבמקומותינו רוב תופסי התורה ומקצת בעלי בתים מניחים דר"ת גם כן ולא מיחזי כיוהרא. אבל של שימושא רבא אין להניח רק המוחזק בחסידות ועיין במח"ב שיש מי שכתב דבקושי התירום. ואמנם מהרח"ו בשערי קדושה כתב בכלל המצוה לעשות תפילין משימושא רבא ומ"מ כתבו בשם הרמ"ז שאין להניח רק במנחה וכן נהג הרמ"ז להניח תפילין אלו של אצבעים כו' ובעת קריאת שמו"ת כ"כ מוהר"ר ישעיה באסאן בתשובותיו הנקראים לחמי תודה עיין שם. ועיין במח"ב בשם מכתם לדוד סי' ד' דאם אין לו של רש"י רק של ר"ת ילבשם גם שחרית בלא ברכה ובמנחה אעפ"י שיש לו של רש"י לא יניח אלא של ר"ת על דרך האמת ולא יברך וכתב במח"ב בשם אור לדיקים קבלתי ממורי ז"ל שלא להניח תפילין בע"ש כי כבר נתנוצץ קדושת שבת עכ"ל. וכ"כ בסוף שומר אמונים בתשובה סימן ז' ומזה מבואר שעל תפילין דר"ת קאמר שג"כ אין להניחם במנחה בע"ש ועיין לקמן סימן ל"ז. וכתב בבר"י מי שנוהג ללבוש תפילין במנחה והושיט ידו אל הכיס ונזדמנו לו תפילין דרש"י לפי מש"ל סימן כ"ה יכול להחזירן לכיס וללבוש של ר"ת כמנהגו ואין בזה משום מעבירין כו': [ג] בכיס אחד. עבה"ט ובמח"ב כתב בשם זרע

באר היטב

בבת אחת כגון שיש לו מכה או שמתביישׁ בפני הבריות מ"א. ועיין דרכי נועם חלק א"ח סימן ב' ובספר בני חייא: (ו) בחסידות. נשאלתי על איש אחד שהיה נוהג להניח תפילין של ר"ת לאחר התפלה בפרהסיא בפני הקהל אי מחזי כיוהרא פסק בתשובת מהר"ש הלוי דמיחזי כיוהרא וצריך שיבטל מנהגו. וכ"כ בתשובת שבות יעקב ח"ב סימן מ"ד שאפילו אם מקצת עושין יש בו משום יוהרא. ואם מניחן בפני אדם גדול שאין נוהג להניחם כי אם בקרב ביתו ודאי מחזי כיוהרא ע"ש: (ז) כיס אחד. אסור להחליף הכיסים וכ"ש הבתים והרצועות

ביאור הלכה

על ידו גופא הלאו דבל תוסיף והכי מוכח פשטא דסוגיא שם להמעיין בו ובמה שפירש הגר"א המימרא דרבי זירא דאיירי אפילו בקישור ולא בחיבור ממש ניחא מאוד מה דקאמר כל בית החיצון שאינו רואה ולא קאמר כל בית הרביעי אלא דאכתי חיצון הוא: * יניח של ר"ת. נ"ל דגם בזה צריך ליזהר לכוין שאינו עושה כן רק משום ספיקא ובזה לכו"ע לא עבר על בל תוסיף ובל תגרע דאם יכוין סתם בזה לקיים מ"ע דתפילין הגם דאין בזה משום ב"ת דהאי לחודיה קאי וכו' עכ"פ שמא באמת הדין כרש"י ותפילין אלו פסולים דהחליף פרשיותיה וכמו שכתב הרא"ש והטור ונמצא דעובר בזה על בל תגרע דהלא מבואר בסמ"ג ל"ת שס"ה דהעושה ג' טוטפות בתפילין עובר על בל תגרע וה"נ דכוותיה דהלא אין לו רק שתי פרשיות שקבועין במקומן ואין לחלק דהתם עכ"פ ג' כשרין הן ויש ע"ז רק שם מגרע משא"כ כאן ע"י שקבועין קצת פרשיות בהקיפה שלא במקומן נאמר דהקיפה כולה מיקרי קיפה פסולה ואין עליה שם מגרע ז"א דהלא שם בודאי אין על הקיפה שם תפילין כלל דהלא קי"ל דארבע טוטפות מעכבין זה את זה ואפ"ה נכלל זה בלאו דלא תגרע. ולהיפך אין לחלק דשם גרע מעיקר התפילין משא"כ כאן דז"א אחד דכיון שלא הניחה במקומה הוי ג"כ כמו שחיסרה ועוד דמי גרע זה מדמים הניתנין במתן אחד במקום דצריכין מתן ב' שהן ד' דאמרינן בעירובין דף ק' ע"א ובר"ה כ"ז[א] דעובר על בל תגרע אף דקי"ל בזבחים בפ' ב"ש דבדיעבד כיפר עכ"פ הלא גרע הלכתחלה במצות השם [הג"ה וזה הוא תוכחת מגולה להאדם הרוצה להתרשל ממ"ע לפעמים במצות בדבר שהוא רק לכתחלה] ק"ו בזה דהוא לעיכובא אף בדיעבד ועוד דהלא כתב הרמב"ם בספר המצות שלו דלאו זה הוא בין אם מגרע מהכתוב בתורה ובין אם הוא מגרע מהמקובל בע"פ וה"נ כיון דמקובל לנו בע"פ שסדר הנחתם הוא כך והוא משנה בודאי הוא מגרע בזה אם לא שנאמר כמש"כ העט"ז בשם המקובלים דאלו ואלו כשרים הם אבל אנו רואין שהטוש"ע וכל הפוסקים לא קיבלו דבר זה להלכה וידוע דכל היכא שהפוסקים חולקים עם המקובלים הדין כהפוסקים וכן הוכיח הגאון ר' ברוך פרענקיל בהגהותיו מן הגמרא ועוד שירא שמים המניח תפילין דר"ת הוא רוצה לצאת ידי כל הדיעות ולא שעי"ז יפול בחשש ספקא דאוריתא ע"כ הנכון לעשות כמו שכתבנו שיכוין בפירוש שאינו מניחן רק משום ספיקא ואפילו סתמא לא מהני בזה דהא קי"ל בר"ה כ"ז ע"ב לעבור בזמנו לא בעי כונה ואף דשם איירי הענין לענין בל תוסיף פשוט דה"ה לענין בל תגרע ועיין בט"ז בסוף סימן תרנ"א ואין לאמר דכאן מיקרי שלא בזמנה משום דכבר יצא בתפילין דרש"י והוא דומה ללולב דפסק שם הט"ז דאינו עובר על בל תגרע אה"כ אם נוטל ג' מינים אם לא שיכוין גם בפירוש לשם מצוה דשאני התם דמדאגבהיה נפיק ביה משא"כ בתפילין דעלם זמנן הוא כל היום והוא מברך עליהן בכל פעם שמניחן ולא גרע עכ"פ מבכור דמסיק שם בר"ה דמיקרי כל היום זמנו או בברכת כהנים אלו מתרמי ליה צבורא אחרינא אף דבדוחק יש לחלק מ"מ הדרך היותר נכון הוא כמו שכתבתי ובפרט דיש דיעות בפוסקים דסברי דחיוב תפילין מן התורה הוא להיותן עליו כל היום עיין בספר ישועות יעקב בודאי מיקרי כל היום זמנו. וכתבתי זה לאפוקי ממה שראיתי לאחד שכתב היפך זה ולא עיין בזה כל הצורך. ויש עוד הרבה דברים שמצאתי אח"כ בפתיחה להפמ"ג בעניגא דבל תוסיף ואכ"מ להעתיקם: * לא יניח. עיין במ"ב והוא מהמג"א ועיין לקמן בסימן מ"ב ס"ג דכל דייהס שייך לכאן ונראה דאפילו אם עשיית הכיס היה על דעת אחד אם קודם שהניח בפעם האחד עקר בפירוש הזמנתו הראשונה דמהני ואין זה בכלל לא אתי דיבור ומבטל מעשה דהעשייה זו לא נחשב רק הזמנה בעלמא עיין סנהדרין מ"ח ואכ"מ להאריך: * שתי הזוגות. ומיירי שהזוג שנתייחד לו הכיס מתחלה הוא בלי תיק ואפילו אם הוא בתיק ופעמים בדרך ערראי הם מונחין בו בלי תיק נתקדש עי"ז וכדאיתא מגילה כ"ו ע"ב בגמרא מריש הו"א וכו' עי"ש אבל אם הוא בתיק תמיד הרי הכיס אין נעשה על ידו כ"א תשמיש דתשמיש ולית בו קדושה. ולכאורה יראה דדוקא אם התיק מכסה גם המעברתא והתיתורא דגם הם מכלל גוף הקדושה דלא חשיב במגילה דף כ"ו לתשמישי קדושה בתפילין רק התיק והרצועה וגם משבת כ"ח ע"ב והא אמר אביי שי"ן של תפילין וכו' ועיין אח"כ מצאתי כעין זה במרדכי בהלכות תפילין: * הוא חול. עיין במ"ב והעתקתי כ"ז מבה"ט בשם תשובת ד"נ ולע"ק לדינא במש"כ דאם[ד] לא הניחן וכו' דיכול להחליפם דפשוט דמקורו

משנה ברורה

ועיין בביאור הלכה שהוכחנו דמאוד צריך להזהר שלא יכוין בהנחתם רק משום ספקא ולא בסתמא לשם מצוה: (יד) ואחר התפלה. היינו כדין המבואר לעיל בסימן כ"ה סי"ג ולא כאלו שחולצין תפילין דרש"י ומניחין דר"ת תיכף לאחר קדושה של י"ח ובאמת מלבד שעושין שלא כדין המבואר לעיל סימן כ"ה סי"ג גם צריך לכוין בתפלת י"ח להש"ץ לא[ב] לעסוק בדבר אחר [פמ"ג]: (טו) שמע והיה א"ש. אבל א"צ [ג]פ' ציצית כי משמע דשמא תעיד עדות שקר (יט) כבר תיקן בג' פרשיות ועיין בפמ"ג דמשמע מיניה דכן יש לנהוג המניח תפילין דר"ת שיניחנו רק לאחר שסילק דרש"י. ופשוט דמי שלובש כל היום תפילין שנכון יותר שילבש תפילין דרש"י: **ג** (טז) כן. היינו אפילו אם ירצה להניחם רק אחר התפלה וכתב הבה"ט באיש אחד שהיה נוהג להניח תפילין דר"ת לאחר התפלה בפרהסיא בפני הקהל אי מחזי כיוהרא פסק בתשובת מהר"ש הלוי דמחזי כיוהרא וצריך שיבטל מנהגו וכ"כ בתשו' שבות יעקב ח"ב סימן מ"ד שאפילו אם מקצת עושין יש בו משום יוהרא ואם מניחן בפני אדם גדול שאין נוהג להניחן כ"א בקרב ביתו ודאי מחזי כיוהרא ע"ש: (יז) בחסידות. שכיון שהעולם נוהגין כרש"י נראה[1] כיוהרא מי שחושש להחמיר ע"ע בזה אם אינו מוחזק שמחמיר ע"ע ג"כ בשאר דברים: **ד** (יח) לא יניח. ומיירי שהוזמן הכיס תחלה רק לדעת אחד מהם (כ) אבל אם נעשה מתחלה להניח בו שניהם שרי: (יט) בכיס אחד. של תפילין כדמסיים אבל בתיק הטלית מותר להניח שניהם אפילו הם בלא תיק דהרי התיק מיוחד גם לדבר חול דהוא הטלית: (כ) הוא

שער הציון

(יט) פמ"ג: (כ) מ"א:

הגהות ותיקונים: א) כ"ח: ב) צ"ל ולא: ג) חסר תבת לומר: ד) ואם:

הערות והארות: 1) עיין בה"ל סי' רס"ב ס"ב ד"ה בגדים נאים וכו' לענין יוהרא כשעושה בבית:

3. One should not act **(16)** in conformance with /the ruling of the previous paragraph/, unless he is renowned **(17)** for piety.
4. **(18)** One should not place both pairs **(19)** in a single bag. /This is/ because one of /the pairs/ **(20)** is /actually/ not sacred and it is forbidden to place it in a

Mishnah Berurah

(16) In conformance with /the ruling of the previous paragraph/. I.e., even if he wishes to don /the *tefilin* which accord with the view of Rabbeinu Tam/ only after the prayer /service/.

The *B.Heyt.* writes /the following/ about a certain person whose practice was to don *tefilin* /which accord with the view/ of Rabbeinu Tam after the prayer /service/ in public, in the presence of the congregation. /The question was raised as to/ whether this appears pretentious /behavior/. It was ruled in a responsum of the *Maharash Ha-Levi* that this /does in fact/ appear pretentious /behavior/ and he must stop his practice. It is likewise written in a responsum of the *Shevus Ya'akov*, Part 2, Sec. 44, that even if a few people do this it constitutes pretentious /behavior for them/. If one dons them before a distinguished person whose practice is to don them only inside his home, it definitely appears pretentious /behavior/. See there.

(17) For piety. This is due to /the fact/ that the public practice accords with /the view of/ *Rashi*. It /therefore/ appears pretentious if someone makes a point of being stringent with himself over this, when he is not reputed to be stringent with himself over other matters as well.

(18) One should not place. /The Shulchan Aruch/ is speaking of /an instance/ when the bag was designated from the outset to /serve/ only for /*tefilin* which conform with/ one[3] /specific view/. However, if it was prepared at the outset for /*tefilin* which conform with/ either /view/ to be placed there, this is /then/ permitted.

(19) In a single bag. /The author of the Shulchan Aruch means in/ a *tefilin* /bag/, as /may be seen/ from his concluding /words/. However, it is permitted to place both /pairs/ in the *talis* bag, even if they are not in a /separate/ bag /of their own/, as that bag is intended also for a non-sacred article, i.e., the *talis*.

(20) Is not sacred. It follows that it is

3 In addition, if the bag was not yet used for *tefilin* which accord with that view, an explicit cancellation of this designation is of avail and one may then use it for *tefilin* which accord with the other view. If the *tefilin* are always inserted first in another bag, it is permitted to use the larger bag in which this other bag is kept for *tefilin* which accord with the other view. (Beyur Halachah)

בכיס תפילין אלא יעשה שני כיסין וסימן לכל כיס שלא יתן של זה בזה:

לה דין מנין השיטין. ובו סעיף א׳:

א (א) ׳נהגו (ב) במנין השיטין לכתוב בשל יד שבעה שיטין בכל פרשה ובשל ראש ארבעה שיטין (ג) ואם שינה לא פסל:

א הרא"ש בסדר תקון תפילין ובספר התרומה

לו דקדוק כתיבתן. ובו ג׳ סעיפים:

א ׳צריך לדקדק (א) בכתיבת האותיות שלא תשתנה (ה) [א] (ב) צורת שום אחת מהן ולא תדמה

א הרא"ש בהלכות ס"ת ובסה"ת בשם תשובת הרשב"א

באר היטב

והפרשיות משל רש"י לר"ת או איפכא דרכי נועם חא"ח סימן ג׳ וכ"כ הרדב"ז והרמ"ע סימן ל"ז. ואם לא הניחם אדם מעולם עליו לשם מצות תפילין יוכל להחליפם. ואם התנה עליהן מעיקרא להחליפן כשירצה לא מהני תנאי כיון שסדרם ע"פ דעת אחד והניחם אפילו פעם אחת לשם מצות תפילין לדעת ר"ת או רש"י אסור להחליפם אח"כ אפי׳ התנה עליהם מתחלה דמקודש לחול לא מהני תנאי. דרכי נועם חא"ח סימן ב׳. אם עשאו כיס התפילין מתחלה להניח בו שניהם שרי דהוי כאלו התנה מ"א. רצועות שנמצאו ואינם יודעים אם הם של רש"י או של ר"ת אם באותו מקום נוהגים להניח שני זוגות יניחן לאיזה שירצה ואם הוא במקום שהרוב מניחים של רש"י יניחם בשל רש"י תשובת יד אליהו סימן ה׳:

(א) צורת. כתב ב"ש דלמ"ד יעשה בראשה כמין וי"ו ולא יו"ד מ"א:

שערי תשובה

אמת שהאריך לבאר שיכול לעשות רצועות לתפילין של רש"י ולהתנות שלכשירצה יוכל להסירה משם ולתלותם בתפילין של רבינו תם וכן להיפך ע"ש דלא כדרכי נועם ומשמע מזה דדוקא ברצועות אבל בפרשיות ובבתים לא מהני תנאי. ובבר"י הביא מרדב"ז בתשובה כת"י שכתב שהורה לעשות משל ר"ת תפילין דרש"י והראו לו בחלומו שלא יפה הורה ולכן חזר. ועיין וראה שיש זלזול בזה לגאונים הסוברים שהתפילין כשרים כו׳ וכתב דמכ"ש לפי מ"ש חכמי האמת שתפילין דר"ת בחינה עליונה מרש"י ודאי אסור שמוריד מקדושתן ולפי זה יש נוהגין להניח שני ראשי רש"י ורבינו תם בכיס אחד ושני ידות בכיס אחר דתרוייהו קדושים ולא כמ"ש מרן שהאחד חול ע"ש. ונראה דקאי אאותן שנהגו להניח השני זוגות בפעם אחד ביחד וכ"כ בסימן מ"ב הטעם דהו"ל כהתנה וכו׳ דהרי הני תרי לובשים תדיר יחד זה אצל זה והמקובלים כתבו דאלו ואלו דא"ח כו׳ ע"ש ומ"מ נראה דגם הם אין להם לעשות כן דלא ליתי לאחלופי וללבוש מה למעלה למטה. ועיין בעטרת זקנים שאין לעשות סימנים של אותיות בגופן של תפילין להכיר בין של רש"י לשל ר"ת ז"ל. ועיין בלבוש ובט"ז שאסור להניח שני זוגות תפילין יחד ממין אחד של רש"י או של רבינו תם משום בל תוסיף: [א] צורת. עבה"ט וכתב הבר"י בשם מהר"מ בן חביב בעל ג"פ בתשובותיו כ"י

משנה ברורה

חול. וממילא דאסור להחליף הכיסים וכ"ש הבתים והרצועות והפרשיות משל רש"י לר"ת או איפכא. ואם לא הניחם אדם מעולם עליו לשם מצות תפילין יוכל להחליפם ואם הניחן אדם עליו אפילו פ"א לשם מצות תפילין והיו מסודרין ע"פ דעת אחד מהם ר"ת או רש"י אסור להחליפן שוב אח"כ ואפילו אם התנה עליהן מעיקרא להחליפן כשירצה לא מהני דמקודש לחול לא מהני תנאי (אחרונים). כ׳ הפ"מ[א] דאם מצא רצועות ואינו יודע אם הם של רש"י או של ר"ת יוכל להניחם לפרשיות של רש"י דרובא מניחין של רש"י ואנן סבירא לן ג"כ דרש"י עיקר ומעלין בקודש. ועיין בבאר היטב ובביאור הלכה. ויש מן האחרונים שמקילין יותר דלדידן דסוברין דרש"י עיקר וכנ"ל יוכל להחליף וליטול רצועה משל ר"ת לרש"י כשאין לו אחרת אבל משל רש"י לר"ת אסור ליטול בכל גווני. ואם נזדמן שהוציא כיס של ר"ת תחלה יעבירם כי לדידן רש"י עיקר ולא הוי בזה אין מעבירין על המצות ואעפ"כ לכתחלה יזהר שלא יבוא לכך. בחוה"מ אין להניח של ר"ת. ובט"ז למנחה יניחם הרוצה:

א (א) נהגו. ע"פ הקבלה ביד סופרים איש מפי איש (טור) : **(ב) במנין השיטין.** וכן יש קבלה בידם בענין התחלת ראשי השורות בשל יד ובשל ראש כמבואר בטור ובב"י והסופרים בזה"ז אין מדקדקין בתחלת ראשי השורות ומשנים כאשר יזדמן להם והרוצה לדקדק לא ימשוך אותיות או יקצר הרבה כדי לכוין ראשי השיטות כי אין נוי לתפילין אבל מעט רשאי (פמ"ג): (ג) ואם שינה. בין בשל יד ובין בש"ר ואם אין לו [illegible] רק קלף קצר וארוך שאין יכול לכתוב עליו שבע שיטין אם לא שיכתוב כתיבה דקה מאד נראה דטוב יותר לשנות מנין השיטין עיין במרדכי בהלכות קטנות סוף ה"ת והובא לעיל סימן ל"ב דבכלל זה [illegible] לכתוב כתיבה גסה במקום שלא יהיו נמחקין מהרה. ובאמת אנו רואין [illegible] דבכתיבות הדקות שרגילין איזה סופרים בעוה"ר מלאי כמה וכמה קלקולים גם בתחילת כתיבתן שלא נכתבו כדין תמונת [illegible] וכמה מנין [illegible] ג"ץ דהוא [illegible] ויש מהגאונים שמחמירין בזה אפילו בדיעבד ואומר נפשי לא יקנה פרשיות כאלה בתוך תפיליו אם לא שיבדוק אותם מתחילה היטב היטב וידע מי כתב הפרשיות דפרשיות כאלו מלאי מאד דכותבין הם עדיין נערים שלא ידעו כלל דיני כתיבת סת"ם:

א (א) בכתיבת. [illegible] אם נשתנה האות מצורתה אחר הכתיבה ע"י נקב או קרע או טשטוש דפסול וכדלעיל בסימן ל"ב: צורת. אפי׳

ביאור הלכה

דמקורו מלקמן בסימן מ"ב בהדתי דיכול לשנותם והלא לפי המבואר שם באחרונים אין מותר רק להוריד מחמורה לקלה אבל לא לחול דהזמנה לגוף הקדושה מילתא הוא והכא הלא המחבר הזה בעצמו ס"ל לקמן דזה הוא בכלל הורדה לחול. גם מש"כ אח"כ ואפילו אם התנה עליהם וכו׳ דמקודש לחול וכו׳ עיין בש"ת דמסיק דברצועות מהני תנאי והוא פשוט דהם רק תשמישי קדושה ומהני תנאי בזה להורידן לחול וכדלקמן בסימן מ"ב ס"ג ואפילו בבתים ופרשיות לענ"ד יש לעיין בזה דהלא בקלף שנתעבד לשם פרשיות דהוא הזמנה לגוף הקדושה ואסור להורידו לחול הוכחתי לקמן בסימן מ"ב דיכול לכתוב עליו שאר ד"ת משום דיש בזה עי"ז עכ"פ קצת קדושה וה"נ בעניינינו הלא גם עתה אף דאין על הפרשיות קדושת תפילין עכ"פ קדושה יש בהן וה"נ הבתים הם תשמישים לקדושה וא"כ ליהני תנאי ואין התשובה בידי לעיין בה ואפשר דיש להקל ע"י תנאי בשל ראש דר"ת לרש"י אם אין לו פרשיות אחרים וצ"ע. עוד כתבתי בשם פמ"ג דאם מצא רצועה וכו׳ והשמטתי תשובת יד אליהו שמובא בבה"ט שבזמנינו רובא של רש"י ועוד עיין בספר פ"ת מש"כ ע"ז. ולפי שדברי הפמ"ג מוקשי ההבנה אמרתי להעתיקו פה ז"ל אם מצא של יד [ט"ס וצ"ל ג"כ או של ראש] ורצועה בלא פרשיות וספק שמא של ר"ת שפיר להניח פרשיות של רש"י ס"ס ורובא של רש"י ומעלין בקודש ואנן בקיאין ורש"י עיקר. ועיבוד צ"ע גם ברצועות מחול לקודש והבן עכ"ל. הנה מה שכתב ס"ס פשוט דשמא הם של רש"י ושמא של רש"י עיקר אך דמשום זה הטעם לבד היה מותר להניחו גם לשל ר"ת או דשמא של שניהם אסור דהספקות הם סותרות אהדדי ולכן סיים דרובא ואנן בקיאין ורש"י עיקר אך סוף דבריו נפלאים הם דבעיבוד אין שייך שמא עידן לשם תפילין דרש"י או דר"ת דהלא העיבוד הוא סתמא לשמה ונלענ"ד דכונתו הוא דלקמן בסימן ל"ט ס"ט איתא דאם לקח תפילין שלא מן המומחה בודק מהם ג׳ קציצות בחסר ויתר ודי בזה ולא חיישינן שמא עיבד המוכרן שלא לשמן דהכל בקיאין בזה ולכן מסתפק הפמ"ג בעניינינו דלו יהי דהכל בקיאין שהפרשיות צריך עיבוד לשמה הלא בעיבוד הבתים והרצועות אין נוכל לאמר שהכל בקיאין עתה בזה דהלא יש בזה מחלוקת בין הפוס׳ וכדלעיל בסימן ל"ג וא"כ שמא אותו שנאבד ממנו עשה הבתים או הרצועות בלא עיבוד לשמה וא"כ הוא מעלה עתה מחול לקודש בלי הזמנה מעלייתא דעיבוד ומה דמתיר הגמרא ליקח תפילין דמשמע אף עם רצועות דוקא בזמניהם שהיה ידוע אם צריך עיבוד או לא וה"נ דבזמנינו אם לוקח ממי שאינו מומחה צריך לדרוש מהמוכר אם היה בהבתים ורצועות עיבוד לשמה משא"כ בעניינינו דאיירי במציאה זהו הנלענ"ד בכונתו. ובאמת לע"ג בזה בזמנינו ברצועה הנמצאת דשמא רק נשחרה לשמה ולא נעבדה לשמה דהרבה יש שמקילין בזה ושלא כדין הוא וכמו שביאר הש"ת לעיל בסימן ל"ג ועי"ש במה שכתבנו שם. ומש"כ אם נזדמן וכו׳ פמ"ג[ב]:

tefilin bag /used for *tefilin* which are in fact sacred/. Instead, one should make two bags with an identification sign on each bag, so that one will not put /the *tefilin*/ of one /pair/ in /a bag used/ for the other.

§35: THE LAW AS REGARDS THE NUMBER OF LINES /REQUIRED IN THE PASSAGES/

(Contains One Paragraph)

1. (1) The practice (2) as regards the number of lines /to be written in the passages/ is to write in the case /of the passages/ of the arm /*tefilin*/ seven lines for each passage and in the case /of the passages/ of the head /*tefilin*/

Mishnah Berurah

forbidden to transfer the bags and certainly the housings, the straps and the passages from /*tefilin* which accord with the view/ of *Rashi* to /*tefilin* which accord with the view/ of Rabbeinu Tam or vice versa.

/However,/ if nobody ever donned /these parts of the *tefilin*/ on himself for the sake of the mitzvah of *tefilin*, one is able to transfer them /from *tefilin* which accord with one view to *tefilin* which accord with the other view/. /On the other hand,/ if someone did don them on himself, even once, for the sake of the mitzvah of *tefilin*, when they were arranged /in *tefilin*/ in accordance with the view of one of these /authorities/, Rabbeinu Tam or *Rashi*, it is henceforth forbidden to transfer them subsequently /to *tefilin* which accord with the view of the other/. Even if one stipulated with them from the beginning that /he should be able/ to transfer them /to *tefilin* which accord with the other view/ when he wishes, this is of no avail. For a stipulation is of no avail /for one to be allowed to transfer anything/ from a sacred to a non-sacred /usage/. ((Acharonim))

The *P.Mg.* writes that if one finds /*tefilin*/ straps and does not know whether they are /of *tefilin* which accord with the view/ of *Rashi* or /of *tefilin* which accord with the view/ of Rabbeinu Tam, he may don them with /*tefilin* which have/ passages /which accord with the view/ of *Rashi*. /The reason is/ because the majority /of *tefilin*/ which are donned /accord with the view/ of *Rashi*. In addition, we are of the opinion that *Rashi*'s /view/ is the prevailing view and one may raise the holiness /of a sacred object/. See the *Ba'eyr Heyteyv* and the Beyur Halachah. There are /authorities/ among the Acharonim who are still more lenient. /They maintain/ that according to us, who are of the opinion that *Rashi*'s /view/ is the prevailing /view/, as /stated/ above, one is allowed to take a strap from /a *tefilin* unit which accords with the view/ of Rabbeinu Tam and transfer it to /a *tefilin* unit which accords with the view of/ *Rashi*, when one does not have another /strap for this purpose/. However, to take /a strap from a *tefilin* unit which accords with the view/ of *Rashi* /and transfer it/ to /a *tefilin* unit which accords with the view of/ Rabbeinu Tam, is forbidden in all circumstances.

If one chances to take out the bag /containing the *tefilin* which accord with the view/ of Rabbeinu Tam first, he should pass over those /*tefilin* and don first *tefilin* which accord with *Rashi*'s view/. For according to our /ruling, the view of/ *Rashi* is the prevailing /view/ and /, therefore,/ this does not involve /a transgression of the prohibition that/ one should not pass over mitzvos. Nevertheless, initially, one should avoid it coming to that.

On Chol Ha-Mo'ed, one should not don /*tefilin* which accord with the view/ of Rabbeinu Tam. On Tishah Be-Av, at Minchah, whoever wishes /to do so/ may /in fact/ don them.

§35

(1) **The practice.** This is based on a tradition of the scribes, /handed down/ orally from one to the other. ((*Tur*))

(2) **As regards the number of lines.** /The

בכיס תפילין אלא יעשה שני כיסין וסימן לכל כיס שלא יתן של זה בזה:

לה דין מנין השיטין. ובו סעיף א':

א (א) ׳נהגו (ב) במנין השיטין לכתוב בשל יד שבעה שיטין בכל פרשה ובשל ראש **ארבעה שיטין** (ג) ואם שינה לא פסל:

א הרא"ש בסדר תקון תפילין ובספר התרומה

לו דקדוק כתיבתן. ובו ג' סעיפים:

א ׳צריך לדקדק (א) בכתיבת האותיות שלא תשתנה (א) [א] (ב) צורת שום אחת מהן ולא תדמה

א הרא"ש בהלכות ס"ת ובפא"ח בשם תשובת הרשב"א

באר היטב

והפרשיות משל רש"י לר"ת או איפכא דרכי נועם חא"ח סימן ג' וכ"כ הרדב"ז והרמ"ע סימן ל"ז. ואם לא הניחם אדם מעולם עליו לשם מצות תפילין יוכל להחליפם. ואם התנה עליהן מעיקרא להחליפן כשירצה לא מהני תנאי כיון שסדרם ע"פ דעת אחד והניחם אפילו פעם אחת לשם מצות תפילין לדעת ר"ת או רש"י אסור להחליפם אח"כ אפי' התנה עליהם מתחלה דמקודש לחול לא מהני תנאי. דרכי נועם חא"ח סימן ב'. אם עשאו כיס התפילין מתחלה להניח בו שניהם שרי דהוי כאלו התנה מ"א. רצועות שנמצאו ואינם יודעים אם הם של רש"י או של ר"ת אם באותו מקום נוהגים להניח שני זוגות יניחן לאיזה שירצה ואם הוא במקום שהרוב מניחים של רש"י יניחם בשל רש"י תשובת יד אליהו סימן ה':

(א) צורת. כתב ב"ש דלמ"ד יעשה בראשה כמין וי"ו ולא יו"ד מ"א:

שערי תשובה

אמת שהאריך לבאר שיכול לעשות רצועות לתפילין של רש"י ולהתנות שלכשירצה יוכל להסירה משם ולתלותם בתפילין של רבינו תם וכן להיפך ע"ש דלא כדרכי נועם ומשמע מזה דדוקא ברצועות אבל בפרשיות ובבתים לא מהני תנאי. ובבר"י הביא מרדב"ז בתשובה כת"י שכתב שהורה לעשות משל ר"ת תפילין דרש"י והראו לו בחלומו שלא יפה הורה ולכן חזר. ועיין וראה שיש זלזול בזה לגאונים הסוברים שהתפילין כשרים כו' וכתב דמכ"ש לפי מ"ש חכמי האמת שתפילין דר"ת בחינה עליונה מרש"י ודאי אסור שמוריד מקדושתן ולפי זה יש נוהגין להניח שני ראשי רש"י ורבינו תם בכיס אחד ושני ידות בכיס אחר דתרוייהו קדושים ולא כמ"ש מרן שהאחד חול ע"ש. ונראה דקאי אאותן שנהגו להניח השני זוגות בפעם אחד ביחד וכ"כ בסימן מ"ב הטעם דהו"ל כהתנה וכו' דהרי הני תרי לובשים תדיר יחד זה אצל זה והמקובלים כתבו דאלו ואלו דא"ח כו' ע"ש ומ"מ נראה דגם הם אין להם לעשות כן דלא ליתי לאחלופי וללבוש מה למעלה למטה. ועיין בעטרת זקנים שאין לעשות סימנים של אותיות בגופן של תפילין להכיר בין של רש"י לשל ר"ת ז"ל. ועיין בלבוש ובט"ז שאסור להניח שני זוגות תפילין יחד ממין אחד של רש"י או של רבינו תם משום בל תוסיף: [א] צורת. עבה"ט וכתב הבר"י בשם מהר"מ בן חביב בעל ג"פ בתשובותיו כ"י

משנה ברורה

סול. וממילא דאסור להחליף הכיסים וכ"ש הבתים והרצועות והפרשיות משל רש"י לר"ת או איפכא. ואם לא הניחם אדם מעולם עליו לשם מצות תפילין יוכל להחליפם ואם הניחן אדם עליו אפילו פ"א לשם מצות תפילין והיו מסודרין ע"פ דעת אחד מהם ר"ת או רש"י אסור להחליפן שוב אח"כ ואפילו אם התנה עליהן מעיקרא להחליפן כשירצה לא מהני דמקודש לחול לא מהני תנאי (אחרונים). כ' הפמ"ג דאם מצא רצועות ואינו יודע אם הם של רש"י או של ר"ת יוכל להניחם לפרשיות של רש"י דרובא מניחין של רש"י ואנן קיי"ל ג"כ דרש"י עיקר ומעלין בקודש. ועיין בבאר היטב ובביאור הלכה. ויש מן האחרונים שמקילין יותר דלדידן דסוברין דרש"י עיקר וכו' יוכל להחליף וליטול רצועה משל ר"ת לרש"י כשאין לו אחרת אבל משל רש"י לר"ת אסור ליטול בכל גווני. ואם נזדמן שהוציא כיס של ר"ת תחלה יעבירם כי לדידן רש"י עיקר ולא הוי בזה אין מעבירין על המצות ואעפ"כ לכתחלה יזהר שלא יבוא לכך. בחוה"מ אין להניח של ר"ת. ובט"ב למנחה יניחם הרוצה:

א (א) נהגו. ע"פ הקבלה ביד סופרים איש מפי איש (טור): (ב) במנין השיטין. וכן יש קבלה בידם בענין התחלת ראשי השורות בשל יד ובשל ראש כמבואר בטור ובב"י וסופרים כהיום אין מדקדקין בתחלת ראשי השורות ומשנים כאשר יזדמן להם והרוצה לדקדק לא ימשוך אותיות או יקצר הרבה כדי לכוין ראשי השיטות כי אין נוי לתפילין אבל מעט רשאי (פמ"ג): (ג) ואם שינה. בין בשל יד ובין בש"ר ואם אין לו לש"י רק קלף קצר וארוך שאין יכול לכתוב עליו שבע שיטין אם לא שיכתוב כתיבה דקה מאד נראה דטוב יותר לשנות מנין השיטין עיין במרדכי בהלכות קטנות סוף ה"ת והובא לעיל סימן ל"ב דבכלל זה אלי ואנוהו לכתוב כתיבה גסה במקצת שלא יהיו נמחקין מהרה. ובאמת אנו רואין בחוש דבכתיבות הדקות שרגילין איזה סופרים כהיום בעו"ה מצוי כמה וכמה קלקולים גם בתחילת כתיבתן שלא נכתבו כדינן מחמת דקותן וברובם חסר כמה וכמה תגין דשעטנ"ז ג"ץ דהוא מדינא דגמרא ויש מהראשונים שמחמירין בזה אפילו בדיעבד ושומר נפשו לא יקנה פרשיות כאלה בתוך תפיליו אם לא שיבדוק אותם מתחילה היטב היטב וידע מי כתב הפרשיות דפרשיות כאלו מצוי מאד דכותביהן הם עדיין נערים שלא ידעו כלל דיני כתיבת סת"ם:

א (א) בכתיבת. וה"ה אם נשתנה האות מצורתה אחר הכתיבה ע"י נקב או קרע או טשטוש דפסול וכדלעיל בסימן ל"ב: צורת. אפי'

ביאור הלכה

דמקורו מלקמן בסימן מ"ב בחדתי דיכול לשנותם והלא לפי המבואר שם באחרונים אין מותר רק להוריד מחמורה לקלה אבל לא לחול דהזמנה לגוף הקדושה מילתא הוא והכא הלא המחבר הזה בעצמו ס"ל לקמן דזה הוא בכלל הורדה לחול. גם מש"כ אח"כ ואפילו אם התנה עליהם וכו' דמקודש לחול וכו' עיין בש"ת דמסיק דברצועות מהני תנאי והוא פשוט דהם רק תשמישי קדושה ומהני תנאי בזה להורידן לחול וכדלקמן בסימן מ"ב ס"ג ואפילו בבתים ופרשיות לענ"ד יש לעיין בזה דהלא בקלף שנתעבד לשם פרשיות דהוא הזמנה לגוף הקדושה ואסור להורידו לחול הוכחתי לקמן בסימן מ"ב דיכול לכתוב עליו שאר ד"ת משום דיש בזה עי"ז עכ"פ קצת קדושה וה"נ בענינינו הלא גם עתה אף דאין על הפרשיות קדושת תפילין עכ"פ קדושה יש בהן וה"נ הבתים הם תשמישים לקדושה וא"כ ליהני תנאי ואין התשובה בידי לעיין בה ואפשר דיש להקל ע"י תנאי בשל ראש דר"ת לרש"י אם אין לו פרשיות אחרים וצ"ע. עוד כתבתי בשם פמ"ג דאם מצא רצועה וכו' והשמטתי תשובת יד אליהו שמובא בבה"ט שבזמנינו רובא של רש"י ועוד עיין בספר פ"ת מש"כ ע"ז. ולפי שדברי הפמ"ג מוקשי ההבנה אמרתי להעתיקו פה ז"ל אם מצא של יד [ט"ס וצ"ל ג"כ או של ראש] ורצועה בלא פרשיות וספק שמא של ר"ת שפיר להניח פרשיות של רש"י ס"ס ורובא של רש"י ומעלין בקודש ואנן בקיאין ורש"י עיקר. ועיבוד צ"ע גם ברצועות מחול לקודש והבן עכ"ל. הנה מה שכתב ס"ס פשוט דשמא הם של רש"י ושמא של רש"י עיקר אך דמשום זה הטעם לבד היה מותר להניחו גם לשל ר"ת או דשמא של שניהם אסור דהספקות הם סותרות אהדדי ולכן סיים דרובא ואנן בקיאין ורש"י עיקר אך סוף דבריו נפלאים הם דבעיבוד אין שייך שמא עיבדן לשם תפילין דרש"י או דר"ת דהלא העיבוד הוא סתמא לשמה ונלענ"ד דכונתו הוא דלקמן בסימן ל"ט ס"ט איתא דאם לקח תפילין שלא מן המומחה בודק מהם ג' קצילות בחסר ויתר ודי בזה ולא חיישינן שמא עיבד המוכרן שלא לשמן דהכל בקיאין בזה ולכן מסתפק הפמ"ג בענינינו דלו יהי דהכל בקיאין שהפרשיות צריך עיבוד לשמה הלא בעיבוד הבתים והרצועות אין נוכל לאמר שהכל בקיאין עתה בזה דהלא יש בזה מחלוקת בין הפוס' וכדלעיל בסימן ל"ג וא"כ שמא אותו שנאבד ממנו עשה הבתים או הרצועות בלא עיבוד לשמה וא"כ הוא מעלה עתה מחול לקודש בלי הזמנה מעלייתא דעיבוד ומה דמתיר הגמרא ליקח תפילין דמשמע אף עם רצועות דוקא בזמניהם שהיה ידוע אם צריך עיבוד או לא וה"נ דבזמנינו אם לוקח ממי שאינו מומחה צריך לדרוש מהמוכר אם היה בהבתים ורצועות עיבוד לשמה משא"כ בענינינו דאיירי במציאה זהו הנלענ"ד בכונתו. ובאמת לע"ג בזה בזמנינו ברצועה הנמצאת דשמא רק נשחרה לשמה ולא נעבדה לשמה דהרבה יש שמקילין בזה ושלא כדין הוא וכמו שביאר הש"ת לעיל בסימן ל"ג ועי"ש במה שכתבנו שם. ומש"כ אם נזדמן וכו' פמ"ג[ב]:

הגהות ותיקונים: א) פמ"ג משב"ז ס"ק ג': ב) צ"ל הוא מפמ"ג:

four lines /for each passage/. (3) If one deviated /from this practice/ he will not have made /the passage/ invalid.

§36: THE ACCURACY /REQUIRED/ FOR THE WRITING OF /THE *TEFILIN* PASSAGES/

(Contains Three Paragraphs)

1. One must be accurate (1) when writing the letters, so that there is no deviation from (2) the form of any one of /the letters/ and /there is

Mishnah Berurah

scribes/ likewise have a tradition as regards the /words/ which start the beginnings of the rows, /both/ in the case /of the passages/ of the arm /*tefilin*/ and in the case /of the passages/ of the head /*tefilin*/, as stated by the *Tur* and by the *B.Y.*

/However,/ nowadays, scribes are not meticulous about the /words/ which start the beginnings of the rows and they deviate /from the traditional start/ in accordance with how /the arrangement of the words/ turns out for them.

If one wishes to be meticulous /about this/, he should not draw out letters or shorten them excessively in order to arrive at the /desired/ beginnings for the lines, as this /makes/ the *tefilin* /passage/ unattractive. However, a little /drawing out or shortening of the letters/ is allowed. ((*P.Mg.*))

(3) If one deviated. /This applies/ both in the case /of the passages/ of the arm /*tefilin*/ and in the case /of the passages/ of the head /*tefilin*/.

If one does not have a parchment /that can serve/ for the arm /*tefilin*/ except for a short and elongated one, so that he is unable to write seven lines on it unless he writes very small script, it appears that it is preferable /for him/ to deviate from the /usual/ number of lines. See the *Mordechai, Halachos Ketanos*, at the end of the laws concerning *tefilin*, that writing a somewhat large script which will not be erased quickly is within the scope of /what is required by the verse/, "This is my God and I will glorify Him".[1] This is quoted above in Sec. 32 /, in the gloss to Par. 4/.

The truth is that we see tangibly that due to the small script that some scribes /use/ nowadays, among our many sins, numerous defects are common /in the passages that they write/. This is also /the case/ at the outset, when they are written. For /the passages/ are not written in accordance with their halachic /requirements/, because of their smallness, and in most of them numerous crownlets are missing from /the letters/ שעטנז גץ. These /crownlets/ are a halachic /requirement/ which /appears/ in the Gemara[2] and there are Rishonim who are stringent about them /and require them on these letters/ even /as regards the ruling/ once it is after the event. A person who safeguards /the well-being of/ his soul should not buy *tefilin* with such passages inside them, unless he first examines them thoroughly. He should /also/ know who wrote the passages, since it is very common in the case of these passages that their writers were still youths, who did not know at all the laws concerning the writing of Torah Scrolls, *tefilin* /passages/ and *mezuzos*.

§36

(1) When writing. Correspondingly, if a letter changed from its /correct/ form after it was written, through a hole, a tear or a blur, it is /now/ invalid, as /ruled/ above in Sec. 32.

(2) The form. /I.e.,/ even if the deviation

1 *Shemos* 15:2.
2 *Menachos* 29b.

(ג) לאחרת: הגה ולכתחלה יכתוב (ד) בכתיבה תמה כמבואר בטור ובשאר פוסקים והוא ידוע אצל הסופרים מיהו (ה) אם שינה בצורת הכתב אינו פסול: ב ׳כל אות צריכה להיות גולם אחד לכך צריך להיות בנקודה שעל האל"ף שהיא כמין יו"ד ובנקודה שתחתיה וביוד"י (ו) השי"ן והעיי"ן ואחורי צד"י שיהיו נוגעות באות (ז) ובאחת (ח) שאינה נוגעת פסולין (ט) וכן בשאר אותיות חוץ מה"א וקו"ף (י) שאין (ב) [ב] ליגע הרגל (יא) בגג ואם נגע פסול: ג ׳צריך (יב) לתייג (ג) [ג] (יג) שעטנ"ז ג"ץ והסופרים (יד) נהגו

ב שם ג מנחות כ"ט בשמושא רבא

שערי תשובה

תפילין מכתב אשכנזי דיש שינוי בצורת אותיות באשורית בין בני אשכנז לבני ספרד התפילין מכתב אשכנזים פסולים לספרדים. וכ"כ הרב החסיד מהר"י מולכו ע"ש: [ב] ליגע. עבה"ט[ג] ומ"ש או שנוגעין זה בזה עיין ביד אפרים ועיין לעיל סימן ל"ב ס"ק י"[ד] מ"ש בזה: [ג] שעטנ"ז ג"ץ. עבה"ט ועיין במג"א בענין התטוטרת של החי"ת וכתב בבר"י בשם מהר"מ בן חביב שאם עשה הסופר החטוטרת באות ה"א ותי"ו כמו שעושין באות חי"ת אין להחליט למעשה להכשיר כיון דלא

באר היטב

(ב) ליגע. בכדי שאדם בינוני יכירנו היטב מעל ס"ת שע"ג הבימה כשקורא בו. וב"ח כתב בשם ב"ש ברחוק אמה. וגם לא ירחיקה יותר מעובי הגג: (ג) שעטנ"ז ג"ץ. צריך שיהיו התגים נוגעים בגוף האותיות. וכל א' נפרד מחבירו מ"ע סימן ל"ה. גם לא ידביקן בסוף האות כ"א באמצעיתן. ואם אינן נוגעים בגוף האותיות או שנוגעין זה בזה פסולים. מיהו אם ידעינן שכתבן מומחה תלינן שנפרד אחר

שנכתב ומכשירים הרמ"ע מ"א. וע"ש שהעלה דאם עשה חית כזה ח כשרה אפילו האריך בה אע"פ שאינה מרובעת כשרה וע"ל סימן ל"ב

משנה ברורה

אם שינוי הצורה היה רק במקצת האות כגון שחסר הראש של האל"ף או (א) קוץ היו"ד או (ב) שנגעו יוד"י האל"ף בגג האל"ף וכדומה ואפילו אם התינוק יקראהו לאות (ג) לא מהני כיון שאנו יודעין שאין צורתה עליה כראוי: (ג) לאחרת. ראיתי בספר מעשה רקח שהביא לדינא בשם תשובת מהראנ"ח סימן א' שכתב דאפילו אם רק מקצת האות נדמה לאות אחר פסול. ומדברי הגר"א לעיל בסימן ל"ב סי"ח לא משמע כן וכן כתב הפר"ח: (ד) בכ"ת. ר"ל כתיבה תמה ושלימה בתמונת האותיות כפי מה שלמדוהו מהתלמוד וקבלת הראשונים וע"פ הסוד וכמבואר בב"י בסימן זה: (ה) אם שינה וכו'. היינו (ד) שלא כתב תמונת האותיות המוזכרים בספרים אבל תמונת האות מיהו צריך כמו שכתב המחבר שלא תשתנה וכו' וכ"ש שלא ישנהו לאות אחר כגון מדלי"ת לרי"ש או מבי"ת לכ"ף וכדומה. והכוונה כמו שכתב הנוב"י סימן פ' דדבר שאין לו שורש בגמ' אין לפסול האות עבור זה. וכדי שידע הקורא איך לכתוב לכתחילה וגם איזה פרט יש לו שורש והוא מעיקר תמונת האותיות שיהיה זה לעיכובא אפילו בדיעבד לכן התחזקתי בעזה"י ועשיתי ע"ז קונטרס מיוחד בסוף סימן זה והעתקתיו מהב"י ופמ"ג ושארי אחרונים תמונת כל האותיות למעשה וקראתיו בשם משנת סופרים. וכללתי בו גם קיצור כללי דיני הקפת גויל וחק תוכות ושלא כסדרן מבעל פמ"ג וש"א: ב (ו) השי"ן והעיי"ן. בכל הראשים: (ז) ובאחת. פי' אפילו (ה) בוי"ד אחד מן השי"ן וה"ה אם יש הפסק באמצע האות: (ח) שאינה נוגעת. אפילו אם הפירוד הוא דק (ו) שאין פרידתו ניכר להדיא (ז) ולא מהני כאן קריאת התינוק כיון שידוע הוא האות ואין לטעות באחר דדוקא אם גריעותו מחמת שיש ספק לדמותו לאות אחר או מועיל קריאת התינוק וכדלעיל בסימן ל"ב סי"ז. וכ"ז בלא תיקון אבל ע"י תיקון מהני דלא ליהוי שלא כסדרן אם התינוק קראו לאות וכדלעיל בסימן ל"ב סכ"ה (ועי"ש מה שכתבנו בשם הגרע"א. ולענין[א] יו"ד שאחורי הצד"י אם נראה כיו"ד ונו"ן) ובכל זה אין חילוק בין אם נעשה בעת הכתיבה או לאחר הכתיבה וכדלעיל בסימן ל"ב: (ט) וכן בשאר אותיות. כגון הנקודה שלמטה שבג' או הנקודה שבפ"א או (ה) הרגל שבתוך המי"ו אם לא נגעו באות או שיש הפסק באמצע איזה אות: (י) שלא[ב] ליגע. ולכתחילה יהיה הפסק (ט) בכדי שאדם בינוני יכירנו היטיב מעל ס"ת שע"ג בימה כשהוא קורא בו גם לא ירחיקו יותר מעובי הגג: (יא) בגג. וה"ה (י) הקו"ף כריכו שבלידו וכ"ז אפילו אם נעשה הנגיעה אחר הכתיבה ואפילו אם הנגיעה דקה כחוט השערה וכמו שנתבאר לעיל בסימן ל"ב סי"ח במ"ב שם ועי"ש בענין תיקון האות אם לא כתב אמ"ז דאל"ה הוי שלא כסדרן: ג (יב) לתייג. אפילו בס"ת וכ"ש בתו"מ. והתגין האלו הם שלשה תגין קטנים (יא) ודקים כחוט השערה וקיפות על אלו האותיות (יב) אחד מימין ואחד משמאל ואחד מלמעלה וי"א דשלשתן מלמעלה וכן נוהגין. וכעין קו דק הוא כל תג ותג כך נוהגין באלו הארצות וטוב יותר לעשות כל אחד כעין (יג) תמונת זיין אך שיהיו קטנים ודקים מאוד: (יג) שעטנ"ז ג"ץ. וה"ה (יד) לד"י כפופה ונו"ן פשוטה. ואם (טו) הוסיף הסופר לעשות תגין חוץ מאותיות שעטנ"ז ג"ץ ומן מאלו המוזכרים בטור ובלבוש שנהגו בהם הסופרים לא עכב אך בתנאי שיהיו מחוברים להאות אבל אם אינו מחובר יש לנותקו ואפילו באותיות שבשם הקודש ולכתחילה אין נכון להוסיף תגין מעצמו כל שלא מוזכר בספרים. ותיוג של שעטנ"ז ג"ץ הוא (טז) בשין על ראש השמאלי של האות ובעי"ן וטי"ת ולד"י על ראש השמאלי וידביקן (יז) באמצעיתו לא בסופו. כתבו האחרונים בשם תשובת הרמ"ע שיזהר שיהיו התגין נפרדין כל אחד מחבירו כדי שלא יראו רק כתמונת זיונין ולא כעיי"ן ושי"ן ולעיכובא הוא. גם צריך שיהיו התגין נוגעין בגוף האות ואל"ה פסולין דאף דאין עיכוב בעשיית התגין כמו שפסק המחבר מ"מ זה גרע דהוי (יח) כיתרון אות קטנה בין השיטין ועיין ביד אפרים שכתב דלא מהני אף אם ימשיכם אח"כ אל האות רק צריך לגוררם ולכותבם מחדש רק אם ידעינן שכתבן מומחה תלינן שנפרד אחר שנכתב ומכשירין בהמשכה אל האות. והלבושי שרד כתב דהרמ"ע ס"ל דלא גרע דבר זה מחסרון הקפת גויל דאינו מעכב רק בתחלה וע"כ אם נפרד אחר שנכתב כשר בלא תיקון כלל ותמילא לדבריו אם לא היו נוגעין מתחלת הכתיבה מהני עכ"פ תיקון דומי' דמ"ש המ"א בסי' ל"ב סקכ"ז לענין הקפת גויל וכן משמע לענ"ד מפשטא דלישניה דהרמ"ע ע"ש. ומ"מ לכתחלה נכון להחמיר כיד אפרי' ועי' פמ"ג: (יד) נהגו לתייג. בתפילין אותיות אחרות מלבד אלו והם מוזכרים בטור בשם השמושא רבא ובשם הרמב"ם. והתגין האלו הם (יט) תגינים גדולים אך שיהיו דקים שלא יתקלקל האות עי"ז ומאוד צריך ליזהר ביותר בתגין שעל הוי"ו או שעל היו"ד כי בקל ישתנה האות עי"ז

שער הציון

(א) מנחות כ"ט ע"א: (ב) לעיל בל"ב סי"ח וכמ"ש בביאור הגר"א שם דזה מיקרי שינוי בצורתה: (ג) ב"י בשם מהרי"ק בסימן זה: (ד) פמ"ג: (ה) כן מוכח מהגר"א וכן מכמה מקומות: (ו) בסי' ל"ב סכ"ה: (ז) ט"ז והגר"א: (ח) ב"י: (ט) מ"א וא"ר: (י) לעיל[ה] בתמונת האותיות עי"ש: (יא) הרמב"ם פ"ז מהלכות ס"ת: (יב) טור"ד והביאו הב"י: (יג) ב"י בשם האגור והרמב"ם: (יד) ב"י בשם רש"י: (טו) תשו' ח"ס: (טז) ב"י בצורת האותיות כמה פעמים דלא כמה שזכר פה בשם הג"י וכן מוכח מספר התרומה שהובא בב"י פה: (יז) מ"א: (יח) היד אפרים והגרע"א בשם המ"ע: (יט) ב"י וד"מ:

הגהות ותיקונים: א) צ"ל לענין: ב) שאין: ג) סק"ג: ד) ה': ה) לקמן:

also/ no /letter/ which resembles (3) another /letter/.

Gloss: Initially, one should write (4) *with impeccable script, as explained by the* Tur *and other Poskim. This /script/ is known by the scribes. However,* (5) *if one deviated from the /required/ form of the script /the letter/ is not /necessarily/ invalid.*

2. Each letter must be a single /coherent/ body. In view of this, it is necessary for the stroke on top of the /letter/ א, which is /formed/ like a /letter/ י, the stroke underneath /the letter א/ and the י /letters forming part/ (6) of the /letter/ ש and of the /letter/ ע and at the back of the /letter/ צ to touch /the

Mishnah Berurah

from the form /of the letter/ is only in part of the letter. For example, if the top of a /letter/ א is missing or the tip of a /letter/ י /is missing/ or if /the bodies of/ the י /letters which form part/ of the /letter/ א touch the roof of the /letter/ א, etc.

/In such cases,/ even if a child /who is neither especially intelligent nor especially simple/ reads the letter /for what it is meant to be/ this is of no avail, since we know that it does not have its proper form.

(3) **Another.** I have seen that /the author of/ the work *Ma'aseh Rokeyach* cites as the halachic /ruling/, on the authority of a responsum written by the *Ra'anach*, Sec. 1, that even if only part of a letter resembles another letter /the letter/ is /also/ invalid. /However,/ from the words of the *Gra* above in Sec. 32, Par. 18, it is implied that this is not so and the *Pr.Ch.* likewise writes this.

(4) **With impeccable script.** I.e., script which is impeccable and complete, with the symbols of the letters in accordance with what has been learned about them from the Talmud, /in accordance with/ the tradition received by the Rishonim and in conformance with the esoteric /law/, as explained by the *B.Y.* in this section.

(5) **If one deviated, etc.** I.e., if one did not write the symbols of the letters /as they are/ described in /the relevant/ books. However, the /basic/ symbol of the letter is at any rate required, as stated by the author /of the Shulchan Aruch/, "so that there is no deviation, etc." One may certainly not alter /the form of a letter/ to /the form of/ another letter, such as /to alter a letter/ from a ד to a ר or from a ב to a כ, etc. The intention /of the gloss is/ as stated by the *No.Biy.* in Sec. 80, that where something /faulty in a letter/ does not /involve a requirement/ which has its roots in the Gemara one should not invalidate a letter because of it.

So that the reader will know how he should write /a letter/, initially, and also what detail has its roots /in the Gemara/ and belongs to the basic symbol of the letter, thus being essential /for its validity/ even once it is after the event /, it is necessary for all this to be clarified./ I have therefore braced myself, with the help of *Ha-Sheym*, may He be blessed, and have prepared a special booklet /which has been printed/ at the end of this section /to explain these matters/. I have taken its /contents/ from the *B.Y.*, the *P.Mg.* and other Acharonim. /It describes/ the /required/ symbol /to be written/ in practice /in the case/ of all the letters. I have called it by the name *Mishnas Soferim* (the teaching of the scribes). I have included in it, in addition, a brief general /account/ of the laws concerning the surrounding /of a letter/ by /blank/ parchment, carving around /a letter to form it/ and /the writing of letters/ in incorrect order. /These laws were taken/ from the author of the *P.Mg.* and other Acharonim.

(6) **Of the ש and of the ע.** /I.e.,/ all the heads /of these letters must touch the rest of the letter/.

(ג) לאחרת: הגה ולכתחלה יכתוב (ד) בכתיבה תמה כמבואר בטור ובשאר פוסקים והוא ידוע אצל הסופרים מיהו (ה) אם שינה בצורת הכתב אינו פסול: ב ‎ב ‏כל אות צריכה להיות גולם אחד לכך צריך להיות בנקודה שעל האל״ף שהיא כמין יו״ד ובנקודה שתחתיה וביוד״י (ו) השי״ן והעיי״ן ואחורי צד״י שיהיו נוגעות באות (ז) ובאחת (ח) שאינה נוגעת פסולין (ט) וכן בשאר אותיות חוץ מה״א וקו״ף (י) שאין (ב) [ב] ליגע הרגל (יא) בגג ואם נגע פסול: ג ‏גצריך (יב) לתייג (ג) [ג] (יג) שעטנ״ז ג״ץ והסופרים (יד) נהגו

ב שם ג מנחות כ״ט בשמושא רבא

שערי תשובה

תפילין מכתב אשכנזי דיש שינוי בצורת אותיות באשורית בין בני אשכנז לבני ספרד התפילין מכתב אשכנזים פסולים לספרדים. וכ״כ הרב החסיד מהר״י מולכו ע״ש: [ב] ליגע. עבה״ט[ג] ומ״ש או שנוגעין זה בזה עיין ביד אפרים ועיין לעיל סימן ל״ב ס״ק י״[ד] מ״ש בזה: [ג] שעטנ״ז ג״ץ. עבה״ט ועיין במג״א בענין התטוטרת של החי״ת וכתב בבר״י בשם מהר״מ בן חביב שאם עשה הסופר התטוטרת באות ה״א ותי״ו כמו שעושין באות חי״ת אין להחליט למעשה להכשיר כיון דלא

באר היטב

(ב) ליגע. בכדי שאדם בינוני יכירנו היטב מעל ס״ת שע״ג הבימה כשקורא בו. ובי״ח כתב בשם ב״ש ברחוק אמה. וגם לא ירחיקה יותר מעובי הגג: (ג) שעטנ״ז ג״ץ. צריך שיהיו התגים נוגעים בגוף האותיות. וכל א׳ נפרד מחבירו מ״ע סימן ל״ה. גם לא ידביקן בסוף האות כ״א באמצעיתן. ואם אינן נוגעים בגוף האותיות או שנוגעין זה בזה פסולים. מיהו אם ידעינן שכתבן מומחה תלינן שנפרד אחר

שנכתב ומכשירים הרמ״ע מ״א. וע״ש שהעלה דאם עשה חית כזה ח כשרה אפילו האריך גג אע״פ שאינה מרובעת כשרה וע״ל סימן ל״ב

משנה ברורה

אם שינוי הצורה היה רק במקצת האות כגון שחסר הראש של האל״ף או (א) קוץ היו״ד או (ב) שנגעו יודי״ן האל״ף בגג האל״ף וכדומה ואפילו אם התינוק יקראהו לאות (ג) לא מהני כיון שאנו יודעין שאין צורתה עליה כראוי: (ג) לאחרת. ראיתי בספר מעשה רקח שהביא לדינא בשם תשובת מהרלנ״ח סימן א׳ שכתב דאפילו אם רק מקצת האות נדמה לאות אחר פסול. ומדברי הגר״א לעיל בסימן ל״ב סי״ח לא משמע כן וכן כתב הפר״ח: (ד) בכ״ת. ר״ל כתיבה תמה ושלימה בתמונת האותיות כפי מה שלמדוהו מהתלמוד וקבלת הראשונים וע״פ הסוד וכמבואר בב״י בסימן זה: (ה) אם שינה וכו׳. היינו (ד) שלא כתב תמונת האותיות המוזכרים בספרים אבל תמונת האות מיהו צריך כמו שכתב המחבר שלא תשתנה וכו׳ וכ״ש שלא ישנהו לאות אחר כגון מדל״ת לרי״ש או מבי״ת לכ״ף וכדומה. והכוונה כמו שכתב הגוב״י סימן פ׳ דדבר שאין לו שורש בגמ׳ אין לפסול האות עבור זה. וכדי שידע הקורא איך לכתוב לכתחילה וגם איזה פרט יש לו שורש והוא מעיקר תמונת האותיות שיהיה זה לעיכובא אפילו בדיעבד לכן התחזקתי בעזה״י ועשיתי ע״ז קונטרס מיוחד בסוף סימן זה והעתקתיו מהב״י ופמ״ג ושארי אחרונים תמונת כל האותיות למעשה וקראתיו בשם משנת סופרים. וכללתי בו גם קיצור כללי דיני הקפת גויל וחק תוכות ושלא כסדרן תמעל פמ״ג וש״א: ב (ו) השי״ן והעיי״ן. בכל הראשים: (ז) ובאחת. פי׳ אפילו (ה) ביו״ד אחד מן השי״ן וה״ה אם יש הפסק באמצע האות: (ח) שאינה נוגעת. אפילו אם הפירוד הוא דק (ו) שאין פרידתו ניכר להדיא (ז) ולא מהני כאן קריאת התינוק כיון שידוע הוא האות ואין לטעות באחר דדוקא אם גריעותו מחמת שיש ספק לדמותו לאות אחר אז מועיל קריאת התינוק וכדלעיל בסימן ל״ב סי״ו. וכ״ז בלא תיקון אבל ע״י תיקון מהני דלא ליהוי שלא כסדרן אם התינוק קראו לאות וכדלעיל בסימן ל״ב סכ״ה (ועי״ש מה שכתבנו בשם הגרע״א. ולענין[א] יו״ד שאחורי הצד״י אם נראה כיו״ד ונו״ן) ובכל זה אין חילוק בין אם נעשה בעת הכתיבה או לאחר הכתיבה וכדלעיל בסימן ל״ב: (ט) וכן בשאר אותיות. כגון הנקודה שלמטה שבג׳ או הנקודה שבפ״א או (ח) הרגל שבתוך התי״ו אם לא נגעו בהאות או שיש הפסק באמצע איזה אות: (י) שלא[ב] ליגע. ולכתחילה יהיה הפסק (ט) בכדי שאדם בינוני יכירנו היטיב מעל ס״ת שע״ג בימה כשהוא קורא בו גם לא ירחיקו יותר מעובי הגג: (יא) בגג. וה״ה (י) הקו״ף בירכו שבצידו וכ״ז אפילו אם נעשה הנגיעה אחר הכתיבה ואפילו אם הנגיעה דקה כחוט השערה וכמו שנתבאר לעיל בסימן ל״ב סי״ח במ״ב שם ועי״ש בענין תיקון האות אם לא כתב אח״ז דאל״ה הוי שלא כסדרן: ג (יב) לתייג. אפילו בס״ת וכ״ש בתו״מ. והתגין האלו הם שלשה תגין קטנים (יא) ודקים כחוט השערה זקופות על אלו האותיות (יב) אחד מימין ואחד משמאל ואחד מלמעלה וי״א דשלשתן מלמעלה וכן נוהגין. וכעין קו דק הוא כל תג ותג כך נוהגין באלו הארצות וטוב יותר לעשות כל אחד כעין (יג) תמונת זיין אך שיהיו קטנים ודקים מאוד: (יג) שעטנ״ז ג״ץ. וה״ה (יד) צד״י כפופה ונו״ן פשוטה. ואם (טו) הוסיף הסופר לעשות תגין חוץ מאותיות שעטנ״ז ג״ץ וחוץ מאלו המוזכרים בטור ובלבוש שנהגו בהם הסופרים לא עכב אך בתגי׳ שיהיו מחוברים לאות. אבל אם אינו מחובר יש לתוקנו ואפילו באותיות שבשם הקודש ולכתחילה אין נכון להוסיף תגין מעצמו כל שלא מוזכר בספרים. ותיוג של שעטנ״ז ג״ץ הוא (טז) בשין על ראש השמאלי של האות ובעי״ן וטי״ת ולד״י על ראש השמאלי וידביקן (יז) באמצעיתו לא בסופו. כתבו האחרונים בשם תשובת הרמ״ע שיזהר שיהיו התגין נפרדין כל אחד מחבירו כדי שלא יראו רק כתמונת זיינין ולא כעיי״ן ושי״ן ולעיכובא הוא. גם צריך שיהיו התגין נוגעין בגוף האות ואל״ה פסולין דאף דאין עיכוב בעשיית התגין כמו שפסק המחבר מ״מ זה גרע דהוי (יח) כיתרון אות קטנה בין השיטין ועיין ביד אפרים שכתב דלא מהני אף אם ימשיכם אח״כ אל האות רק צריך לגוררם ולכותבם מחדש רק אם ידעינן שכתבן מומחה תלינן שנפרד אחר שנכתב ומכשירין בהמשכה אל האות. והלבושי שרד כתב דהרמ״ע ס״ל דלא גרע דבר זה מחסרון הקפת גויל דאינו מעכב רק בתחלה וע״כ אם נפרד אחר שנכתב כשר בלא תיקון כלל ומתילא לדבריו אם לא היו נוגעין מתחלת הכתיבה מהני ע״פ תיקון דומי׳ דמ״ש המ״א בסי׳ ל״ב סקכ״ז לענין הקפת גויל וכן משמע לענ״ד מפשטא דלישניה דהרמ״ע ע״ש. ומ״מ לכתחלה נכון להחמיר כיד אפרי׳ ועי׳ פמ״ג: (יד) נהגו לתייג. בתפילין אותיות אחרות מלבד אלו והם מוזכרים בטור בשם השמושא רבא ובשם הרמב״ם. והתגין האלו הם (יט) תגינים גדולים אך שיהיו דקים שלא יתקלקל האות עי״ז ומאוד צריך ליזהר ביותר בתגין שעל הוי״ו או שעל היו״ד כי בקל ישתנה האות עי״ז

שער הציון

(א) מנחות כ״ט ע״א: (ב) לעיל בל״ב סי״ח וכמ״ש בביאור הגר״א שם דזה מיקרי שינוי בצורתה: (ג) ב״י בשם מהרי״ק בסימן זה: (ד) פמ״ג: (ה) כן מוכח מהגר״א וכן מכמה מקומות: (ו) בסי׳ ל״ב סכ״ה: (ז) ט״ז והגר״א: (ח) ב״י: (ט) מ״א וא״ר: (י) לעיל[ה] בתמונת האותיות עי״ש: (יא) הרמב״ם פ״ז מהלכות ס״ת: (יב) טוי״ד והביאו הב״י: (יג) ב״י בשם רש״י: (יד) ב״י בשם האגור והרמב״ם: (טו) תשו׳ ח״ס: (טז) ב״י בצורת האותיות כמה פעמים דלא כמה שזכר פה בשם הב״י וכן מוכח מספר התרומה שהובא בב״י פה: (יז) מ״א: (יח) היד אפרים והגרע״א בשם המ״ע: (יט) ב״י וד״מ:

הגהות ותיקונים: א) צ״ל לענין: ב) שאין: ג) סק״ג: ד) ה׳: ה) לקמן:

rest of/ the letter. (7) If one /of the י parts/ (8) does not touch, /the letter/ is invalid. (9) This /coherence/ is likewise /necessary/ in the case of the other letters, except for the /letters/ ה and ק. /In the case of the latter/ the leg (10) must not touch (11) the roof and /the letter/ is invalid if it does touch.
3. One must (12) make crownlets /on the letters/ (13) שעטנז גץ. The scribes

Mishnah Berurah

(7) If one /of the י parts/. I.e., even if one of the י /parts/ of the /letter/ ש /does not touch the rest of the letter/.

The same ruling /applies/ if there is an interruption /of blank space/ in the middle of a letter.

(8) Does not touch. /This applies/ even if the separation is narrow, so that the separateness is not clearly noticeable.

/In the case discussed/ here, /the fact that/ a child /who is neither especially intelligent nor especially simple/ reads /the letter correctly/ is of no avail. For the letter /intended/ is manifest and there are no grounds for erring /and thinking it/ to be another /letter/. It is only where the inferiority of /the letter/ is because we are in doubt as to /whether or not/ it resembles another letter /that we get a child to read it/. Then, the reading of /such/ a child is of avail /for the letter to be ruled as valid/, as /described/ above, in Sec. 32, Par. 16.

/However,/ all this /only applies/ if one does not correct /the letter/, but if such a child reads the letter /correctly/, this is of avail for /the letter/ not to be /ruled as having been written/ in incorrect order once one has corrected it, as /explained/ above in Sec. 32, Par. 25. ((See there /in sub-Par. 122/, for what we have written in the name of the *G.R.A.E.*, and /in sub-Par. 118/, as regards the י /part/ behind the /letter/ צ, if /it was written in such a way that the symbol/ appears like a /letter/ י and a /letter/ נ.))

In all cases, it makes no difference whether /the separation/ was made at the time /the letter/ was written or /whether it developed/ after /the letter/ was written, as /explained/ above in Sec. 32.

(9) This is likewise /necessary/ in the case of the other letters. For example, if the stroke at the bottom of the /letter/ ג, the stroke of the /letter/ פ or the leg inside the /letter/ ח does not touch /the rest of/ the letter or if there is an interruption /of blank space/ in the middle of some letter /which divides it, the letter is invalid/.

(10) Must not touch. Initially, there should be an interval /of blank space between the leg and the roof/ which is /large/ enough for an average person to recognize it well on a Torah Scroll on the bimah, when he reads from /the Scroll/. In addition, one should not make /the leg/ further away /from the roof/ than the thickness of the roof /of the letter/.

(11) The roof. The same ruling /applies/ for the /letter/ ק, with respect to /the leg touching/ its thigh on its side.

All this /applies/ even if the touch came about after the writing /of the letter/. /It also applies/ even if the touch is as thin as a hairsbreadth, as explained above in Sec. 32, Par. 18 in the Mishnah Berurah there. See there, as regards the correction of the letter. /However, correction is only relevant/ where one has not /yet/ written after /the letter/. Otherwise /it is impossible as the letters/ will have been /written/ in incorrect order.

(12) Make crownlets. One is even /required to make the crownlets/ when /he writes/ a Torah Scroll and is certainly /required to do so/ when /he writes/ *tefilin* /passages/ or mezuzos.

The crownlets /referred to/ are three small crownlets, as thin as a hairsbreadth, which stand upright on these letters. One is /made/ on the right /of the letter/, one on the left and one on top. There are /authorities/ who say that /all/ three of them should be on top and this is /in fact/ the practice.

Each individual crownlet resembles a thin line. That is how it is the practice /to make them/ in these countries. It is preferable /, however,/ to make each /individual crownlet/ resemble the symbol of a /letter/ ז, but they must be very small and thin.

(13) שעטנז גץ. Correspondingly, /one must

(ג) לאחרת: הגה ולכתחלה יכתוב (ד) בכתיבה תמה כמבואר בטור ובשאר פוסקים והוא ידוע אצל הסופרים מיהו (ה) אם שינה בצורת הכתב אינו פסול: ב בכל אות צריכה להיות גולם אחד לכך צריך להיות בנקודה שעל האל"ף שהיא כמין יו"ד ובנקודה שתחתיה וביוד"י (ו) השי"ן והעיי"ן ואחורי צד"י שיהיו נוגעות באות (ז) ובאחת (ח) שאינה נוגעת פסולין (ט) וכן בשאר אותיות חוץ מה"א וקו"ף (י) שאין (ב) [ב] ליגע הרגל (יא) בגג ואם נגע פסול: ג צריך (יב) לתייג (ג) [ג] (יג) שעטנ"ז ג"ץ והסופרים (יד) נהגו

ב שם ג מנחות כ"ט בשמושא רבא

שערי תשובה

תפילין מכתב אשכנזי דיש שינוי בצורת אותיות באשורית בין בני אשכנז לבני ספרד התפילין מכתב אשכנזים פסולים לספרדים. וכ"כ הרב החסיד מהר"י מולכו ע"ש: [ב] ליגע. עבה"ט[ג] ומ"ש או שנוגעין זה בזה עיין ביד אפרים ועיין לעיל סימן ל"ב ס"ק י"[ד] מ"ש בזה: [ג] שעטנ"ז ג"ץ. עבה"ט ועיין במג"א בענין החטוטרת של החי"ת וכתב בבר"י בשם מהר"מ בן חביב שאם עשה הסופר החטוטרת באות ה"א ותי"ו כמו שעושין באות חי"ת אין להחליט למעשה להכשיר כיון דלא שנכתב ומכשירים הרמ"ע מ"א. וע"ש שהעלה דאם עשה חית כזה ח כשרה אפילו הארוך בה אע"פ שאינה מרובעת כשרה וע"ל סימן ל"ב

באר היטב

(ב) ליגע. בכדי שאדם בינוני יכירנו היטב מעל ס"ת שע"ג הבימה כשקורא בו. ובי"ח כתב בשם ב"ש ברחוק אמה. וגם לא ירחיקה יותר מעובי הגג: (ג) שעטנ"ז ג"ץ. צריך שיהיו התגים נוגעים בגוף האותיות. וכל א' נפרד מחבירו מ"ע סימן ל"ה. גם לא ידביקן בסוף האות כ"א באמצעיתן. ואם אינן נוגעים בגוף האותיות או שנוגעין זה בזה פסולים. מיהו אם ידעינן שכתבן מומחה תלינן שנפרד אחר

משנה ברורה

אם שינוי הצורה היה רק במקצת האות כגון שחסר הראש של האל"ף או (א) קוץ היו"ד או (ב) שנגעו יודי"י האל"ף בגג האל"ף וכדומה ואפילו אם התינוק יקראהו לאות (ג) לא מהני כיון שאנו יודעין שאין צורתה עליה כראוי: (ג) לאחרת. ראיתי בספר מעשה רקח שהביא לדינא בשם תשובת מהרלנ"ח סימן א' שכתב דאפילו אם רק מקצת האות נדמה לאות אחר פסול. ומדברי הגר"א לעיל בסימן ל"ב סי"ח לא משמע כן וכן כתב הפר"ח: (ד) בכ"ת. ר"ל כתיבה תמה ושלימה בתמונת האותיות כפי מה שלמדוהו מהתלמוד וקבלת הראשונים וע"פ הסוד וכמבואר בב"י בסימן זה: (ה) אם שינה וכו'. היינו (ד) שלא כתב תמונת האותיות המוזכרים בספרים אבל תמונת האות מיהו צריך כמו שכתב המחבר שלא תשתנה וכו' וכ"ש שלא ישנהו לאות אחר כגון מדלי"ת לרי"ש או מבי"ת לכ"ף וכדומה. והכוונה כמו שכתב הנוב"י סימן פ' דדבר שאין לו שורש בגמ' אין לפסול האות עבור זה. וכדי שידע הקורא איך לכתוב לכתחילה וגם איזה פרט יש לו שורש והוא מעיקר תמונת האותיות שיהיה זה לעיכובא אפילו בדיעבד לכן התחזקתי בעזה"י ועשיתי ע"ז קונטרס מיוחד בסוף סימן זה והעתקתיו מהב"י ופמ"ג ושארי אחרונים תמונת כל האותיות למעשה וקראתיו בשם משנת סופרים. וכללתי בו גם קיצור כללי דיני הקפת גויל ותוך תוכות ושלא כסדרן מבעל פמ"ג וש"א: ב (ו) השי"ן והעיי"ן. בכל הראשים: (ז) ובאחת. פי' אפילו (ה) ביו"ד אחד מן השי"ן וה"ה אם יש הפסק באמצע האות: (ח) שאינה נוגעת. אפילו אם הפירוד הוא דק (ו) שאין פירודו ניכר להדיא (ז) ולא מהני כאן קריאת התינוק כיון שידוע הוא האות ואין לטעות באחר דדוקא אם גריעותו מחמת שיש ספק לדמותו לאות אחר אז מועיל קריאת התינוק וכדלעיל בסימן ל"ב סי"ו. וכ"ז בלא תיקון אבל ע"י תיקון מהני דלא ליהוי שלא כסדרן אם התינוק קראו לאות וכדלעיל בסימן ל"ב סכ"ה (ועי"ש מה שכתבנו בשם הגרע"א. ולענין[א] יו"ד שאחורי האל"ף אם נראה כיו"ד ונו"ן) ובכל זה אין חילוק בין אם נעשה בעת הכתיבה או לאחר הכתיבה וכדלעיל בסימן ל"ב: (ט) וכן בשאר אותיות. כגון הנקודה שלמטה שבג' או הנקודה שבפ"א או (ח) הרגל שבתוך התי"ו אם לא נגעו באות או שיש הפסק באמצע איזה אות: (י) שלא[ב] ליגע. ולכתחילה יהיה הפסק (ט) בכדי שאדם בינוני יכירנו היטב מעל ס"ת שע"ג בימה כשהוא קורא בו גם לא ירחיקו יותר מעובי הגג: (יא) בגג. וה"ה (י) הקו"ף מריכו שבלידו וכ"ז אפילו אם נעשה הנגיעה אחר הכתיבה ואפילו אם הנגיעה דקה כחוט השערה וכמו שנתבאר לעיל בסימן ל"ב סי"ח במ"ב שם ועי"ש בענין תיקון האות אם לא כתב אח"ז דאל"ה הוי שלא כסדרן: ג (יב) לתייג. אפילו בס"ת וכ"ש בתו"מ. והתגין האלו הם שלשה תגין קטנים (יא) ודקים כחוט השערה וזקופות על אלו האותיות (יב) אחד מימין ואחד משמאל ואחד מלמעלה וי"א דשלשתן מלמעלה וכן נוהגין. וכעין קו דק הוא כל תג ותג כך נוהגין באלו הארצות וטוב יותר לעשות כל אחד כעין (יג) תמונת זיין אך שיהיו קטנים ודקים מאוד: (יג) שעטנ"ז ג"ץ. וה"ה (יד) לד"י כפופה ונו"ן פשוטה. ואם (טו) הוסיף הסופר לעשות תגין חוץ מאותיות שעטנ"ז ג"ץ וחוץ מאלו המוזכרים בטור ובלבוש שנהגו בהם הסופרים לא עכב אך בתנאי שיהיו מחוברים להאות אבל אם אינו מחובר יש למוחקו ואפילו באותיות שבשם הקודש ולכתחילה אין נכון להוסיף תגין מעצמו כל שלא מוזכר בספרים. ותיוג של שעטנ"ז ג"ץ הוא (טז) בשין על ראש השלישי של האות ובעי"ן וטי"ת ולד"י על ראש השמאלי וידביקן (יז) באמצעיתו לא בסופו. כתבו האחרונים בשם תשובת הרמ"ע שיזהר שיהיו התגין נפרדין כל אחד מחבירו כדי שלא יראו רק כתמונת זיונין ולא כעיי"ן וש"ין ולעיכובא הוא. גם צריך שיהיו התגין נוגעין בגוף האות ואל"ה פסולין דאף דאין עיכוב בעשיית התגין כמו שפסק המחבר מ"מ זה גרע דהוי (יח) כיתרון אות קטנה בין השיטין ועיין ביד אפרים שכתב דלא מהני אף אם ימשיכם אח"כ אל האות רק צריך לגוררם ולכותבם מחדש רק אם ידעינן שכתבן מומחה תלינן שנפרד אחר שנכתב ומכשירין בהמשכה אל האות. והלבושי שרד כתב דהרמ"ע ס"ל דלא גרע דבר זה מחסרון הקפת גויל דאינו מעכב רק בתחלה וע"כ אם נפרד אחר שנכתב כשר בלא תיקון כלל וממילא לדבריו אם לא היו נוגעין מתחלת הכתיבה מהני עכ"פ תיקון דומי' דמ"ש המ"א בסי' ל"ב סקכ"ז לענין הקפת גויל וכן משמע לענ"ד מפשטא דלישניה דהרמ"ע ע"ש. ומ"מ לכתחלה נכון להחמיר כיד* אפרי' ועי' פמ"ג: (יד) נהגו לתייג. בתפילין אותיות אחרות מלבד אלו והם מוזכרים בטור בשם השמושא רבא ובשם הרמב"ם. והתגין האלו הם (יט) תגינים גדולים אך שיהיו דקים שלא יתקלקל האות עי"ז ומאוד צריך ליזהר ביותר בתגין שעל הוי"ו או שעל היו"ד כי בקל ישתנה האות עי"ז

שער הציון

(א) מנחות כ"ט ע"א: (ב) לעיל בל"ב סי"ח וכמ"ש בביאור הגר"א שם דזה מיקרי שינוי בצורתה: (ג) ב"י בשם מהרי"ק בסימן זה: (ד) פמ"ג: (ה) כן מוכח מהגר"א וכן מכמה מקומות: (ו) בסי' ל"ב סכ"ה: (ז) ט"ז והגר"א: (ח) ב"י: (ט) מ"א וא"ר: (י) לעיל[ה] בתמונת האותיות עי"ש: (יא) הרמב"ם פ"ז מהלכות ס"ת: (יב) טו"ד והביאו הב"י: (יג) ב"י בשם האגור והרמב"ם: (יד) ב"י בשם רש"י: (טו) תשו' ח"ס: (טז) ב"י בצורת האותיות כמה פעמים כמה שזכר פה בשם הנ"י וכן מוכח מספר התרומה שהובא בב"י פה: (יז) מ"א: (יח) היד אפרים והגרע"א בשם המ"ע: (יט) ב"י וד"מ:

הגהות ותיקונים: א) צ"ל לענין: ב) שאין: ג) סק"ג: ד) ה': ה) לקמן:

(14) have become accustomed to make crownlets on other letters. If one did not

Mishnah Berurah

make crownlets on/ the bent over /letter/ צ[1] and the simple /elongated letter/ ן.[1]

If the scribe made additional crownlets /on letters/ other than the letters שעטנז גץ and other than those /letters/ mentioned in the *Tur* and the *Levush* for which it has become the practice of scribes /to add crownlets/, this does not preclude /the validity of the letters/. However, this is conditional on /the crownlets/ being connected to the letters, but if they are not connected /to them/ they should be erased. This even /applies/ in the case of letters of the Divine Name. /On the other hand,/ initially, it is not proper to add crownlets on one's own /initiative to/ any /letter for/ which /the requirement of crownlets/ has not been mentioned in /Torah/ works.

The crownlets on /the letters/ שעטנז גץ are, in the case of the /letter/ ש, on the third head of the letter and, in the case of the /letters/ ע, ט and צ, on the left head /of the letter/. They should be stuck to the middle /of the head/, not at the end.

The Acharonim write, on the authority of the responsa of the *Rema* /of Fano/, that one must take care that the /individual/ crownlets are all separated from one another, so that they do not appear as anything but ז symbols and not like a/letter/ ע or a /letter/ ש. This is an essential /requirement/. It is also necessary for the crownlets to touch the body of the letter. Otherwise, they are invalid. Although the making of the crownlets is not an essential /requirement/, as ruled by the author /of the Shulchan Aruch, crownlets which do not touch/ nevertheless /cause invalidity, as their presence is/ worse /than the omission of crownlets/. /This is/ because they are like superfluous small letters in between the lines.

See the *Yad Efrayim*, who writes that /when the crownlets do not touch the letter/ it is of no avail even if one subsequently continues /the crownlets/ until /they touch/ the letter, but the only /way to correct this/ is to scrape them off and write them anew. There is an exception /to this ruling/ where one knows that an expert wrote /the crownlets, for then/ we presume that they separated /from the letter/ after it was written and we /, therefore,/ allow them to be /corrected by being/ continued until /they touch/ the letter.

The *Levushey Serad* writes that the *Rema* /of Fano/ is of the opinion that this /fault/ is no worse than the lack of /blank/ parchment surrounding /a letter/, which is not /a fault/ that precludes /validity/ except /if it was there/ at the outset. Consequently, if /the crownlets/ became separated /from the letter/ after it was written /the passage/ is valid without being corrected at all. According to his words, it follows that if /the crownlets/ were not touching at the beginning, when the writing /was done/, correction is at any rate of avail. This would compare with what the *M.A.* writes in Sec. 32, sub-Par. 27 with respect to the /letter being/ surrounded by /blank/ parchment. According to my limited understanding, this is /in fact/ implied by the simple meaning of the wording of the *Rema* /of Fano/; see there. Nevertheless, initially, it is proper to be stringent in conformance with /the words of/ the *Yad Efrayim*. See the *P.Mg.*

(14) Have become accustomed to make crownlets. /I.e., they make crownlets/ in *tefilin* /passages/ on other letters, apart from these. These /other letters/ are mentioned in the *Tur* in the name of the *Shimusha Raba* and in the name of the *Rambam*.

These crownlets are large crownlets, but they must be /made/ thin so that /the form of/ the letter is not spoiled because of them. One must be extremely careful with the crownlets on the /letter/ ו or on the /letter/ י, as these letters easily change /their form/ because of them.

1 I.e., although in this list the elongated letter צ and the bent-over letter נ appear, but not the bent-over letter צ and the simple elongated letter ן.

לתייג אותיות אחרות ^ד^ואם לא תייג אפילו שעטנ"ז ג"ץ (ז) [ז] (טו) לא פסל:

ד הרא"ש וכ"נ מדברי הרמב"ם

באר היטב

ס"ק מ': (ז) לא פסל. והב"ח פוסל אם לא תייג שעטנ"ז ג"ץ. ונ"ל דטוב לתקנם אח"כ ואפי' בתפילין מועיל תיקון. ואין בזה משום שלא כסדרן. וכ"כ ע"ת ובשכנה"ג וע' ט"ז. [ובס' ב"ש מביא פוסקים רבים לפסול אם לא תייגן. וכתב בת' רד"ך דה"ה אם הותירו על הג' זיונין שהוזכרו בש"ס דפסול. כתב בס' אגרת הטיול שעטנ"ז הוא אותיות שטן ע"ז והם ב' מקטרגים גדולים וזהו ג"כ סוד של שעטנ"ז ג"ץ כי ג"ץ ג"כ שם של מקטרג אחד והתגין שעליהם הם כמו חרב וחנית להנצל מהם]:

שערי תשובה

ראינו ולא שמענו מי שעשה כך: [ז] לא פסל. עבה"ט ועיין במח"ב בשם מהר"מ איספיניא ז"ל שהתגין צריכים להיות תמונת זיינין כמ"ש הרמ"ע וכן הוא ברעיא מהימנא ובתקונים וכל מ"ש בשו"ת באר עשק ליתא ע"ש:

משנה ברורה

עי"ז: (טו) לא פסל. והב"ח פוסל בזה וגם הגר"א בביאורו מיישב לכ"א מן השיטות ומביא הרבה פוסקים דמחמירין בזה ע"כ מהנכון מאוד לחוש לזה ולתקנם אח"כ ותיקון מהני אפילו בתו"מ ולא הוי בזה שלא כסדרן דבלא התגין נמי צורתה עליה (אחרונים) ודע עוד דהמחבר מיירי שעשה ראש האות למעלה כתיקונו אך שחיסר התגין שעליו אבל אם עשה למעלה ראשו עגול ג"כ משמע מהב"י דאין להקל אפי' בדיעבד לפי פירוש הרא"ש ול"ע למעשה כי לכאורה להרמב"ם יש להקל בכל גווני [עיין בביאור הגר"א דלהרמב"ם לא איירי הגמרא כלל בתפילין רק במזוזה ולא לענין עיגול והמשכה אך לענין תגין ממש ורק לכתחלה] כתב בספר איגרת הטיול שעטנ"ז הוא אותיות שט"ן ע"ז והם ב' מקטרגים גדולים וזהו ג"כ סוד של שעטנ"ז ג"ץ כי ג"ץ ג"כ שם מקטרג אחד והתגין שעליהם הם כמו חרב וחנית להנצל מהם:

משנת סופרים — קיצור כללי שלא כסדרן מפמ"ג ושארי אחרונים

תפילין ומזוזות צריכין שיהיו כתובין כסדרן מן התורה דכתיב והיו הדברים כסדרן בין הקדים פרשה לפרשה ובין תיבה לתיבה או אות לאות פסול אבל בזה האות גופא לא שייך שלא כסדרן כגון צד"י שמורכב מיו"ד נו"ן וכתב הנו"ן ואח"כ היו"ד לא הוי שלא כסדרן וכל כה"ג. וכן אם כתב מקצת אות ואחר כך כתב האות שמקודם משלים האות ולא הוי שלא כסדרן דכל שאין כותב אות שלם מקרי והיו הדברים כסדרן דדבר שלם בעינן לא חצי דבר אבל אם כתב יו"ד בלא קוצו השמאלי או אל"ף ועיי"ן ושי"ן וכדומה שאין נוגע היו"ד בהאות ואח"כ כתב מקודם יש בו משום שלא כסדרן דהשתא לקולא אמרינן דיכול לתקן אח"כ [כמבואר בט"ז בסימן ל"ו ובסימן ל"ב סכ"ה] משום דעיקר הדברים כסדר נכתבו דשם אות עליה אפילו בלא התיקון וכמו שנכתוב אח"כ כ"ש לחומרא דשם אות עליה והוי שלא כסדרן. וכ"ש אם לא נחסר בהאות רק תגין או שאר דברים שאינם מעכבים ואח"כ כתב מקודם דיש בו משום שלא כסדרן [הג"ה ויש סופרים שנכשלין בענין שלא כסדרן בפסולי דאורייתא והוא רק מחמת חסרון ידיעה שטועין לחשוב ששלא כסדרן נקרא רק אם הוא מתקן איזה דבר אחר גמר הפרשיות וע"כ מתקנים בעת הכתיבה כמה אותיות שכבר חלף ועבר מהן ובאמת לא כן הוא אלא תיכף כשכתב האות שאחריו אסור לתקן האות שלפניו אם לא בדבר שמדינא אפילו בלא התיקון יש עליו שם אותו האות ולאו כו"ע דינא גמירי לידע איזה דבר יש עליו שם אותו האות בלי התיקון ומותר לתקנו אפילו אח"כ ובאיזה דבר אין עליו שם האות בלי התיקון וממילא אסור לתקנו אחר שכתב האות שאחריו ע"כ מהנכון להסופר שיזהר בתו"מ שלא להניף ידו על שום אות לתקנו באיזה תיקון אחר שכתב האות שאחריו אם לא דבר שנמצא כתוב בפירוש בספרי הפוסקים שזה מותר לתקן אפילו אח"כ ולא ידמה בעצמו מילתא למילתא. וכ"ז הוא אפי' תיקון שע"י כתיבה וכ"ש תיקון שע"י מחיקה שיש בו חשש דחק תוכות אפי' לא כתב עדיין שום אות אחר זה שצריך מאד לידע כל פרטי הדינים שיש בזה כי עניניו ארוכין ועיין בח"א שכתב דהוא היה מתנה עם הסופר שלו שלא להניף עליהם ברזל מחמת זה ובאמת עצתו היא טובה מאד אבל איננה מועלת רק לענין להנצל עי"ז מחשש דחק תוכות אבל לא משלא כסדרן אם לא שיזהר הסופר להתנהג במלאכתו מלאכת שמים לאט לאט שלא להעתיק ידו מן האות עד שיעמידנו על תמונתו כדין. וכבר ראיתי אנשים י"א מפזרין ממון רב על תיקון תפיליהן ולוקחין מסופר אומן שיכול לעשות בתים נאים ומהודרים כדין בכל פרטיהם ואשרי חלקם אבל ביותר מזה צריך ליזהר על ענין התפילין מבפנים והם הפרשיות שיעשה הסופר כל אותיותיהם כדין בכל פרטיהם והדוריהם ולזה צריך שיהיה הסופר בקי בדיני כתיבת האותיות וגם שיעשה מלאכתו במתינות כי אפילו אם אות אחד לא נעשה כדין בכל פרטיו הוא מעכב לכל התפילין כדאמרינן מנחות כ"ט]. אם חסר בהכתב התגין או הקוצו של יו"ד מבואר בסימן ל"ו בט"ז ובל"ב במ"א דיש לתקן אפילו אחר שנכתבו דכל שהאות צורתו עליה אע"ג דבלא קוצו של יו"ד השמאלי פסול לר"ת וגם תגין י"א דפסול אם לא תייגן מ"מ והיו הדברים גוף הדברים כסדר נכתבו. וכן להפריד נגיעות בין אות לאות שרי אח"כ ופשוט דדוקא אם לא נשתנה צורתו ע"י הנגיעה וכן יוד"י האל"ף והשי"ן והעי"ן ורגל התי"ו שאין נוגעין ותינוק דלא חכים ולא טיפש קורא אותן בצורתן או בי"ת ודלי"ת וכדומה

make crownlets, even /on the letters/ שעטנז גץ, /the passage/ (15) is not invalid.

Mishnah Berurah

(15) **Is not invalid.** The *Bach* invalidates /the letters/ in such a case. The *Gra*, as well, in his *Beyur*, reconciles every one of the views /in this respect/ and cites many Poskim who are stringent about this. Consequently, it is very proper to take this /view/ into account and correct /the omission of crownlets/ subsequently. Correction is /in fact/ of avail /for the crownlets/ even in the case of *tefilin* /passages/ and mezuzos. /Adding the crownlets later/ is not /regarded as writing the letters/ in incorrect order, since /the letters/ have their form without the crownlets as well. ((Acharonim))

Note further that the author /of the Shulchan Aruch/ is speaking /of an instance/ when one made the top of the letter above correctly, but left out the crownlets /that should be/ on it. If, however, one made the top of /the letter/ above rounded, it is also implied by the *B.Y.*[2] that /then/ one should not be lenient even once it is after the event, according to the explanation of the *Re'eym.* /This ruling/ requires study in practice, as it appears that according to the *Rambam*[3] one can be lenient in all cases. [See the *Beyur Ha-Gra*, that according to the *Rambam* the Gemara[4] /which discusses this question/ is not speaking at all about *tefilin* /passages/, but only about a mezuzah. /It is also/ not /speaking/ with reference to a rounding /of the top of the letter/ or a continuation /of it/, but with reference to the actual crownlets and only /with respect to/ initial /practice/.]

It is written in the work *Igeres Ha-Tiyul*, that /the word/ שעטנז is /comprised of/ the letters שטן עז. These are two great accusers. This is also the esoteric /reason for the requirement/ of /crownlets on the letters/ שעטנז גץ, as גץ is also the name of a certain accuser. The crownlets on these /letters/ are like a sword and a spear, so /that through them/ one will be saved from these /accusers/.

2 The *B.Y.* was written by the author of the Shulchan Aruch and what he writes there forms the background of his decisions in the Shulchan Aruch.
3 See *Rambam, Hilchos Tefilin* 5:3.
4 *Menachos* 29b.

לתייג אותיות אחרות ד ואם לא תייג אפילו שעטנ"ז ג"ץ (ד) [ד] (טו) לא פסל:

ד הרא"ש וכ"נ מדברי הרמב"ם

באר היטב

ס"ק ט': (ד) לא פסל. והב"ח פוסל אם לא תייג שעטנ"ז ג"ץ. ונ"ל דטוב לתקנם אח"כ ואפי' בתפילין מועיל תיקון. ואין בזה משום שלא כסדרן. וכ"כ ע"ת ושכנה"ג וע' ט"ז. [ובס' ב"ש מביא פוסקים רבים לפסול אם לא תייגן. וכתב בס' כד"ך דה"ה אם הוסיפו על הג' זיונין שהוזכרו בש"ס דפסול. כתב בס' אגרת הטיול שעטנ"ז הוא אותיות שטן ע"ז והם ב' מקטרגים גדולים וזהו ג"כ סוד של שעטנ"ז ג"ץ כי ג"ץ ג"כ שם של מקטרג אחד והתגין שעליהם הם כמו חרב וחנית להנצל מהם]:

שערי תשובה

ראינו ולא שמענו מי שעשה כן: [ד] לא פסל. עבה"ט ועיין במח"ב בשם מהר"ת איספינא ז"ל שהתגין צריכים להיות תמונת זיינין כמ"ש הרמ"ע וכן הוא ברעיא מהימנא ובתקונים וכל מ"ש בטו"ת בלא עסק לימא ע"ש:

משנה ברורה

ע"ז: (טו) לא פסל. והב"ח פוסל בזה וגם הגר"א בביאורו מיישב לב"ח מן הקושיות ומביא הרבה פוסקים דמחמירין בזה ע"כ מהנכון מאוד לחוש לזה ולתקנם אח"כ ותיקון מהני אפילו בתו"מ ולא הוי בזה שלא כסדרן דבלא התגין נמי צורתה עליה (אחרונים) ודע עוד דהמחבר מיירי שעשה ראש האות למעלה כתיקונו אך שחיסר התגין שעליו אבל אם עשה למעלה ראשו עגול ג"כ משמע מהב"י דאין להקל אפי' בדיעבד לפי פירוש הרא"ש וצ"ע למעשה כי לכאורה להרמב"ם יש להקל בכל גווני [עיין בביאור הגר"א דלהרמב"ם לא איירי הגמרא כלל בתפילין רק במזוזה ולא לענין עיגול והמשכה אך לענין תגין ממש ורק לכתחלה] כתב בספר אגרת הטיול שעטנ"ז הוא אותיות שטן ע"ז והם ב' מקטרגים גדולים וזהו ג"כ סוד של שעטנ"ז ג"ץ כי ג"ץ ג"כ שם מקטרג אחד והתגין שעליהם הם כמו חרב וחנית להנצל מהם:

משנת   קיצור כללי שלא כסדרן מפמ"ג ושארי אחרונים   סופרים

תפילין ומזוזות צריכין שיהיו כתובין כסדרן מן התורה דכתיב והיו הדברים כסדרן בין הקדים פרשה לפרשה ובין תיבה לתיבה או אות לאות פסול אבל בזה האות גופא לא שייך שלא כסדרן כגון צד"י שמורכב מיו"ד נו"ן וכתב הנו"ן ואח"כ היו"ד לא הוי שלא כסדרן וכל כה"ג. וכן אם כתב מקצת אות ואחר כך כתב האות שמקודם משלים האות ולא הוי שלא כסדרן דכל שאין כותב אות שלם מקרי והיו הדברים כסדרן דדבר שלם בעינן לא חצי דבר אבל אם כתב יו"ד בלא קוצו השמאלי או אל"ף ועיי"ן ושי"ן וכדומה שאין נוגע היו"ד בהאות ואח"כ כתב מקודם יש בו משום שלא כסדרן דהשתא לקולא אמרינן דיכול לתקן אח"כ [כמבואר בט"ז בסימן ל"ו ובסימן ל"ב סכ"ה] משום דעיקר הדברים כסדר נכתבו דשם אות עליה אפילו בלא התיקון וכמו שנכתוב אח"כ כ"ש לחומרא דשם אות עליה והוי שלא כסדרן. וכ"ש אם לא נחסר בהאות רק תגין או שאר דברים שאינם מעכבים ואח"כ כתב מקודם דיש בו משום שלא כסדרן [הג"ה ויש סופרים שנכשלין בענין שלא כסדרן בפסולי דאורייתא והוא רק מחמת חסרון ידיעה שטועין לחשוב ששלא כסדרן נקרא רק אם הוא מתקן איזה דבר אחר גמר הפרשיות וע"כ מתקנים בעת הכתיבה כמה אותיות שכבר חלף ועבר מהן ובאמת לא כן הוא אלא תיכף כשכתב האות שאחריו אסור לתקן האות שלפניו אם לא בדבר שמדינא אפילו בלא התיקון יש עליו שם אותו האות ולאו כו"ע דינא גמירי לידע איזה דבר יש עליו שם אותו האות בלי התיקון ומותר לתקנו אפילו אח"כ ובאיזה דבר אין עליו שם האות בלי התיקון וממילא אסור לתקנו אחר שכתב האות שאחריו ע"כ מהנכון להסופר שיזהר בתו"מ שלא להניף ידו על שום אות לתקנו באיזה תיקון אחר שכתב האות שאחריו אם לא דבר שנמצא כתוב בפירוש בספרי הפוסקים שזה מותר לתקן אפילו אח"כ ולא ידמה בעצמו מילתא למילתא. וכ"ז הוא אפי' תיקון שע"י כתיבה וכ"ש תיקון שע"י מחיקה שיש בו חשש דחק תוכות אפי' לא כתב עדיין שום אות אחר וזה שצריך מאד לידע כל פרטי הדינים שיש בזה כי עניניו ארוכין ועיין בח"א שכתב דהוא היה מתנה עם הסופר שלו שלא להניף עליהם ברזל מחמת זה ובאמת עצתו היא טובה מאד אבל איננה מועלת רק לענין להנצל ע"ז מחשש דחק תוכות אבל לא משלא כסדרן אם לא שיזהר הסופר להתנהג במלאכתו מלאכת שמים לאט לאט שלא להעתיק ידו מן האות עד שיעמידנו על תמונתו כדין. וכבר ראיתי אנשים י"א מפזרין ממון רב על תיקון תפיליהן ולוקחין מסופר אומן שיכול לעשות בתים נאים ומהודרים כדין בכל פרטיהם ואשרי חלקם אבל ביותר מזה צריך ליזהר על ענין התפילין מבפנים והם הפרשיות שיעשה הסופר כל אותיותיהם כדין בכל פרטיהם והדוריהם ולזה צריך שיהיה הסופר בקי בדיני כתיבת האותיות וגם שיעשה מלאכתו במתינות כי אפילו אם אות אחד לא נעשה כדין בכל פרטיו הוא מעכב לכל התפילין כדאמרינן מנחות כ"ט]. אם חסר בהכתב התגין או הקוצו של יו"ד מבואר בסימן ל"ו בט"ז ובל"ב במ"א דיש לתקן אפילו אחר שנכתבו דכל שהאות צורתו עליה אע"ג דבלא קוצו של יו"ד השמאלי פסול לר"ת וגם תגין י"א דפסול אם לא תייגן מ"מ והיו הדברים גוף הדברים כסדר נכתבו. וכן להפריד נגיעות בין אות לאות שרי אח"כ ופשוט דדוקא אם לא נשתנה צורתו ע"י הנגיעה וכן יודי"י האל"ף והשי"ן והעי"ן ורגל התי"ו שאין נוגעין ותינוק דלא חכים ולא טיפש קורא אותן בצורתן או בי"ת ודל"ת וכדומה

MISHNAS SOFERIM

A BRIEF /ACCOUNT/ OF THE RULES CONCERNING /INVALIDITY BECAUSE ONE WROTE/ IN INCORRECT ORDER /TAKEN/ FROM THE *P.MG.* AND OTHER ACHARONIM

/The letters of passages of/ *tefilin* and mezuzos are required according to Torah law to be written in the correct order. /We know this/ because it is stated[1*] /in the passage of *Shema*, which refers both to the writing of *tefilin* passages and of mezuzos/, "And these words should be". /This implies that the words should be written in their actual form/ in the correct order. /Therefore,/ irrespective of whether one /wrote a later/ passage prior to an /earlier/ passage, whether /one wrote/ a /later/ word /prior/ to an /earlier/ word or /whether one wrote/ a /later/ letter /prior/ to an /earlier/ letter, /the passage/ is invalid.

However, as regards /the individual strokes of/ the selfsame letter, /the question of/ incorrect order is not relevant. For example, /in the case of the letter/ צ, which is a compound of the /letter/ י and the /letter/ נ, if one wrote the נ /part first/ and the י /part/ afterwards, this is not /classed as writing/ in incorrect order. /The same ruling applies/ in all similar cases. Likewise, if one wrote part of a letter and subsequently wrote the preceding letter, he may /then/ complete the letter /of which he already wrote a part/ and this is /also/ not /classed as writing/ in incorrect order. /This is/ because as long as one did not write the entire letter /in incorrect order, the writing/ conforms with /the requirement/, "And these words should be"[1*], /i.e., that the writing should be done/ in the correct order. /The reason is/ that a complete /letter/ is required /to be written to be of significance/ and not a part of /a letter/.

On the other hand, if one wrote a /letter/ י without its left tip or a /letter/ א, ע or ש, etc. with a י /part/ not touching /the rest of/ the letter and subsequently wrote the preceding /letter/, this does involve /writing/ in incorrect order. This follows because we /even/ rule leniently /as regards these cases/, that /when the letter was written in this way/ one may correct it subsequently /even though other letters were already written after it/ [as stated by the *Taz* in Sec. 36 and in Sec. 32, Par. 25]. (/The reason is/ that /then/ the essential /part of/ the "words"[1*] was /in fact/ written in /the correct/ order, since /the symbol/ is classed as a letter /in such a case/ even without the correction, as we will write subsequently.) /Therefore,/ it is certainly classed as a letter where this involves stringency, /so that if it was written before a preceding letter the writing/ is /regarded as/ being in incorrect order.

If the letter /which one wrote/ lacked nothing but crownlets or other details which do not preclude /validity/ and one subsequently wrote a preceding /letter/, this is certainly /regarded as writing/ in incorrect order.

[Note: There are scribes who stumble over /the pitfall of writing/ in incorrect order /and they thus cause the passages they write/ to be invalid according to Torah law. This is only due to ignorance, as they erroneously think that /writing/ is only describable as /being/ in incorrect order when one corrects something after /the writing of/ the passages has been completed. They therefore correct several letters which they already left off /writing/ and from which they passed on /to write other letters/, while they are /still engaged in/ writing /the passages/. The truth is that /their understanding/ is not /correct/, but immediately one has written a letter which

1* *Devarim* 6:6.

לתייג אותיות אחרות ד ואם לא תייג אפילו שעטנ״ז ג״ץ (ד) [ד] (טו) לא פסל:

ד הרא״ש וכ״נ מדברי הרמב״ם

באר היטב

ס״ק מ׳: (ד) לא פסל. והב״ח פוסל אם לא תייג שעטנ״ז ג״ץ. ונ״ל דטוב לתקנם אח״כ ואפי׳ בתפילין מועיל תיקון. ואין בזה משום שלא כסדרן. וכ״כ ע״ת ובשכנה״ג וע׳ ט״ז. [ובס׳ נ״ש מביא פוסקים רבים לפסול אם לא תייגן. וכתב בת׳ רד״ך דה״ה אם הותירו על הג׳ זיונין שהוזכרו בש״ס דפסול. כתב בס׳ אגרת הטיול שעטנ״ז הוא אותיות שטן ע״ז והם ב׳ מקטרגים גדולים וזהו ג״כ סוד של שעטנ״ז ג״ץ כי ג״ץ ג״כ שם של מקטרג אחד והתגין שעליהם הם כמו חרב וחנית להנצל מהם]:

שערי תשובה

ראינו ולא שמענו מי שעשה כן: [ד] לא פסל. עבה״ט ועיין במח״ב בשם מהר״מ איספיניא ז״ל שהתגין צריכים להיות תמונת זיינין כמ״ש הרמ״ע וכן הוא ברעיא מהימנא ובתקונים וכל מ״ש בשו״ת באר עשק ליתא ע״ש:

משנה ברורה

ע״ז: (טו) לא פסל. והב״ח פוסל בזה וגם הגר״א בביאורו מיישב לב״ח מן הסיטות ומביא הרבה פוסקים דמחמירין בזה ע״כ מהנכון מאוד לחוש לזה ולתקנם אח״כ ותיקון מהני אפילו בתו״מ ולא הוי בזה שלא כסדרן דבלא התגין נמי צורתה עליה (אחרונים) ודע עוד דהמתחבר איירי שעשה ראש האות למעלה כתיקונו אך שחיסר התגין שעליו אבל אם עשה למעלה ראשו עגול ג״כ משמע מהב״י דאין להקל אפי׳ בדיעבד לפי פירוש הרא״ש ול״ע למעשה כי לכאורה להרמב״ם יש להקל בכל גווני [עיין בביאור הגר״א דלהרמב״ם לא איירי הגמרא כלל בתפילין רק במזוזה ולא לענין עיגול והמשכה אך לענין תגין ממש ורק לכתחלה] כתב בספר איגרת הטיול שעטנ״ז הוא אותיות סט״ן ע״ז והם ב׳ מקטרגים גדולים וזהו ג״כ סוד של שעטנ״ז ג״ץ כי ג״ץ ג״כ שם מקטרג אחד והתגין שעליהם הם כמו חרב וחנית להנצל מהם:

משנת סופרים
קיצור כללי שלא כסדרן מפמ״ג ושארי אחרונים

תפילין ומזוזות צריכין שיהיו כתובין כסדרן מן התורה דכתיב והיו הדברים כסדרן בין הקדים פרשה לפרשה ובין תיבה לתיבה או אות לאות פסול אבל בזה האות גופא לא שייך שלא כסדרן כגון צד״י שמורכב מיו״ד נו״ן וכתב הנו״ן ואח״כ היו״ד לא הוי שלא כסדרן וכל כה״ג. וכן אם כתב מקצת אות ואחר כך כתב האות שמקודם משלים האות ולא הוי שלא כסדרן דכל שאין כותב אות שלם מקרי והיו הדברים כסדרן דדבר שלם בעינן לא חצי דבר אבל אם כתב יו״ד בלא קוצו השמאלי או אל״ף ועיי״ן ושי״ן וכדומה שאין נוגע היו״ד בהאות ואח״כ כתב מקודם י״ש בו משום שלא כסדרן דהשתא לקולא אמרינן דיכול לתקן אח״כ [כמבואר בט״ז בסימן ל״ו ובסימן ל״ב סכ״ה] משום דעיקר הדברים כסדר נכתבו דשם אות עליה אפילו בלא התיקון וכמו שנכתוב אח״כ כ״ש לחומרא דשם אות עליה והוי שלא כסדרן. וכ״ש אם לא נחסר בהאות רק תגין או שאר דברים שאינם מעכבים ואח״כ כתב מקודם דיש בו משום שלא כסדרן [הג״ה ויש סופרים שנכשלין בענין שלא כסדרן בפסולי דאורייתא והוא רק מחמת חסרון ידיעה שטועין לחשוב ששלא כסדרן נקרא רק אם הוא מתקן איזה דבר אחר גמר הפרשיות וע״כ מתקנים בעת הכתיבה כמה אותיות שכבר חלף ועבר מהן ובאמת לא כן הוא אלא תיכף כשכתב האות **שאחריו אסור לתקן האות שלפניו אם לא בדבר שמדינא אפילו בלא התיקון יש עליו שם אותו האות ולאו כו״ע דינא גמירי לידע איזה דבר יש עליו שם אותו האות בלי התיקון ומותר לתקנו אפילו אח״כ ובאיזה דבר אין עליו שם האות בלי התיקון וממילא אסור לתקנו אחר שכתב האות שאחריו ע״כ מהנכון להסופר שיזהר בתו״מ שלא להניף ידו על שום אות לתקנו באיזה תיקון אחר** שכתב האות שאחריו אם לא דבר שנמצא כתוב בפירוש בספרי הפוסקים שזה מותר לתקן אפילו אח״כ ולא ידמה בעצמו מילתא למילתא. וכ״ז הוא אפי׳ תיקון שע״י כתיבה וכ״ש תיקון שע״י מחיקה שיש בו חשש דחק תוכות אפי׳ לא כתב עדיין שום אות אחר זה שצריך מאד לידע כל פרטי הדינים שיש בזה כי עניניו ארוכין ועיין בח״א שכתב דהוא היה מתנה עם הסופר שלו שלא להניף עליהם ברזל מחמת זה ובאמת עצתו היא טובה מאד אבל איננה מועלת רק לענין להנצל עי״ז מחשש דחק תוכות אבל לא משלא כסדרן אם לא שיזהר הסופר להתנהג במלאכתו מלאכת שמים לאט לאט שלא להעתיק ידו מן האות עד שיעמידנו על תמונתו כדין. וכבר ראיתי אנשים י״א מפזרין ממון רב על תיקון תפיליהן ולוקחין מסופר אומן שיכול לעשות בתים נאים ומהודרים כדין בכל פרטיהם ואשרי חלקם אבל ביותר מזה צריך ליזהר על ענין התפילין מבפנים והם הפרשיות שיעשה הסופר כל אותיותיהם כדין בכל פרטיהם והדוריהם ולזה צריך שיהיה הסופר בקי בדיני כתיבת האותיות וגם שיעשה מלאכתו במתינות כי אפילו אם אות אחד לא נעשה כדין בכל פרטיו הוא מעכב לכל התפילין כדאמרינן מנחות כ״ט]. אם חסר בהכתב התגין או הקוצו של יו״ד מבואר בסימן ל״ו בט״ז ובל״ב במ״א דיש לתקן אפילו אחר שנכתבו דכל שהאות צורתו עליה אע״ג דבלא קוצו של יו״ד השמאלי פסול לר״ת וגם תגין י״א דפסול אם לא תייגן מ״מ והיו הדברים גוף הדברים כסדר נכתבו. וכן להפריד נגיעות בין אות לאות שרי אח״כ ופשוט דדוקא אם לא נשתנה צורתו ע״י הנגיעה וכן יודי״ן האל״ף והשי״ן והעי״ן ורגל התי״ו שאין נוגעין ותינוק דלא חכים ולא טיפש קורא אותן בצורתן או בי״ת ודלי״ת וכדומה

follows it is /already/ forbidden to correct /any/ letter that precedes it, unless the detail /involved/ is such that /the symbol/ is halachically classed as that letter even without the correction.

/Now,/ not everyone is versed in the halachah, so that he is aware of the details for which /the symbol/ is classed as that letter /even/ without correction, /in which case/ he is permitted to correct it even after /the following letter has been written/, and the details for which /the symbol/ is not classed as the letter without the correction, from which it follows that he is forbidden to correct /that letter/ after he has written the following letter. It is therefore proper for a scribe to take care when /he writes/ *tefilin* /passages/ and mezuzos not to wave his hand over any letter /in order/ to correct it with some correction, once he has /already/ written the letter which follows it, unless it is written explicitly in the works of the Poskim that it is permitted to correct the detail /involved/ even subsequently. He should not compare one case to another by himself /and conclude that the correction is permitted/.

All /the above considerations/ even apply /with respect to/ a correction by writing. Where the correction /must be done/ by erasure /, however,/ there is /also/ a fear that /the correction will be considered/ carving around /to form the letter/. /If so, the letter will be invalid/ even if one did not yet write any letter after it. /Then/ there is certainly a great need to know all the halachic details that are /relevant to the correction/, as the factors with respect to this /principle/ are extensive.

See the *Ch.A.*, who writes that, in view of this, he would stipulate with his scribe not to wave an iron /tool/ over /the letters in order to erase/. His advice is actually very sound, but it is only of avail as a medium to save one from the fear that /a letter was formed by/ carving around. However, it does not /remove the fear/ that /letters may have been written/ in incorrect order. /There is no solution to this,/ unless the scribe is careful to conduct his work, which is Heavenly work, at a slow pace and does not take his hand away from the letter until it has attained the symbol /required/ halachically.

I have already seen Heaven fearing people spending much money for the perfection of their *tefilin*. They purchase them from a skilled scribe who is able to make attractive and outstanding housings, which accord with halachic /requirements/ in every detail. Happy is their lot. However, one must be /even/ more careful than that with respect to the state of the *tefilin* on the inside, which /means/ the passages. /One should therefore insist/ that the scribe should make all the letters in conformance with halachic /requirements/, with all the /required/ details and embellishments. For this /purpose/ the scribe must be versed in the laws concerning the writing of the letters and he must also do his work patiently. This is because if even a single letter was not formed in accordance with halachic /requirements/ in every detail, this precludes the validity of the entire *tefilin* /unit/, as stated in *Menachos* 29/a/.]

If a written /letter/ lacks crownlets or the /left/ tip of the /letter/ י /is missing/, it is stated in Sec. 36, in the *Taz*, and in /Sec./ 32, in the *M.A.*, that it can be corrected even after /letters which follow it/ have been written. /This is/ because whenever the letter has its form /, the correction is not considered to involve writing in incorrect order/. Although the /letter/ י is invalid without the left tip according to *R.T.* and /as regards/ crownlets, as well, there are /authorities/ who say that /the letter/ is invalid if one did not make the /required/ crownlets, /the writing/ nevertheless /conforms with the requirement/, "and these words should be,"[1*] /despite the correction, since/ the body of the "words" was written in /the correct/ order.

It is likewise allowed to separate touches between one letter and the other after /other letters have been written/. /However,/ it is self-understood, that this only /applies/ if the form of /the letters/ is unchanged by the touch.

Similarly, if the י /parts/ of the /letters/ א, ש and ע or the leg of the /letter/ ת do not touch /the rest of the letter/ and a child who is neither /especially/ intelligent nor /especially/ simple reads /the letters/ in that form /for what they are meant to be/, one is allowed to correct them /even after other letters have been written after them/. /Likewise,/ if /in the case of/ the /letter/ ב or the /letter/ ד, etc. the roof /of the letter/ is not

שאין הגג מחובר לירד למעלה ותינוק קורא אותן בצורתן רשאי לתקן אח״כ. ויראה דכ״ז דוקא אם אין ניכר פרידתו להדיא הא אם ניכר להדיא אע״ג דהתינוק קורא כן כיון שאין צורתה עליה הוי כותב שלא כסדרן [והגרע״א בחי׳ פליג ע״ז וכן בירנו שם בסימן ל״ב להלכה וע״ש שבירנו שבאיזה דבר גם הגרע״א מודה להפמ״ג]. בד״א באלו וכדומה להן שעל ידי שחסר להם איזה דבר לא נדמה על ידי זה תמונתם לאות אחרת אבל יו״ד של צד״י שאין נוגעת להנו״ן שלו ונראה עי״ז כיו״ד נו״ן או חי״ת שברגל שמאלו יש הפרש דק בין הרגל להגג ונראה כה״א אז אפילו אם אירע שהתינוק קראה להאות כצורתה הראויה לה אין מועיל תיקון משום שלא כסדרן. ודע דדעת הפמ״ג בזה דאפילו אם אין ניכר פרידתן להדיא והתינוק קראה ג״כ לאות לא מהני תיקון. ועיין בסימן ל״ב שבירנו שם דעכ״פ בשעת הדחק יש להקל בזה דמהני תיקון.

כתב עוד הפמ״ג כללא דמלתא כל שאין כותב רק מוחק או מושך לא הוי שלא כסדרן המשל לאבותיך מלא וא״ו צריך למחוק הוא״ו ואף דעי״ז יהיה התיבה כשני תיבות ימשוך* [אך צריך להשגיח שלא תתקלקל צורת הבי״ת בשום פעם, שאם ימשוך תחלה את הגג העליון שלה כפי הצורך הרי תתקלקל צורתה, ואף שאחר כך ימשוך גם את הצד התחתון ותחזור לצורת בי״ת הרי תהא שלא כסדרן, לכן צריך לעשות ההוספה במעט מעט קצת כאן וקצת כאן עד כדי הצורך — קסת הסופר בלשכת הסופר סימן ט׳, אות ה׳] *הגה״ה הבי״ת ואע״פ שכותב משיכה לאו כלום עביד דתחלה נמי צורת בי״ת עליה אבל ודאי אם עשה בי״ת מתחלה כצורת נו״ן כפופה ואח״כ משכו לבי״ת הוה שלא כסדרן וכן אפילו אם נכתב האות מתחלה כסדר ואחר כך נתקלקל מחמת איזה דבר שהוא כיון שנתבטל צורת האות כשחוזר אח״כ ומתקן הוה שלא כסדרן דבכל שעה בעינן כסדרן ול״ד למוקף גויל דלא קפיד קרא רק אשעת כתיבה וכמ״ש בפנים באורך. ולפעמים אפילו ע״י כתיבת נקודה אחת יש בזה משום שלא כסדרן כגון שכתב רי״ש במקום דלי״ת וצריך לרבע בדיו כמ״ש בסי׳ ל״ב בט״ז סט״ז תו מיפסיל משום שלא כסדרן. הכלל כל שאין צורתה עליה וכותב נקודה ועי״ז נתכשר האות יש בזה משום שלא כסדרן.

עוד דברים אחרים מענין חק תוכות

כל מקום שנאמר וכתב כגון בתפילין ומזוזות ס״ת גט, פסול בו חק תוכות ואפי׳ אם רק קוצו של יו״ד נגמר ע״י חק תוכות מעכב כיון דבלא הקוץ לא היה מתכשר האות עדיין [וחתימת עדי הגט בחק תוכות עיין ב״ש באה״ע בסימן ק״ל אות כ׳ במקום עיגון כשר אע״ג דלא כתיב בהו וכתב לכתחלה מקפידין כמו בכל הגט, ע״ש]. והנה ענין חק תוכות צריך הסופר ליזהר בו מאד ועניניו ארוכין עיין בל״ב סעיף י״ז י״ח אך נקוט האי כללא בידך כי הפוך הוא משלא כסדרן ששם גורר ומוחק ומושך לא הוי שלא כסדרן וכנ״ל [גורר הוא ביבש ומוחק בלח] ובחק תוכות נהפוך הוא גורר ומוחק ומושך כל שאינו עושה מעשה בגוף האות ומשלימה עדיין הוי חק תוכות. הדמיון בי״ת שנעשית כצורתה או סמ״ך וכ״ף וכדומה שנפל טיפת דיו לתוך החלל אחר שנגמרה בהכשר ונפסד צורתה עי״ז [ואפשר אפי׳ התינוק קורא אותה כל שאנו רואין שאין צורתה עליה] לא מהני לגרור הטיפה ההיא דכל שנפסלה בטלה כתיבה קמייתא ועתה הוי חק תוכות דהא לא עביד מעשה בגופה כ״א ע״י חקיקה בעלמא שחקק תוך האות ואפילו מושך אח״כ הבי״ת גגה ושוליה ג״כ לא מהני דהרי בלא״ה צורתה עליה ופסולה. וגדולה מזו חי״ת במקום ב׳ זייני״ן לא מהני שיגרור החרטום וישארו ב׳ זייני״ן דמה מעשה עשה בגוף האות אבל אם צריך להשלימה אח״כ כשר ולא מיקרי חק תוכות. כן מבואר באה״ע סימן קכ״ה אות ג׳ ומגן אברהם בל״ב אות כ״ג, אבל הט״ז שם פקפק ע״ז, ע״ש באות יו״ד ועי״ל בל״ב סעיף י״ז וסי״ח שמבואר שם הכל באר היטב. וגם ביארנו קצת דיני חק תוכות בכל אות ואות בפרט.

עוד איזה כללים מבעל פמ״ג מדיני הקפת גויל העתקתים בסוף הקונטרס, עי״ש.

צורת אות אל״ף

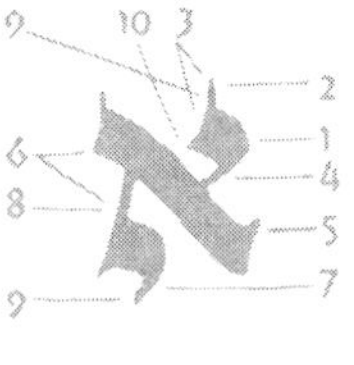

א) [1] תהיה נקודה העליונה כעין יו״ד ב) [2] ועוקץ קטן עליה [3] ויהיה ג) פניה עם העוקץ הפוך קצת כלפי מעלה [4] ויהיה ירך היו״ד דבוק אל גג הגוף ד) באמצע הגג [5] ויהיה סוף הגג של צד ימין ה) לכתחלה עקום למעלה מאחוריו קצת [6] והנקודה שלמטה תהיה רחוקה מן ראש של הגוף ו) כשיעור עובי קולמוס והצי. עובי קולמוס נק׳ רוחב הקו היוצא מן הקולמוס כשהוא כותב. [7] * ולנקודה התחתונה יהיה ז) לכתחילה עוקץ קטן למטה לצד ימין [8] מפני שתמונתה כמו יו״ד שתלוי בתג שלה בגוף האל״ף ח) [9] ויהיה עוקץ שמאל של נקודה עליונה היינו התג שעל גבי היו״ד מכוון כנגד עוקץ ימין של נקודה תחתונה עכ״ל ב״י [10] ומשמע מריהטא דלישניה דא״צ עוקץ שמאל ליו״ד העליון שעל האל״ף אך מפמ״ג בסימן ל״ב בא״א באות

joined to the thigh /of the letter/ above and /such/ a child reads it in that form /for what it is meant to be, one is able to correct it after the other letters have been written/. /However,/ it appears that all this only /applies/ if the separation is not clearly apparent, but if it is clearly apparent /, then/, although such a child reads /the letter correctly/ in that /form a correction/ is /considered/ writing in incorrect order, since /the letter/ does not have its /proper/ form /without the correction/. [The *G.R.A.E.* disputes this in his *Chidushim* and we have likewise explained there in Sec. 32 /, Par. 25 in the Beyur Halachah/ that /his view/ is the /correct/ ruling. See there, that we have explained that in some respect the *G.R.A.E.* also agrees with the *P.Mg.*]

The /above/ remarks apply in these and similar /cases/, where in view of /the fact/ that some element is lacking, the symbol /of the letter nevertheless/ does not seem like /that of/ another letter because of it. However, when the י /like part/ of the /letter/ צ does not touch the נ /like part/ of that /letter/ and in view of this /the symbol/ looks like a /letter/ י and /in addition/ a /letter/ נ or if the /letter/ ח has in its left leg a slight gap between the leg and the roof, /so that the symbol/ looks like the /letter/ ה, then even if /such/ a child happens to read the letter as /if it has/ its proper form, correction will be of no avail /once another letter has been written subsequently/. This is because /then the corrected letter will be classed as having been written/ in incorrect order. Note that with respect to this /matter/, the *P.Mg.* is of the opinion that even if the separation of /the parts of the letter/ is not clearly apparent and /such/ a child also reads it as the letter /it is meant to be/, correction will /nevertheless/ be of no avail /if another letter has been written subsequently/. See /the Beyur Halachah/ in Sec. 32 /, Par. 25/, where we have explained that, at any rate in a time of pressing /need/, one may be lenient in such a case /and rule/ that correction is of avail.

The *P.Mg.* writes a further rule concerning this matter. /This is that/ whenever one does not write /anything more when he corrects/, but merely erases or extends, /the correction/ is not /regarded as writing/ in incorrect order. An example /of this/ is /if one wrote/ לאבותיך with the /letter/ ו /written/ fully, /in which case/ one must erase the ו. Although as a result of this /erasure/ the word will be /written/ like two words, one may /correct this by/ extending the ב. /This is permitted/ despite /the fact/ that it /involves/ writing, /since/ the extension does not do anything at all /to form the letter/, as /the symbol/ has the form of the /letter/ ב at the outset as well. However, if one made the /letter/ ב at the outset with the form of a bent over /letter/ נ and extended /that/ ב /until it had the proper form/ after /the following letter was already written/, this is definitely /regarded as writing/ in incorrect order.

Likewise, even if a letter was written first in /correct/ order and subsequently became spoiled because of whatever /reason, then/, since the form of the letter has /now/ been cancelled, to go back subsequently and correct /the letter/ is regarded as /writing/ in incorrect order. /This is/ because we require /the letters to have been written/ in the correct order at all times. This /requirement/ is not comparable /in this respect/ with /the requirement that the letters must be/ surrounded with /blank/ parchment. The verse /from which that requirement is derived/ is only concerned about /the matter/ at the time when /the letters/ are written, as we have written inside /the Mishnah Berurah/ at length.[2*]

Occasionally, even the writing of a single stroke can involve /writing/ in incorrect order. For example, if one wrote the /letter/ ר instead of the /letter/ ד and needs to square /the letter off/ with ink, as /stated/ in Sec. 32, in the *Taz*, /sub-/Par. 16, then /if one already wrote the following letter the corrected letter/ will be invalid because /it will have been written/ in incorrect order. The rule is that whenever /a letter/ did not have its form /halachically before a subsequent letter was written/ and one /later/ wrote a stroke by means of which the letter became valid, /the correction/ is /ruled/ as /writing/ in incorrect order.

2* See Sec. 32, sub-Par. 34 and 53-59.

שאין הגג מחובר לירד למעלה ותינוק קורא אותן בצורתן רשאי לתקן אח"כ. ויראה דכ"ז דוקא אם אין ניכר פרידתו להדיא הא אם ניכר להדיא אע"ג דהתינוק קורא כן כיון שאין צורתה עליה הוי כותב שלא כסדרן [והגרע"א בחי' פליג ע"ז וכן בירנו שם בסימן ל"ב להלכה וע"ש שבררנו שבאיזה דבר גם הגרע"א מודה להפמ"ג]. בד"א באלו וכדומה להן שעל ידי שחסר להם איזה דבר לא נדמה על ידי זה תמונתם לאות אחרת אבל יו"ד של צד"י שאין נוגעת להנו"ן שלו ונראה עי"ז כיו"ד נו"ן או חי"ת שברגל שמאלו יש הפרש דק בין הרגל להגג ונראה כה"א אז אפילו אם אירע שהתינוק קראה להאות כצורתה הראויה לה אין מועיל תיקון משום שלא כסדרן. ודע דדעת הפמ"ג בזה דאפילו אם אין ניכר פרידתן להדיא והתינוק קראה ג"כ לאות לא מהני תיקון. ועיין בסימן ל"ב שבירנו שם דעכ"פ בשעת הדחק יש להקל בזה דמהני תיקון.

כתב עוד הפמ"ג כללא דמלתא כל שאין כותב רק מוחק או מושך לא הוי שלא כסדרן המשל לאבותיך מלא וא"ו צריך למחוק הוא"ו ואף דעי"ז יהיה התיבה כשני תיבות ימשוך* [אך צריך להשגיח שלא תתקלקל צורת הבי"ת בשום פעם, שאם ימשוך תחלה את הגג העליון שלה כפי הצורך הרי תתקלקל צורתה, ואף שאחר כך ימשוך גם את הצד התחתון ותחזור לצורת בי"ת הרי תהא שלא כסדרן, לכן צריך לעשות ההוספה במעט מעט קצת כאן וקצת כאן עד כדי הצורך — קסת הסופר בלשכת הסופר סימן ט', אות ה'] הבי"ת ואע"פ שכותב משיכה לאו כלום עביד דתחלה נמי צורת בי"ת עליה אבל ודאי אם עשה בי"ת מתחלה כצורת נו"ן כפופה ואח"כ משכו לבי"ת הוה שלא כסדרן וכן אפילו אם נכתב האות מתחלה כסדר ואחר כך נתקלקל מחמת איזה דבר שהוא כיון שנתבטל צורת האות כשחוזר אח"כ ומתקן הוה שלא כסדרן דבכל שעה בעינן כסדרן ול"ד למוקף גויל דלא קפיד קרא רק אשעת כתיבה וכמ"ש בפנים באורך. ולפעמים אפילו ע"י כתיבת נקודה אחת יש בזה משום שלא כסדרן כגון שכתב רי"ש במקום דל"ת וצריך לרבע בדיו כמ"ש בסי' ל"ב בט"ז סט"ז תו מיפסיל משום שלא כסדרן. הכלל כל שאין צורתה עליה וכותב נקודה ועי"ז נתכשר האות יש בזה משום שלא כסדרן.

עוד דברים אחדים מענין חק תוכות

כל מקום שנאמר וכתב כגון בתפילין ומזוזות ס"ת גט, פסול בו חק תוכות ואפי' אם רק קוצו של יו"ד נגמר ע"י חק תוכות מעכב כיון דבלא הקוץ לא היה מתכשר האות עדיין [וחתימת עדי הגט בחק תוכות עיין ב"ש באה"ע בסימן ק"ל אות כ' במקום עיגון כשר אע"ג דלא כתיב בהו וכתב לכתחלה מקפידין כמו בכל הגט, ע"ש]. והנה ענין חק תוכות צריך הסופר ליזהר בו מאד ועניניו ארוכין עיין בל"ב סעיף י"ז י"ח אך נקוט האי כללא בידך כי הפוך הוא משלא כסדרן ששם גורר ומוחק ומושך לא הוי שלא כסדרן וכנ"ל [גורר הוא ביבש ומוחק בלח] ובחק תוכות נהפוך הוא גורר ומוחק ומושך כל שאינו עושה מעשה בגוף האות ומשלימה עדיין הוי חק תוכות. הדמיון בי"ת שנעשית כצורתה או סמ"ך וכ"ף וכדומה שנפל טיפת דיו לתוך החלל אחר שנגמרה בהכשר ונפסד צורתה עי"ז [ואפשר אפי' התינוק קורא אותה כל שאנו רואין שאין צורתה עליה] לא מהני לגרור הטיפה ההיא דכל שנפסלה בטלה כתיבה קמייתא ועתה הוי חק תוכות דהא לא עביד מעשה בגופה כ"א ע"י חקיקה בעלמא שחקק תוך האות ואפילו מושך אח"כ הבי"ת גגה ושוליה ג"כ לא מהני דהרי בלא"ה צורתה עליה ופסולה. וגדולה מזו חי"ת במקום ב' זייני"ן לא מהני שיגרור החרטום וישארו ב' זייני"ן דמה מעשה עשה בגוף האות אבל אם צריך להשלימה אח"כ כשר ולא מיקרי חק תוכות. כן מבואר באה"ע סימן קכ"ה אות ג' ומגן אברהם בל"ב אות כ"ג, אבל הט"ז שם פקפק ע"ז, ע"ש באות יו"ד ועי"ל בל"ב סעיף י"ז וסי"ח שמבואר שם הכל באר היטב. וגם ביארנו קצת דיני חק תוכות בכל אות ואות בפרט.

עוד איזה כללים מבעל פמ"ג מדיני הקפת גויל העתקתים בסוף הקונטרס, עי"ש.

צורת אות אל"ף

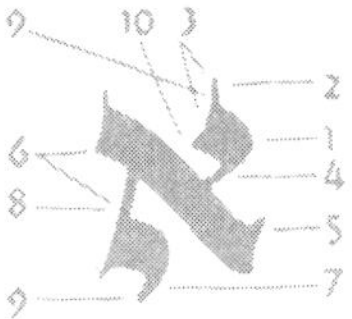

א) [1] תהיה נקודה העליונה כעין יו"ד ב) [2] ועוקץ קטן עליה [3] ויהיה ג) פניה עם העוקץ הפוך קצת כלפי מעלה [4] ויהיה ירך היו"ד דבוק אל גג הגוף ד) באמצע הגג [5] ויהיה סוף הגג של צד ימין ה) לכתחלה עקום למעלה מאחוריו קצת [6] והנקודה שלמטה תהיה רחוקה מן ראש של הגוף ו) כשיעור עובי קולמוס וחצי. עובי קולמוס נק' רוחב הקו היוצא מן הקולמוס כשהוא כותב. [7] * ולנקודה התחתונה יהיה ז) לכתחילה עוקץ קטן למטה לצד ימין [8] מפני שתמונתה כמו יו"ד שתלוי בתג שלה בגוף האל"ף ח) [9] ויהיה עוקץ שמאל של נקודה עליונה היינו התג שעל גבי היו"ד מכוון כנגד עוקץ ימין של נקודה תחתונה עכ"ל ב"י [10] ומשמע מריהטא דלישניה דא"צ עוקץ שמאל ליו"ד העליון שעל האל"ף אך מפמ"ג בסימן ל"ב בא"א באות

A FEW ADDITIONAL POINTS, CONCERNING CARVING AROUND /TO FORM THE LETTER/

Whenever it is stated /in the Torah with respect to a mitzvah matter that one is required/ to write, as /is the case/ with *tefilin* /passages/, mezuzos, Torah Scrolls and a letter of divorce, /if the letters are formed by/ carving out they are invalid. Even if only the /left/ tip of the /letter/ י was completed by carving around /to form the letter/ this precludes /the validity of the writing/, since without the /left/ tip /the form of/ the letter is still not valid.

[/As to whether/ the witnesses of a letter of divorce may sign it by carving around /to form the letters of their signatures/, see the *B.Sh.* in the *Even Ha-Ezer*, in Sec. 130, sub-Par. 20, that where inability to marry would /otherwise/ be involved, /such a signature/ is /ruled as/ valid. /However,/ although with respect to /the signature of the witnesses the Torah/ does not state that they must write, we are insistent initially /that they should not carve around to form the letters of their signature/, just as with /the writing of/ the entire letter of divorce.]

Now the scribe must be very careful about the matter of carving around /to form the letter/. The /relevant/ details are extensive; see /Sec./ 32, Par. 17 and 18. However, /the reader/ should grasp the /general/ rule that the opposite of /what applies for the disqualification of writing because it was written in/ incorrect order /applies as regards disqualification because of carving around to form the letter/. /This is/ because where /the question of writing in incorrect order is involved, a correction merely by/ scraping, erasing or extending /the letter/ is not /classed as writing/ in incorrect order, as /explained/ above. [Scraping is /done/ with dry /writing/ and erasure with damp /writing/.] /On the other hand,/ as regards /invalidity which derives from/ carving around /to form the letter/, the opposite is the case. Scraping, erasing or extending /the letter/, whenever one does not do an action which completes the body of the letter, is still /regarded as/ carving around /to form the letter/.

An illustration /of this/ is /the case of/ a /letter/ ב which was made with the /proper/ form it /requires/, or a /letter/ ט or כ or /some/ similar /letter/, when a drop of ink fell into the empty space /of the letter/ after /the letter/ was completed validly, causing it to lose its /required/ form. [This may even /apply/ if a child /who is neither especially intelligent nor especially simple/ reads /the letter without correction for what it is meant to be/, whenever we see that /in actual fact the letter/ does not have its /proper/ form.] /Then/ it will be of no avail to scrape away that drop, since whenever /a letter/ becomes invalid the original writing is cancelled and /, therefore, if one corrects it/ now /by scraping/ this will be regarded as carving around /to form the letter/. This is because one will not be doing an action to /complete/ the body of /the letter by the scraping/, but only mere carving /around it/, since he will /in fact/ be carving out the inside of the letter.

Even if /in the case of/ the /letter/ ב one will extend the roof and the bottom subsequently, this will also be of no avail, since /after the scraping/ it will have its /required/ form without this and will /nevertheless/ be invalid.

Moreover, /if one wrote/ a /letter/ ח instead of two ז /letters/, it will be of no avail to scrape away the hump /so that/ two ז

שאין הגג מחובר לירך למעלה ותינוק קורא אותן בצורתן רשאי לתקן אח"כ. ויראה דכ"ז דוקא אם אין ניכר פרידתו להדיא הא אם ניכר להדיא אע"ג דהתינוק קורא כן כיון שאין צורתה עליה הוי כותב שלא כסדרן [והגרע"א בחי' פליג ע"ז וכן בירנו שם בסימן ל"ב להלכה וע"ש שבירנו שבאיזה דבר גם הגרע"א מודה להפמ"ג]. בד"א באלו וכדומה להן שעל ידי שחסר להם איזה דבר לא נדמה על ידי זה תמונתם לאות אחרת אבל יו"ד של צד"י שאין נוגעת להנו"ן שלו ונראה ע"ז כיו"ד נו"ן או חי"ת שברגל שמאלו יש הפרש דק בין הרגל להגג ונראה כה"א אז אפילו אם אירע שהתינוק קראה להאות כצורתה הראויה לה אין מועיל תיקון משום שלא כסדרן. ודע דדעת הפמ"ג בזה דאפילו אם אין ניכר פרידתן להדיא והתינוק קראה ג"כ לאות לא מהני תיקון. ועיין בסימן ל"ב שבירנו שם דעכ"פ בשעת הדחק יש להקל בזה דמהני תיקון.

כתב עוד הפמ"ג כללא דמלתא כל שאין כותב רק מוחק או מושך לא הוי שלא כסדרן המשל לאבותיך מלא וא"ו צריך למחוק הוא"ו ואף דע"ז יהיה התיבה כשני תיבות ימשוך[*] [אך צריך להשגיח שלא תתקלקל צורת הבי"ת בשום פעם, שאם ימשוך תחלה את הגג העליון שלה כפי הצורך הרי תתקלקל צורתה, ואף שאחר כך ימשוך גם את הצד התחתון ותחזור לצורת בי"ת הרי תהא שלא כסדרן, לכן צריך לעשות ההוספה במעט מעט קצת כאן וקצת כאן עד כדי הצורך — קסת הסופר בלשכת הסופר סימן ט', אות ה'] הבי"ת ואע"פ שכותב משיכה לאו כלום עביד דתחלה נמי צורת בי"ת עליה אבל ודאי אם עשה בי"ת מתחלה כצורת נו"ן כפופה ואח"כ משכו לבי"ת הוה שלא כסדרן וכן אפילו אם נכתב האות מתחלה כסדר ואחר כך נתקלקל מחמת איזה דבר שהוא כיון שנתבטל צורת האות כשחוזר אח"כ ומתקן הוה שלא כסדרן דבכל שעה בעינן כסדרן ול"ד למוקף גויל דלא קפיד קרא רק אשעת כתיבה וכמ"ש בפנים באורך. ולפעמים אפילו ע"י כתיבת נקודה אחת יש בזה משום שלא כסדרן כגון שכתב רי"ש במקום דלי"ת וצריך לרבע בדיו כמ"ש בסי' ל"ב בט"ז סט"ז תו מיפסיל משום שלא כסדרן. הכלל כל שאין צורתה עליה וכותב נקודה וע"י נתכשר האות יש בזה משום שלא כסדרן.

עוד דברים אחרים מענין חק תוכות

כל מקום שנאמר וכתב כגון בתפילין ומזוזות ס"ת גט, פסול בו חק תוכות ואפי' אם רק קוצו של יו"ד נגמר ע"י חק תוכות מעכב כיון דבלא הקוץ לא היה מתכשר האות עדיין [וחתימת עדי הגט בחק תוכות עיין ב"ש באה"ע בסימן ק"ל אות כ' במקום עיגון כשר אע"ג דלא כתיב בהו וכתב לכתחלה מקפידין כמו בכל הגט, ע"ש]. והנה ענין חק תוכות צריך הסופר ליזהר בו מאד וענינו ארוכין עיין בל"ב סעיף י"ז י"ח אך נקוט האי כללא בידך כי הפוך הוא משלא כסדרן ששם גורר ומוחק ומושך לא הוי שלא כסדרן וכנ"ל [גורר הוא ביבש ומוחק בלח] ובחק תוכות נהפוך הוא גורר ומוחק ומושך כל שאינו עושה מעשה בגוף האות ומשלימה עדיין הוי חק תוכות. הדמיון בי"ת שנעשית כצורתה או סמ"ך וכ"ף וכדומה שנפל טיפת דיו לתוך החלל אחר שנגמרה בהכשר ונפסד צורתה ע"ז [ואפשר אפי' התינוק קורא אותה כל שאנו רואין שאין צורתה עליה] לא מהני לגרור הטיפה ההיא דכל שנפסלה בטלה כתיבה קמייתא ועתה הוי חק תוכות דהא לא עביד מעשה בגופה כ"א ע"י חקיקה בעלמא שחקק תוך האות ואפילו מושך אח"כ הבי"ת גגה ושוליה ג"כ לא מהני דהרי בלא"ה צורתה עליה ופסולה. וגדולה מזו חי"ת במקום ב' זייני"ן לא מהני שיגרור החרטום וישארו ב' זייני"ן **דמה מעשה עשה בגוף האות אבל אם צריך להשלימה אח"כ כשר ולא מיקרי חק תוכות. כן מבואר באה"ע סימן קכ"ה אות ג' ומגן אברהם בל"ב אות כ"ג, אבל הט"ז שם פקפק ע"ז, ע"ש באות יו"ד ועי"ל בל"ב סעיף י"ז וסי"ח שמבואר שם הכל באר היטב. וגם ביארנו קצת דיני חק תוכות בכל אות ואות בפרט.**

עוד איזה כללים מבעל פמ"ג מדיני הקפת גויל העתקתים בסוף הקונטרס, עי"ש.

צורת אות אל"ף

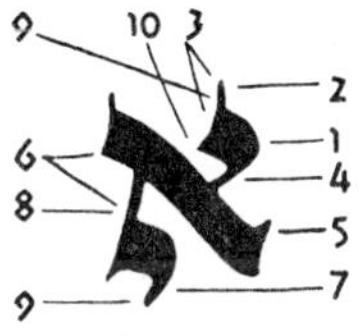

א) [1] תהיה נקודה העליונה כעין יו"ד ב) [2] ועוקץ קטן עליה [3] ויהיה ג) פניה עם העוקץ הפוך קצת כלפי מעלה [4] ויהיה ירך היו"ד דבוק אל גג הגוף ד) באמצע הגג [5] ויהיה סוף הגג של צד ימין ה) לכתחלה עקום למעלה מאחוריו קצת [6] והנקודה שלמטה תהיה רחוקה מן ראש של הגוף ו) כשיעור עובי קולמוס וחצי. עובי קולמוס נק' רוחב הקו היוצא מן הקולמוס כשהוא כותב. [7] * ולנקודה התחתונה יהיה ז) לכתחילה עוקץ קטן למטה לצד ימין [8] מפני שתמונתה כמו יו"ד שתלוי בתג שלה בגוף האל"ף ח) [9] ויהיה עוקץ שמאל של נקודה עליונה היינו התג שעל גבי היו"ד מכוון כנגד עוקץ ימין של נקודה תחתונה עכ"ל ב"י [10] ומשמע מריהטא דלישניה דא"צ עוקץ שמאל ליו"ד העליון שעל האל"ף אך מפמ"ג בסימן ל"ב בא"א באות

/letters/ will remain, as /by doing so/ he will not be doing any act which /completes/ the body of the letters.

However, when it is necessary to complete /the form of the letter with writing/ after /the scraping, the completed letter/ will be valid and /the correction/ will not be classed as carving around /the letter to form it/. This is stated in the *E.Hae.*, Sec. 125, Par. 3 and in the *Magen Avraham* in /Sec./ 32, sub-Par. 23. On the other hand, the *Taz* there questions this /ruling/; see there in sub-Par. 10.

See above in /Sec./ 32, Par. 17 and 18, where all /the details of this requirement/ are explained thoroughly.

/Note that in this booklet/ we have also explained some laws concerning carving around /to form the letter/ for each individual letter separately.

We have recorded some further rules of the author of the *P.Mg.*, /which relate/ to the laws concerning /the need/ to surround /the letter/ with /blank/ parchment, at the end of this booklet; see there.

THE FORM OF THE LETTER א

The upper stroke should be similar to a /letter/ י.[1] It should have a small prickle on it.[2] Its front, with the prickle, should be inverted somewhat /to face/ upwards.[3] The thigh of the י should be stuck to the roof /forming/ the body /of the letter/, in the middle of the roof.[4]

Initially, the end of the roof, on the right side, should be /written/ slanting a little upwards at the back.[5]

The stroke below should be away from the head of the body a length of one and a half /times/ the thickness of a quill.[6] (The thickness of a quill is defined as the breadth of the line that is produced by the quill when it writes.) The lower stroke should have, initially, a small prickle below on the right side,[7] because the symbol for it is like an /inverted letter/ י which is suspended by its crownlet from the body of the א.[8]

/The position of/ the left prickle of the upper stroke, i.e., the crownlet of the י, should correspond with /the position of/ the right prickle of the lower stroke.[9]

This is /all taken from/ the wording of the *B.Y.* It is implied by the flow of his words that a left prickle is not required for the upper י /part/ of the א.[10] However, it is implied by the *P.Mg.* in Sec. 32, in the *E.A.*, sub-Par. 29, that,

כ"ט משמע דלכתחלה צריך להיות גם עוקץ שמאל כמו לשאר יו"ד. אם נגעו יודי"י האל"ף העליון או התחתון בגג האל"ף יותר ממקום דיבוקו דהיינו שאין ניכר הראש אלא קו משוך בשוה וכן יוד"י השי"ן והעי"ן והפ"א והצד"י או ראש השמאלי שבעיי"ן וצד"י שצריך להיות כעין זיי"ן [מס' כתיבה תמה ופשוט] אם נגעו בגוף האות יותר ממקום דיבוקם פסול רק אם לא כתב עדיין יותר בתו"מ מותר להעבות ולהרחיב הראשים כדי שיהא ניכר הראש [פמ"ג בסי' ל"ב במ"ז סק"כ] ואופן התקנה ע"י גרירה עיין בשו"ע סימן ל"ב סוף סי"ח. אם לא היה הנקודה העליונה או שלמטה דבוק אל הגג פסול ועיין לעיל בסימן ל"ב סכ"ה.

צורת אות בי"ת

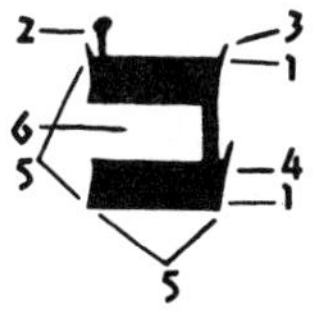

צריך מאד ליזהר א) בריבועה שלא תהא נראית ככ"ף ואם נראית ככ"ף פסולה ואם ספק ב) אזי מראין לתינוק. [1] וצריכה להיות מרובעת בימין בין ג) למעלה בין למטה ואם למעלה עגולה ולמטה מרובעת צ"ע בזה ד) * ואין להקל ה) [2] וצריך לכתחלה שיהא לה בראשה מצד שמאל על פניה תג קטן תמונתו כמו מקל [3] ועוקץ קטן למעלה בצד ימין נוטה לצד האל"ף [כדאמרינן בירושלמי דחגיגה מפני מה יש לב' שני עוקצים אחד למעלה ואחד לאחוריו אומרים לבי"ת מי בראך מראה להם בעוקצו שלמעלה ומה שמו מראה להם בעוקצו שמאחוריה לצד האל"ף ר"ל אחד

הי"א סוף פי"ב

שמו] [4] גם יהיה לה ו) עקב עב למטה כי תמונתה כמו דלי"ת תוך גרון של וא"ו ע"כ צריך להיות לה זוית למעלה שיהיה כדלי"ת ועקב טוב למטה שיהיה במקום ראשה של וא"ו [5] וטוב ז) שאורך ורוחב הבי"ת יהיה כג' קולמוסים [6] ורוחב חללה כעובי קולמוס. ואם קיצר הבי"ת עד שנראה כנו"ן כפופה לתינוק דלא חכים ולא טיפש נראה דיש להחמיר בזה. עיין לקמן בדין אות נו"ן כפופה ובב"י בא"ב שני אות וא"ו. אח"כ מצאתי כן בהדיא בפמ"ג בפתיחה ע"ש שכ' דבתו"מ לא מהני בזה תיקון להמשיכו כמו בי"ת משום שלא כסדרן.

צורת אות גימ"ל

[1] תהיה גופה א) כמו זיי"ן ב) לכתחילה וכן כל ראשי שמאל שבאותיות שעטנ"ז ג"ץ דומה לזיי"ן [2] ויהי' ראשה עב [3] * ורגל ימין ג) דק [4] ויורד מעט למטה יותר מירך שמאל [5] ולא יעשה ירך זה השמאל בשפוע הרבה אלא מעט * וגם ד) לא יהיה עקום אלא ימשוך בשוה ויגביהנו קצת כנגד הדלי"ת [6] והירך שמאל יהיה משוך קצת עב אל הזיי"ן שבצדה ולא בדקות כי תמונתה שתהיה נראית כמין נו"ן כפופה והירך יהיה נמוך כדי להסמיך *[אות] אצל ראשו [7] וג' תגין על ראשה ה) אם נדבק הירך ברגל יגרור הירך ודי בכך כמו שמבואר בסימן ל"ב סי"ח לענין גרירת החרטום ודיני התגין נתבאר בסוף סימן זה במ"ב עי"ש.

* המו"ל

שער הציון

א א) ב"י כל הענין. ב) ג) כל זה לכתחילה. ד) ג"ז לכתחילה אבל עיקר הדביקה הוא לעיכובא. ה) ק"ה בשם נוב"י. ו) לכתחילה. ז) הוא פשוט דרק כעין יו"ד בעינן. ח) לכתחילה. ב א) רא"ש ועיין שם במעיו"ט. ב) ג"ז שם. ג) פמ"ג בדיני צורת אותיות וכן מבואר להדיא באגור ובב"ש וקורא לסופר שאינו עושה כן בשם בור, אך אעפ"כ אין מבואר שם להדיא דהוא לעיכובא עי"ש. ד) פמ"ג ולכאורה ממה שכתב בב"י מרובעת מפני הסוד משמע דהוא רק לכתחילה ויש לדחות דהכוונה דטוב לכתחלה שיהיה האורך והרוחב בשוה כמו דמשמע מד"מ. ה) ב"י. ו) ב"י והיינו לכתחילה כי כן כתב בחתם סופר סימן רס"ה בי"ת בלי עקב אין לפסול כיון שאינה עגולה מאחוריה כעין כ"ף רק כעין דלי"ת ומשמע מזה דכשהיא עגולה ממש למטה יש לפסול. ועיין ברבינו ירוחם דמשמע ג"כ דהעיקר תלוי בלמטה. ז) ד"מ. ג א) כולו בב"י. ב) ממה שכתב הפמ"ג באות טי"ת דאם לא היה ראש שמאלי כזיי"ן כשר וה"ה הכא ועיין לקמן בסוף אות טי"ת ולעיל בסימן זה במ"ב ס"ק ט"ו עי"ש. ג) בדברי הגר"ז משמע דהוא

ביאור הלכה

א * ולנקודה התחתונה תהיה לכתחלה וכו'. וידע המעיין בקונטרס הזה דבכמה מקומות לא ביארתי בפנים וגם בשער הציון אם הדין הוא רק לכתחילה או דיעבד והיא אחת משלשה סיבות או דהוא פשוט דהוא לכתחילה או דיעבד או דיש בזה פרטים המתחלפים דיש בזה לפעמים לכתחילה ולפעמים דיעבד כגון מה שכתוב דצריך האות לעשות כה וכה כדי שיהיה יוכל להסמיך אות אצלו דפשוט דאם לא עשה כן ועי"ז נעשה הפסק בתיבה שנראה כשני תיבות דפסול ואם זה האות הוא בסוף תיבה כשר בדיעבד ועוד הרבה כיוצא בזה ולא רציתי להאריך ע"כ סתמתי הדבר או דהיה אצלי ג"כ ספק והנחתי הדבר כמות שהוא ע"כ אל ימהר האדם להקל בדבר או להחמיר ולהפסיד לאחרים אם לא שימצא ראיה ברורה.

ב * ואין להקל. כ"כ פמ"ג. אמנם מדברי רי"ו [הבאתיו באות כ"ף] מוכח דהעיקר תלוי בלמטה וע"כ נראה דאם התינוק קוראה כהלכה אפשר דיש עכ"פ להקל להוסיף דיו לתקנה בתו"מ ואין בזה משום שלא כסדרן.

ג * ורגל ימין דק. הנה מדברי הגר"ז משמע דהוא רק לכתחילה ולפי מה שכ' בב"י באות זה הטעם לזה עי"ש לכאורה הוא לעיכובא, דהא הברייתא סיימה על הכל דיגנז עי"ש בשבת בגמרא ואולי אפשר דבזה לבד שירך ימין יורד למטה יותר מירך שמאל יש היכר בין הגימ"ל לצדי"ק דלא כב"ש ולפ"ז יורד

initially, there should also be a left prickle /on it/, as /is required/ for other י /symbols/.

If the upper or lower י /part/ touches the roof of the א more than at the point where it should be stuck /to it/, so that the head /of the י/ is not distinguishable, but /the entire stroke consists of/ a line drawn of equal /width, the letter is invalid/. /This applies/ likewise /in the case of/ the י /parts/ of /the letters/ ש, ע, פ and צ or /in the case/ of the left head of the /letters/ ע or צ, which must be like /the letter/ ז. If they touch the body of the letter more than at the point where they should be stuck /to it, the letter/ is invalid. [/This is taken/ from the work *Kesivah Tamah.* It is /also/ self-understood.] Where *tefilin* /passages/ or mezuzos are involved, it is only permitted to thicken and widen the head to make the head distinguishable if one has not yet written /anything/ more /after the faulty letter/. [*P.Mg.*, in Sec. 32, in the *M.Z.*, sub-Par. 20.] /As to/ the method of correction by scraping away, see the Sh.A., Sec. 32, at the end of Par. 18.

If the upper or lower stroke is not stuck to the roof /of the letter א, the letter/ is invalid. See above in Sec. 32, Par. 25.

THE FORM OF THE LETTER ב

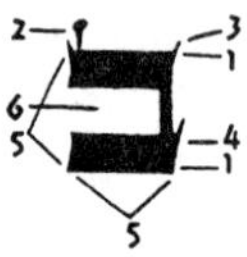

One must be very careful to square the letter ב, so that it does not appear like the /letter/ כ. If it /does/ appear like a כ it is invalid. If this is questionable, it should then be shown to a child /who is neither especially intelligent nor especially simple and if he reads it as a ב it is valid/.

/The letter/ must be square on the right, both above and below.[1] If it is rounded above and square below, study is required /to determine whether or not it is valid/ and one should not be lenient.[3*]

Initially, /the letter/ must have on top on the left side, on its front, a small crownlet, with a symbol which resembles a staff,[2] and /it should have/ a small prickle above on the right side inclined toward[3] the /letter/ א /which precedes it in the alphabet/. [This conforms with what is stated in the /*Talmud*/ *Yerushalmi, Chagigah* /, Chapter 2, Halachah 1/: Why does the ב have two prickles, one /pointing/ above and one /pointing/ to the back? /It is because when people/ say to the ב, "Who created you?", he indicates to them /Who it was/ with his prickle /pointing/ to the back toward the ב further,/ "What is His Name?", he indicates /the answer/ to them with his prickle /pointing/ to the back towards the /letter/ א /, which precedes it in the alphabet and represents the number one/, as if saying, "His Name is One".]

/The letter ב/ must also have a thick heel below.[4] This is because /the letter/ has a symbol which resembles a /letter/ ד inside the throat of a /letter/ ו. In view of this it must have a corner above, so that /that part of the letter/ should be like a ד, and a good heel below to /serve/ instead of the head of a ו.

It is desirable that the length and breadth of the ב should /each/ be approximately /the thickness of/ three[4*] quills[5] and the breadth of its space /inside/ approximately the thickness of a quill.[6]

If one shortened the ב to the extent that it appears like a bent-over /letter/ נ to a child

3* However, the letter may be corrected even in a *tefilin* passage or mezuzah, although other letters have been written after it, provided a child who is neither especially intelligent nor especially simple reads it as a ב. (Beyur Halachah)

4* See the description of the letter א.

כ"ט משמע דלכתחלה צריך להיות גם עוקץ שמאל כמו לשאר יו"ד. אם נגעו יוד"י האל"ף העליון או התחתון בגג האל"ף יותר ממקום דיבוקו דהיינו שאין ניכר הראש אלא קו משוך בשוה וכן יוד"י השי"ן והעי"ן והפ"א והצד"י או ראש השמאלי שבעיי"ן וצד"י שצריך להיות כעין זיי"ן [מס' כתיבה תמה ופשוט] אם נגעו בגוף האות יותר ממקום דיבוקם פסול רק אם לא כתב עדיין יותר בתו"מ מותר להעבות ולהרחיב הראשים כדי שיהא ניכר הראש [פמ"ג בסי' ל"ב במ"ז סק"כ] ואופן התקנה ע"י גרירה עיין בשו"ע סימן ל"ב סוף סי"ח. אם לא היה הנקודה העליונה או שלמטה דבוק אל הגג פסול ועיין לעיל בסימן ל"ב סכ"ה.

צורת אות בי"ת

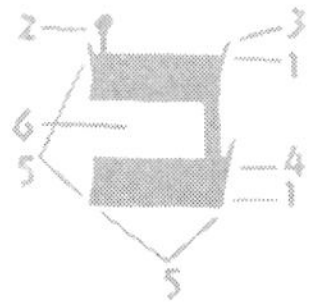

צריך מאד ליזהר א) בריבועה שלא תהא נראית ככ"ף ואם נראית ככ"ף פסולה ואם ספק ב) אזי מראין לתינוק. [1] וצריכה להיות מרובעת בימין בין ג) למעלה בין למטה ואם למעלה עגולה ולמטה מרובעת צ"ע בזה ד) * ואין להקל ה) [2] וצריך לכתחלה שיהא לה בראשה מצד שמאל על פניה תג קטן תמונתו כמו מקל [3] ועוקץ קטן למעלה בצד ימין נוטה לצד האל"ף [כדאמרינן בירושלמי דחגיגה מפני מה יש לב' שני עוקצים אחד למעלה ואחד לאחוריו אומרים לבי"ת מי בראך מראה להם בעוקצו שלמעלה ומה שמו מראה להם בעוקצו שמאחוריה לצד האל"ף ר"ל אחד שמו] [4] גם יהיה לה ו) עקב עב למטה כי תמונתה כמו דלי"ת תוך גרון של וא"ו ע"כ צריך להיות לה זוית למעלה שיהיה כדלי"ת ועקב טוב למטה שיהיה במקום ראשה של וא"ו [5] וטוב ז) שאורך ורוחב הבי"ת יהיה כג' קולמוסים [6] ורוחב חללה כעובי קולמוס. ואם קיצר הבי"ת עד שנראה כנו"ן כפופה לתינוק **דלא חכים ולא טיפש נראה דיש להחמיר בזה. עיין לקמן בדין אות נו"ן כפופה ובב"י בא"ב שני אות וא"ו. אח"כ מצאתי כן בהדיא בפמ"ג בפתיחה ע"ש שכ' דבתו"מ לא מהני בזה תיקון להמשיכו כמו בי"ת משום שלא כסדרן.**

צורת אות גימ"ל

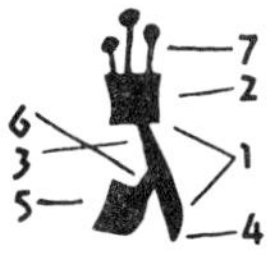

[1] תהיה גופה א) כמו זיי"ן ב) לכתחילה וכן כל ראשי שמאל שבאותיות שעטנ"ז ג"ץ דומה לזיי"ן [2] ויהי' ראשה עב [3] * ורגל ימין ג) דק [4] ויורד מעט למטה יותר מירך שמאל [5] ולא יעשה ירך זה השמאל בשפוע הרבה אלא מעט * וגם ד) לא יהיה עקום אלא ימשוך בשוה ויגביהנו קצת כנגד הדלי"ת [6] והירך שמאל יהיה משוך קצת עב אל הזיי"ן שבצדה ולא בדקות כי תמונתה שתהיה נראית כמין נו"ן כפופה והירך יהיה נמוך כדי להסמיך *[אות] אצל ראשו [7] וג' תגין על ראשה ה) אם נדבק הירך בהרגל יגרור הירך ודי בכך כמו שמבואר בסימן ל"ב סי"ח לענין גרירת החרטום ודיני התגין נתבאר בסוף סימן זה במ"ב עי"ש.

* המר"ל

שער הציון

א א) ב"י כל הענין. ב) ג) כל זה לכתחילה. ד) ג"ז לכתחילה אבל עיקר הדביקה הוא לעיכובא. ה) ק"ה בשם נוב"י. ו) לכתחילה. ז) הוא פשוט דרק כעין יו"ד בעינן. ח) לכתחילה. **ב** א) רא"ש ועיין שם במעיו"ט. ב) ג"ז שם. ג) פמ"ג בדיני צורת אותיות וכן מבואר להדיא באגור ובב"ש וקורא לסופר שאינו עושה כן בשם בור, אך אעפ"כ אין מבואר שם להדיא דהוא לעיכובא עי"ש. ד) פמ"ג ולכאורה ממה שכתב בב"י מרובעת מפני הסוד משמע דהוא רק לכתחילה ויש לדחות דהכוונה דטוב לכתחלה שיהיה האורך והרוחב בשוה כמו דמשמע מד"מ. ה) ב"י. ו) ב"י והיינו לכתחילה כי כן כתב בחתם סופר סימן רס"ה בי"ת בלי עקב אין לפסול כיון שאינה עגולה מאחוריה כעין כ"ף רק כעין דלי"ת ומשמע מזה דכשהיא עגולה ממש למטה יש לפסול. ועיין ברבינו ירוחם דמשמע ג"כ דהעיקר תלוי בלמטה. ז) ד"מ. **ג** א) כולו בב"י. ב) ממה שכתב הפמ"ג באות טי"ת דאם לא היה ראש שמאלי כזיי"ן כשר וה"ה הכא ועיין לקמן בסוף אות טי"ת ולעיל בסימן זה במ"ב ס"ק ט"ו עי"ש. ג) בדברי הגר"ז משמע דהוא

ביאור הלכה

א * **ולנקודה** התחתונה תהיה לכתחלה וכו'. וידע המעיין בקונטרס הזה דבכמה מקומות לא ביארתי בפנים וגם בשער הציון אם הדין הוא רק לכתחילה או דיעבד והיא אחת משלשה סיבות או דהוא פשוט דהוא לכתחילה או דיעבד או דיש בזה פרטים המתחלפים דיש בזה לפעמים לכתחילה ולפעמים דיעבד כגון מה שכתוב דצריך האות לעשות כה וכה כדי שיהיה יוכל להסמיך **אות אצלו דפשוט דאם לא עשה כן ועי"ז** נעשה הפסק בתיבה שנראה כשני תיבות דפסול ואם זה האות הוא בסוף תיבה כשר בדיעבד ועוד הרבה כיוצא בזה ולא רציתי להאריך ע"כ סתמתי הדבר או דהיה אצלי ג"כ ספק והנחתי הדבר כמות שהוא ע"כ אל ימהר האדם להקל בדבר או להחמיר ולהפסיד לאחרים אם לא שימצא ראיה ברורה.

ב * **ואין** להקל. כ"כ פמ"ג. אמנם מדברי רי"ו [הבאתיו באות כ"ף] מוכח דהעיקר תלוי בלמטה וע"כ נראה דאם התינוק קוראה כהלכה אפשר דיש עכ"פ להקל להוסיף דיו לתקנה בתו"מ ואין בזה משום שלא כסדרן.

ג * **ורגל** ימין דק. הנה מדברי הגר"ז משמע דהוא רק לכתחילה ולפי מה שכ' בב"י באות זה הטעם לזה עי"ש לכאורה הוא לעיכובא, דהא הברייתא סיימה על הכל דיגנז עי"ש בשבת בגמרא ואולי אפשר דבזה לבד שירך ימין יורד למטה יותר מירך שמאל יש היכר בין הגימ"ל לצדי"ק דלא כב"ש ולפ"ז יורד

who is neither /especially/ intelligent nor /especially/ simple, it appears that one should be stringent about this /and rule the letter to be invalid/. See below in the laws concerning the bent-over letter נ and in the *B.Y.*, in the second /description of the/ alphabet, letter ו. I afterwards discovered this /stated/ explicitly by the *P.Mg.*, in his introduction. See there, that he writes that in the case of *tefilin* /passages/ and mezuzos correction /of this fault/ by drawing out /the letter until it is/ like the /letter/ ב is of no avail, because of /the fact that in view of the correction the letter will be written/ in incorrect order.

THE FORM OF THE LETTER ג

Initially, the body of the letter ג should be like a /letter/ ז.[1] Likewise, in the case of all the letters /belonging to the group/ שעטנז גץ, the head on the left should resemble a ז.

The head /of the letter/ should be thick.[2]

The right leg should be thin[3] and it should descend a little lower than the left thigh.[4]

One should not make this left thigh very inclined, but only slightly[5] /inclined/. It should also not be slanted, but should be drawn evenly and should be raised somewhat opposite the /letter/ ד /which follows it in the alphabet/. The left thigh should be drawn slightly thickly to the ז /part of the letter/ at its side and not thinly.[6] This is because the symbol /of the letter ג requires it/ to appear like a kind of bent-over נ. The thigh should be low, so that /one will be able/ to put /another letter/ close to the head of /the ג/.

/One should make/ three crownlets on the head[7] /of the letter/.

If the thigh became stuck to the leg /with its full width/, one should scrape away the thigh /and rewrite it/. This /correction/ is adequate, as stated in Sec. 32, Par. 18 with respect to scraping away the nose /of the open letter מ/.

The laws concerning the crownlets are explained at the end of this section /, i.e., Sec. 36,/ in the Mishnah Berurah; see there.

צורת אות דלי"ת

[1] צריך א) שיהא גגה ארוך [2] ורגלה קצרה שאם תהא רגלה ארוכה מגגה תדמה לכ"ף פשוטה ותפסל כשלא יקראנה התינוק ד' ב) [3] * ולכתחלה צריך שתהא הרגל פשוטה בשיפוע קצת לצד ימין ג) [4] ושיהא לה תג קטן בראש גגה מצד שמאל. [5] וצריך מאד ליזהר ד) בריבועה שלא תהא נראית כרי"ש ותפסל ע"י קריאת התינוק [6] ולכתחלה אין די בזה לבד שיהא לה זוית חדה מלאחוריה אלא גם יהא לה שם ה) עקב טוב כי תמונתה הוא כמו ב' ווי"ן סגורים והעקב הוא כנגד ראש הוי"ו האחד והעוקץ שעל פניה הוא כנגד ראש וי"ו השנייה. אם ו) רגל הדלי"ת אין בו רק כמלא יו"ד כשר ועיין בסוף אות תי"ו. אם כתב ה"א במקום דלי"ת אין תקנה לגרור הרגל ולהניח הדלי"ת מאחר שנפסל ודומה לצורת ה"א לא עביד מידי והוי חק תוכות וגם למשוך הגג נמי לא מהני דכל שלא נפסל צורת האות הוי חק תוכות רק צריך לגרור הגג עד שיהא כצורת וי"ו ומשלימה או שיגרור גם הרגל ימין כולו ולא ישאיר בו אפילו כמלא יו"ד ואח"כ ישלימנו [פמ"ג].

צורת אות ה"א

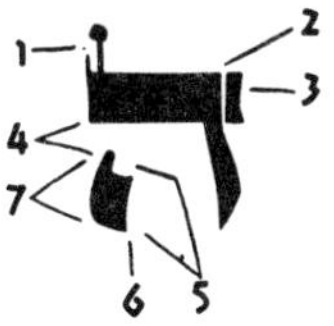

[1] צריך לעשות לה א) לכתחלה תג קטן למעלה מצד שמאל [2] ובאחוריה יזהר ב) לכתחלה שתהי' מרובעת כדלי"ת ולא עגולה כרי"ש [3] וא"צ לעשות לה עקב כמו בד' רק ג) שתהיה אות חדה. [1] והנקודה שבתוכה לא תהיה סמוכה לגגה אלא יהא ביניהם חלק כ"כ בכדי ד) שאדם בינוני יכירנו היטיב מעל ס"ת שע"ג הבימה כשקורא בו. ולא ירחיקה מגגה יותר מעובי הגג. ואם נגע בגגה אפילו נגיעה דקה כחוט השערה פסולה אע"פ שהתינוק יודע שהוא ה"א כדלעיל בסימן ל"ב סי"ח וכ"ה עי"ש. ולא תהיה הנקודה נגד אמצע הגג אלא נגד סופה בצד שמאל ואם עשה באמצע פסולה וצריך לתקנה דהיינו לגררה ולהעמידה בסופה ואם כתב התיבות שאח"ז ואין יכול לתקן משום שלא כסדרן ה) יגרור הגג שיהא שוה לרגל ובמקום שגם תיקון זה אינו יכול לעשות כגון שהה"א באמצע התיבה ואם יגרור הגג יהיה כשתי תיבות אזי יש להכשיר ו) בלא תיקון [כי יש הרבה מהראשונים שסוברים שתמונת ה"א כך. עיין בחידושי הרשב"א על שבת ק"ג ובחידושי הריטב"א שם וברשב"א הנדפס מחדש על מנחות דף כ"ט ובר"ן בפ' הבונה ובחידושי מאירי ובחידושי הר"ן הנדפס מחדש על שבת פ' הבונה, שם מוכח להדיא מדעתם שתמונת הה"א כך]. ועתה נבאר איכות הנקודה. [5] הנקודה תהיה לכתחלה דקה למעלה ועבה קצת למטה כעין יו"ד [6] ותהיה לכתחלה עקומה קצת למטה. ולצד ימין ולא לצד שמאל פן תדמה לתי"ו [7] ואורך הנקודה לא יפחות ג"כ מאורך יו"ד עם עוקץ התחתון שלה ולעיכובא הוא אפי' בדיעבד וכדלעיל בסי' ל"ב סט"ו בהג"ה ע"ש במ"ב וצריך להזהיר הסופרים שנכשלין בזה מאד ונ"ל דעכ"פ תיקון מהני בזה אפילו בתו"מ אם התינוק קוראו לה"א ואין בזה משום שלא כסדרן דומיא דמה שהקיל הפמ"ג לתקן כ"ף פשוטה אם עשאו מרובע להוסיף דיו עליו עי"ש. הפמ"ג בסימן ל"ב ס"ק ל"ג מסתפק אם צריך להיות הנקודה

שער הציון

ד א) ב"י. ב) ב"י ועיין בבה"ל. ג) ב"י. ד) רא"ש בהלכות ס"ת ועיין במעיו"ט שם. ה) ב"י. ו) פמ"ג. **ה** א) כן משמע מרמ"א בהג"ה בתחילת סי' ל"ו. ב) כי רוב הפוסקים סוברים כרש"י וגם הטור לא כתב אלא וטוב וכו' ויותר נראה דאפילו לר"ת הוא רק לכתחילה. אח"כ מצאתי בשם ספר פחד יצחק שגם הוא כתב להקל. ג) כן משמע בב"י ולא תקשה מלשון הטור כמש"כ במעיו"ט בהלכות רק לכתחילה ועיין בבה"ל. ד) ולענין דיעבד עיין בבה"ל. ה) פמ"ג באות גימ"ל בצורת האותיות.

ביאור הלכה

למטה יותר מירך שמאל הוא לעיכובא ולכן לא הזכיר הגר"ז שם לכתחילה ואעפ"כ לדינא הכל צ"ע, דלפי פירוש הרא"ש שם בהלכות ס"ת על הברייתא זו עי"ש [וע"ש ברש"י על הברייתא זו] אין שום ראיה דצריך לדקדק בזה, אך לכתחילה בודאי צריך ליזהר בזה מפני אידך רבוותא כמו שכתב הב"י כעין זה באות אל"ף.

* **ג** וגם לא יהיה עקום. ובדיעבד אם היה עקום צ"ע בזה. עיין בב"י הטעם ממש"כ בגמרא מ"ט פשטא כרעא דגימ"ל לגבי דלי"ת דכה"ג מ"ש בגמרא שם מ"ט פשטא כרעא דדלי"ת לגבי גימ"ל הוא רק לכתחילה [וכמו שיתבאר בביאור הלכה לקמן] ועכ"פ תיקון מהני בזה אפילו בתו"מ וכן אם ירך השמאל שוה לרגל הימין דומיא דמה שהקיל הפמ"ג באות כ' פשוטה שעשאו מרובע ע"ש.

* **ד** ולכתהילה צריך שתהא הרגל פשוטה וכו'. מקור לזה בב"י מהא דשבת ק"ד מ"ט פשטא כרעא דדלי"ת לגבי גימ"ל וכו' ונ"ל דזה רק לכתחילה מהא דאמרינן שם הגיה אות אחת חייב כגון דנטלו לתגא דדלי"ת ועשאו רי"ש ובעירובין י"ג ע"א דילמא יתיב זבוב וכו' עי"ש. ואולי יש לדחות דרי"ש כשר בדיעבד אף אם היה רגלו פשוטה וא"כ ליכא ראיה. ומ"מ לדינא נראה דאין להחמיר בדיעבד מהנ"ל בסימן ל"ב סט"ז בט"ז עי"ש ובקיצור כללי שלא כסדרן שהעתקתי זה מפמ"ג עי"ש.

THE FORM OF THE LETTER ד

The roof of the letter ד is required to be long[1] and its leg /is required to be/ short.[2] If the leg is /made/ longer than its roof, /the letter/ will resemble a simple /elongated letter/ ך and will be invalid if a child /who is neither especially intelligent nor especially simple/ will not read it for the /letter/ ד.

Initially, the leg must be made /as a/ simple /line/, slightly inclined toward the right,[3] and /the letter/ should have a small crownlet at the top of its roof on the left side.[4]

One must be very careful that /the letter/ is squared,[5] so that it will not appear like a /letter/ ר and become invalid through a child /who is neither especially intelligent nor especially simple/ reading /it incorrectly/. Initially, it is insufficient /to rely/ solely on /the roof/ having a sharp angle at the back, but it should also have there a good heel[6] /protruding beyond the leg/. This is because /the letter's/ symbol resembles /a combination of/ two locked ו /letters/. The heel corresponds with the head of one ו and the prickle on the front of /the roof/ corresponds with the head of the second ו.

If the leg of the ד only has the equivalent /length/ of /the letter/ י it is /also/ valid. See /what we have written/ at the end /of the description of the form/ of the letter ח.

If one wrote /a letter/ ה instead of /the letter/ ד, this cannot be remedied by scraping away the /left/ leg and /thus/ leaving a ד. /This is because/ now that /the letter/ became invalid /through the additional leg/ and resembles the form of /the letter/ ה, /this scraping/ will not do anything /to the body of the letter/, but constitutes carving around /to form the letter/. Even if one will /also/ draw out the roof /of the letter subsequently, the scraping/ will also be of no avail. /This is/ because whenever the form of the letter /, following the scraping,/ is not invalid /without the addition, the scraping continues to/ be /classed as/ carving around /to from the letter despite the addition/. /In order to correct the letter validly/ one must scrape off the roof /as well/, until /the resulting form/ is like the form of a /letter/ ו, and /then/ complete /the writing of the letter ד/. Alternatively, one should scrape away the entire right leg as well, without leaving of it even /a length/ which is equivalent /to the length/ of /the letter/ י, and after that he may complete /the ד/. [*P.Mg.*]

THE FORM OF THE LETTER ה

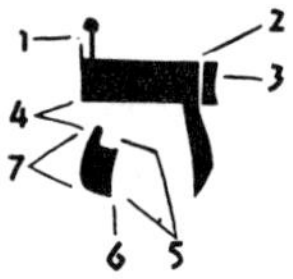

Initially, one should make a small crownlet above on the left side[1] of the letter ה.

One should be careful initially that /the roof/ is square at the back,[2] like /the letter/ ד, and not rounded like /the letter/ ר. It is unnecessary to make a /protruding/ heel[3] for /this letter/, as /is required/ for the /letter/ ד, but /one must/ only /take care/ that the letter should be sharp /at the back of the roof/.

The stroke inside /the letter/ should not be close to the roof[4] of /the letter/, but there should be /a large/ enough blank /space/ between them so that an average person will recognize /the gap/ well from a Torah Scroll

צורת אות דלי"ת

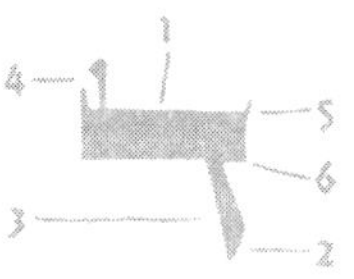

[1] צריך א) שיהא גגה ארוך [2] ורגלה קצרה שאם תהא רגלה ארוכה מגגה תדמה לכ"ף פשוטה ותפסל כשלא יקראנה התינוק ד' ב) [3] * ולכתחלה צריך שתהא הרגל פשוטה בשיפוע קצת לצד ימין ג) [4] ושיהא לה תג קטן בראש גגה מצד שמאל. [5] וצריך מאד ליזהר ד) בריבועה שלא תהא נראית כרי"ש ותפסל ע"י קריאת התינוק [6] ולכתחלה אין די בזה לבד שיהא לה זוית חדה מלאחוריה אלא גם יהא לה שם ה) עקב טוב כי תמונתה הוא כמו ב' ווי"ן סגורים והעקב הוא כנגד ראש הוי"ו האחד והעוקץ שעל פניה הוא כנגד ראש וי"ו השנייה. אם ו) רגל הדלי"ת אין בו רק כמלא יו"ד כשר ועיין בסוף אות תי"ו. אם כתב ה"א במקום דלי"ת אין תקנה לגרור הרגל ולהניח הדלי"ת מאחר שנפסל ודומה לצורת ה"א לא עביד מידי והוי חק תוכות וגם למשוך הגג נמי לא מהני דכל שלא נפסל צורת האות הוי חק תוכות רק צריך לגרור הגג עד שיהא כצורת וי"ו ומשלימה או שיגרור גם הרגל ימין כולו ולא ישאיר בו אפילו כמלא יו"ד ואח"כ ישלימנו [פמ"ג].

צורת אות ה"א

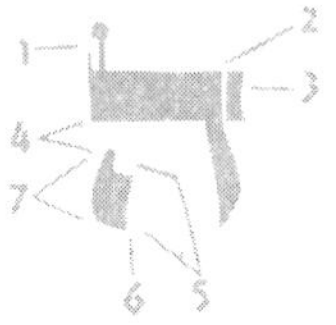

[1] צריך לעשות לה א) לכתחלה תג קטן למעלה מצד שמאל [2] ובאחוריה יזהר ב) לכתחלה שתהי' מרובעת כדלי"ת ולא עגולה כרי"ש [3] וא"צ לעשות לה עקב כמו בד' רק ג) שתהיה אות חדה. [4] והנקודה שבתוכה לא תהיה סמוכה לגגה אלא יהא ביניהם חלק כ"כ בכדי ד) שאדם בינוני יכירנו היטיב מעל ס"ת **שע"ג הבימה כשקורא בו. ולא ירחיקה מגגה יותר מעובי הגג. ואם נגע בגגה אפילו נגיעה דקה כחוט השערה פסולה אע"פ שהתינוק יודע שהוא ה"א כדלעיל בסימן ל"ב סי"ח וכ"ה עי"ש. ולא תהיה הנקודה נגד אמצע הגג אלא נגד סופה בצד שמאל ואם עשה באמצע פסולה וצריך לתקנה דהיינו לגררה ולהעמידה בסופה ואם כתב התיבות שאח"ז ואין יכול לתקן משום שלא כסדרן ה) יגרור הגג שיהא שוה לרגל ובמקום שגם תיקון זה אינו יכול לעשות כגון שהה"א באמצע התיבה ואם יגרור הגג יהיה כשתי תיבות אזי יש להכשיר ו) בלא תיקון [כי יש הרבה מהראשונים שסוברים שתמונת ה"א כך. עיין בחידושי הרשב"א על שבת ק"ג ובחידושי הריטב"א שם וברשב"א הנדפס מחדש על מנחות דף כ"ט ובר"ן בפ' הבונה ובחידושי מאירי ובחידושי הר"ן הנדפס מחדש על שבת פ' הבונה, שם מוכח להדיא מדעתם שתמונת הה"א כך]. ועתה נבאר איכות הנקודה. [5] הנקודה תהיה לכתחלה דקה למעלה ועבה קצת למטה כעין יו"ד [6] ותהיה לכתחלה עקומה קצת למטה. ולצד ימין ולא לצד שמאל פן תדמה לתי"ו [7] ואורך הנקודה לא יפחות ג"כ מאורך יו"ד עם עוקץ התחתון שלה ולעיכובא הוא אפי' בדיעבד וכדלעיל בסי' ל"ב סט"ו בהג"ה ע"ש במ"ב וצריך להזהיר הסופרים שנכשלין בזה מאד ונ"ל דעכ"פ תיקון מהני בזה אפילו בתו"מ אם התינוק קוראו לה"א ואין בזה משום שלא כסדרן דומיא דמה שהקיל הפמ"ג לתקן כ"ף פשוטה אם עשאו מרובע להוסיף דיו עליו עי"ש. הפמ"ג בסימן ל"ב ס"ק ל"ג מסתפק אם צריך להיות הנקודה**

שער הציון

רק לכתחילה ועיין בבה"ל. ד) ולענין דיעבד עיין בבה"ל. ה) פמ"ג באות גימ"ל בצורת האותיות. **ד** א) ב"י. ב) ב"י ועיין בבה"ל. ג) ב"י. ד) רא"ש בהלכות ס"ת ועיין במעיו"ט שם. ה) ב"י. ו) פמ"ג. **ה** א) כן משמע מרמ"א בהג"ה בתחילת סי' ל"ו. ב) כי רוב הפוסקים סוברים כרש"י וגם הטור לא כתב אלא וטוב וכו' ויותר נראה דאפילו לר"ת הוא רק לכתחילה. אח"כ מצאתי בשם ספר פחד יצחק שגם הוא כתב להקל. ג) כן משמע בב"י ולא תקשה מלשון הטור כמש"כ במעיו"ט בהלכות

ביאור הלכה

למטה יותר מירך שמאל הוא לעיכובא ולכן לא הזכיר הגר"ז שם לכתחילה ואעפ"כ לדינא הכל צ"ע, דלפי פירוש הרא"ש שם בהלכות ס"ת על הברייתא זו עי"ש [וע"ש ברש"י על הברייתא זו] אין שום ראיה דצריך לדקדק בזה, אך לכתחילה בודאי צריך ליזהר בזה מפני אידך רבוותא כמו שכתב הב"י כעין זה באות אל"ף.

ג * **וגם** לא יהיה עקום. ובדיעבד אם היה עקום צ"ע בזה. עיין בב"י הטעם ממש"כ בגמרא מ"ט פשטא כרעא דגימ"ל לגבי דלי"ת דכה"ג מ"ש בגמרא שם מ"ט פשטא כרעא דדלי"ת לגבי גימ"ל הוא רק לכתחילה [וכמו שיתבאר בביאור הלכה לקמן] ועכ"פ תיקון מהני בזה אפילו בתו"מ וכן אם ירך השמאל שוה לרגל הימין דומיא דמה שהקיל הפמ"ג באות כ' פשוטה שעשאו מרובע ע"ש.

ד * **ולכתהילה** צריך שתהא הרגל פשוטה וכו'. מקור לזה בב"י מהא דשבת ק"ד מ"ט פשטא כרעא דדלי"ת לגבי גימ"ל וכו' ונ"ל דזה רק לכהחילה מהא דאמרינן שם הגיה אות אחת חייב כגון דנטלו לתגא דדלי"ת ועשאו רי"ש ובעירובין י"ג ע"א דילמא יתיב זבוב וכו' עי"ש. ואולי יש לדחות דרי"ש כשר בדיעבד אף אם היה רגלו פשוטה וא"כ ליכא ראיה. ומ"מ לדינא נראה דאין להחמיר בדיעבד מהנ"ל בסימן ל"ב סט"ז בט"ז עי"ש ובקיצור כללי שלא כסדרן שהעתקתי זה מפמ"ג עי"ש.

on the bimah when he reads from /the Scroll/. /On the other hand,/ one should not make /the stroke/ further away from the roof of /the letter/ than the thickness of the roof. If /the stroke/ touches the roof, even /if it is/ a fine touch like a hairsbreadth, /the letter/ is invalid, even if a child /who is neither especially intelligent nor especially simple/ knows that it is a ה, as /ruled/ above in Sec. 32, Par. 18 and 25; see there.

The stroke should not be against the middle of the roof, but against the end of /the roof/ on the left side. If one made /the stroke/ in the middle /the letter/ is invalid and must be corrected, i.e., one must scrape away /the stroke/ and place it at the end. /In the case of *tefilin* passages and mezuzos,/ if one /already/ wrote the words which follow it and is /therefore/ unable to correct /the letter in this manner/, because /then it will be written/ in incorrect order, he should scrape off /part of/ the roof so that it will /end/ equally with the leg. Where even this /form of/ correction cannot be done, such as when the ה is in the middle of a word and /the word/ will become like two words if one will scrape off /part of/ the roof, one may then rule /the letter/ to be valid /even/ without correcting it. [This is because there are many Rishonim who are of the opinion that this accords with the symbol /required/ for the /letter/ ה. See the *Chidushey Ha-Rashba* on *Shabbos* 103, the *Chidushey Ha-Ritba* there, the *Rashba* newly printed on *Menachos* 29, the *Ran* in the chapter *Ha-Boneh*,[5*] the *Chidushey Ha-Meiri* and the *Chidushey Ha-Ran* on *Shabbos*, which has been newly printed, in the chapter of *Ha-Boneh*. It is clearly evident from their view /given/ there that /in their opinion/ the symbol for the /letter/ ה is of this /form/.]

We will now explain the nature of the stroke /inside the letter/. Initially, the stroke should be fine above and a little thick below,[5] /so that it is/ similar to a /letter/ י. It should be, initially, a little slanted below.[6] /It should be/ towards the right, but not towards the left, to avoid it resembling /the left leg of/ the /letter/ ת. The length of the stroke should also not be less than the length of the /letter/ י, with its underneath prickle,[6] as /ruled/ above in Sec. 32, Par. 15, in the gloss; see there in the Mishnah Berurah. This is essential /for the validity of the letter/, even once it is after the event. One must admonish the scribes /about this/, since they stumble frequently over it. /However,/ it appears to me that, at any rate, correction is of avail /if it was not made sufficiently long/, even in the case of *tefilin* /passages/ and mezuzos /and although one already wrote after it/, if a child /who is neither especially intelligent nor especially simple/ reads /the letter/ for a ה /without the correction/. /We do/ not /rule/ that such /a correction/ is /considered writing the letter/ in incorrect order, because of similar /considerations/ to /those of/ the *P.Mg.*, who rules leniently that one may correct a simple /elongated letter/ ך, if one made it square, by adding ink to it; see there.

In Sec. 32, sub-Par. 33, the *P.Mg.* is in doubt as to whether the end of the /left/ stroke must

5* This is a chapter of *Shabbos*.

בסופה שוה דוקא לירך ימין או אפילו אם נשלמה באמצע הירך ש"ד רק שיהיה בה שיעורה דהיינו כמלא יו"ד וכנ"ל ועיין בתשו' בנין עולם בסימן נ"ד ועכ"פ נראה דיש להקל ע"י קריאת התינוק ועי' לקמן בדין רי"ש שעשהו קצר כוי"ו.

צורת אות וא"ו

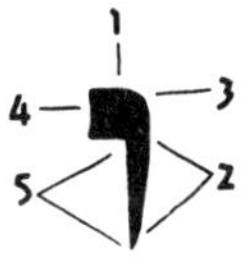

[1] צ"ל א) ראשה קצר לא יותר מעובי קולמוס כדי שלא תדמה לרי"ש [2] ורגלה ארוך כעובי ב' קולמוסים כדי שלא תדמה ליו"ד ולא יעשנה ב) ארוך יותר מדאי פן תדמה לתינוק לנו"ן פשוטה [3] ומטעם זה ג"כ טוב שתהיה ראשה עגולה לצד ימין שלא תדמה לזיי"ן ואע"פ שראש הזיי"ן עובר מב' צדדין מ"מ יש לחוש שמא תינוק דלא חכים ולא טיפש יקראנה זיי"ן ותפסל. [4] ופניה יהיה שוה ולא באלכסון. [5] ורגלה תהיה פשוט תחתיה בשוה לא שבור באמצע. גם טוב שעוביה תתמעט והולך מעט מעט עד שתהיה חדה למטה. אם רגל הוא"ו ג) קצר אם אין בו רק כמלא יו"ד פסול ואם מעט יותר צריך להראות ד) לתינוק וה"ה אם ראש הוא"ו רחב ונדמה קצת לרי"ש. אם כתב דלי"ת במקום וא"ו צריך לגרור כל הגג ה) ואפשר דבעי נמי לגרור כל הירך דדומה לדלי"ת שכתבו במקום רי"ש שצריך למחוק כולו וכנ"ל בסימן ל"ב סי"ח.

צורת אות זיי"ן

א) [1] צריך ליזהר שלא תהיה רגלה ארוכה שלא יתדמה לנו"ן פשוטה ותפסל ע"י קריאת התינוק ע"כ ב) לא יהא רגלה ארוך יותר מב' קולמוסים. [2] וראשה צריך להיות עובר משני צדדין ג) שלא תדמה לוא"ו. [3] ויהיה מרובע [4] וג' תגין על ראשה. [5] ורגלה תהיה ד) פשוט תחתיה לא שבורה [6] ה) ויש שעושין הקו התחתון דק ביציאה והולך ומתעבה עד חציה ומחציה חוזר ומתמעט עד שתהיה חדה למטה.

ואם נתקצרה הרגל מזיי"ן דינו כמו שכתבנו באות וא"ו [מלעיל בסימן ל"ב סט"ז בהג"ה ואף שהפמ"ג מצדד להקל בזה דדי אם נשאר מהרגל כמלא אות יו"ד הדרך החיים בהלכות קה"ת והשערי אפרים סתמו כהשו"ע וכ"ש אם הראו לתינוק ולא קראו לזיי"ן בודאי אין להקל בזה ומוכח ממה שכתב הב"י בא"ב השני באות וא"ו ע"ש ונראה דאפילו תיקון לא מהני בזה בתו"מ משום שלא כסדרן. עיין בסימן ל"ב סכ"ה].

צורת אות חי"ת

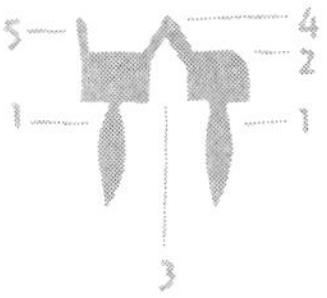

[1] תהיה שתי רגליה א) כתמונת שני זייני"ן. [2] והזיי"ן שבצד ימין ב) נכון לעשות קרן ראשו עגול בצד ימין [3] ויהיו הזייני"ן רחוקים זה מזה ג) לכל היותר כעובי קולמוס. [1] ויהיו מחוברים בחטוטרת יחדיו [הוא כמין גג גבוה].

ומקל ד) [הוא כמין תג גדול] יעשה לה ה) בראש רגל השמאל ולא באמצע. וצריך ליזהר ו) שלא יאריך בגג החי"ת ואם האריך פסול ואין לו תיקון בתפילין ומזוזות משום שלא כסדרן. בד"א שעשה ב' זייני"ן ז) וגג רחב דזה לא הוי כמין חטוטרת ח) שהוא משופע אבל אם עשה החי"ת כדעת רש"י [דהיינו חי"ת פשוטה בלא חטוטרת שעל גגה] אפילו אם האריך הרבה כשר בדיעבד אע"פ שאינה מרובעת. אם עשה החי"ת ט) כתמונת שני ווי"ן או כדלי"ת וא"ו או כדלי"ת זיי"ן וחטוטרת ע"ג כשר בדיעבד, שהרי לא נשתנה לצורת אות אחר עי"ז. ומ"מ אם אפשר לתקן לגרור יתרון האות והחטוטרת ישאר במקומו כגון בחי"ת שתמונתו היה כדלי"ת זיי"ן י) והחטוטרת שלו נעשית באמצע הד' ולא בסופה יגרור מן הד' מקצתו עד שתעשה כמו זיי"ן אבל אם עומד בסופה יחלק האות כשיגרור מן הדלי"ת ולא יהיה לו תיקון אח"כ בתפילין ומזוזות שמעכב בהן שלא כסדרן ע"כ יא) יש להכשיר בלא תיקון אבל בס"ת יב) אם נמצא חי"ת שתמונתו היה

שער הציון

ס"ת אות ש'. ד) מ"א וא"ר. ה) פמ"ג בצורת האותיות שלו. ו) מ"א בסימן ל"ב ס"ק ל"ג. ו א) ב"י. ב) פשוט נלמד מעגולת*הרי"ש ועדיף מניה וכן פסק בספר לדוד אמת שאם רגל הוא"ו הוא כמו נו"ן פשוטה פסול. ג) מסי' ל"ב סט"ז עי"ש. ד) טור בסימן זה. ה) פמ"ג בצורת וא"ו. ז א) ב"י. ב) מדרכי משה וכצ"ל שם וכן איתא בד"מ הארוך. ג) פשוט ומש"כ בב"י בשם ב"ש מפני הסוד אפשר לענין שלא יטה לצד אחד יותר מלצד חבירו וגם בזה אם מטה הרבה עד שנראה כד' פסול. ודע עוד דמה שכתב בב"י על המרובע מפני הסוד היינו לענין הריבוע מכל זויותיה אבל לענין שלא יהיה הראש עגול יש לזה מקור מן התלמוד לפי פי' הב"י שהביא בשם הרא"ם בסימן זה בסוף ד"ה וא"א ז"ל וכו' עי"ש ועיין לקמן בסוף אות טי"ת. ד) לבוש. ה) שם. ח א) ב"י. ב) עיין בב"י ופשוט. ג) ב"ש בא"ב האחרון. ד) ב"ח. ה) חידושי רע"א. ו) מ"א בסימן ל"ו סק"ג. ז) מ"א שם. ח) יד אפרים ובא"ר אות חי"ת מוכח דחטוטרת אינה צריכה להיות משופע כ"כ רק קצת שיפוע וגבהות כגגי הבתים שבא"י ויש לחלק בדוחק. ט) נודע ביהודא בסימן ע"ר ושערי אפרים בשער ה' ולדוד אמת ודלא כהפמ"ג בא"א שמפקפק בזה. ועיין בלבושי שרד ובדה"ח בהלכות קה"ת שחולקין גם כן על הפמ"ג. י) מ"א בסק"ג. יא) כן מוכח מנו"ב הנ"ל עי"ש ואף שראיתי לקצת שמחמירין בזה מ"מ יש לסמוך ע"ז בשעת הדחק אחרי שהשערי אפרים ולדוד אמת

*צ"ל הראש

be specifically at the same /height/ as /the end of/ the right thigh or /whether the letter/ is in order even if /the left stroke/ is completed at /a point which corresponds with/ the middle /of the height/ of the /right/ thigh, provided that it has the /required/ length, i.e., /the length/ which is equivalent /to the length/ of a /letter/ י, as /explained/ above. See the responsa *Binyan Olam*, Sec. 54. At any rate, it appears that one may be lenient /in such a case/ upon the /correct/ reading of a child /who is neither especially intelligent nor especially simple/. See below, as regards the law when one made a /letter/ ר with a short /roof/, like /that of/ a /letter/ ו.

THE FORM OF THE LETTER ו

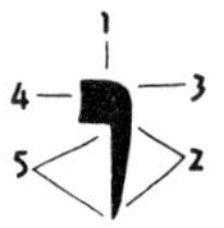

The head of the letter ו should be short, no more than the thickness[4*] of a quill,[1] so that /the letter/ does not resemble a /letter/ ר.

The leg of /the letter/ should have the length of the thickness of two quills,[2] so that /the letter/ does not resemble a /letter/ י. /On the other hand,/ one should not make it more than the appropriate length, in case it will appear like a simple /elongated letter/ ן to a child /who is neither especially intelligent nor especially simple/.

For this reason also, it is desirable for the head of /the ו / to be rounded on the right side,[3] so that it does not resemble a /letter/ ז. Although the head of the /letter/ ז passes over /the leg/ on both sides, there are nevertheless grounds for concern that a child who is neither /especially/ intelligent nor /especially/ simple will read /a ו with a squared roof/ as a /letter/ ז and it will become invalid.

The front of /the head/ should be straight and not sloping.[4]

The leg of /the letter/ should be a simple /line/ underneath /the head/. It should have an even /edge/ and should not be broken in the middle.[5] It is also desirable that the thickness of /the leg/ should diminish progressively until it becomes sharp below.

If the leg of the ו is short /, then/, if it only has /a length/ which is equivalent /to the length/ of a /letter/ י /the ו/ is invalid. If /it is/ a little /longer, the letter/ must be shown to a child /who is neither especially intelligent nor especially simple and will only be valid if he reads it as a ו/. The same ruling /applies/ if the head of a ו is wide and /the letter/ somewhat resembles a /letter/ ר.

If one wrote a /letter/ ד instead of a /letter/ ו, he must scrape away the entire roof. It may be that he is also required to scrape away the entire thigh, since this is comparable to /an instance when/ a /letter/ ד was written instead of a /letter/ ר, in which case /the letter/ must be erased entirely, as /ruled/ above in Sec. 32, Par. 18.

THE FORM OF THE LETTER ז

One must take care that the leg of the letter ז is not /too/ long,[1] so that /the letter/ should not appear like a simple /elongated letter/ ן and become invalid through the reading of a child /who is neither especially intelligent nor especially simple/. Therefore, its leg should not be longer than /the thickness of/ two quills.[4*]

The head /of the letter/ must pass over /the leg/ on both sides,[2] so that /the letter/ does not resemble a /letter/ ו. /The head/ should be square[3] and /should have/ three crownlets on top.[4]

The leg /of the letter/ should be a simple /line/ underneath /the head/ and not broken.[5] There are /scribes/ who make the line underneath /the head/ thin where it goes out /of the head/ and they thicken it progressively until halfway /along the length/. From the halfway /point/ they reduce /the thickness progressively/ until it becomes sharp at the botton.[6]

If the leg was /made/ shorter than /is usual for/ a /letter/ ז, the ruling /which applies/ is the same as /the ruling/ which we have written for a letter ו /whose leg was made short/. [/This is derived/ from /the ruling/ above in Sec. 32, Par. 16 in the gloss. Although the *P.Mg.* adopts a lenient /view/ in this respect, that it is sufficient if there remains of the leg /a length/ which is equivalent /to the length/ of a letter י, the

בסופה שוה דוקא לירך ימין או אפילו אם נשלמה באמצע הירך ש"ד רק שיהיה בה שיעורה דהיינו כמלא יו"ד וכנ"ל ועיין בתשו' בנין עולם בסימן נ"ד ועכ"פ נראה דיש להקל ע"י קריאת התינוק ועי' לקמן בדין רי"ש שעשהו קצר כוי"ו.

צורת אות וא"ו

[1] צ"ל א) ראשה קצר לא יותר מעובי קולמוס כדי שלא תדמה לרי"ש [2] ורגלה ארוך כעובי ב' קולמוסים כדי שלא תדמה ליו"ד ולא יעשנה ב) ארוך יותר מדאי פן תדמה לתינוק לנו"ן פשוטה [3] ומטעם זה ג"כ טוב שתהיה ראשה עגולה לצד ימין שלא תדמה לזיי"ן ואע"פ שראש הזיי"ן עובר מב' צדדין מ"מ יש לחוש שמא תינוק דלא חכים ולא טיפש יקראנה זיי"ן ותפסל. [1] ופניה יהיה שוה ולא באלכסון. [3] ורגלה תהיה פשוט תחתיה בשוה לא שבור באמצע. גם טוב שעוביה תתמעט והולך מעט מעט עד שתהיה חדה למטה. אם רגל הוא"ו ג) קצר אם אין בו רק כמלא יו"ד פסול ואם מעט יותר צריך להראות ד) לתינוק וה"ה אם ראש הוא"ו רחב ונדמה קצת לרי"ש. אם כתב דלי"ת במקום וא"ו צריך לגרור כל הגג ה) ואפשר דבעי נמי לגרור כל הירך דדומה לדלי"ת שכתבו במקום רי"ש שצריך למחוק כולו וכנ"ל בסימן ל"ב סי"ח.

צורת אות זיי"ן

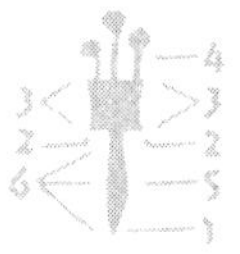

א) [1] צריך ליזהר שלא תהיה רגלה ארוכה שלא יתדמה לנו"ן פשוטה ותפסל ע"י קריאת התינוק ע"כ ב) לא יהא רגלה ארוך יותר מב' קולמוסים. [2] וראשה צריך להיות עובר משני צדדין ג) שלא תדמה לוא"ו. [3] ויהיה מרובע [1] וג' תגין על ראשה. [5] ורגלה תהיה ד) פשוט תחתיה לא שבורה [6] ה) ויש שעושין הקו התחתון דק ביציאה והולך ומתעבה עד חציה ומהציה חוזר ומתמעט עד שתהיה חדה למטה.

ואם נתקצרה הרגל מזיי"ן דינו כמו שכתבנו באות וא"ו [מלעיל בסימן ל"ב סט"ז בהג"ה ואף שהפמ"ג מצדד להקל בזה דדי אם נשאר מהרגל כמלא אות יו"ד **הדרך החיים בהלכות קה"ת והשערי אפרים סתמו כהשו"ע וכ"ש אם הראו לתינוק ולא קראו לזיי"ן בודאי אין להקל בזה ומוכח ממה שכתב הב"י בא"ב השני באות וא"ו עי"ש ונראה דאפילו תיקון לא מהני בזה בתו"מ משום שלא כסדרן. עיין בסימן ל"ב סכ"ה].**

צורת אות חי"ת

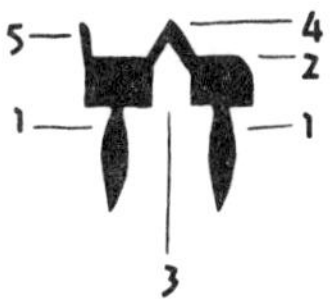

[1] תהיה שתי רגליה א) כתמונת שני זייני"ן. [2] והזיי"ן שבצד ימין ב) נכון לעשות קרן ראשו עגול בצד ימין [3] ויהיו הזייני"ן רחוקים זה מזה ג) לכל היותר כעובי קולמוס. [1] ויהיו מחוברים בחטוטרת יחדיו [הוא כמין גג גבוה]. [5] ומקל ד) [הוא כמין תג גדול] יעשה לה ה) בראש רגל השמאל ולא באמצע. וצריך ליזהר ו) שלא יאריך בגג החי"ת ואם האריך פסול ואין לו תיקון בתפילין ומזוזות משום שלא כסדרן. בד"א שעשה ב' זייני"ן ז) וגג רחב דזה לא הוי כמין חטוטרת ח) שהוא משופע אבל אם עשה החי"ת כדעת רש"י [דהיינו חי"ת פשוטה בלא חטוטרת שעל גגה] אפילו אם האריך הרבה כשר בדיעבד אע"פ שאינה מרובעת. אם עשה החי"ת ט) כתמונת שני ווי"ן או כדלי"ת וא"ו או כדלי"ת זיי"ן וחטוטרת ע"ג כשר בדיעבד, שהרי לא נשתנה לצורת אות אחר עי"ז. ומ"מ אם אפשר לתקן לגרור יתרון האות והחטוטרת ישאר במקומו כגון בחי"ת שתמונתו היה כדלי"ת זיי"ן י) והחטוטרת שלו נעשית באמצע הד' ולא בסופה יגרור מן הד' מקצתו עד שתעשה כמו זיי"ן אבל אם עומד בסופה יחלק האות כשיגרור מן הדלי"ת ולא יהיה לו תיקון אח"כ בתפילין ומזוזות שמעכב בהן שלא כסדרן ע"כ יא) יש להכשיר בלא תיקון אבל בס"ת יב) אם נמצא חי"ת שתמונתו היה

שער הציון

ס"ת אות ש'. ד) מ"א וא"ר. ה) פמ"ג בצורת האותיות שלו. ו) מ"א בסימן ל"ב ס"ק ל"ג. **ו** א) ב"י. ב) פשוט נלמד מעגולת*הרי"ש ועדיף מניה וכן פסק בספר לדוד אמת שאם רגל הוא"ו הוא כמו נו"ן פשוטה פסול. ג) מסי' ל"ב סט"ז עי"ש. ד) טור בסימן זה. ה) פמ"ג בצורת וא"ו. **ז** א) ב"י. ב) מדרכי משה וכצ"ל שם וכן איתא בד"מ הארוך. ג) פשוט ומש"כ בב"י בשם ב"ש מפני הסוד אפשר לענין שלא יטה לצד אחד יותר מלצד חבירו וגם בזה אם מטה הרבה עד שנראה כד' פסול. ודע עוד דמה שכתב בב"י על המרובע מפני הסוד היינו לענין הריבוע מכל זויותיה אבל לענין שלא יהיה הראש עגול יש לזה מקור מן התלמוד לפי פי' הב"י שהביא בשם הרא"ם בסימן זה בסוף ד"ה וא"א ז"ל וכו' עי"ש ועיין לקמן בסוף אות טי"ת. ד) לבוש. ה) שם. **ח** א) ב"י. ב) עיין בב"י ופשוט. ג) ב"ש בא"ב האחרון. ד) ב"ח. ה) חידושי רע"א. ו) מ"א בסימן ל"ו סק"ג. ז) מ"א שם. ח) יד אפרים ובא"ר אות חי"ת מוכח דחטוטרת אינה צריכה להיות משופע כ"כ רק קצת שיפוע וגבהות כגגי הבתים שבא"י ויש לחלק בדוחק. ט) נודע ביהודא בסימן ע"ר ושערי אפרים בשער ה' ולדוד אמת ודלא כהפמ"ג בא"א שמפקפק בזה. ועיין בלבושי שרד ובדה"ח בהלכות קה"ת שחולקין גם כן על הפמ"ג. י) מ"א בסק"ג. יא) כן מוכח מנו"ב הנ"ל עי"ש ואף שראיתי לקצת שמחמירין בזה מ"מ יש לסמוך ע"ז בשעת הדחק אחרי שהשערי אפרים ולדוד אמת

*צ"ל הרא"ש

Derech Ha-Chayim, in his laws of the reading from the Torah, and the *Sha'arey Efrayim* state the view of /the gloss to/ the Shulchan Aruch categorically. /One should/ certainly /follow the ruling of the gloss/ if one showed /the letter/ to a child /who is neither especially intelligent nor especially simple/ and he did not read it as a /letter/ ז. /Then/ one should definitely not be lenient about this. This is evident from what the *B.Y.* writes in the second /description of the/ alphabet with reference to the letter ו; see there. It appears that in such a case even if one corrects /the letter/ this will be of no avail for *tefilin* /passages/ or mezuzos /if one already wrote further/, because /the letter will be written/ in incorrect order. See Sec. 32, Par. 25.]

THE FORM OF THE LETTER ח

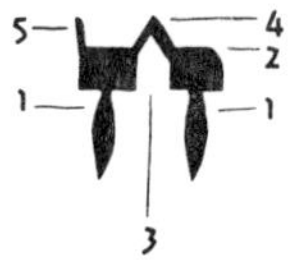

The two legs of the letter ח should have the symbol of two ז[1] /letters/. In the case of the ז on the right side, it is proper to make the corner of its head rounded on its right side.[2] The ז /letters/ should be away from one another at most the thickness[4*] of a quill.[3] They should be joined together with a hump[4] [i.e., a sort of high roof].

One should make a staff [i.e., a sort of large crownlet] for /the letter/ on the head of the left leg and not in the middle[5] /of it/.

One must be careful not to lengthen the roof of the /letter/ ח. If one did lengthen /it the letter/ is invalid and cannot be corrected /if one already wrote further/, where *tefilin* /passages/ or mezuzos are involved, because /then the letter will be written/ in incorrect order.

/The above/ ruling applies when one made the two ז /letters/ with a wide roof /joining them together/, since such /a roof/ does not have the character of a hump, because it is inclined. However, if one made a /letter/ ח in conformance with the view of *Rashi* [i.e., /if one made/ a simple ח without a hump on its roof] /, then/, even if he extended /the roof/ considerably /the letter/ is valid, once it is after the event, even if it is not square.

If one made a ח with the symbol /of a combination/ of two ו /letters, of a combination/ of a /letter/ ד and a /letter/ ו or /of a combination/ of a /letter/ ד and a /letter/ ז, with a hump over /the parts joining them together, the letter/ is valid now that it is after the event. This is because by /using these symbols/ it was not transformed into the form of another letter.

Nevertheless, if it is possible to correct /the form/ by scraping off the superfluous /part of the/ letter with the hump remaining in place /, one should in fact do so/. For example, if the symbol of a /letter/ ח /consists of a combination/ of a /letter/ ד and a /letter/ ז and the hump was made in the middle /of the roof/ of the ד /part/ and not at the end of it, he should scrape off part /of the roof/ of the ד /part/ from it, until it becomes like a ז. However, if /the hump/ stands at the end of /the ד part/ the letter will become divided if one scrapes off /part/ of the ד /part/. /Consequently, it/ will not be correctable subsequently, where *tefilin* /passages/ or mezuzos are involved, since /in their case if a letter was written/ in incorrect order this precludes /their validity/. One should therefore rule /the letter/ to be valid without correction. On the other hand, if a /letter/ ח is discovered in a Torah Scroll which has a symbol of a /letter/

כדלי״ת וזיי״ן או שני ווי״ן אף שאין להוציא אחרת משום זה, מ״מ בחול בכל גווני צריך לתקן האות עד שיעמידו על תמונתו הראויה. וצריך להזהיר הסופרים ע״ז, כי תמונת החי״ת שכתבנו למעלה יש לו עיקר בתלמוד ועמדו עליו גדולי הראשונים ז״ל. ודע עוד דבדיעבד אם עשה להחי״ת יג) מקל לבד או חטוטרת לבד כשר. והגרע״א מסיק בחידושיו דאפילו נחסר להחי״ת החטוטרת וגם המקל שהיה חי״ת פשוטה כחיתי״ן שלנו כשר בדיעבד. רק אם אפשר לתקן בקל לעשות לה מקל יעשה דהוי כלכתחלה. אם נפסק ירך החי״ת ולא נשאר בו רק כמלא יו״ד די בכך בין ירך הימיני או השמאלי [פמ״ג בפתיחה במש״כ יראה לי דה״ה לשאר אותיות וכו׳ ומה דנקט הפמ״ג שם ירך הימיני משום אחריני דזכר שם נקט] ועיין בסוף אות תי״ו מה שכתבנו שם. אם החטוטרת שעל החי״ת לא היה דבוק להחי״ת, אך לא היה ניכר להדיא ההפרדה, מותר לתקנה אפילו בתו״מ ואין בזה משום שלא כסדרן [נלמד מל״ב סכ״ה עי״ש]. אבל אם היה ניכר להדיא נתבטל ממנו שם האות. * ואם נפרד רק מצד אחד החטוטרת מהחי״ת אפשר דיש להקל לתקן אפילו ניכר להדיא ועיין בבה״ל.

צורת אות טי״ת

[1] הראש הימיני יהיה א) כפוף מעט לתוכה * ולא יהיה כפוף הרבה [2] והראש השמאלי יהיה כזיי״ן וג׳ תגין על ראשה [3] אבל הראש הימיני יהיה עגול כוא״ו [4] וגם למטה מצד הימיני ב) תהיה עגולה כי תמונתה כמו כ״ף וזיי״ן וכ״ז אינו מעכב ג) בדיעבד [לבד בענין כפוף הרבה דצ״ע לדינא ועיין בביאור הלכה] ול״נ דאם לא היה כפוף כלל לתוכה צריך להראות לתינוק ובכל גווני צריך לתקנה אח״כ ולא מיקרי בזה שלא כסדרן דבלא״ה תמונתה

שער הציון

הביאוהו להלכה. יב) נו״ב וש״א הנ״ל. יג) פמ״ג בא״א. ט א) ב״י. ב) מוכח מב״י וכן איתא באגור בהדיא. ג) עי׳ בפמ״ג

ביאור הלכה

ח * ואם. דע דהספק אינו רק לפי מה שבררנו בסי׳ ל״ב סכ״ה בבה״ל להלכה כדעת הגאון רע״א דתיקון מועיל באות שאינו נראה. כשתי אותיות אפי׳ בניכר ההפרדה [דלדעת הפמ״ג אין תיקון מועיל בזה בתו״מ] כגון ביו״ד האל״ף שאינו נוגע להאל״ף אף דהיו״ד בפ״ע שם אות אחר עליו מ״מ כיון דיתר האות זה אין שם אחר עליו מועיל זה ג״כ להיו״ד דלא יקרא עליו שם יו״ד אלא שם אל״ף עליו וכמו שזכר שם הפמ״ג ג״כ את עצם הסברא הזו [ורק לשיטתו אין מועיל זה כ״א בלא ניכר ההפרדה להדיא] ובררנו שם ג״כ דאם החטוטרות למעלה בראשו אינם נוגעים זה לזה והיה ניכר ההפרדה אין מועיל תיקון משום דנראה כשני זייני״ן ול״א אמרינן דהחטוטרת יציל את האות שיקרא על ידי החטוטרת עליו שם חי״ת עדיין, ע״כ אפשר דגם בזה עדיין אין תמונת חי״ת עליו משום דאין דבוק מצד אחד להזיי״ן או אפשר דבזה דהחטוטרת למעלה אין נפסק באמצעו שם חטוטרת עליו ומציל על הזיי״ן שתחתיו שלא יקרא עליו שם זיי״ן וכנ״ל ביו״ד האל״ף וצ״ע.

ט * ולא יהיה כפוף הרבה. ומה נקרא כפוף הרבה משמע מברוך שאמר בא״ב א׳ אם נוגע בקרקע הטי״ת וכן משמע מספר האגור אך צ״ע דא״כ מה זה שכתב הב״י הטעם דבזה ידמה לגמרי לפ״א והובא לשון זה בס׳ התרומה והגה״מ [היינו בחצי הצד שמצד ימין דאף שמצד השמאלי והוא הזיי״ן מוכח שאינו פ״א שיטתם הוא דאם האות במקצתו נדמה לאות אחר אין זה כתיבה תמה וכה״ג הוא כל שיטת ס׳ היראים על הברייתא זו באלפי״ן עייני״ן וכדומה עיי״ש ומעשה רקח בשם מהראנ״ח בסימן א׳ והרבה חולקין על סברא זו ואכ״מ להאריך] הלא בפ״א כתבו הב״ש והאגור וכן נפסק הדין לקמן דאם נגעה הנקודה באיזה צד בפנים פסולה וא״כ אדרבה אם לא יכפפנה כ״כ יהיה דומה יותר לפ״א אלא ודאי דאף אם אין נוגע בקרקע הטי״ת כל שכפוף הרבה אסור וה״ה אם נוגע דעכ״פ דמי במקצת לפ״א ובזה ניחא לי מה שהשמיט הב״י והלבוש וכל מפרשי השו״ע לבאר זה דאי הוה ס״ל להא דהב״ש לא היו שותקין מלבאר זה ולא לכתוב סתם כפוף הרבה. עוד ראיתי לבאר במקצת הדין לענין דיעבד דהנה ראיתי בדברי הגר״ז כתוב ולא יהיה כפוף הרבה לכתחילה, משמע דבדיעבד מותר. ובספר לדוד אמת ראיתי שכתב וז״ל לא יכוף הרבה האות ט׳ לתוכה פן ידמה לגמרי לפ״א שאם תגע הקוץ שלה בגופה בפנים פסול והנה אם נאמר דהגר״ז מפרש כפוף הרבה כהב״ש הנ״ל דבר זה במחלוקת שנוי הגר״ז מכשיר ולד״א פוסל. אמנם עיקר דינא לענין דיעבד בין אם נפרש כפירושינו הנ״ל ובין להב״ש והאגור צ״ע לפי מה שכתב בספר היראים והתרומה והגה״מ דבזה ידמה לגמרי לפ״א וכתב שם בספר היראים והתרומה בהדיא דזהו כונת הברייתא שלא יעשה טתי״ן פאי״ן וכו׳ והלא על כולם סיימה הברייתא דיגנז [וכדמוכח שם בגמרא] אכן לפי מה שכתב הרא״ש בהלכות ס״ת בענין זה בשם ר״ת וז״ל וכן טתי״ן פאי״ן שאף על פי שאין דומין לא בכתיבתן ולא בקריאתן כתב ר״ת שתהא צד ימין של טי״ת כפוף ואם תהפך אותה על צד שמאלה יראה פ״א אין שום ראיה לכאן דכוונת הברייתא להשמיענו דאף שהטי״ת דומה באיזה צד לפ״א אפ״ה לא יעשנה פ״א אבל לענין כפוף מעט והרבה לא השמיענו הברייתא דבר וא״כ מנין לנו לאסור. ועוד ראיה גמורה שהרא״ש אין סובר כלל הך נ״מ דכפוף הרבה שהרי שם בהלכות ס״ת העתיק כמעט כל לשון התרומה וד״ז השמיט ש״מ דלא ס״ל וכן הטור ורי״ו

ר /combined/ with a /letter/ ז or /of a combination/ of two ו /letters, then/, even though because of this /fault/ one should not /return that Torah Scroll and/ take out another /Torah Scroll for the reading/, one must nevertheless correct the letter on a weekday in all /such/ cases by adjusting /the letter/ until it has its proper symbol.

One must admonish the scribes over this, as /the requirements for/ the symbol of the /letter/ ח which we have written above have a foundation in the Talmud and the great Rishonim, of blessed memory, insisted on /the letter being written in that way/.

Note further that, once it is after the event, if one made a /letter/ ח with /a straight roof and/ a staff only or with a hump alone /without adding the staff, the letter/ is /nevertheless/ valid. The Gaon, *R.A.E.*, in his *Chidushim*, concludes that even if a /letter/ ח lacks a hump and also a staff, so that it is a simple ח, like /the symbol/ we use /elsewhere/ for a ח, it is /nevertheless/ valid, now that it is after the event. Only, if it is possible to correct /the ח/ easily by making a staff on it, one should /in fact/ make /the staff/, as /then the circumstances/ are like initial /circumstances/.

If a thigh of a /letter/ ח became interrupted and there remained of it only /a length/ which is equivalent /to the length/ of a /letter/ י, this is sufficient. /This applies/ both /in the case of/ the right thigh and /in the case of/ the left /thigh/. [*P.Mg.* in the introduction, /in the paragraph/ where he writes: "It appears to me that the same ruling /applies in the case/ of other letters, etc." /The fact/ that the *P.Mg.* speaks there /specifically/ of the right thigh /is not because the ruling does not apply to the left thigh, but/ he /only/ speaks /of the right thigh/ because /in the case/ of other /letters/ mentioned there /the ruling only applies to the right thigh/.] See at the end of /the description/ of the letter ת, for what we have written there /about this/.

If the hump over the /letter/ ח is not stuck /to the body of/ the ח, but the separation is not clearly apparent, it is permitted to correct /the letter/, even in the case of *tefilin* /passages/ and mezuzos, /because/ this is not /considered writing/ in incorrect order. [This may be derived from /the ruling in Sec./ 32, Par. 25; see there.] However, if /the separation/ is clearly apparent, /the symbol/ ceases to be classified as the letter /ח/. If the hump is separated from the /rest of the letter/ ח only on one side, it may be that one may be lenient /and allow it/ to be corrected even if /the separation/ is clearly apparent. See the Beyur Halachah.

THE FORM OF THE LETTER ט

The right head of the letter ט should be bent slightly inwards,[1] but it should not be bent substantially. The left head should be like /the head of/ a /letter/ ז, with three crownlets on top of it.[2] On the other hand, the right head should be rounded,[3] like /the head of/ the /letter/ ו.

Below, as well, /the letter/ should be rounded on the right side.[4] This is because the symbol of /the letter/ is like /the symbol of a letter/ כ /combined with the symbol of/ a /letter/ ז.

/However,/ all this is not essential once it is after the event [except that as regards an instance where /the head/ is bent substantially, study is required to /determine/ the ruling; see the Beyur Halachah[6*]].

It appears to me that if /the right head/ is not bent inwards at all /the letter/ must be shown to a child /who is neither especially intelligent nor especially simple, to determine its validity/.

It is necessary in all circumstances to correct /the letter/ subsequently and it will not be classed because of this /as having been written/ in incorrect order, since it has its required symbol /even/ without /the

6* The author concludes there that if it is bent substantially, but does not touch below, the ruling is as follows. In the case of a Torah Scroll, one should erase enough to cancel the letter form and then correct it. If one discovers such a letter ט at the reading from the Torah it is unnecessary to take out another Torah Scroll. In the case of *tefilin* passages and mezuzos correction is unnecessary, if one already wrote after the letter. If the bent part touches the floor of the letter, the letter is invalid even in the case of *tefilin* passages and mezuzos. (Beyur Halachah)

עליה ואם לא היה כפוף כלל לתוכה והתינוק לא קראה לאות צ״ע אם יש לה תקנה בתפילין משום שלא כסדרן. ועיין בסימן ל״ב בסעיף כ״ה לענין ח׳ דחטוטרות ואפשר דה״ה בזה דאין מורגל בטי״ת בלי כפיפה ולא מקרי בזה נשתנית צורתה וצ״ע. ויזהר ד) שלא יגעו הראשים זה בזה. ובדיעבד אם יש להם תקנה ע״י גרירה עי׳ לקמן בסוף אות שי״ן מה שכתבנו שם. אם הראש השמאלי לא היה תמונתה כזיי״ן שראשה היתה עגולה, אך שהיתה תגין עליה צ״ע בדיעבד לפי מה שהביא הב״י לקמן בשם הגה״מ בשם הרא״ם דמה שאמרו בגמרא דשעטנ״ז ג״ץ צריכה ג׳ זיוני״ן היינו לא בתגין אלא שלא יעשה ראשיהם עגול אלא משוך שיהא לכל ראש ג׳ פינים ולעיכובא הוא כדמוכח בב״י בסוף סימן ל״ו אם ע״י התגין מתכשרת או לא. ואין להביא ראיה מפמ״ג שכתב דבדיעבד כשר אם לא היה כזיי״ן דאפשר שלא היה עובר מב׳ צדדין כזיי״ן, אבל לא עגולה. וצ״ע להרא״ם וגם אולי אין הלכה כהרא״ם בזה.

ועיין בסי׳ ל״ו במ״ב ס״ק ט״ו בזה.

צורת אות יו״ד

[1] שיעור גופה א) מלא קולמוס אחד ולא יותר שלא תדמה לרי״ש [2] ויכתוב אותה ישרה דהיינו שתהיה ראשה ופניה ב) שוים ולא פניה כלפי מעלה. [3] גם תהיה למעלה ג) עגולה לצד ימין לכתחלה. [4] ד) ויעשה לה רגל מצד ימין ויעקם הרגל לצד שמאל ויהיה הרגל קצר ולא ארוך שלא תדמה לוא״ו ותפסל ע״י קריאת התינוק. [5] * גם צריך להיות להיו״ד תג קטן מלמעלה על פניה [7] וכנגדה עוקץ קטן יורד מלמטה והעוקץ יהיה קצר מן התג. גם יהיה קצר יותר מרגלה שמצד ימיני פן תדמה לחי״ת. ואם האריך העוקץ עד ששוה למטה לרגל ימיני ונראית כחי״ת קטנה פסולה ולא מהני גרירת העוקץ עד שיהיה קצר כהלכתו דה״ל חק תוכות אלא * יגרור כל העוקץ ויחזור ויכתבנו כהלכתו ולא מהני קריאת התינוק בזה [כן הביא בספר משנת אברהם בשם בית יהודה ולדויד אמת ומעשה רוקח וקנאת סופרים סי׳ י״ב] ובס״ת מיירי ולא בתו״מ דהוי שלא כסדרן ויש מי שכתב דלדעת ר״י אכסנדרני [המובא בב״י ד״ה וז״ל הריא״ס נמצא בהגה״מ וכו׳] דקי״ל כוותיה צריך לגרור גם רגל ימיני ואח״כ יתקן [ג״ז שם] [תשובת חב״י בסי׳ ע״ד והובא בפ״ת ליו״ד בסי׳ רע״ד סק״ו] ועיין בביאור הלכה שביארנו דיש להחמיר ברעה זו. וס״ת שנמצאו בה יודי״ן כצורת למ״ד קטנה פסולה וצריך לגרור כל האות ולחזור ולכתוב יו״ד מחדש דבלא״ה הוי חק תוכות. וביודי״ן של שם צריך לסלק כל היריעה, אך אם היו״ד נראה ממש כלמ״ד לעין כל אזי יכול לגרור אפילו בשם באופן שלא ישאר רק גוף הנקודה [*] [רק שיהא נזהר בגרידתו שלא תהא בשום פעם צורת יו״ד עליה] (קסת הסופר י״ב י״ב). ואחר כך יוסיף עליו מלמעלה ולמטה [תשובת חתם סופר סי׳ רס״ט]. על כן יש ליזהר

* המגי״ל

שער הציון

שכ׳ כן לענין כפוף מעט וראש שמאלי כזיי״ן וכ״ש בהשאר שאין להם מקור כ״כ. ד) ב״ש בדף י״ב ע״ג. [י] א) ב״ש

ביאור הלכה

לא הזכירו כלל ד״ז רק כתבו סתמא שיהא כפוף. העולה מדברינו דכפוף הרבה תלוי במחלוקת דלדעת התרומה והיראים והגה״מ פסול אף בדיעבד ולדעת הרא״ש והטור והרי״ו מותר וכיון דהוא מלתא דאורייתא צריך להחמיר ואם כן לפי פירושנו הנ״ל דכפוף הרבה מקרי אף בלא נגיעה למטה יאסר בכל גווני. אמנם קשה מאוד להחמיר בדבר בדיעבד נגד הב״ש והאגור דמשמע מהם דמותר בלא נגיעה, אבל לכתחילה נ״ל דצריך לתקן במקום דאפשר דהיינו בס״ת. אם נמצא כן בעת הקריאה אין להוציא אחרת עבור זה ויסמוך על המכשירים, אבל אח״כ ימחוק הט׳ עד שיבטלנו מצורת אות ויתקננו דאל״ה מיפסל משום ח״ת ובתו״מ דשלא כסדרן פסול יסמוך בזה על המכשירים הנ״ל. ואם נגעה הכפיפה בקרקע הטי״ת אף בתו״מ פסול וכדעת לדוד אמת הנ״ל דאין להקל נגד התרומה והגה״מ הנ״ל. ואפשר דגם הרא״ש בזה מודה דפסול מטעם דנשתנית צורתה בזה ואפילו אם הראוה לתינוק וקראה טי״ת הלא אינו מוקף גויל באותו מקום וכדלקמן באות שי״ן בסופו, אלא דמשום זה לחוד היה מהני גרירא לחודא באותו מקום, משא״כ להתרומה והגה״מ דזהו בכלל טתי״ן פאי״ן בכל גווני צריך לבטל האות מצורתו וזה לא יצוייר בתו״מ וכנ״ל.

* [י] גם צ״ל להיו״ד תג קטן מלמעלה וכו׳. ולענין דיעבד משמע בלבוש דיש להקל, אך לענ״ד צ״ע דבב״ש בא״ב הראשון מוכח בפירוש דלר״ת שוה לענין פסול הקוץ התחתון והתג העליון ומה דנקט המשנה אפילו קוצו של יו״ד מעכב ולא נקט התג אפשר דלרבותא אף שהוא קטן מהתג כדאיתא בב״י. וגם הלא ברא״ש בהלכות ס״ת וכן בהגה״מ ובסה״ת לא פסיקא להו וכתבו דיכול להיות דקוצו של יו״ד היינו התג העליון עי״ש. ועכ״פ נראה אף אם נימא דאינו מעכב בדיעבד לענין שיקרא פסול אבל לכתחלה בודאי צריך לתקן אף אם מצא כן בפרשיות ישנים וכ״ש בעוקץ שמאלי דחייב לתקן ולא לחזור ולהניחן כן בבתים.

* [י] יגרור כל העוקץ וכו׳. תמיה לי הלא כיון דנראית כחי״ת נשתנית צורתה ונפסלה ואם כן אכתי ה״ל חק תוכות ואין לומר דכיון דחסר עדיין עוקצה אינו אות ונכשרה במה דמשלימה ע״י כתיבה זה אינו רק לר״ת דהקוץ מעכב

correction/. If /the right head/ is not bent inwards at all and a child /who is neither especially intelligent nor especially simple/ did not read it for the letter /ט/, study is required /to determine/ whether /or not the letter/ can be corrected in the case of *tefilin* /passages or mezuzos/, because /the correction may be considered writing/ in incorrect order. See Sec. 32, Par. 25, that as regards a /letter/ ח whose hump /parts do not touch one another we take into account the fact that a child is not accustomed to such a form of the letter/. It may be that the same ruling /applies/ here, since /a child/ is not accustomed to a ט which does not /have its right head/ bent /inwards/, and /if so the letter/ is not classed as having a different form because of /the child's reading/. Study is required /to establish the correctness of this reasoning/.

One should take care that the heads /of the letter/ do not touch one another. /In an instance/ where it is after the event /and they do touch/, see below at the end /of the description/ of the letter ש, for what we have written there /as regards/ whether /or not/ this can be corrected by scraping.

If the left head does not have the symbol of a /letter/ ז, as the head is rounded, but it has crownlets /, then/, study is required /to determine/ whether or not it is valid now that it is after the event, in view of the crownlets. This follows from what the *B.Y.* quotes below, in the name of the *Hagah.M.*, on the authority of the *Re'eym*, that when the Gemara[7*] states that /the letters/ שעטנז גץ require ז /letter forms/, this does not mean /that the letters must necessarily have/ crownlets, but that their heads should not be made rounded but drawn out, so that each head has three tips. /The latter/ is an essential /requirement/, as is evident from the *B.Y.*, at the end of Sec. 36. One cannot prove /that the letter is valid/ from what the *P.Mg.* writes, that /the letter/ is valid once it is after the event if /the left head/ is not like a /letter/ ז, because it may be that /the *P.Mg.* means that it is valid/ when the head does not pass over on both sides /of the leg/ like /the head of/ of a /letter/ ז, but not /that it is valid when the head is/ rounded. /This point/ requires study according to /the view of/ the *Re'eym* and, in addition, it may be that the halachic /ruling/ does not /follow/ the *Re'eym* on this /matter/. See Sec. 36, in the Mishnah Berurah, sub-Par. 15, /for what we have written/ about this.

THE FORM OF THE LETTER י

The length of the body of the letter י should be equivalent to /the thickness of/ one[4*] quill,[1] but no more, so that /the letter/ should not resemble a /letter/ ר.

One should write /the letter/ straight, i.e., its head and front should be an even /line/ and the front should not /face/ upwards.[2]

Initially, /the letter/ should also be rounded above on the right side.[3]

One should make a leg to /the letter/ on the

7* *Menachos* 29b.

עליה ואם לא היה כפוף כלל לתוכה והתינוק לא קראה לאות צ״ע אם יש לה תקנה בתפילין משום שלא כסדרן. ועיין בסימן ל״ב בסעיף כ״ה לענין ח׳ דהטוטרות ואפשר דה״ה בזה דאין מורגל בטי״ת בלי כפיפה ולא מקרי בזה נשתנית צורתה וצ״ע. ויזהר ד) שלא יגעו הראשים זה בזה. ובדיעבד אם יש להם תקנה ע״י גרירה עי׳ לקמן בסוף אות שי״ן מה שכתבנו שם. אם הראש השמאלי לא היה תמונתה כזיי״ן שראשה היתה עגולה, אך שהיתה תגין עליה צ״ע בדיעבד לפי מה שהביא הב״י לקמן בשם הגה״מ בשם הרא״ם דמה שאמרו בגמרא דשעטנ״ז ג״ץ צריכה ג׳ זיוני״ן היינו לא בתגין אלא שלא יעשה ראשיהם עגול אלא משוך שיהא לכל ראש ג׳ פינים ולעיכובא הוא כדמוכח בב״י בסוף סימן ל״ו אם ע״י התגין מתכשרת או לא. ואין להביא ראיה מפמ״ג שכתב דבדיעבד כשר אם לא היה כזיי״ן דאפשר שלא היה עובר מב׳ צדדין כזיי״ן, אבל לא עגולה. וצ״ע להרא״ם וגם אולי אין הלכה כהרא״ם בזה.

ועיין בסי׳ ל״ו במ״ב ס״ק ט״ו בזה.

צורת אות יו״ד

[1] שיעור גופה א) מלא קולמוס אחד ולא יותר שלא תדמה לרי״ש [2] ויכתוב אותה ישרה דהיינו שתהיה ראשה ופניה ב) שוים ולא פניה כלפי מעלה. [3] גם תהיה למעלה ג) עגולה לצד ימין לכתחלה. [4] ד) ויעשה לה רגל **מצד ימין** [5] **ויעקם הרגל לצד שמאל ויהיה הרגל קצר ולא ארוך שלא תדמה לוא״ו ותפסל ע״י קריאת התינוק.** [6] *** גם צריך להיות להיו״ד תג קטן מלמעלה על פניה** [7] **וכנגדה עוקץ קטן יורד מלמטה והעוקץ יהיה קצר מן התג. גם יהיה קצר יותר מרגלה שמצד ימיני פן תדמה לחי״ת. ואם האריך העוקץ עד ששוה למטה לרגל ימיני ונראית כחי״ת קטנה פסולה ולא מהני גרירת העוקץ עד שיהיה קצר כהלכתו דה״ל חק תוכות אלא * יגרור כל העוקץ ויחזור ויכתבנו כהלכתו ולא מהני קריאת התינוק בזה** [כן הביא בספר משנת אברהם בשם בית יהודה ולדויד אמת ומעשה רוקח וקנאת סופרים סי׳ י״ב] **ובס״ת מיירי ולא בתו״מ דהוי שלא כסדרן ויש מי שכתב דלדעת ר״י אכסנדרני** [המובא בב״י ד״ה וז״ל הריא״ס נמצא בהגה״מ וכו׳] **דקי״ל כוותיה צריך לגרור גם רגל ימיני ואח״כ יתקן** [ג״ז שם] [תשובת חב״י בסי׳ ע״ד והובא בפ״ת ליו״ד בסי׳ רע״ד סק״ו] **ועיין בביאור הלכה שביארנו דיש להחמיר כדעה זו. וס״ת שנמצאו בה יודי״ן כצורת למ״ד קטנה פסולה וצריך לגרור כל האות ולחזור ולכתוב יו״ד מחדש דבלא״ה הוי חק תוכות. וביודי״ן של שם צריך לסלק כל היריעה, אך אם היו״ד נראה ממש כלמ״ד לעין כל אזי יכול לגרור אפילו בשם באופן שלא ישאר רק גוף הנקודה** *[רק שיהא נזהר בגרידתו שלא תהא בשום פעם צורת יו״ד עליה] (קסת הסופר י״ב י״ב). **ואחר כך יוסיף עליו מלמעלה ולמטה** [תשובת חתם סופר סי׳ רס״ט]. **על כן יש ליזהר**

* המו״ל

שער הציון

א) ב״ש [י] שכ׳ כן לענין כפוף מעט וראש שמאלי כזיי״ן וכ״ש בהשאר שאין להם מקור כ״כ. ד) ב״ש בדף י״ב ע״ג.

ביאור הלכה

לא הזכירו כלל ד״ז רק כתבו סתמא שיהא כפוף. העולה מדברינו דכפוף הרבה תלוי במחלוקת דלדעת התרומה והיראים והגה״מ פסול אף בדיעבד ולדעת הרא״ש והטור והרי״ו מותר וכיון דהוא מלתא דאורייתא צריך להחמיר ואם כן לפי פירושנו הנ״ל דכפוף הרבה מקרי אף בלא נגיעה למטה יאסר בכל גווני. אמנם קשה מאוד להחמיר בדבר בדיעבד נגד הב״ש והאגור דמשמע מהם דמותר בלא נגיעה, אבל לכתחילה נ״ל דצריך לתקן במקום דאפשר דהיינו בס״ת. אם נמצא כן בעת הקריאה אין להוציא אחרת עבור זה ויסמוך על המכשירים, אבל אח״כ ימחוק הט׳ עד שיבטלנו מצורת אות ויתקננו דאל״ה מיפסל משום ח״ת ובתו״מ דשלא כסדרן פסול יסמוך בזה על המכשירים הנ״ל. ואם נגעה הכפיפה בקרקע הטי״ת אף בתו״מ פסול וכדעת לדוד אמת הנ״ל דאין להקל נגד התרומה והגה״מ הנ״ל. ואפשר דגם הרא״ש בזה מודה דפסול מטעם דנשתנית צורתה בזה ואפילו אם הראוה לתינוק וקראה טי״ת הלא אינו מוקף גויל באותו מקום וכדלקמן באות שי״ן בסופו, אלא דמשום זה לחוד היה מהני גרירא לחודא באותו מקום, משא״כ להתרומה והגה״מ דזהו בכלל טתי״ן פאי״ן בכל גווני צריך לבטל האות מצורתו וזה לא יצוייר בתו״מ וכנ״ל.

* **גם** צ״ל להיו״ד תג קטן מלמעלה וכו׳. ולענין דיעבד משמע בלבוש דיש להקל, אך לענ״ד צ״ע דבב״ש בא״ב הראשון מוכח בפירוש דלר״ת שוה לענין פסול הקוץ התחתון והתג העליון ומה דנקט המשנה אפילו קוצו של יו״ד מעכב ולא נקט התג אפשר דלרבותא אף שהוא קטן מהתג כדאיתא בב״י. וגם הלא ברא״ש בהלכות ס״ת וכן בהגה״מ ובסה״ת לא פסיקא להו וכתבו דיכול להיות דקוצו של יו״ד היינו התג העליון עי״ש. ועכ״פ נראה אף אם נימא דאינו מעכב בדיעבד לענין שיקרא פסול אבל לכתחלה בודאי צריך לתקן אף אם מצא כן בפרשיות ישנים וכ״ש בעוקץ שמאלי דחייב לתקן ולא לחזור ולהניחן כן בבתים.

* **יגרור** כל העוקץ וכו׳. תמיה לי הלא כיון דנראית כחי״ת נשתנית צורתה ונפסלה ואם כן אכתי ה״ל חק תוכות ואין לומר דכיון דחסר עדיין עוקצה אינו אות ונכשרה במה דמשלימה ע״י כתיבה זה אינו רק לר״ת דהקוץ מעכב

right side[4] and should slant the leg towards the left.[5] The leg should be short and not long, so that /the letter/ should not resemble /the letter/ ו and become invalid through being /incorrectly/ read by a child /who is neither especially intelligent nor especially simple/.

The י must also have a small crownlet above on its front.[6] Corresponding to /the crownlet/ a small prickle should descend below[7] /the front/. The prickle should be shorter than the crownlet. It must also be shorter than the leg on the right side, lest /the letter/ will appear like a /letter/ ח. If one made the prickle so long that it became even with the right leg below and /the letter therefore/ appears like a small /letter/ ח, /the letter/ is invalid. It is of no avail /in such a case/ to scrape off /some/ of the prickle until it is /sufficiently/ short to conform with the halachic /requirements/ for /the letter י/, since this constitutes carving around /to form the letter/. Instead, one should scrape away the entire prickle and write it again in conformance with halachic /requirements/. If a child /who is neither especially intelligent nor especially simple/ reads /the letter as a י/ this is of no avail when /the prickle is too long/. [This is cited in the work *Mishnas Avraham*, on the authority of the /works/ *Beis Yehudah, Le-David Emes, Ma'aseh Rokey'ach* and *Kin'as Soferim*, Sec. 12.]

/The ruling that one should scrape away the prickle/ applies /when the letter is/ in a Torah Scroll, but not to /the writing of/ a *tefilin* /passage/ or a mezuzah, /when more has been written after it/, since /such a correction/ constitutes /writing/ in incorrect order /, which is invalid in the latter/.

There is an /authority/ who writes that according to the view of the *Ri Aksandarni* [quoted by the *B.Y.* /in the paragraph/ beginning with the words וז״ל הריא״ס נמצא בהגה״מ וכו׳], which the /halachic/ ruling follows, one is required to scrape off the right leg as well /when the scraping is possible/ and /only/ subsequently /can the letter/ be corrected. [This is also /noted/ there.] [Responsa *Ch.B.Y.*, Sec. 74. This is quoted in the *P.T.* to the *Yo.D.*, Sec. 274, sub-Par. 6.] See the Beyur Halachah, where we have explained that one should be stringent in conformance with this view.

If one discovered that a Torah Scroll has י /letters/ with the form of small ל /letters, the Torah Scroll/ is invalid. /When one corrects such a letter/ he must scrape off the entire letter and rewrite the /letter/ י anew, as, otherwise, /the correction/ will constitute carving around /to form the letter/. In the case of י /letters/ of the /Divine/ Name, it is necessary to remove the entire sheet /on which they have been written and rewrite it/. However, if the י looks actually like a ל and this will be discerned by everyone, one may then scrape off /the letter/ even from a /Divine/ Name, in such a manner that only the main stroke /of the letter/ will remain. Subsequently, one may add /the crownlet/ to it above and /the prickle/ below. [Responsum of the *Chasam Sofer*, Sec. 269.]

One must therefore take great care /to act

מאד במ"ש הברוך שאמר דיעשה הקוצות קטנים ודקים שלא יקלקל היו"ד ע"ש כ"א יהיה תג גדול למעלה יהיה נראה כלמ"ד קטן ואם יאריך העוקץ שלמטה יהיה נראה כחי"ת. ובעוו"ה יש מהסופרים שאינם נזהרין בזה כלל או מוסיפין כנ"ל או גורעין שאינם עושין כלל עוקץ לצד שמאלי ובאמת רוב הפוסקים פסקו כר"ת דעוקץ שמאלי מעכב כמו רגל ימיני, אך דיש חילוק ביניהם בדיעבד לענין תיקון, דבשמאלו מועיל תיקון אפילו בתו"מ ולא הוי שלא כסדרן, אבל לא בימינו וכמו שנתבאר בסימן ל"ב וכבר צווח הפמ"ג בזמנו על זה. ע"כ יש ליזהר מאד שלא לחסרם וגם שלא להוסיף עליהם כי העוקץ השמאלי לא יהיה רק כמין נקודה או מעט יותר יוצא מגוף היו"ד כדמוכח בספר התרומה.

צורת אות כ"ף כפופה

[1] יכתבנה א) עגולה מאחריה שלא תדמה לבי"ת. ותהיה עגולה מאחוריה מב' הצדדים [2] וחללה שבפנים יהיה ב) לכל הפחות כעובי קולמוס. [3] ופניה יהיה למעלה ולמטה שוין. גם צריך ליזהר ג) שלא לקצרנה ברחבה כדי שלא תראה כנו"ן כפופה לתינוק דלא חכים ולא טיפש. [עיין בב"י בא"ב שני אות וא"ו] ואם ד) עשה לה זוית מאחוריה למעלה או למטה פסולה ה) ויש מקילין ביש לה זוית מלמעלה כיון שהיא עגולה למטה וכיון שהוא מלתא דאורייתא צריך להחמיר כדעה הראשונה דפסולה ולא יועיל לה תיקון ע"י גרירה דהוי ח"ת אלא ו) יוסיף עליה דיו לעשותה עגול אם לא כתב עדיין יותר כדי דלא ליהוי שלא כסדרן. ואפשר דבזה שיש לה זוית מלמעלה ועגולה מלמטה * אם התינוק קורא כהלכתה צורתה עליה מיקרי ויכול לתקנה בתיקון הנ"ל אף שכתב יותר ואין בזה משום שלא כסדרן וכנ"ל בל"ב סכ"ה.

צורת אות כ"ף פשוטה

[1] רגלה ארוך [2] וגגה קצר א) שלא תדמה לרי"ש. ואעפ"כ לא יקצר גגה יותר מדאי שלא תראה ב) כוי"ו ארוך או כנו"ן פשוטה לתינוק ותפסל. ולכן לא ימשוך אותה בסוף השיטה לעשותה ארוכה כלל ואע"ג דכל אותיות אין למשכן זהו למצוה אבל בדיעבד לא פסול. אבל בכ"ף פשוטה * אם האריך גגה ג) עד שנראה כרי"ש פסול ואם ספק מראין לתינוק דלא חכים ולא טיפש. ומאד צריך הסופר ליזהר עכ"פ לכתחלה שיהיה הירך ד) כפלים מן הגג כדי שאם כופפין אותה תוכל להיות כ"ף כפופה

שער הציון

בא"ב החמישי. ב) ב"י. ג) ב"ש שם. ד) בב"י כל הענין. **כ** א) ב"י. ב) ב"ש. ג) פשוט. ד) פמ"ג. ה) עי' בעבודת היום. ו) לעיל בסי' ל"ב בט"ז ס"ק ט"ז. **ך** א) ב"י. ב) ממה דהבאתי לעיל באות וא"ו בשם הלדוד אמת עי"ש. ג) סידור

ביאור הלכה

אבל לרש"י דכשר בלא עוקץ שמאל נעשה האות ע"י גרירה לבד ודילמא הלכה כרש"י דהלא דינא דר"ת לא ברירא כ"כ להפוסקים [עיין בנו"ב מ"ת בסי' קי"ג דמכשיר בדיעבד בלא עוקץ שמאלי] ורק להחמיר צריך לחוש לדבריו ולא להקל וא"ל דקמיירו דלא נראית כחי"ת קטנה ממש רק דמספקא להו בחי"ת קטנה ותינוק קורא ליו"ד א"כ יועיל זה לבד בלי גרירה כדפסק הטור בכל אות שיש ספק ואמאי כתבו דלא מהני קריאת התינוק [וצריך לעיין בגוף התשובה] ע"כ הנכון כדעת הי"א המובא בפנים.

* **כ אם** התינוק וכו' אפשר וכו'. מה שכתבתי בלשון אפשר אף דבכ"ף פשוטה כתב הפמ"ג ד"ז יש לחלק דשם אריכתו מוכיח על צורתו משא"כ בזה. ואעפ"כ נלענ"ד להקל בשעת הדחק דהלא לפי לשון הרא"ם המובא בב"י באות נו"ן שכ' דכל הכפופות צריכות להיות עגולות למטה וכו' משמע דכלל בזה נמי כ"ף כפופה וא"כ משמע דעיקר ההיכר הוא ע"י עיגולה שלמטה וכן משמע מלשון הד"מ המובא באות ז' בסופו ובפרט שכתב הב"י באות פ' דבכתיבה*אשורית נהגו לכתחלה לעשות לכ"ף זוית מלמעלה א"כ איך נאמר דלדידן אפילו תינוק קורא לאות לא יועיל בזה תיקון משום דאין לה עיקר צורתה. ועוד נ"ל ראיה לזה דעיקר ההיכר תלוי בלמטה מרבינו ירוחם שפירש על הא דאיתא בשבת שלא יכתוב ביתי"ן כפי"ן היינו שיזהר הסופר בעוקץ שאחורי הבי"ת למטה לצד ימין שלא יראה כ"ף א"כ ממילא נמי פשוט דצריך לפרש כפי"ן ביתי"ן נמי כי האי גוונא אצד מטה וכל דברי רי"ו איתא ברא"ש בהלכות קטנות עי"ש, אלא שהוא ביאר לנו דקאי אצד מטה ועכ"פ ע"י תינוק ובהוספת דיו יש להקל.

* צ"ל המאושרה

* **ך אם** האריך גגה וכו'. הוא לשון הדה"ח בהלכות קה"ת ולא הזכיר כלל שיעור דכפלים משום דס"ל דגם בכ"ף הוא רק למצוה [ולזה ציין עי' בד"מ ועיין במרדכי דאכל אותיות אמרן דהוא רק לכתחלה]. וכן מוכח בלבוש בסי' ל"ו ועיין בחידושי רע"א בסי' ל"ב סכ"ה ודלא כהט"ז ביו"ד בסימן רע"ג והש"א שהחזיק בדבריו להחמיר בלא היה כפלים ברגל מן הגג אפילו דיעבד. ודברי הדגמ"ר בסימן ל"ב סקכ"ו במ"א שהחמיר ג"כ בזה אפילו דיעבד מחמת דמוכח כן בב"י בסימן ל"ו נפלאים ממני דהמעיין שם באות ד' בא"ב שני יראה להדיא דלא הזכיר פסול רק באם האריך גגה יותר מרגלה אבל בזה

in accordance/ with what the *Baruch She-Amar* writes, /which is/ to make the tips /of the letter י/ small and thin, so as not to spoil /the form of/ the י; see there. This is because if there will be a large crownlet above /the letter/ will appear like a small ל /letter/ and if one will extend the prickle below /the letter/ will appear like a /letter/ ח.

Among our many sins, there are scribes who are not careful about this at all. They either add /to the tips/ as /described/ above or subtract /from the letter/ by not making a prickle at all on the left side. The truth is that the majority of Poskim rule in accordance with /the opinion of/ *R.T.*, that the prickle on the left is essential /for the validity of the letter/, just like the right leg. (However, once it is after the event, there is a difference between /the leg and the prickle/ as regards correction. For /if the prickle/ on the left of /the letter is lacking/ correction is of avail even in the case of *tefilin* /passages/ and mezuzos and is not /considered writing/ in incorrect order. On the other hand, if the right /leg is missing/ this is not the case. /Then, if one has already written further, correction will be of no avail in the case of *tefilin* passages and mezuzos,/ as stated in Sec. 32 /, in the Mishnah Berurah, sub-Par. 118/.) The *P.Mg.* already cried out against this in his time. Consequently, one must take great care not to omit /the left prickle/ and also not to add to it, because the left prickle should merely be like a dot or a little more coming out of the body of the י, as is evident from the *Sefer Ha-Terumah*.

THE FORM OF THE BENT-OVER LETTER כ

The bent-over /form of the/ letter כ should be written rounded at the back,[1] so that it will not resemble a /letter/ ב. It should be rounded at the back on both sides /, i.e., both at the top and at the bottom/.

The space on the inside should be at least the thickness[4*] of a quill.[2] The front /of the letter/ should be even above and below.[3]

One must also take care not to shorten /the letter/ breadthwise, so that it does not appear like the bent-over /form of the letter/ נ to a child who is neither /especially/ intelligent nor /especially/ simple. [See the *B.Y.* in the second /description of the/ alphabet, letter ו.]

If one made /the letter/ with a corner at the back, above or below, /the letter/ is invalid. There are /authorities/ who are lenient as regards /a bent-over כ/ which has a corner above, once /the letter/ is rounded below. /However,/ since a Torah requirement is involved, one must be stringent in conformance with the first opinion /and regard the letter/ as invalid /in such a case/. Correction by means of scraping away /the corner to round the letter there/ will be of no avail to /make it valid/, as this constitutes carving around /to form the letter/. Instead, one should add ink to /the letter/ to make it rounded. /However, in the case of *tefilin* passages or mezuzos this is only of avail/ if

מאד במ"ש הברוך שאמר דיעשה הקוצות קטנים ודקים שלא יקלקל היו"ד ע"ש כ"א יהיה תג גדול למעלה יהיה נראה כלמ"ד קטן ואם יאריך העוקץ שלמטה יהיה נראה כחי"ת. ובעו"ה יש מהסופרים שאינם נזהרין בזה כלל או מוסיפין כנ"ל או גורעין שאינם עושין כלל עוקץ לצד שמאלי ובאמת רוב הפוסקים פסקו כר"ת דעוקץ שמאלי מעכב כמו רגל ימיני, אך דיש חילוק ביניהם בדיעבד לענין תיקון, דבשמאלו מועיל תיקון אפילו בתו"מ ולא הוי שלא כסדרן, אבל לא בימינו וכמו שנתבאר בסימן ל"ב וכבר צווח הפמ"ג בזמנו על זה. ע"כ יש ליזהר מאד שלא לחסרם וגם שלא להוסיף עליהם כי העוקץ השמאלי לא יהיה רק כמין נקודה או מעט יותר יוצא מגוף היו"ד כדמוכח בספר התרומה.

צורת אות כ"ף כפופה

[1] יכתבנה א) עגולה מאחריה שלא תדמה לבי"ת. ותהיה עגולה מאחוריה מב' הצדדים [2] וחללה שבפנים יהיה ב) לכל הפחות כעובי קולמוס. [3] ופניה יהיה למעלה ולמטה שוין. גם צריך ליזהר ג) שלא לקצרנה ברחבה כדי שלא תראה כנו"ן כפופה לתינוק דלא חכים ולא טיפש. [עיין בב"י בא"ב שני אות וא"ו] ואם ד) עשה לה זוית מאחוריה למעלה או למטה פסולה ה) ויש מקילין בייש לה זוית מלמעלה כיון שהיא עגולה למטה וכיון שהוא מלתא דאורייתא צריך להחמיר כדעה הראשונה דפסולה ולא יועיל לה תיקון ע"י גרירה דהוי ח"ת אלא ו) יוסיף עליה דיו לעשותה עגול אם **לא כתב עדיין יותר כדי דלא ליהוי שלא כסדרן. ואפשר דבזה שיש לה זוית מלמעלה ועגולה מלמטה * אם התינוק קורא כהלכתה צורתה עליה מיקרי ויכול לתקנה בתיקון הנ"ל אף שכתב יותר ואין בזה משום שלא כסדרן וכנ"ל בל"ב סכ"ה.**

צורת אות כ"ף פשוטה

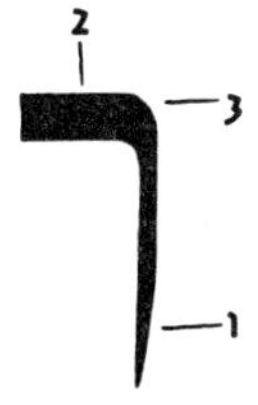

[1] רגלה ארוך [2] וגגה קצר א) שלא תדמה לרי"ש. ואעפ"כ לא יקצר גגה יותר מדאי שלא תראה ב) כוי"ו ארוך או כנו"ן פשוטה לתינוק ותפסל. ולכן לא ימשוך אותה בסוף השיטה לעשותה ארוכה כלל ואע"ג דכל אותיות אין למשכן זהו למצוה אבל בדיעבד לא פסול. אבל בכ"ף פשוטה * אם האריך גגה ג) עד שנראה כרי"ש פסול ואם ספק מראין לתינוק דלא חכים ולא טיפש. ומאד צריך הסופר ליזהר עכ"פ לכתחלה שיהיה הירך ד) כפלים מן הגג כדי שאם כופפין אותה תוכל להיות כ"ף כפופה

שער הציון

בא"ב החמישי. ב) ב"י. ג) ב"ש שם. ד) בב"י כל הענין. כ א) ב"י. ב) ב"ש. ג) פשוט. ד) פמ"ג. ה) עי' בעבודת היום. ו) לעיל בסי' ל"ב בט"ז ס"ק ט"ז. ך א) ב"י. ב) ממה דהבאתי לעיל באות וא"ו בשם הלדוד אמת עי"ש. ג) סידור

ביאור הלכה

אבל לרש"י דכשר בלא עוקץ שמאל נעשה האות ע"י גרירה לבד ודילמא הלכה כרש"י דהלא דינא דר"ת לא ברירא כ"כ להפוסקים [עיין בנו"ב מ"ת בסי' קי"ג דמכשיר בדיעבד בלא עוקץ שמאלי] ורק להחמיר צריך לחוש לדבריו ולא להקל וא"ל דקמיירו דלא נראית כחי"ת קטנה ממש רק דמספקא להו בחי"ת קטנה ותינוק קורא ליו"ד א"כ יועיל זה לבד בלי גרירה כדפסק הטור בכל אות שיש ספק ואמאי כתבו דלא מהני קריאת התינוק [וצריך לעיין בגוף התשובה] ע"כ הנכון כדעת הי"א המובא בפנים.

* **כ אם** התינוק וכו' אפשר וכו'. מה שכתבתי בלשון אפשר אף דבכ"ף פשוטה כתב הפמ"ג ד"ז יש לחלק דשם אריכתו מוכיח על צורתו משא"כ בזה. ואעפ"כ נלענ"ד להקל בשעת הדחק דהלא לפי לשון הרא"ם המובא בב"י באות נו"ן שכ' דכל הכפופות צריכות להיות עגולות למטה וכו' משמע דכלל בזה נמי כ"ף כפופה וא"כ משמע דעיקר ההיכר הוא ע"י עיגולה שלמטה וכן משמע מלשון הד"מ המובא באות ז' בסופו ובפרט שכתב הב"י באות פ' דבכתיבה*אשורית נהגו לכתחלה לעשות לכ"ף זוית מלמעלה א"כ איך נאמר דלדידן אפילו תינוק קוראה לאות לא יועיל בזה תיקון משום דאין לה עיקר צורתה. ועוד נ"ל ראיה לזה דעיקר ההיכר תלוי בלמטה מרבינו ירוחם שפירש על הא דאיתא בשבת שלא יכתוב ביתי"ן כפי"ן היינו שיזהר הסופר בעוקץ שאחורי הבי"ת למטה לצד ימין שלא יראה כ"ף א"כ ממילא נמי פשוט דצריך לפרש כפי"ן ביתי"ן נמי כי האי גווני אצד מטה וכל דברי רי"ו איתא ברא"ש בהלכות קטנות עי"ש, אלא שהוא ביאר לנו דקאי אצד מטה ועכ"פ ע"י תינוק ובהוספת דיו יש להקל.

*צ"ל המאושרה

* **ך אם** האריך גגה וכו'. הוא לשון הדה"ח בהלכות קה"ת ולא הזכיר כלל שיעור דכפלים משום דס"ל דגם בכ"ף הוא רק למצוה [ולזה ציין עי' בד"מ ועיין במרדכי דאכל אותיות אמרן דהוא רק לכתחלה]. וכן מוכח בלבוש בסי' ל"ו ועיין בחידושי רע"א בסי' ל"ב סכ"ה ודלא כהט"ז ביו"ד בסימן רע"ג והש"א שהחזיק בדבריו להחמיר בלא היה כפלים ברגל מן הגג אפילו דיעבד. ודברי הדגמ"ר בסימן ל"ב סקכ"ו במ"א שהחמיר ג"כ בזה אפילו דיעבד מחמת דמוכח כן בב"י בסימן ל"ו נפלאים ממני דהמעיין שם באות ך' בא"ב שני יראה להדיא דלא הזכיר פסול רק באם האריך גגה יותר מרגלה אבל בזה

one has not yet written more /after the letter/, so that /the correction/ will not /constitute writing/ in incorrect order.

It may be that in a case where /the letter/ has a corner above and is rounded below /the letter/ is classed as having its /proper/ form, if a child /who is neither especially intelligent nor especially simple/ reads it as it should be /read/. /If so/ one is able to correct /the letter/ with the aforementioned /method of/ correction even though one has /already/ written more /letters subsequently, since/ it will not be /considered writing/ in incorrect order, as /explained/ above in Sec. 32, Par. 25.

THE FORM OF THE SIMPLE /ELONGATED/ LETTER ך

The leg of the simple /elongated/ letter ך should be long[1] and the roof of /the letter/ should be short,[2] so that /the letter/ will not resemble a /letter/ ר. (Nevertheless, one should not make the roof shorter than necessary, so that /the letter/ will not appear like a long /form of the letter/ ו or like a simple /elongated letter/ ן to a child /who is neither especially intelligent nor especially simple/ and become invalid /through his reading/.) Therefore, one should not extend /the roof of the letter ך/ at the end of a line to lengthen it at all. Although all letters should not be extended, this is /merely/ a mitzvah /requirement/, but once it is after the event they will not be invalid /because of it/. In the case of a simple /elongated/ ך, however, /the letter/ will be invalid if one extends its roof to the extent that /the letter/ looks like a /letter/ ר. If there is a doubt /as to whether it looks like a ר/, one should show /the letter/ to a child who is neither /especially/ intelligent nor /especially/ simple /and if he reads it for a letter ר the letter is invalid/.

The scribe must be extremely careful, at any rate, initially, that /the length of/ the thigh /of the letter/ is double /the length/ of the roof, so that should one bend /the thigh/ over it will be capable of becoming a bent-

שאין חילוק בין פשוטה לכפופה רק שזה פשוטה וזה כפופה כי יש מחמירין ופוסלין בזה אפילו דיעבד [הט"ז ביו"ד סימן רע"ג עי"ש שקרא לאותם הסופרים בורים ושהס"ת פסול בזה] וכן כל הפשוטות צריכות להיות לכתחלה כפלים מן הגג מטעם זה. ובדיעבד אם נמצא בס"ת שהמשיך הגג של ד' עד שנראה כרי"ש אם באפשרו ה) להאריך הרגל למטה יאריך ואם לאו ימחוק הכל ו) ויכתבנו מחדש ויש מקילין ז) דדי בגרירת הרגל או הגג אבל לגרור קצת מן הגג עד שיעמידנו על תמונת כ"ף לא מהני דהו"ל חק תוכות. [3] גם צריך הסופר ליזהר שלא יעשה לכ"ף פשוטה זוית למעלה אלא תהיה עגולה כמו רי"ש שאם כופפין אותה תיעשה כ"ף כפופה. ואם עשה לה זוית למעלה כמו ד' ח) פסולה ודינה שצריך לגרור כולה ולכותבה מחדש או ט) שיוסיף עליה דיו לעשותה עגולה. ועצה זו דהוספת דיו מהני אפילו בתו"מ דלא מיקרי שלא כסדרן דקודם התיקון נמי צורת כ"ף פשוטה עליה וכמבואר לעיל בסימן ל"ב סכ"ה. אך אם נמצא כן בס"ת בעת הקריאה אין להוציא אחרת כי יש מכשירין בזה [עיין בפמ"ג בסי' קמ"ג ובדה"ח בהלכות קה"ת דהיכא דאיכא מחלוקת בין הפוסקים אין להוציא אחרת]. כל אותיות הכפולין בא"ב י) כותב את הראשונים בתחילת התיבה ובאמצעה והאחרונים בסוף. ואם שינה פסול.

צורת אות למ"ד

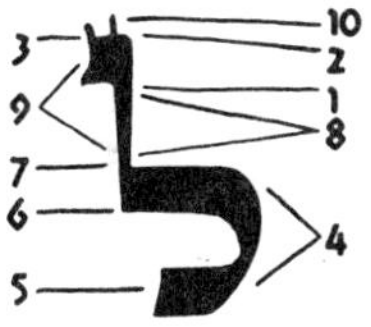

[1] צריך להיות צוארה א) ארוך כוא"ו [2] וראשה של הצואר יהיה עגול לצד ימין למעלה [3] ולצד שמאל זוית לראשה כמו שהוא ראש הוא"ו כי תמונת הלמ"ד היא כמו כ"ף כפופה ועליה וא"ו [4] ומהאי טעמא תהיה ירכה עגולה מאחריה לצד ימין [5] וכפופה היטיב לפניה ב) כצורת כ"ף כפופה. אך אם צריך להמשיך הקו התחתון של הכ"ף שיהיה שוה עם הקו העליון יש דיעות בזה בין הפוסקים די"א דצריך [רדב"ז סימן פ"ב ותורת חיים פ' חלק] וי"א דאדרבה דלא ימשיכו רק מעט [ספר קהלת יעקב בסופו בהשו"ת עיין שם שכתב שגם שמע כן בשם הגר"א]. * ונהגו הסופרים כדעה זו ועיין בביאור הלכה. [6] ולצד שמאל מקום חיבור כ"ף עם וא"ו יהיה בזוית ולא בעיגול [7] ויהא ג) חיבור הוא"ו אל הכ"ף בדקות [8] כי תמונתו כתמונת וא"ו שעוביו מתמעט והולך בסופו וכנ"ל בוא"ו. ויכתוב הראש והצואר כפוף ד) מעט על פניה [10] ועל ראש הצואר צריך להיות ב' תגין ה) מימין גדול ומשמאל קטן. ו) וכ"ז לכתחלה לבד אם עשה צואר הלמ"ד כעין יו"ד יש פוסקים שפוסלין בזה אפילו דיעבד [עיין בתשובת אור ישראל ותמצא שם דיעות בזה ועי' בספר עבודת היום ובספר לדויד אמת]. על כן צריך הסופר ליזהר בזה מאד וז"ל הברוך שאמר לאפוקי מכל הסופרים בורים שמקצרים הצואר של הלמ"ד ועושים על הלמ"ד כמין יו"ד מחמת שאינם עושים ריוח בין שיטה לשיטה כמלא שיטה וכו' כי הרוקח כתב בהדיא שיש לכתוב על הלמ"ד כמו וא"ו ולא כמו יו"ד. וכן מצאתי בהג"ה מפ' גט פשוט וכו'. וכן כתב רבינו שמחה בשם החסיד ז"ל ע"ש. עוד ראיתי סופרים בורים שכשטועין וכותבין קו"ף במקום למ"ד עושין צואר תחלה על ראשו שיהיה למ"ד ואח"כ כשנתייבש הדיו גוררין הרגל וה"ה כשטועין וכותבין למ"ד במקום קו"ף גומרין רגל הקו"ף ואח"כ גוררין הצואר וזה פסול גמור כמו ה' במקום ד' שנתבאר לעיל בצורת ד'. למ"ד שנמצא ע"ג רק כעין קו פשוט כזה ל ולא וא"ו יש להכשיר בשעת הדחק דהיינו אם נמצא כן בשבת א"צ להוציא אחרת ובחול יתקן ובתפילין אם אין לו אחרים יניחם בלא ברכה [ס' החיים וקסת הסופר].

שער הציון

דה"ח בהלכות קה"ת ועי' בבה"ל. ד) ב"י. ה) מ"א בסימן ל"ב סקכ"ו. ו) שער אפרים בשער ה'. ז) מ"א ועי"ש ביד אפרים. ח) ב"י בשם הרי"א. ט) פמ"ג. י) ספ"ב דמסכת סופרים והובא לדינא בסי' ל"ב סי"ח בביאור הגר"א. ל א) ב"י. ב) ב"י.

ביאור הלכה

לא כתב רק דצריך להיות כפלים והכונה למצוה. אח"כ מצאתי בספר ברכת המים להגאון בעה"מ סדר הגט שבאה"ע שכתב ג"כ בהדיא דלא החמירו רק באם האריך גגה יותר מרגלה אבל לא במחצה על מחצה עי"ש. א"כ משמע דכ"ש דכפלים לא הוזכר רק למצוה.

* ונהגו הסופרים כדעה זו. ועיין ג"כ ל בפמ"ג שכתב דמה שאמרו בירכו של ה"א הימיני אם יש בו כמלא אות קטנה והוא היו"ד כשר, נראה לי דה"ה לשאר אותיות כגון ד' למ"ד וכו' אם נשאר מירך הימין כיו"ד די בכך ונ"ל שבלמ"ד כוונתו לענין קו התחתון הזה שאפילו אם לא המשיכו מלמטה רק כיו"ד די דא"ל שכוונתו להקל אפילו בקו העגולה האמצעי שמצד ימין א"כ אין בו תמונת למ"ד כלל.

over כ. /This is/ because there is no difference /in form/ between the simple /elongated ך/ and the bent-over /כ/, except that one is simple /and elongated/ and the other is bent over. /This is important,/ because there are /authorities/ who are stringent about this /ratio/ and invalidate /the letter if it is not conformed with/, even once it is after the event. [The *Taz* in the *Yo.D.*, Sec. 273. See there, that he calls those scribes /who are not careful about this/ know-nothings and /states/ that the Torah Scroll is invalid /if this ratio is lacking/.] (/The thighs of/ all the /other/ simple /elongated letters/ must likewise be, initially, twice /the length/ of the roofs, for this reason.)

/However,/ once it is after the event, if one discovers in a Torah Scroll that /the scribe/ extended the roof of a /simple elongated letter/ ך until it appears like a /letter/ ר/, the ruling is as follows/. If it is possible to lengthen the leg downwards /until the letter looks like a simple elongated ך/, one should /in fact/ lengthen it. Otherwise, he should erase the entire /letter/ and write it anew. There are /authorities/ who are lenient /and rule/ that scraping away the leg or the roof is adequate. However, /they agree that/ to scrape off some of the roof until one has established /the letter/ with the symbol of the /simple elongated/ ך is of no avail, since this constitutes carving around /to form the letter/.

The scribe must also take care that he does not make a corner to the simple /elongated/ ך above, but it must be rounded[3] /there/ like the /letter/ ר, so that if /the thigh is/ bent over /the letter/ will become the bent over /letter/ כ. If one did make a corner to it above, as /one makes for the letter/ ד, /the ך/ is invalid. The ruling in such a case is that one must scrape away /the letter/ entirely and write it anew or one should add ink to /the letter/ and /thus/ make it rounded. This solution of adding ink is of avail even in the case of *tefilin* /passages/ and mezuzos, /although one already wrote after the letter/, since /the correction/ is not classed as /writing/ in incorrect order. /The reason is/ that /the letter/ has the form of a simple /elongated/ ך before the correction as well. This conforms with what is stated above in Sec. 32, Par. 25.

However, if /a simple elongated ך/ like this is discovered in a Torah Scroll at the time when one is reading /from the Torah to the congregation/, one should not take out another /Torah Scroll for the reading/, as there are /authorities/ who rule that /the Scroll/ is valid if /a simple elongated letter ך is written/ like this. [See the *P.Mg.*, in Sec. 143, and the *D.Hach.*, in his laws of the reading from the Torah, that where there is a dispute among the Poskim /concerning the validity of the Torah Scroll/ one should not take out another /Torah Scroll/.]

/In the case of/ all the letters which occur twice in the alphabet, one should write the first /form/ at the beginning and in the middle of the word and the final /form/ at the end /of the word/. If one deviated /from this the letter/ is invalid.

THE FORM OF THE LETTER ל

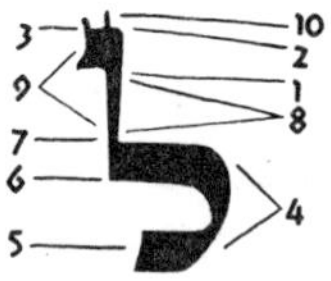

The neck of the letter ל must be as long as a /letter/ ו.[1] The head of the neck should be rounded on the right side above.[2] On the left side, /the neck should have/ a corner on its head.[3] This accords with /the requirements for/ the head of a /letter/ ו. It is /required/ because the symbol of the /letter/ ל is like /that of/ a bent-over /letter/ כ /together/ with a /letter/ ו on /top of/ it.

For this reason the thigh of /the letter/ should be rounded at the back on the right side[4] and /it should be/ well bent over to the front,[5] in conformance with the form of the bent-over /letter/ כ. However, as regards the necessity to continue the lower line of the כ /part/ so that it is even /in length/ with the upper line, there are /conflicting/ views among the Poskim on this /point/. There are /authorities/ who say that it is necessary.

שאין חילוק בין פשוטה לכפופה רק שזה פשוטה וזה כפופה כי יש מחמירין ופוסלין בזה אפילו דיעבד [הט"ז ביו"ד סימן רע"ג עי"ש שקרא לאותם הסופרים בורים ושהס"ת פסול בזה] וכן כל הפשוטות צריכות להיות לכתחלה כפלים מן הגג מטעם זה. ובדיעבד אם נמצא בס"ת שהמשיך הגג של ד' עד שנראה כרי"ש אם באפשרו ה) להאריך הרגל למטה יאריך ואם לאו ימחוק הכל ו) ויכתבנו מחדש ויש מקילין ז) דדי בגרירת הרגל או הגג אבל לגרור קצת מן הגג עד שיעמידנו על תמונת כ"ף לא מהני דהו"ל חק תוכות. [3] גם צריך הסופר ליזהר שלא יעשה לכ"ף פשוטה זוית למעלה אלא תהיה עגולה כמו רי"ש שאם כופפין אותה תיעשה כ"ף כפופה. ואם עשה לה זוית למעלה כמו ד' ח) פסולה ודינה שצריך לגרור כולה ולכותבה מחדש או ט) שיוסיף עליה דיו לעשותה עגולה. ועצה זו דהוספת דיו מהני אפילו בתו"מ דלא מיקרי שלא כסדרן דקודם התיקון נמי צורת כ"ף פשוטה עליה וכמבואר לעיל בסימן ל"ב סכ"ה. אך אם נמצא כן בס"ת בעת הקריאה אין להוציא אחרת כי יש מכשירין בזה [עיין בפמ"ג בסי' קמ"ג ובדה"ח בהלכות קה"ת דהיכא דאיכא מחלוקת בין הפוסקים אין להוציא אחרת]. כל אותיות הכפולין בא"ב י) כותב את הראשונים בתחילת התיבה ובאמצעה והאחרונים בסוף. ואם שינה פסול.

צורת אות למ"ד

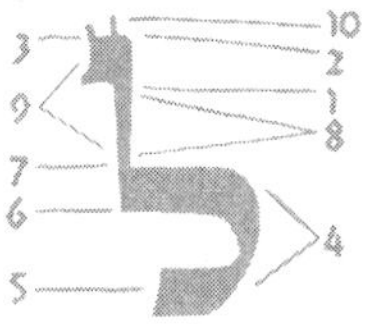

[1] צריך להיות צוארה א) ארוך כוא"ו [2] וראשה של הצואר יהיה עגול לצד ימין למעלה [3] ולצד שמאל זוית לראשה כמו שהוא ראש הוא"ו כי תמונת הלמ"ד היא כמו כ"ף כפופה ועליה וא"ו [4] ומהאי טעמא תהיה יריכה עגולה מאחריה לצד ימין [5] וכפופה היטיב לפניה ב) כצורת כ"ף כפופה. אך אם צריך להמשיך הקו התחתון של הכ"ף שיהיה שוה עם הקו העליון יש דיעות בזה בין הפוסקים די"א דצריך [רדב"ז סימן פ"ב ותורת חיים פ' חלק] וי"א דאדרבה דלא ימשיכו רק מעט [ספר קהלת יעקב בסופו בהשו"ת עיין שם שכתב שגם שמע כן בשם הגר"א]. * ונהגו הסופרים כדעה זו ועיין בביאור הלכה. [6] ולצד שמאל מקום חיבור כ"ף עם וא"ו יהיה בזוית ולא בעיגול [7] ויהא ג) חיבור הוא"ו אל הכ"ף בדקות [8] כי תמונתו כתמונת וא"ו שעוביו מתמעט והולך בסופו וכנ"ל בוא"ו. ויכתוב הראש והצואר כפוף ד) מעט על פניה [10] ועל ראש הצואר צריך להיות ב' תגין ה) מימין גדול ומשמאל קטן. ו) וכ"ז לכתחלה לבד אם עשה צואר הלמ"ד כעין יו"ד יש פוסקים שפוסלין בזה אפילו דיעבד [עיין בתשובת אור ישראל ותמצא שם דיעות בזה ועי' בספר עבודת היום ובספר לדויד אמת]. על כן צריך הסופר ליזהר בזה מאד וז"ל הברוך שאמר לאפוקי מכל הסופרים בורים שמקצרים הצואר של הלמ"ד ועושים על הלמ"ד כמין יו"ד מחמת שאינם עושים ריוח בין שיטה לשיטה כמלא שיטה וכו' כי הרוקח כתב בהדיא שיש לכתוב על הלמ"ד כמו וא"ו ולא כמו יו"ד. וכן מצאתי בהג"ה מפ' גט פשוט וכו'. וכן כתב רבינו שמחה בשם החסיד ז"ל ע"ש. עוד ראיתי סופרים בורים שכשטועין וכותבין קו"ף במקום למ"ד עושין צואר תחלה על ראשו שיהיה למ"ד ואח"כ כשנתייבש הדיו גוררין הרגל וה"ה כשטועין וכותבין למ"ד במקום קו"ף גומרין רגל הקו"ף ואח"כ גוררין הצואר וזה פסול גמור כמו ה' במקום ד' שנתבאר לעיל בצורת ד'. למ"ד שנמצא ע"ג רק כעין קו פשוט כזה ל ולא וא"ו יש להכשיר בשעת הדחק דהיינו אם נמצא כן בשבת א"צ להוציא אחרת ובחול יתקן ובתפילין אם אין לו אחרים יניחם בלא ברכה [ס' החיים וקסת הסופר].

שער הציון

דה"ח בהלכות קה"ת ועי' בבה"ל. ד) ב"י. ה) מ"א בסימן ל"ב סקכ"ו. ו) שער אפרים בשער ה'. ז) מ"א ועי"ש ביד אפרים. ח) ב"י בשם הרי"א. ט) פמ"ג. י) ספ"ב דמסכת סופרים והובא לדינא בסי' ל"ב סי"ח בביאור הגר"א. ל א) ב"י. ב) ב"י.

ביאור הלכה

לא כתב רק דצריך להיות כפלים והכונה למצוה. אח"כ מצאתי בספר ברכת המים להגאון בעה"מ סדר הגט שבאה"ע שכתב ג"כ בהדיא דלא החמירו רק באם האריך גגה יותר מרגלה אבל לא במחצה על מחצה עי"ש. א"כ משמע דכ"ש דכפלים לא הוזכר רק למצוה.

ל * ונהגו הסופרים כדעה זו. ועיין ג"כ בפמ"ג שכתב דמה שאמרו ביריכו של ה"א הימיני אם יש בו כמלא אות קטנה והוא היו"ד כשר, נראה לי דה"ה לשאר אותיות כגון ד' למ"ד וכו' אם נשאר מירך הימין כיו"ד די בכך ונ"ל שבלמ"ד כוונתו לענין קו התחתון הזה שאפילו אם לא המשיכו מלמטה רק כיו"ד די דא"ל שכוונתו להקל אפילו בקו העגולה האמצעי שמצד ימין א"כ אין בו תמונת למ"ד כלל.

[*Radbaz*, Sec. 82 and *Toras Chayim* in the chapter *Cheylek*[8*].] Other /authorities/ say that, on the contrary, one should only continue it a little. [The work *Koheles Ya'akov* at the end, in the responsa. See there, that he writes that he also heard this /ruling given/ in the name of the *Gra*.] The scribes have adopted a practice which accords with this /latter/ view. See the Beyur Halachah.

The place on the left side, where the כ /part/ is connected to the ו /part/, should be in /the form of/ a corner and not rounded.[6] The connection of the ו /part/ to the כ /part/ should be fine,[7] as the symbol of /the ו part of the letter/ should be like the symbol of the /letter/ ו. The thickness /of the letter ו/ diminishes progressively at the end,[8] as /explained/ above /in the description/ of the /letter/ ו.

One should write the head and the neck a little bent over to the front.[9] On the head of the neck there must be two crownlets, a large one on the right and a small one on the left.[10]

/However,/ all this /only applies/ initially, except that if one made the neck of a /letter/ ל resembling a /letter/ י, there are Poskim who invalidate /the ל/ because of this even once it is after the event. [See the responsum of the *Or Yisra'eyl* and you will discover there /that there are conflicting/ opinions about this. See the work *Avodas Ha-Yom* and the work *Le-David Emes*.] Consequently, the scribe must be very careful about this. This is the wording of the *Baruch She-Amar* /on the matter/: "This contradicts /the practice of/ all those know-nothing scribes who shorten the neck of the /letter/ ל and make a kind of י /letter form/ on /top of/ the ל /instead of a ו letter form/, due to /the fact/ that they do not make a /sufficiently large/ space /, i.e./, adequate for /writing/ a line, etc., between one line and the other. For the *Rokeyach* writes explicitly that one should write on /top of/ the ל a ו like /form/ and not a י like /form/." I discovered this likewise in a gloss to the chapter *Get Pashut*,[9*] etc. Rabbeinu Simchah, in the name of the *chasid* (pious person), of blessed memory, likewise writes this; see there.

I saw, in addition, know-nothing scribes, who, when they err and write a /letter/ ק instead of a /letter/ ל, /correct it by/ making a neck first on the head of /the letter/, so that /the letter/ will /have the strokes of/ a ל. They scrape away the /left/ leg /of the ק/ afterwards when the ink has dried. Correspondingly, when they err and write a /letter/ ל instead of a /letter/ ק, they complete the leg of the ק and subsequently scrape away the neck /which served for the ל/. /A ל or ק which was written in/ this /manner/ is completely invalid, just as /a letter ד is invalid if one formed it out of/ a /letter/ ה, /which was written/ instead of a /letter/ ד, /by erasing the left leg/, as explained above in /the description of/ the form of /the letter/ ד.

If a /letter/ ל has on /top of/ it just /a stroke/ that resembles a simple line, but is not /in the form of/ a /letter/ ו, like this ל , one may rule that /the letter/ is valid if /it is/ a time of pressing /need/. I.e., if one discovers /such a ל/ on Shabbos /when the Torah Scroll has been taken out for the reading/, it is unnecessary to take out another /Torah Scroll instead because of this/. On weekdays /, however,/ one should correct /the letter/. In the case of a *tefilin* /passage which has such a ל/, if one does not have other /*tefilin*/ he should don /the *tefilin* which contain this passage, but/ without /making/ a blessing /over the *tefilin*/. [*Sefer Ha-Chayim* and *Keses Ha-Sofer*.]

8* This is a chapter of *Sanhedrin*.
9* This is a chapter of *Bava Basra*.

צורת אות מ"ם פתוחה

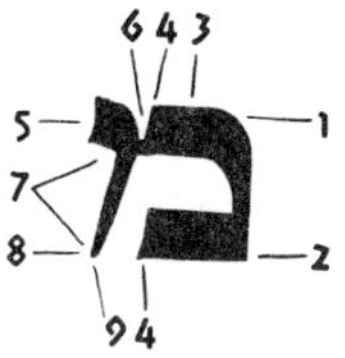

תמונתה קצת א) * כמו כ"ף וא"ו [1] ע"כ תהיה למעלה לצד ימין עגולה [2] אבל למטה יהיה לה זוית ובלא עקב [3] וגגה יהיה למעלה שוה ולא עגול רק לצד ימין יהיה עגול [4] גם יהיה גגה ארוך עד כנגד מושבה התחתון ב) וכ"ז לכתחלה. ג) [5] והחרטום שבצד שמאל יזהר לדבוק אותו לגגו [6] ויהיה לכתחלה כמעט משוך בשוה עם הגג רק ד) שיהיה ביניהם לצד מעלה כמו פגם קטן [7] ה) ותמונת החרטום תהיה כמו וא"ו עומדת מוטה קצת באלכסון ולא הרבה [8] * ויגיע עד כנגד מושב התחתון ועד בכלל. ומאד יזהר שלא יגע בו [9] ומ"מ לא יהיה ביניהם הפסק גדול לכתחלה כדי שלא יהיה עי"ז הוא"ו הרבה באלכסון. ואם לא הדביק החרטום למעלה לגגו ונראה ככ"ף וא"ו פסול ואין מועיל לו תיקון בתו"מ אם כתב אחריו דהוי שלא כסדרן וכדלעיל בסימן ל"ב סכ"ה עי"ש במ"ב. וה"ה אם הדביק החרטום למטה במקום פתיחתו להמ"ם דפסול ומבואר דינו לעיל בסימן ל"ב סי"ח לענין תיקון אם לא כתב עדיין אחריו בתו"מ.

צורת אות מ"ם סתומה

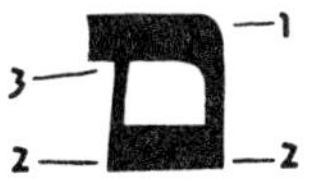

[1] תהיה א) לכתחלה עגולה למעלה לצד ימין [2] ולמטה יהיה לה זוית לימין ולשמאל שלא תהא נראית כסמ"ך. ב) ואם לא עשה כן והתינוק קראה כסמ"ך פסולה. והפמ"ג כתב שטוב יותר שתהיה מרובעת מכל צד כי בקל יוכל לבוא לידי טעות בסמ"ך. ומ"ם זו תהיה סתומה מכל צד. [3] ג) וגגה יהיה עובר ד) לכתחלה מחוץ לסתימה מעט כראש הוא"ו. ה) ולא ימשוך הגג לצד שמאלה הרבה ובדיעבד * יגרור ו) המותר ואין בזה משום חק תוכות ושלא כסדרן ואם נמצא כן בשם הקודש אין לתקנו וישאר כך וכשר. וגם בשבת ז) אין להוציא אחרת עבור זה.

צורת אות נ"ון כפופה

א) [1] יעשה ראשה כמו ראש הזיי"ן [2] וג' תגין עליה ב) ולא יותר רחב מראש הזיי"ן דלא תהוי דומה לבי"ת אם יהיה רחב מעט יותר [3] ומטעם זה יעשה ג"כ מושבה למטה ג) משוך לצד שמאל היטיב יותר מן הראש כדי שלא יתדמה לבי"ת או לכ"ף. [4] וצוארו הנמשך מאמצע ראשו יהיה לכתחלה קצת עב וארוך קצת [5] ומוטה לצד ימין כדי להסמיך אות אצל ראשו. [6] ותהיה הנו"ן ד) לכתחלה עגולה למטה לצד ימין. אם עשה הנו"ן כפופה למעלה צורת וא"ו דהיינו שמשך הצואר מקצה ראשו * הניח הפמ"ג בצ"ע והביאו הגרע"א בחידושיו. ומנחלת דוד בסימן כ"ג משמע דכשר בדיעבד. [וכן משמע לענ"ד לכאורה מהלבוש שחזר בסוף תמונת האותיות שלו הדברים שהם לעיכובא בכל אות ואת וזה דילג] ועכ"פ נ"פ דאף לדעת הפמ"ג מהני תיקון ואפילו בתו"מ דהיינו שיגרור תחלה קצת מראשו לצד שמאל ולא הרבה כדי שישאר עדיין תמונת נו"ן עליו ואח"כ יוסיף עליו דיו לצד ימין לעשותו כמו ראש הזיי"ן ולא מועיל בהוספת דיו מצד ימין לבד דא"כ יהיה ראשו

שער הציון

ג) ב"י בשם הרי"א. ד) ב"י בשם המנהיג. ה) שם בב"י. ו) עבודת היום ופשוט. **מ** א) כולו בב"י. ב) כן משמע מלבוש וש"א ועיין לקמן בבה"ל בנו"ן כפופה בסה"ד דאם עשאו למטה עגולה לא פסיקא כ"כ להכשיר. ג) וכדלקמיה. ד) ב"ש בא"ב האחרון. ה) ב"י. **ם** א) עיין בב"י ופשוט. ב) בס' לד"א. ג) ב"י. ד) נלמד מהנו"ב דבסמוך. ה) דלא יהיה כמו וא"ו. ו) נו"ב בסימן פ' דלא מעכב דבר שאין נמצא בתלמוד וגם לא עדיף מה"א שרגלה באמצע גגה. ז) שערי אפרים בשער ה'

ביאור הלכה

מ * **כמו** כ"ף וא"ו. הכל כתבתי ע"פ המבואר בב"י וכל הפוסקים האחרונים ולאפוקי מהפמ"ג שכתב דתמונתו הוא כמו נו"ן וא"ו כי אין מקור לזה ואפשר דטעמו מסעיף י"ח שכתב המחבר יגרור החרטום עד שתשאר כצורת נו"ן כפופה וג"ז אינו ראיה דאפשר דשם דלא איירי המחבר בדיני כתיבת האותיות לא דקדק לכתוב לפי הנהוג לכתחלה למצוה כיון דאפילו נו"ן וא"ו כשר לכו"ע או דתפס שם לפי מנהג הספרדים שאין ממשיכין הקו שלמעלה עד כנגד מושבה התחתון כמ"ש בספר לדוד אמת א"כ הוא דומה לנו"ן וא"ו וזהו מש"כ שם בס' לד"א דלדידהו המ"ם דומה לטי"ת ובטי"ת כבר ידוע מה שכ' הר"ח דדומה לנו"ן וא"ו וכמש"כ בב"י באות נו"ן אבל לפי מה שאנו נוהגין די בגרירה עד שישאר כצורת כ"ף. תדע דבלבוש וכן באה"ע בסופו בסדר גיטין שסידר מהרמר"י כתוב יגרור עד שתשאר כצורת כ"ף כפופה ומה שכתב שם בט"ז כי המ"ם הוא בב' כתיבות כנו"ן וא"ו כבר תפס עליו בזה הבית אהרן.

מ * **ויגיע** עד כנגד מושב התחתון. ובדיעבד אם לא הגיע עד למטה ותינוק קראו למ"ם צ"ע דאפשר דזהו אינו מעיקר צורת האות רק לכתחלה.

ם * **יגרור** המותר. ומ"מ אם המשיכה כ"כ עד שהתינוק לא הכיר להאות עי"ז לענ"ד צ"ע אם מהני גרירה עיין רמב"ם פ"א מהלכות תפילין הלכה י"ט ואפילו את"ל דבה"א באופן זה ג"כ כשר

THE FORM OF THE OPEN LETTER מ

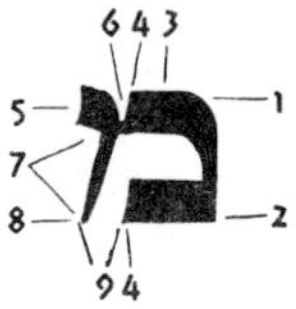

The symbol of the open letter מ is somewhat like that of a /letter/ כ /together with a letter/ ו. Therefore, it should be rounded above on the right side.[1] However, it should have a corner below /on that side/, but without a heel.[2]

The roof on top should be of even /height/ and not round,[3] /but/ should only be rounded on the right side. In addition, the roof should be long, to the extent that /the end of the roof/ will correspond with /the end of/ the base /of the letter/ underneath.[4]

All these are initial /requirements/.

One should take care to adhere the nose on the left side to the roof[5] of /the letter/. Initially, it should be extended almost evenly with the roof, except that there should be /a break/ between them, upwards, like a small notch.[6]

The symbol of the nose should be like /that of/ a /letter/ ו, which stands slightly leaning at a slope, but not excessively.[7] /At the bottom,/ it should reach until opposite the base below, with /the breadth of the base/ also included[8] /in what is opposite it/.

One should take great care that /the nose/ does not touch /the base/. Nevertheless, initially, there should not be a large interval between them,[9] so that the ו /part/ should not be unduly at a slope because of it.

If one did not adhere the nose above to the roof of /the letter/ and /the symbol therefore/ appears like /two letters/ כו, it is invalid. Correction is of no avail /in such a case/ where *tefilin* /passages/ or mezuzos are involved, if one /already/ wrote after /the symbol/, for /the correction/ will /constitute writing/ in incorrect order, as /explained/ above in Sec. 32, Par. 25; see there in the Mishnah Berurah /, sub-Par. 119/.

Correspondingly, if one adhered the nose /of the letter/ below at the point where the /letter/ מ should be open, /the letter/ is invalid. The law as regards correcting /the letter/ (/which is only possible/ if one did not yet write after it, in the case of *tefilin* /passages/ or mezuzos) is stated above in Sec. 32, Par. 18.

THE FORM OF THE CLOSED LETTER ם

Initially, the closed letter ם should be rounded above on the right side.[1] Below, it should have a corner on the right and on the left[2] /side/, so that it does not appear like a /letter/ ס. If one did not /write it/ in this manner and a child /who is neither especially intelligent nor especially simple/ reads it as a /letter/ ס, it is invalid. The *P.Mg.* writes that it is preferable to make /the letter/ square on all sides, since /otherwise/ one could easily come to err /and write it/ as a /letter/ ס.

צורת אות מ"ם פתוחה

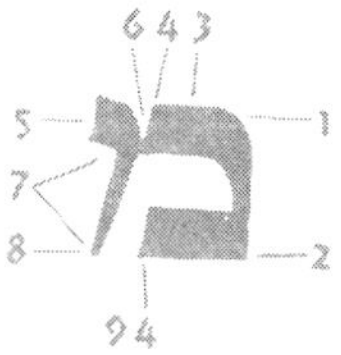

תמונתה קצת א) * כמו כ"ף וא"ו [1] ע"כ תהיה למעלה לצד ימין עגולה [2] אבל למטה יהיה לה זוית ובלא עקב [3] וגגה יהיה למעלה שוה ולא עגול רק לצד ימין יהיה עגול [4] גם יהיה גגה ארוך עד כנגד מושבה התחתון ב) וכ"ז לכתחלה. ג) [5] והחרטום שבצד שמאל יזהר לדבוק אותו לגגו [6] ויהיה לכתחלה כמעט משוך בשוה עם הגג רק ד) שיהיה ביניהם לצד מעלה כמו פגם קטן [7] ה) ותמונת החרטום תהיה כמו וא"ו עומדת מוטה קצת באלכסון ולא הרבה [8] * ויגיע עד כנגד מושב התחתון ועד בכלל. ומאד יזהר שלא יגע בו [9] ומ"מ לא יהיה ביניהם הפסק גדול לכתחלה כדי שלא יהיה עי"ז הוא"ו הרבה באלכסון. ואם לא הדביק החרטום למעלה לגגו ונראה ככ"ף וא"ו פסול ואין מועיל לו תיקון בתו"מ אם כתב אחריו דהוי שלא כסדרן וכדלעיל בסימן ל"ב סכ"ה עי"ש במ"ב. וה"ה אם הדביק החרטום למטה במקום פתיחתו להמ"ם דפסול ומבואר דינו לעיל בסימן ל"ב סי"ח לענין תיקון אם לא כתב עדיין אחריו בתו"מ.

צורת אות מ"ם סתומה

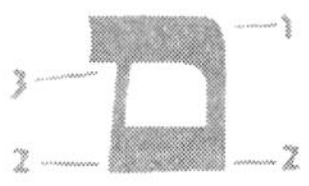

[1] תהיה א) לכתחלה עגולה למעלה לצד ימין [2] ולמטה יהיה לה זוית לימין ולשמאל שלא תהא נראית כסמ"ך. ב) ואם לא עשה כן והתינוק קראה כסמ"ך פסולה. והפמ"ג כתב שטוב יותר שתהיה מרובעת מכל צד כי בקל יוכל לבוא לידי טעות בסמ"ך. **ומ"ם זו תהיה סתומה מכל צד. [3] ג) וגגה יהיה עובר ד) לכתחלה מחוץ לסתימה מעט כראש הוא"ו. ה) ולא ימשוך הגג לצד שמאלה הרבה ובדיעבד * יגרור ו) המותר ואין בזה משום חק תוכות ושלא כסדרן ואם נמצא כן בשם הקודש אין לתקנו וישאר כך וכשר. וגם בשבת ז) אין להוציא אחרת עבור זה.**

צורת אות נ"ון כפופה

א) [1] יעשה ראשה כמו ראש הזיי"ן [2] וג' תגין עליה ב) ולא יותר רחב מראש הזיי"ן דלא תהוי דומה לבי"ת אם יהיה רחב מעט יותר [3] ומטעם זה יעשה ג"כ מושבה למטה ג) משוך לצד שמאל היטיב יותר מן הראש כדי שלא יתדמה לבי"ת או לכ"ף. [4] וצוארו הנמשך מאמצע ראשו יהיה לכתחלה קצת עב וארוך קצת [5] ומוטה לצד ימין כדי להסמיך אות אצל ראשו. [6] ותהיה הנו"ן ד) לכתחלה עגולה למטה לצד ימין. אם עשה הנו"ן כפופה למעלה צורת וא"ו דהיינו שמשך הצואר מקצה ראשו * הניח הפמ"ג בצ"ע והביאו הגרע"א בחידושיו. ומנחלת דוד בסימן כ"ג משמע דכשר בדיעבד. [וכן משמע לענ"ד לכאורה מהלבוש שחזר בסוף תמונת האותיות שלו הדברים שהם לעיכובא בכל אות ואת זה דילג] ועכ"פ נ"פ דאף לדעת הפמ"ג מהני תיקון ואפילו בתו"מ דהיינו שיגרור תחלה קצת מראשו לצד שמאל ולא הרבה כדי שישאר עדיין תמונת נו"ן עליו ואח"כ יוסיף עליו דיו לצד ימין לעשותו כמו ראש הזיי"ן ולא מועיל בהוספת דיו מצד ימין לבד דא"כ יהיה ראשו

שער הציון

ג) ב"י בשם הרי"א. ד) ב"י בשם המנהיג. ה) שם בב"י. ו) עבודת היום ופשוט. מ א) כולו בב"י. ב) כן משמע מלבוש וש"א ועיין לקמן בבה"ל בנו"ן כפופה בסה"ד דאם עשאו למטה עגולה לא פסיקא כ"כ להכשיר. ג) וכדלקמיה. ד) ב"ש בא"ב האחרון. ה) ב"י. ם א) עיין בב"י ופשוט. ב) בס' לד"א. ג) ב"י. ד) נלמד מהנו"ב דבסמוך. ה) דלא יהיה כמו וא"ו. ו) נו"ב בסימן פ' דלא מעכב דבר שאין נמצא בתלמוד וגם לא עדיף מה"א שרגלה באמצע גגה. ז) שערי אפרים בשער ה'

ביאור הלכה

מ * כמו כ"ף וא"ו. הכל כתבתי ע"פ המבואר בב"י וכל הפוסקים האחרונים ולאפוקי מהפמ"ג שכתב דתמונתו הוא כמו נו"ן וא"ו כי אין מקור לזה ואפשר דטעמו מסעיף י"ח שכתב המחבר יגרור החרטום עד שתשאר כצורת נו"ן כפופה וג"ז אינו ראיה דאפשר דשם דלא איירי המחבר בדיני כתיבת האותיות לא דקדק לכתוב לפי הנהוג לכתחלה למצוה כיון דאפילו נו"ן וא"ו כשר לכו"ע או דתפס שם לפי מנהג הספרדים שאין ממשיכין הקו שלמעלה עד כנגד מושבה התחתון כמ"ש בספר לדוד אמת א"כ הוא דומה לנו"ן וא"ו וזהו מש"כ שם בס' לד"א דלדידהו המ"ם דומה לטי"ת ובטי"ת כבר ידוע מה שכ' הר"ח דדומה לנו"ן וא"ו וכמש"כ בב"י באות נו"ן אבל לפי מה שאנו נוהגין די בגרירה עד שישאר כצורת כ"ף. תדע דבלבוש וכן באה"ע בסופו בסדר גיטין שסידר מהרמר"י כתוב יגרור עד שתשאר כצורת כ"ף כפופה ומה שכתב שם בט"ז כי המ"ם הוא בב' כתיבות כנו"ן וא"ו כבר תפס עליו בזה הבית אהרן.

מ * ויגיע עד כנגד מושב התחתון. ובדיעבד אם לא הגיע עד למטה ותינוק קראו למ"ם צ"ע דאפשר דזהו אינו מעיקר צורת האות רק לכתחלה.

ם * יגרור המותר. ומ"מ אם המשיכה כ"כ עד שהתינוק לא הכיר להאות עי"ז לענ"ד צ"ע אם מהני גרירה עיין רמב"ם פ"א מהלכות תפילין הלכה י"ט ואפילו את"ל דבה"א באופן זה ג"כ כשר

The /closed letter/ ם must be closed on all sides.

Initially, its roof should transcend a little beyond the closed[3] /part of the letter on the left/, like the head of the /letter/ ו. One should not continue the roof excessively towards the left. Once it is after the event /and one did do so/, he should scrape off the superfluous /length/. This does not constitute carving around /the letter to form it/ or /writing/ in incorrect order /, where other letters were already written after it/. If this /fault/ is discovered in /a closed ם of/ the Divine Name one should not correct it, but it should remain like that and is valid. In addition, on Shabbos, one should not take out another /Torah Scroll/ because of this /fault/.

THE FORM OF THE BENT-OVER LETTER נ

One should make the head of the bent-over letter נ like the head of the /letter/ ז,[1] with three crownlets on it.[2] /The head/ should not be /made/ wider than the head of the /letter/ ז, so that /the letter/ will not resemble a /letter/ ב, /because it may do so/ if /the head/ is a little wider. For this reason, one should also make the base /of the letter/ below drawn markedly further towards the left than the head,[3] so that /the letter/ should not resemble a /letter/ ב or a /letter/ כ.

The neck of /the letter/, which is drawn from the middle of the head of /the letter/, should be, initially, somewhat thick and somewhat long[4] and leaning towards the right,[5] so that one will be able to put /another/ letter close to the head of /the letter/.

Initially, the /letter/ נ should be rounded below on the right side.[6]

If one made the bent-over /letter/ נ with the form of a /letter/ ו above, i.e., if he drew the neck from the end of the head of /the letter, its validity is then questionable/. The *P.Mg.* deferred /the decision/ for /further/ study. The Gaon *R.A.E.* quotes this in his *Chidushim*. It is implied by the *Nachalas David*, in Sec. 23, that /the letter/ is valid once it is after the event. [This is apparently implied likewise, to my limited understanding, by the *Levush*. At the end of his /description of the/ symbols of the letters, he repeats the points which are essential /for the validity/ in the case of each letter, but omits this /point/.]

At any rate, it seems obvious that even according to the view of the *P.Mg.* correction /of this fault/ is of avail, even in the case of *tefilin* /passages/ and mezuzos /on which one already wrote further/. I.e., one must first scrape off a little of the head on the left side, but not /too/ much, so that it should still retain the symbol of the /letter/ נ, and subsequently he should add ink /to the head/ on the right side to make /the head/ like the head of a /letter/ ז. It is of no avail to add ink to the right side alone, since if /one does/ that

רחב מראש הזיי"ן ואין לעשות כן כנ"ל. ועיין בבה"ל.

צורת אות נו"ן פשוטה

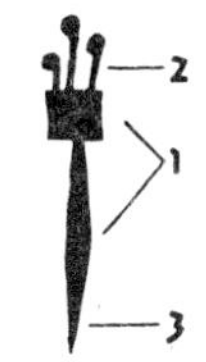

א) [1] תואר צורתה כמו זיי"ן [2] וג' תגין על ראשה, [3] אך שהיא ארוכה כשיעור שתהא ראויה להעשות נו"ן כפופה אם תכפפנה דהיינו לא פחות מד' קולמוסין עם גגה. ואם עשאה קצרה ב) מראין לתינוק דלא חכים ולא טיפש ואם קראה זיי"ן פסולה. ואם משך הקו הארוך מקצה ראשו ועשאו כצורת וא"ו ארוכה, הפמ"ג הניח בצ"ע אך שארי האחרונים [שער אפרים סי' פ"א וגן המלך ולד"א] הסכימו בזה לפסול.

צורת אות סמ"ך

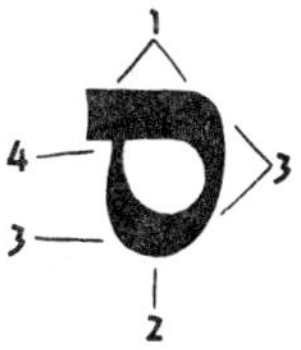

א) [1] תהיה גגה למעלה ארוכה דהיינו שתהא גגה שוה ב) לכתחלה [2] ולמטה מושבה קצר [3] כי צריכה להיות עגולה מג' זויותיה דהיינו למעלה מצד ימין ולמטה משני הצדדים ויסתום אותה לגמרי [4] וגגה למעלה יהיה ג) לכתחלה עובר לחוץ לצד שמאל כשיעור גג הוא"ו.

צורת אות עיי"ן

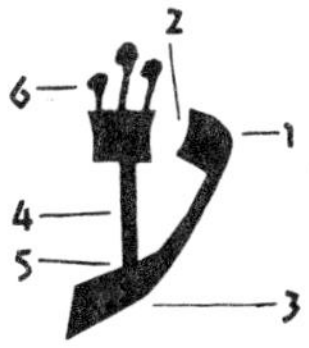

[1] יהיה א) אות ראשון ב) כעין יו"ד [2] ופניה קצת כלפי מעלה ג) לכתחלה [3] וגופה משוך תחתיה בעמידה ד) קצת (דאם ממשיכה הרבה באלכסון לא יהיה יכול להסמיך אות אחר אצל עיי"ן אם יזדמן) [1] ובה תהיה זיי"ן עומדת ה) בשוה [5] ונוגעת בירכה ו) למטה מחציה [6] ויעשה על ראש הזיי"ן ג' תגין. ועיין לעיל בסוף אות א' לענין אם נגעו הראשין יותר ממקום דיבוקם. ומאוד יזהר שלא יגעו הראשים זה בזה ובדיעבד אם נגעו זה בזה כחוט השערה אם מהני גרירה עיין לקמן בסוף אות שי"ן מה שכתבנו שם.

צורת אות פ"א כפופה

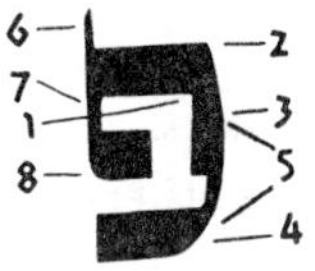

א) [1] צריך להיות לה ב) לכתחלה למעלה בצד ימין זוית מבפנים [2] וגם מבחוץ יהיה כזוית קטן. [3] ותהיה משוכה קצת לאחוריה ג) שתהיה עגולה מבחוץ [4] וכן למטה תהיה עגולה מבחוץ וכמו כל הכפופות שצריך להיות עגולה למטה לכתחלה אבל ד) מבפנים יהיה לה זוית כדי שיהיה בלובן שבפנים צורת בי"ת [5] ותהיה רחבה קולמוס וחצי כדי לתלות בה הנקודה שבפנים שלא תגע בהאות גופה [הג"ה ולא כמה שנהגו איזה סופרים לעשות עקב מבחוץ בצדה כזה *  ואומרים שזה להטיב הבי"ת לבן מבפנים כי הוא ממש אות שבור. ובאמת צריך להיות עגול מבחוץ כמו שכתבנו ורק בפנים צריך להיות בי"ת לבן. ומה שנהגו כך מפני שאינם יודעים ההרגל לעשות לתפוס הקולמוס באלכסון ולהמשיכה מעט לאחוריה הקולמוס בפנים שעי"ז נעשה לה זוית בפנים כמבואר בב"י ע"כ יצא להם הטעות לעשות עקב מבחוץ גם במה שנהגו לכתוב משוכה מסוף גגה מעט והנקודה עושים בזוית ולא עגולה הם מקלקלים הוא"ו לגמרי, עכ"ל ספר כתיבה תמה בקיצור לענינינו. ובאמת מי שאינו יודע לעשות כמש"כ הכתיבה תמה יותר טוב לעשות בי"ת מבפנים בלא עקב רק בזוית לבד ממה שיעשה פ"א שבור מבחוץ כי אפילו בתמונת הבי"ת גופא העקב לא לעיכובא הוא כלל וכ"ש בזה שלא נזכר עקב כלל בב"ש בודאי לא נכון הוא לעשות עי"ז הפ"א שבור, ע"כ הג"ה]. [6] ויהיה לה ה) עוקץ על פניה לצד שמאל ויורד למטה אל הנקודה שבתוכה [7] ותהיה הנקודה תלויה בה כי הנקודה ומשך עוקצה יהיה בתמונת וא"ו כשיהפוך הפ"א. [8] ומה"ט תהיה הנקודה למטה לצד שמאל עגולה כתמונת ראש הוא"ו. ולא תגע הנקודה בשום מקום מבפנים ואם נגעה ו) פסולה. גם יזהר בהנקודה ז) שלא תהיה הפוכה לצד חוץ דאל"ה צ"ע אפילו דיעבד. ואם לא תלה הנקודה ח) בהעוקץ שעל פני הפ"א והרחיקה מקצה הגג לבפנים יש להסתפק בו ודינו כמו בה' שתלה

שער הציון

עי"ש. ן א) ב"י כל הענין. ב) ב"ש בא"ב האחרון. ג) ועיין בתשו' גינת ורדים שכתב לפסול היכי דהמשיך המושב התחתון כ"כ עד שנראה כשני תיבות עי"ש ועיין בפמ"ג ואפשר דגם הוא מודה להג"ו הנ"ל. ד) כן מוכח מהב"י אחר סיום הא"ב שלו בד"ה כתב המרדכי וכו'. ן א) . ב) טור ס א) בב"י. ב) כי היא ככ"ף וא"ו. עיין בב"י וכדלעיל במ"ם פתוחה ולא לעיכובא הוא. ג) עיין באות מ"ם סתומה בשער הציון אות קטן ד'. ע א) ב"י. ב) דאם הקו שוה פסול אפילו בדיעבד. ג) פשוט. ד) דאם לגמרי בעמידה איננה תמונת עיי"ן כראוי וצ"ע אפילו לענין דיעבד ועיין בר"ן פ' הבונה. ה) לכתחלה ונ"ל שגם עיקר תמונת ראשה שהיא כזיי"ן עובר למעלה משני הצדדים אינו מעכב בדיעבד דבעינן רק שיהא ניכר הראש ולא יהיה קו שוה ודומיא דמה שהקיל הפמ"ג בדיעבד בט' בצידו השמאלי שהיא ג"כ כזיי"ן ועיין לעיל בסוף אות טי"ת. ו) לכתחילה. ף א) כולו בב"י. ב) הוא פשוט. ג) ג"ז רק לכתחילה. ד) ג"ז אינו מעכב בדיעבד וכמו שמוכח מנו"ב

* צורה זו צולמה מס' כתיבה תמה ועיין בהערות ובירורים בעמוד 112.

the head of /the נ/ will be wider than the head of a /letter/ ז. One should not make it that /wide/, as /explained/ above. See the Beyur Halachah.

THE FORM OF THE SIMPLE /ELONGATED/ LETTER ן

The description of the form of the simple /elongated/ letter ן resembles /the description of the form of/ a /letter/ ז[1] and it /also has/ three crownlets on its head.[2]

On the other hand, it must be longer /than a ז/, with sufficient length /for the letter/ to be convertible into a bent-over נ if one would /in fact/ bend it over,[3] i.e., /it must have a length of/ no less than /the thickness of/ four quills,[4*] /together/ with its roof. If one made /the letter/ short, it should be shown to a child who is neither /especially/ intelligent nor /especially/ simple and if he reads it as a /letter/ ז it is invalid.

If one drew the long line from the end of the head and made /the letter/ in the form of a long /letter/ ו /, the validity of the letter is then questionable/. The *P.Mg.* defers /the decision/ for /further/ study. However, the other Acharonim [*Sha'ar Efrayim*, Sec. 81, *Gan Ha-Melech* and *Led.E.*] are agreed that in such a case /the letter/ is invalid.

THE FORM OF THE LETTER ס

The roof of the letter ס should be long above,[1] i.e., initially, its roof should be of even /height/.

Its base below /should be/ short,[2] since /the letter/ must be rounded at three of its convergences,[3] i.e., above on the right side and below on both sides.

/The letter/ should be completely closed.

Initially, its roof above should extend outwards towards the left, for the length of the roof of the /letter/ ו.[4]

THE FORM OF THE LETTER ע

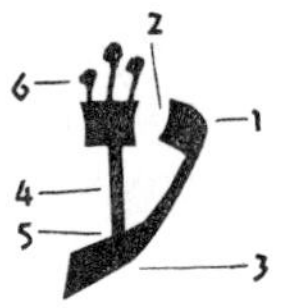

The first character /making up/ the letter ע /, which is the head on the right/, should be similar to the /letter/ י.[1] Initially, the front of it should face somewhat upwards.[2]

The body should be drawn underneath /the head/, somewhat erectly[3] ((since if one will draw it markedly sloping he will be unable to put another letter close to /the letter/ ע if this happens /to be necessary/)).

There should be a /letter/ ז /form/ with even /sides/ standing[4] in /the body/, touching the thigh /of the body/ below half[5] its /length/. One should make three crownlets on the head of the ז[6] /part/.

See above at the end /of the description/ of the letter א, as regards /the ruling/ when the heads touch /the body/ more than at the point where they should be stuck /to the body/.

One must be very careful that the heads do not touch one another. If /the heads/ touch one another /, even/ by a hairsbreadth, see below at the end /of the description/ of the letter ש for what we have written there, /as regards/ whether /or not/ scraping away is of avail /in such a case/ once it is after the event.

THE FORM OF THE BENT-OVER LETTER פ

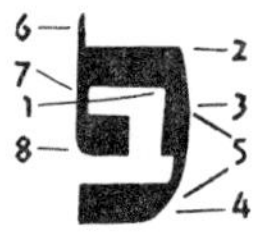

Initially, the bent-over letter פ must have a corner on the inside above on the right side.[1] The outside should be /formed/ like a small corner /there/ as well.[2]

/The letter/ should be drawn a little to the back, so that it is rounded on the outside.[3] It should, likewise, be rounded below on the outside[4] /, at the right/, just as all the /other/ bent-over /letters/ are required to be rounded below, initially.

רחב מראש הזיי"ן ואין לעשות כן כנ"ל. ועיין בבה"ל.

צורת אות נו"ן פשוטה

א) [1] תואר צורתה כמו זיי"ן [2] וג' תגין על ראשה, [3] אך שהיא ארוכה כשיעור שתהא ראויה להעשות נו"ן כפופה אם תכפפנה דהיינו לא פחות מד' קולמוסין עם גגה. ואם עשאה קצרה ב) מראין לתינוק דלא חכים ולא טיפש ואם קראה זיי"ן פסולה. ואם משך הקו הארוך מקצה ראשו ועשאו כצורת וא"ו ארוכה, הפמ"ג הניח בצ"ע אך שארי האחרונים [שער אפרים סי' פ"א וגן המלך ולד"א] הסכימו בזה לפסול.

צורת אות סמ"ך

א) [1] תהיה גגה למעלה ארוכה דהיינו שתהא גגה שוה ב) לכתחלה [2] ולמטה מושבה קצר [3] כי צריכה להיות עגולה מג' זויותיה דהיינו למעלה מצד ימין ולמטה משני הצדדים ויסתום אותה לגמרי [4] וגגה למעלה יהיה ג) לכתחלה עובר לחוץ לצד שמאל כשיעור גג הוא"ו.

צורת אות עיי"ן

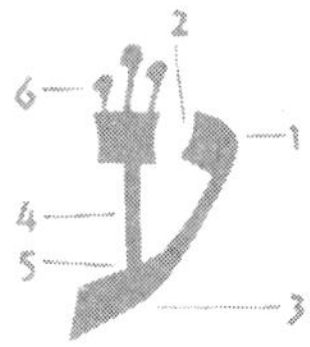

[1] יהיה א) אות ראשון ב) כעין יו"ד [2] ופניה קצת כלפי מעלה ג) לכתחלה [3] וגופה משוך תחתיה בעמידה ד) קצת (דאם ממשיכה הרבה באלכסון לא יהיה יכול להסמיך אות אחר אצל עיי"ן אם יזדמן) [1] ובה תהיה זיי"ן עומדת ה) בשוה [5] ונוגעת בירכה ו) למטה מחציה [6] ויעשה על ראש הזיי"ן ג' תגין. ועיין לעיל בסוף אות א' לענין אם נגעו הראשין יותר ממקום דיבוקם. ומאוד יזהר שלא יגעו הראשים זה בזה ובדיעבד אם נגעו זה בזה כחוט השערה אם מהני גרירה עיין לקמן בסוף אות שי"ן מה שכתבנו שם.

צורת אות פ"א כפופה

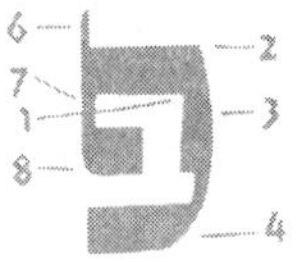

א) [1] צריך להיות לה ב) לכתחלה למעלה בצד ימין זוית מבפנים [2] וגם מבחוץ יהיה כזוית קטן. [3] ותהיה משוכה קצת לאחוריה ג) שתהיה עגולה מבחוץ [4] וכן למטה תהיה עגולה מבחוץ וכמו כל הכפופות שצריך להיות עגולה למטה לכתחלה **אבל ד) מבפנים יהיה לה זוית כדי שיהיה בלובן שבפנים צורת בי"ת [5] ותהיה רחבה קולמוס וחצי כדי לתלות בה הנקודה שבפנים שלא תגע בהאות גופה [הג"ה ולא כמה שנהגו איזה סופרים לעשות עקב מבחוץ בצדה כזה ***  **ואומרים שזה להטיב הבי"ת לבן מבפנים כי הוא ממש אות שבור. ובאמת צריך להיות עגול מבחוץ כמו שכתבנו ורק בפנים צריך להיות בי"ת לבן. ומה שנהגו כך מפני שאינם יודעים ההרגל לעשות לתפוס הקולמוס באלכסון ולהמשיכה מעט לאחוריה הקולמוס בפנים שעי"ז נעשה לה זוית בפנים כמבואר בב"י ע"כ יצא להם הטעות לעשות עקב מבחוץ גם במה שנהגו לכתוב משוכה מסוף גגה מעט והנקודה עושים בזוית ולא עגולה הם מקלקלים הוא"ו לגמרי, עכ"ל ספר כתיבה תמה בקיצור לענינינו. ובאמת מי שאינו יודע לעשות כמש"כ הכתיבה תמה יותר טוב לעשות בי"ת מבפנים בלא עקב רק בזוית לבד ממה שיעשה פ"א שבור מבחוץ כי אפילו בתמונת הבי"ת גופא העקב לא לעיכובא הוא כלל וכ"ש בזה שלא נזכר עקב כלל בב"ש בודאי לא נכון הוא לעשות עי"ז הפ"א שבור, ע"כ הג"ה]. [6] ויהיה לה ה) עוקץ על פניה לצד שמאל ויורד למטה אל הנקודה שבתוכה [7] ותהיה הנקודה תלויה בה כי הנקודה ומשך עוקצה יהיה בתמונת וא"ו כשיהפוך הפ"א. [8] ומה"ט תהיה הנקודה למטה לצד שמאל עגולה כתמונת ראש הוא"ו. ולא תגע הנקודה בשום מקום מבפנים ואם נגעה ו) פסולה. גם יזהר בהנקודה ז) שלא תהיה הפוכה לצד חוץ דאל"ה צ"ע אפילו דיעבד. ואם לא תלה הנקודה ח) בהעוקץ שעל פני הפ"א והרחיקה מקצה הגג לבפנים יש להסתפק בו ודינו כמו בה' שתלה**

שער הציון

עי"ש. **ן** א) ב"י כל הענין. ב) ב"ש בא"ב האחרון. ג) ועיין בתשו' גינת ורדים שכתב לפסול היכי דהמשיך המושב התחתון כ"כ עד שנראה כשני תיבות עי"ש ועיין בפמ"ג ואפשר דגם הוא מודה להג"ו הנ"ל. ד) כן מוכח מהב"י אחר סיום הא"ב שלו בד"ה כתב המרדכי וכו'. **ן** א) . ב) טור **ס** א) בב"י. ב) כי היא ככ"ף וא"ו. עיין בב"י וכדלעיל במ"ם פתוחה ולא לעיכובא הוא. ג) עיין באות מ"ם סתומה בשער הציון אות קטן ד'. **ע** א) ב"י. ב) דאם הקו שוה פסול אפילו בדיעבד. ג) פשוט. ד) דאם לגמרי בעמידה איננה תמונת עיי"ן כראוי וצ"ע אפילו לענין דיעבד ועיין בר"ן פ' הבונה. ה) לכתחלה ונ"ל שגם עיקר תמונת ראשה שהיא כזיי"ן עובר למעלה משני הצדדים אינו מעכב בדיעבד דבעינן רק שיהא ניכר הראש ולא יהיה קו שוה ודומיא דמה שהקיל הפמ"ג בדיעבד בט' בצידו השמאלי שהיא ג"כ כזיי"ן ועיין לעיל בסוף אות טי"ת. ו) לכתחילה. **פ** א) כולו בב"י. ב) הוא פשוט. ג) ג"ז רק לכתחילה. ד) ג"ז אינו מעכב בדיעבד וכמו שמוכח מנו"ב

* צורה זו צולמה מס' כתיבה תמה ועיין בהערות ובירורים בעמוד 112.

However, on the inside, /the letter/ should have a corner /below on the right/, so that the white /forming/ the inside /of the letter/ should have the form of a /letter/ ב.

/The white/ should have a breadth[5] of /the thickness of/ one and a half quills,[4]* so that /one will be able/ to suspend the inside stroke in it, without /that stroke/ touching the letter itself.

[Gloss: /One should/ not /follow/ the practice of some scribes, who make a heel outside /the letter/ at the side like this פ , as this /symbol/ actually /has the form of/ a broken letter. They say that this /should be done/ to improve /the form of/ the white /letter/ ב on the inside /of the letter/. The truth is that /the letter/ must be rounded /at the right/ on the outside, as we have written /above/, and a white ב is only required on the inside.

/The reason/ why they adopted this practice is because they are not aware of the common /device/ used /to overcome the problem of forming the heel of the ב on the inside/. (/This is/ to grasp the quill at an angle and draw /the letter/ a little to the back of the quill inside, so that a corner will thereby be formed in /the letter/ on the inside, as explained by the *B.Y.*) They therefore developed an incorrect /practice/ of making a heel on the outside.

An additional /fault of their's/ is that by their practice of writing /the black stroke, which forms the inside of the white ב,/ drawn away a little from the end of the roof of /the letter/ and to make the stroke with a corner /on the left side at the bottom/ and not rounded, they spoil the /inverted letter/ ו /form that is required at the top left of the letter/ altogether.

Until this point /I have written/ the wording of the work *Kesivah Tamah* concerning this matter in brief.

The truth is that if someone does not know how to act in accordance with what the *Kesivah Tamah* writes, it is better /for him/ to make the /white letter/ ב on the inside without a heel, with only just a corner, rather than to make a /letter/ פ which is broken on the outside. This is because even as regards /the form of/ the symbol of the /letter/ ב itself, the heel is not essential /for its validity/ at all. /Therefore,/ one may certainly /conclude/ that for the sake of /making a heel/ for /the white letter ב required on the inside of the letter פ/, concerning which a heel is not mentioned at all by the *B.Sh.*, it is definitely not proper to make the פ broken. End of gloss.]

/The letter/ should have a prickle on the front of it on the left side[6] and /the prickle/ should descend below to the stroke inside /the letter/. The stroke should be suspended[7] by /the prickle/, as the stroke and the length of the prickle should /form together/ the symbol of a /letter/ ו, when one inverts the פ. For this reason, the stroke should be rounded on the left at the bottom, in conformance with the symbol /required/ for the head of /the letter/ ו.[8]

The stroke should not touch /the rest of the letter at/ any point on the inside. If it does touch, /the letter/ is invalid. One must also take care that the stroke should not be inverted towards the outside. If /one did/ not /avoid this/, study is required /to establish the validity of the letter/, even now that it is after the event.

If one did not suspend the /inside/ stroke on the prickle at the front of the פ, but placed it away from the end of the roof towards the inside /of the roof, the validity of the letter/ is questionable. /Then/ the same ruling /applies/ as for a /letter/ ה in which one

רגל שמאלו באמצע הגג וכנ״ל באות ה״א. ואם לא נגעה הנקודה בגגה ותינוק קראה פ״א יש לתקן ותיקון מועיל אפילו בתו״מ וכנ״ל בסי׳ ל״ב סכ״ה עי״ש. ואם לא עשה הנקודה רק קו שוה, עיין לעיל סוף אות אל״ף.

צורת אות פ״א פשוטה

[1] א) צריך לעשותה ב) לכתחלה בזוית למעלה כמו שהכפופה היא למעלה. [2] גם צריכה להיות ארוכה לכתחלה כשיעור שתהא ראויה לעשות פ״א כפופה אם תכפפנה [3] ובדיעבד אם יש ברגל ימיני מכנגד מקום הנקודה ולמטה כמלא יו״ד די בכך [הפמ״ג כתב סתם כמלא יו״ד מהירך והכוונה כאשר כתבנו דאל״ה אין צורת אות עליו]. ומ״מ אם נמצא כן בס״ת ואפילו בתפילין לכתחלה בודאי חייב לתקן האות ולהשלימו כדין ואין בזה משום שלא כסדרן כיון דבלא התיקון הוא כשר. ועשיית נקודת הפ״א ועוקצה הוא הכל כמו בכפופה. גם יזהר ג) שלא תהיה הנקודה הפוכה לצד חוץ כדי שלא תדמה לתי״ו. אם לא נגעה הנקודה בגג או שהרחיק הנקודה מקצה הגג לבפנים הכל דינו כנ״ל בכפופה.

צורת אות צד״י כפופה

[1] תמונתו כמו נו״ן כפופה [2] ויו״ד על גבה [3] הראש הראשון שמימין שהוא כעין יו״ד א) יהיה פניה ב) נוטה קצת כלפי מעלה. [1] וידבק רגל היו״ד דיבוק טוב בצואר הצד״י ומאוד יזהר להדביק באמצע הצואר ולא למטה שלא תדמה לעיי״ן. [5] וראשה השני יהיה כמין זיי״ן נוטה לכאן ולכאן כי אין להמשיך הצואר מקצה הראש כ״א מאמצעו ג) כמו בנו״ן לעיל. [6] והצואר יהיה קצת עב וארוך קצת [7] ומוטה לצד ימין כדי להסמיך אות אצל ראשה [8] ומושבה התחתון ד) יהיה משוך לכתחלה לצד שמאלה היטיב יותר מן שני הראשים [9] ותהיה לכתחלה עגולה למטה בצד ימין כמו כל הכפופות. [10] וג׳ תגין על ראש השמאלי. ואם לא נגע היו״ד בהנו״ן עיין בסימן ל״ב סכ״ה. ואם הראשים נוגעים יותר ממקום דיבוקם דהיינו שאין ניכר הראש אלא קו שוה, עיין לעיל בסוף אות א׳. ויזהר מאד ה) שלא יגעו הראשים

שער הציון

הנ״ל באות מ׳. ה) ג״ז לכתחילה. ו) ב״ש בא״ב הראשון והאגור. ז) פמ״ג בסוף הפתיחה לל״ב. ח) פמ״ג. ף א) ב״י. ב) עיין בב״י ופשוט. ג) בית יוסף. צ א) ב״י כל הענין. ב) ולכתחילה נ״ל. ג) ומ״מ נ״ל דאפילו הפמ״ג דמסתפק בזה בנו״ן כפופה לענין דיעבד מודה בצד״י דלא מעכב בדיעבד ולא בעינן רק שיהא ניכר הראש ולא יהיה קו שוה ודומיא דטי״ת שגם שם תמונתו כ״ף זיי״ן והקיל שם הפמ״ג ושאני נו״ן דנזכר בגמרא שתמונתו למעלה הוא כעין זיי״ן ועיין לעיל בסוף אות טי״ת. ד) כמו בנו״ן כפופה לעיל ובשלמא שם אפשר דהוא לעיכובא כדי שלא תדמה לכ״ף כפופה או לבי״ת משא״כ כאן ולכך כתבתי לכתחלה.

ביאור הלכה

שם שאני דעיקר תמונתו כן לכמה ראשונים וכנ״ל.

* **הניח נ** הפרי מגדים בצ״ע. וחכם אחד מחכמי הזמן הביא ראיה לדברי המכשירין בזה מהא דאמרינן בשבת ק״ד ע״ב נתכוין לכתוב אות אחת ועלה בידו שתים חייב ולפיר״ח [הובא בהגמיי׳ ובב״י באות זה] קאי זה על אות ט׳ דנתכוין לכתוב טי״ת ולא הדביק הירך לצד שמאל [כן איתא בהגהמ״י וטה״ד בב״י שכתוב ימין] ונעשה נו״ן זיי״ן וא״א דלעיכובא הוא אפי׳ בדיעבד דאין עליו שם נו״ן כלל אמאי חייב בזה בשבת שתים הלא הנו״ן שבטי״ת זה מסתמא עשהו כשאר טי״ת שאין ממשיכין צואר הנו״ן כ״א מצדו ולא מאמצעו ולענ״ד יש לדחות דבלא״ה לפי המסקנא דגמרא שם דמסיק הא דבעי זיוני וכו׳ ע״כ אנו מוכרחין לומר דהברייתא זו מיירי דעשה להטי״ת הנו״ן שבה זקוף למעלה וגם מזויין ודלא כמו שאר טיתי״ן דצריכה להיות הנו״ן שבה בלא זיון וגם כפוף מעט לתוכה כמו דמסקי הפוסקים א״כ נוכל לאמר גם כן דמיירי שעשה להנו״ן שבטי״ת זה משוך מאמצע ראשו כמו נו״ן ממש ולא כשאר טי״ת ולהכי חייב גם משום נו״ן שבו. ולענין תיקון לנו״ן כפופה שעשה ראשו כצורת וא״ו עיין במש״כ בפנים דמהני תיקון אפילו בתו״מ דלא שייך בזה חק תוכות כיון דאין מתכשר ע״י גרירה לחוד ולא שייך בזה שלא כסדרן דצורתן עליה מיקרי דהכל מורגלין בנו״ן כזה ואמינא לה מהא דכתב הפמ״ג באות כ״ף פשוטה שעשאו למעלה מרובע דאפילו להפוס׳ הפוסלים דס״ל דאין לחלק בין הפשוטה להכפופה אפי׳ בדיעבד מודו דמהני הוספת דיו לעשותה עגולה אפי׳ בתו״מ ואין בזה משום שלא כסדרן דצורתה עליה מיקרי דהכל מורגלין בכפי״ן כאלו א״כ פשוט דה״נ בנו״ן כפופה דמהני תיקון כיון דאפילו בלא תיקון נמי הכל קורין אותה נו״ן. ובאמת ק״ו הוא הכא מהתם דשם מה שהכ״ף כפופה צריכה להיות עגולה גמרא מפורשת היא בשבת ק״ג ע״ב ואל״ה אין תמונתה עליה וא״כ להפוסקים דס״ל דאפילו בכ״ף פשוטה שעשאו מרובע יש לפסול אפילו בדיעבד דאין לחלק בהתמונה בין כפופה לפשוטה כיון דשניהן שם כ״ף עליהן היה נראה לן לכאורה דע״י הריבוע אבדה צורתה דתו אין שם כ״ף עליה ואפ״ה כתב הפמ״ג דמהני תיקון דמיקרי עדיין צורתה עליה כיון דהכל מורגלין בכפי״ן כאלו וא״כ כ״ש בענינינו דאפילו בנו״ן פשוטה שהחמיר הר״ן עכ״פ אין לנו מקור מהגמרא דלא ליהני תיקון באם עשאו למעלה כצורת וא״ו עאכ״ו דאין לנו להחמיר בצורת נו״ן כפופה אם עשאו

suspended the left leg /underneath/ the middle of the roof. /The ruling for the latter case is given/ above in /the description of/ the letter ה.

If the stroke does not touch the roof of /the letter/ and a child /who is neither especially intelligent nor especially simple/ reads it as /the letter/ פ, /the letter/ should be corrected. The correction will be of avail even in the case of *tefilin* /passages/ and mezuzos /in which more was already written/. This conforms with /the ruling/ above in Sec. 32, Par. 25; see there.

If one merely made the stroke a straight line, see above at the end /of the description/ of the letter א /for the ruling/.

THE FORM OF THE SIMPLE /ELONGATED/ LETTER ף

The simple /elongated/ letter ף must be made initially with a corner above,[1] just as the bent-over /form of the letter/ is /required to have a corner/ above.

Initially, /the right leg/ must also be /made/ long enough /for the letter/ to be convertible into a bent-over פ if one would bend it over.[2] Once it is after the event, if /the part of/ the right leg from /the point/ corresponding to the point where the /inside/ stroke /ends/ downwards[3] has /a length/ which is equivalent /to the length/ of the /letter/ י, this is adequate. [The *P.Mg.* writes, without qualification, that /a length/ which is equivalent /to the length/ of the /letter/ י /is required/ from the thigh. He means /by this/ what we have written, as, otherwise, /the symbol/ will not have the form of a letter.]

Nevertheless, if one finds in a Torah Scroll /a simple elongated ף with the length of the right leg after this point only as long as the letter י/ or even /if one finds this/ in a *tefilin* /passage/, one is definitely obliged, initially, to correct the letter by completing its /length/ to accord with /initial/ halachic /requirements/. /The correction/ will not involve /writing/ in incorrect order, since /the letter/ is valid without the correction.

/The requirements for/ making the /inside/ stroke of the /simple elongated/ ף and its prickle are entirely the same as /those which we have described/ for /those of/ the bent-over /פ/. One should also take care that the stroke is not inverted /to face/ towards the outside, so that /the letter/ will not resemble a /letter/ ת.

If the /inside/ stroke does not touch the roof or if one placed the stroke away from the end of the roof towards the inside /of the letter/, the ruling is entirely the same as is /explained/ above for /these cases with respect to/ the bent-over /letter פ/.

THE FORM OF THE BENT-OVER LETTER צ

The symbol of the bent-over letter צ is like /the symbol of/ a bent-over /letter/ נ[1] /together/ with a /letter/ י on its back.[2]

The first head /of the letter/, which is on the right and is similar to a /letter/ י, should have its front leaning a little /facing/ upwards.[3] The leg of the י /part/ should be stuck with a good join to the neck of the צ.[4] One must be extremely careful to stick it to the middle of the neck and not below, so that /the letter/ will not resemble a /letter/ ע.

The second head /of the letter/ should be like /the head of/ a /letter/ ז, /so that it should/ extend in both directions.[5] For one should not draw the neck from the end of the head, but from the middle of it, as /is required/ for the /letter/ נ, /described/ above.

The neck should be somewhat thick and somewhat long[6] and it should lean towards the right,[7] so that /one will be able/ to place a letter close to the head of /the צ/.

Initially, the lower base /of the letter/ should be drawn markedly further towards the left than the two heads.[8] It should be /made/, initially, rounded below on the right side,[9] as /is the case for the bases of/ all the bent-over /letters/.

There should be three crownlets on the left head.[10]

If the י /part/ does not touch the נ /part/, see Sec. 32, Par. 25.

If the heads touch more than at the point where they should be stuck /to each other/, meaning that a head is not discernible but /the entire stroke consists of/ a line of equal /width/, see above at the end /of the description/ of the letter א /for the ruling/.

One should be extremely careful that the heads do not touch one another /at the top/.

זה בזה ובדיעבד עיין בסוף אות שי"ן מה שכתבנו שם.

צורת אות צד"י פשוטה

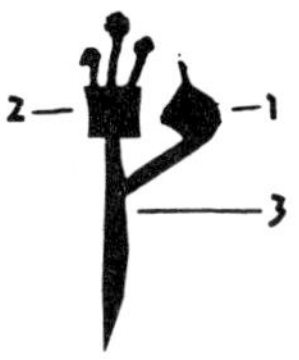

א) יהיו ראשיה כמו בשל כפופה והיא מורכבת ג"כ [1] מיו"ד [2] ונו"ן ואך מנו"ן פשוטה, ע"כ גופה פשוט כמו אות נו"ן פשוטה [3] ושיעור אורכה שתרד למטה מדיבוק הראשים לכתחלה בכדי שיהא ראוי לעשות צד"י כפופה. ובדיעבד פסק הפמ"ג שאם הוציא ממקום דיבוק היו"ד לנו"ן רק כמלא יו"ד כשר אבל אם לא נשאר כמלא יו"ד צ"ע. אם נגעו הראשים יותר ממקום דיבוקם או שנגעו זה בזה או שנפסק בין היו"ד להנו"ן דינו כמו בכפופה וכנ"ל.

צורת אות קו"ף

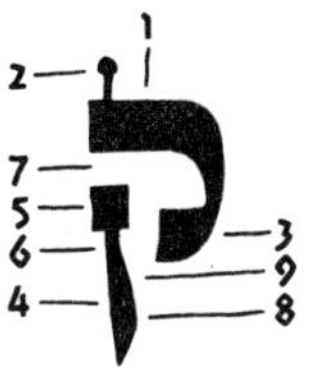

[1] יהיה א) גגה שוה [2] ותג קטן צ"ל על גגה בצד שמאל על פניה לכתחלה ויעשה הקוץ דק כדי שלא יקלקל בזה תמונת הקו"ף דהיינו שלא יראה עי"ז כלמ"ד מצד אחד ובספר מעשה רקח כתב דמטעם זה יעתיק התג מקצה הגג עי"ש. [3] *ויריכה הימנית צ"ל למטה ב) כפוף היטב לצד רגל שמאל כמו צורת כ"ף כפופה אך שתהיה קצרה הרבה מן הגג [4] ורגל השמאלית תלויה בה והיא כצורת נו"ן פשוטה אך שקצרה מעט [5] וע"כ יהיה ראשה עב [6] ומתמעט והולך כמו בנו"ן. [7] ולא ירחיקנו ג) לכתחלה מן הגג יותר מעובי הגג [8] ויש לכתחלה למשוך רגל שמאל התלויה באלכסון קצת לצד ימין. ומאד יזהר שלא יגע הרגל להגג ד) או ליריכו שבצדו ואף לא יהיה סמוך להגג לכתחלה אלא יהא בינו לבין הגג חלק כ"כ בכדי שאדם בינוני ה) יכירנו היטב מעל ס"ת שע"ג בימה כשהוא קורא בו. ולא יהיה הרגל נגד אמצע הגג אלא בסופו בצד שמאל ואם נגע הרגל ו) בגגו וה"ה ביריכו שבצדו או שעשה הרגל באמצע הגג ז) הכל דינו כמו באות ה' וכמבואר שם לעיל באות ה"א. [9] ואם אורך הרגל השמאלי הוא רק כמו יו"ד מכנגד מקום הכפיפה ולמטה כשר בדיעבד [כנ"ל כוונת פמ"ג במה שכתב לענין קו"ף בד"ה קי"ל ניקב רגל הה"א וכו' קו"ף רי"ש וכו' ומה שסיים אם נשאר מירך הימין משום אחריני נקט].

צורת אות רי"ש

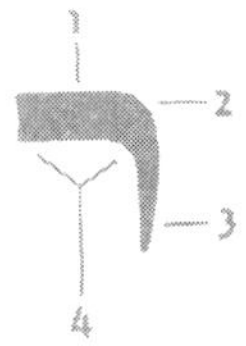

[1] גגה שוה לכתחלה [2] ומאוד יזהר א) שתהיה עגולה ממש מאחוריה כדי שלא תדמה לדלי"ת ואם נראית כדלי"ת פסולה ב) ואם ספק מראין לתינוק [3] ויריכה יהיה קצר כדי שלא תדמה לכ"ף פשוטה. [4] וגגה ארוך כאורך ב' ג) כדי שלא תדמה לוא"ו. ובדיעבד אם יש ספק מראין לתינוק וכנ"ל. ואם עשה רגל הרי"ש קצר כמו יו"ד די בזה בדיעבד פמ"ג. ועיין לקמן בסוף אות תיו.

צורת אות שי"ן

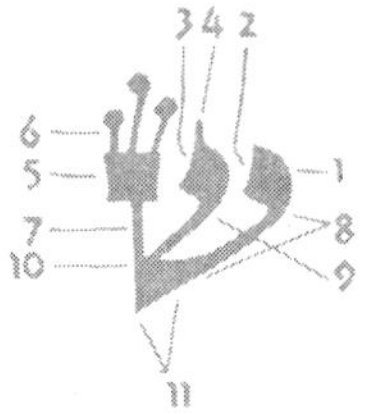

יש לה שלשה ראשים א) [1] ראשה הראשון עם ירך הנמשך ממנו הוא כעין וא"ו [2] ופניה ב) כלפי מעלה קצת [3] והראש השני יהיה כעין יו"ד ופניה ג"כ קצת כלפי מעלה [4] ועוקץ קטן עליה לכתחלה [5] והראש השלישי צריך

שער הציון

ה) ב"ש בדף י"ב. ץ א) הכל מבואר בפשיטות. ק א) ב"י ולכתחילה. ב) כל הענין בב"י. ג) פשוט. ד) מספר כתיבה תמה והדין עמו דאל"ה לא מיקרי הרגל תלויה וכן משמע שבת ק"ג ע"א בגמרא דיש הפסק בין הרגל לגוף הקו"ף. ה) מ"א בסימן ל"ו בשם הרמ"ע וכ"כ הא"ר. ו) לעיל בסימן ל"ב סי"ח עי"ש ובבה"ל. ז) פמ"ג באות ק' בפתיחה. ר א) כל הענין בב"י. ב) טור וכעין זה למעלה באות ב' ע"ש. ג) ב"י בא"ב שלישי. ש א) כל הענין בב"י. ב) ולכתחילה. ג) ב"ש בא"ב

ביאור הלכה

למעלה כצורת וא"ו דלא ליתהני תיקון כנ"ל פשוט. ומ"ש שיגרור קצת דאם יגרור הרבה יאבד תמונתו וכשיתקן אח"כ יהיה בזה שלא כסדרן. ומ"ש ואח"כ יוסיף עליו דיו דאם יעשה בהיפך ויהיה רחב הרבה אפשר דעי"ז יקרא אבד עיקר תמונתו דאין הכל מורגלין בכזה ולא יועיל אח"כ מה שיגרור מצד שמאל. ודע עוד דלדעת הפמ"ג דמחית לתרוייהו בחדא מחתא אפילו לענין דיעבד אלמא דס"ל דאין לחלק בין פשוטה לכפופה כיון דשניהן שם נו"ן עליהן [ותדע דבכ"ף פשוטה שעשאו מרובע נמי מצדד כהפוסקים דס"ל אפילו בדיעבד פסול] א"כ לדבריו יש נמי לומר כה"ג במ"ם פתוחה אם עשאו למטה ג"כ עגולה דיש לפוסלו אפילו בדיעבד מטעם זה כיון דשניהן שם מ"ם עליהן ובמ"ם סתומה ודאי פסול דהוי בכלל ממי"ן סמכין א"כ ה"נ בפתוחה וצ"ע לדינא. ותיקון מהני בזה אפילו בתו"מ דבלא"ה ג"כ עדיין עיקר צורתה עליה.

ק * ויריכה הימנית וכו' כ"ף כפופה. ובדיעבד נראה דאפילו כפוף מעט די, עיין בב"י וכן משמע דעת רש"י בשבת ק"ד ע"א ד"ה ליעול בהך עי"ש. וכן משמע מרבינו ירוחם והאגור שכתבו שיאריך רגל הקו"ף שלא ידמה לה"א. מכל זה משמע דפתוח למטה ועכ"פ כפוף מעט די. ועיין בספר בית אהרן שהביא בשם הרדב"ז שעיקר צורתה רי"ש נו"ן

/For the ruling/ once it is after the event /and they do touch/, see the end /of the description/ of the letter ש, for what we have written there /about this/.

THE FORM OF THE SIMPLE /ELONGATED/ LETTER ץ

The heads of the simple /elongated/ letter ץ should be like those of the bent-over /letter צ/. /This letter/ is also compounded of a /letter/ י[1] /part/ and a /letter/ ן[2] /part/. However, /in its case/ a simple /elongated/ ן /part is involved/. Therefore, the body of /the letter/ is simple /and elongated/, like /the body of/ a simple /elongated/ letter ן.

The required length for this /letter/, initially, is that it should descend /sufficiently/ below /the point/ where the heads are joined /for the letter/ to be convertible into a bent-over צ.[3] Once it is after the event, the *P.Mg.* rules that if one extended it merely for /a length/ which is equivalent /to the length/ of a /letter/ י after the point where the י /part/ is joined to the ן /part, the letter/ is valid. However, if /a length/ which is equivalent /to the length/ of a /letter/ י does not remain /after that point, the ruling/ requires study.

If the heads touch /one another/ at more than the point where they should be stuck /, because one or both of the strokes is a line without a discernible head/, or if they touch one another /at the top/ or if there is a break between the י /part/ and the ן /part/, the same ruling /applies/ as /when this happens/ in the case of the bent-over /צ/, which is /described/ above.

THE FORM OF THE LETTER ק

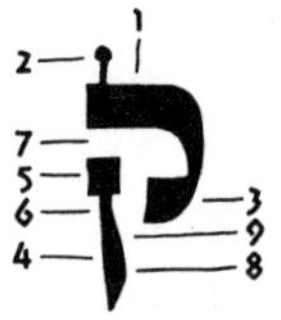

The roof of the letter ק should be of even[1] /height/. Initially, there should be a small crownlet on its roof on the left side, on the front[2] of /the roof/. One should make the prickle /forming the crownlet/ thin, so that its /presence/ should not spoil the symbol of the ק, i.e., so that /the letter/ should not look like a /letter/ ל on one side because of /the prickle/. In the work *Ma'aseh Rokeyach*, /the author/ writes that for this reason one must move the crownlet /along/ away from the end of the roof; see there.

The right thigh of /the letter/ must be pronouncedly bent over below towards the left leg,[3] like /the equivalent stroke in/ the form of a bent-over /letter/ כ.[10*] However, /the base of this thigh/ must be considerably shorter than the roof.

The left leg should be suspended[4] in /the כ part/. /This leg/ should have the form of a simple /elongated letter/ ן, but /should be/ a little shorter. Consequently, its head should be thick[5] and /the thickness of the neck/ should diminish progressively,[6] as /is the case/ with a /simple elongated/ ן.

Initially, one should not place /the left leg/ away from the roof more than the thickness of the roof.[7] /An additional requirement,/ initially, /is that/ one should draw the suspended left leg slightly sloping towards the right.[8] One should be extremely careful that the leg does not touch the roof or the thigh of /the letter/ at its side. It should also not be close to the roof, initially, but there should be /a gap/ between it and the roof of

10* Once it is after the event, even if it is only bent-over a little this is adequate. (Beyur Halachah)

זה בזה ובדיעבד עיין בסוף אות שי"ן מה שכתבנו שם.

צורת אות צד"י פשוטה

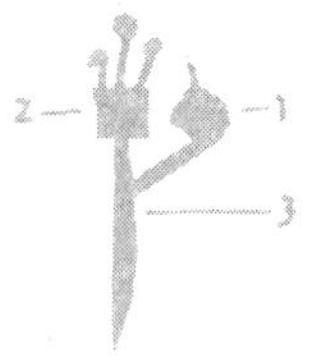

א) יהיו ראשיה כמו בשל כפופה והיא מורכבת ג"כ [1] מיו"ד [2] ונו"ן ואך מנו"ן פשוטה, ע"כ גופה פשוט כמו אות נו"ן פשוטה [3] ושיעור אורכה שתרד למטה מדיבוק הראשים לכתחלה בכדי שיהא ראוי לעשות צד"י כפופה. ובדיעבד פסק הפמ"ג שאם הוציא ממקום דיבוק היו"ד לנו"ן רק כמלא יו"ד כשר אבל אם לא נשאר כמלא יו"ד צ"ע. אם נגעו הראשים יותר ממקום דיבוקם או שנגעו זה בזה או שנפסק בין היו"ד להנו"ן דינו כמו בכפופה וכנ"ל.

צורת אות קו"ף

[1] יהיה א) גגה שוה [2] ותג קטן צ"ל על גגה בצד שמאל על פניה לכתחלה ויעשה הקוץ דק כדי שלא יקלקל בזה תמונת הקו"ף דהיינו שלא יראה עי"ז כלמ"ד מצד אחד ובספר מעשה רקח כתב דמטעם זה יעתיק התג מקצה הגג ע"ש. [3] * ויריכה הימנית צ"ל למטה ב) כפוף היטב לצד רגל שמאל כמו צורת כ"ף כפופה אך שתהיה קצרה הרבה מן הגג [4] ורגל השמאלית תלויה בה והיא כצורת נו"ן פשוטה אך שקצרה מעט [5] וע"כ יהיה ראשה עב [6] ומתמעט והולך כמו בנו"ן. [7] ולא ירחיקנו ג) לכתחלה מן הגג יותר מעובי הגג [8] ויש לכתחלה למשוך רגל שמאל התלויה באלכסון קצת לצד ימין. ומאד יזהר שלא יגע הרגל להגג ד) או ליריכו שבצדו ואף לא יהיה סמוך להגג לכתחלה אלא יהא בינו לבין הגג **חלק כ"כ בכדי שאדם בינוני ה) יכירנו היטב מעל ס"ת שע"ג בימה כשהוא קורא בו. ולא יהיה הרגל נגד אמצע הגג אלא בסופו בצד שמאל ואם נגע הרגל ו) בגגו וה"ה ביריכו שבצדו או שעשה הרגל באמצע הגג ז) הכל דינו כמו באות ה' וכמבואר שם לעיל באות ה"א. [9] ואם אורך הרגל השמאלי הוא רק כמו יו"ד מכנגד מקום הכפיפה ולמטה כשר בדיעבד [כנ"ל כוונת פמ"ג במה שכתב לענין קו"ף בד"ה קי"ל ניקב רגל הה"א וכו' קו"ף רי"ש וכו' ומה שסיים אם נשאר מירך הימין משום אחריני נקט].**

צורת אות רי"ש

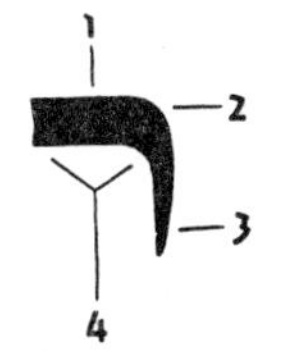

[1] גגה שוה לכתחלה [2] ומאוד יזהר א) שתהיה עגולה ממש מאחוריה כדי שלא תדמה לדלי"ת ואם נראית כדלי"ת פסולה ב) ואם ספק מראין לתינוק [3] ויריכה יהיה קצר כדי שלא תדמה לכ"ף פשוטה. [4] וגגה ארוך כאורך ב' ג) כדי שלא תדמה לוא"ו. ובדיעבד אם יש ספק מראין לתינוק וכנ"ל. ואם עשה רגל הרי"ש קצר כמו יו"ד די בזה בדיעבד פמ"ג. ועיין לקמן בסוף אות תיו.

צורת אות שי"ן

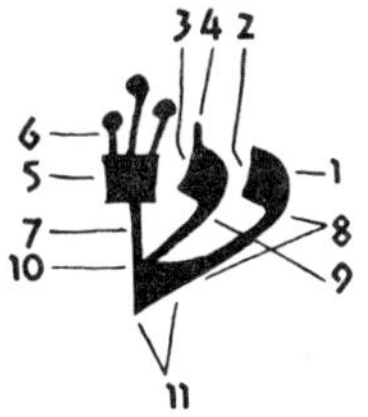

יש לה שלשה ראשים א) [1] ראשה הראשון עם ירך הנמשך ממנו הוא כעין וא"ו [2] ופניה ב) כלפי מעלה קצת [3] והראש השני יהיה כעין יו"ד ופניה ג"כ קצת כלפי מעלה [4] ועוקץ קטן עליה לכתחלה [5] והראש השלישי צריך

שער הציון

ה) ב"ש בדף י"ב. **ץ** א) הכל מבואר בפשיטות. **ק** א) ב"י ולכתחילה. ב) כל הענין בב"י. ג) פשוט. ד) מספר כתיבה תמה והדין עמו דאל"ה לא מיקרי הרגל תלויה וכן משמע שבת ק"ג ע"א בגמרא דיש הפסק בין הרגל לגוף הקו"ף. ה) מ"א בסימן ל"ו בשם הרמ"ע וכ"כ הא"ר. ו) לעיל בסימן ל"ב סי"ח עי"ש ובבה"ל. ז) פמ"ג באות ק' בפתיחה. **ר** א) כל הענין בב"י. ב) טור וכעין זה למעלה באות ב' ע"ש. ג) ב"י בא"ב שלישי. **ש** א) כל הענין בב"י. ב) ולכתחילה. ג) ב"ש בא"ב

ביאור הלכה

למעלה כצורת וא"ו דלא ליתהני תיקון כנ"ל פשוט. ומ"ש שיגרור קצת דאם יגרור הרבה יאבד תמונתו וכשיתקן אח"כ יהיה בזה שלא כסדרן. ומ"ש ואח"כ יוסיף עליו דיו דאם יעשה בהיפך ויהיה רחב הרבה אפשר דעי"ז יקרא אבד עיקר תמונתו דאין הכל מורגלין בכזה ולא יועיל אח"כ מה שיגרור מצד שמאל. ודע עוד דלדעת הפמ"ג דמחית לתרוייהו בחדא מחתא אפילו לענין דיעבד אלמא דס"ל דאין לחלק בין פשוטה לכפופה כיון דשניהן שם נו"ן עליהן [ותדע דבכ"ף פשוטה שעשאו מרובע נמי מצדד כהפוסקים דס"ל אפילו בדיעבד פסול] א"כ לדבריו יש נמי לומר כה"ג במ"ם פתוחה אם עשאו למטה ג"כ עגולה דיש לפוסלו אפילו בדיעבד מטעם זה כיון דשניהן שם מ"ם עליהן ובמ"ם סתומה ודאי פסול דהוי בכלל ממי"ן סמכין א"כ ה"נ בפתוחה וצ"ע לדינא. ותיקון מהני בזה אפילו בתו"מ דבלא"ה ג"כ עדיין עיקר צורתה עליה.

ק * ויריכה הימנית וכו' כ"ף כפופה. ובדיעבד נראה דאפילו כפוף מעט די, עיין בב"י וכן משמע דעת רש"י בשבת ק"ד ע"א ד"ה ליעול בהך עי"ש. וכן משמע מרבינו ירוחם והאגור שכתבו שיאריך רגל הקו"ף שלא ידמה לה"א. מכל זה משמע דפתוח למטה ועכ"פ כפוף מעט די. ועיין בספר בית אהרן שהביא בשם הרדב"ז שעיקר צורתה רי"ש נו"ן

so much blank /space/ that an average person will recognize /the gap/ well from a Torah Scroll on the bimah when he reads from /the Scroll/. The leg should not be against the middle of the roof, but at the end, on the left side. If the leg touches the roof or, correspondingly, /if it touches/ the thigh at its side or if one made the leg /against/ the middle of the roof, the ruling accords fully with /the ruling for the similar case/ where the letter ה is involved. /The rulings with respect to the letter ה/ are stated there above, in /the description of/ the letter ה.

If the length of the left leg is only the same as /the length of/ a /letter/ י, /measuring/ below from /the point/ corresponding to the point where the bent over /part of the thigh ends,[9] the letter/ is valid, now that it is after the event. [This appears to me the meaning of what the *P.Mg.* writes concerning the /letter/ ק in /the paragraph/ beginning with the words .קי"ל ניקב רגל הה"א וכו' קו"ף רי"ש וכו' When he concludes, "If there remains of the right thigh /etc./", he is /giving a ruling/ for the other /letters/.]

THE FORM OF THE LETTER ר

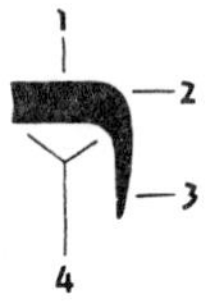

Initially, the roof of the letter ר should be of even[1] /height/. One should be extremely careful that it is actually rounded at the back,[2] so that it will not resemble a /letter/ ד. If it appears like a /letter/ ד it is invalid. If this is in doubt, /the letter/ should be shown to a child /who is neither especially intelligent nor especially simple and his reading will determine the validity/.

The thigh should be short,[3] so that /the letter/ does not resemble the simple /elongated letter/ ך.

The length of the roof should be /the same/ as the length /of the roof/ of the /letter/ ב,[4] so that /the letter/ does not resemble a /letter/ ו. Once it is after the event, if one is in doubt /as to whether or not the letter resembles a letter ו, the letter/ should be shown to a child /to be read/, as /stated/ above /for a similar case/.

If one made /the length of/ the leg of the ר as short as /the length of/ a /letter/ י, this is /ruled as/ adequate now that it is after the event. *P.Mg.* See below at the end /of the description/ of the letter ת.

THE FORM OF THE LETTER ש

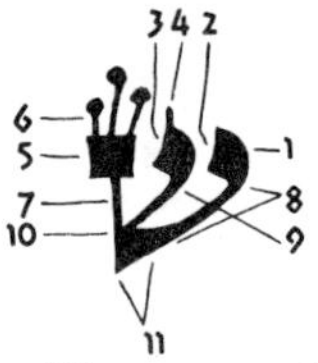

The letter ש has three heads. The first head, with the thigh that is drawn from it, is similar to a /letter/ ו.[1] The front of /the head/ should /face/ slightly upwards.[2]

The second head should be similar to a /letter/ י, with the front of /that head/ also /facing/ slightly upwards,[3] and, initially, /it should have/ a small prickle on it.[4]

The third head must be made with the

שותו בתמונת זיי"ן [6] וג' תגין עליו. וכן כל אותיות ש'ע'ט'נ'ז' ג'ץ' ראשם השמאלי הוא כזיי"ן. ויזהר שלא יגעו הראשים זו בזו. [7] הראש השמאלי הזה יהיה לכתחילה יריכו ממש ג) בעמידה [8] וימשיך אליו הירך מן הראש הראשון בשפוע למטה עד מקום חודו [9] וירך הראש השני ג"כ ימשיך בשפוע לצד שמאל למטה [10] עד שיהיו השלשה ראשים מחוברים למטה במקום אחד. ואם היו"ד האמצעי לא נגעה בשוליה מבואר דינו בל"ב סכ"ה ע"ש. [11] ולא יהיה מושב השי"ן רחב ולא עגול אלא חד ואז יהיו כל הג' ראשים עומדים למטה על רגל אחד כקו"ף ורי"ש.

ובדיעבד אם עשה מושב השי"ן רחב נשאר הפמ"ג בצ"ע. אם כתב שי"ן של ד' ראשים פסולה ולא די בגרירת ראש אחת דהוי חק תוכות אלא צריך לבטל האות ולהשלימה. ובתו"מ אם כתב לאחריה אין מועיל תיקון דהוי שלא כסדרן [פר"ח בא"ע ופמ"ג בפתיחה ולדויד אמת ושארי אחרונים דלא כמהריק"ש]. אם יש הפסק באיזה מהראשים מבואר דינו לעיל בל"ב סכ"ה. אם נגעו איזה מהראשין יותר ממקום דיבוקם דהיינו שאין ניכר הראש אלא קו שוה פסול ואין תינוק מועיל בזה. אם נגעו ד) הראשין זה בזה אפילו כחוט השערה פסול. ולענין תיקון עיין בספר משנת אברהם שכתב דרוב הפוסקים סוברים דמהני בזה גרירה דלא מיקרי נשתנית צורתה עי"ז ורק החסרון הוא משום דאינו מוקף גויל באותו מקום עי"ז ולכך מהני גרירה אח"כ. ול"נ אחרי דיש ג"כ הרבה מהפוסקים שמחמירין בזה אין להקל רק בתו"מ אם כתב אחריו דלא מהני בהו שלא כסדרן משא"כ בס"ת צריך לבטלו מצורת אות ולהשלימו.

צורת אות תי"ו

[1] יהיה א) גגה עם רגל ימין ב) כמו דלי"ת [2] ורגל שמאלו יש שעושין בתוך התי"ו כעין וא"ו הפוכה ויש שעושין כעין דלי"ת קטנה הפוכה וכל מקום שהלכה רופפת בידך הלוך אחר המנהג וכ"ז לכתחלה. [3] ורגל שמאל יגיע למעלה כי כל האותיות שלימות גוף אחד. [4] ורגל ימין יהיה קצר שאם יהיה ארוך שמא תדמה לתינוק דלא חכים ולא טיפש לפ' פשוטה [5] וימשיך להרגל בתוך התי"ו [6] כדי שיהיה סוף רגלה השמאלי כנגד סוף גגה ולא בולט סוף הרגל לחוץ כדי שיהיה יוכל להסמיך אליה אות אחרת מלמעלה למטה. [7] גם לא יהיה הגג בולט להלאה מרגלה.

ובדיעבד ג) אם גגה עוברת להלאה מרגלה והרגל באמצע דינה כמו שנתבאר לעיל באות ה"א. אם ד) עשה רגל השמאלי קצר כיו"ד קטנה הפוכה בתוך התי"ו י"ל שנשתנה כפ"א פשוטה ופסולה ואפילו אם הגג רחב כפלים כירך דפ"א פשוטה אין שיעור לרגלה רק לכ"ף פשוטה יש שיעור לרגלה כפלים כגג שלא תדמה לרי"ש או לדלי"ת. אם עשה רגל התי"ו קו שוה ולא בולט סופו לחוץ. עיין לעיל בסימן ל"ב בסוף סי"ח ובמ"ב שם ס"ק צ"א. אם רגל הימיני של התי"ו נפסק ואין בו רק כמלא יו"ד כשר כ"כ פמ"ג בפתיחה במ"ש יראה לי דה"ה לשאר אותיות וכו' עי"ש. ולפ"ז ה"ה אם לכתחלה לא עשה רק כמלא יו"ד כשר כמו לענין ה"א. ועיין בביאור הלכה בסי' ל"ב לענין ה"א שביארנו שם דאם הראינו לתינוק והתינוק לא קראה לאות צ"ע בזה. כל אות שיש בה ספק שמא אין בה כשיעור הראוי בענין שהיא פסולה או שמא אין צורתה עליה בענין שהיא פסולה מראין לתינוק שאינו לא חכים ולא טיפש ואם יודע לקרותה כהלכתה כשרה וא"צ תיקון, אבל אם ידוע לנו שאין האות כהלכתה אפילו אם הקלקול הזה נעשה לאחר הכתיבה אין קריאת התינוק מועלת כמו שנתבאר בסי' ל"ב סט"ז וע"ש בסכ"ה באיזה דבר מועיל תיקון. אם יש הפסק באותיות הפשוטות כגון וא"ו ונו"ן פשוטה וכדומה שיש הפסק באורך האות וצריך להראות להתינוק ה) צריך לכסות לו מה שלמטה וכ"ש אם נשאר רושם החלודה למטה דכו"ע מודים דצריך לכסות שהתינוק יטעה לצרף זה להאות.

ביאור הלכה

והאריך שם בענין זה. וסיים בזה הלשון ונראה שצורתו כמו רי"ש רק שיהיה הקצה של רי"ש עקום לשמאל כמו למ"ד וכן נראה מספר מגן דוד להרדב"ז ולצאת ידי הכל יעשה למטה כפוף כעין כ"ף וכן נהגו לא כמקצת סופרים שעושים צורתה כמו עיקום של למ"ד כזה ק וזה לא כחד וקוצץ בנטיעות רק כמ"ש עכ"ל.

שער הציון

ת א) כולו בב"י ופמ"ג. ב) ולכתחילה כן מוכח בב"ש בא"ב הראשון. ג) פמ"ג בפתיחה. ד) פמ"ג. ה) מלעיל סימן ל"ב סט"ז.

האחרון. ד) ב"ש בדף י"ב ע"ג.

קצת כללי מוקף גויל מבעל פמ"ג

תחלת הכתיבה צריך מוקף גויל בכל צדדין של האותיות ואפילו בקוצו של יו"ד השמאלי [מנחות דף כ"ט לפיר"ת דפסקו כוותיה רוב הפוסקים] מה"ת דכתיב וכתבתם כתיבה תמה [עיין ב"י וב"ח ודרישה] ומבפנים נמי בענין מוקף גויל [עי' סי' ל"ב סט"ו בבה"ל] ויש להחמיר דאפי' מצד א' בפנים אם אינו מוקף גויל פוסל כמבחוץ [ודלא כט"ז דמיקל שם בזה] וכל זה בתחלת הכתיבה אבל אם לאחר שנכתב ניקב או אכלו עכברים ותולעת כשר אפילו מבחוץ. ומיהו ודאי דיעבד דוקא כשר הא כל מה שיש לתקן הוה כלכתחלה וצריך תיקון, הלכך אם ניקב בצד אות ועב הוא מגרר קצת עוביו ויש לו היקף גויל דאין שיעור לעוביו. ודע עוד דתיקון מועיל אפילו אם נכתב לכתחלה בלא היקף גויל כגון ד' פשוטה בלי היקף וה"ה שאר אותיות בין בארכן או בעוביין אם תשאר צורת האות עליה מוחק וגורר ולא הוי שלא כסדרן בזה.

symbol of a /letter/ ז[5] and it should have three crownlets on it.[6] Likewise, /in the case of/ all the letters /of the group/ שעטנז גץ, the left head should be /formed/ like a /letter/ ז.

One must take care that the heads do not touch one another /at the top/.

Initially, the left head should have its thigh standing actually[7] /erect/. One should draw the thigh of the first head to it at an incline downwards, so that /that thigh reaches/ the sharp point[8] /underneath/ it. The thigh of the second head should also be drawn at an incline towards the left downwards,[9] so that the three heads are joined together below at one point.[10]

If the middle י /part/ does not touch the bottom of /the letter/, the ruling which /applies/ is stated in /Sec./ 32, Par. 25; see there.

The base of the /letter/ ש should neither be wide nor rounded, but sharp.[11] Then all three heads will stand below on one leg, like /the letters/ ק and ר. The *P.Mg.* remains in need of /further/ study /to determine the ruling/ once it is after the event and one made the base of the /letter/ ש wide.

If one wrote a /letter/ ש with four heads, /the letter/ is invalid. It is not sufficient /in such a case/ to scrape away one head, as this constitutes carving around /to form the letter/. Instead, one must cancel /the form of/ the letter /so that it does not even have three heads/ and /then/ complete it. Where *tefilin* /passages/ or mezuzos are involved correction is of no avail, once one has /already/ written after /that ש/, as /when corrected the letter/ will be /written/ in incorrect order. [*Pr.Ch.*, in *Even Ha-Ezer*; *P.Mg.*, in his opening /discourse/; *Le-David Emes* and other Acharonim. This contradicts /the ruling of/ the *Maharikash*.]

If there is an interruption between some of the heads, the ruling which /applies/ is given above in /Sec./ 32, Par. 25.

If any /one/ of the heads touches more than at the point where it should be stuck /to the rest of the letter/, meaning that the head is not discernible but /the entire stroke consists of/ a line of even /width, the letter/ is invalid. In such a case, /even if/ a child /who is neither especially intelligent nor especially simple reads the letter correctly this/ is of no avail.

If the heads touch one another /at the top/, even by a hairsbreadth, /the letter/ is invalid. As regards the correction of /a letter which has heads touching one another/, see the work *Mishnas Avraham*. /The author/ writes /there/ that the majority of Poskim are of the opinion that scraping /away the touch/ is of avail for /the correction of/ this /fault/. /This is/ because /the letter/ will not be classed as having changed its form as a result of /the correction, as/ the fault is only because /, due to the touching, the letter/ is not surrounded by /blank/ parchment at that point. In view of this, scraping is of avail subsequently /and is not classed as carving around the letter to form it/. It appears to me /, though/, that, bearing in mind that there are also many Poskim who are stringent about this, one should not be lenient /and rely on scraping away the touch/, except with respect to *tefilin* /passages/ or mezuzos /in cases/ when one has /already/ written /other letters/ after this /ש/. /If one will cancel the form of the letter before correcting it in the case of the latter, the correction/ will be of no avail for them, /because the corrected letter will be written/ in incorrect order. /However,/ one should not /be lenient about this if one finds such a ש/ in a Torah Scroll, /but/ must /first/ cancel the form of the letter and /then/ complete it /in conformance with halachic requirements/.

THE FORM OF THE LETTER ח

The roof of the letter ח /together/ with its right leg should be /formed/ like /the letter/ ד.[1]

/As for/ the left leg, there are /scribes/ who make inside the /letter/ ח /a stroke/ similar to an inverted /letter/ ו /to serve as this leg/ and other /scribes/ who make /a stroke/ similar to a small inverted /letter/ ד[2] /for this purpose/. Whenever the halachic /ruling/ is unclear one should follow the practice. /However,/ these are all initial /requirements/.

The left leg must reach /the roof/ above,[3] as all the whole letters /consist of/ a single body.

The right leg should be short,[4] as if it is long, /the letter/ may appear to a child who is neither /especially/ intelligent nor /especially/ simple like a simple /elongated letter/ ך.

One should draw the /left/ leg to the inside of the /letter/ ח,[5] so that the end of the left leg /at the bottom/ will correspond with the end

עשותו בתמונת זיי״ן [8]וג׳ תגין עליו. וכן כל אותיות ש׳ע׳ט׳נ׳ז׳ ג׳ץ׳ ראשם השמאלי הוא כזיי״ן. ויזהר שלא יגעו הראשים זו בזו. [7]הראש השמאלי הזה יהיה לכתחילה יריכו ממש ג) בעמידה [8]וימשיך אליו הירך מן הראש הראשון בשפוע למטה עד מקום חודו [9]וירך הראש השני ג״כ ימשיך בשפוע לצד שמאל למטה [10]עד שיהיו השלשה ראשים מחוברים למטה במקום אחד. ואם היו״ד האמצעי לא נגעה בשוליה מבואר דינו בל״ב סכ״ה ע״ש. [11]ולא יהיה מושב השי״ן רחב ולא עגול אלא חד ואז יהיו כל הג׳ ראשים עומדים למטה על רגל אחד כקו״ף ורי״ש.

ובדיעבד אם עשה מושב השי״ן רחב נשאר הפמ״ג בצ״ע. אם כתב שי״ן של ד׳ ראשים פסולה ולא די בגרירת ראש אחת דהוי חק תוכות אלא צריך לבטל האות ולהשלימה. ובתו״מ אם כתב לאחריה אין מועיל תיקון דהוי שלא כסדרן [פר״ת בא״ע ופמ״ג בפתיחה ולדויד אמת ושארי אחרונים דלא כמהריק״ש]. אם יש הפסק באיזה מהראשים מבואר דינו לעיל בל״ב סכ״ה. אם נגעו איזה מהראשין יותר ממקום דיבוקם דהיינו שאין ניכר הראש אלא קו שוה פסול ואין תינוק מועיל בזה. אם נגעו ד) הראשין זה בזה אפילו כחוט השערה פסול. ולענין תיקון עיין בספר משנת אברהם שכתב דרוב הפוסקים סוברים דמהני בזה גרירה דלא מיקרי נשתנית צורתה ע״ז ורק החסרון הוא משום דאינו מוקף גויל באותו מקום ע״ז ולכך מהני גרירה אח״כ. ול״נ אחרי דיש ג״כ הרבה מהפוסקים שמחמירין בזה אין להקל רק בתו״מ אם כתב אחריו דלא מהני בהו שלא כסדרן משא״כ בס״ת צריך לבטלו מצורת אות ולהשלימו.

צורת אות תי״ו

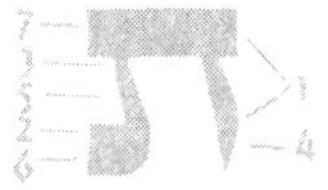

[1]יהיה א) גגה גם רגל ימין ב) כמו דלי״ת [2]ורגל שמאלו יש שעושין בתוך התי״ו כעין וא״ו הפוכה ויש שעושין כעין דלי״ת קטנה הפוכה וכל מקום שהלכה רופפת בידך הלוך אחר המנהג וכ״ז לכתחלה. [3]ורגל שמאל יגיע למעלה כי כל האותיות שלימות גוף אחד. [4]ורגל ימין יהיה קצר שאם יהיה ארוך שמא תדמה לתינוק דלא חכים ולא טיפש לפי פשוטה [5]וימשיך להרגל בתוך התי״ו [6]כדי שיהיה סוף רגלה השמאלי כנגד סוף גגה ולא בולט סוף הרגל לחוץ כדי שיהיה יוכל להסמיך אליה אות אחרת מלמעלה למטה. [7]גם לא יהיה הגג בולט להלאה מרגלה.

ובדיעבד ג) אם גגה עוברת להלאה מרגלה והרגל באמצע דינה כמו שנתבאר לעיל באות ה״א. אם ד) עשה רגל השמאלי קצר כיו״ד קטנה הפוכה בתוך התי״ו י״ל שנשתנה כפ״א פשוטה ופסולה ואפילו אם הגג רחב כפלים כירך דפ״א פשוטה אין שיעור לרגלה רק לכ״ף פשוטה יש שיעור לרגלה כפלים כגג שלא תדמה לרי״ש או לדלי״ת. אם עשה רגל התי״ו קו שוה ולא בולט סופו לחוץ. עיין לעיל בסימן ל״ב בסוף סי״ח ובמ״ב שם ס״ק צ״א. אם רגל הימיני של התי״ו נפסק ואין בו רק כמלא יו״ד כשר כ״כ פמ״ג בפתיחה במ״ש יראה לי דה״ה לשאר אותיות וכו׳ עי״ש. ולפ״ז ה״ה אם לכתחלה לא עשה רק כמלא יו״ד כשר כמו לענין ה״א. ועיין בביאור הלכה בסי׳ ל״ב לענין ה״א שביארנו שם דאם הראינו לתינוק והתינוק לא קראה לאות צ״ע בזה. כל אות שיש בה ספק שמא אין בה כשיעור הראוי בענין שהיא פסולה או שמא אין צורתה עליה בענין שהיא פסולה מראין לתינוק שאינו לא חכים ולא טיפש ואם יודע לקרותה כהלכתה כשרה וא״צ תיקון, אבל אם ידוע לנו שאין האות כהלכתה אפילו אם הקלקול הזה נעשה לאחר הכתיבה אין קריאת התינוק מועלת כמו שנתבאר בסי׳ ל״ב סט״ז וע״ש בסכ״ה באיזה דבר מועיל תיקון. אם יש הפסק באותיות הפשוטות כגון וא״ו ונו״ן פשוטה וכדומה שיש הפסק באורך האות וצריך להראות להתינוק ה) צריך לכסות לו מה שלמטה וכ״ש אם נשאר רושם החלודה למטה דכו״ע מודים דצריך לכסות שהתינוק יטעה לצרף זה להאות.

שער הציון

ת א) כולו בב״י ופמ״ג. ב) ולכתחילה כן מוכח בב״ש בא״ב הראשון. ג) פמ״ג בפתיחה. ד) ב״ש בדף י״ב ע״ג. האחרון. ד) פמ״ג. ה) מלעיל סימן ל״ב סט״ז.

ביאור הלכה

והאריך שם בענין זה. וסיים בזה הלשון ונראה שצורתו כמו רי״ש רק שיהיה הקצה של רי״ש עקום לשמאל כמו למ״ד וכן נראה מספר מגן דוד להרדב״ז ולצאת ידי הכל יעשה למטה כפוף כעין כ״ף וכן נהגו לא כמקצת סופרים שעושים צורתה כמו עיקום של למ״ד כזה ק וזה לא כחד וקוצץ בנטיעות רק כמ״ש עכ״ל.

קצת כללי מוקף גויל מבעל פמ״ג

תחלת הכתיבה צריך מוקף גויל בכל צדדין של האותיות ואפילו בקוצו של יו״ד השמאלי [מנחות דף כ״ט לפיר״ת דפסקו כוותיה רוב הפוסקים] מה״ת דכתיב וכתבתם כתיבה תמה [עיין ב״י וב״ח ודרישה] ומבפנים נמי בעינן מוקף גויל [עי׳ סי׳ ל״ב סט״ו בבה״ל] ויש להחמיר דאפי׳ מצד א׳ בפנים אם אינו מוקף גויל פוסל כמבחוץ [ודלא כט״ז דמיקל שם בזה] וכל זה בתחלת הכתיבה אבל אם לאחר שנכתב ניקב או אכלו עכברים ותולעת כשר אפילו מבחוץ. ומיהו ודאי דיעבד דוקא כשר הא כל מה שיש לתקן הוה כלכתחלה וצריך תיקון, הלכך אם ניקב בצד אות ועב הוא מגרר קצת עוביו ויש לו היקף גויל דאין שיעור לעוביו. ודע עוד דתיקון מועיל אפילו אם נכתב לכתחלה בלא היקף גויל כגון ך׳ פשוטה בלי היקף וה״ה שאר אותיות בין בארכן או בעוביין אם תשאר צורת האות עליה מותק וגורר ולא הוי שלא כסדרן בזה.

of the roof[6] /of the letter/. The end of the leg should not protrude outwards, so that one will be able to put another letter close to /the ת/ from the top to the bottom.

The roof /of the letter/ should also not protrude further than the leg[7] of /the letter/. Once it is after the event, if the roof of /the letter/ continues further than its leg and the leg is in the middle /of the letter/, the ruling which /applies/ is the same as /the ruling/ stated above in /the description of/ the letter ה /as regards the analogous case for that letter/.

If one made the left leg short, like a small inverted /letter/ י, inside the ת, one can argue that /the letter/ has changed /its form and become/ like a simple /elongated letter/ ף and is /therefore/ invalid. This even /applies/ if the roof is twice as wide as /the length of/ the thigh /on the right/. /This is/ because there is no minimum length /required/ for the leg of a simple /elongated letter/ ף. /In fact/ a minimum length for the leg is only /required in the case of/ a simple /elongated letter/ ך. /The leg of that letter must be/ twice /the length of/ the roof, so that /the letter/ will not appear like a /letter/ ר or a /letter/ ד.

/For the ruling/ if one made the /left/ leg of a /letter/ ת a straight line and its end does not project outwards, see above in Sec. 32 at the end of Par. 18 and in the Mishnah Berurah, sub-Par. 91.

If the right leg of a /letter/ ת is interrupted, /so that/ it only has /a length/ which is equivalent /to the length/ of the /letter/ י, /the letter/ is valid. This is what the *P.Mg.* writes in his opening /discourse/ when he writes, "It appears to me that the same ruling /applies/ in the case of other letters, etc."; see there. Accordingly, /even/ if initially one only made /the leg/ of /a length/ which is equivalent /to the length/ of the /letter/ י, /the letter/ is valid, correspondingly, as /is the ruling/ with respect to /the letter/ ה. See the Beyur Halachah in Sec. 32 with respect to /the letter/ ה. There we have explained that if one showed /the letter/ to a child /who is neither especially intelligent nor especially simple/ and the child did not read the letter /for what it is meant to be/, study is required /to determine whether or not we regard the letter as valid/ in such a case.

If there is a question as regards any letter that /one of its strokes/ may not have the proper size (where /this failing would cause the letter/ to be invalid) or that /the letter/ may not have its /required/ form (where /the deviation would cause it/ to be invalid), one should show /the letter/ to a child who is neither /especially/ intelligent nor /especially/ simple. If /this child/ is able to read /the letter/ for what it is /meant/ to be it is valid and does not require correction. However, if we know that the letter does not conform with halachic requirements /, then/, even if the fault /which causes this/ came about after /the letter/ was written, /correct/ reading by /such/ a child will be of no avail /for the letter to be considered valid/, as explained in Sec. 32, Par. 16. See there, in Par. 25, for which matters correction is of avail.

If there is an interruption in the simple letters, such as the /letter/ ו, the simple /elongated letter/ ן or the like, and the interruption is in the length of the letter, it is necessary to show /the letter/ to a child /, who is neither especially intelligent nor especially simple, to determine its validity/. /However,/ one must cover the /part of the letter/ below /the interruption when one shows it/ to him. This certainly /applies/ if the impression of the decayed /ink/ remains below. /Then/ all /authorities/ are agreed that /what is below the interruption/ must be covered /before the letter is shown to the child/, as /, otherwise,/ the child will err and combine it with /what remains of/ the letter.

שותו בתמונת זיי"ן [6] וג' תגין עליו. וכן כל אותיות ש'ע'ט'נ'ז' ג'ץ' ראשם השמאלי הוא כזיי"ן. ויזהר שלא יגעו הראשים זו בזו. [7] הראש השמאלי הזה יהיה לכתחילה יריכו ממש ג) בעמידה [8] וימשיך אליו הירך מן הראש הראשון בשפוע למטה עד מקום חודו [9] וירך הראש השני ג"כ ימשיך בשפוע לצד שמאל למטה [10] עד שיהיו השלשה ראשים מחוברים למטה במקום אחד. ואם היו"ד האמצעי לא נגעה בשוליה מבואר דינו בל"ב סכ"ה ע"ש. [11] ולא יהיה מושב השי"ן רחב ולא עגול אלא חד ואז יהיו כל הג' ראשים עומדים למטה על רגל אחד כקו"ף ורי"ש.

ובדיעבד אם עשה מושב השי"ן רחב נשאר הפמ"ג בצ"ע. אם כתב שי"ן של ד' ראשים פסולה ולא די בגרירת ראש אחת דהוי חק תוכות אלא צריך לבטל האות ולהשלימה. ובתו"מ אם כתב לאחריה אין מועיל תיקון דהוי שלא כסדרן [פר"ח בא"ע ופמ"ג בפתיחה ולדויד אמת ושארי אחרונים דלא כמהריק"ש]. אם יש הפסק באיזה מהראשים מבואר דינו לעיל בל"ב סכ"ה. אם נגעו איזה מהראשין יותר ממקום דיבוקם דהיינו שאין ניכר הראש אלא קו שוה פסול ואין תינוק מועיל בזה. אם נגעו ד) הראשין זה בזה אפילו כחוט השערה פסול. ולענין תיקון עיין בספר משנת אברהם שכתב דרוב הפוסקים סוברים דמהני בזה גרירה דלא מיקרי נשתנית צורתה עי"ז ורק החסרון הוא משום דאינו מוקף גויל באותו מקום עי"ז ולכך מהני גרירה אח"כ. ול"נ אחרי דיש ג"כ הרבה מהפוסקים שמחמירין בזה אין להקל רק בתו"מ אם כתב אחריו דלא מהני בהו שלא כסדרן משא"כ בס"ת צריך לבטלו מצורת אות ולהשלימו.

צורת אות תי"ו

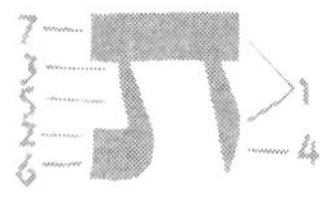

[1] יהיה א) גגה עם רגל ימין ב) כמו דלי"ת [2] ורגל שמאלו יש שעושין בתוך התי"ו כעין וא"ו הפוכה ויש שעושין כעין דלי"ת קטנה הפוכה וכל מקום שהלכה רופפת בידך הלוך אחר המנהג וכ"ז לכתחלה. [3] ורגל שמאל יגיע למעלה כי כל האותיות שלימות גוף אחד. [4] ורגל ימין יהיה קצר שאם יהיה ארוך שמא תדמה לתינוק דלא חכים ולא טיפש לפ' פשוטה [5] וימשיך להרגל בתוך התי"ו [6] כדי שיהיה סוף רגלה השמאלי כנגד סוף גגה ולא בולט סוף הרגל לחוץ כדי שיהיה יוכל להסמיך אליה אות אחרת מלמעלה למטה. [7] גם לא יהיה הגג בולט להלאה מרגלה.

ובדיעבד ג) אם גגה עוברת להלאה מרגלה והרגל באמצע דינה כמו שנתבאר לעיל באות ה"א. אם ד) עשה רגל השמאלי קצר כיו"ד קטנה הפוכה בתוך התי"ו י"ל שנשתנה כפ"א פשוטה ופסולה ואפילו אם הגג רחב כפלים כירך דפ"א פשוטה אין שיעור לרגלה רק לכ"ף פשוטה יש שיעור לרגלה כפלים כגג שלא תדמה לרי"ש או לדלי"ת. אם עשה רגל התי"ו קו שוה ולא בולט סופו לחוץ. עיין לעיל בסימן ל"ב בסוף סי"ח ובמ"ב שם ס"ק צ"א. אם רגל הימיני של התי"ו נפסק ואין בו רק כמלא יו"ד כשר כ"כ פמ"ג בפתיחה במ"ש יראה לי דה"ה לשאר אותיות וכו' עי"ש. ולפ"ז ה"ה אם לכתחלה לא עשה רק כמלא יו"ד כשר כמו לענין ה"א. ועיין בביאור הלכה בסי' ל"ב לענין ה"א שביארנו שם דאם הראינו לתינוק והתינוק לא קראה לאות צ"ע בזה. כל אות שיש בה ספק שמא אין בה כשיעור הראוי בענין שהיא פסולה או שמא אין צורתה עליה בענין שהיא פסולה מראין לתינוק שאינו לא חכים ולא טיפש ואם יודע לקרותה כהלכתה כשרה וא"צ תיקון, אבל אם ידוע לנו שאין האות כהלכתה אפילו אם הקלקול הזה נעשה לאחר הכתיבה אין קריאת התינוק מועלת כמו שנתבאר בסי' ל"ב סט"ז וע"ש בסכ"ה באיזה דבר מועיל תיקון. אם יש הפסק באותיות הפשוטות כגון וא"ו ונו"ן פשוטה וכדומה שיש הפסק באורך האות וצריך להראות להתינוק ה) צריך לכסות לו מה שלמטה וכ"ש אם נשאר רושם החלודה למטה דכו"ע מודים דצריך לכסות שהתינוק יטעה לצרף זה להאות.

שער הציון

ת א) כולו בב"י ופמ"ג. ב) ולכתחילה כן מוכח בב"ש בא"ב הראשון. ג) פמ"ג בפתיחה. ד) ב"ש בדף י"ב ע"ג. האחרון. ד) פמ"ג. ה) מלעיל סימן ל"ב סט"ז.

ביאור הלכה

והאריך שם בענין זה. וסיים בזה הלשון ונראה שצורתו כמו רי"ש רק שיהיה הקצה של רי"ש עקום לשמאל כמו למ"ד וכן נראה מספר מגן דוד להרדב"ז ולצאת ידי הכל יעשה למטה כפוף כעין כ"ף וכן נהגו לא כמקצת סופרים שעושים צורתה כמו עיקום של למ"ד כזה ק וזה לא כחד וקוצץ בנטיעות רק כמ"ש עכ"ל.

קצת כללי מוקף גויל מבעל פמ"ג

תחלת הכתיבה צריך מוקף גויל בכל צדדין של האותיות ואפילו בקוצו של יו"ד השמאלי [מנחות דף כ"ט לפיר"ת דפסקו כוותיה רוב הפוסקים] מה"ת דכתיב וכתבתם כתיבה תמה [עיין ב"י וב"ח ודרישה] ומבפנים נמי בעינן מוקף גויל [עי' סי' ל"ב סט"ו בבה"ל] ויש להחמיר דאפי' מצד א' בפנים אם אינו מוקף גויל פוסל כמבחוץ [ודלא כט"ז דמיקל שם בזה] וכל זה בתחלת הכתיבה אבל אם לאחר שנכתב ניקב או אכלו עכברים ותולעת כשר אפילו מבחוץ. ומיהו ודאי דיעבד דוקא כשר הא כל מה שיש לתקן הוה כלכתחלה וצריך תיקון, הלכך אם ניקב בצד אות ועב הוא מגרר קצת עוביו ויש לו היקף גויל דאין שיעור לעוביו. ודע עוד דתיקון מועיל אפילו אם נכתב לכתחלה בלא היקף גויל כגון ד' פשוטה בלי היקף וה"ה שאר אותיות בין בארכן או בעוביין אם תשאר צורת האות עליה מוחק וגורר ולא הוי שלא כסדרן בזה.

SOME OF THE RULES CONCERNING /THE NEED FOR THE LETTER TO BE/ SURROUNDED BY /BLANK/ PARCHMENT, /TAKEN/ FROM THE AUTHOR OF THE *P.MG.*

At the outset, when they are written, it is necessary for the letters to be surrounded by /blank/ parchment on all sides. This even /applies/ to the left tip of the /letter/ י. [*Menachos* 29/a/, according to the explanation of *R.T.*, whose view is /accepted as/ the /halachic/ ruling by most Poskim.] /This requirement derives/ from Torah law, as it is written,[11*] "And you should write them", /which implies/ impeccable script. [See the *B.Y.*, the *Bach* and the *Derishah.*]

/The letter/ must also be surrounded by /blank/ parchment on the inside. [See Sec. 32, Par. 15 and the Beyur Halachah.] One should /rule/ stringently that even if on one side of the inside /only the letter/ is not surrounded by /blank/ parchment /the letter/ is invalid, just as /a letter is invalid when it is not surrounded completely with blank parchment/ on the outside. [This contradicts /the view of/ the *Taz* who is lenient there about this.]

All the /above remarks apply/ at the outset when one writes. However, if after /a letter/ was written a hole formed /in the parchment/ or /the parchment/ was eaten by mice or a worm, /the passage/ is valid even if /blank parchment surrounding the letter is now lacking/ on the outside. On the other hand, /the passage/ is definitely only /ruled as/ valid /in circumstances/ which are after the event, but whenever there is /a way/ of correcting /this deficiency the circumstances/ are /regarded/ as initial /circumstances/ and /the deficiency/ must /in fact/ be corrected. Therefore, if a hole formed next to a letter and /the letter/ was /written/ thickly, one should scrape away some of its thickness and /then/ it will have /blank/ parchment surrounding it. /This is possible/ because there is no minimum thickness /required for a letter/.

Note further that even if /a letter/ was written initially without being surrounded by /blank/ parchment, correction is of avail. For example, /it is of avail/ if a simple /elongated/ ך /was extended to the bottom of the parchment/ without being surrounded /by blank parchment/ or, correspondingly, if other letters /reached the end of the parchment/ either through their length or through their thickness. /In all cases/ where the form of the letter will /subsequently/ remain, one may erase or scrape away /some of the writing so that the letter will be surrounded by blank parchment/. /Even if other letters have already been written after the letter which must be corrected,/ it will /nevertheless/ not be regarded as /having been written/ in incorrect order /because of this correction/.

11* *Devarim* 6:9.

לז זמן הנחת תפילין. ובו ג׳ סעיפים:

א [א]גדול (א) (א) שכר מצות תפילין וכל מי (ב) שאינו מניחם הוא (ג) בכלל פושעי ישראל (ב) (ד) [ב]בגופן: **ב** * [ג]מצותן להיותם עליו כל היום אבל מפני שצריכים גוף נקי שלא יפיח בהם ושלא יסיח דעתו מהם ואין כל אדם יכול ליזהר בהם נהגו [ד]שלא להניחם כל (ג) [א] היום ומ״מ צריך כל אדם ליזהר בהם (ה) להיותם עליו (ו) * בשעת ק״ש (ז) ותפלה: **ג** * [ה]קטן (ח) היודע לשמור תפילין בטהרה שלא יישן ושלא יפיח בהם: הגה ושלא ליכנס בהן לבית הכסא (רש״י פרק לולב הגזול) חייב

באר הגולה

א מנחות מ״ד
ב ראש השנה י״ז
ג טור ד הרא״ש
ה סוכה מ״ג

באר היטב

(א) שכר. בש״ס איתא דמאריך ימים. ובשמושא רבא איתא שהוא מובטח שהוא בן עה״ב ושאין גיהנם שולטת בו ושעונותיו נמחלים לו. וכתב הרא״ש אם זהיר בתפילין כף זכות מכרעתו. ואם פשע בהם כף חובה מכרעתו שאין לך גדול במצות עשה יותר מתפילין. חרש המדבר ואינו שומע או שומע ואינו מדבר חייב להניח תפילין אבל אינו שומע ואינו מדבר אין מוחין בידו מלהניחם אם רוצה ע״ת וכ״כ בשיורי כנה״ג סימן ל״ח. והבאר היטב אשר לפני לא העתיק היטב ע״ש: (ב) בגופן. ודוקא שאינו מניחם בשביל ביזוי מצוה אבל היראה להניחם משום דבעי גוף נקי ושמא לא יזהר בקדושתן אע״ג דעבירה היא בידו דבקל יוכל ליזהר בהם בשעת ק״ש ותפלה מ״מ לאו בכלל פושעי ישראל הוא הרא״ש: (ג) היום. ומ״ע כתב שתיקן להניחם שנית במנחה. ובערב שבת לא יניחם של״ה. ויניח תפילין דר״ת במנחה:

שערי תשובה

[א] היום. עבה״ט וכבר כתבתי בזה לעיל ס״ס ל״ד ע״ש. ונראה דע״ש לאו דוקא וה״ה ערב יו״ט שא״ל שלפי הטעם שכבר נתווסף קדושת שבת והיינו משום דתוספת שבת דאורייתא דא״כ גם תוספת יו״ט דאורייתא כמ״ש הב״י סי׳ רס״א ע״ש. ועיין בשו״ת שמש צדקה חלק א״ח סי׳ ז׳ וסי׳ ח׳ שהוכיח דליכא איסורא בזה מדינא והנוהג להניחם מבע״י קודם שתחול קדושת שבת אין מוחין בידו אך שם בסימן ז׳ כתב בשם המקובל מהר״ר בנימין כהן ז״ל ששאל לכמה

משנה ברורה

א (א) שכר. שכל המניחן מאריך ימים בעוה״ז שנאמר ד׳ עליהם יחיו כלומר אותם שנושאים שם ה׳ עליהם בתפילין יחיו ומובטח שהוא בן עוה״ב ואין אש של גיהנם שולט בו וכל עונותיו נמחלין לו. טור בשם השמושא רבא: (ב) שאינו מניחם. פי׳ אפילו מניעתו הוא רק לפרקים וכ״ש אם מבטל תמיד ממצוה זו והפמ״ג הביא בשם כ״ל דאפילו מי שביטל מתפילין יום אחד הוא ג״כ בכלל פושעי ישראל: (ג) בכלל פ״י. ודוקא שאינו מניחן בשביל שהמצוה בזויה בעיניו אבל הירא להניחם משום דבעי גוף נקי ושמא לא יזהר בקדושה כראוי אע״ג דעבירה היא דבקל יכול אדם ליזהר בשעת ק״ש ותפלה (א) מ״מ לא הוי בכלל פושעי ישראל. וכ״ש אם המצוה תמיד חביבה עליו ונזהר שיהיה גוף נקי אך עתה אית ליה אונס חולי שאין גופו נקי לכו״ע אין עליו דין פושעי ישראל כלל. ודע דכתב הב״ח דאפילו אם אין המצוה בזויה בעיניו אך ממנע מלהניחם מפני ביטול מלאכה או שאר הפסד ממון או מחמת עצלות (ב) ג״כ הוא בכלל פ״י בגופן אך דיש חילוק ביניהם לענין עונש עי״ש. וד״ז הוא תוכחת מגולה לאותן אנשים שמפני עצלותן מצוי שיהיו תפיליהן מונחין על מצחן ולא על הקרקפתא וגם הש״י אין מונח על מקומו כדין דהלא זה הוא כמי שלא הניח כלל. וכבר זירז ע״ז ג״כ אותנו הפמ״ג בסימן כ״ז שכתב שם דתפילין שמונחין שלא במקומן הרי הם כמונחין בכיסן. ועיין לעיל בסימן כ״ז נבה״ל שהארכנו בזה (ד) בגופן. ודינו פסוק בש״ס ר״ה י״ז דאפילו הוא איש בינוני דדרכו של הקב״ה להטות הכף כלפי חסד מכיון שנמצא בתוך עוונותיו עון זה כף חובה מכרעת והוא מוכרח לירד לגיהנם ואם ח״ו ג״כ עוונותיו מרובין מזכיותיו נידון בגיהנם י״ב חודש ואח״כ גופן כלה ונשמתן נשרפת ורוח מפזרת אפרן תחת כפות רגלי הצדיקים. וע״ש בתוס׳ דכ״ז בשלא עשה תשובה. (ג) ויען כי גדול כח המצוה כ״כ ולהיפך העונש ר״ל לכן יזהר כל אדם לקנות תפילין מסופר מומחה וי״ש ובעל תורה וכן רצועות יקנה מאיש נאמן כדי שיהא בטוח שנעבדו לשמן מעורות טהורות כי מי שהוא מניח תפילין פסולים לא לבד שאינו מקיים המצוה אלא (ד) שמברך כמה וכמה ברכות לבטלה שהוא עון גדול. ובעו״ה רבה המכשלה במה שקונים תפילין ורצועות ממאן דהוא לפי שמוכרים בזול ורובן אינם מרובעין ועוד יתר קלקולים שמצוי בהם בעת כתיבתן וכל ירא שמים יתן אל לבו אם על מלבושיו וכליו הוא מהדר שיהיו בתיקונם תכ״ש בחפצי שמים שלא יקמצם ויחוס על הכסף אלא יהדר לקנות אותן שהם בודאי כשרים אף שמחירם רב. וכתב הד״מ בשם המרדכי יש לאדם להדר אחר תפילין נאים שנאמר זה אלי ואנוהו דהיינו שכתבן לבלר אומן בכתב נאה ובדיו נאה ובקולמוס נאה וקלפים נאים: **ב** (ה) להיותם עליו. דבזמן קצר כזה בקל יכול ליזהר מהפחה ומהסח הדעת: (ו) בשעת ק״ש. דכל הקורא ק״ש בלא תפילין כאלו מעיד עדות שקר בעצמו. ואם לא נזדמן לו אז או שהיה חולה מעיים בשעת מעשה כל היום זמנו ומחויב להניחן עכ״פ כדי שלא יבטל יום אחד ממצות תפילין: (ז) ותפלה. ועיין לעיל סימן כ״ה סי״ג. וזהו לכל אדם אבל אנשי מעשה נוהגין ללמוד אחר התפלה בתפילין (ה) אך יש ליזהר שלא לדבר בהם (ו) דברים בטלים דמלבד איסור דברים בטלים הוא גם לא עי״ז לידי היסח הדעת. ועיין לעיל בסימן כ״ח סק״ג[ג] ובמעשה רב: **ג** (ח) היודע. דקודם לכן אין רשאי להניח תפילין ולאו חינוך

ביאור הלכה

* מצותן וכו׳. עיין בפמ״ג שמסתפק אם מן התורה חייב כל היום או מן התורה די ברגע אחד שמניח ומדרבנן כל היום ובטלוה עכשיו שאין לנו גוף נקי ומסיק דעיקרן של דברים דאם לא הניח יום א׳ כלל לתפילין ביטל מ״ע והניח רגע עליו קיים המצוה אבל מצוה מן המובחר מן התורה להיותן עליו כל היום וכו׳ עיין שם. ובספר ישועות יעקב פסק דמן התורה מצותן כל היום עיין שם. ועיין בספר א״ר שמוכח מדבריו דמי שיודע שיש לו גוף נקי אין לו לפטור א״ע ממצות תפילין כל היום. ופשוט דכונתו אם יודע שיוכל ליזהר א״ע ג״כ מהיסח הדעת דהיינו עכ״פ משחוק וקלות ראש כמו שכתבנו לעיל בכלל[א] כ״ח עי״ש. ועיין בספר מעשה רב שכתב דאם חושש ליוהרא בפני הבריות מותר בשל יד לבד. ומ״מ טוב לעשות של ראש קטן והרצועות יהיה ג״כ מכוסות מלילך בשל יד לבד עכ״ד ואשרי המקיים כדינו כמשאחז״ל במגילה כ״ח שאלו תלמידיו את ר״א[ב] במה הארכת ימים א״ל וכו׳ ולא הלכתי ד״א בלא תורה ובלא תפילין: * בשעת ק״ש ותפלה. ומ״ע כתב בתשובה שתיקן להניחם שנית במנחה ובע״ש לא יניחם של״ה: * קטן וכו׳. נראה פשוט דלדעת המחבר אם מאיזה טעם לא קנה אביו עבורו תפילין כגון שלא היה יכול לשמרם בטהרה וכה״ג ונעשה בנו בן י״ג שנים ויום אחד שוב אין על אביו מצות חינוך דאיש הוא וחייב מעצמו בכל המצות ואם איש עני הוא כל ישראל חייבים בזה וכמו שכתב הפ״מ בסק״ד:

שער הציון

(א) מ״א בשם התוס׳ והרא״ש: (ב) ולע״ק עליו מש״ס דר״ה י״ז ע״א למה צריך לתרץ דאיירי במחלה ע״מ יתרץ בכה״ג וי״ל: (ג) ח״א: (ד) פמ״ג: (ה) ברכי יוסף: (ו) מעשה רב:

הגהות ותיקונים: א) בסימן: ב) ר״ז: ג) סק״א:

§37: THE TIME FOR THE DONNING OF *TEFILIN*

(Contains Three Paragraphs)

1. (1) The reward for /the observance of/ the mitzvah of *tefilin* is substantial. Whoever (2) does not don /*tefilin* when he is obliged to do so/ (3) belongs to

Mishnah Berurah

§37

(1) The reward. For whoever dons /*tefilin*/ lives long in this world. /This is/ because it is stated,[1] "They who have the Lord on them will live". In other words, those who bear the Divine Name on them, by /wearing/ *tefilin*, will live. /A person who dons *tefilin*/ is /also/ assured of being in the world to come. The fire of *Gehinom* will have no control over him and all his sins will be pardoned him. *Tur* in the name of the *Shimusha Raba*.

(2) Does not don. I.e., even if he refrains /from fulfilling this mitzvah/ only on occasion and certainly if he neglects this mitzvah always.

The *P.Mg.* quotes in the name of the *N.Tz.* that even if someone neglected /donning/ *tefilin* for a single day he also belongs to the category of sinful Jews.

(3) Belongs to the category of sinful Jews. This only /applies/ if one does not don /*tefilin*/ because he views the mitzvah with contempt, but /not/ if one is afraid to don them because they require /the wearer to have/ a clean body and he may not be properly heedful of the holiness. Although /a person who does not don them for the latter reason transgresses/ a transgression, since it is easy for a person to be careful /about this/ while /he reads/ "The Reading of Shema" and /prays the eighteen-blessing/ prayer, he nevertheless does not belong to the category of sinful Jews. One certainly /does not belong to this category/ if he always cherishes /the performance of/ the mitzvah and is careful to have a clean body /when he dons *tefilin*/, but /refrains from donning them/ now because of an illness beyond his control, which /has caused/ his body not to be clean. /Then,/ according to all /authorities/, he does not have the ruling of a sinful Jew at all.

Note that the *Bach* writes that even if one does not view the mitzvah /of *tefilin*/ with contempt, but refrains from donning them because /he does not wish to be/ idle from his work or /to avoid some/ other monetary loss or because of neglectfulness, he also belongs to the category of sinful Jews /who have sinned/ with their bodies. However, there is a difference between /contempt for the mitzvah and these reasons for sinning/ as regards the punishment /due/. See there.

/The *Bach*'s words/ are an open rebuke to those people whose /head/ *tefilin* commonly lie on their foreheads and not on the crowns /of their heads/, because of their neglectfulness, and whose arm /*tefilin*/ also do not lie in the place which conforms with halachic /requirements/. For, of course /, if this is the case/, it is as if /the *tefilin*/ were

1 *Yeshaya* 38:16.

א מנחות מ"ד
ב ראש השנה י"ז
ג טור ד הרא"ש
ה סוכה מ"ג

לז זמן הנחת תפילין. ובו ג' סעיפים:

א אגדול (א) (א) שכר מצות תפילין וכל מי (ב) שאינו מניחם הוא (ג) בכלל **פושעי ישראל** **(ב) (ד) בבגופן: ב * גמצותן להיותם עליו כל היום אבל מפני שצריכים גוף נקי שלא יפיח בהם ושלא יסיח דעתו מהם ואין כל אדם יכול ליזהר בהם נהגו דשלא להניחם כל (ג) [א] היום** ומ"מ צריך כל אדם ליזהר בהם (ה) להיותם עליו (ו) * בשעת ק"ש (ז) ותפלה: ג * הקטן (ח) היודע לשמור תפילין בטהרה שלא יישן ושלא יפיח בהם: הגה ושלא ליכנס בהן לבית הכסא (רש"י פרק לולב הגזול) חייב

באר היטב

(א) שכר. בש"ס איתא דמאריך ימים. ובשמושא רבא איתא שהוא מובטח שהוא בן עה"ב ושאין גיהנם שולטת בו ושעונותיו נמחלים לו. וכתב הרא"ש אם זהיר בתפילין כף זכות מכרעתו. ואם פשע בהם כף חובה מכרעתו שאין לך גדול במצות עשה יותר מתפילין. חרש המדבר ואינו שומע או שומע ואינו מדבר חייב להניח תפילין אבל אינו שומע ואינו מדבר אין מוחין בידו מלהניחם אם רוצה ע"ת וכ"כ בשיורי כנה"ג סימן ל"ח. והבאר היטב אשר לפני לא העתיק היטב ע"ש: (ב) בגופן. ודוקא שאינו מניחם בשביל ביזוי מצוה אבל היראה להניחם משום דבעי גוף נקי ושמא לא יזהר בקדושתן אע"ג דעבירה היא בידו דבקל יוכל ליזהר בהם בשעת ק"ש ותפלה מ"מ לאו בכלל פושעי ישראל הוא הרא"ש: (ג) היום. ומ"ע כתב שתיקן להניחם שנית במנחה. ובערב שבת לא יניחם של"ה. ויניח תפילין דר"ת במנחה:

שערי תשובה

[א] היום. עבה"ט וכבר כתבתי בזה לעיל ס"ס ל"ד ע"ש. ונראה דע"ש לאו דוקא וה"ה ערב יו"ט שא"ל שלפי הטעם שכבר נתנוצץ קדושת שבת והיינו משום דתוספת שבת דאורייתא דא"כ גם תוספת יו"ט דאורייתא כמ"ש הב"י סי' רס"א ע"ש. ועיין בשו"ת שמש לדקה חלק א"ח סי' ז' וסי' ח' שהוכיח דליכא איסורא בזה מדינא והנוהג להניחם מבע"י קודם שתחול קדושת שבת אין מוחין בידו אך שם בסימן ז' כתב בשם המקובל מהר"ר בנימין כהן ז"ל ששאל לכמה

משנה ברורה

א (א) שכר. שכל המניחן מאריך ימים בעוה"ז שנאמר ה' עליהם יחיו כלומר אותם שנושאים שם ה' עליהם בתפילין יחיו ומובטח שהוא בן עוה"ב ואין אש של גיהנם שולט בו וכל עונותיו נמחלין לו. טור בשם השמושא רבא: (ב) שאינו מניחם. פי' אפילו מניעתו הוא רק לפרקים וכ"ש אם מבטל תמיד ממצוה זו והפמ"ג הביא בשם כ"ל דאפילו מי שביטל מתפילין יום אחד הוא ג"כ בכלל פושעי ישראל: (ג) בכלל פ"י. ודוקא שאינו מניחן בשביל שהמצוה בזויה בעיניו אבל היראה להניחם משום דבעי גוף נקי ושמא לא יזהר בקדושה כראוי אע"ג דעבירה היא דבקל יכול אדם ליזהר בשעת ק"ש ותפלה (א) מ"מ לא הוי בכלל פושעי ישראל. וכ"ש אם המצוה חביבה עליו ונזהר שיהיה גוף נקי אך עתה אית ליה אונס אולי שאין גופו נקי לכו"ע אין עליו דין פושעי ישראל כלל. ודע דכתב הב"ח דאפילו אם אין המצוה בזויה בעיניו אך ממנע מלהניחם מפני ביטול מלאכה או שאר הפסד ממון או מחמת עצלות (ב) ג"כ הוא בכלל פ"י בגופן אך דיש חילוק ביניהם לענין עונש ע"ש. וד"ז הוא תוכחת מגולה לאותן אנשים שמפני עצלותן מאחרי שיהיו תפיליהן מונחין על תלחן ולא על הקרקע וגם הש"י אין מונח על מקומו כדין דהלא זה הוא **כמי שלא הניח כלל. וכבר זירז ע"ז ג"כ אותנו הפמ"ג בסימן כ"ז שכתב שם דתפילין שמונחין שלא במקומן הרי הם כמונחין בכיסן. ועיין לעיל בסימן כ"ז בבה"ל שהארכנו בזה(ד) בגופן. ודינו פסוק בש"ס ר"ה י"ז דאפילו הוא איש בינוני דדרכו של הקב"ה להטות הכף כלפי חסד מכיון שנמצא בתוך עונותיו עון זה כף חובה מכרעת והוא מוכרח לירד לגיהנם ואם ח"ו ג"כ עונותיו מרובין מזכיותיו נידון בגיהנם י"ב חודש ואח"כ גופן כלה ונשמתן נשרפת ורוח מפזרת אפרן תחת כפות רגלי הצדיקים. וע"ש בתוס' דכ"ז בשלא עשה תשובה. (ג) ויען כי גדול כח המצוה כ"כ ולהיפך העונש ר"ל לכן יזהר כל אדם לקנות תפילין מסופר מומחה וי"ש ובעל תורה וכן רצועות יקנה מאיש נאמן כדי שיהא בטוח שנעבדו לשמן מעורות טהורות כי מי שהוא מניח תפילין פסולים לא לבד שאינו מקיים המצוה אלא (ד) שמברך כמה וכמה ברכות לבטלה שהוא עון גדול. ובעו"ה רבה המכשלה במה שקונים תפילין ורצועות ממאן דהוא לפי שמוכרים בזול ורובן אינם מרובעין ועוד יותר קלקולים שמצוי בהם בעת כתיבתן וכל ירא שמים יתן אל לבו אם על מלבושיו וכליו הוא מהדר שיהיו כתיקונם מכ"ש בחפצי שמים שלא יקמצם ויחוס על הכסף אלא יהדר לקנות אותן שהם בודאי כשרים אף שמחירם רב.** וכתב הד"מ בשם המרדכי יש לאדם להדר אחר תפילין נאים שנאמר זה אלי ואנוהו דהיינו שכתבן לבלר אומן בכתב נאה ובדיו נאה ובקולמוס נאה וקלפים נאים: ב (ה) להיותם עליו. דזמן קצר כזה בקל יכול ליזהר מהפחה ומהסח הדעת: (ו) בשעת ק"ש. דכל הקורא ק"ש בלא תפילין כאלו מעיד עדות שקר בעצמו. ואם לא נזדמן לו אז או שהיה חולה מעיים בשעת מעשה כל היום זמנו ומחויב להניחן עכ"פ כדי שלא יבטל יום אחד ממצות תפילין: (ז) ותפלה. ועיין לעיל סימן כ"ה סי"ג. וזהו לכל אדם אבל אנשי מעשה נוהגין ללמוד אחר התפלה בתפילין (ה) אך יש ליזהר שלא לדבר בהם (ו) דברים בטלים דמלבד איסור דברים בטלים הוא בא ע"י לידי היסח הדעת. ועיין לעיל בסימן כ"ח סק"ג ובמעשה רב: ג (ח) היודע. דקודם לכן אין רשאי להניח תפילין ולאו מינון

ביאור הלכה

* מצותן וכו'. עיין בפמ"ג שמסתפק אם מן התורה חייב כל היום או מן התורה די ברגע אחד שמניח ומדרבנן כל היום ובטלוה עכשיו שאין לנו גוף נקי ומסיק דעיקרן של דברים דאם לא הניח יום א' כלל לתפילין ביטל מ"ע ובהניח רגע עליו קיים המצוה אבל מצוה מן המובחר מן התורה להיותן עליו כל היום וכו' עיין שם. ובספר ישועות יעקב פסק דמן התורה מצותן כל היום עיין שם. ועיין בספר א"ר שמוכח מדבריו דמי שיודע שיש לו גוף נקי אין לו לפטור א"ע ממצות תפילין כל היום. ופשוט דכונתו אם יודע שיוכל ליזהר א"ע ג"כ מהיסח הדעת דהיינו עכ"פ משחוק וקלות ראש כמו שכתבנו לעיל בכלל[א] כ"ח ע"ש. ועיין בספר מעשה רב שכתב דאם חושש ליוהרא בפני הבריות מותר בשל יד לבד. ומ"מ טוב לעשות של ראש קטן והרצועות יהיה ג"כ מכוסות מלילך בשל יד לבד עכ"ד ואשרי המקיים כדינו כמשאחז"ל במגילה כ"ח שאלו תלמידיו את ר"א[ב] במה הארכת ימים א"ל וכו' ולא הלכתי ד"א בלא תורה ובלא תפילין: * בשעת ק"ש ותפלה. ומ"ע כתב בתשובה שתיקן להניחם שנית במנחה ובע"ש לא יניחם של"ה: * קטן וכו'. נראה פשוט דלדעת המחבר אם מאיזה טעם לא קנה אביו עבורו תפילין כגון שלא היה יכול לשמרם בטהרה וכה"ג ונעשה בנו בן י"ג שנים ויום אחד שוב אין על אביו מצות חינוך דאיש הוא וחייב מעצמו בכל המצות ואם איש עני הוא כל ישראל חייבים בזה וכמו שכתב הפ"מ בסק"ד:

שער הציון

(א) מ"א בשם התוס' והרא"ש: (ב) ולע"ק עליו מש"ס דר"ה י"ז ע"א למה צריך לתרץ דאיירי במחלה ע"מ יתרץ בכה"ג וי"ל: (ג) ח"א: (ד) פמ"ג: (ה) ברכי יוסף: (ו) מעשה רב:

הגהות ותיקונים: א) בסימן: ב) ר"ז: ג) סק"א:

the category of sinful Jews /who have sinned/ (4) with their bodies.

2. It is a mitzvah for /the *tefilin*/ to be /worn/ on one's /person/ all day. However, /the wearer is/ required /to have/ a clean body, so that he will not break wind while /he is wearing/ them, and he must not distract his mind from them. Owing to /the fact/ that not everyone is able to be careful about these /requirements/, it has become the practice not to wear /*tefilin*/ all day

Mishnah Berurah

not donned at all. The *P.Mg.*, also, already alerted us to this /pitfall/ in Sec. 27. He writes there that when *tefilin* are not lying in their /correct/ place it is as if they are /still/ lying in their bag. See above in Sec. 27 in the Beyur Halachah, where we have /discussed/ this at length.

(4) With their bodies. The judgment /due/ to such /a person/ is given in the Talmud, *Rosh Ha-Shanah* 17/a/. /It is stated there/ that if one is a medium person /who is neither righteous nor wicked/, it is usual for the Holy One, Blessed be He, to incline the scales towards kindness. Even /for such a person/, if this sin is to be found among his sins his offences tip the scales and he is compelled to descend to *Geyhinom*. If, Heaven forfend, his sins are also in excess of his merits, he is sentenced to /be in/ *Geyhinom* for twelve months. After /the twelve months/ the body will perish and the soul will be burnt and a wind will spread the ash underneath the soles of the feet of the righteous. /However,/ see the *Tosafos* there, that all this /only applies/ if one did not do repentance.

Since the potential of /the performance of/ this mitzvah is so great and, conversely, the punishment /for its neglect so severe/, may the Merciful One save us /from it/, it therefore /befits/ everyone to take care to purchase *tefilin* from a scribe who is competent and Heaven fearing and has Torah /knowledge/. Similarly, he should buy the straps from a trustworthy person, in order to be certain that they were processed for the sake of /the mitzvah/ from the skin of a /halachically/ clean /animal or bird/. (/It should be noted/ that if someone dons invalid *tefilin* he not only does not fulfil the mitzvah, but he /also/ says vain blessings several times over, which is /also/ a grave sin.) Among our many sins, there is much stumbling due to /the fact/ that *tefilin* and /their/ straps are purchased from /just/ anybody, because he sells them cheaply. The majority /of such *tefilin*/ are not /properly/ square and they have in addition other common faults when they are written. Every Heaven fearing person should impress upon his heart that if he is meticulous that his clothes and utensils should be in order, he should certainly /be meticulous/ where his Heavenly articles are concerned. /Therefore,/ he should not stint and spare his money, but should be meticulous to purchase /*tefilin*/ that are definitely valid, although their price is high.

2 *Shemos* 15:2.

לז זמן הנחת תפילין. ובו ג' סעיפים:

א אגדול (א) (א) שכר מצות תפילין וכל מי (ב) שאינו מניחם הוא (ג) בכלל פושעי ישראל (ב) (ד) בבגופן: ב * גמצותן להיותם עליו כל היום אבל מפני שצריכים גוף נקי שלא יפיח בהם ושלא יסיח דעתו מהם ואין כל אדם יכול ליזהר בהם נהגו דשלא להניחם כל (ג) [א] היום ומ"מ צריך כל אדם ליזהר בהם (ה) להיותם עליו (ו) * בשעת ק"ש (ז) ותפלה: ג * הקטן (ח) היודע לשמור תפילין בטהרה שלא יישן ושלא יפיח בהם: הגה ושלא ליכנס בהן לבית הכסא (רש"י פרק לולב הגזול) חייב

באר הגולה

א מנחות מ"ד
ב ראש השנה י"ז
ג טור ד הרא"ש
ה סוכה מ"ג

באר היטב

(א) שכר. בש"ס איתא דמאריך ימים. ובשמושא רבא איתא שהוא מובטח שהוא בן עה"ב ושאין גיהנם שולטת בו ושעונותיו נמחלים לו. וכתב הרא"ש אם זהיר בתפילין כף זכות מכרעתו. ואם פשע בהם כף חובה מכרעתו שאין לך גדול במצות עשה יותר מתפילין. חרש המדבר ואינו שומע או שומע ואינו מדבר חייב להניח תפילין אבל אינו שומע ואינו מדבר אין מוחין בידו מלהניחם אם רוצה ע"ת וכ"כ בשיורי כנה"ג סימן ל"ח. והבאר היטב אשר לפני לא העתיק היטב ע"ש: (ב) בגופן. ודוקא שאינו מניחם בשביל בזוי מצוה אבל היראה להניחם משום דבעי גוף נקי ושמא לא יזהר בקדושתן אע"ג דעבירה היא בידו דבקל יוכל ליזהר בהם בשעת ק"ש ותפלה מ"מ לאו בכלל פושעי ישראל הוא הרא"ש: (ג) היום. ומ"ע כתב שתיקן להניחם שנית במנחה. ובערב שבת לא יניחם של"ה. ויניח תפילין דר"ת במנחה:

שערי תשובה

[א] היום. עבה"ט וכבר כתבתי בזה לעיל ס"ס ל"ד ע"ש. ונראה דע"ש לאו דוקא וה"ה ערב יו"ט שא"ל שלפי הטעם שכבר נתגלה קדושת שבת והיינו משום דתוספת שבת דאורייתא דא"כ גם תוספת יו"ט דאורייתא כמ"ש הב"י סי' רס"א ע"ש. ועיין בשו"ת שמש לדקה חלק א"ח סי' ז' וסי' ח' שהוכיח דליכא איסורא בזה מדינא והנוהג להניחם מבע"י קודם שתחול קדושת שבת אין מוחין בידו אך שם בסימן ז' כתב בשם המקובל מהר"ר בנימין כהן ז"ל ששאל לכמה

משנה ברורה

א (א) שכר. שכל המניחן מאריך ימים בעוה"ז שנאמר ד' עליהם יחיו כלומר אותם שנושאים שם ה' עליהם בתפילין יחיו ומובטח שהוא בן עוה"ב ואין אש של גיהנם שולט בו וכל עונותיו נמחלין לו. טור בשם השמושא רבא: (ב) שאינו מניחם. פי' אפילו מניעתו הוא רק לפרקים וכ"ש אם מבטל תמיד ממצוה זו והפמ"ג הביא בשם כ"ל דאפילו מי שביטל מתפילין יום אחד הוא ג"כ בכלל פושעי ישראל: (ג) בכלל פ"י. ודוקא שאינו מניחן בשביל שהמצוה בזויה בעיניו אבל היראה להניחם משום דבעי גוף נקי ושמא לא יזהר בקדושה כראוי אע"ג דעבירה היא דבקל יכול אדם ליזהר בשעת ק"ש ותפלה (א) מ"מ לא הוי בכלל פושעי ישראל. וכ"ש אם המצוה תמיד חביבה עליו ונזהר שיהיה גוף נקי אך עתה אית ליה אונס חולי שאין גופו נקי לכו"ע אין עליו דין פושעי ישראל כלל. ודע דכתב הב"ח דאפילו אם אין המצוה בזויה בעיניו אך נמנע מלהניחם מפני ביטול מלאכה או שאר הפסד ממון או מחמת עצלות (ב) ג"כ הוא בכלל פ"י בגופן אך דיש חילוק ביניהם לענין עונש ע"ש. וד"ז הוא תוכחת מגולה לאותן אנשים שמפני עצלותן מלוי שיהיו תפליהן מונחין על מלתן ולא על הקרקפתא וגם הש"י אין מונח על מקומו כדין דהלא זה הוא כמי שלא הניח כלל. וכבר זירז ע"ז ג"כ אותנו הפמ"ג בסימן כ"ז שכתב שם דתפילין שמונחין שלא במקומן הרי הם כמונחין בכיס. ועיין לעיל בסימן כ"ז בבה"ל שהארכנו בזה (ד) בגופן. ודינו פסוק בש"ס ר"ה י"ז דאפילו הוא איש בינוני דדרכו של הקב"ה להטות הכף כלפי חסד מכיון שנמצא בתוך עונותיו עון זה כף חובה מכרעת והוא מוכרח לירד לגיהנם ואם ח"ו ג"כ עונותיו מרובין מזכיותיו נידון בגיהנם י"ב חדש ואח"כ גופן כלה ונשמתן נשרפת ורוח מפזרת אפרן תחת כפות רגלי הצדיקים. וע"ש בתוס' דכ"ז בשלא עשה תשובה. (ג) ויען כי גדול כח המצוה כ"כ ולהיפך העונש ר"ל לכן יזהר כל אדם לקנות תפילין מסופר מומחה וי"ש ובעל תורה וכן רצועות יקנה מאיש נאמן כדי שיהא בטוח שנעשו לשמן מעורות טהורות כי מי שהוא מניח תפילין פסולים לא לבד שאינו מקיים המצוה אלא (ד) שמברך כמה וכמה ברכות לבטלה שהוא עון גדול. ובעו"ה רבה המכשלה במה שקונים תפילין ורצועות ממאן דהוא לפי שמוכרים בזול ורובן אינם מרובעין ועוד יתר קלקולים שמצוי בהם בעת כתיבתן וכל ירא שמים יתן אל לבו אם על מלבושיו וכליו הוא מהדר שיהיו כתיקונם מכ"ש במפלי שמים שלא ימנע ויחוס על הכסף אלא יהדר לקנות אומן שהם בודאי כשרים אף שמחירם רב. וכתב הד"מ בשם המרדכי יש לאדם להדר אחר תפילין נאים שנאמר זה אלי ואנוהו דהיינו שכתבן לבלר אומן בכתב נאה ובדיו נאה ובקולמוס נאה וקלפים נאים: ב (ה) להיותם עליו. דבזמן קצר כזה בקל יכול ליזהר מהפפה ומהסח הדעת: (ו) בשעת ק"ש. דכל הקורא ק"ש בלא תפילין כאלו מעיד עדות שקר בעצמו. ואם לא נזדמן לו אז או שהיה חולה מעייס בשעת מעשה כל היום זמנו ומחויב להניחן עכ"פ כדי שלא יבטל יום אחד ממצות תפילין: (ז) ותפלה. ועיין לעיל סימן כ"ה סי"ג. וזהו לכל אדם אבל אנשי מעשה נוהגין ללמוד אחר התפלה בתפילין (ה) אך יש ליזהר שלא לדבר בהם (ו) דברים בטלים דמלבד איסור דברים בטלים הוא בא עי"ז לידי היסח הדעת. ועיין לעיל בסימן כ"ח סק"ג[ג] ובמעשה רב: ג (ח) היודע. דקודם לכן אין רשאי להניח תפילין ולאו חינוך

ביאור הלכה

* מצותן וכו'. עיין בפמ"ג שמסתפק אם מן התורה חייב כל היום או מן התורה די ברגע אחד שמניח ומדרבנן כל היום ובטלוה עכשיו שאין לנו גוף נקי ומסיק דעיקרן של דברים דאם לא הניח יום א' כלל לתפילין ביטל מ"ע ובהניח רגע עליו קיים המצוה אבל מצוה מן המובחר מן התורה להיותן עליו כל היום וכו' עיין שם. ובספר ישועות יעקב פסק דמן התורה מצותן כל היום עיין שם. ועיין בספר א"ר שמוכח מדבריו דמי שיודע שיש לו גוף נקי אין לו לפטור א"ע ממצות תפילין כל היום. ופשוט דכונתו אם יודע שיוכל ליזהר א"ע ג"כ מהיסח הדעת דהיינו עכ"פ משחוק וקלות ראש כמו שכתבנו לעיל בכלל[א] כ"ח ע"ש. ועיין בספר מעשה רב שכתב דאם חושש ליוהרא בפני הבריות מותר בשל יד לבד. ומ"מ טוב לעשות של ראש קטן והרצועות יהיה ג"כ מכוסות מלילך בשל יד לבד עכ"ד ואשרי המקיים כדינו כמשאחז"ל במגילה כ"ח שאלו תלמידיו את ר"א[ב] במה הארכת ימים א"ל וכו' ולא הלכתי ד"א בלא תורה ובלא תפילין: * בשעת ק"ש ותפלה. ומ"ע כתב בתשובה שתיקן להניחם שנית במנחה ובע"ש לא יניחם של"ה: * קטן וכו'. נראה פשוט דלדעת המחבר אם מאיזה טעם לא קנה אביו עבורו תפילין כגון שלא היה יכול לשמרם בטהרה וכה"ג ונעשה בנו בן י"ג שנים ויום אחד שוב אין על אביו מצות חינוך דאיש הוא וחייב מעצמו בכל המצות ואם איש עני הוא כל ישראל חייבים בזה וכמו שכתב הפ"מ בסק"ד:

שער הציון

(א) מ"א בשם התוס' והרא"ש: (ב) ולע"ק עליו מש"ס דר"ה י"ז ע"א למה לריך לתרץ דאיירי במחלה ע"מ יתרץ בכה"ג וי"ל: (ג) ח"א: (ד) פמ"ג: (ה) ברכי יוסף: (ו) מעשה רב:

הגהות ותיקונים: א) בסימן: ב) ר"ז: ג) סק"א:

/long/. Nevertheless, everyone should be careful to /don *tefilin*/ **(5)** and have them on him **(6)** when /he reads/ "The Reading of Shema" **(7)** and /prays the eighteen-blessing/ prayer.

3. If a child **(8)** is capable of looking after *tefilin* in purity, so that he will not sleep /with them on/ and will not break wind with them on *Gloss: and will not*

Mishnah Berurah

The *D.M.* writes in the name of the *Mordechai* that a person should be meticulous to /obtain/ beautiful *tefilin*, as it is stated,[2] "This is my God and I will beautify Him". What is meant is that /the passages/ should be written by an expert calligrapher, with beautiful script, beautiful ink, an excellent quill and beautiful parchment.

(5) And have them on him. /This is/ because during such a brief period /of time/ one is easily able to avoid breaking wind and distracting his mind /from the *tefilin*/.

(6) When /he reads/ "The Reading of Shema". For whenever one reads "The Reading of Shema" without /wearing/ *tefilin*, it is as if he bears false testimony about himself.[3]

If one did not happen to have /*tefilin*/ when /he read "The Reading of Shema" and prayed the eighteen-blessing prayer/ or if one had a disorder in his bowels at the time /when he did so/, he is at any rate obliged to don *tefilin* /later/, in order not to neglect /fulfilling/ the mitzvah of *tefilin* /even/ for a single day. /One should bear in mind that/ the time /which is suitable/ for /the donning of *tefilin*/ is all day.

(7) And prayer. See above in Sec. 25, Par. 13.

This applies for all /classes of/ people, but men of deeds are accustomed to study /Torah/ after the prayer /service/ with the *tefilin* /still on them/. However, they should be careful not to talk idle conversation while /they are wearing/ them. Apart from /the fact that/ idle conversation is forbidden /in any case, if one engages in it/ he will come to distract his mind /from the *tefilin*/ because of it. See above in Sec. 28, sub-Par. 1[4] and in the *Ma'aseh Rav*.

(8) Is capable. For before /he has reached/ this /stage/ he is not allowed to don *tefilin* and there is no education involved /in his having *tefilin*/.

3 See Sec. 25, sub-Par. 14 of the Mishnah Berurah.
4 This is the correct sub-paragraph number.

אביו * לקנות לו תפילין (ט) לחנכו: הגה * וי״א * דהאי קטן (י) דוקא שהוא (יא) בן י״ג (ד) [ג] שנים ויום אחד (בעל העיטור (יב) * וכן נהגו ואין לשנות (דברי עצמו):

לח דין מי הם החייבים בתפילין והפטורים. ובו י״ג סעיפים:

א (א) [א]חולה מעיים (ב) פטור (א) [א] (ג) מתפילין: הגה אפילו אין לו (ג) (ד) צער אבל שאר חולה אם מצטער בחליו ואין דעתו מיושב עליו (ה) פטור וא״ל חייב (מרדכי ה״ת ומיימוני פ״ד): ב (ו) [ב]מי שברי לו שאינו יכול (ז) להתפלל בלא הפחה מוטב שיעבור זמן התפלה ממה שיתפלל בלא גוף נקי (ועיין לקמן סימן פ) ואם יראה לו שיוכל להעמיד עצמו בגוף נקי (ח) בשעת ק״ש יניח תפילין בין אהבה לק״ש (ט) ויברך: ג (י) [ג]נשים ועבדים פטורים מתפילין מפני שהוא מצות עשה (יא) שהזמן גרמא: הגה ואם (יב) הנשים רוצין להחמיר על עצמן (יג) מוחים בידן (כל בו): ד [ד]המניח תפילין צריך (יד) ליזהר מהרהור תאות (ג) אשה: הגה ואם א״א לו בלא הרהורים מוטב (טו) שלא להניחם (כל בו וא״ח):

א חולין ק״י ב תשובת רא״ש כלל ד׳ סימן א׳ ג ברכות כ׳ ד ב״י בפירוש הירושלמי שמביא בא״ח ראיה למה שכתבו בשם הר״מ

שערי תשובה

גדולים בא״י ואמרו לו שאין להניח תפילין בע״ש ע״ש: [ג] שנים. עבה״ט וכל שהגיע לי״ג ויום אחד אף שאין ידוע שהביא[א] שערות חייב בתפילין מדינא מחמת חזקה דרבא דכל שהגיע לכלל שנים חזקה הביא סימנים ועיין לקמן סי׳ נ״ה לענין שנת העיבור ושאר דינים בזה:

[א] מתפילין. עבה״ט ועיין בחו״י שכתב דאפי׳ לא הניח תפילין מעולם אין לברך שהחינו כיון דרגילה ותדירה (עיין בי״ד סי׳ כ״ח ובת״ש שם) וכן בסיום ספר ונשואי בנו ולידת נכדו הראשון אין לברך שהחיינו. ובלידת בן זכר יש מברכין שהחיינו ולכן אין מברכין בשעת המילה ואפילו בלידת בן בכור כמ״ש ש״ך

באר היטב

(ד) שנים. והב״ח חולק וכתב דקטן הלומד תלמוד ויודע לשמור את עצמו חייב אביו לקנות לו תפילין גם הר״ש הלוי חלק א״ח סימן א׳ פסק משהגיע לעשר שנים חייב לחנכו במצות תפילין. ועכשיו נהגו להניח ב׳ או ג׳ חדשים קודם הי״ג שנים מ״א:

(א) מתפילין. מי שביטל מצות תפילין מחמת חולי ועברו עליו למ״ד יום שלא הניחם אם כשחזר והניחם צריך לברך שהחיינו או לא פסק בתשובות חות יאיר סימן רל״ט[ב] דא״צ לברך שהחיינו כיון דאינו מצוה דאתא מזמן לזמן ע״ש: (ב) צער. אפילו הולך בשוקים וברחובות פטור. וכתב המ״א דאם רוצה להחמיר בשעת ק״ש ותפלה מותר כמ״ש בסעיף ב׳: (ג) אשה. עיין ב״י ומ״ש עליו המ״א והיד אהרן מיישבו:

ביאור הלכה

* לקנות לו. ויש לעיין אם יש לו ב׳ בנים אם חייב לקנות תפילין עבור כ״א או שיוצא במה שיחנך מתחלה לבנו האחד ואחר תפלתו יתנם לבנו השני וכן ביש לו בן אחד והוא משיג לשאול עבורו תפילין או שיתן לו את תפליו לק״ש ותפלה בכל עת החינוך דהיינו עד שיעשה לאיש אם יוצא בזה דאפשר מה דנקט הברייתא [סוכה ד׳ מ״ג[ג]] אביו קונה לו תפילין היינו דוקא בזמנם שהיו מניחין תפילין כל היום ואין מצוי שישאיל א׳ לחבירו תפיליו משא״כ בזמנינו תדע דלא נקט כן בלולב שוב מצאתי בב״ח שמשמע קצת כדברינו ויש לדחות ע״ש וצ״ע:* וי״א וכו׳. כתב הפמ״ג וז״ל ואיני יודע אם הוא י״ג שנים איזה חיוב יש על אביו דאיש בפ״ע הוא ואם הוא עני כל ישראל מצווין להחיותו וי״ל יג״ש ולא הביא ב׳ שערות ולפ״ז י״ל דה״ה עד רוב שנותיו אם לא הביא ב׳ שערות חייב לחנכו עכ״ד ואף דאז חייב מדינא מחמת חזקה דרבא וכמו שהביא בש״ת אעפ״כ י״ל דלא פקע מאביו מצות חינוך כ״ז שאין ידוע שהביא ב״ש אבל כ״ז דוחק גדול ועיין לקמן בסימן רכ״ה ס״ב דכשנעשה הבן י״ג אביו מברך ברוך שפטרני והיינו ממצות חינוך לפי מש״כ המ״א שם ולא אישתמיט אחד מהם לומר דדוקא כשידוע שהביא ב׳ שערות אלא בודאי דלענין חינוך שהוא דרבנן נוכל לסמוך על חזקה דרבא. והאמת יורה דרכו שלא ראה הפמ״ג את ספר העיטור ח״ב שבימיו עדיין לא נדפס כי לפי מה שכתב שם מוכח שלדידיה לא נזכר בגמרא האי דינא כלל לענין תקנתא דרבנן ומשמע מיניה דלא היה ע״ז תקנתא כלל רק לענין דאורייתא שאין בן י״ג מחוייב בתפילין כ״א כשיודע לשמור תפיליו והביא ע״ז המכילתא ראיה ממקרא ושמרתם[ד] את החוקה הזאת עי״ש והוא אפילו אם הביא ב״ש דומיא דחיוב מזוזה הנזכר שם עי״ש. ולענין קושית הפמ״ג מה שייך אביו לזה עיין בספר ברכי יוסף ויתיישב לך. וכ״ז לפי שיטת העיטור אבל אנן קי״ל כדעת כל הפוסקים וכמש״כ הב״י דלא נזכר בגמרא האי דינא כלל לענין גדול רק לענין קטן נהגו העולם להחמיר כהעיטור שלא להניח תפילין:* דהאי קטן דוקא. פי׳ ואז תליא באם יודע לשמור תפיליו שזו היא שיטת בה״ע כמו שמפורש שם ומה דאין נוהגין כהיום לדקדק בזה אפשר דהרמ״א לא פסק לנהוג כוותי׳ רק לענין שלא יניח קודם בר מצוה ולא לזה וכן מוכח קצת בד״מ עי״ש א״נ דכ״ז דוקא בזמנם שהיו מניחין תפילין כל היום וקשה ליזהר בשמירתן אבל כהיום שאין מניחין רק בזמן ק״ש ותפלה תלינן מסתמא בשנעשה י״ג שידע לשמור תפיליו דומיא דהמבואר בס״ב אם לא כשנדע שאין יודע לשמור תפיליו: * וכן נהגו. עיין דהא שבת ויו״ט לאו זמן תפילין: (יב) הנשים. עיין בפמ״ג שה״ה לענין עבדים ועיין בספר תוספות[ה] שבת שכתב בהדיא להיפך ועיין בספר תוספות ירושלים: (יג) מוחים בידן. מפני שצריכין גוף נקי ונשים אין זריזות להזהר: ד (יד) ליזהר. דבעינן (ט) גוף נקי גם ממחשבה רעה: (טו) שלא להניחם. ומ״מ ירחה בכל היכולת (י) לכוף את עצמו ולמשוך הלב לירא את שמים כדי להסיח הדעת מדברי הבאי

משנה ברורה

חינוך הוא: (ט) לחנכו. במצות הנחתן וכן ללמדו הדינים הנצרכים לזה: (י) דוקא. וקודם לכן אין מניחו ללבוש תפילין אפילו אם ירצה דבודאי אין יודע לשמור תפילין: (יא) בן י״ג שנים. היינו אפילו אם לא הביא ב׳ שערות (פמ״ג): (יב) וכן נהגו. ועכשיו נהגו להניח ב׳ או ג׳ חדשים קודם הזמן [מ״א] ועיין בבה״ל. חרש המדבר ואינו שומע או שומע ואינו מדבר חייב להניח תפילין אבל אין שומע ואין מדבר אין מוחין בידו מלהניחם אם רוצה [בה״ט]:

א (א) חולה מעיים. וה״ה (א) מי ששתה משקה המשלשל: (ב) פטור. משום דתפילין בעי גוף נקי: (ג) מתפילין. מי (ב) שביטל מצות תפילין מחמת חולי ועברו עליו ל׳ יום שלא הניחם כשחוזר ומניחם א״צ לברך שהחיינו: (ד) צער. אפילו (ג) אם הולך בשווקים וברחובות פטור (ד) ואסור לו להחמיר על עצמו בזה אלא בשעת ק״ש ותפלה אם יודע שיוכל להעמיד א״ע בגוף נקי וכמו שכתב לקמן בס״ב: (ה) פטור. שמא (ה) מתוך הצער יסיח דעתו מהם. ואם רוצה להחמיר ע״ע (ו) רשאי. מי (ז) שלבו ערום דהיינו שהולך במכנסים לבד ולמעלה הוא ערום (ואין בכלל זה מה שבית הצואר פתוח) לא יניח תפילין דאף דלברך רשאי כיון שערותו מכוסה כדמוכח בסימן ע״ד אפ״ה אין נכון שיהא מגולה לבו ויניח תפילין: ב (ו) מי שברי לו. לאפוקי אם אינו יודע בבירור בודאי אין לבטל אפילו תפלה בצבור משום זה: (ז) להתפלל. דוקא תפלה משום דהוא כעומד לפני המלך וגנאי הוא לעמוד להתפלל על דעת שיפסוק באמצע עד שיכלה הריח אבל ק״ש וברכותיה מותר אך בלי תפילין: (ח) בשעת ק״ש. עיין לקמן סימן פ׳ במשנה ברורה כי שם יבואר הכל בעז״ה: (ט) ויברך. ויקרא בהן שמע ואח״כ יחלצן. ואם יודע שאין יכול לעצור עצמו מלהפיח אלא בכדי שיוכל לחלוץ השל ראש אפ״ה מותר להניח לכתחלה את שניהם כ״כ המ״א אבל הפמ״ג מפקפק בזה: ג (י) נשים. (ח) וטומטום ואנדרוגינוס חייבין בתפילין מספק ככל המצות: (יא) שהזמן גרמא.

שער הציון

(א) מ״א: (ב) בה״ט: (ג) מ״א: (ד) מ״א: (ה) פרישה: (ו) פמ״ג: (ז) מ״א ופמ״ג: (ח) פמ״ג בסימן ל״ט: (ט) ב״י: (י) ב״י:

הגהות ותיקונים: א) חסר ב׳: ב) רל״ז: ג) מ״ב: ד) ושמרת: ה) עולת:

go into a lavatory with them on (...), his father is obliged to buy him *tefilin* (9) to educate him.[1*]

Gloss: There are /authorities/ who say that such a child may (10) *only /be given* tefilin/ *if he is* (11) *thirteen years of age /plus/ one day. (...)* (12) *This is /in fact/ the practice and one should not deviate /from it/. (...)*

§38: THE LAW AS REGARDS WHO ARE OBLIGED TO /DON/ *TEFILIN* AND WHO ARE EXEMPT /FROM DOING SO/

(Contains Thirteen Paragraphs)

1. (1) Someone who has a disorder in his bowels (2) is exempt (3) from /donning/ *tefilin.*

Gloss: /I.e., in such a case one is exempt/ even if he is not (4) *suffering. If, however, one has an illness of a different /nature, then/, if he is suffering from*

Mishnah Berurah

(9) **To educate him.** /I.e., he is obliged then to educate him/ towards /the fulfillment of/ the mitzvah of donning /*tefilin*/ and likewise to teach him the laws that it is necessary /to know/ for this /mitzvah/.

(10) **Only.** /According to this opinion,/ before /a child reaches/ this /age/ one may not allow him to wear *tefilin* even if he wishes, since he is definitely incapable of looking after *tefilin.*

(11) **Thirteen years of age.** /Then he may be given *tefilin*/ even if he has not /yet/ produced two /adult/ hairs. ((*P.Mg.*))

(12) **This is the practice.** At present, it is the practice /for children/ to don /*tefilin* already/ two or three months before /they reach/ this /age/. [*M.A.*] See the Beyur Halachah.[5]

A deaf or dumb person who speaks, but does not hear, or hears, but does not speak, is obliged to don *tefilin.* However, if he neither hears nor speaks /the ruling is that/ one need not protest against him donning /*tefilin*/ if he wishes /to do so/. [*B.Heyt.*]

§38

(1) **Someone who has a disorder in his bowels.** The same ruling /applies/ to someone who has drunk a laxative drink.

(2) **Is exempt.** /The reason is/ because a clean body is required /for the donning of/ *tefilin.*

(3) **From *tefilin*.** If someone was idle from the mitzvah of /donning/ *tefilin* because of illness and thirty days passed without him having donned them, he does not need to make the blessing *She-Hecheyanu* when he again dons them.

(4) **Suffering.** Even if he goes about in marketplaces and in the streets /despite the disorder/, he is /nevertheless/ exempt.

One is forbidden to be stringent with himself about this /and don *tefilin*/, except at the time when /he reads/ "The Reading of Shema" and /prays the eighteen-blessing/ prayer /and even then only/ provided he is able to maintain his body clean /for the length of time required/, as stated below in Par. 2.

1* According to the author of the Shulchan Aruch, a father is not obliged to buy *tefilin* for a grown son who has reached the age of thirteen years plus one day. All Jews are obliged to purchase *tefilin* for a poor person. (Beyur Halachah)

5 There the author notes that, at any rate, a child of twelve years of age who studies and understands the Talmud may don *tefilin*, as he may be relied upon to look after the *tefilin* if he is capable of being careful about all the points mentioned.

באר הגולה

א חולין ק"י
ב תשובת רא"ש כלל ד' סימן ח'
ג ברכות כ' ד ב"י בפירוש הירושלמי שמביא בא"ח ראיה למה שכתבו בשם הר"מ.

אביו * לקנות לו תפילין (ט) לחנכו: הגה * וי"א * דהאי קטן (י) דוקא שהוא (יא) בן י"ג (ד) [ג] שנים ויום אחד (בעל העיטור (יב) * וכן נהגו ואין לשנות (דברי עצמו):

לח דין מי הם החייבים בתפילין והפטורים. ובו י"ג סעיפים:

א (א) אחולה מעיים (ב) פטור (א) [א] (ג) מתפילין: הגה אפילו אין לו (ב) (ד) צער אבל שאר חולה אם מצטער בחליו ואין דעתו מיושב עליו (ה) פטור וא"ל חייב (מרדכי ה"ת ומיימוני פ"ד): ב (ו) במי שברי לו שאינו יכול (ז) להתפלל בלא הפחה מוטב שיעבור זמן התפלה ממה שיתפלל בלא גוף נקי (ועיין לקמן סימן פ) ואם יראה לו שיוכל להעמיד עצמו בגוף נקי (ח) בשעת ק"ש יניח תפילין בין אהבה לק"ש (ט) ויברך: ג (י) גנשים ועבדים פטורים מתפילין מפני שהוא מצות עשה (יא) שהזמן גרמא: הגה ואם (יב) הנשים רוצין להחמיר על עצמן (יג) מוחים בידן (כל בו): ד דהמניח תפילין צריך (יד) ליזהר מהרהור תאות (ג) אשה: הגה ואם א"א לו בלא הרהורים מוטב (טו) שלא להניחם (כל בו וא"ח):

שערי תשובה

גדולים בא"י ואמרו לו שאין להניח תפילין בע"ש ע"ש: [ג] שנים. עבה"ט וכל שהגיע לי"ג ויום אחד אף שאין ידוע שהביא[א] שערות חייב בתפילין מדינא מחמת חזקה דרבא דכל שהגיע לכלל שנים חזקה הביא סימנים ועיין לקמן סי' כ"ה לענין שנת העיבור ושאר דינים בזה:

[א] מתפילין. עבה"ט ועיין בחו"י שכתב דאפי' לא הניח תפילין מעולם אין לברך שהחינו כיון דרגילה ותדירה (עיין בי"ד סי' כ"ח ובת"ש שם) וכן בסיום ספר ונשואי בנו ולידת נכדו הראשון אין לברך שהחיינו. ובלידת בן זכר יש מברכין שהחיינו ולכן אין מברכין בשעת המילה ואפילו בלידת בן בכור כמ"ש ש"ך

באר היטב

(ד) שנים. והב"ח חולק וכתב דקטן הלומד תלמוד ויודע לשמור את עצמו חייב אביו לקנות לו תפילין גם הר"ם הלוי חלק א"ח סימן א' פסק משהגיע לעשר שנים חייב לחנכו במצות תפילין. ועכשיו נהגו להניח ב' או ג' חדשים קודם הי"ג שנים מ"א:

(א) מתפילין. מי שביטל מצות תפילין מחמת חולי ועברו עליו למ"ד יום שלא הניחם אם כשחזר והניחם צריך לברך שהחיינו או לא פסק בתשובות חות יאיר סימן רל"ט[ב] דא"צ לברך שהחיינו כיון דאינו מצוה דאתא מזמן לזמן ע"ש: (ב) צער. אפילו הולך בשוקים וברחובות פטור. וכתב המ"א דאם רוצה להחמיר בשעת ק"ש ותפלה מותר כמ"ש בסעיף ב': (ג) אשה. עיין ב"י ומ"ש עליו המ"א והיד אהרן מיישבו:

משנה ברורה

חינוך הוא: (ט) לחנכו. במצות הנחתן וכן ללמדו הדינים הצריכים לזה: (י) דוקא. וקודם לכן אין מניחו ללבוש תפילין אפילו אם ירצה דבודאי אין יודע לשמור תפילין: (יא) בן י"ג שנים. היינו אפילו אם לא הביא ב' שערות (פמ"ג): (יב) וכן נהגו. ועכשיו נהגו להניח ב' או ג' חדשים קודם הזמן [מ"א] ועיין בבה"ל. חרש המדבר ואינו שומע או שומע ואינו מדבר חייב להניח תפילין אבל אין שומע ואין מדבר אין מוחין בידו מלהניחם אם רוצה [בה"ט]:

א (א) חולה מעיים. וה"ה (א) מי שאחזו מכאב המטלטל: (ב) פטור. משום דתפילין בעי גוף נקי: (ג) מתפילין. מי (ב) שביטל מצות תפילין מחמת חולי ועברו עליו ל' יום שלא הניחם כשחוזר ומניחם א"צ לברך שהחיינו: (ד) צער. אפילו (ג) אם הולך בשווקים וברחובות פטור (ד) ואסור לו להחמיר על עצמו בזה אלא בשעת ק"ש ותפלה אם יודע שיוכל להעמיד א"ע בגוף נקי וכמו שכתב לקמן בס"ב: (ה) פטור. שמא (ה) מתוך הצער יסיח דעתו מהם. ואם רוצה להחמיר ע"ע (ו) רשאי. מי (ז) שלבו ערום דהיינו שהולך במכנסים לבד ולמעלה הוא ערום (ואין בכלל זה מה שבית הצואר פתוח) לא יניח תפילין דאף דלברך רשאי כיון שערותו מכוסה כדמוכח בסימן ע"ד אפ"ה אין נכון שיהא מגולה לבו ויניח תפילין: ב (ו) מי שברי לו. לאפוקי אם אינו יודע בבירור בודאי אין לבטל אפילו תפלה בצבור משום זה: (ז) להתפלל. דוקא תפלה משום דהוא כעומד לפני המלך וגנאי הוא לעמוד להתפלל על דעת שיפסוק באמצע עד שיכלה הריח אבל ק"ש וברכותיה מותר אך בלי תפילין: (ח) בשעת ק"ש. עיין לקמן סימן פ' במשנה ברורה כי שם יבואר הכל בעז"ה: (ט) ויברך. ויקרא בהן שמע ואח"כ יחלצן. ואם יודע שאין יכול לעצור עצמו מלהפיח אלא בכדי שיוכל לחלוץ הש"ר ראש אפ"ה מותר להניח לכתחלה את שניהם כ"כ המ"א אבל הפמ"ג מפקפק בזה: ג (י) נשים. (ח) וטומטום ואנדרוגינוס חייבין בתפילין מספק ככל המצות: (יא) שהזמן גרמא. דהא שבת ויו"ט לאו זמן תפילין: (יב) הנשים. עיין בפמ"ג שה"ה לענין עבדים ועיין בספר תוספות[ה] שבת שכתב בהדיא להיפך ועיין בספר תוספות ירושלים: (יג) מוחים בידן. מפני שצריכין גוף נקי ונשים אין זריזות להזהר: ד (יד) ליזהר. דבעינן (ט) גוף נקי גם ממחשבה רעה: (טו) שלא להניחם. ומ"מ יראה בכל היכולת (י) לכוף את עצמו ולמשוך הלב ליראת שמים כדי להסיח הדעת מדברי הבאי:

ביאור הלכה

* לקנות לו. ויש לעיין אם יש לו ב' בנים אם חייב לקנות תפילין עבור כ"א או שיוצא במה שיחנך מתחלה לבנו האחד ואחר תפלתו יתנם לבנו השני וכן ביש לו בן אחד והוא משיג לשאול עבורו תפילין או שיתן לו את תפליו לק"ש ותפלה בכל עת החינוך דהיינו עד שיעשה לאיש אם יוצא בזה דאפשר מה דנקט הברייתא [סוכה ד' מ"ג[ג]] אביו קונה לו תפילין היינו דוקא בזמנם שהיו מניחין תפילין כל היום ואין מצוי שישאיל א' לחבירו תפליו משא"כ בזמנינו תדע דלא נקט כן בלולב שוב מצאתי בב"ח שמשמע קצת כדברינו ויש לדחות ע"ש וצ"ע:* וי"א וכו'. כתב הפמ"ג וז"ל ואיני יודע אם הוא י"ג שנים איזה חיוב יש על אביו דאיש בפ"ע הוא ואם הוא עני כל ישראל מצווין להחיותו וי"ל יג"ש ולא הביא ב' שערות ולפ"ז י"ל דה"ה עד רוב שנותיו אם לא הביא ב' שערות חייב לחנכו עכ"ד ואף דאז חייב מדינא מחמת חזקה דרבא וכמו שהביא בש"ת אעפ"כ י"ל דלא פקע מאביו מצות חינוך כ"ז שאין ידוע שהביא ב"ש אבל כ"ז דוחק גדול ועיין לקמן בסימן רכ"ה ס"ב דכשנעשה הבן י"ג אביו מברך ברוך שפטרני והיינו ממצות חינוך לפי מש"כ המ"א שם ולא אישתמיט אחד מהם לומר דדוקא כשידוע שהביא ב' שערות אלא בודאי דלענין חינוך שהוא דרבנן נוכל לסמוך על חזקה דרבא. והאמת יורה דרכו שלא ראה הפמ"ג את ספר העיטור ח"ב שבימיו עדיין לא נדפס כי לפי מה שכתב שם מוכח שלדידיה לא נזכר בגמרא האי דינא כלל לענין תקנתא דרבנן ומשמע מיניה דלא היה ע"ז תקנתא כלל רק לענין דאורייתא שאין בן י"ג מחוייב בתפילין כ"א כשיודע לשמור תפליו והביא ע"ז המכילתא ראיה ממקרא ושמרתם[ד] את החוקה הזאת עי"ש והוא אפילו אם הביא ב"ש דומיא דחיוב מזוזה הנזכר שם עי"ש. ולענין קושית הפמ"ג מה שייך אביו לזה עיין בספר ברכי יוסף ויתיישב לך. וכ"ז לפי שיטת העיטור אבל אנן קי"ל כדעת כל הפוסקים וכמש"כ הב"י דלא נזכר בגמרא האי דינא כלל לענין גדול רק לענין קטן נהגו העולם להחמיר כהעיטור שלא להניח תפילין:* דהאי קטן דוקא. פי' ואז תליא באם יודע לשמור תפליו שזו היא שיטת בה"ע כמו שמפורש שם ומה דאין נוהגין כהיום לדקדק בזה אפשר דהרמ"א לא פסק לנהוג כוותי' רק לענין שלא יניח קודם בר מצוה ולא לזה וכן מוכח קצת בד"מ עי"ש א"נ דכ"ז דוקא בזמנם שהיו מניחין תפילין כל היום וקשה ליזהר בשמירתן אבל כהיום שאין מניחין רק בזמן ק"ש ותפלה תלינן מסתמא בשנעשה י"ג שידע לשמור תפליו דומיא דהמבואר בס"ב אם לא כשנדע שאין יודע לשמור תפליו:* וכן נהגו. עיין

שער הציון

(א) ת"א: (ב) בה"ט: (ג) מ"א: (ד) מ"א: (ה) פרישה: (ו) פמ"ג: (ז) מ"א ופמ"ג: (ח) פמ"ג בסימן ל"ט: (ט) ב"י: (י) ב"י:

הגהות ותיקונים: א) חסר ב': **ב)** רל"ז: **ג)** מ"ב: **ד)** ושמרת: **ה)** עולת:

his illness, /so that/ he is not composed, (5) *he is exempt /from donning* tefilin*/, but if not, he is obliged /to do so/. (...)*

2. (6) When one is positive that he is unable (7) to pray /the eighteen-blessing prayer/ without breaking wind, it is better that the time for /praying/ the prayer should pass /without him having prayed it/ rather than that he should pray it without a clean body. *(See below in Sec. 80.)* If it appears to him that he will be able to maintain his body clean (8) during the time when /he reads/ "The Reading of Shema", he should don *tefilin* in between /his saying of the blessing/ *Ahavah Rabah* and /his reading of/ "The Reading of Shema" (9) and make a blessing /over the donning of the *tefilin*/.

Mishnah Berurah

(5) **He is exempt.** /He is exempt from donning *tefilin* in such circumstances/ in case through the suffering he will /come to/ distract his mind from /the *tefilin*/. /However,/ if he wishes to be stringent with himself /and don them/ he is allowed /to do so/.

If someone's heart is naked, i.e., if he is going about only in trousers and is naked above ((which does not include /a case/ when /merely/ the neck is open)), he should not don *tefilin.* /In such a case/ one is allowed to say a blessing, in view /of the fact/ that his private parts are covered, as is evident from Sec. 74. Even so, it is nevertheless improper for him to don *tefilin* with an exposed heart.

(6) **When one is positive.** /This wording is meant/ to exclude /from the scope of this ruling an instance/ when one does not know clearly /that he is unable to pray without breaking wind/. In such circumstances one should definitely not even neglect praying with the congregation.

(7) **To pray.** /This ruling/ only /applies with reference to the praying of the eighteen-blessing/ prayer. /The praying of this prayer/ is tantamount to standing before the King and it is /therefore/ censurable /conduct for one/ to stand up and pray it, having in mind to stop in the middle /when he breaks wind and wait/ until the smell comes to an end. However, one is permitted /to read/ "The Reading of Shema" and its blessings /although he is positive that he will break wind/, except /that he must read it/ without /donning/ *tefilin.*

(8) **During the time when /he reads/ "The Reading of Shema".** See below in Sec. 80, in the Mishnah Berurah. There with the help of *Ha-Sheym,* all /the details concerning this law/ will be explained.

(9) **And make a blessing.** He should /then/ read "The Reading of Shema" with them /on/ and afterwards take them off.

If one knows that he will not be able to stop himself breaking wind except for /the length of time/ required to be able to take off the head /*tefilin*/, he is nevertheless permitted initially to don both /units/. This is what the *M.A.* writes, but the *P.Mg.* questions this.

אביו * לקנות לו תפילין (ט) לחנכו: הגה * וי"א * דהאי קטן (י) דוקא שהוא (יא) בן י"ג (ד) [ג] שנים ויום אחד (בעל העיטור (יב) * וכן נהגו ואין לשנות (דברי עצמו):

לח דין מי הם החייבים בתפילין והפטורים. ובו י"ג סעיפים:

א (א) אחולה מעיים (ב) פטור (א) [א] (ג) מתפילין: הגה אפילו אין לו (ג) (ד) צער אבל שאר חולה אם מצטער בחליו ואין דעתו מיושב עליו (ה) פטור וא"ל חייב (מרדכי ה"ח ומיימוני פ"ד): ב (ו) במי שברי לו שאינו יכול (ז) להתפלל בלא הפחה מוטב שיעבור זמן התפלה ממה שיתפלל בלא גוף נקי (ועיין לקמן סימן פ) ואם יראה לו שיוכל להעמיד עצמו בגוף נקי (ח) בשעת ק"ש יניח תפילין בין אהבה לק"ש (ט) ויברך: ג (י) גנשים ועבדים פטורים מתפילין מפני שהוא מצות עשה (יא) שהזמן גרמא: הגה ואם (יב) הנשים רוצין להחמיר על עצמן (יג) מוחים בידן (כל בו): ד דהמניח תפילין צריך (יד) ליזהר מהרהור תאות (ג) אשה: הגה ואם א"א לו בלא הרהורים מוטב (טו) שלא להניחם (כל בו וא"ח):

באר הגולה

א חולין ק"י
ב תשובת רא"ש כלל ד' סימן ח'
ג ברכות כ' ד ב"י בפירוש הירושלמי שמביא בא"ח ראיה למה שכתבו בשם הר"מ

שערי תשובה

[ג] שנים. עבה"ט וכל שהגיע לי"ג ויום אחד אף שאין ידוע שהביאא) שערות חייב בתפילין מדינא מחמת חזקה דרבא דכל שהגיע לכלל שנים חזקה הביא סימנים ועיין לקמן סי' נ"ה לענין שנת העיבור ושאר דינים בזה: [א] מתפילין. עבה"ט ועיין בחו"י שכתב דאפי' לא הניח תפילין מעולם אין לברך שהחינו כיון דרגילה ותדירה (עיין בי"ד סי' כ"ח ובת"ש שם) וכן בסיום ספר ונשואי בנו ולידת נכדו הראשון אין לברך שהחיינו. ובלידת בן זכר יש מברכין שהחיינו ולכן אין מברכין בשעת המילה ואפילו בלידת בן בכור כמ"ש ש"ך גדולים בא"י ואמרו לו שאין להניח תפילין בע"ש ע"ש:

באר היטב

(ד) שנים. והב"ח חולק וכתב דקטן הלומד תלמוד ויודע לשמור את עצמו חייב אביו לקנות לו תפילין גם הר"ש הלוי חלק א"ח סימן א' פסק משהגיע לעשר שנים חייב לחנכו במצות תפילין. ועכשיו נהגו להניח ב' או ג' חדשים קודם הי"ג שנים מ"א: (א) מתפילין. מי שביטל מצות תפילין מחמת חולי ועברו עליו למ"ד יום שלא הניחם אם כשחזר והניחם צריך לברך שהחיינו או לא פסק בתשובות חות יאיר סימן רל"טב) דא"צ לברך שהחיינו כיון דאינו מצוה דאתא מזמן לזמן ע"ש: (ב) נער. אפילו הולך בשוקים וברחובות פטור. וכתב המ"א דאם רוצה להחמיר בשעת ק"ש ותפלה מותר כמ"ש בסעיף ב': (ג) אשה. עיין ב"י ומ"ש עליו המ"א והיד אהרן מיישבו:

ביאור הלכה

* לקנות לו. ויש לעיין אם יש לו ב' בנים אם חייב לקנות תפילין עבור כ"א או שיוצא במה שיחנך מתחלה לבנו האחד ואחר תפלתו יתנם לבנו השני וכן ביש לו בן אחד והוא משיג לשאול עבורו תפילין או שיתן לו את תפליו לק"ש ותפלה בכל עת החינוך דהיינו עד שיעשה לאיש אם יוצא בזה דאפשר מה דנקט הברייתא [סוכה ד' מ"גג)] אביו קונה לו תפילין היינו דוקא בזמנם שהיו מניחין תפילין כל היום ואין מצוי שישאיל א' לחבירו תפיליו משא"כ בזמנינו תדע דלא נקט כן בלולב שוב מצאתי בב"ח שמשמע קצת כדברינו ויש לדחות ע"ש וצ"ע:* וי"א וכו'. כתב הפמ"ג וז"ל ואיני יודע אם הוא י"ג שנים איזה חיוב יש על אביו דאיש בפ"ע הוא ואם הוא עני כל ישראל מצווין להחיותו וי"ל יג"ש ולא הביא ב' שערות ולפ"ז י"ל דה"ה עד רוב שנותיו אם לא הביא ב' שערות חייב לחנכו עכ"ד ואף דאז חייב מדינא מחמת חזקה דרבא וכמו שהביא בש"ת אעפ"כ י"ל דלא פקע מאביו מצות חינוך כ"ז שאין ידוע שהביא ב"ש אבל כ"ז דוחק גדול ועיין לקמן בסימן רכ"ה ס"ב דכשנעשה הבן י"ג אביו מברך ברוך שפטרני והיינו ממצות חינוך לפי מש"כ המ"א שם ולא אישתמיט אחד מהם לומר דדוקא כשידוע שהביא ב' שערות אלא בודאי דלענין חינוך שהוא דרבנן נוכל לסמוך על חזקה דרבא. והאמת יורה דרכו שלא ראה הפמ"ג את ספר העיטור ח"ב שבימיו עדיין לא נדפס כי לפי מה שכתב שם מוכח שלדידיה לא נזכר בגמרא האי דינא כלל לענין תקנתא דרבנן ומשמע מיניה דלא היה ע"ז תקנתא כלל רק לענין דאורייתא שאין בן י"ג מחוייב בתפילין כ"א כשיודע לשמור תפיליו והביא ע"ז המכילתא ראיה ממקרא ושמרתםד) את החוקה הזאת עי"ש והוא אפילו אם הביא ב"ש דומיא דחיוב מזוזה הנזכר שם עי"ש. ולענין קושית הפמ"ג מה שייך אביו לזה עיין בספר ברכי יוסף ויתיישב לך. וכ"ז לפי שיטת העיטור אבל אנן קי"ל כדעת כל הפוסקים וכמש"כ הב"י דלא נזכר בגמרא האי דינא כלל לענין גדול רק לענין קטן נהגו העולם להחמיר כהעיטור שלא להניח תפילין:* דהאי קטן דוקא. פי' ואז תליא באם יודע לשמור תפיליו שזו היא שיטת בה"ע כמו שמפורש שם ומה דאין נוהגין כהיום לדקדק בזה אפשר דהרמ"א לא פסק לנהוג כוותי' רק לענין שלא יניח קודם בר מצוה ולא לזה וכן מוכח קצת בד"מ עי"ש א"כ דכ"ז דוקא בזמנם שהיו מניחין תפילין כל היום וקשה ליזהר בשמירתן אבל כהיום שאין מניחין רק בזמן ק"ש ותפילה תלינן מסתמא בשנעשה י"ג שידע לשמור תפיליו דומיא דהמבואר בס"ב אם לא כשנדע שאין יודע לשמור תפיליו:* וכן נהגו. עיין

משנה ברורה

חינוך הוא: (ט) לחנכו. במצות הנחתן וכן ללמדו הדינים הנצרכים לזה: (י) דוקא. וקודם לכן אין מניחו ללבוש תפילין אפילו אם ירצה דבודאי אין יודע לשמור תפילין: (יא) בן י"ג שנים. היינו אפילו אם לא הביא ב' שערות (פמ"ג): (יב) וכן נהגו. ועכשיו נהגו להניח ב' או ג' חדשים קודם הזמן [מ"א] ועיין בבה"ל. חרש המדבר ואינו שומע או שומע ואינו מדבר חייב להניח תפילין אבל אין שומע ואין מדבר אין מוחין בידו מלהניחם אם רוצה [בה"ט]:

א (א) חולה מעיים. וה"ה (א) מי שותה משקה המשלשל: (ב) פטור. משום דתפילין בעי גוף נקי: (ג) מתפילין. מי (ב) שביטל מצות תפילין מחמת חולי ועברו עליו ל' יום שלא הניחם כשחזר ומניחם א"צ לברך שהחיינו: (ד) צער. אפילו (ג) אם הולך בשווקים וברחובות פטור (ד) ואסור לו להחמיר על עצמו בזה אלא בשעת ק"ש ותפלה אם יודע שיוכל להעמיד א"ע בגוף נקי וכמו שכתב לקמן בס"ב: (ה) פטור. שמא (ה) מתוך הצער יסיח דעתו מהם. ואם רוצה להחמיר ע"ע (ו) רשאי. מי (ז) שלבו ערום דהיינו שהולך במכנסים לבד ולמעלה הוא ערום (ואין בכלל זה מה שבית הצואר פתוח) לא יניח תפילין דאף דלברך רשאי כיון שערותו מכוסה כדמוכח בסימן ע"ד אפ"ה אין נכון שיהא מגולה לבו ויניח תפילין: ב (ו) מי שברי לו. לאפוקי אם אינו יודע בבירור בודאי אין לבטל אפילו תפלה בצבור משום זה: (ז) להתפלל. דוקא תפלה משום דהוא כעומד לפני המלך וגנאי הוא לעמוד להתפלל על דעת שיפסוק באמצע עד שיכלה הריח אבל ק"ש וברכותיה מותר אך בלי תפילין: (ח) בשעת ק"ש. עיין לקמן סימן פ' במשנה ברורה כי שם יבואר הכל בעז"ה: (ט) ויברך. ויקרא בהן שמע ואח"כ יחלצן. ואם יודע שאין יכול לעצור עצמו מלהפיח אלא בכדי שיוכל להלוך הש"ל ראש אפ"ה מותר להניח לכתחלה את שניהם כ"כ המ"א אבל הפמ"ג מפקפק בזה: ג (י) נשים. (ח) וטומטום ואנדרוגינוס חייבין בתפילין מספק ככל המצות: (יא) שהזמן גרמא. דהא שבת ויו"ט לאו זמן תפילין: (יב) הנשים. עיין בפמ"ג סה"ה לענין עבדים ועיין בספר תוספותה) שבת שכתב בהדיא להיפך ועיין בספר תוספות ירושלים: (יג) מוחים בידן. מפני שצריכין גוף נקי ונשים אין זריזות להזהר: ד (יד) ליזהר. דבעינן (ט) גוף נקי גם ממחשבה רעה: (טו) שלא להניחם. ומ"מ יראה בכל היכולת (י) לכוף את עצמו ולמשוך הלב ליראת שמים כדי להסיח הדעת מדברי הבאי

שער הציון

(א) ח"א: (ב) בה"ט: (ג) מ"א: (ד) מ"א: (ה) פרישה: (ו) פמ"ג: (ז) מ"א ופמ"ג: (ח) פמ"ג בסימן ל"ט: (ט) ב"י: (י) ב"י:

הגהות ותיקונים: א) חסר ב': ב) רל"ז: ג) מ"ב: ד) ושמרת: ה) עולת:

3. (10) Women and /non-Jewish/ slaves are exempt from /the donning of/ *tefilin*, because /the mitzvah of *tefilin*/ is a positive commandment (11) which relates to specific times.[1*]

Gloss: If (12) *women wish to be stringent with themselves /and don* tefilin/ (13) *we should protest to them. (...)*

4. While /wearing/ *tefilin* one must (14) avoid thoughts of lust for a woman.

Gloss: If one cannot be without /such/ thoughts it is better (15) *for him not to don* /tefilin/. *(...)*

Mishnah Berurah

(10) Women. A person of unidentified sex and a hermaphrodite are obliged /to don/ *tefilin*, in view of the doubt /in their case as to whether or not they have the obligations of a man/, just as /they are required to observe/ all /other/ mitzvos /which do not apply to women/.

(11) Which relate to specific times. This is because Shabbos and Yom Tov are times when /the mitzvah of/ *tefilin* does not /apply/.

(12) Women. See the *P.Mg.*, that the same ruling /applies/ as regards /non-Jewish/ slaves. See the work *Olas Shabbos*, where the opposite is stated explicitly. See the work *Tosafos Yerushalayim*.

(13) We should protest to them. /The reason is/ that a clean body is required /for the donning of *tefilin*/ and women are not on the alert to be careful /about this/.

(14) Avoid. For it is necessary for the body to be clean even of bad thoughts.

(15) For him not to don /*tefilin*/. Nevertheless, he should see that /he uses/ all his ability to force himself /to correct this/ and induce his heart to fear Heaven, in order to divert his mind from frivolous matters

1* I.e., the obligation to perform the mitzvah only applies at certain specific times, but at other times there is no obligation whatsoever to perform it. Women and non-Jewish slaves are exempt from such a mitzvah.

ה ה‏אבל (טז) ביום (ד) [ג] ראשון (יז) אסור להניח תפילין (יח) מכאן ואילך (ה) (יט) חייב אפי׳ באו (כ) פנים (ו) חדשות: ו ‏בתשעה באב (כא) חייבין בתפילין: (וע"ל סימן תקנ"ה): ז (ז) ‏חתן ושושביניו (פי׳ ריעיו השמחים עמו) (כב) וכל בני חופה (כג) פטורים משום דשכיח שכרות וקלות ראש: ח * ‏כותבי תפילין ומזוזות * הם (ח) (כד) ותגריהם (כה) ותגרי תגריהם וכל העוסקים במלאכת שמים פטורים ‏מהנחת תפילין כל היום זולת בשעת ק"ש ותפלה: הגה * ואם היו (כו) * צריכים לעשות

באר הגולה

ה מ"ק כ"א וכדעת הרי"ף שם ו רא"ש פ"ב דתענית ז סוכה כ"ה ח שם כ"ו ט ר׳ ירוחם בשם ר׳ ניסים והג"א בשם א"ז ור׳ יונה

באר היטב

(ד) ראשון. פי׳ ביום הקבורה דביום המיתה פטור מכל המצות כל זמן שלא נקבר דאז מיקרי אונן. וה"ה אם שמע שמועה קרובה אסור ג"כ להניח תפילין ביום ראשון כמו יום הקבורה. ע"ז בי"ד סימן ת"ב ס"ק א׳. ומהריט"ן בחידושיו לפרק איזהו נשך[א] דף י"ב כתב דנקטינן דדוקא יום המיתה ויום הקבורה פטור מן התפילין יום ראשון אבל כשהמיתה היה יום אחד והקבורה יום אחר חייב בתפילין אפילו ביום ראשון ע"ש: (ה) חייב. משמע דחייב מיד אבל בי"ד סימן שפ"ח כתב אחר הנץ החמה עמ"א וע"ת. כתב הא"י ז"ל דאין להניח תפילין דר"ת כל ז׳ ימי אבילות: (ו) חדשות. פי׳ מנחמים חדשים. ומ"א פסק דאם באו פנים חדשות אינו מניח לכתחלה עד שילכו אבל אם מניח אינו חולץ ע"ש: (ז) חתן ושושביניו. בתשובת רמ"א סי׳ קל"ב כתב דחתן בזמן הזה חייב בתפלה ובתפילין וכן נתפשט המנהג בזמן הזה בארצות אלו דחתן וכל בני חופה קורין ומתפללין. וכתב המג"א ול"נ המיקל לא הפסיד אם החתן מיסב אצלם ע"ש ובכנה"ג: (ח) ותגריהם. דוקא הלוקחים כדי להמציאם למכור למי שצריך להם אבל אם עושה

שערי תשובה

ביו"ד סי׳ רס"ה עכ"ל ועי"ל בט"ז ס"ס כ"ג: [ג] ראשון. עבה"ט ומ"ש בשמועה קרובה כתב בש"ל בשם ספר שבט יהודה למהר"י עייאש ביו"ד שהפוסקים לא גילו דעתם על יום ב׳ קודם הנץ החמה ויש פנים לכאן ולכאן ועביד עובדא בנפשיה

משנה ברורה

הבאי המזיקים לגוף ולנפש ולפנות הלב לקבל עליו עול מ"ש בקדושה: ה (טז) ביום ראשון. פי׳ אפילו ביום שנקבר (יא) שאינו יום המיתה כיון שהוא יום ראשון לאבילות ולמנחמים וע"כ אפילו אם נקבר (יב) בלילה לא יניח תפילין ביום אבל אם מת או נקבר בחוה"מ מניח תפילין בין בחוה"מ [והפמ"ג בסימן ע"א מפקפק בזה דמ"מ יום מר הוא לו היום הראשון ועכ"פ צריך ליזהר שלא לברך עליהן ובלא"ה המנהג שלא לברך על תפילין בחוה"מ] ובין לאחר המועד אף שהוא יום ראשון לאבילות מ"מ כבר נחמוהו מנחמים במועד וכן כשנקבר ביו"ט שני יניח תפילין בא"ח דיו"ט שני עולה למנין שבעה ויום שאחר המועד יחשב לשני וכן אם שמע שמועה קרובה [דהיינו בתוך שלשים אפילו ביום ל׳ עצמו] ג"כ דינו כיום הקבורה ולכן אפילו אם שמע בלילה לא יניח תפילין ביום ואפילו בא לו שמועה קרובה כשכבר הניח תפילין והתחיל להתפלל חולצן. ואם שמע שמועה רחוקה דהיינו לאחר שלשים שאין האבילות רק שעה אחת מותר להניח תפילין וכ"ש שא"צ לחלצן וע"כ אם בא לו השמועה באמצע פסוקי דזמרה וכה"ג לא יחלוץ התפילין רק יחלוץ מנעליו משום אבילות ואם ע"י השמועה בא לידי בכי צריך לחלצן כדמוכח מיו"ד סימן שפ"ח ס"ב וסימן ת"ב בש"ך סק"ב ועיין לקמן בס"ט: (יז) אסור. דתפילין נקראין פאר בפסוק ואבל מעולל באפר ואין נאה לתת פאר תחת אפר. (יח) מכאן ואילך. דכתיב ואחריתה כיום מר ש"מ דעיקר מרירות הוא יום ראשון: (יט) חייב. משמע דחייב מיד ויש פוסקים (יג) דביום ב׳ אין להניח קודם הנץ ע"כ מהנכון להמתין מלהניח עד אחר הנץ: (כ) פנים חדשות. לנחם אותו ומשמע דמניח לכתחלה אבל (יד) האחרונים מסקי דאין להניח בפניהם תפילין עד שילכו להם אלא דאין חולץ אם הניח קודם שבאו פנים חדשות: ו (כא) חייבין בתפילין. דלא תמיר ת"ב משאר ימי אבילות: ז (כב) וכל בני חופה וכו׳. ודוקא (טו) במקום החופה דשם שכיח שכרות וקלות ראש: (כג) פטורים. בתשובת רמ"א סימן קל"ב כתב דהאידנא שאף החתן חייב בק"ש ותפלה [כמו שכתב בסימן ע׳] ממילא חייבין החתן וכל בני החופה גם בתפילין עי"ש ועיין במ"א שמפקפק בדינו ומצדד לפסוק כהשו"ע דפטורין מתפילין בעת המשתה וגם לענין תפלה המיקל כדעת רש"י לפטור בעת המשתה לא הפסיד אם החתן מיסב אצלם דאז הוי מצוה לדעת רש"י אבל מדברי הגר"א בביאורו משמע שאין להקל לענין תפלה וכמו שכתב בב"י בסימן רל"ב ועיין בעולת תמיד ובברכי יוסף שכתבו דנתפשט המנהג כהרמ"א שהחתן וכל ריעיו קורין ומניחין תפילין ומתפללין מיום הראשון עד יום השביעי: ח (כד) ותגריהם. אף שמרויחין מזה ודוקא אם עיקר כוונתם כדי להמציאן למכור למי שצריך להם אבל אם עיקר כוונתם רק להשתכר לא מיקרי עוסק במצוה [מ"א]: (כה) ותגרי תגריהם. הקונים מן הקונים למכור על יד על יד: (כו) צריכים וכו׳. כגון שנזדמן לו קונה שרוצה לקנות סת"ם והקונה רוצה לפרוש בים או בשיירא עכשיו ואי

ביאור הלכה

במ"ב ועיין בפמ"ג שמצדד לפסוק כמש"כ הב"ח דעכ"פ קטן בן י"ב שנה הלומד תלמוד ומבין יכול להניח תפילין דעליו בודאי נוכל לסמוך אם יודע לשמור את עצמו מהדברים הנזכרים בסמוך:

* כותבי ספרים תפילין ומזוזות וכו׳. כצ"ל הכי איתא בגמרא ובכל הראשונים:

* הם ותגריהם וכו׳. עיין במשנה ברורה מש"כ בשם המ"א ולענ"ד צ"ע מב"מ דף פ"ב ע"ב מר סבר מצוה קעביד שהלוהו ומ"ס לאו מצוה קעביד שלהנאתו מתכוין ועיין ברש"י שם ד"ה במצוה צריך וכו׳ אפ"ה איכא מצוה עכ"ל הרי דס"ל לר"ע דהלכה כמותו דאפי׳ היכא שהוא מכוין להנאתו ג"כ מיקרי עוסק במצוה ופטור מלמיתב ריפתא לעניא דעי"ז הוי ש"ש ואולי דכונת הגמרא במ"ש מ"ס מצוה קעביד שהלוהו היינו שמסתמא מכוין בזה לקיים מצות בוראו ומכוין להנאתו ג"כ ור"א סבר דלהנאתו לבד מכוין וכעין מה שפירש רש"י בפסחים דף ט׳[ב] ע"ב ד"ה הרי זה צ"ג וכו׳ ומתכוין אף וכו׳ ושם בע"א ד"ה וכה"ג וכו׳ עיי"ש אבל אם אנו יודעין שכונתו רק כדי להרויח לא מיקרי עוסק במצוה ומ"מ נ"ל דאם כונתו לשניהם בשוה מיקרי עוסק במצוה וכענין מה שפסק הא"ר בסימן תקפ"ט סק"ח דאם תקע בשופר להתלמד וגם לצאת בו ידי מצוה יצא ידי חובתו ודע עוד דלענין כתיבת סת"ם גופא כמו שמצוי שהכותב כונתו להשתכר מסתפיקנא לומר דאפ"ה מיקרי בכלל עוסק במצוה אף דלכאורה הוא היינו הך דהמ"א שהביא מפירש"י נלענ"ד לחלק אף דעי"ז יפול ממילא ג"כ הקושיא של המ"א והוא דלענין כתיבה גופא דהיא בודאי עצם מצוה כדכתיב וכתבתם ורק דאינה גמר מצוה קודם הקשירה וכדמוכח במנחות מ"א[ג] ע"כ הוא תמיד בכלל עוסק במצוה ואפילו אם אנו יודעין שעיקר התחלתו לכתוב היה רק בשביל שכר ולולי זה לא היה מתחיל מ"מ אמרינן דהשתא שכותב אין מכוין כלל רק שכותב סתם לשם מצות תפילין כדין ומה שפירש"י הלוקחין כדי להמציאן וכו׳ הלא רק על ותגריהם פירש וכונתו דשם הלא המסחור בעניני תפילין לא נזכר בשום מקום למצוה ואפילו אם נאמר דמה שהוא מוכר לאיזה אדם הצריך תפילין הוא בכלל עוסק במצוה עכ"פ בשעה שהוא קונה התפילין מהסופר כדי לסחור בהם אין שם לע"ע עצם פעולת המצוה כלל בהמעשה גופא והגמרא פטרן בכל גווני לכן פירש"י הלוקחין כדי להמציאן למכור למי שצריך להם ור"ל דאז ע"י מחשבתו שהוא לשם מצוה מחשיב פעולתו לעוסק במצוה משא"כ בעניני מחזיר אבידה וכתיבת סת"ם וכה"ג הפעולה גופא הוא בכלל עוסק במצוה: * ואם היו וכו׳. עיין בע"ת ובמ"א ובביאור הגר"א ושארי אחרונים דדעת הרמ"א לפסוק כתלמודא דידן ולא כהירושלמי ע"כ פטרו אף מק"ש ותפילה גופא ולא כהמחבר דלדידיה בכל גווני חייב בק"ש ותפילה ומשמע מע"ת ומ"א דהלכה כהרמ"א: * צריכים לעשות

שער הציון

(יא) ט"ז וא"ר ודגמ"ר ביו"ד סימן שפ"ח ודה"ח וכן הסכים בשע"ת דלא כמהריט"ן ומ"א: (יב) א"ר ודה"ח וכן כל הס"ק: (יג) יו"ד סימן שפ"ח: (יד) מ"א ופמ"ג: (טו) ל"ח:

הגהות ותיקונים: א) אלו מגלחין: ב) ח׳: ג) מ"ב:

5. **(16)** On the first day /of his mourning/ a mourner **(17)** is forbidden to don

Mishnah Berurah

which are harmful to the body and to the soul. He should empty his heart /of all immodest thought, so that he will be able/ to accept the yoke of the Kingdom of Heaven upon himself in holiness.

(16) On the first day. I.e., even if /it is merely/ the day when /his dead/ was buried, but is not the day when he died, since the /day of burial/ is the first day of /post-burial/ mourning and for the comforters /to comfort him/. Consequently, even if /his dead/ was buried at night he should not don *tefilin* on the day /which follows/.

However, if /his dead/ died or was buried on Chol Ha-Mo'ed he should don *tefilin*, both during Chol Ha-Mo'ed and after the festival, although /, then, the day following the festival/ is the first day of /post-burial/ mourning. /This is because,/ nevertheless, comforters will already have comforted him during the festival. [The *P.Mg.* in Sec. 71 questions /the ruling as regards Chol Ha-Mo'ed/, since the first day is nevertheless a bitter day for him. He must at least take care not to make a blessing over /the *tefilin* then/. It is in any case the practice not to make a blessing over *tefilin* on Chol Ha-Mo'ed.] Likewise, if /one's dead/ was buried on the second day of Yom Tov /which is observed in the exile/, he should don *tefilin* on the day following Yom Tov, since this second day of Yom Tov counts towards the number of seven /days of mourning required/ and the day after the festival is /thus/ considered the second /of these days/.

Similarly, if one hears within a short time news /of the death of a relative whom he must mourn/ [i.e., /if he hears it/ within thirty /days of the death/ and even /if he hears it/ on the thirtieth day itself], /the day when he hears it/ also has the ruling of the day of burial. Therefore, even when /a mourner/ heard /such news/ at night, he should not don *tefilin* during the day /which follows/. Even if news /of the death/ reaches /a relative who is required to mourn/ when he has already donned *tefilin* and begun praying, he should take them off /if it is/ within a short time /of the death/.

If one hears news /of the death of a relative for whom he is required to mourn when it is already/ long after /the death/, i.e., /if he hears the news more than/ thirty /days/ after /the death/, in which case the mourning /required/ is only for a moment, he is permitted to don *tefilin* and is certainly not required to take them off /if he has already donned them/. Consequently, if /such/ news reaches /a relative who is required to mourn when he is/ in the middle of /saying/ the song verses or something like that, he should not take off the *tefilin*, but should merely take off his shoes because of the mourning /required of him/. /However,/ if the news causes him to weep he must /then/ take off /the *tefilin*/, as is evident from the *Yoreh De'ah*, Sec. 388, Par. 2 and from the *Shach* /there in/ Sec. 402, sub-Par. 2. See below in Par. 9.

(17) Is forbidden. /This is/ because *tefilin* are described as glory by the verse,[1] whereas a mourner rolls in ashes. It is unbecoming to put glory underneath ashes.

1 *Yechezkeyl* 24:17.

ה מ״ק כ״א וכדעת הרי״ף שם ז רא״ש פ״ב דתענית ז סוכה כ״ה ח שם כ״ז ט ר׳ ירוחם בשם ר׳ ניסים והג״א בשם א״ז ור׳ יונה

ה אבל (טז) ביום (ד) [ב] ראשון (יז) אסור להניח **תפילין (יח) מכאן ואילך (ה) (יט) חייב אפי׳ באו (כ) פנים (ו) חדשות: ו בתשעה באב (כא) חייבין בתפילין: (וע״ל סימן תקנ״ה): ז (ז) חתן ושושביניו (פי׳ ריעיו השמחים עמו) (כב) וכל בני חופה (כג) פטורים משום דשכיח שכרות וקלות ראש:** ח * כותבי תפילין ומזוזות * הם (ח) (כד) ותגרי תגריהם (כה) וכל העוסקים במלאכת שמים פטורים מהנחת תפילין כל היום זולת בשעת ק״ש ותפלה: הגה * ואם היו (כו) * צריכים לעשות

באר היטב

(ד) ראשון. פי׳ ביום הקבורה דביום המיתה פטור מכל המצות כל זמן שלא נקבר דאז מיקרי אונן. וה״ה אם שמע שמועה קרובה אסור ג״כ להניח תפילין ביום ראשון כמו יום הקבורה. ט״ז בי״ד סימן ת״ב ס״ק א׳. ומהריט״ץ בחידושיו לפרק איזהו נשך[א] דף י״ב כתב דנקטינן דדוקא יום המיתה ויום הקבורה פטור מן התפילין יום ראשון אבל כשהמיתה היה יום אחר והקבורה יום אחר חייב בתפילין אפילו ביום ראשון ע״ש: (ה) חייב. משמע דחייב מיד אבל בי״ד סימן שפ״ח כתב אחר הנץ החמה עמ״א וע״ת. כתב האר״י ז״ל דאין להניח תפילין דר״ת כל ז׳ ימי אבילות: (ו) חדשות. פי׳ מנחמים חדשים. ומ״א פסק דאם באו פנים חדשות אינו מניח לכתחלה עד שילכו אבל אם מניח אינו חולץ ע״ש: (ז) חתן ושושביניו. בתשובת רמ״א סי׳ קל״ב כתב דחתן בזמן הזה חייב בתפלה ובתפילין וכן נתפשט המנהג בזמן הזה בארצות אלו דחתן וכל בני חופה קורין ומתפללין. וכתב המג״א ול״נ המיקל לא הפסיד אם החתן מיסב אצלם ע״ש ובכנה״ג: (ח) ותגריהם. דוקא הלוקחים כדי להמציאם למכור למי שצריך להם אבל אם עושה

שערי תשובה

ביו״ד סי׳ רס״ה עכ״ל ועי״ל בט״ז ס״ם כ״ב: [ב] ראשון. עבה״ט ומ״ש בשמועה קרובה כתב בש״ל בשם ספר שבט יהודה למהר״י עייאש ביו״ד שהפוסקים לא גילו דעתם על יום ב׳ קודם הנץ החמה ויש פנים לכאן ולכאן ועביד עובדא בנפשיה

משנה ברורה

הבאי המזיקים לגוף ולנפש ולפנות הלב לקבל עליו עול מ״ש בקדושה: ה (טז) ביום ראשון. פי׳ אפילו יום שנקבר (יא) שאינו יום המיתה כיון שהוא יום ראשון לאבילות ולמנחמים וע״כ אפילו אם נקבר (יב) בלילה לא יניח תפילין ביום אבל אם מת או נקבר בחוה״מ מניח תפילין בין בחוה״מ [והפמ״ג בסימן ע״א מסתפק בזה דמ״מ יום מר הוא לו היום הראשון ועכ״פ צריך ליזהר שלא לברך עליהן ונלא״ה המנהג שלא לברך על תפילין בחוה״מ] ובין לאחר המועד אף שהוא יום ראשון לאבילות מ״מ כבר נחמוהו מנחמים במועד וכן כשנקבר בי״ט שני יניח תפילין בא״ח דיו״ט שני עולה למנין שבעה ויום שאחר המועד יחשב לשני וכן אם שמע שמועה קרובה [דהיינו בתוך שלשים אפילו ביום ל׳ עצמו] ג״כ דינו כיום הקבורה ולכן אפילו אם שמע בלילה לא יניח תפילין ביום ואפילו בא לו שמועה קרובה כשכבר הניח תפילין והתחיל להתפלל חולץ. ואם שמע שמועה רחוקה דהיינו לאחר שלשים שאין האבילות רק שעה אחת מותר להניח תפילין וכ״ש שא״צ לחלצן וע״כ אם בא לו השמועה באמצע פסוקי דזמרה וכה״ג לא יחלוץ התפילין רק יחלוץ מנעליו משום אבילות ואם ע״י השמועה בא לידי בכי צריך לחלצן כדמוכח מיו״ד סימן שפ״ח ס״ב וסימן ת״ב בש״ך סק״ב ועיין לקמן בס״ע: (יז) אסור. דתפילין נקראין פאר כפסוק ואבל מעולל בעפר ואין נאה לתת פאר תחת אפר. **(יח) מכאן ואילך. דכתיב ואחריתה כיום מר ש״מ דעיקר מרירות הוא יום ראשון: (יט) חייב. משמע דחייב מיד ויש פוסקים (יג) דביום ב׳ אין להניח קודם הנץ ע״כ מהנכון להמתין מלהניח עד אחר הנץ: (כ) פנים חדשות. לנחם אותו ומשמע דמניח לכתחלה אבל (יד) האחרונים מסקי דאין להניח בפניהם תפילין עד שילכו להם אלא דאין חולץ אם הניח קודם שבאו פנים חדשות: ו (כא) חייבין בתפילין. דלא חמיר ת״ב משאר ימי אבילות: ז (כב) וכל בני חופה וכו׳. ודוקא (טו) במקום החופה דשם שכיח שכרות וקלות ראש: (כג) פטורים. בתשובת רמ״א סימן קל״ב כתב דהאידנא שאף החתן חייב בק״ש ותפלה [כמו שכתב בסימן ע׳] ממילא חייבין החתן וכל בני החופה גם בתפילין עי״ש ועיין במ״א שמפקפק בדינו ומצדד לפסוק כהשו״ע דפטורין מתפילין בעת המשתה וגם לענין תפלה** המיקל כדעת רש״י לפטור בעת המשתה לא הפסיד אם החתן מיסב אצלם דאז הוי מצוה לדעת רש״י אבל מדברי הגר״א בביאורו משמע שאין להקל לענין תפלה וכמו שכתב בב״י בסימן רל״ב ועיין בעולת תמיד ובברכי יוסף שכתבו דנתפשט המנהג כהרמ״א שהחתן וכל סייעתו קורין ומניחין תפילין ומתפללין מיום הראשון עד יום השביעי: ח (כד) ותגריהם. אף שמרויחין מזה ודוקא אם עיקר כוונתם כדי להמציאן למכור למי שצריך להם אבל אם עיקר כוונתם רק להשתכר לא מיקרי עוסק במצוה [מ״א]: (כה) ותגרי תגריהם. הקונים מן הקונים למכור על יד על יד: (כו) צריכים וכו׳. כגון שנזדמן לו קונה שרוצה לקנות סת״ם והקונה רוצה לפרוע בים או בשיירא עכשיו ואי

ביאור הלכה

במ״ב ועיין בפמ״ג שמצדד לפסוק כמש״כ הב״ח דעכ״פ קטן בן י״ב שנה הלומד תלמוד ומבין יכול להניח תפילין דעליו בודאי נוכל לסמוך אם יודע לשמור את עצמו מהדברים הנזכרים בסמוך:

* כותבי ספרים תפילין ומזוזות וכו׳. כצ״ל הכי איתא בגמרא ובכל הראשונים:

* הם ותגריהם וכו׳. עיין במשנה ברורה מש״כ בשם המ״א ולענ״ד צ״ע מב״מ דף פ״ב ע״ב מר סבר מצוה קעביד שהלוהו ומ״ס לאו מצוה קעביד שלהנאתו מתכוין ועיין ברש״י שם ד״ה במצוה צריך וכו׳ אפ״ה איכא מצוה עכ״ל הרי דס״ל לר״ע דהלכה כמותו דאפי׳ היכא שהוא מכוין להנאתו ג״כ מיקרי עוסק במצוה ופטור מלמיתב ריפתא לעניא דעי״ז הוי ש״ש ואולי דכונת הגמרא במ״ש מ״ס מצוה קעביד שהלוהו היינו שמסתמא מכוין בזה לקיים מצות בוראו ומכוין להנאתו ג״כ ור״א סבר דלהנאתו לבד מכוין וכעין מה שפירש רש״י בפסחים דף ט׳[ב] ע״ב ד״ה הרי זה צ״ג וכו׳ ומתכוין אף וכו׳ ושם בע״א ד״ה וכה״ג וכו׳ עיי״ש אבל אם אנו יודעין שכונתו רק כדי להרויח לא מיקרי עוסק במצוה ומ״מ נ״ל דאם כונתו לשניהם בשוה מיקרי עוסק במצוה וכענין מה שפסק הא״ר בסימן תקפ״ט סק״ח דאם תקע בשופר להתלמד וגם לצאת בו ידי מצוה יצא ידי חובתו ודע עוד דלענין כתיבת סת״ם גופא כמו שמצוי שהכותב כונתו להשתכר מסתפיקנא לומר דאפ״ה מיקרי בכלל עוסק במצוה אף דלכאורה הוא היינו הך דהמ״א שהביא מפירש״י נלענ״ד לחלק אף דעי״ז יפול ממילא ג״כ הקושיא של המ״א והוא דלענין כתיבה גופא דהיא בודאי עצם מצוה כדכתיב וכתבתם ורק דאינה גמר מצוה קודם הקשירה וכדמוכח במנחות מ״א[ג] ע״ב הוא תמיד בכלל עוסק במצוה ואפילו אם אנו יודעין שעיקר התחלתו לכתוב היה רק בשביל שכר ולולי זה לא היה מתחיל מ״מ אמרינן דהשתא שכותב אין מכוין כלל רק שכותב סתם לשם מצות תפילין כדין ומה שפירש״י הלוקחין כדי להמציאן וכו׳ הלא רק על ותגריהם פירש וכונתו דשם הלא המסחור בעניני תפילין לא נזכר בשום מקום למצוה ואפילו אם נאמר דמה שהוא מוכר לאיזה אדם הצריך תפילין הוא בכלל עוסק במצוה עכ״פ בשעה שהוא קונה התפילין מהסופר כדי לסחור בהם אין שם לע״ע עצם פעולת המצוה כלל בהמעשה גופא והגמרא פטרן בכל גווני לכן פירש״י הלוקחין כדי להמציאן למכור למי שצריך להם ור״ל דאז ע״י מחשבתו שהוא לשם מצוה מחשיב פעולתו לעוסק במצוה משא״כ בעניני מחזיר אבידה וכתיבת סת״ם וכה״ג הפעולה גופא הוא בכלל עוסק במצוה: * ואם היו וכו׳. עיין בע״ת ובמ״א ובביאור הגר״א ושארי אחרונים דדעת הרמ״א לפסוק כתלמודא דידן ולא כהירושלמי ע״כ פטרו אף מק״ש ותפילה גופא ולא כהמחבר דלדידיה בכל גווני חייב בק״ש ותפילה ומשמע מע״ת ומ״א דהלכה כהרמ״א: * צריכים לעשות

שער הציון

(יא) ט״ז וא״ר ודגמ״ר ביו״ד סימן שפ״ח ודה״ח וכן הסכים בשע״ת דלא כמהריט״ץ וח״א: (יב) א״ר ודה״ח וכן כל הס״ק: (יג) יו״ד סימן שפ״ח: (יד) מ״א ופמ״ג: (טו) ל״ח:

הגהות ותיקונים: א) אלו מגלחין: **ב)** ח׳: **ג)** מ״ב:

tefilin. **(18)** From then onwards **(19)** he is obliged /to don *tefilin*/, even if **(20)** fresh faces arrive.

6. On Tishah Be-Av **(21)** one is obliged to /don/ *tefilin (see below in Sec. 555).*

7. A bridegroom and his groomsmen (i.e., his friends who rejoice with him) **(22)** and all the participants at the wedding ceremony **(23)** are exempt /from donning *tefilin*/, because drunkenness and light-headedness are common /there/.

Mishnah Berurah

(18) From then onwards. For it is written,[2] "and its end is like a bitter day", from which one can derive that the principal bitterness is /on/ the first day.

(19) He is obliged. It is implied that he is obliged /to don *tefilin*/ right away.

There are /authorities/ who rule that on the second day /of his mourning a mourner/ should not don /*tefilin*/ before /sun/rise. Consequently, it is proper /for him/ to wait until after /sun/rise /of the second day/ before he dons /*tefilin*/.

(20) Fresh faces. /I.e.,/ to comfort him.

/The wording of the Shulchan Aruch/ implies that he may don /*tefilin*/ initially /even in the presence of the fresh faces/. However, the Acharonim conclude that he should not don *tefilin* in front of them, /but should wait/ until they have gone away. /According to them, what is meant/ is only that he is not /required/ to take off /the *tefilin*/ if he donned them before the fresh faces arrived.

(21) One is obliged to /don/ *tefilin*. For /the mourning required on/ Tishah Be-Av is not more severe than /the mourning required/ on the other days of mourning.

(22) And all the participants at the wedding ceremony, etc. This only /applies/ at the site of the wedding ceremony, as that is where drunkenness and light-headedness are common.

(23) Are exempt. In a responsum of the *Rema*, Sec. 132 he writes that nowadays, when even the bridegroom is obliged to /read/ "The Reading of Shema" and /pray the eighteen-blessing/ prayer [as stated in Sec. 70 /, Par. 3/], it follows that the bridegroom and all the participants at the wedding ceremony are also obliged to /don/ *tefilin*; see there.

/However,/ see the *M.A.*, who questions his ruling and adopts the decision of /the author of/ the Shulchan Aruch, that they are /in fact/ exempt from /donning/ *tefilin* at the time of the /wedding/ feast /even nowadays/. /He states that/ even as regards the /praying of the eighteen-blessing/

2 *Amos* 8:10.

ה

ה ^אבל (טז) ביום (ד) [ג] ראשון (יז) (ה) אסור להניח תפילין (יח) מכאן ואילך (ה) (יט) חייב אפי' באו (כ) פנים (ו) חדשות: ו ^יבתשעה באב (כא) חייבין בתפילין: (וע"ל סימן תקנ"ה): ז (ז) ^יחתן ושושבינין (פי' ריעיו השמחים עמו) (כב) וכל בני חופה (כג) פטורים משום דשכיח שכרות וקלות ראש: ח * ^חכותבי תפילין ומזוזות * הם (ח) (כד) ותגריהם (כה) ותגרי תגריהם וכל העוסקים במלאכת שמים פטורים ^טמהנחת תפילין כל היום זולת בשעת ק"ש ותפלה: הגה * ואם היו (כו) * לריכים לעשות

באר הגולה: ה מ"ק כ"א וכדעת הרי"ף שם ו רא"ש פ"ב דתענית ז סוכה כ"ה ח שם כ"ו ט ר' ירוחם בשם ר' ניסים והג"א בשם א"ז ור' יונה

באר היטב

(ד) ראשון. פי' ביום הקבורה דביום המיתה פטור מכל המצות כל זמן שלא נקבר דאז מיקרי אונן. וה"ה אם שמע שמועה קרובה אסור ג"כ להניח תפילין ביום ראשון כמו יום הקבורה. ט"ז בי"ד סימן ת"ב ס"ק א'. ומהריט"ץ בחידושיו לפרק איזהו נשך^א) דף י"ב כתב דנקטינן דדוקא יום המיתה ויום הקבורה פטור מן התפילין יום ראשון אבל כשהמיתה היה יום אחר והקבורה יום אחר חייב בתפילין אפילו ביום ראשון ע"ש: (ה) חייב. משמע דחייב מיד אבל בי"ד סימן שפ"ח כתב אחר הנץ החמה עמ"א וע"ת. כתב האר"י ז"ל דאין להניח תפילין דר"ת כל ז' ימי אבילות: (ו) חדשות. פי' מנחמים חדשים. ומ"א פסק דאם באו פנים חדשות אינו מניח לכתחלה עד שילכו אבל אם מניח אינו חולץ ע"ש: (ז) חתן ושושביניו. בתשובת רמ"א סי' קל"ב כתב דחתן בזמן הזה חייב בתפלה ובתפילין וכן נתפשט המנהג בזמן הזה בארצות אלו דחתן וכל בני חופה קורין ומתפללין. וכתב המג"א ול"נ המיקל לא הפסיד אם החתן מיסב אצלם ע"ש ובכנה"ג: (ח) ותגריהם. דוקא הלוקחים כדי להמציאם למכור למי שצריך להם אבל אם עושה

שערי תשובה

ביו"ד סי' רס"ה עכ"ל ועי"ל בט"ז ס"ם כ"ב: [ג] ראשון. עבה"ט ומ"ש בשמועה קרובה כתב בס"ל בשם ספר שבט יהודה למהר"י עייאש ביו"ד שהפוסקים לא גילו דעתם על יום ב' קודם הנץ החמה ויש פנים לכאן ולכאן ועביד עובדא בנפשיה

משנה ברורה

הבאי המזיקים לגוף ולנפש ולפעמים הלב נקל עליו עול מ"ש בקדושה: ה (טז) ביום ראשון. פי' אפילו ביום שנקבר (יא) שאינו יום המיתה כיון שהוא יום ראשון לאבילות ולמנחמים וע"כ אפילו אם נקבר (יב) בלילה לא יניח תפילין ביום אבל אם מת או נקבר בחוה"מ מניח תפילין בין בחוה"מ [והפמ"ג בסימן ע"א מסתפק בזה דמ"מ יום מר הוא לו כיום הראשון ועכ"פ צריך ליזהר שלא לברך עליהן ובלא"ה המנהג שלא לברך על תפילין בחוה"מ] וכן לאחר המועד אף שהוא יום ראשון לאבילות מ"מ כבר נתמעטו מנחמים במועד וכן כשנקבר בי"ט שני יניח תפילין בא"ה דיו"ט שני עולה למנין שבעה ויום שלאחר המועד יחשב לשני וכן אם שמע שמועה קרובה [דהיינו בתוך שלשים אפילו ביום ל' עצמו] ג"כ דינו כיום הקבורה ולכן אפילו אם שמע בלילה לא יניח תפילין ביום ואפילו בא לו שמועה קרובה כשכבר הניח תפילין והתחיל להתפלל חולצן. ואם שמע שמועה רחוקה דהיינו לאחר שלשים שאין האבילות רק שעה אחת מותר להניח תפילין וי"א שא"צ לחלצן וע"כ אם בא לו השמועה באמצע פסוקי דזמרה וכה"ג לא יחלוץ התפילין רק יחלוץ מנעליו משום אבילות ואם ע"י השמועה בא לידי בכי צריך לחלצן כדמוכח מיו"ד סימן שפ"ח ס"ב וסימן ת"ב בש"ך סק"ב ועיין לקמן בס"ט: (יז) אסור. דתפילין נקראין פאר בפסוק ואבל מגולל באפר ואין נאה לתת פאר תחת אפר. (יח) מכאן ואילך. דכתיב ואחריתה כיום מר ש"מ דעיקר מרירות הוא יום ראשון: (יט) חייב. משמע דחייב מיד ויש פוסקים (יג) דביום ב' אין להניח קודם הנץ ע"כ מהנכון להמתין מלהניח עד אחר הנץ: (כ) פנים חדשות. לנחם אותו ומשמע דמניח לכתחלה אבל (יד) האחרונים תפסו דאין להניח בפניהם תפילין עד שילכו להם אלא דאין חולץ אם הניח קודם שבאו פנים חדשות: ו (כא) חייבין בתפילין. דלא התיר ת"ב משאר ימי אבילות: ז (כב) וכל בני חופה וכו'. ודוקא (טו) במקום החופה דשם שכיח שכרות וקלות ראש: (כג) פטורים. בתשובת רמ"א סימן קל"ב כתב דהאידנא שאף החתן חייב בק"ש ותפלה [כמו שכתב בסימן ע'] ממילא חייבין החתן וכל בני החופה גם בתפילין עי"ש ועיין במ"א שמסתפק בדינו ומצדד לפסוק כהשו"ע דפטורין מתפילין בעת המשתה וגם לענין תפלה המיקל כדעת רש"י לפטור בעת המשתה לא הפסיד אם החתן מיסב אצלם דאז הוי מצוה לדעת רש"י אבל מדברי הגר"א בביאורו משמע שאין להקל לענין תפלה וכמו שכתב בב"י בסימן רל"ב ועיין בעולת תמיד ובברכי יוסף שכתבו דנתפשט המנהג כהרמ"א שהחתן וכל סייעתו קורין ומניחין תפילין ומתפללין מיום הראשון עד יום השביעי: ח (כד) ותגריהם. אף שמרויחין מזה ודוקא אם עיקר כוונתם כדי להמציאן למכור למי שצריך להם אבל אם עיקר כוונתם רק להשתכר לא מיקרי עוסק במצוה [מ"א]: (כה) ותגרי תגריהם. הקונים מן הקונים למכור על יד על יד: (כו) צריכים וכו'. כגון שנזדמן לו קונה שרוצה לקנות סת"ס והקונה רוצה לפרוש בים או בשיירא עכשיו ואי

ביאור הלכה

במ"ב ועיין בפמ"ג שמצדד לפסוק כמש"כ הב"ח דעכ"פ קטן בן י"ב שנה הלומד תלמוד ומבין יכול להניח תפילין דעליו בודאי נוכל לסמוך אם יודע לשמור את עצמו מהדברים הנזכרים בסמוך:

* כותבי ספרים תפילין ומזוזות וכו'. כצ"ל הכי איתא בגמרא ובכל הראשונים:

* הם ותגריהם וכו'. עיין במשנה ברורה מש"כ בשם המ"א ולענ"ד צ"ע מב"מ דף פ"ב ע"ב מר סבר מצוה קעביד שהלוהו ומ"ס לאו מצוה קעביד שלהנאתו מתכוין ועיין ברש"י שם ד"ה במצוה צריך וכו' אפ"ה איכא מצוה עכ"ל הרי דס"ל לר"ע דהלכה כמותו דאפי' היכא שהוא מכוין להנאתו ג"כ מיקרי עוסק במצוה ופטור מלמיתב ריפתא לעניא דעי"ז הוי ש"ש ואולי דכונת הגמרא במ"ש מ"ס מצוה קעביד שהלוהו היינו שמסתמא מכוין בזה לקיים מצות בוראו ומכוין להנאתו ג"כ ור"א סבר דלהנאתו לבד מכוין וכעין מה שפירש רש"י בפסחים דף ט'^ב) ע"ב ד"ה הרי זה צ"ג וכו' ומתכוין אף וכו' ושם בע"א ד"ה וכה"ג וכו' עיי"ש אבל אם אנו יודעין שכונתו רק כדי להרויח לא מיקרי עוסק במצוה ומ"מ נ"ל דאם כונתו לשניהם בשוה מיקרי עוסק במצוה וכענין מה שפסק הא"ר בסימן תקפ"ט סק"ח דאם תקע בשופר להתלמד וגם לצאת בו ידי מצוה יצא ידי חובתו ודע עוד דלענין כתיבת סת"ס גופא כמו שמצוי שהכותב כונתו להשתכר מסתפיקנא לומר דאפ"ה מיקרי בכלל עוסק במצוה אף דלכאורה הוא היינו הך דהמ"א שהביא מפירש"י נלענ"ד לחלק אף דעי"ז יפול ממילא ג"כ הקושיא של המ"א והוא דלענין כתיבה גופא דהיא בודאי עצם מצוה כדכתיב וכתבתם ורק דאינה גמר מצוה קודם הקשירה וכדמוכח במנחות מ"א^ג) ע"כ הוא תמיד בכלל עוסק במצוה ואפילו אם אנו יודעין שעיקר התחלתו לכתוב היה רק בשביל שכר ולולי זה לא היה מתחיל מ"מ אמרינן דהשתא שכותב אין מכוין כלל רק שכותב סתם לשם מצות תפילין כדין ומה שפירש"י הלוקחין כדי להמציאן וכו' הלא רק על ותגריהם פירש וכונתו דשם הלא המסחור בעניני תפילין לא נזכר בשום מקום למצוה ואפילו אם נאמר דמה שהוא מוכר לאיזה אדם הצריך תפילין הוא בכלל עוסק במצוה עכ"פ בשעה שהוא קונה התפילין מהסופר כדי לסחור בהם אין שם לע"ע עצם פעולת המצוה כלל בהמעשה גופא והגמרא פטרן בכל גווני לכן פירש"י הלוקחין כדי להמציאן למכור למי שצריך להם ור"ל דאז ע"י מחשבתו שהוא לשם מצוה מחשיב פעולתו לעוסק במצוה משא"כ בעניני מחזיר אבידה וכתיבת סת"ס וכה"ג הפעולה גופא הוא בכלל עוסק במצוה: * ואם היו וכו'. עיין בע"ת ובמ"א ובביאור הגר"א ושארי אחרונים דדעת הרמ"א לפסוק כתלמודא דידן ולא כהירושלמי ע"כ פטרו אף מק"ש ותפילה גופא ולא כהמחבר דלדידיה בכל גווני חייב בק"ש ותפילה ומשמע מע"ת ומ"א דהלכה כהרמ"א: * צריכים לעשות

שער הציון

(יא) ט"ז וא"ר ודגמ"ר ביו"ד סימן שפ"ח ודה"ח וכן הסכים בשע"ת דלא כמהריט"ץ ומ"א: (יב) א"ר ודה"ח וכן כל הס"ק: (יג) יו"ד סימן שפ"ח: (יד) מ"א ופמ"ג: (טו) ל"ח:

הגהות ותיקונים: א) אלו מגלחין: ב) ח': ג) מ"ב:

8. Those who write /Torah/ Scrolls,[2*] *tefilin* /passages/ or mezuzos /are also exempt from donning *tefilin*/. They, **(24)** their brokers **(25)** and their brokers' brokers and all those who engage in Heavenly work are exempt from donning *tefilin* all day, except at the time when /they read/ "The Reading of Shema" and /pray the eighteen-blessing/ prayer.

Gloss: If they **(26)** *need to do their work at the time when /they are required*

Mishnah Berurah

prayer, if someone is lenient /about it/ in accordance with the view of *Rashi* and exempts /the participants at the wedding from praying it/ at the time of the /wedding/ feast, he will not lose /by it/. (/This reasoning only applies/ if the bridegroom is dining with them, in which case a mitzvah[3] is involved in *Rashi's* view.) On the other hand, from the words of the *Gra* in his *Beyur*, it is implied that one should not be lenient as regards /the eighteen-blessing/ prayer, as the *B.Y.* writes in Sec. 232.

See the *Olas Tamid* and the *Birkei Yosef*, who write that it has become the widespread practice /to act/ in accordance with /the view of/ the *Rema*. The bridegroom and all his entourage read /"The Reading of Shema"/, don *tefilin* and pray /the eighteen-blessing prayer/, from the first day /of the wedding celebrations/ until the seventh day.

(24) Their brokers. /This applies/ even if they profit from it. /However,/ it is only the case if their main purpose is to make them available for sale to whoever requires them, but if their main purpose is only gain, this is not classed as being occupied with /the performance of/ a mitzvah. [*M.A.*]

(25) And their brokers' brokers. /I.e.,/ those who buy from the purchaser to sell them individually.

(26) Need, etc. For example, when they chance to have a buyer /then/ who wishes to acquire a Torah Scroll, a *tefilin* /passage/ or a mezuzah and the buyer wishes to set sail by sea or /leave/ with a caravan now and is

2* Corrected in conformance with the Beyur Halachah.

3 Accordingly, they are exempt from the mitzvah of *tefilin* or of prayer because they are occupied with the mitzvah of making the bridegroom rejoice.

מלאכתן בשעת ק"ש ותפלה (כז) * אז פטורין מק"ש ותפלה ותפילין (כח) * דכל העוסק במצוה פטור ממצוה (ט) אחרת (כט) * אם צריך לטרוח אחר האחרת אבל אם יכול לעשות שתיהן כאחת בלא טורח יעשה שתיהן (הגהת אשרי בשם א"ז ור"ן פ' הישן): **ט** (י) (ל) ימצטער ומי (לא) שאין דעתו מיושבת (יא) עליו ונכונה פטור כמפני שאסור להסיח דעתו מהם: י * להקורא (יב) [ג] (לב) בתורה (לג) פטור (לד) מהנחת תפילין כל היום זולת בשעת ק"ש ותפלה: **יא** מלא יחלוץ תפילין (לה) בפני רבו נאלא יפנה לצד אחר (לו) מפני אימתו ויחלוץ שלא (יג) בפניו: **יב** סהיה צריך לתפילין ומזוזה ואין ידו משגת לקנות

י הרמב"ם בפ"ד מה"ת ב הר"ר מנוח ל מכילתא לפי' ר' יונה בפ"ב דברכות מ בשימושא רבא וסנהד' ק"א ג רש"י שם ס ירושלמי שילהי מגילה וכרב הונא כ"כ הרא"ש בה"ר

שערי תשובה

ונתעכב ביום ב' שלא להניח תפילין עד הנץ החמה כדי להסתלק מן הספק ע"ש ואם מת לו מת ברגל או שמע שמועה רחוקה ברגל שאינו נוהג אבילות ומתחיל למנות אחר הרגל כתב בכנה"ג שאסור להניח תפילין ביום ראשון. ובבר"י חלק עליו וכתב דחייב ואפי' אי הוה ספיקא אין לבטל מצוה רבה כזו מספק. וכ"כ בבית לחם יהודה ביו"ד סי' שפ"ח וחלק על הכנה"ג ע"ש. וגם במ"ש בבה"ט בשם מהריט"ץ חולק עליו בבר"י ובמח"ב וסיים בה סוף דבר נ"ל דיום הקבורה אעפ"י שאינו יום מיתה אסור בתפילין וע"ש שכתב שכן מוכח מהט"ז ומ"ב וכן הא"ר ע"ש. ובש"ן כתב ג"כ בשם ספר דרך המלך דלא כמהריט"ץ: [ג] בתורה.

באר היטב

כדי להשתכר לא מיקרי עוסק במצוה מ"א: (ט) אחרת. כל זה מיירי שכבר התחיל לכתוב קודם שהגיע זמן ק"ש אבל משהגיע אסור להתחיל עיין סימן ע"ב ס"ב: (י) מצטער. אפילו מפני הצנה. מגן אברהם: (יא) עליו. דוקא כשא"א לו ליישב דעתו. ב"ח: (יב) בתורה. אבל העוסק בגמרא אפשר דלא מיפטר עיין ב"י: (יג) בפניו. ולא יחלוץ

ביאור הלכה

מלאכתן וכו'. עיין במ"ב סקכ"ו שהעתקתי מלבוש לדינא וכן משמע לכאורה מלשון נריכין שכתב הרמ"א אך קשה דכיון דדעת הרמ"א הוא כשיטת הר"ן וכמו שמחייב בעצמו ולהר"ן פטור בכל גווני אם כבר התחיל לכתוב כמו שמוכח בב"י ואולי אפשר לאמר דבכה"ג שאחד רוצה לפרוש ליס או לשיירא ששם לא ישיג תפילין כמה ימים מותר אפילו לכתחילה להתחיל לכתוב אפילו אחר שהגיע זמן ק"ש אפילו אם עי"ז יעבור הזמן ומ"מ לא נהירא דלמה יחוייב להכניס עצמו לזה להתחיל לכתוב או למכור להיות עליו שם עוסק במצוה ולסלק מעצמו עי"ז המ"ע דק"ש ותפילין וכדומה וכי אומרים לו לאדם חטא וכו' וצ"ע. גם מדברי המ"א סוף סק"י שכתב דכ"ז מיירי וכו' לא משמע כן אך יש לומר דהוא לא איירי בכה"ג דהלבוש ולולי דברי הלבוש היה אפשר לומר דכונת הרמ"א במה שכתב שהיו נריכין ר"ל דהסופר משער שיבוא היום לידו קונים הרבה ע"כ הוא מקדים ומזרז עצמו לזה דאל"ה מסתמא לא יעשה הסופר כן לכתוב תמיד יום ולילה שלא ישאר לו מעט פנאי לשום מצוה ואף לקבלת מ"ש ולתפילין וכן משמע בעבודת היום: * אז פטורין. עיין במ"ב מש"כ בשם המ"א ובדיעבד אפילו אם התחיל באיסור אעפ"כ אין נריך להפסיק דמ"מ הרי עוסק במצוה וכדאיתא שם בסי' ע"ב דאם התחילו להוציאו אין מפסיקין ואפילו אחר שהגיע זמן ק"ש כמו שכתב הפר"ח שם: * דכל העוסק וכו'. עיין בסוכה כ"ו דשלוחי מצוה כגון שהולך להקביל פני רבו או לפדות שבויים הוא ג"כ בכלל עוסק במצוה ופטור מכל המצות: * אם צריך לטרוח. עיין במ"ב וכן כתב הר"ן ואף דהתוספות והרא"ש ורי"ו מחמירין בזה מ"מ משמע מהב"י והרמ"א דמסכימים להלכה להר"ן והג"א בשם או"ז מפני הראיות העצומות שהביאו לזה וכן המ"א הביא בשם הה"מ שהרמב"ם והגאונים ג"כ סוברים דפטור אפילו דיכול לקיים שתיהן וטעם הדבר כתב הר"ן לפי שכל שעוסק במלאכתו של מקום לא חייבתו תורה לטרוח ולקיים מצות אחרות אע"פ שאפשר לו, ולכן המשמר את המת פטור מתפילין ומק"ש ומכל המצוות אע"פ שיכול אז לקיים כמה מצות וכן החופר קבר למת פטור מכולם אע"פ שנח מעט שגם בשעת נוחו נקרא עדיין עוסק במצוה שעי"ז יתחזק כוחו לחזור ולחפור ולכן הוא פטור אז אע"פ שיכול אז לתת פרוטה לעני העומד אצלו אבל מי שלבוש בתפילין אע"פ שמקיים מצוה אינו נקרא עוסק במצוה להפטר מכל המצות אלא בשעה שלובשן אבל לא אח"כ וכן לענין משמר אבידה וכמו שכתבתי במ"ב כ"ז מתבאר מדברי הר"ן ואו"ז ומש"כ הרמ"א אבל אם וכו' בלא טורח ר"ל שאינו מוסיף טרחה כלל בשביל מצוה השניה אלא טורח אחד לשתיהן וכדרכו במצוה הראשונה יכול לצאת ידי שתיהן אז בודאי יראה לצאת ידי שתיהן דמהיות טוב אל יקרא רע כן כתב הר"ן שם ומהראיה שהביא שם ע"ז מהגמרא משמע דחיובא הוא מצד הדין דאל"ה לא מקשי הגמרא שם מידי ועיין: * הקורא בתורה פטור וכו'. עיין במ"ב ס"ק ל"ג דקודם לזה חייב כן איתא בביאור

משנה ברורה

ואי אפשר לו להמתין עד שהסופר או התגר יקיים מצוה אחת שבאה לידו כגון הנחת תפילין או ק"ש וה"ה שאר כל המצות ע"כ מותר לכתוב ולמכור לזה אע"פ שעי"ז יעבור זמן המצוה [לבוש] ועי' בבה"ל: (כז) אז פטורין וכו'. ומיירי שכבר התחיל לכתוב קודם שהגיע זמן ק"ש אבל משהגיע הזמן אסור להתחיל לכתוב כמש"כ סי' ע"ב ס"ב כ"כ המ"א אכן לפי מה שציירנו מתחלה בשם הלבוש שהקונה צריך לעבור בים או בשיירא וא"א לו להמתין עד שהסופר יקיים[א] ק"ש ותפלה פשוט דלכו"ע מותר הסופר לעשות לו מלאכתו אם הוא משער שישאר לו זמן לקרות ואם יוכל לקרוא פרשה אחת מקודם יקרא: (כח) דכל העוסק וכו'. ודוקא עוסק במצוה כגון בשעה שהוא לובש התפילין או עוסק בתיקוני האבידה כגון לשוטחה לצורכה או להשיבה לבעליה וכל כה"ג אבל בשעה שהוא מקיים מצוה כגון שהוא כבר לבוש תפילין או שומר אבידה שהיא מונחת כבר בתיבתו וכל כה"ג אע"פ שהוא מקיים מצוה אינו עוסק במצוה ולא מיפטר ממצוה אחרת עי"ז ועיין בבה"ל שביארתי יותר: (כט) אם צריך וכו'. ר"ל ואפילו אם עי"ז לא יתבטל המצוה הראשונה ואפילו אם המצוה השניה יותר גדולה כיון שכבר התחיל לעסוק בראשונה [או"ז וריטב"א]: **ט** (ל) מצטער. אפילו (טז) מפני הצינה. ועיין בסמוך: (לא) שאין דעתו וכו'. ומיירי (יז) בשא"א לו ליישב דעתו אבל אם אפשר לו חייב ליישב דעתו ולהניחן: י (לב) בתורה. אפשר (יח) דדוקא בתורה שבכתב אבל לא בעוסק בגמרא דתורה י"ל שהיא עצמה אות שנזכר בה יציאת מצרים: (לג) פטור. ר"ל שא"צ לפסוק מלימודו כדי להניחם אבל קודם לזה (יט) חייב. גם מתלמע אם רוצה לפסוק ולהניח ג"כ (כ) רשאי ויכול (כא) לברך עליהן שאע"פ שפטור מלהפסיק בשבילן מ"מ כיון שרוצה להפסיק מלימודו הרי חייב בתפילין מיד שמפסיק: (לד) מהנחת תפילין. ואע"ג שמחוייב להפסיק מת"ת כדי לקיים כל המצות שמוטלין עליו כדאיתא ביו"ד סימן ר"מ[ב] (כב) שאני מצות תפילין שעיקר מוצאתה הוא לתורה כדכתיב ולזכרון בין עיניך למען תהיה תורת ה' בפיך ע"כ מכיון שכבר עוסק בתורה מקודם אין צריך לבטל תורה בשביל זה זולת בשעת ק"ש ותפלה כדי לקבל עליו עול מלכות שמים וגם שאז עדיין אינו עוסק בתורה ומחוייב להיות עליו תפילין. והגר"א פסק בביאורו דדוקא מי שתורתו אומנתו כגון רשב"י וחבריו אבל כגון אנו צריכין להפסיק אף לתפילין: **יא** (לה) בפני רבו. היינו רבו מובהק דרוב חכמתו הימנו: (לו) מפני אימתו. ר"ל (כג) דזלזול הוא שמגלה ראשו בפניו ולפ"ז (כד) אפילו אם כבר הלך רבו תחלה אסור ואם מטה עצמו קצת לצד אחר וחזיר מלגלות ראשו בפניו נראה דיש להקל בכל גווני כ"כ הפמ"ג ועי"ש עוד דמשמע מיניה דאם הולכן סמוך לתשיבה יש להחמיר בכל גווני מלחלוץ אותם קודם שהלך רבו דנראה

שער הציון

(טז) מ"א: (יז) ב"ח ומ"א והגר"א וש"א דלא כהפמ"ג: (יח) כ"כ המ"א והעולם לא נהגו לחלק בזה גם בביאור הגר"א משמע דלא ס"ל חילוק זה אלא מי שתורתו אומנתו פטור בכל גווני: (יט) כן מוכח מהגר"א ע"ש: (כ) הגר"א: (כא) ב"י: (כב) הגר"א: (כג) ט"ז: (כד) אף דבטור מקיל בזה כבר כתב הב"י דלמעשה נכון לחוש להחמיר:

הגהות ותיקונים: א) חסר תיבה מצות: ב) סימן רמ"ו:

to read/ "The Reading of Shema" and /pray the eighteen-blessing/ prayer (27) *they are then exempt from /reading/ "The Reading of Shema", /praying the eighteen-blessing/ prayer and /donning/* tefilin. (28) */This is/ because whoever is occupied*[3*] *with /the performance of/ a mitzvah is exempt from /performing/ another mitzvah,* (29) *if he needs to exert himself over /the performance of/ the other /mitzvah/. However, if one is able to perform both /mitzvos/ simultaneously without exertion,*[4*] *he should /in fact/ perform both of them. (...)*

9. (30) Someone who is distressed or someone (31) whose mind is not at ease and composed is exempt /from donning *tefilin*/; as it is forbidden for one to distract his mind from them /while he is wearing them/.

Mishnah Berurah

unable to wait until the scribe or the broker will have fulfilled /even/ a single mitzvah which has come to hand, such as the donning of *tefilin*, /the reading of/ "The Reading of Shema" or, correspondingly, any other mitzvah. In view of this, they are permitted to write and to sell to this /person/, even though because of it the time during which the /other/ mitzvah /can be fulfilled/ will pass. [*Levush*] See the Beyur Halachah.

(27) They are then exempt, etc. /The gloss/ is referring to /an instance/ when /the scribe/ already began to write before the time for /reading/ "The Reading of Shema" arrived. However, once this time has arrived he is forbidden to begin writing,[4] as /follows from what is/ stated in Sec. 72, Par. 2. This is what the *M.A.* writes.

On the other hand, bearing in mind what we have portrayed in the beginning in the name of the *Levush*, that /we are speaking of an instance when/ the buyer must travel by sea or /join/ a caravan and is unable to wait until the scribe will fulfil /the mitzvah of reading/ "The Reading of Shema" and /praying the eighteen-blessing/ prayer, it is self-understood that, according to all /authorities/, the scribe is permitted to do the work for him if he judges that there will be /sufficient/ time left for him to read /"The Reading of Shema" later/. If /the scribe/ is able to read one passage /of "The Reading of Shema"/ beforehand, he should /in fact/ read it.

(28) /This is/ because whoever is occupied, etc. /This applies/ specifically when one is /actually/ occupied with the mitzvah. For example, /it applies/ when one is putting on *tefilin* or is occupied with attending to a lost article, such as when one is spreading out /the article/ because it requires this or returning it to its owner or /doing/ anything of a comparable character. However, when one is /merely/ fulfilling a mitzvah, such as when he is already wearing *tefilin* or is safeguarding a lost article which is already lying in his cabinet or /doing/ anything of a similar nature /, then/, although he is fulfilling a mitzvah he is not /in fact/ occupied with the mitzvah. /Consequently,/ he is not exempt from /fulfilling/ another mitzvah because of that /mitzvah/. See the Beyur Halachah, where I have explained this more.

(29) If he needs, etc. I.e., even if because of /the second mitzvah/ the first mitzvah will not be set aside and even if the second mitzvah is more important, since he already began to occupy himself with the first /mitzvah/. [*O.Z.* and *Ritba*]

(30) Someone who is distressed. /I.e.,/ even /if it is/ because of the cold. See /what we have written/ nearby.

(31) Whose mind is not, etc. /The Shulchan Aruch/ is referring to /an instance/ when he cannot calm his mind, but if he is able /to do so/ he is obliged to calm his mind and don /*tefilin*/.

3* Someone who is on a mitzvah mission, such as to redeem captives, is also classed as such. (Beyur Halachah)

4* I.e., if they can be performed without any additional exertion being necessary for the second mitzvah. (Beyur Halachah)

4 If one did begin to write in transgression, he does not need to interrupt the writing. (Beyur Halachah)

מלאכתן בשעת ק"ש ותפלה (כז) * אז פטורין מק"ש ותפלה ומתפילין (כח) * דכל העוסק במצוה פטור ממצוה (ע) אחרת (כט) * אם צריך לטרוח אחר האחרת אבל אם יכול לעשות שתיהן כאחת בלא טורח יעשה שתיהן (הגהת אשרי בשם א"ז ור"ן פ' הישן): **ט** (י) (ל) ˙מצטער ומי (לא) שאין דעתו מיושבת (יא) עליו ונכונה פטור ˙מפני שאסור להסיח דעתו מהם: **י** * ˡהקורא (יב) [ג] (לב) בתורה (לג) פטור (לד) מהנחת תפילין כל היום זולת בשעת ק"ש ותפלה: **יא** ᵐלא יחלוץ תפילין (לה) בפני רבו ˢאלא יפנה לצד אחר (לו) מפני אימתו ויחלוץ שלא (יג) בפניו: **יב** ˢהיה צריך לתפילין ומזוזה ואין ידו משגת לקנות

י הרמב"ם בפ"ד מה"ת ב הר"ר מנוח ל מכילתא לפי' ר' יונה בפ"ב דברכות מ בשימושא רבא וסנהד' ק"א נ רש"י שם ס ירושלמי שילהי מגילה וכרב הונא כ"כ הרא"ש בה"ר

שערי תשובה

ונתעכב ביום ב' שלא להניח תפילין עד הנץ החמה כדי להסתלק מן הספק ע"ש ואם מת לו מת ברגל או שמע שמועה רחוקה ברגל שאינו נוהג אבילות ומתחיל למנות אחר הרגל כתב בכנה"ג שאסור להניח תפילין ביום ראשון. ובבר"י חלק עליו וכתב דחייב ואפי' אי הוה ספיקא אין לבטל מצוה רבה כזו מספק. וכ"כ בבית לחם יהודה ביו"ד סי' שפ"ח וחלק על הכנה"ג ע"ש. וגם במ"ש בבה"ט בשם מהריט"ץ חולק עליו בבר"י ובמח"ב וסיים בה סוף דבר נ"ל דיום הקבורה אעפ"י שאינו יום מיתה אסור בתפילין וע"ש שכתב שכן מוכח מהט"ז ומ"ב וכן הא"ר ע"ש. ובש"ן כתב ג"כ בשם ספר דרך המלך דלא כמהריט"ץ: [ג] בתורה.

באר היטב

כדי להשתכר לא מיקרי עוסק במצוה מ"א: (ט) אחרת. כל זה מיירי שכבר התחיל לכתוב קודם שהגיע זמן ק"ש אבל משהגיע אסור להתחיל עיין סימן ע"ב ס"ב: (י) מצטער. אפילו מפני הצנה. מגן אברהם: (יא) עליו. דוקא כשא"א לו ליישב דעתו. ב"ח: (יב) בתורה. אבל העוסק בגמרא אפשר דלא מיפטר עיין ב"י: (יג) בפניו. ולא יחלוץ

ביאור הלכה

מלאכתן וכו'. עיין במ"ב סקכ"ו שהעתקתי מלבוש לדינא וכן משמע לכאורה מלשון נריכין שכתב הרמ"א אך קשה דכיון דדעת הרמ"א הוא כשיטת הר"ן וכמו שמחייב בעצמו ולהר"ן פטור בכל גווני אם כבר התחיל לכתוב כמו שמוכח בב"י ואולי אפשר לאמר דבכה"ג שאחד רוצה לפרוש ליס או לשיירא שאם לא ישיג תפילין כמה ימים מותר אפילו לכתחילה להתחיל לכתוב אפילו אחר שהגיע זמן ק"ש אפילו אם עי"ז יעבור הזמן ומ"מ לא נהירא דלמה יחוייב. להכניס עצמו לזה להתחיל לכתוב או למכור להיות עליו שם עוסק במצוה ולסלק מעצמו עי"ז המ"ע דק"ש ותפילין וכדומה וכי אומרים לו לאדם חטא וכו' וצ"ע. גם מדברי המ"א סוף סק"י שכתב דכ"ז מיירי וכו' לא משמע כן אך יש לומר דהוא לא איירי בכה"ג דהלבוש ולולי דברי הלבוש היה אפשר לומר דכונת הרמ"א במה שכתב שהיו נריכין ר"ל דהסופר משער שיבוא היום לידו קונים הרבה ע"כ הוא מקדים ומזרז עצמו לזה דאל"ה מסתמא לא יעשה הסופר כן לכתוב תמיד יום ולילה שלא ישאר לו מעט פנאי לשום מצוה ואף לקבלת מ"ש ולתפילין וכן משמע בעבודת היום: * אז פטורין. עיין במ"ב מש"כ בשם המ"א ובדיעבד אפילו אם התחיל באיסור אעפ"כ אין נריך להפסיק דמ"מ הרי עוסק במצוה וכדאיתא שם בסי' ע"ב דאם התחילו להוליאו אין מפסיקין ואפילו אחר שהגיע זמן ק"ש כמו שכתב הפר"ח שם: * דכל העוסק וכו'. עיין בסוכה כ"ו דשלוחי מצוה כגון שהולך להקביל פני רבו או לפדות שבויים הוא ג"כ בכלל עוסק במצוה ופטור מכל המצות: * אם צריך לטרוח. עיין במ"ב וכן כתב הר"ן ואף דהתוספות והרא"ש ורי"ו מחמירין בזה מ"מ משמע מהב"י והרמ"א דמסכימים להלכה להר"ן והג"א בשם או"ז מפני הראיות העצומות שהביאו לזה וכן המ"א הביא בשם הה"מ שהרמב"ם והגאונים ג"כ סוברים דפטור אפילו ביכול לקיים שתיהן וטעם הדבר כתב הר"ן לפי שכל שעוסק במלאכתו של מקום לא חייבתו תורה לטרוח ולקיים מצות אחרות אע"פ שאפשר לו, ולכן המשמר את המת פטור מתפילין ומק"ש ומכל המצוות אע"פ שיכול אז לקיים כמה מצות וכן החופר קבר למת פטור מכולם אע"פ שנח מעט שגם בשעת נוחו נקרא עדיין עוסק במצוה שעי"ז יתחזק כוחו לחזור ולחפור ולכן הוא פטור אז אע"פ שיכול אז לתת פרוטה לעני העומד אצלו אבל מי שלבוש בתפילין אע"פ שמקיים מצוה אינו נקרא עוסק במצוה להפטר מכל המצות אלא בשעה שלובשן אבל לא אח"כ וכן לענין משמר אבידה וכמו שכתבתי במ"ב כ"ז מתבאר מדברי הר"ן ואו"ז ומש"כ הרמ"א אבל אם וכו' בלא טורח ר"ל שאינו מוסיף טרחה כלל בשביל מצוה השניה אלא טורח אחד לשתיהן וכדרכו במצוה הראשונה יכול לצאת ידי שתיהן אז בודאי יראה לצאת ידי שתיהן דמהיות טוב אל יקרא רע כן כתב הר"ן שם ומהראיה שהביא שם ע"ז מהגמרא משמע דחיובא הוא מצד הדין דאל"ה לא מקשי הגמרא שם מידי ועיין: * הקורא בתורה פטור וכו'. עיין במ"ב ס"ק ל"ג דקודם לזה חייב כן איתא בביאור

משנה ברורה

ואי אפשר לו להמתין עד שהסופר או התגר יקיים מצוה אחת שבאה לידו כגון הנחת תפילין או ק"ש וה"ה שאר כל המצות ע"כ מותר לכתוב ולמכור לזה אע"פ שעי"ז יעבור זמן המצוה [לבוש] ועי' בבה"ל: (כז) אז פטורין וכו'. ומיירי שכבר התחיל לכתוב קודם שהגיע זמן ק"ש אבל משהגיע הזמן אסור להתחיל לכתוב כמש"כ סי' ע"ב ס"ב כ"כ המ"א אכן לפי מה שביארנו מתחלה בשם הלבוש שהקונה צריך לעבור בים או בשיירא וא"א לו להמתין עד שהסופר יקיים ק"ש ותפלה משום דלכו"ע מותר הסופר לעשות לו מלאכתו אם הוא משער שישאר לו זמן לקרות ואם יוכל לקרות פרשה אחת מקודם יקרא: (כח) דכל העוסק וכו'. ודוקא עוסק במצוה כגון בשעה שהוא לובש התפילין או עוסק בתיקוני האבידה כגון לשוטחה לצורכה או להשיבה לבעליה וכל כה"ג אבל בשעה שהוא מקיים מצוה כגון שהוא כבר לבוש תפילין או שומר אבידה שהיא מונחת כבר בביתו וכל כה"ג אע"פ שהוא מקיים מצוה איננו עוסק במצוה ולא מיפטר ממצוה אחרת עי"ז ועיין בבה"ל שביארתי יותר: (כט) אם צריך וכו'. ר"ל ואפילו אם עי"ז לא יתבטל המצוה הראשונה ואפילו אם המצוה השניה יותר גדולה כיון שכבר התחיל לעסוק בראשונה [או"ז וריטב"א]: ט (ל) מצטער. אפילו (עז) מפני הצינה. ועיין בסמוך: (לא) שאין דעתו וכו'. ומיירי (יז) כשא"א לו ליישב דעתו אבל אם אפשר לו חייב ליישב דעתו ולהניחן: י (לב) בתורה. אפשר (יח) דדוקא בתורה שבכתב אבל לא בעוסק בגמרא דתורה י"ל שהיא עצמה אות שנזכר בה יציאת מצרים: (לג) פטור. ר"ל שא"ל לפסוק מלימודו כדי להניחם אבל קודס לזה (יט) חייב. גם באמצע אם רוצה לפסוק ולהניח ג"כ (כ) רשאי ויכול (כא) לברך עליהן שאע"פ שפטור מלהפסיק בשבילן מ"מ כיון שרוצה להפסיק מלימודו הרי חייב בתפילין מיד שמפסיק: (לד) מהנחת תפילין. ואע"ג שמחוייב להפסיק מת"ת כדי לקיים כל המצות שחיובן עליו כדאיתא ביו"ד סימן ר"מ[ב] (כב) שאני מצות תפילין שעיקר תועלתה הוא לתורה כדכתיב ולזכרון בין עיניך למען תהיה תורת ה' בפיך ע"כ מכיון שכבר עוסק בתורה מקודם אין צריך לבטל תורה בשביל זה זולת בשעת ק"ש ותפלה כדי לקבל עליו עול מלכות שמים וגם שאז עדיין אינו עוסק בתורה ומחוייב להיות עליו תפילין. והגר"א פסק בביאורו דדוקא מי שתורתו אומנתו כגון רשב"י וחבריו אבל כגון אנו צריכין להפסיק אף לתפילין: **יא** (לה) בפני רבו. היינו רבו מובהק דרוב חכמתו הימנו: (לו) מפני אימתו. ר"ל (כג) דזלזול הוא שמגלה ראשו בפניו ולפ"ז (כד) אפילו אם כבר חלץ רבו תחלה אסור ואם מטה עצמו קצת לצד אחר וזהיר מלגלות ראשו בפניו נראה דיש להקל בכל גווני כ"כ הפמ"ג ועי"ש עוד דמשמע מיניה דאם חולצן סמוך לחשיכה יש להחמיר בכל גווני מלחלוץ אותם קודם שחלץ רבו דנראה

שער הציון

(עז) מ"א: (יז) ב"ח ומ"א והגר"א וש"א דלא כהפמ"ג: (יח) כ"כ המ"א והעולם לא נהגו לחלק בזה גם בביאור הגר"א משמע דלא ס"ל חילוק זה אלא מי שתורתו אומנתו פטור בכל גווני: (יט) כן מוכח מהגר"א ע"ש: (כ) הגר"א: (כא) ב"י: (כב) הגר"א: (כג) ט"ז: (כד) אף דבטור מקיל בזה כבר כתב הב"י דלמעשה נכון לחוש להחמיר:

הגהות ותיקונים: **א)** חסר תיבה מצות: **ב)** סימן רמ"ו:

10. Someone who reads (32) Torah (33) is exempt (34) from donning *tefilin* all day, except at the time when /he reads/ "The Reading of Shema" and /prays the eighteen-blessing/ prayer.

11. One should not take off *tefilin* (35) facing his /Torah/ teacher, but should /first/ turn in another direction (36) out of fear of him and /then/ take them off without facing him.

12. If one is in need of *tefilin* and of a mezuzah and does not have enough

Mishnah Berurah

(32) Torah. It may be that this only /applies/ in the case of written Torah, but not when one is occupied with /the study of/ Gemara. For one could argue that the /written/ Torah is itself a sign[5] /, just like *tefilin*/, since the exodus from Egypt is mentioned in it.

(33) Is exempt. I.e., he is not required to interrupt his study in order to don /*tefilin*/, but before /he actually studies/ he is obliged /to don *tefilin*/. /In fact,/ even when he is in the middle /of his Torah study/, if he wishes to interrupt it and don /*tefilin*/ he is allowed /to do so/ and may make a blessing over them. /This is/ because although he is exempt from interrupting /his study/ for the sake of /donning *tefilin*/, he is nevertheless obliged /to don/ *tefilin* as soon as he /does/ interrupt /his study/, since he wishes to interrupt the study /for this purpose/.

(34) From donning *tefilin*. Although one is obliged to interrupt Torah study in order to fulfil all the mitzvos which are incumbent upon him, as stated in the *Yo.D.*, Sec. 240, the mitzvah of *tefilin* differs /from other mitzvos/ in that its main avail is for Torah /study/. For it is stated[6] /with respect to the mitzvah/, "And for a reminder between your eyes, in order that the Torah of the Lord will be in your mouth". Consequently, once one is already engaged in Torah /study/ which /he began/ earlier, he does not need to neglect Torah /study/ for the sake of /donning *tefilin*/. /He is therefore exempt from donning *tefilin*/ except at the time when /he must read/ "The Reading of Shema" and /pray the eighteen-blessing/ prayer, in order to accept upon himself the yoke of the Kingdom of Heaven. In addition, he is not yet occupied with Torah /study/ then and is obliged to have *tefilin* on him.

The *Gra* rules in his *Beyur* that /the ruling of the Shulchan Aruch/ only /applies to/ a person for whom Torah study is his profession, such as *Rashbi* and his fellows, but /people/ like us must interrupt /our Torah study/ even for /donning/ *tefilin.*

(35) Facing his teacher. I.e., his main /Torah/ teacher, from whom /he received/ most of his knowledge.

(36) Out of fear of him. What is meant by this is that /it is disrespectful/ for him to expose his head before his /Torah teacher/. Accordingly, even if his /Torah/ teacher already took off /his own *tefilin*/ first it is /also/ forbidden.

If one inclines himself somewhat in another direction and is careful not to expose his head before /his Torah teacher/, it appears that he may be lenient in all cases. This is what the *P.Mg.* writes.

See there further, that it is implied by him that if one takes off /*tefilin*/ close to the onset of darkness he should be stringent in all cases and avoid taking /his *tefilin*/ off before his /Torah/ teacher has taken /his own

5 The Torah describes *tefilin* as serving as a sign. In view of this, they may not be donned on Shabbos or Yom Tov, since these days also serve as a sign (see Sec. 31, Par. 1). It is suggested that the reason why one does not need to interrupt Torah study in order to don *tefilin* is that the Torah is also a sign and that this is the case only where the written Torah is involved.

6 *Shemos* 13:9.

שניהם (לז) תפילין (יד) [ד] קודמים: **יג** (לח) ⁽ע⁾מנודה ומצורע אסורים להניח תפילין:

לט מי הם הכשרים לכתוב תפילין ולקנות מהם. ובו י' סעיפים:

א (א) ⁽א⁾תפילין שכתבן עבד (ב) או אשה (א) [א] (ג) * או קטן ⁽ב⁾אפילו הגיע (ד) לחנוך (ג) (ה) ⁽ג⁾או כותי

ע איבעיא במ"ק ובעיטור אוסר
א גיטין מ"ה
ב מרדכי שם
ג נמוקי יוסף

באר היטב

קמי ס"ת עי"ל סימן כ"ה ס"ג[א]: (יד) קודמים. ואם אפשר בשאלה מזוזה קודמת דא"א בשאלה. מ"א:

(א) או קטן. ובעינן שיהא דוקא גדול ממש דהיינו שהביא שתי שערות אחר שהוא בן י"ג שנה אבל מספיקא פסול לכתוב עד שיהא בן י"ח שנה. מ"א: (ב) או כותי. כצ"ל דעובד כוכבים בלא"ה פסול

שערי תשובה

עבה"ט והם דברי המג"א ומ"ש עיין ב"י ר"ל דבב"י מבואר שאף שכתב ליישב דברי בעה"ע דמחלק דדוקא בתורה משום זכרון יציאת מצרים כו' דלא תקשי עליו ממ"ש הטור מ"מ סיים בה שאין דברי בעה"ע נראים וכן בש"ע כאן נראה שמסכים לדברי רבינו יונה ע"ש וכן נראה מהירושלמי ריש שבת גבי מפסיקין לק"ש כו'. ועיין בשו"ת בית אפרים חלק א"ח וכתב במח"ב בקו"א בשם אור לדיקים שמ"כ בשם הרמב"ן ומהרח"ו שחייב כל אדם לומר ד' פרשיות תפילין בעודן עליו והב' פ' אומרם בק"ש וקדש והיה כי יביאך ל"ל קודם ברוך שאמר שהם קודמות לשמע והיה אם שמוע עכ"ד. ונראה שאם א"א לאומרם קודם ב"ש יאמרם אחר עלינו קודם שמסיר התפילין עכ"ל. והעולם נהגו לומר קדש והיה כי יביאך וק"ש בתפילין של ר"ת שמניחים אחר התפלה. ויש מדקדקים לומר גם בתפילין של רש"י קדש והיה כי יביאך קודם ב"ש והנוהג כן אם לא אמר קודם ב"ש אין לסמוך על מה שיאמר אחר כך בתפילין של ר"ת אלא יקרא קדש והיה כי יביאך קודם שיחלוץ של רש"י: [ד] קודמים. עבה"ט ועיין לעיל ר"ס כ"ה לענין תפילין וציצית ומשם נלמד לכאן:

[א] או קטן. עבה"ט וכתב בבכור שור בגיטין דף מ"ה דתפילין שכתבן חרש או שוטה פסולין אע"ג דבש"ע לא הזכיר אלא קטן לחוד וע"ש שכתב לתרץ קושיית המג"א על הב"י מיו"ד סי' קנ"ח וכתב בנודע ביהודה מ"ת סי' א' תפילין שכתבן נער בן י"ג שנה ויום אחד או יותר קצת ולא בדקוהו אם יש לו סימני גדלות ואינו לפנינו התפילין כשרים דסמכינן אחזקה כיון שהגיע לכלל שנים הביא סימנים אבל לכתחלה לא. ויש לגעור בסופרים שמניחים לנערים לכתוב תפילין ואין מדקדקים אם הביאו סימני גדלות או לא ע"ש. וכתב במח"ב בשם דברי יוסף סי' י"ב דאם כתב טומטום או אנדרוגינוס פסול ואם טומטום שנקרע

משנה ברורה

דנראה שמורה הלכה בפני רבו שהגיע זמנו לחלוץ ועיין לעיל סימן כ"ה ס"ק כ"ח מ"ש שם בשם הפמ"ג: **יב** (לז) תפילין קודמים. דהיא מצוה שבגופו ועוד דקדושת תפילין למעלה מקדושת מזוזה וכדלעיל בסימן ל"ב ס"ח. מיהו לדידן שאין מניחין רק בשעת ק"ש ותפלה אם אפשר בשאלה מזוזה קודמת דא"א בשאלה [מ"א]: **יג** (לח) מנודה ומצורע וכו'. עיין בל"ח ובש"ך ביו"ד סי' של"ד ס"ב ובשארי אחרונים דפוסקים להיפך וכתב הפמ"ג דיניחו בלי ברכה אבל מביאור הגר"א משמע לכאורה דצריכין לברך ג"כ:

א (א) תפילין. וה"ה (א) ס"ת ומזוזה: (ב) או אשה. וה"ה (ב) טומטום ואנדרוגינוס דהם בכלל ספק אשה: (ג) או קטן. וכיון דילפינן מקרא בעינן שיהא דוקא גדול ממש דהיינו שהביא ב"ש אחר שהוא בן י"ג שנה אבל אם ספק לנו אם הביא ב"ש (ג) פסול לכתוב אם לא שנתמלא זקנו דהיינו שיש ריבוי שער בזקנו אף שהם קטנים מאד [סמ"ע בח"מ סימן ל"ה] או שעברו רוב שנותיו או שנולדו בו סימני סריס וכדלקמן בסימן נ"ה ס"ה. ויש לגעור (ד) בסופרים שמניחין לנערים לכתוב תפילין ואין מדקדקין אם הביאו סימני גדלות או לא. ועיין לעיל בסימן ל"ב סעיף קטן ק"ג מ"ש שם בשם הלבוש מענין זה ועיין בבה"ל: (ד) לחינוך. באמת אפילו גדול לא כל זמן שלא ידעינן שהביא ב"ש אך לענין גדול אם אח"כ בדקוהו ומצאו שיש לו ב"ש תלינן שהיה לו ג"כ בעת הכתיבה [ח"מ סימן ל"ה] משא"כ בקטן דאינו מועיל אז שערות: (ה) או כותי. כצ"ל דעו"ג (ה) בלא"ה פסול

ביאור הלכה

הגר"א והעולם נוהגין להקל בזה ואפשר שטעמם שסומכין על הא דסימן ל"ז ס"ב ועיין מה שכתבתי שם בביאור הלכה ועיין עוד בביאור הגר"א שמשמע מדבריו שאפילו לדעת השו"ע דלא מחלק לענין תורתו אומנתו לא מקילינן רק לענין שא"צ לפסוק מלימודו כדי להניחה אבל אם הם כבר עליו שלבשן לק"ש ותפלה או קודם שהתחיל ללמוד אז צריך שיהיו עליו אף בעת הלימוד ולא יסלקם באמצע דומיא דמאי דפסק בהג"ה בסעיף הקודם דהיכא דבלי טורח יוכל לעשות שתיהן דצריך לעשות שתיהן:

* או קטן. ואם כתבן חרש או שוטה הניח הפמ"ג בפתיחה בצ"ע דאפשר דעדיפי מקטן ומהני אם אחרים עומדין ע"ג ומרמזין לחרש ושוטה שיכתוב לשמן. וסימני שוטה מבואר ביו"ד בסימן א' ס"ה. ולענין קטן אימת נעשה גדול אם לא ידעינן שהביא ב"ש כתבתי במ"ב אם נתמלא זקנו והוא מח"מ סימן ל"ה והשמטתי דברי המ"א שכתב עד י"ח שכל האחרונים השיגו עליו [הלא המה הא"ר והב"מ ודגמ"ר ומחה"ש ולבו"ש ותשו' רע"א בחא"ח סימן ז'] ומ"מ אין בידינו לפוסלם אחרי שהח"א וגם השלחן שלמה מקילין לכתחלה. וראיתי בפמ"ג שסתר ליישב דברי המג"א והביא מסימן נ"ג ס"ח בהג"ה דמי"ח והלאה קרוי נתמלא זקנו וכונת הפמ"ג דמבואר שם דמי"ח והלאה אף אם יש לו זקן מעט קרוי נתמלא זקנו וה"נ כונת המג"א דיש לו זקן מעט ומ"מ באמת לע"ג בזה דאפשר דשם שאני דהלא שם איירי שהביא ב"ש דהוא גדול מן התורה ולא בעינן הזקן רק מפני כבוד הצבור תדע דשם מהני ג"כ אם הוא בן כ' ואין לו זקן כלל מקרי ג"כ עי"ז נתמלא זקנו כמבואר שם בשו"ע והכל מטעם זה דהוא רק מפני כבוד הצבור משא"כ בענינינו דלא ידעינן אם הביא ב"ש והזקן מהני לעשותו גדול עי"ז אפשר דבעינן מלוי זקנו ממש הא פשיטא לי דע"י סיכי דיקני [שיש לו במקומות מיוחדות שער בזקנו] בודאי לא קרוי נתמלא זקנו וראיה מוכרחת מיבמות פ' ע"ב בתוספות ד"ה דהביא ב"ש בסופו ואור"י דאין חשוב וכו' וה"ה דסיכי דיקני ג"כ אינו בכלל מלוי זקן דאל"ה ישאר קושית התוספות על רבה בר אבוה לפי תירוץ הגמרא שם וידוע דדין נתמלא זקנו דלא צריך שוב בדיקה נובע מאותו התוספות כמבואר בטור אה"ע בסי' קס"ט בב"י שם הגם דבב"י בח"מ סימן ל"ה בראשו משמע דהטוח"מ סובר דאפילו לא נתמלא זקנו מהני עכ"ז בהשו"ע שלו העתיק דדוקא אם נתמלא זקנו כי מיבעי לי לענין זקן מעט המבואר בסימן נ"ג דאפשר לפי מה שביארנו שם בשם מהרש"ל שהעתיק מתשובות הגאונים דהיינו שיהיו נמלאים שערות גדולות משני לידי הפנים ומלד הסנטר אפשר דזהו בכלל נתמלא זקנו בכל מקום אפילו לענין דאורייתא או דילמא שם שאני דהוא רק מפני כבוד הצבור ומ"מ אפשר שיש להקל בזה לפי מה שביאר הגר"א שם בח"מ דטעם הטור הוא לפי שע"פ רוב רגיל לבוא סימן התחתון קודם שבא סימן זה העליון לכן תלינן דמסתמא כבר בא התחתון א"כ לפ"ז בודאי דברי הטור שכתב באה"ע נתמלא זקנו הוא לאו דוקא ובח"מ שכתב למח זקנו בדיוק כתבו דגם זה רגיל לבוא זמן הרבה אחר הבאת ב' שערות ולפ"ז אפשר לומר שגם סיכי דיקנא מהני להשוותו גדול לכל דבר דמסתמא כבר הביא ב' שערות ושם ביבמות פ' ע"ב לענין ר"ג שאני שידעו שלא הביא ר"ג ב' שערות וצ"ע. היוצא מדברינו עכ"פ קודם שיש לו קצת זקן בודאי אין להניחו לכתוב תפילין כ"ז שלא ידעינן שהביא ב' שערות אפילו אם הוא כבר בן י"ח שנה ויותר וכמו שכתבתי במ"ב. אך בדיעבד אם כתבן נער בר מצוה ואין לפנינו לבדקו צ"ע למעשה דהנ"ב מ"ת בסימן א' מכשיר וכן בפמ"ג בסימן ל"ט ובסימן נ"ה אות ז' ג"כ מוכח הכי דמדמה שם לענין בדיקת הריאה ובריאה קי"ל דאם נאבדה בלי בדיקה כשר ובתשובת רע"א תא"ח סימן ז' פוסל וכן בספר ישועות יעקב בסימן ל"ג ג"כ מחמיר אך בבן י"ח שכתבן בדיעבד נראה דאין להחמיר אחרי שיש מקילין אפילו

שער הציון

(א) הסכמת האחרונים דלא כדרישה ביו"ד שרצה להקל: (ב) פמ"ג: (ג) מ"א: (ד) ש"ת בשם הנו"ב: (ה) מ"א:

הגהות ותיקונים: א) סי"ג:

means to buy both of them, (37) *tefilin* have priority.
13. (38) A banned person or a person who is suffering from *tzara'as*[5*] is forbidden to don *tefilin.*

§39: WHO ARE FIT TO WRITE *TEFILIN* /PASSAGES/ AND FROM WHOM THEY MAY BE BOUGHT

(Contains Ten Paragraphs)

1. (1) *Tefilin* /passages/ which were written by a /non-Jewish/ slave, (2) a woman, (3) a child (even if /the child/ had /already/ reached /the age then/

Mishnah Berurah

tefilin/ off. /Otherwise,/ he will appear to be giving a halachic ruling in the presence of his teacher, that the time has arrived when /*tefilin*/ must be taken off.

See above in Sec. 25, sub-Par. 58, for what we have written there in the name of the *P.Mg.*

(37) *Tefilin* have priority. /The reason is/ because /the mitzvah of *tefilin*/ is a mitzvah which is /performed/ with one's body. Furthermore, the holiness of *tefilin* is superior to the holiness of a mezuzah, as /follows from what is ruled/ above in Sec. 32, Par. 8.

However, for us, who don /*tefilin*/ only at the time when /we read/ "The Reading of Shema" and /pray the eighteen-blessing/ prayer, /the ruling is that/ if one is able to borrow /*tefilin*/ a mezuzah has priority, as /a mezuzah/ is not borrowable. [*M.A.*]

(38) A banned person or a person who is suffering from *tzara'as*, etc. See the *L.Ch.* and the *Shach*, in the *Yo.D.*, Sec. 334, Par. 2, and other Acharonim, who rule the opposite. The *P.Mg.* writes that they should don /*tefilin*, but/ without making a blessing /over them/. However, it is apparently implied by the *Beyur Ha-Gra* that they must also make the blessings /over the *tefilin*/.

§39

(1) *Tefilin* /passages/. The same ruling /applies with respect to/ a Torah Scroll or a mezuzah.

(2) A woman. The same ruling /applies to *tefilin* passages written by/ a person of unidentified sex or a hermaphrodite, since in their case there is a doubt as to /whether or not they are in fact/ women.

(3) A child. Since we derive from a verse[1] /that one is required to write *tefilin* passages/, it is necessary that /they should be written/ specifically by an actual adult, i.e., /the writer/ must have produced two /adult/ hairs after having become thirteen years of age.

However, if we are in doubt /as to/ whether /or not the writer/ has produced two /adult/ hairs /after having become thirteen years of age/, he is not fit for the writing /of *tefilin* passages/. /In such a case he has the ruling of a child/ unless his beard has filled out (i.e., if he has abundant hair in his beard, even if they are very small /hairs/ [*Sema* in the *Ch.M.*, Sec. 35]) or /unless/ the majority of his years /have gone by/ or the signs of a eunichoid have developed on him, in conformance with /the ruling/ below in Sec. 55, Par. 5.

5* I.e., a person who is unclean because his body exhibits the symptoms described in *Va-Yikra* 13:1-46.

1 *Devarim* 6:9.

שניהם (לז) תפילין (יד) [ד] קודמים: יג (לח) מנודה ומצורע אסורים להניח תפילין:

לט מי הם הכשרים לכתוב תפילין ולקנות מהם. ובו י׳ סעיפים:

א (א) תפילין שכתבן עבד (ב) או אשה (א) [א] (ג) * או קטן אפילו הגיע (ד) לחנוך (ג) (ה) או כותי

ע איבעיא במ"ק ובעיטור אוסר
א גיטין מ"ה
ב מרדכי שם
ג נמוקי יוסף

באר היטב

קמי ס"ת עי"ל סימן כ"ה ס"ג: (יד) קודמים. ואם אפשר בשאלה מזוזה קודמת דא"א בשאלה. מ"א:

(א) או קטן. ובעינן שיהא דוקא גדול ממש דהיינו שהביא שתי שערות אחר שהוא בן י"ג שנה אבל מספיקא פסול לכתוב עד שיהא בן י"ח שנה. מ"א: (ב) או כותי. כצ"ל דעובד כוכבים בלא"ה פסול

שערי תשובה

עבה"ט והם דברי המג"א ומ"ש עיין ב"י ר"ל דבב"י מבואר שאף שכתב ליישב דברי בעה"ע דמחלק דדוקא בתורה משום זכרון יציאת מצרים כו׳ דלא תקשי עליו ממ"ש הטור מ"מ סיים בה שאין דברי בעה"ע נראים וכן בש"ע כאן נראה שמסכים לדברי רבינו יונה ע"ש וכן נראה מהירושלמי ריש שבת גבי מפסיקין לק"ש כו׳. ועיין בשו"ת בית אפרים חלק א"ח וכתב במח"ב בקו"א בשם אור לדיקים שמ"כ בשם הרמב"ן ומהרח"ו שחייב כל אדם לומר ד׳ פרשיות תפילין בעודן עליו והב׳ פ׳ אומרים בק"ש וקדש והיה כי יביאך צ"ל קודם ברוך שאמר שהם קודמות לשמע והיה אם שמוע עכ"ד. ונראה שאם א"א לאומרם קודם ב"ש יאמרם אחר עלינו קודם שמסיר התפילין עכ"ל. והעולם נהגו לומר קדש והיה כי יביאך וק"ש בתפילין של ר"ת שמניחים אחר התפלה. ויש מדקדקים לומר גם בתפילין של רש"י קדש והיה כי יביאך קודם ב"ש והנוהג כן אם לא אמר קודם ב"ש אין לסמוך על מה שיאמר אחר כך בתפילין של ר"ת אלא יקרא קדש והיה כי יביאך קודם שיחלוץ של רש"י: [ד] קודמים. עבה"ט ועיין לעיל ר"ס כ"ה לענין תפילין וציצית ומשם נלמד לכאן:

[א] או קטן. עבה"ט וכתב בבכור שור בגיטין דף מ"ה דתפילין שכתבן חרש או שוטה פסולין אע"ג דבש"ע לא הזכיר אלא קטן לחוד וע"ש שכתב לתרץ קושיית המג"א על הב"י מיו"ד סי׳ קנ"ח וכתב בנודע ביהודה מ"ת סי׳ א׳ תפילין שכתבן נער בן י"ג שנה ויום אחד או יותר קצת ולא בדקוהו אם יש לו סימני גדלות ואינו לפנינו התפילין כשרים דסמכינן אחזקה כיון שהגיע לכלל שנים הביא סימנים אבל לכתחלה לא. ויש לגעור בסופרים שמניחים לנערים לכתוב תפילין ואין מדקדקים אם הביאו סימני גדלות או לא ע"ש. וכתב במח"ב בשם דברי יוסף סי׳ י"ב דאם כתב טומטום או אנדרוגינוס פסול ואם טומטום שנקרע

משנה ברורה

דגדלה שמורה הלכה בפני רבו שהגיע זמנו לחלוץ ועיין לעיל סימן כ"ה ס"ק כ"ח מ"ש שם בשם הפמ"ג: יב (לז) תפילין קודמים. דהיא מצוה שבגופו ועוד דקדושת תפילין למעלה מקדושת מזוזה וכדלעיל בסימן ל"ב ס"ח. מיהו לדידן שאין מניחין רק בשעת ק"ש ותפלה אם אפשר בשאלה מזוזה קודמת דא"א בשאלה [מ"א]: יג (לח) מנודה ומצורע וכו׳. עיין בל"ח וכש"ך ביו"ד סי׳ של"ד ס"ב ובשארי אחרונים דפוסקים להיפך וכתב הפמ"ג דינוחו בלי ברכה אבל מביאור הגר"א משמע דאורייתא דצריכין לברך ג"כ:

א (א) תפילין. וה"ה (א) ס"ת ומזוזה: (ב) או אשה. וה"ה (ב) טומטום ואנדרוגינוס דהם בכלל ספק אשה: (ג) או קטן. וכיון דילפינן מקרא בעינן שיהא דוקא גדול ממש דהיינו שהביא ב"ש אחר שהוא בן י"ג שנה אבל אם ספק לנו אם הביא ב"ש (ג) פסול לכתוב אם לא שנתמלא זקנו דהיינו שיש ריבוי שער בזקנו אף שהם קטנים מאד [פמ"ג בח"מ סימן ל"ה] או שעברו רוב שנותיו או שנולדו בו סימני סריס וכדלקמן בסימן נ"ה ס"ה. ויש לגעור (ד) בסופרים שמניחין לנערים לכתוב תפילין ואין מדקדקין אם הביאו סימני גדלות או לא. ועיין לעיל בסימן ל"ב סעיף קטן ק"ג מש"כ שם בשם הלבוש מענין זה ועיין בבה"ל: (ד) לחינוך. באמת אפילו גדול לא כל זמן שלא ידעינן שהביא ב"ש אך לענין גדול אם אח"כ בדקנוהו ומצאנו שיש לו ב"ש תלינן שהיה לו ג"כ בעת הכתיבה [ח"מ סימן ל"ה] משא"כ בקטן דאינו מועיל אז שערות: (ה) או כותי. כצ"ל דעו"ג (ה) בלא"ה פסול

ביאור הלכה

הגר"א והעולם נוהגין להקל בזה ואפשר שטעמם שסומכין על הא דסימן ל"ז ס"ב ועיין מה שכתבתי שם בביאור הלכה ועיין עוד בביאור הגר"א שמשמע מדבריו שאפילו לדעת השו"ע דלא מחלק לענין תורתו אומנתו לא מקילין רק לענין שא"צ לפסוק מלימודו כדי להניחה אבל אם הם כבר עליו שלבשן לק"ש ותפלה או קודם שהתחיל ללמוד אז צריך שיהיו עליו אף בעת הלימוד ולא יסלקם באמצע דומיא דמאי דפסק בהג"ה בסעיף הקודם דהיכא דבלי טורח יוכל לעשות שתיהן דצריך לעשות שתיהן:

* או קטן. ואם כתבן חרש או שוטה הניח הפמ"ג בפתיחה בצ"ע דאפשר דעדיפי מקטן ומהני אם אחרים עומדין ע"ג ומרמזין לחרש ושוטה שיכתוב לשמן. וסימני שוטה מבואר ביו"ד בסימן א׳ ס"ה. ולענין קטן אימת נעשה גדול אם לא ידעינן שהביא ב"ש כתבתי במ"ב אם נתמלא זקנו והוא מח"מ סימן ל"ה והשמטתי דברי המ"א שכתב עד י"ח שכל האחרונים השיגו עליו [הלא המה הא"ר והב"מ ודגמ"ר ומחה"ש ולבו"ש ותשו׳ רע"א בתא"ח סימן ז׳] ומ"מ אין בידינו לפוסלם אחרי שהח"א וגם השלחן שלמה מקילין לכתחלה. וראיתי בפמ"ג שסתר ליישב דברי המג"א והביא מסימן נ"ג ס"ח בהג"ה דמי"ח והלאה קרוי נתמלא זקנו וכונת הפמ"ג דמבואר שם דמי"ח והלאה אף אם יש לו זקן מעט קרוי נתמלא זקנו וה"נ כונת המג"א ביש לו זקן מעט ומ"מ באמת לע"ג בזה דאפשר דשם שאני דהלא שם איירי שהביא ב"ש דהוא גדול מן התורה ולא בעינן הזקן רק מפני כבוד הצבור תדע דשם מהני ג"כ אם הוא בן כ׳ ואין לו זקן כלל מקרי ג"כ עי"ז נתמלא זקנו כמבואר שם בשו"ע והכל מטעם זה דהוא רק מפני כבוד הצבור משא"כ בעניינו דלא ידעינן אם הביא ב"ש והזקן מהני לעשותו גדול עי"ז אפשר דבעינן מלוי זקנו ממש הא פשיטא לי דע"י סיכי דיקני [שיש לו במקומות מיוחדות שער בזקנו] בודאי לא קרוי נתמלא זקנו וראיה מוכרחת מיבמות פ׳ ע"ב בתוספות ד"ה דהביא ב"ש בסופו ואור"י דאין חשוב וכו׳ וה"ה דסיכי דיקני ג"כ אינו בכלל מלוי זקן דאל"ה ישאר קושית התוספות על רבה בר אבוה לפי תירוץ הגמרא שם וידוע דדין נתמלא זקנו דלא צריך שוב בדיקה נובע מאותו התוספות כמבואר בטור אה"ע בסי׳ קס"ט בב"י שם הגם דבב"י בח"מ סימן ל"ה בראשו משמע דהטוח"מ סובר דאפילו לא נתמלא זקנו מהני עכ"ז בהשו"ע שלו העתיק דדוקא אם נתמלא זקנו כי מיבעי לי לענין זקן מעט המבואר בסימן נ"ג דאפשר לפי מה שביארנו שם בשם מהרש"ל שהעתיק מתשובות הגאונים דהיינו שיהיו נמצאים שערות גדולות משני לידי הפנים ומצד הסנטר אפשר דזהו בכלל נתמלא זקנו בכל מקום אפילו לענין דאורייתא או דילמא שם שאני דהוא רק מפני כבוד הצבור ומ"מ אפשר שיש להקל בזה לפי מה שביאר הגר"א שם בח"מ דטעם הטור הוא לפי שע"פ רוב רגיל לבוא סימן התחתון קודם שבא סימן זה העליון לכן תלינן דמסתמא כבר בא התחתון א"כ לפ"ז בודאי דברי הטור שכתב באה"ע נתמלא זקנו הוא לאו דוקא ובח"מ שכתב צמח זקנו בדיוק כתבו דגם זה רגיל לבוא זמן הרבה אחר הבאת ב׳ שערות ולפ"ז אפשר לומר שגם סיכי דיקנא מהני להשוותו גדול לכל דבר דמסתמא כבר הביא ב׳ שערות ושם ביבמות פ׳ ע"ב לענין ר"נ שאני שידעו שלא הביא ר"נ ב׳ שערות וצ"ע. היוצא מדברינו עכ"פ קודם שיש לו קצת זקן בודאי אין להניחו לכתוב תפילין כ"ז שלא ידעינן שהביא ב׳ שערות אפילו אם הוא כבר בן י"ח שנה ויותר וכמו שכתבתי במ"ב. אך בדיעבד אם כתבן נער בר מצוה ואין לפנינו לבדקו צ"ע למעשה דהנ"ב מ"ת בסימן א׳ מכשיר וכן בפמ"ג בסימן ל"ט ובסימן נ"ה אות ז׳ ג"כ מוכח הכי דמדמה שם לענין בדיקת הריאה ובריאה קי"ל דאם נאבדה בלי בדיקה כשר ובתשובת רע"א תא"ח סימן ז׳ פוסל וכן בספר ישועות יעקב בסימן ל"ב ג"כ מחמיר אך בבן י"ח שכתבן בדיעבד נראה דאין להחמיר אחרי שיש מקילין אפילו

שער הציון

(א) הסכמת האחרונים דלא כדרישה ביו"ד שרצה להקל: (ב) פמ"ג: (ג) מ"א: (ד) ש"ת בשם הנו"ב: (ה) מ"א:

הגהות ותיקונים: א) סי"ג:

(4) when he had to be educated /to observe the mitzvos/), (5) a Cuthean,[1*]

Mishnah Berurah

One must rebuke the scribes who leave youths to write *tefilin* /passages/ without being concerned as to whether or not they have produced signs that they have grown. See above in Sec. 32, sub-Par. 103 for what we have written there in the name of the *Levush* about this matter. See the Beyur Halachah.[2]

(4) When he had to be educated. Actually, even /someone who has reached the age of/ a grown person may not /write *tefilin* passages/, as long as we do not know that he has /already/ produced two /adult/ hairs. However, where /someone who has reached the age of/ a grown person is involved /, then/, if we examine him after /he wrote the *tefilin* passages/ and discover that he has two /adult/ hairs, we assume that he also had /two adult hairs/ when he wrote /the passages/. [*Ch.M.*, Sec. 35] This is not the case when a child /wrote *tefilin* passages/, as /in childhood the appearance of adult/ hairs is of no avail /for him to be considered a grown person/.

(5) A Cuthean. This is the correct /reading and the term is not a substitute term for a gentile/. An idol-worshipper is in any case invalid /for the writing of *tefilin*

1* A descendant of the gentiles who were settled by the Assyrians in the land of Israel after the exile of the ten tribes. They later converted to Judaism, but there is a dispute among the Tanaim as to whether or not the conversion was a valid one. See 2 *Melachim* 17:24-41 and *Kidushin* 75b.

2 There the author rules that if someone wrote *tefilin* passages when he was eighteen years of age and we are unable to examine whether or not he has produced two adult hairs, one need not be stringent about the validity of the passages now that it is after the event.

(ו) * או (ג) [ג] מומר לעבודת גלולים (ז) או מוסר לאנסין פסולים משום דדכתיב וקשרתם וכתבתם כל (ח) * שאינו בקשירה או אינו מאמין בה אינו (ד) בכתיבה: ב * הכל שפסול לכותבן פסול (ט) * בכל תיקון (ה) (י) עשייתן: ג וגר שחזר לדתו מחמת (ו) (יא) יראה

ד רש"י שם והרמב"ם בפ"ג מה"ת הרמב"ם שם ו גיטין שם

שערי תשובה

ונמלא זכר כשרים ע"ש ובדיניס אלו לא מהני גדול וכשר עומד ע"ג כיון שהטעם הוא דכל שישנו בקשירה ישנו בכתיבה: [ג] מומר. עבה"ט ועיין בגט פשוט סי' קכ"ג שכתב שמי שאמר אלך ואמסור אם כתב תפילין מכשירין בדיעבד ובשעת הדחק:

באר היטב

שאינו כותב לשמה. מ"א: (ג) מומר. לכל התורה או להכעיס אפילו לעבירה א' או מסור לאנס אפילו לתיאבון פסול. עמ"א: (ד) בכתיבה. מי שנקטעה ידו השמאלית אע"פ שאינו בקשירה כשר לכתוב תפילין דגברא בר חיובא הוא אלא פומא הוא דכאיב ליה. מ"א: (ה) עשייתן. היינו שעושה מעשה בגוף התפילין אבל לעבדן כשר. ואם תפר וחיפה התפילין פסול שזהו בכלל תיקון עשייתן אבל אם גרר דבק שבין אות לאות או עשה שאר תיקון כשר בדיעבד בתפילין דבעי כסדרן. ובס"ת אם אפשר לגרור לדדי האותיות במקום שנגעו ולחזור ולכתבן יעשה דזה מיקרי לכתחלה מהר"ס לובלין סימן ס"ח. מ"א: (ו) יראה. המ"א העלה דאין להקל ע"ש ועיין מ"ש היד אהרן. כתב הד"מ אע"ג דבס"ת

ביאור הלכה

אפילו לכתחילה וכנ"ל: * או מומר לעבו"ג. ומיירי שאינו אדוק בה דאל"ה ה"ל אפיקורס וצריך שריפה [ע"ת] ועיין במ"ב שכתבנו דאם הוא מומר להכעיס דינו כעו"ג ולהכעיס מקרי היכא דהתירא ואיסורא קמיה ושביק התירא ואכיל איסורא דזה הוא בכלל להכעיס אבל אם אינו מקפיד לברור ההיתר והוא לוקח מן הבא בידו או היתר או איסור עדיין אינו בכלל מומר להכעיס ורק לגבי שחיטה פסק הרמ"א ביו"ד סימן ב' ס"ה בהג"ה דנחשב כלהכעיס משום דתו אינו בר זביחה עי"ש בב"י ובפמ"ג בש"ד[א] בסק"ח ומזה למד המ"א דה"ה גבי תפילין כה"ג וכמש"כ במ"ב דאם אינו חושש למצות תפילין אף שלא להכעיס תו אינו בר קשירה [ולדעת הר"ן דמיקל שם בזה כמבואר שם בב"י ובר"ן גופא באריכות יהיה ה"ה הכא וראיתי לאחד דכתב היפך זה ולא נהירא] וע"ש עוד בביאור הגר"א בס"ק ט"ז דמשמע מניה דדעת רש"י הוא דאפילו אם אינו עושה להכעיס ובשאר עבירות ג"כ תו לאו בכלל בר קשירה הוא. ודע עוד דכל אלו פסולים דחשבינן להכעיס או לעבו"ג או חילול שבת בפרהסיא פסק שם בש"ך ביו"ד דאפילו בפ"א פסול אם לא עשה תשובה ולכאורה ה"ה בענינינו באם אינו חושש למצות תפילין ואין להביא ראיה מדנקט מומר משמע דוקא במומר ורגיל לכך דהרי כתב ב"י דמיירי בלהכעיס ושם אפילו בפ"א וכנ"ל*א"כ אפשר דאם אינו חושש ג"כ דהוא כלהכעיס ג"כ תיכף מיפסל וזה הספק יפול ג"כ על מה שפסק שם ביו"ד דאם אינו חושש בזביחה דהוא כלהכעיס וצ"ע. ומ"ש בפנים דיש מחמירין אפילו בלתיאבון הוא דעת התוספות הביאם המג"א דסוברים דלענין כתיבת סת"ם חמור מלשאר דברים וגם הפמ"ג בפתיחה בסי' ל"ב כתב דבמומר לתיאבון יש לעיונא ביה טובא ע"ש. ובפרט אם הוא מומר לתפילין לתיאבון נ"ל דבאיש כזה עכ"פ צריך שידעו בו שיודע הלכות כתיבות סת"מ לענין חק תוכות וכדומה וכמו בשם לענין שחיטה דדוקא אם ידעו בו שיודע ה"ש וכדאיתא ביו"ד שם דבאיש כזה לא אמרינן ביה רוב מצוין מומחין הן. ודע עוד דנראה פשוט דאם הוא מומר לתפלה אחת ש"ר או ש"י ג"כ תו לא הוי בכלל בר קשירה דהרי כתיב בקרא אחד וקשרתם וגו' והיו לטוטפות וגו' ואיתקש לוכתבתם. ואעפ"כ אם הסופר רגיל לישא תמיד ש"ר על המלא והתרו בו ואינו שומע לדבריהם אף דעבירה גדולה עושה בזה אפשר דאין למנעו מלכתוב סת"מ דאולי רגע א' היו על מקומן כדין וא"כ תו הוי בכלל בר קשירה. ומ"ש במ"ב במסור אפילו בפ"א כן איתא בפמ"ג ביו"ד עי"ש ועיין בפ"ת יו"ד בסימן רפ"א דכתב בשם חומות ירושלים היפך זה וצ"ע ומ"ש במ"ב אפילו לתיאבון כן סתמו הרבה מהאחרונים אך בפמ"ג מפקפק בזה: * שאינו בקשירה וכו'. וכותים אפילו אם נימא דגירי אמת הן ומוזהרין על הקשירה מ"מ כבר פרקו מעליהן העול ואינן מאמינין במצות ומיקרי שאינו בקשירה והוא הטעם בשארי דברים דקחשיב: * כל שפסול וכו'. עיין בב"י ועיין בט"ז שכתב לפי שיש בעשייתן ש"ן לפיכך פסול לכל העשיות ועיין בפמ"ג שכתב דעשיית ש"ן הוא מדאורייתא והשאר הוא מדרבנן עי"ש הנה המ"א פליג ע"ז וסובר דחיפוי ותפירה הוא ג"כ כעשיית ש"ן ולא מטעם גזירה ולכאורה לפי מה שביאר הפמ"ג את דברי הט"ז יוכשר להט"ז קטן שהגיע לחינוך דגם הוא חייב בתפילין מדרבנן ולישנא דכל הפסול משמע דלדלעיל קאי. ובאמת הנכון כמש"כ מהרמ"ל בתשובה סימן ס"ח דאין כונת הב"י משום דגזרינן שאר תיקונין אטו עשיית השין אלא דכיון דשאר תיקונין ועשיית הש"ן כולם נקראין עשיית תפילין והכל עשייה אחת היא אין לחלק בין קלתם לקלתם עכ"ל ומ"מ נ"ל דקטן בן י"ג שנה שלא ידעינן אם הביא ב"ש אין להחמיר בו בדיעבד לענין חיפוי ותפירה אם עשיית הש"ן היה ע"י גדול דבלא"ה הנו"ב מקיל בדיעבד אפי' בכתיבה וכנ"ל: * בכל תיקון עשייתן. עיין במ"ב במה שכתבנו כגון חיפוי הבתים ותפירתן ונ"ל פשוט דה"ה כריכת שער על הפרשיות דזה מעכב אפילו בדיעבד כדאיתא ברמב"ם פ"ג מהלכות תפילין ה"א וכ"ש לימלוס הבתים והתיתורא שיהיו מרובעין וכל כה"ג דכ"ז הוא בכלל תיקון עשייתן וכן מוכח ממהר"מ לובלין בתשובה סי' ס"ח שכתב דכל שאר המלאכות חוץ מתיקון העור הן בכלל חיפוי הבתים ותפירתן ומה שכתב המ"א בשם מהר"ס דאם גרר דבק שבין אות לאות או עשה שאר תיקון כשר בדיעבד כונתו בענין הכתיבה כגון שהיה הפסק גדול בתיבה עד שהיה נראה כשני תיבות והמשיך האות לפניה (כגון בתיבת לאבותיך

משנה ברורה

שאין כותב לשמה: (ו) או מומר לעבו"ג. דזה הוא כמומר לכל התורה וה"ה אם הוא מומר לחלל שבת בפרהסיא אבל אם הוא מומר (ו) לשאר עבירות קי"ל דמומר לדבר אחד לא הוי מומר לכל התורה כולה לבד אם הוא עושה להכעיס דבזה אפילו לד"א דינו ככותי וכדאיתא ביו"ד סימן ב'. ויש מחמירין יותר (ז) דצריך גניזה. וכ"ז אם הוא מומר לשאר עבירות אבל אם (ח) הוא מומר לתפילין שאינו מניח תפילין אפילו אם אינו עושה זה להכעיס פסול דתו איננו בר קשירה לבד אם היה לזה רק מומר לתיאבון כגון שהלך אחר עסקיו עדיין הוא בכלל בר קשירה וכ"ז הוא לענין דיעבד אבל לכתחלה יש להחמיר שלא להניח לאיש כזה לכתוב סת"ס כי (ט) יש מחמירין אפילו במומר לתיאבון ואפילו* באחרים (י) עומדין ע"ג ואומרין לו שיכתוב לשמה ועיין בבה"ל. וכתב הפמ"ג (יא) דאפילו הוא מומר לחלל שבת בפרהסיא באיסור דרבנן כגון מוקצה והוצאה לכרמלית יש להחמיר עכ"פ לכתחלה שלא* להניחו לכתוב סת"ס ואפילו בדיעבד צ"ע: (ז) או וכו'. עיין בה"ט דאפילו בלתיאבון לבד ואפילו פ"א: (ח) שאינו בקשירה וכו'. ועבד ואשה וכותי אין מוזהר על הקשירה וקטן אף שהגיע לחינוך מדרבנן בעלמא הוא [ב"י] ועיין בבה"ל. ובכל אלו (יב) לא מהני אפי' גדול עומד על גבו ורואהו שיהיו לשמן: ב (ט) בכל[ב]. ומי (יג) שנקטעה ידו השמאלית אע"פ שאינו בקשירה יכול לכתוב תפילין דגברא בר חיובא הוא אלא פומא הוא דכאיב ליה: (י) עשייתן. ודוקא שעושה מעשה (יד) בגוף התפילין כגון חיפוי הבתים ותפירתן וכ"ש עשיית הש"ן בעור הבתים או (טו) להגיה איזה אות דעתה הוא פסול וע"י הגהתו יוכשר דזה הוא כתיבה ממש אבל עיבוד הקלף איננו בכלל זה וכשר ע"י עו"ג וכ"ש ע"י אשה רק דבעו"ג בעינן שיהיה ישראל עוע"ג ויראה שיהיה לשמה וכדלעיל בסימן ל"ב ס"ט וה"ה בקטן. והשחרת הבתים והרצועות עיין לעיל בסימן ל"ג[ג] שבררנו שם דינם בעו"ג. וגרירת דבק שבין אות לאות לכתחלה יש ליזהר שלא לעשות על ידם ובדיעבד אין להחמיר דגרירה לא מיקרי כתיבה ועיין היטב לעיל בסימן ל"ב סק"פ. וכ"ז (טז) בתפילין דבעינן כסדרן אבל בס"ת אם אפשר לגרור לדדי האותיות במקום שנגעו ולחזור ולכותבן יעשה דזה מיקרי לכתחלה: ג (יא) יראה. שלא יהרגוהו ואף דבאמת הי"ל למסור

שער הציון

(ו) ב"י ומ"א: (ז) עיין במ"א: (ח) מ"א: (ט) מ"א בשם התוספות: (י) ש"ת ופשוט: (יא) פמ"ג בפתיחה בסימן ל"ב: (יב) ש"ת ופשוט: (יג) מ"א: (יד) מ"א בשם מהר"ס לובלין: (טו) שם: (טז) שם:

הגהות ותיקונים: א) במשב"ז: ב) נ"ל דס"ק זה הוא המשך מס"ק ח': ג) ס"ק כ"ג:

הערות והארות: 1) סק"ט אינו ענין בפ"ע:

(6) a confirmed sinner over the worship of idols **(7)** or an informer to robbers are invalid. /This is/ because it is written,[2*] "And you should bind them ... and

Mishnah Berurah

passages/, as he does not write them for the sake of /the mitzvah/.

(6) A confirmed sinner over the worship of idols. /This is/ because such /a sinner/ is like a confirmed sinner over the entire Torah. The same ruling /applies/ if one is a confirmed sinner over desecration of the Shabbos publicly.

However, if one is a confirmed sinner over other transgressions, we rule that a confirmed sinner over one /transgression/ is not /ruled as/ a confirmed sinner over all /the mitzvos/ of the Torah in its entirety, except if he does /the transgression in order/ to offend. In the /latter/ case, even /if he is a confirmed sinner merely/ over one /transgression/ he has the ruling of a gentile, as stated in the *Yo.D.*, Sec. 2. There are /authorities/ who are more stringent /and rule/ that /*tefilin* passages written by a person who transgresses to offend/ require *genizah*.

/On the other hand,/ all this /only applies/ if one is a confirmed sinner over other transgressions, but if one is a confirmed sinner over /the mitzvah of/ *tefilin* and does not don *tefilin*, he is not fit /for the writing of *tefilin* passages/ even if he does not do it to offend, since he can no longer be /considered/ a binder /of *tefilin*/. There is an exception /to this rule/ where one is only a confirmed sinner in this respect when /satisfying/ his desire is involved. For example, if one pursued his business /and did not don *tefilin* because of that/, he is still ruled as a binder /of *tefilin*/. /It should be noted, however, that/ all these /remarks/ apply /only/ as regards /the ruling/ once it is after the event, but, initially, one should be stringent and not allow such a person to write a Torah Scroll, a *tefilin* /passage/ or a mezuzah. This is because there are /authorities/ who /rule/ stringently /about this/ even with respect to a confirmed sinner /who sins only/ when /satisfying/ his desire is involved, even /as regards an instance/ when others stand over him and instruct him to write for the sake of /the mitzvah/.

See the Beyur Halachah.[3]

The *P.Mg.* writes that even if /a person/ is a confirmed sinner over desecration of the Shabbos publicly /merely/ in /a matter/ which involves /the transgression of/ a Rabbinical prohibition, one should be stringent, at any rate /as regards/ initial /practice/, and not allow him to write a Torah Scroll, a *tefilin* /passage/, or a mezuzah. For example, /one should be stringent about this if he is a confirmed sinner over the handling of/ *muktzeh* or the taking out /of something from a private or a public domain/ into a *karmelis*. Even /with respect to the ruling/ once it is after the event /, if he did write them/, study is required /to determine the ruling to be followed/.

(7) Or, etc. See the *B.Heyt.*, that this even /applies/ where /he did it/ solely to /satisfy/ his desire and even if /he only did it/ once.

2* *Devarim* 6:8-9.

3 There the author gives the following rulings. If the writer of *tefilin* passages is a devout idolator the passages must be burnt. One is considered a confirmed sinner to offend if he chooses the prohibited article in preference to the permitted article, but not if he does not mind which one of them he takes. One is disqualified as a confirmed sinner from writing *tefilin* even if he did the transgression only once and has not repented from it. In the case of a confirmed sinner over the mitzvah of *tefilin* who sins only where satisfying his desire is involved, it must be known that he is familiar with all the laws for the writing of *tefilin* passages. A person is not regarded as a binder of *tefilin* even if he is only a confirmed sinner over the donning of one of the *tefilin* units.

(ו) * אך (ג) [ג] מומר לעבודת גלולים (ז) או מוסר לאנסין פסולים משום ^דכתיב וקשרתם וכתבתם כל (ח) * שאינו בקשירה או אינו מאמין בה אינו (ד) בכתיבה: **ב** * ^הכל שפסול לכותבן פסול (ט) * בכל תיקון (ה) (י) עשייתן: **ג** ^יגר שחזר לדתו מחמת (ו) (יא) יראה

ד רש"י שם והרמב"ם בפ"ג מה"ת ה רמב"ם שם ו גיטין שם

שערי תשובה

ונמלא זכר כשרים ע"ש ובדיניס אלו לא מהני גדול וכשר עומד ע"ג כיון שהטעם הוא דכל שישנו בקשירה ישנו בכתיבה: [ג] מומר. עבה"ט ועיין בגט פשוט סי' קכ"ג שכתב שמי שאמר אלך ואמסור אם כתב תפילין מכשירין בדיעבד ובשעת הדחק:

באר היטב

שאינו כותב לשמה. מ"א: (ג) מומר. לכל התורה או להכעיס אפילו לעבירה א' או מסור לאנס אפילו לתיאבון פסול. עמ"א: (ד) בכתיבה. מי שנקטעה ידו השמאלית אע"פ שאינו בקשירה כשר לכתוב תפילין דגברא בר חיובא הוא אלא פומא הוא דכאיב ליה. מ"א: (ה) עשייתן. היינו שעושה מעשה בגוף התפילין אבל לעבדן כשר. ואם תפר וחיפה התפילין פסול שזהו בכלל תיקון עשייתן אבל אם גרר דבק שבין אות לאות או עשה שאר תיקון כשר בדיעבד בתפילין דבעי כסדרן. ובס"ת אם אפשר לגרור לדדי האותיות במקום שנגעו ולחזור ולכתבן יעשה דזה מיקרי לכתחלה מהר"ס לובלין סימן ס"ח. מ"א: (ו) יראה. המ"א העלה דאין להקל ע"ש ועיין מ"ש היד אהרן. כתב הד"מ אע"ג דבס"ת

ביאור הלכה

אפילו לכתחילה וכנ"ל: * או מומר לעבו"ג. ומיירי שאינו אדוק בה דאל"ה ה"ל אפיקורס וצריך שריפה [ע"ת] ועיין במ"ב שכתבנו דאם הוא מומר להכעיס דינו כעו"ג ולהכעיס מקרי היכא דהתירא ואיסורא קמיה ושביק התירא ואכיל איסורא דזה הוא בכלל להכעיס אבל אם אינו מקפיד לברור ההיתר והוא לוקח מן הבא בידו או היתר או איסור עדיין אינו בכלל מומר להכעיס ורק לגבי שחיטה פסק הרמ"א ביו"ד סימן ב' ס"ה בהג"ה דנחשב כלהכעיס משום דתו אינו בר זביחה עי"ש בב"י ובפמ"ג בש"ד^[א] בסק"ח ומזה למד המ"א דה"ה גבי תפילין כה"ג וכמש"כ במ"ב דאם אינו חושש למצות תפילין אף שלא להכעיס תו אינו בר קשירה [ולדעת הר"ן דמיקל שם בזה כמבואר שם בב"י ובר"ן גופא באריכות יהיה ה"ה הכא וראיתי לאחד דכתב היפך זה ולא נהירא] וע"ש עוד בביאור הגר"א בס"ק ט"ז דמשמע מניה דלדעת רש"י הוא דאפילו אם אינו עושה להכעיס ובשאר עבירות ג"כ תו לאו בכלל בר קשירה הוא. ודע עוד דכל אלו פסולים דחשבינן להכעיס או לעבו"ג או חילול שבת בפרהסיא פסק שם בש"ך ביו"ד דאפילו בפ"א פסול אם לא עשה תשובה ולכאורה ה"ה בענינינו באם אינו חושש למצות תפילין ואין להביא ראיה מדנקט מומר משמע דוקא במומר ורגיל לכך דהרי כתב ב"י דמיירי בלהכעיס ושם אפילו בפ"א וכנ"ל*א"כ אפשר דאם אינו חושש ג"כ דהוא כלהכעיס ג"כ תיכף מיפסל וזה הספק יפול ג"כ על מה שפסק שם ביו"ד דאם אינו חושש בזביחה דהוא כלהכעיס וצ"ע. ומ"ש בפנים דיש מחמירין אפילו בלתיאבון הוא דעת התוספות הבאים המג"א דסוברים דלענין כתיבת סת"מ חמור מלשאר דברים וגם הפמ"ג בפתיחה בסי' ל"ב כתב דבמומר לתיאבון יש לעיונא ביה טובא ע"ש. ובפרט אם הוא מומר לתפילין לתיאבון נ"ל דבאיש כזה עכ"פ צריך שידעו בו שיודע הלכות כתיבות סת"מ לענין חק תוכות וכדומה וכמו בשם לענין שחיטה דדוקא אם ידעו בו שיודע ה"ש וכדאיתא ביו"ד שם דבאיש כזה לא אמרינן ביה רוב מצויין מומחין הן. ודע עוד דנראה פשוט דאם הוא מומר לתפלה אחת ש"ר או ש"י ג"כ תו לא הוי בכלל בר קשירה דהרי כתיב בקרא אחד וקשרתם וגו' והיו לטוטפות וגו' ואיתקש לוכתבתם. ואעפ"כ אם הסופר רגיל לישא תמיד ש"ר על המצח והתרו בו ואינו שומע לדבריהם אף דעבירה גדולה עושה בזה אפשר דאין למנעו מלכתוב סת"מ דאולי רגע א' היו על מקומן כדין וא"כ תו הוי בכלל בר קשירה. ומ"ש במ"ב במסור אפילו בפ"א כן איתא בפמ"ג ביו"ד עי"ש ועיין בפ"ת יו"ד בסימן רפ"א דכתב בשם חוות ירושלים היפך זה וצ"ע ומ"ש במ"ב אפילו לתיאבון כן סתמו הרבה מהאחרונים אך בפמ"ג מפקפק בזה: * שאינו בקשירה וכו'. וכותים אפילו אם נימא דגירי אמת הן ומוזהרין על הקשירה מ"מ כבר פרקו מעליהן העול ואינן מאמינין במצות ומיקרי שאינו בקשירה והוא הטעם בשארי דברים דקחשיב: * כל שפסול וכו'. עיין בב"י ועיין בט"ז שכתב לפי שיש בעשייתן שי"ן לפיכך פסול לכל העשיות ועיין בפמ"ג שכתב דעשיית שי"ן הוא מדאורייתא והשאר הוא מדרבנן עי"ש הנה המ"א

משנה ברורה

שאין כותב לשמה: (ו) או מומר לעבו"ג. דבזה הוא כמומר לכל התורה וה"ה אם הוא מומר לחלל שבת בפרהסיא אבל אם הוא מומר (ו) לשאר עבירות קי"ל דמומר לדבר אחד לא הוי מומר לכל התורה כולה לבד אם הוא עושה להכעיס דבזה אפילו לד"א דינו ככותי וכדאיתא ביו"ד סימן ב'. ויש מחמירין יותר (ז) דלריך גניזה. וכ"ז אם הוא מומר לשאר עבירות אבל אם (ח) הוא מומר לתפילין שאינו מניח תפילין אפילו אם אינו עושה זה להכעיס פסול דתו אינו בר קשירה לבד אם היה לזה רק מומר לתיאבון כגון שהלך אחר עסקיו עדיין הוא בכלל בר קשירה וכ"ז הוא לענין דיעבד אבל לכתחלה יש להחמיר שלא להניח לאיש כזה לכתוב סת"ם כי (ט) יש מחמירין אפילו במומר לתיאבון ואפילו* באחרים (י) עומדין ע"ג ואומרין לו שיכתוב לשמה ועיין בבה"ל. וכתב הפמ"ג (יא) דאפילו הוא מומר לחלל שבת בפרהסיא באיסור דרבנן כגון מוקצה והוצאה לכרמלית יש להחמיר עכ"פ לכתחלה שלא* להניחו לכתוב סת"ם ואפילו בדיעבד צ"ע: (ז) או וכו'. עיין בה"ט דאפילו בלתיאבון לבד ואפילו פ"א: (ח) שאינו בקשירה וכו'. ועבד ואשה וכותי אין מוזהר על הקשירה וקטן אף שהגיע לחינוך מדרבנן בעלמא הוא [ב"י] ועיין בבה"ל. ובכל אלו (יב) לא מהני אפי' גדול עומד על גבו ורואהו שיהיו לשמן: **ב** (ט)[1]בכל^[ב]. ומי (יג) שנקטעה ידו השמאלית אע"פ שאינו בקשירה יכול לכתוב תפילין דגברא בר חיובא הוא אלא פומא הוא דכאיב ליה: (י) עשייתן. ודוקא שעושה מעשה (יד) בגוף התפילין כגון חיפוי הבתים ותפירתן וכ"ש עשיית השי"ן בעור הבתים או (טו) להגיה איזה אות דעתה הוא פסול וע"י הגהתו יוכשר דזה הוא כתיבה ממש אבל עיבוד הקלף איננו בכלל זה וכשר ע"י עו"ג וכ"ש ע"י אשה רק דבעו"ג בעינן שיהיה ישראל עומד על גבו ויראה שיהיה לשמה וכדלעיל בסימן ל"ב ס"ט וה"ה בקטן. והשחרת הבתים והרלועות עיין לעיל בסימן ל"ג^[ג] שבררנו שם דינם בעזה"י. וגרירת דבק שבין אות לאות לכתחלה יש ליזהר שלא לעשות על ידם ובדיעבד אין להחמיר דגרירה לא מיקרי כתיבה ועיין היטב לעיל בסימן ל"ב סק"פ. וכ"ז (טז) בתפילין דבעינן כסדרן אבל בס"ת אם אפשר לגרור לדדי האותיות במקום שנגעו ולחזור ולכותבן יעשה דזה מיקרי לכתחלה: **ג** (יא) יראה. שלא יהרגוהו ואף דבאמת הי"ל למסור

פליג ע"ז וסובר דחיפוי ותפירה הוא ג"כ כעשיית שי"ן ולא מטעם גזירה ולכאורה לפי מה שביאר הפמ"ג את דברי הט"ז יוכשר להט"ז קטן שהגיע לחינוך דגם הוא חייב בתפילין מדרבנן ולישנא דכל הפסול משמע דאלדלעיל קאי. ובאמת הנכון כמש"כ מהרמ"ל בתשובה סימן ס"ח דאין כונת הב"י משום דגזרינן שאר תיקונין אטו עשיית השין אלא דכיון דשאר תיקונין ועשיית השי"ן כולם נקראין עשיית תפילין והכל עשייה אחת היא אין לחלק בין קצתם לקצתם עכ"ל ומ"מ נ"ל דקטן בן י"ג שנה שלא ידעינן אם הביא ב"ש אין להחמיר בו בדיעבד לענין חיפוי ותפירה אם עשיית השי"ן היה ע"י גדול דבלא"ה הנו"ב מקיל בדיעבד אפי' בכתיבה וכנ"ל: * בכל תיקון עשייתן. עיין במ"ב במה שכתבנו כגון חיפוי הבתים ותפירתן ונ"ל פשוט דה"ה כריכת שער על הפרשיות דזה מעכב אפילו בדיעבד כדאיתא ברמב"ם פ"ג מהלכות תפילין ה"א וכ"ש לימלוס הבתים והתיתורא שיהיו מרובעין וכל כה"ג דכ"ז הוא בכלל תיקון עשייתן וכן מוכח ממהר"מ לובלין בתשובה סי' ס"ח שכתב דכל שאר המלאכות חוץ מתיקון העור הן בכלל חיפוי הבתים ותפירתן ומה שכתב המ"א בשם מהר"ס דאם גרר דבק שבין אות לאות או עשה שאר תיקון כשר בדיעבד כונתו בענין הכתיבה כגון שהיה הפסק גדול בתיבה עד שהיה נראה כשני תיבות והמשיך האות לפניה (כגון בתיבת לאבותיך

שער הציון

(ו) ב"י ומ"א: (ז) עיין במ"א: (ח) מ"א: (ט) מ"א בשם התוספות: (י) ש"ת ופשוט: (יא) פמ"ג בפתיחה בסימן ל"ב: (יב) ש"ת ופשוט: (יג) מ"א: (יד) מ"א בשם מהר"ס לובלין: (טו) שם: (טז) שם:

הגהות ותיקונים: א) במשב"ז: **ב)** נ"ל דס"ק זה הוא המשך מס"ק ח': **ג)** ס"ק כ"ג:

הערות והארות: 1) סק"ט אינו ענין בפ"ע:

you should write them", /from which we derive that/ whoever **(8)** is not a binder of /*tefilin*/ or does not believe in /the mitzvah of *tefilin*/ is not /fit/ to write /*tefilin* passages/.

2. Whoever is not fit for the writing of /*tefilin* passages/ is not fit **(9)** for doing anything in **(10)** the production of /*tefilin*/.

3. A convert /to Judaism/ who returned to his /former/ religion out of **(11)** fear is fit for the writing of *tefilin* /passages/.

Mishnah Berurah

(8) Is not a binder, etc. Slaves, women and Cutheans are not enjoined to bind /*tefilin*/. /As for/ a child, even if he has reached /the age/ when he must be educated /towards the observance of mitzvos/, he is merely /obliged to don *tefilin*/ by Rabbinical law. [*B.Y.*] See the Beyur Halachah.[4]

For all these /categories of people/, even if a grown /Jewish/ man stands over them and sees that /they write/ for the sake of /the mitzvah of *tefilin*/, this is of no avail /for what they write to be ruled as valid/.

(9) For ... anything. Someone whose left hand has been severed may write *tefilin* /passages/, even though he is not a binder /of *tefilin*/. /This is/ because such a person is /in fact/ obliged /to bind *tefilin*/, but /is comparable to someone who cannot do something because/ his mouth hurts him.

(10) The production of /*tefilin*/. This only /applies/ to doing an action to the body of the *tefilin*. For example, /it applies to/ covering the housings or sewing them and certainly to making the /letter/ ש[5] in the skin of the housings or to emending some letter which is now invalid and will become valid through his emendment, as that involves actual writing.

However, the processing of the parchment is not in this category and is valid if /done/ by a non-Jew and certainly if /done/ by a /Jewish/ woman. Only, in the case of a non-Jew, it is necessary for a Jew to stand over him and see that /he does/ it for the sake of /use for the mitzvah of *tefilin*/, as /explained/ above in Sec. 32, Par. 9. The same ruling /applies/ with respect to a child.

/As to/ the blackening of the housings and the straps, see above in Sec. 33 /, sub-Par. 23/, where we have explained the /relevant/ laws, with the help of *Ha-Sheym*, may He be blessed.

/As regards/ the scraping off of a sticking between one letter and the other, one should be careful initially that it should not be done by them. Once it is after the event /and it was done by them/ one need not be stringent /about this/, as scraping off is not describable as writing. Note carefully /what we have written/ above in Sec. 32, sub-Par. 80. /However,/ all this /only applies/ in the case of *tefilin* /passages/, for which it is necessary /that the letters be written/ in /the correct/ order, but where a Torah Scroll is involved, if it is possible to scrape away the sides of the letters where they touched and write them again one should /in fact/ do /so/, since /in the case of a Torah Scroll/ these are classed as initial /circumstances/.

(11) Fear. /I.e.,/ that he should not be killed.

Although he should in fact have sacrificed his life for faith in *Ha-Sheym*, he has

4 The author explains there that even if Cutheans have the ruling of genuine converts they are nevertheless not fit to write *tefilin* passages. This is because they have pushed off the yoke of Torah observance and are therefore not to be regarded as binders of *tefilin*.

5 The knots resembling the letter ד and י of the straps must also be done for the sake of the mitzvah and not by a woman or a child. One may be lenient if they were done by a youth of thirteen years of age, although we do not know whether he has produced adult hairs, provided an adult guided him to do it for the sake of the mitzvah. (Beyur Halachah)

* כשר לכתוב תפילין: **ד** [י]תפילין * שכתבם (יב) אפיקורוס (יג) ישרפו: (יד) [ח]וי"א יגנזו: **ה** [ט]נמצאו ביד אפיקורוס ואין ידוע מי כתבם (טו) יגנזו: **ו** [י]נמצאו ביד א"י ואין ידוע מי כתבם (טז) כשרים:

ז * [כ]אין לוקחין תפילין ומזוזות וספרים מן הכותים (יז) יותר מכדי דמיהן

ז הרמב"ם בפ"א שם ח טור ור' ירוחם ט גיטין שם י שם וכלישנא בתרא ורמב"ם שם פ"א ור"ן כ גיטין שם

משנה ברורה

נפשו על אמונת ה' מ"מ לא יצא מכלל ישראל עי"ז כיון דהיה באונס ועי' במ"א שהעלה דאין להקל בזה אפי' אם בצינעא הוא שומר את התורה רק שבהנחת תפילין הוא מתעצל דהלא עכ"פ אינו בקשירה וכ"ש אם הוא מומר לכל התורה כולה אם לא שמחמת פחד שלא יהרגוהו הוא ירא לקיים את התורה אפילו בצינעא. ועיין בביאור הגר"א שמסכים ג"כ להמ"א. עוד כתב המ"א בשם הד"מ דאף דבס"ת ממזר וגר תושב [היינו שקיבל עליו שבע מצות בני נח] פסולים לכתוב כמו שכתב ביו"ד סימן רפ"א אפ"ה בתפילין ומזוזות אין לחוש וכל האחרונים הסכימו דגר תושב פסול לכתיבת סת"ס דהא אינו בקשירה ועיין בבה"ל: **ד** (יב) אפיקורס. ועיין בבה"ל: (יג) ישרפו. עם אזכרותיהן וכדלקמן בסימן של"ד סכ"א עי"ש דסתמו כשכותב לשם עבו"ג הוא כותב: (יד) וי"א יגנזו. דאין דרך אפיקורס (יז) להניח תפילין ובודאי כתבו למכור לישראל ואפשר שלא כתבו לשם עבו"ג. ודעת המחבר לפסוק כדעה א' לכן כתבו בסתמא וכן דעת הט"ז והפרישה והגר"א בביאורו: **ה** (טו) יגנזו. מספק שמא הוא כתבן אבל אין לשרוף מספק דהלא כתיב לא תעשון כן לה' אלהיכם: **ו** (טז) כשרים. דסתם עו"ג (יח) אין בקיאין לכתוב ובודאי ישראל כתבו. ובפרט במקומותינו שידוע שאין א"י יודעין לכתוב אפילו בס"ת שנמצא בידן מסיק הש"ך [ביו"ד בסימן רפ"א סק"ד[א]] דלכו"ע כשרה דתלינן דהא"י בזוז אותה: **ז** (יז) יותר וכו'. אבל במעט יותר מסוין [דהיינו עד כדי (יט) חצי דינר בתפילין ולפי ערך זה בס"ת] חייבין לקנות מהן ואף דס"ת שנמצא ביד א"י י"א דיגנז [ביו"ד סימן רפ"א] אעפ"כ חייבין לקנות מהם ואפילו במעט יותר וכדי לגונזן בכדי שלא יבואו העו"ג לזלזל בהם ופשוט דה"ה אם הם פסולין מחמת עצמם ג"כ חייבין לקנות מהעו"ג כדי לגונזן אבל (כ) בכתבן אפיקורס

ביאור הלכה

לאבותיך המשיך הבי"ת וכל כה"ג) כדי שיהי' נראה כתיבה אחת דזה מותר מדינא אפילו בתפילין דבעינן כסדרן דזה אינו בכלל כתיבה וכדלעיל בסימן ל"ב לכן מותר זה אפילו ע"י פסולין כמו גרירה. ומה שכתבנו עוד או להגיה איזה אות דעתה הוא פסול כונתינו לאפוקי עשיית התגין שעל שעטנ"ז ג"ץ דגם בלא זה כשר בדיעבד וכבסימן ל"ו אין להחמיר בדיעבד גם בזה וה"ה העברת קולמוס על איזו אות דגם עתה יש שם אות עליו שרישומו ניכר אלא ששומרו שלא יתמחק יותר ויפסל דכ"ז אינו בכלל כתיבה. ולכאורה יש להסתפק ביוד"י האלף והשין והעין שאין נוגעין ותינוק דלא חכים ולא טיפש מכירם וכן אם חסר קוץ השמאלי ביו"ד אם מהני תיקון ע"י אלו הפסולין בדיעבד מי נימא כמו דלענין שלא כסדרן מקילינן ואמרינן דאין זה כתיבה חדשה כיון דעיקר צורתו עליו ה"נ לענין זה ולא קרינן ביה כל שאינו בקשירה אינו בכתיבה או דילמא כיון דעכ"פ עתה האות פסול וע"י תיקונן של אלו הפסולין יוכשר האות פסול אפילו בדיעבד ולא דמי לגרירה דשם אינו עושה מעשה בגוף צורת האות כלל ואין להביא ראיה להקל בזה מדנקט המהר"ם בסוף דבריו וז"ל אכן אם היו הנגיעות בגוף האותיות עצמן כגון ברגלי הה"א והקו"ף או רגלי האלף בגגות או פני האלף היו נוגעים בגג שתחתיה והאשה הפרידה אותן פשיטא דהס"ת פסולה דהא א"א לתקנס כ"א בגרירת כל מה שנעשה בפסול לחזור ולכותבו מחדש וזה מיקרי כתיבה גמורה עכ"ל ולא נקט יותר רבותא דאפי' בזה שהיה קודם תיקון האשה ג"כ עיקר צורתו עליו דפסול כל שהוסיף בכתיבה ועל ידו הוכשר האות דאפשר משום דהמהר"מ רצה להשיב להשואל בשאלתו ששאל לפניו בגרירת האשה אם כשר והשיבו דיש חילוק בין גרירה לגרירה וכדאיתא שם לכך לא נקט רבותא זו וכן מסתבר. כתב הפמ"ג דקשר של דלי"ת ואף של יו"ד שבתפילין ש"י יראה דאין לעשותם כ"א לשמה ושלא לעשותם ע"י אשה וקטן דבכלל כתיבה הוה כמו השי"ן שבשל ראש עיין שם. וכ"ל דאין להחמיר בזה בקטן שהוא בן י"ג שנה אם גדול עומד ע"ג ומצוהו לעשות לשמה אף שלא ידעינן שהביא ב"ש דבלא"ה יש הרבה מקילין בזה וכנ"ל וגם לדברי התוספות שבת ס"ב ע"א ד"ה שי"ן עי"ש אין מקום לזה וכ"ש דא"ל להחמיר הקטן הזה לעצמו בזה דאם לא הביא ב"ש ואינו חייב במצות רק מדרבנן הלא גם בתפילין אין חייב רק מדרבנן אך הקשר שעשה הקטן הזה לעצמו קודם שנעשה בן י"ג נ"ל דצריך להתירו לאחר שנעשה בן י"ג ולחזור לעשותו דהרי יש הרבה פוסקים שסוברים דעתה מן התורה הוא בכלל איש וחייב במצות מחמת חזקה דרבא דכיון שהגיע לכלל שנים מסתמא הביא סימנים וגם הלא עכ"פ כשיבדק אח"כ וימצא שיש לו ב"ש הלא צריך לתלות שהביאם תיכף בזמנו ונעשה גדול למפרע וכדאיתא בח"מ סימן ל"ה. ודע עוד דלענין תפירת ס"ת ע"י נשים וה"ה כל אלו הפסולין יש הרבה מפקפקין בזה ע"כ יש להזהיר מאד ע"ז דלא כמו שנהגו איזה סופרים להקל בתפירת ס"ת ע"י נשים בעת סיום הספר ובדיעבד אם אפשר בקלות להתיר התפירות שתפרן האשה ולחזור ולתופרן בהכשר יחזור ויתקנם דכיון דיודע המקומות ואפשר לו לתקנם הוי כלכתחלה גמור אבל בלא"ה אין להחמיר בדיעבד כן פסק המהר"ם לובלין בתשובה ובעל מגן האלף חולק עליו ומצריך להתיר התפירות אפילו בדיעבד. ובמקום שהמנהג שנותנין לנשים לתפור הס"ת וא"א לשנות המנהג צריך להזהיר וליזהר שהתפירה ראשונה ואחרונה וגם באמצע יעשה הסופר מקודם ואח"כ יתן לנשים לתפור. [פ"ת יו"ד סימן רפ"א]: * **כשר לכתוב תפילין.** כ"ז איירי בגר לדק. ולענין גר תושב הסכימו הפמ"ג ול"ש ומחה"ש [ועוד הרבה] דפסול מטעם דהא אינו בקשירה והשע"ת[ב] המציא דבר חדש דאיירי הד"מ דמכשיר בגר תושב דקיבל עליו כל המצות חוץ מאיסור נבלה וא"כ הלא ישנו בקשירה ובאמת נלענ"ד שגם זה אינו דהלא עכ"פ אינו מוזהר על הקשירה ותדע דאטו אם אשה ועבד יקבלו עליהן מצות תפילין יהיו כשרים לכתיבת תפילין ואם תדחה משום דמוחין לנשים על הנחת תפילין וכדלעיל בסימן ל"ח ז"א דכל זה רק מחמת חומרא בעלמא שחוששין להפסיקתא אבל ש"ס דילן סובר דאין מוחין ע"ז וכדאיתא שם בב"י ועוד עבדים יוכיחו דאין מוחין בהן וכמו שכתבתי לעיל במ"ב בשם התו"ש[ג]. וגם לפ"ז אם האשה תקבל על עצמה מצות ציצית תהיה כשירה אף לר"ת לעשות ציצית לאנשים וז"א דא"כ בזה יודה ר"ת יהיה אודא הוכחת הרא"ש [בגיטין מ"ה ע"ב] מהא דקרטליתא דדביתהו דרחב"ד דעתידא למישדי בה תכלתא לצדיקי דעלמא דאתי. ולבר כ"ז אין גירות לחצאין עיין במס' גרים ועוד דא"כ בגר שמל ולא טבל דכתב הרא"ש בע"ז דאינו גרע מגר תושב דהרי קבל עליו כל המצות וא"כ לפ"ז יהיה כשר לכתיבת סת"ס ויהיה כשר לזביחה כישראל לשיטת הר"י דתלי בבר זביחה דהרי הוא מחזיק לעצמו במצות זביחה וסתמא דגמרא ביבמות מ"ו דאמר שם וכיון דלא טביל עו"ג הוא לא משמע כן: * **שכתבם אפיקורס.** הוא האדוק לעבודת כוכבים כן איתא בב"י בשם רש"י וכ"מ ברמב"ם הלכות תפילין פ"א הי"ג לאפוקי ממה שהוגה באיזה דפוס ברש"י גיטין מ"ה ע"ב אפיקורס יהודי שאינו מאמין לדברי רז"ל שזה אינו מפירש"י כידוע הגם שלעניים אחרים ג"ז הוא בכלל אפיקורס אבל לא לענין זה דישרף. ולענין דינא סופר כזה נ"ל פשוט דצריך לגנוז פרשיותיו דשמא לא עיבד הקלף לשמה ושמא לא כתב הפרשיות והאזכרות לשמה ושמא לא היה זהיר בדין חק תוכות כיון דאינו מאמין בדחז"ל וגם חשוד הוא להכשיל לאחרים מיהו אי איתרמי שעמדו אחרים ע"ג וראו שנעשה הכל כהלכה כגון שהוא לא כתב אלא איזו אותיות בהפרשיות אלו בפניהם או בהיריעות של הס"ת אפ"ה יש לעיין אם איש כזה הוא בכלל בר קשירה ולכאורה יש להביא ראיה להתיר דהלא לענין זביחה ג"כ מידריש מי שהוא בכלל בר זביחה אכול מזבחו ולא ממי שאינו בר זביחה וכדאיתא בחולין ג' ע"ב תוד"ה קסבר ואפ"ה פסק ביו"ד סימן ב' ס"ט דלדוקי וביתוסי אם נבדק סכינם ואחרים עומדים על גבם שחיטתם כשרה אלמא דכיון דאחזיק במצוה זו אף דלא כתיבה קרינן בהו שהם בני זביחה ומאמינים במצות זביחה וכדפירש הפמ"ג שם עי"ש א"כ ה"נ בענינו לכאורה אם אחרים עומדים ע"ג ורואין שלא היה בו חסרון דחק תוכות שמצוי מאד במלאכת הכתיבה וגם שנכתב לשמה אין לפוסלו דהוי עדיין בכלל בר קשירה אבל יש לדחות דהלא ידוע דאם שביק התירא ואכיל איסורא אף בדבר אחד תו הוי בכלל אפיקורס ואנשים כאלו בזמנינו ידוע שאינם חוששין כלל למצות ומצוי אצלם חילול שבת בפרהסיא ג"כ וא"כ דינם כמו שמסיק הש"ך שם לענין קראים ע"כ יותר טוב שימחקם ויכתוב אחרים תחתיהם אך אם אינו יכול למחקם מחמת כסדרן או באותיות השם צ"ע למעשה: * **אין לוקחין וכו' מכדי דמיהן וכו'.** עיין במ"ב במה שכתב וה"ה[ד] אם

שער הציון

(יז) ב"י: (יח) מ"א: (יט) עיין בתוס' שם ד"ה מעלין ולכך סתם השו"ע: (כ) ע"ת:

הגהות ותיקונים: **א)** סק"ה: **ב)** וביד אפרים: **ג)** הערו"ש: **ד)** דה"ה:

4. *Tefilin* /passages/ which were written by (12) a heretic (13) must be burnt. (14) There are /authorities/ who say that they require *genizah.*
5. If /*tefilin* passages/ were found in the possession of a heretic and it is unknown who wrote them, (15) they require *genizah.*

Mishnah Berurah

nevertheless not ceased to belong to the Jewish community because of this, since he is under duress.

See the *M.A.*, who contends that one should not be lenient in such a case, even if /the convert/ observes the Torah in private and is only slack about the donning of *tefilin*, since one must bear in mind that he is at any rate not a binder /of *tefilin*/. This is certainly /the case/ if he is a confirmed sinner over all /the mitzvos/ of the Torah in its entirety, unless due to dread of being killed he is afraid to fulfil /the mitzvos of/ the Torah even in private. See the *Beyur Ha-Gra*, who also agrees with the *M.A.*

The *M.A.* writes further, on the authority of the *D.M.*, that although a *mamzeyr*[6] or a *geyr toshav* [i.e., someone who has accepted upon himself the seven Noachian mitzvos] are not fit to write a Torah Scroll, as stated in the *Yo.D.*, Sec. 281, there is nevertheless no need to be concerned /if they write/ *tefilin* /passages/ or mezuzos. /However,/ all the Acharonim are agreed that a *geyr toshav* is not fit to write a Torah Scroll, a *tefilin* /passage/ or a mezuzah, since he is not a binder /of *tefilin*/. See the Beyur Halachah.

(12) A heretic. See the Beyur Halachah.[7]

(13) Must be burnt. /I.e.,/ with the mentions of the Divine Name, as /ruled/ below in Sec. 334, Par. 21; see there. For, ordinarily, when they write, they write for the sake of their idol.

(14) There are /authorities/ who say that they require *genizah.* /They reason/ that it is not usual for a heretic to don *tefilin.* /Consequently,/ he will definitely have written them to sell to a Jew and /, therefore,/ it may be that he did not write them for the sake of an idol.

The author /of the Shulchan Aruch/ is of the opinion that the first view is the ruling /to be followed/ and therefore wrote it without ascribing it /to specific authorities/. This is likewise the opinion of the *Taz* and of the *Perishah* and of the *Gra* in his *Beyur.*

(15) They require *genizah.* /This is because/ we are in doubt /as to/ whether he wrote them. However, one may not burn them in view of the doubt involved, as one must bear in mind that it is written,[8] "You should not do this to the Lord, your God".

6 I.e., someone born to a couple for whom union was halachically inconceivable.
7 The author explains there that a devout idol worshipper is meant. He adds that if *tefilin* passages were written by someone who has no faith in the teachings of the Sages the passages require *genizah*, as he may not have been careful to observe the necessary laws. If others stood over him and saw that he did everything as required, it is better, nevertheless, to erase and rewrite what he wrote. Where this is not possible, the ruling to be followed requires study.
8 *Devarim* 12:4.

* כשר לכתוב תפילין: ד ז תפילין * שכתבם (יב) אפיקורוס (יג) ישרפו: (יד) ח וי"א יגנזו: ה ט נמצאו ביד אפיקורוס ואין ידוע מי כתבם (טו) יגנזו: ו י נמצאו ביד א"י ואין ידוע מי כתבם (טז) כשרים:

ז * כ אין לוקחין תפילין ומזוזות וספרים מן הכותים (יז) יותר מכדי דמיהן

ז הרמב"ם בפ"א שם ח טור ור' ירוחם ט גיטין שם י שם וכלישנא בתרא ורמב"ם שם פ"א ור"ן כ גיטין שם

משנה ברורה

נפשו על אמונת ה' מ"מ לא יצא מכלל ישראל עי"ז כיון דהיה באונס ועי' במ"א שהעלה דאין להקל בזה אפי' אם בצינעא הוא שומר את התורה רק שבהנחת תפילין הוא מתעצל דהלא עכ"פ אינו בקשירה וכ"ש אם הוא מומר לכל התורה כולה אם לא שמחמת פחד שלא יהרגוהו הוא ירא לקיים את התורה אפילו בצינעא. ועיין בביאור הגר"א שמסכים ג"כ להמ"א. עוד כתב המ"א בשם הד"מ דאף דבס"ת ממזר וגר תושב [היינו שקיבל עליו שבע מצות בני נח] פסולים לכתוב כמו שכתב ביו"ד סימן רפ"א אפ"ה בתפילין ומזוזות אין לחוש וכל האחרונים הסכימו דגר תושב פסול לכתיבת סת"ם דהא אינו בקשירה ועיין בבה"ל: ד (יב) אפיקורס. ועיין בבה"ל: (יג) ישרפו. עם אזכרותיהן וכדלקמן בסימן של"ד סכ"א עי"ש דסתמו כשכותב לשם עבו"ג הוא כותב: (יד) וי"א יגנזו. דאין דרך אפיקורס (יז) להניח תפילין ובודאי כתבו למכור לישראל ואפשר שלא כתבו לשם עבו"ג. ודעת המחבר לפסוק כדעה א' לכן כתבו בסתמא וכן דעת הט"ז והפרישה והגר"א בביאורו: ה (טו) יגנזו. מספק שמא הוא כתבן אבל אין לשרוף מספק דהלא כתיב לא תעשון כן לה' אלהיכם: ו (טז) כשרים. דסתם עו"ג (יח) אין בקיאין לכתוב ובודאי ישראל כתבו. ובפרט במקומותינו שידוע שאין א"י יודעין לכתוב אפילו בס"ת שנמצא בידן מסיק הש"ך [ביו"ד בסימן רפ"א סק"ד [א]] דלכו"ע כשרה דתלינן דהא"י בזוז אותה: ז (יז) יותר וכו'. אבל במעט יותר משוין [דהיינו עד כדי (יט) חצי דינר בתפילין ולפי ערך זה בס"ת] חייבין לקנות מהן ואף דס"ת שנמצא ביד א"י י"א דיגנז [ביו"ד סימן רפ"א] אעפ"כ חייבין לקנות מהם ואפילו במעט יותר וכדי לגונזן בכדי שלא יבואו העו"ג לזלזל בהם ופשוט דה"ה אם הם פסולין מחמת עצמם ג"כ חייבין לקנות מהעו"ג כדי לגונזן אבל (כ) בכתבן אפיקורס

ביאור הלכה

לאבותיך המשיך הבי"ת וכל כה"ג) כדי שיהי' נראה כתיבה אחת דזה מותר מדינא אפילו בתפילין דבעינן כסדרן דזה אינו בכלל כתיבה וכדלעיל בסימן ל"ב לכן מותר זה אפילו ע"י פסולין כמו גרירה. ומה שכתבנו עוד או להגיה איזה אות דעתה הוא פסול כונתינו לאפוקי עשיית התגין שעל שעטנ"ז ג"ץ דגם בלא זה כשר בדיעבד וכבסימן ל"ו אין להחמיר בדיעבד גם בזה וה"ה העברת קולמוס על איזו אות דגם עתה יש שם אות עליו שרישומו ניכר אלא שמשמרו שלא יתמחק יותר ויפסל דכ"ז אינו בכלל כתיבה. ולכאורה יש להסתפק ביוד"י האלף והשין והעין שאין נוגעין ותינוק דלא חכים ולא טיפש מכירם וכן אם חסר קוץ השמאלי ביו"ד אם מהני תיקון ע"י אלו הפסולין בדיעבד מי נימא כמו דלענין שלא כסדרן מקילינן ואמרינן דאין זה כתיבה חדשה כיון דעיקר צורתו עליו ה"נ לענין זה ולא קרינן ביה כל שאינו בקשירה אינו בכתיבה או דילמא כיון דעכ"פ עתה האות פסול וע"י תיקונן של אלו הפסולין יוכשר האות פסול אפילו בדיעבד ולא דמי לגרירה דשם אינו עושה מעשה בגוף צורת האות כלל ואין להביא ראיה להקל בזה מדנקט המהר"ם בסוף דבריו וז"ל אכן אם היו הנגיעות בגוף האותיות עצמן כגון ברגלי הה"א והקו"ף או רגלי האלף בגגות או פני האלף היו נוגעים בגג שתחתיה והאשה הפרידה אותן פשיטא דהס"ת פסולה דהא א"א לתקנם כ"א בגרירת כל מה שנעשה בפסול לחזור ולכותבו מחדש וזה מיקרי כתיבה גמורה עכ"ל ולא נקט יותר רבותא דאפי' בזה שהיה קודם תיקון האשה ג"כ עיקר צורתו עליו דפסול כל שהוסיף בכתיבה ועל ידו הוכשר האות דאפשר משום דהמהר"מ רצה להשיב להשואל בשאלתו ששאל לפניו בגרירת האשה אם כשר והשיבו דיש חילוק בין גרירה לגרירה וכדאיתא שם לכך לא נקט רבותא זו וכן מסתבר. כתב הפמ"ג דקשר של דלי"ת ואף של יו"ד שבתפילין ס"י יראה דאין לעשותם כ"א לשמה ושלא לעשותם ע"י אשה וקטן דבכלל כתיבה הוה כמו השי"ן שבשל ראש עיין שם. ונ"ל דאין להחמיר בזה בקטן שהוא בן י"ג שנה אם גדול עומד ע"ג ומלוהו לעשות לשמה אף שלא ידעינן שהביא ב"ש דבלא"ה יש הרבה מקילין בזה וכנ"ל וגם לדברי התוספות שבת ס"ב ע"א ד"ה שי"ן עי"ש אין מקום לזה וכ"ש דא"ל להחמיר הקטן הזה לעצמו בזה דאם לא הביא ב"ש ואינו חייב במצות רק מדרבנן הלא גם בתפילין אין חייב רק מדרבנן אך הקשר שעשה הקטן הזה לעצמו קודם שנעשה בן י"ג נ"ל דצריך להתירו לאחר שנעשה בן י"ג ולחזור לעשותו דהרי יש הרבה פוסקים שסוברים דעתה מן התורה הוא בכלל איש וחייב במצות מחמת חזקה דרבא דכיון שהגיע לכלל שנים מסתמא הביא סימנים וגם הלא עכ"פ כשיבדק אח"כ וימצא שיש לו ב"ש הלא צריך לתלות שהביאם תיכף בזמנו ונעשה גדול למפרע וכדאיתא בח"מ סימן ל"ה. ודע עוד דלענין תפירת ס"ת ע"י נשים וה"ה כל אלו הפסולין יש הרבה מפקפקין בזה ע"כ יש להזהיר מאד ע"ז דלא כמו שנהגו איזה סופרים להקל בתפירת ס"ת ע"י נשים בעת סיום הספר ובדיעבד אם אפשר בקלות להתיר התפירות שתפרן האשה ולחזור ולתופרן בהכשר יחזור ויתקנם דכיון דיודע המקומות ואפשר לו לתקנם הוי כלכתחלה גמור אבל בלא"ה אין להחמיר בדיעבד כן פסק המהר"ם לובלין בתשובה ובעל מגן האלף חולק עליו ומצריך להתיר התפירות אפילו בדיעבד. ובמקום שהמנהג שנותנין לנשים לתפור הס"ת וא"א לשנות המנהג צריך להזהיר וליזהר שהתפירה ראשונה ואחרונה וגם באמצע יעשה הסופר מקודם ואח"כ יתן לנשים לתפור. [פ"ת יו"ד סימן רפ"א]: * **כשר לכתוב תפילין**. כ"ז איירי בגר צדק. ולענין גר תושב הסכימו הפמ"ג ול"ש ומחה"ש [ועוד הרבה] דפסול מטעם דהא אינו בקשירה והשע"ת [ב] המציא דבר חדש דאיירי הד"מ דמכשיר בגר תושב דקיבל עליו כל המצות חוץ מאיסור נבלה וא"כ הלא ישנו בקשירה ובאמת נלענ"ד שגם זה אינו דהלא עכ"פ אינו מוזהר על הקשירה ותדע דאטו אם אשה ועבד יקבלו עליהן מצות תפילין יהיו כשרים לכתיבת תפילין ואם תדחה משום דמוחין לנשים על הנחת תפילין וכדלעיל בסימן ל"ח ז"א דכל זה רק מחמת חומרא בעלמא שחוששין להפסיקתא אבל ש"מ דילן סובר דאין מוחין ע"ז וכדאיתא שם בב"י ועוד עבדים יוכיחו דאין מוחין בהן וכמו שכתבתי לעיל במ"ב בשם התו"ש [ג]. וגם לפ"ז אם האשה תקבל על עצמה מצות ציצית תהיה כשירה אף לר"ת לעשות ציצית לאנשים וז"א דא"כ בזה יודה ר"ת יהיה אודא הוכחת הרא"ש [בגיטין מ"ה ע"ב] מהא דקרטליתא דדביתהו דרחב"ד דעתידא למישדי בה תכלתא לצדיקי דעלמא דאתי. ולבד כ"ז אין גירות לחצאין עיין במס' גרים ועוד דא"כ בגר שמל ולא טבל דכתב הרא"ש בע"ז דאינו גרע מגר תושב דהרי קבל עליו כל המצות וא"כ לפ"ז יהיה כשר לכתיבת סת"ם ויהיה כשר לזביחה כישראל לשיטת הר"י דתלי בבר זביחה דהרי הוא מחזיק לעצמו במצות וזביחה וסתמא דגמרא ביבמות מ"ו דאמר שם וכיון דלא טביל עו"ג הוא לא משמע כן: * **שכתבם אפיקורס**. הוא האדוק לעבודת כוכבים כן איתא בב"י בשם רש"י וכ"מ ברמב"ם הלכות תפילין פ"א הי"ג לאפוקי ממה שהוגה באיזה דפוס ברש"י גיטין מ"ה ע"ב אפיקורס יהודי שאינו מאמין לדברי רז"ל שזה אינו מפירש"י כידוע הגם שלעניינים אחרים ג"ז הוא בכלל אפיקורס אבל לא לענין זה דישרף. ולענין דינא סופר כזה נ"ל פשוט דצריך לגנוז פרשיותיו דשמא לא עיבד הקלף לשמה ושמא לא כתב הפרשיות והאזכרות לשמה ושמא לא היה זהיר בדין חק תוכות כיון דאינו מאמין בדחז"ל וגם חשוד הוא להכשיל לאחרים מיהו אי איתרמי שעמדו אחרים ע"ג וראו שנעשה הכל כהלכה כגון שהוא לא כתב אלא איזו אותיות בהפרשיות אלו בפניהם או בהיריעות של הס"ת אפ"ה יש לעיין אם איש כזה הוא בכלל בר קשירה ולכאורה יש להביא ראיה להתיר דהלא לענין זביחה ג"כ מידריש מי שהוא בכלל בר זביחה אכול מזבחו ולא ממי שאינו בר זביחה וכדאיתא בחולין ג' ע"ב תוד"ה קסבר ואפ"ה פסק ביו"ד סימן ב' ס"ט דלדוקי וביתוסי אם נבדק סכינם ואחרים עומדים על גבם שחיטתם כשרה אלמא דכיון דאחזיק במצוה זו אף דלא כתיבה קרינן בהו שהם בני זביחה ומאמינים במצות זביחה וכדפירש הפמ"ג שם עי"ש א"כ ה"נ בענינינו לכאורה אם אחרים עומדים ע"ג ורואין שלא היה בו חסרון דחק תוכות שמצוי מאד במלאכת הכתיבה וגם שנכתב לשמה אין לפוסלו דהוי עדיין בכלל בר קשירה אבל יש לדחות דהלא ידוע דאם שביק התירא ואכיל איסורא אף בדבר אחד תו הוי בכלל אפיקורס ואנשים כאלו בזמנינו ידוע שאינם חוששין כלל למצות ומצוי אצלם חילול שבת בפרהסיא ג"כ וא"כ דינם כמו שמסיק הש"ך שם לענין קראים ע"כ יותר טוב שימחקם ויכתוב אחרים תחתיהם אך אם אינו יכול למחקם מחמת כסדרן או באותיות השם צ"ע למעשה: * **אין לוקחין וכו' מכדי דמיהן וכו'**. עיין במ"ב במה שכתב וה"ה [ד] אם

שער הציון

(יז) ב"י: (יח) מ"א: (יט) עיין בתוס' שם ד"ה מעלין ולכך סתם השו"ע: (כ) ע"ת:

הגהות ותיקונים: א) סק"ה: ב) וביד אפרים: ג) הערו"ש: ד) דה"ה:

6. If /*tefilin* passages/ were found in the possession of a non-Jew and it is unknown who wrote them, **(16)** they are /ruled as/ valid.
7. One should not buy *tefilin,* mezuzos or /Torah/ Scrolls from gentiles **(17)** for

Mishnah Berurah

(16) They are valid. /This is/ because non-Jews, generally, are not capable of writing /*tefilin* passages/ and they must definitely have been written by a Jew. /This applies/ especially in our localities, where it is well known that the non-Jews are incapable of writing /*tefilin* passages, etc./.

The *Shach* concludes [in the *Yo.D.*, Sec. 281, sub-Par. 5] that even if a Torah Scroll was found in the possession of /non-Jews/ it is valid according to all /authorities/, as we assume that the non-Jew looted it.

(17) For ... more. However, for a little more than their value [i.e., up to a half a dinar in the case of *tefilin* and a proportionate amount in the case of a Torah Scroll] one is obliged to buy them from them.

Although [in the *Yo.D.*, Sec. 281] /authorities are quoted/ who say that a Torah Scroll which was found in the possession of a non-Jew requires *genizah*, we are nevertheless obliged to purchase /Torah Scrolls/ from them, even for a little more /than their value/, in order to put them in the *genizah*, so that the non-Jews will not come to trifle with them. It is self-understood that, correspondingly, /even/ if they are invalid in themselves /because of a fault/ we are also obliged to purchase them from non-Jews, in order to put them in the *genizah*. However, if a heretic wrote them, in which case they are required to be burnt, it is unnecessary to purchase them from them.

(ז) (יח) הרבה כדי שלא להרגיל לגנבן ולגזלן: **ח** לאין נקחין אלא (יט) מן המומחה שבקי בחסירות ויתירות: **ט** (כ) מלקח ממי שאינו מומחה צריך (כא) לבדקן לקח ממנו מאה קציצות בודק מהם שלשה (ח) קציצות שתים של ראש ואחת של יד או שתים של יד ואחת של ראש אם מצאן כשרים הוחזק זה האיש והרי כולם כשרים (כב) ואין השאר צריך בדיקה ואם לקחן צבתים צבתים חזקתם מאנשים הרבה הם לקוחים לפיכך בודק מכל צבת ב׳ של ראש ואחד של יד או ב׳ של יד וא׳ של ראש נהמוכר תפילין ואמר שהיו של אדם (כג) גדול (כד) נאמן (כה) ואינם צריכין (ט) בדיקה:

י סתפילין שהוחזקו בכשרות אינם צריכים בדיקה (י) (כו) לעולם עואם אינו מניחן אלא (כז) לפרקים צריכים (יא) בדיקה פעמים בשבוע: הגה ואם אין לו מי שיוכל לבדוק ולחזור ולתופרן (כח) יניחם כך בלא בדיקה (ב"י בשם א"ח):

ל מנחות מ"ב כפי׳ התוספות והרא"ש מ עירובין צ"ז ורמב"ם בפ"ב שם נ תשובת הרא"ש ס ירושלמי בפרק בתרא דעירובין ורמב"ם בפ"ב ע טור וסמ"ה

מ דין איך לנהוג בקדושת התפילין. ובו ח׳ סעיפים:

א (א) אאסור לתלות (א) תפילין (ב) בין בבתים בין ברצועות אבל מותר לתלותן (ג) [א] (ג) בכיסן:

א ברכות כ"ד

שערי תשובה

[א] בכיסן. עבה"ט ובא"ר בשם מהר"י מברונה דאם נפלו לו תפילין בכיס שלהם יתן פרוטה לצדקה ע"ש. וכתב בתשובת חיים שאל (והוא בעהמ"ח בר"י

באר היטב

ממזר וגר תושב פסולין לכתוב כמ"ש בי"ד ר"ס רפ"א אפ"ה בתפילין ומזוזות אין לחוש: (ז) הרבה. אבל מעט יותר חייבים לקנות שלא יזלזלו בהם ואפילו במקום דטעונין גניזה אבל במקום דצריך שריפה א"צ ליקח מהם. ע"ת. מבואר בש"ס דאסור לומר לא"י שיתנם בזול יותר מדאי דילמא ירגז הא"י וינהג מנהג בזיון וכמעשה דטייעי: (ח) קלילות. ולא חיישינן שמא עיבדן שלא לשמן דהכל בקיאין בזה. תוספות. ועיין מ"ש היד אהרן: (ט) בדיקה. דעד אחד נאמן באיסורין ועכ"פ בעי שיהא מוחזק בכשרות עיין יו"ד סימן קי"ט: (י) לעולם. מיהו נכון לבודקה דמתקלקלין מזיעה. כנה"ג מ"א: (יא) בדיקה. דחיישינן שמא נתעפשו וה"ה אם נפלו למים צריך בדיקה. המוצא תפילין מושלכים בגניזה בלא רצועות ופתוחים יש לחוש שיש להם פסול נסתר אבל אם מצאם דרך הינוח בכיסן ליכא למיחש. הלק"ט ח"ב סי׳ קס"ו ע"ש:

(א) תפילין. אבל באקראי בעלמא שאוחז התפילין בידו והרצועות תלויות לית לן בה אבל אם התפילין תלויות אסור מ"א וט"ז כתב דאין בכלל זה מה שהתפילין של ראש תלוים באויר ומחזיקם ביד ברצועה ומשימם על הראש כי זהו צורך הנחתם ואין בזה בזיון ע"ש: (ב) בכיסן.

ביאור הלכה

אם הם פסולין מחמת עצמם והוא פשוט לדעה זו דמאי שנא אם הוא פסול מחמת חשש שכתבו פסול או חסרון חק תוכות ואולם לדעת הרמב"ם דפסק דקורין בספר שניקח מיד עו"ג אין ראיה דצריך ליקח כדי לגנוז ע"ש בגמרא ולענין כדי דמיהן לכאורה דצריך לחשוב כמו אם היו התפילין כשרין דהלא אם כתבו עו"ג ג"כ אין כדי דמיו שוה כלום וע"כ מה דאיתא בש"ס כדי דמיו ליגנז היינו כמו אם היה ס"ת כשר ומחמת זה לא יתרגל העו"ג דהוא אין יודע שהס"ת זו אין שוה אצלנו כלום [וכמו שפסק הט"ז ביו"ד רפ"א דאפילו ביחיד אין קורין בה] א"כ פשוט דה"ה נמי בענינינו. ולע"ק:

משנה ברורה

דטעונין שריפה א"צ ליקח מהם: (יח) הרבה. ואעפ"כ (כא) לא יסלק עצמו הישראל תיכף ממנו אף שאומר הרבה ומחוייב לעסוק אתו פן ישוה עמו. אך כשהעו"ג עומד על דבריו מניחן בידו. ומבואר בש"ס דאסור לומר לעו"ג שיתנם בזול יותר מדאי דלמא ירגז העו"ג וינהג בהם מנהג בזיון: **ח** (יט) מן המומחה. אבל לא ממי שאינו מומחה אע"פ שהלוקח רוצה לבדקן לפי שיש לחוש שמא יתעצל בבדיקתן מפני (כב) שטורח הוא לו להסיר התפירה ולחזור ולתופרן. ופשוט דמי שהוא סופר קבוע לרבים הוא בכלל מומחה. (כג) ומזוזה וה"ה פרשיות של תפילין ניקחות אפילו שלא מן המומחה ובתנאי שיבדקנה אח"כ: **ט** (כ) לקח. בדיעבד (כד) או שאין שם מומחה בעיר: (כא) לבדקן. (כה) בחסירות ויתירות וה"ה בתמונת האותיות אם הם כהלכה וכנ"ל בסי׳ ל"ו ס"א ואין לחוש שמא עיבדן שלא לשמן דהכל בקיאין בזה: (כב) ואין השאר. והוא שאומר שכתבן בעצמו או שאומר שלקחן מאדם אחד ותלינן שאותו האדם כתבן הכל בעצמו כיון שהם בצבת א׳ וכמש"כ הפרישה: (כג) גדול. נראה דה"ה אם אמר שלקחן ממומחה: (כד) נאמן. דעד אחד נאמן באיסורין וכתב המ"א דעכ"פ בעינן שמכירין אותו שהוא מוחזק בכשרות עיין יו"ד סימן קי"ט ס"ב בהג"ה. ולפי המבואר שם מוכח דאם ראינוהו שלבשן בעצמו נאמן בכל גווני דלעבור בעצמו בודאי אינו חשוד. וע"ש בש"ך סק"ה: (כה) וא"צ בדיקה. שמוקם על חבר שאינו מוציא מת"י דבר שאינו מתוקן: **י** (כו) לעולם. שכל זמן שתיפורין שלם (כו) הרי הן בחזקתן מן הדין ואין חוששין שמא נתמקה אות מתוכן או ניקבה. ומ"מ (כז) נכון לבדקן מפני שמתקלקלין מפני הזיעה. ואם (כח) נקרע תיפור הבתים או שנשרו במים צריכין בדיקה תיכף שמא נמחק הכתב או נתקלקל. וכל שצריך בדיקה מן הדין ואין לו מי שיבדוק ויתפור אותם (כט) מניחם בלא ברכה דלא שייך אוקמיה אחזקה כה"ג וכתב הח"א דה"ה אם מונחים במקום לח והכל לפי הענין: (כז) לפרקים. דחיישינן (ל) שמא נתעפשו לכך יבדקם שני פעמים בשמיטה: (כח) יניחם כך. ולענין ברכה משמע מח"א דצריך לברך והטעם נראה משום דלא ראינו עליהן ריעותא ברורה תשא"כ בנשרו במים או שנתקלקל העור וכנ"ל ולמעשה צ"ע. המוצא תפילין (לא) מושלכין בגניזה בלא רצועות ופתוחים יש לחוש שיש להם פסול נסתר אבל אם מצאן דרך הינוח בכיסן ליכא למיחש:

א (א) אסור לתלות. על היתד מפני שהוא דרך בזיון: (ב) בין בבתים. שהבתים תלויות למטה ובין שהרצועות תלויות למטה. ומ"מ (א) באקראי בעלמא שאוחז התפילין בידו והרצועות תלויות למטה אין להקפיד אבל אם התפילין תלויין אסור בכל גווני ואין בכלל זה מה (ב) שהתש"ר תלוי באויר ומחזיקן ביד ברצועות ומשימם על הראש כי זהו צורך הנחתן. ויש מניחין הש"ר על הדף וכדומה בשעה שלובשין: (ג) בכיסן. וס"ת אסור לתלותה (ג) בכל גווני אפילו כשהיא בתה"ק ותולה האה"ק ועיין בח"א כלל ל"א שכתב דאפילו כשאה"ק מחובר ביתידות לכותל אסור כל שאין תחתיו עומד דבר מה (ד) וספרים כגון ספרי תלמוד וכדומה דומה לתפילין. ומ"מ ספרים או סידורי תפלות (ה) הקבועים בלוחות שבהם שלשלת של כסף אסור לתלותן גם שהלוחות אין דומות לכיס לפי שהן מחוברות לסידור והרי הן כסידור עצמו.

מותר

שער הציון

(כא) ט"ז יו"ד סי׳ רפ"א: (כב) תוספות והרא"ש: (כג) ברייתא שם: (כד) פמ"ג: (כה) תוספות והרא"ש: (כו) הרמב"ם והובא בב"י: (כז) מ"א: (כח) ב"ח: (כט) פמ"ג: (ל) מ"א: (לא) בה"ט בשם הלק"ט: (א) מ"א: (ב) ט"ז ופמ"ג: (ג) מ"א: (ד) (ה) ממ"א ופמ"ג:

הערות והארות: 1) עיין במ"ב סי׳ קנ"ד סק"ט לענין תיבה המיוחדת לספרים המכורכים דמקרי תשמיש דתשמיש:

(18) considerably more than their value, so as not to get them into the habit of stealing or robbing them.

8. /*Tefilin*/ should only be acquired **(19)** from a qualified person who is familiar with the /letters which must be/ left out and the /letters which must be/ added.

9. **(20)** If one purchased /*tefilin*/ from an unqualified person, he must **(21)** examine them. If he purchased from him a hundred /*tefilin*/ capsules, he should examine /the passages of/ three capsules among them, /either/ of two head /*tefilin* capsules/ and one arm /*tefilin* capsule/ or of two arm /*tefilin* capsules/ and one head /*tefilin* capsule/. If he finds them valid, this person may be presumed /reliable/ and /the passages/ of all /the capsules/ are /therefore ruled as/ valid **(22)** and the other /capsules/ do not need examination.

/However,/ if he purchased /the *tefilin*/ in separate bundles, they are presumed to have been purchased from many people. Therefore, he must examine from every bundle /either the passages/ of two head /*tefilin* capsules/ and one arm /*tefilin* capsule/ or of two arm /*tefilin* capsules/ and one head /*tefilin* capsule/.

Mishnah Berurah

(18) Considerably. Nevertheless, the Jew should not go away from /the non-Jew/ immediately, even if he speaks of a considerable /price/, but he is obliged to deal with him in case he will /be able to/ come to terms with him. However, if the non-Jew insists on his demands, he should leave them in his possession.

It is clear from the Talmud[9] that it is forbidden to tell the non-Jew to hand them over too cheaply, in case the non-Jew will get angry and treat them in a disrespectful manner.

(19) From a qualified person. However, they may not /be acquired/ from an unqualified person, even though the purchaser wishes to examine them. This is because there are grounds for concern that he may be slack about examining them, because it is burdensome for one to remove the sewing and sew them up again.

It is self-understood that if someone is an established scribe /who writes *tefilin* passages/ for the public, he belongs to the category of /people/ who are qualified /to do so/.

A mezuzah and likewise /uninserted/ *tefilin* passages may be purchased even from an unqualified person, on condition that one examines them subsequently.

(20) If one purchased. /In view of what is stated in the previous paragraph this ruling applies/ once it is after the event /and one transgressed/ or when there is no qualified person there in the city.

(21) Examine them. /I.e., to check that the passages have been written correctly/ as regards the /letters which must be/ left out and the /letters which must be/ added. He must likewise /examine/ the symbols of the letters,/ to check/ whether they conform with halachic /requirements/, as /follows from what is ruled/ above in Sec. 36, Par. 1.

One need not be concerned in case /the parchment/ was not processed for the sake of /the mitzvah of *tefilin*/, as everyone is familiar with this /requirement/.

(22) And the other /capsules/ do not. /This ruling applies/ provided that /the seller/ says that he wrote them himself or says that he purchased them from one person. /In the latter case,/ we assume that the person wrote them all himself, in view /of the fact/ that they are in a single bundle, as stated by the *Perishah*.

9 *Gitin* 45b.

(ז) (יח) הרבה כדי שלא להרגיל לגנבן ולגזלן: **ח** ^ל אין נקחין אלא (יט) מן המומחה שבקי בחסירות ויתירות: **ט** (כ) ^מ לקח ממי שאינו מומחה צריך (כא) לבדקן לקח ממנו מאה קציצות בודק מהם שלשה (ח) קציצות שתים של ראש ואחת של יד או שתים של יד ואחת של ראש אם מצאן כשרים הוחזק זה האיש והרי כולם כשרים (כב) ואין השאר צריך בדיקה ואם לקחן צבתים צבתים חזקתם מאנשים הרבה הם לקוחים לפיכך בודק מכל צבת ב' של ראש ואחד של יד או ב' של יד וא' של ראש ^נ המוכר תפילין ואמר שהיו של אדם (כג) גדול (כד) נאמן (כה) ואינם צריכין (ט) בדיקה: **י** ^ס תפילין שהוחזקו בכשרות אינם צריכים בדיקה (י) (כו) לעולם ^ע ואם אינו מניחן אלא (כז) לפרקים צריכים (יא) בדיקה פעמים בשבוע: הגה ואם אין לו מי שיוכל לבדוק ולחזור ולתופרן (כח) יניחם כך בלא בדיקה (ב"י בשם א"ח):

ל מנחות מ"ב כפי' התוספות והרא"ש מ עירובין צ"ז ורמב"ם בפ"ג שם נ תשובת הרא"ש ס ירושלמי בפרק בתרא דעירובין ורמב"ם בפ"ב ע טור וסמ"ג

מ דין איך לנהוג בקדושת התפילין. ובו ח' סעיפים:

א (א) ^א אסור לתלות (א) תפילין (ב) בין בבתים בין ברצועות אבל מותר לתלותן (ג) [א] (ג) בכיסן:

א ברכות כ"ד

שערי תשובה

[א] בכיסן. עבה"ט ובא"ר בשם מהר"י מברונה דאם נפלו לו תפילין בכיס שלהם יתן פרוטה לצדקה ע"ש. וכתב בתשובת חיים שאל (והוא בעהמ"ח בר"י

באר היטב

ממזר וגר תושב פסולין לכתוב כמ"ש בי"ד ר"ס רפ"א אפ"ה בתפילין ומזוזות אין לחוש: (ז) הרבה. אבל מעט יותר חייבים לקנות שלא יזלזלו בהם ואפילו במקום דטעונין גניזה אבל במקום דצריך שריפה א"צ ליקח מהם. ע"ת. מבואר בש"ס דאסור לומר לא"י שיתנם בזול יותר מדאי דילמא ירגז הא"י וינהג מנהג בזיון וכמעשה דטייעי: (ח) קצילות. ולא חיישינן שמא עיבדן שלא לשמן דהכל בקיאין בזה. תוספות. ועיין מ"ש היד אהרן: (ט) בדיקה. דעד אחד נאמן באיסורין ועכ"פ בעי שיהא מוחזק בכשרות עיין יו"ד סימן קי"ט: (י) לעולם. מיהו נכון לבודקה דמתקלקלין מזיעה. כנה"ג מ"א: (יא) בדיקה. דחיישינן שמא נתעפשו וה"ה אם נפלו למים צריך בדיקה. המוצא תפילין מושלכים בגניזה בלא רצועות ופתוחים יש לחוש שיש להם פסול נסתר אבל אם מצאם דרך הינוח בכיסן ליכא למיחש. הלק"ט ח"ב סי' קס"ו ע"ש:

(א) תפילין. אבל באקראי בעלמא שאוחז התפילין בידו והרצועות תלויות לית לן בה אבל אם התפילין תלויות אסור מ"א וט"ז כתב דאין בכלל זה מה שהתפילין של ראש תלויים באויר ומחזיקם ביד ברצועה ומשימם על הראש כי זהו צורך הנחתם ואין בזה בזיון ע"ש: (ב) בכיסן.

ביאור הלכה

אם הם פסולין מחמת עצמם והוא פשוט לדעה זו דמאי שנא אם הוא פסול מחמת חשש שכתבו פסול או חסרון חק תוכות ואולם לדעת הרמב"ם דפסק דקורין בספר שניקח מיד עו"ג אין ראיה דצריך ליקח כדי לגנוז ע"ש בגמרא ולענין כדי דמיהן לכאורה דצריך לחשוב כמו אם היו התפילין כשרין דהלא אם כתבו עו"ג ג"כ אין כדי דמיו שוה כלום וע"כ מה דאיתא בש"ס כדי דמיו ליגנז היינו כמו אם היה ס"ת כשר ומחמת זה לא יתרגל העו"ג דהוא אין יודע שהס"ת זו אין שוה אצלנו כלום [וכמו שפסק הט"ז ביו"ד רפ"א דאפילו ביחיד אין קורין בה] א"כ פשוט דה"ה נמי בענינינו. ולע"ק:

משנה ברורה

דטעונין שריפה א"צ ליקח מהם: (יח) הרבה. ולענ"ד (כא) לא ימלך עצמו הישראל מיקח ממנו אף שאומר הגוי ומחייב לגנוק אתו כן ישוה עמו. אך כשהעו"ג עומד על דבריו מניחן בידו. ומבואר בש"ס דאסור לומר לעו"ג שיתנם בזול יותר מדאי דלמא ירגז העו"ג וינהג בהם מנהג בזיון: ח (יט) מן המומחה. אבל לא ממי שאינו מומחה אע"פ שהלוקח רוצה לבדקן לפי שיש לחוש שמא יתקלקל בבדיקתן מפני (כב) שטורח הוא לו להסיר התפירה ולחזור ולתופרן. ומשוע דמי שהוא סופר קבוע לרבים הוא בכלל מומחה. (כג) ומזוזה וה"ה פרשיות של תפילין ניקחות אפילו שלא מן המומחה ובתנאי שיבדקנה אח"כ: (כא) לבדקן. (כה) בחסירות ויתירות וה"ה בתמונת האותיות אם הם כהלכה וכנ"ל בסי' ל"ו ס"א ואין לחוש שמא עיבדן שלא לשמן דהכל בקיאין בזה: ט (כ) לקח. בדיעבד (כד) או שאין שם מומחה כנ"ל: (כב) ואין השאר. והוא שאומר שכתבן בעצמו או שאומר שלקחן מאדם אחד ותלינן שאותו האדם כתבן הכל בעצמו כיון שהם נמצאו א' וכמש"כ הפרישה: **(כג) גדול. נראה דה"ה אם אמר שלקחן ממומחה: (כד) נאמן. דעד אחד נאמן באיסורין וכתב המ"א דעכ"פ בעינן שמכירין אותו שהוא מוחזק בכשרות עיין יו"ד סימן קי"ט ס"ב בהג"ה. ולפי המבואר שם מוכח דאם ראינוהו שלבשן בעצמו נאמן בכל גווני דלעבור בעצמו בודאי אינו חשוד. וע"ש בש"ך סק"א: (כה) וא"צ בדיקה. שחזקה על חבר שאינו מוציא מת"י דבר שאינו מתוקן: י (כו) לעולם. שכל זמן שחיפויין שלם (כו) הרי הן בחזקתן מן הדין ואין חוששין שמא נמחקה אות מתוכן או ניקבה. ומ"מ (כז) נכון לבדקן מפני שמתקלקלין מפני הזיעה. ואם (כח) נקרע חיפוי הבתים או שנשרו במים צריכין בדיקה תיכף שמא נמחק הכתב או נתקלקל. וכל שצריך בדיקה מן הדין ואין לו מי שיבדוק ויתפור אותם (כט) מניחם בלא ברכה דלא שייך אוקמיה אחזקה כה"ג וכתב הח"א דה"ה אם מונחים במקום לח והכל לפי הענין: (כז) לפרקים. דחיישינן (ל) שמא נתעפשו לכך יבדקם שני פעמים בשמיטה:** (כח) יניחם כך. ולענין ברכה משמע מח"א דצריך לברך והטעם נראה משום דלא ראינו עליהן ריעותא ברורה תשא"כ נשרו במים או שנתקלקל העור וכנ"ל ולמעשה צ"ע. המוצא תפילין (לא) מושלכין בגניזה בלא רצועות ופתוחים יש לחוש שיש להם פסול נסתר אבל אם מצאן דרך הינוח בכיסן ליכא למיחש:

א (א) אסור לתלות. על היתד מפני שהוא דרך בזיון: (ב) בין בבתים. שהבתים תלוים למטה וכן שהרצועות תלויות למטה. ומ"מ (א) באקראי בעלמא שאוחז התפילין בידו והרצועות תלויות למטה אין להקפיד אבל אם התפילין תלוין אסור בכל גווני ואין בכלל זה מה (ב) שהתש"ר תלוי באויר ומחזיקן ביד ברצועות ומשימם על הראש כי זהו צורך הנחתן. ויש מניחין הש"ר על הדף וכדומה בשעה שלובשין: (ג) בכיסן. ומ"מ אסור לתלותם (ג) בכל גווני אפילו בשהיא בתה"ק ומולה התה"ק ועיין במ"א כלל ל"א שכתב דאפילו כשתה"ק מחובר ביתידות לכותל אסור כל שאין תחתיו עומד דבר מה (ד) וספרים כגון ספרי תלמוד וכדומה דומה לתפילין. ומ"מ ספרים או סידורי תפלות (ה) הקבועים בלוחות שהם תלויות של כסף אסור לתלותן גם שהלוחות אין דומות לכיס לפי שהן מחוברות לסידור והריהן כסידור עצמו. מותר

שער הציון

(כא) ט"ז יו"ד סי' רפ"א: (כב) תוספות והרא"ש: (כג) ברייתא שם: (כד) פמ"ג: (כה) תוספות והרא"ש: (כו) הרמב"ם והובא בב"י: (כז) מ"א: (כח) ב"ח: (כט) פמ"ג: (ל) מ"א: (לא) בה"ט בשם הלק"ט: (א) מ"א: (ב) ט"ז ופמ"ג: (ג) מ"א: (ד) (ה) ממ"א ופמ"ג:

הערות והארות: 1) עיין במ"ב סי' קנ"ד סק"ט לענין תיבה המיוחדת לספרים המכורכים דמקרי תשמיש דתשמיש:

If someone who sells *tefilin* says that they are /the work/ of (23) a distinguished person, (24) he may be trusted (25) and /the *tefilin* passages/ do not need to be examined.

10. *Tefilin* /passages/ which /according to the halachah/ are presumed valid do not need to be examined (26) ever. /However,/ if they are only donned (27) occasionally, they must be examined twice in a seven year cycle.

Mishnah Berurah

(23) A distinguished person. It appears /logical/ that the same ruling /applies/ if he says that he acquired them from a qualified person.

(24) He may be trusted. /This is/ because where /a question of/ prohibition is involved the evidence of one person can be trusted.

The *M.A.* writes that it is at any rate necessary for us to know that /the seller/ is held to be reliable. See the *Yo.D.*, Sec. 119, in the gloss to Par. 2. According to what is stated there, it is clear that if one saw him wear them himself he is trusted in all cases, since he is definitely not suspected of transgressing himself. See there in the *Shach*, sub-Par. 1.

(25) And /the *tefilin* passages/ do not need to be examined. /This is/ because in the case of a staunch observer it may be presumed that he does not allow an article which is not in order out of his possession.

(26) Ever. /This is/ because as long as their cover is whole they continue to be presumed /valid/ halachically and we are not afraid that a letter in them has become erased or perforated. Nevertheless, it is proper to examine them, since they get spoiled by sweat.

If the cover of the housings became torn or if /the housings/ were soaked in water, /the passages/ require immediate examination, in case the script became erased or spoiled.

Whenever /*tefilin* passages/ require examination halachically and one does not have anyone who can examine them and sew up /the *tefilin* again/, he should don /the *tefilin*/ without /making/ a blessing /over them/. /This is/ because in such circumstances there is no question of relying on their presumed /validity/. The *Ch.A.* writes that the same ruling /applies/ if the *tefilin* are lying in a damp place. Everything depends on the /particular/ circumstances.

(27) Occasionally. /Then/ we are afraid that they may have become moldy. Therefore, one should examine them twice in a seven year cycle.

באר הגולה

ל מנחות מ"ב כפי' התוספות והרא"ש
מ עירובין ל"ז ורמב"ם בפ"ב שם
נ תשובת הרא"ש
ס ירושלמי בפרק בתרא דעירובין ורמב"ם בפ"ב ע טור וסא"ח

(ז) (יח) הרבה כדי שלא להרגיל לגנבן ולגזלן: ח לאין נקחין אלא (יט) מן המומחה שבקי בחסירות ויתירות: ט (כ) מלקח ממי שאינו מומחה צריך (כא) לבדקן לקח ממנו מאה קציצות בודק מהם שלשה (ח) קציצות שתים של ראש ואחת של יד או שתים של יד ואחת של ראש אם מצאן כשרים הוחזק זה האיש והרי כולם כשרים (כב) ואין השאר צריך בדיקה ואם לקחן צבתים צבתים חזקתם מאנשים הרבה הם לקוחים לפיכך בודק מכל צבת ב' של ראש ואחד של יד או ב' של יד וא' של ראש נהמוכר תפילין ואמר שהיו של אדם (כג) גדול (כד) נאמן (כה) ואינם צריכין (ט) בדיקה: י סתפילין שהוחזקו בכשרות אינם צריכים בדיקה (י) (כו) לעולם עואם אינו מניחן אלא (כז) לפרקים צריכים (יא) בדיקה פעמים בשבוע: הגה ואם אין לו מי שיוכל לבדוק ולחזור ולתופרן (כח) יניחם כך בלא בדיקה (ב"י בשם א"ח):

מ דין איך לנהוג בקדושת התפילין. ובו ח' סעיפים:

א (א) אאסור לתלות (א) תפילין (ב) בין בבתים בין ברצועות אבל מותר לתלותן (ב) [א] (ג) בכיסן: א ברכות כ"ד

שערי תשובה

[א] בכיסן. עבה"ט ובא"ר בשם מהר"י מברונה דאם נפלו לו תפילין בכים שלהם יתן פרוטה לצדקה ע"ש. וכתב בתשובת חיים שאל (והוא בעהמ"ח בר"י

באר היטב

ממזר וגר תושב פסולין לכתוב כמ"ש בי"ד ר"ס רפ"א אפ"ה בתפילין ומזוזות אין לחוש: (ז) הרבה. אבל מעט יותר חייבים לקנות שלא יזלזלו בהם ואפילו במקום דטעונין גניזה אבל במקום דצריך שריפה א"צ ליקח מהם. ע"ת. מבואר בש"ס דאסור לומר לא"י שיתנם בזול יותר מדאי דילמא ירגז הא"י וינהג מנהג בזיון וכמעשה דטייעי: (ח) קצילות. ולא חיישינן שמא עיבדן שלא לשמן דהכל בקיאין בזה. תוספות. ועיין מ"ש היד אהרן: (ט) בדיקה. דעד אחד נאמן באיסורין ועכ"פ בעי שיהא מוחזק בכשרות עיין יו"ד סימן קי"ט: (י) לעולם. מיהו נכון לבודקה דמתקלקלין מזיעה. כנה"ג מ"א: (יא) בדיקה. דחיישינן שמא נתעפשו וה"ה אם נפלו למים צריך בדיקה. המוצא תפילין מושלכים בגניזה בלא רצועות ופתוחים יש לחוש שיש להם פסול נסתר אבל אם מצאם דרך הינוח בכיסן ליכא למיחש. הלק"ט ח"ב סי' קס"ו ע"ש:

(א) תפילין. אבל באקראי בעלמא שאוחז התפילין בידו והרצועות תלויות לית לן בה אבל אם התפילין תלויות אסור מ"א וט"ז כתב דאין בכלל זה מה שהתפילין של ראש תלוים באויר ומחזיקם ביד ברצועה ומשימם על הראש כי זהו צורך הנחתם ואין בזה בזיון ע"ש: (ב) בכיסן.

ביאור הלכה

אם הם פסולין מחמת עצמם והוא פשוט לדעה זו דמאי שנא אם הוא פסול מחמת חשש שכתבו פסול או חסרון חק תוכות ואולם לדעת הרמב"ם דפסק דקורין בספר שניקח מיד עו"ג אין ראיה דצריך ליקח כדי לגנוז ע"ש בגמרא ולענין כדי דמיהן לכאורה דצריך לחשוב כמו אם היו התפילין כשרין דהלא אם כתבו עו"ג ג"כ אין כדי דמיו שוה כלום וע"כ מה דאיתא בש"ס כדי דמיו ליגנז היינו כמו אם היה ס"ת כשר ומחמת זה לא יתרגל העו"ג דהוא אין יודע שהס"ת זו אין שוה אצלנו כלום [וכמו שפסק הט"ז ביו"ד רפ"א דאפילו ביחיד אין קורין בה] א"כ פשוט דה"ה נמי בענינינו. ולע"ק:

משנה ברורה

דטעונין שריפה א"צ ליקח מהם: (יח) הרבה. ואעפ"כ (כא) לא יסלק עצמו הישראל מיכף ממנו אף שאומר הרבה ומחויב לעסוק אתו מן ישוה עמו. אך כשהעו"ג עומד על דבריו מניחן בידו. ומבואר בש"ס דאסור לומר לעו"ג שיתנם בזול יותר מדאי דלמא ירגז העו"ג וינהג בהם מנהג בזיון: ח (יט) מן המומחה. אבל לא ממי שאינו מומחה אע"פ שהלוקח רוצה לבדקן לפי שיש לחוש שמא יתעצל בבדיקתן מפני (כב) שטורח הוא לו להסיר התפירה ולחזור ולתופרן. ופשוט דמי שהוא סופר קבוע לרבים הוא בכלל מומחה. (כג) ומזוזה וה"ה פרשיות של תפילין ניקחות אפילו שלא מן המומחה ובתנאי שיבדקנה אח"כ: ט (כ) לקח. בדיעבד (כד) או שאין שם מומחה בעיר: (כא) לבדקן. (כה) בחסירות ויתירות וה"ה בתמונת האותיות אם הם כהלכה וכנ"ל בסי' ל"ו ס"א ואין לחוש שמא עיבדן שלא לשמן דהכל בקיאין בזה: (כב) ואין השאר. והוא שאומר שכתבן בעצמו או שאומר שלקחן מאדם אחד ותלינן שאותו האדם כתבן הכל בעצמו כיון שהם בצבת א' וכמש"כ הפרישה: (כג) גדול. נראה דה"ה אם אמר שלקחן ממומחה: (כד) נאמן. דעד אחד נאמן באיסורין וכתב המ"א דעכ"פ בעינן שמכירין אותו שהוא מוחזק בכשרות עיין יו"ד סימן קי"ט ס"ב בהג"ה. ולפי המבואר שם מוכח דאם ראינוהו שלבשן בעצמו נאמן בכל גווני דלעבור בעצמו בודאי אינו חשוד. וע"ש בש"ך סק"א: (כה) וא"צ בדיקה. שחזקה על חבר שאינו מוציא מת"י דבר שאינו מתוקן: י (כו) לעולם. שכל זמן שתיפורין שלם (כו) הרי הן בחזקתן מן הדין ואין חוששין שמא נמחקה אות מתוכן או ניקבה. ומ"מ (כז) נכון לבדקן מפני שמתקלקלין מפני הזיעה. ואם (כח) נקרע תיפור הבתים או שנשרו במים צריכין בדיקה תיכף שמא נמחק הכתב או נתקלקל. וכל שצריך בדיקה מן הדין ואין לו מי שיבדוק ויתפור אותם (כט) מניחם בלא ברכה דלא שייך אוקמיה אחזקה כה"ג וכתב המ"א דה"ה אם מונחים במקום לח והכל לפי הענין: (כז) לפרקים. דחיישינן (ל) שמא נתעפשו לכך יבדקם שני פעמים בשמיטה: (כח) יניחם כך. ולענין ברכה משמע מס"א דצריך לברך והטעם נראה משום דלא ראינו עליהן ריעותא ברורה משא"כ בנשרו במים או שנתקלקל העור וכנ"ל ולמעשה צ"ע. המוצא תפילין (לא) מושלכין בגניזה בלא רצועות ופתוחים יש לחוש שיש להם פסול נסתר אבל אם מצאן דרך הינוח בכיסן ליכא למיחש:

א (א) אסור לתלות. על היתד מפני שהוא דרך בזיון: (ב) בין בבתים. שהבתים תלויות למטה ובין שהרצועות תלויות למטה. ומ"מ (א) באקראי בעלמא שאוחז התפילין בידו והרצועות תלויות למטה אין להקפיד אבל אם התפילין תלויין אסור בכל גווני ואין בכלל זה מה (ב) שהתש"ר תלוי באויר ומחזיקן ביד ברצועות ומשימם על הראש כי זהו צורך הנחתן. ויש מניחין הש"ר על הדף וכדומה בשעה שלובשין: (ג) בכיסן. וס"ת אסור לתלותה (ג) בכל גווני אפילו כשהיא בארגז ותולה הארגז ועיין בח"א כלל ל"א שכתב דאפילו כשהארגז מחובר ביתידות לכותל אסור כל שאין תחתיו עומד דבר מה (ד) וספרים כגון ספרי תלמוד וכדומה דומה לתפילין. ומ"מ ספרים או סידורי תפלות (ה) הקבועים בלוחות שבהם שלשלת של כסף אסור לתלותן גם שהלוחות אין דומות לכים לפי שהן מחוברות לסידור והרי[1] הן כסידור עצמו.

מותר

שער הציון

(כא) ט"ז יו"ד סי' רפ"א: (כב) תוספות והרא"ש: (כג) ברייתא שם: (כד) פמ"ג: (כה) תוספות והרא"ש: (כו) הרמב"ם והובא בב"י: (כז) מ"א: (כח) ב"ח: (כט) פמ"ג: (ל) מ"א: (לא) בה"ט בשם הלק"ט: (א) מ"א: (ב) ט"ז ופמ"ג: (ג) מ"א: (ד) (ה) ממ"א ופמ"ג:

הערות והארות: 1) עיין במ"ב סי' קנ"ד סק"ט לענין תיבה המיוחדת לספרים המכורכים דמקרי תשמיש דתשמיש:

Gloss: If one does not have someone who is able to examine them and sew up /the tefilin/ *again,* (28) *he may don them as they are without examination. (...)*

§40: THE LAW AS REGARDS HOW ONE SHOULD ACT WITH RESPECT TO THE HOLINESS OF *TEFILIN*

(Contains Eight Paragraphs)

1. (1) It is forbidden to hang up *tefilin* (2) either by the housings or by the straps, but it is permitted to hang them up (3) in their bag.

Mishnah Berurah

(28) **He may don them as they are.** As regards /making/ a blessing /over them/, it is implied by the *Ch.A.* that it is necessary to make the blessing. The reason seems /to be/ that /if the reason for the examination is merely that they are only donned occasionally,/ clear grounds for concern have not been observed on them. This is not the case when /*tefilin*/ were soaked in water or where the skin /of the housings/ became spoiled, which is /discussed/ above. /Further/ study is required as regards /the ruling to be followed/ in practice.

If one finds *tefilin* cast in the *genizah* without straps and open, there are grounds for fear that they have a hidden invalidity. However, if one finds them placed normally in their bag there is no basis for concern.

§40

(1) **It is forbidden to hang up.** /I.e.,/ on a peg.

/The reason is/ because this is a disrespectful manner /in which to treat the *tefilin*/.

(2) **Either by the housings.** /I.e.,/ either with the housings suspended below or with the straps suspended below.

Nevertheless, one need not be particular /to avoid/ holding the *tefilin* in his hand with the straps suspended below on a mere isolated occasion. Suspending the *tefilin* units, however, is forbidden in all circumstances. /However,/ suspending the head *tefilin* in the air and holding them in one's hand by the straps and /then/ placing them on the head is not classed as /a transgression of/ this /prohibition/, as this is necessary for donning them. There are /people/ who place the head /*tefilin*/ on a shelf or something similar when they put them on.

(3) **In their bag.** A Torah Scroll may not be hung in any manner, even if it is in a Holy Ark and one hangs the Holy Ark. See the *Ch.A.* in Sec. 31, where he writes that it is even forbidden for a Holy Ark /which contains a Torah Scroll/ to be joined to the wall with pegs, whenever there is nothing standing underneath /supporting/ it.

/Holy/ books, such as the books of the Talmud and similar /books/, are comparable to *tefilin* /in this respect/. Nevertheless, /holy/ books or prayer sidurim which are bound in covers which have a silver chain are forbidden to be hung in these /covers/. /This is/ because the covers are not comparable to a bag as they are joined to the sidur /etc./ and are like the sidur itself.

ב * בבית שיש בו (ג) [ג](ד) תפילין * אסור לשמש בו (ה) מטתו (ו) עד שיוציאם או שיניחם (ז) בכלי תוך כלי והוא (ח) שאין השני מיוחד (ד) להם שאם הוא מיוחד אפי' מאה חשובים כא': הגה ואם שניהם אינם מיוחדים להם או שהפנימי אינו מיוחד להם והחיצון מיוחד להם מותר (וע"ל סי' ר"מ סעיף ו) (ב"י): ג * גאפי' להניחם בכלי תוך כלי אסור להניחם תחת מרגלותיו דוכן אסור להניחם תחת מראשותיו (ט) כנגד ראשו האפילו

ב שם כ"ה ג שם ד שם ה ר' יונה שם

באר היטב

אבל ס"ת אסור לתלות אפילו בכיס חידושי הרשב"א. הסידורים שקבועים בהם שלשלת של כסף אסור לתלות בהם מ"א. ומותר לכתוב פסוקים בנייר ולתלותן בבהכ"נ כנה"ג בשם מהרי"ט. נוהגים להתענות מי שנופלים לו תפילין וה"ה כשנפל ס"ת ובתשו' משפטי שמואל סימן י"ב תמלא סמך למנהג. וכתב המ"א בסי' מ"ד ס"ק ה' נ"ל דמיירי בלא נרתיקן. אבל בס"ת אפילו בנרתיקן ע"ש ועיין כנה"ג ובס' שמות בארץ בקונטרס כפות תמרים דף י"ג: (ג) תפילין. ואם פירס טלית על הכיס של תפילין אף ע"פ שאין כרוך מלמטה שרי שהטלית לא מיקרי כליין מיהו אותן המניחין כיס התפילין והטלית לתוך כיס גדול גם הכיס גדול מיקרי כליין וצריך עוד כלי על גביו. ומיהו אם כיס התפילין מחובר למעלה על כיס הטלית. הצד השני של הכיס גדול לא מיקרי כליין מ"א. ותשובת מהריט"ץ סימן קל"א כתב הכיס שאנו מניחין טלית והתפילין מיקרי כלי שאין כליין ומותר לשמש מטתו והיינו דוקא כשלא הכין הכיס אלא לטלית ואחר כך הניח תפילין אז מותר אבל אם מתחלה הכין הכיס לטלית ותפילין אסור דמיקרי כליין ע"ש. אם כרך הכיס במטפחת בשעת הדחק מיקרי גם המטפחת כלי אחד מהריט"ץ שם. אם המזוזה בפנים בחדר צריך ג"כ כלי בתוך כלי ואם יש זכוכית על השם די בפריסת סודר עליה מ"א וט"ז ביו"ד סימן רפ"ו כתב דכיסוי זכוכית לא מהני ע"ש משמע דמיירי אפילו פרס סודר ע"ג דאסור דבכלי א' פשיטא דאסור ומ"א חולק עליו: (ד) להם. ר"ל דהכלי בתוך כלי לא בעינן שיהא שניהם כלים שאינם מיוחדים רק א' מהם והכלי שהוא מיוחד מצטרף עם הכלי שאינו מיוחד והרב רמ"א לא בא רק לפרש דברי המחבר ב"י דלא תימא דאם תרווייהו אינם מיוחדים להם או שהפנימי אינו מיוחד והחיצון מיוחד יהא אסור הואיל ונקיט המחבר בלישנא והוא שאין השני מיוחד להם קמ"ל דמותר. אבל כלי

שערי תשובה

ומח"ב) שיש שרצו להתענות מפני שראו נפילת תפילין ודחו דבריהם דנפל מידו שאני ע"ש הביאו בקצרה במח"ב: [ג] תפילין. עיין בה"ט ובש"ל כתב דמה שמניחים הטלית ע"ג תפילין אינו יודע על מה סמכו העולם להתיר דלכ"ע קדושת תפילין חמורה מצילית וראוי שיהא הטלית בכיס אחד ותפילין בכיס אחר דלהניח התפילין על הטלית אינו נכון שלא יצטרך לעבור על המצות כו' עיין שם. ונראה דאם אין לו כיס לתפילין ומניח הטלית עליהם לשמירה שלא יתלכלכו וכה"ג הרי הטלית נעשה כאילו הוא כליין ושרי. ובשו"ת תשב"ץ ח"ג סימן כ"ו כיס של תפילין יש לעשותו צר קצת כדי שיפגע תחילה בש"י ולא יצטרך לעבור על המצות ומה שאמרו כיס של תפילין טפח היינו לענין הנחה על גבי קרקע דבכלי שהוא כליין אם אין בו טפח יש זלזול אבל אין צריך שיהיה בו חלל טפח אחר שהכניס התפילין שיהיה חוצץ או מגין בפני ערוה או תינוקות שבבית. אף על גב דבכיסוי כל דהו מהני לענין והיה מחנך קדוש עיין שם. ולענין כלי בתוך כלי לענין תשה"מ יתבאר

משנה ברורה

מותר לכתוב (ו) פסוקים בנייר ולתלותן בפתח ביהכ"נ. נוהגים העולם (ז) להתענות כשנופל תפילין מידו על הארץ בלא נרתיקן וה"ה כשנופל ס"ת אפילו בנרתיקן. ועיין בא"ר שכתב דאפילו תפילין בנרתיקן יתן פרוטה לצדקה: ב (ד) תפילין. וה"ה (ח) חומשים או סדורי תפילות או שאר ספרים בין בכתיבה או (ט) בדפוס הכל יש בהם קדושה ובעינן כלי תוך כלי ואפילו אם הן כתב משיט"א [היינו שאינה כתיבת סת"ס והוא רק כתב אשורי] וכריכת (י)[1]הספר אינה נחשבת לכיסוי דהיא מגוף הספר ובעינן עוד שני כיסוין. ועיין ביו"ד בסי' רע"א בט"ז שם סק"ח שכתב כל המיקל בקדושת ספרים הנדפסין עתיד ליתן את הדין דדפוס הוי כמו כתיבה. אך בתשובת חו"י סי' קפ"ז[א] נוטה להקל בזה (יא) בשעת הדחק כשאין לו במה לכסות: (ה) מטתו. או (יב) לעשות צרכיו: (ו) עד שיוציאם. בחדר אחר או שמפסיק בפניהם במחיצה גבוה יו"ד טפחים. ועיין לקמן בסי' ר"מ במ"א סקט"ו: (ז) בכלי תוך כלי. ל"ד כלים (יג) דה"ה שני כיסוין (יד) ואם פירס טלית או שאר כיסוי על הכיס של תפילין אע"פ שהכיסוי אין מכסה רק למעלה ומן הצדדין ולא למטה אפ"ה שרי. ועיין בבה"ל. ואותן המניחין כיס התפילין והטלית לתוך כיס אחד גדול הרי גם הכיס הגדול נקרא כליין המיוחד להן וצריך עוד כסוי על גבן (טו) אם לא שמכסה בטלית על התפילין בתוך הכיס דאז שרי דהטלית אינו כליין וה"ה (טז) אם כיס התפילין מחובר למעלה על הכיס הגדול הרי צד הב' של כיס הגדול אין נקרא כליין ומועיל להן (יז) אם הפכן. ועיין בביאור הלכה מה שכתבתי בשם הא"ר. כתב המ"א דה"ה במזוזה הקבועה לפנים בחדר צריך כלי בתוך כלי דהיינו שיכסה אותה בב' כסוין ואחד מהם יהיה עכ"פ אינו מיוחד לה וכדלקמן ואם על המזוזה יש כסוי זכוכית אף שהמזוזה נראית מתוכה אפ"ה נחשבת כסוי אחד ודי בפריסת סודר על המזוזה דהא עתה לא מיתחזיא וכ"כ הדה"ח. אבל לכו"ע לא מהני אם יכסנה עוד בזכוכית מלמעלה אע"ג שמכוסה בשני כסוין דהא המזוזה נראית מתוכן. כתב בחכמת אדם נ"ל דבין במזוזה או שאר ספרים אם עשה מתחלה ב' כלים שיחשב אחד לכלי בתוך כלי כגון שכרך המזוזה בנייר ואח"כ הניחה בתיק שלה מותר כיון שבתחלה כיון לכך. ויתר כל הדינים בזה נבאר לקמן בסימן ר"מ בעזה"י: (ח) שאין השני. לאו דוקא (יח) וה"ה אם הפנימי אינו מיוחד והחיצון מיוחד או ששניהם אינם מיוחדים וכמו שכתוב בהג"ה ואינו אסור כלי בתוך כלי רק אם שניהם מיוחדים אבל אם אחד אינו מיוחד מצטרף עם המיוחד ושרי והגה"ה לא בא רק לפרש דברי המחבר דלא נטעה בלישניה וכלי אחד אפילו אינו מיוחד לא מהני ואסור: ג (ט) כנגד ראשו. שהוא ג"כ דרך בזיון:

ביאור הלכה

* בית שיש בו וכו' בכת"כ. עיין במ"ב במה שכתב ואם פירש טלית וכו' והשמטתי מה שהביא הבה"ט בשם מהריט"ץ שמסתפק בכיס שהי' כרוך עליו מטפחת שכל האחרונים השיגו עליו דודאי שרי מהא דגלימא אקמטרא דשרי רבא בברכות כ"ו אף שהכיסוי העליון אין מכסה מכל הצדדים וכ"ש בזה אך אם שני הכיסויים היה כזה שלא היה מכוסה רק למעלה ולא למטה לע"ק והפוסקים לא הזכירו חילוק בזה. ולענין כיס התפילין שמונח בתוך כיס גדול של הטלית עיין במ"ב שכתבנו דהכיס גדול הוא כליין זהו דעת המג"א והעתיק הדה"ח דבריו. אך הא"ר הביא בשם המהריט"ץ להקל בשעת הדחק בזה והשמטתי זה משום דהא יכול לכסות התפילין בהטלית וכמ"ש בפנים אך נ"מ לכאורה מהא דמהריט"ץ לענין שמותר לצור מעות בשעת הדחק בהכיס של טלית דאינו נקרא מיוחד לתפילין כיון שהוא לשניהם וכ"כ הח"א בכלל י"ד אבל באמת נ"ל דזה לכו"ע מותר וכמו שנבאר אי"ה לקמן בכלל[ב] מ"ב בבה"ל עי"ש: * אסור לשמש מטתו. עיין במ"ב דה"ה לעשות בו צרכיו והוא מהדה"ח ול"ע מנין לו זה ומלקמן סימן מ"ג סעיף ז' אין ראיה לזה ובודאי דבעי כיסוי [ועיין בסימן שט"ו ס"ב[ג]] אבל כלי בתוך כלי מנין: * אפילו וכו' כנגד ראשו אפילו בכלי תוך כלי. ואפילו אם היו כבת"כ קודם שנתנם תחת הכר וכ"ש אם ע"י צירוף הכר נעשה כלי בתוך כלי כן מוכח מן הרמב"ס. ועיין במ"א סק"ד ועכ"פ בדין זה לא פליגי האחרונים על הרמב"ס:

מותר

שער הציון

(ו) הכל ממ"א ופמ"ג: (ז) מ"א בסימן מ"ד סק"ה: (ח) לקמן בסימן ר"מ עי"ש: (ט) פמ"ג בסי' ר"מ עי"ש: (י) פמ"ג: (יא) וכן נוטה הא"ר: (יב) דה"ח: (יג) פשוט: (יד) מ"א: (טו) דה"ח (טז) מ"א: (יז) לבש"ר: (יח) בה"ט וש"א:

הגהות ותיקונים: א) קפ"ד: ב) בסימן: ג) ס"א:

הערות והארות: 1) עיין במ"ב סי' מ"ג ס"ק כ"ה לענין להכניס ספרים שיש בהם שמות בבהכ"ס כשהם תיק בתוך תיק:

2. When a room contains (4) *tefilin*, one is forbidden to have marital (5) relations /there/ (6) until he has taken them out /of the room/.

Alternatively, he may place /the *tefilin*/ (7) in a receptacle which is inside

Mishnah Berurah

It is permitted to write Scriptural verses on paper and hang them at the entrance to the Synagogue.

It is the universal practice /for one/ to fast if *tefilin* fell from his hand to the ground when they were not in their case. /This is the practice,/ correspondingly, when a Torah Scroll fell, even if /it was then/ in its case. See the *E.R.*, who writes that even if *tefilin* /fell when they were/ in their case one should give a *perutah*[1] to charity.

(4) ***Tefilin.*** The same ruling /applies/ to *chumashim*, prayer sidurim or other /holy/ books. Irrespective of whether they are written or printed, they all have holiness and /for one to be permitted to have marital relations with them in the room/ it is necessary /for them to be in/ a receptacle which is inside /another/ receptacle. This is even /the case/ if they are written in fine script [i.e., not with the script /used/ for Torah Scrolls, *tefilin* /passages/ and mezuzos, for which only Assyrian script /may be used/].

The binding of a book is not considered a cover /for this purpose/ as it is /part/ of the body of the book. /Consequently,/ a further two covers are required.

See the *Yo.D.*, Sec. 271 in the *Taz* there, sub-Par. 8. He writes that whoever is lenient with respect to the holiness of printed books is destined to pay the penalty, as print /has the same ruling/ as writing /in this respect/. However, in a responsum of the *Chav. Y.*, Sec. 184, /the author/ is inclined to be lenient about this as regards a time of pressing /need/, when one does not have /anything/ with which to cover /the books/.

(5) Relations. Or to relieve himself.

(6) Until he has taken them out. /I.e., until he has removed them/ to another room or separated from them by means of a partition which is ten handbreadths high. See below in Sec. 240 in the *M.A.*, sub-Par. 15.

(7) In a receptacle which is inside /another/ receptacle. /The use of/ receptacles /for this purpose/ is not imperative, but two covers are of corresponding /avail/. /In fact,/ if one spread a *talis* or /some/ other cover over a bag of *tefilin* /, then/, even if the cover does not cover them except at the top and at the sides, but not at the bottom, /marital relations/ are nevertheless allowed. See the Beyur Halachah.

Those /people/ who place the *tefilin* bag and the *talis* inside one large bag, /should note/ that the large bag is also classed as a "receptacle" which is specifically for /the *tefilin*, so that/ another cover is required over /the *tefilin*/. This is not /the case/ if they cover the *tefilin* inside the bag by means of the *talis*. In such a case /marital relations/ are allowed /in the room where the *tefilin* are lying without an additional cover over the *tefilin*/, since the *talis* is not a "receptacle" /specifically/ for /the *tefilin*/. Correspondingly, if the *tefilin* bag is joined above to the large bag, the other side of the large bag is not classed as a "receptacle" /specifically/ for /the *tefilin*/. /Therefore,/ for /marital relations to be permitted/, it is of avail to turn /the other side of the large bag/ over /the *tefilin*/. See what I have written in the Beyur Halachah in the name of the *E.R.*

The *M.A.* writes that, correspondingly, /a

1 I.e., a small amount.

ב * ^ב^בית שיש בו (ג) [ג](ד) תפילין * אסור לשמש בו (ה) מטתו (ו) עד שיוציאם או שיניחם (ז) בכלי תוך כלי והוא (ח) שאין השני מיוחד (ד) להם שאם הוא מיוחד אפי׳ מאה חשובים כא׳: הגה ואם שניהם אינם מיוחדים להם או שהפנימי אינו מיוחד להם והחיצון מיוחד להם מותר (וע״ל סי׳ ר״מ סעיף ו) (ב״י): ג * ^ג^אפי׳ להניח בכלי תוך כלי אסור להניחם תחת מרגלותיו ^ד^וכן אסור להניחם תחת מראשותיו (ט) כנגד ראשו ^ה^אפילו

ב שם כ״ה ג שם ד שם ה ר׳ יונה שם

באר היטב

אבל ס״ת אסור לתלות אפילו בכיס חידושי הרשב״א. הסידורים שקבועים בהם שלשלת של כסף אסור לתלות בהם מ״א. ומותר לכתוב פסוקים בנייר ולתלותן בבהכ״נ כנה״ג בשם מהרי״ט. נוהגים להתענות מי שנופלים לו תפילין וה״ה כשנפל ס״ת ובתשו׳ משפטי שמואל סימן י״ב תמלא סמך למנהג. וכתב המ״א בסי׳ מ״ד ס״ק ה׳ נ״ל דמיירי בלא נרתיקן. אבל בס״ת אפילו בנרתיקן ע״ש ועיין כנה״ג ובס׳ שמות בארץ בקונטרס כפות תמרים דף י״ג: (ג) תפילין. ואם פירס טלית על הכיס של תפילין אף ע״פ שאין כרוך מלמטה שרי שהטלית לא מיקרי כליין מיהו אותן המניחין כיס התפילין והטלית לתוך כיס גדול גם הכיס גדול מיקרי כליין וצריך עוד כלי על גביו. ומיהו אם כיס התפילין מחובר למעלה על כיס הטלית. הצד השני של הכיס גדול לא מיקרי כליין מ״א. ותשובת מהריט״ץ סימן קל״א כתב הכיס שאנו מניחין טלית והתפילין מיקרי כלי שאין כליין ומותר לשמש מטתו והיינו דוקא כשלא הכין הכיס אלא לטלית ואחר כך הניח תפילין אז מותר אבל אם מתחלה הכין הכיס לטלית ותפילין אסור דמיקרי כליין ע״ש. אם כרך הכיס במטפחת בשעת הדחק מיקרי גם המטפחת כלי אחד מהריט״ץ שם. אם המזוזה בפנים בחדר צריך ג״כ כלי בתוך כלי ואם יש זכוכית על השם די בפריסת סודר עליה מ״א וט״ז ביו״ד סימן רפ״ו כתב דכיסוי זכוכית לא מהני ע״ש משמע דמיירי אפילו פרס סודר ע״ג דאסור דבכלי א׳ פשיטא דאסור ומ״א חולק עליו: (ד) להם. ר״ל דהכלי בתוך כלי לא בעינן שיהא שניהם כלים שאינם מיוחדים רק א׳ מהם והכלי שהוא מיוחד מצטרף עם הכלי שאינו מיוחד והרב רמ״א לא בא רק לפרש דברי המחבר ב״י דלא תימא דאם תרווייהו אינם מיוחדים להם או שהפנימי אינו מיוחד והחיצון מיוחד יהא אסור הואיל ונקיט המחבר בלישנא והוא שאין השני מיוחד להם קמ״ל דמותר. אבל כלי

שערי תשובה

ומח״ב) שיש שרצו להתענות מפני שראו נפילת תפילין ודחו דבריהם דנפל מידו שאני ע״ש הביאו בקצרה במח״ב: [ג] תפילין. עיין בה״ט ובש״ל כתב דמה שמניחים הטלית ע״ג תפילין אינו יודע על מה סמכו העולם להתיר דלכ״ע קדושת תפילין חמורה מצילית וראוי שיהא הטלית בכיס אחד ותפילין בכיס אחר דלהניח התפילין על הטלית אינו נכון שלא יצטרך לעבור על המצות כו׳ עיין שם. ונראה דאם אין לו כיס לתפילין ומניח הטלית עליהם לשמירה שלא יתלכלכו וכה״ג הרי הטלית נעשה כאילו הוא כליין ושרי. ובשו״ת תשב״ץ ח״ג סימן כ״ו כיס של תפילין יש לעשותו צר קצת כדי שיפגע תחילה בש״י ולא יצטרך לעבור על המצות ומה שאמרו כיס של תפילין טפח היינו לענין הנחה על גבי קרקע דבכלי שהוא כליין אם אין בו טפח יש זלזול אבל אין צריך שיהיה בו חלל טפח אחר שהכניס התפילין שיהיה חוצץ או מגין בפני ערוה או תינוקות שבבית. אף על גב דבכיסוי כל דהו מהני לענין והיה מחנך קדוש עיין שם. ולענין כלי בתוך כלי לענין תשה״מ יתבאר

משנה ברורה

מותר לכתוב (ו) פסוקים בנייר ולתלותן בפתח ביהכ״נ. נוהגים העולם (ז) להתענות כשנופל תפילין מידו על הארץ בלא נרתיקן וה״ה כשנופל ס״ת אפילו בנרתיקן. ועיין בא״ר שכתב דאפילו תפילין בנרתיקן יתן פרוטה לצדקה: ב (ד) תפילין. וה״ה (ח) חומשים או סדורי תפילות או שאר ספרים בין בכתיבה או (ט) בדפוס הכל יש בהם קדושה ובעינן כלי תוך כלי ואפילו אם הן כתב משיט״א [היינו שאינה כתיבת סת״ם והוא רק כתב אשורין] וכריכת (י) ^א^הספר אינה נחשבת לכיסוי דהיא מגוף הספר ובעינן עוד שני כיסוין. ועיין ביו״ד בסי׳ רע״א בט״ז שם סק״ח שכתב כל המיקל בקדושת ספרים הנדפסין עתיד ליתן את הדין דדפוס הוי כמו כתיבה. אך בתשובת חו״י סי׳ קפ״ז^א^ נוטה להקל בזה (יא) בשעת הדחק כשאין לו במה לכסות: (ה) מטתו. או (יב) לעשות צרכיו: (ו) עד שיוציאם. בחדר אחר או שמפסיק בפניהם במחילה גבוה יו״ד טפחים. ועיין לקמן בסי׳ ר״מ במ״א סקט״ו: (ז) בכלי תוך כלי. ל״ד כלים (יג) דה״ה שני כיסוין (יד) ואם פירס טלית או שאר כיסוי על הכיס של תפילין אע״פ שהכיסוי אין מכסה רק למעלה ומן הצדדין ולא למטה אפ״ה שרי. ועיין בבה״ל. ואותן המניחין כיס התפילין והטלית לתוך כיס אחד גדול הרי גם הכיס הגדול נקרא כליין המיוחד להן וצריך עוד כסוי על גבן (טו) אם לא שמכסה בטלית על התפילין בתוך הכיס דאז שרי דהטלית אינו כליין וה״ה (טז) אם כיס התפילין מחובר למעלה על הכיס הגדול הרי צד הב׳ של כיס הגדול אין נקרא כליין ומועיל להן (יז) אם הפכן. ועיין בביאור הלכה מה שכתבתי בשם הא״ר. כתב המ״א דה״ה במזוזה הקבועה לפנים בחדר צריך כלי בתוך כלי דהיינו שיכסה אותה בב׳ כסויין ואחד מהם יהיה עכ״פ אינו מיוחד לה וכדלקמן ואם על המזוזה יש כסוי זכוכית אף שהמזוזה נראית מתוכה אפ״ה נחשבת כסוי אחד ודי בפריסת סודר על המזוזה דהא עתה לא מיתחזיא וכ״כ הדה״ח. אבל לכו״ע לא מהני אם יכסנה עוד בזכוכית מלמעלה אע״ג שמכוסה בשני כסויין דהא המזוזה נראית מתוכן. כתב בחכמת אדם נ״ל דבין במזוזה או שאר ספרים אם עשה מתחלה ב׳ כלים שיחשב אחד לכלי בתוך כלי כגון שכרך המזוזה בנייר ואח״כ הניחה בתיק שלה מותר כיון שבתחלה כיון לכך. ויתר כל הדינים בזה נבאר לקמן בסימן ר״מ בעזה״י: (ח) שאין השני. לאו דוקא (יח) וה״ה אם הפנימי אינו מיוחד והחיצון מיוחד או ששניהם אינם מיוחדים וכמו שכתוב בהג״ה ואינו אסור כלי בתוך כלי רק אם שניהם מיוחדים אבל אם אחד אינו מיוחד מצטרף עם המיוחד ושרי והגה״ה לא בא רק לפרש דברי המחבר דלא נטעה בלישניה וכלי אחד אפילו אינו מיוחד לא מהני ואסור: ג (ט) כנגד ראשו. שהוא ג״כ דרך בזיון:

ביאור הלכה

* בית שיש בו וכו׳ בכת״כ. עיין במ״ב במה שכתב ואם פירס טלית וכו׳ והשמטתי מה שהביא הבה״ט בשם מהריט״ץ שמסתפק בכיס שהי׳ כרוך עליו מטפחת שכל האחרונים השיגו עליו דודאי שרי מהא דגלימא אקמטרא דשרי רבא בברכות כ״ו אף שהכיסוי העליון אין מכסה מכל הצדדים וכ״ש בזה אך אם שני הכיסויים היה כזה שלא היה מכוסה רק למעלה ולא למטה צע״ק והפוסקים לא הזכירו חילוק בזה. ולענין כיס התפילין שמונח בתוך כיס גדול של הטלית עיין במ״ב שכתבנו דהכיס גדול הוא כליין זהו דעת המג״א והעתיק הדה״ח דבריו. אך הא״ר הביא בשם המהריט״ץ להקל בשעת הדחק בזה והשמטתי זה משום דהא יכול לכסות התפילין בהטלית וכמ״ש בפנים אך נ״מ לכאורה מהא דמהריט״ץ לענין שמותר לצור מעות בשעת הדחק בהכיס של טלית דאינו נקרא מיוחד לתפילין כיון שהוא לשניהם וכ״כ הח״א בכלל י״ד אבל באמת נ״ל דזה לכו״ע מותר וכמו שנבאר אי״ה לקמן בכלל^ב^ מ״ב בבה״ל עי״ש: * אסור לשמש מטתו. עיין במ״ב דה״ה לעשות בו צרכיו והוא מהדה״ח וצ״ע מנין לו זה ומלקמן סימן מ״ג סעיף ז׳ אין ראיה לזה ובודאי דבעי כיסוי [ועיין בסימן שט״ו ס״ב^ג^] אבל כלי בתוך כלי מנין: * אפילו וכו׳ כנגד ראשו אפילו בכלי תוך כלי. ואפילו אם היו כבת״כ קודם שנתנס תחת הכר וכ״ש אם ע״י צירוף הכר נעשה כלי בתוך כלי כן מוכח מן הרמב״ם. ועיין במ״א סק״ד ועכ״פ בדין זה לא פליגי האחרונים על הרמב״ם:

מותר

שער הציון

(ו) הכל ממ״א ופמ״ג: (ז) מ״א בסימן מ״ד סק״ה: (ח) לקמן בסימן ר״מ עי״ש: (ט) פמ״ג בסי׳ ר״מ עי״ש: (י) פמ״ג: (יא) וכן נוטה הא״ר: (יב) דה״ח: (יג) פשוט: (יד) מ״א: (טו) דה״ח (טז) מ״א: (יז) לבש״ר: (יח) בה״ט וש״א:

הגהות ותיקונים: א) קפ״ד: ב) בסימן: ג) ס״א:

הערות והארות: 1) עיין במ״ב סי׳ מ״ג ס״ק כ״ה לענין להכניס ספרים שיש בהם שמות בבהכ״ס כשהם תיק בתוך תיק:

/another/ receptacle. /However,/ this is /only of avail/ **(8)** if the second /receptacle/ is not specifically for /the *tefilin*/, as if they are specifically /for the *tefilin*/ even a hundred /receptacles/ are considered like a single /receptacle for the purposes of this ruling/.

Gloss: If both /receptacles/ are not specifically for /the tefilin*/ or if the inner /receptacle/ is not specifically /for the* tefilin*/ and the outer receptacle is specifically for them, /marital relations/ are permitted. (See below in Sec. 240, Par. 6.) (...)*

3. Even if /*tefilin*/ have been placed in a receptacle which is inside /another/ receptacle, one is forbidden to place them underneath the foot of his /bed/. He is likewise forbidden to place them underneath the head of his /bed/ **(9)** against his head, even /when they are in a receptacle which is inside

Mishnah Berurah

covering which is equivalent to/ a receptacle which is inside /another/ receptacle is required for a mezuzah, when it is mounted inside the room /and one wishes to have marital relations in that room/. I.e., one must cover /the mezuzah/ with two covers, of which at least one of them is not specifically for /the mezuzah/, as /stated/ below. If there is a glass cover over the mezuzah /, then/, even if the mezuzah is visible through /this cover/ it is nevertheless considered as one cover. It is /therefore/ sufficient to spread a shawl over the mezuzah, as once that /has been done/ it cannot be seen. The *D.Hach.* writes likewise. However, according to all /authorities/, it is of no avail to cover /the mezuzah/ again with glass on top /of the first glass cover/, although it will /then/ be covered with two covers, since the mezuzah will be visible through them.

The *Chachmas Adam* writes that it appears to him that both in the case of a mezuzah and /in the case/ of /holy/ books other /than Scriptural books written on a scroll/, if one made two "receptacles" at the outset, one of which can be considered a "receptacle" inside /another/ "receptacle", /and placed the mezuzah or book in the inner "receptacle"/, he is /then/ permitted /to have marital relations in that room/, since he had this /purpose/ in mind from the outset. For example, /marital relations are permitted in the room/ if one wrapped the mezuzah in paper /first/ and afterwards placed it in its case.

We will explain all the remaining laws concerning this below in Sec. 240, with the help of *Ha-Sheym*, may He be blessed.

(8) If the second is not. /This combination is/ not imperative, but the same ruling /applies/ if the inner /receptacle/ is not specifically /for the *tefilin*/ and the outer /receptacle/ is specifically /for them/ or if both /receptacles/ are not specifically /for them/, as stated by the gloss. /Once the *tefilin* are in/ a receptacle which is inside /another/ receptacle, /marital relations/ are only prohibited when both /receptacles/ are specifically /for the *tefilin*/, but if one of them is not specifically /for them/ it combines with the one which is specifically /for them/ and /marital relations/ are allowed /in that room/. The purpose of the gloss is not /to dispute/ the statement of the author /of the Shulchan Aruch/, but only to explain it, so that one will not err in /understanding/ his wording.

/Placing the *tefilin* in/ a single receptacle, even if it is not specifically /for the *tefilin*/, is of no avail /for this purpose/. /If one did so, marital relations/ are /still/ forbidden /in that room/.

(9) Against his head. For this is also a disrespectful manner /in which to treat them/.

בכלי תוך כלי ואפי' אין אשתו עמו * אבל שלא כנגד ראשו אם אין אשתו עמו (ה) [ג] (י) מותר * ואם אשתו עמו צריך כלי (יא) בתוך (ו) כלי: ד * ואשתו עמו במטה ואינו רוצה לשמש (יב) מקרי אין אשתו (ז) עמו: ה * זלהניחם במטה כנגד (ח) צדו (יג) דינן כתחת מרגלותיו: ו חשכח ושמש מטתו בתפילין לא יאחוז לא בבתים ולא ברצועות (יד) עד שיטול (ט) ידיו מפני שהידים עסקניות הם ושמא נגעו במקום הטנופת: ז טישן בהם וראה קרי לא יאחוז בבתים (טו) אלא יאחוז ברצועה ומסיר אותם: הגה עד שיקנח הקרי מעליו (טז) ויטול ידיו (כ"י): ח * יהנכנס לסעודת קבע (יז) חולצן ומניחן (יח) על השלחן עד זמן ברכה * וחוזר ומניחן (יט) כאבל לאכילת (כ) עראי אין צריך לחלצן:

ו ב"י מההיא דברכות כ"ה ז רבי יונה שם ח סוכה כ"ו ט שם י ברכות כ"ג ב ירוש' שם פ"ב הרמב"ם בפ"ד מהל' תפילין והמרדכי

שערי תשובה

א"ה בסימן ר"מ: [ג] מותר. עבה"ט ועיין באוהל יעקב סימן א' בספסלים של בהכ"נ שיש שעושים במקום המיוחד לישיבתם תחת הספסל תיבה קטנה להצניע שם טלית ותפילין שלהם ויושבים על הספסל ויש שאין בהם חלל גובה טפח בינם לבין התפילין המונחים שם וכתב לאסור ושם בתשובה שאחר זה כתב לצד היתר די"ל דתחת מרגלותיו אסור וה"ה לישב עליהם היינו היכא דליכא גובה וחלל כלל בינם לבין היושב או לבין מרגלותיו משום שהוא מהדקה ברגליו או בכובד משאוי והוי בזיון וכו' וסיים בה ואי לא מיסתפינא אמינא דלמינטרינהו עדיף וכו'. ומכ"ש להרחיקה מביתו ולשומרה בבהכ"נ במקום קדוש להזהר בקדושתה ע"י גובה קצת מרחק דאין לפקפק בדבר ע"ש ונראה דמ"מ יש להחמיר בגובה טפח כמו דמייתי התם פלוגתא דירושלמי לענין ס"ת. ובעל נפש יש לו להחמיר גם בזה כי תפילין יש להזהר בקדושתן מאוד כמו שנתבאר לעיל:

באר היטב

אחד אפילו אינו מיוחד לא מהני ואסור: (ה) מותר. פי' אפילו בלא כלי בתוך כלי רק בכלי א' מותר מ"א ט"ז דלא כב"ח ע"ש וביד אהרן: (ו) כלי. וא"צ אלא כלי אחד והכר מיקרי כלי שני. עיין מ"א וט"ז: (ז) עמו. וט"ז חולק ואוסר דשמא יבא לידי תשמיש ע"ש וביד אהרן סותר הראיות של ט"ז ע"ש: (ח) צדו. אם משתמרים במקום אחר לא יניחם במטה כלל ומיהו אם יש למעלה מראשותיו מקום גבוה ג"ט או נמוך ג' מותר. ש"ס מ"א: (ט) ידיו. ואח"כ יחלצם עד שיקנח הקרי כמ"ש ס"ו[א]:

ביאור הלכה

* אבל שלא וכו' מותר. עיין במ"ב דר"ל בין כר לכסת הכי איתא בגמרא ובכל הפוסקים והיד אפרים שכתב ואפשר דס"ל דדוקא וכו' א"י כונתו שהוא סותר דברי הט"ז ודברי הגמרא ואולי ט"ס יש בדבריו: * ואם אשתו עמו צריך כלי בתוך כלי. עיין במ"ב שכ' דבצירוף הכר נעשה כלי בתוך כלי כ"כ המ"א ובא"ר מחמיר כהרמב"ם דבעינן כלי בתוך כלי לבד הכר אבל בביאור הגר"א משמע כהמ"א וכ"פ הדה"ח וש"א: * אשתו וכו' ואינו רוצה לשמש וכו'. עיין במ"ב בשם הט"ז וראיתי בספר מטה יהודא שכתב דאפילו לדעת השו"ע היינו אם הוסכם אצלו שלא לשמש ס"ל דלא חיישינן שמא ימלך אבל בסתמא לכ"ע מיקרי אשתו עמו עיי"ש: * להניחם במטה כנגד צדו וכו'. עיין במ"ב הטעם והוא מהתר"י ול"ע מתמיד כ"ז ע"א אר"פ ש"מ תפילין מן הצד שריין ולא חיישינן דילמא מיגנדר וכו' ואף אם נפרש כפי' המפרש שם דהכונה בין כר לכסת שלא נגד ראשו מ"מ הרי חזינן דלא חיישינן דילמא מיגנדר ואין לומר דלפי מה שפסק הרמב"ם בגדי כהונה ניתנו ליהנות בהן א"כ הרי אזל הש"מ דר"פ מ"מ הרי מוכח מאותה סוגיא דאם אמרינן דילמא מיגנדר גם שלא נגד ראשו אסור וא"כ כיון דאנן פסקינן בשו"ע דשלא נגד ראשו מותר הרי דלא חיישינן דילמא מיגנדר וא"כ גם מן הצד יהא מותר וצ"ע: * הנכנס לסעודת וכו' עד זמן ברכה. ברמב"ם איתא דלובשן אחר שנטל ידיו מים אחרונים ומסתמא טעמו כדי שלא ילבשם בידים מזוהמות ולא הביאו האחרונים את דבריו ואפשר שטעמם דלפי מה דאנן פסקינן בריש סימן קע"ט דאפילו דיבור בעלמא אסור להפסיק בין מים אחרונים לבהמ"ז עיין שם בב"י כ"ש בזה ועיי"ש בריש סימן קע"ט במ"א. ועיין מה שנכתוב לקמיה לענין ברכה: * וחוזר ומניחן. עיין בירושלמי בפ' היה קורא דמוכח שם עכ"פ לכל הגרסאות [עיין בפ"מ ובספר חרידים] דלסעודת קבע כשמסירן צריך אח"כ בשעת לבישה לחזור ולברך. והנה לדינא להמחבר לעיל בסימן כ"ה סי"ב בודאי צריך לחזור ולברך ואפילו לדעת הרמ"א דדעתו שם דכשמסירן ע"ד להחזיר מיד אין צריך לברך והכא נמי הרי הסירו והניחו אצלו על השולחן ע"ד לחזור ולהניחו בשעת בהמ"ז מ"מ הרי כתבו שם דכשמסירן ע"ד ליכנס בהם לבה"כ צריך לחזור ולברך לכו"ע דמפני שאין רשאי לילך בהם לבה"כ אידחי ליה שעה זו ממצוה וא"כ ה"נ כיון דגזרו חז"ל שלא ילך בעת הסעודה בתפילין א"כ אידחי ממצוה וצ"ע. ומהירושלמי אין ראיה די"ל לפי גירסת הפני משה שם וכן גירסת הגר"א בהגהותיו על הירושלמי דאיירי כשהסיר התפילין דהירושלמי איירי לפי מה דאיתא שם בברייתא [בבבלי ברכות כ"ג ע"ב] דצריך לפנות קודם שנכנס לסעודת קבע א"כ ממילא מוכרח לברך עתה על התפילין וספיקתיו הוא בשלא נפנה מקודם:

משנה ברורה

(י) מותר. אפילו שלא בכלי כלל רק שמניחן בענין שלא יתגלגלו משם לנדדין כגון שמניחן (יט) בין כר התחתון לכר שתחת ראשו שלא כנגד ראשו: (יא) בתוך כלי. דהיינו שמניחן בתוך כלי או כיס המיוחד להן (כ) תחת הכר דהכר מיקרי כלי שני או שיניחן בלי כלי כלל (כא) תחת שני כרין (כב) ולא התירו חכמים להניח תפילין תחת מראשותיו (כג) כשאשתו עמו אפילו בכלי תוך כלי אלא כדי שישתמרו מן הגנבים והעכברים ולפיכך אם יש לו מקום אחר שמשתמרים שם לא יניחם כלל במטה. (כד) ומיהו אם יש למעלה מראשותיו מקום יוצא מן המטה שהוא גבוה ג"ט או נמוך ג' טפחים למטה מראשותיו מותר להניחן עליו: ד (יב) מקרי וכו'. וט"ז אוסר להיות אשתו עמו במטה עד שיניח התפילין כלי בתוך כלי שמא ישכח וישמש וכן משמע בביאור הגר"א ועיין בא"ר: ה (יג) דינן וכו'. (כה) שפעמים מתהפך במטה וישכב עליהן (כו) ספסלים שבבהכ"נ שתחת הספסלים יש תיבה להצניע שם טלית ותפילין י"א דאסור לישב על הספסלין ויש מתירין אבל כשיש חלל טפח בהתיבה פנוי מותר ודאי לישב על הספסלין ובעל נפש ראוי לו להחמיר שלא במקום הדחק גם בזה כי תפילין יש להזהר בקדושתן מאד. ואם קבעו במסמרים לכותל מותר לישב על הספסל: ו (יד) עד שיטול ידיו. ואח"כ (כז) יחלצם עד שיקנח הקרי וכמש"כ ס"ז: ז (טו) אלא יאחוז וכו'. דבזה (כח) לא חיישינן כ"כ שמא נגעו במקום הטינופת ולכך הקילו לאחוז ברצועה ולהסירה כדי שלא להשהות התפילין על עצמו בעוד שהוא מטונף בהקרי: (טז) ויטול ידיו. אבל אח"כ (כט) מותר להניחן אע"פ שהוא טמא: ח (יז) חולצן. דיש (ל) לחוש שמא ישתכר בסעודה ויתגנה בתפיליו: (יח) על השולחן. כדי שיהיו (לא) מזומנים לו לחזור ולהניחן בשעת ברכה: (יט) אבל וכו'. בספר שולחן שלמה מסתפק דאפשר דזהו דוקא מי שמניחן כל היום אבל לא מי שדרכו להניח בשעת ק"ש ותפלה: (כ) עראי. נראה דשיעור אכילת עראי הוא כביצה וכדין סוכה בסימן תרל"ט יע"ש [מטה יהודה]:

שער הציון

(יט) גמרא: (כ) מ"א וש"א: (כא) מוכח מפמ"ג: (כב) מ"א: (כג) הגר"ז וכן מלדד הפמ"ג: (כד) מ"א: (כה) תר"י: (כו) עיין בשע"ת וט"ז ביו"ד סימן רפ"ב וש"א: (כז) מ"א: (כח) פמ"ג: (כט) עט"ז: (ל) רש"י ופרישה: (לא) רש"י:

הגהות ותיקונים: א) ס"ז:

/another/ receptacle[1*] and even when his wife is not with him. However, **(10)** he is permitted /to place them underneath the head of his bed/ not against his head, provided his wife is not with him. If his wife is with him it is necessary /for them to be in/ a receptacle **(11)** which is inside /another/ receptacle.

4. If one's wife is with him in bed but he does not wish to have marital relations, **(12)** it is classed as /if/ his wife is not with him.

5. Placing /*tefilin*/ in the bed against one's side **(13)** has the /same/ ruling as /placing them/ underneath the foot of one's /bed/.

6. If one forgot and had marital relations /wearing/ *tefilin*, he should not take hold of either the housings or the straps **(14)** until he has washed his hands. This is because hands are active and they may have touched a place where there is dirt.

Mishnah Berurah

(10) He is permitted. /I.e.,/ even if they are not in a receptacle at all, except that he must place them in such a way that they will not roll away from there to the sides. For example, he may place them between the bottom cushion and the cushion which is underneath his head, /but/ not against his head.

(11) Which is inside /another/ receptacle. I.e., he must place them inside the receptacle or bag which is specifically for them underneath the cushion, as the cushion is classed as a second "receptacle". Alternatively, he may place them without /any/ receptacle at all underneath two cushions.

Even when /*tefilin*/ are inside a receptacle which is inside /another/ receptacle, the Sages only permitted one to place the *tefilin* underneath the head of his /bed/ when his wife is with him in order that they should be safeguarded from thieves and mice. Therefore, if one has another place where they will be safeguarded he should not place them in the bed at all. On the other hand, if one has above the head of his /bed/ a place which comes out of the bed that is three handbreadths higher or below the head of his /bed a place which comes out of the bed that is/ three handbreadths lower, he is permitted to place /the *tefilin*/ on it.

(12) It is classed, etc. The *Taz* forbids one to have his wife with him in the bed, unless he has placed the *tefilin* in a receptacle which is inside /another/ receptacle, in case he will forget himself and have marital relations. This is likewise implied by the *Beyur Ha-Gra*. See the *E.R.*

(13) Has the ruling, etc. /This is/ because one turns about in the bed and will occasionally /come to/ lie on them.

When the benches of a Synagogue have chests underneath the benches for the *talis* and the *tefilin* to be put away there, there are /authorities/ who forbid sitting on the benches and /authorities/ who permit it. However, when there is an empty space of a handbreadth /above the *tefilin*/ in the chest it is definitely permitted to sit on the bench. It is /nevertheless/ proper for a conscientious person to be stringent about this as well when there is no pressing /need to act otherwise/, as one must be extremely careful /to avoid trifling/ with the holiness of *tefilin*. If /the bench/ has been affixed to the wall with nails it is permitted to sit on the bench.

(14) Until he has washed his hands. Subsequently, he should take off /the *tefilin*/ until he has wiped off the semen, as stated in Par. 7.

1* I.e., even before they are placed underneath the cushion. (Beyur Halachah).

בכלי תוך כלי ואפי' אין אשתו עמו * אבל שלא כנגד ראשו אם אין אשתו עמו (ה) [ג] (י) מותר * ואם אשתו עמו צריך כלי (יא) בתוך (ו) כלי: ד * ואשתו עמו במטה ואינו רוצה לשמש (יב) מקרי אין אשתו (ז) עמו: ה * זלהניחם במטה כנגד (ח) צדו (יג) דינן כתחת מרגלותיו: ו חשכח ושמש מטתו בתפילין לא יאחוז לא בבתים ולא ברצועות (יד) עד שיטול (ט) ידיו מפני שהידים עסקניות הם ושמא נגער במקום הטנופת: ז טישן בהם וראה קרי לא יאחוז בבתים (טו) אלא יאחוז ברצועה ומסיר אותם: הגה עד שיקנח הקרי מעליו (טז) ויטול ידיו (ב"י): ח * יהנכנס לסעודת קבע (יז) חולצן ומניחן (יח) על השלחן עד זמן ברכה * וחוזר ומניחן (יט) כאבל לאכילת (כ) עראי אין צריך לחלצן:

ו ב"י מההיא דברכות כ"ה ז רבי יונה שם ח סוכה כ"ו ט שם י ברכות כ"ג ב ירוש' שם פ"ב הרמב"ם בפ"ד מהל' תפילין והמרדכי

שערי תשובה

א"ה בסימן ר"מ: [ג] מותר. עבה"ט ועיין באוהל יעקב סימן א' בספסלים של בהכ"נ שיש שעושים במקום המיוחד לישיבתם תחת הספסל תיבה קטנה להצניע שם טלית ותפילין שלהם ויושבים על הספסל ויש שאין בהם חלל גובה טפח בינם לבין התפילין המונחים שם וכתב לאסור ושם בתשובה שאחר זה כתב לצד היתר די"ל דתחת מרגלותיו אסור וה"ה לישב עליהם היינו היכא דליכא גובה וחלל כלל בינם לבין היושב או לבין מרגלותיו משום שהוא מהדקה ברגליו או בכובד משאוי והוי בזיון וכו' וסיים בה ואי לא מיסתפינא אמינא דלמיגטרינהו עדיף וכו'. ומכ"ש להרחיקה מביתו ולשומרה בבהכ"נ במקום קדוש להזהר בקדושתה ע"י גובה קצת מרחק דאין לפקפק בדבר ע"ש ונראה דמ"מ יש להחמיר בגובה טפח כמו דמייתי התם פלוגתא דירושלמי לענין ס"ת. ובעל נפש יש לו להחמיר גם בזה כי תפילין יש להזהר בקדושתן מאוד כמו שנתבאר לעיל:

באר היטב

אחד אפילו אינו מיוחד לא מהני ואסור: (ה) מותר. פי' אפילו בלא כלי בתוך כלי רק בכלי א' מותר מ"א ט"ז דלא כב"ח ע"ש וביד אהרן: (ו) כלי. וא"צ אלא כלי אחד והכר מיקרי כלי שני. עיין מ"א וט"ז: (ז) עמו. וט"ז חולק ואוסר דשמא יבא לידי תשמיש ע"ש וביד אהרן סותר הראיות של ט"ז ע"ש: (ח) צדו. אם משתמרים במקום אחר לא יניחם במטה כלל ומיהו אם יש למעלה מראשותיו מקום גבוה ג"ט או נמוך ג' מותר. ש"ס מ"א: (ט) ידיו. ואח"כ יחלצם עד שיקנח הקרי כמ"ש ס"ו[א]:

ביאור הלכה

* אבל שלא וכו' מותר. עיין במ"ב דר"ל בין כר לכסת הכי איתא בגמרא ובכל הפוסקים והיד אפרים שכתב ואפשר דס"ל דדוקא וכו' א"י כונתו שהוא סותר דברי הט"ז ודברי הגמרא ואולי ט"ס יש בדבריו: * ואם אשתו עמו צריך כלי בתוך כלי. עיין במ"ב שכ' דבצירוף הכר נעשה כלי בתוך כלי כ"כ המ"א ובא"ר מחמיר כהרמב"ם דבעינן כלי בתוך כלי לבד הכר אבל בביאור הגר"א משמע כהמ"א וכ"פ הדה"ח וש"א: * אשתו וכו' ואינו רוצה לשמש וכו'. עיין במ"ב בשם הט"ז וראיתי בספר מטה יהודא שכתב דאפילו לדעת השו"ע היינו אם הוסכם אצלו שלא לשמש ס"ל דלא חיישינן שמא ימלך אבל בסתמא לכ"ע מיקרי אשתו עמו עיי"ש: * להניחם במטה כנגד צדו וכו'. עיין במ"ב הטעם והוא מהתר"י ול"ע מתמיד כ"ז ע"א אר"פ ש"מ תפילין מן הצד שריין ולא חיישינן דילמא מיגנדר וכו' ואף אם נפרש כפי' המפרש שם דהכונה בין כר לכסת שלא נגד ראשו מ"מ הרי חזינן דלא חיישינן דילמא מיגנדר ואין לומר דלפי מה שפסק הרמב"ם בגדי כהונה ניתנו ליהנות בהן א"כ הרי אזל הש"ס דר"פ מ"מ הרי מוכח מאותה סוגיא דאם אמרינן דילמא מיגנדר גם שלא נגד ראשו אסור וא"כ כיון דאנן פסקינן בשו"ע דשלא נגד ראשו מותר הרי דלא חיישינן דילמא מיגנדר וא"כ גם מן הצד יהא מותר וצ"ע: * הנכנס לסעודת וכו' עד זמן ברכה. ברמב"ם איתא דלובשן אחר שנטל ידיו מים אחרונים ומסתמא טעמו כדי שלא ילבשם בידים מזוהמות ולא הביאו האחרונים את דבריו ואפשר שטעמם דלפי מה דאנן פסקינן בריש סימן קע"ט דאפילו דיבור בעלמא אסור להפסיק בין מים אחרונים לבהמ"ז עיין שם בב"י כ"ש בזה ועיי"ש בריש סימן קע"ט במ"א. ועיין מה שנכתוב לקמיה לענין ברכה: * וחוזר ומניחן. עיין בירושלמי בפ' היה קורא דמוכח שם עכ"פ לכל הגרסאות [עיין בפ"מ ובספר חרידים] דלסעודת קבע כשמסירן צריך אח"כ בשעת לבישה לחזור ולברך. והנה לדינא להמחבר לעיל בסימן כ"ה סי"ב בודאי צריך לחזור ולברך ואפילו לדעת הרמ"א דדעתו שם דכשמסירן ע"ד להחזיר מיד אין צריך לברך והכא נמי הרי הסירו והניחו אצלו על השולחן ע"ד לחזור ולהניחו בשעת בהמ"ז מ"מ הרי כתבו שם דכשמסירן ע"ד ליכנס בהם לבה"כ צריך לחזור ולברך לכו"ע דמפני שאין רשאי לילך בהם לבה"כ אידחי ליה שעה זו ממצוה וא"כ ה"נ כיון דגזרו חז"ל שלא ילך בעת הסעודה בתפילין א"כ אידחי ממצוה וצ"ע. ומהירושלמי אין ראיה די"ל לפי גירסת הפני משה שם וכן גירסת הגר"א בהגהותיו על הירושלמי דאיירי כשהסיר התפילין דהירושלמי איירי לפי מה דאיתא שם בברייתא [בבבלי ברכות כ"ג ע"ב] דצריך לפנות קודם שנכנס לסעודת קבע א"כ ממילא מוכרח לברך עתה על התפילין וספיקתו הוא בשלא נפנה מקודם:

משנה ברורה

(י) מותר. אפילו שלא בכלי כלל רק שמניחן בענין שלא יתגלגלו משם לגדין כגון שמניחן (יט) בין כר התחתון לכר שתחת ראשו שלא כנגד ראשו: (יא) בתוך כלי. דהיינו שמניחן בתוך כלי או כיס המיוחד לאן (כ) תחת הכר דהכר מיקרי כלי שני או שיניחן בלי כלי כלל (כא) תחת שני כרין (כב) ולא התירו חכמים להניח תפילין תחת מראשותיו (כג) כשאשתו עמו אפילו בכלי תוך כלי אלא כדי שישתמרו מן הגנבים והעכברים ולפיכך אם יש לו מקום אחר שמשתמרים שם לא יניחם כלל במטה. (כד) ומיהו אם יש למעלה מראשותיו מקום יוצא מן המטה שהוא גבוה ג"ט או נמוך ג' טפחים למטה מראשותיו מותר להניחן עליו: ד (יב) מקרי וכו'. וט"ז אוסר להיות אשתו עמו במטה עד שיניח התפילין כלי בתוך כלי שמא ישכח וישמש וכן משמע בביאור הגר"א ועיין בא"ר: ה (יג) דינן וכו'. (כה) שפעמים מתהפך במטה וישכב עליהן (כו) ספסלים שבבהכ"נ שתחת הספסלים יש תיבה להצניע שם טלית ותפילין י"א דאסור לישב על הספסלין ויש מתירין אבל כשיש חלל טפח בהתיבה פנוי מותר ודאי לישב על הספסלין ובעל נפש ראוי לו להחמיר שלא במקום הדחק גם בזה כי תפילין יש להזהר בקדושתן מאד. ואם קבעו במסמרים לכותל מותר לישב על הספסל: ו (יד) עד שיטול ידיו. ואח"כ (כז) יחלצם עד שיקנח הקרי וכמש"כ ס"ז: ז (טו) אלא יאחוז וכו'. דבזה (כח) לא חיישינן כ"כ שמא נגעו במקום הטינופת ולכך הקילו לאחוז ברצועה ולהסירה כדי שלא להשהות התפילין על עצמו בעוד שהוא מטונף בהקרי: (טז) ויטול ידיו. אבל אח"כ (כט) מותר להניחן אע"פ שהוא טמא: ח (יז) חולצן. דיש (ל) לחוש שמא ישתכר בסעודה ויתגנה בתפיליו: (יח) על השולחן. כדי שיהיו (לא) מזומנים לו לחזור ולהניחן בשעת ברכה: (יט) אבל וכו'. בספר שולחן שלמה מסתפק דאפשר דזהו דוקא מי שמניחן כל היום אבל לא מי שדרכו להניח בשעת ק"ש ותפלה: (כ) עראי. נראה דשיעור אכילת עראי הוא כביצה וכדין סוכה בסימן תרל"ט יע"ש [מטה יהודה]:

שער הציון

(יט) גמרא: (כ) מ"א וש"א: (כא) מוכח מפמ"ג: (כב) מ"א: (כג) הגר"ז וכן מלדד הפמ"ג: (כד) מ"א: (כה) תר"י: (כו) עיין בשע"ת וט"ז ביו"ד סימן רפ"ב וש"א: (כז) מ"א: (כח) פמ"ג: (כט) עט"ז: (ל) רש"י ופרישה: (לא) רש"י:

הגהות ותיקונים: א) ס"ז:

7. If one slept in /*tefilin*/ and experienced a chance /ejaculation of/ semen, he should not take hold of the housings, **(15)** but should take hold of the straps and remove them.

Gloss: /I.e.,/ until he has wiped the semen off his /body/ **(16)** *and washed his hands. (...)*

8. If one engages in a set meal, **(17)** he should remove /the *tefilin*/ and place them **(18)** on the table until the time /arrives/ for /saying/ the blessings /for after the meal/ and /then/ he should don them again. **(19)** However, it is unnecessary to remove /the *tefilin*/ for **(20)** snack eating.

Mishnah Berurah

(15) But should take hold, etc. For in such a case we are not so worried that he may have touched a place where there is dirt. Consequently, /the Sages/ were lenient /and allowed him/ to take hold of the strap and remove /the *tefilin*/ so as not to retain the *tefilin* on himself while he is still dirty with semen.

(16) And washed his hands. However, he is permitted to don them subsequently although he is unclean.

(17) He should remove /the *tefilin*/. /The reason is/ because there are grounds for concern that he may become intoxicated at the meal and become disgraced /wearing/ *tefilin*.

(18) On the table. So that they will be ready for him to put on again when /he makes/ the blessings /for after the meal/.

(19) However, etc. In the work *Shulchan Shelomoh*, /the author/ is in doubt /as regards the application of this ruling/. For it may be that it only /relates/ to someone who dons /*tefilin*/ all day, but not to someone who usually dons /*tefilin* only/ when /he reads/ "The Reading of Shema" and /prays the eighteen-blessing/ prayer.

(20) Snack. It appears that the amount which is /regarded as/ snack eating is an egg's bulk. This conforms with the ruling /given/ in Sec. 639 /with respect to eating outside/ a *sukah*; see there. [*Mateh Yehudah*]

באר הגולה

מא דין הנושא משאוי איך ינהג בתפילין. ובו סעיף אחד:

א (א) אהנושא משאוי (ב) על ראשו (ג) * חולץ תפילין של ראש עד שיסיר המשאוי * ואפי' מטפחתו אסור להניח על הראש שיש בו תפילין באבל דבר שדרכו ליתן בראשו כגון כובע או מצנפת (ד) מותר: הגה * ואפילו הכי אם הוא משאוי כבד (א) (ה) ד' קבין והתפילין (ו) נדחקות צריך להסירן (ב"י):

א בבא מציעא ק"ה וכר' שילא ב רמב"ם בפ"ד מהלכות תפילין והסכימו לדבריו ר' יונה והרא"ש

מב אם מותר לשנות תפילין של יד לשל ראש. ובו ג' סעיפים:

א * אאסור לשנות תפילין של ראש לעשותן של (א) (א) יד * באפילו ליקח (ב) רצועה (ג) [א] (ג) * מהם

א מנחות ל"ד ב הרמב"ם בפ"ג מהלכות תפילין

באר היטב

(א) ד' קבין. והוא כ"ה זקוקים כסף משקל פראג ל"ח מ"א:

(א) יד. אפי' אין לו תפלה של יד כ"מ בגמרא מ"א: (ב) מהם. אם נפסקה רצועה של יד סמוך לקשר אסור להפוך ראש האחר למעלה ולעשות בו קשר ש"י והתחתונה שהיה בו הקשר יקשור למטה דמורידו מקדושתו כיון שהיה בו הקשר והיו"ד ועתה יעשה בו כריכות האצבעות. ואם אין הרצועה ארוכה כ"כ אזי לא יעשה כ"כ כריכות סביב היד מ"א ובהלק"ט

שערי תשובה

[א] מהם. עבה"ט וצ"ע מה דנקט המג"א להפוך ראש אחר למעלה דמשמע שמהפך הרצועה הארוכה ממש שהרי אפילו בלא היפוך רק שבאותה הקצה של הרצועה הארוכה במקום שנפסקה שם הוא רוצה לעשות הקשר נמי אסור כיון שלוקח הקצרה שהיה בה הקשר וקושרה למטה הו"ל הורדה מקדושה. ועל כ"פ ממה שמסיים ואם אין הרצועה כו' משמע דאם אין קושר הקצרה למטה אין קפידא בהיפוך לבד. ועיין בא"ר בשם זקנו הגאון מהר"ש שמתיר להפוך וראיה מהא דויקח מאבני וכו' עיין שם שנעשו כולם אבן אחת וקשה דעדיין יש קנאה באיזה צד מונח על האבן וע"כ דליכא קפידא בהכי וע"ש שכתב דמסימן יו"ד לא משמע הכי

ור"ל שגם ס"ק י"ד כתב בשם ל"ח ושל"ה בטעם העטרה שלא להפוך כו' ושם כתב שלפ"ז אין להקל ברצועה להפך אך מסיק שם להקל גם בטלית אם נקרע למעלה וכיוצא בזה ע"ש. וגם בהלק"ט ח"ב סימן נ"א שכתב בה"ט בשמו שמתיר עיין שם אינו מתיר רק מדינא. וכתב שם שהמקפידים לעשות סימן בטלית אפשר דלאלו יש קפידא גם בזה ע"ש. והראיה שמביא הא"ר בשם זקנו אינו ראיה כ"כ דכיון דמעשה ניסים היו שמא לא היו בדרך דביקות זה בזה כי אם נעשה גוש אחד בלול מכולם. אך בלא"ה אין ראיה מדברי אגדה ואסמכתא בעלמא קאמר וקרוב לומר דמ"ש המג"א להפוך ראשו כו' אין כוונתו היפך ממש להפוך התחלתן שתלוי כלפי הארץ ולתתו עליון בתוך המעברתא לעשות בו הקשר אלא כוונתו מה שכתב ראש האחר היינו הראש של הרצועה האחרת שבמקום שנפסק שהיה מתחלה מרוחק מהמעברתא

משנה ברורה

א (א) הנושא משאוי. זה מיירי בכל היום לא בשעת ק"ש ותפלה. ועיין לקמן סימן צ"ז ס"ה: (ב) על ראשו. ואם הוא נושא משאוי על ידו במקום תפילין דמסתמא מכוסין הן וליכא גנאי אין צריך לחלוץ כ"א בשיש בהמשא ארבעה קבין דאז מסתמא התפילין רוצצות עי"ז [פמ"ג ע"ש עוד]: (ג) חולץ תש"ר. ואם יכול לסלק המשאוי לצדדין שלא במקום התפילין משמע מפמ"ג דמותר מ"מ אם יש בהם משא ד' קבין נראה שיש להחמיר אף בכה"ג עיין ב"י ולהוציא זבל על ראשו אפילו מעט ואפילו לצדדין אסור דבכל גווני הוי בזה בזיון לתפילין שעל ראשו אם לא כשמסלק אז התש"ר מעליו שרי אף דנושא הש"י. ואם ירצה להוציא זבל על היד אפשר דאפילו אם התפילין הם מכוסים בבגדיו איכא בזה בזיון להתפילין שעליו [פמ"ג]: (ד) מותר. אף דהוא מונח על התפילין אין בזה בזיון לתפילין כיון שהוא דרך מלבוש אך אם הכובע גדולה יזהר שכובד הכובע לא יסיר את התפילין ממקום הראוי להן [מח"א]: (ה) ד' קבין. הם כ"ה ליטראות שוקלין בו הכסף בפראג [ל"ח]: (ו) נדחקות. אין פי' שהתפילין זזין ממקומן לגמרי ואין מונחין כדין דבזה פשיטא שאסור ואפי' אם משאן קל אלא ר"ל שמונחין במקומן מיהו מחמת המשוי שמונח עליהם ומיצר את מקומם והב"ח מיקל בענין זה במצנפת וכובע [פמ"ג]:

א (א) יד. אפי' (א) אין לו ש"י ויש לו ב' של ראש: (ב) רצועה. ופשוט דה"ה נרתק המיוחד לשל ראש דגם הוא בכלל תשמיש קדושה כמו רצועה [כדאיתא מגילה כ"ו ע"ב] וכן מוכח בביאור הגר"א וכ"כ המ"א לעיל בסוף סימן כ"ח: (ג) מהם. כתב המ"א דאם נפסקה רצועה של יד סמוך לקשר אסור להפוך ראש האחר למעלה [במקום שהוא תוך] ולעשות בו הקשר ש"י והחתיכה שהיה בו הקשר יקשור עתה לו למטה דמורידו מקדושתו כיון שהיה בו הקשר והיוד ועתה יעשה בו כריכות האצבעות אלא אותה החתיכה צריכה גניזה ואם אין הרצועה ארוכה כ"כ אזי לא יעשה כריכות כ"כ סביב היד. וכן (ג) בשל ראש אם נפסק מה שמקיף הראש אסור להפוך מה שבתוך הקשר שיהיה חוץ לקשר מטעם הנ"ל. אמנם אם נפסקה הרצועה ש"ר תנחון להקשר ורוצה למשכה ולהורידה למטה

ביאור הלכה

* חולץ תש"ר. עיין במ"ב מה שכתבנו בשם הפמ"ג ונראה שטעמו משום התירוץ של הב"י שכתב לדעת הטור ודעימיה עי"ש בחד תירוצא אבל לדעת הרמב"ם דלא הביא כלל הא דד' קבין אין שום הכרח לזה וכן ברש"י ב"מ ק"ה ע"ב ד"ה אסור לא משמע כן: * ואפילו מטפחתו. עיין בט"ז שכתב דלדעת הטור אין אסור במטפחת וכן במשא שהיא פחותה מד' קבין כ"א בשרוצץ ודוחק התפילין עי"ז אבל אנו אין לנו אלא דברי השו"ע דבכל גווני אסור דהוי גנאי לתפילין עי"ז [מטה יהודא]: * ואפ"ה אם הוא וכו'. כתב המ"א בשם הד"מ כל מקום וכו' עיין ספר נהר שלום ובספר מאמר מרדכי שכתבו שלא כיון הד"מ לזה. ולדינא בלא"ה כתב המ"א שצ"ע בזה:

* אסור וכו'. עיין בפמ"ג שמסתפק אם דינא דאין מורידין הוא מדאורייתא או מדרבנן ולבסוף צידד לומר דהוא דאורייתא. ועיין בתשובת משכנות יעקב בסי' נ"ה שהביא ג"כ ראיה מירושלמי דהא דאין מורידין מדאורייתא הוא:
* אפילו ליקח רצועה וכו'. וכ"ש ליקח מהש"ר איזה פרשה ליתן בש"י דאסור. ואם נמצא איזה פסול בפרשה אחת אם מותר ליקח מהפרשה שלפניה לתנם בש"י תלוי בזה אם הפסול הוא מחמת שלא היה כתוב מתחלה איזה אות כדין או שאר פסול אחר שהוא פסול מעיקרא א"כ הפרשיות האחרות והרצועות עדיין הם בכלל חולין ואם הפסול נעשה מחמת יושנן או שאר קלקול שנתהוה אח"כ כבר חלה עליהם קדושה החמורה ואסור לשנותם: * מהם. עיין במ"ב במה שכתבנו בסוף והוא הכרעת הש"ת. והח"א מיקל עוד יותר בעני ומכ"ש במקום ביטול מצוה דהותר לחבר בשל יד למטה החתיכה העליונה שנפסקה וכתב דיש לסמוך בזה על הא"ר שהתיר עי"ש אף דלכאורה אין ראית הא"ר ראיה לזה רק דמותר להפוך רצועה אחת מסופה לתחלתה וכמו שהתיר המ"א עצמו ואף לזה אין כ"כ ראיה וכמו שכתב הש"ת אעפ"כ אין למחות במקום ביטול מצוה להמיקל. ולפי האמת טוב יותר שלא לעשות כריכות כ"כ ולא יתבטל המצוה וכמו שכתב המ"א אך נ"מ מדבריו לענין אם נפסק הרצועה ש"ר בתוך השיעור שמקיף הראש שיהא מותר למשוך למטה את מקום שנפסק שיהיה עתה תחת הקשר במקום שהוא עני או שאין לו רצועה אחרת אך לענ"ד הנכון יותר שיחתוך מן רצועה אחת במקום שנפסקת חתיכה קטנה דהיינו מה שהיה מקיף ממנה את הראש ומקום הקשר ויגנז ושאר הרצועה[1] יחברנה בגידין אח"כ ויעשה הקשר במקום השלם אך יצמצם שלא יצא חוץ לקשר ממה שהיה בתחלה בתוך הקשר ויהיה יוצא בזה אף לדעת המ"א:

שער הציון

(א) מ"א: (ב) דה"ח:

הערות והארות: 1) עיין לעיל סי' ל"ג ס"ה במ"ב ס"ק כ"ט לענין לתפור בתוך השיעור:

§41: THE LAW CONCERNING HOW SOMEONE WHO IS CARRYING A BURDEN SHOULD ACT AS REGARDS *TEFILIN*

(Contains One Paragraph)

1. (1) Someone who is carrying a burden (2) on his head (3) must take off the head *tefilin* until he has removed the burden. One is even forbidden to place his scarf on his head when he is /wearing/ *tefilin* /on his head/.

However, (4) one is permitted /without taking off the *tefilin* to place on his

Mishnah Berurah

§41

(1) Someone who is carrying a burden. This /ruling/ relates to /the wearing of *tefilin*/ all day, not /to the wearing of *tefilin*/ at the time /when one reads/ "The Reading of Shema" and /prays the eighteen-blessing/ prayer. See below in Sec. 97, Par. 5.

(2) On his head. If one is carrying a burden on his arm, in the area where /he is wearing/ *tefilin*, /the ruling is different/. /This is/ because /the arm *tefilin*/ are ordinarily covered and /therefore, carrying a burden there does/ not involve contempt /for them/. One does not need to remove /the arm *tefilin* because of a burden/ unless it is a burden of four *kavim*, in which case the *tefilin* are probably under stress because of it. [*P.Mg.*; see further there.]

(3) Must take off the head *tefilin*. If he is able to move away the burden to the sides, beyond the *tefilin* area, it is implied by the *P.Mg.* that he is permitted /to do so and does not need to take off the *tefilin*/. Nevertheless, if it is a burden of four *kavim* it appears that he should be stringent even in such circumstances. See the *B.Y.*

To take out even a little refuse on one's head /while wearing *tefilin*/ is forbidden, even /if one puts the refuse/ at the sides, since this involves disrespect to the *tefilin* on one's head in all cases. This does not /apply/ if one removes the head *tefilin* then from his /head/. /Then/ one is allowed /to take out refuse on his head/ even though he is /still/ carrying the arm /*tefilin* on his arm/. If one wishes to take out refuse on his arm, it may be that even if the /arm/ *tefilin* are covered by his clothes this involves disrespect to the *tefilin* he has on him. [*P.Mg.*]

(4) One is permitted. Even if /such an article/ lies on the *tefilin* this does not involve disrespect for the *tefilin*, since it is /carried/ as clothing. However, if the hat is large, one should be careful that the weight of the hat does not displace the *tefilin* from the area which is appropriate for them. [*Mach.A.*]

מא דין הנושא משאוי איך ינהג בתפילין. ובו סעיף אחד:

א (א) [א]הנושא משאוי (ב) על ראשו (ג) * חולץ תפילין של ראש עד שיסיר המשאוי * ואפי' מטפחתו אסור להניח על הראש שיש בו תפילין [ב]אבל דבר שדרכו ליתן בראשו כגון כובע או מצנפת (ד) מותר: הגה * ואפילו הכי אם הוא משאוי כבד (א) (ה) ד' קבין והתפילין (ו) נדחקות צריך להסירן (ב"י):

א בבא מציעא ק"ה וכר' שילא ב רמב"ם בפ"ד מהלכות תפילין והסכימו לדבריו ר' יונה והרא"ש

מב אם מותר לשנות תפילין של יד לשל ראש. ובו ג' סעיפים:

א * [א]אסור לשנות תפילין של ראש לעשותן של (א) (א) יד * [ב]אפילו ליקח (ב) רצועה (ב) [א] (ג) * מהם

א מנחות ל"ד ב הרמב"ם בפ"ג מהלכות תפילין

באר היטב

(א) ד' קבין. והוא כ"ה זקוקים כסף משקל פראג ל"ח מ"א:

(א) יד. אפי' אין לו תפלה של יד כ"מ בגמרא מ"א: (ב) מהם. אם נפסקה רצועה של יד סמוך לקשר אסור להפוך ראש האחר למעלה ולעשות בו קשר ש"י והתחתונה שהיה בו הקשר יקשור למטה דמורידו מקדושתו כיון שהיה בו הקשר והיו"ד ועתה יעשה בו כריכות האצבעות. ואם אין הרצועה ארוכה כ"כ אזי לא יעשה כ"כ כריכות סביב היד מ"א ובהלק"ט

שערי תשובה

[א] מהם. עבה"ט וצ"ע מה דנקט המג"א להפוך ראש אחר למעלה דמשמע שמהפך הרצועה הארוכה ממש שהרי אפילו בלא היפוך רק שבאותה הקצה של הרצועה הארוכה במקום שנפסקה שם הוא רוצה לעשות הקשר נמי אסור כיון שלוקח הקצרה שהיה בה הקשר וקושרה למטה הו"ל הורדה מקדושה. ועל כ"פ ממה שמסיים ואם אין הרצועה כו' משמע דאם אין קושר הקצרה למטה אין קפידא בהיפוך לבד. ועיין בא"ר בשם זקנו הגאון מהר"ש שמתיר להפוך וראיה מהא דויקח מאבני וכו' עיין שם שנעשו כולם אבן אחת וקשה דעדיין יש קפידא באיזה צד מונח על האבן וע"כ דליכא קפידא בהכי וע"ש שכתב דמסימן יו"ד לא משמע הכי ור"ל שבס"ק י"ד כתב בשם ל"ח ושל"ה בטעם העטרה שלא להפוך כו' ושם כתב שלפ"ז אין להקל ברצועה להפך אך מסיק שם להקל גם בטלית אם נקרע למעלה וכיוצא בזה ע"ש. וגם בהלק"ט ח"ב סימן נ"א שכתב בה"ט בשמו שמתיר עיין שם אינו מתיר רק מדינא. וכתב שם שהמקפידים לעשות סימן בטלית אפשר דלאלו יש קפידא גם בזה ע"ש. והראיה שמביא הא"ר בשם זקנו אינו ראיה כ"כ דכיון דמעשה ניסים היו שמא לא היו בדרך דדיקות זה בזה כי אם נעשה גוש אחד בלול מכולם. אך בלא"ה אין ראיה מדברי אגדה ואסמכתא בעלמא קאמר וקרוב לומר דמ"ש המג"א להפוך ראשו כו' אין כוונתו היפך ממש להפוך התחלתן שתלוי כלפי הארץ ולתתו עליון בתוך המעברתא לעשות בו הקשר אלא כוונתו מה שכתב ראש האחר היינו הראש של הרצועה האחרת שבמקום שנפסק שהיה מתחלה מרוחק מהמעברתא

משנה ברורה

א (א) הנושא משאוי. זה מיירי בכל היום לא בשעת ק"ש ותפלה. ועיין לקמן סימן צ"ז ס"ה: (ב) על ראשו. ואם הוא נושא משאוי על ידו במקום תפילין דמסתמא מכוסין הן וליכא גנאי אין צריך לחלוץ כ"א בשיש בהמשא ארבעה קבין דאז מסתמא התפילין רוצצות עי"ז [פמ"ג ע"ש עוד]: (ג) חולץ תש"ר. ואם יכול לסלק המשאוי לצדדין שלא במקום התפילין משמע מפמ"ג דמותר מ"מ אם יש בהם משא ד' קבין נראה שיש להחמיר אף בכה"ג עיין ב"י ולהוציא זבל על ראשו אפילו מעט ואפילו לצדדין אסור דבכל גווני הוי בזה בזיון לתפילין שעל ראשו אם לא כשמסלק או התש"ר מעליו שרי אף דנושא השל יד. ואם ירצה להוציא זבל על היד אפשר דאפילו אם התפילין הם מכוסים בבגדיו איכא בזה בזיון להתפילין שעליו [פמ"ג]: (ד) מותר. אף דהוא מונח על התפילין אין בזה בזיון לתפילין כיון שהוא דרך מלבוש אך אם הכובע גדולה יזהר שכובד הכובע לא יסיר את התפילין ממקום הראוי להן [מא"א]: (ה) ד' קבין. הם כ"ה ליטראות ששוקלין בו הכסף בפראג [ל"ח]: (ו) נדחקות. אין פי' שהתפילין זזין ממקומן לגמרי ואין מונחין כדין דבזה פשיטא שאסור ואפי' אם משאן קל אלא ר"ל שמונחין במקומן בדוחק מחמת המשוי שמונח עליהם ומקצר את מקומם והב"ח מיקל בענין זה במצנפת וכובע [פמ"ג]:

א (א) יד. אפי' (א) אין לו ש"י ויש לו ב' של ראש: (ב) רצועה. ופשוט דה"ה נרתק המיוחד לשל ראש דגם הוא בכלל תשמיש קדושה כמו רצועה [כדאיתא מגילה כ"ו ע"ב] וכן מוכח בביאור הגר"א וכ"כ המ"א לעיל בסוף סימן כ"ח: (ג) מהם. כתב המ"א דאם נפסקה רצועה של יד סמוך לקשר אסור להפוך ראש האחר למעלה [במקום שהוא חזק] ולעשות בו הקשר ש"י והחתיכה שהיה בו הקשר יקשור עתה לזו למטה דמורידו מקדושתו כיון שהיה בו הקשר והיוד ועתה יעשה בו כריכות האצבעות אלא אותה החתיכה צריכה גניזה ואם אין הרצועה ארוכה כ"כ אזי לא יעשה כריכות כ"כ סביב היד. וכן (ב) בשל ראש אם נפסק מה שמקיף הראש אסור להפוך מה שבתוך הקשר שיהיה חוץ לקשר מטעם הנ"ל. אמנם אם נפסקה הרצועה ש"ר מבחוץ להקשר ורוצה למשכה ולהורידה למטה

ביאור הלכה

* חולץ תש"ר. עיין במ"ב מה שכתבנו בשם הפמ"ג ונראה שטעמו משום התירוץ של הב"י שכתב לדעת הטור ודעימיה עי"ש בחד תירוצא אבל לדעת הרמב"ם דלא הביא כלל הא דד' קבין אין שום הכרח לזה וכן ברש"י ב"מ ק"ה ע"ב ד"ה אסור לא משמע כן: * ואפילו מטפחתו. עיין בט"ז שכתב דלדעת הטור אין אסור במטפחת וכן במשא שהיא פחותה מד' קבין כ"א בשרוצץ ודוחק התפילין עי"ז אבל אנו אין לנו אלא דברי השו"ע דבכל גווני אסור דהוי גנאי לתפילין עי"ז [מטה יהודא]: * ואפ"ה אם הוא וכו'. כתב המ"א בשם הד"מ כל מקום וכו' עיין ספר נהר שלום ובספר מאמר מרדכי שכתבו שלא כיון הד"מ לזה. ולדינא בלא"ה כתב המ"א שצ"ע בזה:

* אסור וכו'. עיין בפמ"ג שמסתפק אם דינא דאין מורידין הוא מדאורייתא או מדרבנן ולבסוף צידד לומר דהוא דאורייתא. ועיין בתשובת משכנות יעקב בסי' נ"ה שהביא ג"כ ראיה מירושלמי דהא דאין מורידין מדאורייתא הוא: * אפילו ליקח רצועה וכו'. וכ"ש ליקח מהש"ר איזה פרשה ליתן בש"י דאסור. ואם נמצא איזה פסול בפרשה אחת אם מותר ליקח מהפרשה שלפניה לתנם בש"י תלוי בזה אם הפסול הוא מחמת שלא היה כתוב מתחלה איזה אות כדין או שאר פסול אחר שהוא פסול מעיקרא א"כ הפרשיות האחרות והרצועות עדיין הם בכלל חדשים ואם הפסול נעשה מחמת יושנן או שאר קלקול שנתהוה א"כ כבר חלה עליהם קדושה החמורה ואסור לשנותם: * מהם. עיין במ"ב במה שכתבנו בסוף והוא הכרעת הש"ת. והא"ר מיקל עוד יותר בעני ומכ"ש במקום ביטול מצוה דהותר לחבר בשל יד למטה החתיכה העליונה שנפסקה וכתב דיש לסמוך בזה על הא"ר שהתיר עי"ש אף דלכאורה אין ראית הא"ר ראיה לזה רק דמותר להפוך רצועה אחת מסופה לתחלתה וכמו שהתיר המ"א עצמו ואף לזה אין כ"כ ראיה וכמו שכתב הש"ת אעפ"כ אין למחות במקום ביטול מצוה להמיקל. ולפי האמת טוב יותר שלא לעשות כריכות כ"כ ולא יתבטל המצוה וכמו שכתב המ"א אך כ"מ מדבריו לענין אם נפסק הרצועה ש"ר בתוך השיעור שמקיף הראש שיהא מותר למשוך למטה את מקום שנפסק שיהיה עתה תחת הקשר במקום שהוא עני או שאין לו רצועה אחרת אך לענ"ד הנכון יותר שיחתוך מן רצועה אחת במקום שנפסקת חתיכה קטנה דהיינו מה שהיה מקיף ממנה את הראש ומקום הקשר ויגנז ושאר הרצועה[1] יחברנה בגידין אח"כ ויעשה הקשר במקום השלם אך ימצא שלא יצא חוץ לקשר ממה שהיה בתחלה בתוך הקשר ויהיה יוצא בזה אף לדעת המ"א:

שער הציון

(א) מ"א: (ב) דה"ח:

הערות והארות: 1) עיין לעיל סי' ל"ג ס"ה במ"ב ס"ק כ"ט לענין לתפור בתוך השיעור:

head/ an article which it is usual for him to put on his head, such as a hat or a turban.

Gloss: Nevertheless, if /the article/ is a heavy burden of (5) *four* kavim[1*] *and the* tefilin (6) *are under pressure, he must remove /the* tefilin, *although it is usual for him to put that article on his head/. (...)*

§42: WHETHER IT IS PERMITTED TO ALTER ARM *TEFILIN* TO HEAD */TEFILIN/*

(Contains Three Paragraphs)

1. It is forbidden to alter /the usage of/ head *tefilin*, by transforming them into (1) arm */tefilin/*. It is even forbidden to take (2) a strap (3) from /head

Mishnah Berurah

(5) **Four *kavim*.** These are /equivalent in weight to/ twenty-five of the pounds with which silver is weighed in Prague. [*L.Ch.*]

(6) **Are under pressure.** One should not interpret this /as referring to an instance when/ the *tefilin* have moved away altogether from their /appropriate/ place and are not lying in conformance with halachic /requirements/. It is obvious that it is forbidden /to keep the *tefilin* on one's head/ in such circumstances, even if the burden is light. /The *Rema*/ is actually referring to /an instance/ when they are barely lying in place, because of the burden which is lying over them and limiting the area /which is appropriate/ for them.

The *Bach* is lenient in this matter, as regards a turban and a hat. [*P.Mg.*]

§42

(1) **Arm.** This even /applies/ if one does not have arm */tefilin/* and has two head */tefilin* units/.

(2) **A strap.** It is self-understood that the same ruling /applies/ to a case which is specifically for head */tefilin/*. Such /a case/ also belongs to the category of holy appurtenances, just like a strap [as stated in *Megilah* 26b]. This is in fact evident from the *Beyur Ha-Gra* and the *M.A.* writes likewise above, at the end of Sec. 28.

(3) **From /head *tefilin*.** The *M.A.* writes that if the strap of arm */tefilin/* became severed close to the knot, it is forbidden to turn over the other end /of the strap/ to /serve at/ the top [where it is strong] and make the arm */tefilin/* knot in that /end/ and now bind the piece of strap which had the knot /formerly/ to /the strap/ at the bottom. /This is/ because one will thereby reduce the /degree of/ holiness /of that piece/, since, /originally,/ it had the knot and the /letter/ י in it and it will now be used /merely/ for the coils around the fingers. Instead, that piece must be put away /in the *genizah*/. In circumstances where /the remaining part of/ the strap is not so long, one should not make that many /nonobligatory/ coils around the arm.

Similarly, in the case of head */tefilin/*, if /the part of the strap/ that surrounds the head became severed, it is forbidden to turn over /the part/ that is inside the knot, so that it will /serve/ outside the knot, for the aforementioned reason.

On the other hand, if the strap of head */tefilin/* became severed outside the knot and one wishes to pull /the strap/ out /of the knot

1* A measure of volume.

וליתן בש"י אסור ג מפני שאין מורידין מקדושה חמורה לקדושה קלה ושל ראש קדושתו חמורה ד שרובו של שדי (ד) בשל ראש * אבל משל יד לשל ראש (ג) (ה) מותר לשנות * ה ואם היו (ד) [נ] * חדשים שעדיין (ו) לא הניחם * מותר לשנות אפילו * משל ראש לשל יד שטולה עליהם מכסה עור אחד ונראים (ז) כבית אחד: ב * ו אם התנה (ה) עליהם (ח) מתחלה אפילו לבשן אדם יכול לשנותם אפי' * משל ראש לשל

ג שם בגמרא ד שם ברש"י ה שם בגמרא ו ר' ירוחם ומהרא"י בשם סה"ח

באר היטב

ח"ב סי' כ"א) פסק להתיר ע"ש: (ג) מותר. היינו כשיעשה לו ד' בתים או על רצועה קאי: (ד) חדשים וכו'. דהזמנה לאו מילתא היא: (ה) עליהם. אפי' אם התנה רק אם יצטרך לעשות ממנו של יד שיעשה

שערי תשובה

עתה יקחהו ישאהו לתתו לתוך המעברתא. וגם כה"ג היפוך קרי ליה וכמ"ש המג"א אחר כך מדברי הב"י בשם הגהות מיימוני שכתב ויהפוך הרצועה תוך המעברתא והתם פשיטא שאין פירושו היפוך ממש רק דכל שהוא נתון בתחלה במקום זה והוא מעלהו או מורידו במקום אחר היפוך קרי ליה ולפ"ז אין ללמוד מדברי המג"א הללו להפוך ממש דמסתברא שאין לעשות כן אפילו שלא מטעם הורדה בשביל הקשר. וכמ"ש לעיל סימן ח' לענין טלית של מצוה. ונראה שאין להפוך כי אם בשעת הדחק שהקלה במקום שנפסק הוא רך וחלוש ואינו ראוי לעשות ממנו הקשירה בזרוע כדינו שיהיה קרוב ליפסק ואין לו רצועה אחרת יש להתיר להפוך וכמ"ש בא"ר ועיין מ"ש ביד אפרים על דברי המג"א. וי"ל דהמג"א סבירא ליה דהכא איכא תרתי שאין הקשר בחתיכה זו וגם מוריד מקדושת קשר לכריכות אצבע. אבל בהא לחוד שאין בה הקשר אין קפידא כיון דלא חזוא ליה. ונ"מ אם ברצועה הארוכה לבד יש די גם לכריכת האצבעות מותר לקושרה כיון שעתה אין משתמש בה קדושה כלל. ואפשר דבכה"ג אסור טפי לקושרה ולכרכה על פס ידו שטוב אין כאן תשמיש קדושה כלל ויש לגנוזה וצ"ע: [נ] חדשים. עבה"ט דהזמנה לאו מלתא היא ועיין בשאלות ותשובות צ"צ סימן פ"א שאם עיבד עור לשם רצועות של תפילין מותר להשתמש במותר דבר חול אף שלא התנה ומכ"ש אם התנה. ועיין לעיל סימן ל"ב בבה"ט ס"ק י"ב שמביא דברי הצ"צ ומשמע דמתיר דוקא בהתנה וליתא. ומה שהביא שם ראיה מגילית דאע"ג דבעי טוויה

משנה ברורה

למטה כדי שיהיה הרצועה שלימה בהשיעור המבואר למעלה בסימן ל"ג י"א (ג) דיכול להורידה אע"פ שמוריד קצת מקדושתה שהרי מקום הקשר יהיה תלוי למטה אין זה הורדה דעכ"פ באותה חתיכה יהיה הקשר. וי"א (ד) דג"ז אינו נכון דעכ"פ איכא קצת הורדת קדושה. ולפי דבריהם (ה) ה"ה בש"י אם נפסקה הרצועה של יד סמוך להקשר אפי' אם לא ירצה לקשור למטה החתיכה שנפסקה אעפ"כ לא יהפוך תחתית הרצועה למעלה לעשות בו הקשר דבזה מוריד העליונית של הרצועה קצת מקדושתה שהיתה מתחלה קרובה אל הקשר ע"כ יש להחמיר (ו) שלא להפוך כ"א בשעת הדחק שאין לו רצועה אחרת ובמקום שנפסק הוא רך וחלוש שאינו ראוי לעשות ממנו הקשירה בזרוע שיהא קרוב ליפסק אז יש להפוך. ועיין בביאור הלכה: (ד) בשל ראש. דשם הוא השין והדלית משא"כ בש"י דאין בו רק הקשר של יוד: (ה) מותר. היינו שיעשה לה ארבעה בתים ויכניס כל פרשה בבית שלה וה"ה דמותר ליקח הפרשיות ורצועות משל יד לשל ראש: (ו) לא הניחם. על ראשו אע"פ שזימנם והכינם לצורך הראש הזמנה לאו מלתא היא: (ז) כבית אחד. ואף שהם כתובים על ד' קלפים ונתונים בד' בתים תפנים אין בכך כלום בדיעבד וכמש"כ בסימן ל"ב סמ"ז ע"ש ועיין בבה"ל: ב (ח) מתחלה. בעת עשיית הש"ר (ז) אפילו אם לא התנה רק אם יצטרך לעשות ממנו של יד שיעשה מהני התנאי וכ"ש אם הוא אומר שאינו עושה

ביאור הלכה

* אבל משל יד וכו'. עיין במ"ב במש"כ וה"ה דמותר ליקח הפרשיות וכו' אף דשל יד רגיל לכתוב בקלף אחד מ"מ יצויר דיכניסה בד' בתים עיין בפמ"ג ובסי' ל"ב בסעיף מ"ה בס"ק ס"ב ובסעיף מ"ז בט"ז שם: * ואם היו וכו'. ופשוט דכ"ז דוקא מדוחק באין לו ש"י ויש לו ב' של ראש כמו שאמרו בגמרא דאל"ה הלא לכתחלה צריך לכתוב ד' פרשיות של יד בקלף אחד ואין צריך המחבר לבאר זה דכבר ביאר בסימן ל"ב סעיף מ"ז. ודברי הפמ"ג בזה מופלאים ממני: * חדשים שעדיין וכו'. עיין במ"ב. ורצועה חדשה שנתנה בתוך תפילין ישנים לכאורה לא הוי זה ג"כ כ"א הזמנה עדיין ושרי לשנותה דלא נקראה בשם תשמיש קדושה כ"א כשהניחה פ"א על הראש ואף דשם במגילה כ"ו ע"ב נשנו בחדא מחתא תשמישי קדושה נרתק של תפילין ורצועותיהן ובנרתק הלא משכר ביה פ"א אחר הזמנה שוב הוי בכלל תשמישי קדושה וכדבסמוך ס"ג וא"כ לכאורה ה"נ ברצועה משנקשרו בהתפילין שוב הוי בכלל תשמישיהן דז"א דשאני התם דהנרתק נקראת תשמיש קדושה משום דהיא משמשת להקדושה שנכנסת בה ע"כ משהכניס בתוכה התפילין כבר שימש להקדושה משא"כ ברצועות דנקראת תשמיש קדושה פשוט משום דהם משמשין להקדושה שעל ידן האדם מניח לתפילין על ראשו ועל ידו כל זמן שלא הניחן עליו עדיין לא נקראו בשם ת"ק ולא הוי כ"א הזמנה ולמעשה צ"ע: * מותר לשנות וכו'. מזה דייק הפמ"ג לעיל בסימן ל"ב סק"י דאם כתב על קלף לס"ת ונפסל ע"י שם וכדומה דמותר לכתוב על הנותר תו"מ דכתיבה ג"כ לא הוי כ"א הזמנה מעלייתא ולא הוי כלר ביה ואזמניה ודלא כא"ר שמחמיר בזה. אח"כ מצאתי בנו"ב מה"ת חיו"ד סי' קע"ד שנשא ונתן בזה והעלה דהמורה להקל לכתוב אח"כ עליה תפילין לא נשתבש אבל במזוזה אין להקל עי"ש הטעם: * מש"ר לשל יד. היינו הפרשיות והבתים דלדבר חול אסור לשנותם (כגון לכתוב על הגליונות ד"ת וכל כה"ג) וכמו שמבואר בס"ג בהג"ה ובמ"ב בס"ק י"ח[א]. ואפילו תנאה לא מהני בזה וכדבסמוך ואפילו לדיעות החולקים על הג"ה וסוברים דהזמנה אפילו לגוף הקדושה לאו מילתא היא[1] זה עדיף וכמו שפסק המ"א דאם התחיל לכתוב על קלף או נייר אסור לכתוב עליו ד"ת והטעם דעדיף מהזמנה אחרת אף דזה לא הוי ג"כ כ"א הזמנה דאל"ה היה אסור להוריד אפילו לקדושה קלה עכ"ז עדיפא דהוא בגוף הקדושה עצמה אבל הרצועות דהוא רק ת"ק כמבואר לקמן בסימן קנ"ב[ב] מותר לשנותם אפילו לדבר חול כיון שהם חדשים וכמו שפסק הצ"ל והביאו הא"ר להלכה דעור המעובד לרצועות מותר לשנותו אפילו לדבר חול אפילו בדלא התנה משום דלא הוי הזמנה רק לת"ק ולאו מילתא היא ועיין בסמוך מה שנכתוב בזה בשם הרז"ה דלפי דבריו הזמנה ברצועות מילתא היא שלא לשנותה עכ"פ לדבר חול ואף דרוב פוסקים חולקים עליו ואין מחלקין בין רצועות לשאר ת"ק מ"מ שלא במקום הדחק יש להחמיר: * ואם[ג] התנה עליהם מתחלה. עיין במ"ב במש"כ דהיינו בעת עשיית הש"ר. הנה אף דמדברי הב"ח משמע דה"ה דמהני אם התנאי היה בפעם ראשונה כשקשרן לכאורה לע"ג דהלא פשוט דעשיית הש"ר עכ"פ לא גרע מההזמנה דעשיית כיס לשם תפילין ובו הלא הכריח המ"א מהטור דאפילו בעת שהוא רק לפי שעה ואח"כ לכאורה כ"ש דלא מהני אם פירש שאם יצטרך לפנות שיהיה יכול לפנות לפי הק"ו שעושה הע"ת [והוא מובא בבה"ט בס"ק ד'[ד] מדברי מהרא"י] כיון דבעת ההזמנה לא היה שום תנאי ומה שהובא לקמן בסי' קנ"ד ס"ח דמהני בהו תנאי איירי ג"כ שהיה בשעת ההזמנה א"נ שם איירי דלר ביה ע"ד קביעותא דהיה ההזמנה והשימוש בפ"א ולכך מועיל שם תנאי משא"כ בענינינו ועיין במנחות ל"ד שם משמע ג"כ דהתנאי הוא בההזמנה אך זה יש לדחות דשם למ"ד הזמנה מילתא משא"כ לדידן דהזמנה בלבד לאו מילתא רק בצירוף הקשירה אפשר דיועיל תנאי אף בעת שקשרן על ראשו ואפשר דהב"ח יפלוג על הק"ו דהע"ת וצ"ע. ודע דמש"כ בס"ג בהג"ה ואם התנה עליו מתחלה וכו' נוכל לומר דאיירי אפילו אם לא היה התנאי רק בעת שלר ביה שאינו לר ביה אלא לפי שעה דמהני דהלא שם לא עשה הכיס לשם תפילין ואם הג"ה מיירי בכל גווני יהיה ג"כ מיירי דהיה התנאי בעת העשיה: * מש"ר לשל יד.[2] הפרשיות וכ"ש הרצועות אלא דלפי המבואר בסי' קנ"ד ובפמ"ג שם יש חילוק ביניהם כמה שאבאר והוא דהפרשיות וה"ה הבתים דהוא גוף הקדושה לא[ה] מהני ביה תנאי כ"א להורידו לקדושה קלה אבל לחול כגון אם ירצה לכתוב על הגליונות דבר חול וכה"ג לא מהני ביה תנאה אפילו אם הם חדשים אבל הרצועות דהוא רק ת"ק מהני ביה תנאה אפילו להורידן לחול ואפי' אם כבר נשתמש בהן וכדבסמוך בס"ג בהג"ה דאפילו לר ביה דהוא מעשה מהני תנאה וכ"ז להשו"ע שם אבל לפי מה שכתבנו שם דלכתחלה יש לחוש למש"כ הב"ח בשיטת רש"י דמקום הקשר והיו"ד הוא קדושה עצמה דינן כפרשיות אם כבר נשתמש בהן דבעשיית הקשר בעלמא מסתברא דלא ירד עליהם הקדושה עדיין:

שער הציון

סודר

(ג) מוכח ממ"א וכ"כ הגר"ז וח"א: (ד) עיין בפמ"ג ובש"ת ובסימן קנ"ד במ"ז אות ב"ת: (ה) דה"ח: (ו) ש"ת: (ז) בה"ט והוא מע"ת:

הגהות ותיקונים: א) י"ז: **ב)** קנ"ד: **ג)** אם: **ד)** ה': **ה)** תיבת לא נמחק (ר"מ): **ו)** נ"א: **ז)** בבה"ט סי' ח' סק"ד:

הערות והארות: 1) עיין במ"ב בס"ק כ"ג: 2) עיין לקמן במ"ב ס"ק י"ח לענין גוף הקדושה ובס"ק כ"ג לענין תנאי (ר"ש):

tefilin/ and put it in arm /*tefilin*/. This is because one may not reduce /a holy article/ from a higher /degree of/ holiness to a lesser /degree of/ holiness. The holiness of head /*tefilin*/ is of a higher /degree than that of arm *tefilin*/ as most of /the Divine Name/ ש־ד־י is (4) in the head /*tefilin*/.

Mishnah Berurah

on the severed side/ and lower it down so that the strap will be whole for the /required/ length stated above in Sec. 33 /, Par. 5 and sub-Par. 29 of the Mishnah Berurah/, there are /authorities/ who say that he may /in fact/ lower it. Even though /by doing so/ he will reduce its /degree of/ holiness a little, as the place in which the knot /was tied/ will be hanging below, this is not /regarded as/ a reduction /in its degree of holiness/, since the knot will at any rate be in that /same/ piece /of strap/. /However,/ there are /authorities/ who say that this is also improper, since it does involve at any rate a little reduction of /the degree/ of holiness. According to their words, a similar ruling /applies/ in the case of arm /*tefilin*/. /I.e.,/ if the strap of arm /*tefilin*/ became severed close to the knot /, then/, even if one does not wish to tie /to it/ below the piece which was severed, he should nevertheless not turn around the bottom of the strap to the top, to make the knot in it. For by /doing/ so /the part that served as/ the upper /part/ of the strap will /now/ be reduced by him a little from the /degree of/ holiness which it had originally, through being close to the knot. Consequently, one should be stringent and should not turn it /around/ except in a time of pressing /need, i.e.,/ when he does not have another strap and /the strap/ is soft and weak in the area where it was severed, so that it is not fit /there/ for the binding on the upper arm to be done with it, because it would be close to severing /if used/. In such a case one should turn /the strap/ around. See the Beyur Halachah.[1]

(4) In the head /*tefilin*/. For the /letter/

1 The author recommends there that when the part of the strap which surrounds the head became severed, a poor person or someone who does not have another strap should cut off a piece of the strap from where it was severed, which includes the part that surrounded the head and was inside the knot, and put it away in the *genizah*. He should then join the rest of the strap with sinews and make a knot in the whole part of the strap, taking care that what was previously inside the knot does not go beyond the knot. As regards arm *tefilin*, the author writes that it is better to make less nonobligatory coils rather than to bind two pieces of strap together.

וליתן בש"י אסור [ג]מפני שאין מורידין מקדושה חמורה לקדושה קלה ושל ראש קדושתו חמורה [ד]שרובו של שדי (ד) בשל ראש * אבל משל יד לשל ראש (ג) (ה) מותר לשנות * [ה]ואם היו (ד) [נ] * חדשים שעדיין (ו) לא הניחם * מותר לשנות אפילו * משל ראש לשל יד שטולה עליהם מכסה עור אחד ונראים (ז) כבית אחד: **ב** * [ו]אם התנה (ה) עליהם (ח) מתחלה אפילו לבשן אדם יכול לשנותם אפי' * משל ראש לשל

ג שם בגמרא ד שם ברש"י ה שם בגמרא ו ר' ירוחם ומהרא"י בשם סא"ח

שערי תשובה

עתה יקחהו ישאהו לתתו לתוך המעברתא. וגם כה"ג היפוך קרי ליה וכמ"ש המג"א אחר כך מדברי הב"י בשם הגהות מיימוני שכתב ויהפוך הרצועה תוך המעברתא והתם פשיטא שאין פירושו היפוך ממש רק דכל שהוא נתון בתחלה במקום זה והוא מעלהו או מורידו במקום אחר היפוך קרי ליה ולפ"ז אין ללמוד מדברי המג"א האלו להפוך ממש דמסתברא שאין לעשות כן אפילו שלא מטעם הורדה בשביל הקשר. וכמ"ש לעיל סימן ח'[י] לענין טלית של מצוה. ונראה שאין להפוך כי אם בשעת הדחק שהקלה במקום שנפסק הוא רך וחלוש ואינו ראוי לעשות ממנו הקשירה בזרוע כדינו שיהיה קרוב ליפסק ואין לו רצועה אחרת יש להתיר להפוך וכמ"ש בא"ר ועיין מ"ש ביד אפרים על דברי המג"א. וי"ל דהמג"א סבירא ליה דהכא איכא תרתי שאין הקשר בחתיכה זו וגם מוריד מקדושת קשר לכריכות אצבע. אבל בהא לחוד שאין בה הקשר אין קפידא כיון דלא חזיא ליה. וכ"מ אם ברצועה הארוכה לבד יש די גם לכריכת האצבעות מותר לקושרה כיון שעתה אין משתמש בה קדושה כלל. ואפשר דבכה"ג אסור טפי לקושרה ולכרכה על פס ידו שסוב אין כאן תשמיש קדושה כלל ויש לגנוזה וצ"ע: [נ] חדשים. עבה"ט דהזמנה לאו מלתא היא ועיין בשאלות ותשובות ל"ל סימן פ"א שאם עיבד עור לשם רצועות של תפילין מותר להשתמש במותר דבר חול אף שלא התנה ומכ"ש אם התנה. ועיין לעיל סימן ל"ב בבה"ט ס"ק י"ב שמביא דברי הל"ל ומשמע דמתיר דוקא בהתנה וליתא. ומה שהביא שם ראיה מציצית דאע"ג דבעי טויה

באר היטב

ח"ב סי' כ"א[י] פסק להתיר ע"ש: (ג) מותר. היינו כשיעשה לו ד' בתים או על רצועה קאי: (ד) חדשים וכו'. דהזמנה לאו מילתא היא: (ה) עליהם. אפי' אם התנה רק אם יצטרך לעשות ממנו של יד שיעשה

ביאור הלכה

* **אבל משל יד וכו'.** עיין במ"ב במש"כ וה"ה דמותר ליקח הפרשיות וכו' אף דשל יד רגיל לכתוב בקלף אחד מ"מ יצוייר דיכניסה בד' בתים עיין בפמ"ג ובסי' ל"ב בסעיף מ"ה בס"ק ס"ב ובסעיף מ"ז בט"ז שם:

* **ואם היו וכו'.** ופשוט דכ"ז דוקא מדוקק באין לו ש"י ויש לו ב' של ראש כמו שאמרו בגמרא דאל"ה הלא לכתחלה צריך לכתוב ד' פרשיות של יד בקלף אחד ואין צריך המחבר לבאר זה דכבר ביאר בסימן ל"ב סעיף מ"ז. ודברי הפמ"ג בזה מופלאים ממני: * **חדשים שעדיין וכו'.** עיין במ"ב. ורצועה חדשה שנתנה בתוך תפילין ישנים לכאורה לא הוי זה ג"כ כ"א הזמנה עדיין ושרי לשנותה דלא נקראה בשם תשמיש קדושה כ"א כשהניחה פ"א על הראש ואף דשם במגילה כ"ו ע"ב נשנו בחדא מחתא תשמישי קדושה נרתק של תפילין ורצועותיהן ובנרתק הלא משכר ביה פ"א אחר הזמנה שוב הוי בכלל תשמישי קדושה וכדבסמוך ס"ג וא"כ לכאורה ה"נ ברצועה משנקשרו בהתפילין שוב הוי בכלל תשמישיהן דז"א דשאני התם דהנרתק נקראת תשמיש קדושה משום דהיא משמשת להקדושה שנכנסת בה ע"כ משהכניס בתוכה התפילין כבר שימש להקדושה משא"כ ברצועות דנקראת תשמיש קדושה פשוט משום דהם משמשין להקדושה שעל ידן האדם מניח לתפילין על ראשו ועל ידו כל זמן שלא הניחן עליו עדיין לא נקראו בשם ת"ק ולא הוי כ"א הזמנה ולמעשה צ"ע: * **מותר לשנות וכו'.** מזה דייק הפמ"ג לעיל בסימן ל"ב סק"י דאם כתב על קלף לס"ת ונפסל ע"י שם וכדומה דמותר לכתוב על הנותר תו"מ דכתיבה ג"כ לא הוי כ"א הזמנה מעלייתא ולא הוי כלר ביה ואזמניה ודלא כא"ר שמחמיר בזה. אח"כ מצאתי בנו"ב מה"ת חיו"ד סי' קע"ד שנשא ונתן בזה והעלה דהמורה להקל לכתוב אח"כ עליה תפילין לא נשתבש אבל במזוזה אין להקל עי"ש הטעם: * **מש"ר לשל יד.** היינו הפרשיות והבתים דלדבר חול אסור לשנותם (כגון לכתוב על הגליונות ד"ת וכל כה"ג) וכמו שמבואר בס"ג בהג"ה ובמ"ב בס"ק י"ח[א]. ואפילו תנאה לא מהני בזה וכדבסמוך ואפילו לדיעות החולקים על הג"ה וסוברים דהזמנה אפילו לגוף הקדושה לאו מילתא היא[1] זה עדיף וכמו שפסק המ"א דאם התחיל לכתוב על קלף או נייר אסור לכתוב עליו ד"ח והטעם דעדיף מהזמנה אחרת אף דזה לא הוי ג"כ כ"א הזמנה דאל"ה היה אסור להוריד אפילו לקדושה קלה עכ"ז עדיפא דהוא בגוף הקדושה עצמה אבל הרצועות דהוא רק ת"ק כמבואר לקמן בסימן קנ"ב[ב] מותר לשנותם אפילו לדבר חול כיון שהם חדשים וכמו שפסק הל"ל והביאו הא"ר להלכה דעור המעובד לרצועות מותר לשנותו אפילו לדבר חול אפילו בדלא התנה משום דלא הוי הזמנה רק לת"ק ולאו מילתא היא ועיין בסמוך מה שנכתוב בזה בשם הרז"ה דלפי דבריו הזמנה ברצועות מילתא היא שלא לשנותה עכ"פ לדבר חול ואף דרוב פוסקים חולקים עליו ואין מחלקין בין רצועות לשאר ת"ק מ"מ שלא במקום הדחק יש להחמיר: * **ואם[ג] התנה עליהם מתחלה.** עיין במ"ב במש"כ דהיינו בעת עשיית הש"ר. הנה אף דמדברי הב"ח משמע דה"ה דמהני אם התנאי היה בפעם ראשונה כשקשרן לכאורה לע"ג דהלא פשוט דעשיית הש"ר עכ"פ לא גרע מההזמנה דעשיית כיס לשם תפילין ובו הלא הכריח המ"א מהטור דאפילו בעת שהוא נר ביה פירש שהוא רק לפי שעה ואח"כ יפנהו אסור וא"כ לכאורה כ"ש דלא מהני אם פירש שאם יצטרך לפנות שיהיה יכול לפנות לפי הק"ו שעושה הע"ת [והוא מובא בבה"ט בס"ק ד'[ד] מדברי מהרא"י] כיון דבעת ההזמנה לא היה שום תנאי ומה שהובא לקמן בסי' קנ"ד ס"ח דמהני בהו תנאי איירי דלר ביה ע"ד קביעותא דהיה ההזמנה והשימוש בפ"א ולכך מועיל שם תנאי משא"כ בענינינו ועיין במנחות ל"ד שם משמע ג"כ דהתנאי הוא בההזמנה אך זה יש לדחות דשם למ"ד הזמנה מילתא משא"כ לדידן דהזמנה בלבד לאו מילתא רק בצירוף הקשירה אפשר דיועיל תנאי אף בעת שקשרן על ראשו ואפשר דהב"ח יפלוג על הק"ו דהע"ת וצ"ע. ודע דמש"כ בס"ג בהג"ה ואם התנה עליו מתחלה וכו' נוכל לומר דאיירי אפילו אם לא היה התנאי רק בעת שנר ביה שאינו נר ביה אלא לפי שעה דמהני דהלא שם לא עשה הכיס לשם תפילין ואם הג"ה מיירי בכל גווני יהיה ג"כ מיירי דהיה התנאי בעת העשיה: * **מש"ר לשל יד.**[2] הפרשיות וכ"ש הרצועות אלא דלפי המבואר בסי' קנ"ד ובפמ"ג שם יש חילוק ביניהם במה שאבאר והוא דהפרשיות וה"ה הבתים דהוא גוף הקדושה לא[ה] מהני ביה תנאי כ"א להורידו לקדושה קלה אבל לחול כגון אם ירצה לכתוב על הגליונות דבר חול וכה"ג לא מהני ביה תנאה אפילו אם הם חדשים אבל הרצועות דהוא רק ת"ק מהני ביה תנאה אפילו להורידן לחול ואפי' אם כבר נשתמש בהן וכדבסמוך בס"ג בהג"ה דאפילו נר ביה דהוא מעשה מהני תנאה וכ"ז להשו"ע שם אבל לפי מה שכתבנו שם דלכתחלה יש לחוש למש"כ הב"ח בשיטת רש"י דמקום הקשר והיו"ד הוא קדושה עצמה דינן כפרשיות אם כבר נשתמש בהן דבעשיית הקשר בעלמא מסתברא דלא ירד עליהם הקדושה עדיין:

משנה ברורה

למטה כדי שיהיה הרצועה שלימה בהשיעור המבואר למעלה בסימן ל"ג י"ח (ג) דיכול להורידה אע"פ שמוריד קצת מקדושתה שהרי מקום הקשר יהיה תלוי למטה אין זה הורדה דעכ"פ באותה חתיכה יהיה הקשר. וי"א (ד) דג"ז אינו נכון דעכ"פ איכא קצת הורדת קדושה. ולפי דבריהם (ה) ה"ה בש"י אם נפסקה הרצועה של יד סמוך להקשר אפי' אם לא ירצה לקשור למטה החתיכה שנפסקה אעפ"כ לא יהפוך תחתית הרצועה למעלה לעשות בו הקשר דבזה מוריד העליונית של הרצועה קצת מקדושתה שהיתה מתחלה קרובה אל הקשר ע"כ יש להחמיר (ו) שלא להפוך כ"א בשעת הדחק שאין לו רצועה אחרת ובמקום שנפסק הוא רך וחלוש שאינו ראוי לעשות ממנו הקשירה בזרוע שיהא קרוב ליפסק אז יש להפוך. ועיין בביאור הלכה: (ד) בשל ראש. דשם הוא השין והדלית משא"כ בש"י דאין בו רק הקשר של יוד: (ה) מותר. היינו שיעשה לה ארבעה בתים ויכניס כל פרשה בבית שלה וה"ה דמותר ליקח הפרשיות ורצועות משל יד לשל ראש: (ו) לא הניחם. על ראשו אע"פ שזימנם והכינס לצורך הראש הזמנה לאו מלתא היא: (ז) כבית אחד. ואף שהם כתובים על ד' קלפים ונתונים בד' בתים מבפנים אין בכך כלום בדיעבד וכמש"כ בסימן ל"ב סמ"ז עי"ש ועיין בבה"ל: **ב** (ח) מתחלה. בעת עשיית הש"ר (ז) אפילו אם לא התנה רק אם יצטרך לעשות ממנו של יד שיעשה מהני התנאי וכ"ש אם הוא אומר שאינו עושה

שער הציון

סודר

(ג) מוכח ממ"א וכ"כ הגר"ז וח"א: (ד) עיין בפמ"ג ובש"ת ובסימן קנ"ד במ"ז אות ב"ת: (ה) דה"ח: (ו) ש"ת: (ז) בה"ט והוא מע"ת:

הגהות ותיקונים: א) י"ז: **ב)** קנ"ד: **ג)** אם: **ד)** ה': **ה)** תיבת לא נמחק (ר"מ): **ו)** נ"א: **ז)** בבה"ט סי' ח' סק"ד:

הערות והארות: 1) עיין במ"ב בס"ק כ"ג: 2) עיין לקמן במ"ב ס"ק י"ח לענין גוף הקדושה ובס"ק כ"ג לענין תנאי (ר"ש):

However, (5) it is permitted to alter /the usage of/ arm /*tefilin*/ to /that of/ head /*tefilin*/.

If /the *tefilin*/ are new, /meaning/ that as yet (6) they have not been donned, it is permitted to alter /the usage/ even of head /*tefilin*/ to /that of/ arm /*tefilin*/, by enveloping them with a cover of a single skin and /thus making/ them appear (7) like a single housing.

2. If one made a stipulation with respect to /the designation of the *tefilin*/ (8) at the outset, he may /then/ alter /their usage/, even though /an alteration/ from /the usage of/ head /*tefilin*/ to /that of/ arm /*tefilin* is involved/ and even if a person has /already/ worn them.

Mishnah Berurah

ש /on the housings/ and the /letter/ ד /of the knot, which form the first two letters of the Divine Name ש-ד-י,/ are there. By contrast, the arm /*tefilin*/ have only the knot /in the form/ of the /letter/ י /, which completes this Divine Name/.

(5) It is permitted. I.e., if one makes four housings to it and inserts each passage in its /appropriate/ housing.

Correspondingly, it is permitted to take passages and straps from arm /*tefilin* and use them/ for head /*tefilin*/.

(6) They have not been donned. /I.e.,/ on his head.

Even though one designated them and prepared them for the sake of /serving as/ head /*tefilin*/, designation is of no significance /by itself/.

(7) Like a single housing. Even though /the passages/ are written on four parchments and were put into four /separate/ housings on the inside, this does not /matter/ at all once it is after the event, as stated in Sec. 32, Par. 47; see there. See the Beyur Halachah.[2]

(8) At the outset. /I.e., if one made a stipulation/ at the time when the head /*tefilin*/ were made.

Even if one merely made a stipulation that if he needs to make /the *tefilin* serve for/ arm /*tefilin*/ he may do so, the stipulation is of avail. It is certainly of avail if one said that

2 The author writes there that this may only be done where one is pressed, when he does not have arm *tefilin* and has two head *tefilin* units. Otherwise, the passages of the arm *tefilin* must be written on a single parchment.

יד: ג * (ט) ⁰סודר (י) דאזמניה * למיצר ביה * (יא) תפילין (ו) [ג] * (יב) ⁰לעולם * (יג) וצר ביה * תפילין

ז ברכות כ"ג וסנהד' מ"ח ח מרדכי פרק בני העיר

באר היטב

מהני התנאי וכ"ש אם מתחלה אומר שאינו עושה של ראש אלא לפי שעה דמהני מהרא"י: (ו) לעולם. ואם עשה כיס לשם תפילין אפי' צר ביה ע"ד

שערי תשובה

לשמה נזרקים ל"ע דהתם הטעם משום דכבר עברה מצותו כמ"ש במקום אחר. וע"ש שכתב דע"י תנאי מהני אף לקלף עצמו אף דהוי הזמנה לגוף הקדושה מ"מ הזמנה זו שוברה עמה מחמת התנאי ומועיל אף לדבר חול. ועיין בשו"ת עבודת הגרשוני סימן ס"ה דס"ל דמעובד לשם ס"ת אין להורידו לתפילין וגם אין לומר בתחלת העיבוד שמעבד לשם ס"ת ולתפילין שיש חשש דדאורייתא אין ברירה. לכן יאמר שמעבד לס"ת ויתנה אם ירצה לשנותה לקדושה קלה שיהא רשות בידו ע"ש. ונראה כוונתו לסברת הנ"ל דאפילו תימא הזמנה לגוף הקדושה מלתא היא מ"מ כשמתנה הוי שוברה עמה. ולפ"ז י"ל דגם לדבר חול שפיר דמי. ומ"ש שם מתחלה לחלק בין קדושה קלה לחול הא מסיק דאין חילוק וא"כ ע"י תנאי י"ל דמודה דשרי גם לחול ואדרבה י"ל דלחול שרי טפי דלתפילין י"ל כיון שע"י התנאי הוא שובר ההזמנה שוב הו"ל כעיבוד שלא לשמה שהרי לא נתעבד לשם תפילין וגם לקדושה חמורה של ס"ת לא בא מה תאמר שע"י התנאי מועיל שוב צריך לומר הוברר הדבר למפרע שנתעבד לשם תפילין וזה לא אמרינן. ועיין בשו"ת בית אפרים חלק אה"ע אם יש שייכות ברירה בדברים שע"י תנאי ע"ש ול"ע. ובמ"א הארכתי בזה ועיין לעיל סימן ל"ב[א] מ"ש שם על דברי העה"ג בזה: [ג] לעולם.

משנה ברורה

ש"ר אלא לפי שעה דמהני: ג (ט) סודר. וה"ה אם עשה כיס (ח) מחדש לצורך תפילין ג"כ אין אסור להשתמש ביה חול עד דצר ביה דהזמנה לאו מילתא היא וה"ה בכל תשמישי קדושה אפילו תיק לס"ת. ותשמיש דתשמיש (ט) אין בו קדושה כלל: (י) דאזמניה. אפילו בדבור בלבד וכ"ש אם נטלו ואמר זה יהיה לתפילין דמהני. ועיין בבה"ל מה שכתבתי בשם הר"ן: (יא) תפילין. ותיק (י) של טלית לא מיקרי תשמיש קדושה רק תשמיש מצוה ולכן מותר להניח בו שאר דברים של חול דאף דמונח בו ג"כ תיק של תפילין לא הוי התיק של טלית כ"א תשמיש דתשמיש ואפי' אם ניתן בתוכו הסידור שלו דיש בו קדושה או התפילין בלא תיק מ"מ בעת הצורך מותר ליתן בתוכו דברים של חול דהלא הוא עשוי מתחלה גם לטלית דהוא דבר של חול והוי כאלו התנה וכדלקמן בהג"ה. ואותן האנשים ההולכין בדרך ומשתמשין בשק של תפילין בדברים של חול אף דמדינא אסור אעפ"כ (יא) יש ללמד עליהן זכות דכיון דרגילין בכך הוי כאלו התנו בתחלה. ואעפ"כ לכתחלה אין נכון לעשות כן: (יב) לעולם. י"א דוקא בפירוש אבל בסתמא לא אמרינן דהזמנתו הוא על עולם כיון דסתם סודר אין מיוחד לתפילין אבל מדברי הגר"א בביאורו משמע דסתמא הוי כלעולם ולא מיעט המחבר בזה אלא היכא דהתנה שלא יהיה רק לפי שעה ולא לעולם ואם עשה כיס להניח תפילין או שאמר לאומן עשה לי כיס של תפילין לכו"ע הוי סתמא כלעולם: (יג) וצר ביה. כ"ז בסודר או כיס שלו (יג) אבל אין אדם אוסר דבר שאינו שלו אא"כ

ביאור הלכה

* סודר דאזמניה וכו'. עיין במ"ב במה שכ' אפילו בדבור בלבד והוא מהדה"ח שכתב כן אף דפמ"ג מסתפק אולי אפי' במחשבה בלבד מהניא לא רציתי לסתום כן משום דבעיני יפלא למה העלימו הפוסקים עיניהם מהתוס' בסנהדרין מ"ח ע"א ד"ה נתנו דמסקי לבסוף דאפילו הזמנה בדיבור לא מהניא אא"כ נטלו ואמר זה יהיה לספר או למת עי"ש. ואין לדחוק דהתוספות לא קאמר אלא למ"ד דהזמנה מילתא היא משא"כ לדידן דבעינן ג"כ צר ביה מהני אפילו הזמנה גרוע אבל פשטא דסוגיא לא משמע שם כן עי"ש בגמרא ולאביי דאמר וכו'. וכן מדנקט הוסיף ביה דימום וכו' משמע דיחוד בעלמא לא מהני אפילו לרבא עי"ש בתוספות ועכ"פ במחשבה בעלמא בודאי אין להחמיר. ודע דמה שכתבנו דאין די ההזמנה במחשבה דוקא אם לא צר ביה תיכף בעת ההזמנה רק לאח"ז ולא חשב אז כלל רק הניח בו בסתמא ופנייה אח"כ אבל אם המחשבה הזו היה בעת שצר ביה הרי צר ביה אדעתא דקביעותא ואסור אפילו אם פנייה אח"כ דמחשיב כמו צר ביה ואזמניה וכדלקמן. אח"כ מצאתי בעזה"י בחדושי רע"א ביו"ד סי' שס"ד בשם חדושי הר"ן שסובר ג"כ כמו שהערנו בתחלת דברינו דלפעמים אפילו הזמנה בדבור לא מהניא ואעתיק מה שכתב שם [לענין מת וה"ה לענין תפילין וכמו שכתב המ"א] דאם כשהניח התפילין באיזה דבר הזמינו בפירוש שיהיה מיוחד לכך או שחשב כך בלבו נאסר אפילו בלא מעשה אפילו אם פנייה אח"כ להתפילין אבל אם ההזמנה היתה מקודם ולא הניח בו אז התפילין ולאח"ז בלא הסכמה אחרת [דאי הסכים אח"כ להניח בו רק אדעתא לפנותו ס"ל להר"ן דשרי בכל גווני וכמו שנכתוב אח"כ בשמו] הניח בו התפילין תלוי בזה אם ההזמנה שמקודם היה ע"י מעשה נאסר בהנחת התפילין סתם שלאח"כ אע"ג דפנייה אח"כ להתפילין אבל אם ההזמנה הוא רק בדבור לא נאסר כיון דההזמנה היה שלא בשעת הנחת התפילין עכ"ד. והנה דין הראשון שלו הוא פשוט ומוסכם כמעט מכל הפוסקים וכמו שכתבנו מתחלה בעצמנו אך בדינו השני התעורר בזה דבר חדש. אח"כ מצאתי גם בא"ר שהעתיק להלכה דברי הש"ג דבדבור בעלמא לא הוי הזמנה ופשוט דמה שכתב המ"א דמדברי הש"ג לא משמע כן לא אהזמנה בדיבור קאי. ע"כ ל"ע למעשה בהזמנה בדבור בלבד. ומ"מ נראה דיודה הר"ן לדברי התוספות דאם נטלו ואמר זה יהיה לתפילין דמהני דזה מחשיב כמו מעשה וכמו שהוכיחו שם התוספות מהא דנתנתו לספר עי"ש: * למיצר ביה. נ"ל דדוקא אם בעת ההזמנה היה לו כבר תפילין אז חל ההזמנה אבל אם עשה כיס לתפילין שיקנה אח"כ לא חל בזה ההזמנה והוי אח"כ כצר ביה ולא אזמניה דמותר אם הוא רק לפי שעה ואמינא לה מהא דסנהדרין מ"ח ע"א דנפש שבנאו לשם חי עי"ש ברש"י ופשוט:

* תפילין וכו'. עיין במ"ב סק"א[ב] במה שכתבתי דאף דניתן בתוכו תפילין וכו' עיין בח"א כלל י"ד סעיף כ"א דמש"כ ונ"ל וכו' ופשוט דט"ס הוא וצ"ל דאע"ג דניתן לתוכו תפילין וכו' דאל"ה הלא לא הוי אלא רק תשמיש דתשמיש אך בלא"ה דבריו לע"ג דמדמי זה לדינא דמ"א הנ"ל בסימן מ' סק"ב ומשמע מדבריו דלמ"א אסור בזה ולא נהירא דהלא הוא עשוי מתחלה גם לטלית דהוא לדבר חול וא"כ אין עליו שם תשמישי קדושה דהוי כאלו התנה בפירוש שיהא מותר להשתמש בו דבר חול וכמו שכתב המ"א כעין זה בסימן ל"ד סק"ו עי"ש ומה דאוסר המ"א בסימן מ' הנ"ל לשמש בהבית עד שיניחנו עוד בתוך כלי שם שאני דסברת המ"א דכיון דהוא מיוחד גם לתפילין שוב הו"ל כליין מה תאמר דכיון דהוא מיוחד גם לטלית תו אין על התיק הזה שום קדושה הלא שם אין תלוי בקדושה כלל דהרי אפי' מאה כלים זה עג"ז דבעלמא תשמיש דתשמיש אין בו שום קדושה ואעפ"כ אסור שם אע"כ דלא חשיב שם כיסוי אלא בדבר שאין מיוחד לה תמיד וע"כ אוסר המ"א שם דהלא בהתיק של הטלית רגיל תמיד לכסות גם התפילין משא"כ בענינינו דהאיסור להשתמש אינו רק בדבר שיש עליו שם ת"ק וזה הלא עשוי מתחלה גם לדבר חול ואולי דהח"א סובר דאף אם התנה שיהא מותר להשתמש בו איזה דבר חול אין מותר רק לאותו דבר: * לעולם. עיין במ"ב סקי"ב במש"כ י"א וכו' הוא דעת הא"ר עי"ש במה שהביא מתשובת חו"י דמשמע הכי ומש"כ מדברי הגר"א וכו' הוא ממש"כ מקור לדין זה דלעולם כמש"כ בהג"ר וכנ"ל ס"ב [דפשוט דהוא להוכיח דהגמרא לא איירי בהתנה שיהא רק לפי שעה או תנאי אחר שהוא למעט ההזמנה ומש"כ וכמש"כ הרא"ש בשם הירושלמי כיון בזה לתרץ קושית הפמ"ג במ"ז מנ"ל דתנאי מהני אפילו להורידן לחול דשם במנחות מיירי לענין להורידו לקדושה קלה וע"ז רמז וכמש"כ הרא"ש וכו' עי"ש דמיירי אפי' להורידו לחול] (ובעל דמשק אליעזר השיא את דברי הגר"א לענין אחר ללא צורך) ולכאורה לדברי הא"ר הנ"ל ל"ל להגמרא לומר בברכות כ"ג ע"ב הא דלא אזמני' עי"ש ויש לדחות: * וצר ביה וכו'. עיין במ"ב במה שכתב לענין קטן שצר וכו' ועיין בפמ"ג שכתב דקטן שצר לא מיתסר אלא בדצר ביה אדעתא דקביעותא או דאביו אזמין לי' דאל"ה ה"ל כצר ביה ולא אזמין דאין לו מחשבה וממ"א לא משמע כן וכן הגר"ז והח"א סתמו כהמ"א וקושית הפמ"ג בקל יש ליישב לכאורה וכמש"ל: * תפילין חד זימנא. ואפילו בעידנא דצר עתה פעם ראשון אחר הזמנה צרר אותם עם מעות ג"כ אעפ"כ חלה הקדושה מאחר שהזמינו בתחלה לתפילין לבד וממילא דאסור לעשות כן אם לא שיחזור בפי' מההזמנה הראשונה ואתי דבור ומבטל דבור וראיה מברכות כ"ג ע"ב ותניא אידך לא יצור עי"ש ואין לדחות דהברייתא איירי דווקא שצר תחלה התפילין אבל בזמן אחד ש"ד א"כ ל"ל להגמרא לתרץ דאידך ברייתא איירי בדלא אזמניה יתרצנה כפשוטה עם מעותיו

שער הציון

(ח) סנהדרין מ"ח ע"ב: (ט) פמ"ג בסימן קנ"ג במ"ז: (י) ח"א כלל י"ד עי"ש ובבה"ל: (יא) ט"ז: (יב) מ"א:

הגהות ותיקונים: א) סק"ז: ב) סקי"א:

3. If (9) a cloth (10) was designated for (11) *tefilin* to be wrapped in it (12) on a

Mishnah Berurah

he is only making them /serve as/ head /*tefilin*/ temporarily.

(9) A cloth. Correspondingly, if one made a new bag for the sake of *tefilin* it is also not forbidden to be used for a secular /purpose/ until he has wrapped /*tefilin*/ in it /once/, as designation /alone/ is of no significance.

The same ruling /applies/ to all holy appurtenances, even to a case for a Torah Scroll. /However,/an appurtenance of an appurtenance /to a holy article/ has no holiness whatsoever.[3]

(10) Was designated. /This ruling applies/ even if /the cloth was designated/ solely by speech. /The designation/ is certainly of avail if one took hold of it and said, "This should be for *tefilin*". See what I have written in the name of the *Ran* in the Beyur Halachah.[4]

(11) *Tefilin.* A *talis* bag is not classed as a holy appurtenance, but only as a mitzvah appurtenance. Consequently, one is permitted to place in it other articles, which are secular. Even if a *tefilin* bag is also lying in it, the *talis* bag is merely /classed as/ an appurtenance of a /holy/ appurtenance /because of this/. /Furthermore,/ even if one's sidur, which does have holiness, is lying in /the bag/ or if the *tefilin* /are lying in it/ without /having been inserted first in their own/ bag, it is nevertheless permitted to put in it secular articles in a time of need. /This is/ because /the bag/ was obviously meant from the outset /to serve/ for a *talis* as well, which is /regarded in this respect as/ a secular article, /so that the same ruling/ applies as if one stipulated /that the bag may be used for secular articles/. /Such a stipulation is of avail,/ as /stated/ below in the gloss.

/Now as regards/ those people who go on the road and use their *tefilin* pouch for secular articles, although /we rule that/ this is forbidden halachically there are nevertheless grounds for justifying /the practice/. /This is/ because they are accustomed to this /practice/ and in view /of this fact/ it is as if they stipulated at the outset /that the pouch may be used for these articles/. Despite this, it is not proper to act in this way initially.

(12) On a permanent /basis/. There are

3 For example, a bag in which a *tefilin* bag is kept.

4 The *Ran* is of the opinion that mere speech is of no avail when the designation was made earlier and the *tefilin* were only wrapped in it later. Therefore, the ruling in practice requires further study. However, the author of the Mishnah Berurah is of the opinion that the *Ran* would concede that if one took the cloth in his hand and said, "This should be for *tefilin*", it would be of avail. In addition, the *Ran* is of the opinion that where one designates the cloth at the time when he wraps *tefilin* in it, the designation is of avail even if done mentally. The author of the Mishnah Berurah is of the opinion that this ruling is in fact self-understood and almost all the Poskim would agree with it.

יד: ג * (ט) ׳סודר (י) דאזמניה * למיצר ביה * (יא) תפילין (ו) [ג] * (יב) ׳לעולם * (יג) וצר ביה * תפילין

ז ברכות כ״ג וסנהד׳ מ״ח ח מרדכי פרק בני העיר

באר היטב

מהני התנאי וכ״ש אם מתחלה אומר שאינו עושה של ראש אלא לפי שעה דמהני מהרא״י: (ו) לעולם. ואם עשה כים לשם תפילין אפי׳ צר ביה ע״ד

שערי תשובה

לשמה נזרקים ל״ע דהתם הטעם משום דכבר עברה מצותו כמ״ש במקום אחר. וע״ש שכתב דע״י תנאי מהני אף לקלף עצמו אף דהוי הזמנה לגוף הקדושה מ״מ הזמנה זו שוברה עמה מחמת התנאי ומועיל אף לדבר חול. ועיין בשו״ת עבודת הגרשוני סימן ס״ה דס״ל דמעובד לשם ס״ת אין להורידו לתפילין וגם אין לומר בתחלת העיבוד שמעבד לשם ס״ת ולתפילין שיש חשש דבדאורייתא אין ברירה. לכן יאמר שמעבד לס״ת ויתנה אם ירצה לשנותה לקדושה קלה שיהא רשות בידו ע״ש. ונראה כוונתו לסברת הנ״ל דאפילו תימא הזמנה לגוף הקדושה מלתא היא מ״מ כשמתנה הוי שוברה עמה. ולפ״ז י״ל דגם לדבר חול שפיר דמי. ומ״ש שם מתחלה לחלק בין קדושה קלה לחול הא מסיק דאין חילוק וא״כ ע״י תנאי י״ל דמודה דשרי גם לחול ואדרבה י״ל דלחול שרי טפי דלתפילין י״ל כיון שע״י התנאי הוא שובר ההזמנה שוב הו״ל כעיבוד שלא לשמה שהרי לא נתעבד לשם תפילין וגם לקדושה חמורה של ס״ת לא בא מה תאמר שע״י התנאי מועיל שוב צריך לומר הוברר הדבר למפרע שנתעבד לשם תפילין וזה לא אמרינן. ועיין בשו״ת בית אפרים חלק אה״ע אם יש שייכות ברירה בדברים שע״י תנאי ע״ש וצ״ע. ובמ״א הארכתי בזה ועיין לעיל סימן ל״ב[א] מ״ש שם על דברי העה״ג בזה: [ג] לעולם.

משנה ברורה

ש״ר אלא לפי שעה דמהני: ג (ט) סודר. וה״ה אם עשה כים (ח) מתחלה לצורך תפילין ג״כ אין אסור להשתמש ביה חול עד דצר ביה דהזמנה לאו מילתא היא וה״ה בכל תשמישי קדושה אפילו תיק לס״ת. ותשמיש דתשמיש (ט) אין בו קדושה כלל: (י) דאזמניה. אפילו בדבור בלבד וכ״ש אם נטלו ואמר זה יהיה לתפילין דמהני. ועיין בבה״ל מה שכתבתי בשם הר״ן: (יא) תפילין. ותיק (י) של טלית לא מיקרי תשמיש קדושה רק תשמיש מצוה ולכן מותר להניח בו שאר דברים של חול דאף דמונח בו ג״כ תיק של תפילין לא הוי התיק של טלית כ״א תשמיש דתשמיש ואפי׳ אם ניתן בתוכו הסידור שלו דיש בו קדושה או התפילין בלא תיק מ״מ בעת הצורך מותר ליתן בתוכו דברים של חול דהלא הוא עשוי מתחלה גם לטלית דהוא דבר של חול והוי כאלו התנה וכדלקמן בהג״ה. ואותן האנשים ההולכין בדרך ומשתמשין בשק של תפילין בדברים של חול אף דמדינא אסור אעפ״כ (יא) יש ללמד עליהן זכות דכיון דרגילין בכך הוי כאלו התנו בתחלה. ואעפ״כ לכתחלה אין נכון לעשות כן: (יב) לעולם. י״א דוקא בפירוש אבל בסתמא לא אמרינן דהזמנתו הוא על עולם כיון דסתם סודר אין מיוחד לתפילין אבל מדברי הגר״א בביאורו משמע דסתמא הוי כלעולם ולא מיעט המחבר בזה אלא היכא דהתנה שלא יהיה רק לפי שעה ולא לעולם ואם עשה כים להניח תפילין או שאמר לאומן עשה לי כים של תפילין לכו״ע הוי סתמא כלעולם: (יג) וצר ביה. כ״ז בסודר או כים שלו (יב) אבל אין אדם אוסר דבר שאינו שלו אא״כ

ביאור הלכה

* סודר דאזמניה וכו׳. עיין במ״ב במה שכ׳ אפילו בדבור בלבד והוא מהדה״ח שכתב כן אף דבפמ״ג מסתפק אולי אפי׳ במחשבה בלבד מהניא לא רציתי לסתום כן משום דבעיני יפלא למה העלימו הפוסקים עיניהם מהתוס׳ בסנהדרין מ״ח ע״א ד״ה נתנו דמסקי לבסוף דאפילו הזמנה בדיבור לא מהניא אא״כ נטלו ואמר זה יהיה לספר או למת עי״ש. ואין לדחוק דהתוספות לא קאמר אלא למ״ד דהזמנה מילתא היא משא״כ לדידן דבעינן ג״כ צר ביה מהני אפילו הזמנה גרוע אבל פשטא דסוגיא לא משמע שם כן עי״ש בגמרא ולאביי דאמר וכו׳. וכן מדנקט הוסיף ביה דימום וכו׳ משמע דיחוד בעלמא לא מהני אפילו לרבא עי״ש בתוספות ועכ״פ במחשבה בעלמא בודאי אין להחמיר. ודע דמה שכתבנו דאין די ההזמנה במחשבה דוקא אם לא צר ביה תיכף בעת ההזמנה רק לאח״ז ולא חשב אז כלל רק הניח בו בסתמא ופנייה אח״כ אבל אם המחשבה הזו היה בעת שצר ביה הרי צר ביה אדעתא דקביעותא ואסור אפילו אם פנייה אח״כ דמחשיב כמו צר ביה ואזמניה וכדלקמן. אח״כ מצאתי בעזה״י בחדושי רע״א ביו״ד סי׳ שס״ד בשם חדושי הר״ן שסובר ג״כ כמו שהערנו בתחלת דברינו דלפעמים אפילו הזמנה בדבור לא מהניא ואעתיק מה שכתב שם [לענין מת וה״ה לענין תפילין וכמו שכתב המ״א] דאם כשהניח התפילין באיזה דבר הזמינו בפירוש שיהיה מיוחד לכך או שחשב כך בלבו נאסר אפילו בלא מעשה אפילו אם פנייה אח״כ להתפילין אבל אם ההזמנה היתה מקודם ולא הניח בו אז התפילין ולאח״ז בלא הסכמה אחרת [דאי הסכים אח״כ להניח בו רק אדעתא לפנותו ס״ל להר״ן דשרי בכל גווני וכמו שנכתוב אח״כ בשמו] הניח בו התפילין תלוי בזה אם ההזמנה שמקודם היה ע״י מעשה נאסר בהנחת התפילין סתם שלאח״כ אע״ג דפנייה אח״כ להתפילין אבל אם ההזמנה הוא רק בדבור לא נאסר כיון דההזמנה היה שלא בשעת הנחת התפילין עכ״ד. והנה דין הראשון שלו הוא פשוט ומוסכם כמעט מכל הפוסקים וכמו שכתבנו מתחלה בעצמנו אך בדינו השני התעורר בזה דבר חדש. אח״כ מצאתי גם בא״ר שהעתיק להלכה דברי הש״ג דבדבור בעלמא לא הוי הזמנה ופשוט דמה שכתב המ״א דמדברי הש״ג לא משמע כן לא אהזמנה בדיבור קאי. ע״כ צ״ע למעשה בהזמנה בדבור בלבד. ומ״מ נראה דיודה הר״ן לדברי התוספות דאם נטלו ואמר זה יהיה לתפילין דמהני דזה מחשיב כמו מעשה וכמו שהוכיחו שם התוספות מהא דנתנתו לספר עי״ש: * למיצר ביה. נ״ל דדוקא אם בעת ההזמנה היה לו כבר תפילין אז חל ההזמנה אבל אם עשה כים לתפילין שיקנה אח״כ לא חל בזה ההזמנה והוי אח״כ כצר ביה ולא אזמניה דמותר אם הוא רק לפי שעה ואמינא לה מהא דסנהדרין מ״ח ע״א דנפש שבנאו לשם חי עי״ש ברש״י ופשוט:

* תפילין וכו׳. עיין במ״ב סק״א[ב] במה שכתבתי דאף דניתן בתוכו תפילין וכו׳ עיין בח״א כלל י״ד סעיף כ״א דמש״כ וכ״ל וכו׳ ופשוט דט״ס הוא וצ״ל דאע״ג דניתן לתוכו תפילין וכו׳ דאל״ה הלא לא הוי אלא רק תשמיש דתשמיש אך בלא״ה דבריו לע״ג דמדמי זה לדינא דמ״א הנ״ל בסימן מ׳ סק״ב ומשמע מדבריו דלמ״א אסור בזה ולא נהירא דהלא הוא עשוי מתחלה גם לטלית דהוא לדבר חול וא״כ אין עליו שם תשמישי קדושה דהוי כאלו התנה בפירוש שיהא מותר להשתמש בו דבר חול וכמו שכתב המ״א כעין זה בסימן ל״ד סק״ו עי״ש ומה דאוסר המ״א בסימן מ׳ הנ״ל לשמש בהבית עד שיניחנו עוד בתוך כלי שם שאני דסברת המ״א דכיון דהוא מיוחד גם לתפילין שוב הו״ל כלייו מה תאמר דכיון דהוא מיוחד גם לטלית תו אין על התיק הזה שום קדושה הלא שם אין תלוי בקדושה כלל דהרי אפי׳ מאה כליס זה עג״ז דבעלמא תשמיש דתשמיש אין בו שום קדושה ואעפ״כ אסור שם אע״כ דלא חשיב שם כיסוי אלא בדבר שאין מיוחד לה תמיד וע״כ אוסר המ״א שם דהלא בהתיק של הטלית רגיל תמיד לכסות גם התפילין משא״כ בענייננו דהאיסור להשתמש אינו רק בדבר שיש עליו שם ת״ק וזה הלא עשוי מתחלה גם לדבר חול ואולי דהמ״א סובר דאף אם התנה שיהא מותר להשתמש בו איזה דבר חול אין מותר רק לאותו דבר: * לעולם. עיין במ״ב סקי״ב במש״כ י״א וכו׳ הוא דעת הא״ר עי״ש במה שהביא מתשובת חו״י דמשמע הכי ומש״כ מדברי הגר״א וכו׳ הוא ממש״כ מקור לדין זה דלעולם כמש״כ בהג״ר וכנ״ל ס״ב [דפשוט דהוא להוכיח דהגמרא לא איירי בהתנה שיהא רק לפי שעה או תנאי אחר שהוא למעט ההזמנה ומש״כ וכמש״כ הרא״ש בשם הירושלמי כיון בזה לתרץ קושית הפמ״ג במ״ז מנ״ל דתנאי מהני אפילו להורידן לחול דשם במנחות מיירי לענין להורידו לקדושה קלה וע״ז רמז וכמש״כ הרא״ש וכו׳ עי״ש דמיירי אפי׳ להורידו לחול] (ובעל דמשק אליעזר השיא את דברי הגר״א לענין אחר ללא צורך) ולכאורה לדברי הא״ר הנ״ל צ״ל להגמרא לומר בברכות כ״ג ע״ב הא דלא אזמני׳ עי״ש ויש לדחות: * וצר ביה וכו׳. עיין במ״ב במה שכתב לענין קטן שצר וכו׳ ועיין בפמ״ג שכתב דקטן שצר לא מיתסר אלא בדצר ביה אדעתא דקביעותא או דאביו אזמין לי׳ דאל״ה ה״ל כצר ביה ולא אזמין דאין לו מחשבה וממ״א לא משמע כן וכן הגר״ז והח״א סתמו כהמ״א וקושית הפמ״ג בקל יש ליישב לכאורה ואכמ״ל: * תפילין חד זימנא. ואפילו בעידנא דצר עתה פעם ראשון אחר הזמנה צרר אותם עם מעות ג״כ אעפ״כ חלה הקדושה מאחר שהזמינו בתחלה לתפילין לבד וממילא דאסור לעשות כן אם לא שיחזור בפי׳ מההזמנה הראשונה ואתי דבור ומבטל דבור וראיה מברכות כ״ג ע״ב ותניא אידך לא יצור עי״ש ואין לדחות דהברייתא איירי דווקא שצר תחלה התפילין אבל בזמן אחד ש״ד א״כ צ״ל להגמרא לתרץ דאידך ברייתא איירי בדלא אזמניה יתרצנה כפשוטה עם מעותיו

שער הציון

(ח) סנהדרין מ״ח ע״ב: (ט) פמ״ג בסימן קנ״ג במ״ז: (י) ח״א כלל י״ד עי״ש ובבה״ל: (יא) ט״ז: (יב) מ״א:

הגהות ותיקונים: א) סק״ז: ב) סקי״א:

permanent /basis/ (13) and one /in fact/ wrapped in /the cloth/ *tefilin*

Mishnah Berurah

/authorities/ who say that /the designation of a cloth for *tefilin* is/ only /considered permanent designation/ if it was explicit, but if one did not specify /that the cloth should be used permanently for *tefilin*/ it is not ruled to be designated permanently /for *tefilin*/, since, generally a cloth is not /meant/ specifically for *tefilin* /only/. However, it is implied by the words of the *Gra* in his *Beyur*, that /even/ if one did not specify /anything the designation/ is /nevertheless regarded/ as permanent /designation/. /According to his view,/ by /speaking of permanent designation/ the author /of the Shulchan Aruch/ only excludes /from the scope of this ruling/ an instance when one stipulated /explicitly/ that /the cloth/ should only /serve for *tefilin*/ temporarily and not permanently.

If one made a bag for placing *tefilin* /in it/ or said to a tradesman, "Make me a bag for *tefilin*", all /authorities/ are agreed that /even/ without /explicitly/ specifying this /the bag/ is regarded as /designated/ permanently /for *tefilin*/.

(13) And one wrapped in /the cloth/. All this /only applies/ where the cloth or bag is one's own. However, a person cannot make something which is not his own become forbidden /because of his designation/, unless /, for example,/ he stole /a piece of/

1* This even applies if on that occasion there were also coins wrapped in it. However, designation is only of avail if one already has *tefilin*. (Beyur Halachah)
2* If a bag has two compartments and only one of them is used for *tefilin*, the other may be used for coins. (Beyur Halachah)

(יד) חד (ז) זימנא * (טו) אסור למיצר ביה (טז) זוזי: הגה ואם התנה עליו מתחלה (יז) בכל ענין (ח) שרי (ב"י בשם רבי ירוחם ומהרי"א) וקלף המעובד (יח) לשם תפילין אסור לכתוב עליו (יט) דברי חול דהזמנה * (כ) כי האי גוונא·(כא) לגוף (כב) הקדושה

שערי תשובה

עבה"ט ועיין בחות יאיר סימן נ"ט דבי"ד סי' שס"ד מוכח דאם אזמניה לעולם אפילו צר ביה ע"ד זמן מה אסור וגם כתב דדוקא בסודר שדרך תשמישו לחול צריך הזמנה לעולם אבל אם עשה לו כיס לתפילין או שאמר לאומן עשה לי כיס תפילין הוי הזמנה בלי דבור ואין צריך לחשוב לעולם עיין שם והביאו הא"ר:

באר היטב

לפנותו אסור. וה"ה אם היה כיס והוסיף בו איזה דבר לשם תפילין וצר ביה ע"ד לפנותו אסור עד שיטול מה שחידש ואם צר ביה חדא זימנא אדעתא למיצר בו לעולם אפילו לא אזמניה אסור מ"א ע"ש. ועי' בתשובת שער אפרים סימן כ"א שהעלה דכל מה שהוא עודף על מקום הנצרך לתפילין לא מיקרי נורך תפילין. לכן התיר שם בכיס התפילין שיש לו ב' כיסין זה תחת זה. דמותר להניח התפילין למטה ומעות בכיס שהוא למעלה ממנו ע"ש: (ז) זימנא. כ"ל דקטן שצר בו תפילין אסור אבל בדבר הנאסר בהזמנה לחוד לא מיתסר בהזמנת קטן דקטן יש לו מעשה ואין לו מחשבה. ופשוט דאין אדם אוסר דבר שאינו שלו. ואם גנב בגד ועשה ממנו כיס תפילין קניא בשינוי מעשה ואסרו מ"א:(ח) שרי. ובסתם

משנה ברורה

גנב בגד (יג) וחתכו ועשה ממנו כיס דאז קניה בשינוי מעשה ואסרו. וקטן שצר ביה תפילין בהכיס שהזמינו לכך ג"כ נאסר אבל דבר הנאסר בהזמנה לחוד כמו שיתבאר לא מיתסר בהזמנת קטן דקטן יש לו מעשה ואין לו מחשבה אפילו גילו מחשבתם בדיבורם: (יד) חד זימנא. אף שהיה רק לפי שעה דהוא דרך ערַאי כיון שהיה בסתמא מצרפינן המעשה להזמנה. אבל (יד) אם פירש בעת הנחה דהוא ע"מ לפנותו שרי להשתמש בו חול אח"כ ואם עשה הכיס לשם תפילין וצר ביה תפילין חדא זימנא אפילו (טו) ע"מ לפנותן אח"כ אסור למיצר ביה זוזי וה"ה אם היה כיס עשוי והוסיף בו איזה דבר לצורך תפילין לנאותו הוי כמי שעשה הכיס לשם תפילין עד שיטול מה שחידש ועיין בבה"ל: (טו) אסור. לעולם אפילו (טז) לאחר שנתקלקל ואין ראוי עוד לתפילין וצריך גניזה: (טז) זוזי. וכן שאר דבר אפילו דבר שיש בה קדושה כל שהוא למטה מתפילין כגון מזוזה וכנ"ל בסימן ל"ב ס"ח ולא נקט זוזי רק משום סיפא. ולפ"ז אין לתת סידור בכיס שהיה מיוחד מתחלה לתפילין לבד ואעפ"כ אין למחות בזה דכיון דרגילין בזה הו"ל כאלו התנו מתחלה וכנ"ל בס"ק י"א: (יז) בכל ענין. אפילו (יז) עשה הכיס לשם תפילין וגם צר ביה (יח) בקביעות שרי כיון דהתנה בעת עשייה שיהיה יוכל לשנות כשירצה ותנאי מהני (יט) להשתמש בהן אפילו בעודן בקדושתן וכמש"כ סימן קנ"ד ס"ח אך לתשמיש מגונה לא מהני תנאי וה"ה אם ירצה לכרוך איזה דבר ברצועה הקבוע בתפילין שעליו דלא (כ) מהני משום ביזוי מצוה: (יח) לשם תפילין. היינו הפרשיות של תפילין וה"ה עור המעובד להבתים ש"ר או (כא) של יד ואף דאין מקוק עליו השין מ"מ גוף קדושה מיקרי וכ"ש עור המעובד לס"ת או מזוזה: (יט) דברי חול. אבל להורידו מקדושתו כגון לכתוב עליו (כב) מזוזה שקדושתה קלה מתפילין או (כג) שאר ד"ת מותר אפילו על עור שנתעבד לס"ת. וגט (כד) הוי דבר של חול ואסור לכתבו על קלף המעובד לס"ת אם לא שהתנה וכדלקמן: (כ) כי האי גוונא. שהוא ע"י מעשה גמור לאפוקי אם היה רק הזמנה בדבור בעלמא או (כה) שהיה רק תיקון הקלף ושרטוטו לשמה: (כא) לגוף וכו'. לאפוקי הזמנה לתשמישי קדושה כגון עשיית כיס לתפילין או (כו) עיבוד עור לרצועות שהוא רק תשמישי קדושה דמותר לשנותו אפי' לחול ועי' בביאור הלכה שביארנו דשלא במקום הדחק יש להחמיר בעיבוד עור לרצועות: (כב) הקדושה. אבל הזמנה לגוף המצוה כגון ציצית שופר לולב סוכה נר חנוכה (כז) אפילו עשאן לכך לא מיתסרי דהזמנה לאו מילתא היא וכדלקמן בסימן תרל"ח ס"א בהג"ה ומותר להשתמש בהו חול אף בלי תנאי. ועיין לעיל בסימן כ"א ולקמן בסימן קנ"ד שיש עוד

ביאור הלכה

ממש בזמן אחד אלא ודאי כמו שכתבנו. ואפשר עוד לומר דאם עשה כיס לשם תפילין ואח"כ צרר ביה מעות ואח"כ צרר ביה תפילין דאסור למיצר ביה זוזי אח"כ כיון דבשעה שצר ביה המעות לא בטליה בפי' מההזמנה. ואולי דזהו חשיב כביטול בפי' וצ"ע. ודע עוד דמה שכתב המ"א בשם הטור דאם עשה הכיס לשם תפילין אפילו בדצר אח"כ ע"מ לפנותו אסור הר"ן בחידושיו פ' נגמר הדין [והובא בחידושי רע"א ביו"ד סי' שס"ד ע"ש] לא ס"ל כן. ואעפ"כ אין להקל למעשה דדברי הטוש"ע שם נובע מהרמב"ן בספר תולדות אדם[א]. ותיק של תפילין של יד עיין בפמ"ג בסימן קנ"ד שמצדד לומר דאין עליו שם תשמישי קדושה כי הבית עצמו אין עליו רק שם ת"ק דאין עליו השין ובמ"א ביארתי בכמה ראיות דאינו כן וגם הפמ"ג עצמו כתב שם לבסוף ע"ז וצ"ע וגם בסימן זה כתב בעצמו בא"א להיפך. ועוד דלא לישתמיט אחד מן הפוסקים להשמיענו דהאי דינא דר"ח דסודר דאזמניה למיצר ביה וכו' איירי דוקא בשל ראש ועוד ממקומו הוא מוכרע בברכות כ"ג ע"ב דקרמי הגמרא שתי ברייתות אהדדי בענין זה וא"כ לישני דהא ברייתא דתניא נורר אדם תפיליו עם מעותיו איירי בשל יד וא"ל דתפיליו משמע תרוייהו דא"ל לתני תפלה א"כ הרי מוכח להדיא דאסור גם הש"י דהא מסתמא באידך ברייתא קתני ג"כ לא יצור אדם תפיליו עם מעותיו כדמשמע פשטיות הגמרא עי"ש ובדוחק יש לומר דהאיסור הוא משום רצועות שעליהן שיש בהן הקשר ש"י לדעת רש"י הוא גוף הקדושה אבל א"כ איך יתרץ הנ"י ואידך פוסקים דסברי דלא כרש"י ש"מ דהאי דינא דר"ח אשל יד נמי קאי: * אסור למיצר ביה וכו'. עיין בתשובת שער אפרים סימן כ"א שהעלה דכל מה שהוא עודף על מקום הנצרך לתפילין לא מיקרי נורך תפילין לכן התיר שם בכיס התפילין שיש לו ב' כיסין זה תחת זה דמותר להניח התפילין למטה ומעות בכיס שהוא למעלה ממנו עי"ש [בה"ט]: * כי האי גוונא.[1]עיין מ"ב ועיין בתשובת משכנות יעקב סי' נ"ה דדיו שנעשה לכתיבת סת"מ הוי ג"כ הזמנה לגוף הקדושה ועדיף מיניה ואסור להשתמש ממנו לחול אם לא התנה מעיקרא וראיתי בספר משנת אברהם שהשיג עליו מהא דיו"ד סי' רע"ד בש"ך וט"ז שם ס"ק ג' ד' ה' עי"ש ובאמת יש לעיין הרבה בזה דכדבריו משמע בהרמב"ן במלחמות פ"ק דסוכה אף דהרמב"ן עצמו מיקל שם ה"ט דאיהו פליג על עיקר דין דהזמנה לגוף הקדושה משא"כ לדידן וקושייתו יש ליישב דאפשר דשם איירי שלא נעשה בכיון לשם סת"ס והכתיבה גופא לא הוי כצר בי' אדעתא דקביעותא דאפשר דלא נתקדש רק הדיו דצריך להכתיבה ושם נשפך דיו יתר מהצורך על האות עי"ש ודומיא דמה שכתב הש"א הנ"ל וצ"ע ע"כ יותר טוב להתנות מתחלה בעת עשיית הדיו: * לגוף הקדושה. עיין במ"ב במה שכתב או עיבוד עור לרצועות הוא מהנ"י שהובא במ"א והביאו הנ"ל והא"ר להלכה אמנם יש לעיין קצת בזה דהנה הפמ"ג נשאר לבסוף בצ"ע על האי דנ"ל לפי דעת רש"י שס"ל דמקום הקשר של הדלית ויו"ד הוא קדושה עצמה נמלא דהעיבוד הוא הזמנה לגוף הקדושה. אולם ראיתי בנ"ל שרמז שם לעיין בתוספות שם במגילה כ"ו ע"ב כי באמת כמעט כל הפוסקים חולקין על רש"י והשו"ע ג"כ לקמן בסימן קנ"ד סתם דלא כוותיה ועוד נ"ל דאפשר דאפילו לדעת רש"י דהיוד והדלית הם הלמ"מ מ"מ כ"ז שלא נקשר הרצועה בהקצילה עדיין אין שם הזמנה עליה ע"י העיבוד דלא דמי לעיבוד של הקלף דהתם העיבוד הוא הכנה שיכתבו עליה ולכך תיכף משנעשה העיבוד הוא הזמנה משא"כ כאן דהעיקר הוא הלבישה על ראשו ועל ידו הקשירה של הרצועה בהקצילה היא הזמנה למצוה זו ולא העיבוד דאפילו אחר העיבוד עדיין אין על העור שום שם רצועה ואפילו אחר שיתחכנה לרצועות עדיין אין הרצועה מזומנת למצוה עד שיקשרנה בהקצילה דאז היא מזומנת לגוף הקדושה דהיינו הלבישה שע"ז נתקדש היו"ד והשי"ן[ב] כי פשוט שע"י העשייה לבד לא נתקדש עדיין האותיות וסברא זו ממש נזכרת בהמאור

שער הציון

(יג) פמ"ג: (יד) פמ"ג ודה"ח. ועיין א"ר ולכאורה פליג ויש לדחות: (טו) מ"א: (טז) פמ"ג: (יז) (יח) מסעיף ב' ומסימן קנ"ד ס"ח: (יט) מ"א: (כ) שו"ע הגר"ז: (כא) פמ"ג וכן הכריחי ע"ז בראיות בבה"ל: (כב) פמ"ג: (כג) ממה דרלה העו"ש להתיר גט משום דיש בו קצת קדושה דמותר לטלטלו בשבת משום דיוכל ללמוד ממנו דינים עי"ש: (כד) ב"ח ומ"א וא"ר דלא כט"ז עי"ש בא"ר: (כה) עיין בביאור הגר"א ובהלכות ס"ת בהרא"ש: (כו) א"ר וצ"ל: (כז) מ"א

הגהות ותיקונים: א) תורת אדם: ב) צ"ל והדלי"ת:

הערות והארות: 1) עיין בסי' ל"ב במ"ב ס"ק ח' אם צריך דיו לשמה (ר"ש):

(14) on one occasion,[1*] **(15)** it is forbidden to wrap **(16)** coins in it.[2*]

Gloss: If one made a stipulation at the outset /that the cloth should be usable for wrapping other articles/, one is /in fact/ allowed /to do so/ **(17)** *in all cases. (...)*

Mishnah Berurah

cloth /from his fellow/ and cut it up and made a bag out of it /for *tefilin*/. /In the latter case/ he will have acquired it /halachically/, in view of the change /in it brought about/ by his action, and /he will therefore have been able to/ make it forbidden.

If a child wrapped up *tefilin* in a bag which was designated for this /purpose/ it will also have become forbidden. However, /in the circumstances/ which are explained below where something will become forbidden through designation alone, it will not become forbidden when it is designated by a child. /This is/ because a child is /ruled as/ capable of /doing/ a /meaningful/ act, but is not /ruled as/ capable of a /meaningful/ mental decision, even if he made his decision known by speech.

(14) On one occasion. Even if they were only /wrapped in the cloth then/ temporarily, which involves a provisional usage, the act is /nevertheless/ combined with the designation /to make the use of the cloth for coins forbidden/, once /the act/ was done without specification. However, if one specified when he placed /the *tefilin* in the cloth/ that /he was doing so/ with a view to taking them out /subsequently/, it is allowed to use /the cloth/ for a secular /purpose/ later.

/On the other hand,/ if one made a bag for the sake of *tefilin* and wrapped *tefilin* in it on one occasion, even with a view to taking them out subsequently, it is forbidden to wrap coins in /the bag/. Correspondingly, if one had a bag that was made /previously not for the sake of *tefilin*/, but added something to /the bag/ to make it attractive, for the sake of /the bag being used for/ *tefilin*, it is /regarded/ as if he made the bag for the sake of *tefilin* /and will continue to have this ruling/ until he removes the new /improvement/. See the Beyur Halachah.

(15) It is forbidden. /I.e.,/ forever, even after /the cloth/ has become spoiled and is no longer fit for *tefilin*. /Then/ it must be put away in the *genizah*.

(16) Coins. /One may/ likewise /not wrap/ other articles /in it/. This even /applies to/ an article which has holiness, whenever it is of a lower /degree of holiness/ than *tefilin*. For example, /it applies to/ a *mezuzah* (as /follows from what is stated/ above in Sec. 32, Par. 8.) /The author of the Shulchan Aruch/ only speaks of coins because of /the cases discussed/ at the end /of the paragraph, to teach us that in those circumstances one is even permitted to wrap coins in it/.

According to this, one should not put a sidur in a bag which was originally /used/ specifically for *tefilin* /only/. Nevertheless, one should not protest against /people when they do/ this, since in view /of the fact/ that they are accustomed to /do/ so it is as if they stipulated at the outset /that it should be permitted/, as /explained/ above in sub-Par. 11.

(17) In all cases. Even if one made a bag for the sake of *tefilin* and wraps /*tefilin*/ in it regularly, he is allowed /to use it for coins/, once he stipulated when it was made that he should be able to alter /its usage/ when he wishes /to do so/.

The stipulation is of avail /for one to be able/ to use /the cloth or bag for other articles/ even when /the cloth or bag/ still has holiness, as /follows from what/ is stated in Sec. 154, Par. 8.

However, a stipulation is of no avail for a

(יד) חד (ז) זימנא * (טו) אסור למיצר ביה (טז) זוזי: הגה ואם התנה עליו מתחלה (יז) בכל ענין (ח) שרי (כ״י בשם רבי ירוחם ומהרי״א) וקלף המעובד (יח) לשם תפילין אסור לכתוב עליו (יט) דברי חול דהזמנה * (כ) כי האי גוונא *(כא) לגוף (כב) הקדושה

שערי תשובה

עבה״ט ועיין בחות יאיר סימן נ״ט דבי״ד סי׳ שמ״ד מוכח דאם אזמניה לעולם אפילו צר ביה ע״ד זמן מה אסור וגם כתב דדוקא בסודר שדרך תשמישו לחול צריך הזמנה לעולם אבל אם עשה לו כיס לתפילין או שאמר לאומן עשה לי כיס תפילין הוי הזמנה בלי דבור ואין צריך לחשוב לעולם עיין שם והביאו הא״ר:

באר היטב

לפנותו אסור. וה״ה אם היה כיס והוסיף בו איזה דבר לשם תפילין וצר ביה ע״ד לפנותו אסור עד שיטול מה שחידש ואם צר ביה חדא זימנא אדעתא למיצר בו לעולם אפילו לא אזמניה אסור מ״א ע״ש. ועי׳ בתשובת שער אפרים סימן כ״א שהעלה דכל מה שהוא עודף על מקום הנצרך לתפילין לא מיקרי נרתק תפילין. לכן התיר שם בכיס התפילין שיש לו ב׳ כיסין זה תחת זה. דמותר להניח התפילין למטה ומעות בכיס שהוא למעלה ממנו ע״ש: (ז) זימנא. נ״ל דקטן שצר בו תפילין אסור אבל בדבר הנאסר בהזמנה לחוד לא מיתסר בהזמנת קטן דקטן יש לו מעשה ואין לו מחשבה. ופשוט דאין אדם אוסר דבר שאינו שלו. ואם גנב בגד ועשה ממנו כיס תפילין קניא בשינוי מעשה ואסרו מ״א:(ח) שרי. ובסתם

ביאור הלכה

ממש בזמן אחד אלא ודאי כמו שכתבנו. ואפשר עוד לומר דאם עשה כיס לשם תפילין ואח״כ צרר ביה מעות ואח״כ צרר ביה תפילין דאסור למיצר ביה זוזי אח״כ כיון דבשעה שצר ביה המעות לא בטליה בפי׳ מההזמנה. ואולי דזהו חשיב כביטול בפי׳ וצ״ע. ודע עוד דמה שכתב המ״א בשם הטור דאם עשה הכיס לשם תפילין אפילו בדצר אח״כ ע״מ לפנותו אסור הר״ן בחידושיו פ׳ נגמר הדין [והובא בחידושי רע״א ביו״ד סי׳ שמ״ד ע״ש] לא ס״ל כן. ואעפ״כ אין להקל למעשה דדברי הטוש״ע שם נובע מהרמב״ן בספר תולדות אדם[א]. ותיק של תפילין של יד עיין בפמ״ג בסימן קנ״ד שמצדד לומר דאין עליו שם תשמישי קדושה כי הבית עצמו אין עליו רק שם ת״ק דאין עליו השין ובמ״א ביארתי בכמה ראיות דאינו כן וגם הפמ״ג עצמו כתב שם לבסוף ע״ז וצ״ע וגם בסימן זה כתב בעצמו בא״א להיפך. ועוד דלא לישתמיט אחד מן הפוסקים להשמיענו דהאי דינא דר״ח דסודר דאזמניה למיצר ביה וכו׳ איירי דוקא בשל ראש ועוד ממקומו הוא מוכרע בברכות כ״ג ע״ב דקרמי הגמרא שתי ברייתות אהדדי בענין זה וא״כ לישני דהא ברייתא דתניא צורר אדם תפיליו עם מעותיו איירי בשל יד וא״ל דתפיליו משמע תרוייהו דאל״ה לתני תפלה א״כ הרי מוכח להדיא דאסור גם הש״י דהא מסתמא באידך ברייתא קתני ג״כ לא יצור אדם תפיליו עם מעותיו כדמשמע פשטיות הגמרא עי״ש ובדוחק יש לומר דהאיסור הוא משום רצועות שעליהן שיש בהן הקשר ש״י לדעת רש״י הוא גוף הקדושה אבל א״כ איך יתרץ הנ״י ואידך פוסקים דסברי דלא כרש״י ש״מ דהאי דינא דר״ח אשל יד נמי קאי: * אסור למיצר ביה וכו׳. עיין בתשובת שער אפרים סימן כ״א שהעלה דכל מה שהוא עודף על מקום הנצרך לתפילין לא מיקרי צורך תפילין לכן התיר שם בכים התפילין שיש לו ב׳ כיסין זה תחת זה דמותר להניח התפילין למטה ומעות בכיס שהוא למעלה ממנו עי״ש [בה״ט]: * כי האי גוונא.[1] עיין מ״ב ועיין בתשובת משכנות יעקב סי׳ כ״ה דדיו שנעשה לכתיבת סת״מ הוי ג״כ הזמנה לגוף הקדושה ועדיף מיניה ואסור להשתמש ממנו לחול אם לא התנה מעיקרא וראיתי בספר משנת אברהם שהשיג עליו מהא דיו״ד סי׳ רע״ד בש״ך וט״ז שם ס״ק ג׳ ד׳ ה׳ עי״ש ובאמת יש לעיין הרבה בזה דכדבריו משמע בהרמב״ן במלחמות פ״ק דסוכה אף דהרמב״ן עצמו מיקל שם ה״ט דאיהו פליג על עיקר דין דהזמנה לגוף הקדושה משא״כ לדידן וקושייתו יש ליישב דאפשר דשם איירי שלא נעשה בכיון לשם סת״ם והכתיבה גופא לא הוי כצר בי׳ אדעתא דקביעותא דאפשר דלא נתקדש רק הדיו דצריך להכתיבה ושם נשפך דיו יתר מהצורך על האות עי״ש ודומיא דמה שכתב הש״א הנ״ל וצ״ע ע״כ יותר טוב להתנות מתחלה בעת עשיית הדיו: * לגוף הקדושה. עיין במ״ב במה שכתב או עיבוד עור לרצועות הוא מהנ״י שהובא במ״א והביאו הנ״ל והא״ר להלכה אמנם יש לעיין קצת בזה דהנה הפמ״ג נשאר לבסוף בצ״ע על האי דנ״ל לפי דעת רש״י שס״ל דמקום הקשר של הדלית ויו״ד הוא קדושה עצמה נמצא דהעיבוד הוא הזמנה לגוף הקדושה. אולם ראיתי בנ״ל שרמז שם לעיין בתוספות שם במגילה כ״ו ע״ב כי באמת כמעט כל הפוסקים חולקין על רש״י והשו״ע ג״כ לקמן בסימן קנ״ד סתם דלא כוותיה ועוד נ״ל דאפשר דאפילו לדעת רש״י דהיוד והדלית הם הלמ״מ מ״מ כ״ז שלא נקשר הרצועה בהקיצה עדיין אין שם הזמנה עליה ע״י העיבוד דלא דמי לעיבוד של הקלף דהתם העיבוד הוא הכנה שיכתבו עליה ולכך תיכף משנעשה העיבוד הוא הזמנה משא״כ כאן דהעיקר הוא הלבישה על ראשו ועל ידו הקשירה של הרצועה בהקיצה היא הזמנה למצוה זו ולא העיבוד דאפילו אחר העיבוד עדיין אין על העור שום שם רצועה ואפילו אחר שיחתכנה לרצועות עדיין אין הרצועה מזומנת למצוה עד שיקשרנה בהקיצה דאז היא מזומנת לגוף הקדושה דהיינו הלבישה שע״ז נתקדש היו״ד והשי״ן[ב] כי פשוט שע״י העשייה לבד לא נתקדש עדיין האותיות וסברא זו ממש נזכרת בהמאור

משנה ברורה

גנב בגד (יג) וחתכו ועשה ממנו כיס דאז קניה בשינוי מעשה ואסרו. וקטן שצר ביה תפילין בהכיס שהזמינו לכך ג״כ נאסר אבל דבר הנאסר בהזמנה לחוד כמו שיתבאר לא מיתסר בהזמנת קטן דקטן יש לו מעשה ואין לו מחשבה אפילו גילו מחשבתם בדיבורם: (יד) חד זימנא. אף שהיה רק לפי שעה דהוא דרך עראי כיון שהיה בסתמא מצרפינן המעשה להזמנה. אבל (יד) אם פירש בעת הנחה דהוא ע״מ לפנותו שרי להשתמש בו חול אח״כ ואם עשה הכיס לשם תפילין וצר ביה תפילין חדא זימנא אפילו (טו) ע״מ לפנותן אח״כ אסור למיצר ביה זוזי וה״ה אם היה כיס עשוי והוסיף בו איזה דבר לצורך תפילין לנאותו הוי כמי שעשה הכיס לשם תפילין עד שיטול מה שחידש ועיין בבה״ל: (טו) אסור. לעולם אפילו (טז) לאחר שנתקלקל ואין ראוי עוד לתפילין וצריך גניזה: (טז) זוזי. וכן שאר דבר אפילו דבר שיש בה קדושה כל שהוא למטה מתפילין כגון מזוזה וכנ״ל בסימן ל״ב ס״ח ולא נקט זוזי רק משום סיפא. ולפ״ז אין לתת סידור בכיס שהיה מיוחד מתחלה לתפילין לבד ואעפ״כ אין למחות בזה דכיון דרגילין בזה הו״ל כאלו התנו מתחלה וכנ״ל בס״ק י״א: (יז) בכל ענין. אפילו (יז) עשה הכיס לשם תפילין וגם צר ביה (יח) בקביעות שרי כיון דהתנה בעת עשייה שיהיה יוכל לשנות כשירצה ותנאי מהני (יט) להשתמש בהן אפילו בעודן בקדושתן וכמש״כ סימן קנ״ד ס״ח אך לתשמיש מגונה לא מהני תנאי וה״ה אם ירצה לכרוך איזה דבר ברצועה הקבוע בתפילין שעליו דלא (כ) מהני משום ביזוי מצוה: (יח) לשם תפילין. היינו הפרשיות של תפילין וה״ה עור המעובד להבתים ש״ר או (כא) של יד ואף דאין חקוק עליו השין מ״מ גוף קדושה מיקרי וכ״ש עור המעובד לס״ת או מזוזה: (יט) דברי חול. אבל להורידו מקדושתו כגון לכתוב עליו (כב) מזוזה שקדושתה קלה מתפילין או (כג) שאר ד״ת מותר אפילו על עור שנתעבד לס״ת. וגט (כד) הוי דבר של חול ואסור לכתבו על קלף המעובד לס״ת אם לא שהתנה וכדלקמן: (כ) כי האי גוונא. שהוא ע״י מעשה גמור לאפוקי אם היה רק הזמנה בדבור בעלמא או (כה) שהיה רק תיקון הקלף ושרטוטו לשמה: (כא) לגוף וכו׳. לאפוקי הזמנה לתשמישי קדושה כגון עשיית כיס לתפילין או (כו) עיבוד עור לרצועות שהוא רק תשמישי קדושה דמותר לשנותו אפי׳ לחול ועי׳ בביאור הלכה שביארנו דשלא במקום הדחק יש להחמיר בעיבוד עור לרצועות: (כב) הקדושה. אבל הזמנה לגוף המצוה כגון ציצית שופר לולב סוכה נר חנוכה (כז) אפילו עשאן לכך לא מיתסרי דהזמנה לאו מילתא היא וכדלקמן בסימן תרל״ח ס״א בהג״ה ומותר להשתמש בהו חול אף בלי תנאי. ועיין לעיל בסימן כ״א ולקמן בסימן קנ״ד שיש עוד

שער הציון

(יג) פמ״ג: (יד) פמ״ג ודה״ח. ועיין א״ר ולכאורה פליג ויש לדחות: (טו) מ״א: (טז) פמ״ג: (יז) (יח) מסעיף ב׳ ומסימן קנ״ד ס״ח: (יט) מ״א: (כ) שו״ע הגר״ז: (כא) פמ״ג וכן הרכיתי ע״ז בראיות בבה״ל: (כב) פמ״ג: (כג) ממה דרלה העו״ש להתיר גט משום דיש בו קצת קדושה דמותר לטלטלו בשבת משום דיוכל ללמוד ממנו דינים עי״ש: (כד) ב״ח ומ״א וא״ר דלא כט״ז עי״ש בא״ר: (כה) עיין בביאור הגר״א ובהלכות ס״ת בהרא״ש: (כו) א״ר ונ״ל: (כז) מ״א

הגהות ותיקונים: א) תורת אדם: **ב)** צ״ל והדלי״ת:

הערות והארות: 1) עיין בסי׳ ל״ב במ״ב ס״ק ח׳ אם צריך דיו לשמה (ר״ש):

If parchment has been processed (18) *for the sake of /use for/* tefilin, *it is forbidden to write on it* (19) *secular matters, since designation* (20) *of that nature,* (21) *for the actual* (22) *holiness,* (23) *is of significance. (...)*

Mishnah Berurah

use /which involves/ disrespect /to be permitted/. Correspondingly, if when one /is wearing *tefilin*/ he wishes to wind something with the strap which is attached to the *tefilin*, /a stipulation/ is of no avail /for this to be permitted/, because /it involves/ disrespect to the mitzvah.

(18) For the sake of *tefilin*. I.e., /for use/ for the passages of *tefilin*.

The same ruling /applies to/ skin processed /for use/ for the housings of the head /*tefilin*/ or of the arm /*tefilin*/. Although /the skin/ does not have the /letter/ ש engraved on it, it is nevertheless classed as /being of/ actual holiness. This is certainly /true of/ skin which has been processed for a Torah Scroll or a mezuzah.

(19) Secular matters. However, it is permitted to reduce its /degree of/ holiness. For example, one may write a mezuzah on it, which has a lesser /degree of/ holiness than *tefilin*, or /any/ other words of Torah. This even /applies/ to skin which was processed for /the sake of/ a Torah Scroll.

A *geyt* (letter of divorce) is a secular document. It is /therefore/ forbidden to write it on parchment which was processed for /the sake of use for/ a Torah Scroll, unless one stipulated /that he should be able to use the parchment for other purposes/, as /explained/ below /in sub-Par. 23/.

(20) Of that nature. /I.e.,/ which is by means of a full act.

/The wording/ excludes designation which was only /done/ by mere speech /from this category/. /It also excludes instances/ where only the preparation of the parchment and the forming of lines on it was /done/ for the sake of /the mitzvah/.

(21) For the actual, etc. /This is meant/ to exclude designation to /serve as/ a holy appurtenance. For example, the making of a bag for *tefilin* or the processing of skin for the straps /of *tefilin*/, which are only holy appurtenances. It is permitted to alter /the usage/ of such /articles/, even to a secular /purpose, where there was only designation without actual use/.

See the Beyur Halachah, where we have explained that where there is no pressing /need/ one should be stringent as regards skin processed for the straps /of *tefilin* and should refrain from using it for a secular purpose/.

(22) Holiness. However, designation /of an article/ for an actual mitzvah, such as /for the mitzvah of/ *tzitzis, shofar, lulav, sukah* or Chanukah lights, does not cause /the article/ to become forbidden /for a secular use/, even when one made /the article/ for /the purposes of/ that /mitzvah/. For /we rule that/ designation /for these purposes/ is of no significance, as /stated/ below in Sec. 638, in the gloss to Par. 1, and it is /subsequently/ permitted to use /the article/ for a secular purpose, even without a stipulation /having been made/.

See above in Sec. 21 and below in Sec. 154, that there are further differences /in this

* (כג) מילתא היא (ר"ן סוף פ' נגמר הדין): [ט]אזמניה ולא צר ביה או (ט) * (כד) צר ביה (כה) ולא אזמניה * (כו) שרי למיצר ביה * זוזי:

ט שם ברכות ושם בסנהדרין

מג דין איך להתנהג בתפילין בהכנסו לבהכ"ס. ובו ט' סעיפים:

א [א]אסור ליכנס לבית הכסא קבוע (א) להשתין (ב) בתפילין (א) שבראשו גזירה שמא יעשה בהם צרכיו [ב]ואם אוחזן. (ג) (ג) בידו מותר להשתין בהם בבית הכסא קבוע: הגה והיינו דוקא כשמשתין מיושב

א ברכות כג ב שם

באר היטב

אסור א"כ לא יפה עושים המשתמשין בשק של תפילין כשהולכין בדרך אלא דנראה ללמוד זכות דאותן אנשים מסתמא הוי כמתנה בפירוש וכן בההוא שכתב רמ"א כאן דקלף המעובד לשם תפילין אסור לכתוב עליו דברי חול ואנו רואין בכל יום שהסופרים כותבים על הקלפים שלהם כתובות וגיטין ושאר דברי רשות אלא ודאי דמסתמא כשהסופרים מתקנים אותו תחלה דעתם להשתמש בהן הן לדבר קדושה הן לדבר רשות. ולפ"ז פשיטא דמותר לכתוב גט על קלף שנעבד לשם ס"ת וכ"מ בא"ע סימן קכ"ד ס"ב. מ"א ט"ז עיין ב"ח וע"ת. ומיהו אם התחיל לכתוב על הקלף או על הנייר דבר קדושה אסור לכתוב אח"כ עליו דברי חול ולא מהני תנאי. וכל זה בקדושה כגון תפילין וס"ת אבל לתשמישי קדושה מהני תנאי להשתמש בהן אפילו בעודן בקדושתן כמ"ש בסי' קנ"ד ס"ת אבל לתשמיש מגונה לא מהני כמ"ש סי' קנ"ד. ותשמישי מצוה כגון ציצית שופר לולב נר חנוכה אפילו עשאן לכך לא מיתסרי ומותר להשתמש בהן חול אפילו בלא תנאי ע"ש: (ט) צר ביה. פירוש לפי שעה ולא אזמניה להיות שם לעולם:

(א) שבראשו. ה"ה דבזרוע נמי אסור מה"ט והא דנקט בראשו בא למעט אם אוחזן בידו. רי"ו מ"א ועיין כ"ל ובתשו' בית יעקב סימן ק"ע כתב דוקא בראשו מפני שהם בגלוי אבל בשל יד שהם מכוסים שרי דלא גרע מאוחזן בבגדו ובידו ע"ש. והמחבר יד אהרן חולק עליו והעלה להלכה בין בשל יד או של ראש אסור ליכנס לב"ה והסכים עם המ"א וכ"ל וכ"כ בספר בני חייא. ועי' תוס' דמנחות דף ל"ה ע"ב בד"ה אלו תפילין שבראש וכו' שהר"י דאורלינ"ש מסופק אם צריך לחלוץ תפילין של יד כשנכנס לב"ה ע"ש [וע' בספר אליהו רבה פלפול ארוך מזה]: (ב) בידו. ר"ל בבגדו ובידו כנגד לבו כמ"ש בסעיף ה' ט"ז:

משנה ברורה

כ"מ בין קדושה למצוה: (כג) מילתא היא. אף דבסעיף א' קי"ל דמותר לשנות הש"ר ולהורידו מקדושתו מטעם דהזמנה לאו מילתא היא אף דשם הוא גוף הקדושה (כח) שאני התם דעכ"פ עושה בהם קדושה קלת אבל הכא הלא רוצה לעשות בהם דבר חול ולזה מהני הזמנה בגוף הקדושה ועיין במג"א שהביא דיעות החולקין ע"ז וס"ל דאף בגוף הקדושה הזמנה אינה כלום ואעפ"כ לענין מעשה יש להחמיר כסברא הא' וכמו שכתבנו בביאור הלכה ועכ"פ מהני (כט) תנאי בזה מיהו אם התחיל לכתוב על הקלף סת"ס או שאר כתבי הקדש אפילו על הנייר אסור לכתוב אח"כ עליו דברי חול לכו"ע שזה עשה מעשה של גוף הקדושה (ל) ואפי' תנאי לא מהני בזה: (כד) צר ביה. פי' (לא) לפי שעה וגם בסתמא אפי' אם עשה כן פעמים הרבה אך שבכל פעם היה לפי שעה דרך עראי לא נתקדש עי"ז אבל אם צר ביה בקביעות או שצר ביה אפילו פ"א אך שצר ביה אדעתא דקביעותא דהיינו שהיה אז בדעתו (לב) למיצר ביה תמיד אפילו לא אזמניה מעיקרא ג"כ אסור דהוי כאזמניה וצר ביה. ואם פי' ע"מ לפנותו אפילו צר ביה (לג) כמה פעמים וגם אזמניה מעיקרא מותר כל שלא עשה כים לשם תפילין וכנ"ל בסקי"ד: (כה) ולא אזמניה. מעולם לשם תפילין: (כו) שרי. י"א דהיינו דהסודר לא נתקדש ע"י שצר ביה פ"א בלי הזמנה אבל כל זמן שהתפילין שם אין מדרך הכבוד (לד) להניח יחד שם גם מעות אלא (לה) יקשרם בקשר בפני עצמו:

א (א) להשתין. המג"א בסק"ע כתב דמה שכתב המחבר להשתין לרבותא נקט דאפילו להשתין אע"פ שהוא חיי של אדם אסור לכנס וכ"ש שלא לצורך: (ב) בתפילין שבראשו. ה"ה (א) דבזרוע נמי אסור מה"ט והא דנקט בראשו בא למעוטי אם אוחזן בידו: (ג) בידו. ר"ל (ג) בבגדו

ביאור הלכה

בהמאור במסכת סוכה וז"ל וה"ה לרצועות של תפילין אם בא לשנותן אחר העיבוד קודם שיתברס לקיילה הרשות בידו שאינן נאסרות בהזמנה אע"פ שעבדן לשמן עכ"ל ועיי"ש יותר אלמא דהמאור ס"ל דאין עליה שם הזמנה למצוה כ"ז שלא קשרה בהקיילה וה"נ לדידן דס"ל דהויא הזמנה לגוף הקדושה כ"ז שלא קשרה בהקיילה אין שם הזמנה עליה ומ"מ שלא במקום הצורך יותר טוב להחמיר בזה לצאת כל החששות כי לכאורה מהנ"י שמחמיר בעור המעובד להבתים לא משמע כסברא זו ובמקום הדחק יש להקל בכל גווני כי הרז"ה יחידאה הוא שמחמיר בהזמנה לרצועה: * מילתא היא. עיין במ"א שמצדד לפסוק כהרמב"ן שחולק ע"ז ולפי דברי הגר"א בביאורו שמתרץ היטיב שיטת הרז"ה והנ"י בעלי סברא זו וגם הביא שהריטב"א ג"כ ס"ל דהזמנה לגוף הקדושה מילתא היא קשה מאוד להקל נגד כל הני רבוותא שוב מצאתי לאחד מן האחרונים שכתב ג"כ דלמעשה יש להחמיר כסברא הא' וכן בתשובת משכנות יעקב בסימן נ"ה מכריע ג"כ לפסוק כהרמ"א ודלא כמ"א. ודע דמה שכתבתי במ"ב מיהו אם התחיל לכתוב וכו' ואפילו תנאי לא מהני בזה כן מוכח מא"ר ופמ"ג ושארי אחרונים ובאמת שכן מוכח ג"כ מהמג"א להמעיין בו והח"א מיקל בתנאי גם בזה ולא ידעתי מנ"ל. * צר בי'. עיין במ"ב במש"כ או שצר ביה וכו' שהיה אז בדעתו למיצר וכו' אף דבפמ"ג משמע דבעינן צר בפירוש ע"מ למיצר לעולם השמטתי זה דכל האחרונים לא הזכירו זה רק כתבו סתמא אדעתא למיצר ביה תמיד ועל כולם בהר"ן שהעתקתיו למעלה כתוב בפירוש דמחשבה ג"כ מהני לזה. ועוד אפשר לומר דהפמ"ג ג"כ מודה לזה ולא נקט האי לישנא אלא משום דרוצה לסיים שם דאם צר בפי' ע"מ לפנותו מותר אפילו צר כמה וכמה פעמים כל דלא תפר כים לתפילין עי"ש נקט בזה ג"כ בפי' ודוחק: * שרי למיצר וכו'. עיין במ"ב במה שכתב י"א וכו' הוא מרש"י ברכות כ"ג ע"ב ד"ה עם מעותיו וכו' עיי"ש ועיין בנ"י בפ' נגמר הדין שכתב ג"כ דכ"ז בשניטל התפילין אבל כ"ז שהתפילין עליהם אסור והעתיקו ג"כ הא"ר והגר"ז העתיק דשרי למיצר זוזי עם תפילין יחד ולין ע"ז ברכות כ"ג ע"ב ולפלא שלא זכר כלל דעת רש"י בזה: ודע דנ"ל דמה שכתב הנ"י אסור היינו רק שאין מדרך הכבוד וכמו שכתבנו בפנים אבל לא איסור ממש דאל"ה יתרץ הגמרא הרומיא דהברייתא דלא יצור היינו עם המעות ממש ובדלא אזמניה ואפשר שזה טעם הגר"ז שהשמיטו. וביו"ד סימן שס"ד ס"א דאם נתנו בו המת אדעתא לפנותו ולא הזמינו מתחלה מותר לאחר שפינהו משמע דבעוד שהמת שם אסור ליהנות מהקבר והגמרא מדמה אותם שם [בסנהדרין מ"ח] להדדי ולכאורה צ"ע על השו"ע בזה דמדהשמיט דעת הנ"י בזה משמע דס"ל עכ"פ דמדינא לא נאסר הסודר להשתמש בו חול אפי' בעת שהתפילין שם ושם סתם דאסור ואפשר דאורחא דמילתא נקט שם השו"ע א"נ דמשום סיפא נקט שם עי"ש ודוחק וצ"ע: * זוזי. עיין בספר נהר שלום שכתב דה"ה דמותר להשתמש בו תשמיש מגונה ודוקא לאחר שניטלו התפילין משם והביא ראיה לדבר עי"ש:

שער הציון

ובבה"כ

(כח) עי"ש ופמ"ג: (כט) ל"ח ומ"א: (ל) א"ר ופמ"ג: (לא) מ"א: (לב) מ"א סק"ה: (לג) אחרונים: (לד) נ"י בפ' נגמר הדין: (לה) רש"י ברכות כ"ג ע"ב ד"ה עם: (א) מ"א וש"א המובאים בבה"ט ופמ"ג בסימן מ"ד דלא כא"ר: (ג) ט"ז והגר"א וש"א:

If one designated /a cloth for wrapping *tefilin* in it/ but did not /actually/ wrap /*tefilin*/ in it or (24) if one wrapped /*tefilin*/ in /a cloth/ (25) but did not

Mishnah Berurah

respect/ between holiness and mitzvah which are of practical /significance/.

(23) Is of significance. Although we rule in Par. 1 that it is permitted to alter /the usage of/ head /*tefilin* in such circumstances/ and to reduce it from its /degree of/ holiness, for the reason that designation /alone/ is of no significance, despite /the fact/ that in such a case the actual holiness is involved /, the ruling here is nevertheless understandable/. /This is because the case discussed/ there is different, since one will at any rate be making /the designated article serve with/ some /degree of/ holiness, whereas here, /we are/ of course /referring to a case where/ one wishes to use /the designated article/ for a secular purpose. Designation for actual holiness is of avail for /secular use to become forbidden/.

See the *M.A.*, who cites authorities who dispute this and are of the opinion that even designation for actual holiness is of no /significance/. Even so, as regards /actual/ practice, one should be stringent in accordance with the other opinion, as we have written in the Beyur Halachah. At any rate, a stipulation is of avail in such a case.

Nevertheless, if one began to write on a parchment a Torah Scroll, a *tefilin* /passage/ or a mezuzah or /some/ other Holy Writing and even if /one did so/ on paper, it is subsequently forbidden to write secular matters on /the parchment or paper/, according to all /authorities/. /This is/ because by that /writing/ one did an act for the actual holiness. Even stipulation is of no avail in such a case.

(24) If one wrapped in /a cloth/. I.e., temporarily and also without specifying /anything with respect to the cloth/.

Even if one /wrapped *tefilin* in the cloth/ many times, but /did it/ temporarily every time and provisionally, /the cloth/ will not have become holy because of this.

However, /the ruling is different/ if one wrapped /*tefilin*/ in /the cloth/ regularly or even if one wrapped /*tefilin*/ in /the cloth only/ once, but wrapped them in it having in mind /that it should serve/ regularly /for this purpose/, i.e., if /when one wrapped *tefilin* in it/ he had in mind to wrap /*tefilin*/ in it always. /Then,/ even though he did not designate /the cloth/ originally /for *tefilin*/ it is also forbidden /to use it for coins/, as /it has the ruling/ of having been designated and wrapped in.

If one specified /that he was wrapping *tefilin* in the cloth/ with a mind to taking them out /, then/, even if he wrapped /the *tefilin*/ in it several times and also designated /the cloth/ originally /for wrapping *tefilin* in it/, he is /nevertheless/ permitted /to use the cloth for a secular article/. /However, this ruling only applies/ as long as he did not make a bag /out of the cloth/ for the sake of *tefilin*, as /explained/ above in sub-Par. 14.

(25) But did not designate it. /I.e., if he

* (כג) מילתא היא (ר"ן סוף פ' נגמר הדין): ט אזמניה ולא צר ביה או (ע) * (כד) צר ביה (כה) ולא אזמניה * (כו) שרי למיצר ביה * זוזי:

ט שם ברכות ושם בסנהדרין

מג דין איך להתנהג בתפילין בהכנסו לבהכ"ס. ובו ט' סעיפים:

א א אסור ליכנס לבית הכסא קבוע (א) להשתין (ב) בתפילין (א) שבראשו גזירה שמא יעשה בהם צרכיו ב ואם אוחזן (ב) (ג) בידו מותר להשתין בהם בבית הכסא קבוע: הגה והיינו דוקא כשמשתין מיושב

א ברכות כג ב שם

באר היטב

אסור א"כ לא יפה עושים המשתמשין בשק של תפילין כשהולכין בדרך אלא דנראה ללמוד זכות דאותן אנשים מסתמא הוי כמתנה בפירוש וכן בההוא שכתב רמ"א כאן דקלף המעובד לשם תפילין אסור לכתוב עליו דברי חול ואנו רואין בכל יום שהסופרים כותבים על הקלפים שלהם כתובות וגיטין ושאר דברי רשות אלא ודאי דמסתמא כשהסופרים מתקנים אותו תחלה דעתם להשתמש בהן הן לדבר קדושה הן לדבר רשות. ולפ"ז פשיטא דמותר לכתוב גט על קלף שנעבד לשם ס"ת וכ"מ בא"ע סימן קכ"ד ס"ב. מ"א ט"ז עיין ב"ח וע"ת. ומיהו אם התחיל לכתוב על הקלף או על הנייר דבר קדושה אסור לכתוב אח"כ עליו דברי חול ולא מהני תנאי. וכל זה בקדושה כגון תפילין וס"ת אבל לתשמישי קדושה מהני תנאי להשתמש בהן אפילו בעודן בקדושתן כמ"ש בסי' קנ"ד ס"ח אבל לתשמיש מגונה לא מהני כמ"ש סי' קנ"ד. ותשמישי מצוה כגון ציצית שופר לולב נר חנוכה אפילו עשאן לכך לא מיתסרי ומותר להשתמש בהן חול אפילו בלא תנאי ע"ש: (ט) צר ביה. פירוש לפי שעה ולא אזמניה להיות שם לעולם:

(א) שבראשו. ה"ה דבזרוע נמי אסור מה"ט והא דנקט בראשו בא למעט אם אוחזן בידו. רי"ו מ"א ועיין נ"ל ובתשו' בית יעקב סימן ק"ע כתב דוקא בראשו מפני שהם בגלוי אבל בשל יד שהם מכוסים שרי דלא גרע מאוחזן בבגדו ובידו ע"ש. והמחבר יד אהרן חולק עליו והעלה להלכה בין בשל יד או של ראש אסור ליכנס לב"ה והסכים עם המ"א ונ"ל וכ"כ בספר בני חייא. ועי' תוס' דמנחות דף ל"ה ע"ב בד"ה אלו תפילין שבראש וכו' שהר"י דאורלינ"ש מסופק אם צריך לחלוץ תפילין של יד כשנכנס לב"ה ע"ש [וע' בספר אליהו רבה פלפול ארוך מזה]: (ב) בידו. ר"ל בבגדו ובידו כנגד לבו כמ"ש בסעיף ה' ט"ז:

משנה ברורה

נ"ת בין קדושה למצוה: (כג) מילתא היא. אף דבסעיף א' קי"ל דמותר לשנות הש"ר ולהורידו מקדושתו מטעם דהזמנה לאו מילתא היא אף דשם הוא גוף הקדושה (כח) שאני התם דעכ"פ עושה בהם קדושה קלת אבל הכא הלא רוצה לעשות בהם דבר חול ולזה מהני הזמנה בגוף הקדושה ועיין במג"א שהביא דיעות החולקין ע"ז וס"ל דאף בגוף הקדושה הזמנה אינה כלום ואעפ"כ לענין מעשה יש להחמיר כסברא הא' וכמו שכתבנו בביאור הלכה ועכ"פ מהני (כט) תנאי בזה מיהו אם התחיל לכתוב על הקלף סת"ס או שאר כתבי הקדש אפילו על הנייר אסור לכתוב אח"כ עליו דברי חול לכו"ע שזה עשה מעשה של גוף הקדושה (ל) ואפי' תנאי לא מהני בזה: (כד) צר ביה. פי' (לא) לפי שעה וגם בסתמא אפי' אם עשה כן פעמים הרבה אך שבכל פעם היה לפי שעה דרך עראי לא נתקדש ע"ז אבל אם צר ביה בקביעות או שצר ביה אפילו פ"א אך שצר ביה אדעתא דקביעותא דהיינו שהיה אז בדעתו (לב) למיצר ביה תמיד אפילו לא אזמניה מעיקרא ג"כ אסור דהוי כאזמניה וצר ביה. ואם פי' ע"מ לפנותו אפילו צר ביה (לג) כמה פעמים וגם אזמניה מעיקרא מותר כל שלא עשה כים לשם תפילין וכנ"ל בסקי"ד: (כה) ולא אזמניה. מעולם לשם תפילין: (כו) שרי. י"א דהיינו דהסודר לא נתקדש ע"י שצר ביה פ"א בלי הזמנה אבל כל זמן שהתפילין שם אין מדרך הכבוד (לד) להניח יחד שם גם מעות אלא (לה) יקשרם בקשר בפני עצמו:

א (א) להשתין. המג"א בסק"ט כתב דמה שכתב המחבר להשתין לרבותא נקט דאפילו להשתין אע"פ שהוא חייו של אדם אסור לכנס וכ"ש שלא לצורך: (ב) בתפילין שבראשו. ה"ה (א) דבזרוע נמי אסור מה"ט והא דנקט בראשו בא למעוטי אם אוחזן בידו: (ג) בידו. ר"ל (ב) בבגדו

ביאור הלכה

בהמאור במסכת סוכה וז"ל וה"ה לרצועות של תפילין אם בא לשנותן אחר העיבוד קודם שיתחברו לקציצה הרשות בידו שאינן נאסרות בהזמנה אע"פ שעבדן לשמן עכ"ל ועיי"ש יותר אלמא דהמאור ס"ל דאין עליה שם הזמנה למצוה כ"ז שלא קשרה בהקציצה וה"נ לדידן דס"ל דהויא הזמנה לגוף הקדושה כ"ז שלא קשרה בהקציצה אין שם הזמנה עליה ומ"מ שלא במקום הצורך יותר טוב להחמיר בזה לצאת כל החששות כי לכאורה מהנ"י שמחמיר בעור המעובד להבתים לא משמע כסברא זו ובמקום הדחק יש להקל בכל גווני כי הרז"ה יחידאה הוא שמחמיר בהזמנה לרצועה: * מילתא היא. עיין במ"א שמלדד לפסוק כהרמב"ן שחולק ע"ז ולפי דברי הגר"א בביאורו שמתרץ היטיב שיטת הרז"ה והנ"י בעלי סברא זו וגם הביא שהריטב"א ג"כ ס"ל דהזמנה לגוף הקדושה מילתא היא קשה מאוד להקל נגד כל הני רבוותא שוב מצאתי לאחד מן האחרונים שכתב ג"כ דלמעשה יש להחמיר כסברא הא' וכן בתשובת משכנות יעקב בסימן נ"ה מכריע ג"כ לפסוק כהרמ"א ודלא כמ"א. ודע דמה שכתבתי במ"ב מיהו אם התחיל לכתוב וכו' ואפילו תנאי לא מהני בזה כן מוכח מא"ר ופמ"ג ושארי אחרונים ובאמת שכן מוכח ג"כ מהמג"א להמעיין בו והח"א מיקל בתנאי גם בזה ולא ידעתי מנ"ל. * צר בי'. עיין במ"ב במש"כ או שצר ביה וכו' שהיה אז בדעתו למיצר וכו' אף דבפמ"ג משמע דבעינן צר בפירוש ע"מ למיצר לעולם השמטתי זה דכל האחרונים לא הזכירו זה רק כתבו סתמא אדעתא למיצר ביה תמיד ועל כולם בהר"ן שהעתקתיו למעלה כתוב בפירוש דמחשבה ג"כ מהני לזה. ועוד אפשר לומר דהפמ"ג ג"כ מודה לזה ולא נקט האי לישנא אלא משום דרוצה לסיים שם דאם צר בפי' ע"מ לפנותו מותר אפילו צר כמה וכמה פעמים כל דלא תפר כים לתפילין עי"ש נקט בזה ג"כ בפי' ודוחק:

* שרי למיצר וכו'. עיין במ"ב במה שכתב י"א וכו' הוא מרש"י ברכות כ"ג ע"ב ד"ה עם מעותיו וכו' עיי"ש ועיין בנ"י בפ' נגמר הדין שכתב ג"כ דכ"ז בשניטל התפילין אבל כ"ז שהתפילין עליהם אסור והעתיקו ג"כ הא"ר והגר"ז העתיק דשרי למיצר זוזי עם תפילין יחד ועיין ע"ז ברכות כ"ג ע"ב ולפלא שלא זכר כלל דעת רש"י בזה: ודע דנ"ל דמה שכתב הנ"י אסור היינו רק שאין מדרך הכבוד וכמו שכתבנו בפנים אבל לא איסור ממש דאל"ה יתרץ הגמרא הרומיא דהברייתא דלא יצור היינו עם המעות ממש ובדלא אזמניה ואפשר שזה טעם הגר"ז שהשמיטו. וביו"ד סימן שס"ד ס"א דאם נתנו בו המת אדעתא לפנותו ולא הזמינו מתחלה מותר לאחר שפינהו משמע דבעוד שהמת שם אסור ליהנות מהקבר והגמרא מדמה אותם שם [בסנהדרין מ"ח] להדדי ולכאורה צ"ע על השו"ע בזה דמהשמיט דעת הנ"י בזה משמע דס"ל עכ"פ דמדינא לא נאסר הסודר להשתמש בו חול אפי' בעת שהתפילין שם ושם סתם דאסור ואפשר דאורחא דמילתא נקט שם השו"ע א"נ דמשום סיפא נקט שם עי"ש ודוחק וצ"ע:

* זוזי. עיין בספר נהר שלום שכתב דה"ה דמותר להשתמש בו תשמיש מגונה ודוקא לאחר שניטלו התפילין משם והביא ראיה לדבר עי"ש:

ובבה"כ

שער הציון

(כח) עי"ש ופמ"ג: (כט) ל"ח ומ"א: (ל) א"ר ופמ"ג: (לא) מ"א: (לב) מ"א סק"ה: (לג) אחרונים: (לד) נ"י בפ' נגמר הדין: (לה) רש"י ברכות כ"ג ע"ב ד"ה עם: (א) מ"א וש"א המובאים בבה"ט ופמ"ג בסימן מ"ד דלא כא"ר: (ב) ט"ז והגר"א וש"א:

designate it /for this purpose/, **(26)** one is allowed to wrap coins in it.[3*]

§43: THE LAW AS REGARDS HOW ONE SHOULD CONDUCT HIMSELF WITH *TEFILIN* WHEN HE ENTERS A LAVATORY

(Contains Nine Paragraphs)

1. It is forbidden to enter a permanent lavatory **(1)** to urinate **(2)** with *tefilin* on one's head. /This prohibition was/ decreed /out of fear/ that one may /come to/ relieve himself with them on. If one holds them **(3)** in his hand, he is permitted to urinate with them /on his person/ in a permanent lavatory.

Gloss: It is only /permitted/ for him to urinate sitting, in which case there is

Mishnah Berurah

did not designate it/ ever for the sake of *tefilin*.

(26) One is allowed. There are /authorities/ who say that what is meant is that the cloth will not have become holy by virtue /of the fact/ that he wrapped /*tefilin*/ in it once without having designated /it for *tefilin*/. However, as long as the *tefilin* are there it is disrespectful to place money there as well together with /the *tefilin* in the same bundle/, but he should bundle /the money/ in an independent bundle /and the *tefilin* in an independent bundle/.

§43

(1) To urinate. The *M.A.* writes in sub-Par. 9 that when the author /of the Shulchan Aruch/ writes, "to urinate", he uses this wording to /give/ a wider /ruling/. /This is/ that it is forbidden to enter /a lavatory with *tefilin* on one's head/ even /in order/ to urinate, although a person's life is /dependent on/ it. /It is, however,/ certainly /forbidden to enter a lavatory/ unnecessarily /with *tefilin* on one's head/.

(2) With *tefilin* on one's head. Correspondingly, it is also forbidden /to enter with *tefilin*/ on one's arm, for the same reason. /The reason why the author of the Shulchan Aruch/ speaks of /*tefilin*/ on the head /is not because one is allowed to have them on his arm, but it/ is meant to except /an instance/ when one holds them in his hand.

(3) In his hand. What is meant is inside his garment and in his right /hand/ against his heart, as stated in Par. 5.

3* The cloth may even be used for a repugnant purpose, provided that the *tefilin* are no longer there. (Beyur Halachah)

דליכא למיחש לניצוצות אבל משתין מעומד (ד) פשיטא דאסור דלא עדיף מבית הכסא עראי וה"ה אם משתין מיושב או בעפר (ה) תחוח דליכא ניצוצות בבית הכסא עראי (ו) נמי שרי ואין חילוק בין קבע לעראי לענין זה אלא דבה"כ קבוע מסתמא עושה צרכיו (ג) מיושב ובה"כ עראי מסתמא עושה מעומד הואיל ואינו נפנה (ד) לגדולים (ב"י בשם כ"י ומגדל עוז) * (ז) גובבית הכסא עראי מותר להשתין בהם כשהם בראשו דאבל אם אוחזן בידו אסור להשתין בהם מעומד אפילו אם תופס אותם בבגדו (ח) מפני שצריך לשפשף בידו ניצוצות שברגליו אלא (ט) חולצן ברחוק (ה) ד' אמות ונותנם (י) לחבירו ה ומדברי הרמב"ם נראה שאסור להשתין (יא) כשהם בראשו בין בבית הכסא קבוע בין בבית הכסא עראי ויש לחוש (יב) לדבריו: ב * ו בית הכסא קבוע היינו שיש בו צואה והוא על פני השדה (יג) בלא (ו) חפירה: ג * (יד) ז בית הכסא עראי (ז) היינו כגון להשתין מים שאין אדם הולך בשבילם לבית הכסא והפעם הזאת נעשה המקום הזה (טו) בית הכסא תחלה: ד (טז) ח אם הם בחיקו וחגור חגורה (יז) או בבגדו בידו מותר בין להשתין בין (ס) לפנות: ה ט אם רוצה ליכנס (יח) לבית הכסא י קבוע לעשות צרכיו חולצן ברחוק ארבע אמות: הגה ויש אומרים אפילו בלא (ע) צרכיו (ב"י בשם רבי אלי) (יט) וטוב להחמיר: וגוללן ברצועות שלהן

באר היטב

(ג) מיושב. לכן כשהם בראשו אסור אפי' להשתין גזירה שמא יעשה צרכיו: (ד) לגדולים. לכן בבה"כ עראי מותר דלא גזרינן שמא יפנה בהם: (ה) ד"א. וכ"כ הטור וקאי ארישא דהיינו בבה"כ קבוע דאסור להשתין כשהם בראשו אלא חולצן ברחוק ד"א וממילא שמעינן בבה"כ עראי דאסור כשהם בידו אין תקנה רק שיתנם לחבירו אבל מ"מ א"צ להסיר מידו ברחוק ד"א. ט"ז מ"א. ובתשובת מטה יוסף ח"ב סימן ה' הבין שמ"ש הטור אלא חולצן ברחוק ד"א קאי נמי לבה"כ עראי ומש"ה הרבה להקשות ע"ש ולא דק. ועיין ב"ח: (ו) חפירה. אבל כשהוא בחפירה חולץ ומשתין לאלתר וא"צ להרחיק ד"א. מ"א ע"ש: (ז) היינו. ר"ל הא דאמרינן לעיל דמותר להשתין בו בתפילין שבראשו היינו במקום שאין רגילות לפנות שם: (ח) לפנות. נ"ע דבס"א כתב אפי' תופס אותם בבגדו אסור וי"ל דהכא מיירי שקשורים בבגדו שאף אם ישפשף בידו לא יפלו התפילין מ"א וע' ט"ז: (ט) צרכיו. והא דנקט הטור והש"ע סעיף א' אסור ליכנס להשתין וכו' לרבותא נקט להשתין אע"פ שהוא חייו של

ביאור הלכה

* ובבה"כ עראי מותר להשתין בהם כשהם בראשו. פשוט דה"ה לענין תפילין של זרועו וכן איתא להדיא בספר התרומה ודלא כהפמ"ג ונראה שיסיר הכריכות מעל כף ידו שלא יבוא לשפשף בם: * בה"כ קבוע היינו שיש בו וכו'. נראה לכאורה דאפילו אם עתה אין בו צואה כלל כיון דהוא מקום שרגילין לפנות שם גזרינן שמא יעשה צרכיו ולא נקט המחבר לשון זה רק להורות לנו דאם יש צואה במקום הזה תו חיישינן שמא הוא יעשה צרכיו ג"כ במקום הזה ואפילו אם עד עתה לא היה זה המקום מיוחד לפנות ובזה ניחא מה דסיים המחבר בלי חפירה להורות דאם הוא בחפירה חשוב כמאן דליתא ומותר אם אותו המקום אינו מיוחד לפנות עד עתה ועין במ"א סק"ו מה שתמה על המחבר ולפ"ז ניחא הכל: * בה"כ עראי וכו' בה"כ תחלה. עין במ"ב בשם הפמ"ג ואם הוא מקום המסריח מפני מי רגלים המצוי תמיד שם לכאורה המקום הזה דין בה"כ קבוע יש לו דלא גרע מעביט של מי רגלים המסריח דדינו כצואה

משנה ברורה

וביד (ג) ימינו כנגד לבו כמש"כ בס"ה: (ד) פשיטא דאסור. באוחזן בידו שמא יקנח הניצוצות וה"ה כשהם בראשו דאסור דחיישינן שמא ישב ויעשה בהם צרכיו [פמ"ג]: (ה) תיחוח. או במקום (ד) מדרון: (ו) נמי שרי ואין חילוק וכו'. ומ"מ (ה) יש חילוק קצת דבקבע דיש חשש שמא יעשה צרכיו צריך שיהיה בבגדו ובידו כמ"ש בסק"ג ובעראי אפילו בידו לבד נמי מותר בזה דליכא חשש ניצוצות: (ז) ובבה"כ עראי וכו'. דלא גזרינן ביה שמא יפנה בהם ורק שיזהר שלא יפיח בהם: (ח) מפני שצריך וכו'. וחיישינן (ו) שמא ישפשף הניצוצות שנופלין על רגליו ביד שאוחז בה התפילין: (ט) חולצן ברחוק וכו'. עיין מ"א שכתב דמש"כ המחבר מתחלה אסור להשתין בהן מעומד מיירי בין בעראי ובין בקבוע וכמו שכ' בהג"ה ומש"כ אלא חולצן ברחוק ד"א מיירי בקבוע דאי בבה"כ ערלאי חולץ ומשתין לאלתר וכ"כ הט"ז: (י) לחבירו. דהוא בעצמו אסור לאחוז בהן או (ז) אף דמיירי בקבוע ומבואר לקמן בס"ה דיאחזו בבגדו ובידו כיון דמיירי כשמשתין מעומד וחיישינן משום ניצוצות: (יא) כשהן בראשו. (ח) וה"ה בזרועו דס"ל דגזרינן שמא יפיח בהם אבל כשהן בכיסן ואוחז הכיס בידו מותר להשתין בהן לד"ה שבכסן בכיסן אין איסור בהפחה כמו שיתבאר בסימן מ"ד: (יב) לדבריו. ולעת הצורך כגון שיתבטל עי"ז מתפלה בצבור יכול לסמוך אדיעה ראשונה אך שיזהר הרבה שלא יבוא לידי הפחה כ"כ הח"א ומ"מ נוהגין לחלוץ הש"ר. וגם הש"י (ט) נכון להסיר הרצועות מכף היד שלא יבוא לשפשף הניצוצות בהם: ב (יג) בלא חפירה. ר"ל אז צריך לחלוץ ברחוק ד"א אבל אם הוא בחפירה הרי החפירה היא רשות לעצמו ובה"כ שלמעלה רשות לעצמו ואין לו דין בה"כ כלל כמו שיתבאר בסימן ע"ג ומותר ליכנס בתוכו בתפילין שעליו ומ"מ קודם שישתין צריך לחלוץ לד"ה כמו בשאר בה"כ קבוע כן מסיק המ"א בד"א להשתין אבל לעשות צרכיו משמע מדברי הב"י דיש להחמיר לחלוץ ברחוק ד"א ממקום שרוצה לעשות צרכיו (י) אפילו נפנה במקום שאינו בה"כ כלל אלא בחצירו או ע"פ השדה: ג (יד) בה"כ עראי וכו'. פי' הא דאמרינן לעיל דמותר להשתין בו בתפילין שבראשו היינו במקום שאין בו צואה וגם הוא מקום שאין רגילין לפנות שם ולכן לא גזרינן שמא יפנה בהתפילין (יא) ואפילו אם הוא מקום נגוע: (טו) בה"כ תחלה. עיין בפמ"ג דס"ל דהאי לישנא לאו דוקא דאפילו מיוחד מכמה זמנים להשתין מ"מ ערלאי יחשב: ד (טז) אם הם בחיקו וכו'. דתו ליכא למיחש משום ניצוצות וגם משום שמא יפלו ממנו ומותר בין בבה"כ קבוע (יב) ובין בערלאי: (יז) או בבגדו בידו. נ"ע דבס"א כתב אפילו תופס אותם בבגדו אסור ועיין בט"ז ומ"א שנדחקו בזה מאד ובביאור הגר"א כתב דסעיף זה שכתב בעל התרומות הוא שיטה אחרת החולק על הא דס"א וס"ל דבבגדו וידו תו לא חיישינן לשפשוף הניצוצות וכן הכריע בספר מאמר מרדכי. ובקשורין בבגדו (יג) לכו"ע מותר: ה (יח) לבה"כ קבוע. (יד) נקט קבוע משום סיפא דאשמועינן דאפילו בקבוע מכניס התפילין עמו משום שמירה אבל לה"ג דאפילו באינו קבוע כלל צריך לחלוץ ברחוק ד"א ממקום שרוצה לפנות וכדלעיל בסוף ס"ק י"ג. וכן מה דנקט לעשות צרכיו ג"כ משום רבותא דסיפא אבל באמת ה"ה להשתין צריך לחלוץ ברחוק ד"א וכדלעיל בס"א: (יט) וטוב להחמיר. המ"א מסיק דמדינא אסור לכנס לבהכ"ס בתפילין דלא גרע מגרתק לקמן בסימן מ"ה ס"ב ועיין בפמ"ג ובמאמר מרדכי שכתבו דמדברי הרא"ש לא משמע הכי גם מדברי

שער הציון

(ג) ע"ת וא"ר: (ד) רמב"ס וב"י: (ה) פמ"ג: (ו) ב"י: (ז) ממ"א ופמ"ג: (ח)מסתימת לשון הרמב"ס וכן משמע בשו"ע של הגר"ז אכן מלאתי בסוף הסימן בפמ"ג שמלדד להיתר בשם הא"ר: (ט) מישועות יעקב: (י) הגר"ז: (יא) הגר"ז: (יב) מט"ז: (יג) מ"א: (יד) מאמר מרדכי:

באר הגולה

ג תוס' שם והרא"ש בה"ת וסמ"ג וספר התרומה ד שם בגמ' ה בפרק ד' מהלכות תפילין ו רש"י שם בגמרא ז שם ברש"י ח ס' התרומה ט שם בגמרא י כן הוא בגמרא שם אבל הב"י כתב שהטור לפי גירסתו שלפניו והרמב"ס והרי"ף והרא"ש לא חלקו בין קבוע לעראי

no fear of /sprinkling/ drops /of urine/. However, /for him/ to urinate standing is **(4)** *obviously forbidden, since /the ruling for a permanent lavatory/ cannot be more /lenient/ than /the ruling for/ a provisional lavatory. Correspondingly, if one /wishes to/ urinate in a provisional lavatory sitting or into* **(5)** *loose earth, in which case there are no /sprinkling/ drops,* **(6)** *it is also permitted /for him to do so with* tefilin *in his hand/ and there is /in fact/ no difference between a permanent /lavatory/ and a provisional /lavatory/ in this respect. /Different rulings are given/ only because in a permanent lavatory one generally relieves himself sitting and in a provisional lavatory one generally /urinates/ standing, /the reason/ being that one does not excrete solids /in a provisional lavatory/. (...)*

(7) In a provisional lavatory, it is permitted /for one/ to urinate with /*tefilin* on his person/ when they are on his head.[1*] /However,/ if he holds /the *tefilin*/ in his hand he is forbidden to urinate standing with them, even if he grasps them with his garment. **(8)** This is because he will need to wipe /sprinkling/ drops off his feet with his hand.

Instead, **(9)** he should take them off at a distance of four cubits /from the

Mishnah Berurah

(4) Obviously forbidden. /I.e.,/ if he holds them in his hand. /It is forbidden then/ in case he will /come to/ wipe off the /sprinkling/ drops.

/It is, however,/ forbidden likewise when /the *tefilin*/ are on his head, for we are afraid that he may sit /there/ and relieve himself with them on. [*P.Mg.*]

(5) Loose. Or onto an area which slopes.

(6) It is also permitted and there is no difference, etc. There is at any rate a slight difference. For when /one enters/ a permanent /lavatory/, where there are grounds for fear that he may relieve himself, /the *tefilin*/ must be inside his garment and in his /right/ hand, as we have written in sub-Par. 3. /On the other hand,/ in a provisional lavatory, even if they are merely in his hand /and not inside his garment/ it is also permitted in such cases, since /then/ there are no grounds for fear of /sprinkling/ drops.

(7) In a provisional lavatory, etc. For /the Sages/ did not decree /a prohibition against this/ in such /a lavatory, as they were not afraid/ that one may /come to/ excrete /there/ with them on. Only, one must avoid breaking wind with them on.

(8) This is because he will need, etc. We are /therefore/ afraid that he may wipe off the /sprinkling/ drops which fall on to his feet with the hand in which he is holding the *tefilin*.

(9) He should take them off at a distance, etc. See the *M.A.*, who writes that when the author /of the Shulchan Aruch/ writes first that it is forbidden to urinate standing with them, he is referring both to /when one is in/ a provisional /lavatory/ and to /when one is in/ a permanent /lavatory/, in conformance with what is stated by the gloss. /However,/ when he writes, "Instead, he should take them off at a distance of four cubits", he is referring /only/ to /a case when one wishes to urinate in/ a permanent /lavatory/. For in the case of a provisional lavatory, one may take them off /and hand them to his fellow/ and urinate forthwith /on that spot/. The *Taz* likewise writes this.

1* Or on his arm. He should remove the coils from his hand if he has *tefilin* on his arm, so that he should not come to wipe himself with them. (Beyur Halachah)

דליכא למיחש לנצוצות אבל משתין מעומד (ד) פשיטא דאסור דלא עדיף מבית הכסא עראי וה"ה אם משתין מיושב או בעפר (ה) תחוח דליכא נצוצות בבית הכסא עראי (ו) נמי שרי ואין חילוק בין קבע לעראי לענין זה אלא דבה"כ קבוע מסתמא עושה צרכיו (ג) מיושב ובה"כ עראי מסתמא מעומד עושה הואיל ואינו נפנה (ד) לגדולים (ב"י בשם כ"י ומגדל עוז) * (ז) ובבית הכסא עראי מותר להשתין בהם כשהם בראשו אבל אם אוחזן בידו אסור להשתין בהם מעומד אפילו אם תופס אותם בבגדו (ח) מפני שצריך לשפשף בידו ניצוצות שברגליו אלא (ט) חולצן ברחוק (ה) ד' אמות **ונותנם (י) לחבירו ומדברי הרמב"ם נראה שאסור להשתין (יא) כשהם בראשו בין בבית הכסא קבוע בין בבית הכסא עראי ויש לחוש (יב) לדבריו: ב * בית הכסא קבוע היינו שיש בו צואה והוא על פני השדה (יג) בלא (ו) חפירה:** ג * (יד) בית הכסא עראי (ז) היינו כגון להשתין מים שאין אדם הולך בשבילם לבית הכסא והפעם הזאת נעשה המקום הזה (טו) בית הכסא תחלה: ד (טז) אם הם בחיקו וחגור חגורה (יז) או בבגדו בידו מותר בין להשתין בין (ח) לפנות: ה אם רוצה ליכנס (יח) לבית הכסא קבוע לעשות צרכיו חולצן ברחוק ארבע אמות: הגה ויש אומרים אפילו בלא (ט) צרכיו (ב"י בשם רבי האי) (יט) וטוב להחמיר: וגוללן ברצועות שלהן

באר הגולה

ג תוס' שם והרא"ש נה"ת וסמ"ג וספר התרומה ד שם בגמ' ה בפרק ד' מהלכות תפילין ו רש"י שם בגמרא ז שם ברש"י ח ס' התרומה ט שם בגמרא י כן הוא בגמרא שם אבל הב"י כתב שהטור לפי גירסתו שלפניו והרמב"ם והרי"ף והרא"ש לא חלקו בין קבוע לעראי

באר היטב

(ג) מיושב. לכן כשהם בראשו אסור אפי' להשתין גזירה שמא יעשה צרכיו: (ד) לגדולים. לכן בבה"כ עראי מותר דלא גזרינן שמא יפנה בהם: (ה) ד"א. וכ"כ הטור וקאי ארישא דהיינו בבה"כ קבוע דאסור להשתין כשהם בראשו אלא חולצן ברחוק ד"א וממילא שמעינן בבה"כ עראי דאסור כשהם בידו אין תקנה רק שיתנם לחבירו אבל מ"מ א"צ להסיר מידו ברחוק ד"א. ט"ז מ"א. ובתשובת מטה יוסף ח"ב סימן ה' הבין שמ"ש הטור אלא חולצן ברחוק ד"א קאי נמי לבה"כ עראי ומש"ה הרבה להקשות ע"ש ולא דק. ועיין ב"ח: (ו) חפירה. אבל כשהוא בחפירה חולץ ומשתין לאלתר וא"צ להרחיק ד"א. מ"א ע"ש: (ז) היינו. ר"ל הא דאמרינן לעיל דמותר להשתין בו בתפילין שבראשו היינו במקום שאין רגילות לפנות שם: (ח) לפנות. נ"ע דבס"א כתב אפי' תופס אותם בבגדו אסור וי"ל דהכא איירי שקשורים בבגדו שאף אם ישפשף בידו לא יפלו התפילין מ"א וע' ט"ז: (ט) צרכיו. והא דנקט הטור והש"ע סעיף א' אסור ליכנס להשתין וכו' לרבותא נקט להשתין אע"פ שהוא חייו של

ביאור הלכה

* ובבה"כ עראי מותר להשתין בהם כשהם בראשו. פשוט דה"ה לענין תפילין של זרועו וכן איתא להדיא בספר התרומה ודלא כהפמ"ג ונראה שיסיר הכריכות מעל כף ידו שלא יבוא לשפשף בם: * בה"כ קבוע היינו שיש בו וכו'. נראה לכאורה דאפילו אם עתה אין בו צואה כלל כיון דהוא מקום שרגילין לפנות שם גזרינן שמא יעשה צרכיו ולא נקט המחבר לשון זה רק להורות לנו דאם יש צואה במקום הזה תו חיישינן שמא הוא יעשה צרכיו ג"כ במקום הזה ואפילו אם עד עתה לא היה זה המקום מיוחד לפנות ובזה ניחא מה דסיים המחבר בלי חפירה להורות דאם הוא בחפירה חשוב כמאן דליתא ומותר אם אותו המקום אינו מיוחד לפנות עד עתה ועין במ"א סק"ו מה שתמה על המחבר ולפ"ז ניחא הכל: * בה"כ עראי וכו' בה"כ תחלה. עין במ"ב בשם הפמ"ג ואם הוא מקום המסריח מפני מי רגלים המצוי תמיד שם לכאורה המקום הזה דין בה"כ קבוע יש לו דלא גרע מעביט של מי רגלים המסריח דדינו כצואה

משנה ברורה

וכיד (ג) ימינו כנגד גבו כמש"כ בס"ה: (ד) פשיטא דאסור. באוחזן בידו שמא יקנח הניצוצות וה"ה כשהם בראשו דאסור דחיישינן שמא ישב ויעשה בהם צרכיו [פמ"ג]: (ה) תיחוח. או במקום (ו) מדרון: (ו) נמי שרי ואין חילוק וכו'. ומ"מ (ז) יש חילוק קצת דבקבע יש חשש שמא יעשה צרכיו צריך שיהיה בבגדו ובידו כמ"ש בסק"ג ובעראי אפילו בידו לבד נמי מותר בזה דליכא חשש ניצוצות: (ז) ובבה"כ עראי וכו'. דלא גזרינן ביה שמא יפנה בהם ורק שיזהר שלא יפיח בהם: (ח) מפני שצריך וכו'. וחיישינן (ט) שמא ישפשף הניצוצות שנופלין על רגליו ביד שאוחז בה התפילין: (ט) חולצן ברחוק וכו'. עיין מ"א שכתב דמש"כ המחבר מתחלה אסור להשתין בהן מעומד איירי בין בעראי ובין בקבוע וכמו שכ' בהג"ה ומש"כ אלא חולצן ברחוק ד"א איירי בקבוע דאי בבה"כ עראי חולץ ומשתין לאלתר וכ"כ הט"ז: **(י) לחבירו. דהוא בעצמו אסור לאחוז בהן אז (ז) אף דמיירי בקבוע ומבואר לקמן בס"ה דיאחוז בבגדו ובידו כיון דמיירי כשמשתין מעומד וחיישינן משום ניצוצות: (יא) כשהן בראשו. (ח) וה"ה בזרועו דס"ל דגזרינן שמא יפיח בהם אבל כשהן בכיסן ואוחז הכיס בידו מותר להשתין בהן לד"ה שכשהן בכיסן אין איסור בהפחה כמו שיתבאר בסימן מ"ד: (יב) לדבריו. ולעת הצורך כגון שיתבטל עי"ז מתפלה בצבור יכול לסמוך אדיעה ראשונה אך שיזהר הרבה שלא יבוא לידי הפחה כ"כ הח"א ומ"מ נוהגין לחלוץ הש"ר. וגם הש"י (ט) נכון להסיר הרצועות מכף היד שלא יבוא לשפשף הניצוצות בהם: ב (יג) בלא חפירה. ר"ל אז צריך לחלצן ברחוק ד"א אבל אם הוא בחפירה הרי החפירה היא רשות לעצמו ובה"כ שלמעלה רשות לעצמו ואין לו דין בה"כ כלל כמו שיתבאר בסימן פ"ג ומותר ליכנס בתוכו בתפילין שעליו ומ"מ קודם שישתין צריך לחלצן לד"ה כמו בשאר בה"כ קבוע כן מסיק המ"א בד"א להשתין אבל לעשות צרכיו משמע מדברי הב"י דיש להחמיר לחלוץ ברחוק ד"א ממקום שרוצה לעשות צרכיו (י) אפילו נפנה במקום שאינו בה"כ כלל אלא בחצירו או ע"פ השדה:** ג (יד) בה"כ עראי וכו'. פי' הא דאמרינן לעיל דמותר להשתין בו בתפילין שבראשו היינו במקום שאין בו צואה וגם הוא מקום שאין רגילין לפנות שם ולכך לא גזרינן שמא יפנה בהתפילין (יא) ואפילו אם הוא מקום נגוע: (טו) בה"כ תחלה. עיין בפמ"ג דס"ל דהאי ליגנא לאו דוקא דאפילו מיוחד מכמה זמנים להשתין מ"מ עראי יחשב: ד (טז) אם הם בחיקו וכו'. דתו ליכא למיחש משום ניצוצות וגם משום שמא יפלו ממנו ומותר בין בבה"כ קבוע (יב) ובין בעראי: (יז) או בבגדו בידו. נ"ע דבס"א כתב אפילו תופס אותם בבגדו אסור ועיין בט"ז ומ"א שנדחקו בזה מאד ובביאור הגר"א כתב דסעיף זה שהוא מבעל התרומות הוא שיטה אחרת החולק על הא דס"א וס"ל דבבגדו וידו תו לא חיישינן לשפשוף הניצוצות וכן הכריע בספר מאמר מרדכי. ובקשורין בבגדו (יג) לכו"ע מותר: ה (יח) לבה"כ קבוע. (יד) נקט קבוע משום סיפא לאשמועינן דאפילו בקבוע מכניס התפילין עמו משום שמירה אבל הה"נ דאפילו באינו קבוע כלל צריך לחלוץ ברחוק ד"א ממקום שרוצה לפנות וכדלעיל בסוף ס"ק י"ג. וכן מה דנקט לעשות צרכיו ג"כ משום רבותא דסיפא אבל באמת ה"ה להשתין צריך לחלוץ ברחוק ד"א וכדלעיל בס"א: (יט) וטוב להחמיר. המ"א מסיק דמדינא אסור לכנס לבה"כ בתפילין דלא גרע ממרחץ לקמן בסימן מ"ה ס"ב ועיין בפמ"ג ובמאמר מרדכי שכתבו דמדברי הרא"ש לא משמע הכי גם מדברי

שער הציון

(ג) ע"ת וא"ר: (ד) רמב"ם וב"י: (ה) פמ"ג: (ו) ב"י: (ז) ממ"א ופמ"ג: (ח)מסתימת לשון הרמב"ם וכן משמע בשו"ע של הגר"ז אכן מצאתי בסוף הסימן בפמ"ג שמצדד להיתר בשם הא"ר: (ט) מישועות יעקב: (י) הגר"ז: (יא) הגר"ז: (יב) מט"ז: (יג) מ"א: (יד) מאמר מרדכי:

lavatory/ and hand them (10) to his fellow /until he returns/.

It appears from the words of the *Rambam*[2*] that /in his opinion/ it is forbidden to urinate (11) when /*tefilin*/ are on one's head, both in a permanent lavatory and in a provisional lavatory. One should have regard (12) for his words.

2. By a permanent lavatory is meant /a lavatory/ that has excrement in it[3*] /with the place for the excrement/ being on the surface of the field (13) without having been dug out.

Mishnah Berurah

(10) **To his fellow.** For he himself is forbidden to hold /the *tefilin*/ then.

Although /the ruling/ is referring to /a case where/ a permanent /lavatory/ is involved and it is stated below in Par. 5 that one may hold them /there/ inside his garment and in his hand, /the Shulchan Aruch/ is speaking of /an instance/ when he /wishes to/ urinate standing, in view of which we are afraid of /sprinkling/ drops.

(11) **When /*tefilin*/ are on one's head.** The same ruling /applies/ when /*tefilin*/ are on one's arm. For /the *Rambam*/ is of the opinion that /the Sages/ made a decree /forbidding this, for fear/ that one may /come to/ break wind with them on.

On the other hand, if /the *tefilin*/ are in their bag and one holds the bag in his hand, he is permitted to urinate with them /on his person/ according to all /authorities/. For when /*tefilin*/ are in their bag there is no /transgression of a/ prohibition involved if one breaks wind, as will be explained in Sec. 44.

(12) **For his words.** At a time of need, such as when one would have to neglect praying with the congregation because of this, he may rely on the first opinion. However, he must be very careful that he does not come to break wind. This is what the *Ch.A.* writes.

Nevertheless, it is the practice to take off the head /*tefilin* even in such a case/. /In the case of/ the arm /*tefilin*/ as well, it is proper to remove the straps from the palm, so that one will not come to wipe off the /sprinkling/ drops with them.

(13) **Without having been dug out.** /The author of the Shulchan Aruch/ means by this that in the case of such /a lavatory/ one is required to take off /*tefilin*/ at a distance of four cubits /away/.

On the other hand, if /the place for the excrement/ has been dug out /, as described in Sec. 83, Par. 4 below/, the dug out /area/ is of course an independent area and /the part of/ the lavatory above is an independent area. /In view of this, the part above/ does not have the ruling of a lavatory at all, as will be explained in Sec. 83 /, Par. 4/ below. It is /therefore/ permitted /for one/ to enter into it with *tefilin* on him. Nevertheless, according to all /authorities/, one must take off /the *tefilin* even in such a lavatory/ before he may urinate, just as /one is required to do/ in /any/ permanent lavatory. This is the conclusion of the *M.A.*

/However, it should be noted that/ this ruling only applies as regards urinating, but it is implied by the words of the *B.Y.* that /if one wishes/ to relieve himself he should be stringent and take off /the *tefilin*/ at a distance of four cubits /away/ from the place where he wishes to relieve himself. /In fact, one is required to do so/ even if he excretes in a place which is not a lavatory at all, but in his courtyard or in a field.

2* *Rambam, Hilchos Tefilin* 4:17.

3* In the Beyur Halachah, the author writes that it appears that if it is usual to relieve oneself in that lavatory, it has the ruling of a permanent lavatory even when it does not have excrement.

דליכא למיחש לניצוצות אבל משתין מעומד (ד) פשיטא דאסור דלא עדיף מבית הכסא עראי וה"ה אם משתין מיושב או בעפר (ה) תחוח דליכא ניצוצות בבית הכסא עראי (ו) נמי שרי ואין חילוק בין קבע לעראי לענין זה אלא דבה"כ קבוע מסתמא עושה צרכיו (ג) מיושב ובה"כ עראי מסתמא עושה מעומד הואיל ואינו נפנה (ד) לגדולים (ב"י בשם נ"י ומגדל עוז) * (ז) [ג]ובבית הכסא עראי מותר להשתין בהם כשהם בראשו [ד]אבל אם אוחזן בידו אסור להשתין בהם מעומד אפילו אם תופס אותם בבגדו (ח) מפני שצריך לשפשף בידו ניצוצות שברגליו אלא (ט) חולצן ברחוק (ה) ד' אמות ונותנם (י) לחבירו [ה]ומדברי הרמב"ם נראה שאסור להשתין (יא) כשהם בראשו בין בבית הכסא קבוע בין בבית הכסא עראי ויש לחוש (יב) לדבריו: **ב** * [ו]בית הכסא קבוע היינו שיש בו צואה והוא על פני השדה (יג) בלא (ו) חפירה: **ג * (יד) [ז]בית הכסא עראי (ז) היינו כגון להשתין מים שאין אדם הולך בשבילם לבית הכסא והפעם הזאת נעשה המקום הזה (טו) בית הכסא תחלה: ד (טז) [ח]אם הם בחיקו וחגור חגורה (יז) או בבגדו בידו מותר בין להשתין בין (ח) לפנות: ה [ט]אם רוצה ליכנס (יח) לבית הכסא [י]קבוע לעשות צרכיו חולצן ברחוק ארבע אמות:** הגה ויש אומרים אפילו בלא (ט) צרכיו (ב"י בשם רבי האי) (יט) וטוב להחמיר: **וגוללן ברצועות שלהן**

באר הגולה

ג תוס' שם והרא"ש בה"ת וסמ"ג וספר התרומה ד שם בגמ' ה בפרק ד' מהלכות תפילין ו רש"י שם בגמרא ז שם ברש"י ח ס' התרומה ט שם בגמרא י כן הוא בגמרא שם אבל הב"י כתב שהטור לפי גירסתו שלפניו והרמב"ם והרי"ף והרא"ש לא חלקו בין קבוע לעראי

באר היטב

(ג) מיושב. לכן כשהם בראשו אסור אפי' להשתין גזירה שמא יעשה צרכיו: (ד) לגדולים. לכן בבה"כ עראי מותר דלא גזרינן שמא יפנה בהם: (ה) ד"א. וכ"כ הטור וקאי ארישא דהיינו בבה"כ קבוע דאסור להשתין כשהם בראשו אלא חולצן ברחוק ד"א ומתילא שמעינן בבה"כ עראי דאסור כשהם בידו אין תקנה רק שיתנם לחבירו אבל מ"מ א"צ להסיר מידו ברחוק ד"א. ט"ז מ"א. ובתשובת מטה יוסף ח"ב סימן ה' הבין שמ"ש הטור אלא חולצן ברחוק ד"א קאי נמי לבה"כ עראי ומש"ה הרבה להקשות ע"ש ולא דק. ועיין ב"ח: (ו) חפירה. אבל כשהוא בחפירה חולץ ומשתין לאלתר וא"צ להרחיק ד"א. מ"א ע"ש: (ז) היינו. ר"ל הא דאמרינן לעיל דמותר להשתין בו בתפילין שבראשו היינו במקום שאין רגילות לפנות שם: (ח) לפנות. צ"ע דבס"א כתב אפי' תופס אותם בבגדו אסור וי"ל דהכא מיירי שקשורים בבגדו שאף אם ישפשף בידו לא יפלו התפילין מ"א וע' ט"ז: (ט) צרכיו. והא דנקט הטור והש"ע סעיף א' אסור ליכנס להשתין וכו' לרבותא נקט להשתין אע"פ שהוא חייו של

ביאור הלכה

* ובבה"כ עראי מותר להשתין בהם כשהם בראשו. פשוט דה"ה לענין תפילין של זרועו וכן איתא להדיא בספר התרומה ודלא כהפמ"ג ונראה שיסיר הכריכות מעל כף ידו שלא יבוא לשפשף בם: * בה"כ קבוע היינו שיש בו וכו'. נראה לכאורה דאפילו אם עתה אין בו צואה כלל כיון דהוא מקום שרגילין לפנות שם גזרינן שמא יעשה צרכיו ולא נקט המחבר לשון זה רק להורות לנו דאם יש צואה במקום הזה תו חיישינן שמא הוא יעשה צרכיו ג"כ במקום הזה ואפילו אם עד עתה לא היה זה המקום מיוחד לפנות ובזה ניחא מה דסיים המחבר בלי חפירה להורות דאם הוא בחפירה חשוב כמאן דליתא ומותר אם אותו המקום אינו מיוחד לפנות עד עתה ועין במ"א סק"ו מה שתמה על המחבר ולפ"ז ניחא הכל: * בה"כ עראי וכו' בה"כ תחלה. עין במ"ב בשם הפמ"ג ואם הוא מקום המסריח מפני מי רגלים המצוי תמיד שם לכאורה המקום הזה דין בה"כ קבוע יש לו דלא גרע מעביט של מי רגלים המסריח דדינו כצואה

משנה ברורה

ובי"ד (ג) ימינו כנגד לבו כמש"כ בס"ה: (ד) פשיטא דאסור. באוחזן בידו שמא יקנח הניצוצות וה"ה כשהם בראשו דאסור דחיישינן שמא ישב ויעשה בהם צרכיו [פמ"ג]: (ה) תיחוח. או במקום (ד) מדרון: (ו) נמי שרי ואין חילוק וכו'. ומ"מ (ה) יש חילוק קצת דבקבע דיש חשש שמא יעשה צרכיו צריך שיהיה בבגדו ובידו כמ"ש בסק"ג ובעראי אפילו בידו לבד נמי מותר כיון דליכא חשש ניצוצות: (ז) ובבה"כ עראי וכו'. דלא גזרינן ביה שמא יפנה בהם ורק שיזהר שלא יפיח בהם: (ח) מפני שצריך וכו'. וחיישינן (ו) שמא ישפשף הניצוצות שנופלין על רגליו ביד שאוחז בה התפילין: (ט) חולצן ברחוק וכו'. עיין מ"א שכתב דמש"כ המחבר מתחלה אסור להשתין בהן מעומד מיירי בין בעראי ובין בקבוע וכמו שכ' בהג"ה ומש"כ אלא חולצן ברחוק ד"א מיירי בקבוע דאי בבה"כ עראי הולך ומשתין לאלתר וכ"כ הט"ז: (י) לחבירו. דהוא בעצמו אסור לאחוז בהן או (ז) אף דמיירי בקבוע ומבואר לקמן בס"ה דיאחזו בבגדו וידו כיון דמיירי כשמשתין מעומד וחיישינן משום ניצוצות: (יא) כשהן בראשו. (ח) וה"ה בזרועו דס"ל דגזרינן שמא יפיח בהם אבל כשהן בכיסן ואוחז הכיס בידו מותר להשתין בהן לד"ה שכשהן בכיסן אין איסור בהפחה כמו שיתבאר בסימן מ"ד: (יב) לדבריו. ולעת הצורך כגון שיתבטל ע"ז תפלה בצבור יכול לסמוך אדיעה ראשונה אך שיזהר הרבה שלא יבוא לידי הפחה כ"כ הח"א ומ"מ נוהגין לחלוץ הש"ר. וגם הש"י (ט) נכון להסיר הרצועות מכף היד שלא יבוא לשפשף הניצוצות בהם: **ב (יג) בלא חפירה.** ר"ל או צריך לחלוץ ברחוק ד"א אבל אם הוא בחפירה הרי החפירה היא רשות לעצמו ובה"כ שלמעלה רשות לעצמו ואין לו דין בה"כ כלל כמו שיתבאר בסימן ע"ג ומותר ליכנס בתוכו בתפילין שעליו ומ"מ קודם שישתין צריך לחלוץ לד"ה כמו בשאר בה"כ קבוע כן מסיק המ"א בד"א להשתין אבל לעשות צרכיו משמע מדברי הב"י דיש להחמיר לחלוץ ברחוק ד"א ממקום שרוצה לעשות צרכיו (י) אפילו נפנה במקום שאינו בה"כ כלל אלא בתליו או ע"פ השדה: **ג (יד) בה"כ עראי וכו'.** פי' הא דאמרינן לעיל דמותר להשתין בו בתפילין שבראשו היינו במקום שאין בו צואה וגם הוא מקום שאין רגילין לפנות שם ולכך לא גזרינן שמא יפנה בהתפילין (יא) ואפילו אם הוא מקום גנוע: **(טו) בה"כ תחלה.** עיין בפמ"ג דס"ל דהאי לישנא לאו דוקא דאפילו מיוחד מכמה זמנים להשתין מ"מ עראי יחשב: **ד (טז) אם הם בחיקו וכו'.** דתו ליכא למיחש משום ניצוצות וגם משום שמא יפלו ממנו ומותר בין בבה"כ קבוע (יב) ובין בעראי: **(יז) או בבגדו בידו.** צ"ע דבס"א כתב אפילו תופס אותם בבגדו אסור ועיין בט"ז ומ"א שנדחקו בזה מאד ובביאור הגר"א כתב דסעיף זה שהוא מבעל התרומות הוא שיטה אחרת החולק על הא דס"א וס"ל דבבגדו וידו תו לא חיישינן לשפשוף הניצוצות וכן הכריח בספר מאמר מרדכי. ובקשורין בבגדו (יג) לכו"ע מותר: **ה (יח) לבה"כ קבוע.** (יד) נקט קבוע משום סיפא לאשמועינן דאפילו בקבוע מכניס התפילין עמו משום שמירה אבל אה"נ דאפילו באינו קבוע כלל צריך לחלוץ ברחוק ד"א ממקום שרוצה לפנות וכדלעיל בסוף ס"ק י"ג. וכן מה דנקט לעשות צרכיו ג"כ משום רבותא דסיפא אבל באמת ה"ה להשתין צריך לחלוץ ברחוק ד"א וכדלעיל בס"א: **(יט) וטוב להחמיר.** המ"א מסיק דמדינא אסור לכנס לבהכ"ס בתפילין דלא גרע ממרחץ לקמן בסימן מ"ה ס"ב ועיין בפמ"ג ובמאמר מרדכי שכתבו דמדברי הרא"ש לא משמע הכי גם מדברי

שער הציון

(ג) ע"ת וא"ר: (ד) רמב"ם וב"י: (ה) פמ"ג: (ו) ב"י: (ז) ממ"א ופמ"ג: (ח) מסתימת לשון הרמב"ם וכן משמע בשו"ע של הגר"ז אכן מצאתי בסוף הסימן בפמ"ג שמצדד להיתר בשם הא"ר: (ט) מישועות יעקב: (י) הגר"ז: (יא) הגר"ז: (יב) מט"ז: (יג) מ"א: (יד) מאמר מרדכי:

3. By **(14)** a provisional lavatory is meant /a place which one uses/ in an instance /when he wishes/ to urinate, since a person does not go to a /permanent/ lavatory /just/ to /urinate/ and the place becomes /used as/ **(15)** a lavatory for the first /time/, on that occasion.

4. **(16)** If /the *tefilin*/ are inside one's bosom and one's belt is fastened **(17)** or are in one's garment in one's hand, it is permitted both to urinate and to excrete.

5. If one wishes to enter **(18)** a permanent lavatory to relieve himself he should take off /the *tefilin*/ at a distance of four cubits /from the lavatory/.

Gloss: There are /authorities/ who say /that one should do so/ even when he does not /enter to/ relieve himself. (...) **(19)** *It is desirable to be stringent.*

Mishnah Berurah

(14) A provisional lavatory, etc. I.e., when we rule above that it is permitted to urinate in /a provisional lavatory/ with *tefilin* on one's head, what is meant is a place which does not have excrement and it /must also be/ a place where it is not usual to excrete. That is why /the Sages/ did not decree /a prohibition against this for fear/ that one may /come to/ excrete with *tefilin* on him, even if /the provisional lavatory/ is in a secluded spot.

(15) A lavatory for the first /time/. See the *P.Mg.*, who is of the opinion that this wording is not /meant to be taken/ literally, but even if /the place has been used/ specifically on several occasions for urinating it is nevertheless considered a provisional /lavatory/.

(16) If /the *tefilin*/ are inside one's bosom, etc. For there are thenceforth no grounds to fear /anything/ because of /sprinkling/ drops and /one need/ also /have no fear/ that they may fall from him.

/In these cases/ it is permitted both in a permanent and in a provisional lavatory.

(17) Or are in one's garment in one's hand. /This ruling/ requires /further/ study, as it is stated in Par. 1 that it is forbidden even if one grasps them with his garment. See the *Taz* and the *M.A.* who give very forced /explanations/ to /reconcile/ this. /However, the *Gra*/ writes in the *Beyur Ha-Gra* that /the wording of/ this paragraph, which is /taken/ from the author of the /*Sefer*/ *Ha-Terumah*, /follows/ a different view, which disputes that /ruling/ of Par. 1. /The author of that work/ is of the opinion that /when the *tefilin* are/ in one's garment in one's hand we are no longer afraid about the wiping off of the /sprinkling/ drops. This is likewise proved in the work *Ma'amar Mordechai*.

When /the *tefilin*/ are tied inside one's garment it is permitted according to all /authorities/.

(18) A permanent lavatory. /The author of the Shulchan Aruch/ speaks of a permanent /lavatory/ because of the latter /part/ of the ruling, which teaches us that one may take *tefilin* with him even into a permanent /lavatory/ because of /the need to/ safeguard them. However, even in the case of /a lavatory/ which is not permanent in any way, one is indeed also required to take off /the *tefilin*/ at a distance of four cubits /away/ from where he wishes to excrete, as /stated/ above at the end of sub-Par. 13.

Likewise, /when the author of the Shulchan Aruch/ speaks of "to relieve himself", this is also /done/ to /give/ a wider /ruling/ in the latter part /of the ruling/. However, in actual fact, one must take off /the *tefilin*/, correspondingly, at a distance of four cubits /away, even when he merely wishes/ to urinate, as /stated/ above in Par. 1.

(19) It is desirable to be stringent. The *M.A.* concludes that it is prohibited from /the point of view of binding/ halachah to enter a lavatory with *tefilin* on. /He argues that/ this must be no less /forbidden/ than /having *tefilin* on in/ a bathhouse /, which is forbidden, as ruled/ below in Sec. 45, Par. 2.

See the *P.Mg.* and the *Ma'amar Mordechai*, who write /with respect to this ruling of the *M.A.*/ that the words of the *Rosh* indicate

* ואוחזן (י) (כ) בימינו [כ] ובבגדו כנגד לבו [ל] ויזהר שלא תהא רצועה יוצאה מתחת ידו טפח וכשיוצא מרחיק ארבע אמות ומניחן: ו [מ] היה לבוש בתפילין והוצרך לבית הכסא בלילה או סמוך לחשיכה שאין שהות להניחם עוד אחר שיצא לא יכנס בהם (כא) גלולין בבגדו * ואפילו להשתין מים *בבית הכסא קבוע אלא כיצד יעשה חולצן * ומניחן בכלי (כב) אם היה בו טפח או בכלי שאינו כליין אע"פ שאין בו טפח [נ] ואוחז הכלי (כג) בידו ונכנס: ז [ס] בד"א בבית הכסא שבשדה אבל בבית הכסא שבבית לא יכניסם (כד) כלל כיון שיכול להניחם במקום (יא) [א] (כה) המשתמר: ח [ע] אם שכח תפילין בראשו ועשה בהם צרכיו מניח ידו עליהן (כו) עד שיגמור עמוד (יב) הראשון ויוצא וחולצן וחוזר ונכנס: ט [פ] מותר (כז) לרופא ליקח עביט של מי רגלים בידו ותפילין בראשו ובעל נפש יחמיר לעצמו:

כ כר"ע שם הרמב"ם שם והטור ור' יונה ל שם בגמרא מ שם נ רמב"ם שם פ"ד ס ספר התרומה והטור ור' ירוחם ע שם בגמרא כ"ה פ תשובת הרשב"א

מד איסור שינה בתפילין ובו סעיף א':

א [א] כל זמן שהתפילין בראשו או בזרועו אסור לישן בהם * אפילו שינת (א) עראי [ב] אלא אם הניח עליהם

א ברכות כ"ג וסוכה כ"ו ב שם בגמרא

באר היטב

אדם אפ"ה אסור ליכנס וכ"ש שלא לצורך עמ"א: (י) בימינו. אבל לא בשמאלו מפני שצריך לקנח בה כמ"ש סימן ג'[א] והכא ליכא נילוצות כיון שמיירי בב"ה קבוע מסתמא עושה צרכיו מיושב. כתב הרמ"ע סי' נ"ט דמותר ליכנס בתפילין למבואות המטונפות אפי' יש מקום מטונף להדיא וטוב לכסותו בכובע ואם רוצה לחלצן ולחזור ולהניחן ש"ד. עמ"א: (יא) המשתמר. משמע אפי' בכים לא יכניסם אבל להשתין בב"ה עראי אם הם בכיסן שרי אף להרמב"ם עמ"א. ומשמע בגמרא דכל הני שריותא אינן אלא בתפילין שלובשן כל היום וא"א להטריח אבל שאר ספרים אסור להכניסן אפי' בב"ה שבשדה מיהו אם הם בכים שרי להכניסן חוץ מס"ת שאסור מ"א: (יב) הראשון. דעמוד החוזר מביא האדם לידי הדרוקן וסילון החוזר מביא האדם לידי ירקון:

שערי תשובה

[א] המשתמר. עבה"ט ובא"ר בשם נ"צ[ב] דתפילין וכתבים שיש בהם שמות צריך ליתן תיק בתוך תיק אם צריך ליכנס לבה"כ ונהגו לקנות כליס של עור ובי"ד סימן רפ"ב[ג] קמיע מחופה בעור מותר וע"ש בשם ש"ג בקמיען[ד] שעושין לתינוקות מחופין וחקוק עליהם אותיות של שם נ"ע ובא"ר כתב הטעם לפי שהוא חקיקה ולא כתיבה ונראה דאותן שמלבישין התינוקות בקמיע שכתוב שמות בקלף צריך ליזהר שיהיה כלי בתוך כלי כיון שהתינוקות נפנים בהם בעודם עליהם ועיין בסי' רפ"ב:

משנה ברורה

מדברי רב האי לא משמע הכי ע"ש ובספר האשכול בשם הגאון משמע כתירוצו דהמג"א עי"ש: (כ) בימינו. אבל לא בשמאלו מפני שצריך לקנח בה כמש"כ בס"ג[א] והכא ליכא למיחש לניצוצות שיבוא לשפשף ביד שאוחז בה התפילין דכיון שמיירי בבה"כ קבוע מסתמא עושה צרכיו מיושב. כתב הרמ"ע סימן נ"ט דמותר לכנס בתפילין למבואות המטונפות אפי' יש שם מקום מטונף להדיא וטוב לכסותו בכובע ואם רוצה לחלצן ולחזור ולהניחן שפיר דמי והמג"א מלמד לומר דכשיודע שיכנס דרך מבואות המטונפות לא יניחם בביתו אלא בבהכ"נ או שיניחם בביתו ויכסם במבואות המטונפות ונסתפק המחה"ש דאפשר דצריך לכסות ג"כ הרצועות וכ"ש ג' כריכות שעל האצבע ובתשובות רדב"ז ח"ד סימן ל"ו משמע ג"כ שסובר דמדינא צריך לכסות התפילין במקומות המטונפות וכל שאי אפשר לו לכסותם מוטב שיניחם בבהכ"נ ומשמע שם דהדלי"ת והיו"ד שברצועות אין צריך לכסות שהם דרך קשירה לא דרך כתיבה עי"ש: ו (כא) גלולין בבגדו. ר"ל (טו) מה שהותר בסעיף הקודם לאוחזן בימינו בבגדו דוקא כשיש לו שהות להניחם עוד אח"כ לא הטריחוהו להניחם בכלי משא"כ באין שהות (כב) אם היה בו טפח. אבל כשאין בו טפח בטל לגבי התפילין כיון שהוא כליין ואסור להכניסם לבה"כ: (כג) בידו ונכנס. שלא יטלו אותם עוברי דרכים [גמרא עי"ש]: ז (כד) כלל. משמע (טז) דאפילו בכים לא יכניסם ועיין במנחת השקל שכתב דאם הם בכיסן ונותן בכים התפור במלבושו דאותו כים אינו כליין והוי כלי תוך כלי ומותר: (כה) המשתמר. ושאר ספרים וכתבים שיש בהן שמות (יז) אם הם בכים שרי להכניסן (יח) ויש אומרים דבעינן דוקא תיק בתוך תיק. אם צריך ליכנס לבה"כ וכדלעיל לענין תפילין וס"ת אסור בכל גווני. וכתב בס"ת דאותן המלבישין התינוקות בקמיע שכתוב שמות בקלף צריך ליזהר שיהיה כלי בתוך כלי כיון שהתינוקות נפנים בהם בעודם עליהם: ח (כו) עד שיגמור. דעמוד החוזר מביא האדם לידי הדרוקן וסילון החוזר מביא האדם לידי ירקון:

ט (כז) לרופא ליקח וכו'. לבדוק בו החולה וא"ל לחלוץ או התפילין ועובדא הוי ברופא וה"ה בכל אדם:

א (א) עראי. דגזרינן (א) שמא יבוא להפיח בהם וע"י הנחת הסודר עליהן

ביאור הלכה

מדאורייתא כמ"ש תר"י ולא גרע ממים סרוחים או מי משרה וכו' המבואר בסימן פ"ו דדינו כצואה עי"ש ואפשר דלענין זה לא מחלקינן בזה ובכל גווני מותר להשתין בו בתפילין שעליו ולא חיישינן בו שמא יפנה בו כיון דאינו מיוחד רק להשתין ואין לאסור מטעם המי רגלים גופא כיון דהוא מיוחד שם דינו כצואה דז"א דא"כ הא מי רגלים נגד העמוד ג"כ דינו כצואה ואפ"ה בבה"כ עראי מותר להשתין בתפילין שבראשו ואפילו בקבוע היה מותר אי לאו דחיישינן שמא יפנה בהם וא"כ אפשר דבזה לא חיישינן שמא יפנה ומותר:

* ואוחזן בימינו. עיין במ"ב מש"כ בשם הרמ"ע להקל והרדב"ז מחמיר. ובספר אור זרוע אשר זכינו מקרוב לאורו משמע כהרמ"ע דכתב בסי' תקפ"ו דמותר לעבור בבית הכסא לפי דרכו שלא לצורך נקביו ותפילין בראשו. ומשמע מלשונו שהוא מחלק בין אם הוא עובר או שהוא קובע עצמו להיות שם ובזה יש ליישב קצת קושית המג"א בסק"ט ממרחץ דמולך כמ"ש סימן מ"ה סעיף ב' ואע"ג דלענין ד"ת לא מחלקינן בין מהלך או עומד בברכות כ"ד ע"ב לענין זה מחלקינן: * ואפילו להשתין מים. ר"ל במיושב או בעפר תיחוח דליכא משום ניצוצות וכדלעיל בס"א: * בבה"כ קבוע. וה"ה לענין בה"כ עראי ותפילין שבראשו. [ביאור מהרמ"כ על המרדכי]: * ומניחן בכלי אם היה בו טפח וכו'. עיין במ"ב והמ"א הביא עוד בשם רש"י דאם הכלי היה טפח חשיב הכלי אוהל להפסיק בינם לקרקע ומותר להניחם בביתו ע"ג קרקע ובכלי שאינו כליין אפילו פחות מטפח:

* אפילו שינת עראי. דלא כהרא"ש ור"י שמתירין שינת עראי ובביאור הגר"א בריש הסימן משמע שדעתו לפסוק כמותם להקל אך לדעתו לא מיקרי שינת עראי כ"א כדי הילוך ק' אמה ואף בזה דוקא אם הניח ראשו בין ברכיו

יזכור

שער הציון

(טו) לבש"ר: (טז) מ"א: (יז) מ"א ועיין בפמ"ג דאפילו בבה"כ שבבית והגר"ז מחמיר וברדב"ז משמע להקל: (יח) א"ר: (א) מפמ"ג:

הגהות ותיקונים: א) בסימן ג' סקי"ז: ב) כתב: ג) ס"ו: ד) בקמיעין:

הערות והארות: 1) עיין במ"ב סי' ש"א ס"ק ק"א לענין לפנות בקמיע כשהוא מחופה בעור:

He should roll them up in their straps and hold them **(20)** in his right /hand/ and inside his garment against his heart. He must take care that a strap does not protrude underneath his hand for /as much as/ a handbreadth.

When he goes out /of the lavatory/ he should move away /from it/ four cubits and may /then/ don /the *tefilin*/.

6. If one is wearing *tefilin* and needs /to go/ to a lavatory at night or close to dark, so that there will be no time /left for him/ to don them additionally after he has left /the lavatory/, he should not enter a permanent lavatory[4*] with them **(21)** rolled up in his garment, even if /only/ to urinate.

Instead, he should act as follows. He should take them off and put them in a receptacle, **(22)** provided /that the receptacle/ has /a space the height of/ a handbreadth. Alternatively, /he may put them/ in a receptacle which is not a

Mishnah Berurah

differently. The implication of the words of *Rav Hai* also differs /from the *M.A.*'s ruling/; see there. /However,/ the explanation of the *M.A.* is implied in the *Sefer Ha-Eshkol*, in the name of a Gaon; see there.

(20) In his right. However, /he should/ not /hold them/ in his left /hand/, because he needs to wipe with it, as stated in Sec. 3 /, Par. 10./

In these circumstances there are no grounds for fear /because/ of /sprinkling/ drops /, i.e.,/ that one would come to wipe off /sprinkling drops/ with the hand with which he is holding the *tefilin*. For in view /of the fact/ that a permanent lavatory is being referred to he will probably relieve himself sitting.

The *Rema* /of Fano/ writes in Sec. 59 that one is permitted to enter with *tefilin* on into dirty alleyways, even if there is obviously a dirty place there. It is desirable to cover /the *tefilin* then/ with a hat. If one wishes to take them off /beforehand/ and put them on again /subsequently/ this is in order. The *M.A.* adopts the view that where one knows that he will be entering through dirty alleyways he should not don /*tefilin*/ at home, but /only when he arrives/ at the Synagogue. Alternatively, he should don them at home and cover them /while he is/ in the dirty alleyways. The *Mach. Hash.* is in doubt as /to whether/ one may also be required to cover the straps and, all the more so, the three coils on the finger. It is also implied in a responsum of the *Radbaz*, Part 4, Sec. 36, that he is of the opinion that the halachah binds one to cover the *tefilin* /while he is/ in dirty places and whenever one will be unable to cover them /there/ it is preferable for him to don them /only when he arrives/ at the Synagogue. It is implied there that it is unnecessary to cover the /letter/ ד and the /letter/ י /formed/ in the straps, as they are /formed/ by tying and not by writing. See there.

(21) Rolled up in his garment. I.e., when /the author of the Shulchan Aruch/ permits one in the previous paragraphs to hold /*tefilin*/ in his right /hand/ inside his garment /when he goes into a lavatory/, this only /applies/ when he will have time /left/ to don them additionally subsequently. /Then, the Sages/ did not burden him with putting them in a receptacle. /The ruling/ does not apply /, however,/ when one will not have time /to don them again/.

(22) Provided /that the receptacle/ has /a space the height of/ a handbreadth. However, when it does not have a /space the height of/ a handbreadth it becomes secondary to the *tefilin*, since it is a receptacle which is /specifically used/ for them. It is /therefore/ forbidden to take /*tefilin*/ into the lavatory /in that receptacle/.

4* The same ruling applies if one wishes to enter a provisional lavatory and has *tefilin* on his head. (Beyur Halachah)

* ואוחזן (י) (כ) בימינו ^ו^ ובבגדו כנגד לבו ^ל^ ויזהר שלא תהא רצועה יוצאה מתחת ידו טפח וכשיוצא מרחיק ארבע אמות ומניחן: ו ^מ^ היה לבוש בתפילין והוצרך לבית הכסא בלילה או סמוך לחשיכה שאין שהות להניחם עוד אחר שיצא לא יכנס בהם (כא) גלולין בבגדו * ואפילו להשתין מים *בבית הכסא קבוע אלא כיצד יעשה חולצן * ומניחן בכלי (כב) אם היה בו טפח או בכלי שאינו **כליין אע"פ שאין בו טפח ^נ^ ואוחז הכלי (כג) בידו ונכנס: ז ^ס^ בד"א בבית הכסא שבשדה אבל בבית הכסא שבבית לא יכניסם (כד) כלל כיון שיכול להניחם במקום (יא) [א] (כה) המשתמר:** ח ^ע^ אם שכח תפילין בראשו ועשה בהם צרכיו מניח ידו עליהן (כו) עד שיגמור עמוד (יב) הראשון ויוצא וחולצן וחוזר ונכנס: ט ^פ^ מותר (כז) לרופא ליקח עביט של מי רגלים בידו ותפילין בראשו ובעל נפש יחמיר לעצמו:

כ כר"ע שם הרמב"ם שם והטור ור' יונה ל שם בגמרא מ שם נ רמב"ם שם פ"ד ס ספר התרומה והטור ור' ירוחם ע שם בגמרא כ"ה פ תשובת הרשב"א

מד איסור שינה בתפילין ובו סעיף א':

א ^א^ כל זמן שהתפילין בראשו או בזרועו אסור לישן בהם * אפילו שינת (א) עראי ^ב^ אלא אם הניח עליהם

א ברכות כ"ג וסוכה כ"ו ב שם בגמרא

באר היטב

אדם אפ"ה אסור ליכנס וכ"ש שלא לצורך עמ"א: (י) בימינו. אבל לא בשמאלו מפני שצריך לקנח בה כמ"ש סימן ג' ^א^ והכא ליכא ניצוצות כיון שמיירי בב"ה קבוע מסתמא עושה צרכיו מיושב. כתב הרמ"ע סי' נ"ט דמותר ליכנס בתפילין למבואות המטונפות אפי' יש מקום מטונף להדיא וטוב לכסותו בכובע ואם רוצה לחלצן ולחזור ולהניחן ש"ד. עמ"א: (יא) המשתמר. משמע אפי' בכיס לא יכניסם אבל להשתין בב"ה עראי אם הם בכיסן שרי אף להרמב"ם עמ"א. ומשמע בגמרא דכל הני שריותא אינן אלא בתפילין שלובשן כל היום וא"א להטריח אבל שאר ספרים אסור להכניסן אפי' בב"ה שבשדה מיהו אם הם בכיס שרי להכניסן חוץ מס"ת שאסור מ"א: (יב) הראשון. דעמוד החוזר מביא האדם לידי הדרוקן וסילון החוזר מביא האדם לידי ירקון:

שערי תשובה

[א] המשתמר. עבה"ט ובא"ר בשם נ"צ ^ב^ דתפילין וכתבים שיש בהם שמות צריך ליתן תיק בתוך תיק אם צריך ליכנס לבה"כ ונהגו לקנות כליס של עור ובי"ד סימן רפ"ב ^ג^ קמיע מחופה בעור מותר וע"ש בשם ש"ג בקמיען ^ד^ שעושין לתינוקות מחופין וחקוק עליהם אותיות של שם ל"ע ובא"ר כתב הטעם לפי שהוא חקיקה ולא כתיבה ונראה דאותן שמלבישין התינוקות בקמיע שכתוב שמות בקלף צריך ליזהר שיהיה כלי בתוך כלי כיון שהתינוקות נפנים בהם בעודם עליהם ועיין בסי' רפ"ב:

משנה ברורה

מדברי רב האי לא משמע הכי ע"ש ובספר האשכול בשם הגאון משמע כפירושו דהמג"א ע"ש: (כ) בימינו. אבל לא בשמאלו מפני שצריך לקנח בה כמש"כ בס"ג ^א^ והכא ליכא למיחש לניצוצות שיבוא לשפשף ביד שאוחז בה התפילין דכיון שמיירי בבה"כ קבוע מסתמא עושה צרכיו מיושב. כתב הרמ"ע סימן נ"ט דמותר לכנס בתפילין למבואות המטונפות אפי' יש שם מקום מטונף להדיא וטוב לכסותו בכובע ואם רוצה לחלצן ולחזור ולהניחן שפיר דמי והמג"א מלמד לומר דכשיודע שיכנס דרך מבואות המטונפות לא יניחם בביתו אלא בבהכ"נ או שיניחם בביתו ויכסם במבואות המטונפות ונסתפק המחה"ש דאפשר דצריך לכסות ג"כ הרצועות וכ"ש ג' כריכות שעל האצבע ובתשובות רדב"ז ח"ד סימן ל"ו משמע ג"כ שסובר דמדינא צריך לכסות התפילין במקומות המטונפות וכל שאי אפשר לו לכסותם מוטב שיניחם בבהכ"נ ומשמע שם דהדלי"ת והיו"ד שברצועות אין צריך לכסות שהם דרך קשירה לא דרך כתיבה ע"ש: ו (כא) גלולין בבגדו. ר"ל (טו) מה שהותר בסעיף הקודם לאוחזן בימינו בבגדו דוקא כשיש לו שהות להניחם עוד אח"כ לא הטריחוהו להניחם בכלי משא"כ באין שהות (כב) אם היה בו טפח. אבל כשאין בו טפח בטל לגבי התפילין כיון שהוא כליין ואסור להכניסם לבה"כ: **(כג) בידו ונכנס. שלא יטלו אותם עוברי דרכים [גמרא עי"ש]: ז (כד) כלל. משמע (טז) דאפילו בכיס לא יכניסם ועיין במחצית השקל שכתב דאם הם בכיסן ונותן בכיס התפור במלבושו דאותו כיס אינו כליין והוי כלי תוך כלי ומותר: (כה) המשתמר. ושאר ספרים וכתבים שיש בהן שמות (יז) אם הם בכיס שרי להכניסן (יח) ויש אומרים דבעינן דוקא תיק בתוך תיק ^1)^ אם צריך ליכנס לבה"כ וכדלעיל לענין תפילין וס"ת אסור בכל גווני. וכתב בש"ת דאותן המלבישין התינוקות בקמיע שכתוב שמות בקלף צריך ליזהר** שיהיה כלי בתוך כלי כיון שהתינוקות נפנים בהם בעודם עליהם: ח (כו) עד שיגמור. דעמוד החוזר מביא האדם לידי הדרוקן וסילון החוזר מביא האדם לידי ירקון: ט (כז) לרופא ליקח וכו'. לבדוק בו החולה וא"צ לחלוץ אז התפילין ועובדא הוי ברופא וה"ה בכל אדם:

א (א) עראי. דגזרינן (א) שמא יפוח להפיח בהם וע"י הנחת הסודר עליהן

ביאור הלכה

מדאורייתא כמ"ש תר"י ולא גרע ממים סרוחים או מי משרה וכו' המבואר בסימן פ"ו דדינו כצואה עי"ש ואפשר דלענין זה לא מחלקינן בזה ובכל גווני מותר להשתין בו בתפילין שעליו ולא חיישינן בו שמא יפנה בו כיון דאינו מיוחד רק להשתין ואין לאסור מטעם המי רגלים גופא כיון דהוא מיוחד שם דינו כצואה דז"א דא"כ הא מי רגלים נגד העמוד ג"כ דינו כצואה ואפ"ה בבה"כ עראי מותר להשתין בתפילין שבראשו ואפילו בקבוע היה מותר אי לאו דחיישינן שמא יפנה בהם וא"כ אפשר דבזה לא חיישינן שמא יפנה ומותר:

* ואוחזן בימינו. עיין במ"ב מש"כ בשם הרמ"ע להקל והרדב"ז מחמיר. ובספר אור זרוע אשר זכינו מקרוב לאורו משמע כהרמ"ע דכתב בסי' תקפ"ו דמותר לעבור בבית הכסא לפי דרכו שלא לצורך נקביו ותפילין בראשו. ומשמע מלשונו שהוא מחלק בין אם הוא עובר או שהוא קובע עצמו להיות שם ובזה יש ליישב קצת קושית המג"א בסק"ט ממרחץ דאולך כמ"ש סימן מ"ה סעיף ב' ואע"ג דלענין ד"ת לא מחלקינן בין מהלך או עומד בברכות כ"ד ע"ב לענין זו מחלקינן: * ואפילו להשתין מים. ר"ל במיושב או בעפר תיחוח דליכא משום ניצוצות וכדלעיל בס"א: * בבה"כ קבוע. וה"ה לענין בה"כ עראי ותפילין שבראשו. [ביאור מהרמ"כ על המרדכי]: * ומניחן בכלי אם היה בו טפח וכו'. עיין במ"ב והמ"א הביא עוד בשם רש"י דאם הכלי היה טפח חשיב הכלי אוהל להפסיק בינם לקרקע ומותר להניחם בביתו ע"ג קרקע ובכלי שאינו כליין אפילו פחות מטפח:

* אפילו שינת עראי. דלא כהרא"ש ור"י שמתירין שינת עראי ובביאור הגר"א בריש הסימן משמע שדעתו לפסוק כמותם להקל אך לדעתו לא מיקרי שינת עראי כ"א כדי הילוך ק' אמה ואף בזה דוקא אם הניח ראשו בין ברכיו

שער הציון

(טו) לבו"ר: (טז) מ"א: (יז) מ"א ועיין בפמ"ג דאפילו בבה"כ שבבית והגר"ז מחמיר ורדב"ז משמע להקל: (יח) א"ר: (א) מפמ"ג:

הגהות ותיקונים: א) בסימן ג' סקי"ז: ב) כתב: ג) ס"ו: ד) בקמיעין:

הערות והארות: 1) עיין במ"ב סי' ש"א ס"ק ק"א לענין לפנות בקמיע כשהוא מחופה בעור:

receptacle /that is specifically used/ for them, even if it does not have /a space the height of/ a handbreadth. He may /then/ take hold of the receptacle (23) in his hand and enter[5*] /the lavatory/.

7. This ruling applies as regards a lavatory which is in a field, but where the lavatory is in a house one should not take /*tefilin*/ into /the lavatory/ (24) at all, since he can leave them in a place (25) which is safeguarded.

Mishnah Berurah

(23) In his hand and enter. So that passers-by will not take them. [Gemara;[1] see there.]

(24) At all. It is implied that one should not take /*tefilin*/ into /such a lavatory/ even in a bag. See the *Machatzis Ha-Shekel*, who writes that if they are in their bag one can put them in a pocket which is sewn into his clothing and /then/ it is permitted. /This is/ because the pocket is not a receptacle /specifically used/ for /the *tefilin*/ and /the *tefilin*/ will /therefore be ruled as being in/ a receptacle which is /itself/ inside a receptacle.

(25) Which is safeguarded. /As for/ other books and writings which contain /Divine/ Names, it is permitted to take them into /a lavatory/ if they are in a bag. /However,/ there are /authorities/ who say that they are required /to be in/ a case which is /itself/ inside a case if one must enter /with them/ into a lavatory, as /ruled/ above with respect to *tefilin*. It is forbidden /to take/ a Torah Scroll /into a lavatory/ in any manner.

It is stated in the *Sh.T.*, that those /people/ who put on children amulets of /Divine/ Names written on parchment, must take care

5* Once one has put *tefilin* in a receptacle which has a space of a handbreadth or is not specifically used for *tefilin*, he may also place the receptacle on the ground with the *tefilin* in it. (Beyur Halachah)

1 *Berachos* 23a.

* ואוחזן (י) (כ) בימינו [כ] ובבגדו כנגד לבו [ל] ויזהר שלא תהא רצועה יוצאה מתחת ידו טפח וכשיוצא מרחיק ארבע אמות ומניחן: ו [מ] היה לבוש בתפילין והוצרך לבית הכסא בלילה או סמוך לחשיכה שאין שהות להניחם עוד אחר שיצא לא יכנס בהם (כא) גלולין בבגדו * ואפילו להשתין מים *בבית הכסא קבוע אלא כיצד יעשה חולצן * ומניחן בכלי (כב) אם היה בו טפח או בכלי שאינו כליין אע"פ שאין בו טפח [נ] ואוחז הכלי (כג) בידו ונכנס: ז [ס] בד"א בבית הכסא שבשדה אבל בבית הכסא שבבית לא יכניסם (כד) בלל כיון שיכול להניחם במקום (יא) [א] (כה) המשתמר: **ח** [ע] אם שכח תפילין בראשו ועשה בהם צרכיו מניח ידו עליהן (כו) עד שיגמור עמוד (יב) הראשון ויוצא וחולצן וחוזר ונכנס: **ט** [פ] מותר (כז) לרופא ליקח עביט של מי רגלים בידו ותפילין בראשו ובעל נפש יחמיר לעצמו:

כ כר"ע שם הרמב"ם שם והטור ור' יונה
ל שם בגמרא מ שם
נ רמב"ם שם פ"ד
ס ספר התרומה והטור ור' ירוחם
ע שם בגמרא כ"ה
פ תשובת הרשב"א

מד איסור שינה בתפילין ובו סעיף א':

א [א] כל זמן שהתפילין בראשו או בזרועו אסור לישן בהם * אפילו שינת (א) עראי [ב] אלא אם הניח עליהם

א ברכות כ"ג וסוכה כ"ו ב שם בגמרא

באר היטב

אדם אפ"ה אסור ליכנס וכ"ש שלא לצורך עמ"א: (י) בימינו. אבל לא בשמאלו מפני שצריך לקנח בה כמ"ש סימן ג' [א] והכא ליכא ניצוצות כיון שמיירי בב"ה קבוע מסתמא עושה צרכיו מיושב. כתב הרמ"ע סי' נ"ט דמותר ליכנס בתפילין למבואות המטונפות אפי' יש מקום מטונף להדיא וטוב לכסותו בכובע ואם רוצה לחלצן ולחזור ולהניחן ש"ד. עמ"א: (יא) המשתמר. משמע אפי' בכיס לא יכניסם אבל להשתין בב"ה עראי אם הם בכיסן שרי אף להרמב"ם עמ"א. ומשמע בגמרא דלכל הני שריותא אינן אלא בתפילין שלובשן כל היום וא"א להטריח אבל שאר ספרים אסור להכניסן אפי' בב"ה שבשדה מיהו אם הם בכיס שרי להכניסן חוץ מס"ת שאסור מ"א: (יב) הראשון. דעמוד החוזר מביא האדם לידי הדרוקן וסילון החוזר מביא האדם לידי ירקון:

שערי תשובה

[א] המשתמר. עבה"ט ובא"ר בשם נ"צ [ב] דתפילין וכתבים שיש בהם שמות צריך ליתן תיק בתוך תיק אם צריך ליכנס לבה"כ ונהגו לקנות כליס של עור ובי"ד סימן רפ"ב [ג] קמיע מחופה בעור מותר וע"ש בשם ש"ג בקמיען [ד] שעושין לתינוקות מחופין וחקוק עליהם אותיות של שם ל"ע ובא"ר כתב הטעם לפי שהוא חקיקה ולא כתיבה ונראה דאותן שמלבישין התינוקות בקמיע שכתוב שמות בקלף צריך ליזהר שיהיה כלי בתוך כלי כיון שהתינוקות נפנים בהם בעודם עליהם ועיין בסי' רפ"ב:

משנה ברורה

מדברי רב האי לא משמע הכי ע"ש ובספר האשכול בשם הגאון משמע כפירושו דהמג"א ע"ש: (כ) בימינו. אבל לא בשמאלו מפני שצריך לקנח בה כמש"כ בס"ג [א] והכא ליכא למיחש לניצוצות שיבוא לשפשף ביד שאוחז בה התפילין דכיון שמיירי בבה"כ קבוע מסתמא עושה צרכיו מיושב. כתב הרמ"ע סימן נ"ט דמותר לכנס בתפילין למבואות המטונפות אפי' יש שם מקום מטונף להדיא וטוב לכסותו בכובע ואם רוצה לחלצן ולחזור ולהניחן שפיר דמי והמג"א מלמד לומר דכשיודע שיכנס דרך מבואות המטונפות לא יניחם בביתו אלא בבהכ"נ או שיניחם בביתו ויכסם במבואות המטונפות ונסתפק המחה"ש דאפשר דצריך לכסות ג"כ הרצועות וכ"ש ג' כריכות שעל האצבע ובתשובות רדב"ז ח"ד סימן ל"ו משמע ג"כ שסובר דמדינא צריך לכסות התפילין במקומות המטונפות וכל מה שאפשר לו לכסותם מוטב שיניחם בבהכ"נ ומשמע שם דהדלי"ת והיו"ד שברצועות אין צריך לכסות שהם דרך קשירה לא דרך כתיבה עי"ש: ו (כא) גלולין בבגדו. ר"ל (טו) מה שהותר בסעיף הקודם לאוחזן בימינו ובבגדו דוקא כשיש לו שהות להניחם עוד אח"כ לא הטריחוהו להניחם בכלי משא"כ באין שהות (כב) אם היה בו טפח. אבל כשאין בו טפח בטל לגבי התפילין כיון שהוא כליין ואסור להכניסם לבה"כ: (כג) בידו ונכנס. שלא יטלו אותם עוברי דרכים [גמרא עי"ש]: ז (כד) כלל. משמע (טז) דאפילו בכיס לא יכניסם ועיין במחצית השקל שכתב דאם הם בכיסן ונותן בכיס התפור במלבושו דאותו כיס אינו כליין והוי כלי תוך כלי ומותר: (כה) המשתמר. ושאר ספרים וכתבים שיש בהן שמות (יז) אם הם בכיס שרי להכניסן (יח) ויש אומרים דבעינן דוקא תיק בתוך תיק: אם צריך ליכנס לבה"כ וכדלעיל לענין תפילין וס"ת אסור בכל גווני. וכתב בש"ת דאותן המלבישין התינוקות בקמיע שכתוב שמות בקלף צריך ליזהר שיהיה כלי בתוך כלי כיון שהתינוקות נפנים בהם בעודם עליהם: ח (כו) עד שיגמור. דעמוד החוזר מביא האדם לידי הדרוקן וסילון החוזר מביא האדם לידי ירקון: ט (כז) לרופא ליקח וכו'. לבדוק בו החולה וא"צ לחלוץ אז התפילין ועובדא הוי ברופא וה"ה בכל אדם:

א (א) עראי. דגזרינן (א) שמא יבוא להפיח בהם וע"י הנחת הסודר עליהן

יזכור

ביאור הלכה

מדאורייתא כמ"ש תר"י ולא גרע ממים סרוחים או מי משרה וכו' המבואר בסימן פ"ו דדינו כצואה עי"ש ואפשר דלענין זה לא מחלקינן בזה ובכל גווני מותר להשתין בו בתפילין שעליו ולא חיישינן בו שמא יפנה בו כיון דאינו מיוחד רק להשתין ואין לאסור מטעם המי רגלים גופא כיון דהוא מיוחד שם דינו כצואה דז"א דא"כ הא מי רגלים נגד העמוד ג"כ דינו כצואה ואפ"ה בבה"כ עראי מותר להשתין בתפילין שבראשו ואפילו בקבוע היה מותר אי לאו דחיישינן שמא יפנה בהם וא"כ אפשר דבזה לא חיישינן שמא יפנה ומותר:

* ואוחזן בימינו. עיין במ"ב מש"כ בשם הרמ"ע להקל והרדב"ז מחמיר. ובספר אור זרוע אשר זכינו מקרוב לאורו משמע כהרמ"ע דכתב בסי' תקפ"ו דמותר לעבור בבית הכסא לפי דרכו שלא לצורך נקביו ותפילין בראשו. ומשמע מלשונו שהוא מחלק בין אם הוא עובר או שהוא קובע עצמו להיות שם ובזה יש ליישב קצת קושית המג"א בסק"ט ממרחץ דמולך כמ"ש סימן מ"ה סעיף ב' ואע"ג דלענין ד"ת לא מחלקינן בין מהלך או עומד בברכות כ"ד ע"ב לענין זה מחלקינן: * ואפילו להשתין מים. ר"ל במיושב או בעפר תיחוח דליכא משום ניצוצות וכדלעיל בס"א: * בבה"כ קבוע. וה"ה לענין בה"כ עראי ותפילין שבראשו. [ביאור מהרמ"ב על המרדכי]: * ומניחן בכלי אם היה בו טפח וכו'. עיין במ"ב והמ"א הביא עוד בשם רש"י דאם הכלי היה טפח חשיב הכלי אוהל להפסיק בינם לקרקע ומותר להניחם בביתו ע"ג קרקע ובכלי שאינו כליין אפילו פחות מטפח:

* אפילו שינת עראי. דלא כהרא"ש ור"י שמתירין שינת עראי ובביאור הגר"א בריש הסימן משמע שדעתו לפסוק כמותם להקל אך לדעתו לא מיקרי שינת עראי כ"א כדי הילוך ק' אמה ואף בזה דוקא אם הניח ראשו בין ברכיו

שער הציון

(טו) לבש"ר: (טז) מ"א: (יז) מ"א ועיין בפמ"ג דאפילו בבה"כ שבבית והגר"ז מחמיר ורדב"ז משמע להקל: (יח) א"ר: (א) מפמ"ג:

הגהות ותיקונים: א) בסימן ג' סקי"ז: ב) כתב: ג) ס"ו: ד) בקמיעין:

הערות והארות: 1) עיין במ"ב סי' ש"א ס"ק ק"א לענין לפנות בקמיע כשהוא מחופה בעור:

8. If one forgot /that he had/ *tefilin* on his head and /started to/ relieve himself with them on, he should place his hand over them **(26)** until he has finished the first column. /Then/ he should go out and take them off and go back into /the lavatory/.

9. It is permitted **(27)** for a doctor to take a urine bowl in his hand with *tefilin* on his head, but a conscientious person should be stringent with himself /about this/.

§44: THE PROHIBITION AGAINST SLEEPING /WEARING/ *TEFILIN*

(Contains One Paragraph)

1. As long as *tefilin* are on his head or on his arm, one is forbidden to sleep even **(1)** a momentary sleep /wearing/ them.

On the other hand, if one put a cloth over /the *tefilin*/ and he does not have

Mishnah Berurah

that they /are in/ a receptacle which is inside /another/ receptacle, since the children excrete with them still on them.

(26) Until he has finished. For if the column /of excrement/ returns it will cause a person to have a swollen belly and if the stream /of urine/ returns it will cause a person to have jaundice.

(27 For a doctor to take, etc. /I.e., in order/ to examine a patient with it. It is unnecessary for him to take off the *tefilin* then.

/The reason why the Shulchan Aruch speaks of a doctor is only because/ in the incident /where this question arose/ a doctor was involved, but /in fact/ the same ruling /applies/ for everybody.

§44

(1) A momentary. /This is/ because /the Sages/ decreed /a prohibition against this, for fear/ that one may come to break wind /wearing/ them. By putting a cloth over them one will remember that he is /wearing/ *tefilin* and will not come to break wind.

סודר ג ולא היתה (ב) עמו אשה * (ג) ישן בהם (ד) שינת (א) עראי וכיצד הוא עושה מניח ראשו (ה) בין ברכיו והוא יושב וישן ד היו תפילין כרוכין בידו (ו) מותר לישן בהם אפילו שינת קבע ה ואם אוחזן בידו ואינם כרוכים בידו (ז) אסור לישן בהם אפי' שינת (ב) עראי: הגה ודוקא כשאוחזן בלא נרתקן אבל בנרתקן (ח) בכל ענין (ג) שרי (ב"י בשם העיטור):

ג לשון הרמב"ם פ"ד מה"ת ד שם לפי פירושו שם בגמרא ה לפי רש"י שם בגמ'

מה דין תפילין בבית הקברות ובבית המרחץ ובו ב' סעיפים:

א * א אסור לכנוס א) (א) בבית הקברות או (ב) בתוך ארבע אמות של (א) מת ותפילין בראשו משום לועג לרש ב ואם הם מכוסים (ב) (ג) מותר: ב ג בבית (ג) המרחץ (ד) בית החיצון שכל העומדים בו

א ברכות י"ח ב ב"י וכן מצא בתשובת הרשב"א ג שבת י

באר היטב

(א) עראי. ולא חשיב היסח הדעת אלא כשהוא עומד בשחוק או בקלות ראש. טור. וז"ל הר"ר יונה דלא חשיב היסח הדעת אלא כשעומד בקלות ראש ובשחוק אבל מתעסק בצרכיו אע"פ שמתעסק במלאכתו ואומנתו ואין דעתו עליהם ממש אין זה נקרא היסח הדעת. לכאורה צ"ע הא דאמרי' בשבת יוצא אדם בתפילין ע"ש עם חשיכה וכו'. ע"ש. ושמא הואיל ומצוה מן המובחר הוא שלא יסיח דעתו מהם כלל לא חיישי' שילא בהם בשבת לר"ה עי' יד אהרן. והאר"י ז"ל החמיר מאוד בזה אפי' בשעת התפלה זולת בשעת תפלת י"ח ובשעה שלומד. עמ"א: (ב) עראי. דחיישי' שמא יפלו מידו. עי' ב"י וברמב"ם פ"ד מה"ת. והמחבר מגדול עוז כתב שם וז"ל ואני אומר שזה הלשון לא נמצאת בגמ' שלנו אלא ה"ג לה בפרק הישן וכו' ע"ש. נראה דאשתמיט מיניה להא דת"ר לא יאחוז וכו' ברכות דף כ"ג ע"ב. עיין סוכה דף מ"ב ע"א ודו"ק: (ג) שרי. וע"ל סי' מ' ס"ק ב' מש"ש:

(א) מת. משמע דבבה"ק אסור אפי' חוץ לד"א מן הקבר ובריש פרק מי שמתו אמרי' תוך ד' אמות אסור חוץ לד' אמות שרי לקרות ק"ש וכ' הט"ז דהטור ס"ל דודאי עיקר האיסור הוא תוך ד"א לקבר אלא משום גדר לא יכנס לבה"ק ותפילין בראשו דשמא יתקרב לתוך ד"א של קבר ולאו אדעתיה אבל מ"מ אם אירע שהלך לבה"ק והוא חוץ לד"א מקבר ודאי חייב לקרות ע"ש, וכ"כ הב"ח וע"ת דהאיסור הוא דוקא בתוך ד"א של קבר ע"ש. ועיין ט"ז בסימן ע"א ס"ק ה'. ודברי המ"א בכאן צל"ע. עיין סי' ע"א ס"ק ד' במ"א. ובי"ד סי' רפ"ב ס"ד וסי' שס"ו ס"ג ודו"ק. אפי' קבר של קטן שעדיין לא הגיע לכלל מצות אפ"ה אסור להניח תפילין ולקרות ק"ש אצלו. מהריט"ץ בחידושיו לפרק איזהו נשך ב) דף י"ב ע"ד. עיין עט"ז שכתב כל החדר שהמת מונח בו חשיב כד' אמות ע"ש: (ב) מותר. נראה דגם הרצועות צריכים להיות מכוסים ט"ז: (ג) המרחץ. עיין מ"א שהעלה דבמקוה מותר כשאין שם אדם

ביאור הלכה

וכמ"ש לקמיה באותו הסימן: * ישן בהם וכו'. עיין במשנה ברורה סק"ג מה שכ' זולת בשעת התפלה והלימוד וכו' אף דבפמ"ג כתב דמצוה מן המובחר שלא יסיח דעתו כלל מתפילין אפילו בשעת ק"ש ותפלה לא סתמתי כן כי הבה"ט בשם האר"י ז"ל כתב להיפך ובפרט שמצאתי בספר אור זרוע וז"ל בסימן תקפ"ה וצריך אדם כשהוא לבוש תפילין לזכור שתפילין עליו ולא להסיח דעתו מהם שלא יישן בהם ולא יפיח בהם כי מחמת שזוכר שנושא שם הנכבד עליו אינו בא לידי קלות ראש ותופס יראת שמים בלבו כדאמרינן פרק א"ע וכו' הלכך כשאדם מכוין לבו בתפלתו או בהלכה שלו אין זה היסח הדעת דכ"ש דאיכא יראת השם עכ"ל:
* אסור לכנוס לבה"ק וכו'. עיין בפמ"ג שכתב דג' מחלוקת בדבר הב"ח סובר דבקברות נמי תוך ד"א לקבר הוא דאסור הא חוץ לד"א של קבר אע"פ שעומד באמצע בה"ק שרי כל שאין סביבו קבר תוך ד"א וט"ז פירש מדינא אין איסור כ"א תוך ד"א לקבר והטור החמיר משום גדר חוץ לד"א של קבר כל שעומד בבה"ק [היינו מקום שהוקצה לקברות אבל חוץ לבה"ק אין להחמיר כלל לדידיה וכמו שפירש בא"א דאין עושין גדר לגדר] והמ"א פירש דתוך ד"א של בה"ק נמי אסור ולדבריו קשה לערבינהו וליתניהו אסור לכנוס לתוך ד"א של בה"ק או של מת עכ"ל אבל במחצית השקל בסימן ע"א פירש דהמ"א סובר ג"כ בזה כהט"ז דאינו אסור ממקום שהותחל הבה"ק [היינו הקרקע שהוקצה לקברות] ולחוצה אפילו אמה אחת אפילו אי ליכא מחיצה מפסקת בנתיים רק דבזה פליג עם הט"ז וסובר דממקום בה"ק ולפנים כגון שיש מחיצה סביב בה"ק או אפילו ליכא מחיצה כלל רק שהוקצה לקברות אסור מדינא אפילו רחוק ד"א מן הקברים [ובזה יוסר קושית הפמ"ג מעל מ"א] ומ"א שכתב בעניינו דאסור אפילו בתוך ד"א של בה"ק היינו אם הקברים מתחילין תיכף ממקום התחלת בה"ק ומה שלא הזכיר בהמחבר האיסור רק בבה"ק היינו דהוא בא לרבות בזה דממקום התחלת הקרקע של בה"ק ולפנים אסור אפילו חוץ לד"א מן הקברים. ודע עוד דהגר"א שסובר בסי' כ"ג בביאורו דתוך ד"א של בה"ק אסור ורמז ג"כ לעיין במ"א בעניינו

משנה ברורה

יזכור שיש תפילין עליו ולא יבוא להפיח: (ב) עמו אשה. אבל אם אשתו עמו (ג) אסור גזירה שמא ישמש בהן: (ג) ישן בהם. ולא חשיב היסח הדעת אלא כשהוא עומד בשחוק וקלות ראש (ג) אבל כשהוא עוסק במלאכתו ואומנתו ואין דעתו עליהן ממש אין זה נקרא היסח הדעת [(ד) אם לא שמטריד דעתו כ"כ לצרכי הגוף עד שלבבו פונה מי"ש מחמת טרדתו] וכן כשהוא ישן שוכח הבלי העולם. ומ"מ מצוה מן המובחר שיהא דעתו תמיד על התפילין ושלא יסיח דעתו מהן למשוך ולהרהר במחשבות רעות שמטעם זה חייב למשמש כל שעה שלא יסיח דעתו מהן [ב"ח] זולת (ה) בשעת התפלה והלימוד א"צ ליתן דעתו בהתפילין: (ד) שינת עראי.[1] (ו) ואין שיעור לזה וי"א כדי הילוך ק' אמה והוא חלק ס"ז משעה בקירוב וכן פסק הגר"א בביאורו: (ה) בין ברכיו. דאל"ה (ז) חיישינן שמא יבוא להשתקע בשינת קבע: (ו) מותר לישן. דלא חיישינן בזה להפחה כיון שאינם עליו: (ז) אסור לישן. דחיישינן שמא יפלו מידו: (ח) בכל ענין שרי. דאפילו אם יפלו על הקרקע אין חשש כ"כ ועיין בביאור הגר"א שכתב דדוקא אם הנרתק מחזיק טפח אז חשיב חצילה להפסיק בינו לקרקע[2]:

א (א) בבה"ק. ואפילו תוך ד"א של מקום התחלת הקברים ג"כ אסור אי ליכא מחיצה מפסקת ביניהם והא דלא עירב ביחד ויאמר אסור לילך תוך ד"א של קבר או של מת דעת המ"א דבא לרמז דממקום בה"ק ולפנים אסור אפי' רחוק ד"א מן הקבר ויש מקילין בזה ועיין בבה"ל דבאמצע בה"ק שיש קברים סביב נראה דיש להחמיר אפילו רחוק ד"א מן הקבר משא"כ בסוף בה"ק דאין שם קברים רק דהוקצה הקרקע לקברים אין להחמיר מדינא ברחוק ד"א מן הקבר ואעפ"כ נכון שלא יכנוס כלל בתפילין שבראשו כל שהוא לפנים מתחלת בה"ק שמא יתקרב בתוך ד"א של איזה קבר בלי דעת: (ב) בתוך ד"א וכו'. וכתב העט"ז דכל אותו חדר שהמת מונח בו חשוב כד"א של מת ומגן גיבורים חולק עליו וכתב דאינו תופס רק ד"א עי"ש ואפילו קבר של קטן שעדיין לא הגיע לכלל מצות אפ"ה אין לכנוס שם בתפילין בראשו משום לועג לרש: (ג) מותר. וצריך שגם הרצועות תהיינה מכוסות לפיכך אע"פ שמותר לכנוס בתש"י לנדה הואיל והוא מכוסה צריך ליזהר ברצועה שעל אצבעו שתהיה ג"כ מכוסה [ט"ז]: ב (ד) בית החיצון. שדרכם היה (א) לאחר שלבשו החלוק בבית האמצעי לילך

שער הציון

(ב) גמרא: (ג) תר"י והרשב"א בחידושיו דסוכה והרא"ש והטור ועי"ל בסי' כ"ח בשע"ת: (ד) הגר"ז: (ה) עיין בה"ל: (ו) מ"א: (ז) גמרא: (א) רש"י:

הגהות ותיקונים: א) ליכנס: ב) צ"ל אלו מגלחין:

הערות והארות: 1) עיין סי' ל' במ"ב סק"ז לענין שינת עראי בלילה: 2) עיין בה"ל סי' מ"ג ס"ו לענין אם אין הנרתק מיוחד להם:

(2) his wife with him, (3) he may sleep (4) a momentary sleep /wearing/ them. He must act as follows. He should put his head (5) in between his knees and sleep sitting.

If *tefilin* are /held by one/ bound to his hand, (6) he is permitted to sleep even a settled sleep with them. If one is holding *tefilin* in his hand, but they are not bound to his hand, (7) he is forbidden to sleep with them even a momentary sleep.

Gloss: This only /applies/ if he is holding them without their case, but /if they are/ in their case (8) *all forms /of sleep/ are allowed. (...)*

Mishnah Berurah

(2) **His wife with him.** However, if one's wife is with him it is forbidden. /The Sages/ decreed /a prohibition in such a case for fear/ that one may /come to/ have marital relations /wearing/ them.

(3) **He may sleep ... /wearing/ them.** One is only considered to have diverted his mind /from the *tefilin*/ if he amuses himself and /acts/ lightheartedly. If, however, one engages in his work and trade and does not have /the *tefilin*/ actually in mind, this is not classed as a distraction of his mind /from them/ [unless he preoccupies his mind so much with his bodily requirements that his heart turns aside from the fear of Heaven due to his preoccupation]. When one sleeps, he likewise forgets the world's vanities.

Nevertheless, /one performs/ the mitzvah choicely if his mind is on the *tefilin* continually and he does not divert his mind from them to /engage in/ prolonged /idle talk/ and think bad thoughts. It is for this reason that one is obliged to feel /the *tefilin*/ all the time, so that he should not divert his mind from them [*Bach*], except that when he is praying or studying /Torah/ he does not need to direct his thoughts to the *tefilin.*

(4) **A momentary sleep.** There is no maximum duration /for the sleep/ to be /considered as/ such. There are /authorities/ who say that /there is such a maximum duration and/ it is as long as /it takes/ to walk a hundred cubits, which is approximately a sixty-seventh of an hour. The *Gra* rules in accordance with this /latter view/ in his *Beyur.*

(5) **In between his knees.** Otherwise, we are afraid that he may come to sink into a settled sleep.

(6) **He is permitted to sleep.** Then we are not concerned about him breaking wind, since /the *tefilin*/ are not on him.

(7) **He is forbidden to sleep.** Then we are afraid that they may fall from his hand.

(8) **All forms are allowed.** For /in such a case/ even if they will /in fact/ fall to the ground there is not so much /reason/ to be concerned.

See the *Beyur Ha-Gra,* who writes that this only /applies/ if the case has a capacity of a handbreadth. Then it is considered as an interposition which will separate between /the *tefilin*/ and the ground.

סודר [ג]ולא היתה (ב) עמו אשה * (ג) ישן בהם (ד) שינת (א) עראי וכיצד הוא עושה מניח ראשו (ה) בין ברכיו והוא יושב וישן [ד]היו תפילין כרוכין בידו (ו) מותר לישן בהם אפילו שינת קבע [ה]ואם אוחזן בידו ואינם כרוכים בידו (ז) אסור לישן בהם אפי' שינת (ב) עראי: הגה ודוקא כשאוחזן בלא נרתקן אבל בנרתקן (ח) בכל ענין (ג) שרי (ב"י בשם העיטור):

ג לשון הרמב"ם פ"ד מה"ת ד שם לפי פירושו שם בגמרא ה לפי רש"י שם בגמ'

מה דין תפילין בבית הקברות ובבית המרחץ ובו ב' סעיפים:

א * [א]אסור לכנוס[א] (א) בבית הקברות או (ב) בתוך ארבע אמות של (א) מת ותפילין בראשו משום לועג * לרש [ב]ואם הם מכוסים (ב) (ג) מותר: **ב** [ג]בבית (ג) המרחץ (ד) בית החיצון שכל העומדים בו

א ברכות י"ח ב ב"י וכן מלא בתשובת הרשב"א ג שבת י

באר היטב

(א) עראי. ולא חשיב היסח הדעת אלא כשהוא עומד בשחוק או בקלות ראש. טור. וז"ל הר"ר יונה דלא חשיב היסח הדעת אלא כשעומד בקלות ראש ובשחוק אבל מתעסק בצרכיו אע"פ שמתעסק במלאכתו ואומנתו ואין דעתו עליהם ממש אין זה נקרא היסח הדעת. לכאורה ל"ע הא דאמרי' בשבת יולא אדם בתפילין ע"ש עם חשיכה וכו'. ע"ש. ושמא הואיל ומלוה מן המובחר הוא שלא יסיח דעתו מהם כלל לא חיישי' שילא בהם בשבת לר"ה עי' יד אהרן. והאר"י ז"ל החמיר מאוד בזה אפי' בשעת התפלה זולת בשעת תפלת י"ח ובשעה שלומד. עמ"א: (ב) עראי. דחיישי' שמא יפלו מידו. עי' ב"י והרמב"ם פ"ד מה"ת. והמחבר מגדול עוז כתב שם וז"ל ואני אומר שזה הלשון לא נמלאת בגמ' שלנו אלא ה"ג לה בפרק הישן וכו' ע"ש. נראה דאשתמיט מיניה להא דת"ר לא יאחוז וכו' ברכות דף כ"ג ע"ב. עיין סוכה דף מ"ב ע"א ודו"ק: (ג) שרי. וע"ל סי' מ' ס"ק ב' מש"ש:

(א) מת. משמע דבבה"ק אסור אפי' חוץ לד"א מן הקבר וברים פרק מי שמתו אמרי' תוך ד' אמות אסור חוץ לד' אמות שרי לקרות ק"ש וכ' הט"ז דהטור ס"ל דודאי עיקר האיסור הוא תוך ד"א לקבר אלא משום גדר לא יכנס לבה"ק ותפילין בראשו דשמא יתקרב לתוך ד"א של קבר ולאו אדעתיה אבל מ"מ אם אירע שהלך לבה"ק והוא חוץ לד"א מקבר ודאי חייב לקרות ע"ש, וכ"כ הב"ח וע"ת דהאיסור הוא דוקא בתוך ד"א של קבר ע"ש. ועיין ט"ז בסימן ע"א ס"ק ה'. ודברי המ"א בכאן צ"ע. עיין סי' ע"א ס"ק ד' במ"א. ובי"ד סי' רפ"ב ס"ד וסי' שס"ו ס"ג ודו"ק. אפי' קבר של קטן שעדיין לא הגיע לכלל מלות אפ"ה אסור להניח תפילין ולקרות ק"ש אצלו. מהריט"ץ בחידושיו לפרק איזהו נשך[ב] דף י"ב ע"ד. עיין עט"ז שכתב כל החדר שהמת מונח בו חשיב כד' אמות ע"ש: (ב) מותר. נראה דגם הרלועות לריכים להיות מכוסים ט"ז: (ג) המרחץ. עיין מ"א שהעלה דבמקוה מותר כשאין שם אדם

ביאור הלכה

וכמ"ש לקמיה באותו הסימן: * ישן בהם וכו'. עיין במשנה ברורה סק"ג מה שכ' זולת בשעת התפלה והלימוד וכו' אף דבפמ"ג כתב דמלוה מן המובחר שלא יסיח דעתו כלל מתפילין אפילו בשעת ק"ש ותפלה לא סמכתי כן כי הבה"ט בשם האר"י ז"ל כתב להיפך ובפרט שמלאתי בספר אור זרוע וז"ל בסימן תקפ"ה ולריך אדם כשהוא לבוש תפילין לזכור שתפילין עליו ולא להסיח דעתו מהם שלא יישן בהם ולא יפיח בהם כי מחמת שזוכר שנושא שם הנכבד עליו אינו בא לידי קלות ראש ותופש יראת שמים בלבו כדאמרינן פרק א"ע וכו' הלכך כשאדם מכוין לבו בתפלתו או בהלכה שלו אין זה היסח הדעת דכ"ש דאיכא יראת השם עכ"ל: * אסור לכנוס לבה"ק וכו'. עיין בפמ"ג שכתב דג' מחלוקת בדבר הב"ח סובר דבקברות נמי תוך ד"א לקבר הוא דאסור הא חוץ לד"א של קבר אע"פ שעומד באמלע בה"ק שרי כל שאין סביבו קבר תוך ד"א וט"ז פירש מדינא אין איסור כ"א תוך ד"א לקבר והטור החמיר משום גדר חוץ לד"א של קבר כל שעומד בבה"ק [היינו מקום שהוקלה לקברות אבל חוץ לבה"ק אין להחמיר כלל לדידיה וכמו שפירש בא"א דאין עושין גדר לגדר] והמ"א פירש דתוך ד"א של בה"ק נמי אסור ולדבריו קשה לערבינהו וליתניניהו אסור לכנוס לתוך ד"א של בה"ק או של מת עכ"ל אבל במחלית השקל בסימן ע"א פירש דהמ"א סובר ג"כ בזה כהט"ז דאינו אסור ממקום שהותחל הבה"ק [היינו הקרקע שהוקלה לקברות] ולחולה אפילו אמה אחת אפילו אי ליכא מחילה מפסקת בנתיים רק דבזה פליג עם הט"ז וסובר דממקום בה"ק ולפנים כגון שיש מחילה סביב בה"ק או אפילו ליכא מחילה כלל רק שהוקלה לקברות אסור מדינא אפילו רחוק ד"א מן הקברים [ובזה יוסר קושית הפמ"ג מעל מ"א] ומ"א שכתב בענינינו דאסור אפילו בתוך ד"א של בה"ק היינו אם הקברים מתחילין תיכף ממקום התחלת בה"ק ומה שלא הזכיר המחבר האיסור רק בבה"ק היינו דהוא בא לרבות בזה דממקום התחלת הקרקע של בה"ק ולפנים אסור אפילו חוץ לד"א מן הקברים. ודע עוד דהגר"א שסובר בסי' כ"ג בביאורו דתוך ד"א של בה"ק אסור ורמז ג"כ לעיין במ"א בענינינו

משנה ברורה

יזכור שיש תפילין עליו ולא יבוא להפיח: (ב) עמו אשה. אבל אם אשתו עמו (ג) אסור גזירה שמא ישמש בהן: (ג) ישן בהם. ולא חשיב היסח הדעת אלא כשהוא עומד בשחוק וקלות ראש (ג) אבל כשהוא עוסק במלאכתו ואומנתו ואין דעתו עליהן ממש אין זה נקרא היסח הדעת [(ד) אם לא שמטריד דעתו כ"כ לצרכי הגוף עד שלבנו פונה מי"ש מחמת טרדתן] וכן כשהוא ישן שוכח הבלי העולם. ומ"מ מלוה מן המובחר שיהא דעתו תמיד על התפילין ושלא יסיח דעתו מהן למשוך ולהרהר במחשבות רעות שמטעם זה חייב למשמש כל שעה שלא יסיח דעתו מהן [ב"ח] זולת (ה) בשעת התפלה והלימוד א"ל ליתן דעתו בהתפילין: (ד) שינת עראי.[1] (ו) ואין שיעור לזה וי"א כדי הילוך ק' אמה והוא הלך ס"ו משעה בקירוב וכן פסק הגר"א בביאורו: (ה) בין ברכיו. דאל"ה (ז) חיישינן שמא יבוא להשתקע בשינת קבע: (ו) מותר לישן. דלא חיישינן בזה להפחה כיון שאימת עליו: (ז) אסור לישן. דחיישינן שמא יפלו מידו: (ח) בכל ענין שרי. דאפילו אם יפלו על הקרקע אין חשש כ"כ ועיין בביאור הגר"א שכתב דדוקא אם הנרתק מחזיק טפח או חשיב מחילה להפסיק בינו לקרקע[2]:

א (א) בבה"ק. ואפילו תוך ד"א של מקום התחלת הקברים ג"כ אסור אי ליכא מחילה מפסקת ביניהם והא דלא עירב ביחד ויאמר אסור לילך תוך ד"א של קבר או של מת דעת המ"א דבא לרמז דממקום בה"ק ולפנים אסור אפי' רחוק ד"א מן הקבר ויש מקילין בזה ועיין בבה"ל דבאמלע בה"ק שיש קברים סביב נראה דיש להחמיר אפילו רחוק ד"א מן הקבר משא"כ בסוף בה"ק דאין שם קברים רק דהוקלה הקרקע לקברים אין להחמיר מדינא ברחוק ד"א מן הקבר ואעפ"כ נכון שלא יכנוס כלל בתפילין שבראשו כל שהוא לפנים ממחילת בה"ק שמא יתקרב בתוך ד"א של איזה קבר בלי דעת: (ב) בתוך ד"א וכו'. וכתב העט"ז דכל אותו חדר שהמת מונח בו חשוב כד"א של מת ומגן גיבורים חולק עליו וכתב דאינו תופס רק ד"א עי"ש ואפילו קבר של קטן שעדיין לא הגיע לכלל מלות אפ"ה אין לכנוס שם בתפילין בראשו משום לועג לרש: (ג) מותר. ולריך שגם הרלועות תהיינה מכוסות לפיכך אע"פ שמותר לכנוס בתש"י לבדה הואיל והוא מכוסה לריך ליזהר ברלועה שעל אלבעו שתהיה ג"כ מכוסה [ט"ז]: **ב** (ד) בית החיצון. שדרכם היה (א) לאחר שלבשו החלוק בבית האמלעי לילך

שער הציון

(ב) גמרא: (ג) תר"י והרשב"א בחידושיו דסוכה והרא"ש והטור וע"ל בסי' כ"ח בשע"ת: (ד) הגר"ז: (ה) עיין בה"ל: (ו) מ"א: (ז) גמרא: (א) רש"י:

הגהות ותיקונים: א) ליכנס: ב) צ"ל אלו מגלחין:

הערות והארות: 1) עיין סי' ל' במ"ב סק"ז לענין שינת עראי בלילה: 2) עיין בה"ל סי' מ"ג ס"ו לענין אם אין הנרתק מיוחד להם:

§45: THE LAW AS REGARDS /WEARING/ *TEFILIN* /WHEN ONE IS/ IN A GRAVEYARD OR A BATHHOUSE

(Contains Two Paragraphs)

1. One is forbidden to enter (1) a graveyard or (2) within four cubits of a dead person with *tefilin* on his head, because /this involves/ mockery of the destitute.[1*] If /the *tefilin*/ are covered (3) it is permitted.

2. /When one is/ in a bathhouse /the ruling is as follows/.

(4) In the outer room, since all /the people who/ stand in it are dressed, he may don *tefilin* there initially.

Mishnah Berurah

§45

(1) A graveyard. Even /to enter/ with *tefilin* on one's head within four cubits of the area where the graves begin is also forbidden, if there is no partition separating between /one and the graves/.

In the opinion of the *M.A.*, the reason why /the author of the Shulchan Aruch/ does not amalgamate /the two cases/ and say that one is forbidden to go within four cubits of a grave or of a dead person is because he wishes to indicate that from /the beginning of/ the area of the graveyard /where there are graves and/ inwards this is forbidden even /when one is/ at a distance of four cubits away from /any/ grave. There are /authorities/ who are lenient about this.

See the Beyur Halachah, /where we have concluded/ that in the middle of a graveyard, where one is surrounded by graves, it seems /logical/ that one should be stringent even /when he is at least/ four cubits away from /any/ grave. By contrast, at the end of a graveyard, where there are no graves, but the ground has merely been assigned /to be used/ for graves, one need not be stringent, from the /point of view of binding/ halachah, when he is four cubits away from /any/ grave. Nevertheless, it is proper not to enter /into a graveyard/ any /distance/ at all with *tefilin* on one's head, within the partition of the graveyard, in case one will approach unwittingly within four cubits of some grave.

(2) Within four cubits. The *At.Z.* writes that /when the dead person is in a room/ the entire room where the dead person is lying is considered /to have the ruling/ of /within/ four cubits of the dead person. The *Magen Giborim* disputes this and writes that /halachically the dead person/ is only /considered to/ occupy /the area within/ four cubits /of him, even in a room/; see there.

Even when a grave is that of a child who did not yet reach /the age/ when /one is obliged to perform/ mitzvos, one should nevertheless not enter there with *tefilin* on his head, because /the need to avoid/ mockery of the destitute /is relevant even in such a case/.

(3) It is permitted. It is necessary for the straps to be covered as well. Therefore, although it is permitted to enter /wearing/ arm *tefilin* alone, since they are covered, one must be careful that the strap on his finger is also covered. [*Taz*]

(4) In the outer room. It was their habit that after they put on the undergarment in the middle room they would go to the outer room and finish dressing.

1* See Sec. 24, sub-Par. 1 of the Mishnah Berurah.

הם לבושים יכולין להניח שם תפילין לכתחלה ובבית האמצעי שמקצת בני אדם עומדים שם לבושים (ה) ומקצתן ערומים אינו יכול להניחם לכתחלה ואם היו בראשו אינו צריך לחלצן (ו) ובבית הפנימי שכל העומדים שם ערומים אפילו היו בראשו צריך לחלצן: א ברכות ס׳

באר היטב

דדוקא במרחץ החמירו אע״פ שאין שם אדם משום זוהמא דאית ביה אבל לא במקוה ע״ש ועי׳ סי׳ פ״ד ס״ק א׳:

משנה ברורה

לילך לבית החיצון ולגמור הלבישה: (ה) ומקצתן ערומים. י״א דאם עתה אין שם אדם ערום (ב) מותר להניח בו תפילין ולברך (ג) ויש אוסרין כיון דהמקום מיוחד לזה דין מרחץ עליו במקלתו. ובית הטבילה משמע בט״ז סי׳ פ״ד דדין בית אמצעי יש לו לכל דבר ורק ברכת הטבילה מותר לברך בה עי״ש טעמו. ומהמ״א בסימן זה משמע דבאין בה אדם ערום מותר להניח בה תפילין ולברך דדוקא במרחץ החמירו אע״פ שאין שם אדם[ג] משום שזוהמתו רבה מהבל החמין שמשתמשין בה משא״כ במקוה [ואם שופכין בה ג״כ חמין (ד) יש לעיין] אבל אם יש שם אדם ערום אסור לכנס בה בתפילין וכתבי הקודש דאסור לעמוד לפני השם ערום ועיין לקמן בסימן פ״ד במ״ב בענין זה: (ו) ובבית הפנימי. בזה (ה) לכו״ע אפילו אין שם אדם ערום (ו) דנפישא זוהמיה וכבית הכסא דמיא:

ביאור הלכה

משמע ג״כ דהוא מפרש בהמ״א כהמתלית השקל הנ״ל ואיירי ג״כ באופן זה דוקא דהא ציין שם זה למקור על הא דכתב המחבר שם דתוך ד״א לקבר אסור ותדע דאין דוחק כלל לפרש כן דהא הט״ז גופא דאין מחמיר כלל חוץ לבה״ק כתב ג״כ ביו״ד בסי׳ רפ״ב סק״ג דתוך ד״א לבה״ק אסור וע״כ דמיירי באופן דכתב המחה״ש הנ״ל. היוצא מזה דמקרקע שהוקצה לקברות ולחוצה בודאי אין אסור כלל אפילו אמה אחת כל שיש ד״א מן הקבר אמנם אפילו במה דהחמיר המ״א בבה״ק עצמה מדינא חוץ לד״א של קבר ג״כ יש לעיין בזה דהב״ח והע״ת בחדא שיטתא קיימי להקל וגם הט״ז סובר כוותייהו מעיקרא דדינא גם הפמ״ג הקשה עליו לדבריו שקרקע שהוקצה לקברות אסור אפילו רחוק הרבה מקברים א״כ איך נהגו לומר קדיש בבה״ק עיו״ד סי׳ שע״ו וכן כתב בספר נהר שלום דחומרא יתירא היא להחמיר חוץ לד״א דא״כ נצטרך להחמיר כל הקרקע שהוקצה לקברות ואפילו רחוק כמה אך ממקום הקברות ולפנים אפילו אי איתרמי שיש יותר מד״א רחוק מן הקבר כתב הנה״ש שם דיש מקום להחמיר בזה:

שער הציון

(ב) מב״י וא״ר לקמן בסי׳ פ״ד: (ג) ב״ח וע״ת ופרישה: (ד) פמ״ג: (ה) בסי׳ פ״ד: (ו) מ״א שם:

הגהות ותיקונים: ג) חסר תיבה ערום:

In the middle room, where some of the people stand dressed (5) and some of them /stand/ naked, he may not don /*tefilin*/ initially, but if they are /already/ on his head he is not required to take them off.

(6) In the inner room, where all /the people/ who stand there are naked, even if /the *tefilin*/ are /already/ on his head he is required to take them off.

Mishnah Berurah

(5) **And some of them naked.** There are /authorities/ who say that if there is nobody naked present now one is permitted to don *tefilin* in /that room/ and make the blessing. Other /authorities/ forbid it /even then/. /They reason that,/ since the place is designated for /nakedness/, it has the ruling of a bathhouse to some extent.

It is implied by the *Taz*, in Sec. 84, that the room where people immerse /in a *mikveh*/ has the ruling of the middle room /of a bathhouse/ for all purposes. It is only permitted to say the blessing over immersion in it /, but no other blessing/. See his reason there. It is implied by the *M.A.* in this section that when there is no naked person present it is permitted /for one/ to don *tefilin* there and make the blessing. /According to him, the Sages/ were only stringent /about this/ even when there is nobody present with respect to a bathhouse, because /a bathhouse/ abounds in filth from the steam of the hot /water/ which is used there. This is not the case in a *mikveh* /room/. [If hot /water/ is poured in /a *mikveh*/ as well, study /is required to determine the ruling in this respect/.] However, if there is a naked person present, it is forbidden to enter there with *tefilin* or Holy Writings, as it is forbidden to stand before the /Divine/ Name naked. See below in Sec. 84, in /sub-Par. 4 of/ the Mishnah Berurah, as regards this matter.

(6) **In the inner room.** As regards /the inner room/, all /authorities/ are agreed that /it is forbidden to don *tefilin* there/, even if there is no naked person present. /This is/ because filth abounds /in the inner room/ and it is /therefore/ comparable to a lavatory.

GLOSSARY

Acharon (pl. ***Acharonim***): A later halachic authority, contemporary with or after the time of the Shulchan Aruch.
After-blessing: A blessing to be made after the performance of an action, for example, after eating or drinking or saying the song verses.
Aleynu: A prayer said after the eighteen-blessing prayer of the prayer service.
Al Keyn Nekaveh Lecha: A passage of the prayer *Aleynu*.
Al Mitzvas Tefilin: A blessing made over the donning of *tefilin*; according to the Ashkenazic practice, regularly, and according to the Sephardic practice, when one made an interruption between the donning of the arm *tefilin* and of the head *tefilin*.
Amora (pl. ***Amoraim***): A halachic authority of the times of the Gemara.
Ascription: A verse given as the source of a law, when this is not the true implication of the verse.
Ashkenazic: Pertaining to the Ashkenazim.
Ashkenazim: The Jews who are descended from the communities of Central and Eastern Europe.
Ashrey: A prayer consisting of the verses, *Tehilim* 84:5; 144:15; 145; 115:18. It is part of the song verses and is also said after the Shacharis eighteen-blessing prayer and before the Minchah eighteen-blessing prayer.
Ban: A ban is imposed on a person for various transgressions, for lack of observance of community regulations or to combat an undesirable practice rife among community members.

A banned person must observe laws similar to those of a mourner, contact with him is restricted and in certain cases he is not counted to complete a *minyan*.
Barechu: The call to bless, made primarily before the saying of the blessings of "The Reading of Shema." Someone who is called up to read from the Torah also makes this call.
Bar Mitzvah: The age when one becomes obliged to fulfil mitzvos.
Baruch She-Amar: The blessing said before the song verses in the Shacharis prayer service.
Beyn Ha-Shemashos: The period between sunset and the appearance of the stars, when it is doubtful as to whether it is daytime or nighttime.
Beys Din: A Jewish court of law.
Beys Ha-Midrash (pl. ***Batei Midrashos***): A place used for the study of Torah.
Beys Ha-Mikdash: The Holy Temple of Jerusalem.
Blessings for mitzvos: Blessings relating to the performance of mitzvos.
Blessings for "The Reading of Shema": Blessings which were ordained to be said together with "The Reading of Shema."
Blessings of the kohanim: The verses *Ba-Midbar* 6:24-26, which are said by the *kohanim* when they bless the people.
Bridge: The skin covering the opening of the housing of the *tefilin* passage or passages. See Sec. 32, Par. 44.
Call of Barechu: See *Barechu*.
Carving around to form the letter: Forming a letter by scraping or erasing around it until what remains has the required form.

Chanukah: The holiday commemorating the miracles when the Jews were delivered from the Greeks who had suppressed Torah observance. See Sec. 670, sub-Par. 1 of the Mishnah Berurah.
Chanukah lights: The lights which are lit on Chanukah to publicize the miracle which occurred then. After the Jews prevailed and entered the *Beys Ha-Mikdash*, the small amount of oil they found which was not unclean should only have sufficed for *Beys Ha-Mikdash* use for one day, but lasted eight days until fresh oil could be produced.
Chazan (pl. ***Chazanim***): A community prayer. See Sec. 53, sub-Par. 87 of the Mishnah Berurah.
Chirik: The Hebrew vowel sign written as a single dot underneath the letter. See Transliteration Key at the beginning of the volume.
Cholam: The Hebrew vowel sign written as a dot over the top left of the letter or over a letter ו added following the letter. See Transliteration Key at the beginning of the volume.
Chol Ha-Mo'ed: The weekdays of Pesach and of Sukkos.
Chumash: One of the five books of the Torah.
Community Prayer: The person who leads the prayers of the congregation and says those prayers which must be said for the congregation.
Complete Kadish: A *kadish* which has the full wording, with or without the passage תתקבל וכו'.
Cubit: A measure of length, ±57.6 cm (22.7 inches), according to the *Chazon Ish*, and ±48 cm (18.9 inches), according to Rabbi Avraham Chayim Na'eh.
Dagesh: A dot in the middle of a Hebrew letter, changing or strengthening its pronunciation.
Daily offering: The burnt-offering which must be offered daily, morning and afternoon.
Descend before the Holy Ark: To act as community prayer. The expression derives from the practice of making the place where the community prayer stands lower than the rest of the Synagogue. (Mishnah Berurah, Sec. 90, sub-Par. 5)
Dinar: A coin used in Mishnaic and Talmudic times.
Egg's bulk: A measure of volume, ±100 c.c., according to the *Chazon Ish*, and ±57.6 c.c., according to Rabbi Avraham Chayim Na'eh. The measurements refer to an egg with its shell.
Eighteen-blessing prayer: The principal prayer. It is prayed three times daily on weekdays. It originally consisted of eighteen blessings, but a nineteenth blessing was added later.
Erev Shabbos: The day hours before the inception of Shabbos.
Erev Yom Tov: The day hours before the inception of Yom Tov.
Falling on one's face in supplication: To say the supplicatory prayer which follows immediately after the eighteen-blessing prayer. One falls on his face when he says it.
Fingerbreadth: A measure of length. There are twenty-four fingerbreadths in a cubit. See *Cubit*.
Gaon (pl. ***Ge'onim***): Great scholar from after the time of the Gemara but before the period of the Rishonim; also, any outstanding scholar.
Genizah: The putting away of holy articles which are no longer fit for use in a place where their sanctity will be protected. Also, the place where these articles are put away.
Geyhinom: The place where the wicked are punished after death.
Great Assembly: A body of scholars set up by Ezra and Nechemyah (Nehemiah). They made many ordainments and precautionary decrees and are responsible for the form and formula of the prayers and blessings.
Haftarah: The portion from the Prophets, read in the Synagogue after the reading of the Torah.
Halachah: Jewish law.
Halachically: From the point of view of Jewish law.
Haleyl: The songs of praise said on Festivals, Rosh Chodesh and Chanukah. They are *Tehilim* 113-118. They are said with a prior-blessing and an after-blessing.
Handbreadth: A length equivalent to a sixth of a cubit.
Ha-Sheym: Lit., "The Name." Used as a substitute for the actual Divine Name.
Holy tongue: Hebrew.
Initially: When it is stated that something may or should be done initially, this implies that one may or should choose to do it in the first instance.
Kadesh: A *tefilin* passage. *Shemos* 13:1-10.
Kadesh Li Chal Bechor: Same as *Kadesh*.
Kadish (pl. ***Kadishim***): A prayer which is

said in sanctification of the Divine Name.
Kadish for an orphan: The *kadish* after the prayer *Aleynu*, which is usually said by an orphan who is in mourning. See the gloss in Sec. 132, Par. 2 and the Mishnah Berurah there, sub-Par. 10.
Kadish Tiskabal: A *kadish* which is said following a prayer and contains the additional request, *Tiskabal*, etc., for the acceptance of the prayer.
Kamatz: The Hebrew vowel sign written like a small T underneath the letter. See Transliteration Key at the beginning of the volume.
Kamatz Katan: A kamatz which is a short vowel.
Karaites: A sect who do not accept the Rabbinical law and oral law.
Karmelis: A domain with respect to the laws of carrying on Shabbos, intermediate in character between a private domain and a public domain.
Kav (pl. ***Kavim***): A measure of volume, equivalent to twenty-four times the bulk of an egg.
Kedushah: A prayer of sanctification said at the repetition of the eighteen-blessing prayer of the community prayer. There is also a *kedushah* prayer in the first blessing of "The Reading of Shema" of the morning and in the prayer *U-Va Le-Tziyon.*
Kedushah Service: The *kedushah* of the prayer *U-Va Le-Tziyon.*
Keser: The *kedushah* of the Musaf service according to the Sephardic tradition. It begins with this word.
Koheyn (pl. ***Kohanim***): A descendant of Aharon (Aaron) through an uninterrupted male line, none of whom became disqualified from performing the holy duties required of *kohanim* and the enjoyment of their privileges.
Kosher: Valid and permitted.
Kubutz: The Hebrew vowel sign, written as three dots placed in a diagonal line descending from left to right underneath the letter. See Transliteration Key at the beginning of the volume.
Large Talis: The large *talis* worn during the prayer service.
Lehani'ach Tefilin: A blessing said over the donning of *tefilin.*
Lehisateyf: The blessing made over the large *talis.*
Levite: A member of the tribe of Levi. The Levites are required to assist the *kohanim* in the *Beys Ha-Mikdash* and are entitled to certain privileges.
Lulav: An unopened palm branch. One of the four species one must take hold of on Sukkos.
Ma'ariv: The nighttime prayer service.
Mamzeyr: A person who is descended from a union of two people whose union is halachically inconceivable.
Mapik: A dot which appears in the letter ה at the end of a word. It is a sign that the letter should be pronounced as an audible consonant.
Matzah: Unleavened bread.
Megilah: Lit., "a scroll." Usually, what is meant is a scroll of the Book of *Esteyr* (Esther), which is read on Purim. However, scrolls of the Book of *Shir Ha-Shirim* (Song of Songs), *Rus* (Ruth), *Eychah* (Lamentations) and *Koheles* (Ecclesiastes) are also referred to as a *megilah.*
Mezuzah: The Torah passages *Devarim* 6:4-9 and *Devarim* 11:13-21 written on parchment for mounting on the doorpost, in accordance with the requirement of the Torah. See *Devarim* 6:9 and 11:20.
Mikveh (pl. ***Mikva'os***): A body of standing water which satisfies the halachic requirements for removing uncleanness from an unclean person or utensil that is immersed in it. The sea, the waters of a fountain or a river may also be of avail for this purpose.
Mil (pl. ***Milin***): A measure of distance, equivalent to two thousand cubits.
Minchah: The afternoon prayer service.
Minyan: Ten grown Jewish males, collected together.
Mitzvah (pl. ***Mitzvos***): A commandment of God or of the Sages; also, a meritorious deed.
Morning Blessings: The various blessings ordained to be said in the morning. They relate mainly to the blessing one receives from the creation of the world, one's own creation and the conduct of the creation.
Motza'ey Shabbos: The night after Shabbos.
Muktzeh: An article that may not be handled or eaten on Shabbos or Yom Tov because it has been set aside from use.
Musaf: The additional principal prayer which is prayed on Shabbos, Yom Tov, Rosh Chodesh and Chol Ha-Mo'ed to correspond with the additional offerings that should be sacrificed on those days.
Negative injunction: A mitzvah of the Torah, expressed in the form of an

instruction not to do something.

Neveylah: A dead animal or bird which is either unclean or was not slaughtered in accordance with halachic requirements.

Noachian mitzvos: The mitzvos which were commanded to all mankind and not only to Israel.

Numerical Value: Each letter of the Hebrew alphabet also serves as a numeral. This numeral is the numerical value of the letter. The total of the numerical values of the letters of a word or expression is considered significant.

Olive's bulk: A half of the bulk of an egg, according to one opinion, and a third of the bulk of an egg, according to another.

Once it is after the event: A situation which should not have arisen had one fulfilled his required duty as he should have done initially.

Partial kadish: A *kadish* which does not have the full wording, but stops at the words דאמירן בעלמא ואמרו אמן.

Pasach: The Hebrew vowel sign written as a line underneath the letter. See Transliteration Key at the beginning of the volume.

Passage of Shema: Passage of "The Reading of Shema."

Passageway: The extension of the bridge of the *tefilin* unit, through which the strap passes. See Sec. 32, Par. 44.

Pelag Ha-Minchah: The time of ten and three quarters seasonal hours of the day.

Pesach: The holiday of Passover, celebrating the Exodus from Egypt.

Pesach-Offering: The offering which must be brought on Erev Pesach and eaten on Pesach night, once the Beys Ha-Mikdash will be rebuilt. May this happen speedily in our days.

Poseyk (pl. ***Poskim***): Halachic authority.

Positive injunction: A mitzvah of the Torah, expressed in the form of an instruction to do something.

Prayer יהי רצון מלפניך וכו' שנשמר חקיך וכו': The final part of the prayer *U-Va Le-Tziyon.*

Prior-blessing: A blessing to be made prior to the performance of an action, for example, before eating or drinking or saying the song verses.

Quiet eighteen-blessing prayer: The eighteen-blessing prayer prayed by the congregation. It is called that because they must pray it quietly.

Rabbeinu: A title of respect. Lit., "our Rabbi."

Rabbinical law: The enactments or requirements of the Sages.

Rabbinical requirement: A requirement which is incumbent by Rabbinical law.

Rabbis' Kadish: A *kadish* which contains an additional prayer for the Rabbis and their pupils.

Reading from the Torah: The reading from the Torah Scroll in the Synagogue.

Respond אָמֵן: To say אָמֵן in endorsement and confirmation of what has been said.

Respond אמן יהא שמה רבא וכו': The principal response to the *kadish*, whereby the listener joins in the blessing of the Holy Name. There is a similar response in *Dani'eyl* 2:20.

Respond to the call of Barechu: I.e., to respond ברוך ד' המברך לעולם ועד upon hearing the call of *Barechu.*

Responsum (pl. ***Responsa***): An answer by a halachic authority to a halachic problem, often involving a detailed discussion of the problem.

Revi'is (pl. ***Revi'iyos***): A measure of volume, ±150 c.c., according to the *Chazon Ish*, and ±86 c.c., according to Rabbi Avraham Chayim Na'eh.

Rishon (pl. ***Rishonim***): An early halachic authority, inbetween the time of the Ge'onim and the time of the Shulchan Aruch.

Rosh Chodesh: The day which begins the new Jewish month. When a month has thirty days, the final day is also a Rosh Chodesh.

Rosh Ha-Shanah: The holiday at the beginning of the Jewish year.

Se'ah (pl. ***Se'ah***): A measure of volume, ±14.4 liters, according to the *Chazon Ish*, and ±8.3 liters, according to Rabbi Avraham Chayim Na'eh.

Seasonal hours: Hours arrived at for any day by dividing the actual daytime into twelfths. Each twelfth is a seasonal hour.

Selichos: Prayers for forgiveness. They are said from before Rosh Hashanah until Yom Kippur and on fast days.

Sephardic: Pertaining to the Sephardim.

Sephardim: The Jews who are descended from the communities of Spain and Portugal.

Shabbos: The seventh day of the week. It is a day of rest for the Jewish people, in memory of the creation.

Shacharis: The morning prayer service.

Shavu'os: The holiday commemorating the giving of the Torah to Israel.

Shechinah: The Divine Presence.

She-Hecheyanu: A blessing made upon hearing good reports which are only good for the hearer himself; upon acquiring new articles of use; upon seeing a friend, whom one rejoices to see, after an interval of thirty days; for fruit which reappears from year to year; for the arrival of a festival and in the case of the fulfillment of certain mitzvos.

Shema: A *tefilin* passage. It is also the first passage of "The Reading of Shema". *Devarim* 6:4-9.

Shemini Atzeres: The holiday which follows immediately after Sukkos.

Sheva: The Hebrew vowel sign consisting of two dots, underneath the letter, one below the other. See Transliteration Key at the beginning of the volume.

Shofar: The ram's horn blown on Rosh Hashanah.

Sidur (pl. ***Sidurim***): Prayer book.

Small Talis: The small *talis* worn all day.

Song verses: A collection of verses said in the Shacharis prayer service before "The Reading of Shema" and its blessings.

Sukah: A dwelling with at least three partitions, which has a covering of materials which grew from the ground. One is obliged to dwell in a *sukah* on *Sukkos*.

Sukkos: The holiday when Jews dwell in a *sukah* and take the four species.

Supplication prayer: A prayer of humble entreaty; especially the prayer said falling on one's face after the Shacharis and Minchah eighteen-blessing prayer and the prayer said following every eighteen-blessing prayer or its equivalent while one is still standing before the Shechinah.

Talis: A four-cornered garment, worn in order to fulfil the mitzvah of *tzitzis*.

Tana (pl. ***Tanaim***): A halachic authority of the times of the Mishnah.

Targum: Translation. Usually the Aramaic translation.

Tefilin: Also called phylacteries. They consist of skin capsules containing the Torah passages *Shemos* 13:1-10; *Shemos* 13:11-16; *Devarim* 6:4-9 and *Devarim* 11:13-21 written on parchment. They are bound with straps to the head and the arm.

Tereyfah (pl. ***Tereyfos***): Meat of a slaughtered kosher animal or bird when the animal or bird had one of the eighteen defects which make it forbidden to be eaten.

"The Reading of Shema": Torah passages which one is obliged to read twice daily, in the morning and at night. They are *Devarim* 6:4-9; *Devarim* 11:13-21 and *Ba-Midbar* 15:37-41.

Tishah Be-Av: The ninth of Av. On that day Jews fast and mourn the destruction of the *Beys Ha-Mikdash*.

Torah law: Law that derives from the Torah itself, as it was given.

Torah requirement: A requirement which is incumbent by Torah law.

Tzeyreh: The Hebrew vowel sign consisting of two dots, underneath the letter, one alongside the other. See Transliteration Key at the beginning of the volume.

Tzitzis: The threads which must be worn on the corners of a four-cornered garment, for example, a *talis*.

Unclean: A halachic state. Certain objects are regarded as sources of uncleanness. There are also persons who are regarded as sources of uncleanness, because of certain bodily symptoms or a discharge, etc., or as a result of the performance of certain actions. Uncleanness may be contracted by persons, utensils, food or drink, through contact with a source of uncleanness, and they can also pass on the uncleanness in certain cases.

Also, an animal, bird or fish which is forbidden to be eaten.

U-Va Le-Tziyon: A prayer said in the Shacharis service, which also contains a *kedushah*.

Vain blessing: A blessing which does not relate to anything. It is forbidden to say such a blessing if one uses the Divine Name and mentions His Kingship.

Ve-Hayah Im Shamo'a: A *tefilin* passage. It is also the second passage of "The Reading of Shema". *Devarim* 11:13-21.

Ve-Hayah Ki Yevi'acha: A *tefilin* passage. *Shemos* 13:11-16.

Weak letter: A letter which does not have a *dagesh*.

Weekly portion: The portion of the Torah which is read that week in the Synagogue on Shabbos.

Woman with whom union is inconceivable: A woman with whom relations are forbidden to one by *kareys* (Divine capital punishment) or death.

Yishtabach: The blessing said after the song verses.

Yom Kippur: The Day of Atonement.

Yom Tov (pl. ***Yamim Tovim***): A holiday on which it is forbidden to do labor.

BIBLIOGRAPHY

Works and authors (including abbreviations) cited in this volume

(Dates given are Jewish dates with common era equivalents in parentheses)
b. = born; B. = Ben (son of); c. = circa (approximately); d. = died; p. = published; pl. = plural; R. = Rabbi

Acharon (pl. **Acharonim**): A later halachic authority contemporary with or after the time of the Shulchan Aruch.
Agadah (pl. **Agados**): The non-halachic part of the Talmud, which is mainly homiletic.
Amora (pl. **Amora'im**): A halachic authority of the times of the Gemara.
Ar.Hach. = **Artzos Ha-Chayim**: Novellae to the Shulchan Aruch, *Orach Chayim* and its commentaries; by R. Meir Leybush Malbim; 5569-5639 (1809-1879); p. Breslau, 5597 (1837).
Ari = **R. Yitzchak Luria**: Great kabalist and halachic authority; 5294-5332 (1534-1572).
At.Z. = **Atzeres Zekeynim**: Glosses to the Shulchan Aruch, *Orach Chayim*; by R. Menachem Mendel Auerbach; 5380-5449 (1620-1689); p. Dyhernfürth, 5452 (1692).
Avodas Ha-Yom: Laws of daily conduct; by R. Yisachar Doberish Apisdorf; p. Lwow, 5628 (1868).
Bach = **Bayis Chadash**: Commentary on the *Tur*; by R. Yo'el Sirkes; 5321-5400 (1561-1640); p. Krakow, 5391-5400 (1631-1640).
Ba-Midbar: The Book of Numbers.
Bava Basra: A Talmudic tractate.
Beis Meir: Commentary to the Shulchan Aruch; by R. Meir Pozner; 5489-5567 (1729-1807); p. Frankfort-on-the-Main, 5547 (1787).
Beis Yehudah: Responsa; by R. Yehuda Ayash; Algerian Rabbi; d. 5520 (1760); p. Leghorn 5506 (1746).
Benei Yonah: Novel laws concerning a Torah Scroll and writing it; by R. Yonah Landsofer; 5438-5472 (1678-1712); p. Prague 5563 (1803).
Berachos: A Talmudic tractate.
Beraysa: A Tanaitic ruling that was not incorporated in the Mishnah.
Bereyshis: The Book of Genesis.
Beyurey Ha-Gaon Maharam Banet = **Beyur Mordechai**: See *Beyur Mordechai.*
Beyur Ha-Gra: Commentary on the Shulchan Aruch; by R. Eliyahu of Vilna ("The Vilna Gaon"); 5480-5558 (1720-1797); p. Shklov, 5563 (1803).
Beyur Halachah: Additional comments and more detailed studies by the author of the Mishnah Berurah.
Beyur Mordechai: Commentary to the *Mordechai*; by the Gaon Mordechai Benet (Banet); 5513-5589 (1753-1829); p. Vienna, 5565-5573 (1805-1813).
B.Heyt. = **Ba'eyr Heyteyv**: Commentary to the Shulchan Aruch; by R. Yehudah Ashkenazi; p. Amsterdam, 5502 (1742).
Binyan Olam: Responsa; by R. Yitzchak Issac (Haver) Wildmann; 5549-5613 (1789-1853); p. Warsaw, 5611 (1851).
Birk.Y. = **Birkey Yosef**: Commentary on the Shulchan Aruch, *Orach Chayim*; by R. Chayim Yosef David Azulai ("The *Chida*"); 5484-5566 (1724-1806); p. Leghorn, 5534 (1774).
B.Sh. = **Baruch She-Amar**: Laws concerning the writing of *tefilin* passages, the preparation of *tefilin* and the form of the letters; by R. Shimshon B. Eliezer; 14th century.
B.Sh. = **Beis Shemu'el**: Commentary on the Shulchan Aruch, *Even Ha-Ezer*; by R. Shemu'el B. Uri Shraga Faibish; p. Dyhernfürth, 5449 (1689).
B.Y. = **Beis Yosef**: Commentary on the *Tur*; by R. Yosef Karo, author of the Shulchan Aruch; 5248-5335 (1488-1575); p. Venice, 5310-5311 (1550-1551).
Ch.A. = **Chayei Adam**: Laws concerning daily conduct, prayers, blessings, Shabbos and Holidays, etc.; by R. Avraham Danzig; 5508-5580 (1748-1820); p. Vilna, 5570 (1810).
Chach.A. = **Chachm.A.** = **Chachmas Adam**: Laws concerning forbidden foods, idolatory, vows, family life, etc.; by R. Avraham Danzig; 5508-5580 (1748-1820); p. Vilna, 5572 (1812).

Chasid = **R. Yehudah B. Shemu'el Ha-Chasid**: Author of *Sefer Chasidim*; c. 4910-4977 (1150-1217).

Chav.Y. = **Chavos Ya'ir**: Responsa; by R. Chaim Ya'ir Bacharach; 5398-5462 (1638-1702); p. Frankfort-on-the-Main, 5459 (1699).

Chazon Ish: A great scholar of modern times, R. Avraham Yeshayah Karelitz; 5638-5713 (1878-1953). His writings appeared under that name.

Ch.B.Y. = **Chinuch Beis Yehudah**: Responsa; by R. Yehudah Leyb, R. Chanoch Henich and R. Yehudah Leyb, the elder; p. Frankfort-on-the-Main, 5468 (1708).

Chidushey Ha-Meiri: Commentary to the Talmud; by the *Meiri*; see *Meiri.*

Chidushey Ha-Ran: Commentary to the Talmud; by the *Ran*; see *Ran.*

Chidushey Ha-Rashba: Commentary to the Talmud; by the *Rashba*; see *Rashba.*

Chidushey Ha-Ritba: Commentary to the Talmud; by the *Ritba*; see *Ritba.*

Chidushey R.A.E. = **Chidushey Rabbi Akiva Eiger**: Commentary and glosses on the Shulchan Aruch; by R. Akiva Eiger (Eger); 5521-5597 (1761-1837); p. Berlin, 5622 (1862).

Ch.M. = **Choshen Mishpat**: One of the four parts of the Shulchan Aruch.

Ch.S. = **Chasam Sofer**: Responsa; by R. Mosheh Sofer; 5522-5599 (1762-1839); p. Pressburg and Munkács, 5615-5672 (1855-1912).

Chumash: One of the five Books of the Torah.

Chut Ha-Shani: Responsa; by R. Mosheh Shimshon Bacharach; 5367-5430 (1607-1670) and father; R. Shemu'el Bacharach; p. Frankfort-on-the-Main, 5439 (1679).

Damesek Eliezer: Novellae on the *B.Y.*, printed together with responsa, called *Heyshiv R. Eliezer Ve-Si'ach Ha-Sadeh*; by R. Eliezer Lipschuetz; 18th century scholar; p. Nevewirth, 5509 (1749).

Derishah: A twin work of the *Perishah*; see *Perishah.*

Devarim: The Book of Deuteronomy.

Dev.Sh. = **D.Sh.** = **Devar Shemu'el**: Responsa; by R. Shemu'el Aboab; 5370-5454 (1610-1694); p. Venice, 5462 (1702).

D. Hach. = **Derech Ha-Chayim**: Glosses to the sidur (prayer book) containing laws pertaining to daily conduct, prayers, blessings, Shabbos and Holidays, etc.; by R. Ya'akov Lorbeerbaum; 5520-5592 (1760-1832); p. Berlin, 5600 (1840).

D.M. = **Darkei Mosheh**: Commentary on the *Tur*; by R. Mosheh Isserles ("The *Rema*"); c. 5290-5332 (1530-1572); p. Fürth, 5520 (1760).

E.A. = **Eyshel Avraham**: One of the twin works comprising the *P.Mg.*; see *P.Mg.*

E.Hae. = **Even Ha-Ezer**: One of the four parts of the Shulchan Aruch.

E.R. = **Elyah Rabba** = **Eliyahu Rabba**: Commentary on the *Levush* and Shulchan Aruch; by R. Eliyahu Shapira; 5420-5472 (1660-1712); p. Sulzbach, 5517 (1757).

Esteyr: The Book of Esther.

Eychah: The Book of Lamentations.

Gan Ha-Melech: Halachic decisions and rules in brief; by R. Avraham B. Mordechai Ha-Levi; Egyptian Rabbi; late 17th century; p. Istanbul, 5476-7 (1716-7).

Gaon (pl. **Ge'onim**): The great scholars after the time of the Gemara until the period of the Rishonim; also, any outstanding scholar.

Gemara: The part of the Talmud which discusses and interprets the Mishnah and related matters.

Geyt Mekushar: The laws concerning a letter of divorce; by R. Refa'el Mosheh Di Bula; d. 5533 (1773); p. Istanbul, 5527 (1767).

Gra = **Gaon Rabbeinu Eliyahu** ("The Vilna Gaon"): Halachic authority and author; 5480-5558 (1720-1797). References are usually to his *Beyur Ha-Gra* (see entry).

G.R.A.E. = **Gaon R. Akiva Eiger (Eger)**: 5521-5597 (1761-1837).

Hagah.M. = **Hagahos Maimoniyos**: by R. Meir *Ha-Koheyn*; pupil of the Maharam of Rothenburg; end of 13th century.

Igeres Ha-Tiyul: Esoteric work by R. Chayim B. Betzaleyl; c. 5280-5348 (1520-1588); p. Prague, 5365 (1605).

Ikrey Dinim: Anthology of halachic rulings; by R. Daniel Terni (late eighteenth and early nineteenth century); p. Florence, 5563 (1803).

Kabala: The secret mystical teachings.

Kavanos Ha-Ari = **P.E.Ch.**: See *P.E.Ch.*

Keses Ha-Sofer: Laws of writing Torah Scrolls, *tefilin* passages and mezuzos; by R. Shelomoh Ganzfried; 5564-5646 (1804-1886); p. Ofen, 5595 (1835).

Kesivah Tamah = **Kasuv Le-Chayim**: The symbols of all the letters of the alphabet and the laws for writing them; by R. Avraham Chayim B. Yitzchak Ya'akov; p. Vilna, 5618 (1858).

K.Hag. = **Kn.Hag.** = **Kneses Ha-Gedolah**: Collection of halachic rulings; by R. Chaim Benveniste; 5363-5433 (1603-1673); p. Leghorn, 5418 (1658).
Kidushin: A Talmudic tractate.
Kin'as Soferim: The laws for scribes; by R. Shelomoh Kluger; 5545-5629 (1785-1869); p. Lwow, 5620 (1860).
Koheles: The Book of Ecclesiastes.
Koheles Ya'akov: Novellae and responsa; by R. Ya'akov Beruchim; p. Vilna, 5607 (1847).
L.Ch. = **Lechem Chamudos**: Commentary to the *Rosh*; by R. Yom Tov Lipman Heller; 5339-5415 (1579-1654); p. Prague, 5388 (1628).
Le-David Emes: Laws of the reading from the Torah and the writing of a Torah Scroll; by R. Chayim Yosef David Azulai ("The *Chida*"); 5484-5566 (1724-1806); p. Leghorn, 5546 (1786).
Levush: Code of laws following the framework of the Shulchan Aruch; by R. Mordechai Jaffe; c. 5295-5372 (1535-1612); p. Lublin, Prague, Krakow, 5350-5364 (1590-1604).
Levu.Sr. = **Levushey Serad**: Commentary on the Shulchan Aruch; by R. David Shelomoh Eybeschuetz; d. 5570 (1809); p. Mahlow, 5578 (1818).
M.A. = **Magen Avraham**: Commentary on the Shulchan Aruch; by R. Avraham Abeli Gombiner; c. 5397-5443 (1637-1683); p. Dyhernfürth, 5452 (1692).
Ma'aseh Rav: Practices of the *Gra*; by R. Yissachar Ber B. Tanchum; p. Zholkva, 5568 (1808).
Ma'aseh Rokeyach: Commentary to the *Rambam*; by R. Masud Chay Rokeyach; p. Venice, Leghorn, 5502-5623 (1742-1863).
Machazeh Avraham: Responsa and novellae; by R. Avraham Di Boton; ?5470-5540 (1710-1780); p. Salonika, 5555 (1795).
Mach. Hash. = **Machatzis Ha-Shekel**: Commentary on the *Magen Avraham*; by R. Shemu'el Ha-Levi Kelin; 5480-5566 (1720-1806); p. Vienna, 5567 (1807).
Magen Giborim: Commentary on the Shulchan Aruch; by R. Mordechai Ze'ev Ettinger, 5564-5623 (1804-1863) and R. Yosef Sha'ul Nathanson, 5570-5635 (1810-1875); p. Lwow, 5594 (1834) and Zholkva, 5599 (1839).
Maharam of Rothenburg = **R. Meir B. Baruch of Rothenburg**: Halachic authority; c. 4975-5053 (1215-1293).
Maharash Ha-Levi = **R. Shelomoh B. Yitzchak Ha-Levi**: Author of responsa; p. Salonika, 5412 (1652).
Maharikash = **R. Ya'akov Kastro**: Halachic authority and author; ?5285-5370 (1525-1610).
Maharil = **R. Ya'akov Ha-Levi Molin**: Halachic authority and author; 5120-5187 (1360-1427).
Maharim of Brisk (Brest-Litovsk) = **R. Ya'akov Meir Padua**: Author of responsa and other works; d. 5615 (1854).
Maharit = **R. Yosef Trani**: Author of responsa, novellae, etc.; 5328-5399 (1568-1639).
Mahariy = **R. Yehudah Ayash**: Algerian Rabbi; d. 5520 (1760).
Mahariya = **R. Yitzchak Abohav**: Spanish scholar at the time of the exile, who taught the teacher of the author of the Shulchan Aruch; 5193-5253 (1433-1493).
Mahariy Ben Chaviv = **Ri Ben Chaviv**: See *Ri Ben Chaviv*.
Maharshal = **R. Shelomoh Luria**: Halachic authority and author and contemporary of the *Rema*; c. 5270-5334 (1510-1574).
Mateh Yehudah: Commentary on the Shulchan Aruch; by Rabbi Yehudah Ayash; d. 5520 (1760); p. Leghorn, 5543 (1783).
Megilah: A Talmudic tractate.
Meiri: R. Menachem B. Shelomoh, author of a commentary to the Talmud; 5009-5076 (1249-1316).
Melachim: The Book of Kings.
Menachos: A Talmudic tractate.
Meshivas Nafesh: Responsa; by R. Aryeih Leyb B. Mosheh Tzinz; p. Warsaw, 5609 (1849).
Michah: The Book of Micah.
Midrash: Any of several works consisting of expositions of the Scriptures by the Tanaim and Amoraim.
Mishkenos Ya'akov: Responsa; by R. Ya'akov B. Aharon; d. 5604 (1844); p. Vilna, 5598 (1838).
Mishnah: The oral law, compiled and committed to writing by the Tana Rabbi Yehudah *Ha-Nasi* ("Rabbi").
Mishnas Avraham: Laws for writing Torah Scrolls, *tefilin* passages and mezuzos; by R. Avraham Jaffe; p. Zhitomir, 5628 (1868).
M.M. = **Ma'amar Mordechai**: Commentary on the Shulchan Aruch; by R. Mordechai Karmi; 5509-5585 (1749-1825); p. Leghorn, 5544 (1784).

Mordechai: Halachic digest of the Talmud and early authorities; by R. Mordechai B. Hilel Ashkenazi; 5000-5058 (1240-1298).
M.Z. = **Mishbetzos Zahav**: One of the twin works comprising the *P.Mg.*; see *P.Mg.*
N.A. = **Nishmas Adam**: The rationale of the author of the *Chayei Adam* underlying his original decisions in the latter work; p. Vilna, 5570 (1810); see *Chayei Adam*.
Nachalas David: Responsa and novellae; by R. David Tevil; p. Vilna, 5624 (1864).
Nesiv Chayim: Glosses and corrections to the Shulchan Aruch; by R. Nesanel Weil; 5447-5529 (1687-1769); p. Fürth, 5539 (1779).
Nidah: A Talmudic tractate.
No.B. = **No.Biy.** = **Noda Bi-Yehudah**: Responsa; by R. Yechezkeyl Landau; 5473-5553 (1713-1793); p. Prague, 5536-5571 (1776-1811).
N.Tz. = **Nachalas Tzevi**: Commentary to the Shulchan Aruch; by R. Tzevi Hirsh B. Yosef Ha-Koheyn; p. Krakow, 5406 (1646).
Olas Shabbos: Commentary to the Shulchan Aruch, Laws of Shabbos; by R. Shemu'el B. Yosef; d. 5460 (1700); p. Amsterdam, 5434 (1674).
Or Yisra'eyl: Responsa; by R. Yisra'eyl Lipschuetz; d. 5542 (1782); p. Cleves, 5530 (1770).
O.T. = **Olas Tamid** = **Olas Ha-Tamid**: Commentary on the Shulchan Aruch; by R. Shemu'el B. Yosef; d. 5460 (1700); p. Amsterdam, 5434 (1674).
O.Z. = **Or Zaru'a**: Commentary on the Talmud; by R. Yitzchak of Vienna; c. 4940-5010 (1180-1250).
P.E.Ch. = **Peri Eytz Chayim**: Kabalistic work describing what one should have in mind for prayer, etc. and inner meanings; by R. Chayim Vital; 5303-5380 (1543-1620); p. Korets, 5545 (1785).
Perishah: Commentary on the *Tur*; by R. Yehoshua Ha-Koheyn Falk; 5315-5374 (1565-1614); p. Berlin and Lublin, 5395-5527 (1635-1767).
P.M. = **Panim Me'iros**: Responsa and commentary to the Talmud; by R. Meir Eisenstadt; c. 5430-5504 (1670-1744); p. Amsterdam, Sulzbach, 5475-5489 (1715-1729).
P.Mg. = **Peri Megadim**: A pair of commentaries, *Eyshel Avraham*, on the *Magen Avraham*, and *Mishbetzos Zahav*, on the *Turey Zahav*; by R. Yosef Teomim; c. 5487-5552 (1727-1792); p. Frankfort-on-the-Oder, 5545 (1785).
Poseyk (pl. **Poskim**): Halachic authority.
Pr.Ch. = **Peri Chadash**: Commentary to the Shulchan Aruch; by R. Chizkiyah Da Silva; 5419-5455 (1659-1695); p. Amsterdam, 5452-5490 (1692-1730).
P.T. = **Pischey Teshuva**: A collection of responsa on the Shulchan Aruch, *Orach Chayim*; by R. Yisra'el Isar Isserlein; p. Vilna, 5635 (1875).
P.T. = **Pischey Teshuvah**: A digest of responsa, etc. relevant to the Shulchan Aruch; by R. Tzvi Hirsch Eisenstadt; p. Vilna, 5596 (1836).
Ra'ah = **R. Aharon Ha-Levi of Barcelona**: c. 4995-5060 (1235-1300).
Ra'anach = **R. Eliyahu B. Chayim**: Author of responsa and novellae; ?5290-?5370 (1530-1610).
Rabbeinu Simchah = **R. Simchah B. Shemu'el of Speyer**: A Rishon of the second half of the twelfth century and the first half of the thirteenth century.
Rabbi Avraham Chayim Na'eh: Author of several halachic works; d. 5714 (1954).
Rabbi Elazar: A Tana.
Rabbi Yitzchak of Posen = **R. Yitzchak B. Avraham**: Author of novellae and responsa; d. 5445 (1685).
Rabbi Yosef Karo: Author of the Shulchan Aruch and other works; 5248-5335 (1488-1575).
Radach = **R. David B. Chayim Ha-Koheyn of Corfu**: Author of responsa; d. 5290 (1530); responsa p. Istanbul, 5297 (1537).
Radbaz = **R. David B. Zimra**: Author of responsa and a commentary on the Rambam; 5240-5334 (1480-1574).
R.A.E. = **Rabbi Akiva Eiger (Eger)**: Halachic authority and author; 5521-5597 (1761-1837).
Rambam = **R. Mosheh B. Maimon**: Author of a code of laws that covers every field of Jewish law and many other works; also described as Maimonides; 4895-4964 (1135-1204).
Ramban = **R. Mosheh B. Nachman**: Halachic authority and author; also described as Nachmanides; 4954-5030 (1194-1270).
Ran = **R. Nisim B. Reuven of Gerona**: Halachic authority, author of a commentary on the *Rif* and novellae; 5070-5135 (1310-1375).
Rashal = **R. Shelomoh Luria**: See *Maharshal*.
Rashba = **R. Shelomoh B. Avraham Adret**: Halachic authority and author; c. 4995-c. 5070 (1235-1310).

Rashbi = **R. Shimon B. Yochaiy**: A Tana.
Rashi = **R. Shelomoh Yitzchaki**: Author of the basic commentary to the Scriptures and the Talmud; 4800-4865 (1040-1105).
Rash of Chinon = **R. Shimshon B. Yitzchak of Chinon**: Fourteenth century French scholar and tosafist.
Re'eym = **Rabbeinu Eliezer B. Shemu'el of Metz**: A pupil of Rabbeinu Tam and author of a halachic work; c. 4875-c. 4958 (c. 1115-c. 1198).
Rema = **R. Moshe Isserles**: Author of the glosses to the Shulchan Aruch and numerous other works; 5290-5332 (1530-1572).
Rema of Fano = **Rabbi Menachem Azaryah of Fano**: Author of responsa; 5308-5380 (1548-1620); p. Venice, 5360 (1600).
Revid Ha-Zahav: Responsa; by R. Ze'ev Valf Avreich; 5605-5682 (1845-1921); p. Vilna, 5658 (1898).
Ri = **R. Yitzchak**: One of the main authorities of the *Tosafos*, a nephew and pupil of Rabbeinu Tam; d. c. 4945 (1185).
Ri Aksandarni = **Ri Askandarni**: Scholar quoted by the *B.Y.* whom the *Radbaz* knew in Safed.
Ri Ben Chaviv = **R. Ya'akov B. Chaviv**: Author of responsa and compiler of *Eyn Ya'akov*, the Aggadic material of the Talmud, with a commentary; ?5205-5275/6 (1445-1515/6).
Ri Chasid = **Rabbi Yehudah *Ha-Chasid* (the pious)**: Author of *Sefer Chasidim*; c. 4910-4977 (1150-1217).
Rif = **R. Yitzchak Al-Fasi**: Early Rishon, who gave the rulings of the discussions in the Talmud; 4773-4863 (1013-1103).
Rishon (pl. **Rishonim**): An early halachic authority. The period of the Rishonim stretches from the time of the Ge'onim until the time of the Shulchan Aruch.
Ritba = **R. Yom Tov B. Avraham Ashbili**: Halachic authority, author of novellae; c. 5010-5090 (1250-1330).
Rokeyach: Halachic work; by R. Elazar of Worms; c. 4925-c. 4990 (1165-1230).
Rosh = **Rabbeinu Asher B. Yechi'el**: Halachic authority and author; c. 5010-5087 (1250-1327).
Rosh Ha-Shanah: A Talmudic tractate.
R.T. = **Rabbeinu Tam**: R. Ya'akov B. Meir; one of the early authorities of the *Tosafos*; c. 4860-4931 (c. 1100-1171).
Rus: The Book of Ruth.
Sanhedrin: A Talmudic tractate.
S. Ch. = **Sefer Chasidim**: Mystical, ethical and halachic work; by R. Yehudah B. Shemu'el *Ha-Chasid* (the pious); c. 4910-4977 (c. 1150-1217).
Sefer Ha-Chareydim: An inspiring work on the mitzvos; by R. Elazar Azikri; 5293-5360 (1533-1600); Venice, 5361 (1601).
Sefer Ha-Chayim: Novellae on the Shulchan Aruch; by R. Shelomoh Kluger; 5545-5629 (1785-1869); p. Zholkva, 5585 (1825).
Sefer Ha-Chinuch: An account and explanation of the mitzvos; authorship uncertain, but ascribed mainly to the *Ra'ah*; see *Ra'ah*.
Sefer Ha-Eshkol: Halachic work; by R. Avraham B. Yitzchak of Narbonne; c. 4870-4939 (1110-1179).
Sefer Ha-Kavanos: Same as *P.E.Ch.*; see *P.E.Ch.*
Sefer Ha-Terumah: Halachic work; by R. Baruch B. Yitzchak of Worms (12th and 13th century).
Sema = **Sefer Me'iras Eynayim**: Commentary to the Shulchan Aruch *Choshen Mishpat*; by R. Yehoshua Wolk Katz; c. 5300-5374 (1540-1614); p. Prague, 5366 (1606).
Sh.A. = **Sha'agas Aryeih**: Responsa; by R. Aryeh Leib Gunzberg; 5455-5545 (1695-1785); p. Frankfort-on-the Oder, 5515 (1755).
Sh.A. = **Shulchan Aruch**: A work which contains the halachic decisions deriving from the longer discussions by the same author in the *Beis Yosef*, his commentary to the *Tur*. It was written by R. Yosef Karo, who divided it into four parts, *Orach Chayim, Yoreh De'ah, Choshen Mishpat* and *Even Ha-Ezer*; p. Venice, 5325 (1565).
Sha'ar Efrayim: Responsa; by R. Efrayim B. Ya'akov Ha-Koheyn of Vilna; 5376-5438 (1616-1678); p. Sulzbach, 5448 (1688).
Sha'ar Ha-Tziyun: Sources and notes to the Mishnah Berurah; by its author.
Shabbos: A Talmudic tractate.
Shach = **Sifsey Kohen**: Commentary to the Shulchan Aruch, *Yoreh De'ah* and *Choshen Mishpat*; by R. Shabsay B. Meir Ha-Koheyn; 5381-5422 (1621-1662); p. Krakow, 5406 (1646).
Shamay: A Tana, who founded a school whose opinions conflicted with the opinions of the school of Hileyl.

Sh.E. = **Sha'arey Efrayim**: Laws of the Reading of the Torah; by R. Efrayim Zalman Margolioth; 5520-5588 (1760-1828); p. Dubno, 5580 (1820).
Shelah = **Sheney Luchos Ha-Bris**: Esoteric, ethical and halachic work; by R. Yeshayah Ha-Levi Horowitz; c. 5325-5390 (1565-1630); p. Amsterdam, 5408 (1648).
Shemos: The Book of Exodus.
Shevus Ya'akov: Responsa; by R. Ya'akov Reischer; c. 5430-5493 (1670-1733); p. Halle, 5470 (1710).
Shimushah Raba: Work on the laws of *tefilin* from the time of the Geonim.
Shir Ha-Shirim: The Book of "The Song of Songs".
Sh.Kn.Hag. = **Shiyurey Kneses Ha-Gedolah**: Addenda to the *Kn.Hag.* (see *Kn.Hag.*); p. Smyrna, 5431 (1671).
Sh.T. = **Sha. T.** = **Sha'arey Teshuvah**: Digest of responsa, etc. relating to the Shulchan Aruch; by R. Chayim Mordechai Margolis; p. Dubno, 5580 (1820).
Shulchan Shelomoh: Laws of the Shulchan Aruch, *Orach Chayim* in brief; by R. Shelomoh Zalman Mirkish; eighteenth century Rabbi; p. Frankfort-on-the-Oder, 5531 (1771).
Soferim: A minor tractate which was not composed on the Mishnah. It contains laws concerning the writing of holy books and passages, the public reading from the Torah, sanctification, elements of the prayer service, fasting and other matters.
Talmud: The Mishnah together with the expanded discussions and interpretations of the Gemara.
Talmud Yerushalmi: The Jerusalem Talmud, as opposed to the Babylonian Talmud which is the Talmud ordinarily referred to.
Tana (pl. **Tanaim**): A halachic authority of the times of the Mishnah.
Taz = **Turey Zahav**: Commentary to the Shulchan Aruch; by R. David Ha-Levi of Lwow; 5346-5427 (1586-1667); p. Dyhernfürth, 5452 (1692). Also called *Magen David.*
Teshuvah Mey-Ahavah: Responsa; by R. Elazar Fleckeles; 5514-5586 (1754-1826); p. Prague, 5569-5581 (1809-1821).
Tif'eres Aryeih: On the laws of *tefilin*; by R. Mosheh Leib Litsh Segal Rosenbaum; p. Pressburg, 5628 (1868).
Toras Chayim: Novellae on the Talmud and its commentaries; by R. Avraham Chayim Schor; on the tractate Sanhedrin, p. Krakow, 5394 (1634).
Tosafos: Talmudic commentary, containing the views of the early European Rishonim, especially of the first few generations after *Rashi.*
Tosafos Yerushalayim = **Tosefes Yerushalayim**: Laws from the *Tosefta* and *Talmud Yerushalmi* not quoted in the Shulchan Aruch; by R. Yisra'el Isar Isserlein; p. Vilna, 5631 (1871).
Tur: Code of laws which formed the basis for the Shulchan Aruch; by R. Ya'akov B. Asher, son of the *Rosh*; c. 5030-5100 (1270-1340).
Va-Yikra: The Book of Leviticus.
Yad Aharon: Commentary to the Shulchan Aruch; by R. Aharon Alfandari; c. 5450-5534 (1690-1774); p. Izmir, 5495 (1735).
Yad Efrayim: Commentary to the Shulchan Aruch, *Orach Chayim*; by R. Efrayim Zalman Margolios; 5520-5588 (1760-1828); p. Dubno, 5580 (1820).
Yo.D. = **Yoreh De'ah**: One of the four parts of the Shulchan Aruch.
Yechezkeyl: The Book of Ezekiel.
Yerushalmi = **Talmud Yerushalmi**: See *Talmud Yerushalmi.*
Yeshayah: The Book of Isaiah.
Yeshu'os Ya'akov: Commentary on the Shulchan Aruch; by R. Ya'akov Ornstein; 5535-5599 (1775-1839); p. Zholkva, 5588 (1828).
Yoma: A Talmudic tractate.
Zohar: An early kabalistic work ascribed to the Tana Rabbi Shimon B. Yochaiy.